July 23–25, 2013
Montréal, Québec, Canada

Association for Computing Machinery

Advancing Computing as a Science & Profession

I0006888

SPAA'13

Proceedings of the 25th ACM

Symposium on Parallelism in Algorithms and Architectures

Sponsored by:
ACM SIGACT and ACM SIGARCH

Supported by:
Akamai, IBM Research, Sandia National Laboratories, Oracle Labs, Intel, and Concordia University

The Association for Computing Machinery
2 Penn Plaza, Suite 701
New York, New York 10121-0701

Notice to Past Authors of ACM-Published Articles
ACM intends to create a complete electronic archive of all articles and/or other material previously published by ACM. If you have written a work that has been previously published by ACM in any journal or conference proceedings prior to 1978, or any SIG Newsletter at any time, and you do NOT want this work to appear in the ACM Digital Library, please inform permissions@acm.org, stating the title of the work, the author(s), and where and when published.

ISBN: 978-1-4503-1572-2

ACM Order Number : 417130

Additional copies may be ordered prepaid from:

ACM Order Department
PO Box 30777
New York, NY 10087-0777, USA

Phone: 1-800-342-6626 (USA and Canada)
+1-212-626-0500 (Global)
Fax: +1-212-944-1318
E-mail: acmhelp@acm.org
Hours of Operation: 8:30 am – 4:30 pm ET

Printed in the USA

Foreword

This volume consists of papers that were presented at the 25th ACM Symposium on Parallelism in Algorithms and Architectures (SPAA 2013), held on 23–25 July 2013, in Montreal, Canada, co-located with PODC. It was sponsored by the ACM Special Interest Groups on Algorithms and Computation Theory (SIGACT) and Computer Architecture (SIGARCH) and organized in cooperation with the European Association for Theoretical Computer Science (EATCS). Financial support was provided by Akamai, IBM Research, Sandia National Laboratories, Oracle Labs and ACM SIGARCH.

The program committee selected 31 regular presentations following electronic discussions. Of these papers, the papers "IRIS: A Robust Information System Against Insider DoS-Attacks" by Martina Eikel and Christian Scheideler and "Fast Greedy Algorithms in MapReduce and Streaming" by Ravi Kumar, Benjamin Moseley, Sergei Vassilvitskii, and Andrea Vattani were selected to receive the best paper award.

The regular presentations were selected out of 130 submitted manuscripts. The mix of selected papers reflects the unique nature of SPAA in bringing together the theory and practice of parallel computing. SPAA defines parallelism very broadly to encompass any computational device or scheme that can perform multiple operations or tasks simultaneously or concurrently. The technical papers in this volume are to be considered preliminary versions, and authors are generally expected to publish polished and complete versions in archival scientific journals.

In addition to the regular presentations, this volume includes 8 brief announcements. The committee's decisions in accepting brief announcements were based on the perceived interest of these contributions, with the goal that they serve as bases for further significant advances in parallelism in computing. Extended versions of the SPAA brief announcements may be published later in other conferences or journals. Finally, this year's program also included the ACM Athena lecture given by Nancy Lynch of the Massachusetts Institute of Technology and additional keynote addresses by Marc Snir of Argonne National Laboratory and the University of Illinois at Urbana-Champaign and by Philipp Woelfel of the University of Calgary.

The program committee would like to thank all who submitted papers and who helped the committee in the review process. The names of these external reviewers appear later in the proceedings. We would very much like to thank the program committee for all of their hard work during the paper selection process. The authors, the external reviewers, and the program committee together made it possible to come up with a great collection of papers for the conference.

Berthold Vöcking　　　　**Guy Blelloch**
RWTH Aachen University　　　*Carnegie Mellon University*
SPAA 2013 Program Chair　　　*SPAA General Chair*

Table of Contents

Session 4
Session Chair: Hagit Attiya *(Technion)*

Session 5
Session Chair: Marc Snir *(Argonne National Laboratory & University of Illinois at Urbana-Champaign)*

Session 6
Session Chair: Christian Scheideler *(University of Paderborn)*

Session 7
Session Chair: Robert Elsässer *(Salzburg University)*

Session 8
Session Chair: Michael Bender *(Stony Brook University)*

Author Index

SPAA 2013 Symposium Organization

General Chair: Guy Blelloch *(Carnegie Mellon University, USA)*

Program Chair: Berthold Vöcking *(RWTH Aachen University, Germany)*

Program Committee: Matthew Andrews *(Bell Labs, USA)*
Hagit Attiya *(Technion, Israel)*
Zhaojun Bai *(University of California, Davis, USA)*
Michael Bender *(Stony Brook University, USA)*
George Bosilca *(University of Tennessee, USA)*
Michael Dinitz *(Weizmann Institute, Israel)*
Robert Elsässer *(Salzburg University, Austria)*
Thomas Erlebach *(University of Leicester, Great Britain)*
Magnus M. Halldorsson *(Reykjavik University, Iceland)*
Torsten Hoefler *(ETH Zürich, Switzerland)*
Giuseppe Persiano *(University of Salerno, Italy)*
Cynthia A. Phillips *(Sandia Labs, USA)*
Rajmohan Rajaraman *(Northeastern University, USA)*
Andréa W. Richa *(Arizona State University, USA)*
André Schiper *(EPFL Lausanne, Switzerland)*
Stefan Schmid *(TU Berlin and T-Labs, Germany)*
Ravi Sundaram *(Northeastern University, USA)*
Peter Varman *(Rice University, USA)*
Jennifer Welch *(Texas A&M University, USA)*
Norbert Zeh *(Dalhousie University, Canada)*

Publicity Chair: Jeremy Fineman *(Georgetown University, USA)*

Treasurer and Registration Chair: David Bunde *(Knox College, USA)*

Secretary: Christian Scheideler *(University of Paderborn, Germany)*

Local Arrangements Chairs: Lata Narayanan *(Concordia University, Canada)*
Jaroslav Opatrny *(Concordia University, Canada)*

Steering Committee: Guy Blelloch *(Carnegie Mellon University, USA)*
David Culler *(University of California, Berkeley, USA)*
Frank Dehne *(Carleton University, Canada)*
Pierre Fraigniaud *(University of Paris-Sud, France)*
Phil Gibbons *(Intel Research, USA)*
Maurice Herlihy *(Brown University, USA)*
Tom Leighton *(MIT and Akamai Technologies, USA)*
Charles Leiserson *(Massachusetts Institute of Technology, USA)*
Fabrizio Luccio *(University of Pisa, Italy)*

Steering Committee:
(cont'd)

Friedhelm Meyer auf der Heide *(University of Paderborn, Germany)*
Gary Miller *(Carnegie Mellon University, USA)*
Burkhard Monien *(University of Paderborn, Germany)*
Franco Preparata *(Brown University, USA)*
Vijaya Ramachandran *(University of Texas, Austin, USA)*
Arnold Rosenberg *(University of Massachusetts, Amherst, USA and Colorado State University, USA)*
Paul Spirakis *(CTI, Greece)*
Uzi Vishkin *(University of Maryland, USA)*

Additional reviewers:

Umut Acar
Henry Adams
Deepak Ajwani
Venkatesh Akella
Kamal Al-Bawani
Susanne Albers
Maya Arbel
Holger Arndt
Vincenzo Auletta
Chen Avin
Amotz Bar-Noy
Stefano Basagni
Petra Berenbrink
Jonathan Berry
Macicj Bcsta
Martin Biely
Erik Boman
Vincenzo Bonifaci
Aurelien Bouteiller
Joshua Brody
Rodrigo Carrasco
Sixia Chen
Rezaul Chowdhury
Hyun Chul Chung
Andrea Clementi
Peter Cogan
Johannes Dams
Anthony Danalis
Maciej Drozdowski
Swan Dubois
Pascal Felber
Diodato Ferraioli
Jeremy Fineman

Chien-Chung Huang
Csanád Imreh
Riko Jacob
Zahra Jafargholi
Mitesh Jain
Dominik Kaaser
Thomas Kesselheim
Shuji Kijima
Shiva Kintali
Kirill Kogan
Nitish Korula
Andreas Koutsopoulos
Dariusz Kowalski
Evangelos Kranakis
Ravishankar Krishnaswamy
Petr Kuznetsov
Silvio Lattanzi
Hyunyoung Lee
I-Ting Angelina Lee
Christoph Lenzen
Mihai Letia
Yossi Lev
Li Lu
Piotr Luszczek
Lin Ma
Aleksander Madry
Fredrik Manne
Virendra Marathe
Xavier Martorell
Henning Meyerhenke
Maged Michael
Matus Mihalak
Pradipta Mitra

SPAA 2013 Sponsors and Supporters

Sponsors:

 **IBM Research**

Supporters:

 Oracle Labs

Fast Greedy Algorithms in MapReduce and Streaming

Ravi Kumar[*]
Google
Mountain View, CA
ravi.k53@gmail.com

Benjamin Moseley[*†]
Toyota Technological Institute
Chicago, IL
moseley@ttic.edu

Sergei Vassilvitskii[*]
Google
Mountain View, CA
sergeiv@google.com

Andrea Vattani[*]
University of California
San Diego, CA
avattani@cs.ucsd.edu

ABSTRACT

Greedy algorithms are practitioners' best friends—they are intuitive, simple to implement, and often lead to very good solutions. However, implementing greedy algorithms in a distributed setting is challenging since the greedy choice is inherently sequential, and it is not clear how to take advantage of the extra processing power.

Our main result is a powerful sampling technique that aids in parallelization of sequential algorithms. We then show how to use this primitive to adapt a broad class of greedy algorithms to the MapReduce paradigm; this class includes maximum cover and submodular maximization subject to p-system constraints. Our method yields efficient algorithms that run in a logarithmic number of rounds, while obtaining solutions that are arbitrarily close to those produced by the standard sequential greedy algorithm. We begin with algorithms for modular maximization subject to a matroid constraint, and then extend this approach to obtain approximation algorithms for submodular maximization subject to knapsack or p-system constraints. Finally, we empirically validate our algorithms, and show that they achieve the same quality of the solution as standard greedy algorithms but run in a substantially fewer number of rounds.

Categories and Subject Descriptors

F.2.2 [**Analysis of Algorithms and Problem Complexity**]: Nonnumerical Algorithms and Problems

Keywords

Distributed computing, Algorithm analysis, Approximation algorithms, Greedy algorithms, Map-reduce, Submodular function

[*]Part of this work was done while the author was at Yahoo! Research.

[†]Partially supported by NSF grant CCF-1016684.

1. INTRODUCTION

Greedy algorithms have been very successful in practice. For a wide range of applications they provide good solutions, are computationally efficient, and are easy to implement. A typical greedy algorithm repeatedly chooses an action that maximizes the objective given the previous decisions that it has made. A common application of greedy algorithms is for (sub)modular maximization problems, such as the MAXCOVER[1] problem. For this rich class of problems, greedy algorithms are a panacea, giving near-optimal solutions.

Submodular maximization. Submodular maximization has received a significant amount of attention in optimization; see [8] and [38] for pointers to relevant work. Examples of its numerous applications include model-driven optimization [21], skyline representation [36], search result diversification [1, 9], string transformations [2], social networks analysis [11, 12, 23, 28, 31], the generalized assignment problem [8], and auction theory [3]. In submodular maximization, we are given a submodular function f and a universe U, with the goal of selecting a subset $S \subseteq U$ such that $f(S)$ is maximized. Typically, S must satisfy additional feasibility constraints such as cardinality, knapsack, matroid, or p-systems constraints (see Section 2).

Maximizing a submodular function subject to these types of constraints generalizes many well-known problems such as the maximum spanning tree problem (modular maximization subject to a single matroid constraint), the maximum weighted matching problem in general graphs (modular maximization subject to a 2-system), and MAXCOVER (submodular maximization subject to a cardinality constraint). For this class of problems there is a natural greedy algorithm: iteratively add the best feasible element to the current solution. This simple algorithm turns out to be a panacea for submodular maximization. It is optimal for modular function maximization subject to one matroid constraint [17] and achieves a $(1/p)$-approximation for p matroid constraints [26]. For the submodular coverage problem, it achieves a $(1 - 1/e)$-approximation for a single uniform matroid constraint [33], and a $(1/(p+1))$-approximation for p matroid constraints [8, 20]; for these two cases, it is known that it is NP-hard to achieve an approximation factor better than $(1 - 1/e)$ and $\Omega(\frac{\log p}{p})$, respectively [19, 25].

The case of big data. Submodular maximization arises in data management, online advertising, software services, and online inventory control domains [7, 13, 14, 30, 35], where the data sizes are

---

[1]In the MAXCOVER problem we are given a universe U and a family of sets $\mathcal{S}$. The goal is to find a set $S' \subset \mathcal{S}$ of size k that maximizes the total union, $|\cup_{X \in S'} X|$.

routinely measured in tens of terabytes. For these problem sizes, the MapReduce paradigm [16] is standard for large-scale parallel computation. An instantiation of the BSP model [37] for parallel computing, a MapReduce computation begins with data randomly partitioned across a set of machines. The computation then proceeds in rounds, with communication between machines taking place only between successive rounds. A formal model of computation for this paradigm was described in [27]. It requires both the number of machines and the memory per machine to be sublinear in the size of the input, and looks to reduce the total number of rounds necessary.

The greedy algorithm for submodular maximization does not appear to be useful in this setting due to its inherently sequential nature. The greedy choice made at each step critically depends on the its previous actions, hence a naive MapReduce implementation would perform one action in each round, and gain little advantage due to parallelism. A natural question arises: *is it possible to realize an efficient version of the greedy algorithm in a distributed setting?* The challenge comes from the fact that to reduce the number of rounds, one is forced to add a large number of elements to the solution in every round, even though the function guiding the greedy selection can change dramatically with every selection. Moreover, the selection must be done in parallel, without any communication between the machines. An affirmative answer to this question would open up the possibility of using these algorithms for large-scale applications. In fact, the broader question looms: which greedy algorithms are amenable to MapReduce-style parallelization?

There have been some recent efforts to find efficient algorithms for submodular maximization problems in the parallel setting. For the MAXCOVER problem Chierichetti et al. [13] obtained a MapReduce algorithm that achieves a factor of $1 - 1/e - \epsilon$ by adapting an algorithm for parallel set cover of Berger et al. [6]; the latter was improved recently by Blelloch et al. [7]. Cormode et al. [14] also consider improving the running time of the natural greedy algorithm for large datasets in the sequential setting. For the densest subgraph problem, Bahmani et al. [4] obtained a streaming and MapReduce algorithm by adapting a greedy algorithm of Charikar [10]. Lattanzi et al. [30] considered the vertex cover and maximal matching problems in MapReduce. The recent work Ene et al. [18] adapted the well-known greedy algorithm for the k-center problem and the local search algorithm for the k-median problem to MapReduce. Beyond these, not much is known about maximizing general submodular functions under matroid/knapsack constraints—in particular the possibility of adapting the greedy algorithm—in the MapReduce model.

1.1 Main contributions

We show that a large class of greedy algorithms for non-negative submodular maximization with hereditary constraints can be efficiently realized in MapReduce. (We note that all of our results can be extended to the streaming setting, but defer the complete proofs to a full version of this paper.) We do this by defining an approximately greedy approach that selects a feasible element with benefit at least $1/(1+\epsilon)$ of the maximum benefit. This ϵ-greedy algorithm works almost as well as the standard algorithm for many important problems (Theorem 5), but gives the algorithm designer some flexibility in selecting which element to add to the solution.

We then show how to simulate the ϵ-greedy algorithm in a distributed setting. If Δ is a bound on the maximum increase in the objective any element can offer and k is the size of the optimal solution, then the MapReduce algorithm runs in $O(\frac{1}{\epsilon\delta} \log \Delta)$ rounds when the memory per machine is $O(kn^\delta)$ for any $\delta > 0$. In fact, all

of the algorithms we propose display a smooth tradeoff between the maximum memory per machine and the total number of rounds before the computation finishes. Specifically, when each machine has roughly $O(kn^\delta)$ memory, the computation takes $O(1/\delta)$ rounds. We present a summary of the results in Table 1. Recall that any simulation of PRAM algorithms requires $\Omega(\log n)$ rounds, we improve on this bound whenever the memory per machine is $\omega(k)$.

At the heart of the simulation lies the main technical contribution of this paper. We describe a sampling technique called SAMPLE&PRUNE that is quite powerful for the MapReduce model. The high level idea is to find a candidate solution to the problem on a sample of the input and then use this intermediate solution to repeatedly prune the elements that can no longer materially contribute to the solution. By repeating this step we can quickly home in on a nearly optimal (or in some cases optimal) solution. This *filtering* approach was used previously in [30] for the maximal matching problem, where it was argued that a matching on a sample of edges can be used to drop most of the edges from consideration. Here we abstract and extend the idea and apply to a large class of greedy algorithms. Unlike the maximal matching case, where it is trivial to decide when an element can be discarded (it is adjacent to an already selected edge), this task is far less obvious for other greedy algorithms such as for set cover. We believe that the technique is useful for scaling other algorithms in the MapReduce model and is one of the first *rules of thumb* for this setting.

Improvements on previous work. While we study parallelizations of greedy algorithms and give the first results for general submodular function maximization, for some specific problems, we improve over previous MapReduce algorithms provided that the memory per machine is polynomial. In [13] an $O(\text{poly} \log(n, \Delta))$-round $(1 - 1/e - \epsilon)$-approximate algorithm was given for the MAXCOVER problem. In this work, the approximate greedy algorithm reduces the number of rounds to $O(\log \Delta)$ and achieves the same approximation guarantees. Further, the algorithm for submodular maximization subject to 1-knapsack constraint implies an even faster *constant*-round algorithm that achieves a slightly worse approximation ratio of $1/2 - \epsilon$. For the maximum weighted matching problem previously a $1/8$-approximate constant-round algorithm was known [30]. Knowing that maximum matching can be represented as a 2-system, our algorithm for p-systems implies a constant-round algorithm for the maximum matching problem that achieves an improved approximation of $\frac{1}{3+\epsilon}$.

Organization. We begin in Section 2 by introducing necessary definitions of the problems and the MapReduce model. In Section 3 we introduce the SAMPLE&PRUNE technique and bound its guarantees. Then we apply this technique to simulate a broad class of greedy algorithms in Section 4. In Section 5 we introduce an $O(1)$ round algorithm for maximizing a modular function subject to a matroid constraint. In Section 6 we consider maximizing a submodular function subject to knapsack or matroid constraints. We present an experimental evaluation of our algorithm in Section 8.

2. PRELIMINARIES

Let U be a universe of $n = |U|$ elements, let $f : 2^U \to \mathbb{R}^+$ be a function, and let $\mathcal{I} \subseteq 2^U$ be a given family of feasible solutions. We are interested in solving the following optimization problem:

$$\max\{f(S) \mid S \in \mathcal{I}\}. \tag{1}$$

We will focus on the case when f and $\mathcal{I}$ satisfy some nice structural properties. For simplicity, we use the notation $f'_S(u)$ to denote the incremental value in f of adding u to S, i.e., $f'_S(u) = f(S \cup \{u\}) - f(S)$.

Problem		Approximation	Rounds	Reference
Objective	Constraint			
Modular	1-matroid	1	$O(1/\delta)$	Section 5
Submodular		$1/(2+\epsilon)$	$O(\frac{1}{\epsilon\delta}\log\Delta)$	Section 4
	1-knapsack	$1/2 - \epsilon$		
	d-knapsacks	$\Omega(1/d)$	$O(1/\delta)$	Section 6
	p-system	$\frac{1}{p+1}\lceil 1/\delta\rceil^{-1}$		
		$\frac{1}{p+1+\epsilon}$	$O(\frac{1}{\epsilon\delta}\log\Delta)$	Section 4

Table 1: **A summary of the results. Here, n denotes the total number of elements and Δ, the maximum change of the function under consideration. Our algorithms use $O(n/\mu)$ machines with μ, the memory per machine, $\mu = O(kn^\delta \log n)$, where k is the cardinality of the optimum solution.**

DEFINITION 1 (MODULAR AND SUBMODULAR FUNCTIONS). *A function* $f : 2^U \to \mathbb{R}^+$ *is said to be* submodular *if for every* $S' \subseteq S \subseteq U$ *and* $u \in U \setminus S$, *we have* $f'_{S'}(u) \geq f'_S(u)$; *it is said to be* modular *if* $f'_{S'}(u) = f'_S(u)$.

A function f is said to be *monotone* if $S' \subseteq S \implies f(S) \geq f(S')$. A family $\mathcal{I}$ is *hereditary* if it is downward closed, i.e., $A \in \mathcal{I} \wedge B \subseteq A \implies B \in \mathcal{I}$. The greedy simulation framework we introduce will only be restricted to submodular functions for a hereditary feasible family. We now define more specific types on constraints on the feasible family.

DEFINITION 2 (MATROID). *The pair* $\mathcal{M} = (U, \mathcal{I})$ *is a matroid if* $\mathcal{I}$ *is hereditary and satisfies the following* augmentation property: $\forall A, B \in \mathcal{I}, |A| < |B| \implies \exists u \in B \setminus A$ *such that* $A \cup \{u\} \in \mathcal{I}$.

Given a matroid $(U, \mathcal{I})$, a set $A \subseteq U$ is called *independent* if and only if $A \in \mathcal{I}$. Throughout the paper, we will often use the terms feasible and independent interchangeably, even for more general families $\mathcal{I}$ of feasible solutions. The *rank* of a matroid is the number of elements in a maximal independent set.

We next recall the notion of p-systems, which is a generalization of intersection of p matroids (e.g., see [8, 26, 29]). Given $U' \subseteq U$ and a hereditary family $\mathcal{I}$, the maximal independent sets of $\mathcal{I}$ contained in U' are given by $\mathcal{B}(U') = \{A \in \mathcal{I} \mid A \subseteq U' \wedge \nexists A' \in \mathcal{I}, A \subsetneq A' \subseteq U'\}$.

DEFINITION 3 (p-SYSTEM). *The pair* $\mathcal{P} = (U, \mathcal{I})$ *is a* p-system *if* $\mathcal{I}$ *is hereditary and for all* $U' \subseteq U$, *we have* $\max_{A \in \mathcal{B}(U')} |A| \leq p \cdot \min_{A \in \mathcal{B}(U')} |A|$.

Given $\mathcal{F} = (U, \mathcal{I})$, where $\mathcal{I}$ is hereditary, we will use the notation $\mathcal{F}[X]$, for $X \subseteq U$, to denote the pair $(X, \mathcal{I}[X])$, where $\mathcal{I}[X]$ is the restriction of $\mathcal{I}$ to the sets over elements in X. We observe that if $\mathcal{F}$ is a matroid (resp., p-system), then we have that $\mathcal{F}[X]$ is a matroid (resp., p-system) as well.

2.1 Greedy algorithms

A natural way to solve (1) is to use the following sequential *greedy* algorithm: start with an empty set S and grow S by iteratively adding the element $u \in U$ such that greedily maximizes the benefit:

$$u = \arg\max_{\substack{u' \in U \\ S \cup \{u'\} \in \mathcal{I}}} f'_S(u').$$

It is known that this greedy algorithm obtains a $(1 - 1/e)$ approximation for the maximum coverage problem, a $(1/p)$-approximation for maximizing a modular function subject to p-system constraints [26] and a $(1/(p+1))$-approximation for maximizing a submodular function [8, 20]. Recently, for $p = 1$, Calinescu et al. [8] obtained

a $(1 - 1/e)$-approximation algorithm for maximizing a submodular function; this result generalizes the maximum coverage result.

We now define an approximate greedy algorithm, which is a modification of the standard greedy algorithm. Let $0 \leq \epsilon \leq 1$ be a fixed constant.

DEFINITION 4 (ϵ-GREEDY ALGORITHM). *Repeatedly, add an element* u *to the current solution* S *such that* $S \cup \{u\} \in \mathcal{I}$ *and*

$$f'_S(u) \geq \frac{1}{1+\epsilon}\left(\max_{\substack{u' \in U \\ S \cup \{u'\} \in \mathcal{I}}} f'_S(u')\right), \text{ with ties broken in an}$$

arbitrary but consistent way.

The usefulness of this definition is evident from the following.

THEOREM 5. *The ϵ-greedy algorithm achieves a: (i) $\frac{1}{2+\epsilon}$ approximation for maximizing a submodular function subject to a matroid constraint; (ii) $\frac{1-1/e}{1+\epsilon}$ approximation for maximizing a submodular function subject to choosing at most k elements; and (iii) $\frac{1}{p+1+\epsilon}$ (resp., $\frac{1}{p+\epsilon}$) approximation for maximizing submodular (modular) function subject to a p-system.*

The proof follows by definition and from the analysis of Calinescu et al. [8]. Finally, without loss of generality, we assume that for every $S \subseteq U$ and $u \in U$ such that $f'_S(u) \neq 0$, we have $1 \leq f'_S(u) \leq \Delta$, i.e., Δ represents the "spread" of the non-zero incremental values.

2.2 MapReduce

We describe a high level overview of the MapReduce computational model; for more details see [16, 18, 27, 30]. In this setting all of the data is represented by $\langle \text{key}; \text{value} \rangle$ pairs. For each pair, the key can be seen as the logical address of the machine that contains the value, with pairs sharing the same key being stored on the same machine.

The computation itself proceeds in rounds, which each round consisting of a *map*, *shuffle*, and *reduce* phases. Semantically, the map and shuffle phases distribute the data, and the reduce phase performs the computation. In the map phase, the algorithm designer specifies the desired location of each value by potentially changing its key. The system then routes all of the values with the same key to the same machine in the shuffle phase. The algorithm designer specifies a reduce function that takes as input all $\langle \text{key}; \text{value} \rangle$ pairs with the same key and outputs either the final solution or a set of $\langle \text{key}; \text{value} \rangle$ pairs to be mapped in a subsequent MapReduce round.

Karloff et al. [27] introduced a formal model, designed to capture the real world restrictions of MapReduce as faithfully as possible. Specifically, their model insists that the total number of machines available for a computation of size n is at most $n^{1-\epsilon}$, with each machine having $n^{1-\epsilon}$ amount of memory, for some constant $\epsilon > 0$. The overall goal is to reduce the number of rounds necessary for the computation to complete. Later refinements on the model [18, 30, 34] allow for a specific tradeoff between the memory per machine the number of machines and the total number of rounds.

The MapReduce model of computation is incomparable to the traditional PRAM model where an algorithm can use a polynomial number of processors that share an unlimited amount of memory. The authors of [27] have shown how to simulate T-step EREW PRAM algorithms in $O(T)$ rounds of MapReduce. This result has subsequently been extended by [22] to CRCW algorithms with an additional overhead of $\log_\mu M$, where μ is the memory per machine and M is the aggregate memory used by the PRAM algorithm. We note that only a few special cases of the problems we consider have efficient PRAM algorithms and, the MapReduce simulation of these cases requires at least logarithmic factor larger running time than our algorithms.

3. SAMPLE&PRUNE

In this section we describe a primitive that will be used in our algorithms to progressively reduce the size of the input. A similar *filtering* method was used in [30] for maximal matchings and in [18] for clustering. Our contribution is to abstract this method and significantly expand the scope of its applications.

At a high level, the idea is to identify a large subset of the data that can be safely discarded without changing the value of the optimum solution. As a concrete example, consider the MAXCOVER problem. We are given a universe of elements U, and a family of subsets $\mathcal{S}$. Given an integer k, the goal is to choose at most k subsets from $\mathcal{S}$ such that the largest number of elements are covered. Say that the sets in U are $S_1 = \{a, b, c\}, S_2 = \{a\}, S_3 = \{a, c\}$, and $S_4 = \{b, d\}$. If S_1 has been selected as part of the solution, then both S_2 and S_3 are redundant and can be clearly removed thus reducing the problem size. We refer to S_1 above as a *seed* solution. We show for a large family of optimization functions that a seed solution computed on a *sample* of all of the elements can be used to reduce the problem size by a factor proportional to the size of the sample.

Formally, consider a universe U and a function $\mathcal{G}_k$ such that for $A \subseteq U$, the function $\mathcal{G}_k(A)$ returns a subset of A of size at most k and $\mathcal{G}_k(A) \subseteq \mathcal{G}_k(B)$, for $A \subseteq B$. The algorithm SAMPLE&PRUNE begins by running $\mathcal{G}_k$ on a sample of the data to obtain a seed solution S. It then examines every element $u \in U$ and removes it if it appears to be redundant under $\mathcal{G}_k$ given S.

SAMPLE&PRUNE$(U, \mathcal{G}_k, \ell)$
1: $X \leftarrow$ sample each point in U with probability $\min\{1, \frac{\ell}{|U|}\}$
2: $S \leftarrow \mathcal{G}_k(X)$
3: $M_S \leftarrow \{u \in U \setminus S \mid u \in \mathcal{G}_k(S \cup \{u\})\}$
4: **return** (S, M_S)

The algorithm is sequential, but can be easily implemented in the MapReduce setting, since both lines (1) and (3) are trivially parallelizable. Further, the set X at line (2) has size at most $O(\ell \log n)$ with high probability. Therefore, for any $\ell > 0$ the algorithm can be implemented in two rounds of MapReduce using $O(n/\mu)$ machines each with $\mu = O(\ell \log n)$ memory.

Finally, we show that the number $|M_S|$ of non-redundant elements is smaller than $|U|$ by a factor of ℓ/k. Thus, a repeated call to SAMPLE&PRUNE terminates after $O(\log_{\ell/k} n)$ iterations, as shown in Corollary 7.

LEMMA 6. *After one round of* SAMPLE&PRUNE *with* $\ell = kn^\delta \log n$, *we have* $\Pr\left[|M_S| \le 2n^{1-\delta}\right] \ge 1 - 2n^{-k}$ *when* $\mathcal{G}_k(A)$ *is a function that returns a subset of* A *of size at most* k *and* $\mathcal{G}_k(A) \subseteq \mathcal{G}_k(B)$, *for* $A \subseteq B$.

PROOF. First, observe that when $n \le \ell$, we have $M_S = \emptyset$ and hence we are done. Therefore, assume $n > \ell$. Call the set S obtained in step 2 a *seed* set. Fix a set S and let $\mathcal{E}_S$ be the event that S was selected as the seed set. Note that when $\mathcal{E}_S$ happens, by the hereditary property of $\mathcal{G}_k$, none of the elements in M_S is part of the sample X, since any element $x \in X$ discarded in step 2 would be discarded in step 3 as well. Therefore, for each S such that $|M_S| \ge m = (2k/\ell)n \log n$, we have $\Pr[\mathcal{E}_S] \le \left(1 - \frac{\ell}{n}\right)^{|M_S|} \le \left(1 - \frac{\ell}{n}\right)^m \le n^{-2k}$.

Since each seed set S has at most k elements, there are at most $2n^k$ such sets, and hence $\sum_{S:|M_S| \ge m} n^{-2k} \le 2n^k \cdot n^{-2k} = 2n^{-k}$ □

COROLLARY 7. *Suppose we run* SAMPLE&PRUNE *repeatedly for* T *rounds, that is: for* $1 \le i \le T$, *let* $(S_i, M_i) =$ SAMPLE&PRUNE$(M_{i-1}, \mathcal{G}_k, \ell)$, *where* $M_0 = U$. *If* $\ell = kn^\delta \log n$ *and* $T > 1/\delta$, *then we have* $M_T = \emptyset$, *with probability at least* $1 - 2Tn^{-k}$.

PROOF. By Lemma 6, assuming that $M_i \le n(2n^{-\delta})^i$ we can prove that $M_{i+1} \le n\left(2n^\delta\right)^{i+1}$ with probability at least $1 - 2n^{-k}$. The claim follows from a union bound. □

We now illustrate how Corollary 7 generalizes some prior results [18, 30]. Note that the choice of the function $\mathcal{G}_k$ affects both the running time and the approximate ratio of the algorithm. Since Corollary 7 guarantees convergence, the algorithm designer can focus on judiciously selecting a $\mathcal{G}_k$ that offers approximation guarantees for the problem at hand. For finding maximal matchings, Lattanzi et al. [30] set $\mathcal{G}_k(X, S)$ to be the maximal matching obtained by streaming all of the edges in X, given that the edges in S have already been selected. Setting $k = n/2$, as at most k edges can ever be in a maximum matching, and the initial edge size to m, we see that using nm^δ memory, the algorithm converges after $O(\frac{1}{\delta})$ rounds. For clustering, Ene et al. [18] first compute the value v of the distance of the (roughly) n^δth furthest point in X to a predetermined set S and the function $\mathcal{G}_k(X, S)$ returns all of the points that have distance to S further than v. Since $\mathcal{G}_k$ returns at most $k = n^\delta$ points, using $n^{2\delta}$ memory, the algorithm converges after $O(\frac{1}{\delta})$ rounds.

In addition to these two examples, we will show below how to use the power of SAMPLE&PRUNE to parallelize a large class of greedy algorithms.

4. GREEDY ALGORITHMS

In this section we consider a generic submodular maximization problem with hereditary constraints. We first introduce a simple scaling approach that simulates the ϵ-greedy algorithm. The scaling algorithm proceeds in phases: in phase $i \in \{1, \dots, \log_{1+\epsilon} \Delta\}$, only the elements that improve the current solution by an amount in $\left[\frac{\Delta}{(1+\epsilon)^{i+1}}, \frac{\Delta}{(1+\epsilon)^i}\right)$ are considered (recall that no element can improve the solution by more than Δ). These elements are added one at a time to the solution as the algorithm scans the input. We will show that the algorithm terminates after $O(\frac{\log \Delta}{\epsilon})$ iterations, and effectively simulates the ϵ-greedy algorithm. We note that somewhat similar scaling ideas have proven to be useful for submodular problems such as in [5, 24]. We first describe the sequential algorithm (GREEDYSCALING) and then show how it can be parallelized.

```
GREEDYSCALING
1: S ← ∅
2: for i = 1, . . . , log_{1+ε} Δ do
3:     for all u ∈ U do
4:         if S ∪ {u} ∈ 𝓘 and f'_S(u) ≥ Δ/(1+ε)^i then
5:             S ← S ∪ {u}
6:         end if
7:     end for
8: end for
```

LEMMA 8. *For the submodular maximization problem with hereditary constraints,* GREEDYSCALING *implements the ε-greedy method.*

PROOF. Given the current solution, call an element u *feasible* if $S \cup \{u\} \in 𝓘$. We use induction to prove the following claim: at the beginning of phase i, the marginal benefit of any feasible element is at most $\frac{\Delta}{(1+\epsilon)^{i-1}}$. The base case is clear. Suppose the claim is true at the beginning of phase j. At the end of this phase, no feasible element with a marginal benefit of more than $\frac{\Delta}{(1+\epsilon)^j}$ to the solution remains. By the hereditary property of $𝓘$, the set of feasible elements at the end of the phase is a subset of feasible elements at the beginning and, by submodularity of f, the marginal benefit of any element could only have decreased during the phase. Therefore, the marginal benefit of any element added by GREEDYSCALING is within $(1+\epsilon)$ of that of the best element, completing the proof. □

For realizing in MapReduce, we use SAMPLE&PRUNE in every phase of the outer **for** loop to find all elements with high marginal values. Recall that SAMPLE&PRUNE takes a function $\mathcal{G}_k : 2^U \to U^k$ as input, and returns a pair of sets (S, M). Note that k is a bound on the solution size. We will show how to define $\mathcal{G}_k$ in each phase so that we can emulate the behavior of the scaling algorithm. Our goal is to ensure that every element not returned by SAMPLE&PRUNE was rightfully discarded and does not need to be considered in this round.

Let $\tau_i = \frac{\Delta}{(1+\epsilon)^i}$ be the threshold used in the ith round. Let $\mathcal{G}_{S,i} : 2^U \to U^k$ be the function implemented in lines (3) through (7) of GREEDYSCALING during the ith iteration of the outer loop. In other words, the function $\mathcal{G}_{S,i}(A)$ maintains a solution S', and for every element $a \in A$ adds it to the solution if $f'_{S \cup S'}(a) \geq \tau_i$ (the marginal gain is above the threshold), and $S \cup S' \cup \{a\} \in 𝓘$ (the resulting solution is feasible). Note that the procedure of $\mathcal{G}_{S,i}$ can change in each iteration of the loop since S can change and $\mathcal{G}_{S,i}$ may return a set of size less than k, but never larger than k. Consider the algorithm GREEDYSCALINGMR that repeatedly calls SAMPLE&PRUNE while adding the sampled elements into the solution set.

```
GREEDYSCALINGMR(Phase i)
1: S ← ∅, M ← U
2: while M ≠ ∅ do
3:     (S', M) ← SAMPLE&PRUNE(M, 𝒢_{S,i}, ℓ)
4:     S ← S ∪ S'
5: end while
6: return S
```

Observe that every element added to S has a marginal value of at least τ_i by definition of $\mathcal{G}_{S,i}$. We show the converse below.

LEMMA 9. *Let S be the result of the ith phase of* GREEDYSCALINGMR *on U. For any element $u \notin S$ either $S \cup \{u\} \notin 𝓘$ or $f'_S(u) \leq \tau_i$.*

PROOF. Suppose not, and consider the iteration of the algorithm immediately before u is removed from M. We have sets S, M with $u \in M$, but $u \notin S' \cup M$ after an additional iteration of SAMPLE&PRUNE. If u were removed, then $u \notin \mathcal{G}_{S,i}(S' \cup \{u\})$ and therefore the addition of S' to the solution either resulted in u being infeasible (i.e., $S \cup S' \cup \{u\} \notin 𝓘$) or its marginal benefit becoming inadequate (i.e., $f'_{S \cup S'}(u) \leq \tau_i$). Since the constraints are hereditary, once u becomes infeasible it stays infeasible, and the marginal benefit of u can only decrease. Therefore, at the end of the iteration, either $S \cup \{u\} \notin 𝓘$ or $f'_S(u) \leq \tau_i$, a contradiction. □

The following is then immediate given Lemma 9, Corollary 7, and that SAMPLE&PRUNE can be realized in two rounds of MapReduce.

THEOREM 10. *For any hereditary family $𝓘$ and submodular function f,* GREEDYSCALING *emulates the ε-greedy algorithm on $(U, f, 𝓘)$ and can be realized in $O(\frac{1}{\epsilon\delta} \log \Delta)$ rounds of MapReduce using $O(n/\mu \log n)$ machines with $\mu = O(kn^\delta \log n)$ memory, with high probability.*

To put the above statement in perspective, consider the classical greedy algorithm for the maximum k-coverage problem. If the largest set covers $\Delta = O(\text{poly} \log n)$ elements, then by setting $\ell = \sqrt{n}$ and $k = O(\text{poly} \log n)$, we obtain an $1 - 1/e - \epsilon$ approximate algorithm that uses $O(\sqrt{n})$ machines each with $\sqrt{n} \log n$ memory in $O(\frac{\log \log n}{\epsilon})$ rounds, improving on the comparable PRAM algorithms [6, 7]. Further, in [13] an $O(\text{poly} \log(n, \Delta))$ round MapReduce algorithm for the maximum k-coverage problem was given and our algorithm achieves the same guarantees while reducing the number of rounds to be $O(\log \Delta)$ when δ and ϵ are constants.

5. MODULAR MAXIMIZATION WITH A MATROID CONSTRAINT

In this section we consider the problem of finding the maximum weight independent set of a matroid $\mathcal{M} = (U, 𝓘)$ of rank k with respect to a modular function $f : U \to \mathbf{R}^+$. We assume that k is given as input to the algorithm. Note that when the function is modular, it is sufficient to define the function only on the elements, as the value of a solution S is $\sum_{u \in S} f(u)$. It is a well-known fact that the greedy procedure that adds the maximum weight feasible element at each step solves the problem optimally. Indeed, the set obtained at the end of the ith step is an independent set that is maximum among those of size i. Henceforth, we will assume that f is injective; note that this is without loss of generality, as we can make f injective by applying small perturbations to the values of f. We observe that when the weights are distinct, the greedy algorithm has only one optimal choice at each step.

The following claim directly follows by the greedy property.

FACT 11. *Let $\mathcal{M} = (U, 𝓘)$ be a matroid of rank k and $f : U \to \mathbf{R}^+$ be an injective weight function. Let $S^* = \{s_1^*, \ldots, s_k^*\}$, where $f(s_1^*) > \cdots > f(s_k^*)$ is the greedy solution. Then, for every $1 \leq i < k$ and any $u \in U \setminus \{s_1^*, \ldots, s_{i+1}^*\}$, we have that either $\{s_1^*, \ldots, s_i^*, u\} \notin 𝓘$ or $f(u) < f(s_{i+1}^*)$.*

Our analysis will revolve around the following technical result, which imposes additional structure on the greedy solution. Fix a function f and consider a matroid, $\mathcal{M} = (U, 𝓘)$. Let S be the greedy solution under f and consider an element $u \in S$. For any $X \subseteq U$ it is the case that u is in the greedy solution for $\mathcal{M}[X \cup \{u\}]$ under f. In other words, no element u in the (optimal) greedy solution can be blocked by other elements in a submatroid. This property of the greedy algorithm is known in the literature and, we give a proof here for completeness.

LEMMA 12. *Let $\mathcal{M} = (U, \mathcal{I})$ be a matroid of rank k and $f : U \to \mathbf{R}^+$ be an injective weight function. For any $X \subseteq U$, let $\mathcal{G}(X)$ be the greedy solution for $\mathcal{M}[X]$ under f. Then, for any $X \subseteq U$ and $u \in \mathcal{G}(U)$, it holds that $u \in \mathcal{G}(\mathcal{G}(X) \cup \{u\})$.*

PROOF. Let $u \in \mathcal{G}(U)$ and let X be any subset of U such that $u \in X$. Let A contain an element $u' \in U$ such that $f(u') > f(u)$ and let $A' = A \cap X$. We define $r(S)$ to be the rank of the matroid $M[S]$ for any $S \subseteq U$ and let $r(S, u') = r(S \cup \{u\}) - r(S)$ for any $u' \in U$. It can be easily verified that $r(S)$ is a submodular function. Notice that $r(A, u) = 1$ because u is in $\mathcal{G}(U)$. Knowing that r is submodular and $A' \subseteq A$ we have that $r(A', u) \geq r(A, u) = 1$. Thus, it must be the case that $u \in \mathcal{G}(X \cup \{u\})$ □

To find the maximum weight independent set in MapReduce we again turn to the SAMPLE&PRUNE procedure. As in the case of the greedy scaling solution, our goal will be to cull the elements not in the global greedy solution, based on the greedy solution for the sub-matroid induced by a set of sampled elements. Intuitively, Lemma 12 guarantees that no optimal element will be removed during this procedure.

MATROIDMR$(U, \mathcal{I}, f, \ell)$
1: $S \leftarrow \emptyset, M \leftarrow U$
2: **while** $M \neq \emptyset$ **do**
3: $\quad (S, M) \leftarrow$ SAMPLE&PRUNE$(S \cup M, \mathcal{G}, \ell)$
4: **end while**
5: **return** S

Algorithm MATROIDMR contains the formal description. Given the matroid $\mathcal{M} = (U, \mathcal{I})$, the weight function f, and a memory parameter ℓ, the algorithm repeatedly (a) computes the greedy solution S on a submatroid obtained from $\mathcal{M}$ by restricting it to a small sample of elements that includes the solution computed in the previous iteration and (b) prunes away all the elements that cannot individually improve the newly computed solution S. We remark that, unlike in the algorithm for the greedy framework of Section 4, the procedure $\mathcal{G}$ passed to SAMPLE&PRUNE is invariant throughout the course of the whole algorithm and corresponds to the classical greedy algorithm for matroids. Note that $\mathcal{G}$ always returns a solution of size at most k, as no feasible set has size more than the rank.

The correctness of the algorithm again follows from the fact that no element in the global greedy solution is ever removed from consideration.

LEMMA 13. *Upon termination, the algorithm* MATROIDMR *returns the optimal greedy solution S^*.*

PROOF. It is enough to show inductively that after each call of SAMPLE&PRUNE, we have $S^* \subseteq S \cup M$. Indeed, this implies that after each call, the greedy solution of $S \cup M$ is exactly S^*. Let $s^* \in S^* \subseteq S \cup M$, and suppose by contradiction that after a call of SAMPLE&PRUNE$(S \cup M, \mathcal{G}, \ell)$, we have $s^* \notin S' \cup M'$, where (S', M') is the new pair returned by the call. By definition of SAMPLE&PRUNE and $\mathcal{G}$, it must be that s^* was pruned since it was not a part of the greedy solution on $S' \cup \{s^*\}$. But then Lemma 12 guarantees that s^* is not part of the greedy solution of $S \cup M$. By induction, $s^* \notin S^*$, a contradiction. □

For the running time of the algorithm, we bound the number of iterations of the **while** loop using a slight variant of Corollary 7. The reason Corollary 7 is not directly applicable is that S is added to M after each iteration of the while loop in MATROIDMR.

LEMMA 14. *Let $\ell = kn^\delta \log n$. Then, the* **while** *loop of the algorithm* MATROIDMR *is executed at most $T = 1 + 1/\delta$ times, with probability at least $1 - 2Tn^{-k}$.*

PROOF. Let (S_i, M_i) be the pair returned by SAMPLE&PRUNE in the ith iteration of the **while** loop, where $S_0 = \emptyset$ and $M_0 = U$. Also, let $n_i = |S_i \cup M_i|$ and $\gamma = n^{-\delta}$. Note that $n_0 = |U| = n$. We want to show that the sequence of n_i decreases rapidly. Assuming $n_i \leq \gamma^i n + k(1 + \gamma + \cdots + \gamma^{i-1})$, Lemma 6 implies that, with probability at least $1 - 2n^{-k}$,

$$n_{i+1} \leq |M_i| + |S_i| \leq \gamma n_i + |S_i| \leq \gamma n_i + r \leq \gamma^{i+1} n + k \sum_{j=0}^{i} \gamma^j.$$

Therefore, for every $i \geq 1$, we have $n_i \leq \gamma^i n + k \frac{1-\gamma^i}{1-\gamma} < \gamma^i n + \frac{k}{1-\gamma^i}$, with probability at least $1 - 2in^{-k}$. For $i = T - 1 = \frac{1}{\delta}$, we have $n_{T-1} \leq \frac{k}{1-\gamma}$. Therefore, at iteration T, SAMPLE&PRUNE will sample with probability one all elements in $S_{T-1} \cup M_{T-1}$, and hence $S_T = \mathcal{G}(S_{T-1} \cup M_{T-1})$. By Lemma 13, $S_T = S^*$ and therefore $M_T = \emptyset$. □

Given that SAMPLE&PRUNE is realizable in MapReduce the following is immediate from Lemma 14.

COROLLARY 15. MATROIDMR *can be implemented to run in $O(1/\delta)$ MapReduce rounds using $O(n/\mu \log n)$ machines with $\mu = O(kn^\delta \log n)$ memory with high probability.*

6. MONOTONE SUBMODULAR MAXIMIZATION

In this section we consider the problem of maximizing a monotone submodular function under a cardinality constraint, knapsack constraints and p-system constraints. We first consider the special case of a single cardinality constraint, i.e., 1-knapsack constraint with unit weights. In this case, we provide a $(1/2 - \epsilon)$-approximation using a simple threshold argument. Then, we observe that the same ideas can be applied to achieve a $(1/d)$-approximation for d knapsack constraints. This is essentially the best achievable as Dean et al. [15] show a $(1/d^{(1-\epsilon)})$-hardness.

6.1 Cardinality constraint

We consider maximizing a submodular function subject to a cardinality constraint. The general techniques have the same flavor as the greedy algorithm described in Section 4. At a high level, we observe that for these problems a *single* threshold setting leads to an approximate solution and hence we do not need to iterate over the $\log_{1+\epsilon} \Delta$ thresholds. We will show the following theorem.

THEOREM 16. *For the problem of maximizing a submodular function under a k-cardinality constraint, there is a MapReduce algorithm that produces a $(\frac{1}{2} - \epsilon)$-approximation in $O(\frac{1}{\delta})$ rounds using $O(n/\mu \log n)$ machines with $\mu = O(kn^\delta \log n)$ memory, with high probability.*

Given a monotone submodular function f and an integer $k \geq 1$, we would like to find a set $S \subset U$ of size at most k that maximizes f. We show how to achieve a $1/2 - \epsilon$ approximation in a constant number of MapReduce rounds. Also our techniques will lead to a one-pass streaming algorithms that use $\tilde{O}(k)$ space. Details of the streaming algorithm are omitted in this version of the paper. The analysis is based on the following lemma.

LEMMA 17. *Fix any $\gamma > 0$. Let* OPT *be the value of an optimal solution S^* and $\tau =$ OPT $\cdot \frac{\gamma}{2k}$. Consider any $S = \{s_1, \ldots, s_t\} \subseteq U, |S| = t \leq k$, with the following properties.*

(i) There exists an ordering of elements $s_1, \ldots, s_t$ such that for all $0 \le i < t$, $f'_{\{s_1,\ldots,s_i\}}(s_{i+1}) \ge \tau$.

(ii) If $t < k$, then $f'_S(u) \le \tau$, for all $u \in U$.

Then, $f(S) \ge \text{OPT} \cdot \min\left\{\frac{\gamma}{2}, 1 - \frac{\gamma}{2}\right\}$.

PROOF. If $t = k$, then $f(S) = \sum_{i=0}^{k-1} f'_{S_i}(s_{i+1}) \ge \sum_{i=0}^{k-1} \tau = k\tau = \text{OPT}\gamma/2$. If $t < k$, we know that $f'_S(u^*) \le \tau$, for any element $u^* \in S^*$. Furthermore, since f is submodular, $f(S \cup S^*) - f(S) \le \tau \cdot |S^* \setminus S| \le \gamma\text{OPT}/2$. We have $f(S) \ge f(S \cup (S^* \setminus S)) - \frac{\gamma\text{OPT}}{2} \ge \text{OPT} - \frac{\gamma\text{OPT}}{2} = \left(1 - \frac{\gamma}{2}\right)\text{OPT}$, where the third step follows from the monotonicity of f. $\square$

We now show how to adapt the algorithm to MapReduce. We will again make use of the SAMPLE&PRUNE procedure. As in the case of the greedy scaling solution, our goal will be to prune the elements with marginal gain below τ with respect to a current solution S. Moreover, only elements with marginal gain above τ will be added to S, so that Lemma 17 can be applied.

The algorithm THRESHOLDMR shares similar ideas with the MapReduce algorithm for greedy framework. In particular, the procedure $\mathcal{G}_{S,\tau,k}$ passed to SAMPLE&PRUNE changes throughout different calls, and is defined as follows: $\mathcal{G}_{S,\tau,k}(X)$ maintains a solution S' and for every element $u \in X$ adds it to the solution S' if $f'_{S \cup S'}(u) \ge \tau$ (the marginal gain is above the threshold) and $|S \cup S'| < k$ (the solution is feasible). The output of $\mathcal{G}_{S,\tau,k}(X)$ is the resulting set $S \cup S'$.

Algorithm 1 THRESHOLDMR(U, f, k, τ, ℓ)

1: $S \leftarrow \emptyset$, $M \leftarrow U$
2: **while** $M \ne \emptyset$ **do**
3: $\quad (S', M) \leftarrow$ SAMPLE&PRUNE$(M, \mathcal{G}_{S,\tau,k}, \ell)$
4: $\quad S \leftarrow S \cup S'$
5: **end while**
6: **return** S

Observe that all of the elements that were added to S had their marginal value at least τ by definition of $\mathcal{G}_{S,\tau,k}$. The following claim guarantees the applicability of Lemma 17. The proof is substantially a replica of that of Lemma 9 and is omitted.

LEMMA 18. *Let S be the solution returned by the algorithm* THRESHOLD. *Then, either $|S| = k$, or $f'_S(u) \le \tau$, for all $u \in U$.*

Finally, observe that an upper bound on Δ (and therefore on OPT) can be computed in one MapReduce round. Hence, we can easily run the algorithm in parallel on different thresholds τ. This observation along with Lemma 18, Corollary 7 and the fact that SAMPLE&PRUNE can be implemented in two rounds of MapReduce, yield the following corollary.

COROLLARY 19. THRESHOLD *produces* $\left(\frac{1}{2} - \epsilon\right)$-*approximation and can be implemented to run in $O(\frac{1}{\delta})$ rounds using $O(n \log n/\mu)$ machines with $\mu = O(kn^\delta \log n)$ memory with high probability.*

6.2 Knapsack constraints

For the case of d knapsack constraints we are given a submodular function f and would like to find a set $S \subseteq U$ of maximum value with respect to f with the property that its characteristic vector $\mathbf{x}_S$ satisfies $C\mathbf{x}_S \le \mathbf{b}$. Here, $C_{i,j}$ is the "weight" of the element u_j with respect to the ith knapsack, and b_i is the capacity of the ith knapsack, for $1 \le i \le d$. Our goal is to show the following theorem. Let k be a given upper bound on the size of the smallest optimal solution.

Algorithm 2 THRESHOLDSTREAM(f, k, τ)

1: $S \leftarrow \emptyset$
2: **for all** $u \in U$ **do**
3: $\quad$ **if** $|S| < k$ and $f'_S(u) \ge \tau$ **then**
4: $\quad\quad S \leftarrow S \cup \{u\}$
5: $\quad$ **end if**
6: **end for**
7: **return** S

THEOREM 20. *For the problem of maximizing a submodular function under d knapsack constraints, there exists a MapReduce algorithm that produces a $\Omega(1/d)$-approximation in $O(\frac{1}{\delta})$ rounds using $O(n/\mu \log n)$ machines with $\mu = O(kn^\delta \log n)$ memory with high probability.*

Without loss of generality, we will assume that there is no element that individually violates a knapsack constraint, i.e., there is no u_j such that $c_{i,j} > b_i$, for every $1 \le i \le d$. We begin by providing an analog of Lemma 17.

LEMMA 21. *Fix any $\gamma > 0$. Let OPT be the value of an optimal solution S^* and $\tau_i = \frac{\gamma\text{OPT}}{2b_i d}$, for $1 \le i \le d$. Consider any feasible solution $S \subseteq U$ with the following properties:*

(i) There exists an ordering of its elements $a_{j_1}, \ldots, a_{j_t}$ such that for all $0 \le m < t$ and $1 \le i \le d$, it holds that $f'_{S_m}(a_{j_{m+1}}) \ge \tau_i c_{i,j_{m+1}}$, where $S_m = \{a_{j_1}, \ldots, a_{j_m}\}$.

(ii) Assuming that for all $1 \le i \le d$, $\sum_{m=1}^t c_{i,j_m} \le \frac{b_i}{2}$, then for all $a_j \in U$ there exists an index $1 \le h(j) \le d$ such that $f'_S(a_j) \le \tau_{h(j)} c_{h(j),j}$.

Then, $f(S) \ge \text{OPT} \cdot \min\left\{\frac{\gamma}{4(d+1)}, 1 - \frac{\gamma}{2}\right\}$.

PROOF. Consider first the case that the solution S fills at least half of a knapsack, i.e., for some $1 \le i \le d$, $\sum_{m=1}^t c_{i,j_m} \ge \frac{b_i}{2}$; since each element $a_{j_m} \in S$ added a marginal value of at least $\tau_i c_{i,j_m}$, we have $f(S) \ge \tau_i \sum_{m=1}^t c_{i,j_m} = \frac{\gamma\text{OPT}}{4d}$.

Now assume that the solution S does not fill half of any knapsack. Then, using (ii), define S_i^* to be the set of elements $a_j \in S^* \setminus S$ such that $h(j) = i$, for $1 \le i \le d$. Because of the knapsack constraints, submodularity, and the fact that $f'_S(a_j) \le \tau_{h(j)} c_{h(j),j}$, we must have that $f(S \cup S_i^*) - f(S) \le \frac{\gamma\text{OPT}}{2d}$, for every $1 \le i \le d$. Therefore, we have $f(S \cup (S^* \setminus S)) - f(S) \le \frac{\gamma\text{OPT}}{2}$. Therefore, by monotonicity of f, we have $f(S) \ge f(S^*) - \frac{\gamma\text{OPT}}{2} = (1 - \frac{\gamma}{2})\text{OPT}$. $\square$

Now we show how the algorithm can be implemented in MapReduce. We assume the algorithm is given an estimate γOPT to compute all τ_i's for some γ and an upper bound k on the size of the smallest optimal solution. The algorithm will simulate the presence of an extra knapsack constraint stating that no more than k elements can be picked. (Note that the value of the optimum value for this new system is not changed, as S^* is feasible in this new system.)

We say that an element $a_j \in U$ is *heavy profitable* if $c_{i,j} \ge \frac{b_i}{2}$ and $f(\{a_j\}) \ge \tau_i c_{i,j}$ for some i. The algorithm works as follows: if there exists a heavy profitable element (which can be detected in a single MapReduce round), the algorithm returns it as solution. Otherwise, the algorithm is identical to THRESHOLD, except for the procedure $\mathcal{G}_{S,\tau,k}$ which is now defined as follows: $\mathcal{G}_{S,\tau,k}(X)$ maintains a solution S' and for every element $a_j \in X$ adds it to S' if, for all $1 \le i \le d$, $f'_{S \cup S'}(a_j) \ge \tau_i c_{i,j}$, and $S \cup S' \cup \{a_j\}$ is feasible w.r.t. the knapsack constraints; the output of $\mathcal{G}_{S,\tau,k}(X)$ is the resulting set $S \cup S'$.

We now analyze the quality of the solution returned by the algorithm. In the presence of a heavy profitable element, then the returned solution has value at least $\frac{\gamma \text{OPT}}{4d}$. Otherwise, we argue that S satisfies the properties of Lemma 17: the first property is satisfied trivially by definition of the algorithm and the second property is valid by submodularity and the fact that there is no heavy profitable element.

Similarly to the algorithm THRESHOLD, we can run the algorithm in parallel on different values of the estimate γOPT. We can conclude the following.

THEOREM 22. *There exists a MapReduce algorithm that produces a $\Omega(1/d)$ approximation in $O(\frac{1}{\delta})$ rounds using $O(n \log n/\mu)$ machines with $\mu = O(kn^\delta \log n)$ memory with high probability.*

6.3 p-system constraints

Finally, consider the problem of maximizing a monotone submodular function subject to a p-system constraint. This generalizes the question of maximizing a monotone submodular function subject to p matroid constraints. Although one could try to extend the threshold algorithm for submodular functions to this setting, simple examples show that the algorithm can result in a solution whose value is arbitrarily smaller than the optimal due to the p-system constraint. The algorithms in this section are more closely related to the algorithm for the modular matroid; however, in this case, we will need to store all of the intermediate solutions returned by SAMPLE&PRUNE and choose the one with the largest value. Our goal is to show the following theorem.

THEOREM 23. SUBMODULAR-p-SYSTEM *can be implemented to run in $O(\frac{1}{\delta})$ rounds of MapReduce using $O(n/\mu \log n)$ machines with memory $\mu = O(kn^\delta \log n)$ with high probability, and produces a $\left(\frac{1}{p+1}\lceil\frac{1}{\delta}\rceil^{-1}\right)$-approximation.*

The algorithm SUBMODULAR-p-SYSTEM is similar to the algorithm for the modular matroid as the procedure $\mathcal{G}$ passed to SAMPLE&PRUNE is simply the greedy algorithm. However, unlike MATROIDMR, all intermediate solutions are kept and the largest one is chosen as final solution. The following lemma provides a bound on the quality of the returned solution.

LEMMA 24. *If T is the number of iterations of the **while** loop in SUBMODULAR-p-SYSTEM, then SUBMODULAR-p-SYSTEM gives a $\frac{1}{(1+p)T}$-approximation.*

PROOF. Let R_i be the elements of U that are removed during the ith iteration of the **while** loop of SUBMODULAR-p-SYSTEM. Let O denote the optimal solution and $O_i := O \cap R_i$. Let S_i be the set returned by SAMPLE&PRUNE during the ith iteration. Note that the algorithm $\mathcal{G}$ used in SUBMODULAR-p-SYSTEM is known to be a $1/(p+1)$-approximation for maximizing a monotone submodular function subject to a p-system if the input to $\mathcal{G}$ is the entire universe [8].

Let $\mathcal{I}_i$ denote the p-system induced on only the elements in $R_i \cup S_i$. Note that by definition of p-systems $\mathcal{I}_i$ exists. By definition of $\mathcal{G}$ and SAMPLE&PRUNE, an element e is in the set R_i because the algorithm $\mathcal{G}$ with input $\mathcal{I}_i$ and f returns S_i and $e \notin S_i$. This is because for each element $e \in R_i$, SAMPLE&PRUNE runs the algorithm $\mathcal{G}$ on the set $(S_i \cup \{e\})$ and e was not chosen to be in the solution. Thus if we run $\mathcal{G}$ on $S \cup R_i$ still no element in R_i will be chosen to be in the output solution. Therefore, $f(S_i) \geq \frac{1}{p+1} f(O_i)$ since $\mathcal{G}$ is a $1/(p+1)$ approximation algorithm for the

instance consisting of $\mathcal{I}_i$ and f. By submodularity we have that $\sum_{i=1}^{t} f(S_i) \geq \frac{1}{p+1} \sum_{i=1}^{t} f(O_i) \geq \frac{1}{p+1} f(O)$. Since there are only T such sets S_i if we return the set $\arg\max_{S \in \mathcal{F}} f(S)$ then this must give a $\frac{1}{(1+p)T}$-approximation. Further, by definition of $\mathcal{G}$, we know that for all i the set S_i is in $\mathcal{I}$, so the set returned must be a feasible solution. $\square$

Algorithm 3 SUBMODULAR-p-SYSTEM$(U, \mathcal{I}, k, f, \ell)$

1: For $X \subseteq U$, let $\mathcal{G}(X, k)$ be the greedy procedure running on the subset X of elements: that is, start with $A := \emptyset$, and greedily add to A the element $a \in X \setminus A$, with $A \cup \{a\} \in \mathcal{I}$, maximizing $f(A \cup \{a\}) - f(A)$. The output of $\mathcal{G}(X, k)$ is the resulting set A.
2: $\mathcal{F} = \emptyset$
3: **while** $U \neq \emptyset$ **do**
4: $\quad (S, M_S) \leftarrow$ SAMPLE&PRUNE$(U, \mathcal{G}, \ell)$
5: $\quad \mathcal{F} \leftarrow \mathcal{F} \cup \{S\}$
6: $\quad U \leftarrow M_S$
7: **end while**
8: **return** $\arg\max_{S \in \mathcal{F}} f(S)$

---

7. ADAPTATION TO STREAMING

In this section we discuss how the algorithms given in this paper extend to the streaming setting. In the data stream model (cf. [32]), we assume that the elements of U arrive in an arbitrary order, with both f and membership in $\mathcal{I}$ available via oracle accesses. The algorithm makes one or more passes over the input and has a limited amount of memory. The goal in this setting is to minimize the number of passes over the input and to use as little memory as possible.

ϵ-**greedy.** We can realize each phase of GREEDYSCALING with a pass over the input in which an element is added to the current solution if the marginal value of adding the element is above the threshold for the phase. If k is the desired solution size, the algorithm will require $O(k)$ space and will terminate after $O(\frac{\log \Delta}{\epsilon})$ phases. The approximation guarantees are given in Theorem 5. For the case of modular function maximization subject to a p-system constraint, the approximation ratio achieved by GREEDYSCALING is $\frac{1}{p+\epsilon}$; we show that the approximation ratio achieved in the streaming setting cannot be improved without drastically increasing either the memory or the number of passes. The proof is omitted from this version of the paper.

THEOREM 25. *Fix any $p \geq 2$ and $\epsilon > 0$. Then any ℓ-pass streaming algorithm achieving a $\frac{1}{p-\epsilon}$ approximation for maximizing a modular function subject to a p-system constraint requires $\Omega(n/(\ell p^2 \log p))$ space.*

Matroid optimization. Lemma 12 leads to a very simple algorithm in the streaming setting. The algorithm keeps an independent set and, when a new element comes, updates it by running the greedy algorithm on the current solution and the new element. Observe that the algorithm uses only $k + 1$ space. Lemma 12 implies that no element in the global greedy solution will be discarded when examined. Therefore, we have:

THEOREM 26. *Algorithm MATROIDSTREAM finds an optimal solution in a single pass using $k + 1$ memory.*

Submodular maximization. The algorithms and analysis for these settings are omitted from this version of the paper.

THEOREM 27. *There exists a one-pass streaming algorithm that uses $O(k/\epsilon \log(n\Delta))$ (resp. $O(k\log(n\Delta))$ memory and produces a $\frac{1}{2} - \epsilon$ (resp. $(1/d)$) approximation for the problem of maximizing a submodular function subject to a k-cardinality constraint (resp. d knapsack constraints).*

THEOREM 28. *There exists a streaming algorithm that uses $O(kn^\delta \log n)$ memory and produces a $\frac{1}{p+1}\lceil \frac{1}{\delta}\rceil^{-1}$ approximation in $O(\frac{1}{\delta})$ passes, where k is the size of the largest independent set.*

8. EXPERIMENTS

In this section we describe the experimental results for our algorithm outlined in section 4 for the MAXCOVER problem. Recall the MAXCOVER problem: given a family S of subsets and a budget k, pick at most k elements from S to maximize the size of their union. The standard (sequential) greedy algorithm gives a $(1-1/e)$-approximation to this problem. We measure the performance of our algorithm, focusing on two aspects: the quality of approximation with respect to the greedy algorithm and the number of rounds; note that the latter is k for the straightforward implementation of the greedy algorithm. On real-world datasets, our algorithms perform on par with the greedy algorithm in terms of approximation, while obtaining significant savings in the number of rounds.

For our experiments, we use two publicly available datasets from `http://fimi.ua.ac.be/data/`: ACCIDENTS and KOSARAK. For ACCIDENTS, $|S| = 340, 183$ and for KOSARAK, $|S| = 990, 002$.

Figure 1 shows the performance of our algorithm for $\epsilon = \delta = 0.5$ for various values of k, on these two datasets. It is easy to see that the approximation factor is essentially same as that of Greedy once k grows beyond 40 and we obtain a significant factor savings in the number of rounds (more than an order of magnitude savings for KOSARAK.)

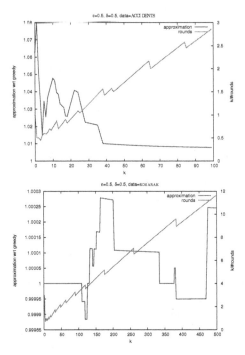

Figure 1: Approximation and number of rounds with respect to Greedy for KOSARAK **and** ACCIDENTS **datasets as a function of** k.

The first pane of Figure 2 shows the role of ϵ (Theorem 5). Even for large values of ϵ, our algorithm performs almost on par with greedy in terms of approximation (note the scale on the y-axis), while the number of rounds is significantly less. Though Theorem 5 only provides a weak guarantee of $(1 - 1/e)/(1 + \epsilon)$, these results show that one can use $\epsilon \gg 1$ in practice without sacrificing much in approximation, while gaining significantly in the number of rounds.

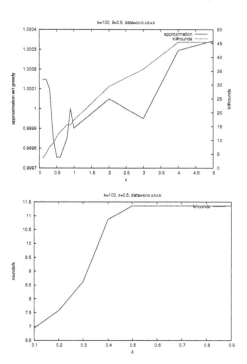

Figure 2: Approximation and number of rounds with respect to Greedy for KOSARAK **datasets as a function of** ϵ **and** δ.

Finally, the lower pane of Figure 2 shows the role of δ on the number of rounds. Smaller values of δ require more iterations of SAMPLE&PRUNE to achieve the memory requirement, thus requiring a larger number of rounds overall. However even for $\delta = 1/2$, with memory requirement only $k\sqrt{n}\log n$, is already enough to achieve the best possible speedup. Once again, a higher value of δ results in a larger savings in the number of rounds. The approximation factor is unchanged.

9. CONCLUSIONS

In this paper we presented algorithms for large-scale submodular optimization problems in the MapReduce and streaming models. We showed how to realize the classical and inherently sequential greedy algorithm in these models and allow algorithms to select more than one element at a time in parallel without sacrificing the quality of the solution. We validated our algorithms on real world datasets for the maximum coverage problem and showed that they yield an order of magnitude improvement in reducing the number of rounds, while producing solutions of the same quality. Our work opens up the possibility of solving submodular optimization problems at web-scale.

Many interesting questions remain. Not all greedy algorithms fall under the framework presented in this paper. For example the augmenting-paths algorithm for maximum flow, or the celebrated Gale-Shapley matching algorithm cannot be phrased as submodular function optimization. Giving efficient MapReduce or streaming algorithms for those problems is an interesting open question.

More generally, understanding what classes of algorithms can and cannot be efficiently implemented in the MapReduce setting is a challenging open problem.

Acknowledgments. We thank Chandra Chekuri for helpful discussions and pointers to relevant work. We thank Sariel Har-Peled for advice on the presentation of this paper.

10. REFERENCES

[1] R. Agrawal, S. Gollapudi, A. Halverson, and S. Ieong. Diversifying search results. In *WSDM*, pages 5–14, 2009.

[2] A. Arasu, S. Chaudhuri, and R. Kaushik. Learning string transformations from examples. *PVLDB*, 2(1):514–525, 2009.

[3] M. Babaioff, N. Immorlica, and R. Kleinberg. Matroids, secretary problems, and online mechanisms. In *SODA*, pages 434–443, 2007.

[4] B. Bahmani, R. Kumar, and S. Vassilvitskii. Densest subgraph in streaming and MapReduce. *PVLDB*, 5(1), 2012.

[5] M. Bateni, M. Hajiaghayi, and M. Zadimoghaddam. Submodular secretary problem and extensions. In *APPROX-RANDOM*, 2010.

[6] Berger, Rompel, and Shor. Efficient NC algorithms for set cover with applications to learning and geometry. *JCSS*, 49:454–477, 1994.

[7] G. E. Blelloch, R. Peng, and K. Tangwongsan. Linear-work greedy parallel approximate set cover and variants. In *SPAA*, pages 23–32, 2011.

[8] G. Calinescu, C. Chekuri, M. Pal, and J. Vondrak. Maximizing a submodular set function subject to a matroid constraint. *SICOMP*, To appear.

[9] G. Capannini, F. M. Nardini, R. Perego, and F. Silvestri. Efficient diversification of web search results. *PVLDB*, 4(7):451–459, 2011.

[10] M. Charikar. Greedy approximation algorithms for finding dense components in a graph. In *APPROX*, pages 84–95, 2000.

[11] W. Chen, C. Wang, and Y. Wang. Scalable inﬄuence maximization for prevalent viral marketing in large-scale social networks. In *KDD*, pages 1029–1038, 2010.

[12] W. Chen, Y. Wang, and S. Yang. Efficient influence maximization in social networks. In *KDD*, pages 199–âĂŞ208, 2009.

[13] F. Chierichetti, R. Kumar, and A. Tomkins. Max-cover in Map-reduce. In *WWW*, pages 231–240, 2010.

[14] G. Cormode, H. J. Karloff, and A. Wirth. Set cover algorithms for very large datasets. In *CIKM*, pages 479–488, 2010.

[15] B. C. Dean, M. X. Goemans, and J. Vondrák. Adaptivity and approximation for stochastic packing problems. In *SODA*, pages 395–404, 2005.

[16] J. Dean and S. Ghemawat. MapReduce: Simplified data processing on large clusters. In *OSDI*, page 10, 2004.

[17] J. Edmonds. Matroids and the greedy algorithm. *Mathematical Programming*, 1:126–136, 1971.

[18] A. Ene, S. Im, and B. Moseley. Fast clustering using MapReduce. In *KDD*, pages 85–94, 2011.

[19] U. Feige. A threshold of ln n for approximating set cover. *JACM*, 45(4):634–652, 1998.

[20] M. L. Fisher, G. L. Nemhauser, and L. A. Wolsey. An analysis of approximation for maximizing submodular set functions II. *Math. Prog. Study*, 8:73–87, 1978.

[21] A. Goel, S. Guha, and K. Munagala. Asking the right questions: model-driven optimization using probes. In *PODS*, pages 203–212, 2006.

[22] M. T. Goodrich, N. Sitchinava, and Q. Zhang. Sorting, searching, and simulation in the MapReduce framework. In *ISAAC*, pages 374–383, 2011.

[23] A. Goyal, F. Bonchi, and L. V. S. Lakshmana. A data-based approach to social influence maximization. *PVLDB*, 5(1), 2012.

[24] A. Gupta, A. Roth, G. Schoenebeck, and K. Talwar. Constrained non-monotone submodular maximization: Offline and secretary algorithms. In *WINE*, pages 246–257, 2010.

[25] E. Hazan, S. Safra, and O. Schwartz. On the complexity of approximating k-set packing. *Computational Complexity*, 15(1):20–39, 2006.

[26] T. A. Jenkyns. The efficacy of the "greedy" algorithm. In *Proceedings of 7th South Eastern Conference on Combinatorics, Graph Theory and Computing*, pages 341–350, 1976.

[27] H. J. Karloff, S. Suri, and S. Vassilvitskii. A model of computation for MapReduce. In *SODA*, pages 938–948, 2010.

[28] D. Kempe, J. M. Kleinberg, and É. Tardos. Maximizing the spread of influence through a social network. In *KDD*, pages 137–146, 2003.

[29] B. Korte and D. Hausmann. An analysis of the greedy heuristic for independence systems. *Annals of Discrete Math.*, 2:65–74, 1978.

[30] S. Lattanzi, B. Moseley, S. Suri, and S. Vassilvitskii. Filtering: a method for solving graph problems in MapReduce. In *SPAA*, pages 85–94, 2011.

[31] J. Leskovec, A. Krause, C. Guestrin, C. Faloutsos, J. VanBriesen, and N. Glance. Cost-effective outbreak detection in networks. In *KDD*, pages 420–429, 2007.

[32] S. Muthukrishnan. Data streams: Algorithms and applications. *Foundations and Trends in Theoretical Computer Science*, 1(2), 2005.

[33] G. L. Nemhauser, L. A. Wolsey, and M. L. Fisher. An analysis of approximation for maximizing submodular set functions I. *Math. Prog.*, 14:265–294, 1978.

[34] A. Pietracaprina, G. Pucci, M. Riondato, F. Silvestri, and E. Upfal. Space-round tradeoffs for mapreduce computations. *CoRR*, abs/1111.2228, 2011.

[35] B. Saha and L. Getoor. On maximum coverage in the streaming model & application to multi-topic blog-watch. In *SDM*, pages 697–708, 2009.

[36] A. D. Sarma, A. Lall, D. Nanongkai, R. J. Lipton, and J. J. Xu. Representative skylines using threshold-based preference distributions. In *ICDE*, pages 387–398, 2011.

[37] L. G. Valiant. A bridging model for parallel computation. *Commun. ACM*, 33(8):103–111, 1990.

[38] J. Vondrak. *Submodularity in Combinatorial Optimization*. PhD thesis, Charles University, Prague, 2007.

Reduced Hardware Transactions: A New Approach to Hybrid Transactional Memory

Alexander Matveev
Tel-Aviv University
matveeva@post.tau.ac.il

Nir Shavit
MIT and Tel-Aviv University
shanir@csail.mit.edu

ABSTRACT

For many years, the accepted wisdom has been that the key to adoption of best-effort hardware transactions is to guarantee progress by combining them with an all software slow-path, to be taken if the hardware transactions fail repeatedly. However, all known generally applicable hybrid transactional memory solutions suffer from a major drawback: the coordination with the software slow-path introduces an unacceptably high instrumentation overhead into the hardware transactions.

This paper overcomes the problem using a new approach which we call *reduced hardware* (RH) transactions. Instead of an all-software slow path, in RH transactions part of the slow-path is executed using a smaller hardware transaction. The purpose of this hardware component is not to speed up the slow-path (though this is a side effect). Rather, using it we are able to eliminate almost all of the instrumentation from the common hardware fast-path, making it virtually as fast as a pure hardware transaction. Moreover, the "mostly software" slow-path is obstruction-free (no locks), allows execution of long transactions and protected instructions that may typically cause hardware transactions to fail, allows complete concurrency between hardware and software transactions, and uses the shorter hardware transactions only to commit.

Finally, we show how to easily default to a mode allowing an all-software slow-slow mode in case the "mostly software" slow-path fails to commit.

Categories and Subject Descriptors

D.4.1 [**Process Management**]: Concurrency, Synchronization, Multiprocessing, Threads

Keywords

Multicore Software, Hybrid Transactional Memory, Obstruction-freedom

1. INTRODUCTION

IBM and Intel have recently announced hardware support for best-effort hardware transactional memory (HTM) in upcoming processors [16, 17]. Best-effort HTMs impose limits on hardware transactions, but eliminate the overheads associated with loads and stores in software transactional memory (STM) implementations. Because it is possible for HTM transactions to fail for various reasons, a hybrid transactional memory (HyTM) approach has been studied extensively in the literature. It supports a best effort attempt to execute transactions in hardware, yet always falls back to slower all-software transactions in order to provide better progress guarantees and the ability to execute various systems calls and protected instructions that are not allowed in hardware transactions.

The first HyTM [7, 10] algorithms supported concurrent execution of hardware and software transactions by instrumenting the hardware transactions' shared reads and writes to check for changes in the STM's metadata. This approach, which is the basis of all the generally applicable HyTM proposals, imposes severe overheads on the hardware transaction – the HyTM's frequently executed *fast-path*.

Riegel et al. [13] provide an excellent survey of HyTM algorithms to date, and the various proposals on how to reduce the instrumentation overheads in the hardware fast-path. There are three key proposed approaches, each with its own limitations.

The first is Phased TM [11], in which transactions are executed in phases, each of which is either all hardware or all software. Phased TM performs well when all hardware transactions are successful, but has poor performance if even a single transaction needs to be executed in software, because it must switch all transactions to a slower all-software mode of execution. Though this is a good approach for some workloads, in general it is not clear how to overcome frequent switches between phases.

The second approach, Hybrid Norec [5], is a hybrid version of the efficient Norec STM [6]. In it, write transactions' commits are executed sequentially and a global clock is used to notify concurrent read transactions about the updates to memory. The write commits trigger the necessary revalidations and aborts of the concurrently executing transactions. The great benefit the Norec HyTM scheme over classic HyTM proposals is that no metadata per memory location is required and instrumentation costs are reduced significantly. However, as with the original Norec STM, scalability is limited because the conflicts cannot be detected at a sufficiently low granularity.

The third approach, by Riegel et al. [13], effectively reduces the instrumentation overhead of hardware transactions in HyTM algorithms based on both the LSA [15] and Norec [6] STMs. It does so by using non-speculative operations inside the hardware transactions. Unfortunately, these operations are supported by AMD's proposed ASF transactional hardware [4] but are not supported in the best-effort HTMs that IBM and Intel are bringing to the marketplace.

1.1 The Big "If" in Hybrid Transactional Memory

What will the cost of the instrumentation of the hardware transactions in HyTM be in upcoming hardware?

Unfortunately, access to such processors is not available yet. Thus, in an attempt to answer the question, we conducted a number of "emulation" benchmarks on todays Intel processors. We emulated an idealized HTM execution by running virtual transactions that execute the same sets of instructions but modify the shared data structure in a way that does not affect the logic of the concurrently executing transactions.

For example, to implement an update method of a red-black tree as a transaction, the method searches for a node with a key chosen from a given distribution and writes a dummy value to this node. The dummy value is read by concurrent readers, but it is not logically used for decisions during the tree traversals. In this way, the transactions can run correctly and not crash, and still pay the cache coherence traffic that is associated with the writes. To make this emulation more precise, we also introduce an abort ratio similar to that known from past STM-based benchmarks.

What we found in our emulated benchmarks is that in a traditional HyTM implementation, as opposed to the ideal HTM, the overhead in hardware transactions of loading and conditionally branching on the shared STM meta data, is excessively high. This conforms with findings in prior work that stated that the overhead of traditional HyTM implementations is high [5, 13]. As can be seen from the graph of the red-black tree benchmark in Figure 1, with meta data loading, testing and branching, the performance of an HTM goes from 5-6x faster to being only 2x faster than a TL2 STM [8]. In other words, adding the meta data loads and "if" branches to the HTM transactions eliminates much of the benefits of running in hardware.

Obviously, the results of our benchmarks should be taken with a large grain of salt, in particular because processors with HTM support (such as Intel's Haswell) will most likely have caching and speculation paths that differ from those we used, and yet, we believe our emulations have a chance of proving true, at least qualitatively.

The conclusion to be taken from this data – consistent with the arguments made by others (See [5, 13]) – is that HyTM makes sense only if we can remove the meta-data accesses and conditional branches from as much of the HTM code as possible. As we noted above, existing algorithms that provide this on standard architectures, despite their good performance on some benchmarks, suffer from scalability issues or have overall limited applicability. Thus, the question is if one can devise a broadly applicable HyTM algorithm that will have reduced conditional branching and meta data access along the hardware fast-path, and will thus be scalable.

1.2 Reduced Hardware Transactions

This paper presents a new broadly applicable approach: *reduced hardware* (RH) transactions. RH transactions allow an extensive reduction of the instrumentation overhead of the hardware fast-path transactions on all upcoming architectures, without impairing concurrency among hardware and software transactions, and with various other scalability benefits. We present the RH1 reduced hardware HyTM protocol in the body of this paper, and provide the RH2 protocol in the appendix, to be viewed at the committee's discretion.

As we noted earlier, all known HyTMs have the best-effort hardware fast-path default to a *purely software* slow-path if they fail repeatedly due to hardware constraints (These constraints can be the result of transactions that are simply too long, or because they call protected or OS related instructions that are simply not allowed in HTM). In an RH transaction protocol, instead of having the hardware fast-path default to a pure software slow-path, it defaults to a "mixed" path that consists mostly of software but also includes a shorter best-effort hardware transaction during the commit. Though others have proposed STMs that have hardware elements [14, 2], unlike them, the goal here is not to improve the slow-path software's performance. Rather, by introducing this shorter hardware transaction into the software slow-path, we are able to remove most of the meta-data accesses and conditional branches from the common hardware fast-path, making it virtually as fast as pure hardware.

Here, in a nutshell, is how the RH1 HyTM protocol works. (We assume familiarity with global-time based STM algorithms such as TL2 [8] or LSA [15]). The RH1 protocol has a multi-level fallback mechanism: for any transaction it first tries a pure hardware fast path; If this fails it tries a new "mixed" slow-path, and if this fails, it tries an all software *slow-slow-path*.

On the slow-path, RH1 runs a global-time based STM transaction (such as TL2 [8] or TinySTM [12]) in which each memory location has an associated time-stamp that will be updated when written. The transaction body is executed purely in software, collecting read and write sets, and postponing the actual data writes to the commit phase. The key new element in RH1, is that the commit phase is executed in a single speculative hardware transaction: the read and write locations are validated based on an earlier read of the global clock, and if successful, the actual writes are applied to memory together with an updating of the time-stamps based on a new read of the global clock. Unlike TL2 or TinySTM, there are no locks (only time-stamps), and the transaction is obstruction-free.

Perhaps surprisingly, this change in the slow-path allows us to completely remove all of the testing and branching in the hardware fast-path for both reads and writes. The hardware fast-path transaction needs only to read the global clock (which is updated only rarely by concurrent slow-path transactions that happen to fail) and use it to update the time-stamps of locations it writes. Intuitively, this suffices because for any slow-path transaction, concurrent hardware transactions will either see all the new values written, or all the old ones, but will fail if they read both new and old versions because this means they overlapped with the slow-path's hardware commit. The writing of the new timestamps on the fast path makes sure to fail inconsistent slow-path transactions.

How likely to fail is the hardware part of the mixed slow-path transaction? Because in the slow-path the transaction body is executed purely in software, any system calls and protected instructions that might have failed the original hardware transaction can now complete in software before the commit point. Moreover, the RH1 slow-path hardware transaction simply validates the time-stamps of each location in the read-set (not the data itself), and writes each location in the write-set. The number of locations it accesses is thus linear in the size of the meta-data accessed, which is typically much smaller than the number of data locations accessed. For example, for the red-black tree, the read-set time-stamp meta-data is 1/4 the size of the locations actually read, and we would thus expect the mixed slow-path to accommodate transactions that are 4x longer than the all-hardware fast-path.

If some slow-path transaction still fails to complete, we show that it is easy to fall back briefly to a slow-slow-path mode, in which concurrent hardware and software both run a more complex protocol that allows software TL2 style transactions. Alternately, once could default first to a mode of running an alternative RH2 protocol which has a shorter hardware transaction on the slow-path rather than a full STM, and manages to avoid instrumenting reads in the fast-path hardware transactions. We note that in our slow-path and slow-slow-path we have not added an implicit privatization mechanism (see for example [1]) which would be necessary in unmanaged environments, and leave this for future work.

In summary, the RH1 protocol allows virtually uninstrumented hardware transactions and mixed hardware-software slow-path transactions that (1) execute the transaction body fully in software (2), significantly extend the length of the transaction, (3) run concurrently with hardware fast-path transactions, and (4) provide obstruction-free progress guarantees. Our emulation results suggest that the RH1 protocol performs as well as pure HTM transactions on a variety of benchmarks including red-black trees, hash-tables, and linked lists, spanning the parallelism and transaction-length range.

2. REDUCED HARDWARE TRANSACTIONS

We begin with an overview of our obstruction-free RH1 hybrid transactional memory protocol.

2.1 RH1 Algorithm Overview

Our algorithm is a variation of the TL2 or LSA-style STM algorithms [8, 15], and we will assume the reader's familiarity with these algorithms. In a similar way to TL2, the shared memory range is divided into logical stripes (partitions), each with an associated metadata entry. The software and hardware transactions communicate by inspecting and updating the metadata entries for the memory locations they read and write. In our hybrid TM every transaction has a pure hardware fast-path implementation, a mostly software slow-path implementation that uses a shorter hardware transaction for its commit protocol, and an all software slow-slow-path in case both of the others fail repeatedly.

Transactions must maintain a consistent snapshot of the locations read during their execution. To this end a global version clock is introduced, used by both fast and slow-path transactions to update local version time-stamps upon writing. Slow-path transactions identify conflicts by reading this shared global version clock on start, and comparing it against the stripe version for every location read. If a location is overwritten after a transaction started, then its timestamp will reflect this causing the transaction to abort, and otherwise the locations read form a consistent snapshot. In TL2 the transaction body is executed collecting a read set and a write set, then validating the time-stamps of all the locations in these sets, and writing the new values with increased time stamps. The TL2 software commit is executed after taking locks on all locations to be updated, but one of the advantages of the scheme here is that we will not need them.

Now, to achieve our goal of making the fast-path hardware transactions execute at hardware speed, we make two observations about a TL2 style Hybrid protocol executed in both hardware and software modes.

The first observation is that if we execute all the commit-time writes of the slow-path in a single hardware transaction, then in order to be consistent the fast-path hardware transaction does not need to do any testing of locations it accesses: it will either see all of them or none of them, since if it sees only part of them then the other transaction must have written concurrently and the hardware transaction will have a cache invalidation and abort.

The second observation is that if we have the hardware transaction update the time-stamps of the locations it writes using the latest value of the global version clock, then it will cause any concurrent software transaction that reads these locations to fail its commit time validation of the timestamps of its read and write sets.

There is one little caveat to this simple approach. The hardware transaction might manage to slip in the middle of the commit and write immediately after a successful validation and before all the updated writes are executed atomically in hardware. Traditionally, as in TL2 or TinySTM, this is prevented by holding locks on the locations to be written. In RH1 we do not wish to use locks since they would have to be updated also in the hardware transaction, introducing an overhead. Instead, the solution is to have the validation and the write-back of the write-set values be part of one hardware transaction. With this change, we are guaranteed that the slow-path is also consistent. (In the appendix we show the RH2 protocol that uses locks, requires only the writes of data to be executed in a single hardware transaction, but introduces the added overhead into the hardware path in order to update the locks.).

2.2 The RH1 Algorithm Details

The global *stripe_version_array* holds the stripe versions (time-stamps). Each thread is associated with a thread local context that includes; *tx_version*, the global version counter value read on transaction start, *read_set*, a buffer of the locations read, and a *write_set*, a buffer of the locations written. All of the versions are 64bit unsigned integers, initialized to 0, and the *read_set* with the *write_set* can be any list implementation.

The global version counter is manipulated by the *GVRead()* and *GVNext()* methods, for reading and "advancing" it, and we use the GV6 [8, 3] implementation that does not modify the global counter on *GVNext()* calls, but only on transactional aborts. This design choice avoids unnecessary aborts

Algorithm 1 RH1 fast-path transaction implementation

```
 1: function RH1_FASTPATH_START(ctx)
 2:    HTM_Start()
 3:    ctx.next_ver ← GVNext()
 4: end function
 5:
 6: function RH1_FASTPATH_WRITE(ctx, addr, value)
              ▷ update write location version
 7:    s_index ← get_stripe_index(addr)
 8:    stripe_version_array[s_index] ← ctx.next_ver
              ▷ write value to memory
 9:    store(addr, value)
```

```
10: end function
11:
12: function RH1_FASTPATH_READ(ctx, addr)
              ▷ no instrumentation - simply read the location
13:    return load(addr)
14: end function
15:
16: function RH1_FASTPATH_COMMIT(ctx)
17:    HTM_Commit()
18: end function
```

Algorithm 2 RH1 slow-path transaction implementation

```
 1: function RH1_SLOWPATH_START(ctx)
 2:    ctx.tx_version ← GVRead()
 3: end function
 4:
 5: function RH1_SLOWPATH_WRITE(ctx, addr, value)
              ▷ add to write-set
 6:    ctx.write_set ← ctx.write_set ∪ {addr, value}
 7: end function
 8:
 9: function RH1_SLOWPATH_READ(ctx, addr)
              ▷ check if the location is in the write-set
10:    if addr ∈ ctx.write_set then
11:       return the value from the write-set
12:    end if
              ▷ log the read
13:    ctx.read_set ← ctx.read_set ∪ {addr}
              ▷ try to read the memory location
14:    s_index ← get_stripe_index(addr)
15:    ver_before ← stripe_version_array[s_index]
16:    value ← load(addr)
17:    ver_after ← stripe_version_array[s_index]
18:    if  ver_before  ≤  ctx.tx_version  and
       ver_before = ver_after then
19:       return value
20:    else
21:       stm_abort(ctx)
22:    end if
23: end function
24:
```

```
25: function RH1_SLOWPATH_COMMIT(ctx)
              ▷ read-only transactions commit immediately
26:    if ctx.write_set is empty then
27:       return
28:    end if
              ▷ a single hardware transaction that performs read-set
       revalidation and write-back
29:    HTM_Start()
              ▷ read-set revalidation
30:    for addr ∈ ctx.read_set do
31:       s_index ← get_stripe_index(addr)
32:       version ← stripe_version_array[s_index]
33:       if version > ctx.tx_version then
34:          HTM_Abort(ctx)
35:       end if
36:    end for
              ▷ perform the actual writes and update the locations'
       versions
37:    next_ver ← GVNext()
38:    for addr, new_value ∈ ctx.write_set do
39:       s_index ← get_stripe_index(addr)
40:       stripe_version_array[s_index] ← next_ver
41:       store(addr, new_value)
42:    end for
43:    HTM_Commit()
44:    if the HTM failed then
45:       fallback to RH2
46:    end if
47: end function
```

---

of the hardware transactions that call for *GVNext()* (speculate on the global clock), in order to install it to the write locations.

Algorithm 1 shows the implementation of the RH1 fast-path transaction. The fast-path starts by initiating a hardware transaction (line 2). It performs the reads without any instrumentation (line 13), and the writes with minimal instrumentation that only updates write location's version on every write (lines 6 - 8). On commit, it simply performs the hardware transaction commit instruction (line 17).

Algorithm 2 shows the implementation of the RH1 slow-path. The slow-path starts by reading the global version to its local *tx_version* variable (line 2). During the execution, the writes are deferred to the commit by buffering them to a local write-set (line 6), and scanning this write-set on every read operation (lines 10-11). If the read location is not found in the local write-set, then it is read directly from the memory, followed by a consistency check (lines 14-18). This check verifies that the read location has not been overwritten since the transaction has started, based on the following invariant:

If the read location has been already updated from the time the current transaction started, then the location's version must be greater than the transaction's version, *tx_version*. The fast-path and slow-path commits ensure this invariant. Finally, the slow-path commit executes a single hardware transaction that first performs the read-set revalidation, and then the write-back, that includes making the actual memory updates and installing of the next global version to the stripe versions of the write locations (lines 29 - 42).

2.3 RH1 Algorithm Limitations - Fallback to RH2 and the all-software slow-slow-path

The RH1 slow-path commit executes a single hardware transaction that performs the read-set revalidation and the write-back. This hardware transaction may fail for various reasons. In the common-case, the failure reason will be contention, and some kind of contention management mechanism can be applied to handle the transactional retries. In more rare situations, the hardware transaction may fail due to some hardware limitation. Note, that this hardware transaction accesses a predefined memory range (the meta-data range), and it performs only simple memory reads and writes. Therefore, on Intel architectures with RTM [17], the most likely reason for a constant failure of this transaction is a capacity overflow of the hardware reads buffer. In other words, the transaction metadata cannot fit in the L1 cache of the processor. To handle these cases, the algorithm performs fallback to RH2 that we describe in Appendix A and Appendix B.

RH2 reduces the HTM requirements of the slow-path transactions by performing only the commit-time write-back in a single hardware transaction (not including the read-set revalidation). The core idea is to introduce locks to the fast-path and the slow-path, and force the slow-path "expose" its read-set for the duration of the slow-path commit.

Still, one might worry about the progress guarantees of RH2, because the slow-path commit-time hardware transaction that performs the write-back atomically may fail. This would mean that the transaction's write-set cannot be accommodated inside the L1 cache of the processor, which is unlikely for real-world transactions. We show that in any case RH2 can easily fallback to a fully pure software slow-path in which it performs an all software commit and the fast-path transactions inspect the metadata for every read and write, in a similar way to the standard hybrid TMs. The switch to fully software RH2 slow-path aborts the current RH2 fast-path transactions and restarts them in the RH2 *fast-path-slow-read* mode. We call this special mode the *all software slow-slow-path*.

3. PERFORMANCE EVALUATION

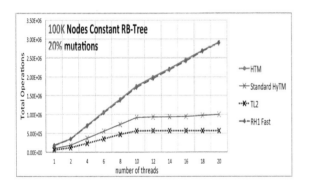

Figure 1: The graphs show the throughput of 100K sized Red-Black Tree for 20% writes. In this test we can see that the standard Hybrid TMs eliminate the benefit that HTMs can achieve, because they instrument the reads and writes of the hardware transactions. In contrast, *RH1* preserves the HTMs benefit by avoiding hardware reads instrumentation.

We evaluate our hybrid TM by constructing a set of special benchmarks that can be executed on current multicore processors, that is, without the (yet unavailable) HTM support. Our results should thus be taken with a grain of salt, and if you will, skeptic minds should treat our quantitative results as being mostly qualitative.

Our idea is to emulate an HTM transaction execution by running its logic and its reads and writes using plain loads

and stores. There is no speculation, and the cache performance is obviously not the same as with an HTM mechanism, but we believe that the transaction with plain reads and writes is close to being a lower-bound on the performance of a real HTM system; we would be surprised if an all-hardware HTM, with its added functionality, can perform better.

The problem with executing non-instrumented transactions is that they cannot detect concurrent conflicts and maintain a consistent snapshot of the locations read. As a result, the non-instrumented transactions may crash and get into deadlocks. To avoid this problem, for every benchmark, we constrain the set of possible executions to the ones that will work correctly, and report the performance results for these specific executions. We try to make these executions as realistic as possible by emulating the expected abort ratio for every number of threads.

3.1 Red-Black Tree Emulation Overview

Our red-black tree implementation, the *Constant Red-Black Tree*, must allow only executions that are correct with non-instrumented transactions that simulate the HTM. We populate the RB-Tree with 100K nodes, and execute concurrent operations that do not modify the structure of the tree. Update operations only modify dummy variables inside the tree's nodes, while the lookups traverse the nodes and read these dummy variables, paying the cache-coherence traffic for their fake updates.

More precisely, we expose a read-only and a write operation: *rb-lookup(key)*, and *rb-update(key, value)*. The *rb-lookup(key)* makes the usual tree traversal, looking for the node with the given key, and making 10 dummy shared reads per node visited. The *rb-update(key, value)* also executes the usual tree traversal to find the node with the given key, and then makes fake modifications. It writes a dummy value to the dummy variable in the node it found and its two children; it does not touch the pointers or the key value. To make the modifications mimic tree rotations, the operation makes the same fake modifications to triplets of nodes, going up from the node it found to the root. The number of nodes climbed up the tree is selected at random, so that getting to the upper levels and the root will happen with diminishing probability, as in a real tree implementation.

We estimate the expected abort ratio for a given execution by first executing with the usual TL2 STM implementation. Then, we force the same abort ratio for the hybrid execution by aborting HTM transactions when they arrive at the commit. Obviously the STM abort ratio is only an estimate of the HTM abort ratio. Real HTM may add more aborts because of the internal hardware implementation limitations, or may reduce the number of aborts because of the reduced transaction execution window (hardware transactions execute faster); making them less vulnerable to conflict. Therefore, the STM abort ratio is probably somewhere in the middle.

3.2 Red-Black Tree Emulation Execution

The benchmark first creates a 100K node red-black tree, and then spawns the threads that execute the *rb-lookup(key)* and *rb-update(key, value)* operations as transactions. We vary the number of threads and the write ratio (the percentage of update transactions).

We execute the benchmarks on Intel 20-way Xeon E7-4870

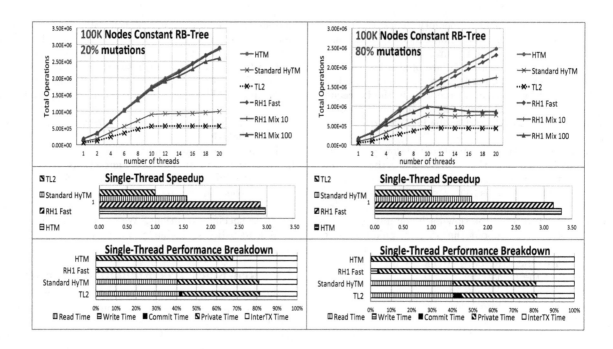

Figure 2: The top graphs show the throughput of 100K sized Red-Black Tree for varying number of writes; 20% and 80%. The middle and the bottom graphs show the single-thread speedup and performance breakdown.

chip with 10 2.40GHz cores, each multiplexing 2 hardware threads (HyperThreading). Each core has a private write-back L1 and L2 caches and the L3 cache is shared.

The algorithms we benchmark are:

HTM *Hardware Transactional Memory without any instrumentation:* all of the transactions are executed without instrumenting the reads and the writes. This represents the best performance that HTM can achieve.

Standard HyTM *The Standard Hybrid Transactional Memory*: This represents the best performance that can be achieved by current state-of-the-art hybrid TMs [13]. To make the hybrid as fast as possible, we execute only the hardware mode implementation, by executing and retrying transactions only in hardware, without any software fallback. We implement the hardware mode transaction with instrumented read and write operations, and make the commit immediate without any work. The hardware transaction reads and writes are minimally instrumented; each read and write accesses the STM metadata and creates a fake "if" condition check on its contents. The "if" condition does not change the execution logic; its only purpose is to show the resulting instrumentation overheads that occur for the standard hybrid TMs.

RH1 Mixed *Reduced Hardware Transactions 1:* Our new hybrid TM with hardware commit in the slow-path and uninstrumented hardware reads. This implementation uses both the all hardware fast-path and the mixed hardware-software slow-path.

RH1 Fast This is the RH1 fast-path only. All of the aborts are retried in hardware mode.

TL2 This is the usual TL2 STM implementation [8], that uses a GV6 global clock.

The standard hybrid TM algorithms instrument the read and write operations of the hardware transaction. In contrast, our new hybrid TM executes the reads with no instrumentation and the writes with an additional write. Therefore, our first benchmark goal is to measure the cost of adding instrumentation to the hardware operations. Figure 1 shows the penalties introduced by instrumenting the reads of the hardware transactions. Since, we are only interested in the hardware instrumentation overhead, this test is not using the RH1 slow-path mode, and retries the hardware transactions in fast-path mode only. The *TL2* and *HTM* graphs show the results for STM and HTM executions respectively. We can see that HTM performs 5-6x better than STM, and by adding instrumentation to the hardware reads in *Standard HyTM*, a dramatic performance penalty is introduced that makes HTM only 2x better than STM. In contrast, *RH1 Fast* with the non-instrumented hardware reads, executes approximately at the same speed as HTM, and preserves the 5x speedup of the HTM.

Figure 2 shows the performance of our *RH1 Mixed* that first tries the fast-path, and on abort, retries the transaction in the slow-path. *RH1 Fast*, *RH1 Mixed 10*, and *RH1 Mixed 100* mean that 0%, 10%, and 100% of the aborted transactions are retried in the slow-path mode respectively. We compare the different variants of the *RH1 Mixed* to the best case *Standard HyTM* that uses only a hardware mode for its aborted transactions. For 20% writes, the *RH1 Mixed* slow-path mode penalty is not significant, because the abort ratio is low (approximately 5%). But for the 80% writes case, where the abort ratio is high (approximately 40%), the software fallback introduces a significant penalty. De-

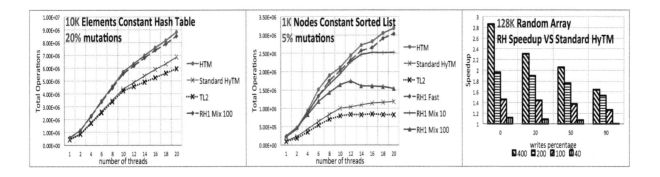

Figure 3: The results for the hash-table, sorted-list, and random-array benchmarks (from left to right).

spite this, *RH1 Mixed 100* performs slightly better than the same *Standard HyTM* for the mix of 80% writes. Recall, that *Standard HyTM* uses only the hardware mode for its execution and retries, but still is slightly slower than *RH1 Mixed 100*.

In order to understand the factors that affect the performance, we measured the single-thread speedups and the single-thread performance breakdowns of the different algorithms involved in Figure 2. The single-thread speedup is normalized to the *TL2* performance. They show the relative time used for the transactional read, write and commit operations, with the time used for the transaction's private code execution (local computations inside the transaction), and the time used for the inter-transactional code (code not inside a transaction). We can see that there is a correlation between the single-thread speedup and the algorithm's overall performance. Also, the single-thread breakdown shows that the read time is the dominating reason for the slowdown of the *Standard HyTM* relative to *RH1*.

3.3 Hash Table Emulation

We implemented a *Constant Hash Table* benchmark using an approach similar to the one we used in the *Constant Red-Black Tree*. The benchmark inserts 1000K distinct elements into the hash table. Then, the benchmark spawns the threads that execute the *hash_query(key)* and the *hash_update(key, val)* operations, where the number of updates is defined by the writes ratio parameter. The *hash_update* makes a query for the given key, and when the node with the key is found, it updates to the dummy variables inside this node, without touching the structure (pointers) of the hash table.

In Figure 3, the left graph shows the hash table results for 20% writes. In contrast to the red-black tree, the hash table transactions are much shorter and introduce less STM overhead relative to the non-transactional code. As a result, for the hash table, *HTM* improves the *TL2* STM performance by approximately 40%, where in the red-black tree it provides a 5x factor improvement. Additionally, the abort ratio is very small (approximately 3%) due to the highly distributed nature of hash table access. Still, the throughput of the *Standard HyTM* remains as low as that of the STM, while the *RH1 Mixed 100* preserves the HTM's advantage over STM.

3.4 Sorted List Emulation

The *Constant Sorted List* benchmark creates a 1K sorted list of distinct elements, and spawns the threads that execute the *list_search(key)* and the *list_update(key, val)* operations. The *list_update* searches for the node with the given key by a linear scan, and then, makes updates to the dummy variables inside this node, without touching the structure of the list.

In Figure 3, the middle graph shows the sorted list results for a mix that includes 5% writes. This benchmark represents a heavy-contended case for the STM. The transactions are long, introducing a significant STM overhead, and are prone to aborts because the *list_search(key)* operation makes a linear scan that implies in a shared list prefix by all currently executing transactions. The abort ratio is approximately 50% for 20 threads. We can see that the *HTM* is 4x faster than the *TL2* STM. As in the previous benchmarks, the *Standard HyTM* eliminates the HTM benefit and improves on the TL2 STM by only 50%, while the *RH1 Fast* preserves the HTM speedup. The introduction of the software mode aborts in *RH1 Mixed 10* and *RH1 Mixed 100* degrades the hybrid performance for high number of threads.

3.5 Random Array Emulation - Measuring the Effect of the Reads/Writes Ratio

The RH1 fast-path executes instrumented writes with non-instrumented reads. A common rule is that in real-world applications with transactions, the ratio of reads to writes is approximately 4 to 1 (20% writes). Still, since in the RH1 fast-path writes are not free, it is interesting to see the effect of increasing their number inside a transaction.

The *Random Array* is a shared array with 128K entries. Transactions simply access random array locations to read and write, without any special additional logic. This setup allows us to control the transaction length and the number of reads and writes inside a transaction. All of the executions have 20 threads.

In Figure 3, the right hand graph shows the speedup that *RH1 Fast* gains over *Standard HyTM* for different transaction lengths (400, 200, 100 and 40 shared accesses) and different write percentages inside a transaction (0%, 20%, 50% and 90% of writes). We can see that for long transactions the speedup decreases as the fraction of writes increases. For short transactions, the speedup change is less significant, because the overall effect of the small transactions on the benchmark is much less than that of the long ones. The interesting result is that even with mixes of 90%

writes, *RH1* with sufficiently long transactions provides a good speedup of 1.3-1.7x relative to the *Standard HyTM*. The reason is the different cache-coherence behavior of the two algorithms. RH1 does not read metadata on hardware reads, and only writes metadata on hardware writes. In contrast, *Standard HyTM* reads and writes the metadata on hardware reads and writes respectively. This introduces significantly more cache traffic between concurrently executing transactions, resulting in a performance degradation.

4. ACKNOWLEDGEMENTS

This work was supported in part by NSF grant CCF-1217921, ISF grant 1386/11, DoE ASCR grant ER26116/DE-SC0008923, and by grants from the Oracle and Intel corporations.

5. REFERENCES

[1] D. Dice A. Matveev and N. Shavit. Implicit privatization using private transactions. In *Transact 2010*, Paris, France, 2010.

[2] Hagit Attiya and Eshcar Hillel. A single-version stm that is multi-versioned permissive. *Theory Comput. Syst.*, 51(4):425–446, 2012.

[3] Hillel Avni and Nir Shavit. Maintaining consistent transactional states without a global clock. In *SIROCCO*, pages 131–140, 2008.

[4] Dave Christie, Jae-Woong Chung, Stephan Diestelhorst, Michael Hohmuth, Martin Pohlack, Christof Fetzer, Martin Nowack, Torvald Riegel, Pascal Felber, Patrick Marlier, and Etienne Rivière. Evaluation of amd's advanced synchronization facility within a complete transactional memory stack. In *Proceedings of the 5th European conference on Computer systems*, pages 27–40, New York, NY, USA, 2010. ACM.

[5] Luke Dalessandro, François Carouge, Sean White, Yossi Lev, Mark Moir, Michael L. Scott, and Michael F. Spear. Hybrid norec: a case study in the effectiveness of best effort hardware transactional memory. *SIGPLAN Not.*, 46(3):39–52, March 2011.

[6] Luke Dalessandro, Michael F. Spear, and Michael L. Scott. Norec: streamlining stm by abolishing ownership records. In *Proceedings of the 15th ACM SIGPLAN Symposium on Principles and Practice of Parallel Programming*, PPoPP '10, pages 67–78, New York, NY, USA, 2010. ACM.

[7] Peter Damron, Alexandra Fedorova, Yossi Lev, Victor Luchangco, Mark Moir, and Daniel Nussbaum. Hybrid transactional memory. *SIGPLAN Not.*, 41(11):336–346, October 2006.

[8] D. Dice, O. Shalev, and N. Shavit. Transactional locking II. In *Proc. of the 20th International Symposium on Distributed Computing (DISC 2006)*, pages 194–208, 2006.

[9] D. Dice and N. Shavit. Tlrw: Return of the read-write lock. In *Transact 2009*, Raleigh, North Carolina, USA, 2009.

[10] Sanjeev Kumar, Michael Chu, Christopher J. Hughes, Partha Kundu, and Anthony Nguyen. Hybrid transactional memory. In *Proceedings of the eleventh ACM SIGPLAN symposium on Principles and practice of parallel programming*, PPoPP '06, pages 209–220, New York, NY, USA, 2006. ACM.

[11] Yossi Lev, Mark Moir, and Dan Nussbaum. Phtm: Phased transactional memory. In *In Workshop on Transactional Computing (Transact), 2007. research.sun.com/scalable/pubs/ TRANSACT2007PhTM.pdf*, 2007.

[12] C. Fetzer P. Felber and T. Riegel. Dynamic performance tuning of word-based software transactional memory. In *PPoPP '08: Proceedings of the 13th ACM SIGPLAN Symposium on Principles and practice of parallel programming*, pages 237–246, New York, NY, USA, 2008. ACM.

[13] Torvald Riegel, Patrick Marlier, Martin Nowack, Pascal Felber, and Christof Fetzer. Optimizing hybrid transactional memory: the importance of nonspeculative operations. In *Proceedings of the 23rd ACM symposium on Parallelism in algorithms and architectures*, SPAA '11, pages 53–64, New York, NY, USA, 2011. ACM.

[14] Arrvindh Shriraman, Virendra J. Marathe, Sandhya Dwarkadas, Michael L. Scott, David Eisenstat, Christopher Heriot, William N. Scherer III, and Michael F. Spear. Hardware acceleration of software transactional memory. Technical report, DEPT. OF COMPUTER SCIENCE, UNIV. OF ROCHESTER, 2006.

[15] P. Felber T. Riegel and C. Fetzer. A lazy snapshot algorithm with eager validation. In *20th International Symposium on Distributed Computing (DISC)*, September 2006.

[16] Amy Wang, Matthew Gaudet, Peng Wu, José Nelson Amaral, Martin Ohmacht, Christopher Barton, Raul Silvera, and Maged Michael. Evaluation of blue gene/q hardware support for transactional memories. In *Proceedings of the 21st international conference on Parallel architectures and compilation techniques*, PACT '12, pages 127–136, New York, NY, USA, 2012. ACM.

[17] Web. Intel tsx http://software.intel.com/en-us/blogs/2012/02/07/transactional-synchronization-in-haswell, 2012.

APPENDIX

A. RH1 FALLBACK TO RH2

In this section we present the RH1 code modifications that implement the fallback to RH2.

RH1 uses a global *is_RH2_fallback* counter variable to perform the switch to the RH2 mode. The RH1 slow-path atomically increments this global counter before executing the fallback RH2 slow-path commit code, and decrements it on fallback finish. As a result, the *is_RH2_fallback* counter indicates the number of currently executing RH2 slow-path transactions, and the RH1 fast-path transactions can use this global counter to decide when to execute the RH2 fast-path transactions. Upon the first *is_RH2_fallback* increment, all currently executing RH1 fast-path transactions must abort and restart in RH2 fast-path mode. For this purpose, the RH1 fast-path monitors this global counter for

Algorithm 3 RH1 fast-path and slow-path modifications for switching to RH2

```
 1: function RH1_FastPath_start(ctx)
 2:    if is_RH2_fallback > 0 then
 3:       RH2_FastPath_start(ctx)
 4:       return
 5:    end if
 6:    HTM_Start()
          ▷ RH1 fast-path monitors the is_RH2_fallback global
       counter to be 0 for the duration of the hardware transaction
 7:    if is_RH2_fallback > 0 then    ▷ speculative load of the
       global value
 8:       HTM_Abort(ctx)
 9:    end if
10: end function
11:
12: function RH1_SlowPath_commit(ctx)
          ▷ read-only transactions commit immediately
13:    if ctx.write_set is empty then
14:       return
15:    end if
          ▷ a single hardware transaction that performs read-set
       revalidation and write-back
16:    HTM_Start()
          ▷ read-set revalidation
17:    for addr ∈ ctx.read_set do
18:       s_index ← get_stripe_index(addr)
19:       version ← stripe_version_array[s_index]
20:       if version > ctx.tx_version then
21:          HTM_Abort(ctx)
22:       end if
23:    end for
          ▷ perform the actual writes and update the locations'
       versions
24:    next_ver ← GVNext()
25:    for addr, new_value ∈ ctx.write_set do
26:       s_index ← get_stripe_index(addr)
27:       stripe_version_array[s_index] ← next_ver
28:       store(addr, new_value)
29:    end for
30:    HTM_Commit()
31:    if the HTM failed then
32:       fetch_and_add(is_RH2_fallback)
33:       RH2_SlowPath_commit(ctx)
34:       fetch_and_dec(is_RH2_fallback)
35:    end if
36: end function
```

the duration of the transaction by speculatively reading this global counter and verifying its value is zero, immediately after the hardware transaction starts. In addition, before the hardware transaction starts, the RH1 fast-path checks this global counter to be greater than 0, and if so, then it executes the RH2 fast-path, else it runs the RH1 fast-path. Algorithm 3 presents the RH1 fast-path and slow-path modifications that support the switching to the RH2 algorithm.

B. RH2 ALGORITHM OVERVIEW

In this section we give a brief overview of the *RH2* hybrid protocol. Our main RH1 protocol falls back to RH2 upon persistent failure of the RH1 slow-path commit-time hardware transaction. RH2 reduces the HTM requirements of the slow-path transactions by performing only the commit-time write-back in a single hardware transaction (not including the read-set revalidation). The core idea is to introduce locks to the fast-path and the slow-path, and force the slow-path "expose" its read-set for the duration of its commit.

Still, one might worry about the progress guarantees of RH2, because the slow-path commit-time hardware transaction that performs the write-back may fail. This would mean that the transaction's write-set cannot be accommodated inside the L1 cache of the processor, yet as we show even in this case, RH2 can easily fallback to a fully pure software slow-path that performs the whole commit in the software, and the fast-path transactions inspect the metadata for every read and write, in a similar way to the standard hybrid TMs. The switch to full software RH2 slow-path aborts the current RH2 fast-path transactions and restarts them in the RH2 *fast-path-slow-read* mode. We call this special mode the *all software slow-slow-path.*

The main difference between RH1 and RH2 is the fact that RH2 uses locks for synchronization between the fast-path and the slow-path. The RH2 slow-path commit locks the write-set, revalidates the read-set, and then executes a small hardware transaction that performs the write-back. The RH2 fast-path writes inspect these locks, while the reads execute without any instrumentation. Now, since the RH2 slow-path is not executing the read-set revalidation inside a hardware transaction, a problematic scenario may occur between the fast-path and the slow-path as follows: a slow-path transaction arrives at the commit, locks its write-set and revalidates its read-set. Now, before the new values are actually written to the memory, a fast-path transaction starts, reads a location that is currently locked, and decides to overwrite a location inside the read-set of this slow-path transaction. Then, the fast-path transaction commits successfully, and the slow-path finalizes the commit using an atomic memory write-back. In this scenario, one of the transactions must abort, yet both commit successfully.

The problem is that the un-instrumented fast-path transaction reads cannot see that a location is currently being locked by a concurrent slow-path transaction. To overcome this race, during the slow-path commit, the transaction makes its read-set visible to the writes of the fast-path transaction. In this way, fast-path transactions cannot write to a read-set of a concurrently committing slow-path transaction.

The read-set visibility is implemented by adding a read mask for every memory stripe. The bits of the read mask are associated with threads: the transaction of thread K makes its read-set visible by setting the K-th bit of every read location's read mask. To set the K-th bit on and off, we use a non-blocking fetch-and-add synchronization primitive. In our implementation, we use a 64bit read mask to represent 64 active threads, and a fetch-and-add atomic primitive to turn the read mask's bits on and off. For larger thread numbers, additional read masks are required. See [9] for a discussion of the scalability of the mask array approach.

A fast-path hardware transaction collects the write-set, and on commit, detects if there is a concurrent slow-path transaction executing. If so, it inspects the read masks of the locations in the write-set before committing. It sums up the total of all mask bits and aborts the transaction if this sum is greater than zero, that is, one of the mask's bits was made non-zero by some concurrent slow-path transaction.

Usually, making an STM's reads visible results in poor

performance, since every STM read is augmented with a write to shared memory. In our implementation the read visibility works differently, because it is applied only during the commit phase of the software write transactions. Any other transactions, hardware or software read-only, are not performing this visibility procedure, and do not pay any additional overhead for their reads. Additionally, we use an efficient fetch-and-add synchronization primitive to update locations' read masks, instead of using a compare-and-swap (CAS) operation that can fail multiple times before turning on the required bit. As a result, our software transactions with a commit-time visible read-set have nearly the same performance as that of state-of-the-art STMs.

C.   RH2 ALGORITHM DETAILS

Here we present the implementation details of RH2 hybrid protocol. Algorithm 4 and Algorithm 5 show the RH2 fast-path and slow-path. Algorithm 6 presents the fast-path-slow-read mode implementation for the pure software slow-path execution, and Algorithm 7 presents slow-path additional helper functions, that implement the locking and visibility mechanisms.

In a similar way to RH1, the memory range is divided into logical stripes (partitions), each with a stripe version and a stripe read mask. Additionally, a global version counter is used to coordinate the transactions, and each thread is associated with a thread local context that includes; $tx\_version$, the global version read on transaction start, $read\_set$, a buffer of the locations read, and a $write\_set$, a buffer of the locations written. All of the versions are 64bit unsigned integers, initialized to 0, and the $read\_set$ and $write\_sets$ can be any list implementation.

The global version counter is manipulated by the $GVRead()$ and $GVNext()$ methods, for reading and "advancing" it, which can be implemented in different ways. We use the GV6 [3, 8] implementation that does not modify the global counter on $GVNext()$ calls, but only on transactional aborts. This design choice avoids unnecessary aborts of the hardware transactions that call $GVNext()$ (speculate on the global clock) in order to install it to the write locations.

The RH2 slow-path commit protocol is based on two basic mechanisms: (1) locking a location, and (2) making the location visible. The location's stripe version lowest order bit is reserved for locking. Transactions lock a location by setting the stripe version to the thread's lock value $ctx.thread\_id *$ $2 + 1$: that turns on the lowest order bit and encodes the thread id into the lock. The visibility of a location is represented by its read mask. Every bit of the read mask is associated with some active thread, so a 64bit read mask can hold information for 64 threads. In our implementation the threads are assigned ids from 0 to 63, and these ids are used to "index" the read masks (more threads require more read masks per stripe). A thread with id K will turn on the K-th bit in the location's read mask to indicate that it's reading it, and will reset this bit to remove this indication. We use the fetch_and_add() synchronization primitive to turn on and off bits in read masks, instead of using a CAS operation that can fail multiple times before actually succeeding (implementation in Algorithm 7).

Algorithm 5 shows the implementation of the RH2 slow-path. The slow-path starts by reading the global version to its local $tx\_version$ variable (line 2). During the execution, the writes are deferred to the commit by buffering them to a local write-set (line 6), and scanning this write-set on every read operation (lines 10-11). If the read location is not found in the local write-set, then it is read directly from the memory, followed by a consistency check (lines 14-18). This check verifies that the read location has not been overwritten since the transaction has started, based on the following invariant: If the read location has been already updated from the time the current transaction started, then the location's version must be greater than the transaction's version, $tx\_version$. The fast-path and slow-path commits ensure this invariant.

Upon RH2 slow-path commit, the write-set locations are locked and the read-set is made visible (lines 29 - 30). Locking is done by setting the location's stripe version to the thread's lock value $ctx.thread\_id * 2 + 1$. This value turns on the lowest order bit, the one reserved for locking, and encodes the thread that locked the location. Location visibility is done by turning on the thread-associated bit in the location's read mask (shown in Algorithm 7). Then, the next global version is generated (line 44), and the read locations are revalidated (line 31), ensuring they have not been overwritten from the transaction's start. After a successful revalidation, the new values are written-back to the memory by using a hardware transaction (line 32 - 43). On a successful write-back, the write locations are unlocked, by updating their versions to the new next global version, and the read locations' visibility is removed, by turning off the thread-associated bit in every read location's read mask.

Now, if the RH2 slow-path commit-time small hardware transaction fails due to contention reasons, then it is retried again. Else, aborts all of the current fast-path transactions and restarts them in the fast-path-slow-read mode, and performs the slow-path write-back in pure software (lines 36 - 42). RH2 implements this switch through a global integer $is\_all\_software\_slow\_path$ variable, that counts the number of slow-paths that currently execute the commit-time write-back in pure software. Current fast-path transactions monitor this global variable to be 0 during their execution (by speculatively loading it), and on its modification (by the slow-path) automatically abort. On fast-path start, the transactions check this global variable, and if its not zero, they switch to the fast-path-slow-read mode.

Algorithm 4 shows the implementation of the RH2 fast-path hardware transaction. The fast-path performs speculative reads and writes, where the writes are augmented with logging the addresses written (line 13) and the reads proceed as is, without any instrumentation. These reads cannot be inconsistent, because, as we said, the slow-path transactions perform the actual memory writes atomically.

Finally, the fast-path commit verifies that the read masks of the write locations are all 0 (lines 25 - 33), before initiating the HTM commit instruction. Additionally, the write locations are speculatively locked (lines 34 - 45), by verifying that they are not locked by others, and by writing the special thread lock-mask value to each one of them. Then the HTM commit instruction is executed, and upon success, the write locations are updated and locked atomically. Finally, it gets the next global version, and installs it to the write location (lines 48 - 52).

Algorithm 4 RH2 fast-path transaction implementation

1: **function** RH2_FASTPATH_START(ctx)
2: **if** $is\_all\_software\_slow\_path > 0$ **then**
3:    RH2_FastPath_SR_start(ctx)
4:    **return**
5: **end if**
6: HTM_Start()
   ▷ Fast-Path monitors the is_all_software_slow_path global counter to be 0 for the duration of the hardware transaction
7: **if** $is\_all\_software\_slow\_path > 0$ **then** ▷ speculative load of the global value
8:    HTM_Abort(ctx)
9: **end if**
10: **end function**
11:
12: **function** RH2_FASTPATH_WRITE($ctx, addr, value$)
    ▷ log the write
13: $ctx.write\_set \leftarrow ctx.write\_set \cup \{addr\}$
    ▷ write value to memory
14: $store(addr, value)$
15: **end function**
16:
17: **function** RH2_FASTPATH_READ($ctx, addr$)
    ▷ no instrumentation - simply read the location
18: **return** $load(addr)$
19: **end function**
20:
21: **function** RH2_FASTPATH_COMMIT(ctx)
    ▷ read-only transactions commit immediately
22: **if** ctx.write_set is empty **then**
23:    **return**
24: **end if**
    ▷ verify the write-set locations are not read by concurrent software transactions
25: $total\_mask \leftarrow 0$
26: **for** $addr \in ctx.write\_set$ **do**

27:    $s\_index \leftarrow get\_stripe\_index(addr)$
28:    $mask\_arr \leftarrow stripe\_read\_mask\_array$
      ▷ ∥ - bitwise OR operation
29:    $total\_mask \leftarrow total\_mask \parallel mask\_arr[s\_index]$
30: **end for**
31: **if** $total\_mask \neq 0$ **then**
32:    HTM_Abort()   ▷ there is a concurrent software reader
33: **end if**
    ▷ put locks on the write-set locations.
34: $lock\_mask \leftarrow (ctx.thread\_id * 2) + 1$
35: **for** $addr \in ctx.write\_set$ **do**
36:    $s\_index \leftarrow get\_stripe\_index(addr)$
37:    $cur\_ver \leftarrow stripe\_version\_array[s\_index]$
38:    **if** is_locked_by_me(ctx, cur_ver) **then**
39:      **continue**
40:    **end if**
41:    **if** is_locked(cur_ver) **then**
42:      HTM_Abort()
43:    **end if**
44:    $stripe\_version\_array[s\_index] \leftarrow lock\_mask$
45: **end for**
46: HTM_Commit()
47: **if** HTM commit successful **then**
      ▷ now the write-set locations are updated and locked - unlock the write-set locations by updating their versions to the next one.
48:    $next\_version \leftarrow GVNext()$
49:    **for** $addr \in ctx.write\_set$ **do**
50:      $s\_index \leftarrow get\_stripe\_index(addr)$
51:      $stripe\_version\_array[s\_index] \leftarrow next\_version$
52:    **end for**
53:    **return**
54: **end if**
55: **end function**

Algorithm 5 RH2 slow-path transaction implementation

1: **function** RH2_SLOWPATH_START(ctx)
2: $ctx.tx\_version \leftarrow GVRead()$
3: **end function**
4:
5: **function** RH2_SLOWPATH_WRITE($ctx, addr, value$)
    ▷ add to write-set
6: $ctx.write\_set \leftarrow ctx.write\_set \cup \{addr, value\}$
7: **end function**
8:
9: **function** RH2_SLOWPATH_READ($ctx, addr$)
    ▷ check if the location is in the write-set
10: **if** $addr \in ctx.write\_set$ **then**
11:   return the value from the write-set
12: **end if**
    ▷ log the read
13: $ctx.read\_set \leftarrow ctx.read\_set \cup \{addr\}$
    ▷ try to read the memory location
14: $s\_index \leftarrow get\_stripe\_index(addr)$
15: $ver\_before \leftarrow stripe\_version\_array[s\_index]$
16: $value \leftarrow load(addr)$
17: $ver\_after \leftarrow stripe\_version\_array[s\_index]$
18: **if** $ver\_before \leq ctx.tx\_version$ and $ver\_before = ver\_after$ **then**
19:   **return** $value$
20: **else**
21:   stm_abort(ctx)
22: **end if**
23: **end function**
24:

25: **function** RH2_SLOWPATH_COMMIT(ctx)
    ▷ read-only transactions commit immediately
26: **if** ctx.write_set is empty **then**
27:   **return**
28: **end if**
    ▷ set locking and visibility
29: lock_write_set(ctx)
30: make_visible_read_set(ctx)
    ▷ commit validation
31: revalidate_read_set(ctx)
    ▷ perform the writes atomically
32: **while** $True$ **do**
33:   HTM_Start()
34:   write the write-set values to memory
35:   HTM_Commit()
36:   **if** the HTM transaction failed due to contention **then**
37:     **continue**   ▷ retry HTM transaction
38:   **else**
39:     fetch_and_add($is\_all\_software\_slow\_path$)
40:     write-back the write-set using regular store instructions.
41:     fetch_and_dec($is\_all\_software\_slow\_path$)
42:   **end if**
43: **end while**
    ▷ reset locking and visibility
44: $next\_version \leftarrow GVNext()$
45: release_locks($addr, next\_version$)
46: reset_visible_read_set(ctx)
47: **end function**

Algorithm 6 RH2 fast-path-slow-read transaction implementation

```
 1: function RH2_FASTPATH_SR_START(ctx)
 2:    ctx.tx_version ← GVRead(ctx, global_version)
 3:    HTM_Start()
 4: end function
 5:
 6: function RH2_FASTPATH_SR_WRITE(ctx, addr, value)
           ▷ log the write
 7:    ctx.write_set ← ctx.write_set ∪ {addr}
           ▷ write value to memory
 8:    store(addr, value)
 9: end function
10:
11: function RH2_FASTPATH_SR_READ(ctx, addr)
           ▷ try to read the memory location
12:    s_index ← get_stripe_index(addr)
13:    version ← stripe_version_array[s_index]
14:    value ← load(addr)
15:    if ¬ is_locked(version) and version ≤ ctx.tx_version
       then
16:       return value
17:    else
18:       HTM_abort(ctx)
19:    end if
20: end function
21:
22: function RH2_FASTPATH_SR_COMMIT(ctx)
           ▷ read-only transactions commit immediately
23:    if ctx.write_set is empty then
24:       HTM_Commit()
25:    end if
           ▷ put locks on the write-set locations.
26:    lock_mask ← (ctx.thread_id ∗ 2) + 1
27:    for addr ∈ ctx.write_set do
28:       s_index ← get_stripe_index(addr)
29:       cur_ver ← stripe_version_array[s_index]
30:       if is_locked_by_me(ctx, cur_ver) then
31:          continue
32:       end if
33:       if is_locked(cur_ver) then
34:          HTM_Abort()
35:       end if
36:       stripe_version_array[s_index] ← lock_mask
37:    end for
38:    HTM_Commit()
39:    if HTM commit successful then
           ▷ now the write-set locations are updated and locked -
       unlock the write-set locations by updating their versions to
       the new one.
40:       next_version ← GVNext()
41:       for addr ∈ ctx.write_set do
42:          s_index ← get_stripe_index(addr)
43:          stripe_version_array[s_index] = next_version
44:       end for
45:       return
46:    end if
47: end function
```

Algorithm 7 RH2 slow-path transactions: additional functions

```
 1: function IS_LOCKED(stripe_version)
 2:    return (stripe_version & 1) = 1   ▷ checks if the low order
       bit is 1
 3: end function
 4:
 5: function IS_LOCKED_BY_ME(ctx, stripe_version)
 6:    lock_mask ← (ctx.thread_id ∗ 2) + 1
 7:    return version = lock_mask
 8: end function
 9:
10: function LOCK_WRITE_SET(ctx)
11:    lock_mask ← (ctx.thread_id ∗ 2) + 1
12:    for addr ∈ ctx.write_set do
13:       s_index ← get_stripe_index(addr)
14:       ver ← stripe_version_array[s_index]
15:       if is_locked_by_me(ctx, ver) then
16:          continue                ▷ to next - already locked
17:       end if
18:       if is_locked(ver) then
19:          stm_abort(ctx)          ▷ someone else locked
20:       end if
21:       if ver ≠ CAS(stripe_version_array[s_index], ver, lock_mask)
       then
22:          stm_abort(ctx)          ▷ someone else locked
23:       end if
24:    end for
25: end function
26:
27: function REVALIDATE_READ_SET(ctx)
28:    for addr ∈ ctx.read_set do
29:       s_index ← get_stripe_index(addr)
30:       version ← stripe_version_array[s_index]
31:       if is_locked_by_me(ctx, version) then
32:          continue
33:       end if
34:       if is_locked(ctx, version) then
35:          stm_abort(ctx)
36:       end if
37:       if version > ctx.tx_version then
38:          stm_abort(ctx)
39:       end if
40:    end for
41: end function
42:
43: function RELEASE_LOCKS(addr, new_version)
44:    for addr ∈ ctx.write_set do
45:       s_index ← get_stripe_index(addr)
46:       stripe_version_array[s_index] ← new_version
47:    end for
48: end function
49:
50: function MAKE_VISIBLE_READ_SET(ctx)
51:    for addr ∈ ctx.read_set do
52:       s_index ← get_stripe_index(addr)
53:       mask_arr ← stripe_read_mask_array
54:       id ← ctx.thread_id
55:       if (mask_arr[s_index] & 2^{id}) = 0 then
           ▷ turn ON the id-th bit of the read mask
56:          fetch_and_add(mask_arr[s_index], 2^{id})
57:       end if
58:    end for
59: end function
60:
61: function RESET_VISIBLE_READ_SET(ctx)
62:    for addr ∈ ctx.read_set do
63:       s_index ← get_stripe_index(addr)
64:       mask_arr ← stripe_read_mask_array
65:       id ← ctx.thread_id
66:       if (mask_arr[s_index] & 2^{id}) ≠ 0 then
           ▷ turn OFF the id-th bit of the read mask
67:          fetch_and_add(mask_arr[s_index], (−2^{id}))
68:       end if
69:    end for
70: end function
```

Recursive Design of Hardware Priority Queues

Yehuda Afek
Tel Aviv University
Tel Aviv, Israel
afek@post.tau.ac.il

Anat Bremler-Barr
The Interdisciplinary Center
Hertzelia, Israel
bremler@idc.ac.il

Liron Schiff[*]
Tel Aviv University
Tel Aviv, Israel
schiffli@post.tau.ac.il

ABSTRACT

A recursive and fast construction of an n elements priority queue from exponentially smaller hardware priority queues and size n RAM is presented. All priority queue implementations to date either require $O(\log n)$ instructions per operation or exponential (with key size) space or expensive special hardware whose cost and latency dramatically increases with the priority queue size. Hence constructing a priority queue (PQ) from considerably smaller hardware priority queues (which are also much faster) while maintaining the $O(1)$ steps per PQ operation is critical. Here we present such an acceleration technique called the Power Priority Queue (PPQ) technique. Specifically, an n elements PPQ is constructed from $2k - 1$ primitive priority queues of size $\sqrt[k]{n}$ ($k = 2, 3, ...$) and a RAM of size n, where the throughput of the construct beats that of a single, size n primitive hardware priority queue. For example an n elements PQ can be constructed from either three $\sqrt{n}$ or five $\sqrt[3]{n}$ primitive H/W priority queues.

Applying our technique to a TCAM based priority queue, results in TCAM-PPQ, a scalable perfect line rate fair queuing of millions of concurrent connections at speeds of 100 Gbps. This demonstrates the benefits of our scheme when used with hardware TCAM, we expect similar results with systolic arrays, shift-registers and similar technologies.

As a by product of our technique we present an $O(n)$ time sorting algorithm in a system equipped with a $O(w\sqrt{n})$ entries TCAM, where here n is the number of items, and w is the maximum number of bits required to represent an item, improving on a previous result that used an $\Omega(n)$ entries TCAM. Finally, we provide a lower bound on the time complexity of sorting n elements with TCAM of size $O(n)$ that matches our TCAM based sorting algorithm.

Categories and Subject Descriptors

D.1.3 [**Programming Techniques**]: Concurrent Programming—*Parallel programming*; F.2.2 [**Analysis of Algorithms and Prob-**

lem Complexity]: Nonnumerical Algorithms and Problems—*Sequencing and scheduling, Sorting and searching*

Keywords

Sorting; TCAM; Priority Queue; WFQ

1. INTRODUCTION

A priority queue (PQ) is a data structure in which each element has a priority and a dequeue operation removes and returns the highest priority element in the queue. PQs are the most basic component for scheduling, mostly used in routers, event driven simulators and is also useful in shortest path and navigation (e.g. Dijkstra's algorithm) and compression (Huffman coding). In routers (or event driven simulators) the PQ is intensively accessed, at least twice per packet (or event) and the throughput of the system is mostly dictated by the PQ.

Since PQs share the same time bounds as sorting algorithms [1], in high throughput scenarios, (e.g., backbone routers) special hardware PQs are used. Hardware PQs are usually implemented by ASIC chips that are specially tailored and optimized to the scenario and do not scale well [2–7].

We present a new construction for large hardware PQs, called Power Priority Queue (PPQ), which recursively uses small hardware priority queues in parallel as building blocks to construct a much larger one. The size of the resulting PQ is a power of the smaller PQs size, specifically we show that an n elements priority queue can be constructed from only $2k - 1$ copies of any base (hardware) $\sqrt[k]{n}$ elements (size) priority queue. Our construction benefits from the optimized performance of small hardware PQs and extends these benefits to high performance, large size PQ.

We demonstrate the applicability of our construction in the case of the Ternary Content Addressable Memory (TCAM) based PQ, that was implied by Panigrahy and Sharma [8]. The TCAM based PQ, as we investigate and optimize in [9], has poor scalability and become impractical when it is required to hold 1M items. But by applying our construction with relatively tiny TCAM based PQ, we achieve a PQ of size 1M with throughput of more than 100M operations per second, which can be used to schedule packets at a line rate of 100Gb/s. The construction uses in parallel 10 TCAMs (or TCAM blocks) of size 110Kb and each PQ operation requires 3.5 sequential TCAM accesses (3 for Dequeue and 4 for Insert).

Finally this work also improves the space and time performance of the TCAM based sorting scheme presented in [8]. As we show in Section 4 an n elements sorting algorithm is constructed from two $w\sqrt{n}$ entries TCAM's, where w is the number of bits required to represent one element (in [8] two n entries TCAM's are used). The time complexity to sort n elements in our solution is the same as in [8], $O(n)$ when counting TCAM accesses, however our algorithm accesses much smaller TCAM's and thus is expected to be

*Supported by European Research Council (ERC) Starting Grant no. 259085

faster. Moreover, in Section 4.2 we prove a lower bound on the time complexity of sorting n elements with a TCAM of size n (or $\sqrt{n}$) that matches our TCAM based sorting algorithm.

2. PRIORITY QUEUES BACKGROUND

2.1 Priority queues and routing

One of the most complex tasks in routers and switches, in which PQ's play a critical role is that of scheduling and deciding the order by which packets are forwarded [10–12]. Priority Queues is the main tool with which the schedulers implement and enforce fairness combined with priority among the different flows. Guaranteeing that flows get a weighted (by their relative importance) fair share of the bandwidth independent of packet sizes they use.

For example, in the popular Weighted Fair Queueing (WFQ) scheduler, each flow is given a different queue, ensuring that one flow does not overrun another. Then, different weights are associated with the different flows indicating their levels of quality of service and bandwidth allocation. These weights are then used by the WFQ scheduler to assign a time-stamp to each arriving packet indicating its virtual finish time according to emulated Generalized Processor Sharing (GPS). And now comes the critical and challenging task of the priority queue, to transmit the packets in the order of the lowest timestamp packet first, i.e., according to their assigned timestamps[1]. For example, in a 100Gbps line rate, hundreds of thousands of concurrent flows are expected[2]. Thus the priority queue is required to concurrently hold more than million items and to support more than 100 million insert or dequeue operations per second. Note that the range of the timestamps depends on the router's buffer size and the accuracy of the scheduling system. For best accuracy, the timestamps should atleast represent any offset in the router's buffer. Buffer size is usually set proportional to $RTT \cdot lineRate$, and for a 100Gbps line rate and RTT of 250ms, timestamp size can get as high as 35 bits.

No satisfactory software PQ implementation exists due to the inherent $O(\log n)$ step complexity per operation in linear space solutions, or alternatively $O(w)$ complexity but then with $O(2^w)$ space requirement, where n is the number of keys (packets) in the queue and w is the size of the keys (i.e., timestamps in the example above). These implementations are mostly based on binary heaps or Van De Boas Trees [4]. None of these solutions is scalable, nor can it handle large priority queues with reasonable performances.

Networking equipment designers have therefore turned to two alternatives in the construction of efficient high rate and high volume PQ's, either to implement approximate solutions, or to build complex hardware priority queues. The approximation approach has light implementation and does not require a PQ [14]. However the inaccuracy of the scheduler hampers its fairness, and is thus not applicable in many scenarios. The hardware approaches, described in detail in the next subsection, are on the other hand not scalable.

2.2 Hardware priority queue implementations

Here we briefly review three hardware PQ implementations, Pipelined heaps [5, 15], Systolic Arrays [2, 3] and Shift Registers [7]. ASIC implementations, based on pipelined heaps, can reach $O(1)$ amortized time per operation and $O(2^w)$ space [5, 15], using pipeline depth that depends on w, the key size, or $\log n$ the number of elements. Due to the strong dependence on hardware design and key

size, most of the ASIC implementations use small key size, and are not scalable for high rate. In [16] a more efficient pipelined heap construction is presented, and our technique resembles some of the principals used in their work, however their result is a complex hardware implementation requiring many hardware processors or special elements and is very specific to pipelined heaps and of particular size, while the technique presented here is general, scalable with future technologies and works also with simpler hardware such as the TCAM.

Other hardware implementations are Systolic Arrays and Shift Registers . They are both based on an array of $O(n)$ comparators and storing units, where low priority items are gradually pushed to the back and highest priority are kept in front allowing to extract the highest priority item in $O(1)$ step complexity. In shift register based implementations new inputs are broadcasted to all units where as in systolic arrays the effect of an operation (an inserted item, or values shift) propagates from the front to the back one step in each cycle. Shift Registers require a global communication board that connects with all units while systolic arrays require bigger units to hold and process propagated operations. Since both of them requires $O(n)$ special hardware such as comparators, making them cost effective or even feasible only for low n values and therefore again not scalable.

Another forth approach, which is mostly theoretical is that of Parallel Priority Queues. It consists of a pipeline or tree of processors [17], each merges the ordered list of items produced by its predecessor processor(s). The number of processors required is either $O(n)$ in a simple pipeline or $O(\log n)$ in a tree of processors, where n is the maximal number of items in the queue. The implementations of these algorithms [18] is either expensive in case of multi-core based architectures or unscalable in the case of ASIC boards.

3. PPQ - THE POWER APPROACH

The first and starting point idea in our Power Priority Queue (PPQ) construction is that to sort n elements one can partition them into $\sqrt{n}$ lists of size $\sqrt{n}$ each, sort each list, and merge the lists into one sorted list. Since a sorted list and a PQ are essentially the same, we use one $\sqrt{n}$ elements PQ to sort each of the sublists (one at a time), and a second $\sqrt{n}$ elements PQ in order to merge the sublists. Any $\sqrt{n}$ elements (hardware) PQ may be used for that. In describing the construction we call each PQ that serves as a building block, Base Priority Queue (BPQ). This naive construction needs two $\sqrt{n}$ elements BPQ's to construct an n element PPQ.

The BPQ building block expected API is as follows:

- Insert(item) - inserts an item with priority item.key.
- Delete(item) - removes an item from the BPQ, item may include a pointer inside the queue.
- Dequeue() - removes and returns the item with the highest priority (minimum key).
- Min() - like a peek, returns the BPQ item with the minimum key.

Note that the Min operation can easily be constructed by caching the highest priority item after every Insert and Dequeue operation, introducing an overhead of a small and fixed number of RAM accesses.

In addition our construction uses a simple in memory (RAM) FIFO queue, called RList, implemented by a linked list that supports the following operations:

- Push(item) - inserts an item at the tail of the RList.
- Pop() - removes and returns the item at the head of the RList.

---

[1]Note that it's enough to store the timestamp of the first packet per flow.
[2]Estimated by extrapolating the results in [13] to the current common rate.

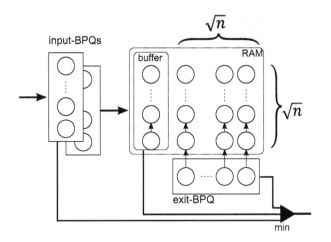

Figure 1: The basic (and high level) Power Priority Queue (PPQ) construction. Note that the length of sublists in the RAM may reach $2\sqrt{n}$ (after merging).

Notice that an RList FIFO queue, due to its sequential data access, can be mostly kept in DRAM while supporting SDRAM like access speed (more than 100Gb/s). This is achieved by using SRAM based buffers for the head and tail parts of each list, and storing internal items in several interleaved DRAM banks [19].

3.1 Power Priority Queue

To construct a PPQ (see Figures 1 and 2) we use one BPQ object, called input-BPQ, as an input sorter. It accepts new items as they are inserted into the PPQ and builds $\sqrt{n}$ long lists out of them. When a new $\sqrt{n}$ list is complete it is copied to the merging area and the input BPQ starts constructing a new list. A second BPQ object, called exit-BPQ, is used to merge and find the minimum item among the lists in the merge area. The pseudo-code is given in [9]. The minimum element from each list in the merge area is kept in the exit-BPQ. When the minimum element in the exit-BPQ is dequeued as part of a PPQ dequeue, a new element from the corresponding list in the merging area is inserted into the exit-BPQ object. Except for the minimum of each RList sorted list the elements in the merging area are kept in a RAM (see notice at the end of the previous subsection). Each PPQ Dequeue operation extracts the minimum element from the exit-BPQ (line 37) or the input-BPQ (line 46), depending on which one contains the smallest key.

The above description suffers from two inherent problems (bugs); first, the construction may end up with more than $\sqrt{n}$ small RLists in the merging area which in turn would require an exit-BPQ of size larger than $\sqrt{n}$, and second, how to move $\sqrt{n}$ sorted elements from a full input-BPQ to an RList while maintaining an $O(1)$ worst case time per operation. In the next subsections we explain how to overcome these difficulties (the pseudo-code of the full algorithm is given in [9]).

3.1.1 Ensuring at most $\sqrt{n}$ RLists in the RAM

As items are dequeued from the PPQ, RAM lists become shorter, but the number of RAM lists might not decrease and we could end up with more than $\sqrt{n}$ RLists many of which with less than $\sqrt{n}$ items. This would cause the exit-BPQ to become full, even though the total number of items in the PPQ is less than n. To overcome this, any time a new list is ready (when the input-BPQ is full) we find another RAM list of size at most $\sqrt{n}$ (which already has a

representative in the exit-BPQ) and we start a process of merging these two lists into one RList in the RAM (line 22 in the pseudo-code) keeping their mutual minimum in the exit-BPQ (lines 25-28), see Figure 2(c). In case their mutual minimum is not the currently stored item in the exit-BPQ, the stored item should be replaced using exit-BPQ.Delete operation, followed by an Insert of the mutual minimum.

This RAM merging process is run in the background interleaving with the usual operation of the PPQ. In every PPQ.Insert or PPQ.Dequeue operation we make two steps in this merging (line 13), extending the resulting merged list (called *fused-sublist* in the code) by two more items. Considering the fact that it takes at least $\sqrt{n}$ insertions to create a new RAM sublist, we are guaranteed that at least $2\sqrt{n}$ merge steps complete between two consecutive RAM lists creations, ensuring that the two RAM lists are merged before a new list is ready. Note that since the heads of two merged lists and the tail of the resulting list are buffered in SRAM the two merging steps have small, if any at all, influence on the overall completion time of the operation.

If no RAM list smaller than $\sqrt{n}$ exists then either there is free space for the new RAM list and there is no need for a merge, or the exit-BPQ is full, managing $\sqrt{n}$ RAM lists of size larger than $\sqrt{n}$, i.e., the PPQ is overfull. If however such a smaller than $\sqrt{n}$ RLists exists we can find one such list in $O(1)$ time by holding a length counter for each RList, and managing an *unordered* set of small RLists (those with length at most $\sqrt{n}$). This set can easily be managed as a linked list with $O(1)$ steps per operation.

3.1.2 Moving a full input-BPQ into an RList in the RAM in $O(1)$ steps

When the input-BPQ is full we need to access the $\sqrt{n}$ sorted items in it and move them into the RAM (either move or merge with another RList as explained above). At the same time we also need to use the input-BPQ to sort new incoming items. Since the PPQ is designed for real time scheduling systems, we should carry out these operations while maintaining $O(1)$ worst case steps per insert or dequeue operations. As the BPQ implementation might not support an operation "copy all items and reset" in one step, the items should be deleted (using dequeue) and copied to the RAM one by one. Such an operation consumes too much time ($\sqrt{n}$) to be allowed during a single Insert operation. Therefore, our solution is to use two input-BPQs with flipping roles, while we insert a new item to the first we evacuate one from the second into an RList in the RAM. Since their size is the same, by the time we fill the first we have emptied the second and we can switch between them. Thus our construction uses a total of three BPQ objects, rather than two. Note that when removing the highest-priority element, we have to consider the minimums of the queues and the list we fill, i.e., one input-BPQ, one RList and the exit-BPQ.

The pseudo-code of the full algorithm is provided in [9]. The two input-BPQs are called input-BPQ[0] and input-BPQ[1], where input-BPQ[in] is the one currently used for insertion of new incoming items and input-BPQ[out] is evacuated in the background into an RList named buffer[out]. The RList accessed by buffer[in] is the one being merged with another small sublist already in the exit-BPQ.

3.2 PPQ Complexity Analysis

Here we show that each PPQ.Insert operation requires at most 3 accesses to BPQ objects, which can be performed in parallel, thus adding one sequential access time, and each PPQ.dequeue operation requires at most 2 sequential accesses to BPQ objects.

The most expensive PPQ operation is an insert in which exactly

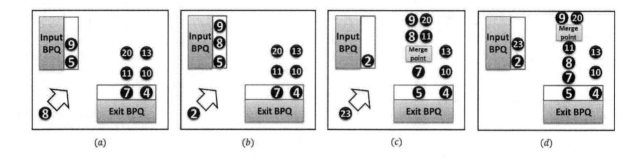

(a)   (b)   (c)   (d)

Figure 2: A sequence of operations, Insert(8), Insert(2), and Insert(23), and the Power Priority Queue (PPQ) state after each ((b)-(d)). Here $n = 9$ and the Merge in state (c) is performed since there is a sublist whose size is at most $\sqrt{n}$.

the input-BPQ[in] becomes full. In such an operation the following 4 accesses (A1-A4) may be required; A1: An insert on input-BPQ[in], A2: a Delete and A3: Insert in the exit-BPQ, and A4: A dequeue from the input-BPQ[out]. Accesses A2& A3 are in the case that the head item in the new list that starts its merge with an RList needs to replace an item in the exit-BPQ. However, notice that accesses A1, A2 and A4 may be executed in parallel, and only access A3 sequentially follows access A2. Thus the total sequential time of this PPQ.Insert is 2. Since such a costly PPQ.Insert happens only once every $\sqrt{n}$ Insert operations, we show in [9] how to delay access A3 to a subsequent PPQ.Insert thus reducing the worst case sequential access time of PPQ.Insert to 1.

The PPQ.Dequeue operation performs in the worst case a Dequeue followed by an Insert to the exit-BPQ and in the background merging process, a Dequeue in one input-BPQ. Therefore the PPQ Dequeue operation requires in the worst case 3 accesses to the BPQ objects which can be performed in two sequential steps.

Both operations can be performed with no more than 7 RAM accesses per operation (which can be made to the SRAM whose size can be about 8MB), and by using parallel RAM accesses, can be completed within 6 sequential RAM accesses. Thus, since each packet is being inserted and dequeued from the PPQ the total number of sequential BPQ accesses per packet is 3 with 6 sequential SRAM accesses. This can be farther improved by considering that the BPQ accesses of the PPQ.Insert are to a different base hardware object than those of the PPQ.Dequeue. In a balanced Insert-Dequeue access pattern, when both are performed concurrently, this reduces to 2 the number of sequential accesses to BPQ objects per packet.

3.3 The TCAM based Power Priority Queue (TCAM-PPQ)

The powering technique can be applied to several different hardware PQ implementations, such as, Pipelined heaps [5,15], Systolic Arrays [2,3] and Shift Registers [7]. Here we use a TCAM based PQ building block, called TCAM Ranges based PQ (RPQ), to construct a TCAM based Power Priority Queue called TCAM-PPQ, see Figure 3. The RPQ construction is described in [9], it is an extension of the TCAM based set of ranges data structure of Panigrhay and Sharma [8] and features a constant number of TCAM accesses per RPQ operation using two $w \cdot m$ entries TCAMs (each entry of w bits) to handle m elements. Thus a straightforward naive construction of an n items TCAM-PPQ requires 6 TCAM's of size $w\sqrt{n}$ entries.

Let us examine this implementation in more detail. According to the RPQ construction in [9] 1 sequential access to TCAMs is required in the implementation of RPQ.Insert, 1 in the implemen-

tation of RPQ.Dequeue and 3 for RPQ.delete(item). Combining these costs with the analysis in the previous subsection yields that the worst case cost of TCAM-PPQ.Insert is 3 sequential accesses to TCAMs, and also 3 for TCAM-PPQ. Dequeue. However, TCAM-PPQ.Insert costs 3 only once every $\sqrt{n}$ inserts, i.e., its amortized cost converges to 2, and the average of the two operations together is thus 2.5 sequential TCAM accesses. Note that it is possible to handle priorities' (values of the PQ) wrap around by a simple technique as described in our technical report [9].

Consider for example the following use case of the TCAM-PPQ. It can handle million keys in a range of size 2^{35} (reasonable 100 Gbps rate [20]) using 6 TCAMs, each smaller than 1 Mb. Considering a TCAM rate of 500 millions accesses per second (reasonable rate for 1 Mb TCAM [21]), and 2.5 accesses per operation (Insert or Dequeue) this TCAM-PPQ works at a rate of 100 million packets per second. Assuming average packet size of 140 bytes [5,22], then the TCAM-PPQ supports a line rate of 112 Gbps.

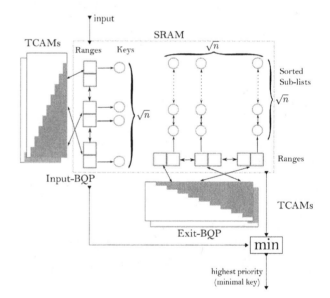

Figure 3: The TCAM based Priority Queue (TCAM-PPQ) construction.

3.4 The Power k Priority Queue - PPQ(k)

The PPQ scheme describes how to build an n elements priority queue from three $\sqrt{n}$ elements priority queues. Naturally this calls for a recursive construction where the building blocks are built from smaller building blocks. Here we implement this idea in the following way; (see Figure 5) we fix the size of the exit-BPQ to be x, the size of the smallest building block. In the RAM area x lists each of size n/x are maintained. The input-BPQ is however constructed recursively. In general if the recursion is applied k times, a PPQ with capacity n is constructed from $\cdot 2^k$ BPQs each of size $\sqrt[k]{n}$.

However, a closer look at the BPQ's used in each step of the recursion reveals that each step requires only 2 size x exit-BPQ and each pair of input-BPQs is replaced by a pair of input-BPQs whose size is x times smaller as illustrated in Figure 4. Thus each step of the recursion adds only 2 size x BPQ's objects (the exit-BPQs) and the corresponding RAM space (see Figure 4). At the last level 2 size x input-BPQs are still required. Consider the top level of the recursion as illustrated in Figure 4, where a size n PPQ is constructed from two input-BPQs, Q_0 and Q_1 each of size n/x and each with size n/x RAM (the RAM and the exit-BPQs are not shown in the figure at any level). Each of Q_0 and Q_1 is in turn constructed from two size n/x^2 input-BPQs ($Q_{0,0}$, $Q_{0,1}$, $Q_{1,0}$, and $Q_{1,1}$) and the corresponding RAM area and size x exit-BPQ. As can be seen, at any point of time only two n/x^2 input-BPQs are in use. For example moving from state (b) to state (c) in Figure 4, $Q_{0,0}$ is already empty when we just switch from inputting into Q_0 to inputting to Q_1, and Q_1 needs only $Q_{1,0}$ for n/x^2 steps. When Q_1 starts using $Q_{1,1}$, moving from (c) to (d), $Q_{0,1}$ is already empty, etc. Recursively, these two size n/x^2 input-BPQs may thus be constructed by two n/x^3 input-BPQs. Moreover notice that since only two input-BPQs are used at each level, also only two exit-BPQs are required at each level. The construction recurses k times until the size of the input-BPQ equals x, which can be achieved by selecting $x = \sqrt[k]{n}$. Thus the whole construction requires $2k - 1$, size $\sqrt[k]{n}$ BPQs. In our construction in Section 3.4.1 we found that $k = 3$ gives the best performance for a TCAM based PQ with 100GHz line rate.

We represent the time complexity of an operation $OP \in \{ins, deq\}$ on a size n PPQ(k) built from base BPQs of size $x = \sqrt[k]{n}$, $T(OP, n, x)$, by a three dimensional vector $(N_{ins}, N_{deq}, N_{del})$ that represents the number of BPQ Insert, the number of BPQ Dequeue and the number of BPQ Delete operations (respectively) required to complete OP in the worst case. BPQ operations, for for moderate size BPQ, are expected to dominate other CPU and RAM operations involved in the algorithm. In what follows we show that the amortized cost of an Insert operation is (1,1,1/x) (i.e., all together at most 3 sequential BPQ operations), and (1,1,0) for a Dequeue operation.

If we omit the Background routine, each PPQ(k) Dequeue operation either performs a Dequeue from input-BPQ[in] (a PPQ $(k-1)$ of size n/x), extract an item from the exit-BPQ (using one BPQ Dequeue and one Insert operations) or fetch it from a buffer[out] (no BPQ operation). Therefore we can express the time complexity of PPQ(k) Dequeue operation (without Background), $t(deq, n, x)$ or in shorter form $t_{deq}(n)$, by the following recursive function:

$$t_{deq}(n) = \begin{cases} (0,0,0) & \text{min. is in buffer}[out] \\ (1,1,0) & \text{min. is in exit-BPQ} \\ t_{deq}(n/x) & \text{otherwise} \end{cases} \quad (1)$$

Considering the fact that a priority queue of capacity x is the BPQ itself, $t_{deq}(x) = t(deq, x, x) = (0, 1, 0)$. Therefore the worst case time for any Dequeue is (1, 1, 0), i.e. $t(deq, n, x) = (1, 1, 0)$ when $n > x$.

Note that the equation $t(deq, n, x) = (1, 1, 0)$ expresses the fact that Dequeue essentially updates at most one BPQ (holding the minimum item), which neglects the RAM and CPU operations re-

quired to find that BPQ within the $O(k)$ possible BPQs and buffers. Neglecting these operations is reasonable when k is small, or when we use additional BPQ-like data structure of size $O(k)$ that holds the minimums of all input-BPQ[in] and buffers and can provide their global minimum in $O(1)$ time.

The Background() routine, called at the end of the Dequeue operation, recursively performs a Dequeue from all input-BPQ[out]s. Since there are $k - 1$ input-BPQ[out]s, the Background()'s time cost, $B(n, x)$, equals $(k-1, k-1, 0)$. Therefore the total time complexity of PPQ(k) Dequeue (by definition $T(deq, n, x) = t(deq, n, x) + B(n, x)$) equals k BPQ Dequeues and k BPQ Inserts in the worst case, i.e.

$$T(deq, n, x) = (k, k, 0). \quad (2)$$

If we omit the Background routine, each PPQ(k) Insert operation performs an Insert to one of its two n/x-sub-queues (the input-BPQ[in]) and sometimes (when the input-BPQ[in] is full) also starting merging of a new RList with existing one which might require a Delete and Insert to the exit-BPQ. Therefore we can express the time complexity of PPQ(k) Insert operation (without Background), $t(ins, n, x)$ or in shorter form $t_{ins}(n)$, by the following recursive function:

$$t_{ins}(n) = \begin{cases} t_{ins}(n/x) + (1,0,1) & \text{input-BPQ}[in] \text{ is full} \\ t_{ins}(n/x) & \text{otherwise} \end{cases} \quad (3)$$

Considering the fact that a priority queue of capacity x is the BPQ itself, $t_{ins}(x) = t(ins, x, x) = (1, 0, 0)$. Therefore the worst case time of any Insert is $(k, 0, k-1)$, i.e. $t(ins, n, x) = (k, 0, k-1)$ when $n > x$. When we include the cost of the Background, we get that

$$T(ins, n, x) = (2k-1, k-1, k-1). \quad (4)$$

Moreover, since the probability that at least one input-BPQ[in] is full is approximately $1/x$, the amortized cost of a PPQ(k) Insert without Background is $(1, 0, 0) + \frac{1}{x}(1, 0, 1)$, and with background it is $(k, k - 1, 0) + \frac{1}{x}(1, 0, 1)$.

An important property of the Background() routine is that it only accesses input-BPQ[out]s while the rest of the operations of Insert and Dequeue access input-BPQ[in]s, therefore it can be executed in parallel with them. Moreover, since Background performs a Dequeue on input-BPQ[out]s, and since in input-BPQ[out] minimum key can be found locally (no input-BPQ[in] is used by input-BPQ[out]), all Dequeue calls belonging to a Background can be performed concurrently, thereby achieving parallel time cost of $(1,1,0)$ for the Background routine. As a consequence, putting it all together, in a fully parallel implementation the amortized cost of Insert is $(1, 1, 1/x)$ and $(1, 1, 0)$ for Dequeue.

3.4.1 The generalized TCAM-PPQ(k)

When applying the PPQ(k) scheme with the RPQ (Ranges based Priority Queue), we achieve a priority queue with capacity n which uses $O(wk \sqrt[k]{n})$ entries TCAM (each entry of size w bits) and $O(k)$ TCAM accesses per operation. More precisely, using the general analysis of PPQ(k) above and the RPQ analysis in [9], TCAM-PPQ(k) requires $2k-1$ RPQs of size $\sqrt[k]{n}$ each and achieves Insert with amortized cost of $3k - 1$ TCAM accesses and Dequeue with $3k$ TCAM accesses. As noted above these results can be farther improved, by using parallel execution of independent RPQ operations, which when fully applied can results in this case with only 3 TCAM accesses.

Since access time, cost and power consumption of TCAMs decreases as the TCAM gets smaller, the TCAM-PPQ(k) scheme can be used to achieve an optimized result based on the goals of the cir-

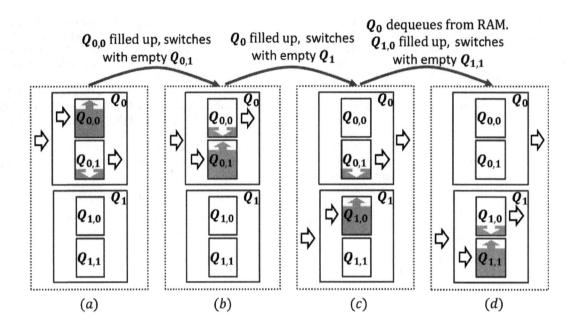

$Q_{0,0}$ filled up, switches with empty $Q_{0,1}$

Q_0 filled up, switches with empty Q_1

Q_0 dequeues from RAM. $Q_{1,0}$ filled up, switches with empty $Q_{1,1}$

(a)　　　　　　(b)　　　　　　(c)　　　　　　(d)

Figure 4: A scenario in which four n/x^2 input-BPQs construct two size n/x input-BPQs that in turn are used in the construction of one size n input-BPQ. As explained in the text it illustrates that only $2\,n/x^2$ input-BPQs are required at any point of time.

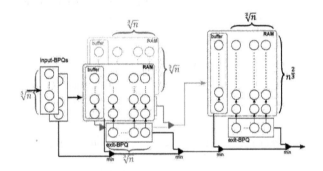

Figure 5: High level diagram of the Power $k = 3$ Priority Queue - PPQ(3) construction.

cuit designer. Note that large TCAMs also suffer from long sequential operation latency which leads to pipeline based TCAM usage. The reduction of TCAM size with TCAM-PPQ(k) allows a simpler and straightforward TCAM usage. Considering the TCAM size to performance tradeoffs the best TCAM based PQ is the TCAM-PPQ (3) whose performance exceeds RPQ and simple TCAM based lists implementations.

Let $T(S)$ be the access time of a size S TCAM, then another interesting observation is that for any number of items n, the time complexity of each operation on TCAM-PPQ(k) is $O\left(k \cdot T(\theta \sqrt[k]{n})\right)$, where θ is either w or w^2 depending on whether the TCAM returns the longest prefix match or not, respectively. This time complexity can be also expressed by $O\left(\log n \cdot \frac{T(S)}{\log S - \log \theta}\right)$. This implies that faster scheduling can be achieved by using TCAMs with lower $T(S)$ to $(\log S - \log \theta)$ ratio, suggesting a design objective for future TCAMs.

The new TCAM-PPQ(3) can handle million keys in a range of size 2^{35} (reasonable 100 Gbps rate) using 10 TCAMs (5 BPQs) each smaller than 110 Kb with access time 1.1 ns. A TCAM of this size has a rate of 900 millions accesses per second, and 3.5 accesses per operation (Insert or Dequeue) this TCAM-PPQ(3) works at a rate of 180 million packets per second (assuming some parallelism between Insert and Dequeue operations steps). Assuming average packet size of 140 bytes [5,22], TCAM-PPQ(3) supports a line rate of 200 Gbps.

4. POWER SORTING

We present the *PowerSort* algorithm (code is given in [9]), that sorts n items in $O(n)$ time using one BPQ with capacity $\sqrt{n}$. In order to sort n items, PowerSort considers the n items input as $\sqrt{n}$ sublists of size $\sqrt{n}$ each, and using the BPQ to sort each one of them apart (lines 3-13). Each sorted sublist is stored in a RList (see Section 3). Later on the $\sqrt{n}$ sublists are merged to one sorted list of n items (by calling PowerMerge on line 14). We use $PowerMerge_{s,t}$ to refer to the function responsible for the merging phase, this function merges a total of t keys divided to s ordered sublists using a BPQ with capacity s. The same BPQ previously used for sorting is used in the merge phase for managing the minimal unmerged keys one from each sublist, we call such keys local minimum of their sublists.

The merge phase starts by initialization of the BPQ with the smallest keys of the sublists (lines 17-20). From now on until all keys have been merged, we extract the smallest key in the list (line 23), put it in the output array, deletes it from the BPQ and insert a new one, taken from the corresponding sublist which the extracted key originally came from (line 27), i.e. this new key is the new local minimum in the sublist of the extracted key.

When running this algorithm with a RPQ, we can sort n items in $O(n)$ time requiring only $O(w \cdot \sqrt{n})$ TCAM entries. As can be seen from Section 4.2 these results are in some sense optimal.

4.1 The Power k Sorting

The PPQ(k) scheme can also be applied for the sorting problem. An immediate reduction is to insert all items to the queue and then dequeuing them one by one according to the sorted order. A more space efficient scheme can be obtained by using only one BPQ with capacity $\sqrt[k]{n}$ for all the functionalities of the $O(k)$ BPQs in the previous method. We use k phases, each phase $0 \leq i < k$, starts with $n^{\frac{k-i}{k}}$ sorted sublists each contains $n^{\frac{i}{k}}$ items, and during the phase the BPQ is used to merge each $\sqrt[k]{n}$ of the sublists resulting with $n^{\frac{k-i-1}{k}}$ sorted sublists each with $n^{\frac{i+1}{k}}$. Therefore the last phase completes with one sorted list of n items.

This sorting scheme inserts and deletes each item k times from the BPQ (one time in every phase), therefore the time complexity remains $O(kn)$, but it uses only one BPQ. When using this method with TCAM based BPQ, this method will sort n items in $O(kn)$ TCAM accesses using $O(kw\sqrt[k]{n})$ TCAM space (in term of entries). Similar to the TPQ(k) priority queue implementation, this sorting scheme presents an interesting time and TCAM space tradeoffs that can have big importance to TCAMs and scheduling systems designers.

4.2 Proving $\Omega(n)$ queries lower bound for TCAM sorting

Here we generalize Ben Amram's [23] lower bound and extend it to the TCAM assisted model. We consider a TCAM of size M as a black box, with a $query(v)$ - an operation that searches v in the TCAM resulting with one out of M possible outcomes, and a $write(p, i)$ - an operation that writes the pattern value p to the entry $0 \leq i < M$ in the TCAM but has no effect on the RAM.

Following [23], we use the same representation of a program as a tree in which each node is labeled with an instruction of the program. Instructions can be assignment, computation, indirect-addressing, decision and halt where we consider TCAM query as M outputs decision instruction and omit TCAM writes from the model. The proof of the next lemma is the same as in [23].

LEMMA 4.1. *In the extended model, for any tree representation of a sorting program of n elements, the number of leafs is at least $n!$.*

DEFINITION 4.2. *An M,q-Almost-Binary-Tree ($ABTree_{M,q}$) is a tree where the path from any leaf to the root contains at most q nodes with M sons each, the rest of the nodes along the path are binary (have only two sons).*

LEMMA 4.3. *The maximal height of any $ABTree_{M,q}$ with N leafs is at least $\lfloor \log_2 N \rfloor - q \lceil \log_2 M \rceil$.*

PROOF. we simply replace each M-node with a balanced binary tree of M leafs [3]. Each substitution adds at most $\lceil \log_2 M \rceil - 1$ nodes across all the paths from the root to any predecessor of the replaced M-node. In the resulting tree T', the maximal hight H' is at least $\log_2 N$. By the definition of q, at most $q \cdot (\lceil \log M \rceil - 1)$ nodes along the maximal path in T' are the result of nodes replacements. Therefore the maximal height H of the original tree T (before replacement) must satisfy:

$$H \geq H' - q\lceil \log M \rceil \geq \frac{n}{2} \log n - q\lceil \log M \rceil, \quad (5)$$

□

THEOREM 4.4. *Any sorting algorithm that uses standard operators, polynomial size RAM and M size TCAMs, must use at least $\frac{n}{2} \log n - q \log M$ steps (in the worst case) to complete where q is the maximum number of TCAM queries per execution and n is the number of sorted items.*

[3]if M is not a power of 2 then the sub tree should be as balanced as possible

PROOF. Let T be the computation tree of the sorting algorithm as defined in [23], considering TCAM queries as M-nodes. A simple observation is that T is an $ABTree_{M,q}$ with at least $n!$ leafs. Therefore by Lemma 4.3 the maximal height of the tree is at least $\lfloor \log_2 n! \rfloor - q\lceil \log_2 M \rceil$. As $\log n! > \frac{n}{2} \log n$ we get that the worst case running time of the sorting algorithm is at least: $\frac{n}{2} \log n - q \log M$. □

COROLLARY 4.5. *Any $o(n \log n)$ time sorting algorithm that uses standard operators, polynomial size RAM and $O(n^r)$ size TCAMs, must use $\Omega(\frac{n}{r})$ TCAM queries.*

PROOF. From Theorem 4.4, $\frac{n}{2} \log n - q \log M = o(n \log n)$, therefore

$$q = \Omega\left(\frac{n \log n}{\lceil \log M \rceil}\right).$$

By setting $M = O(n^r)$ we obtain that

$$q = \Omega\left(\frac{n}{r}\right).$$

□

COROLLARY 4.6. *Any $o(n \log n)$ time sorting algorithm that uses standard operators, polynomial size RAM and $O(n^r)$ size BPQs, must use $\Omega(\frac{n}{r})$ BPQ operations.*

PROOF. A BPQ of size $O(n^r)$ can be implemented with TCAMs of size $O(n^r)$ when considering TCAMs that return the most accurate matching line (the one with fewest '*'s). Such implementation performs O(1) TCAM accesses per operation, therefore, if there was a sorting algorithm that can sort n items using $O(n^r)$ size BPQs with $o(\frac{n}{r})$ BPQ operations then it was contradicting Corollary 4.5. □

Note that the model considered here matches the computation model used by the PPQ algorithm and also the implementation of the TCAM-PPQ. However one may consider a model that includes more CPU instructions such as shift-right and more, that are beyond the scope of our bound.

5. TCAM-PPQ ANALYTICAL RESULTS

We compare our scheme TCAM-PPQ and TCAM-PPQ(3) to the optimized TCAM based PQ implementations RPQ, RPQ-2 and RPQ-CAO that are described in [9]. We calculate the required TCAM space and resulting packet throughput for varying number n of elements in the queue (i.e., n is the maximal number of concurrent flows). We set w, the key width to 36 bits which is above the minimum required in the current high end traffic demands.

In Figure 6 we present the total TCAM space (over all TCAMs) required by each scheme . We assume that the TCAM chip size is limited to $72Mb$, which as far as we know is the largest TCAM available today [21]. Each of the lines in the graph is cut when the solution starts using infeasible TCAM building block sizes (i.e., larger than 72Mb). Clearly TCAM-PPQ and TCAM-PPQ(3) have a significant advantage over the other schemes since they require much smaller TCAM building blocks (and also total size) than the other solutions for the same PQ size. Moreover they are the only ones that use feasible TCAM size when constructing a one million elements PQ. All the other variations of RPQ require TCAM of size 1Gb for million elements in the queue, which is infeasible in any aspect (TCAM price, or power consumption, or speed).

In Figure 7 we present the potential packet throughput of the schemes in the worst case scenario. Similar to [21] and [24], we calculate the throughput considering only the TCAM accesses and

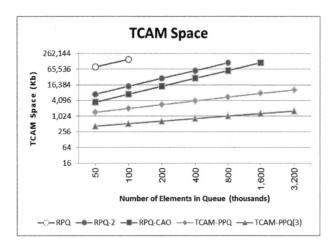

Figure 6: Total TCAM space (size) requirement for different number of elements PQ for the different implementation methods.

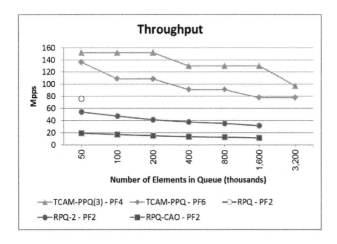

Figure 7: Packet throughput as a function of the number of elements. For each implementation we specify its Parallel Factor (PF) which stands for the maximal number of parallel accesses to different TCAMs.

not SRAM memory accesses. The rational is that the TCAM accesses dominate the execution time and power consumption and it is performed in pipeline with the SRAM accesses. The TCAM access time is a function of the basic TCAM size. Recall that the TCAM speed increases considerably as its size reduces, [21, 24]. Next to each scheme we print the Parallelization Factor(PF), which is defined as the number of TCAM chips the scheme accesses in parallel. As can be seen in Figure 7, TCAM-PPQ and TCAM-PPQ (3) are the only schemes with reasonable throughput, of about 100Mpps for one millions timestamps, i.e., they can be used to construct a PQ working at a rate of 100Gbps. This is due to two major reasons: First, they use smaller TCAM chips and thus the TCAM is faster, and Secondly, have high Parallelization Factor and hence reducing the number of sequential accesses and thus increase the throughput. Note that the RPQ scheme achieves 75Mbps but it may be used with 50 elements, due to its high space requirement. Comparing TCAM-PPQ to TCAM-PPQ(3) we see that the later is more space efficient and reach higher throughput levels. Table 1

summarizes the requirement of the different schemes.

Method	Insert	Dequeue	space (#entries)
RPQ	2	1	$2w \cdot N$
RPQ-2	$\log w + 1$	1	$4N$
RPQ-CAO	$w/2 + 1$	1	$2N$
TCAM-PPQ	2	3	$6w \cdot \sqrt{N}$
TCAM-PPQ(3)	4	3	$10w \cdot \sqrt[3]{N}$

Table 1: Number of sequential TCAM accesses for the different TCAM based priority queues in an Insert and Dequeue operations (parallel access scheme is assumed).

In [7] a PQ design based on shift registers is presented which supports similar throughput as RPQ but cannot scale beyond 2048 items. By applying the PPQ scheme (results summarized in [9]) we can extend it to hold one million items while supporting a throughput of 100 million packets per second as with TCAM-PPQ.

6. CONCLUSIONS

This paper presents a sweet spot construction of a priority queue. A construction that enjoys the throughput and speed of small hardware priority queues without the size limitations they impose. It requires small hardware priority queues as building blocks of size cube root of the resulting priority queue size. We demonstrate the construction on the TCAM parallel technology, that when the size reduces works even faster. Combining these two together results in the first feasible and accurate solution to the packets scheduling problem while using commodity hardware. Thus avoiding the special, complex and inflexible ASIC design, and avoiding the alternative slow software solution (slow due to the inherent logarithmic complexity of the problem).

Our work shows that TCAMs can be used to solve a data structure problem more efficiently than it is possible in a software based system. This is another step in the direction of understanding the power of TCAMs and the way they can be used to solve basic computer science problems such as sorting and priority queue.

Acknowledgments. We thank David Hay for helpful discussions, and the anonymous referees for their comments.

7. REFERENCES

[1] M. Thorup, "Equivalence between priority queues and sorting," in *IEEE Symposium on Foundations of Computer Science*, 2002, pp. 125–134.

[2] P. Lavoie, D. Haccoun, and Y. Savaria, "A systolic architecture for fast stack sequential decoders," *Communications, IEEE Transactions on*, vol. 42, no. 234, pp. 324 –335, feb/mar/apr 1994.

[3] S.-W. Moon, K. Shin, and J. Rexford, "Scalable hardware priority queue architectures for high-speed packet switches," in *Real-Time Technology and Applications Symposium, 1997. Proceedings., Third IEEE*, jun 1997, pp. 203 –212.

[4] H. Wang and B. Lin, "Pipelined van emde boas tree: Algorithms, analysis, and applications," in *IEEE INFOCOM*, 2007, pp. 2471–2475.

[5] K. Mclaughlin, S. Sezer, H. Blume, X. Yang, F. Kupzog, and T. G. Noll, "A scalable packet sorting circuit for high-speed wfq packet scheduling," *IEEE Transactions on Very Large Scale Integration Systems*, vol. 16, pp. 781–791, 2008.

[6] A. Ioannou and M. Katevenis, "Pipelined heap (priority queue) management for advanced scheduling in high-speed

networks," *Networking, IEEE/ACM Transactions on*, vol. 15, no. 2, pp. 450 –461, april 2007.

[7] R. Chandra and O. Sinnen, "Improving application performance with hardware data structures," in *Parallel Distributed Processing, Workshops and Phd Forum (IPDPSW), 2010 IEEE International Symposium on*, april 2010, pp. 1 –4.

[8] R. Panigrahy and S. Sharma, "Sorting and searching using ternary cams," *IEEE Micro*, vol. 23, pp. 44–53, January 2003.

[9] Y. Afek, A. Bremler-Barr, and L. Schiff, "Recursive design of hardware priority queues." [Online]. Available: http://www.cs.tau.ac.il/~schiffli/PPQfull.pdf

[10] L. Zhang, "Virtualclock: a new traffic control algorithm for packet-switched networks," *ACM Transactions on Computer Systems (TOCS)*, vol. 9, no. 2, pp. 101 –124, may 1991.

[11] P. Goyal, H. Vin, and H. Cheng, "Start-time fair queueing: a scheduling algorithm for integrated services packet switching networks," *Networking, IEEE/ACM Transactions on*, vol. 5, no. 5, pp. 690 –704, oct 1997.

[12] S. Keshav, *An engineering approach to computer networking: ATM networks, the Internet, and the telephone network*. Boston, MA, USA: Addison-Wesley Longman Publishing Co., Inc., 1997.

[13] A. Kortebi, L. Muscariello, S. Oueslati, and J. Roberts, "Evaluating the number of active flows in a scheduler realizing fair statistical bandwidth sharing," in *Proceedings of the 2005 ACM SIGMETRICS international conference on Measurement and modeling of computer systems*, ser. SIGMETRICS '05. New York, NY, USA: ACM, 2005, pp. 217–228. [Online]. Available: http://doi.acm.org/10.1145/1064212.1064237

[14] M. Shreedhar and G. Varghese, "Efficient fair queueing using deficit round-robin," *IEEE/ACM Trans. Netw.*, vol. 4, pp. 375–385, June 1996. [Online]. Available: http://dx.doi.org/10.1109/90.502236

[15] H. Wang and B. Lin, "Succinct priority indexing structures for the management of large priority queues," in *Quality of Service, 2009. IWQoS. 17th International Workshop on*, july 2009, pp. 1 –5.

[16] X. Zhuang and S. Pande, "A scalable priority queue architecture for high speed network processing," in *INFOCOM 2006. 25th IEEE International Conference on Computer Communications. Proceedings*, april 2006, pp. 1 –12.

[17] G. S. Brodal, J. L. TrÃd'ff, and C. D. Zaroliagis, "A parallel priority queue with constant time operations," *Journal of Parallel and Distributed Computing*, vol. 49, no. 1, pp. 4 – 21, 1998.

[18] A. V. Gerbessiotis and C. J. Siniolakis, "Architecture independent parallel selection with applications to parallel priority queues," *Theoretical Computer Science*, vol. 301, no. 1âĂŞ3, pp. 119 – 142, 2003.

[19] J. Garcia, M. March, L. Cerda, J. Corbal, and M. Valero, "On the design of hybrid dram/sram memory schemes for fast packet buffers," in *High Performance Switching and Routing, 2004. HPSR. 2004 Workshop on*, 2004, pp. 15 – 19.

[20] H. J. Chao and B. Liu, *High Performance Switches and Routers*. John Wiley & Sons, Inc., 2006.

[21] J. Patel, E. Norige, E. Torng, and A. X. Liu, "Fast regular expression matching using small tcams for network intrusion detection and prevention systems," in *USENIX Security Symposium*, 2010, pp. 111–126.

[22] *Packet size distribution comparison between Internet links in 1998 and 2008*, CAIDA. [Online]. Available: http://www.caida.org/research/traffic-analysis/pkt_size_distribution/graphs.xml

[23] A. M. Ben-amram, "When can we sort in o(n log n) time?" *Journal of Computer and System Sciences*, vol. 54, pp. 345–370, 1997.

[24] B. Agrawal and T. Sherwood, "Ternary cam power and delay model: Extensions and uses," *IEEE Transactions on Very Large Scale Integration Systems*, vol. 16, pp. 554–564, 2008.

APPENDIX

A.   THE PPQ ALGORITHM

1: **function** PPQ.INIT(n)
2:     $in \leftarrow 0$
3:     $out \leftarrow 1$
4:     input-BPQ[in] $\leftarrow$ new BPQ ($\sqrt{n}$)
5:     input-BPQ[out] $\leftarrow$ new BPQ ($\sqrt{n}$)
6:     exit-BPQ $\leftarrow$ new BPQ ($\sqrt{n}$)
7:     buffer[in] $\leftarrow$ new RList ($\sqrt{n}$)
8:     buffer[out] $\leftarrow$ new RList ($\sqrt{n}$)
9:     small-sublists $\leftarrow$ new RList ($\sqrt{n}$)
10:     fused-sublist $\leftarrow$ null
11: **end function**

12: **function** BACKGROUND
13:     Do 2 steps in merging buffer[in] with fused-sublist   ▷ fused-sublist is merged with buffer[in], both are in the SRAM; In this step two merge steps are performed.
14:     **if** input-BPQ[out].count > 0 **then**
15:         item $\leftarrow$ input-BPQ[out].Dequeue()
16:         buffer[out].Push(item)
17:     **end if**
18: **end function**

19: **function** PPQ.INSERT(item)
20:     **if** input-BPQ[in].count $= \sqrt{N}$ **then**
                              ▷ A new full list is ready
21:         swap in with out
22:         fused-sublist $\leftarrow$ small-sublists.Pop()
23:         input-BPQ[in].Insert (item)
24:         Background()
25:         **if** fused-sublist.head > buffer[in].head **then**
                 ▷ Need to replace the head item of fused-sublist which is in the exit-BPQ, head of buffer[in] is going to be the new head of fused-sulist
26:             exit-BPQ.Delete(fused-sublist.head)
27:             exit-BPQ.Insert (buffer[in].head)
28:         **end if**
29:     **else**
30:         Background()
31:         input-BPQ[in].Insert (item)
32:     **end if**
33: **end function**

34: **function** PPQ.DEQUEUE
35:     min1 $\leftarrow$ min(input-BPQ[in].Min, buffer[out].Min)
36:     **if** exit-BPQ.Min < min1 **then**
37:         min $\leftarrow$ exit-BPQ.Dequeue()
38:         remove min from min.sublist

```
                          ▷ min.sublist is the RList that contained min.
39:        local-min ← new head of min.sublist
40:        exit-BPQ.Insert (local-min)
41:        if min.sublist.count = √N then
42:            small-sublists.Push(min.sublist)
43:        end if
44:    else
45:        if input-BPQ[in].min < buffer[out].head then
46:            min ← input-BPQ[in].Dequeue()
47:        else
48:            min ← buffer[out].Pop()
49:        end if
50:    end if
51:    Background()
52:    return min
53: end function
```

B. REDUCING THE WORST CASE NUMBER OF BPQ ACCESSES IN A PPQ.INSERT OPERATION FROM 3 TO 2

In this appendix we explain how to reduce the worst case number of BPQ accesses in a PPQ.insert operation from 3 to 2. A careful look at the PPQ.insert algorithm reveals that only once every $\sqrt{n}$, when the input-BPQ is exactly full may this operation require 3 sequential accesses, in all other cases this operation requires only 1 sequential access. It requires 3 operation if the head of the buffer[in] is smaller than the head of the sublist marked to be merge with it (the fused-list in code). This 3 sequential accesses consist of Insert to the input-BPQ and Delete and Insert to the exit-BPQ, can be broken by delaying the last access in the sequence (line 27) to the next Insert operation. Notice that now each dequeue operation needs to check whether the minimum that needs to be returned is this delayed value, as in the pseudo-code below. Implementing this delay requires the following changes to the algorithm:

- Delaying the insert (in line 27) - the existing line should be replaced by:

```
1:  wait-head ← new-sublist.head
```

- Performing delayed insertion - the following code should be added just before line 31:

```
1:  if wait-head ≠ null then
2:      exit-BPQ.Insert(wait-head)
3:      wait-head ← null
4:  end if
```

- Check if delayed item should be dequeued - we need to ensure that Insert() doesn't miss the minimum item when it is the delayed new-sublist head. By comparing the delayed head to other minimums the Dequeue can decide whether it should be used. This change is implemented by adding the following lines at the beginning of Dequeue:

```
1:  if wait-head ≠ null then
2:      if wait-head < input-BPQ.min &&
3:  wait-head < merge-list.min then
4:          min ← wait-head
5:          remove wait-head from wait-head.sublist
6:          local-min ← new head of wait-head.sublist
7:          exit-BPQ.Insert(local-min)
8:          wait-head ← null
9:          Background()
10:         return min
11:     end if
12: end if
```

C. THE POWER SORTING SCHEME

```
1: function POWERSORT(Array In, List Out, n)
2:     q ← new BPQ (√n)
3:     for i = 0 to √n − 1 do
4:         for j = 0 to √n − 1 do
5:             q.Insert(In[i · √n + j])
6:         end for
7:         Subs[i] ← new RList (√n)
8:         for j = 0 to √n − 1 do
9:             item ← q.Dequeue()
10:            item.origin-id ← i
11:            Subs[i].Push(item)
12:        end for
13:    end for
14:    PowerMerge(Subs, Out, q, √n, √n)
15: end function

16: function POWERMERGE(RList Subs[], RList Out, BPQ q, s, t)
17:     for i = 0 to s do            ▷ s is the number of sublists
18:         local-min ← Subs[i].Pop()
19:         q.Insert(local-min)
20:     end for
21:     count ← 0
22:     for count = 1 to t do        ▷ t is the total num. of items
23:         min ← q.Dequeue()
24:         id ← min.origin-id
25:         if Subs[id] not empty then
26:             local-min ← Subs[id].Pop()
27:             q.Insert(local-min)
28:         end if
29:         Out.Push(min)
30:     end for
31: end function
```

Drop the Anchor: Lightweight Memory Management for Non-Blocking Data Structures[*]

Anastasia Braginsky[†]
Computer Science
Technion
anastas@cs.technion.ac.il

Alex Kogan[‡]
Oracle Labs
alex.kogan@oracle.com

Erez Petrank
Computer Science
Technion
erez@cs.technion.ac.il

ABSTRACT

Efficient memory management of dynamic non-blocking data structures remains an important open question. Existing methods either sacrifice the ability to deallocate objects or reduce performance notably. In this paper, we present a novel technique, called *Drop the Anchor*, which significantly reduces the overhead associated with the memory management while reclaiming objects even in the presence of thread failures. We demonstrate this memory management scheme on the common linked list data structure. Using extensive evaluation, we show that Drop the Anchor significantly outperforms Hazard Pointers, the widely used technique for non-blocking memory management.

Categories and Subject Descriptors

E.1 [**Data**]: Data Structures—*lists, stacks, and queues*; D.1.3 [**Software**]: Programming Techniques—*Concurrent Programming*

General Terms

Algorithms, Design, Theory

Keywords

Concurrent data structures, progress guarantee, lock-freedom, parallel programming, linked list, memory management, hazard pointers, timestamps, freezing

[*]Supported by the Israeli Science Foundation (grant No. 283/10).

[†]Supported by the Ministry of Science and Technology, Israel.

[‡]The work on this paper was done while the author was with the Department of Computer Science, Technion.

1. INTRODUCTION

Non-blocking data structures [9, 11] are fast, scalable and widely used. In the last two decades, many efficient non-blocking implementations for almost any common data structure have been developed. However, when designing a dynamic non-blocking data structure, one must address the non-trivial issue of how to manage its memory. Specifically, one has to ensure that whenever a thread removes some internal node from the data structure, then (a) the memory occupied by this node will be eventually deallocated (i.e., returned to the memory manager for arbitrary reuse), and (b) no other concurrently running thread will access the deallocated memory, even though some threads might hold a reference to the node.

Previous attempts to tackle the memory management problem had limited success. Existing non-blocking algorithms usually take two standard approaches. The first approach is to rely on automatic garbage collection (GC), simply deferring the problem to the GC. By doing this, the designers hinder the algorithm from being ported to environments without GC [5]. Moreover, the implementations of these designs with currently available (blocking) GC's cannot be considered non-blocking.

The second approach taken by designers of concurrent data structures is to adopt one of the available non-blocking memory management schemes. The most common schemes are probably the Hazard Pointers technique by Michael [14] or the similar Pass the Buck method by Herlihy et al. [10]. In these schemes, each thread has a pool of global pointers, called *hazard pointers* in [14] or *guards* in [10], which are used to mark objects as "live" or ready for reclamation. When a thread t reclaims a node, t adds the node to a special local reclamation buffer. Once in a while, t scans its buffer and for each node it checks whether some other thread has a hazard pointer[1] to the node. If not, that node can be safely deallocated. Special attention must be given to the time interval after a thread obtains a reference to an object and before it registers this object in a hazard pointer. During this time, the object may be reclaimed and reallocated. Thus, by the time it gets protected by a hazard pointer, it could have become a completely different entity. This delicate point enforces validation of the object's state after assigning it with a hazard pointer.

Although these techniques are not universal (i.e., there is no automatic way to incorporate them into a given algorithm), they are relatively simple. Moreover, a failure

[1]In this paper we will use the term "hazard pointers", but guard pointers are equally relevant.

of one thread prevents only a small number of nodes (to which the failed thread has references in its hazard pointers) from being deallocated. The major drawback of these techniques, however, is their significant runtime overhead, caused mainly by the management and validation of the global pointers required before accessing *each* internal node for the first time [8]. Along with that, expensive instructions, such as memory fences or compare-and-swap (CAS) instructions [14, 10, 8], are required for correctness of those schemes. Moreover, if the validation fails, the thread must restart its operation on the data structure, harming the performance further.

Another known method for memory management uses per-thread timestamps, as in [7], which are incremented by threads before every access to the data structure. When a thread removes a node, it records the timestamps of other threads. Later, it can deallocate the node once all threads increase their timestamps beyond the recorded values. Although this method is very lightweight, it is vulnerable to thread delays and failures. In such cases, memory space of an unbounded size may become impossible to reclaim [14].

In this paper, we concentrate on the linked list, one of the most fundamental data structures, which is particularly prone to the shortcomings of previous approaches [8]. The presented technique eliminates the performance overhead associated with the memory management without sacrificing the ability to deallocate memory in case of thread failures. The good performance of our technique stems from the assumption that thread failures are typically very uncommon in real systems, and if they do occur, this is usually indicative of more serious problems than being unable to deallocate some small part of memory. Our approach provides a flexible tradeoff between the runtime overhead introduced by memory management and the size of memory that might be lost when some thread fails.

Our memory management technique builds on a combination of three ideas: timestamps, anchors and freezing. As in [7], we use per-thread timestamps to track the activity of each thread on the data structure. Similarly to [14], we use global pointers, which we call anchors. Unlike [14], however, a thread drops the anchor (i.e., records a reference in the anchor) every bunch of node accesses, e.g., every one thousand nodes it traverses. As a result, the amortized cost of anchor management is spread across multiple node accesses and is thus very low. To recover the data structure from a failure of a thread t, we apply freezing [3]. That is, using t's anchors, other threads mark nodes that t may hold a reference to, as frozen. Then they copy and replace the frozen part of the data structure, restoring the ability of all threads to deallocate memory. The recovery operation is relatively expensive, but it is required only in the uncommon case in which a thread fails to make progress for a long while. Thus, the overall cost of the memory management remains very low.

We have implemented our scheme in C and compared its performance to the widely used implementation of the linked list based on Hazard Pointers (HP) [14]. Our performance results show that the total running time, using the anchor-based memory management, is about 250–500% faster the one based on HP. We also discuss how to apply our technique on other data structures, where the use of other approaches for memory management is more expensive.

2. RELATED WORK

Memory management can be fairly considered as the Achilles heel of many dynamically sized non-blocking data structures. In addition to the techniques mentioned in the introduction (that use per-thread timestamps [7] or global pointers [14, 10]), one can also find an approach based on reference counting [16, 6, 4, 15]. There, the idea is to associate a counter with every node, which is updated atomically when a thread gains or drops a reference to the node. Such atomic updates are typically performed with a fetch-and-add instruction, and the node can be safely removed once its reference count drops to zero. This approach suffers from several drawbacks, such as requiring each node to keep the reference count field even after the node is reclaimed [16, 15] or using uncommon atomic primitives, such as double compare-and-swap (DCAS) [4]. The major problem, however, remains performance [14, 8], since even when applying a read-only operation on the data structure, this approach requires atomic reference counter updates on every node access.

In a related work, Hart et al. [8] compare several memory management techniques, including hazard pointers, reference counters, and so-called quiescent-state-based reclamation. In the latter, the memory can be reclaimed when each thread passes through at least one quiescent state [13], in which it does not hold any reference to shared nodes, and in particular, to nodes that have been removed from the data structure. In fact, the timestamp-based technique [7] discussed in the introduction can be seen as a special case of the quiescent-state approach. Hart et al. [8] find that when using hazard pointers or reference counters, expensive atomic instructions, such as fences and compare-and-swaps (CAS) executed for every traversed node, dominate the performance cost. Quiescent-state reclamation usually performs better, but it heavily depends on how often quiescent states occur. Moreover, if a thread fails before reaching the quiescent state, no memory can be safely reclaimed from that point.

Dragojevic et al. [5] consider how hardware transactional memory (HTM) can help to alleviate the performance and conceptual difficulties associated with memory management techniques. In contrast to [5], our algorithm does not rely on special hardware support, such as HTM.

The freezing idea was previously used in the context of concurrent data structures by Braginsky and Petrank in their recent work on chunk-based linked lists [3]. There, list nodes are grouped into chunks for better cache locality and list traversal performance. The freezing technique is used in [3] for list restructuring to notify threads that the part of the data structure they are currently using is obsolete. This is done by setting a special freeze-bit on pointers belonging to nodes in the obsolete part, making the pointers/nodes unsuitable for traversing. A thread that fails to use a frozen pointer realizes that this part of the data structure is obsolete and it restarts its operation, usually after helping to accomplish the list restructuring procedure that froze that part.

3. AN OVERVIEW OF DROP THE ANCHOR

As mentioned in the introduction, our technique relies on three building blocks, namely timestamps, anchors, and freezing. A thread t manages a monotonically increasing

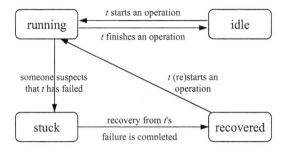

Figure 1: Transition diagram for possible states of the thread t

timestamp in the following way. When t starts its operation on a list data structure, it reads the timestamps of all threads and sets its timestamp to the maximal value it read plus one. When t finishes its operation, it simply marks its timestamp as idle.

The timestamp of t is associated with two flags, STUCK and IDLE. These flags specify one of the following states of the timestamp (and of the corresponding thread): *running* (both flags are turned off, meaning that t has a pending operation on the data structure), *idle* (only the IDLE flag is on, meaning that t does not have any pending operation on the data stucture), *running, but stuck*, which we call for brevity simply *stuck* (only the STUCK flag is on, meaning that t with a pending operation is suspected by other thread(s) to be stuck) and *recovered* (both flags are turned on, meaning that other threads have frozen and copied the memory that might be accessed by t). The transition between these states is captured in Figure 1. Normally, t moves between running and idle states. Once some thread suspects t to be stuck, t's timestamp is marked as stuck. The only way for t to return to the running state is to go through the recovered state (cf. Figure 1).

The timestamps are also used to mark the insertion and deletion times of list nodes. That is, each node in the list has two additional fields, which are set as follows. When t decides to insert (remove) a node into (from) the list, it sets the node's insertion (deletion, respectively) timestamp field to be higher by one from the maximal timestamp value that it observes among the timestamps of all threads.

The nodes deleted by t are stored in t's special reclamation buffer, which is scanned by t once in a while (as in [14]). During each scan, and for each deleted node n, t checks whether the deletion time of n is smaller than the current timestamps of other threads (plus an additional condition described later), and if so, deallocates the node. This check ensures that all threads have started a new list operation since the time this node was removed from the list, and therefore, no thread can be viewing this node at this time.

If threads did not fail, this would be everything needed to manage the memory of non-blocking lists by a traditional epoch-based approach [7]. Unfortunately, thread failures may happen. In the design described so far, if a thread fails during its operation on the list, no additional node can be deallocated, since the timestamp of the failed thread would not advance.

To cope with the problem of thread failures, we use two additional concepts, namely anchors and freezing. Anchors are simply pointers used by threads to point to list nodes. In fact, hazard pointers[14] can be seen as a special case of

anchors. The difference between the two is that the anchor is not dropped (set) before accessing every internal node in the list, but rather every ten, one hundred, or several thousands of node accesses (the frequency is controlled by the ANCHOR_THRESHOLD parameter). As a result, the amortized cost of anchor management is significantly reduced and spread across the traversal of (controllably) many nodes in the list data structure. The downside of our approach, however, is that when a thread t is suspected of being stuck, other threads do not know for sure which object t may access when (and if) it revives. They only know a range of nodes where t might be, which includes the node pointed by t's anchor plus additional nodes reachable from that anchored node. The suspecting threads use this range to recover the list from the failure of t. Specifically, they freeze all nodes in the range by setting the special *freeze-bit* of all pointers in these nodes[2]. Next, they copy all frozen nodes into a new sub-list. Finally, they replace the frozen nodes with the new sub-list and mark t's timestamp as recovered. This mark tells other threads that the list was recovered from t's failure. In other words, threads may again deallocate nodes they remove from the data structure, disregarding t's timestamp.

The recovery procedure is relatively heavy performance-wise and has certain technical issues, but in return, the common path, i.e., the traversal of the data structure, incurs virtually no additional operations related to memory management. Since the recovery is expected to be very infrequent, we believe (and show in our performance measurements) that the complication associated with the recovery procedure pays off by eliminating the overhead in the common path. In the next section, we provide technical details of the application of this general idea into the concrete non-blocking implementation of the linked list.

4. DETAILED DESCRIPTION

4.1 Auxiliary fields and records

We use the singly linked list of Harris [7] as a basis for our construction. To support our scheme, each thread maintains two records where it stores information related to the memory management. The first record is global, i.e., it can be read and written by any thread (not just the owner of the record), and used to manage the thread's timestamp and anchor. The second record is local, and is used during object reclamations and for deciding whether the recovery procedure is necessary.

The structure of the records is given in Listing 1. The global record contains two fields, `timestampAndAnchor` and `lowTimeStamp`. The `timeStampAndAnchor` field contains the timestamp, the anchor, and the IDLE and STUCK bits of the thread, combined into one word so that all can be modified atomically. The width and the actual internal structure of the field depends on the underlying machine. In certain settings of 64-bit Linux-based architectures, the virtual memory addressing requires 48 bits; the two least significant bits in a pointer are typically zeroed due to memory alignment. Moreover, most existing architectures support wide-CAS instruction, which operates atomically on two adjacent memory words (i.e., 128 bits). In such settings, we allocate 64

---

[2]The freeze-bit is one of the least significant bits of a pointer, which are normally zeroed due to memory alignment.

Listing 1: Auxiliary records

```
struct GlobalMemoryManagementRec{
    uint128_t timeStampAndAnchor;
    uint64_t lowTimeStamp;
};

struct LocalMemoryManagementRec{
    list_t reclamationBuffer;
    uint64_t minTimeStamp;
    uint32_t minTimeStampThreadID;
    uint32_t minTimeStampThreadCnt;
};
```

bits for the timestamp and 64 bits for the anchor pointer, including two bits for two flags, which specify the state of the thread (i.e., running, idle, stuck and recovered). In the settings where only 64 bits can be a target for a CAS instruction, one can use 48 bits or fewer for the anchor pointer and, respectively, 16 bits for timestamp. However, different allocation techniques can be used to require fewer bits for the pointer.

When a thread t accesses the list, it reads the timestamps of all threads in the system and sets its own timestamp to one plus the maximum among all the timestamp values that were read. It writes its new timestamp in the **timeStampAndAnchor** field, simultaneously setting the IDLE bit to zero. When t completes its operation, it simply turns the IDLE bit on (leaving the same timestamp value). The exact details of the manipulation of this field are provided in subsequent sections.

In addition to the **timeStampAndAnchor** field, the global record contains a field called **lowTimeStamp**. This field is set by t to the minimal timestamp observed by t when it starts an operation on the list. As described in Section 4.4, the **lowTimeStamp** field is used by other threads when they try to recover the list from the failure of t (to identify nodes that were inserted into the list before t started its current operation).

The local record has four fields. The description of their role is given in Section 4.3.

Along with adding auxiliary records for each thread, we also augment each node in the linked list with two fields having self-explanatory names, **insertTS** and **retireTS**. These fields are set to the current maximal timestamp plus one when a node is inserted into or deleted from the list, respectively.

4.2 Anchor maintenance

Anchor maintenance is carried out when threads traverse the list, looking for a particular key. The simplified pseudo-code for this traversal composes the **find** method given in the full version of this paper [2]. Recall that this method is used by all list operations in [7].

A thread counts the number of list nodes it has passed through and updates its anchor every ANCHOR_THRESHOLD nodes (where ANCHOR_THRESHOLD is some preset number). The anchor points to the first node in the list that can be accessed by the thread (which is the node pointed by **prev** in the **find** method). Anchor updates are made in the auxiliary **setAnchor** function also shown in [2]. An anchor update

may fail for thread t_i if some other thread t_j has marked the **timeStampAndAnchor** field of t_i as stuck, as explained in Section 4.4.

It is important to note that the actual update of the anchor is done with CAS (and not with a simple write operation) to avoid races with concurrently running threads that might suspect t_i being stuck and try to set the STUCK bit in t_i's **timeStampAndAnchor**. From a performance standpoint, however, the write operation of a hazard pointer, made on accessing every node, requires an expensive memory fence right after it [14, 8]. In contrast, the CAS in our approach is performed only every ANCHOR_THRESHOLD node accesses, and its amortized cost is negligible.

We note that the **find** function is allowed to traverse the frozen nodes of the list. A node is frozen if the second least significant bit in its **next** pointer is turned on (while the first least significant bit is used to mark the node as deleted [7]). If there is a need to update the **next** pointer of the frozen node, the update operation fails (as in [3]) and retries after invoking the **helpRecovery** method (pseudo-code can be found in [2]). As its name suggests, the latter method is used to help the recovery process of some stuck thread. This method is also called when a thread fails to update its anchor in **setAnchor**.

Finally, we note that at any time instant, list operations have references to at most two adjacent list nodes. (Recall that for the linked list data structure two hazard pointers are required [14]). As we require that a stuck thread will be able to access nodes only between its current anchor and (but not including) the next potential anchor, the ANCHOR_THRESHOLD parameter for the linked lists has to be at least 2.

4.3 Node reclamation

When a thread t_i removes a node from the list, it calls the **retireNode** method, which sets the deletion timestamp of the node (i.e., the **retireTS** field) to the current maximal timestamp plus one. Then, similarly to [14], the **retireNode** method adds the deleted node to a reclamation buffer. The latter is simply a local linked list (cf. Listing 1) where t_i stores nodes deleted from the list data structure, but not deallocated yet. When the size of the buffer reaches a predefined bound (controlled by the RETIRE_THRESHOLD parameter), t_i runs through the buffer and deallocates all nodes with the retire timestamp smaller than the current minimal timestamp (plus an additional condition elaborated in Section 4.4). Note that if the deletion time of a node n is smaller than the timestamp of a thread t_j, t_j started its last operation on the list after n was removed from the list; thus, t_j will never access n. Obviously, if this holds for any t_j, it is safe to deallocate n.

When t_i finds that some thread t_j exists such that the timestamp of t_j is smaller than or equal to the timestamp of one of the nodes in t_i's reclamation buffer, t_i stores the ID of that thread (i.e., j) in the **minTimeStampThreadID** field of its local memory management record (cf. Listing 1) and t_j's timestamp in the **minTimeStamp** field of that record. It also sets the **minTimeStampThreadCnt** field to 1. It is important to note that if several threads have the same minimal timestamp, t_i will store the smallest ID in **minTimeStampThreadID**. This will ensure that even if several threads are stuck with the same timestamp, all threads will consider the same thread in the recovery procedure.

On later scans of the reclamation buffer, if t_i finds that the thread t_j (whose ID is stored in t_i's `minTimeStampThreadID`) still has the same timestamp, t_i will increase the `minTime-StampThreadCnt` counter. Once the counter reaches the pre-defined RECOVERY_THRESHOLD parameter, t_i will suspect that t_j has failed and will start the recovery procedure described in Section 4.4.

4.4 Recovery procedure

The recovery procedure is invoked in one of the following three cases. First, it is invoked by a thread t_i that tries to deallocate an object n from its reclamation buffer, but repeatedly finds a running thread t_j whose timestamp remains smaller than or equal to the timestamp of n (cf. Section 4.3). The second case is when a thread t_i tries to modify the `next` pointer of one of the nodes in the list, but finds that this node is frozen (cf. Section 4.2). Finally, the third case happens when a thread tries to update its anchor by modifying its `timeStampAndAnchor` field, but finds that some other thread turned the STUCK bit on in this field (cf. Section 4.2). In two last cases t_i invokes the `helpRecovery` method. There, t_i scans through global records of the threads, looking for a thread t_j with the STUCK bit in t_j's `timeStampAndAnchor` field turned on.

The recovery procedure consists of four phases (the code can be found in [2]). We explain these phases using the example in Figure 2. Assume that at some point in time the list data structure is in the state depicted in Figure 2(a), and thread t_0 decides to recover the list from the failure of thread t_1. Before invoking the first phase of the recovery procedure, t_0 stores locally the current value of t_1's `timeStampAndAnchor` field. Then, in the first phase of the recovery procedure, t_0 attempts to modify t_1's `timeStampAndAnchor` field by turning the STUCK bit on using CAS operation (cf. Figure 2(b)). If this operation fails, t_0 rereads t_1's `timeStampAndAnchor` field and checks whether it was marked as stuck by some other thread. If not, it aborts the recovery procedure (since either t_1 is actually alive and has modified its `timeStampAndAnchor` field, or some other thread, i.e., t_2, has finished the recovery of t_1 and, as we will see later, turned both STUCK and IDLE bits on). Otherwise, if the CAS operation that turns the STUCK bit on succeeds, or if it fails, but t_1 is marked as stuck by another thread, t_0 proceeds to the second phase.

In the second phase of the recovery procedure, t_0 freezes and copies all nodes that t_1 might access if t_1 revived and traversed the list until realizing at the next anchor update that its anchor is marked as stuck. To identify such nodes, t_0 extracts t_1's anchor pointer out of the value stored in t_1's `timeStampAndAnchor` field (which points to node 25 in our example in Figure 2(a)). Then, t_0 starts setting the freeze-bit in the `next` pointers of reachable nodes, starting from node 25. It copies the frozen nodes (with the freeze-bit set off) into a new list. Note that some of the nodes may already be deleted from the list (e.g., node 25, 27 and 42 in Figure 2), but not disconnected or reclaimed yet. Such nodes are frozen, but they do not enter the new copied part of the list. The thread t_0 keeps freezing and copying until it passes through ANCHOR_THRESHOLD nodes having an insertion timestamp smaller than the value of t_1's `lowTimeStamp` field. In our example in Figure 2, let us assume that these are nodes 25, 27, 40, 41 and 42. Note that for traversing those nodes, t_0 had to update its own anchor to be the same

as t_1's anchor in order to handle t_0's failure during the recovery procedure. At the end of the second phase the list looks as depicted in Figure 2(c). The pseudo-code for how we freeze the nodes and create the copies can be found in [2].

In the third phase, t_0 attempts to replace the frozen nodes with a locally copied part of the list. To this end, it runs from the beginning of the list data structure and looks for the first (not-deleted) node m whose `next` pointer either points to the not-deleted frozen nodes or it is followed by a sequence of one or more deleted nodes such that the `next` pointer of the last node in the sequence points to a not-deleted frozen node (in Figure 2(c), m is the node 12). If such m were not found by reaching the end of the list data structure, t_0 would finish this phase, as it would assume that some other thread has replaced the frozen part of the list with the new list created by that thread. Otherwise, t_0 attempts to update m's `next` pointer to point to the corresponding copied node in the new list. If it fails, it restarts this phase from the beginning. Otherwise, t_0 inserts all nodes between m and the first frozen node (i.e., node 20 in Figure 2(c)) into its reclamation buffer in order to deallocate them later, bringing the list to the state exhibited in Figure 2(d). The code of the procedure for replacing frozen nodes can also be found in [2].

One subtlety that is left out of the code for lack of space, is the verification that the new local list indeed matches the frozen nodes being replaced. It is crucial to ensure that if a thread running the recovery procedure gets delayed, it does not replace another frozen part of the list when it resumes. To this end, we record the sources of the new nodes, when they are copied, and CAS the new list into the data structure only if it replaces the adequate original nodes that can be found in the recorded sources.

In the final, fourth phase, t_0 sets the IDLE bit in the t_1's `timeStampAndAnchor` field, marking t_1 as recovered. Additionally, t_0 promotes t_1's timestamp, recording the (logical) time when t_1 was recovered (cf. Figure 2(e)). Note that t_0 does not need to check whether its CAS has succeeded, since if it hasn't, some other thread has performed this operation. We denote a timestamp of a thread with IDLE and STUCK flags turned on as *recovery timestamp*.

4.5 The refined reclamation procedure

Thread t_1, considered stuck, might actually have a pointer to a node n which is already not a part of the list. For instance, in the state of the list shown in Figure 2(a), t_1 might be stopped while inspecting node 25 (or 27). If this node is currently in the reclamation buffer of some other thread t_k (i.e., t_0 or t_2), and if t_k does not consider t_1 after the recovery is done (i.e., t_k only checks that node 25's `retireTS` is smaller than the timestamp of any *running* thread), t_k might deallocate node 25 and t_1 might erroneously access this memory if and when it revives. Note that node 27 may already be unreachable from the node pointed by t_1's anchor by the time of t_1's recovery, if, e.g., the next pointer of node 25 was updated while t_1 was inspecting node 27. In this case, node 27 will not be frozen and copied at all. In order to cope with such situations, before deallocating a node we require its retire timestamp (`retireTS`) to be larger than the timestamp of any thread in the *recovered* state (in addition to being smaller than the timestamp of any running thread). This way we prevent nodes removed from the list

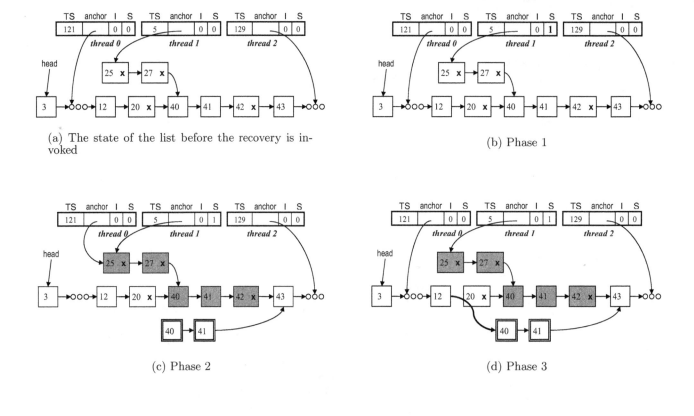

(a) The state of the list before the recovery is invoked

(b) Phase 1

(c) Phase 2

(d) Phase 3

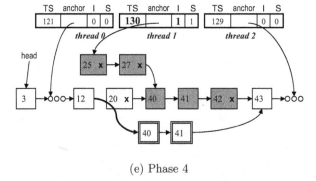

(e) Phase 4

Figure 2: Recovery phases. Nodes marked with 'x' are deleted, i.e., the delete-bit of their next pointer is turned on [7]. Shaded nodes are frozen, i.e., the freeze-bit of their next pointer is turned on.

before some thread got recovered from being deallocated, as the thread being recovered might hold a pointer to such node. When (and if) the recovered thread becomes running again, it will be possible to reclaim those nodes. To summarize, when a thread wants to deallocate a node n, it checks that n is not frozen (i.e., the freeze-bit in its `next` pointer is not set) and that the following condition holds:

$$\mathrm{MAX}(\{\text{timestamp of } t_x \mid t_x \text{ is recovered}\}) < n.\text{retireTS} <$$
$$\mathrm{MIN}(\{\text{timestamp of } t_x \mid t_x \text{ is running}\})$$

It should be noted that when calculations of the retire timestamp and the recovery timestamp are done simultaneously (by different threads), the retire timestamp can erroneously be higher than the recovery timestamp, and wrong reclamation can happen. Therefore, when calculating the retire timestamp for a node, we require a thread to pass twice over the timestamps of the threads verifying that no thread was marked stuck or recovered concurrently. If such thread(s) is found, the node is inserted into the reclamation stack as frozen.

For simplicity of presentation, in the algorithm described above frozen nodes are not reclaimed. Such nodes can only appear if threads fail and such a solution may be acceptable. However, frozen nodes can be easily reclaimed for recovered threads that have resumed operation. A recovered thread can reclaim nodes according to the recovery timestamps. Also, a frozen node that appears in a reclamation stack can be reclaimed using its `retireTS` field and the `lowTimeStamp` field of all stuck threads. Details are omitted.

4.6 Correctness argument

In this section we give high-level arguments behind the proofs of correctness. We start by outlining the assumed memory model and defining linearization points for the modified list operations. Then we argue that any internal node deleted after the last recovery was finished (or deleted any time if no thread has been suspected being stuck) will be eventually reclaimed (we call this property *eventual conditional reclamation*). Next, we argue that our technique guarantees the safety of memory references. In other words, no thread t accesses the memory that has been reclaimed since the time t obtained a reference to it. Finally, we argue that our technique is non-blocking, meaning that whenever a thread t starts the recovery procedure, then after a finite number of t's steps either t completes the recovery, or some other thread completes an operation on the list. In addition, we show that the system-wide progress with respect to the list operations is preserved, that is after a finite number of completed recovery procedures there is at least one completed list operation.

Due to space limitation, the proof sketch of all lemmas appears in the full version of this paper [2].

4.6.1 Model and linearizability

Our model for concurrent multi-threaded computation follows the linearizability model of [12]. In particular, we assume an asynchronous shared memory system where n deterministic threads communicate by executing atomic operations on some finite number of shared variables. Each thread performs a sequence of steps, where in each step the tread may perform some local computation or invoke a single atomic operation on a shared variable. The atomic operations allowed in our model are reads, writes, or compare-and-swaps (CAS). The latter receives a memory address of

a shared variable v and two values, *old* and *new*. It sets the value of v to *new* only if the value of v right before CAS is applied is *old*; in this case CAS returns *true*. Otherwise, the value of v does to change and CAS returns *false*. We assume that each thread has an ID, denoted as tid, which is a value between 0 and $n-1$. In systems where tid may have values from arbitrary range, known non-blocking renaming algorithms can be applied (e.g., [1]). In addition, we assume each thread can access its tid and n.

The original implementation of all operations of the non-blocking linked list by Harris [7] is linearizable [12]. We argue that after applying Drop the Anchor memory management technique, all list operations remain linearizable. Recall that all list operations invoke the `find` method, which returns pointers to two adjacent nodes, one of which holds the value smaller than the given key. For further details, see [7]). Denote this node as *prev*. Furthermore, recall that list operations may invoke `find` several times. For instance, `insert` will invoke `find` again if the `next` pointer of *prev* has being concurrently modified (in particular, in our case, frozen). Thus, we define the linearization points for a list operation *op* with respect to the *prev* returned from the last invocation of `find` by *op*. If this *prev* node is not frozen (i.e., the freeze-bit of its `next` pointer is not set), the linearization point of *op* is exactly as in [7]. However, if this *prev* node is frozen, we set the linearization point of *op* at the time instance defined as following. Consider the sequence of frozen nodes read by the corresponding `find` operation starting from a frozen node m and including the (frozen) node *prev* (where m and *prev* might be the same node). The linearization point of *op* is defined at the latest of the two events: (a) the corresponding `find` traversed m (i.e., read the `next` pointer of the node previous to m in the list) and (b) the latest time at which some node between (and including) m and *prev* was inserted or marked as deleted. The intuition is that when `find` returns a result from a frozen part of the list, this part no longer reflects the actual state of the list at the moment *prev* node is read. Thus, we have to linearize the corresponding operation at some earlier time instance, at which the nodes read by `find` are still consistent with the actual keys stored in the list.

4.6.2 Eventual conditional reclamation

LEMMA 4.1. *Let T_s and T_f be the time when a thread t starts and finishes, respectively, the call to `retireNode(node)` and $T_r > T_f$ is the time when t finishes to scan its reclamation buffer. Then at least one of the following events occurs in the time interval $[T_s, T_r]$:*

1. *Some thread remains running throughout $[T_f, T_r]$, and its timestamp changes at most once in $[T_f, T_r]$.*

2. *Some thread becomes recovered at some point in time in $[T_s, T_r]$.*

3. *The memory allocated to `node` is reclaimed by the time T_r.*

Based on the lemma above, we prove that when a thread removes a node from the list, as long as that tread keeps applying (delete) operations on the list and particularly "bad" things do not happen to other threads (e.g., they are not suspected to be failed), the memory of that node will be eventually reclaimed.

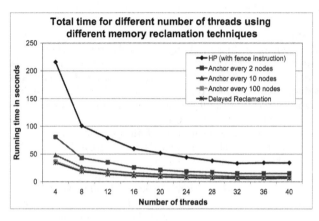

(a) The total running time comparison for searches only.

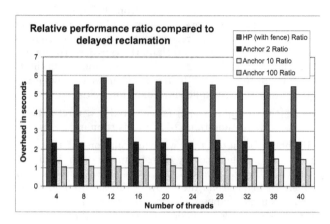

(b) Memory management overhead referred to delayed reclamation for searches only.

Figure 3: Drop the Anchor vs. Hazard Pointers for lists with the initial size of 100k keys, the read-only workload results.

LEMMA 4.2. *Let T_s be the time when a thread t starts the call to* `retireNode(node)`. *Then* `node` *will be eventually reclaimed as long as t keeps removing nodes from the list and there is no thread that is stuck or recovered at or after T_s.*

Note that even if some thread t_x gets stuck or recovered after T_s as above, it may have impact only on nodes being removed *before* (or concurrently to) t_x's recovery.

4.6.3 Safety of memory references

First, we prove that access to any node that can be reached from t's anchor (for any thread t) is safe, i.e., such node cannot be reclaimed.

LEMMA 4.3. *No node reachable from an anchor of some thread can be reclaimed.*

Using the lemma above, we show that with the Drop the Anchor memory management, no thread will access a reclaimed memory.

LEMMA 4.4. *No thread t accesses the memory that has been reclaimed since the time t obtained a reference to it.*

4.6.4 Progress guarantees

The original implementation of all operations of the non-blocking linked list by Harris [7] is lock-free [12] . We argue that after applying Drop the Anchor memory management technique, all list operations remain lock-free. We say that a thread t_i *starts the recovery* of a thread t_j when t_i sets the STUCK bit on in t_j's `timestampAndAnchor` field. Similarly, we say a thread t_i *completes the recovery* of a stuck thread t_j when t_i sets the IDLE bit on in t_j's `timestampAndAnchor` field.

LEMMA 4.5. *If a thread t_i starts the recovery of t_j at T_s, then the recovery of t_j will be completed at $T_f > T_s$ (by possibly another thread t_k) and/or infinitely many list operations will be linearized after T_s.*

Next, we show that despite recovery operations, the system-wide progress is preserved, i.e., threads never keep recovering one another forever without completing list operations.

LEMMA 4.6. *Consider $n+1$ recovery operations completed at times $T_1 < T_2 < ... < T_{n+1}$. Then there must be at least one list (delete) operation linearized in the time interval $[T_1, T_{n+1}]$.*

5. PERFORMANCE EVALUATION

We have implemented the non-blocking linked list data structure of Harris [7] with several memory management techniques. First, we have implemented the Hazard Pointers technique following the pseudo-code presented in [14], but with the additional memory fence instruction added just after the write of a new value to the hazard pointer of a thread [8]. Second, we have implemented our new Drop the Anchor technique presented in this paper. Finally, we have also implemented a simple technique, where nodes removed by a thread t from the list are added to t's reclamation stack and reclaimed later once 64 nodes are collected in the reclamation stack. We refer to this implementation as *delayed reclamation*. We note that this scheme is incorrect in a sense that it allows threads to access deallocated memory, but we used this implementation to represent a memory management scheme with a minimal performance impact. All our implementations were coded in C and compiled with -O3 optimization level.

We have run our experiments on the machine with two AMD Opteron(TM) 6272 16-core processors, operated by Linux OS (Ubuntu 12.04). We have varied the number of threads between 1 and 40, slightly above the number of threads that can run concurrently on this machine (32). If not stated otherwise, each test starts by building an initial list with 100k random keys. After that, we measure the total time of 320k operations divided equally between all threads. The keys for searches and insertions are randomly chosen 20-bit sized keys. For deletion operations, we ensure that randomly chosen keys actually exist in the list in order to make the reclamation process substantial. The values of RECOVERY_THRESHOLD and RETIRE_THRESHOLD were always 64. All threads are synchronized to start their operations immediately after the initial list is built and we

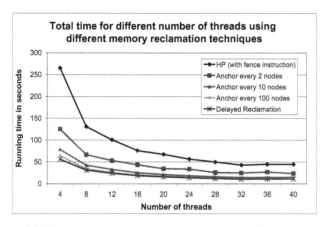

(a) The total running time comparison for 20% inserts, 20% deletes and 60% searches.

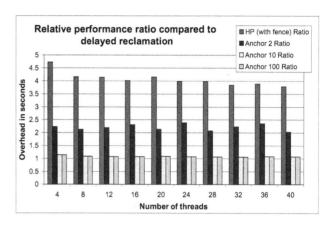

(b) Memory management overhead referred to delayed reclamation for 20% inserts, 20% deletes and 60% searches.

Figure 4: Drop the Anchor vs. Hazard Pointers for lists with the initial size of 100k keys, the mixed workload results.

measure the time it takes to complete all operations by all threads. We run each test 10 times and present the average results. The variance of all reported results is below 1.5% of the average.

Figures 3 and 4 show the measurements of the total time required to complete our benchmark using the HP memory management, the delayed reclamation and the Drop the Anchor method. For the latter, we have used three versions with different values for the ANCHOR_THRESHOLD value. Specifically, in the first version the anchor is dropped every second node (which is the lowest legitimate value for ANCHOR_THRESHOLD in the case of the linked list), in the second version the anchor is dropped every 10 nodes, and in the third – every 100 nodes. We show the results for read-only workload where all operations are searches (Figure 3(a)) and for the mixed workload, where 20% of all operations are insertions, 20% are deletions, and the remaining 60% are searches (Figure 4(a)).

Our measurements show that in the mixed workload the Drop the Anchor-based implementation is faster in about 150–250% than the HP-based one, even if the anchor is dropped every second node. When increasing the ANCHOR_TH-RESHOLD parameter from 2 to 100, we get even higher improvement of 300–450% over the performance of HPs.

In read-only workload we can see even better performance improvement (400% on average) due to anchors usage compared to HP usage (cf. Figure 3(a)). Finally, we can see that for substantial amount of threads, the Drop the Anchor-based linked list performance is very close to the linked list implementation based on the simple delayed reclamation. This suggests that the amortized cost of the memory management in the Drop the Anchor technique is very small.

Additionally, Figures 3(b), 4(b) present the relative performance ratio of each memory management technique, explained above, compared to delayed reclamation. When the ratio is close to 1 it means that the memory management technique adds almost no overhead over the delayed reclamation. The HP memory management shows 400–550% slowdown, where Anchor-based implementation shows 7–

10% slowdown for anchors dropped every 100 nodes, and 200–250% slowdown for anchors dropped every 2 nodes, all compared to delayed reclamation results.

In another set of experiments, we measure the impact of the initial size of the list on the performance of the HP-based and Drop the Anchor-based implementations, while the number of threads is constant (16) and the workload is mixed. The results are depicted in Figure 5(a). It can be seen that the running time of both implementations increases linearly with the size of the list as threads need to traverse more nodes per operation on average. The slope of the HP-based implementation is much steeper, however, suggesting that the overhead introduced by fences is much more significant than the cost of the anchor management.

In Figure 5(b) we can see the performance impact of the recovery procedure in the Drop the Anchor technique. We use the version of the technique with the ANCHOR_THRESHOLD value equals 100 for more significant impact. We explicitly delay one of the threads, thus causing this thread to be considered as stuck and recovered by other threads. The stuck thread returns to run after 2 seconds and the presented total time is measured until all threads finish their runs. The results show that the recovery procedure has 15–50% impact on the performance, even when the ANCHOR_THRESHOLD value is high. In any case, the Anchors-based implementation's performance (with the delay and recovery) is much better than the HP-based one.

6. DISCUSSION

We presented a new method for memory management of non-blocking data structures called *Drop the Anchor*. Drop the Anchor is a novel combination of the time-stamping method (which cannot handle thread failures) with the anchors and freezing techniques that provide a fallback allowing reclamation even when threads fail. Non-blocking algorithms must be robust to thread failures and so coping with thread failures in the memory manager is crucial. We have applied Drop the Anchor for the common non-blocking linked list implementation and compared it with

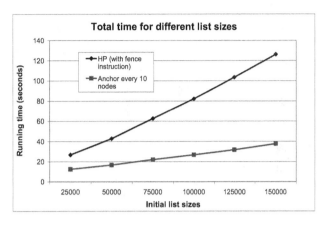

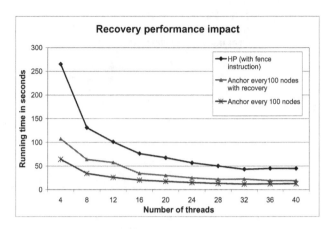

(a) Drop the Anchor vs. Hazard Pointers when 16 threads are run on lists with different initial sizes. In the Anchor-based implementation, the anchor is dropped every 10 nodes.

(b) The impact of the recovery on the performance of lists with the initial size of 100k keys.

Figure 5: Drop the Anchor vs. Hazard Pointers for lists with the different initial sizes and the recovery performance impact.

the standard Hazard Pointers method. Measurements show that Drop the Anchor drastically reduces the memory management overhead, while robustly reclaiming objects in all executions.

We believe our technique can be applied for other non-blocking data structures. Specifically, assume a data structure represented by a directed graph, where vertices correspond to internal nodes and edges correspond to pointers between these nodes. When recovering a thread t, we need to freeze and copy the sub-graph containing all internal nodes at the distance that depends on the ANCHOR_THRESHOLD parameter, from the node pointed by t's anchor. Essentially, although the copying operation might be expensive and even involve the whole data structure, the scalability bottleneck associated with the memory fences will be removed from the common node access step.

7. ACKNOWLEDGMENTS

We want to thank Tim Harris for his helpful comments on the earlier version of this paper.

8. REFERENCES

[1] H. Attiya and A. Fouren. Adaptive and efficient algorithms for lattice agreement and renaming. *SIAM J. Comput.*, 31(2):642–664, 2001.

[2] A. Braginsky, A. Kogan, and E. Petrank. Drop the anchor: Lightweight memory management for non-blocking data structures (full version). http://www.cs.technion.ac.il/ erez/Papers/-DropTheAnchorFull.pdf.

[3] A. Braginsky and E. Petrank. Locality-conscious lock-free linked lists. In *ICDCN*, pages 107–118, 2011.

[4] D. Detlefs, P. A. Martin, M. Moir, and G. L. Steele. Lock-free reference counting. *Distributed Computing*, 15(4):255–271, 2002.

[5] A. Dragojevic, M. Herlihy, Y. Lev, and M. Moir. On the power of hardware transactional memory to simplify memory management. In *PODC*, pages 99–108, 2011.

[6] A. Gidenstam, M. Papatriantafilou, H. Sundell, and P. Tsigas. Efficient and reliable lock-free memory reclamation based on reference counting. *TPDS*, 20(8):1173–1187, 2009.

[7] T. L. Harris. A pragmatic implementation of non-blocking linked-lists. In *DISC*, pages 300–314, 2001.

[8] T. E. Hart, P. E. McKenney, A. D. Brown, and J. Walpole. Performance of memory reclamation for lockless synchronization. *Journal of Parallel and Distributed Computing*, 67(12):1270–1285, 2007.

[9] M. Herlihy. Wait-free synchronization. *ACM Trans. Program. Lang. Syst.*, 13(1):124–149, 1991.

[10] M. Herlihy, V. Luchangco, P. Martin, and M. Moir. Nonblocking memory management support for dynamic-sized data structures. *ACM Trans. Comput. Syst.*, 23(2):146–196, 2005.

[11] M. Herlihy and N. Shavit. *The Art of Multiprocessor Programming*. Morgan Kaufmann Publishers Inc., 2008.

[12] M. P. Herlihy and J. M. Wing. Linearizability: a correctness condition for concurrent objects. *ACM Trans. Program. Lang. Syst.*, 12(3):463–492, 1990.

[13] P. E. McKenney and J. D. Slingwine. Read-copy update: Using execution history to solve concurrency problems. In *PDCS*, pages 509–518, 1998.

[14] M. M. Michael. Hazard pointers: Safe memory reclamation for lock-free objects. *TPDS*, 15:491–504, 2004.

[15] H. Sundell. Wait-free reference counting and memory management. In *IPDPS*, 2005.

[16] J. D. Valois. Lock-free linked lists using compare-and-swap. In *PODC*, pages 214–222, 1995.

Scalable Statistics Counters

Dave Dice
Oracle Labs
dave.dice@oracle.com

Yossi Lev
Oracle Labs
yossi.lev@oracle.com

Mark Moir
Oracle Labs
mark.moir@oracle.com

ABSTRACT

Statistics counters are important for purposes such as detecting excessively high rates of various system events, or for mechanisms that adapt based on event frequency. As systems grow and become increasingly NUMA, commonly used naive counters impose scalability bottlenecks and/or such inaccuracy that they are not useful. We present both precise and statistical (probabilistic) counters that are nonblocking and provide dramatically better scalability *and* accuracy properties. Crucially, these counters are competitive with the naive ones even when contention is low.

Categories and Subject Descriptors

D.1.3 [**Programming Techniques**]: Concurrent Programming; E.1 [**Data Structures**]; E.2 [**Data Storage Representations**]; G.3 [**Probability and Statistics**]

Keywords

Statistical counters, performance, scalability, accuracy

1. INTRODUCTION

Most large software systems use statistics counters for performance monitoring and diagnostics. While single-threaded statistics counters are trivial, commonly-used naive concurrent implementations quickly become problematic, especially as thread counts grow, and as they are used in increasingly Non-Uniform Memory Access (NUMA) systems. Designers face difficult tradeoffs involving latency of lightly contended counters, scalability—and in some cases accuracy—of heavily contended ones, and probe effects.

Although counters are almost as simple a data structure as one can imagine, there is a wide variety of use cases, assumptions and constraints that can significantly impact the range of implementations that are acceptable and/or effective. In this paper, we mostly concentrate on statistics counters that are used to count events that may occur with high frequency,

while the value of the counter is read infrequently, as is common for performance monitoring and diagnostics. Another interesting use case is data structures that employ counters to monitor access patterns, allowing the data structure to be reorganized to improve performance (see [1], for example).

In discussing shared counters with both theoretical and practical colleagues, we find good understanding of some issues, but confusion and misinformation about others. It is widely understood that simply incrementing a shared counter without synchronization does not work for multiple threads, because one thread's update can overwrite another's, thereby losing the effects of one or more increments. It is also well known that such counters can be made thread-safe by protecting them with a lock, but that in most modern shared memory multiprocessors, it is better to increment the counter using an atomic instruction such as compare-and-swap (CAS). CAS increments the counter—and indicates success—only if the counter has the value the incrementing thread "expects". Otherwise, it is retried, perhaps after some backoff.

This solution is simple, correct, and nonblocking but does not scale to large, NUMA systems. A common "solution" is to use the single-threaded version, eliminating the overhead of using CAS, as the precise value of the counter is not important, so losing "occasional" updates is acceptable.

This approach is flawed in two crucial ways. First, using separate load and store instructions to update the counter may *slightly* reduce the latency, as compared to using CAS, but it does not avoid the dominant cost of resolving the remote cache miss that is likely to occur when a variable is modified by many threads in a NUMA system. But most importantly, when contention on the counter increases, it is not just "occasional" updates that are lost: *many* increments can be lost due to a single delayed update. In our experiments, such counters consistently lost over 90% of increments when shared by 32 or more threads. Ironically, this problem becomes worse as contention increases: exactly the scenario many counters are intended to detect.

Some minor variations can mitigate the poor scalability and/or inaccuracy of naive counters to some degree. Examples include prefetching to avoid unnecessary cache state upgrades, ignoring CAS failures or using atomic add instructions to avoid retry loops and branch mispredicts, etc. Most of these are architecture-specific and—more importantly—none of them changes the fact that updating a single variable on every increment of a statistics counter will not scale to large, NUMA systems. Experiments confirm our intuition that they do not adequately addresses the shortcomings of the commonly used naive counters.

This paper explores scalable implementations of two kinds of counters: precise and statistical. Although statistical counters may not provide an exact count, to be useful, they should have reasonable statistical properties such that, with high probability, they do not deviate from the precise count by "too much", as explained in more detail later. In both categories, we present implementations that are substantially better than those in common use.

We focus on counters that are incremented only by one and are never decremented. We exploit these assumptions to improve our algorithms, though many of the techniques we describe can be generalized to weaken or avoid them.

We cannot explore all possible implementations. In this paper, we investigate a variety of existing and new counter implementations, concentrating on those we believe are most likely to be used in practice in large software systems. We aim to highlight shortfalls of some counters that are widely used, and to offer practical alternatives that overcome them.

We present precise counters in Section 2 and statistical counters in Sections 3 and 4. In Section 5, we present experimental results showing that our algorithms can provide dramatically better throughput than the naive counters discussed above. Furthermore, our statistical counter algorithms are very accurate, even under heavy contention. We conclude in Section 6.

2. PRECISE COUNTERS

A simple and well-known approach to making counters scalable is to split them into per-thread components, with each thread incrementing its own component without synchronization. This increases space requirements by a factor of the number of threads that use it. While this space overhead may be acceptable in many modern systems, and per-thread components may be acceptable in monolithic applications with fixed sets of threads, modern application structures are often more dynamic, executing tasks via a dynamic pool of worker threads, for example. In such caoses, use of per-thread components is inconvenient at best. In this section, we present several algorithms that mitigate these disadvantages to varying degrees.

2.1 Minimal space overhead

If additional space overhead is unacceptable, and counters must be precise, well-known randomized backoff techniques [2] can at least avoid a complete meltdown under heavy contention; we call this version RBO.

We have also explored some approaches that are inspired by previous NUMA lock algorithms, such as the HBO algorithm due to Radovic and Hagersten [10] and the cohort locks of Dice et al. [5]. These locks significantly improve performance and scalability under contention by handing off the lock multiple times within a NUMA node before it is acquired on another node. One simple approach based on this idea is to use a cohort lock to improve contention management for RBO: when a thread fails an attempt to increment the counter using CAS, it retries after acquiring a cohort lock, thereby encouraging multiple updates on one NUMA node before an update on another when contention arises. We have implemented this algorithm and found it to be effective in improving performance over RBO. However, because of the space overhead of the cohort lock, this algorithm has no particular advantage over others we introduce later (particularly MultilineAdapt).

Another approach that is similar in spirit to the above-mentioned NUMA locks, but does not add significant space overhead, is to use a few bits of the counter's value to identify which node currently has "priority": threads on other nodes delay retrying after a failed update, making it more likely that threads on the priority node can perform consecutive updates. Of course, the bits used to identify the priority node should not include the lowest-order bits that change frequently, but should be chosen so that the priority changes often enough to avoid unreasonable delays. This approach is simple, adds no space overhead, and performs well when increment operations are evenly spread across all nodes. But it does not adapt well to less uniform workloads.

This shortcoming is addressed by RBONuma, which augments the counter with a few bits (or alternatively steals bits from the counter, thereby restricting its range). It requires only enough additional bits to store the ID of a NUMA node plus one more bit. Thus, it can accommodate a counter that ranges from 0 to $2^{(N-1)-\lceil \log_2(\#NODES) \rceil}-1$ using N bits. Our implementation—for a 4-node system—uses 32 bits, thus supporting counting up to $2^{29} - 1$.

RBONuma stores the ID of the node on which the counter was last incremented with the counter, allowing threads on other nodes to hold off in order to encourage consecutive increments on that node. A thread that waits too long can become "impatient", at which point it stores its node ID into an *anti-starvation variable*.[1] This tells threads on other nodes to wait before attempting to update the counter, thus enabling threads on the node with the impatient thread to fetch the cache line and increment the counter. Unlike the HBO lock [10], we do not *prevent* other threads from incrementing the counter before the impatient thread because we did not want to sacrifice the non-blocking property of the counter, and the heuristic approach described above avoids starvation in practice, even under heavy contention.

In RBONuma, threads on the same node as an impatient thread abort their "slow" backoff, and attempt to increment the counter immediately. Regardless of which thread on a node increments the counter, this has the effect of bringing the relevant cache line to that node, which gives all threads on that node a better chance to increment the counter. Thus, we do not attempt to ensure that the thread that becomes impatient is the next to increment the counter, but rather allow nearby threads whose increments will help the impatient thread to increment the counter before it. We found that this approach gave the best performance.

Although RBONuma can yield an order of magnitude better throughput than RBO under heavy contention (see Section 5), it imposes significant overhead in low-contention scenarios. Part of the reason is the need to test the anti-starvation flag before even trying to increment the counter. We therefore implemented RBONumaAdapt, which begins as a regular counter that does not record the node of the most recent increment; while there is no node recorded, there is no need to check the anti-starvation variable. If a thread retries more than a certain number of times (our implementation tries three times quickly, followed by 16 times with randomized backoff) before successfully incrementing the counter, then it records its node ID in the counter. Thereafter, the slower but more scalable algorithm described above is used. Al-

---

[1] Each counter must be associated with an anti-starvation variable, but it is not necessary to have one per counter. Our implementation uses a single, global anti-starvation variable.

though we did not do so, it would be straightforward to reset the counter to an ordinary counter occasionally, so that the effects of occasional contention do not persist forever. The results in Section 5 show that `RBONumaAdapt` is competitive with the best of `RBO` and `RBONuma` at all contention levels.

The counters described so far achieve good single-thread performance and scalability under heavy contention. However, their advantage over simple `RBO` is reduced under moderate load, because there is less opportunity to perform consecutive increments on the same node. Furthermore, these algorithms tend to be sensitive to system-specific tuning, making them less stable. Next, we explore counters that overcome these issues by using a little more space.

2.2 Using a little more space

To avoid expensive cross-node communication without suffering the above-mentioned disadvantages of per-thread counter components, our `Multiline` algorithm uses a counter component *per NUMA node*; each component occupies a separate cache line to avoid false sharing. Synchronization on per-node components is again via CAS increments with randomized backoff. CAS synchronization is not as problematic as is often assumed, as there is no cross-node contention. (Somewhat analogously, Dice and Garthwaite [4] used per-processor allocation buffers in their memory allocator, achieving good scalability while avoiding the pitfalls of using per-thread allocation buffers.)

`GetVal` reads each component in turn, with no synchronization, and returns the sum of the values read. (The correctness of this approach depends on our assumption that increments only add one; other techniques are available for more general cases [7].)

Although the space blow-up is limited by the number of nodes, we prefer to avoid it for counters that are incremented rarely. Our `MultilineAdapt` implementation begins with a regular counter, and "inflates" it to use the above-described technique only if more than a certain number (four in our implementation) of attempts to increment it fail. Other policies are possible, such as inflating the counter if it frequently causes remote cache misses. To inflate a counter, we allocate a structure with one counter per node and replace the counter with a pointer to that structure (we reserve one bit to distinguish such pointers from counter values).

With this solution, low-contention counters use just the reserved bit (in practice cutting the range of the counter by half), and we only pay higher space overhead for contended counters. `MultilineAdapt` introduces an extra level of indirection for contended counters. The resulting slowdown to the increment operation is not a problem if the counter is contended (on the contrary, reduces the rate of CAS attempts on the counter, hence reducing contention).

The result is a counter that is competitive in both space overhead and throughput with the basic `RBO` counter at low levels of contention, scales well with increasing contention, and yields more than 700x higher throughput than `RBO` under high contention (see Section 5). Despite this encouraging data, our results show that `Multiline` and `MultilineAdapt` suffer under high contention levels because of contention between threads on the same node using a single component.

This contention can be alleviated by using more components per node. While per-node components must be in separate cache lines to avoid false sharing between nodes, if we use more than one component per node, it may not be unreasonable to locate multiple components for a single node in the same cache line. While false sharing may still arise in this case, it will be only within one NUMA node, and there is still benefit from using multiple components, as fewer CAS failures will occur. Thus, it may be possible to improve performance without increasing space usage.

The additional space overhead used by `Multiline` may be problematic in systems with large numbers of statistics counters, most of which are not heavily contended. While `MultilineAdapt` allows us to incur the space overhead only for contended counters, if different counters are contended at different times, this may result in excessive overhead over time. Furthermore, these algorithms increase `GetVal` latency (see Section 5.5), and in some contexts, they may be unacceptable due to their use of dynamically allocated memory. In Section 3, we show how we can avoid all of these issues if counters are not required to be precise.

3. STATISTICAL COUNTERS

Simple *unsynchronized* counters lose significant fractions of counter updates, even at moderate levels of contention (see Section 5). Because counters are often used to detect excessive rates of various system events, these naive implementations are ironically least effective exactly when the data they should provide is most important. Nonetheless, precise counts are often not required. In this section, we explore counters that exploit this flexibility while still aiming to maintain a prescribed level of accuracy that is not achieved by the naive implementations.

We begin with background on a counter algorithm published by Morris [9] in 1978, from which we borrow some ideas. Morris's primary motivation was to maintain a large number of counters, each of which could represent large numbers using only 8 bits. He did not address concurrent counters, much less scalability in the NUMA systems of the (then) distant future. Our key observation, however, is that Morris's technique has the effect of substantially reducing the frequency of updates to the counter, which lends itself perfectly to our purposes.

3.1 Morris's algorithm

Morris's counter [9] represents a larger range than 8 bits usually does by storing a probabilistic approximation of the following value, where n is the precise count (i.e., number of times increment has been invoked):

$$v(n) = \log(1 + n/a)/\log(1 + 1/a),$$

where a is a parameter that controls the accuracy of the counter, as explained below. Adding one to n/a ensures that the function is well defined and equals zero when $n = 0$, and dividing by $\log(1 + 1/a)$ ensures that the function is one when $n = 1$. As we will see, this ensures that the counter contains accurate values at least for values zero and one. It follows from this definition that, when the value stored in the counter is v, the counter value it represents is:

$$n(v) = a((1 + 1/a)^v - 1).$$

We call the value v that is physically stored in the counter the *stored value*, and the value $n(v)$ that it represents the *projected value*.

The algorithm stores a *probabilistic approximation* of $v(n)$, where n is the precise count, because the stored value must be an integer, as Morris assumed only 8 bits. As a result, the precise count cannot be determined from the stored value. Therefore, there is no deterministic way to know when to increment the value stored in the counter to reflect that enough increments have occurred that the counter's value should now be represented by a higher stored value.

To address these issues, Morris's algorithm increments the stored value with probability

$$p(v) = 1/(n(v+1) - n(v))$$

when it contains the value v. Intuitively, this means that on average the value stored in the counter will be incremented once out of the $n(v+1) - n(v)$ increment operations after value v is stored. This ensures that the value projected by the stored value is a random variable whose expected value is equal to the precise count.

To avoid computing probabilities on each increment, Morris's algorithm precomputes all 256 probabilities for a given value of a and stores them in a lookup table; this table does not need to be replicated for each counter, only for each accuracy class (i.e., each choice of a).

The parameter a determines both the range that the counter can represent and the expected error between the projected and actual counts (measured as the ratio between the STDV of the projected value and the actual count, a.k.a. relative STDV, or RSTDV). The variance of the projected value when the precise count is n is given by $\sigma^2 = n(n - 1)/2a$ [6, 9] from which it follows that the RSDTV is bounded by $1/\sqrt{2a}$. Thus, taking an example from [9], choosing $a = 30$ yields an RSTDV of about $1/8$. Furthermore, this choice of a allows the counter to represent $n(255)$, which is about 130,000. While impressive for using only 8 bits, this is not satisfactory—either in terms of range or accuracy—for counters to be used in today's systems. We next discuss how we have adapted Morris's ideas to implement scalable counters with much larger ranges and higher accuracy.

3.2 Our statistical counter algorithms

Because $n(v)$ is exponential in v, counter updates become less frequent as the precise count grows. This is the key property we borrow from Morris in order to reduce contention on frequently updated shared counters, while bounding expected error. However, we wish to implement counters with a higher range and with higher accuracy than is possible using Morris's algorithm with 8 bits per counter. While the basic principles behind Morris's algorithm extend to counters that use more bits, it becomes significantly less desirable to precompute update probabilities for all possible stored values as more bits are used. In this section, we explain how we have extended Morris's ideas to avoid this requirement.

First, we observe that the probability to increment the stored count from v to $v + 1$ is a geometric series in v with a factor of $a/(a+1)$. To see this, we observe that

$$n(v+1) - n(v) = a((1 + 1/a)^{v+1} - (1 + 1/a)^v)$$
$$= a((1 + 1/a)^v(1 + 1/a - 1))$$
$$= (1 + 1/a)^v$$
$$\Rightarrow p(v) = 1/(1 + 1/a)^v = (a/(a+1))^v$$

Therefore, given $p(v)$ we can compute $p(v + 1)$ simply by multiplying by $a/(a+1)$. We can precompute this constant to avoid performing the floating point division repeatedly.

We further observe from above that $n(v) = a(1/p(v) - 1)$. Therefore, we can compute the projected value $n(v)$ of the stored counter value v directly from $p(v)$, without knowing v (in fact, it turns out that doing so is about 5 times faster than computing $n(v)$ directly from v). Therefore, we decided not to store v in the counter, as Morris's algorithm does, but instead store the floating point value $p(v)$. (Our implementation uses 32-bit floats, but the range and/or accuracy could be extended further using 64-bit doubles.)

On each increment, we read the value p stored in the counter, and with probability p replace it with $p * a/(a+1)$. The advantage of this approach, besides faster evaluation of the projected counter value, is that we avoid precomputing and storing values for all 2^b bits when using a b bits to represent a counter. Instead, we need only precompute the value of a for the desired RSTDV and $a/(a+1)$.

Practical implementation details.

During each increment operation, we update the stored value with probability p, which is determined by the stored value. To do so, we use a thread-local Marsaglia xor shift pseudorandom number generator (PRNG) [8] using parameters $(6, 21, 7)$, which returns an integer i between 1 and Max-Int $(= 2^{32} - 1)$, and we update the stored value if $i/\texttt{MaxInt} \leq p$. As a practical matter, our implementation stores $\texttt{MaxInt} * p$ (as a float), so that we only need to compare i to the stored value to make this decision. We call this stored value a "threshold". The initial threshold $T_0 = \texttt{Max-Int}$. When we update the stored value, we replace the current value T_i with T_{i+1} $(= T_i * a/(a+1))$ if and only if the number returned by the PRNG is at most T_i. Pseudocode for this algorithm is presented in Figure 1.

With this implementation, care is needed to avoid updating T_i when it becomes too small, as the properties of the counter may be lost. In particular, we note that, because we use an integer PRNG, if an update does not reduce the integer part of the stored threshold, this does not actually affect the probability of update. For our implementation, we have observed that $T_i - T_{i+1} \geq 1$ at least while $T_i \geq a + 1$. We therefore reset the counter when this is no longer true (it is straightforward to instead raise an error if this is preferable). For our choice of $a = 5000$ to achieve a 1% RSTDV, and using a 32 bit counter, we cross this threshold when the projected value is about 0.02% below $\texttt{MaxInt}$. Thus, we achieve low relative error and much better scalability (see Section 5) without significantly reducing the range of the implemented counter as compared to naive 32-bit counters.

Variations.

The algorithm as described thus far performs very well when the counter becomes contended and reaches higher values, but it is significantly slower than a regular CAS-based counter when contention is low and the projected counter value is low. We therefore developed a hybrid version— MorrisAdapt—that starts with the implementation of a regular concurrent counter, using CAS, but if the CAS fails multiple times it switches to the probabilistic counting scheme described above. Our implementation stores a regular counter in one half of a 64-bit word, and a probabilistic counter in the other half. When contention is encountered, we switch from updating the regular counter to updating the probabilistic one; to read the counter, we add the value projected by the probabilistic counter to the value stored by the regular one. This is especially important when the application has thousands of counters, only a few of which are contended.

```
1   template <int Accuracy> // RSTDV as percentage
2   class MorrisCounter {
3   private:
4     float threshold;

6     // Static (global per accuracy class) info
7     //
8     static float s_a;
9     static float s_probFactor;   // a/(a+1)

11  public:
12    static StaticInit () {
13      // a = 1/(2*err^2)
14      //
15      float tmp = ((float)Accuracy/100.0);
16      s_a = 1/(2*tmp*tmp);
17      s_probFactor = s_a/(s_a+1.0);
18    }

20    MorrisCounter() {
21      threshold = (double)MaxInt;
22    }

24    unsigned int GetVal() {
25      float pr = threshold/MaxInt;
26      float val = (1.0/pr - 1.0)*s_a;
27      return lroundf(val);
28    }

30    void Inc() {
31      unsigned int r = rand();
32      float seenT = threshold;

34      while(true) {
35        if (r > (unsigned int)seenT) return;

37        bool overflow = (seenT < s_a + 1.0);
38        float newT = seenT * s_probFactor;
39        if (overflow) newT = (float)MaxInt;

41        float expected = seenT;
42        seenT = CAS(&threshold, seenT, newT));
43        if (seenT == expected) return;
44      }
45    }
46  }
```

Figure 1: Pseudocode for the counter based on Morris's algorithm.

4. AVOIDING FLOATING POINT

The counters presented above are appealing in terms of accuracy, performance under low contention, scalability under higher contention, and space usage. However, we received feedback from a group that would like to use such counters, but floating point operations cannot be used in their context. Even when floating point operations can be used, it is useful to avoid them so that, for example, they can be powered down if not in use by the application itself. We were therefore motivated to explore counters that provide similar properties without using floating point operations.

The key idea behind the counters discussed in this section is to constrain update probabilities to non-positive powers of two. We have developed two such algorithms, which are instances of a more general approach. We describe the general approach, and then present two specific instances of it.

4.1 The general approach

Using non-positive powers of two for update probabilities means that we can decide whether to update the counter with probability $1/2^k$ simply by checking whether the low-order k bits of an integer random number are all zero, thus avoiding any floating point computation. This approach re-

```
1   template <int Accuracy> // RSTDV as percentage
2   class BFPCounter {
3   private:
4     // BFP Counter type: 4 bits for the exponent,
5     //                   28 bits for the mantissa.
6     //
7     struct Counter {
8       int mantissa : 28;
9       int exp: 4;
10      enum {MaxExp = (1<<4) − 1 , MaxMant = (1<<28) − 1};
11    };

13    Counter bfpData;

15    enum {
16      MantThreshold = 2*((30000/(Accuracy*Accuracy) + 3)/8)
17    };

19  public:
20    BFPCounter() {
21      bfpData = {0,0};
22    }

24    // Note: represented value could be larger than MaxInt,
25    // so we use 64bit return value
26    //
27    unsigned long long GetVal() {
28      Counter data = bfpData;
29      return (unsigned long long)(data.mantissa << data.exp);
30    }

32    void Inc() {
33      int r = rand();
34      int numFailures = 0;
35      while (true) {
36        ExpBackoff(numFailures);
37        Counter oldData = bfpData;
38        int e = oldData.exp, m = oldData.mantissa;

40        // Choose to update the counter with probability 1/2^e
41        //
42        if ((r & ((1<<e)−1)) != 0) return;

44        // We assume that the mantissa field can hold
45        // MantThreshold−1, so we do not check for mantissa
46        // overflow unless the exponent is saturated.
47        //
48        bool overflow = (e == Counter::MaxExp &&
49                        m == Counter::MaxMant);
50        Counter newData = {0,0};
51        if (!overflow) {
52          if ((m == MantThreshold − 1) &&
53              (e < Counter::MaxExp)) {
54            newData = {e+1, (m+1)>>1};
55          } else {
56            newData = {e, m+1};
57          }
58        }
59        if (CAS(&bfpData, oldData, newData) == oldDdata)
60          return;
61        numFailures++;
62      }
63  }
```

Figure 2: Pseudocode for the Deterministic Update Policy BFP counter (BFP-DUP).

quires us to use coarser-grained update probabilities: we can only halve the update probability, in contrast to reducing it by a factor of $a/(a+1)$ in the previous section. Reducing the update probability is important for performance and scalability (up to a point, as discussed later). However, if we halve the update probability after every update, it becomes small too quickly, harming accuracy. Thus, we must use the same update probability repeatedly before eventually reducing it, so there is a tradeoff to manage; we discuss this later.

The algorithms in this section represent counter values

using *binary floating point* (BFP): we store a pair (m, e), which represents a projected value $m \cdot 2^e$ (m is the mantissa and e is the exponent). We use bitfields in the counter variable to store m and e. For example, if we use four bits for e and 28 bits for m, we can represent a counter value of up to $(2^{28} - 1) \cdot 2^{15}$, about 2K times `MaxInt`.

When the exponent is e, we update the counter with probability 2^{-e}. As in the previous section, in order to keep the expected projected value of the counter equal to the total number of increments, we add 2^e to the projected value when incrementing the counter with probability 2^{-e}.

Observe that we can add 2^e to the projected value of a counter represented by (m, e) in two ways. The first is to update it to $(m + 1, e)$. The second way, which applies only when m is odd and the exponent field is not saturated, is to update the counter to $((m + 1)/2, e + 1)$. The first way leaves the update probability unchanged, and the second way halves it. The two algorithms we have implemented based on this general approach differ in the policy that controls which method to use when updating the counter.

4.2 Deterministic update policy

For our first BFP counter, BFP-DUP, we aimed for similar properties as the counters presented in the previous section, namely that we could specify a desired bound on the RSTDV, and reduce update probabilities as quickly as possible in order to improve scalability, while ensuring the desired RSTDV bound. Ensuring this bound requires that we do not reduce the update probability too quickly.

The policy we chose increments the mantissa by default, but if it would become `MantissaThreshold`, which is required to be even, we instead halve the mantissa (after incrementing it) and increment the exponent. This way, the first `MantissaThreshold` increments update the counter with probability $2^0 = 1$, thus ensuring that the counter reaches `MantissaThreshold` without introducing any error. Thereafter, the exponent is incremented (and the mantissa halved) every `MantissaThreshold`/2 counter updates. The choice for `MantissaThreshold` determines how quickly the exponent grows (and thus the update probability reduces); we explain how its value is chosen later.

BFP-DUP is shown in Figure 2. The `BFPCounter` class accepts as a template argument the desired bound on RSTDV as a percentage (e.g., if `Accuracy` is 1, then a 1% bound is desired). The value of `MantissaThreshold` is determined based on the desired `Accuracy`, as explained below. The `Inc` operation decides with probability $1 - 1/2^e$ not to update the counter, where e is the exponent currently stored in the counter (lines 33–42). If the decision is to update the counter, we first check if the counter has reached its maximum value (line 48), in which case we attempt to update the counter to zero (it is easy to signal an error if that is preferable). Otherwise, a new pair is determined based on the current pair, as described above (lines 52–57). Finally, the algorithm attempts to store the new pair to the counter, using CAS to confirm that the counter has not changed (line 59). If the CAS fails, the operation is retried.

Details and optimizations.

Figure 2 elides several optimizations that are included in the implementation used for the experiments in the next section. For example, our implementation code inlines the common update case in which the CAS succeeds, and uses

the return value of a failed CAS to avoid the need to reread `bfpData` before retrying. Furthermore, when a CAS fails due to a concurrent update, the test to determine whether an update should be applied based on the new value is performed before backing off, as this will almost never be the case. We also note that all calculations are performed using bit shifting and masking operations.

Accuracy analysis and choice of parameters.

While exploring methods for analyzing the accuracy properties of our BFP-DUP algorithm, we found closely related work by Csűrös [3], who presents a sequential approximate counting algorithm. This algorithm does not support concurrent updates, and is less flexible than ours, but the results Csűrös developed and used to analyze the accuracy properties of the counter enabled us to analyze our algorithm easily. The algorithm in [3] is similar in spirit to ours but, rather than explicitly updating the mantissa and exponent, whenever it updates the counter, it does so simply by incrementing the stored value. When the mantissa part of the counter is incremented past its maximum value, the overflow naturally increments the exponent field (which is placed appropriately to ensure this).

As a result of this choice, the update function used in Csűrös's algorithm is slightly simpler than ours, but this has little performance impact because the counter is updated less and less frequently over time. Another implication is that the frequency with which an update increments the exponent (and thus reduces the update probability for subsequent operations) is required to be a power of two. Finally, a slightly different way of computing the projected value from the counter's stored data is needed, because the mantissa part becomes zero when the exponent is incremented.

Nonetheless, the Markov chain used in Csűrös's analysis is easily modified to model our BFP-DUP algorithm. The only substantive difference is due to BFP-DUP performing twice as many increments to the mantissa before incrementing the exponent for the first time as it does between subsequent increments of the exponent. The Markov chain used to model our algorithm thus has a deterministic chain of length `MantissaThreshold`/2 before a chain that is otherwise identical to the one used by Csűrös [3]. This does not change the result in the limit, because these deterministic increments of the mantissa occur with probability 1, and therefore do not increase the inaccuracy of the counter. Thus we can use similar techniques as Csűrös did to apply his theorems to in order to determine a bound on RSTDV for our algorithm.

In contrast to the algorithms presented in the previous section, this analysis does not yield a bound on RSTDV that is independent of the number of increment operations performed. Rather, using the techniques presented in [3], we establish that the algorithm provides a bound on expected RSTDV in the limit as the number of increments n approaches infinity. More precisely, we have

$$\limsup_{n \to \infty} A_n \leq \sqrt{\frac{3}{8M - 3}}$$

where A_n is the expected RSTDV after n `Inc` operations, and M is the number of increments of the mantissa between increments of the exponent (i.e., `MantissaThreshold`/ 2).

This formula yields a bound on RSTDV only in the limit, unlike the one in the previous section, which provides a bound that holds for all counter values. Nonetheless, we can use it heuristically to guide our choice of M for a given desired bound. Because the `BFPCounter` class accepts its accuracy argument as a percentage (e.g., if we desire a 1% bound, the `Accuracy` argument is 1), this equation implies

$$M \leq ((30,000/\texttt{Accuracy}^2) + 3)/8$$

hence the formula for `MantissaThreshold` at line 16 (recall that `MantissaThreshold=`$2M$).

Because `BFP-DUP` does not constrain the number of increments to the mantissa between increments of the exponent to be a power of two, as Csűrös's algorithm does, we have the flexibility to choose `MantissaThreshold` based on this calculation, giving us finer-grained control over the accuracy-performance tradeoff. For the experiments presented in the next section, we used a 1% bound, resulting in `MantissaThreshold` being set to 7500.

4.3 Contention-sensitive update policy

The deterministic update policy used by `BFP-DUP` is attractive because it lends itself to the analysis described above. However, while it is important for scalability and performance to reduce the update probability as the counter grows, at some point for a given system and workload, contention on the counter variable will be insignificant, and the overhead of updating the counter occasionally will be unnoticeable. Thereafter, reducing the update probability further only increases the inaccuracy of the counter. Therefore, we explored a different policy, whereby we choose to update the exponent (thereby reducing the update probability) only in response to contention. In particular, we always try to increment the mantissa once using a CAS (unless it would overflow), and only if that CAS fails, we decide whether to update the exponent and halve the mantissa using a similar policy to that used in `BFP-DUP`. We call this algorithm Contention-Sensitive Update Policy (`BFP-CSUP`). As the experiments presented in the next section show, `BFP-CSUP` yields similar performance to the `BFP-DUP` algorithm, while achieving higher accuracy in practice.

5. EVALUATION

We have evaluated both throughput and relative error of our counters under a variety of workloads via experiments conducted on an Oracle T5440 series machine. The T5440 consists of 4 Niagara T2+ SPARC chips, each containing 8 cores, with each core containing 2 pipelines with 4 hardware thread contexts per pipeline, for a total of 256 hardware thread contexts, running at a 1.4 GHz. Each chip has a 4MB L2 cache, and each core has a shared 8KB L1 data cache. Each Niagara T2+ chip is a NUMA node, and the nodes are connected via a central coherence hub.

Thread distribution is controlled solely by the operating system (Solaris 10) scheduler, which typically spreads threads out across nodes, then across cores, and finally across hardware threads within each core. Each run consists of a two-second warmup period to allow thread placement to settle, after which we reset the counter(s), and then measure throughput during a further eight seconds of execution. Each data point is the median throughput from five runs.

In all of our experiments, each thread alternates between performing an increment operation and doing some "external work" (modeling other work of the application). External work is implemented by executing a short `Pause` routine some number of times that is chosen uniformly at random

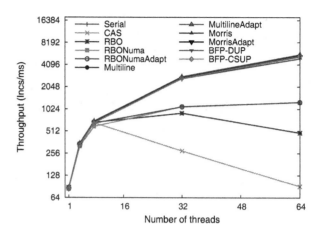

Figure 3: Single counter, low contention (99.02% external work) up to 64 threads.

from a range controlled by a parameter. To give some intuitive meaning to this parameter, we reflect it as the fraction of time spent executing external work in a single-thread run using the CAS counter. For example, 99% external work means that the single-thread throughput is $1/100$ of the throughput achieved when run with no external work.

5.1 Single counter, low contention

Figure 3 shows throughput (increment operations per millisecond) on the log-scale y axis, varying the number of threads on the x axis. This experiment has 99.02% external work, resulting in low contention, at least for low thread counts. The counters perform similarly up to 8 threads, but with higher numbers of threads, contention starts to arise, and the behavior of the algorithms becomes more important.

RBO's backoff mitigates the poor scalability of CAS considerably, but it still shows negative scalability. Both RBONuma and `RBONumaAdapt` provide positive scalability, but are not competitive with the remaining algorithms, which all perform similarly and show significantly better scalability. These algorithms are: `Serial`, `Multiline`, `MultilineAdapt`, `Morris`, `MorrisAdapt`, `BFP-DUP` and `BFP-CSUP`.

`Serial`, which uses simple load-increment-store sequences to avoid the overhead of CAS, provides *slightly* lower throughput than the other algorithms that show similar performance in Figure 3. However, the others all entail significantly more algorithmic complexity, and in some cases significant space overhead too. One might therefore conclude that `Serial` is the best choice on balance.

However, we believe this conclusion is seriously flawed. First, Figure 3 shows data only up to 64 threads. As we will see, the scalability of `Serial` falls off at higher thread counts because every operation updates the single counter, so it becomes a bottleneck.

More important, however, is that `Serial` does *not* lose only "occasional" updates. In fact, the relative error exhibited by `Serial` can be dramatic. Under heavy contention (e.g., 0% external work, 256 threads), we consistently observe relative error of more than 99% meaning that fewer than 1% of increments on the counter are actually reflected in the count. The effect is not limited to such extreme cases: even with low contention (99.01% external work), we observe over 75% relative error for 64 threads and above, and over

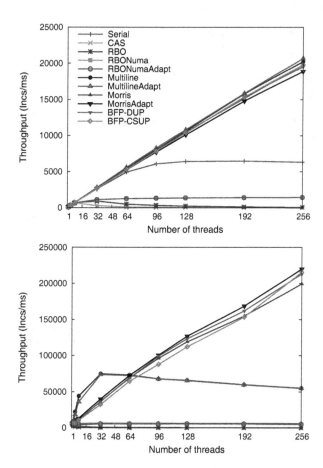

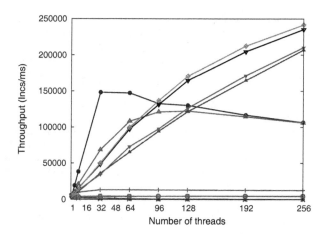

Figure 5: 7500 counters, one highly contended, 0% external work.

eAdapt, Morris, MorrisAdapt, BFP-DUP and BFP-CSUP all exhibit good scalability, achieving at least 3x the throughput of Serial, more than 13x the throughput of any of the other precise counters at 256 threads, and more than 260x the throughput of RBO. Amongst these good performers, the precise counters (Multiline and MultilineAdapt) have a slight edge in throughput over the probabilistic ones (Morris and MorrisAdapt), although they use 256 bytes of additional space (one cache line for each of four nodes) to do so.

5.2   Single counter, high contention

We also performed a similar experiment with no external work. Although this may not be a realistic workload, it is important to understand the behavior of these algorithms under extreme conditions. Furthermore, as the number of cores per chip and the number of chips per system grows, realistic workloads may move closer to the levels of contention exhibited by this workload on this machine. Results are shown in Figure 4 (bottom).

We first observe that, although Serial yields two orders of magnitude higher throughput with one thread than before (because it is no longer spending 99% of its time doing "external work"), it again fails to scale, this time flattening out at about 32 threads. The other nonscalable counters all perform similarly poorly. Morris, MorrisAdapt, BFP-DUP and BFP-CSUP again scale well, and yield over 33x throughput compared to Serial at 256 threads. However, in this scenario, Multiline and MultilineAdapt peak around 32 threads, and scale negatively thereafter, due to contention on the per-node counter components. As discussed in Section 2, we could further partition these components to avoid this problem at the cost of additional space overhead; this cost would apply only to counters that experience heavy contention in the case of MultilineAdapt.

All algorithms except Morris, MorrisAdapt, BFP-DUP and BFP-CSUP either use significantly more space, or exhibit poor scalability in the above results, or both. Therefore, these algorithms appear to be the best choice, provided their error properties are acceptable for the application.

5.3   Many counters, mixed contention

It is common for an application to have many counters, of

Figure 4: Single counter throughput, full thread range. Top: low contention (99% external work), bottom: high contention (0% external work).

10% error for 8 threads and above. The reason is that, from the time a thread reads the counter until the time that it stores its new value, it is guaranteed that the counter will increase by only one, regardless of how many other increment operations are performed by other threads in the interim.

Such counters are worse than useless: they impede scalability *and* fail to fulfil their purpose exactly when they are needed most, i.e., when the counter is being incremented more frequently. We also note that, with Serial, the counter regularly "goes backwards", which may be very undesirable in some cases, even when an accurate count is not required. Thus, we believe Serial is simply unacceptable as a statistics counter. Nonetheless, it is widely used in practice. We hope our paper brings this pitfall to the attention of practitioners, and helps them to choose another counter implementation that provides much better scalability *and* accuracy.

Figure 4 (top) shows the same data as Figure 3 up to 256 threads, with a linear *y* axis. None of Serial, CAS, RBO, RBONuma, and RBONumaAdapt is scalable. Nonetheless, we observe that, at 256 threads, RBONuma and RBONumaAdapt both provide about 20x the throughput of RBO, the most commonly used implementation, while requiring minimal space overhead. Although Serial provides higher throughput, it is not useful due to its egregious error properties, as discussed above. On the other hand, Multiline, Multilin-

which only a small number are contended. We performed an experiment in which threads alternate between incrementing a counter chosen uniformly at random from an array of 7500 counters, and incrementing one specific counter.

In the low contention case (e.g., 98.89% external work), the results (not shown) were qualitatively similar to the single-counter experiment except that `Serial` performed significantly better in this scenario because there was little contention on counters other than the central one. Results with no external work were more interesting (see Figure 5). As before, the probabilistic counters (`Morris`, `MorrisAdapt`, `BFP-DUP` and `BFP-CSUP`) all scaled well and produced low relative error (see Section 5.4). However, whereas `Multiline` and `MultilineAdapt` performed about the same in the single-counter experiment, in the array experiment, `Multiline` provided significantly higher throughput than `MultilineAdapt` for low thread counts (more than 2x at 32 threads), though this gap mostly disappeared with higher thread counts. The reason is that, with `Multiline`, counter components can be accessed directly, without a level of indirection or associated checks to determine whether a counter is inflated. On the other hand, `Multiline` pays a significant space overhead for all counters, while `MultilineAdapt` inflates only the contended counters, so the space overhead associated with the additional level of indirection is paid only by the counters that benefit from it.

The adaptive probabilistic counters (`MorrisAdapt` and `BFP-CSUP`) both outperformed their non-adaptive counterparts significantly because most of the counters are not heavily contended. For `MorrisAdapt`, the half of the operations that access non-contended counters avoid the expense of generating a random number and deciding whether to update the counter. Similarly, `BFP-CSUP` need not generate a random number when the update probability is 1, which is usually the case for the uncontended counters. `BFP-DUP` and `BFP-CSUP` outperform `Morris` and `MorrisAdapt`, respectively, probably due to their avoidance of floating point operations. (Despite our efforts to eliminate floating point operations from the common case, `Morris` performs a floating point conversion in every `Inc` operation in order to compare the integer random number to the floating point update probability; see line 35 in Figure 1.)

For a conservative comparison, we padded `RBO` counters to eliminate false sharing and packed the `Morris` counters as tightly as possible (16 32-bit counters per cache line). Despite these conservative choices, `Morris` dramatically outperformed `RBO`, as discussed above. `Morris` avoids the pitfalls of false sharing by reducing the frequency of updates to counters as the number of increments to them increases.

The components of `Multiline`, and of `MultilineAdapt` when inflated, are padded to avoid false sharing. However, in our experiments, the initial counters used by `MultilineAdapt` were packed with multiple counters per cache line; false sharing is avoided by inflating (only) contended counters. Because counters become read-only pointers when inflated, `MultilineAdapt` will perform well even if *multiple* highly contended counters are in the same cache line; this scenario is a certain performance disaster for the more naive, nonscalable counters.

5.4 Accuracy in practice

Next we examine the accuracy of the probabilistic counters in practice. Figure 6 shows the absolute value of the rel-

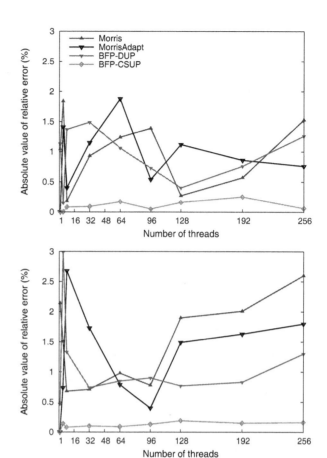

Figure 6: Relative error (absolute value). Top: low contention (99% external work), bottom: high contention (0% external work).

ative error for low-contention (99% external work) and high-contention (0% external work) workloads. These graphs show the *worst* relative error from five runs for each data point. No relative error higher than 3% is observed, and in most cases, the worst relative error is within 1.5%.

The maximum relative error exhibited by `BFP-CSUP` was often close to zero, and was never higher than 0.25% in these tests. In contrast, all of the other probabilistic counters typically exhibit relative error in the 0.75-2% range, and sometimes up to 3%. Together with performance data already presented, this shows that `BFP-CSUP`'s approach of not increasing the exponent unnecessarily achieves similar performance while reducing maximum error in practice.

We note that, in the high-contention case, most of the probabilistic counters exhibit somewhat higher relative error. This is because they count to higher values in this case (they provide higher throughput during our 8-second measurement period; see Figure 4). Therefore, they reduce the update probability more in the high-contention experiment. In contrast, `BFP-CSUP` increments the exponent only when contention is observed (or the mantissa is saturated). Thus its relative error does not increase simply due to executing more `Inc` operations, as is the case with all of the others.

5.5 `GetVal` overhead

We have targeted scenarios in which there are many counters, some of which may be incremented frequently. Our main goals have thus been low space overhead, low overhead in the absence of contention, and good scalability under heavy contention. We have not optimized for `GetVal` performance, but we believe that the costs discussed below are reasonably low for most of the algorithms.

The cost of `GetVal` comprises reading the necessary data and computing a return value from it. In the scenarios that have motivated our work, the cost of reading the data is likely to dominate, because it is likely not to be in cache for the thread executing `GetVal`: it may need to be fetched from memory, or from another—likely remote—cache.

`GetVal` for `Serial`, `CAS`, and `RBO` simply reads the underlying data and returns the value read, costing a single cache miss. `RBONuma`, `RBONumaAdapt`, `BFP-DUP`, and `BFP-CSUP` similarly require a single cache miss, but also entail some simple masking and/or shifting to determine the counter's value. `Multiline` requires multiple cache lines to be read. We note, however, that these are independent reads, so the cache misses will be resolved largely in parallel on most modern architectures. Read operations with `MultilineAdapt` are like the simple counters unless the counter is inflated, in which case `GetVal` must read not only the multiple cache lines for the counter, but also the pointer that determines where they are. The reads of the allocated cache lines *do* depend on the value of the pointer, and therefore the latency of `GetVal` likely includes at least two cache misses in series, even if all of the allocated lines are read in parallel.

For `Morris` and `MorrisAdapt`, `GetVal` entails mutliple floating point operations that will add noticeable overhead if executed often, in which case BFP-based counters may be preferable. Alternatively, projected values calculated from recent stored value(s) could be cached, as (eventually) the stored value of a counter changes infrequently.

6. CONCLUDING REMARKS

We have shown that nonatomic, centralized counters scale poorly *and* yield highly inaccurate counts. We have explored a variety of counters, some of which provide a precise count, while others aim for reasonable relative error, such that they are still useful for the purpose of detecting counters that are incremented many times. We present and evaluate several counters that dramatically outperform commonly used counters in terms of both throughput and accuracy, especially in NUMA systems, while keeping space overhead low.

The algorithms in this paper are easily seen to be lock-free. Furthermore, the probabilistic counters retry less often over time because the update probability becomes smaller over time (particularly in the case of contention in the case of `BFP-CSUP`). Modifying the counters in this paper to be wait-free while preserving their accuracy properties would likely add significant overhead and complexity. It would also introduce constraints such as needing to know the maximum number of threads in advance, or more overhead and complexity to avoid such constraints. In practice, lock-freedom is usually a strong enough progress property, provided back-off is used in case of contention.

Finally, we note the value of scalable statistics counters when used with transactional memory (hardware, software, or hybrid). Counters are used for many purposes, such as recording the number of entries in a hash table, or maintaining code execution frequencies, etc. The use of counters within transactions often causes all pairs of transactions to conflict because they all update the counter. The key to making the counters in this paper scalable has been to reduce contention on them, either by splitting them up so that multiple updates can occur in parallel (as in `Multiline`) or reducing the frequency of updates (as in the probabilistic counters). These techniques therefore reduce conflicts between transactions relative to using the naive nonscalable counters. We therefore expect them to be particularly valuable when used in transactions.

Acknowledgments.
Sumanta Chatterjee, Paul Loewenstein, and Steve Sistare gave useful input that motivated this work.

7. REFERENCES

[1] Yehuda Afek, Haim Kaplan, Boris Korenfeld, Adam Morrison, and Robert E. Tarjan. Cbtree: a practical concurrent self-adjusting search tree. In *Proceedings of the 26th international conference on Distributed Computing*, DISC'12, pages 1–15, Berlin, Heidelberg, 2012. Springer-Verlag.

[2] A. Agarwal and M. Cherian. Adaptive backoff synchronization techniques. In *Proceedings of the 16th annual international symposium on Computer architecture*, ISCA '89, pages 396–406, New York, NY, USA, 1989. ACM.

[3] Miklós Csűrös. Approximate counting with a floating-point counter. In *Proceedings of the 16th annual international conference on Computing and combinatorics*, COCOON'10, pages 358–367, Berlin, Heidelberg, 2010. Springer-Verlag.

[4] Dave Dice and Alex Garthwaite. Mostly lock-free malloc. In *Proceedings of the 3rd international symposium on Memory management*, ISMM '02, pages 163–174, New York, NY, USA, 2002. ACM.

[5] David Dice, Virendra J. Marathe, and Nir Shavit. Lock cohorting: a general technique for designing numa locks. In *Proceedings of the 17th ACM SIGPLAN symposium on Principles and Practice of Parallel Programming*, PPoPP '12, pages 247–256, New York, NY, USA, 2012. ACM.

[6] Philippe Flajolet. Approximate counting: a detailed analysis. *BIT*, 25(1):113–134, June 1985.

[7] Yossi Lev and Mark Moir. Lightweight parallel accumulators using c++ templates. In *Proceedings of the 4th International Workshop on Multicore Software Engineering*, IWMSE '11, pages 33–40, New York, NY, USA, 2011. ACM.

[8] George Marsaglia. Xorshift rngs. *Journal of Statistical Software*, 8(14):1–6, 7 2003.

[9] Robert Morris. Counting large numbers of events in small registers. *Commun. ACM*, 21(10):840–842, October 1978.

[10] Zoran Radovic and Erik Hagersten. Hierarchical backoff locks for nonuniform communication architectures. In *Proceedings of the 9th International Symposium on High-Performance Computer Architecture*, HPCA '03, pages 241–, Washington, DC, USA, 2003. IEEE Computer Society.

Storage and Search in Dynamic Peer-to-Peer Networks

John Augustine
Department of Computer
Science and Engineering
Indian Institute of Technology
Madras, Chennai, India.
augustine@cse.iitm.ac.in

Anisur Rahaman Molla
Division of Mathematical
Sciences
Nanyang Technological
University, Singapore 637371
anisurpm@gmail.com

Ehab Morsy
Department of Mathematics
Suez Canal University
Ismailia 22541, Egypt
ehabmorsy@gmail.com

Gopal Pandurangan[*]
Division of Mathematical
Sciences
Nanyang Technological
University
Singapore 637371
gopalpandurangan@gmail.com

Peter Robinson[†]
Division of Mathematical
Sciences
Nanyang Technological
University, Singapore 637371
peter.robinson@ntu.edu.sg

Eli Upfal[‡]
Department of Computer
Science
Brown University
Providence, RI 02912, USA
eli@cs.brown.edu

ABSTRACT

We study robust and efficient distributed algorithms for searching, storing, and maintaining data in dynamic Peer-to-Peer (P2P) networks. P2P networks are highly dynamic networks that experience heavy node *churn* (i.e., nodes join and leave the network continuously over time). Our goal is to guarantee, despite high node churn rate, that a large number of nodes in the network can store, retrieve, and maintain a large number of data items. Our main contributions are fast randomized distributed algorithms that guarantee the above with high probability even under high *adversarial* churn. In particular, we present the following main results:

1. A randomized distributed search algorithm that with high probability guarantees that searches from as many as $n - o(n)$ nodes (n is the stable network size) succeed in $O(\log n)$-rounds despite $O(n/\log^{1+\delta} n)$ churn, for any small constant $\delta > 0$, *per round*. We assume that the churn is controlled by an oblivious adversary (that has complete knowledge and control of what nodes join

and leave and at what time and has unlimited computational power, but is oblivious to the random choices made by the algorithm).

2. A storage and maintenance algorithm that guarantees, with high probability, data items can be efficiently stored (with only $\Theta(\log n)$ copies of each data item) and maintained in a dynamic P2P network with churn rate up to $O(n/\log^{1+\delta} n)$ per round. Our search algorithm together with our storage and maintenance algorithm guarantees that as many as $n - o(n)$ nodes can efficiently store, maintain, and search even under $O(n/\log^{1+\delta} n)$ churn *per round*. Our algorithms require only polylogarithmic in n bits to be processed and sent (per round) by each node.

To the best of our knowledge, our algorithms are the first-known, fully-distributed storage and search algorithms that provably work under highly dynamic settings (i.e., high churn rates per step). Furthermore, they are localized (i.e., do not require any global topological knowledge) and scalable. A technical contribution of this paper, which may be of independent interest, is showing how random walks can be provably used to derive scalable distributed algorithms in dynamic networks with adversarial node churn.

*G. Pandurangan is also affiliated with Dept. of Computer Science, Brown University Providence, RI 02912, USA. Research supported in part by the following grants: Nanyang Technological University grant M58110000, Singapore Ministry of Education (MOE) Academic Research Fund (AcRF) Tier 2 grant MOE2010-T2-2-082, and a grant from the US-Israel Binational Science Foundation (BSF).

†Research supported in part by the following grants: Nanyang Technological University grant M58110000, Singapore Ministry of Education (MOE) Academic Research Fund (AcRF) Tier 2 grant MOE2010-T2-2-082

‡Work supported in part by NSF award IIS-1247581.

Categories and Subject Descriptors

F.2.2 [**Theory of Computation**]: [Analysis of Algorithms and Problem Complexity—Nonnumerical Algorithms and Problems]

Keywords

Peer-to-peer network; dynamic network; search, storage; distributed algorithm; randomized algorithm; expander graph.

1. INTRODUCTION

Peer-to-peer (P2P) computing is emerging as one of the key networking technologies in recent years with many application systems, e.g., Skype, BitTorrent, Cloudmark, Crash-Plan, Symform etc. For example, systems such as Crash-Plan [13] and Symform [46] are relatively recent P2P-based storage services that allow data to be stored and retrieved among peers [40]. Such data sharing among peers avoids costly centralized storage and retrieval, besides being inherently scalable to millions of peers. However, many of these systems are not fully P2P; they also use dedicated centralized servers in order to guarantee high availability of data — this is necessary due to the highly dynamic and unpredictable nature of P2P. Indeed, a key reason for the lack of fully-distributed P2P systems is the difficulty in designing highly robust algorithms for large-scale dynamic P2P networks.

P2P networks are highly dynamic networks characterized by high degree of node *churn* — i.e., nodes continuously join and leave the network. Connections (edges) may be added or deleted at any time and thus the topology changes very dynamically. In fact, measurement studies of real-world P2P networks [19, 24, 43, 45] show that the churn rate is quite high: nearly 50% of peers in real-world networks can be replaced within an hour. (However, despite a large churn rate, these studies also show that the total number of peers in the network is relatively *stable*.) P2P algorithms have been proposed for a wide variety of tasks such as data storage and retrieval [40, 17, 16, 11, 25], collaborative filtering [8], spam detection [12], data mining [15], worm detection and suppression [36, 48], privacy protection of archived data [22], and recently, for cloud computing services as well [46, 5]. However, all algorithms proposed for these problems have no theoretical guarantees of being able to work in a dynamically changing network with a very high churn rate, which can be as much as linear (in the network size) per round. This is a major bottleneck in implementation and wide-spread use of P2P systems.

In this paper, we take a step towards designing provably robust and scalable algorithms for large-scale dynamic P2P networks. In particular, we focus on the fundamental problem of storing, maintaining, and searching data in P2P networks. Search in P2P networks is a well-studied fundamental application with a large body of work in the last decade or so, both in theory and practice (e.g., see the survey [34]). While many P2P systems/protocols have been proposed for efficient search and storage of data (cf. Section 1.3), a major drawback of almost all these is the lack of algorithms that work with provable guarantees under a large amount of churn per round. The problem is especially challenging since the goal is to guarantee that almost all nodes[1] are able to efficiently store, maintain, and retrieve data, even under high churn rate. In such a highly dynamic setting, it is non-trivial to even just store data in a persistent manner; the churn can simply remove a large fraction of nodes in just one time step. On the other hand, it is costly to replicate too many copies of a data item to guarantee persistence. Thus the challenge is to use as little storage as possible and maintain the data for a long time, while at the same time designing efficient search algorithms that find the data quickly, despite high churn rate. Another complication to this challenge is designing algorithms that are also scalable, i.e., nodes that process and send only a small number of (small-sized) messages per round.

1.1 Our Main Results

We provide a rigorous theoretical framework for the design and analysis of storage, maintenance, and retrieval algorithms for highly dynamic distributed systems with churn. We briefly describe the key ingredients of our model here. (Our model is described in detail in Section 2). Essentially, we model a P2P network as a bounded-degree expander graph whose topology — both nodes and edges — can change arbitrarily from round to round and is controlled by an adversary. However, we assume that the total number of nodes in the network is stable. The number of node changes *per round* is called the *churn rate* or *churn limit*. We consider a churn rate of up to some $O(n/\log^{1+\delta} n)$[2], where $\delta > 0$ is any small constant and n is the stable network size. Note that our model is quite general in the sense that we only assume that the topology is an expander at every step; no other special properties are assumed. Indeed, expanders have been used extensively to model dynamic P2P networks[3] in which the expander property is preserved under insertions and deletions of nodes (e.g., [2, 33, 39]). Since we do not make assumptions on how the topology is preserved, our model is applicable to all such expander-based networks. (We note that various prior work on dynamic network models (e.g., [3, 31, 2, 14]) make similar assumptions on preservation of topological properties — such as connectivity, high expansion etc. — at every step under insertions/deletions — cf. Section 1.3. The issue of how such properties are preserved are abstracted away from the model, which allows one to focus on the dynamism. Indeed, this abstraction has been a feature of most dynamic models e.g., see the survey of [9].)

Our main contributions are efficient randomized distributed algorithms for searching, storing, and maintaining data in dynamic P2P networks. Our algorithms succeed with high probability (i.e., with probability $1 - 1/n^{\Omega(1)}$, where n is the stable network size)) even under high adversarial churn in a polylogarithmic number of rounds. In particular, we present the following results (the precise theorem statements are given in Section 4):

1. (cf. Theorem 3) A storage and maintenance algorithm that guarantees, with high probability, that data items can be efficiently stored (with only $\Theta(\log n)$ copies of each data item [4]) and maintained in a dynamic P2P network with churn rate up to $O(n/\log^{1+\delta} n)$ *per round*, assuming that the churn is controlled by an oblivious adversary (that has complete knowledge and control of what nodes join and leave and at what time and has unlimited computational power, but is oblivious to the random choices made by the algorithm).

2. (cf. Theorem 4) A randomized distributed search algorithm that with high probability guarantees that

---

[1]In sparse, bounded-degree networks, as assumed in this paper, an adversary can always isolate some number of nodes due to churn, hence "almost all" is the best one can hope for in such networks.

[2]Throughout this paper, we use log to represent natural logarithm unless explicitly specified otherwise.

[3]A number of works on static networks have used expander graph topologies to solve the agreement and related problems [28, 18, 47]. Here we show that similar expansion properties are beneficial in the more challenging setting of dynamic networks (cf. Section 1.3).

[4]Using erasure coding techniques, the number of bits stored can be reduced even further, so as to incur only a constant factor overhead. We discuss this in in the full version of the paper.

searches from as many as $n - o(n)$ nodes succeed in $O(\log n)$-rounds under up to $O(n/\log^{1+\delta} n)$ churn *per round*. Our search algorithm together with the storage and maintenance algorithm guarantees that as many as $n - o(n)$ nodes can efficiently store, maintain, and search even under $O(n/\log^{1+\delta} n)$ churn *per round*. Our algorithms require only polylogarithmic in n bits to be processed and sent (per round) by each node.

To the best of our knowledge, our algorithms are the first-known, fully-distributed storage and search algorithms that work under highly dynamic settings (i.e., high churn rates per step). Furthermore, they are localized (i.e., do not require any global topological knowledge) and scalable.

1.2 Technical Contributions

We derive techniques (cf. Section 3) for doing scalable distributed computation in highly dynamic networks. In such networks, we would like distributed algorithms to work correctly and efficiently, and terminate even in networks that keep changing continuously over time (not assuming any eventual stabilization). The main technical tool that we use is random walks. Flooding techniques (which proved useful in solving the agreement problem under high adversarial churn [2]) are not useful for search as they generate lot of messages and hence are not scalable. We note that random walks have been used before to perform search in P2P networks (e.g., [37, 35, 49, 23]) as well for other applications such as sampling (e.g., [21, 7]), but these are not applicable to dynamic networks with large churn rates.

One of the main technical contributions of this paper is showing how random walks can be used in a dynamic network with high adversarial *node churn* (cf. Section 3). The basic idea is quite simple and is as follows. All nodes generate tokens (which contain the source node's ids) and send it via random walks continuously over time. These random walks, once they "mix" (i.e., reach close to the stationary distribution), reach essentially "random" destinations in the network; we (figuratively) call these simultaneous random walks as a *soup of random walks*. Thus the destination nodes receive a steady stream of tokens from essentially random nodes, thereby allowing them to sample nodes uniformly from the network. While this is easy to establish in a static network, it is no longer true in a dynamic network with adversarial churn — the churn can cause many random walks to be lost and also might introduce bias. We show a technical result called the "Soup Theorem" (cf. Theorem 1) that shows that "most" random walks do mix (despite large adversarial churn) and have the usual desirable properties as in a static network. We use the Soup theorem crucially in our search, storage, and maintenance algorithms. We note that our technique can handle churn only up to $n/\text{polylog}\, n$. Informally, this is due to the fact that at least $\Omega(\log n)$ rounds are needed for the random walks to mix, before which any non-trivial computation can be performed. This seems to be a fundamental limitation of our random walk based method. We come close to this limit in that we allow churn to be as high as $O(n/\log^{1+\delta} n)$ for *any* fixed $\delta > 0$.

Another technique that we use as a building block in our algorithms is construction and maintenance of (small-sized) committees. A committee is a clique of small ($\Theta(\log n)$) size composed of essentially "random" nodes. We show how such a committee can be efficiently constructed, and more importantly, *maintained* under large churn. A committee can be used to "delegate" a storage or a search operation; its small size guarantees scalability, while its persistence guarantees that the operation will complete successfully despite churn. Our techniques (the Soup Theorem and committees) can be useful in other distributed applications as well, e.g., leader election.

Due to space limitation, full proofs and omitted details are in the full version of the paper.

1.3 Related Work

There has been significant prior work in designing P2P networks that are provably robust to a large number of Byzantine faults (e.g., see [20, 26, 38, 42, 4]). These focus on robustly enabling storage and retrieval of data items under adversarial nodes. However, these algorithms will not work in a highly dynamic setting with *large, continuous, adversarial* churn (controlled by an all-powerful adversary that has full control of the network topology, including full knowledge and control of what nodes join and leave and at what time and has unlimited computational power). Most prior works develop algorithms that will work under the assumption that the network will eventually stabilize and stop changing. (An important aspect of our algorithms is that they will work and terminate correctly even when the network keeps continually changing.) There has been a lot of work on P2P algorithms for maintaining desirable properties (such as connectivity, low diameter, bounded degree) under churn (see e.g., [39, 27, 32], but these don't work under large adversarial churn rates. In particular, there has been very little work till date that rigorously addresses distributed computation in dynamic P2P networks under high node churn. The work ([29]) raises the open question of whether one can design robust P2P protocols that can work in highly dynamic networks with a large adversarial churn. The recent work of [2] was one of the first to address the above question; its focus was on solving the fundamental agreement problem in P2P networks with very large adversarial churn. However, the paper does not address the problem of search and storage, which was a problem left open in [2].

There has been works on building fault-tolerant Distributed Hash Tables (which are classified as "structured" P2P networks unlike ours which are "unstructured" e.g., see [39]) under different deletion models — adversarial deletions and stochastic deletions. The structured P2P network described by Saia *et al.* [41] guarantees that a large number of data items are available even if a large fraction of *arbitrary* peers are deleted, under the assumption that, at any time, the number of peers deleted by an adversary must be smaller than the number of peers joining.

The dynamic network model of [31, 3, 14] allows only edge changes from round to round while the nodes remain fixed. In our work, we study a dynamic network model where *both* nodes and edges can change by a large amount. Therefore, the framework we study in Section 2 (and first introduced in [2]) is more general than the model of [31], as it is additionally applicable to dynamic settings with node churn. We note that the works of [3, 14] study random walks under a dynamic model where the nodes are fixed (and only edges change) and hence not applicable to systems with churn. The surveys of [30, 10] summarizes recent work on dynamic networks.

Expander graphs and spectral properties have already been applied extensively to improve the network design and fault-tolerance in distributed computing in general ([47, 18, 6]) and P2P networks in particular [29, 2]. The problem of achieving almost-everywhere agreement among nodes in P2P networks — modeled as an expander graph — is considered by King et al. in [29] in the context of the leader election problem. However, the algorithm of [29] does not work for dynamic networks. The work of [2] addresses the agreement problem in a dynamic P2P network under an adversarial churn model where the churn rates can be very large, up to linear in the number of nodes in the network. It also crucially makes use of expander graphs. (More related work can be found in the full paper [1].)

2. MODEL AND PROBLEM STATEMENT

We consider a synchronous dynamic network with churn represented by a dynamically changing graph whose edges represent connectivity in the network. Our model is similar to the one introduced in [2]. The computation is structured into synchronous rounds, i.e., we assume that nodes run at the same processing speed and any message that is sent by some node u to its (current) neighbors in some round $r \geq 1$ will be received by the end of r. To ensure scalability, we restrict the number of bits sent per round by each node to be polylogarithmic in n, the stable network size. In each round, up to $O(n/\log^{1+\delta} n)$ nodes can be replaced by new nodes, for any small constant $\delta > 0$. Furthermore, we allow the edges to change arbitrarily in each round, but the underlying graph must be a D-regular non-bipartite expander graph (D can be a constant). (The regularity assumption can be relaxed, e.g., it is enough for nodes to have approximately equal degrees, and our results can be extended.) The churn and edge changes are made by an adversary that is *oblivious* to the state of the nodes. (In particular, it does not know the random choices made by the nodes.) More precisely, the dynamic network is represented by a sequence of graphs $\mathcal{G} = (G^0, G^1, \dots)$. We assume that the adversary commits to this sequence of graphs before round 0, but the algorithm is unaware of the sequence. Each $G^r = (V^r, E^r)$ has n nodes. We require that for all $r \geq 0$, $|V^r \setminus V^{r+1}| = |V^{r+1} \setminus V^r| \leq O(n/\log^{1+\delta} n)$. Furthermore, each G^r must be a D-regular non-bipartite expander with a fixed upper bound of λ on the second largest eigenvalue in absolute value.

A node u can communicate with any node v if u knows the id of v.[5] When a new node joins the network, it has only knowledge of the ids of its current neighbors in the network and thus can communicate with them. We note that communication can be highly unreliable due to churn, since when u sends a message to v there is no guarantee that v is still in the network. However, each node in the network is guaranteed to have D neighbors in the network at any round with whom it can reliably communicate in that round. We note that random walks always use the neighbor edges.

The network is synchronous, so nodes operate under a common clock. The following sequence events occur in each round or time step r. Firstly, the adversary makes the nec-

---

essary changes to the network, so the algorithm is presented with graph G^r. So each node becomes aware of its neighbors in G^r. Each node then exchanges messages with its neighbors. The nodes can perform any required computation at any time. Each node u has a unique identifier and is *churned in* at some round r_i and *churned out* at some $r_o > r_i$. More precisely, for each node u, there is a maximal range $[r_i, r_o - 1]$ such that for every $r \in [r_i, r_o - 1]$, $u \in V^r$ and for every $r \notin [r_i, r_o - 1]$, $u \notin V^r$. Any information about the network at large is only learned through the messages that u receives. It has no a priori knowledge about who its neighbors will be in the future. Neither does u know when (or whether) it will be churned out. For all r, we assume that $|V^r| = n$, where n is a suitably large positive integer. This assumption simplifies our analysis. Our algorithms can be adapted to work correctly as long as the number of nodes is reasonably stable. Also, we assume that $\log n$ and $\log \log n$ (or constant factor estimates bounding these values from above) are common knowledge among the nodes in the network.

2.1 The Storage and Search Problem.

In simple terms, we want to build a robust distributed solution for the storage and retrieval of data items. Nodes can produce data items. Each data item is uniquely identified by an id (such as its hash value). When a node produces a data item, the network must be able to place and maintain copies of the data item in several nodes of the network. To ensure scalability, we want to upper bound the number of copies of each data item, but more importantly, we must also replicate the data sufficiently to ensure that, with high probability, the churn does not destroy all copies of a data item. When a node u requires a data item (whose id, we assume, is known to the node), it must be able to access the data item within a bounded amount of time. To keep things simple, we only require that u knows the id of *a* node (currently in the network) that has the data item u needs. We ideally want an arbitrarily large number of data items to be supported.

3. RANDOM WALKS UNDER CHURN

As a building block for our solution to the storage and search problem, we study some basic properties of random walks in dynamic networks with churn. It is well-known that random walks on expander graphs exhibit fast mixing time, thus allowing near uniform sampling of nodes in the network. This behavior quite easily extends to expander networks in which edges change dynamically, but nodes are fixed [14]. It is more challenging to obtain such characteristics under networks under adversarial node churn. One issue is that random walks may not survive. The more challenging issue is that adversarial churn may bias the random walks, which in turn will bias sampling of nodes. We address both issues in our analysis. In particular, we show that for any time t, most of the random walks that were generated at time t survive up to time $t + O(\log n)$ and at that time the surviving walks are close to uniformly distributed among the existing nodes.

Let $\frac{1}{n}\mathbf{1}$ be the uniform distribution vector that assigns probability $1/n$ to each of the n nodes in G^t. We define $\pi(\mathcal{G}, s, t, t_0)$, $t \geq t_0 \geq 0$, to be the probability distribution vector of the position of a random walk in round t, given that the random walk started at $s \in G^{t_0}$ in round t_0 and proceeded to walk in the dynamic network $\mathcal{G}$. For our purposes, we will restrict our attention to random walks that start in round 0, so, for convenience, we use $\pi(\mathcal{G}, s, t)$ to refer to $\pi(\mathcal{G}, s, t, 0)$. The component $\pi_d(\mathcal{G}, s, t)$ refers to the probability that the random walk is at $d \in V^t$ in round t. Since the random walk could have been terminated because of churn, we use $\pi_*(\mathcal{G}, s, t) = 1 - \sum_{d \in V^t} \pi_d(\mathcal{G}, s, t)$ to denote the probability that the random walk did not survive until round t. We are now ready to present a key ingredient in our algorithms, namely the Soup Theorem, which may also be of independent interest in dynamic graphs (and not just P2P [6]) with churn.

THEOREM 1 (SOUP THEOREM). *Suppose that the churn is limited by $4n/\log^k n$, where $k = 1 + \delta$ for any fixed $\delta > 0$. With high probability, there exists a set of nodes* CORE $\subseteq V^0 \cap V^{2\tau}$, *with cardinality at least $n - \frac{8n}{\log^{(k-1)/2} n}$ such that for any $s \in$ CORE and $d \in$ CORE, a random walk that starts in s terminates in d (in round 2τ) with probability in $[1/17n, 3/2n]$.*

We present a high level sketch of the proof and defer the details to the full version of the paper [1].

PROOF SKETCH. With near linear churn per round, we cannot assume that a random walk will survive in the network, let alone distribute evenly throughout the network. Therefore, for analysis purposes, we construct a dynamic graph $\bar{\mathcal{G}}$ that mimics $\mathcal{G}$, but with the (artificially) added advantage that random walk in $\bar{\mathcal{G}}$ survive with probability 1. When a node $v \in \mathcal{G}^i$ is churned out, all the random walks at v are killed. Recall that we have assumed that the number of nodes churned in at any round equals the number of nodes churned out. To obtain $\bar{\mathcal{G}}$, for each v that is churned out, we pick a unique node $v' \in \mathcal{G}^{i+1}$ that was churned in at round $i + 1$ and place all the random walks previously at v on v'. The dynamic network $\bar{\mathcal{G}}$ thus obtained satisfies the type of network studied in [14], i.e., the edges are rewired arbitrarily but the nodes are unaffected. The dynamic mixing time of a random walk starting from some initial distribution over the nodes of a network at time step 0 is the time it takes for the random walk to be distributed nearly uniformly over the nodes of the network. More formally, the dynamic mixing time

$$T(\bar{\mathcal{G}}, \frac{1}{2n}) \triangleq \min \left\{ t : \max_s ||\pi(\bar{\mathcal{G}}, s, t) - \frac{1}{n}\mathbf{1}||_\infty \leqslant \frac{1}{2n} \right\}.$$

In [14], Sarma *et al.* show that $T(\bar{\mathcal{G}}, 1/2n) \in O\left((\log n)/(1 - \lambda)\right)$, where λ is an upper bound on the second largest eigenvalue in absolute value for all $\bar{G} \in \bar{\mathcal{G}}$. Moreover, the expected number of random walks that are at any specific node at any point in time is the same as the initial token distribution. Thus, with high probability, all tokens are able to take T steps within $\tau \in O(\log n)$ rounds. For the rest of the analysis, we use this fast mixing behavior of random walks in $\bar{\mathcal{G}}$ to make inferences on the behavior of random walks in $\mathcal{G}$. The sequence of inferences we make are as follows.

1. Given a dynamic graph process $\mathcal{G}$, we show that there is a large set of nodes $S \subseteq V^0$ of cardinality at least $n -$

$4n/\log^{(k-1)/2} n$ such that every random walk generated in each of these nodes at time 0 survives up to the mixing time with probability $1 - 1/\log^{(k-1)/2} n$.

We then show that for every $s \in S$ there is a set $D(s) \in V^\tau$ also of cardinality at least $n - 4n/\log^{(k-1)/2} n$ such that a random walk that starts from s at time step 0 is almost uniformly distributed in $D(s)$. More precisely, for any $d \in D(s)$, $1/4n \leqslant \pi_d(\mathcal{G}, s, \tau) \leqslant 3/2n$.

2. Taking advantage of the reversibility of random walks in $\bar{\mathcal{G}}$, we show that there is a set $D \subseteq V^\tau$ such that for every $d \in D$, there is a set $S(d) \subseteq V^0$ again of cardinality at least $n - 4n/\log^{(k-1)/2} n$ such that the origin of every random walk that terminated in d is almost uniformly distributed in $S(d)$, i.e., for any specific $s \in S(d)$, the random walk the probability that the random walk originated from s lies in the range $[1/4n, 3/2n]$.

3. Carefully combining two τ round phases, we show that there is a large set of nodes CORE $\subseteq V^0 \cap V^{2\tau}$ of cardinality at least $n - 8n/\log^{(k-1)/2} n$ such that, for any fixed pair $s, d \in$ CORE, a random walk that starts from s in round 0 will reach d in round 2τ with probability in $\Theta(1/n)$ and likewise a random walk that started in round 0 and terminated at d in round 2τ originated in s with probability in $\Theta(1/n)$, thus proving the theorem. $\square$

The upshot of Theorem 1 is that for any fixed period of 2τ rounds we are guaranteed a large set CORE of cardinality at least $n - o(n)$ such that random walks starting and ending in CORE are well mixed.

4. STORAGE AND SEARCH OF DATA

In this section we describe a mechanism that enables all but $o(n)$ nodes to persistently store data in the network. We will assume that churn rate is $4n/\log^k n$. A key goal is to tolerate as much churn as possible, hence we would like k to be as small as possible. With this in mind, we again show in the analysis that k can be of the form $1 + \delta$ for any fixed $\delta > 0$.

A naïve solution is to flood the data through the network and store it at a linear number of nodes, which guarantees fast retrieval and persistence with probability 1. Clearly, such an approach does not scale to large peer-to-peer networks due to the congestion caused by flooding and the costs of storing the item at almost every node. As we strive to design algorithms that are useful in large scale P2P-networks, we limit the amount of communication by using random walks instead of flooding and require only a sublinear number of nodes to be responsible for the storage of an item — only $\Theta(\log n)$ of these nodes will actually store the item[7] whereas the other nodes serve as landmarks pointing to these $\Theta(\log n)$ nodes.

Suppose that node u wants to store item $\mathcal{I}$ and assume that u is part of the large set of nodes CORE provided by Theorem 1, which consists of nodes that are able to obtain (almost uniform) node id samples from the same set, despite churn. A well known solution is to make use of the birthday paradox: If node u is able to select $\Theta(\sqrt{n} \log n)$ sample ids and assign these so called *data nodes* to store $\mathcal{I}$, then $\mathcal{I}$ can be retrieved within $\sqrt{n}$ rounds by most nodes, with

---

[6]In particular, the Soup theorem applies to any expander topology model with churn. It can also be extended to general connected networks, although the bounds will depend on the dynamic mixing time [14] of the underlying dynamic network.

[7]In fact (as we noted earlier) using erasure coding techniques, the overall storage can be limited to a constant factor overhead; see the full version of the paper [1].

high probability. In our dynamic setting, up to $O(n/\log^k n)$ nodes per round can be affected by churn, which means that the number of data nodes might decrease rapidly. Care must be taken when replenishing the number of data nodes, as we need to ensure that the data nodes are chosen randomly and their total number does not exceed $\tilde{O}(\sqrt{n})$. A simple algorithm for estimating the actual number of data nodes is to require data nodes first to generate a random value from the exponential distribution with rate 1, then to aggregate the minimum generated value z by flooding it through the network (cf. [2]), and finally to compute the estimate as $1/z$. The simplicity of the above approach comes at the price of requiring every node to participate (by flooding) in the storage of the item.

We now describe an approach that avoids the above pitfalls and provides fast data retrieval and persistence with high probability, while limiting the actual number of nodes needed for storing a data item to $\Theta(\log n)$, while a large set of $\Omega(\sqrt{n})$ nodes serve as so-called "landmarks". That is, a node v is a *landmark for item $\mathcal{I}$ in r*, if v knows the id of some node $w \in V^r$ that stores $\mathcal{I}$. Note that even if v was a landmark in r, it might no longer be a landmark in round $r+1$ if w has been churned out at the beginning of r; moreover, v itself will not be aware of this change until it attempts to contact w. To facilitate the maintenance of a large set of randomly distributed landmarks, our algorithms construct a committee of $\Theta(\log n)$ nodes via the overlay network. In the context of the storage procedure, the committee is responsible for storing some data item $\mathcal{I}$ and creating sufficiently many (i.e. $\Omega(\sqrt{n})$) randomly distributed *storage landmarks* for allowing fast retrieval of $\mathcal{I}$ by other nodes. If, on the other hand, u wants to retrieve item $\mathcal{I}$, having a large number of *search landmarks* will significantly increase the probability of finding a sample of a storage landmark in short time. Due to churn, the number of landmark nodes (and the number of committee members) might be decreasing rapidly. Thus the committee members continuously need to replenish the committee and rebuild the landmark set. Note that we guarantee that the number of landmarks involved with a storage or search request remains in $\tilde{O}(n^{1/2+\delta})$, for any constant $\delta > 0$, which ensures that our algorithms are scalable to large networks.

4.1 Building Block: Electing and Maintaining a Committee

We will now study how a node u can elect and maintain a committee of nodes in the network. Such a committee can be entrusted with some task that might need to be performed persistently in the network even after u is churned out. We for instance use such a committee in Section 4.3 to enable u to store a data item $\mathcal{I}$ so that some other node that needs the data may be able to access it well into the future without relying on u's presence in the network. While electing a committee is easy, we need to be careful to maintain the committee for a longer (polynomial in n) period of time because, without maintenance, the members can be churned out in $O(\log^k n)$ rounds.

Towards this goal, we make each node initiate $\alpha \log n$ random walks every round. Depending on how long we want the committee to last, we can fix an appropriately large α. Each random walk travels for 2τ rounds; the node at which the random walk stops is called its destination. The destination node can use the source of the random walk as a

sample from the set of nodes in the network. Since every node initiates some $\alpha \log n$ random walks every round, Theorem 1 is applicable in every round $r \geqslant 2\tau$. To formalize this application of Theorem 1, we parameterize CORE with respect to time. We define CORE^r to be the largest subset of $V^{r-2\tau} \cap V^r$ such that for any $s \in \text{CORE}^r$ and $d \in \text{CORE}^r$, a random walk that starts from s (in round $r-2\tau$) terminates in d (in round r) with probability in $[1/17n, 3/2n]$. From Theorem 1, we know that CORE^r has cardinality at least $n - O(n/\log^{(k-1)/2} n)$. When the value of r is clear from the context, we may avoid the explicit superscript.

Algorithm 1 presents an algorithm that

1. enables a node $u \in \text{CORE}^r$, $r \geqslant 2\tau$, to elect a committee of $\Theta(\log n)$ nodes and
2. enables the committee to maintain itself at a cardinality of $\Theta(\log n)$ nodes despite $O(n/\log^k n)$ churn. Moreover, the committee must comprise of at least $\Theta(\log n)$ nodes from the current CORE.

In Algorithm 1, we assume that u is in the CORE when it needs to create the committee. We show that, if $u \in \text{CORE}$, then, u will receive a sufficient number of random samples, so it chooses some $h \log n$ samples to form the committee. To ensure that churn does not decimate the committee, every $\Theta(\log n)$ rounds, we re-form the committee, i.e., the current committee members choose a suitable leader that chooses a new set of committee members. The old committee members hand over their task to the new committee members and "resign" from the committee and the new members join the committee and resume the task they are called to perform.

Let COM^r, $r \geqslant r_1$, denote the set of nodes that consider themselves to be committee members in round r. We say that COM^r is *good* if $|\text{COM}^r \cap \text{CORE}^r| \geqslant (1 - \varepsilon) h \log n$ for any fixed $\varepsilon > 0$. In the following theorem states that the committee that is created by u will be good for a suitably long period of time.

THEOREM 2. *Fix ε to be a small positive number in $(0, 1]$. Recall that u creates the committee in round r_1. Let $R \geqslant r_1$ be a random variable denoting the smallest value of r when COM^r is not good and let Y be a geometrically distributed random variable with parameter $p = (1/n^{\ell_1} + 2/n^{2h}) \in n^{-\Omega(1)}$. Then, Y is smaller than $R - r_1 + 1$ in the usual stochastic order [44]. In other words, for every positive integer i, $Pr[Y \geqslant i] \leqslant Pr[R - r_1 + 1 \geqslant i]$.*

PROOF SKETCH. When a new set of nodes are elected to form the committee, they perform this role for 2τ rounds and then elect a new committee. We thus show that either (i) a newly formed committee does not last for 2τ rounds (with probability at most $1/n^{2h}$) or is incapable of electing a new committee (with probability at most $1/n^{\ell_1} + 1/n^{2h}$). Thus a newly formed committee fails to survive and elect a successor committee with probability at most $p = (1/n^{\ell_1} + 2/n^{2h}) \in n^{-\Omega(1)}$. $\square$

COROLLARY 1. *Let ℓ be a suitably large number that respects the inequality $p \leqslant n^{-\ell}$. Suppose at some round $r + 2$, a new set of committee members have been selected by $c^r \in \text{CORE}^r$. Let $g \geqslant 0$ be a random variable such that $r + g + 2$ is the first round after $r + 2$ when the committee ceases to be good. Then, $E(g) \geqslant n^\ell$. Furthermore, for any $0 \leqslant i \leqslant \ell$, $Pr[g \leqslant n^{\ell-i}] \leqslant n^{-i}$.*

Algorithm 1 Committee Maintenance and Construction for node u.

Committee Creation.

⟪*Let $r_1 \geq 2\tau$ be the round when u must create* Com. *We assume that $u \in \text{Core}^{r_1}$. Let $h \leq \alpha/36$ be a fixed constant.*⟫

At round r_1: Node u chooses $h \log n$ sample ids and requests each node to join the committee Com. Therefore, Com $\leftarrow \{v | (v \in V^{r_1}) \wedge v$ received an invitation from $u\}$. Along with the request, u sends all the ids in Com to every node in Com. This enables the nodes in Com to form a clique interconnection.

Committee Maintenance.

⟪*For every round r that is $2\gamma\tau$ rounds after* Com *is created for every positive integer γ.*⟫

At round r: The nodes in Com record the random walks they receive along with the source of each random walk.

At round $r + 1$: The nodes in Com exchange the number of random walks they received in round r with each other.

At the end of round $r + 1$: The number of random walks received by each node in Com is common knowledge among the members of Com. The node c^r with the largest number of random walks is chosen to initiate the new committee (breaking ties arbitrarily yet unanimously). The choice of c^r is now common knowledge among the nodes in Com.

At round $r + 2$: The node c^r chooses $h \log n$ random walks that stopped at c^r in round r and invites[8] their source nodes to form the new committee in round $r + 3$. Let Com* be the set of invited source nodes. Along with the invitation, the $h \log n$ id's of all members of Com* are included. Therefore, the id's of nodes in Com* becomes common knowledge among the nodes in Com*. The nodes in Com cease to be members of the committee at the end of round $r + 2$. (If the situation calls for it, we may postpone the "resignation" of the current committee members; the overlap in membership can be used for ensuring smooth transition of the task performed by the committee.)

At round $r + 3$: The members in Com* formally take over the committee. I.e. Com $\leftarrow$ Com*.

Each member of the new Com uses the id's of all other members to form a clique interconnection.

4.2 Building Block: Constructing a Set of Randomly Distributed Landmarks

Once we have succeeded in constructing a committee of $\Theta(\log n)$ nodes, we can extend the "reach" of this committee by creating a randomly distributed set of nodes that know about the committee members. An easy but inefficient solution is to simply flood the ids of the committee members through the network, which requires a linear number of messages to be sent. In this section, we will describe a more scalable approach (cf. Algorithm 2) that constructs a set of $\Omega(\sqrt{n})$ randomly distributed nodes that know the ids of the committee members and thus serve as "landmarks" for the committee. The basic idea is that every current committee member selects 2 of its received samples and adds them as children. These child nodes in turn then attempt to select 2 child nodes each and so forth. Taking into account churn, and the fact that only $n - o(n)$ nodes are able to select *random* child nodes, we choose a tree depth that ensures with high probability that the committee members will succeed to construct a landmark set of size at least $\Omega(\sqrt{n})$, but containing no more than $O(n^{1/2+\delta} \log n)$ nodes.

Due to the high amount of churn and the fact that the committee members change over time, the committee nodes are responsible for rebuilding the set of landmarks every $O(\log n)$ rounds, which will also ensure that the landmarks are randomly distributed among the nodes *currently* in Core. We define Core$^{[r_1,r_2]}$ as a shorthand for Core$^{r_1} \cap \cdots \cap$ Core^{r_2}.

Lemma 1. *Consider any round $r \geq 2\tau$ and suppose that some node $u \in \text{Core}^r$ executes Algorithm 2 for storing item $\mathcal{I}$ and let T be the set of landmarks created for $\mathcal{I}$. Then the following holds with high probability for a polynomial number of rounds starting at any round $r_1 \geq r + 2\tau$. For $r_2 = r_1 + 4\tau$, there exists a set $M_{\mathcal{I}} \subseteq T \cap \text{Core}^{[r_1,r_2]}$ of landmarks such that every node in $M_{\mathcal{I}}$ is distributed with probability in $[1/17n, 3/2n]$ among the nodes in $\text{Core}^{[r_1,r_2]}$ and $\sqrt{n} \leq |M_{\mathcal{I}}| \leq |T| \leq O(n^{1/2+\delta} \log n)$.*

4.3 Storage and Retrieval Algorithms

Now that we have general techniques for maintaining a committee of nodes and creating a randomly distributed set of landmarks for this committee (cf. Sections 4.1 and 4.2), we will use these methods to implement algorithms for storage and retrieval of data items.

Definition 1. *We say that a data item $\mathcal{I}$ is available in round r, if the probability of any node in $\text{Core}^{[r,r+\tau]}$ to be in the current set of landmarks $M_{\mathcal{I}}^r$ is at least $\frac{1}{\Theta(\sqrt{n})}$.*

It follows immediately from Corollary 1 and Lemma 1 that if a data item $\mathcal{I}$ is stored by a node $u \in \text{Core}^{r_1}$ in some round r_1, then $\mathcal{I}$ will be available in the network for a polynomial number of rounds starting from r_1, with high probability.

For storing some data item $\mathcal{I}$ by some node $u \in$ Core, we combine the committee maintenance and landmark construction. In more detail, node u first creates a committee of $\Theta(\log n)$ nodes (cf. Algorithms 1), which will be responsible for storing the data item, i.e., every committee member will store a copy of $\mathcal{I}$. The committee immediately starts creating a set of $\Omega(\sqrt{n})$ landmark nodes, which know the ids of the committee members, but do *not* store $\mathcal{I}$ itself. Choosing these landmark nodes almost uniformly at random (cf. Lemma 1) from the current Core set, ensures that

---

[8]In our algorithm description, we assume for simplicity that c^r is not churned out in round $r + 2$. We can handle the case where c^r *is* churned out, by having the set S of the $\Theta(\log n)$ committee members that have received the largest number of random walks all perform the task of c^r in parallel, i.e., each of them builds a new committee. Once these committee constructions are complete, the (survived) nodes in S agree

on a single member c^* of S and its committee Com*, and all other committees are dissolved.

Algorithm 2 Constructing a Random Set of Landmarks

Assumption: There is a committee of $\Theta(\log n)$ nodes each of which is carrying out some task $\mathcal{T}$ that requires all committee nodes to simultaneously start executing this algorithm. Task $\mathcal{T}$ can either be a data retrieval or a storage request of some item $\mathcal{I}$.

Every τ rounds do:
1: Every committee node v tries to add $\Omega(\sqrt{n})$ randomly chosen nodes to the landmark set of $\mathcal{I}$ by constructing a tree:
2: Node v contacts its $\Theta(\log n)$ received sample nodes and adds 2 nodes v_1 and v_2 that are not yet part of the tree as its children (if possible).
3: Nodes v_1 and v_2 in turn each select 2 (unused) nodes among their own samples as their children and so on. The nodes in the tree keep track of a tree depth counter μ that is initialized to 0 and increased every time a new level is added to the tree. The construction stops at a tree depth of

$$\mu = \left\lceil \frac{\log_2 n - 2\left(\log_2 \log n + \log 2\right)}{2 \log_2 \left(2\left(1 - \frac{1}{\log^{(k-1)/2} n}\right)\left(1 - \frac{1}{\log^{k-1} n}\right)\left(1 - \frac{1}{n^3}\right)\right)} \right\rceil . \tag{1}$$

Note that nodes do not need to remember the actual tree structure. Every time a new level of v's tree is created, the parent nodes send all $O(\log n)$ committee ids to its newly added children.
4: Every node that has become a landmark for $\mathcal{I}$, remains a landmark for 2τ rounds and then simply discards any information about $\mathcal{I}$.

---

the committee members can be found efficiently by the data retrieval mechanism described below

It follows immediately from Corollary 1 and Lemma 1 that if a data item $\mathcal{I}$ is stored by a node $u \in \textsc{Core}^{r_1}$ in some round r_1, then $\mathcal{I}$ will be available in the network for a polynomial number of rounds starting from r_1, with high probability. Owing to the memoryless nature of the persistence of the committee (cf. Theorem 2 and Corollary 1), the same holds with high probability for any later interval of polynomial number of rounds if the data was stored in a good committee at the start of the interval.

Algorithm 3 Persistently Storing a Data Item

Node u issues an insertion request in round r for data $\mathcal{I}$.

1: Node u initiates Algorithm 1 to create a committee $\textsc{Com}$ and requests the committee nodes to store $\mathcal{I}$. Note that the committee nodes will continue to store $\mathcal{I}$ on u's behalf, even if u has long been churned out.
2: Moreover, u instructs the committee members to execute Algorithm 2 and repeatedly create landmark sets of $\Omega(\sqrt{n})$ nodes that will respond to retrieval requests of $\mathcal{I}$.

THEOREM 3 (DATA STORAGE). *Consider any round $r \geqslant 2\tau$. There is a set A of at least $n - o(n)$ nodes, such that any data item $\mathcal{I}$ stored by a node in A via Algorithm 3 in round r is available for a polynomial number of rounds starting from round $r + 2\tau$, with high probability, in a network with churn rate up to $O(n/\log^{1+\delta} n)$ per round.*

Conditioning on the fact that a data item $\mathcal{I}$ is available in some round r_i, gives us a high probability bound that $\mathcal{I}$ will be available for another polynomial number of rounds, for any $r_i \geqslant r_1$.

COROLLARY 2. *Suppose that Algorithm 3 is executed for some data item $\mathcal{I}$ since round r_1. If $\mathcal{I}$ is available in some round $r_i \geqslant r_1$, then $\mathcal{I}$ will be available for a polynomial number of rounds starting from r_i with high probability.*

For efficient retrieval of an available data item, we will again use the committee maintenance and landmark construction techniques. To distinguish between the nodes that are serving as landmarks or committee members for the storage procedures from the committee and landmark sets that are created for data retrieval, we will call the former *storage landmarks*, resp. *storage committee* and the latter *search landmarks* resp. *search committee*.

When a node $u \in \textsc{Core}^r$ executes Algorithm 4 to retrieve some available data item $\mathcal{I}$, it first creates a search committee via Algorithm 1, which in turn is responsible for creating a set of $\Omega(\sqrt{n})$ search landmarks. These search landmarks have high probability to be reached by any of the random walks originating from one of the storage landmarks that were previously created by the storage committee members. In more detail, we can show that with high probability, $\Omega(\sqrt{n})$ search landmark nodes are from the same core set from which the $\Omega(\sqrt{n})$ storage landmarks have been chosen and therefore, within $O(\log n)$ rounds, a search landmark is very likely to get to know the id of one of the storage landmarks.

Algorithm 4 Retrieval of a Data Item

Node u issues a retrieval request in round r_1 for data $\mathcal{I}$.

1: Node u initiates Algorithm 1 to create a committee $\textsc{Com}$ which will automatically dissolve itself after $\Theta(\log n)$ rounds.
2: Node u instructs the committee members to execute Algorithm 2 and repeatedly create a landmark set of $\Omega(\sqrt{n})$ nodes. Every landmark node w contacts all nodes of received samples and inquires about $\mathcal{I}$. If $\mathcal{I}$ is found, w directly reports this to u.

THEOREM 4 (DATA RETRIEVAL). *Consider any round $r_1 \geqslant 2\tau$. There is a set A of at least $n - o(n)$ nodes, such that any available data item $\mathcal{I}$ can be retrieved by any $u \in A$ via Algorithm 4 in $O(\log n)$ rounds, with high probability, in a network with churn rate up to $O(n/\log^{1+\delta} n)$ per round.*

5. CONCLUSION

We have presented efficient algorithms for robust storage and retrieval of data items in a highly dynamic setting where a large number of nodes can be subject to churn in every round and the topology of the network is under control of the adversary. An important open problem is finding lower bounds for the maximum amount of churn that is tolerable by any algorithm with a sublinear message complexity. For random walks based approaches, we conjecture that there is a fundamental limit at $o(n/\log n)$ churn, for the simple reason that if churn can be in order $\Omega(n/\log n)$, the adversary can subject a constant fraction of the nodes to churn by the time a random walk has completed its course. In this context, it will be interesting to determine exact tradeoff between message complexity and tolerable amount of churn per round.

6. REFERENCES

[1] John Augustine, Anisur Rahaman Molla, Ehab Morsy, Gopal Pandurangan, Peter Robinson, and Eli Upfal. Storage and search in dynamic peer-to-peer networks. *CoRR*, abs/1305.1121, 2013.

[2] John Augustine, Gopal Pandurangan, Peter Robinson, and Eli Upfal. Towards robust and efficient computation in dynamic peer-to-peer networks. In *ACM-SIAM*, SODA 2012, pages 551–569. SIAM, 2012.

[3] C. Avin, M. Koucký, and Z. Lotker. How to explore a fast-changing world (cover time of a simple random walk on evolving graphs). In *Proc. of 35th Coll. on Automata, Languages and Programming (ICALP)*, pages 121–132, 2008.

[4] Baruch Awerbuch and Christian Scheideler. Towards a scalable and robust DHT. *Theory of Computing Systems*, 45:234–260, 2009.

[5] Ozalp Babaoglu, Moreno Merzolla, and Michele Tamburini. Design and implementation of a p2p cloud system. *SAC*, March, 2012.

[6] Amitabha Bagchi, Ankur Bhargava, Amitabh Chaudhary, David Eppstein, and Christian Scheideler. The effect of faults on network expansion. *Theory Comput. Syst.*, 39(6):903–928, 2006.

[7] Edward Bortnikov, Maxim Gurevich, Idit Keidar, Gabriel Kliot, and Alexander Shraer. Brahms: Byzantine resilient random membership sampling. *Computer Networks*, 53, March, 2009.

[8] John F. Canny. Collaborative filtering with privacy. In *IEEE Symposium on Security and Privacy*, pages 45–57, 2002.

[9] Arnaud Casteigts, Paola Flocchini, Walter Quattrociocchi, and Nicola Santoro. Time-varying graphs and dynamic networks. *CoRR*, abs/1012.0009, 2010. Short version in ADHOC-NOW 2011.

[10] Arnaud Casteigts, Paola Flocchini, Walter Quattrociocchi, and Nicola Santoro. Time-varying graphs and dynamic networks. *CoRR*, abs/1012.0009, 2010.

[11] Yu-Wei Chan, Tsung-Hsuan Ho, Po-Chi Shih, and Yeh-Ching Chung. Malugo: A peer-to-peer storage system. *Int. J. ad hoc and ubiquitous computing*, 5(4), 2010.

[12] Website of Cloudmark Inc. http://cloudmark.com/.

[13] Website of Crashplan Inc. http://www.crashplan.com/.

[14] Atish Das Sarma, Anisur Rahaman Molla, and Gopal Pandurangan. Fast distributed computation in dynamic networks via random walks. In *DISC*, pages 136–150, 2012.

[15] Souptik Datta, Kanishka Bhaduri, Chris Giannella, Ran Wolff, and Hillol Kargupta. Distributed data mining in peer-to-peer networks. *IEEE Internet Computing*, 10(4):18–26, 2006.

[16] P. Druschel and A. Rowstron. Past: A large-scale, persistent peer-to-peer storage utility. In *HotOS VIII*, pages 75–80, 2001.

[17] P. Druschel and A. Rowstron. Storage management and caching in past, a large-scale, persistent peer-to-peer storage utility. *In Proc. of ACM SOSP*, 2001.

[18] Cynthia Dwork, David Peleg, Nicholas Pippenger, and Eli Upfal. Fault tolerance in networks of bounded degree. *SIAM J. Comput.*, 17(5):975–988, 1988.

[19] Jarret Falkner, Michael Piatek, John P. John, Arvind Krishnamurthy, and Thomas E. Anderson. Profiling a million user dht. In *Internet Measurement Comference*, pages 129–134, 2007.

[20] Amos Fiat and Jared Saia. Censorship resistant peer-to-peer content addressable networks. In *SODA*, pages 94–103, 2002.

[21] A.J. Ganesh, A.-M. Kermarrec, E. Le Merrer, and L. Massoulié. Peer counting and sampling in overlay networks based on random walks. *Distributed Computing*, 20:267–278, 2007.

[22] Roxana Geambasu, Tadayoshi Kohno, Amit A. Levy, and Henry M. Levy. Vanish: Increasing data privacy with self-destructing data. In *USENIX Security Symposium*, pages 299–316, 2009.

[23] Christos Gkantsidis, Milena Mihail, and Amin Saberi. Hybrid search schemes for unstructured peer-to-peer networks. In *IEEE INFOCOM*, 2005.

[24] P. Krishna Gummadi, Stefan Saroiu, and Steven D. Gribble. A measurement study of napster and gnutella as examples of peer-to-peer file sharing systems. *Computer Communication Review*, 32(1):82, 2002.

[25] Ragib Hasan, Zahid Anwar, William Yurcik, Larry Brumbaugh, and Roy Campbell. A survey of peer-to-peer storage techniques for distributed file systems. In *Proc of ITCC*, pages 205–213. IEEE Computer Society, 2005.

[26] Kirsten Hildrum and John Kubiatowicz. Asymptotically efficient approaches to fault-tolerance in peer-to-peer networks. In *DISC*, volume 2848 of *Lecture Notes in Computer Science*, pages 321–336. Springer, 2003.

[27] T. Jacobs and G. Pandurangan. Stochastic analysis of a churn-tolerant structured peer-to-peer scheme. *Peer-to-Peer Networking and Applications*, 2012.

[28] Bruce M. Kapron, David Kempe, Valerie King, Jared Saia, and Vishal Sanwalani. Fast asynchronous byzantine agreement and leader election with full information. *ACM Transactions on Algorithms*, 6(4), 2010.

[29] Valerie King, Jared Saia, Vishal Sanwalani, and Erik Vee. Towards secure and scalable computation in peer-to-peer networks. In *FOCS*, pages 87–98, 2006.

[30] F. Kuhn and R. Oshman. Dynamic networks: Models and algorithms. *SIGACT News*, 42(1):82–96, 2011.

[31] Fabian Kuhn, Nancy Lynch, and Rotem Oshman. Distributed computation in dynamic networks. In *ACM STOC*, pages 513–522, 2010.

[32] Fabian Kuhn, Stefan Schmid, and Roger Wattenhofer. Towards worst-case churn resistant peer-to-peer systems. *Distributed Computing*, 22(4):249–267, 2010.

[33] C. Law and K.-Y. Siu. Distributed construction of random expander networks. In *INFOCOM 2003. Twenty-Second Annual Joint Conference of the IEEE Computer and Communications. IEEE Societies*, volume 3, pages 2133 – 2143 vol.3, march-3 april 2003.

[34] Eng Keong Lua, Jon Crowcroft, Marcelo Pias, Ravi Sharma, and Steven Lim. A survey and comparison of peer-to-peer overlay network schemes. *IEEE communications survey and tutorial*, 2004.

[35] Q. Lv, P. Cao, E. Cohen, K. Li, and S. Shenker. Search and replication in unstructured peer-to-peer networks. *In Proceedings of the 16th international conference on Supercomputing*, pages 84–95, 2002.

[36] David J. Malan and Michael D. Smith. Host-based detection of worms through peer-to-peer cooperation. In Vijay Atluri and Angelos D. Keromytis, editors, *WORM*, pages 72–80. ACM Press, 2005.

[37] Ruggero Morselli, Bobby Bhattacharjee, Michael A. Marsh, and Aravind Srinivasan. Efficient lookup on unstructured topologies. *IEEE Journal on selected areas in communications*, 15(1), January 2007.

[38] Moni Naor and Udi Wieder. A simple fault tolerant distributed hash table. In *IPTPS*, pages 88–97, 2003.

[39] Gopal Pandurangan, Prabhakar Raghavan, and Eli Upfal. Building low-diameter P2P networks. In *FOCS*, pages 492–499, 2001.

[40] Arjan Peddemors. Cloud storage and peer-to-peer storage - end-user considerations and product overview. *http://www.novay.nl/okb/publications/152*, 2010.

[41] J. Saia, A. Fiat, S. Gribble, A. Karlin, and S. Saroiu. Dynamically fault-tolerant content addressable networks. *In the Proceedings of the 1st International Workshop on Peer-to-Peer Systems*, March 2002.

[42] Christian Scheideler. How to spread adversarial nodes?: rotate! In *STOC*, pages 704–713, 2005.

[43] Subhabrata Sen and Jia Wang. Analyzing peer-to-peer traffic across large networks. In *Proceedings of the 2nd ACM SIGCOMM Workshop on Internet measurment*, IMW '02, pages 137–150, New York, NY, USA, 2002. ACM.

[44] Moshe Shaked and J. George Shanthikumar. *Stochastic Orders*. Springer, 2007.

[45] Daniel Stutzbach and Reza Rejaie. Understanding churn in peer-to-peer networks. In *Proceedings of the 6th ACM SIGCOMM conference on Internet measurement*, IMC '06, pages 189–202, New York, NY, USA, 2006. ACM.

[46] Website of Symform:. http://www.symform.com/.

[47] Eli Upfal. Tolerating a linear number of faults in networks of bounded degree. *Inf. Comput.*, 115(2):312–320, 1994.

[48] Vasileios Vlachos, Stephanos Androutsellis-Theotokis, and Diomidis Spinellis. Security applications of peer-to-peer networks. *Comput. Netw.*, 45:195–205, June 2004.

[49] Ming Zhong and Kai Sheng. Popularity biased random walks for peer to peer search under the squareroot principle. In *IPTPS*, 2006.

Broadcasting in Logarithmic Time
for Ad Hoc Network Nodes on a Line Using MIMO

Thomas Janson
University of Freiburg
Department of Computer Science
Georges-Koehler-Allee 51
79110 Freiburg, Germany
janson@informatik.uni-freiburg.de

Christian Schindelhauer
University of Freiburg
Department of Computer Science
Georges-Koehler-Allee 51
79110 Freiburg, Germany
schindel@informatik.uni-freiburg.de

ABSTRACT

We consider n wireless ad hoc network nodes with one antenna each and equidistantly placed on a line. The transmission power of each node is just large enough to reach its next neighbor. For this setting we show that a message can be broadcasted to all nodes in time $\mathcal{O}(\log n)$ without increasing each node's transmission power. Our algorithm needs $\mathcal{O}(\log n)$ messages and consumes a total energy which is only a constant factor larger than the standard approach where nodes sequentially transmit the broadcast message to their next neighbors. We obtain this by synchronizing the nodes on the fly and using MIMO (multiple input multiple output) techniques.

To achieve this goal we analyze the communication capacity of multiple antennas positioned on a line and use a communication model which is based on electromagnetic fields in free space. We extend existing communication models which either reflect only the sender power or neglect the locations by concentrating only on the channel matrix. Here, we compute the scalar channel matrix from the locations of the antennas and thereby only consider line-of-sight-communication without obstacles, reflections, diffractions or scattering.

First, we show that this communication model reduces to the SINR power model if the antennas are uncoordinated. We show that n coordinated antennas can send a signal which is n times more powerful than the sum of their transmission powers. Alternatively, the power can be reduced to an arbitrarily small polynomial with respect to the distance. For coordinated antennas we show how the well-known power gain for MISO (multiple input single output) and SIMO (single input multiple output) can be described in this model. Furthermore, we analyze the channel matrix and prove that in the free space model no diversity gain can be expected for MIMO.

Finally, we present the logarithmic time broadcast algorithm which takes advantage of the MISO power gain by self-coordinating wireless nodes.

Categories and Subject Descriptors

C.2.1 [**Computer-Communication Networks**]: Network Architecture and Design—*Wireless communication, Network topology, Network communications, Distributed networks*

Keywords

MIMO, Shannon's theorem, signal-to-noise ratio, channel capacity

1. INTRODUCTION

The broadcast problem is to distribute a single message to all nodes in a wireless network. When the transmission power is limited it seems obvious that the time to deliver the message is lower bounded by the diameter of a graph of wireless point-to-point connections. We show that without additional power we can deliver a message in logarithmic time, if one uses so-called MIMO (multiple input multiple output) communication. In order to establish this result we need an accurate model for radio communication.

1.1 Modeling Radio Communication

The capacity of radio communication is strongly influenced by the locations of the radio stations and this influence has been modeled and studied for a long time in computer science. Since computer scientists concentrate on the algorithmic aspects, the communication models have been chosen mostly for simplicity while neglecting physical accuracy.

In the algorithmic networking community first considerations started with graph based models where nodes represent radio stations and edges indicate connections [3, 11]. There is a long line of research in the area of radio broadcasting which consists of handling the problem of interference in an unknown graph in order to broadcast a message.

Later on, geometric graphs were used to model this communication graph. Starting with unit-disk graphs [4], which reflect the power fading around a transmitter and the signal-to-noise ratio, this model was further developed. For a geometric modeling the delay, energy and dilation of routing in networks have been investigated in [9] and approximative solutions as well as trade-offs between these measures have been presented. Further works [2, 12, 13, 14] also considered variable disk ranges around senders. Different disk sizes indicated safe, unsure and no message receipt. This research was motivated by the path-loss model, where a communication between two radio stations takes place if the signal to interference and noise ratio, defined as $\frac{S}{I+N}$ is larger than a given constant. In this term S denotes the signal power proportional to $d^{-\alpha}$ where d is the distance and α is the path loss exponent, usually in the range between 2 and 5. One can find an overview for different indoor and outdoor path loss models in [19]. The term I denotes the sum of all interfering signal powers approximated as $\sum_{i=1}^{m}(d_i)^\alpha$ and N is a constant, which describes the noise coming from the medium and the receiver's hardware. Recent work has described the geometric behavior of senders and interfering radio stations [1] and the complexity of solving communication tasks [6].

Initially, Gupta and Kumar derive in [7] the capacity of a wireless network from the signal-to-noise ratio (SNR). They determine the network throughput for n arbitrarily or randomly placed nodes with single antennas. The path loss exponent is $\alpha > 2$ and they consider interference as boolean property: if the SNR is above a given threshold the signal can be received with a constant not mentioned channel capacity. The capacity is in the order of $\sqrt{n}$. Kumar et al. [8] extend their work from two to three dimensions and then generalize their result for two dimensions by using Shannons law to estimate the channel capacity with $\Theta(\log(1 + \mathrm{SNR}))$.

However this approach completely fails to describe the phenomena with coupled antennas, better known as smart antennas or MIMO (multiple input and multiple output). While there are models that are derived from experimental research in communication, there is little mathematical understanding about these communication models. Furthermore, the relationship of the signal-to-noise ratio in MIMO to the communication bandwidth, which has been theoretically founded for single antennas by Claude Shannon [20], is also not completely understood.

1.2 Related Work

Özgür, Leveque, and Tse show in [17] that linear capacity in the number of nodes n is possible when $\sqrt{A}/\lambda > n$ where A denotes the area A for node placing and λ denotes the wavelength. To achieve linear scaling they use MIMO techniques by allowing several nodes with single antennas to join into a coordinated antenna array. We also arrive at the same precondition $\sqrt{A}/\lambda > m$ for our model to receive a SNR gain of $1/m$ for MIMO and nodes with m antennas in [10]. In [16] they further divide wireless networks in working regimes with the main parameters short-distance SNR, long-distance SNR, and the path loss exponent α of the environment.

In a recent work [15], Özgür et al. present a hierarchical broadcast scheme for n nodes in an one-dimensional network. The basic scheme distributes information in clusters of size M and the beamforming gain of the the M nodes is used to transmit the messages to the target. This recursion step is repeated in a hierarchical strategy. Their analysis assumes a path-loss exponent $1 \leq \alpha < 2$ in the line-of-sight case. At the same time, they demand low SNR $\ll 0$ dB and for small-range communication between neighboring nodes a $\mathrm{SNR}_s \leq n^{\alpha-2}$. In this paper, we assume a path-loss exponent $\alpha = 2$.

On the other hand MIMO is already a standard in use in IEEE WLAN 802.11n and there have been a series of considerations describing the bandwidth gain, which have been theoretically predicted up to a factor of n for n senders and n receivers. However, these predictions rely on the presence of a complex environment where radio signals are reflected from many points which are scattered around. Counterintuitively, such environments are helpful and for sometimes even necessary for MIMO communication. So, we consider here the worst case, which is the free space model.

1.3 Contribution

In this paper, we derive a theoretic model for the communication bandwidth for MIMO. This is based on the fundamentals of physics for electromagnetic waves combined with the theorem of Claude Shannon. We can reduce our model to the standard SINR (signal to interference and noise ratio) model in the plane for the path loss exponent $\alpha = 2$ but with the enhancement of describing bandwidth limits and multiple synchronized senders and receivers. Thereby, we approve the superposition of power of unsynchronized interferences in the SINR model.

Then, we consider the case where multiple senders and receivers are placed on a line. If n senders are synchronized, then the transmission range can be extended by MIMO (multiple input multiple output) communication to a distance of a factor $\sqrt{n}$ compared to a single sender when using the same transmission power of all senders combined. A similar observation can be made for SIMO (single input multiple output) communication. For MIMO we predict a range increase of a factor of n without increasing the power. Regarding the bandwidth only little improvement can be expected if only one pair of MIMO senders and receivers is active. However, it is possible to have multiple communication links in parallel, when multiple MIMO pairs are communicating. From these observations, we propose a broadcasting scheme in $\mathcal{O}(\log n)$ time and the same energy consumption as direct-neighbor communication. We also show the ability of parallelism of this broadcast algorithm in intervals on the line.

2. THE COMMUNICATION MODEL

We consider radio stations R in the plane with antennas oriented perpendicular to a plane and therefore neglect the effects of polarization. The antennas are used for sending and receiving signals, which essentially hold binary strings, called messages. These messages are modulated on the same carrier wave with some frequency f. We assume a line-of-sight communication model without obstacles and neglect the influence of the nodes to the radio communication.

The antennas are placed on a line of this plane. A radio station may use more than one antenna for sending or receiving. The set of antennas of a radio station v are identified by their positions on the line. This position knowledge allows a radio station to send coordinated signals. However, it is also possible that antennas of different radio stations are coordinated.

DEFINITION 2.1. *A set of sending antennas are coordinated if their locations are known at their radio stations, the carrier waves and signal encoding are synchronized and they perform the same task, e.g. send the same message. Receiving antennas are coordinated if they share these properties and the signal can be decoded without further wireless transmission.*

Note that it is conceivable to consider decoding using further wireless communication. However, this causes an increased message size. In the seminal work of [17] and subsequent article [16] this factor is expressed by a so called *observation* of a message. The increase of the message size limits multi-hop routing with uncoordinated MIMO communication because the message size grows exponentially with each hop when observations are forwarded instead of decoding them right away.

We assume that uncoordinated radio stations use unsynchronized clocks, which can be modeled by independently identically distributed random variables describing the relative phase shift of the carrier waves.

The key term to model the reception of a signal is the signal power, while the key of understanding how the signal is transmitted is the electric field. In Appendix A you can find a detailed derivation of our model, which we now shortly summarize.

At the sending antenna u signals are described by the function $s_u(t)$ modulated over a carrier wave described by $a_u \mathrm{e}^{j(2\pi ft+\phi_u)}$ where a_u describes the amplitude of the field and ϕ_u some random phase shift (we denote j as the imaginary unit). Now $a_u^2 f^2$ is proportional to the transmission power P and for coordinated senders we can adjust the amplitude and phase shifts to values $a_u' \leq a_u$ and arbitrary ϕ_u'. The complex value $s_u = a_u' \mathrm{e}^{j\phi_u'}$ describes the full information of the carrier wave with $|s_u| \leq \sqrt{P}/f$ and transmission power P at antenna u. Note that for coordinated senders these complex numbers can be freely chosen and adjusted.

DEFINITION 2.2. *The electric field E_u at sending antenna u is characterized by $E_u(t) = s_u\mathrm{e}^{j2\pi ft}$, where $s_u = |s_u|\mathrm{e}^{j\phi}$ describes the amplitude $|s_u| \leq \sqrt{P}/f$ for maximum transmission power P and ϕ the phase shift of the sender u.*

The propagation of the electromagnetic wave is described by the channel matrix which takes two terms into account – the decrease of the electric field of a sinusoidal wave, which is proportional to $\frac{1}{d}$ where d is the distance, and the phase shift induced by the time the signal needs to travel with the speed of light c.

DEFINITION 2.3. *The received electric field $E_v(t)$ at a receiver antenna v is described by*

$$E_v(t) = \sum_{i=1}^{n} s_i \cdot \frac{\mathrm{e}^{j2\pi f(t+|u_i-v|/c)}}{|u_i-v|} = \mathrm{e}^{j2\pi ft} \cdot \sum_{i=1}^{n} s_i \cdot h_{i,k}$$

where $u_1,\ldots,u_n$ are the sender antennas with characteristic scalar s_i.

This modification between sender and receiver can be described by a multiplication with the complex number $h_{i,k} = \frac{\mathrm{e}^{j2\pi f|u_i-v_k|/c}}{|u_i-v_k|}$, where u_i and v_k denote the positions of sender and receiver on the line. The resulting matrix $H = (h_{i,k})_{i,k}$ is called the channel matrix.

Similarly, at the receiver it is possible to amplify and phase shift signals. This is denoted by the multiplication with r_i. However, the amplification also changes the received noise and possibly interfering messages by a factor of $|g_i|$.

So, for (coordinated or uncoordinated) senders $u_1,\ldots,u_n$ the receiver antennas $v_1,\ldots,v_m$ receive an electric field which consists of the linear combination of the signals

$$E(t) = \sum_{i=1}^{n}\sum_{k=1}^{m} g_k \cdot E_{u_i,v_k}(t)$$

where $g_k \in \mathbb{C}$ is chosen for each receiver antenna which consists of a phase shift and an amplification. Furthermore, some noise N will be received which we will take care of soon. Whenever a phase shift occurs the constant factor $2\pi f/c$ occurs. For readability, we omit it and set $2\pi f/c = 1$ for the rest of this paper. We also omit the carrier wave function $\mathrm{e}^{j2\pi ft}$, since the characteristics are solely described by the factors. So, the electric field is no longer a function of time. The power of the coordinated signal can be described by $(E_S)^2$ as well as the power of the uncoordinated signal is $(E_I)^2$. Since we assume independent choices of the phase shifts we can simplify this term.

LEMMA 2.4. *The expected power of uncoordinated senders $w_1,\ldots,w_\ell$ with signal $s_1',\ldots,s_\ell'$ at the coordinated receivers $v_1,\ldots,v_m$ is*

$$\mathbb{E}[P] = \mathbb{E}\left[|E|^2\right] = \sum_{k=1}^{m}\sum_{i=1}^{\ell} |g_k|^2 \frac{|s_i'|^2}{|w_i-v_k|^2}$$

where g_k denotes the signal gain of the k-th receiver.

The following proof of Lemma 2.4 approves the superposition of power of unsynchronized interferences in the SINR model.

Proof of Lemma 2.4: Given n senders with characteristic scalars $s_i' = a_i\mathrm{e}^{j\phi_i}$ and distance $|w_i-r|$ to a receiver r. The sender antennas are not synchronized with phase angle ϕ_i and produce interference at r. The electrical field strength of sender w_i with far field approximation is

$$E_{s_i} = \frac{a_i \cdot \mathrm{e}^{j\phi_i}}{|w_i-r|} .$$

The power of the field produced by sender w_i at r alone is

$$P_{w_i,r} = \left|\frac{a_i \cdot \mathrm{e}^{j\phi_i}}{|w_i-r|}\right|^2 = \frac{a_i^2}{|w_i-r|^2} .$$

The superposition principle can be applied to the electrical field strength and not to the power.

$$E_r = \sum_{i=1}^{n} E_{w_i}$$

The power of the superposed field is then

$$P_r = \left(\sum_{i=1}^{n} E_{w_i}\right)^2 . \tag{1}$$

The expected power of the noise is then

$$
\begin{aligned}
\mathbb{E}\left[P\right] &= \mathbb{E}\left[\left|\sum_{i=1}^{n}\frac{a_i \cdot \mathrm{e}^{j\phi_i}}{|w_i - r|}\right|^2\right] \\
&= \mathbb{E}\left[\sum_{i=1}^{n}\frac{a_i \cdot \mathrm{e}^{j\phi_i}}{|w_i - r|} \cdot \sum_{i=1}^{n}\frac{a_i \cdot \mathrm{e}^{-j\phi_i}}{|w_i - r|}\right] \\
&= \mathbb{E}\left[\sum_{i\in\{1..n\}}\left(\frac{a_i}{|w_i - r|}\right)^2\right] \\
&\quad + \underbrace{\mathbb{E}\left[\sum_{i=1}^{n}\sum_{k=1,i\neq k}^{n}\mathrm{e}^{j(\phi_i-\phi_k)}\right]}_{=0}\frac{a_i}{|w_i - r|}\cdot\frac{a_k}{|w_k - r|} \\
&= \mathbb{E}\left[\sum_{i=1}^{n}\frac{a_i^2}{|w_i - r|^2}\right] .
\end{aligned}
$$

□

This corresponds to the well known SINR model. The noise power is amplified like all other signals at the m coordinated receivers by a factor of $|g_k|^2$ with signal gain g_k at the k-th receiver. Since electric fields superpose we get the following signal-to-noise ratio.

DEFINITION 2.5. *For n coordinated senders at positions $u_1,\ldots,u_n$ and m coordinated receivers at positions $v_1,\ldots,v_m$ the signal-to-noise-ratio (SINR) can be determined as*

$$
SINR = \frac{\left|\sum_{i=1}^{n}\sum_{k=1}^{m}s_i \cdot \frac{\mathrm{e}^{j|u_i-v_k|}}{|u_i-v_k|}\cdot g_k\right|^2}{\sum_{k=1}^{m}|g_k|^2\left(N+\sum_{i=1}^{\ell}\frac{P_i'}{|w_i-v_k|^2}\right)} = \frac{|s\cdot H\cdot g|^2}{N'+I}
$$

where $u = (u_1,\ldots,u_n) \in \mathbb{R}^n$ is the set of the coordinated sending antenna positions, $v = (v_1,\ldots,v_m) \in \mathbb{R}^m$ is the set of the coordinated receiving antenna positions, and $w = (w_1,\ldots,w_\ell) \in \mathbb{R}^\ell$ is the set of uncoordinated sender antenna positions on the line. N is the power equivalent of the noise level at each receiving antenna v_k. P_i' describes the power of the interfering antenna w_i. The positions of the coordinated senders and receivers describe the channel matrix in free space

$$
H_{i,k} = \frac{\mathrm{e}^{j|u_i-v_k|}}{|u_i - v_k|} \quad i\in[n],\ k\in[m] .
$$

$$
I = \sum_{i\in[\ell],k\in[m]}|g_k|^2\frac{P_i'}{|w_i-v_k|^2}
$$

is the sum of the received signal power from uncoordinated senders. And the received noise is given by

$$
N' = N\sum_{k\in[m]}|g_k|^2 .
$$

The vectors $s = (s_1,\ldots,s_n) \in \mathbb{C}^n$ with $|s_i|^2 \leq P_{u_i}$ and $g = (g_1,\ldots,g_m) \in \mathbb{C}^m$ can be chosen arbitrarily.

For the bandwidth we follow Shannon's theorem. We also assume that a minimum SINR is necessary to establish communication.

DEFINITION 2.6. *If the SINR is above a certain threshold, then communication can be established. For higher SINR values the bandwidth of the transmission is modeled by $f\cdot\log(1+SINR)$ where f is the carrier frequency.*

The *threshold effect* [20] causes the error rate to increase drastically when the noise is over a certain threshold of the system design.

3. POWER GAIN AND DELIBERATE ATTENUATION OF COORDINATED SENDERS IN MISO

For senders on a line, this results in a power gain when the senders are in sync, e.g. all senders emit the same signal and a receiver on the line receives the signal of all senders in the same phase (Theorem 3.1). The coordinated senders produce noise in the opposite of the receiver's direction and we can also attenuate this noise by increasing the path loss exponent at the expense of decreasing power gain towards the receiver. We call this *deliberate attenuation* (Theorem 3.3).

THEOREM 3.1. *If n coordinated senders send with transmission power $P_i = P/n$ each, at positions $u_i \geq 0$, they can always produce a signal at a receiver $v_k \geq \max_\ell\{u_\ell\}$, which is n times more powerful than a single sender at position 0 with transmission power P when m receiver antennas are positioned at $v_1,\ldots,v_m \geq u_n$.*

PROOF. Choose $s_i = \mathrm{e}^{ju_i}\sqrt{P/n}$ and $g_k = \mathrm{e}^{-jv_k}$. This results in

$$
\begin{aligned}
SINR_{n,m} &= \frac{\left|\sum_{i=1}^{n}\sum_{k=1}^{m}\mathrm{e}^{ju_i}\sqrt{P/n}\cdot\frac{\mathrm{e}^{j|u_i-v_k|}}{|u_i-v_k|}\mathrm{e}^{-jv_k}\right|^2}{\sum_{k=1}^{m}|\mathrm{e}^{-jv_k}|^2\cdot(N+I)} \\
&= \frac{\frac{P}{n}\cdot\left|\sum_{i=1}^{n}\sum_{k=1}^{m}\frac{1}{|u_i-v_k|}\right|^2}{m\cdot(N+I)} \\
&\geq \frac{n\cdot P\cdot\left|\sum_{k=1}^{m}\frac{1}{|v_k|}\right|^2}{m\cdot(N+I)} .
\end{aligned}
$$

The same equation for one sender at the origin yields for $s_1 = \sqrt{P}$ and $g_k = \mathrm{e}^{-jv_k}$.

$$
\begin{aligned}
SINR_{1,m} &= \frac{\left|\sum_{k=1}^{m}\sqrt{P}\cdot\frac{\mathrm{e}^{j|v_k|}}{|v_k|}\cdot\mathrm{e}^{-jv_k}\right|^2}{\sum_{k=1}^{m}|\mathrm{e}^{-jv_k}|^2(N+I)} \\
&= P\frac{\left|\sum_{k=1}^{m}\frac{1}{v_k}\right|^2}{m(N+I)} \\
&\leq \frac{1}{n}\,SINR_{n,m} .
\end{aligned}
$$

□

This implies that although the overall transmission power is the same, the signal range with n coordinated antennas extends by a factor of $\sqrt{n}$. This phenomenon is long known and is called power gain in MISO [21].

COROLLARY 3.2. *Any n coordinated senders can send $\sqrt{n}$ times farther than a single sender consuming the same power.*

This is not contradicting the principle of conservation of power, since we consider only the power on the line, whereas the power distribution in the rest of the space changes drastically.

While the factor n power gain is well known, the observation, that one can deliberately attenuate the signal in one direction, is new to our knowledge.

THEOREM 3.3. *Any n coordinated antennas in general positions on the line can produce a fast fading signal on the line which decreases with SINR $\mathcal{O}\left(1/d^{2n}\right)$ in distance d.*

PROOF. To increase the path-loss exponent to $\alpha = 2n$ or a field strength decreasing with $1/d^n$ we want to ensure that

$$h\left(x\right) = \sum_{i=1}^{n} s_i \cdot \frac{e^{j(x-x_i)}}{x-x_i} = \frac{\gamma}{\mathcal{O}\left(x^n\right)}$$

for the complex antenna characteristics s_i and some constant γ. W.l.g. we only consider x-values outside the sender group with $x > x_i$. We extend all summands to the same denominator and the goal is to simplify the nominator to a constant γ to decrease the signal strength to $\mathcal{O}\left(x^{-n}\right)$.

$$
\begin{aligned}
h\left(x\right) &= \sum_{i=1}^{n} \frac{s_i\, e^{j(x-x_i)} \cdot \prod_{k=1,k\neq i}^{n}\left(x-x_k\right)}{\left(x-x_i\right) \cdot \prod_{k=1,k\neq i}^{n}\left(x-x_k\right)} \\
&= \frac{\sum_{i=1}^{n} s_i\left(d_{0,i}x^{n-1} + d_{1,i}x^{n-2} + \cdots + d_{n-1,i}\right)}{\prod_{k=1}^{n}\left(x-x_k\right)} \quad (2) \\
&= \frac{\gamma}{\prod_{k=1}^{n}\left(x-x_k\right)} \quad (3)
\end{aligned}
$$

There is a choice for $(s_1,\ldots,s_n)$ resolving (2) to (3), since there is a solution to the following equation

$$
\begin{pmatrix}
d_{0,1} & \cdots & d_{0,n} \\
\cdots & & \cdots \\
d_{n-1,1} & \cdots & d_{n-1,n}
\end{pmatrix}
\cdot
\begin{pmatrix}
s_1 \\
\vdots \\
s_n
\end{pmatrix}
=
\begin{pmatrix}
0 \\
\vdots \\
0 \\
\gamma
\end{pmatrix}.
$$

Because n vectors of length $(n-1)$ are linear dependent there is always a non-trivial solution $(s_1,\ldots,s_n) \neq (0,\ldots,0)$ to this equation.

$\square$

One may object that the neglected near-field components have stronger asymptotics than this attenuated signal. However, this proof technique also applies to a more accurate model chosen, which reflects far-field and near-field, and yields the same result, i.e. a near-field component for the electromagnetic field of $\mathcal{O}\left(\frac{1}{d^2}\right)$ with distance d to the sender (see Equation 5 in the appendix).

THEOREM 3.4. *Given $n = \rho \cdot \beta$ (for $\rho \geq 2$) coordinated senders with power P each, we can obtain in opposite directions a power gain $\mathcal{O}\left(\beta P/d^2\right)$ and a deliberate power attenuation of $\mathcal{O}\left(\beta P/d^{2\rho-2}\right)$.*

Proof Sketch. Let $u = (u_1,\ldots,u_n)$ be the sender antennas divided into β groups of ρ antennas.

Each group of the ρ antennas will deliberately attenuate for a position $x > \max\{u_i\}$ and distance $d = (x - \max\{u_i\})$ with a power of $\mathcal{O}(\frac{P}{d^{2\rho-2}})$ and send a signal of power of at least P/d^2 to a position $x < \min\{u_i\}$ and the distance $d = (\min\{u_i\} - x)$ to the group of antennas. In order to achieve this claim the linear equation in the proof of Theorem 3.3 needs to be combined with an inequality preventing the attenuation to the left. The probabilistic method shows that the additional degree of freedom by attenuating only to $O(P/d^{2\rho-2})$ allows this property. Now we multiply each of the β groups with a random phase shift.

By the argument of Lemma 2.4 the expected power will be the sum of all signal powers of the sub-groups. From this, we can induce the existence of a choice such that the signal is attenuated by $O(\rho\beta/d^2)$ to the left and $\mathcal{O}\left(\beta P/d^{2\rho-2}\right)$ to the right. $\square$

COROLLARY 3.5. *Among many others the following combination of deliberate attenuation and power gain to different directions are possible for antennas with power P each.*

1. $\mathcal{O}\left(P/d^2\right)$ to the left and $\mathcal{O}\left(P/d^{2n-2}\right)$ to the right ($\rho = n$, $\beta = 1$)

2. $\mathcal{O}\left(\sqrt{n}P/d^2\right)$ to the left and $\mathcal{O}\left(\sqrt{n}P/d^{2\sqrt{n}-2}\right)$ to the right ($\rho = \sqrt{n}$, $\beta = \sqrt{n}$)

3. $\mathcal{O}\left(nP/d^2\right)$ to the left and $\mathcal{O}\left(nP/d^{2c}\right)$ to the right for any integer $c \geq 1$ ($\rho = c+1$, $\beta = n/(c+1)$).

4. POWER GAIN AND DIVERSITY GAIN OF SIMO AND MIMO

For a single sender we can also experience a power gain of a factor n if we use coordinated antennas for receiving (SIMO).

THEOREM 4.1. *Given m coordinated receivers $0 < v_1 < \ldots < v_m$ and a sender at the origin 0. Let $SINR_{1,m}$ be the SINR of these receivers and let $SINR_{1,1}$ be the SINR of a single receiver at v_m. Then, $SINR_{1,1} \leq \frac{1}{m} SINR_{1,m}$.*

PROOF. Choose $s_1 = \sqrt{P}$ and $g_k = e^{-j2\pi f v_k}$. This results in

$$
\begin{aligned}
\mathrm{SINR}_{1,m} &= \frac{\left|\sum_{k=1}^{m} \sqrt{P} \cdot \frac{e^{j|v_k|}}{|v_k|} \cdot e^{-jv_k}\right|^2}{\sum_{k=1}^{m} \left|e^{-jv_k}\right|^2 (N+I)} \\
&= P \cdot \frac{\left|\sum_{k=1}^{m} \frac{1}{|v_k|}\right|^2}{m(N+I)} \\
&\geq m\frac{P}{(v_m)^2 \cdot (N+I)} \\
&= m \cdot \mathrm{SINR}_{1,1}
\end{aligned}
$$

$\square$

Again this results in an extension of the transmission range.

COROLLARY 4.2. *Any n coordinated receivers can get a message from a distance $\sqrt{n}$ times farther than a single receiver.*

With the same calculation one can see a power gain in MIMO.

THEOREM 4.3. *Given n coordinated senders $u_1 < \ldots < u_n < 0$ and m coordinated receivers $0 < v_1 < \ldots < v_m$. Let $SINR_{n,m}$ be the SINR of these senders and receivers and let $SINR_{1,1}$ be the SINR of a single sender at u_1 and a single receiver at v_m. Then, $SINR_{n,m} \geq nm \cdot SINR_{1,1}$.*

These power gains help to extend the communication reach. However, there is also a direct possibility to increase the bandwidth using the so-called diversity gain.

It is often mentioned in literature (e.g. in [18]) that angular spread is essential for MIMO transmission. Our first observation is that in principle such a diversity gain is possible on the line even in free space.

LEMMA 4.4. *For coordinated senders $u_1 < \ldots < u_n$ and coordinated receivers $v_1 < \ldots < v_m$ on a line with $u_n < v_1$ or $v_m < u_1$ the channel matrix H has rank $\min\{n, m\}$.*

PROOF. Without loss of generality we consider the only the case $u_n < v_1$. Let $n = m$, then the channel matrix is

$$
\begin{aligned}
H &= \left(\frac{e^{j|u_i - v_k|}}{|u_i - v_k|} \right)_{i,k \in [n]} = \left(\frac{e^{j(v_k - u_i)}}{v_k - u_i} \right)_{i,k \in [n]} \\
&= D\left(\left(e^{-ju_i} \right)_{i \in [n]} \right) \left(\frac{1}{v_k - u_i} \right)_{i,k \in [n]} D\left(\left(e^{jv_k} \right)_{k \in [n]} \right)
\end{aligned}
$$

where $D(a)$ denotes the diagonal matrix of vector a, which has full rank if a has no zero entry. The matrix $\left(\frac{1}{v_k - u_i} \right)_{i,k \in [n]}$ is a Cauchy matrix and thus is invertible for all u, v if for all i, k: $u_i \neq v_k$. $\square$

THEOREM 4.5. *For coordinated senders $u_1 < \ldots < u_n$ and non coordinated receivers $v_1 < \ldots < v_m$ with $m < n$ on a line with $u_n < v_1$ or $v_m < u_1$ it is possible to send to any subset of receivers without producing a signal at the other receivers.*

PROOF. Consider the vector $a_1, \ldots, a_m$ such that $a_i = 1$ if i is in the subset of aimed receivers and $a_i = 0$ otherwise. Now, we use only m senders. Then let H^{-1} be the inverse of H, which exists because of Lemma 4.4. Then each sender u_i uses the parameter $qH^{-1}a$, where $q = P/\max\{|(H^{-1}a)_i|\}$, where P denotes the maximum possible transmission power. The resulting signal is therefore $qHH^{-1}a = qa$. $\square$

Using this theorem it is possible to send n messages in parallel from n coordinated senders to n uncoordinated receivers, which can be seen as parallel MISO. For this, we choose a receiver and modulate a signal, which can be received at this receiver only, while the other receivers get no signal. Now, we repeat this for all receivers and send the superposed signal from the n coordinated senders. As a result each uncoordinated receiver gets only "his message". This seems to increase the bandwidth between senders and receivers on the line by a factor of n. However, the delimiting factor is the attenuation of the signals imposed by the maximum transmission power P and the entries of the inverse channel matrix H^{-1}.

LEMMA 4.6. *Fix a set of n senders $u_1, \ldots, u_n$ and n receivers $v_1, \ldots, v_n$. Consider the channel matrix of u and $(v_1 + d, \ldots, v_n + d)$ for increasing distance d on the line. Then, the maximum absolute value of the inverse of the channel matrix is $\Theta(d^{2n-1})$.*

PROOF. The absolute values of the channel matrix are described by the Cauchy matrix

$$
M = \left(\frac{1}{v_k - u_i} \right)_{i,k \in [n]}.
$$

The determinant of a Cauchy matrix is

$$
\begin{aligned}
\det M &= \frac{\prod_{i=2}^{n} \prod_{k=1}^{i-1} (v_i - v_k)(u_i - u_k)}{\prod_{i=1}^{n} \prod_{k=1}^{n} (v_i - u_k)} \\
&= \frac{\prod_{i=2}^{n} \prod_{k=1}^{i-1} (v_i - v_k)(u_i - u_k)}{\prod_{i=1}^{n} \prod_{k=1}^{n} (d + v_i - u_k)} \\
&= \Theta\left(\frac{1}{d^{n^2}} \right).
\end{aligned}
$$

The inverse $D = (d_{ik})_{i,k \in [n]}$ of a matrix can be computed as

$$
d_{ik} = (-1)^{i+k} \frac{\det(M_{ik})}{\det(M)}
$$

where M_{ik} is the submatrix of M without the i-th row and k-th column. Note that M_{ik} is also a Cauchy matrix. Therefore

$$
|d_{ik}| = \Theta\left(\frac{d^{n^2}}{d^{(n-1)^2}} \right) = \Theta\left(d^{2n-1} \right)
$$

$\square$

So, the usage of Theorem 4.5 leads to an attenuation by a factor of $O(1/d^{2n-2})$, which is close to the deliberate attenuation which we have discussed before. On the positive side, we show that it is possible to send n message in parallel from n coordinated senders to n uncoordinated receivers even in free space. However, the power of each antenna must be chosen extremely large with respect to the noise, interference power, and distance, i.e. $P \geq (N + I)d^{4n+2}$. For such powerful senders the diversity gain of MIMO is larger than the bandwidth increase using the classic Shannon bounds even in the free space communication model.

5. BROADCASTING ON A LINE

We now concentrate on the main problem, which is the broadcast problem where n nodes with one antenna each are placed equidistantly on a line. Assume the first node of the line is the originator of the broadcast message. The broadcast scheme works in rounds. In the first round the only informed node u_1 transmits the message to neighbor u_2. The informed node synchronizes with the first node and thus becomes coordinated. In the subsequent rounds all coordinated senders use the MISO power gain to reach the next neighbors and synchronize them. This process continues until all nodes are informed. Using our previous observations of the MISO power gain we can prove that this way the number of coordinated nodes increases exponentially inducing a logarithmic time for the broadcast.

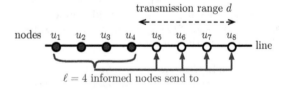

Figure 1: Four coordinated nodes $u_1, .., u_4$ broadcast and double the the number of informed nodes.

THEOREM 5.1. *The broadcast problem of n equidistant nodes on a line where each node can establish a point-to-point connection to each neighbor, can be solved in time $\mathcal{O}(\log n)$ and energy $\mathcal{O}(n)$ using MISO and wireless self-coordination.*

PROOF. Without loss of generality the nodes have unit distance. For a given noise N and a required threshold SNR_0, the minimum power P_0 to reach a neighbor in unit distance is $P_0 \geq N \cdot \text{SNR}_0$.

First let us analyze the transmission range d of ℓ adjacent, coordinated, and informed nodes. Each informed node u_i uses the characteristic $s_i = \sqrt{P_0}e^{-ji}$. If all ℓ nodes send with unit power P_0 the signal power they produce in distance d is

$$
\begin{aligned}
|h(\ell,d)|^2 &= \left| \left(\sum_{i=1}^{\ell} \underbrace{\sqrt{P_0} \cdot e^{-ji} \cdot \frac{e^{j(d+i)}}{d+i}}_{s_i} \right)^2 \right| \\
&= P_0 \cdot \left(\sum_{i=1}^{\ell} \frac{1}{d+i} \right)^2 \\
&= P_0 \cdot \left(\Psi(d+\ell+1) - \Psi(d+1) \right)^2 \\
&> P_0 \cdot \ln\left((d+\ell)/d \right)^2 .
\end{aligned}
$$

where $\Psi(x)$ is the digamma function.

Now, if $\frac{|h(\ell,d)|^2}{N} \geq \mathrm{SNR}_0$, then the receiver in distance d gets the message and can be coordinated.

$$
\frac{|h(\ell,d)|^2}{N} \geq \mathrm{SNR}_0 \cdot \ln\left((d+\ell)/d \right)^2
$$

So, for $\ln\left((d+\ell)/d \right)^2 \geq 1$ the node in distance d can be reached. This is the case for $d \leq \frac{1}{e-1}\ell$. If the number of informed and coordinated nodes in round i is ℓ_i then in the next round

$$
\ell_{i+1} \geq \ell_i + \max\left\{ 1, \left\lfloor \frac{1}{e-1}\ell_i \right\rfloor \right\}
$$

nodes are informed. Clearly $\ell_i = \Omega(\kappa^i)$ for any $\kappa < \frac{e}{e-1}$. Hence, after $T = \mathcal{O}(\log n)$ rounds all n nodes are informed.

The energy is bounded by

$$
\begin{aligned}
\mathcal{O}\left(\sum_{i=1}^{T} P_0 \ell_i \right) &= \mathcal{O}\left(P_0 \sum_{i=1}^{T} \kappa^i \right) \\
&= \mathcal{O}\left(P_0 \sum_{i=0}^{T-1} \frac{n}{\kappa^i} \right) \\
&= \mathcal{O}(nP_0) .
\end{aligned}
$$

$\square$

An interesting feature of this broadcasting process is that it can be performed in parallel, since we can bound the interfering energy by the following theorem.

THEOREM 5.2. *For an infinite number of equidistant nodes on the line the broadcasting algorithm above can be performed for each contiguous group of n nodes if the minimum distance between these groups is $\mathcal{O}(n)$.*

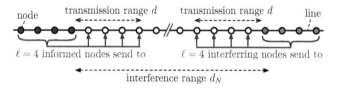

Figure 2: parallel transmissions: $\ell = 4$ nodes (blue) send to range d with interference in distance d_N (red).

The following proof shows Theorem 5.2 that the noise produced by unsynchronized simultaneous sending antenna groups is independent from the number of nodes in the network n.

Proof of Theorem 5.2: Let $\ell \leq n$ be the number of active senders and let d denote the distance between the groups. Using the upper bound for the signal strength of one sender group with ℓ antennas with $(s \cdot \ell/d)$ we get a noise level of

$$
|h_N| \leq \sum_{i=0}^{\infty} \frac{s \cdot \ell}{i \cdot d} e^{j\beta_i} = \frac{\ell}{d_N} \cdot \sum_{i=0}^{\infty} \frac{e^{j\beta_i}}{i} = \frac{\ell}{d_N} \cdot c_N .
$$

Let $\overline{c_N}$ denote the complex conjugate of c_N.

$$
\begin{aligned}
|c_N|^2 &= c_N \cdot \overline{c_N} \\
&= \sum_{i=1}^{\infty} \frac{e^{j\beta_i}}{i} \cdot \sum_{k=1}^{\infty} \frac{e^{-j\beta_k}}{k} \\
&= \left(\sum_{i=1}^{\infty} \frac{1}{i^2} \right) + \left(\sum_{i=1}^{\infty} \sum_{k=1, i\neq k}^{\infty} \frac{e^{j(\beta_i - \beta_k)}}{i \cdot k} \right) \\
&= \frac{\pi^2}{6} + \sum_{i=1}^{\infty} \sum_{k=1, i\neq k}^{\infty} \frac{e^{j(\beta_i - \beta_k)}}{i \cdot k}
\end{aligned}
$$

For each index tuple (i,k) with $i \neq k$ there exists a symmetric (k,i) with the negated imaginary value.

$$
\forall i \neq k: \quad \Im\left(e^{j(\beta_i - \beta_k)} \right) + \Im\left(e^{j(\beta_k - \beta_i)} \right) = 0
$$

So, we get only a sum of real numbers.

$$
\sum_{i=1}^{\infty} \sum_{k=1, i\neq k}^{\infty} \frac{e^{j(\beta_i - \beta_k)}}{i \cdot k} = \sum_{i=1}^{\infty} \sum_{k=1, i\neq k}^{n} \frac{\cos(\beta_i - \beta_k)}{i \cdot k}
$$

We have assumed that angles $\beta_i \in [0, 2\pi)$ are independently, identically, and uniformly distributed over $[0, 2\pi)$. So the expectation of $\cos(\beta_i)$ is $\left(\frac{1}{2\pi} \int_{\beta=0}^{2\pi} \cos\beta \, d\beta \right) = 0$ And, the expected value of the sum is

$$
\mathbb{E}\left[|c_N|^2 \right] = \frac{\pi^2}{6} + \sum_{i=1}^{\infty} \sum_{k=1, i\neq k}^{\infty} \frac{\overbrace{\mathbb{E}[\cos\beta_i - \beta_k]}^{0}}{i \cdot k} = \frac{\pi^2}{6} .
$$

The root mean square of h_N is therefore

$$
|h_N|_{\mathrm{rms}} = \frac{\ell}{d_N} \frac{\pi}{\sqrt{6}} = \mathcal{O}\left(\frac{\ell}{d_N} \right) . \tag{4}
$$

$\square$

Figure 3 illustrates the result of Theorem 5.2 for the noise strength $|h_N|_{\mathrm{rms}} = \frac{\ell}{d_N} \frac{\pi}{\sqrt{6}}$. In the experiment, $\frac{\ell}{d_N}$ was set to 1 and the phase angles of the interfering sender groups are chosen uniform at random with $\beta_i \in [0, 2\pi)$. Each number of

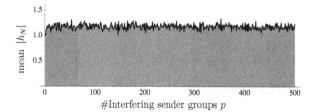

Figure 3: Experimental result for the signal strength $|h_N|$ varying the number of sender groups p.

interfering sender groups was tested 100 times and averaged.

The total average measured strength of noise was ≈ 1.17 whereas the factor in the proof is $\frac{\pi}{\sqrt{6}} \approx 1.28$.

6. CONCLUSION

We present a communication model for the bandwidth in MIMO communication in free space which enhances the SINR model. Exploiting MISO power gain of n coordinated senders increases the transmission power by factor n compared to a single sender with same power. We show how to obtain a deliberate attenuation in MISO for n coordinated senders on a line with factor $1/\mathcal{O}\left(d^{2n}\right)$. While theoretically diversity gain of MISO/MIMO communication with n independent data streams is possible, we show that this works in the free space model only for high SINR and for short distances. We present a logarithmic time MISO broadcast scheme for n nodes placed on a line in time $\mathcal{O}\left(\log n\right)$ which needs only a constant times more energy than the sequential direct-neighbor communication. We show that this algorithm broadcasting to $\mathcal{O}\left(n\right)$ nodes does not influence simultaneous broadcasts which are in distance $\Omega(n)$.

Note that the communication model is deduced from analyzing Hertz dipole antennas and basic physical observation. So, the model has a solid foundation, which can be understood even by non-physicists. The complete derivation can be found in the Appendix.

Outlook

A straight-forward question is how this approach generalizes to two dimensions. This question is not easy to be answered. The power gain in MISO and SIMO results from the beam forming. In a preceding paper we have analyzed the angle of the main beam [10] for the case of randomly placed antennas in a disk of radius r. It turns out that besides the main beam a small number of side beams appears next to it, while in the residual directions the power behaves like a Gaussian distribution. A next step is an understanding of free space MIMO effects in equidistant grid networks, and how broadcasting can be improved.

Note that the polarization does not play a role in the two-dimensional case, since we assume antennas perpendicular to the plane. Clearly this effect cannot be ignored anymore in three dimensions. Then, the channel matrix cannot be described by a single complex value. A more sophisticated model is needed, which is also part of future research.

In this work we have only considered the free space model. It is well known that the channel matrix allows a diversity gain, if the environment provides reflections and multiple path diffraction. The relationship of the environment to the channel matrix is not fully understood so far. So, many research papers simply assume the best possible channel matrix, the existence of which is not clear. Here, further research may help to a better understanding of the influence of a limited number of obstacles to the possible positive impact on communication.

7. REFERENCES

[1] C. Avin, Y. Emek, E. Kantor, Z. Lotker, D. Peleg, and L. Roditty. SINR Diagrams: Convexity and Its Applications in Wireless Networks. *J. ACM*, 59(4):18, 2012.

[2] L. Barrière, P. Fraigniaud, L. Narayanan, and J. Opatrny. Robust Position-Based Routing in Wireless Ad Hoc Networks with Irregular Transmission Ranges. *Wireless Communications and Mobile Computing*, 3(2):141–153, 2003.

[3] I. Chlamtac and S. Kutten. On Broadcasting in Radio Networks–Problem Analysis and Protocol Design. *IEEE Transactions on Communications*, 33(12):1240 – 1246, dec 1985.

[4] B. N. Clark, C. J. Colbourn, and D. S. Johnson. Unit disk graphs. *Discrete Mathematics*, 86(1–3):165–177, 1990.

[5] R. P. Feynman, R. B. Leighton, and M. Sands. *The Feynman Lectures on Physics*, volume 1. Pearson Addison-Wesley, 2006.

[6] O. Goussevskaia, Y. A. Oswald, and R. Wattenhofer. Complexity in Geometric SINR. In *Proceedings of the 8th ACM international symposium on Mobile ad hoc networking and computing*, MobiHoc '07, pages 100–109, New York, NY, USA, 2007. ACM.

[7] P. Gupta and P. R. Kumar. The Capacity of Wireless Networks. *IEEE Transactions on Information Theory*, 46:388–404, 2000.

[8] P. Gupta and P. R. Kumar. Internets in the Sky: The Capacity of Three Dimensional Wireless Networks. *Communications in Information and Systems*, 1:33–50, 2001.

[9] F. M. Heide, C. Schindelhauer, K. Volbert, and M. Grünewald. Congestion, Dilation, and Energy in Radio Networks. *Theory of Computing Systems*, 37:343–370, 2004.

[10] T. Janson and C. Schindelhauer. Analyzing Randomly Placed Multiple Antennas for MIMO Wireless Communication. In *Fifth International Workshop on Selected Topics in Mobile and Wireless Computing (IEEE STWiMob'2012)*, Barcelona, Spain, October 2012.

[11] L. M. Kirousis, E. Kranakis, D. Krizanc, and A. Pelc. Power consumption in packet radio networks. *Theoretical Computer Science*, 243(1-2):289–305, july 2000.

[12] F. Kuhn, T. Moscibroda, and R. Wattenhofer. Unit Disk Graph Approximation. In *Proceedings of the 2004 joint workshop on Foundations of mobile computing*, DIALM-POMC '04, pages 17–23, New York, NY, USA, 2004. ACM.

[13] E. Lebhar and Z. Lotker. Unit disk graph and physical interference model: Putting pieces together. In *IEEE International Symposium on Parallel Distributed Processing (IPDPS 2009)*, pages 1–8, may 2009.

[14] X.-Y. Li, W.-Z. Song, and Y. Wang. Efficient Topology Control for Ad-hoc Wireless Networks with Non-uniform Transmission Ranges. *Wireless Networks*, 11(3):255–264, May 2005.

[15] A. Merzakreeva, O. Leveque, and A. Özgür. Hierarchical Beamforming for Large One-Dimensional Wireless Networks. In *Information Theory Proceedings (ISIT), 2012 IEEE International Symposium on*, pages 1533 –1537, july 2012.

[16] A. Özgür, R. Johari, D. Tse, and O. Leveque. Information Theoretic Operating Regimes of Large Wireless Networks. *IEEE Transactions on Information Theory*, 56(1):427–437, 2010.

[17] A. Özgür, O. Leveque, and D. Tse. Hierarchical

Cooperation Achieves Optimal Capacity Scaling in Ad Hoc Networks. *IEEE Transactions on Information Theory*, 53(10):3549–3572, October 2007.

[18] T. S. Pollock, T. D. Abhayapala, and R. A. Kennedy. Introducing Space into MIMO Capacity Calculations. *Journal on Telecommunications Systems*, 24:415–436, 2003.

[19] J. S. Seybold. *Introduction to RF Propagation*. Wiley, 2005.

[20] C. Shannon. Communication in the Presence of Noise. *Proceedings of the IRE*, 37(1):10–21, 1949.

[21] B. Widrow, P. Mantey, L. Griffiths, and B. B. Goode. Adaptive antenna systems. *Proceedings of the IEEE*, 55(12):2143–2159, 1967.

APPENDIX

A. APPENDIX: DERIVATION OF THE COMMUNICATION MODEL

In this appendix, we present the physical basis for our communication model of Section 2 starting at electromagnetic fields of antennas to data transmission, and the derived transmission capacity.

A.1 Electric Fields

We briefly summarize essentials for radio communication based on Maxwell's equations. You can find the following observations in much greater detail in Physics textbooks. Here, we now present a compilation of "The Feynman Lectures on Physics" Vol. I. [5], chapter 28 and 29. An electric field **E** is a vector at each point describing the force on a charged particle. It is described for a single particle with charge q as

$$\mathbf{E} = \frac{-q}{4\pi\varepsilon_0} \left(\frac{e_{r'}}{r'^2} + \frac{r'}{c} \frac{d}{dt}\left(\frac{\mathbf{e_{r'}}}{r'^2}\right) + \frac{1}{c^2}\frac{d^2}{dt^2}\mathbf{e_{r'}} \right) \qquad (5)$$

where $c \approx 3.000 \times 10^6 m/s$ is the speed of light, and $\varepsilon_0 \approx 8.854 \times 10^{-12} F/m$ is the electric constant, r' is the distances to the particle where it has been considering the speed of light and the distance. $\mathbf{e_{r'}}$ denotes the unit factor in the direction.

Note that this equation already combines the electric and magnetic field which is described by (the Maxwell-Faraday equation)

$$\mathbf{B} = -\mathbf{e_{r'}} \times \mathbf{E}/c .$$

In the far-field for large distances r the last component in Eq. 5 prevails, rendering the equation to

$$\mathbf{E} = \frac{-q}{4\pi\varepsilon_0 \cdot c^2} \cdot \frac{d^2}{dt^2}\mathbf{e_{r'}} . \qquad (6)$$

If a particle moves vertically along a line according where charged particles are moved with acceleration function $a(t)$ the electric field has an approximated magnitude of

$$E(t) = \frac{-q}{4\pi\varepsilon_0 \cdot c^2 r} \cdot \sin\theta \cdot a(t - r/c)$$

and the orientation of the vector is as been shown in Figure 4.

The electric fields have the superposition property. For two electric fields $\mathbf{E_1}$ and $\mathbf{E_2}$ the resulting electric field is

$$\mathbf{E} = \mathbf{E_1} + \mathbf{E_2} . \qquad (7)$$

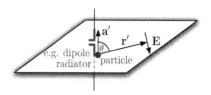

Figure 4: Electric field E in distance r' of a dipole radiator in the plane with a charge q accelerated with a.

This of course applies for single charges in antennas as well as the different currents of multiple antennas.

Radio signals are modulated as sine curves with $x_0 \cos\omega t$, which leads to an acceleration of

$$a(t) = -\omega^2 x_0 \cos\omega t = a_0 \cos\omega t$$

where $\omega = 2\pi f$ with frequency f, x_0 is the amplitude of the charged particle, ω denotes the frequency, and $a_0 = -\omega^2 x_0$. This results in the well-known Hertz dipole equation

$$E(t) = \frac{-q}{4\pi\varepsilon_0 \cdot c^2 r} \cdot \sin\theta \cdot a_0 \cos\omega(t - r/c) . \qquad (8)$$

Of course the orientation of the antennas plays a major role. However, if we restrict ourselves to a two-dimensional plane with perpendicular antennas all electric fields are oriented perpendicular to the plane. This allows us to simplify the dynamic electric field to a scalar field. The far-field approximation of Equation 6 holds for a distance r of a few wavelengths $\lambda = c/f$.

A.2 Power

The power or energy per second of an electric wave through an unit area is

$$S = \varepsilon_0 c \cdot E^2$$

with the impedance of free space $1/(\varepsilon_0 c) \approx 376.7$ ohms. Thus, the power increases inversely to the square of the distance with

$$S = \frac{q^2 \cdot a(t)^2 \cdot \sin^2\theta}{16\pi^2\varepsilon_0 \cdot r^2 \cdot c^3} .$$

Therefore the power through the enveloping surface of radius r produced of a charge q oscillating with ω is

$$P = \frac{q^2\omega^4 x_0^2}{12\pi\varepsilon_0 c^3} .$$

The length of the antenna is described by x_0 which is proportional to $c/f = 2\pi c/\omega$.

At a receiver antenna parallel to the movement of the particle this causes a voltage proportional in E. Also the current is proportional according to Ohm's law, however the inductances plays a major role. Summarizing we observe that the received power P at the antenna is

$$P = kE^2 \qquad (9)$$

where k is a suitable constant for a fixed frequency. This also holds for the combination of antennas, since the electric fields increase each voltage and each current.

This leads to two interesting observations, which has been proved useful in antenna design for a long time.

1. Two antennas in sync produce an electric field twice the size. So, four times the power arrives at the receiver antenna.

2. Two receivers can reproduce four times the power of a sender antenna if the induced current is time shifted accordingly.

A.3 Modulation

This observation is only possible if one carefully considers the interplay of the locations of the antennas and the time shift to achieve the constructive interference. For this we introduce the following notations. Let $\mathbf{s_1}, \ldots, \mathbf{s_n}$ denote the locations of sender antennas in two dimensional space, likewise $\mathbf{r_1}, \ldots, \mathbf{r_n}$ denote the receiver antennas.

If we assume a amplitude/phase shift key modulation with function $a_{\mathrm{am}}(t)$, $a_{\mathrm{pm}}(t)$, so the movement of a particle can be described as:

$$a_{\mathrm{am}}(t) \cdot \cos\left(\omega t + a_{\mathrm{pm}}(t)\right) = \Re\left(a_{\mathrm{am}}(t) \cdot e^{j a_{\mathrm{pm}}(t)} e^{j\omega t}\right)$$

For simplicity we use the complex number

$$a(t) = a_{\mathrm{am}}(t) \cdot e^{j a_{\mathrm{pm}}(t)}$$

as the combined signal emitted at s over time (while $\mathbf{s}$ denotes the location).

A.4 Superposition

So, at receiver r we have the following electric field for one sender s.

$$
\begin{aligned}
E &\propto \Re\left(a(t) \cdot \frac{e^{j\omega(t - |\mathbf{s}-\mathbf{r}|/c)}}{|\mathbf{s}-\mathbf{r}|}\right) \\
&= \Re\left(a(t) \cdot \frac{e^{-j\omega|\mathbf{s}-\mathbf{r}|/c}}{|\mathbf{s}-\mathbf{r}|} \cdot e^{j\omega t}\right)
\end{aligned}
$$

We denote by $h_{i,k} = e^{-j|\mathbf{s_i}-\mathbf{r_j}|/c} \cdot |\mathbf{s_i}-\mathbf{r_k}|^{-1}$ the amplitude shift transformation of the signal from sender s_i to receiver r_k. Hence, the electric field received at receiver r_k is therefore

$$E_k \propto \Re\left(\sum_{i=1}^{n} a_i(t) \cdot h_{i,k} \cdot e^{j\omega t}\right).$$

This describes the MISO case (multiple input/single output). For true MIMO all antennas are combined. This could be a simple addition of the electric fields. However, more likely is that a time shift t_k and a dampening $d_k \leq 1$ is applied. These terms can be adjusted to increase the sensitivity and we combine these terms to $r_k = d_k e^{j t_k}$.

Now the combined received electrical field is

$$E = \sum_{k=1}^{m} E_k = \Re\left(\sum_{k=1}^{m}\sum_{i=1}^{n} a_i(t) \cdot h_{i,k} \cdot r_k \cdot e^{j\omega t}\right). \quad (10)$$

A.5 Signal to Interference + Noise Ratio (SINR)

For the successful radio reception of the information in $a(t)$ from sender s_i to receiver r, the magnitude of the also undesirably received noise is crucial. The standard measure in literature is the Signal-to-Noise Ratio (SNR) or Signal-to-Interference+Noise Ratio (SINR). The second measure SINR (see [7]) also includes – besides environmental noise and noise in the receiver (e.g. amplifier stage) N – the noise produced by interfering senders s_k involved in parallel transmissions

$$\mathrm{SINR}(r) = \frac{\frac{P(s_i)}{|\mathbf{s_i}-\mathbf{r}|^\alpha}}{N + \sum_{k\neq i} \frac{P(s_k)}{|\mathbf{s_k}-\mathbf{r}|^\alpha}}. \quad (11)$$

The path-loss exponent is here α which is $\alpha = 2$ for free-space and $\alpha > 2$ including obstacles absorbing the energy. The power P is in Eq. 11 exclusive the path-loss factor. Here we answer the question why we sum up the receive power when the superposition principle is applied for the field strengths.

A.6 Data Rate in Presence of Noise

The maximum possible data rate in a channel with white noise was derived by Shannon in 1949 [20]. In the presence of noise with power N, each modulation scheme with power P uses a limited number of distinguishable signals. The maximum power of the received signal is then $(P + N)$ and since each transmitted signal can be perturbed by noise power N there are $K \cdot \sqrt{(P+N)/N} = K \cdot \sqrt{1 + P/N}$ distinguishable signals for some constant K near unity. Given a bandwidth W in Hertz we can transmit in a time unit up to $\left(K\sqrt{1 + P/N}\right)^{2W}$ distinct signals. Since we can decode in m possible states $\log_2 m$ binary digits this gives a maximum capacity in bits per second of the well-known Shannon-Hartley theorem

$$C = W \cdot \log_2\left(1 + \frac{P}{N}\right) = W \cdot \log_2\left(1 + \mathrm{SINR}\right). \quad (12)$$

For a low SNR ≈ 0 we can approximate

$$C \approx W \cdot \mathrm{SINR} \cdot \log_2(e). \quad (13)$$

Expected Sum and Maximum of Displacement of Random Sensors for Coverage of a Domain

[Extended Abstract]

Evangelos Kranakis [*]
School of Comp. Sci.
Carleton University
Ottawa, ON, Canada
kranakis@scs.carleton.ca

Danny Krizanc
Dept. Math. & Comp. Sci.
Wesleyan University
Middletown CT, USA
dkrizanc@wesleyan.edu

Oscar Morales-Ponce [†]
Dept. Comp. Sci. & Engg.
Chalmers Univ. of Tech.
Gothenburg, Sweden
mooscar@chalmers.se

Lata Narayanan [‡]
Dept. Comp. Sci. & Soft.Engg.
Concordia University
Montréal, QC, Canada
lata@cs.concordia.ca

Jaroslav Opatrny [§]
Dept. Comp. Sci. & Soft.Engg.
Concordia University
Montréal, QC, Canada
opatrny@cs.concordia.ca

Sunil Shende
Dept. of Comp. Sci.
Rutgers University
Camden, NJ, USA
shende@camden.rutgers.edu

ABSTRACT

Assume that n sensors with identical range $r = \frac{f(n)}{2n}$, for some $f(n) \geq 1$ for all n, are thrown randomly and independently with the uniform distribution in the unit interval $[0, 1]$. They are required to move to new positions so as to cover the entire unit interval in the sense that every point in the interval is within the range of a sensor. We obtain tradeoffs between the expected sum and maximum of displacements of the sensors and their range required to accomplish this task. In particular, when $f(n) = 1$ the expected total displacement is shown to be $\Theta(\sqrt{n})$. For sensors with larger ranges we present two algorithms that prove the upper bound for the sum drops sharply as $f(n)$ increases. The first of these holds for $f(n) \geq 6$ and shows the total movement of the sensors is $O(\sqrt{\ln n / f(n)})$ while the second holds for $12 \leq f(n) \leq \ln n - 2 \ln \ln n$ and gives an upper bound of $O(\frac{\ln n}{f(n)e^{f(n)/2}})$. Note that the second algorithm improves upon the first for $f(n) > \ln \ln n - \ln \ln \ln n$. Further we show a lower bound, for any $1 < f(n) < \sqrt{n}$ of $\Omega(\epsilon f(n)e^{-(1+\epsilon)f(n)}), \epsilon > 0$.

For the case of the expected maximum displacement of a sensor when $f(n) = 1$ our bounds are $\Omega(n^{-1/2})$ and for any $\epsilon > 0$, $O(n^{-1/2+\epsilon})$. For larger sensor ranges (up to $(1 - \epsilon)\frac{\ln n}{n}, \epsilon > 0$) the expected maximum displacement is shown to be $\Theta(\frac{\ln n}{n})$.

We also obtain similar sum and maximum displacement and range tradeoffs for area coverage for sensors thrown at random in a unit square. In this case, for the expected maximum displacement our bounds are tight and for the expected sum they are within a factor of $\sqrt{\ln n}$. Finally, we investigate the related problem of the expected total and maximum displacement for perimeter coverage (whereby only the perimeter of the region need be covered) of a unit square. For example, when n sensors of radius $> 2/n$ are thrown randomly and independently with the uniform distribution in the interior of a unit square, we can show the total expected displacement required to cover the perimeter is $\frac{n}{12} + o(n)$.

Categories and Subject Descriptors

F.2.2 [**Analysis of Algorithms and Problem Complexity**]: Nonnumerical Algorithms and Problems—*Geometrical problems and computations*

Keywords

Barrier; Coverage; Displacement; Mobile; Sensors; Random

[*]Supported in part by NSERC and MITACS grants.

[†]Research supported by MITACS.

[‡]Supported in part by NSERC grant.

[§]Supported in part by NSERC grant.

1. INTRODUCTION

Mobile sensors are being deployed in a variety of application areas in order to enable easy access and information retrieval in diverse communication environments, ranging from habitat monitoring, sensing and diagnostics to critical infrastructure monitoring. Random deployments of sensors are becoming more feasible with current reductions in manufacturing costs. Existing sensor deployment scenarios cannot ensure precise placement of sensors. Their initial deployment may be somewhat random either because the sensors were originally randomly scattered over the region or have drifted to new positions over time or due to random failures. Therefore in order to increase the coverage provided by the set of sensors it is necessary to redeploy them by displacing them along the domain. By displacing the sensors to new positions one can improve the overall coverage (points within some sensor's range) of a given region.

A basic instance of the problem considered in this paper is the expected cost of moving mobile sensors with a given circular (but bounded) sensing range from their original positions to new positions so as to achieve full coverage of a region, i.e., every point of the region is within the range of at least one sensor. Given a geometric region in the plane there are two basic formulations of the problem: displace the sensors so as to either ensure 1) full coverage of the region, or 2) coverage of the perimeter of the region. The first problem is referred as *area coverage* and the second as *perimeter or barrier coverage*. In both instances it is assumed the sensors are deployed initially in the domain uniformly and independently at random. Since such a random deployment does not necessarily guarantee full coverage it is important to displace the sensors so as to ensure all points are covered while at the same time minimizing the transportation cost. The two cost parameters we choose to optimize are the expected sum and maximum of the sensor's displacements, the former being an approximation of the total energy consumed while the latter of the time required to complete the task by the entire system of deployed sensors.

1.1 Results of the paper

More formally, in this paper, we consider the following problem concerning the movement of sensors. n mobile sensors of range r are thrown randomly and independently in a region and move from their current location to positions that cover the region. We assume that r and n are chosen so as to allow full coverage of the region. Among all choices of positions, we assume the sensors move in such a way as to minimize the total displacement of the sensors. We want to know what is the expected sum of distances traversed by all n sensors under the above assumption. We are also interested in the expected maximum traversed by the sensors again under the assumption that this is minimized. Similar expected sum and maximum problems arise when considering the experiment above where one is only required to cover the perimeter of the region. In this paper, we consider as our regions the unit interval and the unit square. We obtain tradeoffs between the expected sum and maximum of displacements and the range of the sensors in each case. In particular, we show that as the range of the sensors increases from the minimum needed to cover the region, the expected displacement drops off precipitously.

For the case of the unit interval we show the following. If the sensor range is $1/2n$ the expected sum of displacements of the sensors is $\Theta(\sqrt{n})$. If the range is $r = f(n)/2n$ where $f(n) \geq 6$ for all n, the expected sum of displacements is $O(\sqrt{\frac{\ln n}{f(n)}})$. If the range is $r = f(n)/2n$ where $12 \leq f(n) \leq \ln n - 2\ln\ln n$, the expected sum of displacements is $O(\frac{\ln n}{f(n)e^{f(n)/2}})$. Note this improves upon the above bound for $f(n) > \ln\ln n - \ln\ln\ln n$. If the range is $r = f(n)/2n$ where $1 < f(n) < \sqrt{n}$, then for any $\epsilon > 0$, the expected sum of displacements is $\Omega(\epsilon f(n)e^{-(1+\epsilon)f(n)})$. If the range is $1/2n$, the expected maximum displacement is $\Omega(1/\sqrt{n})$ and $O(1/n^{1/2-\epsilon})$, for any $\epsilon > 0$. If the range is $r = f(n)/2n$, $6 \leq f(n) \leq (1 - \epsilon)\ln n, \epsilon > 0$, the expected maximum displacement is $\Theta(\frac{\ln n}{n})$.

For the case of the unit square we show the following. For any $c \geq 4$, if the sensor range is $c/\sqrt{n}$, the expected sum of displacements required to cover the square is $O(\sqrt{n \ln n})$. For any $c \geq 1/\sqrt{\pi}$, if the sensor range is $c/\sqrt{n}$, the expected sum of displacements required to cover the square is $\Omega(\sqrt{n})$. For sensors of range $2/n$, the expected sum of displacements required to cover the perimeter is $n/12 + o(n)$ and the expected maximum displacement is at least $1/12$. Finally we show, for any $c \geq 4$, if the sensor range is $c/\sqrt{n}$, the expected maximum displacement is $\Theta(\sqrt{\ln/n})$.

1.2 Related Work

There is an extensive literature on sensor positioning and repositioning. [24] provides a survey of models, requirements and strategies that would affect sensor deployment and repositioning so as to optimize various computation, energy and communication constraints. [17] presents stable control strategies for groups of vehicles to move and reconfigure cooperatively in response to a sensed, distributed environment. [12] addresses the problem of deploying relay nodes to provide fault-tolerance with higher network connectivity in heterogeneous wireless sensor networks, where sensor nodes possess different transmission radii. Distributed actor recovery algorithms are studied in [2] so as to address the 1- and 2-connectivity requirements of the actor network. The problem they study is how to identify the least set of actors that should be repositioned in order to reestablish a particular level of connectivity; generally they are interested in localizing the scope of the recovery process and minimizing the movement overhead imposed on the actors involved.

There is also an extensive literature on area and barrier or perimeter coverage by a set of sensors (e.g., see [15, 22]). The deterministic sensor movement problem for planar domains with pre-existing anchor (or destination) points was introduced in [4] and for a linear domain (or interval) in [7]. Interestingly enough, the complexity of the problem (i.e., finding an algorithm that optimizes the total or maximum displacement) depends on the types of the sensors, the type of the domain and whether one is minimizing the sum or maximum of the sensor movements. For example, for the unit interval the problem of minimizing the sum is NP-complete if the sensors may have different ranges but is polynomial time in the case where all the sensor ranges are the same[8]. The problem of minimizing the maximum is NP-complete if the region consists of two intervals[7] but is polynomial time for a single interval even when the sensors may have different ranges[6]. Related work on deterministic algorithms for minimizing the total and maximum movement of sensors for barrier coverage of a planar region may be found in [4].

Related to the problem of random sensor displacement in a line segment is the concept of spacings in Poisson arrivals. It is known that for a homogeneous Poisson process $\{N(t) : t \geq 0\}$ with parameter λ the successive times of successive arrivals are distributed like the order statistics of a sample of n observations taken from the uniform distribution on $[0, t]$ (see [19]). In a way, this represents a natural relationship between the Poisson process, random points on a line, and the uniformly distributed, random points on an interval (see [1]). If $Y_1, Y_2, \ldots, Y_n$ are the *spacings* (or consecutive distances) between n points drawn randomly and independently with the uniform distribution in the interval $[0, 1]$ then it is known (see [9]) that

$\lim_{n\to\infty} \Pr\left[\max_j Y_j \le \frac{\ln n + x}{n}\right] = e^{-e^{-x}}$ (see also [1, 14] for related work on spacings, as well as in [18] for points in the plane). Related work on extremes of interarrival times of a Poisson process can also be found in [9, 20, 21]. For an analysis of the structure of the intervals (e.g., expected size of largest collection of pairwise disjoint subintervals, number of edges, degrees, Hamiltonicity, chromatic number and independence number) we refer the reader to [13] and [23].

1.3 Organization of the paper

The organization of the paper is as follows. In Section 2 we address the expected total and maximum displacement problem in a unit segment. We parametrize our results with respect to the given sensor range (assumed to be identical for all sensors) and give upper and lower bounds on the expected sum and maximum displacement. In Section 3 we address the same questions when the deployment domain is a unit square. For the square, we also consider the problem of the expected sum and maximum displacement to achieve barrier (perimeter) coverage.

2. DISPLACEMENT IN 1D

In this section we study the total and maximum displacement required to achieve coverage when n mobile sensors are thrown uniform at random and independently in the unit interval $[0, 1]$.

2.1 Tight bound for total displacement when $r = 1/2n$

The first problem we address concerns the total displacement required to cover a unit interval when n mobile sensors with range $1/2n$ are thrown uniformly at random and independently in the interval. As it never makes sense for sensors to change their relative position when minimizing the sum of their moves and, in this case, the sensors exactly cover the interval, we consider the following equivalent problem. Assume that n sensors are thrown randomly and independently in the unit interval $[0, 1]$ and move from their current location to the new *anchor* locations $t_i = \frac{i}{n} - \frac{1}{2n}$, for $i = 1, \ldots, n$, respectively (i.e., equidistant locations in the unit interval). What is the expected sum of distances (or total displacement) traversed by all n sensors?

A similar problem arises when considering the experiment above either on the perimeter of a circle or in the interior of a circle. Obviously, this formulation of the problem does not require mention of the sensor range since regardless of their range the sensors have to move to the anchor points specified. An equivalent formulation is to assume that the sensors have range $\frac{1}{2n}$ each. It follows that the only way to attain complete coverage is for the sensors to occupy the positions $t_i := \frac{i}{n} - \frac{1}{2n}$, for $i = 1, \ldots, n$. We often refer to the latter positions as *anchors*.

We prove the following tight bound on the displacement in this case:

THEOREM 1. *Assume that n mobile sensors are thrown uniformly and independently at random in the unit interval. The expected sum of displacements of all n sensors to move from their current location to anchor locations $\frac{i}{n} - \frac{1}{2n}$, for $i = 1, \ldots, n$, respectively is $\Theta(\sqrt{n})$.*

Before providing the proof of the theorem we will give two lemmas. Let X_i be the ith order statistic, i.e., the position

of the ith sensor when ordered from 0 to 1. It turns out that the sum of distances is a very compact formula. We know that the density function and the distribution function for X_i are:

$$f_{X_i}(x) = i\binom{n}{i} x^{i-1}(1-x)^{n-i},$$

$$F_{X_i}(x) = \sum_{k=i}^{n} \binom{n}{k} x^k (1-x)^{n-k}$$

For example, see [3]. Let D_i be the expected distance between X_i and the ith target sensor position, $t_i = \frac{2i-1}{2n}$, on the unit interval, hence given by:

$$\begin{aligned} D_i &= \int_0^{t_i} (t_i - x) f_{X_i}(x) dx + \int_{t_i}^1 (x - t_i) f_{X_i}(x) dx \\ &= t_i \left(\int_0^{t_i} f_{X_i}(x) dx - \int_{t_i}^1 f_{X_i}(x) dx \right) + \\ &\quad \left(\int_{t_i}^1 x\, f_{X_i}(x) dx - \int_0^{t_i} x\, f_{X_i}(x) dx \right) \\ &= t_i \left(2 F_{X_i}(t_i) - 1\right) + \left(2 \int_{t_i}^1 x\, f_{X_i}(x) dx - E[X_i]\right) \\ &= 2 t_i F_{X_i}(t_i) + 2 \int_{t_i}^1 x\, f_{X_i}(x) dx - t_i - E[X_i] \end{aligned}$$

We will prove the following lemma.

LEMMA 1. *The sum of distances, $D = \sum_{1 \le i \le n} D_i$, is given by:*

$$\frac{2}{n+1} \sum_{i=1}^{n} \sum_{j=i+1}^{n+1} (j-i) \cdot \binom{n+1}{j} t_i^j (1-t_i)^{n+1-j} \quad (1)$$

PROOF. The proof is given in the Appendix. □

In the sequel we find the asymptotic value of Formula (1). Let $N_i^{(n)}$ be the random variable that counts the number of successes in n i.i.d. Bernoulli trials with each trial taking the value 1 with probability t_i and 0 with probability $1 - t_i$. We will need the identities:

$$\Pr[N_i^{(n)} = i] = \binom{n}{i} t_i^i (1-t_i)^i,$$

$$\Pr[N_i^{(n)} \ge i] = \sum_{j=i}^{n} \binom{n}{j} t_i^j (1-t_i)^{n-j}$$

We will prove the following lemma.

LEMMA 2. *The sum of distances, $D = \sum_{1 \le i \le n} D_i$, is asymptotically:*

$$\frac{2}{n} \sum_{i=1}^{n} i \cdot \Pr[N_i^{(n)} = i] - \frac{2}{n^2} \sum_{i=1}^{n} i^2 \cdot \Pr[N_i^{(n)} = i] \quad (2)$$

PROOF. The proof is given in the Appendix. □

PROOF. (Theorem 1) We use Stirling's formula to determine the asymptotic of Formula (2). Recall, [11][page 54] that

$$\sqrt{2\pi} m^{m+\frac{1}{2}} e^{-m+\frac{1}{12m+1}} < m! < \sqrt{2\pi} m^{m+\frac{1}{2}} e^{-+\frac{1}{12m}}.$$

We now consider Formula (2); we drop the nth summand because it does not change the asymptotics of the formula.

$$\sum_{i<n}\left(\frac{i}{n}-\frac{i^2}{n^2}\right)\cdot \Pr[N_i^{(n)}=i]= \qquad (3)$$

$$= \sum_{i<n}\frac{i(n-i)}{n^2}\binom{n}{i}t_i^i(1-t_i)^{n-i}$$

$$\sim \frac{1}{\sqrt{2\pi}}\sum_{i<n}\frac{i(n-i)}{n^2}\sqrt{\frac{n}{i(n-i)}}\left(\frac{nt_i}{i}\right)^i\left(\frac{n(1-t_i)}{n-i}\right)^{n-i}$$

$$= \frac{1}{\sqrt{2\pi}}\sum_{i<n}\frac{i(n-i)}{n^2}\sqrt{\frac{n}{i(n-i)}}\left(1-\frac{1}{2i}\right)^i\left(1+\frac{1}{2(n-i)}\right)^{n-i}$$

$$\sim \frac{1}{\sqrt{2\pi}}\sum_{i<n}\frac{i(n-i)}{n^2}\sqrt{\frac{n}{i(n-i)}}$$

$$= \frac{1}{n^{3/2}\sqrt{2\pi}}\sum_{i<n}\sqrt{i(n-i)}.$$

This completes the proof of Theorem 1 since the last sum is in $\Theta(\sqrt{n})$. $\square$

2.2 Upper bounds for total displacement when $r > 1/2n$

We now study a more general version of the sensor movement problem the main difference being that in this case there are no anchors predetermined in advance. Rather, the sensors need move to any positions as long as the whole segment is fully covered. A simple intuitive argument indicates improvements in the total displacement are possible by increasing the radius of the sensors. Suppose n such sensors with radius $r = f(n)/2n$ are thrown randomly and independently with the uniform distribution in the unit interval. Select any $n/f(n)$ among these sensors at random and have them move to $n/f(n)$ equally spaced anchors in the unit interval (the rest of the sensors do not have to move). By Theorem 1, the expected sum of movements of the sensors is $O(\sqrt{n/f(n)})$, an improvement over Theorem 1 for large $f(n)$. A natural question to ask is: can we do better?

In the sequel we look at sensor range and movement trade-offs so as to accomplish full coverage. We present two upper bounds, one which holds for all functions $f(n)$ where $f(n) \geq 6$ for all n, and a second one that improves upon the first for $f(n)$ bounded in the range $\ln\ln n - \ln\ln\ln n \leq f(n) \leq \ln n - 2\ln\ln n$.

We begin with a simple lemma which indicates how to scale the result of Theorem 1 to intervals of arbitrary length.

LEMMA 3. Assume that m sensors are thrown randomly and independently with the uniform distribution on an interval of length x. The sensors are to be moved to equidistant positions (within this interval) at distance x/m from each other. The total expected movement of the sensors is $\Theta(x\sqrt{m})$.

PROOF. Consider m sensors in the interval $[0,x]$ (of length x). Multiply their coordinates by $1/x$ to normalize the problem over the unit interval. By our previous result the total movement in the unit interval is in $O(\sqrt{m})$. Now "scale this back" by multiplying by x and we get $x\sqrt{m}$, which is the desired result. $\square$

Our first upper bound on the total sensor movement is based on the following algorithm.

Algorithm 1.

1. Divide the interval into subintervals of length $6\ln n/n$;

2. If there is a subinterval with fewer than $\ln n$ sensors then use the standard algorithm that moves all n sensors to positions that are equidistant and stop;

3. Otherwise, in each subinterval choose $\lceil 6\ln n/f(n)\rceil$ ($\leq \ln n$ since $f(n) \geq 6$) sensors at random and move the chosen sensors to equidistant positions $f(n)/n$ apart;

Its analysis is based on the following result.

THEOREM 2. Let $r = f(n)/2n$ where $f(n) \leq 6$, for all n. n sensors of radius r are thrown randomly and independently with uniform distribution on a unit interval. The total expected movement of sensors required to cover the interval is $O(\sqrt{\ln n/f(n)})$.

PROOF. The bound is based on Algorithm 1 which uses $O(\sqrt{\ln n/f(n)})$ expected total movement. Since an optimal algorithm must use at most this movement the result follows.

Clearly the algorithm yields positions for the sensors that cover the entire interval. We now upper bound the expected total distance the sensors are moved. There are two cases to consider.

Case 1: There exists a subinterval with fewer than $\ln n$ sensors. In this case the total expected movement is $O(\sqrt{n})$ by Theorem 1.

Case 2: All subintervals contain at least $\ln n$ sensors. By the independence of the sensor positions, the $6\ln n/f(n)$ chosen sensors in any given subinterval are distributed randomly and independently with uniform distribution over the interval of length $6\ln n/n$. By Lemma 3, the expected movement inside each interval is $O\left(\ln n/n\sqrt{\ln n/f(n)}\right)$. Since there are $n/(6\ln n)$ intervals, the total expected displacement over all intervals must be $O(\sqrt{\ln n/f(n)})$.

It remains to consider the probability with which each of these cases occurs. The proof of the theorem will be a consequence of the following claim.

CLAIM 1. The probability that fewer than $\ln n$ sensors fall in any subinterval is $< 1/n$.

PROOF. The number of sensors falling in a subinterval is a Bernoulli process with probability of success $6\ln n/n$. By Chernoff bounds, the probability that a given subinterval has fewer than $\ln n$ sensors is less than $e^{\frac{-25\ln n}{12}} < 1/n^2$. (Specifically we use the Chernoff bound $\Pr[X < (1-\delta)m] < e^{-\delta^2 m/2}, \delta = 5/6; m = 6\ln n$.) As there are $n/(6\ln n)$ subintervals, the probability that at least one has fewer than $\ln n$ sensors occurs with probability less than $1/n$. This completes the proof of the claim. $\square$

Using Claim 1 we can upper bound the total expected sensor movement as follows:

$$(1-1/n)O(\sqrt{\ln n/f(n)}) + (1/n)O(\sqrt{n}) = O(\sqrt{\ln n/f(n)}),$$

which proves Theorem 2.

The above theorem can be improved for large enough radii using occupancy estimates (see [16]). In particular, the upper bound they provide is better for $\ln\ln n - \ln\ln\ln n \leq f(n)$.

THEOREM 3. *Let $r = f(n)/2n$ where $12 \leq f(n) \leq \ln n - 2\ln\ln n$, for all n. n sensors of radius r are thrown randomly and independently with the uniform distribution on a unit interval. The total expected movement of sensors required to cover the interval is $O(\frac{\ln n}{f(n)e^{f(n)/2}})$.*

PROOF. As before, to prove the bound we present an algorithm that uses $O(\frac{\ln n}{f(n)e^{f(n)/2}})$ expected total movement. Here is an outline of the algorithm specifying how the sensors should move so as to attain coverage of the interval:

Algorithm 2.

1. Divide the interval into subintervals of length $\frac{6\ln n}{n}$;

2. If there is a subinterval with fewer than $\ln n$ sensors then use the standard algorithm that moves all n sensors to positions that are equidistant and stop;

3. Otherwise, divide subintervals into "bins" (i.e., sub-subintervals) of size $\frac{f(n)}{2n}$;

   (a) If the total number of *empty* bins (containing the center of no sensor) over all subintervals is greater than $\frac{4n}{f(n)e^{f(n)/2}}$ then use the standard moving algorithm as above and stop;

   (b) Otherwise, within each subinterval find a matching of extra sensors to empty bins and move the sensors accordingly; Note that each subinterval has at least $\ln n \geq 12\ln n/f(n)$ $(f(n) \geq 12)$ sensors and at most $12\ln n/f(n)$ bins in any subinterval.

Clearly the algorithm results in complete coverage of the interval. Our analysis of the total expected movement will depend upon Claim 1 along with the following claim:

CLAIM 2. *The probability that the number of empty bins is $> \frac{4n}{f(n)e^{f(n)/2}}$ is at most $1/n$.*

PROOF. The proof follows from [16][Theorem 4.18] which in turn is based on the analysis of the number of empty bins when throwing M balls into N bins using Azuma's Inequality. Namely, if $x = M/N$ and Z is the number of empty bins when M balls are thrown randomly into N bins then $\mu = E[Z] = N(1 - 1/N)^M \approx Ne^{-x}$, and, for $\lambda > 0$,

$$\Pr[|Z - \mu| \geq \lambda] \leq 2\exp\left(-\frac{\lambda^2(N-1/2)}{N^2-\mu^2}\right).$$

In our case, we have $\lambda = \mu = \frac{2n}{f(n)e^{f(n)/2}}$ and we are throwing $M = n$ balls (centers of sensors) into $N = 2n/f(n)$ bins, i.e., $x = f(n)/2$, and we derive

$$\begin{aligned} \Pr[|Z - \mu| \geq \mu] &\leq 2\exp\left(-\frac{\mu^2(N-1/2)}{N^2-\mu^2}\right) \\ &= 2\exp\left(-\frac{2n/f(n) - 1/2}{e^{f(n)}-1}\right) \leq \frac{1}{n}, \end{aligned}$$

which proves the claim. $\square$

Now we can analyze the total displacement of the sensors so as to attain coverage of the unit interval. There are three cases to consider.

Case 1: We stop after Step 2 of the algorithm. Then by Claim 1 the probability that this case can occur is $\leq 1/n$ and

this adds to the total expected movement at most $O(\frac{\sqrt{n}}{n}) = O(\frac{1}{\sqrt{n}})$.

Case 2: We stop after Step 3a of the algorithm. Then by Claim 2 the probability that this case can occur is $\leq 1/n$ and this adds to the total expected movement at most $O(\frac{\sqrt{n}}{n}) = O(\frac{1}{\sqrt{n}})$.

Case 3: We stop after Step 3b of the algorithm. In this case we have at most $\frac{4n}{f(n)e^{f(n)/2}}$ sensors that each move at most $\frac{6\ln n}{n}$ for a total movement of $O(\frac{\ln n}{f(n)e^{f(n)/2}})$.

Adding these three cases we obtain a total displacement of $O(\frac{\ln n}{f(n)e^{f(n)/2}})$. This completes the proof of Theorem 3.

2.3 Lower bounds for total displacement when $r > 1/2n$

In this section, we prove a lower bound on the total displacement when the range of the sensors is larger than $1/2n$, the minimum required to achieve full coverage.

The process we are studying is equivalent to the following much studied process: n arcs of equal length $r < 1$ are placed uniformly and independently at random on an interval of length 1 (so that all arcs lie within the interval). This process comes up in the analysis of the size and number of *contigs* in "shotgun" sequencing of DNA. Note that the only distinction is the requirement that the arcs lie within the given interval.

After the random placement of sensors, there remain regions of the interval that are not covered by any sensors. We refer to these regions as *gaps*. Using well-known results from the analysis of the process above (see for example [10][Chapter 5]) it is easy to establish the following:

FACT 1. *If the sensor radius is $1/2n < r \leq 1/\sqrt{n}$ then the expected number of gaps is at least $ne^{-2rn}/2$.*

THEOREM 4. *If the sensor radius is $r = f(n)/2n$, $1 < f(n) \leq \sqrt{n}$, then for any $\epsilon > 0$, the expected total movement of the sensors so as to cover the whole unit interval is at least $\Omega(\epsilon f(n)e^{-(1+\epsilon)f(n)})$.*

PROOF. We think of our process as choosing n points uniformly at random and placing the centers of arcs of length $2r$ at those points. Let $r' = (1+\epsilon)r$. By Fact 1, the expected number of gaps is at least $ne^{-2r'n}/2$ if sensors of radius r' are distributed at random. Certainly, if we now shrink the radius of our sensors to r, all of these gaps remain (as well as possibly new gaps being formed) and they are each of size at least $2r\epsilon$. For our sensors to cover the entire interval at least one sensor must move at least $r\epsilon$ to fill each of the gaps. I.e., a total at least $r\epsilon ne^{-2r'n}/2$ movement is required. This completes the proof of Theorem 4. $\square$

2.4 Maximum displacement

In this section we determine the expected maximum displacement of n sensors required to achieve coverage of a unit interval.

As above, we first consider the case of $r = 1/2n$ where the sensors must move to their anchor points. Recall the notation from section 2.1. We prove the following theorem.

THEOREM 5. *Assume that n sensors of radius $r = 1/2n$ are thrown uniformly at random and independently in the unit interval. For any $\epsilon > 0$, the expected maximum displacement of a sensor required to cover the interval satisfies*

$$\Omega\left(\frac{1}{\sqrt{n}}\right) \leq E\left[\max_{1 \leq i \leq n}\left|X_i - \frac{2i-1}{2n}\right|\right] \leq O\left(\frac{1}{n^{1/2-\epsilon}}\right)$$

PROOF. First of all, we discuss the proof of the lower bound. Observe that

$$E\left[\max_{1\le i\le n}\left|X_i - \frac{2i-1}{2n}\right|\right] \ge \max_{1\le i\le n} E\left[\left|X_i - \frac{2i-1}{2n}\right|\right],$$

where the righthand side in the last inequality is in $\Omega\left(\frac{1}{\sqrt{n}}\right)$. This follows from Theorem 1. Indeed, since the sum for $i = 1, 2, \ldots, n$ of the displacements $E\left[\left|X_i - \frac{2i-1}{2n}\right|\right]$ is in $\Omega\left(\sqrt{n}\right)$ there must exist at least one term in the sum which is in $\Omega\left(\frac{1}{\sqrt{n}}\right)$.

Let ϵ be a sufficiently small constant > 0. To prove the upper bound

$$E\left[\max_{1\le i\le n}\left|X_i - \frac{2i-1}{2n}\right|\right] \in O\left(\frac{1}{n^{1/2-\epsilon}}\right)$$

we argue as follows. If the event

$$\max_{1\le i\le n}\left|X_i - \frac{2i-1}{2n}\right| > n^{-1/2+\epsilon}$$

is true then for some $1 \le i \le n$, we have that $|X_i - \frac{2i-1}{2n}| > n^{-1/2+\epsilon}$; i.e., some sensor i must have moved distance more than $n^{-1/2+\epsilon}$ towards its anchor point $\frac{2i-1}{2n}$. In turn, this implies that the number of sensors which lie in one of the intervals $[0, \frac{2i-1}{2n}]$ or $[\frac{2i-1}{2n}, 1]$ differs by more than $n^{-1/2-\epsilon}$ from its expected value, i.e, there is a $n^{-1/2-\epsilon}$ "deficit" of sensors in at least one of the two previous intervals.

Consider a subinterval I of length x and let N_I be the random variable that counts the number of sensors that lie inside I. The expected number of sensors inside I is xn. Therefore, using Chernoff bounds we see that $\Pr[|N_I - xn| > a] \le 2e^{-2a^2/n}$. Assuming that $a = n^{1/2+\epsilon}$ we see that

$$\Pr[|N_I - xn| > n^{1/2+\epsilon}] \le 2e^{-2n^{2\epsilon}}.$$

Thus, using Chernoff bounds, we see that with high probability, the number of sensors in any interval of length x is at most $xn \pm n^{1/2+\epsilon}$. In particular, with high probability the number of sensors in the interval $[0, \frac{2i-1}{2n}]$ is at most $\frac{2i-1}{2} \pm n^{1/2+\epsilon}$ and in the interval $[\frac{2i-1}{2n}, 1]$ it is at most $1 - \frac{2i-1}{2} \pm n^{1/2+\epsilon}$. It follows from the above that

$$\Pr\left[\max_{1\le i\le n}\left|X_i - \frac{2i-1}{2n}\right| > n^{-1/2+\epsilon}\right] \le 4e^{-2n^{2\epsilon}}.$$

This proves the theorem. $\square$

Theorem 5 is valid for sensor range $\frac{1}{2n}$, which, as explained before, amounts to having the sensors move from their current location to specific anchors $t_i = \frac{2i-1}{2n}$, for $i = 1, 2, \ldots, n$. We next prove a tight bound on the expected maximum sensor movement for a more general sensor range.

THEOREM 6. Assume that n sensors of radius $r = f(n)/2n$ such that $6 \le f(n) < (1-\epsilon)\ln n$, for all n, for any $\epsilon > 0$, are thrown randomly and independently with uniform distribution on a unit interval. The expected maximum displacement required to cover the interval is $\Theta(\frac{\ln n}{n})$.

PROOF. The upper bound follows from the proof of Theorem 2. Recall in the Algorithm 1, the first thing we do is divide the unit interval into subintervals of size $6\ln n/n$. With probability at least $1 - 1/n$ all sensor movement takes place entirely within these subintervals so no sensor moves

more than $6\ln n/n$. With probability at most $1/n$ the expected maximum displacement is $O(1)$. The upper bound follows.

For the lower bound, we use the well known results on the spacing of points (centers of the sensor ranges) thrown uniformly at random on the unit interval. (See [9].) In particular, it is easy to show that with probability at least $1/e$ there are two points at distance at least $\frac{\ln n}{n}$. Thus with constant probability, in order for this interval between the centers of the neighboring sensors to be covered at least one sensor must move at least distance $\frac{\ln n - f(n)}{2n} = \Omega(\frac{\ln n}{n})$ assuming $f(n) < (1-\epsilon)\ln n$, $\epsilon > 0$. $\square$

3. DISPLACEMENT IN 2D

In this section we consider the total and maximum displacement required to achieve coverage when sensors are randomly distributed in a unit square. First we consider total displacement for area coverage, then for perimeter coverage and finally maximum displacement for both.

3.1 Total displacement for area coverage

Our first result is an upper bound on the total displacement for the case where $r = c/\sqrt{n}$ for a sufficiently large c. Clearly c must be $> 1/\sqrt{\pi}$ in order for the sensors to be able to cover the square. We can prove the following theorem:

THEOREM 7. Let $c \ge 4$. Assume that n sensors of radius $\le \frac{c}{\sqrt{n}}$ are thrown randomly and independently with the uniform distribution on a unit square. The total expected displacement required for the sensors to cover the unit square is $O(\sqrt{n}\ln n)$.

PROOF. To prove the upper bound we present an algorithm that uses $O(\sqrt{n\ln n})$ expected total movement. Here is an outline of the algorithm.

Algorithm 3: Sensor displacement on a square.

1. Divide the unit square into subsquares of side $\sqrt{\frac{c^2\ln n}{2n}}$;

2. If there is a subsquare with fewer then $c\ln n$ sensors then use any algorithm that moves all n sensors to positions that are equidistant apart and sufficient to cover the square and stop;

3. Otherwise, choose $c\ln n$ sensors in each subsquare (arbitrarily) and move them to equidistant points that are sufficient to cover the square.

The proof follows from the following claim:

CLAIM 3. For $c \ge 4$, with probability at least $1-1/n$ every subsquare has at least $c\ln n$ sensors.

PROOF. We use the Chernoff bound $\Pr[X < (1-\delta)m] < e^{-\delta^2 m/2}$; $\delta = 1/2$; $m = \frac{c^2\ln n}{2}$ to show that any subsquare has fewer than $c\ln n$ sensors with probability at most $1/n^2$. The result now follows. $\square$

Now we can prove the theorem. Observe that with probability $\le 1/n$ we stop after step 2 and the total movement in this case is $O(n)$. With probability at least $1 - 1/n^2$ we finish after step 3 in which case no sensor moves more than $\sqrt{\frac{c^2\ln n}{2n}}$ for a total movement of $O(\sqrt{n\ln n})$, which proves the theorem.

Now we prove a lower bound which matches the upper bound to within a factor $\sqrt{\ln n}$.

THEOREM 8. *Let $c \geq 1/\sqrt{\pi}$. Assume that n sensors of radius $\frac{c}{\sqrt{n}}$ are thrown randomly and independently with the uniform distribution on a unit square. The total distance required for moving the sensors to cover the unit square is $\Omega(\sqrt{n})$.*

PROOF. Divide the square into subsquares of side $\frac{3c}{\sqrt{n}}$. The number of such squares is $\frac{n}{9c^2}$ and using [16][Theorem 4.18], with high probability the expected number of empty squares is $\frac{n}{9c^2}e^{-9c^2} \in \Theta(n)$. Clearly, for each of the empty subsquares a sensor has to move distance at least $\frac{c}{2\sqrt{n}}$ just to cover the centre of the sub square. It follows the total movement required to cover the entire square is $\frac{n}{9c^2}e^{-9c^2}\frac{c}{2\sqrt{n}} \in \Theta(\sqrt{n})$. This proves the lower bound. □

3.2 Total displacement for perimeter coverage

In this subsection we consider perimeter coverage of a unit square. Consider a unit square with n equidistant anchors on its perimeter and suppose that n sensors are thrown randomly and independently with the uniform distribution in the unit square. We compare three algorithms for sensors to move from their initial position to the perimeter of the square 1) the Hungarian Algorithm (see [5]), and 2) the Rectilinear Algorithm. We use the following notation.

- HA: The "Hungarian Algorithm" is the well-known algorithm for solving the minimum weight matching problem in the bipartite graph. It provides an optimal algorithm for the total movement of sensors to anchors.

- SDA: The "Shortest Distance Algorithm" whereby each sensor moves to its shortest distance point on the perimeter of the square. Note: this does not necessarily result in coverage of the perimeter but it does define a displacement amount.

- RA: the "Rectilinear Algorithm" whereby each sensor moves according to first, shortest distance algorithm SDA, and second according to the natural generalization to the perimeter of the square of the algorithm defined on the interval above. We refer to this algorithm as IA.

In the sequel we show that the Rectilinear Algorithm is asymptotically optimal in that it has the same asymptotic for the expected total displacement as the Hungarian Algorithm.

THEOREM 9. *Assume that n sensors of radius $2/n$ are thrown randomly and independently with uniform distribution on a unit square. The optimal algorithm for moving the (centre of the) sensors (to the perimeter) so as to cover the perimeter of the unit square uses expected total movement $\frac{n}{12} + o(n)$.*

PROOF. Before proving the theorem, we prove a lemma.

LEMMA 4. *The following inequalities hold*

$$E[SDA] \leq E[HA] \leq E[RA] = E[SDA] + E[IA].$$

PROOF. The lower bound follows from the fact the length of an edge from a sensor to an anchor point always exceeds the distance between the sensor and the shortest distance point on the perimeter of the square. The upper bound is also easy to prove because the length of edge assigned to the sensor by the Hungarian Algorithm cannot exceed the sum of the lengths of the two movements assigned by the IA and SDA algorithm. □

LEMMA 5. *For a unit square, $E[SDA] = \frac{n}{12}$.*

PROOF. (Lemma 5) Consider a unit square $Q = [0,1] \times [0,1]$ with vertices $(0,0),(0,1),(1,0),(1,1)$. Consider a random point (X,Y) in the unit square and let $D := \min\{X,Y\}$. We compute $E[D]$ as follows. Partition Q into four squares $Q_{00} = [0,1/2] \times [0,1/2]$, $Q_{10} = [1/2,1] \times [0,1/2]$, $Q_{01} = [0,1/2] \times [1/2,1]$, $Q_{11} = [1/2,1] \times [1/2,1]$. Let S_{ij} denote the event that the random point lies in the quadrant Q_{ij}, for $i,j = 0,1$. Observe that

$$E[D] = \sum_{i,j=0,1} E[D|S_{ij}]\Pr[S_{ij}]] = \frac{1}{4}\sum_{i,j=0,1} E[D|S_{ij}].$$

It remains to compute $E[D|S_{ij}]$. Observe that from the definitions above we have that

$$D = \begin{cases} X & \text{if } (X,Y) \in Q_{01} \\ Y & \text{if } (X,Y) \in Q_{10} \\ \min\{X,Y\} & \text{if } (X,Y) \in Q_{00} \\ \min\{1-X,1-Y\} & \text{if } (X,Y) \in Q_{11}. \end{cases}$$

This implies easily $\Pr[D > r|S_{01}] = 1/2 - r$ and therefore

$$E[D|S_{01}] = \int_0^{1/2} \Pr[D > r|S_{01}]dr = \int_0^{1/2}(1/2 - r)dr = \frac{1}{8}.$$

Similarly, $E[D|S_{10}] = 1/8$. Now consider the quadrant S_{00}. Observe that $\Pr[D > r|S_{00}] = (1/2 - r)^2$ and therefore

$$E[D|S_{00}] = \int_0^{1/2} \Pr[D > r|S_{00}]dr = \int_0^{1/2}(1/2 - r)^2 dr = \frac{1}{24}.$$

Similarly, $\Pr[D > r|S_{11}] = (1-r)^2$ and therefore

$$E[D|S_{11}] = \int_{1/2}^1 \Pr[D > r|S_{11}]dr = \int_{1/2}^1(1-r)^2 dr = 1/24.$$

From this we conclude that $E[D] = 1/12$. Since the points are chosen independently with the same distribution, we conclude that $E[SDA] = n/12$. This completes the proof of Lemma 5. □

Now we return to the proof of Theorem 9. Recall that for the unit interval we have proved that $E[IA] \in \Theta(\sqrt{n})$. The perimeter of the unit square is 4. By Lemma 5, $E[SDA] = n/12$. Hence, the theorem follows from the main inequality in Lemma 4.

3.3 Maximum displacement in 2D

We investigate separately the maximum displacement for area coverage and perimeter coverage of a unit square.

THEOREM 10. *Let $c \geq 4$. Assume that n sensors of radius $\frac{c}{\sqrt{n}}$ are thrown randomly and independently with the uniform distribution on a unit square. The expected maximum displacement required for moving the sensors to cover the unit square is in $\Theta(\sqrt{\ln n/n})$.*

PROOF. The upper bound follows easily from the proof of correctness of the main algorithm in Theorem 7 since no sensor ever has to move more than $O(\sqrt{\ln n/n})$ with probability at least $1 - 1/n$. For the lower bound recall from [18] that if M_n denotes the maximum edge length in the MST on the set of n randomly distributed points on a unit square (or centers of our sensors), then the distribution of $n\pi M_n^2 - \ln n$ converges weakly to the double exponential distribution, i.e.,

$$\lim_{n \to \infty} \Pr[n\pi M_n^2 - \ln n \leq x] = e^{-e^{-x}}, \text{ for all reals } x.$$

Substituting $x = -\ln\ln(1/\epsilon)$ in this formula we see that the event "$n\pi M_n^2 > \ln n - \ln\ln(1/\epsilon)$" holds with high probability (at least $1 - \epsilon$). Since a sensor must move to cover the centre of the maximum edge of the MST, the proof of the theorem is complete. □

We now look at the maximum displacement for random sensors in a unit square.

THEOREM 11. *Assume that n sensors of radius $\frac{2}{n}$, are thrown randomly and independently with the uniform distribution on a unit square. The expected maximum displacement required for moving the sensors to cover the perimeter of the unit square is at least $1/12$.*

PROOF. Since the total displacement is $n/12$ there is a sensor with displacement at least $1/12$. It follows that the expected maximum displacement of a sensor is at least $1/12$, which proves the theorem. □

4. CONCLUSION

In this paper we obtained tradeoffs between the expected sum and maximum of displacements and the range of the sensors for the total/max displacement problem. It is not difficult to see that similar results may be obtained for other domains, like the unit disk, as well as in higher dimensions.

There are several interesting questions arising, aside from tightening the bounds of the results already obtained. These include measuring the expected sum and maximum of the displacement required to attain k-coverage, for some $k \geq 2$. Another interesting question is concerned with the displacement necessary so as to improve sender and/or receiver interference of the sensor network. Finally, there is the question of the expected minimum number of sensors that must be moved to achieve coverage.

5. REFERENCES

[1] A. Abay. Extremes of interarrival times of a poisson process under conditioning. *Applicationes Mathematicae*, 23(1):73–82, 1995.

[2] A.A. Abbasi, M. Younis, and K. Akkaya. Movement-assisted connectivity restoration in wireless sensor and actor networks. *Parallel and Distributed Systems, IEEE Trans. on*, 20(9):1366–1379, 2009.

[3] B. C. Arnold, N. Balakrishnan, and H. N. Nagaraja. *A first course in order statistics*, volume 54. SIAM, 2008.

[4] B. Bhattacharya, M. Burmester, Y. Hu, E. Kranakis, Q. Shi, and A. Wiese. Optimal movement of mobile sensors for barrier coverage of a planar region. *TCS*, 410(52):5515–5528, 2009.

[5] J.A. Bondy and U.S.R. Murty. *Graph theory with applications*, volume 244. Springer, GTM, 2008.

[6] D. Chen, Y. Gu, J. Li, and H. Wang. Algorithms on minimizing the maximum sensor movement for barrier coverage of a linear domain. *Algorithm Theory–SWAT 2012*, pages 177–188, 2012.

[7] J. Czyzowicz, E. Kranakis, D. Krizanc, I. Lambadaris, L. Narayanan, J. Opatrny, L. Stacho, J. Urrutia, and M. Yazdani. On minimizing the maximum sensor movement for barrier coverage of a line segment. *ADHONOW*, pages 194–212, 2009.

[8] J. Czyzowicz, E. Kranakis, D. Krizanc, I. Lambadaris, L. Narayanan, J. Opatrny, L. Stacho, J. Urrutia, and M. Yazdani. On minimizing the sum of sensor movements for barrier coverage of a line segment. *ADHOCNOW*, pages 29–42, 2010.

[9] D. A. Darling. On a class of problems related to the random division of an interval. *The Annals of Mathematical Statistics*, pages 239–253, 1953.

[10] W. J. Ewens and G. R. Grant. *Statistical methods in bioinformatics: an introduction*, volume 10. Springer, 2005.

[11] W. Feller. *An Introduction to Probability Theory and its Applications*, volume 1. John Wiley, NY, 1968.

[12] X. Han, X. Cao, E.L. Lloyd, and C.C. Shen. Fault-tolerant relay node placement in heterogeneous wireless sensor networks. In *INFOCOM 2007*, pages 1667–1675. IEEE, 2007.

[13] J. Justicz, E.R. Scheinerman, and P.M. Winkler. Random intervals. *American Mathematical Monthly*, 97(10):881–889, 1990.

[14] B. Kopochinski. The extreme gap in the multivariate poisson process. *Zestos Mat.*, 21:137–141, 1991.

[15] S. Kumar, T. H. Lai, and A. Arora. Barrier coverage with wireless sensors. In *Proceedings of the 11th annual international conference on Mobile computing and networking*, pages 284–298. ACM, 2005.

[16] R. Motwani and P. Raghavan. *Randomized algorithms*. Cambridge University Press, 1995.

[17] P. Ogren, E. Fiorelli, and N.E. Leonard. Cooperative control of mobile sensor networks: Adaptive gradient climbing in a distributed environment. *Automatic Control, IEEE Trans. on*, 49(8):1292–1302, 2004.

[18] M.D. Penrose. The longest edge of the random minimal spanning tree. *The annals of applied probability*, 7(2):340–361, 1997.

[19] R. Pyke. Spacings. *J. of the Royal Statistical Society. Series B (Methodological)*, pages 395–449, 1965.

[20] R. Pyke. Spacings revisited. In *Proc. 6th Berkeley Symp. Math. Stat. Prob.*, volume 1, pages 417–427, 1972.

[21] R. Pyke. The asymptotic behavior of spacings under Kakutani's model for interval subdivision. *The Annals of Probability*, 8(1):157–163, 1980.

[22] A. Saipulla, C. Westphal, B. Liu, and J. Wang. Barrier coverage of line-based deployed wireless sensor networks. In *INFOCOM*, pages 127–135. IEEE, 2009.

[23] E.R. Scheinerman. Random interval graphs. *Combinatorica*, 8(4):357–371, 1988.

[24] M. Younis and K. Akkaya. Strategies and techniques for node placement in wireless sensor networks: A survey. *Ad Hoc Networks*, 6(4):621–655, 2008.

Appendix

PROOF. (Lemma 1) We first compute D_i. The definite integral on the right hand side of the expression for D_i can be evaluated using integration by parts (as a by-product, we can derive $E[X_i] = \frac{i}{n+1}$ if we let the limits go from 0 to 1). Let E_i denote the definite integral $\int_{t_i}^1 x f_{X_i}(x)dx$. We will assume that the evaluation limits are always t_i (lower) and 1 (upper). Then, using integration by parts to successively reduce the exponent of the x term, we get:

$$
\begin{aligned}
E_i &= i\binom{n}{i}\int x^i(1-x)^{n-i}dx \\
&= i\binom{n}{i}\left(\left[-\frac{1}{(n-i+1)}x^i(1-x)^{n-i+1}\right]+\right. \\
&\qquad \left.\frac{i}{(n-i+1)}\int x^{i-1}(1-x)^{n-i+1}dx\right) \\
&= i\binom{n}{i}\cdot\frac{1}{(n-i+1)}\left(t_i^i(1-t_i)^{n-i+1}+\right. \\
&\qquad \left[-\frac{i}{(n-i+2)}x^{i-1}(1-x)^{n-i+2}\right] \\
&\qquad \left.+\frac{i(i-1)}{(n-i+2)}\int x^{i-2}(1-x)^{n-i+2}dx\right) \\
&\qquad\vdots \\
&= \binom{n}{i}\cdot\frac{i}{(n-i+1)}\cdot\left(t_i^i(1-t_i)^{n-i+1}+\right. \\
&\qquad \frac{i}{(n-i+2)}t_i^{i-1}(1-t_i)^{n-i+2}+\ldots \\
&\qquad +\left[-\frac{i(i-1)\ldots 2}{(n-i+2)\ldots n}x(1-x)^n\right]+ \\
&\qquad \left.\frac{i(i-1)\ldots 2}{(n-i+2)\ldots n}\int(1-x)^n dx\right) \\
&= \frac{n!\,i}{i!(n-i)!(n-i+1)} \\
&\qquad \sum_{k=0}^{i}\left(\frac{i!(n-i+1)!}{(i-k)!(n-i+k+1)!}t_i^{i-k}(1-t_i)^{n-i+k+1}\right) \\
&= \sum_{k=0}^{i}i\cdot\frac{n!}{(n-i+k+1)!(i-k)!}t_i^{i-k}(1-t_i)^{n-i+k+1} \\
&= \sum_{k=0}^{i}\frac{i}{(n+1)}\cdot\binom{n+1}{i-k}t_i^{i-k}(1-t_i)^{n-i+k+1} \\
&\qquad \text{and, substituting } j=(i-k) \\
&= \sum_{j=0}^{i}\frac{i}{(n+1)}\cdot\binom{n+1}{j}t_i^j(1-t_i)^{n+1-j}
\end{aligned}
$$

So, putting everything together, we obtain

$$
\begin{aligned}
D_i &= 2t_i F_{X_i}(t_i)+2\int_{t_i}^1 x f_{X_i}(x)dx - t_i - E[X_i] \\
&= \left(\sum_{k=i}^{n}2\binom{n}{k}t_i^{k+1}(1-t_i)^{n-k}\right. \\
&\qquad \left.+\frac{2i}{n+1}\sum_{j=0}^{i}\binom{n+1}{j}t_i^j(1-t_i)^{n+1-j}\right) \\
&\qquad -\frac{i}{n+1}-\frac{2i-1}{2n}
\end{aligned}
$$

Substitute $j=k+1$ in the first sum and with appropriate rearrangement of terms, this leads to the following formula for D_i:

$$
\begin{aligned}
&\left(\sum_{j=0}^{i}\frac{2i}{n+1}\cdot\binom{n+1}{j}t_i^j(1-t_i)^{n+1-j}\right. \\
&\qquad \left.+\sum_{j=i+1}^{n+1}2\binom{n}{j-1}t_i^j(1-t_i)^{n+1-j}\right) \\
&\qquad -\frac{i}{n+1}-\frac{2i-1}{2n} \\
&= \left(\sum_{j=0}^{i}\frac{2i}{n+1}\cdot\binom{n+1}{j}t_i^j(1-t_i)^{n+1-j}\right. \\
&\qquad \left.+\sum_{j=i+1}^{n+1}\frac{2j}{n+1}\binom{n+1}{j}t_i^j(1-t_i)^{n+1-j}\right) \\
&\qquad -\frac{i}{n+1}-\frac{2i-1}{2n} \\
&= \frac{2i}{n+1}\left(\sum_{j=0}^{n+1}\binom{n+1}{j}t_i^j(1-t_i)^{n+1-j}\right) \\
&\qquad +\sum_{j=i+1}^{n+1}\frac{2(j-i)}{n+1}\binom{n+1}{j}t_i^j(1-t_i)^{n+1-j} \\
&\qquad -\frac{i}{n+1}-\frac{2i-1}{2n} \\
&= \frac{2i}{n+1}-\frac{i}{n+1}-\frac{2i-1}{2n}+ \\
&\qquad \sum_{j=i+1}^{n+1}\frac{2(j-i)}{n+1}\binom{n+1}{j}t_i^j(1-t_i)^{n+1-j} \\
&= \frac{1}{n+1}\left(\frac{n+1-2i}{2n}+\right. \\
&\qquad \left.\sum_{j=i+1}^{n+1}2(j-i)\cdot\binom{n+1}{j}t_i^j(1-t_i)^{n+1-j}\right)
\end{aligned}
$$

Summed over all $1\le i\le n$, we get $\sum_i \frac{n+1-2i}{2n}=0$, and hence:

$$
\begin{aligned}
D &= \sum_{1\le i\le n}D_i \\
&= \frac{2}{n+1}\sum_{i=1}^{n}\sum_{j=i+1}^{n+1}(j-i)\cdot\binom{n+1}{j}t_i^j(1-t_i)^{n+1-j}
\end{aligned}
$$

thus proving Lemma 1. $\square$

PROOF. (Lemma 2) Since $\binom{n+1}{j} = \frac{n+1}{j}\binom{n}{j-1}$, we can now simplify the inner sum in Formula (1) as follows:

$$\sum_{j=i+1}^{n+1} (j-i) \cdot \binom{n+1}{j} t_i^j (1-t_i)^{n+1-j}$$

$$= \sum_{j=i+1}^{n+1} j \cdot \binom{n+1}{j} t_i^j (1-t_i)^{n+1-j} -$$
$$i \sum_{j=i+1}^{n+1} \binom{n+1}{j} t_i^j (1-t_i)^{n+1-j}$$

$$= (n+1)t_i \sum_{j=i+1}^{n+1} \binom{n}{j-1} t_i^{j-1} (1-t_i)^{n-(j-1)} -$$
$$i \sum_{j=i+1}^{n+1} \binom{n+1}{j} t_i^j (1-t_i)^{n+1-j}$$

$$= (n+1)t_i \sum_{j=i}^{n} \binom{n}{j} t_i^j (1-t_i)^{n-j} -$$
$$i \sum_{j=i+1}^{n+1} \binom{n+1}{j} t_i^j (1-t_i)^{n+1-j}$$

We can simplify this further by rewriting $\binom{n+1}{j} = \binom{n}{j-1} + \binom{n}{j}$ in the second term above; as a result, the RHS becomes:

$$(n+1)t_i \sum_{j=i}^{n} \binom{n}{j} t_i^j (1-t_i)^{n-j}$$
$$-i \sum_{j=i+1}^{n+1} \binom{n}{j-1} t_i^j (1-t_i)^{n+1-j}$$
$$-i \sum_{j=i+1}^{n+1} \binom{n}{j} t_i^j (1-t_i)^{n+1-j}$$

$$= (n+1)t_i \cdot \Pr[N_i^{(n)} \geq i]$$
$$-it_i \sum_{j=i+1}^{n+1} \binom{n}{j-1} t_i^{j-1} (1-t_i)^{n-(j-1)}$$
$$-i(1-t_i) \sum_{j=i+1}^{n} \binom{n}{j} t_i^j (1-t_i)^{n-j}$$

$$= ((n+1)t_i - it_i) \cdot \Pr[N_i^{(n)} \geq i]$$
$$-i(1-t_i) \sum_{j=i}^{n} \binom{n}{j} t_i^j (1-t_i)^{n-j}$$
$$+i(1-t_i) \binom{n}{i} t_i^i (1-t_i)^{n-i}$$

$$= ((n+1)t_i - it_i - i(1-t_i)) \cdot \Pr[N_i^{(n)} \geq i]$$
$$+i(1-t_i) \cdot \Pr[N_i^{(n)} = i]$$

$$= \left((n+1)\frac{2i-1}{2n} - i\right) \Pr[N_i^{(n)} \geq i]$$
$$+i \cdot \frac{2n-2i+1}{2n} \cdot \Pr[N_i^{(n)} = i]$$

$$= \frac{2i-(n+1)}{2n} \Pr[N_i^{(n)} \geq i]$$
$$+\frac{i(2n+1)-2i^2}{2n} \Pr[N_i^{(n)} = i]$$

Now, we substitute Identity (4) into Formula (1) to obtain

$$\frac{2}{n+1} \sum_{i=1}^{n} \sum_{j=i+1}^{n+1} (j-i) \cdot \binom{n+1}{j} t_i^j (1-t_i)^{n+1-j}$$

$$= \frac{2}{n+1} \sum_{i=1}^{n} \left(\frac{2i-(n+1)}{2n} \Pr[N_i^{(n)} \geq i]+\right.$$
$$\left.\frac{i(2n+1)-2i^2}{2n} \Pr[N_i^{(n)} = i]\right)$$

$$= \frac{2}{n(n+1)} \sum_{i=1}^{n} i \cdot \Pr[N_i^{(n)} \geq i]$$
$$-\frac{1}{n} \sum_{i=1}^{n} \Pr[N_i^{(n)} \geq i] +$$
$$\frac{2n+1}{n(n+1)} \sum_{i=1}^{n} i \cdot \Pr[N_i^{(n)} = i]$$
$$-\frac{2}{n(n+1)} \sum_{i=1}^{n} i^2 \cdot \Pr[N_i^{(n)} = i]$$

The first two summands contribute $\Theta(1)$ terms: the inner sum of the first summand is at most $\sum_{1 \leq i \leq n} i = n(n+1)/2$ while the inner sum of the second is exactly $n/2$. Thus the asymptotics depends on the expression given by the last two summands, viz.

$$\frac{2n+1}{n(n+1)} \sum_{i=1}^{n} i \cdot \Pr[N_i^{(n)} = i] - \frac{2}{n(n+1)} \sum_{i=1}^{n} i^2 \cdot \Pr[N_i^{(n)} = i]$$

This easily completes the proof of Lemma 2. $\square$

On Dynamics in Selfish Network Creation

Bernd Kawald
Department of Computer Science
Humboldt-Universität zu Berlin
Berlin, Germany
kawald@informatik.hu-berlin.de

Pascal Lenzner
Department of Computer Science
Humboldt-Universität zu Berlin
Berlin, Germany
lenzner@informatik.hu-berlin.de

ABSTRACT

We consider the dynamic behavior of several variants of the Network Creation Game, introduced by Fabrikant et al. [PODC'03]. Equilibrium networks in these models have desirable properties like low social cost and small diameter, which makes them attractive for the decentralized creation of overlay-networks. Unfortunately, due to the non-constructiveness of the Nash equilibrium, no distributed algorithm for *finding* such networks is known. We treat these games as sequential-move games and analyze if (uncoordinated) selfish play eventually converges to an equilibrium. Thus, we shed light on one of the most natural algorithms for this problem: distributed local search, where in each step some agent performs a myopic selfish improving move.

We show that fast convergence is guaranteed for all versions of Swap Games, introduced by Alon et al. [SPAA'10], if the initial network is a tree. Furthermore, we prove that this process can be sped up to an almost optimal number of moves by employing a very natural move policy. Unfortunately, these positive results are no longer true if the initial network has cycles and we show the surprising result that even one non-tree edge suffices to destroy the convergence guarantee. This answers an open problem from Ehsani et al. [SPAA'11] in the negative. Moreover, we show that on non-tree networks no move policy can enforce convergence. We extend our negative results to the well-studied original version, where agents are allowed to buy and delete edges as well. For this model we prove that there is no convergence guarantee – even if all agents play optimally. Even worse, if played on a non-complete host-graph, then there are instances where no sequence of improving moves leads to a stable network. Furthermore, we analyze whether cost-sharing has positive impact on the convergence behavior. For this we consider a version by Corbo and Parkes [PODC'05] where bilateral consent is needed for the creation of an edge and where edge-costs are shared among the involved agents. We show that employing such a cost-sharing rule yields even worse dynamic behavior.

Finally, we contrast our mostly negative theoretical results by a careful empirical study. Our simulations indicate two positive facts: (1) The non-convergent behavior seems to be confined to a small set of pathological instances and is unlikely to show up in practice. (2) In all our simulations we observed a remarkably fast convergence towards a stable network in $\mathcal{O}(n)$ steps, where n is the number of agents.

Categories and Subject Descriptors

F.2.2 [**Theory of Computation**]: Analysis of Algorithms and Problem Complexity—*Nonnumerical Algorithms and Problems*; G.2.2 [**Mathematics of Computing**]: Discrete Mathematics—*Graph Theory, Network Problems*

General Terms

Algorithms, Design, Theory, Experimentation

Keywords

Network Creation Games, Game Dynamics, Convergence, Stabilization, Distributed Local Search

1. INTRODUCTION

Understanding Internet-like networks and their implications on our life is a recent endeavor undertaken by researchers from different research communities. Such networks are difficult to analyze since they are created by a multitude of selfish entities (e.g. Internet Service Providers) which modify the infrastructure of parts of the network (e.g. their Autonomous Systems) to improve their service quality. The classical field of Game Theory provides the tools for analyzing such decentralized processes and from this perspective the Internet can be seen as an equilibrium state of an underlying game played by selfish agents.

Within the last decade several such games have been proposed and analyzed. We will focus on the line of works which consider Network Creation Games, as introduced by Fabrikant et al. [11]. These games are very simple but they contain an interesting trade-off between an agent's investment in infrastructure and her obtained usage quality. Agents aim to invest as little as possible but at the same time they want to achieve a good connection to all other agents in the network. Network Creation Games and several variants have been studied intensively, but, to the best of our knowledge, almost all these works exclusively focus on properties of the equilibrium states of the game. With this focus, the game is usually considered to be a one-shot simultaneous-move game. However, the Internet was not created in "one shot". It has rather evolved from an initial network, the ARPANET, into its current shape by repeated infrastructural changes performed by selfish agents who entered or left the stage at some time in the process. For this reason, we focus on a more dynamic point of view: We analyze the properties of the network creation *processes* induced by the sequential-move version of the known models of selfish network creation.

It is well-known that Network Creation Games have low price of anarchy, which implies that the social cost of the worst stable states arising from selfish behavior is close to the cost of the social optimum. Therefore these games are appealing for the decentralized and selfish creation of networks which optimize the service quality for all agents at low infrastructural cost, e.g. overlay networks created by selfish peers. But, to the best of our knowledge, it is not known how a group of agents can collectively *find* such a desirable stable state. Analyzing the game dynamics of Network Creation Games is equivalent to analyzing a very natural search strategy: (uncoordinated) distributed local search, where in every step some agent myopically modifies the network infrastructure to better suit her needs. Clearly, if at some step in the process no agent wants to modify her part of the network, then a stable network has emerged.

1.1 Models and Definitions

We consider several versions of a network creation process performed by n selfish agents. In all versions we consider networks, where every node corresponds to an agent and undirected links connect nodes in the network. The creation process is based on an underlying Network Creation Game (NCG) and can be understood as a dynamic process where agents sequentially perform strategy-changes in the NCG. In such games, the strategies of the agents determine which links are present in the network and any strategy-profile, which is a vector of the strategies of all n agents, determines the induced network. But this also works the other way round: Given some network $G = (V, E, o)$, where V is the set of n vertices, E is the set of edges and $o : E \to V$ is the *ownership-function*, which assigns the ownership of an edge to one of its endpoints, then G completely determines the current strategies of all n agents of the NCG. Starting from a network G_0, any sequence of strategy-changes by agents can thus be seen as a sequence of networks $G_0, G_1, G_2, \ldots$, where the network G_{i+1} arises from the network G_i by the strategy-change of exactly one agent. In the following, we will write xy or yx for the undirected edge $\{x, y\} \in E$. In figures we will indicate edge-ownership by directing edges away from their owner.

The creation process starts in an initial state G_0, which we call the *initial network*. A step from state G_i to state G_{i+1} consists of a *move* by one agent. A move of agent u in state G_i is the replacement of agent u's pure strategy in G_i by another *admissible* pure strategy of agent u. The induced network after this strategy-change by agent u then corresponds to the state G_{i+1}. We consider only improving moves, that is, strategy-changes which strictly decrease the moving agent's cost. The cost of an agent in G_i depends on the structure of G_i and it will be defined formally below. If agent u in state G_i has an admissible new strategy which yields a strict cost decrease for her, then we call agent u *unhappy in network G_i* and we let U_i denote the set of all unhappy agents in state G_i. Only one agent can actually

move in a state of the process and this agent $u \in U_i$, whose move transforms G_i into G_{i+1}, is called *the moving agent in network G_i*. In any state of the process the *move policy* determines which agent is the moving agent. The process stops in some state G_j if no agent wants to perform a move, that is, if $U_j = \emptyset$, and we call the resulting networks *stable*. Clearly, stable networks correspond to pure Nash equilibria of the underlying NCG.

Depending on what strategies are admissible for an agent in the current state, there are several variants of this process, which we call *game types*:

- In the *Swap Game* (SG), introduced as "Basic Network Creation Game" by Alon et al. [2], the strategy S_u of an agent u in the network G_i is the set of neighbors of vertex u in G_i. The new strategy S_u^* is admissible for agent u in state G_i, if $|S_u| = |S_u^*|$ and $|S_u \cap S_u^*| = |S_u| - 1$. Intuitively, admissible strategies in the SG are strategies which replace one neighbor x of u by another vertex y. Note, that this corresponds to "swapping" the edge ux from x towards y, which is the replacement of edge ux by edge uy. Furthermore, observe, that in any state both endpoints of an edge are allowed to swap this edge. Technically, this means that the ownership of an edge has no influence on the agents' strategies or costs.

- The *Asymmetric Swap Game* (ASG), recently introduced by Mihalák and Schlegel [16], is similar to the SG, but here the ownership of an edge plays a crucial role. Only the owner of an edge is allowed to swap the edge in any state of the process. The strategy S_u of agent u in state G_i is the set of neighbors in G_i to which u owns an edge and the strategy S_u^* is admissible for agent u in state G_i, if $|S_u| = |S_u^*|$ and $|S_u \cap S_u^*| = |S_u| - 1$. Hence, in the ASG the moving agents are allowed to swap one own edge.

- In the *Greedy Buy Game* (GBG), recently introduced by us [14], agents have more freedom to act. In any state, an agent is allowed to buy or to delete or to swap one own edge. Hence, the GBG can be seen as an extension of the ASG. The strategy S_u of agent u in state G_i is defined as in the ASG, but the set of admissible strategies is larger: S_u^* is admissible for agent u in state G_i if (1) $|S_u^*| = |S_u| + 1$ and $S_u \subset S_u^*$ or (2) if $|S_u^*| = |S_u| - 1$ and $S_u^* \subset S_u$ or (3) if $|S_u| = |S_u^*|$ and $|S_u \cap S_u^*| = |S_u| - 1$.

- The *Buy Game* (BG), which is the original version of an NCG and which was introduced by Fabrikant et al. [11], is the most general version. Here agents can perform arbitrary strategy-changes, that is, agents are allowed to perform any combination of buying, deleting and swapping of own edges. The strategy S_u of agent u in G_i is defined as in the ASG, but an admissible strategy for agent u is any set $S_u^* \subseteq V \setminus \{u\}$.

The *cost* of an agent u in network G_i has the form $c_{G_i}(u) = e_{G_i}(u) + \delta_{G_i}(u)$, where $e_{G_i}(u)$ denotes the *edge-cost* and $\delta_{G_i}(u)$ denotes the *distance-cost* of agent u in the network G_i. Each edge has cost $\alpha > 0$, which is a fixed constant, and this cost has to be paid fully by the owner, if not stated otherwise. Hence, if agent u owns k edges in the network

G_i, then $e_{G_i}(u) = \alpha k$. In the (A)SG we simply omit the edge-cost term in the cost function.

There are two variants of distance-cost functions capturing the focus on average or worst-case connection quality. In the SUM-version, we have $\delta_{G_i}(u) = \sum_{v \in V(G_i)} d_{G_i}(u,v)$, if the network G_i is connected and $\delta_{G_i}(u) = \infty$, otherwise. In the MAX-version, we have $\delta_{G_i}(u) = \max_{v \in V(G_i)} d_{G_i}(u,v)$, if G_i is connected and $\delta_{G_i}(u) = \infty$, otherwise. In both cases $d_{G_i}(u,v)$ denotes the shortest path distance between vertex u and v in the undirected graph G_i.

The move policy specifies for any state of the process, which of the unhappy agents is allowed to perform a move. From a mechanism design perspective, the move policy is a way to enforce coordination and to guide the process towards a stable state. We will focus on the *max cost policy*, where the agent having the highest cost is allowed to move and ties among such agents are broken arbitrarily. Sometimes we will assume that an adversary chooses the worst possible moving agent. Note, that the move policy only specifies who is allowed to move, not which specific move has to be performed. We do not consider such strong policies since we do not want to restrict the agents' freedom to act.

Any combination of the four game types, the two distance functions and some move policy together with an initial network completely specifies a network creation process. We will abbreviate names, e.g. by calling the Buy Game with the SUM-version of the distance-cost the SUM-BG. If not stated otherwise, edge-costs cannot be shared.

A cyclic sequence of networks $C_1, \ldots, C_j$, where network $C_{i+1 \bmod j}$ arises from network $C_{i \bmod j}$ by an improving move of one agent is called a *better response cycle*. If every move in such a cycle is a *best response move*, which is a strategy-change towards an admissible strategy which yields the largest cost decrease for the moving agent, then we call such a cycle a *best response cycle*. Clearly, a best response cycle is a better response cycle, but the existence of a better response cycle does not imply the existence of a best response cycle.

1.2 Classifying Games According to their Dynamics

Analyzing the convergence processes of games is a very rich and diverse research area. We will briefly introduce two well-known classes of finite strategic games: *games having the finite improvement property* (FIPG) [17] and *weakly acyclic games* (WAG) [20].

FIPG have the most desirable form of dynamic behavior: Starting from any initial state, every sequence of improving moves must eventually converge to an equilibrium state of the game, that is, such a sequence must have finite length. Thus, in such games distributed local search is guaranteed to succeed. It was shown by Monderer and Shapley [17] that a finite game is a FIPG if and only if there exists a *generalized ordinal potential function* Φ, which maps strategy-profiles to real numbers and has the property that if the moving agent's cost decreases, then the potential function value decreases as well. Stated in our terminology, this means that $\Phi : \mathcal{G}_n \to \mathbb{R}$, where $\mathcal{G}_n$ is the set of all networks on n nodes, and we have

$$c_{G_i}(u) - c_{G_{i+1}}(u) > 0 \Rightarrow \Phi(G_i) - \Phi(G_{i+1}) > 0,$$

if agent u is the moving agent in the network G_i. Clearly, no FIPG can admit a better response cycle. An especially nice subclass of FIPG are games that are guaranteed to converge

to a stable state in a number of steps which is polynomial in the size of the game. We call this subclass poly-FIPG.

Weakly acyclic games are a super-class of FIPG. Here it is not necessarily true that *any* sequence of improving moves must converge to an equilibrium but we have that from any initial state there exists *some* sequence of improving moves which enforces convergence. Thus, with some additional coordination distributed local search may indeed lead to stable states for such games. A subclass of WAG are games where from any initial state there exists a sequence of best response moves, which leads to an equilibrium. We call those games *weakly acyclic under best response*, BR-WAG for short. Observe, that if a game is not weakly acyclic, then there is *no* way of enforcing convergence if agents stick to playing improving moves.

The above mentioned classes of finite strategic games are related as follows:

$$\text{poly-FIPG} \subset \text{FIPG} \subset \text{BR-WAG} \subset \text{WAG}.$$

The story does not end here. Very recently, Apt and Simon [3] have classified WAG in much more detail by introducing a "scheduler", which is a moderating super-player who guides the agents towards an equilibrium.

1.3 Related Work

The original model of Network Creation Games, which we call the SUM-BG, was introduced a decade ago by Fabrikant et al. [11]. Their motivation was to understand the creation of Internet-like networks by selfish agents without central coordination. In the following years, several variants were proposed: The MAX-BG [9], the SUM-SG and the MAX-SG [2], the SUM-ASG and the MAX-ASG [16], the SUM-GBG and the MAX-GBG [14], a bounded budget version [10], an edge-restricted version [8, 4], a version with bilateral equal-split cost-sharing [6] and a version considering points in a metric space using a different distance measure [18]. All these works focus on properties of stable networks or on the complexity of computing an agent's best response. To the best of our knowledge, the dynamic behavior of most of these variants, including best response dynamics in the well-studied original model, has not yet been analyzed.

Previous work, e.g. [11, 1, 9, 15], has shown that the price of anarchy for the SUM-BG and the MAX-BG is constant for a wide range of α and in $2^{\mathcal{O}(\sqrt{\log n})}$ in general. For the SUM-(A)SG the best upper bound is in $2^{\mathcal{O}(\sqrt{\log n})}$ as well [2, 16], whereas the MAX-SG has a lower bound of $\Omega(\sqrt{n})$ [2]. Interestingly, if played on trees, then the SUM-SG and the MAX-SG have constant price of anarchy [2], whereas the SUM-ASG and the bounded budget version on trees has price of anarchy in $\Theta(\log n)$ [10, 16]. Moreover, it is easy to show that the MAX-ASG on trees has price of anarchy in $\Theta(n)$. Thus, we have the desirable property that selfish behavior leads to a relatively small deterioration in social welfare for most of the proposed versions.

In earlier work [13] we studied the game dynamics of the SUM-SG and showed that if the initial network G_0 is a tree on n nodes, then the network creation process is guaranteed to converge in $\mathcal{O}(n^3)$ steps. By employing the max cost policy, this process can be sped up significantly to $\mathcal{O}(n)$ steps, which is asymptotically optimal. For the SUM-SG on general networks we showed that there exists a best response cycle, which implies that the SUM-SG on arbitrary initial networks is not a FIPG.

Very recently, Cord-Landwehr et al. [7] studied a variant of the MAX-SG, where agents have communication interests, and showed that this variant admits a best response cycle on a tree network as initial network. Hence the restricted-interest variant of the MAX-SG is not a FIPG – even on trees.

Brandes et al. [5] were the first to observe that the SUM-BG is not a FIPG and they prove this by providing a better response cycle. Very recently, Bilò et al. [4] gave a better response cycle for the MAX-BG which implies the same statement for this version. Note, that both proofs contain agents who perform a sub-optimal move at some step in the better response cycle. Hence, these two results do not address the convergence behavior if agents play optimally.

1.4 Our Contribution

In this work, we study Network Creation Games, as proposed by Fabrikant et al. [11], and several natural variants of this model from a new perspective. Instead of analyzing properties of equilibrium states, we apply a more constructive point of view by asking if and how fast such desirable states can be found by selfish agents. For this, we turn the original model and its variants, which are originally formulated as one-shot simultaneous-move games, into more algorithmic models, where moves are performed sequentially.

For the MAX Swap Game on trees, we show that the process must converge in $\mathcal{O}(n^3)$ steps, where n is the number of agents. Furthermore, by introducing a natural way of coordination we obtain a significant speed-up to $\Theta(n \log n)$ steps, which is almost optimal. We show that these results, combined with results from our earlier work [13], give the same bounds for the Asymmetric Swap Game on trees in both the SUM- and the MAX-version.

These positive results for initial networks which are trees are contrasted by several strong negative results on general networks. We show that the MAX-SG, the SUM-ASG and the MAX-ASG on general networks are *not* guaranteed to converge if agents repeatedly perform best possible improving moves and, even worse, that *no* move policy can enforce convergence. We show that these games are not in FIPG, which implies that there cannot exist a generalized ordinal potential function which "guides" the way towards an equilibrium state. For the SUM-ASG we show the even stronger negative result that it can happen that *no* sequence of best response moves may enforce convergence, that is, the SUM-ASG is not even weakly acyclic under best response. If not all possible edges can be created, that is if we have a non-complete *host graph* [8, 4], then we show that the SUM-ASG and the MAX-ASG on non-tree networks is not weakly acyclic. Moreover, we map the boundary between convergence and non-convergence in ASGs and show the surprising result that cyclic behavior can already occur in n-vertex networks which have n edges. That is, even one non-tree edge suffices to completely change the dynamic behavior of these games. In our constructions we have that every agent owns exactly one edge, which is equivalent to the uniform-budget case introduced by Ehsani et al. [10]. In their paper [10] the authors raise the open problem of determining the convergence speed for the bounded-budget version. Thus, our results answer this open problem – even for the simplest version of these games – in the negative, since we show that no convergence guarantee exists.

We provide best response cycles for all versions of the Buy Game, which implies that these games have no convergence guarantee – even if agents have the computational resources to repeatedly compute best response strategies. To the best of our knowledge, the existence of *best* response cycles for all these versions was not known before. Furthermore, we investigate the version where bilateral consent is needed for edge-creation and where the edge-cost is shared equally among its endpoints. We show that this version exhibits a similar undesirable dynamic behavior as the unilateral version. Quite surprisingly, we can show an even stronger negative result in the SUM-version which implies the counter-intuitive statement that cost-sharing may lead to worse dynamic behavior. Our findings nicely contrast a result of Corbo and Parkes [6] who show guaranteed convergence if agents repeatedly play best response strategies against *perturbations* of the other agents' strategies. We show, that these perturbations are necessary for achieving convergence.

Finally, we present a careful empirical study of the convergence time in the ASG and in the GBG. Interestingly, our simulations show that our negative theoretical results seem to be confined to a small set of pathological instances. Even more interesting may be that our simulations show a remarkably fast convergence towards stable networks in $\mathcal{O}(n)$ steps, where n is the number of agents. This indicates that despite our negative results distributed local search may be a suitable method for selfish agents for collectively finding equilibrium networks.

2. MAX SWAP GAMES

In this section we focus on the game dynamics of the MAX-SG. Interestingly, we obtain results which are very similar to the results shown in our earlier work [13] but we need entirely different techniques to derive them. Omitted proofs can be found in the full version [12].

2.1 Dynamics on Trees

We will analyze the network creation process in the MAX-SG when the initial network is a tree. We prove that this process has the following desirable property:

THEOREM 1. *The MAX-SG on trees is guaranteed to converge in $\mathcal{O}(n^3)$ steps to a stable network. That is, the MAX-SG on trees is a poly-FIPG.*

Before proving Theorem 1, we analyze the impact of a single edge-swap. Let $T = (V, E)$ be a tree on n vertices and let agent v be unhappy in network T. Assume that agent v can decrease her cost by performing the edge-swap vu to vw, for some $u, w \in V$. This swap transforms T into the new network $T' = (V, (E \setminus \{vu\}) \cup \{vw\})$. Let $c_T(v) = \max_{x \in V(T)} d_T(v, x)$ denote agent v's cost in the network T. Let $c_{T'}(u)$ denote her respective cost in T'. Let A denote the tree of $T'' = (V, E \setminus \{vu\})$ which contains v and let B be the tree of T'' which contains u and w. It is easy to see, that we have $d_T(x, y) = d_{T'}(x, y)$, if $x, y \in V(A)$ or if $x, y \in V(B)$.

LEMMA 1. *For all $x \in V(A)$ there is no $y \in V(A)$ such that $c_T(x) = d_T(x, y)$.*

Lemma 1 directly implies the following statement:

COROLLARY 1. *For all $x \in V(A)$: $c_T(x) > c_{T'}(x)$.*

Hence, we have that agent v's improving move decreases the cost for all agents in $V(A)$. For agents in $V(B)$ this may not be true: The cost of an agent $y \in V(B)$ can increase by agent v's move. Interestingly, the next result guarantees that such an increase cannot be arbitrarily high.

LEMMA 2. *Let $x \in V(A)$, $y \in V(B)$ such that $d_{T'}(x,y) = c_{T'}(y)$. It holds that $c_T(x) > c_{T'}(y)$.*

PROOF. In tree T we have $c_T(x) = d_T(x,v) + d_T(u,z) + 1$. Furthermore, in tree T' we have $c_{T'}(y) = d_{T'}(x,v) + d_{T'}(w,y) + 1$. Since $c_T(v) > c_{T'}(v)$, we have $d_{T'}(w,y) < d_T(u,z)$, where $z \in V(B)$ is a vertex having maximum distance to v in T. Hence, this implies $c_T(x) - c_{T'}(y) = d_T(u,z) - d_T(w,y) > 0$. $\square$

Towards a generalized ordinal potential function we will need the following:

Definition 1. (Sorted Cost Vector and Center-Vertex) Let G be any network on n vertices. The *sorted cost vector* of G is $\overrightarrow{c_G} = (\gamma_G^1, \ldots, \gamma_G^n)$, where γ_G^i is the cost of the agent, who has the i-th highest cost in the network G. An agent having cost γ_G^n is called *center-vertex* of G.

LEMMA 3. *Let T be any tree on n vertices. The sorted cost vector of T induces a generalized ordinal potential function for the MAX-SG on T.*

PROOF. Let v be any agent in T, who performs an edge-swap which strictly decreases her cost and let T' denote the network after agent v's swap. We show that $c_T(v) - c_{T'}(v) > 0$ implies $\overrightarrow{c_T} >_{\text{lex}} \overrightarrow{c_{T'}}$, where $>_{\text{lex}}$ is the lexicographic order on $\mathbb{N}^n$. The existence of a generalized ordinal potential function then follows by mapping the lexicographic order on $\mathbb{N}^n$ to an isomorphic order on $\mathbb{R}$.

Let the subtrees A and B be defined as above and let $c_T(v) - c_{T'}(v) > 0$. By Lemma 1 and Lemma 2, we know that there is an agent $x \in V(A)$ such that $c_T(x) > c_{T'}(y)$, for all $y \in V(B)$. By Lemma 1 and Corollary 1, we have that $c_T(x) > c_{T'}(x)$, which implies that $\overrightarrow{c_T} >_{\text{lex}} \overrightarrow{c_{T'}}$. $\square$

In the following, a special type of paths in the network will be important.

Definition 2. (Longest Path) Let G be any connected network. Let v be any agent in G having cost $c_G(v) = k$. Any simple path in G, which starts at v and has length k is called a *longest path of agent v*.

As we will see, center-vertices and longest paths are closely related.

LEMMA 4. *Let T be any connected tree and let v^* be a center-vertex of T. Vertex v^* must lie on all longest paths of all agents in $V(T)$.*

PROOF. Let P_{xy} denote the path from vertex x to vertex y in T. We assume towards a contradiction that there are two vertices $v, w \in V(T)$, where $c_T(v) = d_T(v,w)$, and that $v^* \notin V(P_{vw})$. Let $z \in V(T)$ be the only shared vertex of the three paths $P_{vv^*}, P_{wv^*}, P_{vw}$. We have $d_T(v,z) < d_T(v,v^*) \leq c_T(v^*)$ and $d_T(w,z) < d_T(w,v^*) \leq c_T(v^*)$. We show that $c_T(z) < c_T(v^*)$, which is a contradiction to v^* being a center-vertex in T.

Assume that there is a vertex $u \in V(T)$ with $d_T(u,z) \geq c_T(v^*)$. It follows that $V(P_{vz}) \cap V(P_{zu}) = \{z\}$, since otherwise $d_T(v^*, u) = d_T(v^*, z) + d_T(z,u) > c_T(v^*)$. But now, since $d_T(z,w) < c_T(v^*) \leq d_T(z,u)$, we have $d_T(v,u) > c_T(v)$, which clearly is a contradiction. Hence, we have $d_T(z,u) < c_T(v^*)$, for all $u \in V(T)$, which implies that $c_T(z) < c_T(v^*)$. $\square$

Lemma 4, leads to the following observation.

OBSERVATION 1. *Let G be any connected network on n nodes and let $\overrightarrow{c_G} = (\gamma_G^1, \ldots, \gamma_G^n)$ be its sorted cost vector. We have $\gamma_G^1 = \gamma_G^2$ and $\gamma_G^n = \left\lceil \frac{\gamma_G^1}{2} \right\rceil$.*

Now we are ready to provide the key property which will help us upper bound the convergence time.

LEMMA 5. *Let $T = (V,E)$ be a connected tree on n vertices having diameter $D \geq 4$. After at most $\frac{nD - D^2}{2}$ moves of the MAX-SG on T one agent must perform a move which decreases the diameter.*

PROOF. Let $v, w \in V$ such that $d_T(v,w) = D \geq 4$ and let P_{vw} be the path from v to w in T. Clearly, if no agent in $V(P_{vw})$ makes an improving move, then the diameter of the network does not change. On the other hand, if the path P_{vw} is the unique path in T having length D, then any improving move of an agent in $V(P_{vw})$ must decrease the diameter by at least 1. The network creation process starts from a connected tree having diameter $D \geq 4$ and, by Lemma 3, must converge to a stable tree in a finite number of steps. Moreover, Lemma 3 guarantees that the diameter of the network cannot increase in any step of the process. It was shown by Alon et al. [2] that any stable tree has diameter at most 3. Thus, after a finite number of steps the diameter of the network must strictly decrease, that is, on all paths of length D some agent must have performed an improving move which reduced the length of the respective path. We fix the path P_{vw} to be the path of length D in the network which survives longest in this process.

It follows, that there are $|V \setminus V(P_{vw})| = n - (D+1)$ agents which can perform improving moves without decreasing the diameter. We know from Observation 1 and Lemma 4 that each one of those $n - (D+1)$ agents can decrease her cost to at most $\left\lceil \frac{D}{2} \right\rceil + 1$ and has to decrease her cost by at least 1 for each edge-swap. We show that an edge-swap of such an agent does not increase the cost of any other agent and use the minimum possible cost decrease per step to conclude the desired bound.

Let $u \in V(T) \setminus V(P_{vw})$ be an agent who decreases her cost by swapping the edge ux to uy and let T' be the tree after this edge-swap. Let $a, b \in V(T)$ be arbitrary agents. Clearly, if $\{u,y\} \not\subseteq V(P_{ab})$ in T', then $d_T(a,b) = d_{T'}(a,b)$. Let A be the tree of $T'' = (V, E \setminus \{uy\})$ which contains u and let B be the tree of T'' which contains y. W.l.o.g. let $a \in V(A)$ and $b \in V(B)$. By Corollary 1, we have $c_T(z) > c_{T'}(z)$ for all $z \in V(A)$ and it follows that $V(A) \cap V(P_{vw}) = \emptyset$. Hence, it remains to analyze the change in cost of all agents in $V(B)$.

If no vertex on the path P_{ab} is a center-vertex in T', then, by Lemma 4, we have that $d_{T'}(a,b) < c_{T'}(b)$. It follows that every longest path of agent b in T' lies entirely in subtree B which implies that $c_{T'}(b) \leq c_T(b)$.

If there is a center-vertex of T' on the path P_{ab} in T', then let v^* be the last such vertex on this path. We have assumed that the diameters of T' and T are equal, which implies that P_{vw} is a longest path of agent v in T'. Since, by Lemma 4, any center-vertex of T' must lie on all longest paths, it follows that v^* is on the path P_{vw} and we have $v^* \in V(B)$. W.l.o.g. let $d_{T'}(v,b) \geq d_{T'}(w,b)$. We have $d_{T'}(a,b) = d_{T'}(a,v^*) + d_{T'}(v^*,b) \leq d_{T'}(v,v^*) + d_{T'}(v^*,b)$. Hence, we have $d_{T'}(a,b) \leq c_{T'}(b)$. Since the path P_{bv} is in subtree B, we have $c_{T'}(b) \leq c_T(b)$.

Now we can easily conclude the upper bound on the number of moves which do not decrease the diameter of T. Each of the $n - (D+1)$ agents with cost at most D may decrease their cost to $\lceil \frac{D}{2} \rceil + 1$. If we assume a decrease of 1 per step, then this yields the following bound:

$$(n - (D+1)) \left(D - \left(\left\lceil \frac{D}{2} \right\rceil + 1 \right) \right) < \frac{nD - D^2}{2}. \quad \square$$

PROOF OF THEOREM 1. By Lemma 3, we know there exists a generalized ordinal potential function for the MAX-SG on trees. Hence, we know that this game is a FIPG and we are left to bound the maximum number of improving moves needed for convergence. It was already shown by Alon et al. [2], that the only stable trees of the MAX-SG on trees are stars or double-stars. Hence, the process must stop at the latest when diameter 2 is reached.

Let $N_n(T)$ denote the maximum number of moves needed for convergence in the MAX-SG on the n-vertex tree T. Let $D(T)$ be the diameter of T. Let $D_{i,n}$ denote the maximum number of steps needed to decrease the diameter of any n-vertex tree having diameter i by at least 1. Hence, we have

$$N_n(T) \leq \sum_{i=3}^{D(T)} D_{i,n} \leq \sum_{i=3}^{n-1} D_{i,n},$$

since the maximum diameter of a n-vertex tree is $n - 1$. By applying Lemma 5 and adding the steps which actually decrease the diameter, this yields

$$N_n(T) \leq \sum_{i=3}^{n-1} D_{i,n} < \sum_{i=3}^{n-1} \left(\frac{ni - i^2}{2} + 1 \right)$$

$$< n + \frac{n}{2} \left(\sum_{i=1}^{n} i \right) - \frac{1}{2} \left(\sum_{i=1}^{n} i^2 \right) \in \mathcal{O}(n^3). \quad \square$$

The following result shows that we can speed up the convergence time by employing a very natural move policy. The speed-up is close to optimal, since it is easy to see that there are instances in which $\Omega(n)$ steps are necessary.

THEOREM 2. *The MAX-SG on trees with the max cost policy converges in $\Theta(n \log n)$ moves.*

We prove Theorem 2, by proving the lower and the upper bound separately, starting with the former. Since we analyze the max cost policy, we need two additional observations.

OBSERVATION 2. *An agent having maximum cost in a tree T must be a leaf of T.*

OBSERVATION 3. *Let u be an unhappy agent in the tree $T = (V, E)$ and let u be a leaf of T and let v be u's unique neighbor. Let B be the tree of $T' = (V, E \setminus \{uv\})$ which contains v. The edge-swap uv to uw, for some $w \in V(B)$ is a best possible move for agent u if w is a center-vertex of B.*

LEMMA 6. *There is a tree T on n vertices where the MAX-SG on T with the max cost policy needs $\Omega(n \log n)$ moves for convergence.*

PROOF. We will consider the path on n-vertices $P_n = v_1 v_2 \ldots v_n$ of length $n - 1$. We apply the max cost policy and for breaking ties we will always choose the vertex having the smallest index among all vertices having maximum cost. If a maximum cost vertex has more than one best response move,

then we choose the edge-swap towards the new neighbor having the smaller index. With these assumptions and with Observation 2 and Observation 3, we have that the center-vertex having the smallest index will "shift" towards a higher index, from $v_{\lceil n/2 \rceil}$ to v_{n-2}. Finally, agent v_n is the unique agent having maximum cost and her move transforms the tree to a star.

We start by analyzing the change in costs of agent v_1. Clearly, $c_0 = c_{P_n}(v_1) = n - 1$. By Observation 3, we know that v_1's best swap connects to the minimum index center-vertex of the tree without vertex v_1. Hence after the best move of v_1 this agent has cost $c_1 = \lceil \frac{c_0 - 1}{2} \rceil + 1 > \frac{c_0}{2}$. When v_1 is chosen to move again, her cost can possibly decrease to $\lceil \frac{c_1 - 1}{2} \rceil + 1 > \frac{c_0}{4}$. After the i-th move of v_1 her cost is at least $\lceil \frac{c_{i-1} - 1}{2} \rceil + 1 > \frac{c_0}{2^i}$. Thus, the max cost policy allows agent v_1 to move at least $\log \frac{c_0}{3}$ times until she is connected to vertex v_{n-2}, the center of the final star, where she has cost 3.

The above implies, that the number of moves of every agent allowed by the max cost policy only depends on the cost of that agent when she first becomes a maximum cost agent. Moreover, since all moving agents are leaves, no move of an agent increases the cost of any other agent. By construction, the cost of every moving agent is determined by her distance towards vertex v_n. Since agent v_n does not move until in the last step of the process, we have that a move of agent v_i does not change the cost of any other agent $v_j \neq v_n$ who moves after v_i. It follows, that we can simply add up the respective lower bounds on the number of moves of all players, depending on the cost when they first become maximum cost agents. It is easy to see, that agent v_i becomes a maximum cost agent, when the maximum cost is $n - i$. Let $M(P_n)$ denote the number of moves of the MAX-SG on P_n with the max cost policy and the above tie-breaking rules. This yields

$$M(P_n) > \sum_{c_0 = n-1}^{4} \log \frac{c_0}{3} \in \Omega(n \log n). \quad \square$$

LEMMA 7. *The MAX-SG on a n-vertex tree T with the max cost policy needs $\mathcal{O}(n \log n)$ moves to converge to a stable tree.*

PROOF. Consider any tree T on n vertices. By Observation 2, we know that only leaf-agents are allowed to move by the max cost policy, which implies that no move of any agent increases the cost of any other agent. Observation 3 guarantees that the best possible move of a leaf-agent u having maximum cost c decreases agent u's cost to at most $\lceil \frac{c}{2} \rceil + 1$. Hence, after $\mathcal{O}(\log n)$ moves of agent u her cost must be at most 3. If the tree converges to a star, then agent u may move one more time. If we sum up over all n agents, then we have that after $\mathcal{O}(n \log n)$ moves the tree must be stable. $\square$

2.2 Dynamics on General Networks

In this section we show that allowing cycles in the initial network completely changes the dynamic behavior of the MAX-SG.

THEOREM 3. *The MAX-SG on general networks admits best response cycles. Moreover, no move policy can enforce convergence. The first result holds even if agents are allowed to perform multi-swaps.*

3. ASYMMETRIC SWAP GAMES

In this section we consider the Sum-ASG and the Max-ASG. Note, that now we assume that each edge has an owner and only this owner is allowed to swap the edge. We show that we can directly transfer the results from above and from [13] to the asymmetric version if the initial network is a tree. On general networks we show even stronger negative results. Omitted proofs can be found in the full version [12].

Observe, that the instance used in the proof of Theorem 3 and the corresponding instance in [13] show that best response cycles in the Swap Game are not necessarily best response cycles in the Asymmetric Swap Game. We will show the rather counter-intuitive result that this holds true for the other direction as well.

3.1 Dynamics in ASGs on Trees

The results in this section follow from the respective theorems in [13] and from the results in Section 2.1 and are therefore stated as corollaries.

COROLLARY 2. *The* Sum-*ASG and the* Max-*ASG on n-vertex trees are both a poly-FIPG and both must converge to a stable tree in $\mathcal{O}(n^3)$ steps.*

COROLLARY 3. *Using the max cost policy and assuming a n-vertex tree as initial network, we have that*

- *the* Sum-*ASG converges in $\max\{0, n-3\}$ steps, if n is even and in $\max\{0, n + \lceil n/2 \rceil - 5\}$ steps, if n is odd. Moreover, both bounds are tight and asymptotically optimal.*

- *the* Max-*ASG converges in $\Theta(n \log n)$ steps.*

3.2 Dynamics in ASGs on General Graphs

If we move from trees to general initial networks, we get a very strong negative result for the Sum-ASG: There is no hope to enforce convergence if agents stick to playing best responses even if multi-swaps are allowed.

THEOREM 4. *The* Sum-*ASG on general networks is not weakly acyclic under best response. Moreover, this result holds true even if agents can swap multiple edges in one step.*

PROOF. We give a network which induces a best response cycle. Additionally, we show that in each step of this cycle exactly one agent can decrease her cost by swapping an edge and that the best possible swap for this agent is unique in every step. Furthermore, we show that the moving agent cannot outperform the best possible single-swap by a multi-swap. This implies that if agents stick to best response moves then *no* best response dynamic can enforce convergence to a stable network and allowing multi-swaps does not alter this result.

Fig. 1 shows the best response cycle consisting of the networks G_1, G_2, G_3 and G_4. We begin with showing that in $G_1, \ldots, G_4$ all agents, except agent b and agent f, cannot perform an improving strategy change even if they are allowed to swap multiple edges in one step.

In $G_1, \ldots, G_4$ all leaf-agents do not own any edges and the agents c and e cannot swap an edge since otherwise the network becomes disconnected. For the same reason, agent d cannot move the edge towards d_1. Agent d owns three other edges, but they are optimally placed since they are connected to the vertices having the most leaf-neighbors.

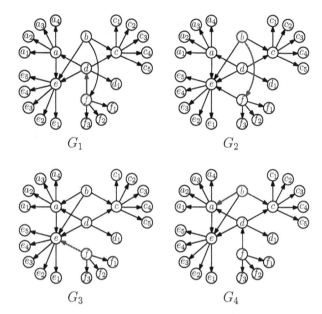

Figure 1: The steps of a best response cycle for the Sum-ASG on general networks. Edge directions indicate edge-ownership. All edges are two-way.

It follows, that agent d cannot decrease her cost by swapping one edge or by performing a multi-swap. Note, that this holds true for all networks $G_1, \ldots, G_4$, although the networks change slightly. Agent a cannot move her edges towards a_i, for $1 \leq i \leq 4$. On the other hand, it is easy to see that agent a's edge towards vertex e cannot be swapped to obtain a strict cost decrease since the most promising choice, which is vertex c, yields the same cost in G_1 and G_4 and even higher cost in G_2 and G_3. Trivially, no multi-swap is possible for agent a.

Now, we consider agent b and agent f. First of all, observe that in $G_1, \ldots, G_4$ agent f owns exactly one edge which is not a bridge. Thus, agent f cannot perform a multi-swap in any step of the best response cycle. Agent b, although owning three edges, is in a similar situation: Her edges to vertex c and e can be considered as fixed, since swapping one or both of them does not yield a cost decrease in $G_1, \ldots, G_4$. Hence, agent b and agent f each have one "free" edge to operate with. In G_1 agent b's edge towards f is placed optimally, since swapping towards a or d does not yield a cost decrease. In G_3, agents b's edge towards a is optimal, since swapping towards d or f does not decrease agent b's cost. Analogously, agent f's edge towards e in G_2 and her edge towards d in G_4 are optimally placed.

Last, but not least, we describe the best response cycle: In G_1 agent f can improve and her unique best possible edge-swap in G_1 is the swap from d to e, yielding a cost decrease of 4. In G_2 agent b has the swap from f to a as unique best improvement which yields a cost decrease of 1. In G_3 have agent f being unhappy with her strategy and the unique best swap is the one from e to d yielding an improvement of 1. In G_4 it is agent b's turn again and her unique best swap is from a to f which decreases her cost by 3. After agent b's swap in G_4 we arrive again at network G_1, hence $G_1, \ldots, G_4$ is a best response cycle where in each step exactly one agent has a single-swap as unique best possible improvement. □

Note, that the best response cycle presented in the proof of Theorem 4 is not a best response cycle in the Sum-SG. The swap fb to fe of agent f in G_1 yields a strictly larger cost decrease than her swap fd to fe.

Compared to Theorem 4, we show a slightly weaker negative result for the max-version.

THEOREM 5. *The* MAX-*ASG on general networks admits best response cycles. Moreover, no move policy can enforce convergence.*

If played on a non-complete host-graph, then we get the worst possible dynamic behavior.

COROLLARY 4. *The* SUM-*ASG and the* MAX-*ASG on a non-complete host graph are not weakly acyclic.*

3.3 The Boundary between Convergence and Non-Convergence

In this section we explore the boundary between guaranteed convergence and cyclic behavior. Quite surprisingly, we can draw a sharp boundary by showing that the undesired cyclic behavior can already occur in n-vertex networks having exactly n edges. Thus, one non-tree edge suffices to radically change the dynamic behavior of Asymmetric Swap Games. Our constructions are such that each agent owns exactly one edge, which corresponds to the uniform unit budget case, recently introduced by Ehsani et al. [10]. Hence, even if the networks are build by identical agents having a budget the cyclic behavior may arise. This answers the open problem raised by Ehsani et al. [10] in the negative.

THEOREM 6. *The* SUM-*ASG and the* MAX-*ASG admit best response cycles on a network where every agent owns exactly one edge.*

PROOF OF THEOREM 6, SUM-VERSION. The network inducing a best response cycle and the steps of the cycle are shown in Fig. 2. Let n_k denote the number of vertices having the form k_j, for some index j.

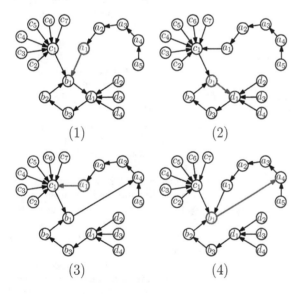

(1)   (2)

(3)   (4)

Figure 2: The steps of a best response cycle for the Sum-ASG where each agent owns exactly one edge.

In the first step, depicted in Fig. 2 (1), agent a_1 has only one improving move, which is the swap from b_1 to c_1. This swap reduces agent a_1's cost by 1, since $n_c = n_b + n_d + 1$. After

this move, shown in Fig. 2 (2), agent b_1 is no longer happy with her edge towards d_1, since by swapping towards a_4 she can decrease her cost by 2. This is a best possible move for agent b_1 (note, that a swap towards a_3 yields the same cost decrease). But now, in the network shown in Fig. 2 (3), by swapping back towards vertex b_1, agent a_1 can additionally decrease her distances to vertices a_4 and a_5 by 1. This yields that agent a_1's swap from c_1 to b_1 decreases her cost by 1. This is true, since all distances to c_j vertices increase by 1 but all distances to b_i and d_l vertices and to a_4 and a_5 decrease by 1 and since we have $n_c = n_b + n_d + 1$. Note, that this swap is agent a_1's unique improving move. By construction, we have that after agent a_1 has swapped back towards b_1, depicted in Fig. 2 (4), agent b_1's edge towards a_4 only yields a distance decrease of 7. Hence, by swapping back towards d_1, agent b_1 decreases her cost by 1, since her sum of distances to the d_j vertices decreases by 8. This swap is the unique improving move of agent b_1 in this stage. Now the best response cycle starts over again, with agent a_1 moving from b_1 to c_1. □

3.4 Empirical Study of the Bounded-Budget Version

We have conducted extensive simulations of the convergence behavior and the obtained results provide a sharp contrast to our mostly negative theoretical results for both versions of the ASG. Our experiments show for the bounded-budget version a surprisingly fast convergence in at most $5n$ steps under the max cost policy or by choosing the moving agents uniformly at random. Despite millions of trials we have not found any best response cycle in our experiments. This indicates that our negative results may be only very rare pathological examples. We refer to the full version [12] for a detailed description of our simulations and results.

4. (GREEDY) BUY GAMES

We focus on the dynamic behavior of the Buy Game and the Greedy Buy Game. Remember, that we assume, that each edge can be created for the cost of $\alpha > 0$.

4.1 Convergence Results

We show that best response cycles exist, even if arbitrary strategy-changes are allowed. However, on the positive side, we were not able to construct best response cycles where only one agent is unhappy in every step. Hence, the right move policy may have a substantial impact in (Greedy) Buy Games. In contrast to this, we rule out this glimmer of hope if played on a non-complete host-graph.

THEOREM 7. *The* SUM-*(G)BG and the* MAX-*(G)BG admit best response cycles.*

We sketch the proof by providing the best response cycle for the SUM-(G)BG in Fig. 3 and for the MAX-(G)BG in Fig. 4. See the full version [12] for the complete proof.

If we restrict the set of edges which can be build, then we get the worst possible dynamic behavior. In this case there is no hope for convergence if agents are only willing to perform improving moves.

COROLLARY 5. *The* SUM-*(G)BG and the* MAX-*(G)BG on general host graphs is not weakly acyclic.*

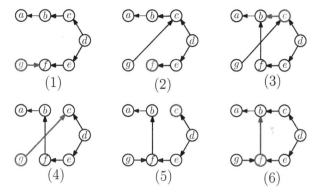

(1) (2) (3)

(4) (5) (6)

Figure 3: The steps of a best response cycle for the Sum-(G)BG for $7 < \alpha < 8$.

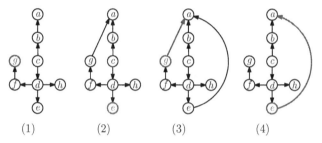

(1) (2) (3) (4)

Figure 4: The steps of a best response cycle for the Max-(G)BG for $1 < \alpha < 2$.

4.2 Empirical Study of Greedy Buy Games

We give empirical results for the convergence time for both versions of the GBG. Our focus is on the GBG, since a best response for both versions of the GBG can be computed in polynomial time [14], whereas this problem is well-known [11, 15] to be NP-hard for the BG. Due to space constraints we can only sketch the setup and give a glimpse of the results. See the full version [12] for a detailed discussion and additional plots.

4.2.1 Experimental Setup

One run of our simulations consists of the generation of a random initial network and then the max cost or the random policy is employed in the GBG until the process converges to a stable network. We measure the number of steps needed for this convergence to happen and take the maximum over 5000 such runs for each configuration.

The initial networks are generated as follows: Starting from an empty graph on n vertices we first generate a random spanning tree to enforce connectedness of our networks. Then we randomly insert edges until the desired number of edges is present. Note, that we do not allow multi-edges. The ownership of every edge is chosen uniformly at random among the endpoints.

We have considered networks having n agents, where n ranges between 10 and 100. In order to investigate the impact of the density of the initial network on the convergence time, we fix the number of edges in the initial network to be n, $2n$ and $4n$, respectively. The impact of the edge-cost parameter α is investigated by setting α to $n/10$, $n/4$, $n/2$ and n, respectively. Demaine et al. [9] argue that this is the most interesting range for α, since implies that the average distance is roughly on par with the creation cost of an edge.

4.2.2 Experimental Results

We have observed a remarkably small number of steps needed for convergence in these games, which indicates that distributed local search is a practical method for selfishly creating stable networks. For the SUM-GBG no run took longer than $7n$ steps to converge, whereas for the MAX-version we always observed less than $8n$ steps until convergence, see Fig. 5. It can be seen that the convergence time grows roughly linear in n for all configurations, which implies that these processes scale very well.

The number of edges in the initial network has an impact on the convergence time: All curves for $m = 4n$ are well above the respective curves for $m = n$. The reason for this may be the relatively high value for α compared to the diameter of the resulting networks. We have not found any stable network having a diameter larger than 4.

The choice of α influences the convergence time in the SUM-version but not in the MAX-version. In the former we see that a smaller α generally yields a higher convergence time. In the latter, there may be no influence since the relatively high values of α yield that the edge-cost dominates the distance-cost for most of the agents.

Moreover, as in the simulations for the ASG, despite several millions of trials we did not encounter a cyclic instance. This indicates that such instances are rather pathological and may never show up in practice.

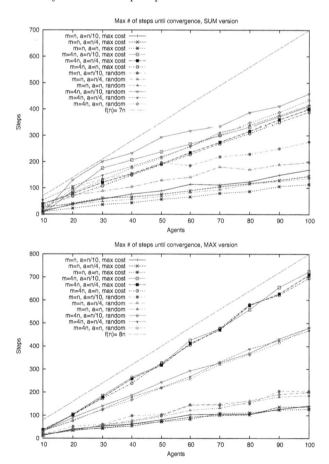

Figure 5: Experimental results for both versions of the GBG. Each point is the maximum over the steps needed for convergence of 5000 trials with random initial networks having m edges and $\alpha = a$.

5. BILATERAL BUY GAMES WITH COST-SHARING

We consider "bilateral network formation", as introduced by Corbo and Parkes [6], which we call the *bilateral equal-split BG*. This version explicitly models that bilateral consent is needed in order to create an edge, which is a realistic assumption in some settings. The cost of an edge is split equally among its endpoints and edges are build only if *both* incident agents are willing to pay half of the edge-price. This model implicitly assumes coordination among coalitions of size two and the corresponding solution concept is therefore the pairwise Nash equilibrium, which can be understood as the minimal coalitional refinement of the pure Nash equilibrium. The authors of [6] show that this solution concept is equivalent to Meyerson's proper equilibrium [19], which implies guaranteed convergence if the agents repeatedly play best response strategies against *perturbations* of the other players' strategies, where costly mistakes are made with less probability. We show in this section that these perturbations are necessary for achieving convergence by proving that the bilateral equal-split BG is not weakly acyclic in the Sum-version and that it admits best response cycles in the Max-version. Interestingly, the first result is stronger than the result for the Sum-(G)BG, which yields the counter-intuitive observation, that sharing the cost of edges can lead to worse dynamic behavior.

THEOREM 8. *The* Sum *bilateral equal-split Buy Game is not weakly acyclic.*

For the Max-version, we can show a slightly weaker result.

THEOREM 9. *The* Max *bilateral equal-split Buy Game admits best response cycles.*

6. REFERENCES

[1] S. Albers, S. Eilts, E. Even-Dar, Y. Mansour, and L. Roditty. On nash equilibria for a network creation game. In *Proceedings of the seventeenth annual ACM-SIAM Symposium on Discrete Algorithms*, SODA '06, pages 89–98, New York, NY, USA, 2006. ACM.

[2] N. Alon, E. D. Demaine, M. Hajiaghayi, and T. Leighton. Basic network creation games. In *SPAA '10: Proceedings of the 22nd ACM Symposium on Parallelism in Algorithms and Architectures*, pages 106–113, New York, NY, USA, 2010. ACM.

[3] K. Apt and S. Simon. A classification of weakly acyclic games. In M. Serna, editor, *Algorithmic Game Theory*, volume 7615 of *Lecture Notes in Computer Science*, pages 1–12. Springer Berlin / Heidelberg, 2012.

[4] D. Bilò, L. Guàlâ, S. Leucci, and G. Proietti. The max-distance network creation game on general host graphs. In P. Goldberg, editor, *Internet and Network Economics*, Lecture Notes in Computer Science, pages 392–405. Springer Berlin Heidelberg, 2012.

[5] U. Brandes, M. Hoefer, and B. Nick. Network creation games with disconnected equilibria. In C. Papadimitriou and S. Zhang, editors, *Internet and Network Economics*, volume 5385 of *Lecture Notes in Computer Science*, pages 394–401. Springer Berlin Heidelberg, 2008.

[6] J. Corbo and D. Parkes. The price of selfish behavior in bilateral network formation. In *Proceedings of the twenty-fourth annual ACM symposium on Principles of distributed computing*, PODC '05, pages 99–107, New York, NY, USA, 2005. ACM.

[7] A. Cord-Landwehr, M. Hüllmann, P. Kling, and A. Setzer. Basic network creation games with communication interests. In M. Serna, editor, *Algorithmic Game Theory*, volume 7615 of *Lecture Notes in Computer Science*, pages 72–83. Springer Berlin / Heidelberg, 2012.

[8] E. D. Demaine, M. T. Hajiaghayi, H. Mahini, and M. Zadimoghaddam. The price of anarchy in cooperative network creation games. *SIGecom Exch.*, 8(2):2:1–2:20, Dec. 2009.

[9] E. D. Demaine, M. T. Hajiaghayi, H. Mahini, and M. Zadimoghaddam. The price of anarchy in network creation games. *ACM Trans. on Algorithms*, 8(2):13, 2012.

[10] S. Ehsani, M. Fazli, A. Mehrabian, S. S. Sadeghabad, M. Safari, M. Saghafian, and S. ShokatFadaee. On a bounded budget network creation game. In *SPAA*, pages 207–214, 2011.

[11] A. Fabrikant, A. Luthra, E. Maneva, C. H. Papadimitriou, and S. Shenker. On a network creation game. In *Proceedings of the twenty-second annual Symposium on Principles of Distributed Computing*, PODC '03, pages 347–351, New York, NY, USA, 2003. ACM.

[12] B. Kawald and P. Lenzner. On dynamics in selfish network creation. *CoRR*, abs/1212.4797, 2012.

[13] P. Lenzner. On dynamics in basic network creation games. In G. Persiano, editor, *Algorithmic Game Theory*, volume 6982 of *Lecture Notes in Computer Science*, pages 254–265. Springer Berlin / Heidelberg, 2011.

[14] P. Lenzner. Greedy selfish network creation. In P. Goldberg, editor, *Internet and Network Economics*, Lecture Notes in Computer Science, pages 142–155. Springer Berlin Heidelberg, 2012.

[15] M. Mihalák and J. C. Schlegel. The price of anarchy in network creation games is (mostly) constant. In *Proceedings of the Third international conference on Algorithmic Game Theory*, SAGT'10, pages 276–287, Berlin, Heidelberg, 2010. Springer-Verlag.

[16] M. Mihalák and J. C. Schlegel. Asymmetric swap-equilibrium: A unifying equilibrium concept for network creation games. In B. Rovan, V. Sassone, and P. Widmayer, editors, *Mathematical Foundations of Computer Science 2012*, volume 7464 of *LNCS*, pages 693–704. Springer Berlin / Heidelberg, 2012.

[17] D. Monderer and L. S. Shapley. Potential games. *Games and Economic Behavior*, 14(1):124 – 143, 1996.

[18] T. Moscibroda, S. Schmid, and R. Wattenhofer. On the topologies formed by selfish peers. In *Proceedings of the twenty-fifth annual ACM symposium on Principles of distributed computing*, PODC '06, pages 133–142, New York, NY, USA, 2006. ACM.

[19] R. Myerson. *Game theory: analysis of conflict*. Harvard University Press, 1997.

[20] H. P. Young. The evolution of conventions. *Econometrica*, 61(1):pp. 57–84, 1993.

Brief Announcement: Truly Parallel Burrows-Wheeler Compression and Decompression * †

James A. Edwards
University of Maryland
College Park, Maryland
jedward5@umd.edu

Uzi Vishkin
University of Maryland
College Park, Maryland
vishkin@umiacs.umd.edu

ABSTRACT

We present novel work-optimal PRAM algorithms for Burrows-Wheeler (BW) compression and decompression of strings over a constant alphabet. For a string of length n, the depth of the compression algorithm is $O(\log^2 n)$, and the depth of the corresponding decompression algorithm is $O(\log n)$. These appear to be the first polylogarithmic-time work-optimal parallel algorithms for any standard lossless compression scheme.

The algorithms for the individual stages of compression and decompression may also be of independent interest: 1. a novel $O(\log n)$-time, $O(n)$-work PRAM algorithm for Huffman decoding; 2. original insights into the stages of the BW compression and decompression problems, bringing out parallelism that was not readily apparent. We then mapped such parallelism in interesting ways to elementary parallel routines that have $O(\log n)$-time, $O(n)$-work solutions, such as: (i) prefix-sums problems with an appropriately-defined associative binary operator for several stages, and (ii) list ranking for the final stage of decompression (inverse block-sorting transform).

Companion work reports empirical speedups of up to 25x for compression and up to 13x for decompression. This reflects a speedup of 70x over recent work on BW compression on GPUs.

Categories and Subject Descriptors

D.1.3 [**Programming Techniques**]: Concurrent Programming—Parallel programming

Keywords

parallel; PRAM; Burrows-Wheeler; lossless compression

---

*Supported by NSF grants CCF-0811504 and CNS1161857

†For the missing details in this brief announcement, see the technical report [4].

1. INTRODUCTION

In [1], Burrows and Wheeler describe their eponymous lossless compression algorithm and corresponding decompression algorithm. The *Burrows-Wheeler (BW) Compression problem* is to compute the lossless compression function defined by the algorithm of [1], and the *BW Decompression problem* is to compute its inverse. The algorithms of [1] solve the BW Compression problem in $O(n \log^2 n)$ serial time and the BW Decompression problem in $O(n)$ serial time. Later work reduced a critical step of the compression algorithm to the problem of computing the suffix array of S, for which linear-time algorithms are known, so both problems can now be solved in $O(n)$ serial time.

In passing, we note the common practical compromise of partitioning the input string into uniformly-sized blocks, using a serial algorithm separately for the BW Compression problem on each block. Such independent compression of the blocks trades off lower compression for some parallelism. However, it does not solve the BW Compression problem for the original input and thus is not a parallel algorithm for solving it. It is worth noting that our parallel-algorithmic approach can be combined with the foregoing block-based approach, since they are orthogonal.

1.1 Contributions

The primary contributions of this paper are an $O(\log^2 n)$-time, $O(n)$-work PRAM algorithm for solving the BW Compression problem and a $O(\log n)$-time, $O(n)$-work PRAM algorithm for solving the BW Decompression problem. These algorithms appear to be the first polylogarithmic-time work-optimal parallel algorithms for any standard lossless compression scheme. Also, the algorithms for the individual stages of compression and decompression may be of independent interest. We present a novel $O(\log n)$-time, $O(n)$-work PRAM algorithm for Huffman decoding (Section 3.2.1).

This paper also provides original insights into the BW compression and decompression problems. The original serial algorithms for these problems were presented in such a way that their potential parallelism was not readily apparent. Here, we reexamine them in a way that allows them to be mapped to elementary parallel routines. Of particular interest are insights on properly-defined associative binary operators that allow most of the compression and decompression stages to be cast as prefix-sums problems, as seen in the following sections:
- MTF encoding (Section 3.1.2)
- Huffman decoding (Section 3.2.1)
- MTF decoding (Section 3.2.2)

The prefix-sums problem has a known $O(\log n)$-time, $O(n)$-work solution.

1.2 Related Work

A commonly-used, serial implementation of the block-based approach noted above is bzip2 [14]; the algorithm it applies to each block is based on the original BW compression algorithm of [1]. There are also variants of bzip2 [7, 10] that compress multiple blocks simultaneously. However, these variants do not achieve speedup on single blocks. Also, breaking into blocks limits compression.

The survey paper [6] articulates some of the issues involved in parallelizing BW for a GPU; decompression is not discussed. The author gives an outline of an approach for making some parts of the algorithm parallel and claims that the remaining parts would not work well on GPUs due to exhibiting poor locality.

[12] reports such parallelization, and indeed was unable to demonstrate a speedup for compression using the GPU, instead obtaining a slowdown of 2.78x. Parallelization of decompression was left as future work, and no speedups or slowdowns are reported. Furthermore, no asymptotic complexity analysis is given, and our own analysis shows their algorithm to be non-work-optimal. To their credit, they appear to be the first to formulate MTF encoding (Section 3.1.2) in terms of a binary associative operator. However, two challenges, (i) work-optimal parallelization of BW and (ii) feasibility of speedups on buildable hardware, remained unmet. Our empirical results reflect a speedup of 70x over [12].

In fact, the companion paper [5] reports up to 25x speedups for compression and up to 13x speedups for decompression. These results were obtained using the Extensible Multi-threaded (XMT) architecture developed at the University of Maryland to provide good performance on algorithms with fine-grained, irregular parallelism such as the one described herein.

A parallel algorithm for Huffman decoding is given in [9]. However, the algorithm is not analyzed therein as a PRAM algorithm, and its worst case run time is $O(n)$. Our PRAM algorithm for Huffman decoding runs in $O(\log n)$ time.

2. PRELIMINARIES: SERIAL ALGORITHM

In their original paper, Burrows and Wheeler [1] describe a lossless data compression algorithm consisting of three stages in the following order: a reversible block-sorting transform (BST)[1], move-to-front (MTF) encoding, and Huffman coding. The corresponding decompression algorithm performs the inverses of these stages in reverse order: Huffman decoding, MTF decoding and inverse BST (IBST).

Given a string S, the BST stage computes S^{BST}, an invertible permutation of S; as explained in [1], repeated occurrences of a character in S tend to appear near one another in S^{BST}. The MTF stage assigns an integer to each character of S based on the number of distinct characters between the character and its prior occurrence in S, yielding S^{MTF}. Finally, Huffman coding assigns bit strings to integers such that more frequent integers have shorter bit strings, yielding the final output S^{BW}.

---

[1]This transform is also known as the Burrows-Wheeler Transform (BWT). We refrain from using this name to avoid confusion with the similarly-named Burrows-Wheeler compression algorithm which employs it as a stage.

Given an input string of length n, their original decompression algorithm runs in $O(n)$ serial time, as do all stages of their compression algorithm except the (forward) BST, which requires $O(n \log^2 n)$ serial time [15]. More recently, linear-time serial algorithms [8, 11] have been developed to compute suffix arrays, and the problem of finding the BST of a string can be reduced to that of computing its suffix array, so BW compression and decompression can be performed in $O(n)$ serial time.

3. NEW CONTRIBUTION: PARALLEL ALGORITHM

The parallel BW compression and decompression algorithms follow the same sequence of stages as the foregoing serial algorithms, but the sequential algorithm of each stage is replaced by an equivalent PRAM algorithm.

3.1 Compression

As in the serial algorithm, the input is a string S of length n over an alphabet Σ, where $|\Sigma|$ is constant with respect to n. The overall PRAM compression algorithm consists of the following three steps.

3.1.1 Block-Sorting Transform (BST)

The BST of a string S of length n can be computed using its suffix array. The suffix array can be derived from a depth-first search (DFS) traversal of the suffix tree of S (see Figure 1). The suffix tree of S can be computed in $O(\log^2 n)$ time and $O(n)$ work using the algorithm of [13]. The order that leaves are visited in a DFS traversal of the suffix tree can be computed using the Euler tour technique [16] within the same complexity bounds yielding the suffix array of S. Given the suffix array SA of S, we derive S^{BST} from S in $O(1)$ time and $O(n)$ work as follows:

$$S^{BST}[i] = S[(SA[i] - 1)_{\bmod n}], 0 \leq i < n$$

Overall, computing the BST takes $O(\log^2 n)$ time using $O(n)$ work. This is the only stage whose time complexity is not upper bounded by $O(\log n)$.

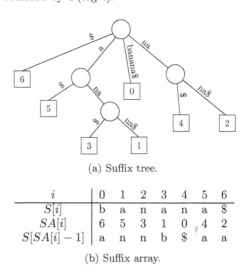

(a) Suffix tree.

i	0	1	2	3	4	5	6
$S[i]$	b	a	n	a	n	a	\$
$SA[i]$	6	5	3	1	0	4	2
$S[SA[i] - 1]$	a	n	n	b	\$	a	a

(b) Suffix array.

Figure 1: Suffix tree and suffix array (SA) for the string $S =$ "banana\$".

3.1.2 Move-to-Front (MTF) Coding

Let $S_{i,j}^{BST}$, $0 \le i \le j \le n$ be the substring $[S_i^{BST}, ..., S_{j-1}^{BST}]$; $S_{i,j}^{BST}$ is defined to be the null string when $i = j$. Let $\sigma_{i,j}$ be the set of characters contained within $S_{i,j}^{BST}$ and $M_{i,j}$ be the listing of the characters in $\sigma_{i,j}$ in order of last occurrence in $S_{i,j}^{BST}$ (i.e., in MRU order); this is the empty list when $i = j$. Denote by $x \oplus y$ the list formed by concatenating to the end of y the list formed by removing from x all elements that are contained in y.

Observation: The operator $\oplus$ can be used to reduce the problem of MTF coding to a prefix-sums operation over an array of lists as follows.

L_i is the MRU listing of the characters of $S_{0,i}^{BST}$ followed by the remaining characters of Σ in their originally defined order. That is, $L_i = L_0 \oplus M_{0,i}$. Observe that $M_{i,j} = M_{i,k} \oplus M_{k+1,j}$ for all k, $i \le k < j$. This implies that $M_{i,j} = \oplus_{k=i}^{j-1} M_{k,k+1}$. By definition, $M_{k,k+1}$ is simply the list $[S_k^{BST}]$. Furthermore, $\oplus$ is associative, and assuming $|\Sigma|$ is constant, takes $O(1)$ time and work to compute. Therefore, $M_{0,i}$, and thus L_i, for $0 \le i < n$ can be computed in $O(\log n)$ time using $O(n)$ work by the standard PRAM algorithm for computing all prefix-sums with respect to the operation $\oplus$. The prefix-sums algorithm works in two phases:

1. Adjacent pairs of MTF lists are combined using $\oplus$ in a balanced binary tree approach until only one list remains (see Figure 2).
2. Working back down the tree, the prefix-sums corresponding to the rightmost leaves of each subtree are computed using the lists computed in phase 1.

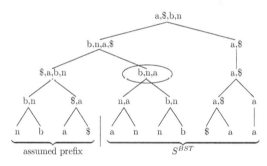

Figure 2: Phase 1 of prefix-sums: Computing local MTF lists for "annb\$aa", the output of the BST stage, using the operator $\oplus$. The "assumed prefix" is a listing of the characters of Σ in some arbitrary, predefined order. Each node in the tree is the $\oplus$-sum of its children. For example, the circled node is (n, a) $\oplus$ (b, n).

Given L_i, S_i^{MTF} is simply the index in L_i of S_i^{BST}, which can be found for all characters independently in $O(1)$ time and $O(n)$ work. Therefore, MTF coding can be performed in $O(\log n)$ time using $O(n)$ work.

3.1.3 Huffman Coding

The PRAM algorithm for Huffman coding follows readily from the serial algorithm. In step 1, the frequency table F is constructed using the integer sorting algorithm outlined in [2], which sorts a list of n integers in the range $[0, r - 1]$ in $O(r + \log n)$ time using $O(n)$ work. Because $r = |\Sigma|$ is constant, step 1 runs in $O(\log n)$ time and $O(n)$ work. Step 2 of the serial algorithm, constructing the Huffman table T from F, already runs in $O(1)$ time (and work). Step 3 is per-

formed as follows. First, the prefix-sums of the code lengths $|T(S_i^{MTF})|$ are computed into the array U in $O(\log n)$ time and $O(n)$ work. Then, in parallel for all i, $0 \le i < n$, $T(S_i^{MTF})$ is written to S^{BW} starting at position U_i in $O(1)$ time using $O(n)$ work. Therefore, the overall Huffman coding stage runs in $O(\log n)$ time using $O(n)$ work.

The above discussion proves the following theorem:

THEOREM 3.1. *The above algorithm solves the BW Compression problem in $O(\log^2 n)$ time using $O(n)$ work.*

3.2 Decompression

3.2.1 Huffman Decoding

The main obstacle to decoding S^{BW} in parallel is that, because Huffman codes are variable-length codes, we do not know where the boundaries between codewords in S^{BW} lie. We cannot simply begin decoding from any position, as the result will be incorrect if we begin decoding in the middle of a codeword. Thus, we must first identify a set of valid starting positions for decoding. Then, we can trivially decode the substrings of S^{BW} corresponding to those starting positions in parallel.

Our algorithm for locating valid starting positions for Huffman decoding is as follows. Let l be the length of the longest codeword in T, the Huffman table used to produce S^{BW}; l is constant because $|\Sigma|$ is. Without loss of generality, we assume that $|S^{BW}|$ is divisible by l. Divide S^{BW} into partitions of size l. Our goal is to identify one bit in each partition as a valid starting position.

Observation: Every partition of size l must have at least one valid starting position, and the partial decoding of S^{BW} starting from any position always terminates in the immediately following partition. Therefore, prefix-sums can be used to identify a sequence of valid starting positions.

The computation will proceed in two steps: (1) initialization and (2) prefix-sums computation. For the initialization stage, we consider every bit i, $0 \le i < |S^{BW}|$, in S^{BW} as if it were the first bit in a string to be decoded, henceforth S_i^{BW}. In parallel for all i, we decode S_i^{BW} (using the standard serial algorithm) until we cross a partition boundary, at which point we record a pointer from bit i to the stopping point. Now, every bit i has a pointer $i \to j$ to a bit j in the immediately following partition, and if i happens to be a valid starting position, then so is j. See Figure 3(a).

For the prefix-sums stage, we define the associative binary operator $\oplus$ to be the merging of adjacent pointers (that is, $\oplus$ merges $A \to B$ and $B \to C$ to produce $A \to C$). See Figure 3(b). The result is that there are now pointers from each bit in the *first* partition to a bit in every other partition. Finally, we identify all bits with pointers from bit 0 as valid starting positions for Huffman decoding (see Figure 3(c)); we refer to this set of positions as V. All this takes $O(\log n)$ time and $O(n)$ work. The actual decoding is straightforward:

1. Employ $|S^{BW}|/l$ (which is $O(n)$) processors, assign each one a different starting position from the set V, and have each processor run the serial Huffman decoding algorithm until it reaches another position in V in order to find the number of decoded characters. Do not actually write the decoded output to memory yet. This takes $O(1)$ time because the partitions are of size $O(1)$.
2. Use prefix-sums to allocate space in S^{MTF} for the output of each processor. ($O(\log n)$ time, $O(n)$ work)

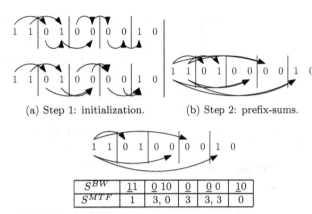

(a) Step 1: initialization.

(b) Step 2: prefix-sums.

S^{BW}	<u>11</u>	<u>0</u> 10	<u>0</u>	<u>0</u> 0	10
S^{MTF}	1	3, 0	3	3, 3	0

(c) Pointers from bit 0, corresponding to valid staring positions in S^{BW} (underlined).

Figure 3: Huffman decoding of S^{BW} = "1101000010" where $T = \{$ "0" → 3, "10" → 0, and "11" → 1 $\}$.

3. Repeat step (1) to actually write the output to S^{MTF}. ($O(1)$ time, $O(n)$ work)

These three steps, and thus the entire Huffman decoding algorithm, take $O(\log n)$ time and $O(n)$ work.

3.2.2 Move-to-Front (MTF) Decoding

The parallel MTF decoding algorithm is similar to the parallel MTF encoding algorithm but uses a different operator for the prefix sums step. MTF decoding uses the characters of S^{MTF} directly as indices into the MTF lists L_i; L_i is the listing of characters in backward order of appearance relative to position i in S^{BST}. Therefore, for every character in S^{MTF}, we know the effect of the immediately preceding character on the L_i. We want to know, for every character in S^{MTF}, the cumulative effect of all the preceding characters.

Observation: The local effects of the characters can be combined pairwise to compute the L_i using prefix sums.

Formally, $S^{MTF}[i]$ defines a permutation function mapping L_i to L_{i+1}; this function reproduces the effect of iteration i of the serial algorithm on L_i (i.e., it moves $L_i[S^{MTF}[i]]$ to the front of the list). Denote by $P_{i,j}$ the permutation function mapping L_i to L_j. Given $P_{0,1}$, $P_{1,2}$, $P_{2,3}$, etc., we want to find $P_{0,1}$, $P_{0,2}$, $P_{0,3}$, etc.. We can do this using prefix sums with function composition as the associative binary operator. A permutation function for a list of constant size can be represented by another list of constant size, so composing two permutation functions takes $O(1)$ time and work. Therefore, the prefix sums computation, as well as the overall MTF decoding algorithm, takes $O(\log n)$ time and $O(n)$ work.

3.2.3 Inverse Block-Sorting Transform (IBST)

The parallel IBST algorithm proceeds in two steps, analogous to the serial algorithm. In step 1, the integer sorting algorithm of [2] is used to sort the characters of S^{BST}. Because $|\Sigma|$ is constant, the characters have a constant range, and so this step takes $O(\log n)$ time and $O(n)$ work. In step 2, and the list ranking algorithm of [3] is used to rank the linked list in $O(\log n)$ time and $O(n)$ work. Finally, the characters of S^{BST} are written to S according to their rank in

the linked list; this takes $O(1)$ time and $O(n)$ work. Overall, the IBST takes $O(\log n)$ time and $O(n)$ work.

The above discussion proves the following theorem:

THEOREM 3.2. *The above algorithm solves the BW Decompression problem in $O(\log n)$ time using $O(n)$ work.*

4. CONCLUSION

We present novel, optimal PRAM algorithms for the BW Compression and Decompression problems. This is particularly significant since PRAM parallelism has been all but absent from lossless compression problems. The observations in Sections 3.1.2, 3.2.1, and 3.2.2 are of independent interest.

5. REFERENCES

[1] M. Burrows and D. J. Wheeler. A block-sorting lossless data compression algorithm. TR, DEC SRC, 1994.

[2] R. Cole and U. Vishkin. Deterministic coin tossing with applications to optimal parallel list ranking. *Inf. Control*, 70(1):32–53, July 1986.

[3] R. Cole and U. Vishkin. Faster optimal parallel prefix sums and list ranking. *Information and Computation*, 81(3):334–352, 1989.

[4] J. A. Edwards and U. Vishkin. Parallel algorithms for Burrows-Wheeler compression and decompression. TR, UMD, 2012. http://hdl.handle.net/1903/13299.

[5] J. A. Edwards and U. Vishkin. Empirical speedup study of truly parallel data compression. TR, UMD, 2013. http://hdl.handle.net/1903/13890.

[6] A. Eirola. Lossless data compression on GPGPU architectures. *ArXiv e-prints*, 2011.

[7] J. Gilchrist and A. Cuhadar. Parallel lossless data compression based on the Burrows-Wheeler transform. *Proc. Advanced Information Networking and Applications*, 877–884, May 2007.

[8] J. Kärkkäinen, P. Sanders, and S. Burkhardt. Linear work suffix array construction. *J. ACM*, 53(6):918–936, Nov. 2006.

[9] S. T. Klein and Y. Wiseman. Parallel Huffman decoding with applications to JPEG files. *The Computer Journal*, 46(5):487–497, 2003.

[10] S. Lewin-Berlin. A parallel bzip2. http://software.intel.com/en-us/articles/a-parallel-bzip2, 2010.

[11] G. Nong, S. Zhang, and W. H. Chan. Linear suffix array construction by almost pure induced-sorting. *Proc. Data Compression Conference*, 193–202, 2009.

[12] R. Patel, Y. Zhang, J. Mak, A. Davidson, and J. Owens. Parallel lossless data compression on the GPU. *Proc. Innovative Parallel Computing*, 1–9, 2012.

[13] S. C. Sahinalp and U. Vishkin. Symmetry breaking for suffix tree construction. *Proc. STOC'94*, 300–309.

[14] J. Seward. bzip2, a program and library for data compression. http://www.bzip.org/.

[15] J. Seward. On the performance of BWT sorting algorithms. *Proc. Data Compression Conference*, 173–182, 2000.

[16] R. E. Tarjan and U. Vishkin. Finding biconnected components and computing tree functions in logarithmic parallel time. *Proc. FOCS'84*, 12–20.

Brief Announcement: Locality in Wireless Scheduling *

Magnús M. Halldórsson

ICE-TCS, School of Computer Science, Reykjavik University, Iceland

mmh@ru.is

Categories and Subject Descriptors

C.2.1 [**Computer-Communication Networks**]: Network Architecture and Design—*Wireless communication*; F.2.2 [**Analysis of Algorithms and Problem Complexity**]: Nonnumerical Algorithms and Problems—*Sequencing and scheduling*

Keywords

Wireless networks, conflict graphs, scheduling

1. LOCALITY

Locality is one of the fundamental issues in computing, with particular resonance in distributed settings. When it comes to wireless communication, it is not only an issue of what can be computed by consulting with your neighbors, but whether what happens far away can adversely affect whether you can actually do your work.

With increasing attention to fading models of interference, such as the SINR model, lack of locality in communication has risen to the fore. When models take into account and accumulate arbitrarily far away transmissions, everyone seems to be affected by everyone else. This apparently unavoidable non-locality effect has been frequently cited as an impediment to effective analysis of SINR algorithms, especially distributed (see, e.g., [5, 1, 3]).

Our main result is that a useful form of locality can actually be achieved in the SINR model. Specifically, we define locality to mean that the combined interference of any reasonably sparse (say, feasible) instance on any link that is "well-separated" from the instance must be low. It turns out that this locality property depends directly on the power assignment used: locality holds if power increases strictly faster than the square of the intended transmission distance (but not beyond the so-called path-loss factor), and fails otherwise.

We then leverage the locality property to address a version of the fundamental *(Link) Scheduling* problem. Whereas the related throughput variant has been found to be efficiently solvable, the scheduling problem has largely resisted solution, with an apparently impenetrable logarithmic approximation barrier.

The *Balanced Scheduling* problem that we address adds the constraint that links scheduled simultaneously cannot be too close, relative to their lengths. Effectively it finesses the curious asymmetry in the model, where a short link can be much closer to say the receiver of another link than to its sender and still be feasible with the appropriate power control. This restricted problem is still NP-hard, since the instances constructed in [2] for the general problem actually satisfy the balanced criteria. This condition is natural and realistic, but still allows for a significant structural complexity in the link distribution. For instance, it allows for any set that is feasible (modulo constant factors) under uniform power, as well as arbitrarily nested links, which are hard both for uniform and linear power [5].

Our algorithm is actually obtained by formulating and coloring the appropriate graph on the links. From the point of view of algorithm analysis, it is clearly preferable to deal with the simpler binary, symmetric, and pairwise models of graphs, but it has been well documented that traditional disk-based graphs are unsatisfactory for capturing SINR-like fading and additivity (e.g., [4]). The exponentially increasing nested instances are actually a prototypical example of the latter [5]. Since our proposed class, *dual-disc graphs*, can properly capture nested instances, as well as all those handled by ordinary disc graphs, they can be said to strictly dominate any single-disc based graph representation.

Seen in the light of the budding theory of SINR algorithms, the results of this paper answer a few other interesting questions. For one, the locality/non-locality dichotomy illustrates that *the choice of a power assignment does matter.* It was known that the uniform and linear power assignments perform worse than other oblivious (i.e., dependent only on the link length) assignments whose growth is intermediate. We see that the dimension of the metric (here, 2) is a tipping point when it comes to scheduling. The results show a separation in the approximability of the capacity vs. the scheduling problem. Finally, we show that the usual assumption in scheduling problems – that the input is free of *weak* links – is warranted, since their inclusion in the balanced scheduling problem makes it as hard as the general problem.

Formal Definitions

Given is a set $L = \{l_1, l_2, \ldots, l_n\}$ of *links*, where each link $l_v = (s_v, r_v)$ represents a communication request from a sender s_v to a receiver r_v, both points in the plane. The distance between points x and y is denoted $d(x, y)$. The length of link l_v is denoted as $\ell_v = d(s_v, r_v)$. Denote $d_{vw} = d(s_v, r_w)$, for links l_v and l_w.

Let P_v denote the power assigned to link l_v, i.e., the power with which s_v transmits. We focus on power assignments $\mathcal{P}_\rho$, for $0 \le \rho \le \alpha$, where the P_v on link l_v is proportional to ℓ_v^ρ.

The *affectance* $a_w^P(v)$ of link l_v caused by another transmitting link l_w, with a given power assignment P, is the interference of l_w on l_v relative to the power received, or

$$a_w^P(v) = c_v^P \frac{P_w / d_{wv}^\alpha}{P_v / \ell_v^\alpha} = c_v^P \frac{P_w}{P_v} \cdot \left(\frac{\ell_v}{d_{wv}} \right)^\alpha,$$

where $c_v^P = \beta / (1 - \beta N \ell_v^\alpha / P_v)$ and α, β, N are universal constants. Let $a_v^P(v) = 0$. For a set S of links and a link ℓ_v, let $a_S^P(v) = \sum_{w \in S} a_w^P(v)$. A link l_v is *weak* if $c_v \ge 2\beta$.

In the presence of a set S of transmitting links, the receiver of link l_v can decode its intended transmission iff

$$a_S^P(v) \le 1 . \tag{1}$$

A set S is *feasible* if (1) holds for each link l_v in S.

The *scheduling* problem is that of both partitioning a link set into fewest possible slots and choosing a power assignment to make each slot feasible.

Locality Property

Let $d(l_v, l_w) = \min(d(s_v, s_w), d_{vw}, d_{wv}, d(r_v, r_w))$ denote the distance between two links. Links l_v and l_w are said to be: κ-*separated* if $d(l_v, l_w) \ge \kappa(\ell_w + \ell_v)$; *independent* if $d_{vw} \cdot d_{wv} \ge \ell_w \ell_v$, and *weakly feasible* if independent or if they differ in length by a factor of at least 2. A set of links satisfies a property if all pairs do, and a partition satisfies it if all the sets in it do. Separatedness is more restrictive than feasibility, while the other two properties are strictly looser.

Our definition of locality in SINR is the following.

DEFINITION 1.1. *A power assignment $\mathcal{P}$ is* local *(for a problem space Π) if, for any $\kappa > 0$, any link l_v and any weakly-feasible set S (in Π) that is κ-separated from l_v, $a_S^\mathcal{P}(v) = O(\kappa^{-\nu})$, for some absolute constant $\nu > 0$.*

Somewhat surprisingly, we find that locality is possible when using the right power assignment.

THEOREM 1.2. *$\mathcal{P}_\tau$ is local for instances in the plane, when τ satisfies $2 < \tau < \alpha$.*

2. DUAL DISC GRAPHS & BALANCED SCHEDULING

Our locality result suggests a new type of conflict graphs, parameterized by a constant κ. To each link l_v we associate a *dual disc*, a pair of discs of radius $\kappa \ell_v$: disc D_{s_v} centered at s_v and D_{r_v} centered at r_v. Given a set L of links and constant κ, we form the graph $G_{L,\kappa}$ on the links as the geometric intersection graph of the dual discs. Namely, $G_{L,\kappa}$ has a vertex v for each link l_v, with two nodes u and v adjacent if the dual-discs overlap (i.e., if $(D_{s_v} \cup D_{r_v}) \cap (D_{s_u} \cup D_{r_u}) \ne \emptyset$).

We say that a conflict graph representation is *conservative* if every independent set in the graph is schedulable in $O(1)$ slots (using some power assignment in the SINR model). Observe that a subset $S \subseteq L$ of links corresponds to an independent set in $G_{L,\kappa}$ iff S is κ-separated.

THEOREM 2.1. *Dual-disc graphs are conservative. Namely, for any fixed $\kappa > 0$, independent sets in $G_{L,\kappa}$ correspond to $O(1)$-schedulable sets of links, and correspond to feasible sets when κ is sufficiently large.*

These graphs correctly capture feasible instances that no single-disc representation can do.

THEOREM 2.2. *There is an infinite family $\{L_n\}$ of feasible instances that are independent sets in $G_{L_n, 1/4}$ but a clique in any conservative disc graph representation.*

Dual-disc graphs are easily seen to be *10-inductive independent*: in any subgraph, the node corresponding to the dual-disc of smallest radius intersects at most 10 mutually non-adjacent vertices.

This means that we obtain constant-factor approximation algorithms for a special class of the Scheduling problem. The Balanced Scheduling problem is to find a κ-balanced schedule of a given set of links (and the appropriate power assignment), meaning that each slot in the schedule is both κ-separated and feasible.

THEOREM 2.3. Balanced Scheduling *is 10-approximable.*

3. REFERENCES
[1] D. M. Blough, C. Canali, G. Resta, and P. Santi. On the impact of far-away interference on evaluations of wireless multihop networks. In *MSWiM*, pages 90–95, 2009.

[2] O. Goussevskaia, Y. A. Oswald, and R. Wattenhofer. Complexity in geometric SINR. In *Mobihoc*, pages 100–109, 2007.

[3] H. Liang, H. S. Kim, W. L. Yeow, and H.-P. Tan. So near, and yet so far: Managing 'far-away' interferers in dense femto-cell networks. In *Globecom*, 2012.

[4] T. Moscibroda, R. Wattenhofer, and Y. Weber. Protocol Design Beyond Graph-based Models. In *Hotnets*, 2006.

[5] T. Moscibroda, R. Wattenhofer, and A. Zollinger. Topology control meets SINR: The scheduling complexity of arbitrary topologies. In *Mobihoc*, pages 310–321, 2006.

Brief Announcement: Universally Truthful Secondary Spectrum Auctions[*]

Martin Hoefer
Max-Planck-Institut für Informatik
Saarland University, Saarbrücken, Germany
mhoefer@mpi-inf.mpg.de

Thomas Kesselheim
Dept. of Computer Science
Cornell University, Ithaca, NY, USA
kesselheim@cs.cornell.edu

ABSTRACT

We present algorithms for implementing local spectrum redistribution in wireless networks using a mechanism design approach. For example, in single-hop request scheduling, secondary users are modeled as rational agents that have private utility when getting assigned a channel for successful transmission. We present a simple algorithmic technique that allows to turn existing and future approximation algorithms and heuristics into truthful mechanisms for a large variety of networking problems. Our approach works with virtually all known interference models in the literature, including the physical model of interference based on SINR. It allows to address single-hop and multi-hop scheduling, routing, and even more general assignment and allocation problems. Our mechanisms are randomized and represent the first universally-truthful mechanisms for these problems with rigorous worst-case guarantees on the solution quality. In this way, our mechanisms can be used to obtain guaranteed solution quality even with risk-averse or risk-seeking bidders, for which existing approaches fail.

Categories and Subject Descriptors

F.2.2 [**Analysis of Algorithms and Problem Complexity**]: Nonnumerical Algorithms and Problems

General Terms

Algorithms, Economics, Theory

Keywords

Mechanism Design; Secondary Usage; SINR Model; Universal Truthfulness

[*]Supported by DFG through Cluster of Excellence MMCI, UMIC Research Center at RWTH Aachen University, and by a fellowship within the Postdoc-Programme of the German Academic Exchange Service (DAAD).

1. INTRODUCTION

A major challenge in the development of future wireless networking technology lies in spectrum scarcity, i.e., the limited availability of frequency bands for existing and new devices or services. To a large extent this problem results from the static allocation and licensing rules currently in use, where licenses for frequency bands are given to large service providers for entire countries. There is a major research effort underway in computer science and engineering to overcome this static allocation approach. The main idea is to motivate the licensed *primary users* to open up their bands in local areas and enable *secondary users* to use these local spectrum opportunities.

An attractive approach to implement secondary usage are *auctions*. There is a rich theory in economics showing that auctions allow to implement global objectives in a market with rational participants and private information. Auction mechanisms allow to implement secondary spectrum usage as a market, in which primary users can sell access to their unused licensed spectrum bands to secondary users [1]. Secondary users are assumed to be selfish and try to misreport their valuation to obtain a desired channel with smaller payments. Therefore, we desire a *truthful* mechanism that computes allocation and payments in a way that every user maximizes his utility by reporting the true valuation. For decades, the most prominent technique to design truthful mechanisms was VCG, which applies only if the chosen allocation optimizes social welfare exactly. Unfortunately, for non-trivial spectrum auctions social welfare maximization is NP-hard. The challenge is thus to find mechanisms that (1) are truthful, (2) run in polynomial time, and (3) provide allocations with near-optimal social welfare.

Our Contribution. We introduce a unified framework to design simple polynomial-time mechanisms for a large variety of problems within secondary spectrum usage and prove non-trivial worst-case guarantees on their social welfare. We heavily extend the current literature on secondary spectrum auctions in several ways.

Many existing secondary spectrum auctions model interference as a binary property using, e.g., unit-disk graphs, interference boundaries, or are otherwise based on local binary conflicts [3, 11]. These approaches lack many important features of realistic signal propagation. Instead, we here use realistic interference models based on the signal-to-interference-plus-noise ratio (SINR).

While there exist approaches to secondary spectrum auctions with SINR [6, 8], they are mostly unsuitable for practical use because of time-intensive use of randomized meta-rounding and the ellipsoid method for convex optimization. In contrast, our mechanisms are fast, surprisingly simple to grasp and implement, without complicated convex optimization techniques. Nevertheless, we prove non-trivial worst-case bounds on their allocation quality.

All existing randomized spectrum auctions use meta-rounding and are *truthful in expectation*, i.e., if users care only about the *expectation* of utility, they have no incentive to lie. Such mechanisms lose their truthfulness if users are, e.g., risk-averse or risk-seeking or consider further parameters of the utility distribution. In contrast, our mechanisms are *universally truthful*, randomization has no effect on incentives.

Our approach is applicable to a large variety of mechanism design problems in (wireless) networks. The main criterion is that feasibility in the underlying allocation problem is downward closed. This holds, e.g., for all allocation problems modeled via packing linear or integer programs.

Related Work. In recent years, there have been numerous studies of different flavors of the problem of maximizing the number of successful transmissions in a wireless network with interference. A variety of approximation algorithms have been proposed for variant of interference models based on SINR [4,5,9,10]. In addition to algorithm design, mechanisms for secondary spectrum markets have attracted research interest. Usually, socially optimal channel assignment poses NP-hard graph coloring and maximum independent set problems. In these cases, the classic approach of VCG for designing truthful mechanisms cannot be applied efficiently. Most approaches to spectrum auctions are single-parameter problems, where each user has a single numerical value for getting any one of a set of channels. Recently, Gopinathan et al. [3] studied truthful-in-expectation mechanisms based on meta-rounding with worst-case approximation bounds that allow to incorporate additional objectives like fairness. In addition, Zhu et al. [11] proposed deterministic monotone mechanisms for a single-parameter multi-hop routing model. They also provided truthful-in-expectation mechanisms based on meta-rounding with provable worst-case performance.

In contrast to these works on single-parameter domains, the case of multi-parameter domains, where each user has a valuation for each subset of acquired channels, was studied in our work [8]. Very recently, we provided improved results for the popular subclasses of symmetric and submodular user valuations [6]. In both papers, we proposed truthful-in-expectation mechanisms based on randomized meta-rounding with provable worst-case guarantees.

2. PRELIMINARIES

Network Model. Let us explain our approach in the context of single-hop wireless transmission scheduling. We assume there is a primary user that holds a set $\mathcal{C}$ of k channels in a local area. There is a set $\mathcal{N}$ of n secondary users that strive to obtain a channel. Each user corresponds to a communication request or *link* between points in a metric space. Link i consists of sender s_i and receiver r_i.

For each channel, the primary user assigns licenses to allow a subset $\mathcal{L} \subseteq \mathcal{N}$ of users to use the channel. If link i gets a license, sender s_i transmits on the channel. User i

gets benefit $w_i > 0$ if and only if he gets a license for at least one channel on which he is *successful*. Otherwise, its benefit is 0. Successful transmission is defined by being conflict-free in an interference model, e.g., by obtaining a minimum SINR in the SINR model [8]. The goal of the primary user is to compute an allocation $\mathcal{A} = (\mathcal{L}_1, \ldots, \mathcal{L}_k)$ of secondary users in $\mathcal{N}$ to channels to maximize *social welfare*, i.e., the sum of benefits of successful users. Such an allocation determines a set W of winners that become successful in the solution, we will say they are assigned a "license" for successful transmission. The social welfare of the allocation is given by $\sum_{i \in W} w_i$.

Our results rely on the fact that for all well-known interference models, social welfare maximization in this context poses a packing problem with a *downward-closed structure*: If a subset $S \cup \{i\}$ of users is assigned to a channel j and user i is successful, then i remains successful if any subset $S' \subseteq S$ is removed from channel j.

Our general approach is based solely on this property as follows. We introduce a family $\mathcal{W} \subseteq 2^{\mathcal{N}}$ consisting of sets of bidders. Each $W \in \mathcal{W}$ represents a subset of bidders that are assigned a license in a particular feasible solution. That is, if we consider a fixed allocation, each $i \in W$ obtains a license, whereas no $i \notin W$ gets a license. If a scenario has a packing structure, the family $\mathcal{W}$ is *downward closed*: For any $W \in \mathcal{W}$ all subsets are contained in $\mathcal{W}$ as well, i.e., if $W \in \mathcal{W}$ and $W' \subseteq W$, then also $W' \in \mathcal{W}$.

For the single-hop scenario described above, $\mathcal{W}$ contains all sets $W \subseteq \mathcal{N}$ of links that can be allocated to the channels in $\mathcal{C}$ such that the considered interference model labels them conflict-free. In general, there are a variety of network (packing) problems in routing and scheduling that have a downward-closed structure and for which we can define the set system $\mathcal{W}$. By adjusting the meaning of "being successful" and "getting a license" to the respective setting (e.g., obtaining a routing path, being scheduled before the deadline, etc.), we can handle all these problems using our approach.

Mechanism Design. Benefits are private information of secondary users. Before the allocation each user i must report its benefit w_i for getting a license; we say user i makes *bid* b_i. Users are rational and selfish, they would like to obtain a license at the lowest possible cost. Depending on the channel allocation algorithm, user i might benefit from misreporting its value and have an incentive to lie $b_i \neq w_i$. This fundamental problem has been studied for several decades in the area of *mechanism design*. To avoid manipulation and set incentives for truthful bids, we design a *truthful mechanism*. It collects the vector of bids $b = (b_i)_{i \in \mathcal{N}}$, allocates users to channels, and charges payments $p_i(b)$ to user $i \in \mathcal{N}$. User $i \in \mathcal{N}$ has a quasi-linear *utility*

$$u_i(b) = \begin{cases} w_i - p_i(b) & i \text{ is successful} \\ 0 & \text{otherwise .} \end{cases}$$

A deterministic mechanism is *truthful* if no user profits from lying. More formally, we require that

$$u_i(b_i, b_{-i}) \leq u_i(w_i, b_{-i}) \quad \text{for all } b_i \geq 0 \text{ and } b_{-i} , \quad (1)$$

where we use b_{-i} to denote the vector b of bids excluding bid b_i. The classic technique to compose deterministic truthful mechanisms is VCG, but it applies only when the allocation maximizes social welfare exactly. We have to find other ways to obtain truthful mechanisms with good social welfare guarantees that run in polynomial time.

Towards this end, we study randomized mechanisms, which are *universally truthful*. We can interpret a universally truthful mechanism as having a number of deterministic truthful mechanisms and initially making one randomized decision which one of the deterministic mechanisms to apply. Here truthfulness is independent of randomization, so the mechanism could make the random decision in public before collecting bids. The reason we use randomization is to obtain a better approximation of social welfare.

3. UNIVERSALLY TRUTHFUL AUCTIONS

Based on the downward-closed property, we introduce a mechanism design framework as shown in Algorithm 1. We first adjust the set of bidders $\mathcal{N}$ to remove all bidders that can never be part of a feasible allocation. Because $\mathcal{W}$ is downward closed, it suffices to check for each single $i \in \mathcal{N}$ if there is a feasible allocation with $W = \{i\}$.

The general idea of our approach is as follows. Similar to [2], we first determine a "representative" valuation of the users by independently at random moving each user into a statistics group with small probability. The users in this group are asked their valuation and discarded. Based on their reports, a representative valuation is determined, from which we obtain a random take-it-or-leave-it price p. Each surviving user is asked if he would want to buy a channel at price p. If not, the user leaves the auction, otherwise he survives. For the set of surviving users, we then determine an allocation using an arbitrary polynomial-time approximation algorithm for the underlying optimization problem. Finally, each winning user pays p, all others pay nothing. While truthfulness of this scheme can be shown rather directly, the challenge is proving that this approach allows to obtain non-trivial worst-case guarantees on social welfare.

In the main routine, our mechanism relies on an algorithm `UnweightedPacking(M)`. Given at set M of candidate bidders, it calculates a feasible allocation $\mathcal{A}$, in which only the bidders in W are served. Here algorithm `UnweightedPacking` neglects the bids.

Theorem 1. *Algorithm 1 is universally truthful.*

In addition, we can show an approximation guarantee based on the applied algorithm `UnweightedPacking(M)`. We assume that this algorithm is a ψ-approximation, meaning that for the winning set W, we have

$$|W| \geq \psi \cdot \max_{W' \in \mathcal{W} \cap 2^M} |W'|.$$

Given this guarantee, we can show the following approximation factor for the complete mechanism.

Theorem 2. *Let $\mathcal{A}$ be the allocation returned by the mechanism and $\mathcal{A}^*$ be the allocation optimizing social welfare. Then we have*

$$\mathbf{E}\left[b(\mathcal{A})\right] = \Omega\left(\frac{\varepsilon\psi}{\log n}\right) \cdot b(\mathcal{A}^*) \ .$$

Proofs can be found in the full version of this paper [7].

Algorithm 1: Universally-truthful framework

1 For each bidder i: If there is no allocation that yields i as winner, remove i from $\mathcal{N}$;

2 Set *SEC-PRICE* to 1 with probability ε, otherwise to 0;

3 **if** *SEC-PRICE* = 1 **then**

4   Let i^* be a bidder such that $b_{i^*} = \max_{i \in \mathcal{N}} b_i$;

5   Compute the allocation in which only i^* is a winner;

6   Charge $p_{i^*}(b) := \max_{i \in \mathcal{N} \setminus \{i^*\}} b_i$;

7   All other bidders i are charged $p_i(b) := 0$;

8 **else**

9   **forall the** $i \in \mathcal{N}$ **do**

10   add i to STAT with probability ε, otherwise to FIXED

11   Set $B := \max_{i \in \text{STAT}} b_i$;

12   Choose X uniformly at random from $\{0, 1, \ldots, \lceil \log n \rceil + 1\}$;

13   Set $p := 2^{-X} \cdot B$;

14   Set $M := \{i \in \text{FIXED} \mid b_i \geq p\}$;

15   Run `UnweightedPacking(M)` which returns allocation $\mathcal{A}$;

16   If i contained in $\mathcal{A}$, charge $p_i(b) := p$, otherwise $p_i(b) := 0$;

---

4. REFERENCES

[1] R. Berry, M. Honig, and R. Vohra. Spectrum markets: Motivation, challenges, and implications. *IEEE Communications Magazine*, 2010.

[2] S. Dobzinski, N. Nisan, and M. Schapira. Truthful randomized mechanisms for combinatorial auctions. *J. Comput. Syst. Sci.*, 78(1):15–25, 2012.

[3] A. Gopinathan, Z. Li, and C. Wu. Strategyproof auctions for balancing social welfare and fairness in secondary spectrum markets. In *INFOCOM*, pp. 3020–3028, 2011.

[4] M. Halldórsson, S. Holzer, P. Mitra, and R. Wattenhofer. The power of non-uniform wireless power. In *SODA*, pp. 1595–1606, 2013.

[5] M. Halldórsson and R. Wattenhofer. Wireless communication is in APX. In *ICALP*, vol. 1, pp. 525–536, 2009.

[6] M. Hoefer and T. Kesselheim. Secondary spectrum auctions for symmetric and submodular bidders. In *EC*, pp. 657–671, 2012.

[7] M. Hoefer and T. Kesselheim. Universally truthful secondary spectrum auctions. CoRR, 2013.

[8] M. Hoefer, T. Kesselheim, and B. Vöcking. Approximation algorithms for secondary spectrum auctions. In *SPAA*, pp. 177–186, 2011.

[9] T. Kesselheim. A constant-factor approximation for wireless capacity maximization with power control in the SINR model. In *SODA*, pp. 1549–1559, 2011.

[10] T. Kesselheim. Approximation algorithms for wireless link scheduling with flexible data rates. In *ESA*, pp. 659–670, 2012.

[11] Y. Zhu, B. Li, and Z. Li. Truthful spectrum auction design for secondary networks. In *INFOCOM*, pp. 873–881, 2012.

Brief Announcement:
Online Batch Scheduling for Flow Objectives

Sungjin Im
Duke University
Durham, NC 27708
sungjin@cs.duke.edu

Benjamin Moseley
Toyota Technological Institute
Chicago, IL 60637
moseley@ttic.edu

ABSTRACT

Batch scheduling gives a powerful way of increasing the throughput by aggregating multiple homogeneous jobs. It has applications in large scale manufacturing as well as in server scheduling. In batch scheduling, when explained in the setting of server scheduling, the server can process requests of the same type up to a certain number simultaneously. Batch scheduling can be seen as *capacitated* broadcast scheduling, a popular model considered in scheduling theory. In this paper, we consider an online batch scheduling model. For this model we address flow time objectives for the *first* time and give positive results for average flow time, the k-norms of flow time and maximum flow time. For average flow time and the k-norms of flow time we show algorithms that are $O(1)$-competitive with a small constant amount of resource augmentation. For maximum flow time we show a 2-competitive algorithm and this is the best possible competitive ratio for any online algorithm.

Categories and Subject Descriptors

F.2.2 [**Analysis of Algorithms and Problem Complexity**]: Nonnumerical Algorithms and Problems

Keywords

Online Algorithms; Scheduling Algorithms

1. INTRODUCTION

A majority of works in scheduling literature studies the case where all jobs/requests must be processed sequentially and only on a single machine at any point in time. However, more general problems arise practice. For instance, jobs could be parallelizable. In this setting a job can be decomposed into multiple pieces and can be processed on multiple machines simultaneously. Scheduling parallelizable jobs has received a significant amount of attention in theoretical scheduling literature, for instance [12, 8, 14, 20, 13]. The reason to address the parallelizability of a job is to be able to process more work per unit time by using more machines.

Another way to increase the work being done per time unit is to batch homogeneous jobs. In a batch scheduling setting, jobs of the same type can be aggregated and processed together *simultaneously*. Thus, one unit of processing can decrease the work that needs to be performed on more than one job. Batch scheduling arises in many real work systems. For example, if jobs require the same code, then the server can let the jobs share the code loaded into the memory. Or in a multicast network, many different clients can receive a communication simultaneously. Batch scheduling is not restricted to computers and networks. In particular, in manufacturing lines, such as semiconductor manufacturing, tasks are grouped together to be processed simultaneously. See [19], for a variety of industry applications of batched scheduling.

A special type of batch scheduling, known as broadcast scheduling, has received a significant amount of attention recently in scheduling literature. In the broadcast scheduling model, there are n pages of data stored at a server. Over time requests arrive for specific pages. When the server broadcasts a page p, *all* unsatisfied/outstanding requests are satisfied simultaneously. Broadcast scheduling finds applications in multicast systems, LAN and wireless networks [21, 1, 2]. Notice that here any number of requests can be satisfied simultaneously. This can be viewed as having an infinite batch size. In practice, however, there could be a limit on the number of requests that a server can handle simultaneously, as was pointed out in [7].

In this paper, we consider online batch scheduling where there is possibly some limit on the number of jobs that can be processed simultaneously. In the *online* setting, the scheduler becomes aware of a request only when it arrives at the system. Inspired by the broadcast model, we consider a generalization of this model to the batched setting. As in the broadcast model, there are n pages of information stored at the server. Requests arrive over time for different pages. The server can satisfy up to B_p requests for page p simultaneously. Here B_p is different for each page p and takes some integral value in $(0, \infty]$. We note that the model we consider is not only restricted to applications in wireless networks. Indeed, one can think of the n pages as n different types of jobs. Over time requests come for a specific type of job p to be done and up to B_p requests of type p can be done simultaneously. This model accurately captures a variety of batched settings, for instance batch scheduling tasks in an assembly line.

The *flow time* of a request is the amount of time it takes the server to satisfy the request. A client is interested in having the flow time of their request minimized. Let $J_{p,i}$ be the ith request for page p and say that this request arrives at time $r_{p,i}$. Each page p has a size ℓ_p which specifies the amount of work on page p that is required to complete a request for page p. We assume that a page consists of a sequence of unit sized pieces $(p, 1), (p, 2), \ldots, (p, \ell_p)$. The server can broadcast/schedule one piece of a page at each time step. A request will need to be in a batch for each piece of a page it requested to be completed. A request $J_{p,i}$ is satisfied at the first time when the request, since its release time $r_{p,i}$, receives all pieces of information $(p,1),(p,2),...,(p,\ell_p)$ in *sequential* order. However, such a sequence of transmissions does not have to be contiguous, and can be interrupted by other transmissions. For a given schedule, let $C_{p,i}$ be the time $J_{p,i}$ is completed in the system. The flow time of a request is $C_{p,i} - r_{p,i}$. The scheduler's goal is to determine how requests should be processed so that the clients are given good service. That is, the schedule's goal is to optimize a quality of service metric. Perhaps the most popular quality of service metrics are based on the flow time of the requests. In this paper, we study flow time objectives for the *first* time in batch scheduling.

The most popular flow time based quality of service metric is minimizing the total or *average flow time*. Here the schedule's goal is to minimize $\sum_{p,i}(C_{p,i} - r_{p,i})$ and this objective essentially minimizes the average quality of service. Unfortunately, by optimizing average flow time, the scheduler could give a few clients poor quality of service to optimize the flow time of other jobs. Thus, it can be seen that optimizing average flow time is not necessarily 'fair' to all of the jobs. An objective that focuses on ensuring no job is given poor quality of service is minimizing the *maximum flow time*. Finally, an objective that is also used to ensure fairness while not being as stringent as maximum flow time is minimizing the *k-norms of flow time*. Here the objective is to minimize $\sqrt[k]{\sum_{p,i}(C_{p,i} - r_{p,i})^k}$ for some $k \in [1,\infty)$. By focusing on minimizing the k-norms for small values of k greater than one the scheduler is forced to reduce the variance in the requests flow time, which enforces fairness [6]. It can be noted that average flow time is equivalent to setting $k = 1$ and maximum flow time is equivalent to setting $k = \infty$. Each of these objectives are widely considered in scheduling theory and the scheduling objective of choice depends on the underlying system requirements.

In theoretical scheduling literature, batch scheduling has been studied only for the objective of maximizing the total throughput [7, 16]. For this objective, each request $J_{p,i}$ has a release time $r_{p,i}$ and deadline $d_{p,i}$. If a request $J_{p,i}$ is completed by its deadline, then the scheduler receives some profit $w_{p,i}$. The goal of the scheduler is to maximize the profit obtained. Flow objectives are quite different from the throughput objective, and the algorithms that perform well for the throughput objective do not necessarily for the flow objectives. For example, there exists a simple 2-competitive greedy algorithm for the total throughput [7].[1] However, it is known that any randomized online algorithm is $\Omega(\sqrt{n})$-competitive for the average flow time objective [3]. This strong lower bound holds even in the special case of broadcast scheduling.

Due to this strong lower bound, we consider analyzing algorithms in the popular resource augmentation [18]. In the resource augmentation model, an algorithm is given extra resources over the adversary and then the competitive ratio is bounded. In previous work, the resource augmentation usually comes in the form of being able to process requests at a faster rate. An algorithm is said to be s-speed c-competitive if it can process requests s times faster than the adversary. In our setting, we will consider algorithms that possibly have resource augmentation on how fast jobs can be processed as well as resource augmentation on the number of jobs that can be satisfied together. We will say that an algorithm is s-speed d-capacity c-competitive if the algorithm can process jobs s times faster than the adversary, the batches can be d times larger and the

---

[1] We note that [7] studies a more general batch scheduling problem in the offline setting.

algorithm achieves a competitive ratio of c. The ultimate goal of a resource augmentation analysis is to find a constant competitive algorithm even with a minimum amount of extra resource augmentation.

Our Results: As mentioned, we consider minimizing flow time objectives for the first time in the batched scheduling setting. First we consider the problems of minimizing average flow time and the k-norms of flow time. For both of these problems we consider a generalization of an algorithm that was considered in the broadcast scheduling setting [5]. Both of these results will follow a similar framework. We will specify two different cases depending on the size of pages. One is when pages are all unit sized (i.e. $\ell_p = 1$ for all p) and the other is when pages are varying sized. We are able to show the following theorems for the case of unit sized pages.

Theorem 1.1 *For any $\varepsilon > 0$, there exists an online algorithm that is $(1 + \varepsilon)$-speed 2-capacity $O(1/\varepsilon^3)$-competitive for minimizing average flow time when pages are unit-sized.*

Theorem 1.2 *For any $\varepsilon > 0$ and any fixed integer $k \in [1,\infty)$, there exists an online algorithm that is $(1 + \varepsilon)$-speed 2-capacity $O(1/\varepsilon^4)$-competitive algorithm for minimizing the k-norm of flow time when pages are unit-sized.*

We extend these result for varying sized pages. Here we require a further relaxation on the capacity constraints.

Theorem 1.3 *For any $\varepsilon > 0$, there exists an online algorithm that is $(1 + \varepsilon)$-speed 6-capacity $O(1/\varepsilon^3)$-competitive for minimizing average flow time when pages are varying-sized.*

Theorem 1.4 *For any $\varepsilon > 0$ and any fixed integer $k \in [1,\infty)$, there exists an online algorithm that is $(1 + \varepsilon)$-speed 6-capacity $O(1/\varepsilon^4)$-competitive algorithm for minimizing the k-norm of flow time when pages are varying-sized.*

Finally, we consider the problem of minimizing the maximum flow time. In this case we do not use resource augmentation at all, neither on the processing speed nor the capacity of the batch size. In this case the algorithm considered is the natural extension of the algorithm first-in-first-out which always prioritizes the request that arrived the earliest.

Theorem 1.5 *There exists a 2-competitive algorithm for minimizing the maximum flow time.*

This result is tight, since any randomized online algorithm was shown to have a competitive ratio larger than $2 - \varepsilon$ for any fixed constant $\varepsilon > 0$ even in the special case of $B_p = \infty$ [9, 10].

Our Technical Contributions: As mentioned before, our algorithm and analysis are inspired by the previous work in broadcast scheduling [5, 13, 11]. We first give a high-level view of the approach in [5, 13] for the k norms objectives, $1 \le k < \infty$. The main difficulty of broadcast scheduling comes from the fact that an optimal schedule can be very effective in processing multiple requests simultaneously compared the the online scheduler. This is the case particularly since the optimal scheduler knows the future input while our algorithm does not. Hence it is challenging for an online algorithm to decide when and what to broadcast. That is, the online algorithm may want to wait more hoping for a chance to aggregate more requests, however, it increases the flow time of such waiting requests.

The key idea that was used in [5, 13] is to first obtain a fractionally good schedule. To illustrate the idea, we assume that all pages are unit sized, requests arrive at integer times, and it takes a unit time to broadcast a page p. In the real (aka *integral*) schedule, the scheduler is allowed to broadcast only one page per time step. However, in the fractional schedule, at each instantaneous time, multiple pages can be broadcasted fractionally, up to a total of one unit. Then in fractional schedule, a request $J_{p,i}$ is satisfied, if page p is broadcasted by one unit since its release time $r_{p,i}$. Finally, the schedule for the fractional case is converted to a valid real schedule, where only one page is broadcasted in a time step, in a online manner.

Until this, our algorithm and analysis are fairly similar to the previous work. We will also consider a fractional schedule and convert it to a valid schedule in an online manner. However, in batch scheduling, one has to decide which requests get satisfied in a batch; whereas, in the broadcast schedule all requests get satisfied together. Deciding which requests get satisfied makes the problem more challenging. Our algorithm at any point in time, will decide a *single* request that it wants to satisfy. However, now it also needs to decide which requests to group in a batch with this request. Our algorithm will define 'balls' around each request where a ball consists of the requests that get satisfied (in the batch) if this request is chosen to be satisfied. The ball will be defined on requests for the same page that arrived the most closely to this request. Using this, we will obtain a fractionally good scheduler. However, the online conversion to a valid schedule is much more challenging in our case. For the online conversion, we will need use a more intricate analysis particularly when pages are varying sized. This is because the batch a request is in can change over time since the algorithm may have to restart to broadcast the same page from the beginning to satisfy more newly arriving requests together. For this reason, we will need to be careful about how the algorithm and optimal solution group requests. To do this, we will determine some structural properties of the optimal solution that we can compare against.

Related Work: Broadcast scheduling for minimizing average flow time is NP-hard [15, 9]. It is also NP-hard to optimize the maximum flow objecttive [9]. Since broadcast scheduling is a special case of the problems considered in this paper, each of the problems we consider is NP-hard. The best known approximation for average flow time in broadcast scheduling is a $O(\log^2 n / \log \log n)$-approximation [4]. The first $(1 + \varepsilon)$-speed $O(1)$-competitive algorithm for average flow time was given in [17] for unit sized pages and an algorithm with similar guarantees was given in [5] for varying sized pages. For the k-norms objective, [13] gave the first algorithm that is $(1 + \varepsilon)$-speed $O(1)$-competitive. For the problem of minimizing the maximum flow time, [9, 11] gave a 2-competitive algorithm, which was shown to be tight [9, 10].

Acknowledgements: This work was partially supported by NSF grant CCF-1008065.

2. REFERENCES

[1] S. Acharya, M. Franklin, and S. Zdonik. Dissemination-based data delivery using broadcast disks. *Personal Communications, IEEE [see also IEEE Wireless Communications]*, 2(6):50–60, Dec 1995.

[2] D. Aksoy and M. J. Franklin. R x W: A scheduling approach for large-scale on-demand data broadcast. *IEEE/ACM Trans. Netw.*, 7(6):846–860, 1999.

[3] N. Bansal, M. Charikar, S. Khanna, and J. S. Naor. Approximating the average response time in broadcast scheduling. In *SODA '05*, pages 215–221, 2005.

[4] N. Bansal, D. Coppersmith, and M. Sviridenko. Improved approximation algorithms for broadcast scheduling. *SIAM J. Comput.*, 38(3):1157–1174, 2008.

[5] N. Bansal, R. Krishnaswamy, and V. Nagarajan. Better scalable algorithms for broadcast scheduling. In *ICALP '10*, pages 324–335. Springer, 2010.

[6] N. Bansal and K. Pruhs. Server scheduling to balance priorities, fairness, and average quality of service. *SIAM J. Comput.*, 39(7):3311–3335, 2010.

[7] A. Bar-Noy, S. Guha, Y. Katz, J. S. Naor, B. Schieber, and H. Shachnai. Throughput maximization of real-time scheduling with batching. *ACM Trans. Algorithms*, 5(2):18:1–18:17, Mar. 2009.

[8] H.-L. Chan, J. Edmonds, and K. Pruhs. Speed scaling of processes with arbitrary speedup curves on a multiprocessor. In *SPAA '09*, pages 1–10, 2009.

[9] J. Chang, T. Erlebach, R. Gailis, and S. Khuller. Broadcast scheduling: algorithms and complexity. In *SODA '08*, pages 473–482, 2008.

[10] C. Chekuri, A. Gal, S. Im, S. Khuller, J. Li, R. M. McCutchen, B. Moseley, and L. Raschid. New models and algorithms for throughput maximization in broadcast scheduling - (extended abstract). In *WAOA '10*, pages 71–82. Springer, 2010.

[11] C. Chekuri, S. Im, and B. Moseley. Online scheduling to minimize maximum response time and maximum delay factor. *Theory of Computing*, 8(7):165–195, 2012.

[12] J. Edmonds, D. D. Chinn, T. Brecht, and X. Deng. Non-clairvoyant multiprocessor scheduling of jobs with changing execution characteristics. *J. Scheduling*, 6(3):231–250, 2003.

[13] J. Edmonds, S. Im, and B. Moseley. Online scalable scheduling for the ℓ_k-norms of flow time without conservation of work. In *SODA '11*, pages 109–119, 2011.

[14] J. Edmonds and K. Pruhs. Scalably scheduling processes with arbitrary speedup curves. In *SODA '09*, pages 685–692, 2009.

[15] T. Erlebach and A. Hall. Np-hardness of broadcast scheduling and inapproximability of single-source unsplittable min-cost flow. *J. Scheduling*, 7(3):223–241, 2004.

[16] R. Y. S. Hung and H.-F. Ting. Design and analysis of online batching systems. *Algorithmica*, 57(2):217–231, 2010.

[17] S. Im and B. Moseley. An online scalable algorithm for average flow time in broadcast scheduling. *ACM Trans. Algorithms*, 8(4):39:1–39:17, Oct. 2012.

[18] B. Kalyanasundaram and K. Pruhs. Speed is as powerful as clairvoyance. *J. ACM*, 47(4):617–643, 2000.

[19] M. Mathirajan and A. Sivakumar. A literature review, classification and simple meta-analysis on scheduling of batch processors in semiconductor. *The International Journal of Advanced Manufacturing Technology*, 29(9-10):990–1001, 2006.

[20] K. Pruhs, J. Robert, and N. Schabanel. Minimizing maximum flowtime of jobs with arbitrary parallelizability. In *WAOA '10*, pages 237–248, 2010.

[21] J. Wong. Broadcast delivery. *Proceedings of the IEEE*, 76(12):1566–1577, 1988.

Brief Announcement: Set It and Forget It–Approximating the Set Once Strip Cover Problem[*]

Amotz Bar-Noy
Dept. Computer Science,
Graduate Center, CUNY
New York, NY 10016, USA
amotz@sci.brooklyn.cuny.edu

Ben Baumer
Dept. of Mathematics &
Statistics, Smith College
Northampton, MA 01063, USA
bbaumer@smith.edu

Dror Rawitz
School of Electrical
Engineering, Tel Aviv Univ.
Tel-Aviv 69978, Israel
rawitz@eng.tau.ac.il

ABSTRACT

In the SET ONCE STRIP COVER problem n wireless sensors are deployed over a one-dimensional region. Each sensor has a battery that drains in inverse proportion to a radius that can be set just once, but activated at any time. The problem is to find an assignment of radii and activation times that maximizes the length of time during which the entire region is covered. We show that this problem is NP-hard. We also show that the approximation ratio of ROUNDROBIN, the algorithm in which the sensors take turns covering the entire region, is $\frac{3}{2}$ in both SET ONCE STRIP COVER and the more general STRIP COVER problem, in which each radius may be set finitely-many times. Moreover, we show that the more general class of *duty cycle* algorithms, in which groups of sensors take turns covering the entire region, can do no better. Finally, we give an polynomial time algorithm that solves the related SET RADIUS STRIP COVER problem, in which sensors must be activated immediately.

Categories and Subject Descriptors

F.2.2 [**Analysis of Algorithms and Problem Complexity**]: Nonnumerical Algorithms and Problems—*Sequencing and scheduling*; C.2.1 [**Computer-Communication Networks**]: Network Architecture and Design—*Wireless Communication*

Keywords

wireless sensor networks; strip cover; barrier coverage; network lifetime

1. BACKGROUND

SET ONCE STRIP COVER (ONCESC) is defined as follows. Let $[0, 1]$ be the interval that we wish to cover. Given is a vector $x = (x_1, \ldots, x_n) \in [0, 1]^n$ of n sensor locations, and a corresponding vector $b = (b_1, \ldots, b_n) \in \mathbb{Q}_+^n$ of battery

charges, with $b_i \geq 0$ for all i. We assume that $x_i \leq x_{i+1}$ for every i. An instance of the problem thus consists of a pair $I = (x, b)$, and a solution is an assignment of radii and activation times to sensors. More specifically a solution is a pair $S = (\rho, \tau)$ where ρ_i is the *radius* of sensor i and τ_i is the *activation time* of i. Since the radius of each sensor cannot be reset, this means that sensor i becomes active at time τ_i, covers the *range* $[x_i - \rho_i, x_i + \rho_i]$ for b_i/ρ_i time units, and then becomes inactive since it has exhausted its battery.

Any schedule can be visualized by a space-time diagram in which each coverage assignment can be represented by a rectangle. It is customary in such diagrams to view the sensor locations as forming the horizontal axis, with time extending upwards vertically. In this case, the coverage of a sensor located at x_i and assigned the radius ρ_i beginning at time τ_i is depicted by a rectangle with lower-left corner $(x_i - \rho_i, \tau_i)$ and upper-right corner $(x_i + \rho_i, \tau_i + b_i/\rho_i)$. Let the set of all points contained in this rectangle be denoted as $R(\rho_i, \tau_i)$. A point (u, t) in space-time is *covered* by a schedule (ρ, τ) if $(u, t) \in \bigcup_i R(\rho_i, \tau_i)$. The *lifetime* of the network in a solution $S = (\rho, \tau)$ is the maximum value T such that every point $(u, t) \in [0, 1] \times [0, T]$ is covered. In ONCESC our goal is to find a schedule S that maximizes T. Depictions of two schedules are shown in Figure 1.

Motivation. Scheduling problems of this ilk arise in many applications, particularly when the goal is *barrier coverage* (see [9, 22] for surveys, or [14] for motivation). Suppose that we have a highway, supply line, or fence in territory that is either hostile or difficult to navigate. While we want to monitor activity along this line, conditions on the ground make it impossible to systematically place wireless sensors at specific locations. However, it is feasible and inexpensive to deploy adjustable range sensors along this line by, say, dropping them from an airplane flying overhead (e.g. [8, 19, 21]). Once deployed, the sensors send us their location via GPS, and we wish to send a single radius-time pair to each sensor as an assignment. Replacing the battery in any sensor is infeasible. How do we construct an assignment that will keep this vital supply line completely monitored for as long as possible?

Models. While the focus of this paper is the ONCESC problem, we touch upon three closely related problems. In each problem the location and battery of each sensor are fixed, and a solution can be viewed as a finite set of radius-time pairs. In ONCESC, both the radii and the activation times are variable, but can be set only once. In the more gen-

---

[*]A detailed version of this paper can be found in [4].

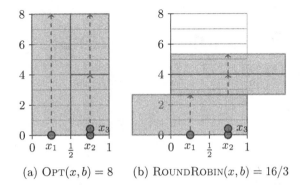

(a) $\text{OPT}(x,b) = 8$ (b) $\text{ROUNDROBIN}(x,b) = 16/3$

Figure 1: Best schedule vs. best duty cycle schedule. Here $x = (\frac{1}{4}, \frac{3}{4}, \frac{3}{4})$ and $b = (2, 1, 1)$. The sensors are indicated by dots. Each of the rectangles represents the active coverage region for one sensor. The dashed arrow helps to clarify which sensor is active at a particular point in time.

eral STRIP COVER problem, the radius and activation time of each sensor can be set finitely many times. On the other hand, if the radius of each sensor is fixed and given as part of the input, then we call the problem of assigning an activation time to each sensor so as to maximize network lifetime SET TIME STRIP COVER (TIMESC). SET RADIUS STRIP COVER (RADSC) is another variant of ONCESC in which all of the sensors are scheduled to activate immediately, and the problem is to find the optimal radial assignment.

Related work. STRIP COVER was first considered by Bar-Noy and Baumer [3], who gave a $\frac{3}{2}$ lower bound on the performance of ROUNDROBIN, the algorithm in which the sensors take turns covering the entire region, but were only able to show a corresponding upper bound of 1.82. The similar CONNECTED RANGE ASSIGNMENT (CRA) problem, in which radii are assigned to points in the plane in order to obtain a connected disk graph, was studied by Chambers et al. [12]. They showed that the best one circle solution to CRA also yields a $\frac{3}{2}$-approximation guarantee, and in fact, the instance that produces their lower bound is simply a translation of the instance used in [3].

The TIMESC problem, which is known as RESTRICTED STRIP COVERING, was shown to be NP-hard by Buchsbaum et al., who also gave an $O(\log \log n)$-approximation algorithm [7]. Later, a constant factor approximation algorithm was discovered by Gibson and Varadarajan [13].

Close variants of RADSC have been the subject of previous work. Whereas RADSC requires *area* coverage, Peleg and Lev-Tov [15] studied *target* coverage. In this problem the input is a set of n sensors and a finite set of m points on the line that are to be covered, and the goal is to find the radial assignments with the minimum sum of radii. They used dynamic programming to devise a polynomial time algorithm. Bar-Noy et al. [6] improved the running time to $O(n + m)$.

The notion of *duty cycling* as a mean to maximize network lifetime was also considered in the literature of discrete geometry. In this context, maximizing the number of covers t serves as a proxy for maximizing the actual network lifetime. Pach [16] began the study of decomposability of multiple coverings. Pach and Tóth [17] showed that a t-fold cover of

translates of a centrally-symmetric open convex polygon can be decomposed into $\Omega(\sqrt{t})$ covers. This was later improved to the optimal $\Omega(t)$ covers by Aloupis et al. [2], while Gibson and Varadarajan [13] showed the same result without the centrally-symmetric restriction.

Motivated by prior invocations of duty cycling [20, 18, 1, 8, 10, 11], Bar-Noy et al. [5] studied a *duty cycle* variant of ONCESC in which sensors must be grouped into shifts of size at most k that take turns covering $[0, 1]$. (ROUNDROBIN is the only possible algorithm when $k = 1$.) For the unit batteries case they presented a polynomial-time algorithm for $k = 2$ and showed that the approximation ratio of this algorithm is $\frac{35}{24}$ for $k > 2$. It was also shown that its approximation ratio is at least $\frac{15}{11}$, for $k \geq 4$, and $\frac{6}{5}$, for $k = 3$. A fault-tolerance model, in which smaller shifts are more robust, was also proposed.

2. OUR RESULTS

We introduce the SET ONCE model that corresponds to the case where the scheduler does not have the ability to vary the sensor's radius once it has been activated.

We show that ONCESC is NP-hard using a reduction from PARTITION:

THEOREM 1. ONCESC *is NP-hard.*

Given this hardness result we turn our attention to approximation algorithms. While ROUNDROBIN is among the simplest possible algorithms (note that its running time is exactly n), the precise value of its approximation ratio is not obvious (although it is not hard to see that 2 is an upper bound). We show that the approximation ratio of ROUNDROBIN is exactly $\frac{3}{2}$. This closes a gap between the best previously known lower and upper bounds ($\frac{3}{2}$ and 1.82, resp.) on the performance of this algorithm.

THEOREM 2. ROUNDROBIN *is a $\frac{3}{2}$-approximation algorithm for* ONCESC.

The structure of the proof is as follows. We start with an optimal schedule S, and cut it into disjoint time intervals, or strips, such that the same set of sensors is active within each time interval. (See Figure 2.) Each strip induces a RADSC instance I_j and a corresponding solution S_j. Next, we show that for any such instance I_j, there exists a unit-battery instance I'_j with the same optimum lifetime. Finally, we prove a lower bound on the performance of ROUNDROBIN on such unit battery instances. By combining these results, we prove that $\text{RR}(x, b) \geq \frac{3}{2}T$.

Theorem 2 readily extends to the STRIP COVER problem.

THEOREM 3. ROUNDROBIN *is a $\frac{3}{2}$-approximation algorithm for* STRIP COVER.

We show that, in the worst case, no duty cycle algorithm outperforms ROUNDROBIN. More specifically, we show that the approximation ratio of any duty cycle algorithm is at least $\frac{3}{2}$. (The construction is given in Figure 1.)

THEOREM 4. *The approximation ratio of any duty cycle algorithm is at least $\frac{3}{2}$.*

Finally, we provide an algorithm that solves RADSC.

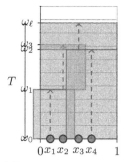 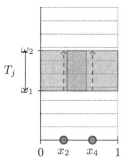

(a) An optimal schedule. (b) One strip of that schedule.

Figure 2: Cutting an optimal schedule into strips. Note that coverage overlaps may occur in both the horizontal and vertical directions in the optimal schedule, but only horizontally in a strip.

THEOREM 5. *There exists an $O(n^2 \log n)$-time algorithm for solving* RADSC.

This is obtained by showing that the network lifetime is determined by two sensors that are the "weakest link" of the network. Since each sensor pair induces a candidate lifetime, the search can be limited to $O(n^2)$ possible candidates.

3. DISCUSSION AND OPEN PROBLEMS

We show that ROUNDROBIN, which is perhaps the simplest possible algorithm, has a tight approximation ratio of $\frac{3}{2}$ for both ONCESC and STRIP COVER. We also show that ONCESC is NP-hard, but it remains to be seen whether the same is true for STRIP COVER. Future work may include finding algorithms with better approximation ratios for either problem. However, we have eliminated duty cycle algorithms as candidates. Observe that both ONCESC and TIMESC are NP-hard, while RADSC can be solved in polynomial time. This suggests that hardness comes from setting the activation times.

We have assumed that the battery charges dissipate in direct inverse proportion to the assigned sensing radius. It is natural to suppose that an exponent could factor into this relationship, so that, say, the radius drains in quadratic inverse proportion to the sensing radius (e.g. $\tau = b/\rho^2$). One could expand the scope of the problem to higher dimensions. Before moving both the sensor locations and the region being covered to the plane, one might consider moving one but not the other. This yields two different problems: 1) covering the line with sensors located in the plane; and 2) covering a region of the plane with sensors located on a line.

4. REFERENCES

[1] Z. Abrams, A. Goel, and S. A. Plotkin. Set k-cover algorithms for energy efficient monitoring in wireless sensor networks. In *IPSN*, pages 424–432, 2004.

[2] G. Aloupis, J. Cardinal, S. Collette, S. Langerman, D. Orden, and P. Ramos. Decomposition of multiple coverings into more parts. *Discrete & Computational Geometry*, 44(3):706–723, 2010.

[3] A. Bar-Noy and B. Baumer. Maximizing network lifetime on the line with adjustable sensing ranges. In *ALGOSENSORS*, volume 7111 of *LNCS*, pages 28–41, 2011.

[4] A. Bar-Noy, B. Baumer, and D. Rawitz. Set it and forget it: Approximating the set once strip cover problem. http://arxiv.org/abs/1204.1082.

[5] A. Bar-Noy, B. Baumer, and D. Rawitz. Changing of the guards: Strip cover with duty cycling. In *SIROCCO*, volume 7355 of *LNCS*, pages 36–47, 2012.

[6] A. Bar-Noy, T. Brown, M. Johnson, and O. Liu. Cheap or Flexible Sensor Coverage. In *DCOSS*, pages 245–258, 2009.

[7] A. Buchsbaum, A. Efrat, S. Jain, S. Venkatasubramanian, and K. Yi. Restricted strip covering and the sensor cover problem. In *SODA*, pages 1056–1063, 2007.

[8] M. Cardei and D. Du. Improving wireless sensor network lifetime through power aware organization. *Wireless Networks*, 11(3):333–340, 2005.

[9] M. Cardei and J. Wu. Coverage in wireless sensor networks. *Handbook of Sensor Networks*, 2004.

[10] M. Cardei, J. Wu, and M. Lu. Improving network lifetime using sensors with adjustable sensing ranges. *Int. J. Sensor Networks*, 1(1/2):41–49, 2006.

[11] M. Cardei, J. Wu, M. Lu, and M. Pervaiz. Maximum network lifetime in wireless sensor networks with adjustable sensing ranges. In *WiMob (3)*, pages 438–445, 2005.

[12] E. W. Chambers, S. P. Fekete, H.-F. Hoffmann, D. Marinakis, J. S. B. Mitchell, V. Srinivasan, U. Stege, and S. Whitesides. Connecting a set of circles with minimum sum of radii. In *WADS*, volume 6844 of *LNCS*, pages 183–194, 2011.

[13] M. Gibson and K. Varadarajan. Decomposing coverings and the planar sensor cover problem. In *FOCS*, pages 159–168, 2009.

[14] S. Kumar, T.-H. Lai, and A. Arora. Barrier coverage with wireless sensors. *Wireless Networks*, 13(6):817–834, 2007.

[15] N. Lev-Tov and D. Peleg. Polynomial time approximation schemes for base station coverage with minimum total radii. *Computer Networks*, 47(4):489–501, 2005.

[16] J. Pach. Covering the plane with convex polygons. *Discrete & Computational Geometry*, 1(1):73–81, 1986.

[17] J. Pach and G. Tóth. Decomposition of multiple coverings into many parts. *Computational Geometry: Theory and Applications*, 42(2):127–133, 2009.

[18] M. A. Perillo and W. B. Heinzelman. Optimal sensor management under energy and reliability constraints. In *WCNC*, pages 1621–1626, 2003.

[19] A. Saipulla, C. Westphal, B. Liu, and J. Wang. Barrier coverage of line-based deployed wireless sensor networks. In *INFOCOM*, pages 127–135, 2009.

[20] S. Slijepcevic and M. Potkonjak. Power efficient organization of wireless sensor networks. In *ICC*, pages 472–476, 2001.

[21] Y. Taniguchi, T. Kitani, and K. Leibnitz. A uniform airdrop deployment method for large-scale wireless sensor networks. *IJSNet*, 9(3/4):182–191, 2011.

[22] L. Wang and Y. Xiao. A survey of energy-efficient scheduling mechanisms in sensor networks. *Mobile Networks and Applications*, 11(5):723–740, 2006.

Brief Announcement: Between All and Nothing—Versatile Aborts in Hardware Transactional Memory

Stephan Diestelhorst
TU Dresden, Germany
stephan.diestelhorst@
gmail.com

Martin Nowack
TU Dresden, Germany
martin@se.inf.tu-
dresden.de

Michael Spear
Lehigh University, Bethlehem,
PA
spear@cse.lehigh.edu

Christof Fetzer
TU Dresden, Germany
christof.fetzer@tu-
dresden.de

ABSTRACT

Hardware Transactional Memory (HTM) implementations are becoming available in commercial, off-the-shelf components. While generally comparable, some implementations deviate from the strict all-or-nothing property of pure Transactional Memory. We analyse these deviations and find that with small modifications, they can be used to accelerate and simplify both transactional and non-transactional programming constructs. At the heart of our extensions we enable access to the transaction's full register state in the abort handler in an existing HTM without extending the architectural register state. Access to the full register state enables applications in both transactional and non-transactional parallel programming: hybrid transactional memory; transactional escape actions; transactional suspend/resume; and alert-on-update.

Categories and Subject Descriptors

C.1.2 [**Computer Systems Organization**]: Processor Architectures—*Multiprocessors*; D.1.3 [**Software**]: Programming Techniques—*Parallel Programming*

Keywords

computer architecture, synchronisation, transactional memory, cross thread communication

1. INTRODUCTION

Hardware Transactional Memory [4] (HTM) has at last gained traction in industry, and leading microprocessors are soon [8, 10, 1] to incorporate HTM support [6, 5, 7]. However, these products provide a much less exotic flavor of HTM than those proposed by researchers [11, 12]: a comparable best-effort HTM with strong isolation, but very loose capacity specifications. We claim that it

is possible to extend an industry HTM proposal to bridge this gap, adding features such as alert-on-update [13], escape actions [9], and transactional suspend/resume. We enable these features without increasing hardware verification costs or changes to existing system software by extending the state that survives the transactional abort and is available to the abort handler. In particular, we do not extend the architectural state of applications, and thus the operating system and hypervisor can remain oblivious of the extensions, e.g., when performing context switches. Our hardware modifications are non-invasive in nature and do not require any additional associative tracking structures or other deep changes to the processor pipeline or the cache coherence / memory subsystem.

Our extensions are in line with the variation in various HTM proposals and forthcoming products. Despite the similarities in their core feature set, the proposals differ on the periphery, for example how they treat the register state, and in the availability and design of mechanisms that allow code to escape through the transactional layer. Comparing, for example, Intel's Transactional Synchronization Extension (TSX) and AMD's Advanced Synchronization Facility (ASF), both provide best-effort transactional memory, but differ in (1) the way they treat the snapshot/rollback of a transaction's register state, (2) nontransactional accesses from within a transaction, and (3) the availability of a minimum capacity guarantee.

TSX snapshots all registers on transaction start, and restores them automatically on abort; it also does not provide instructions to bypass the transactional mechanisms (untracked loads or immediate, escaping stores). ASF provides the opposite: registers are not automatically saved and restored, but instead software needs to manually save live registers on transaction start and restore them on abort. Additionally, ASF allows programs to bypass the transactional mechanisms through the application of an existing instruction prefix to mark memory operations as *nontransactional*, these operations will appear to take effect immediately, rather than at the end of the transaction. A similar feature was present in the cancelled Rock processor [2].

For our design we extend AMD's Advanced Synchronization Facility (ASF) [3], because its design already covers parts of our mechanism. We add four new instructions to ASF that extend the transaction abort logic and simplify the specification of nontransactional operations. The result suffices to enable transaction suspend/resume, multi-location alert-on-update, and escape actions.

2. BACKGROUND: ASF

ASF transactions are started with the SPECULATE instruction, which creates a partial checkpoint of the thread state and serves as the entry to an abort handler, if a transaction fails to commit. The COMMIT instruction ends a transaction, making all transactional updates immediately and atomically visible to memory. Within a transaction, regular x86 MOV instructions and prefixed LOCK MOV instructions (which can be either loads or stores) are used to distinguish between immediate, irrevocable accesses that escape the transaction and transactional accesses (i.e., stores are buffered until commit, and loads are tracked in the cache).[1]

ASF provides strong isolation: transactions detect conflicts with concurrent accesses from outside a transaction. Conflicts are resolved through a requester-wins policy that always aborts the transaction that added the conflicting item to its working set first.

In case of an abort, ASF will undo any transactional memory writes but will not restore the processor registers and all other memory updates. The CPU redirects the control flow to the instruction following SPECULATE and stores the abort reason and error code in register rax. The application checks rax to take appropriate measures (e.g., backoff and restart the transaction) in an abort handler. Aborts in ASF happen synchronously with the abort condition and may occur between any two instructions in the transaction.

3. ABORTS WITH CONTINUATION

The ASF abort handler can access all of the transaction's register state, except those registers that are overwritten at abort: rax conveys the abort cause; rflags is set according to rax; rsp (stack pointer) is restored to the value it had at transaction start; and rip (instruction pointer) points to the instruction after the SPECULATE instruction. We cannot use shadow registers to hold the values of these overwritten registers across an abort; operating systems and hypervisors would then have to be aware of these registers and save/restore them on context switches. To avoid affecting systems software, the register state must go elsewhere: we let the programmer allocate a buffer to hold the old values of these registers and provide its location as a parameter to SPECULATE. We enhance SPECULATE so it accepts this parameter, translates the virtual to a physical address, stores it in an internal register, and checks write permissions to the location. Any page faults are thus already resolved before the transaction starts.

In case of an abort, rax, rip, rsi, rflags, and rsp (old value at SPECULATE) are stored in the buffer. The abort handler runs as before, with rsi holding the buffer address. Furthermore, rsp will no longer be restored, preventing stack smashing due to signals or interrupt handlers running within the abort handler.

The abort handler can simply restore rsi and rsp from the buffer to reenable the original ASF functionality. However, it can also resume the code in the transaction by restoring all overwritten registers. Since existing assembly primitives cannot restore all registers without overwriting an additional temporary register, we provide a new CONTINUE instruction that performs a simple micro-code sequence to restore the registers.

With these modifications, it is easy to translate ASF's *synchronous* aborts into *asynchronous* aborts. The abort handler will simply set a thread local variable signalling an abort and will then execute CONTINUE. We also provide RDINVMODE and WRINVMODE instructions for detecting and changing the behavior of MOV and LOCK MOV within transactions.

From a hardware perspective, the required changes are minimal:

---

[1]SPECULATE or SPECULATE_INV determine the polarity of the LOCK prefix. We omit the specifics for brevity.

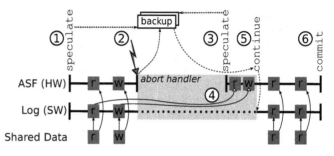

Figure 1: Overall Suspend/Resume mechanism based on the proposed extension: (1) A transaction and its ASF counterpart is started (SPECULATE with "backup" as argument); (2) In case of an abort, ASF stores the instruction pointer rax and executes the abort handler; (3) if the transaction can be recovered, the handler starts the hardware transaction; (4) the working set is replayed; (5) the transaction resumes the normal execution (CONTINUE) until it commits (6).

memorising an additional pointer during the execution of the transaction is easily achieved in either an internal register or in scratchpad memory. The changes to SPECULATE, CONTINUE, and the changed behaviour of aborts can be coded in microcode effectively.

4. OS-TRANSPARENT SUSPEND / RESUME

Suspend/resume appears in the new IBM POWER8 HTM proposal [5], but relies on additional registers and special handling in the OS when dealing with suspended transactions. We now show how to enable it in ASF given the simple extensions from Section 3.

Clearly, making available all register state of the transaction to the abort handler is not enough to resurrect an aborted transaction, because the transactional working set in memory is rolled back in ASF for all aborts. We note that this is not strictly necessary. For aborts other than violations of the integrity of the working set (certain types of contention or capacity evictions), it may be possible to keep the transactional state tentatively in the cache and make it available to the resurrecting SPECULATE/CONTINUE pair. To keep the OS unmodified, the speculative state however needs to be cleared when the processor sees an event that causes a TLB flush, usually indicating a context switch. However, the proposed suspension/resurrection mechanism can tolerate brief kernel invocations, e.g. due to interrupts or system calls from within the transaction.

When lazy clearing of transactional state proves too complex for an HTM, or support to survive full context switches is desired, we propose a lightweight hybrid TM approach: transactional accesses can be manually logged (with *nontransacional* stores) in a thread local log, which is employed to validate and replay the hardware transaction upon resurrection, see Figure 1. For normal transactional exection, the HTM is responsible for conflict detection and versioning, so the log is append-only.

5. MULTI-LOCATION ALERT-ON-UPDATE

Alert-on-update (AOU) is a mechanism that uses transactional read set tracking to generate user-level signals upon certain cache evictions [13]. To synthesise alert-on-update on top of our extended abort behaviour, we begin an ASF transaction and emulate AOU-marking loads with transactional loads and use nontransactional accesses for all other program data accesses, so that changes to program state will not roll back on transaction abort. We also nontransactionally log all AOU locations. Whenever an AOU-marked location is evicted from the cache, the ASF transaction jumps to the abort handler, which serves as (or chains to) the alert handler.

After the handler finishes resolving the alert, it starts a new transaction, adds again the monitored location(s) to the working set and continues execution at the previously aborted location through `CONTINUE`. Due to the overlapping nature of starting a transaction before executing `CONTINUE` to restore the state of the preceding transaction, we must take care to use alternating buffers for the storage of the clobbered registers. An additional complication is to flatten aborts in the overlap region, in order to prevent unbounded recursion. The abort handler will also be invoked for other reasons than changes in the monitored location(s), but those cases can be discerned through the abort condition codes presented to the abort handler. Continuing the transaction is usually enough to continue execution, but some cases require simple emulation of instructions illegal within transactions (such as system calls).

Because ASF will initiate the abort before switching contexts, the operating system / hypervisor does not need to be aware of additional information about the location of abort handlers, or the state of the aborted code. This is an improvement over the original alert-on-update proposal [13].

6. ESCAPE ACTIONS FROM HARDWARE TRANSACTIONS

ASF already supports escaping from a transaction with single loads / stores. Composing longer code blocks escaping these mechanisms (as in [14]) is complicated by the synchronous nature of aborts in ASF: whenever a condition for abort is detected, execution of the local control flow is redirected to the abort handler. This is usually not an issue with transactional code since all side-effects are tracked and rolled back. However, interrupting an escape action while it has not finished executing can leave escaped data in an inconsistent state. We therefore need to turn these synchronous aborts into asynchronous ones by updating a thread-local field F prior to beginning the escape action. The abort handler first checks F: if set, the handler memorises information about the abort in another field H, and then uses `CONTINUE` to immediately resume the aborted escape action. In this manner, the (nontransactional) escape action code will not be aborted while holding locks, or at some point where invariants may not hold. Upon completion of the escape action, the code registers any related undo actions, clears F, and checks H. If H indicates that an abort occurred during the escape action, the program uses the additional information saved by the handler to complete the abort, closely resembling an explicit abort in a software TM implementation.

7. CONCLUSION

In this paper, we presented small modifications to ASF that modify abort handling and managing the polarity of transactional / nontransactional accesses. Using only these two minor extensions, we support Alert-on-Update, Escape Actions, and Suspend/Resume in a simple hardware TM without changes to complex hardware structures and the system software stack. We believe that our modifications lie in the same complexity realm as the differences between the various HTM industry proposals, incur little added verification cost, and can also be implemented in other HTM proposals, for example extending first generation HTM support in TSX or POWER. This is a promising direction that can turn these *synchronization* extensions into *synchronization and speculation* extensions that support a rich transactional programming environment. Stephan received funding from the European Community's Seventh Framework Programme [FP7/2007-2013] under the ParaDIME Project,

grant agreement No. 318693, and developed related, initial ideas while employed at Advanced Micro Devices, Inc. At Lehigh University, this work was supported by the US National Science Foundation under grant CNS-1016828. Martin received funding by Deutsche Forschungsgemeinschaft (grant agreement No. FE 1035/1-2.)

8. REFERENCES

[1] Joanna Brewer. IBM Unveils zEnterprise EC12, a Highly Secure System for Cloud Computing and Enterprise Data. `http://www-03.ibm.com/press/us/en/pressrelease/38653.wss`, August 2012.

[2] Shailender Chaudhry, Robert Cypher, Magnus Ekman, Martin Karlsson, Anders Landin, and Sherman Yip. Rock: A High-Performance Sparc CMT Processor. *IEEE Micro*, 29(2):6–16, March–April 2009.

[3] Jaewoong Chung, Luke Yen, Stephan Diestelhorst, Martin Pohlack, Michael Hohmuth, Dan Grossman, and David Christie. ASF: AMD64 Extension for Lock-free Data Structures and Transactional Memory. In *Proceedings of the 43rd IEEE/ACM International Symposium on Microarchitecture*, Atlanta, Ga., December 2010.

[4] Maurice P. Herlihy and J. Eliot B. Moss. Transactional Memory: Architectural Support for Lock-Free Data Structures. In *Proceedings of the 20th International Symposium on Computer Architecture*, San Diego, Calif., May 1993.

[5] IBM(R). *Power ISA(tm) Transactional Memory*, 2.07 edition, December 2012.

[6] Intel Corp. *Intel(R) Architecture Instruction Set Extensions Programming Reference*, 319433-012a edition, February 2012.

[7] Christian Jacobi, Timothy Slegel, and Dan Greiner. Transactional Memory Architecture and Implementation for IBM System z. In *45th Int. Symp. On Microarchitecture*, 2012.

[8] Steve Chen Monica Chen. Intel Releases Updated Haswell CPU Roadmaps to Production Partners, Say Sources. `http://www.digitimes.com/news/a20130118PD210.html`, January 2013.

[9] Michelle Moravan, Jayaram Bobba, Kevin Moore, Luke Yen, Mark Hill, Ben Liblit, Michael Swift, and David Wood. Supporting Nested Transactional Memory in LogTM. In *Proceedings of the 12th International Conference on Architectural Support for Programming Languages and Operating Systems*, San Jose, Calif., October 2006.

[10] Timothy Prickett Morgan. Some Insight Into Those Future Power7+ Processors. `http://www.itjungle.com/tfh/tfh070912-story01.html`, July 2012.

[11] Ravi Rajwar, Maurice Herlihy, and Konrad Lai. Virtualizing Transactional Memory. In *Proceedings of the 32nd International Symposium on Computer Architecture*, Madison, Wis., June 2005.

[12] Hany E Ramadan, Christopher J Rossbach, and Emmett Witchel. Dependence-aware Transactional Memory for Increased Concurrency. In *Proceedings of the 41st annual IEEE/ACM International Symposium on Microarchitecture*, pages 246–257. IEEE Computer Society, 2008.

[13] Michael F. Spear, Arrvindh Shriraman, Luke Dalessandro, Sandhya Dwarkadas, and Michael L. Scott. Nonblocking Transactions Without Indirection Using Alert-on-Update. In *Proceedings of the 19th ACM Symposium on Parallelism in Algorithms and Architectures*, San Diego, Calif., June 2007.

[14] Craig Zilles and Lee Baugh. Extending Hardware Transactional Memory to Support Non-Busy Waiting and Non-Transactional Actions. In *Proceedings of the 1st ACM SIGPLAN Workshop on Languages, Compilers, and Hardware Support for Transactional Computing*, Ottawa, Ont., Canada, June 2006.

Brief Announcement: Towards a Fully-Articulated Pessimistic Distributed Transactional Memory [*]

Konrad Siek
Institute of Computing Science
Poznań University of Technology
Poznań, Poland
konrad.siek@cs.put.edu.pl

Paweł T. Wojciechowski
Institute of Computing Science
Poznań University of Technology
Poznań, Poland
pawel.t.wojciechowski@cs.put.edu.pl

ABSTRACT

Transactional memory, an approach aiming to replace cumbersome locking mechanisms in concurrent systems, has become a popular research topic. But due to problems posed by irrevocable operations (e.g., system calls), the viability of pessimistic concurrency control for transactional memory systems is being explored, in lieu of the more typical optimistic approach. However, in a distributed setting, where partial transaction failures may happen, the inability of pessimistic transactional memories to roll back is a major shortcoming. Therefore, this paper presents a novel transactional memory concurrency control algorithm that is both fully pessimistic and rollback-capable.

Categories and Subject Descriptors

D.1.3 [**Programming Techniques**]: Concurrent Programming—*Distributed programming*

Keywords

Concurrency control; Software transactional memory

1. INTRODUCTION

Transactional Memory (TM) [8, 13] is an increasingly popular research topic and a promising way to reduce the effort overhead introduced by concurrent programming by using the *transaction* abstraction. This approach is also applied to distributed systems, although additional issues like partial failures need to be addressed there.

In TM emphasis is placed on optimistic concurrency control. There are variations, but generally speaking in this approach a transaction executes regardless of other transactions and performs validation only when it finishes executing (at commit-time). If two transactions try to access the same object, and one of them writes to it, they conflict and one of them aborts and restarts. When a transaction aborts, it should not change the system state, so aborting transactions must revert the objects they modified to a checkpoint. Alternatively, they work on local copies and merge them with the original object on a successful commit.

Unfortunately, there is a problem with irrevocable operations in the optimistic approach. Such operations as system calls, I/O operations, or network messages, once executed, cannot be canceled and so, cause aborted transactions to have a visible effect on the system. In a distributed context these operations are common. The problem was avoided by using irrevocable transactions that run sequentially, and so cannot abort [16], or providing multiple versions of transaction view for reads [1, 12]. In other cases, irrevocable operations are just forbidden in transactions (e.g., in Haskell).

A different approach, as suggested by [10] and our earlier work [17, 18], is to use fully-pessimistic concurrency control. This involves transactions waiting until they have permission to access shared objects. In effect, conflicting operations are postponed and transactions avoid forced aborts. And therefore, transactions naturally avoid the problems stemming from irrevocable operations.

However, distributed transactional memory, pessimistic or optimistic, must still support rollback, because it is possible for partial failures to occur in the system. More precisely, rollback is ideal for reverting the system to a consistent state as part of a recovery procedure. Moreover, rollback makes a TM more expressive. That is, there are situations where the programmer wants to abort transactions as part of program logic. If there is no rollback and the programmer implements an *ad hoc* stand-in within the transaction, this detract from readability and is inefficient due to extra network communication with objects. To make it efficient, the programmer has to make changes to the object code (i.e., allow object-local backup copies).

In this paper we propose the *Supremum Versioning Algorithm* (SVA) with rollback support, a novel algorithm for fully-pessimistic concurrency control aimed for distributed wide-area transactions. Given precise information on object use within transactions, SVA provides optimal scheduling of transaction operations comparable to manually-designed fine-grained locking. This is due to its ability to release objects before committing (after the object was used for the last time). The ability to use rollback allows SVA to react to failures and makes it more expressive and easier to use from the point of view of the programmer. SVA preserves opacity and strong progressiveness guarantees while supporting both rollbacks and the early release mechanism.

[*]This work was funded in part by NCN grant 2012/06/M/ST6/00463.

$$
\begin{array}{lll}
O & \subseteq & \text{Objects} \\
T & \subseteq & \text{Transactions} \\
L & \subseteq & \text{Objects} \to \text{Locks} \\
V_g, V_l, V_{lt}, V_c & \subseteq & \text{Objects} \to \mathbb{N}_0 \\
V_p, C, V_r & \subseteq & \text{Objects} \times \text{Transactions} \to \mathbb{N}_0 \\
O_s & \subseteq & \text{Objects} \times \text{Transactions} \to \\
& & \quad \text{ObjectData} \cup \{\texttt{null}\}
\end{array}
$$

Figure 1: SVA structures.

2. RELATED WORK

Several distributed TM systems were proposed (see e.g., [2, 5, 9, 19]). Most of them replicate a non-distributed TM on many nodes and guarantee that replicas are consistent. Their programming model is different from our distributed transactions. Other systems extend non-distributed TMs with a communication layer, e.g., DiSTM [9] extends [7] with distributed coherence protocols. HyFlow [15] uses a similar model to ours. However, these are optimistic TMs.

Distributed transactions are successfully used where requirements for strong consistency meet wide-area distribution, e.g., in Google's Percolator [11] and Spanner [4]. Percolator supports multi-row, ACID-compliant, pessimistic database transactions that guarantee snapshot isolation. A drawback in comparison to TM is that writes must follow reads. Spanner provides semi-relational replicated tables with general purpose distributed transactions. It uses real-time clocks and Paxos to guarantee consistent reads. Spanner defers commitment like SVA, but buffers writes and aborts on conflict. Irrevocable operations are banned in Spanner.

Matveev and Shavit [10] propose pessimistic non-distributed TM that runs transactions sequentially (as in [16]) but allows parallel read-only transactions (a plausible extension of SVA). Operations are synchronized by delaying writes of the write-set location (with busy waiting). This is done using version numbers of transactions. In contrast, SVA uses object versions for similar purposes, which enables early release. However, direct comparison is difficult, because [10] aims at non-distributed environments with fast access, while SVA assumes network communication with overheads.

In [3], the authors prove that in a TM with faulty processes, local progress (analogous to wait-freedom) and opacity cannot both be ensured. Faulty processes either crash or are *parasitic*—they run without ever attempting to commit or abort. This is also evident for SVA.

There is no rigorous performance comparison of pessimistic and optimistic (or hybrid) distributed TM. However, our previous work [19] can shed some light. We compared pessimistic state-machine–based and optimistic deferred-update replication schemes in a faulty system. We showed that neither scheme is clearly superior, but performance of the former is less dependent on workload and contention.

3. SVA WITH ROLLBACK

The *Supremum Versioning Algorithm* (SVA) is a pessimistic concurrency control algorithm with rollback support; it builds on our rollback-free variant in [18]. The *modus operandi* of SVA is that transactions receive a version number during initialization and use it to determine whether they can access a shared object or whether they must wait until another transaction finishes using that object. Finally a transaction

```
1   proc @t start(t ∈ T, S ⊆ O → ℕ₀ ∪ {ω}) ≜
2     for each o ∈ dom(S) according to ≺_L do
3       @o lock L(o)
4     for each o ∈ dom(S) in parallel do
5       @o V_g[o ↦ V_g(o) + 1]
6       @o V_p[(o, t) ↦ V_g(o)]
7     for each o ∈ dom(S) according to ≺_L do
8       @o unlock L(o)

9   proc @t call(t ∈ T, S ⊆ O → ℕ₀ ∪ {ω}, o ∈ O) ≜
10    @o wait until V_p(o, t) − 1 = V_l(o)
11    @o checkpoint(t, o)
12    if V_r(o, t) ≠ V_c(o) then
13      @t rollback(t, S) and exit
14    @o call o
15    @o C[(o, t) ↦ C(o, t) + 1]
16    if C(o, t) = S(o) then
17      @o V_c[o ↦ V_p(o, t)]
18      @o V_l[o ↦ V_p(o, t)]

19  proc @t rollback(t ∈ T, S ⊆ O → ℕ₀ ∪ {ω}) ≜
20    for each o ∈ dom(S) in parallel do
21      @o dismiss(t, o)
22      @o restore(t, o)

23  proc @t commit(t ∈ T, S ⊆ O → ℕ₀ ∪ {ω}) ≜
24    for each o ∈ dom(S) in parallel do
25      @o dismiss(t, o)
26    if ∃o ∈ dom(S), V_r(o, t) > V_c(o) then
27      @t rollback(t, S) and exit
28    for each o ∈ dom(S) in parallel do
29      @o O_s(o, t) ← null
30      @o V_lt[o ↦ V_p(o, t)]

31  proc @o checkpoint(t ∈ T, o ∈ O) ≜
32    if C(o, t) = 0 then
33      @o O_s(o, t) ← copy o
34      @o V_r[(o, t) ↦ V_c(o)]

35  proc @o dismiss(t ∈ T, o ∈ O) ≜
36    @o wait until V_p(o, t) − 1 = V_lt(o)
37    if C(o, t) ≠ 0 ∧ V_r(o, t) = V_c(o) then
38      @o V_c[o ↦ V_p(o, t)]
39    if V_p(o, t) − 1 = V_l(o) then
40      @o V_l[o ↦ V_p(o, t)]

41  proc @o restore(t ∈ T, o ∈ O) ≜
42    if C(o, t) ≠ 0 ∧ V_r(o, t) < V_c(o) then
43      @o revert o ← O_s(o, t)
44      @o V_c[o ↦ V_r(o, t)]
45    @o O_s(o, t) ← null
46    @o V_lt[o ↦ V_p(o, t)]
```

Figure 2: SVA with rollback.

commits, which means it releases its objects—other transactions can start using them and this transaction no longer will. Alternatively, the transaction can roll back (abort). This reverts the state of all shared objects as if the transaction never modified them and finally releases them.

SVA supports an early release mechanism. That is, a transaction can release any objects after it used them for the last time (even before committing). This is possible because every transaction knows the upper bounds on the number of accesses to each object. (For our purposes this information comes from an oracle, but in practice, it may be extracted through static analysis [14] or typing [17].) However, while this development significantly improves the number of transactions executing simultaneously, it leads to a more complex rollback mechanism. A transaction must defer commit until the preceding transaction finishes, in case the current transaction uses objects that were released early and the preceding transaction rolls back. This is detailed below.

SVA Structures Before discussing the algorithm we describe the structures it uses. They are defined in Fig. 1. SVA works on sets of shared objects O and transactions T.

Since SVA works in a distributed system, objects are located and transactions spawn at arbitrary locations (or sites).

The basic premise of versioning algorithms is that counters are associated with transactions and used to allow or deny access by these transactions to shared objects (rather than only for recovery). SVA uses several version counters. *Private version counters* V_p uniquely define the version of a transaction with respect to an object. *Global version counters* show which transaction last started on a given object (this is used to initialize V_p). *Local version counters* V_l show which transaction can use a given object. *Local terminal version counters* V_{lt} show which transaction can commit or roll back a specific object. *Current version counters* V_c and *recovery version counters* V_r are used as a pair to detect if a preceding transaction rolled back an object that the current transaction is already using and to determine which transaction is responsible for reverting the object's state.

In order to detect the last use of an object, SVA requires that suprema (or infinity ω) on accesses S be given for each object used by a transaction. Then, *call counter* C is used to track actual accesses and to release objects early. In order be able to revert the state of objects SVA also uses a *stored object map* O_s, where transactions store copies of objects before modifying them. Also, SVA uses a map of locks L, one lock for each object during transaction start. These locks must always be used in order $\prec_L$ to prevent deadlocks.

The version counters and other structures are distributed among shared objects. Specifically, for any object o, values of V_p, V_l, V_{lt}, V_g, V_c, V_l, L, and O_s associated with o are located at o. Initially, all the locks are unlocked, all counters are set to zero, and the stored object map is empty.

SVA Transactions The life cycle of every SVA transaction begins with procedure start (we also refer to this part as initialization). Following that, a transaction may execute one or more accesses (calls) to a shared object. After any call or right after start a transaction may then either proceed to commit or rollback, which ends a transaction's life cycle. All procedures are shown in Fig. 2 and described below.

Note that accesses to shared objects can be interleaved with accesses to non-shared, transaction-local objects. However, those objects are only visible to the transaction they are local to, so they do not influence other transaction. So, we omit them for clarity. We also assume that transactions are executed in a single fresh dedicated thread. We also do not allow nested transactions and recurrency.

The pseudocode in Fig. 2 indicates where particular procedures and operations are located in the distributed system. If an operation is run on the host where object o is located, we mark it as @o. By analogy, @t means the operation is executed at the client running t. This gives a picture of network communication that transactions need to engage in.

The initialization of a transaction is shown in start at line 1. When a transaction starts it uses V_g to assign itself a unique version for each object it will access (V_p). This must be done atomically and in isolation, so these operations are guarded by locks—one lock l_o for each object used.

Objects are accessed via procedure call at line 9. Before accessing an object, the transaction waits for the preceding transaction to release it (line 10). When this happens, the transaction makes a backup copy to O_s using checkpoint (line 31)—a backup copy is made only before the first access to the object. If meanwhile no transaction modified the

object by rolling back, it is accessed. Otherwise, the transaction also rolls back, because it would access inconsistent state. After accessing an object, transaction checks whether this was the last access using C. If so, the object is released early—i.e, V_l is set to the version of the transaction V_p.

A transaction can attempt to commit using the procedure at line 23. A commit first releases all objects used by the transaction (procedure dismiss at line 35). To do this, the transaction waits for the previous transaction to commit the object. Then, V_c and V_l are set to indicate the object is released and who is responsible for reverting it. This may not be necessary if the object was not used or was released early. Second, the transaction checks whether any transaction rolled back and modified its objects. If so, it is forced to roll back. Otherwise the transaction erases backup copies from O_s and completes the commit by setting V_{lt}.

If the programmer decides to roll back a transaction, or if a rollback is forced in an aforementioned situation, procedure rollback (line 19) is used. In that case, objects are released using dismiss (as described above). Afterwards, the transaction restores its objects using restore (line 41). If an object was accessed at least once, this procedure reverts it to a copy from O_s and sets V_c to show that this transaction is now responsible for rolling the object back (e.g., so a simultaneously aborting younger transaction won't override the copy). Finally, the transaction cleans up O_s and finishes rolling back by setting V_{lt}.

4. PROPERTIES AND CORRECTNESS

In this section, we show that SVA guarantees safety (opacity) and liveness (strong progressiveness). The property of opacity is defined as follows (after [6]):

DEFINITION 1. *A finite TM history H is final-state opaque if there exists a sequential TM history S equivalent to any completion of H, such that (1) S preserves the real-time order of H, (2) every transaction $t \in T$ in S is legal in S.*

DEFINITION 2. *A TM object o is opaque if, and only if, every finite history of o is final-state opaque.*

Before defining strong progressiveness, it is necessary to define sets $CTrans(H)$, $CObj_H(t_i)$, and $CObj_H(Q)$. $CTrans(H)$ is a set of all subsets Q of all transactions in a history H, such that Q is not empty and no transaction in Q conflicts with any transaction not in Q. $CObj_H(t_i)$ is a set of shared objects, such that object o is included in the set if there exists a transaction t_j ($i \neq j$) in history H that conflicts with transaction t_i on shared object o. Given a set of transactions Q, $CObj_H(Q)$ is a union $\bigcup_{t_k \in Q} CObj_H(t_k)$.

Given this, strong progressiveness is defined as follows:

DEFINITION 3. *A TM history H is strongly progressive if, for every set $Q \in CTrans(H)$ such that $|CObj_H(Q)| \leq 1$, at least one transaction in Q is not forcibly aborted in H.*

DEFINITION 4. *A TM object o is strongly progressive if every history of o is strongly progressive.*

4.1 Opacity

THEOREM 1. *A finite SVA history is final-state opaque.*

PROOF. Since all SVA transactions access each object o only when the guard condition $V_p(o, t) - 1 = V_l(o)$ (line 10 in Fig. 2) they have exclusive access to o and they do so according to total order $\prec_{T'}$.

An SVA transaction t can access o when a previous transaction t' releases o early. In that case the upper bound on its use by t' was reached, so the state of o is the same as if t' committed. Also, t will wait on condition $V_p(o,t) - 1 = V_{lt}(o)$ (line 36 in Fig. 2) until t' finishes and if t' aborts, t will also abort. So no SVA transaction sees an inconsistent state of the system, nor does any committing transaction see changes from an aborting transaction.

Let H' be a completion of any SVA history H such that every live or commit-pending transaction in H is aborted. Since accesses to each o are totally ordered, this imposes a partial order $\preceq_{H'}$ on H'. Given this, we can construct a sequential witness history S equivalent to completion H' ($H'|t = S|t$ for every t), where there is a total order $\prec_S$ on S, such that $\preceq_{H'} \subseteq \prec_S$. Thus, we can construct an equivalent sequential history S that preserves the real-time order of H'.

Since committing transactions do no see the effects of aborted transactions and have exclusive access to objects they use for the duration of their execution, and since live transactions do not see an inconsistent state of the system, then for any H', transactions will behave as if they were executed sequentially, so as transactions in the sequential history S will conform to a sequential specification of the shared objects. Therefore, every transaction will be legal in S.

Since there exists a sequential history S equivalent to H that preserves the real time order of H and every transaction t in S is legal in S. Therefore H is final-state opaque. □

THEOREM 2. *SVA is opaque.*

PROOF. By Definition 1 and Definition 2 any transactional object o is opaque if, and only if, every finite history of o is final-state opaque. Since the latter follows from Theorem 1, then it is true that SVA objects are opaque, and therefore SVA is opaque. □

4.2 Strong progressiveness

THEOREM 3. *Every SVA history is strongly progressive.*

PROOF. Note also that an SVA transaction t may only be forcibly aborted if for some object o, $V_r(o,t) \neq V_c(o)$ or $V_r(o,t) > V_c(o)$ (line 13 and line 27 in Fig. 2). This happens if there is another transaction t' that also accesses object o, t' accesses o prior to t and releases it early so that t can access it, and finally t' aborts.

If there is a set of transactions $Q \in CTrans(H)$ such that $|CObj_H(Q)| = 0$ then no two transactions in Q attempt to access the same object. Therefore no transaction can force another to abort. If there is a set of transactions $Q \in CTrans(H)$ such that $|CObj_H(Q)| = 1$ then all transactions in Q share exactly one remote object o. Since all transactions in Q are ordered using a total order $\prec_Q$ it then follows that there is some transaction $t \in Q$ such that t is not preceded by any transaction, and therefore no transaction can cause it to abort. Therefore, there exists in Q a transaction that cannot be forcibly aborted.

Since transactions in $Q \in CTrans(H)$ such that $|CObj_H(Q)| = 0$ cannot be forcibly aborted and since there exists at least one transaction t in $Q \in CTrans(H)$ where $|CObj_H(Q)| = 1$ such that t cannot be aborted, then it is true that for any set Q where $|CObj_H(Q)| \leq 1$ some transaction is not forcibly aborted in H. Therefore every SVA history H is strongly progressive in accordance with Definition 3. □

THEOREM 4. *SVA is strongly progressive.*

PROOF. Since Theorem 3 shows that every SVA history is strongly progressive, it follows from Definition 4 that SVA objects are strongly progressive. □

5. REFERENCES

[1] H. Attiya and E. Hillel. Single-version STMs can be multi-version permissive. In *Proc. ICDCD'11*, 2011.

[2] R. L. Bocchino, V. S. Adve, and B. L. Chamberlain. Software transactional memory for large scale clusters. In *Proc. PPoPP'08*, Feb. 2008.

[3] V. Bushkov, R. Guerraoui, and M. Kapałka. On the liveness of transactional memory. In *Proc. PODC'12*, July 2012.

[4] J. C. Corbett and et al. Spanner: Google's globally-distributed database. In *Proc. OSDI'12*, 2012.

[5] M. Couceiro, P. Romano, N. Carvalho, and L. Rodrigues. D2STM: Dependable distributed software transactional memory. In *Proc. PRDC'09*, Nov. 2009.

[6] R. Guerraoui and M. Kapałka. *Principles of Transactional Memory.* Morgan & Claypool, 2010.

[7] M. Herlihy, V. Luchangco, and M. Moir. A flexible framework for implementing software transactional memory. In *Proc. OOPSLA'06*, Oct. 2006.

[8] M. Herlihy and J. E. B. Moss. Transactional memory: Architectural support for lock-free data structures. In *Proc. ISCA'93*, May 1993.

[9] C. Kotselidis, M. Ansari, K. Jarvis, M. Luján, C. C. Kirkham, and I. Watson. DiSTM: A software transactional memory framework for clusters. In *Proc. ICPP'08*, Sept. 2008.

[10] A. Matveev and N. Shavit. Towards a fully pessimistic STM model. In *Proc. TRANSACT'12*, Aug. 2012.

[11] D. Peng and F. Dabek. Large-scale incremental processing using distributed transactions and notifications. In *Proc. OSDI'10*, Oct. 2010.

[12] D. Perelman, R. Fan, and I. Keidar. On maintaining multiple versions in STM. In *Proc. PODC'10*, 2010.

[13] N. Shavit and D. Touitou. Software transactional memory. In *Proc. PODC'95*, Aug. 1995.

[14] K. Siek and P. T. Wojciechowski. A formal design of a tool for static analysis of upper bounds on object calls in Java. In *Proc. FMICS'12*, LNCS 7437, Aug. 2012.

[15] A. Turcu and B. Ravindran. On open nesting in distributed transactional memory. In *Proc. SYSTOR'12*, June 2012.

[16] A. Welc, B. Saha, and A.-R. Adl-Tabatabai. Irrevocable transactions and their applications. In *Proc. SPAA'08*, June 2008.

[17] P. T. Wojciechowski. Isolation-only transactions by typing and versioning. In *Proc. PPDP '05*, July 2005.

[18] P. T. Wojciechowski. *Language Design for Atomicity, Declarative Synchronization, and Dynamic Update in Communicating Systems.* Poznań University of Technology Press, 2007.

[19] P. T. Wojciechowski, T. Kobus, and M. Kokociński. Model-driven comparison of state-machine-based and deferred-update replication schemes. In *Proc. SRDS'12*, Oct. 2012.

Brief Announcement: A Game-Theoretic Model Motivated by the DARPA Network Challenge[*]

Rajesh Chitnis   MohammadTaghi Hajiaghayi   Jonathan Katz   Koyel Mukherjee

Department of Computer Science
University of Maryland, College Park
{rchitnis, hajiagha, jkatz, koyelm}@cs.umd.edu

ABSTRACT

In this paper we propose a game-theoretic model to analyze events similar to the 2009 *DARPA Network Challenge*, which was organized by the Defense Advanced Research Projects Agency (DARPA) for exploring the roles that the Internet and social networks play in incentivizing wide-area collaborations. The challenge was to form a group that would be the first to find the locations of ten moored weather balloons across the United States. We consider a model in which N people (who can form groups) are located in some topology with a fixed coverage volume around each person's geographical location. We consider various topologies where the players can be located such as the Euclidean d-dimension space and the vertices of a graph. A balloon is placed in the space and a group wins if it is the first one to report the location of the balloon. A larger team has a higher probability of finding the balloon, but we assume that the prize money is divided equally among the team members. Hence there is a competing tension to keep teams as small as possible.

Risk aversion is the reluctance of a person to accept a bargain with an uncertain payoff rather than another bargain with a more certain, but possibly lower, expected payoff. In our model we consider the *Isoelastic* utility function derived from the Arrow-Pratt measure of relative risk aversion. The main aim is to analyze the structures of the groups in Nash equilibria for our model. For the d-dimensional Euclidean space ($d \geq 1$) and the class of bounded degree regular graphs we show that in any Nash Equilibrium the *richest* group (having maximum expected utility per person) covers a constant fraction of the total volume. The objective of events like the DARPA Network Challenge is to mobilize a large number of people quickly so that they can cover a big fraction of the total area. Our results suggest that this objective can be met under certain conditions.

---

[*]A full version of the paper is available at arXiv.org [2]. R.C. and M.H were supported in part by NSF CAREER award 1053605, NSF grant CCF-1161626, ONR YIP award N000141110662, DARPA/AFOSR grant FA9550-12-1-0423, and a University of Maryland Research and Scholarship Award (RASA)

Categories and Subject Descriptors

F.2 [**Analysis of Algorithms and Problem Complexity**]: General

General Terms

Theory

Keywords

Crowdsourcing, Nash Equilibrium, Risk Aversion

1. INTRODUCTION

With the advent of communication technologies, and the Web in particular, we can now harness the collective abilities of large groups of people to accomplish tasks with unprecedented speed, accuracy, and scale. In the popular culture and the business literature, this process has come to be known as crowdsourcing [12]. Crowdsourcing has been used in various tasks such as labeling of images [16], predicting protein structures [10], and posting and solving Human Intelligence Tasks in Amazon's *Mechanical Turk* [14]. An important class of crowdsourcing problems demand a large recruitment along with an extremely fast execution. Examples of such *time-critical social mobilization* tasks include search-and-rescue operations in the times of disasters, evacuation in the event of terrorist attacks, and distribution of medicines during epidemics.

The DARPA Network Challenge: A good example of collaboratition is The 2009 *DARPA Network Challenge* [1], an event organized by the Defense Advanced Research Projects Agency (DARPA) for exploring the roles that the Internet and social networks play in incentivizing wide-area collaborations. The strategy of the winning team from MIT is outlined in [6]. Their main focus is on the mechanics of the group formation process in the DARPA Network Challenge whereas in this paper we try to analyze the structures of the groups which form in Nash Equilibria.

Related Work: Douceur and Moscibroda [3] addressed a problem close to the spirit of the DARPA Network Challenge. They address the problem of motivating people to install and run a distributed service, like peer-to-peer systems. Their focus is on incentivizing the growth of a single group whereas in this paper we take a bird's-eye view and try to analyze the structures of the groups in Nash equilibria.

Some recent results [9, 5] analyze the structures of Nash Equilibria. A well-studied parameter related to Nash equilibria is the *price of anarchy* [13]. However as observed in [9, 5], bounds on the structures of Nash equilibria lead to approximate bounds on the price of anarchy as well but not necessarily the other way around.

Therefore trying to analyze the structures of groups in Nash equilibria is more general than trying to bound the price of anarchy.

There is an entire body of literature in Economics which is closely related to the model we consider in this paper. There have also been studies on how the rules of coalition formation affect the stability of environmental agreements between countries [11]. In the last year there have been two papers which consider events similar to the DARPA Network Challenge [8, 7].

2. OUR MODEL

There is a set of N players, each covering a region of space within the total volume A. In particular, in the Euclidean space, we assume each player covers a ball of radius one centered at his location; in the discrete case we view the players as occupying the vertices of a graph and assume each player covers himself and his neighbors. Players are allowed to organize themselves into a collection of disjoint *groups* partitioning the set of players. In this work, we do not consider the precise dynamics of group formation, but instead we focus on analyzing the structures of the groups in Nash equilibria. Once the groups are formed, we envision the balloon being placed in the space. [1] We say the balloon *falls within* a group S if the location of the balloon is in the coverage of S; a group S *wins* if it is the first one to report the location of the balloon. To model this we assume the probability that the balloon *falls within* a group S is A_S/A, where A_S is the total volume covered by the players in S and A is the total volume. The prize money M is given to the group that wins, and the money received by a group is split equally among all members of that group. We note the balloon can be placed anywhere in the space, and we do not know where it will be placed. Hence the probability of any of the groups (which might form) finding the balloon first is the same and we do not consider this common factor hereafter.

Risk aversion [15] is the reluctance of a person to accept a bargain with an uncertain payoff rather than another bargain with a more certain, but possibly lower, expected payoff [15]. Risk aversion is a natural assumption when we consider money and people: most of us would accept a guaranteed payment of say X dollars than a 50% chance of receiving 2X and a 50% chance of getting nothing, especially if X is large (the DARPA Challenge had a prize money of $40,000). *Constant relative risk aversion* means that the ratio of the increase in the utility to the increase in the risk taken is constant. Assuming that the Arrow-Pratt measure of relative risk aversion is constant, the *isoelastic* utility function for money x is given by $u(x) = \frac{x^{1-r}}{1-r}$ where $0 \leq r < 1$ is the risk aversion factor [4]. For $r = 1$ we take the utility to be the natural logarithm. Here $r = 0$ means there is no risk aversion. For simplicity we scale up everything by a factor of $1 - r$ to get a concave utility function given by $u(x) = x^{1-r}$ where $0 < r < 1$. The *expected* utility for a player who is a member of a group S is given by $p(S) \cdot u(\frac{M}{|S|})$, where $p(S) = \frac{A_S}{A}$ is the probability that the balloon fall within S. Consider two players who have disjoint area of coverage. If they are on their own, then their expected utility is $u = \left(\frac{|M|}{1}\right)^{1-r} \cdot \frac{a}{A}$ where a is the area they can cover. If they join together to form a group then their expected utility is $u' = \left(\frac{|M|}{2}\right)^{1-r} \cdot \frac{2a}{A} = 2^r \cdot u > u$ since $1 > r > 0$. Therefore two people whose coverage areas are disjoint will always join together, not matter what the risk aversion factor r is. The intuition is that the value of r affects how much overlapping coverage areas is allowed for it to be beneficial for people to join together. The smaller the value of r the lesser the

overlap must be between the coverage areas of the players for it to make sense for them to merge.

We assume that the balloon is placed in a location covered by at least one player. Given a partition $S_1, \ldots, S_\ell$ of all the players into groups, we now ask whether it forms an equilibrium. More formally, we allow two types of actions:

1. Two groups S_i and S_j can decide to *merge*. We say this operation is *incentivized* only if each player in S_i and S_j would increase their expected utility by merging.

2. A member x of group S_i may *defect* to join a different group S_j. We say this operation is *incentivized* only if both x's expected utility and the expected utility of each player in S_j increase after the defect.

A given partition is a *Nash Equilibrium* if no merge or defect operation is incentivized, i.e., no player can do better by unilaterally changing his group.

3. OUR RESULTS

We consider the *social welfare* from the viewpoint of the agency which hosts the event described by our model. First we show that the hosting agency needs to offer prize money proportional to the desired size of a largest group or to the desired fraction of the total volume covered if each person must receive a minimum threshold expected utility.

THEOREM 3.1. $[\star]$[2] *If there exists a Nash Equilibrium in which at least one group S covers a λ-fraction of the total volume, and each player in S covers volume V and has an expected utility of at least c, then $M \geq \lambda Ac^{\frac{1}{1-r}}$.*

THEOREM 3.2. $[\star]$ *If there exists a Nash Equilibrium in which there is at least one group S of size k, and each player in S covers volume V and has an expected utility of at least c, then $M \geq k\left(\frac{cA}{N}\right)^{\frac{1}{1-r}}$.*

DEFINITION 3.3. *Given a partition of the people into groups, we say a group G is a **richest** group if its expected utility per person value is at least that of any other group in the partition.*

We note that given any partition of people into groups, there always exists at least one richest group. We show the following interesting and unexpected phenomenon: for various different topologies, in every Nash Equilibrium any richest group covers a constant fraction of the total volume. We assume that each point in the space belongs to coverage area of at least one player.

3.1 The One-Dimensional (Line) Case

In this section the players are located along a line. We assume each person has a coverage length of one on both sides. Recall for each person x in a group S the expected utility is $E[u(x)] = \left(\frac{M}{|S|}\right)^{1-r} \cdot \frac{A_S}{A}$ where M is the total money, A_S is the length covered by group S and A is the total length. We contract the points not covered by any player. Therefore every point in the total length has at least one person whose coverage length contains it.

LEMMA 3.4. $[\star]$ *For the line case, let S be a richest group in a Nash Equilibrium. Then there is no player $i \notin S$ who can add a length of at least $2(1-r)$ to the length A_S currently covered by S.*

---

[1] In fact, we may assume without loss of generality the ten balloons are placed uniformly in the space covered by all the players.

[2] The proofs of the results labeled with $\star$ have been deferred to the full version [2]

THEOREM 3.5. [⋆] *For the one dimensional (line) case, in any Nash Equilibrium a richest group which covers a constant fraction of the total length where the constant is $\frac{1}{1+2(1-r)}$.*

3.2 The Euclidean d-dimensional Case

In this section we consider the case in which the players are located in a Euclidean d-dimensional space and each person covers a unit ball around himself. The next lemma bounds the ratio of volumes of the union of the two families of balls with the same set of centers but different radii.

LEMMA 3.6. *Let A be a finite family of balls of radius one in a Euclidean d-dimensional space. Let B be a family of balls with the same set of the centers but radius $t \geq 1$. Let A_U, B_U denote the union of balls in A and B respectively. Then $Vol(B_U) \leq t^d \cdot Vol(A_U)$ where $Vol(A_U), Vol(B_U)$ denotes the volume of A_U and B_U respectively.*

PROOF. Let $C = \{c_1, c_2, \ldots, c_n\}$ be the centers of the balls in A. For $x \in B_U$ define $c(x) = \min\{ d(c_j, x) \mid 1 \leq j \leq n \}$. Consider the partition $P_1, P_2, \ldots, P_n$ of B_U into n parts: $x \in B_U$ is placed in P_i if and only if $i = \min\{ j \mid d(x, c_j) = c(x) \}$.

We claim $y \in P_j$ implies $[c_j, y] \in P_j$. Suppose there is a point $z \in [c_j, y]$ such that $z \in P_k$ for $k \neq j$. By the triangle inequality $d(c_k, y) \leq d(c_k, z) + d(z, y) \leq d(c_j, z) + d(z, y) = d(c_j, y)$ where we used $z \in P_k$ implies $d(c_k, z) \leq d(c_j, z)$. So $d(c_k, y) \leq d(c_j, y)$. But $y \in P_j$ implies $d(c_k, y) = d(c_j, y)$, $d(c_k, z) = d(c_j, z)$ and $j < k$. This contradicts the membership of z in P_k. So we can apply homothecy: for every $1 \leq i \leq n$ we contract each P_i w.r.t point c_i by a factor of $\frac{1}{t}$ to get a region say P_i'. We note $P_i' \subseteq A_U$ as $x \in P_i$ implies $d(x, c_i) \leq t$ and if we denote by x' the point to which x is mapped under the contraction, then $d(x', c_i) = \frac{1}{t} \cdot d(x, c_i) \leq \frac{1}{t} \cdot t = 1$.

The next claim is $P_i' \cap P_j' = \emptyset$ for any $i \neq j$. Suppose not and say $y \in P_i' \cap P_j'$. Let y_i, y_j be the points in P_i and P_j respectively which get mapped to y under the contraction. Let $d(c_j, y) = \alpha$ and $d(c_i, y) = \beta$. By the triangle inequality we have $d(c_i, y_j) \leq d(c_i, y) + d(y, y_j) = \beta + (t-1)\alpha$. Also $y_j \in P_j$ implies $d(c_i, y_j) \geq d(c_j, y_j) = t\alpha$. So $\beta + (t-1)\alpha \geq d(c_i, y_j) \geq d(c_j, y_j) \geq t\alpha$, i.e., $\beta \geq \alpha$. Similarly we have $\alpha \geq \beta$ which implies $\alpha = \beta$. Therefore $t\alpha = d(c_j, y_j) \leq d(c_i, y_j) \leq d(c_i, y) + d(y, y_j) = \beta + (t-1)\alpha = t\alpha$. Equality in the triangle inequality gives c_i, y_j, y_i are on the same line and $d(c_i, y_j) = d(c_i, y_i)$ which implies $y_i = y_j$ which is a contradiction. So we have the following two conditions :

1. $P_i' \subseteq A_U$ for every $1 \leq i \leq n$.

2. $P_i' \cap P_j' = \emptyset$ for any $i \neq j$.

Therefore, $Vol(A_U) \geq \sum_{i=1}^{n} Vol(P_i') = \frac{1}{t^d} \cdot \sum_{i=1}^{n} Vol(P_i) = \frac{1}{t^d} \cdot Vol(B_U)$. We note the bound is tight when all the balls in B are disjoint. □

We now give a generalization of Lemma 3.4 for a Euclidean d-dimensional space. Let V_d denote the volume of a unit ball in the Euclidean d-dimensional space.

LEMMA 3.7. *Let S be a richest group in a Nash Equilibrium. There is no player $i \notin S$ who can add a volume of at least $(1-r)V_d$ to the volume A_S currently covered by S.*

PROOF. Suppose there is a player $i \notin S$, who can add a volume of at least $(1 - r)V_d$ to the volume covered by S. However, since it is a Nash Equilibrium, either the new expected utility of S on adding this player is less than or equal to the current expected utility

of S, hence S would have no incentive in adding the player i. Or else the player i would not have any incentive to move to S, as the projected new expected utility of i is less than or equal to his current expected utility. Since S is a richest group, both these conditions combine to give:

$$\left(\frac{M}{|S|+1}\right)^{1-r} \cdot \frac{A_S + (1-r)V_d}{A} \leq \left(\frac{M}{|S|}\right)^{1-r} \cdot \frac{A_S}{A} \quad (1)$$

As each player has a coverage volume of V_d we have $|S|V_d \geq A_S$ (with equality only if the coverage volumes of the members of S are pairwise disjoint). The function $f(x) = \frac{x}{x+1}$ is increasing on $(0, \infty)$ and hence $\frac{|S|}{|S|+1} \geq \frac{\beta}{\beta+1}$ where $\beta = \frac{A_S}{V_d}$. Combining with Equation 1 gives $\left(\frac{\beta}{\beta+1}\right)^{1-r} \leq \left(\frac{|S|}{|S|+1}\right)^{1-r} \leq \frac{A_S}{A_S+(1-r)V_d}$ Rearranging and setting $1 - r = \frac{1}{t}$ implies

$$\frac{A_S + (1-r)V_d}{A_S} \leq \left(\frac{\beta+1}{\beta}\right)^{\frac{1}{t}} \implies \left(1 + \frac{(1-r)V_d}{A_S}\right)^t \leq 1 + \frac{1}{\beta}$$

Bernoulli's inequality states if $x, q \in \mathbb{R}$ and $x > -1, q > 1$ then $(1 + x)^q > 1 + qx$. Applying the inequality for $x = \frac{(1-r)V_d}{A_S}$ and $q = t = \frac{1}{1-r} > 1$ gives $1 + \frac{1}{\beta} = 1 + \frac{t(1-r)V_d}{A_S} < \left(1 + \frac{(1-r)V_d}{A_S}\right)^t \leq 1 + \frac{1}{\beta}$ which is a contradiction. □

A simple proof shows that if S is any richest group in a Nash Equilibrium then $\frac{A_S}{A} \geq \frac{1}{3^d}$ where A_S is the volume covered by the group S and A is the total volume.

THEOREM 3.8. [⋆] *If the players are located in a d-dimensional Euclidean space then in any Nash Equilibrium every richest group covers at least a $\frac{1}{3^d}$-fraction of the total volume.*

The above bound of $\frac{1}{3^d}$ is independent of the risk aversion factor r. We now give a better bound which depends on r. To this end, the following lemma shows how to bound the volume of intersection of two unit balls in a Euclidean d-dimensional space.

LEMMA 3.9. [⋆] *Let B_1 and B_2 be two unit balls in a Euclidean d-dimensional space. For $a \leq 1$, if the distance between the centers of B_1 and B_2 is $2a$, then the volume of intersection of B_1 and B_2 is at most $2(1-a^2)^{\frac{d-1}{2}} \cdot V_{d-1}$ where V_{d-1} is the volume of a unit ball in a Euclidean $(d-1)$-dimensional space.*

The next lemma gives a lower bound on the ratio of the volumes of unit balls in Euclidean spaces of consecutive dimensions.

LEMMA 3.10. [⋆] *For $d \geq 2$ let V_{d-1}, V_d be the volumes of unit balls in the $d-1$ and d-dimensional Euclidean spaces respectively. Then $\frac{V_d}{V_{d-1}} \geq \frac{1}{d}$.*

We are now ready to give a better bound than $\frac{1}{3^d}$ on the fraction of the total volume covered by any richest group in a Nash Equilibrium.

THEOREM 3.11. *If the players are located in a d-dimensional Euclidean space, then in any Nash Equilibrium there always is a group which covers at least a $\frac{1}{(2\delta+1)^d}$-fraction of the total volume where $\delta = \sqrt{1 - \left(\frac{r}{2d}\right)^{\frac{2}{d-1}}}$. We note $\frac{1}{(2\delta+1)^d} > \frac{1}{3^d}$ as $\delta < 1$ and therefore this improves on Theorem 3.8.*

PROOF. Consider a richest group S in a Nash Equilibrium. By Lemma 3.7, no player outside of S can get his coverage ball to contribute at least $(1 - r)V_d$ volume to S, i.e, for every $x \notin S$ there is a player $s \in S$ such that volume of intersection of balls B_x, B_s of x and s respectively is at least rV_d. Let the distance between centers of B_x and B_s be $2a$. Lemma 3.9 gives $2(1 - a^2)^{\frac{d-1}{2}} V_{d-1} \geq \text{Vol}(B_s \cap B_x) \geq r \cdot V_d$ which implies $2(1 - a^2)^{\frac{d-1}{2}} \geq r\frac{V_d}{V_{d-1}} \geq \frac{r}{d}$ by Lemma 3.10. Rearranging we get $a \leq \sqrt{1 - \left(\frac{r}{2d}\right)^{\frac{2}{d-1}}} =$ say δ. So each player not in S is at a distance of at most 2δ from some player of S. Therefore the total volume A is covered by the volume A'_S of the union of the family of balls of radius $2\delta + 1$ centered at members of S. By Lemma 3.6 we have $\frac{A_S}{A} \geq \frac{A_S}{A'_S} \geq \frac{1}{(2\delta+1)^d}$. $\square$

3.3 The Graph Case

In the discrete version of the problem we assume that the players form the vertex set of an undirected graph. The coverage of a vertex is its closed neighborhood, i.e., a vertex covers itself and all its neighbors. We assume the same utility function as before: Each member x belonging to a group S has expected utility given by $E[u(x)] = \left(\frac{M}{|S|}\right)^{1-r} \cdot \frac{|A_S|}{|A|}$ where M is the total money, A_S is the union of the closed neighborhoods of the vertices in S and A is the vertex set of the graph. We first show a preliminary lemma which bounds the contribution to a richest group in a Nash Equilibrium by any vertex which is not in the richest group. This lemma can be viewed as a discrete version of Lemma 3.7.

LEMMA 3.12. $[\star]$ *Let $G = (V, E)$ be an undirected graph with maximum degree Δ. Let S be a richest group in a Nash Equilibrium. Then there is no player $i \notin A_S$ who can add at least $(1 - r)(\Delta + 1)$ vertices to the set A_S currently covered by S.*

In the next theorem we show if the topology is the class of bounded-degree regular graphs, then in any Nash Equilibrium there always exists a group which covers a constant fraction of the total number of vertices.

THEOREM 3.13. $[\star]$ *Let $G = (A, E)$ be a f-regular graph. In any Nash Equilibrium there always exists a group covering a constant fraction of the total number of vertices where the constant is $\frac{1}{\frac{f-1}{r(f+1)} + 1}$.*

The general graph case does not seem to be hopeful. Recall in all the three topologies (the one-dimensional (line) space, the d-dimensional Euclidean space and the bounded-degree regular graphs) considered so far, we were able to show the surprising phenomenon that any *richest* group in a Nash Equilibrium covers a constant fraction of the total volume/vertices. We show this approach fails for general graphs, i.e., there exist graphs having a Nash Equilibrium in which no richest group covers a constant fraction of the total number of vertices.

THEOREM 3.14. $[\star]$ *There exist graphs which have a Nash Equilibrium in which no richest group covers a constant fraction of the total number of vertices.*

Theorem 3.14 implies we need different ideas than those we use previously to tackle the general graph case. In collaboratition events we think it is reasonable to allow a person to defect to another group but not back to his original state of being alone. Under this assumption, we can show there exist graphs which have a Nash Equilibrium in which no group covers a constant fraction of the total number of vertices.

THEOREM 3.15. $[\star]$*Given any constant $0 < c < 1$, under the **assumption that defecting to an empty group is not allowed**, there exists a graph G_c and a Nash Equilibrium in G_c such that each group in the Nash Equilibrium covers strictly less than a c-fraction of the total number of vertices.*

4. CONCLUSIONS

In this paper we have suggested a game-theoretic model motivated by the DARPA Network Challenge. We analyze the structures of the groups in Nash equilibria. We show for various topologies: a one-dimensional space (line), a d-dimensional Euclidean space, and bounded-degree regular graphs; in any Nash Equilibrium there always exists a group which covers a constant fraction of the total volume. The objective of events like the DARPA Network Challenge is to mobilize a large number of people quickly so that they can cover a big fraction of the total area. Our results suggest that this objective can be met under certain conditions.

The most important open question is to show the existence of Nash equilibria in our model, maybe under some additional assumptions.

5. REFERENCES

[1] The 2009 DARPA Network Challenge (http://archive.darpa.mil/networkchallenge/).

[2] Rajesh Hemant Chitnis, MohammadTaghi Hajiaghayi, Jonathan Katz, and Koyel Mukherjee. A game-theoretic model motivated by the darpa network challenge. *CoRR*, abs/1204.6552, 2012.

[3] J.R. Douceur and T. Moscibroda. Lottery Trees: Motivational Deployment of Networked Systems. *ACM SIGCOMM Computer Communication Review*, 37(4):121–132, 2007.

[4] Charles Holt et al. Risk Aversion and Incentive Effects . *The American Economic Review*, 92(5), 2002.

[5] Erik D. Demaine et al. The Price of Anarchy in Cooperative Network Creation Games. In *STACS*, 09.

[6] Galen Pickard et al. Time Critical Social Mobilization: The DARPA Network Challenge Winning Strategy. *CoRR*, abs/1008.3172, 2010.

[7] Manuel Cebrián et al. Finding red balloons with split contracts: robustness to individuals' selfishness. In *STOC*, 2012.

[8] Moshe Babaioff et al. On bitcoin and red balloons. In *EC*, 2012.

[9] Noga Alon et al. Basic Network Creation Games. In *SPAA*, 2010.

[10] Seth Cooper et al. Predicting protein structures with a multiplayer online game. *Nature*, 466(7307):756–760, 2010.

[11] Michael Finus and Bianca Rundshagen. How Rules of Coalition Formation Affect Stability of International Environmental Agreements. Technical Report 2003.62, Fondazione Eni Enrico Mattei, 2003.

[12] Jeff Howe. *Crowdsourcing: Why the Power of the Crowd Is Driving the Future of Business*. Crown Business, 2008.

[13] Elias Koutsoupias and Christos H. Papadimitriou. Worst-case Equilibria. In *STACS*, 1999.

[14] Jason Pontin. Artificial Intelligence, With Help From the Humans . *The New York Times*, 2007.

[15] J.W. Pratt. Risk aversion in the small and in the large. *Econometrica*, pages 122–136, 1964.

[16] Luis von Ahn. Games with a Purpose. *IEEE Computer*, 39(6):92–94, 2006.

IRIS: A Robust Information System Against Insider DoS-Attacks*

[Extended Abstract]

Martina Eikel
University of Paderborn
martinah@upb.de

Christian Scheideler
University of Paderborn
scheideler@upb.de

ABSTRACT

In this work we present the first scalable distributed information system, i.e., a system with low storage overhead, that is provably robust against Denial-of-Service (DoS) attacks by a *current insider*. We allow a current insider to have *complete* knowledge about the information system and to have the power to block *any ε-fraction* of its servers by a DoS-attack, where ε can be chosen up to a constant. The task of the system is to serve any collection of lookup requests with at most one per non-blocked server in an efficient way despite this attack. Previously, scalable solutions were only known for DoS-attacks of past insiders, where a past insider only has complete knowledge about some *past* time point t_0 of the information system. Scheideler et al. [2, 3] showed that in this case it is possible to design an information system so that any information that was inserted or last updated *after* t_0 is safe against a DoS-attack. But their constructions would not work at all for a current insider. The key idea behind our IRIS system is to make extensive use of coding. More precisely, we present two alternative distributed coding strategies with an at most logarithmic storage overhead that can handle up to a constant fraction of blocked servers.

Categories and Subject Descriptors

C.2.4 [**Computer-Communication Networks**]: Distributed Systems; H.3.4 [**Information Storage and Retrieval**]: Systems and Software—*Distributed systems*

General Terms

Theory

Keywords

Distributed systems; Denial-of-Service attacks; DHT

*This work was partially supported by the German Research Foundation (DFG) within the Collaborative Research Center "On-The-Fly Computing" (SFB 901)

1. INTRODUCTION

Distributed denial-of-service (DoS) attacks are one of the biggest threats in the Internet. The basic idea behind a DoS-attack is to make a service unavailable to its intended users. There are various ways of achieving that, like causing computationally expensive operations [13], downloading large files [24], exploiting protocol bugs, or just overloading servers with junk. Information services like Google and Akamai are frequently under attack, and also the Domain Name System has been involved in many attacks, either as a victim itself, or as a means to raise reflected or DNS amplification attacks [33].

The predominant approaches in information systems to deal with the threat of DoS-attacks are to use *redundancy* and *information hiding*: information which is replicated on multiple servers is more likely to remain accessible during a DoS-attack, in particular, if the attacker does not know the servers resp. how the data items are distributed among the servers. For example, if $\Theta(\log n)$ copies of a data item are placed randomly among n servers, and these random positions are not known to the attacker, then it is easy to show that any strategy of the attacker to block half of the servers will not block all of the copies with high probability[1]. The situation is completely different, however, when considering an insider, i.e., someone that has complete knowledge about the system. Since information cannot be hidden any more in this case, it seems unavoidable to replicate a data item across more than t servers to remain accessible under a DoS-attack that can block up to t servers, which creates a huge storage overhead. This is why in our previous work we just focused on past insiders [2, 3]. However, it turns out that this dilemma can be circumvented when using coding, which is the key idea of the IRIS system presented in this paper ("IRIS" is a short form of "Insider-Resistant Information System").

1.1 Model

To keep the presentation of our ideas clean and simple, we will use a simple model. We assume that the information system consists of a static set V of n reliable servers of identical type. (We deliberately use the word "server" here since assuming a static set of nodes is unrealistic for peer-to-peer solutions; we focus instead on solutions based on dedicated equipment provided by one or more institutions or companies.) The servers are responsible for storing the data as

---

[1]"With high probability", or short, "w.h.p.", means a probability of at least $1 - 1/n^c$ where the constant c can be made arbitrarily large.

well as handling the user requests. We assume that all data items are of the same size, and a data item x is uniquely identified by a key $key(x)$. The universe of all possible keys is denoted by U, and we set $m = |U|$. The only type of user requests that we consider are lookup(k) requests, where k is any key in U (i.e., the purpose of the system is just to deliver information, not to let users update it). Given a lookup(k) request, the system is supposed to either return the data item x with $key(x) = k$, or to return $NULL$ if no such data item exists.

Every server knows about all other servers and can therefore directly communicate with any one of them. This does not endanger scalability since millions of IP addresses can easily be stored in main memory in any reasonable computer today and we assume the set of servers to be static. We will use the standard synchronous message passing model for the communication between the servers. That is, time proceeds in synchronized *communication rounds*, or simply *rounds*, and in each round each server first receives all messages sent to it in the previous round, processes all of them, and then sends out all messages that it wants to send out in this round. A message will never get lost, unless it is sent to a blocked server. We assume that the time needed for internal computations is negligible (the IRIS protocols are simple enough to satisfy this property). Note however that using local synchronizers [23], our algorithms also work in asynchronous settings. All we need is a bounded transmission time between two non-attacked servers.

The competition between the information system and the attacker works as follows. Initially, the attacker can inspect the entire system and selects, based on that, an arbitrary ε-fraction of the servers to be blocked (where ε depends on the limitations of the given system). A server that is blocked will not react to messages from the other servers. We assume that the servers have a failure detector that allows them to determine whether a server is blocked so that statements like "if server i is blocked then..." are allowed in the protocol.

The attacker may then select an arbitrary collection of lookup requests, one per non-blocked server (the most simple case of an even request distribution among servers). That is, the keys selected by the attacker may or may not be associated with data items stored in the system, and the attacker is also allowed to issue multiple lookup requests for the same key. The task of the system is to correctly serve *all* of these requests.

In order to measure the quality of the information system, we introduce the following notation. A storage strategy is said to have a *redundancy* of r if r times more storage (including any control storage) is used for the data than storing the plain data. We call an information system

- *scalable* if its redundancy is at most polylog(n),

- *efficient* if any collection of lookup requests specified by the attacker can be processed correctly in at most polylog(n) many communication rounds in which every server sends and receives at most polylog(n) many messages of at most polylog(n) size, and

- *robust* if this is possible even if up to an ε-fraction of the servers is blocked by an insider.

Our goal is to design an information system that is scalable, efficient, and robust for an ε that is as large as possible. As we will see, the IRIS system satisfies all of these properties.

1.2 Related Work

Due to their importance, DoS-attacks are a well-studied problem (e.g., [8, 17] for an overview). Unfortunately, it is often difficult to distinguish DoS traffic from legitimate traffic, which limits the effectiveness of network-layer and transport-layer DoS prevention tools [31], such as filtering out anomalies [16], blacklisting particular IP addresses, using TCP SYN cookies [4], and pushback [12]. This has led some researchers to follow alternative means like letting legitimate clients "speak up" [31, 32].

In this paper, we do not seek to prevent DoS-attacks but rather focus on how to maintain a good availability and performance during the attack. Our system is based on the distributed hash table (DHT) paradigm (e.g., [5, 10, 11, 25, 30]), with the new twist of using coding. Various DoS-resistant systems based on DHTs have already been proposed [14, 15, 18]. For instance, the Secure Overlay Services approach [15] uses proxies on Chord to defend against DoS-attacks. A Chord overlay is also used by the Internet Indirection Infrastructure *i3* [29] to achieve resilience to DoS-attacks. Other DoS limiting architectures have been proposed in [20, 34]. Many of these systems are based on traffic analysis or some indirection approach.

Non-malicious DoS-attacks like flash crowds have also been studied in the context of DHTs. Examples in the systems community include CoopNet [21], Backslash [27], and PROOFS [28], and there is also theoretical work [19]. However, these works only consider scenarios where many requests are targeted to the same data item, but there are harder instances like many requests to different items *at the same location* (which can be set up by an attacker when the hash functions are known). These instances can still be handled in DHTs using techniques originally proposed for CRCW PRAMs [1] but these techniques cannot protect the system against DoS-attacks that can block specific servers.

The first DHTs that are robust against past-insider DoS-attacks were proposed in [2, 3]. A past insider only has complete knowledge about some *past* time point t_0 of the information system. For this kind of insider it is possible to design an information system so that any information that was inserted or last updated *after* t_0 is safe against a DoS-attack [2, 3]. But the constructions proposed in these papers would not work at all for a current insider because they are heavily based on randomization to ensure unpredictability.

1.3 Our Contribution

When considering a current insider who knows *everything* about the information system, standard replication and information hiding techniques are useless to protect the system against DoS-attacks. However, it turns out that distributed coding techniques can achieve that goal, which is our main contribution. More precisely, we present two variants of the IRIS system, the basic IRIS system and the enhanced IRIS system, with the following properties given that m is at most polynomial in n.

THEOREM 1.1. *The basic IRIS system and the enhanced IRIS system are both scalable and efficient. Whereas the basic IRIS system just needs a constant redundancy to protect itself against insider DoS-attacks blocking up to $\gamma \cdot n^{1/\log\log n}$ servers for a constant $\gamma > 0$, the enhanced IRIS system needs $O(\log n)$ redundancy but can protect itself against insider DoS-attacks blocking up to a constant fraction of the servers.*

In the following we assume that the data items we are dealing with have a size of $\Omega(\log n \log m)$. Due to space constraints, we will only give a detailed description of the basic IRIS system and just present a sketch of the enhanced system.

2. BASIC IRIS

In this section we present the basic IRIS system. First we present the coding strategy and then the lookup protocol and we show that with these two strategies the IRIS system is scalable, efficient and robust.

2.1 Coding strategy

We are using a block-based distributed coding strategy that follows the topology of a k-ary butterfly. In the following, let $[k]$ denote the set $\{0, \ldots, k-1\}$.

DEFINITION 2.1   (k-ARY BUTTERFLY). *For any $d, k \in \mathbb{N}$, the d-dimensional k-ary butterfly $BF(k,d)$ is a graph $G = (V_k, E)$ with node set $V_k = [d+1] \times [k]^d$ and edge set E with*

$$E = \{\{(i, x), (i+1, (x_1, \ldots, x_i, b, x_{i+2}, \ldots, x_d))\}$$
$$\mid x = (x_1, \ldots, x_d) \in [k]^d, \ i \in [d], \ and \ b \in [k]\}.$$

A node u of the form (ℓ, x) is said to be on level ℓ of G. For a node $u = (\ell, x)$, $LT(u)$ is the unique k-ary tree of nodes reached from u when going downwards the butterfly (i.e., to nodes on levels $\ell' > \ell$) and $UT(u)$ is the unique k-ary tree of nodes reached from u when going upwards the butterfly. Moreover, let $BF(u)$ be the unique k-ary sub-butterfly of dimension ℓ ranging from level 0 to ℓ in $BF(k,d)$ that contains u. Finally, $B(u)$ is the unique k-ary sub-butterfly of dimension 1 (which is just a bipartite graph of k nodes on each side) ranging from level ℓ to $\ell+1$ in $BF(k,d)$ that contains u. We also call $B(u)$ a k-block at level ℓ.

See Figure 1 for a visualization.

Consider any $BF(k,d)$, and let $n = k^d$. The encoding works as follows for a set of data items $d_0, \ldots, d_{n-1}$ of uniform size. Initially, d_i is placed in node $(0, i)$ for every $i \in \{0, \ldots, n-1\}$. Given that in level ℓ we have already assigned data items $d(\ell, x)$ to the nodes (ℓ, x), we use the following coding strategy to assign data items $d(\ell+1, x)$ to the nodes at level $\ell + 1$:

Consider any k-block B at level ℓ with nodes $(\ell, x_1), \ldots, (\ell, x_k)$ that store data items $d(\ell, x_1), \ldots, d(\ell, x_k)$. We first compute $D = d(\ell, x_1) \oplus d(\ell, x_2) \oplus \ldots \oplus d(\ell, x_k)$ where "$\oplus$" is the bit-wise parity operation. Then we cut D into $k-1$ pieces $D_1, \ldots, D_{k-1}$ of equal size (up to an additive 1) and assign the bit string $d(\ell+1, x_i) = d(\ell, x_i) \circ D_i$ to node $(\ell+1, x_i)$ where "$\circ$" is the concatenation operator. Finally, we compute $D_k = D_1 \oplus D_2 \oplus \cdots \oplus D_{k-1}$ and assign $d(\ell+1, x_k) = d(\ell, x_k) \circ D_k$ to node $(\ell+1, x_k)$. Our coding strategy satisfies the following lemma.

LEMMA 2.2. *For any k-block B with node sets $(\ell, x_1), \ldots, (\ell, x_k)$ and $(\ell+1, x_1), \ldots, (\ell+1, x_k)$ in which at most one $(\ell+1, x_j)$ is blocked, the information in the remaining nodes $(\ell+1, x_i)$ suffices to recover $d(\ell, x_1), \ldots, d(\ell, x_k)$.*

PROOF. Since every non-blocked $(\ell+1, x_i)$ contains $d(\ell, x_i)$, the information in any corresponding (ℓ, x_i) can be recovered directly. Suppose that node $(\ell+1, x_j)$ is blocked. Then the parity coding strategy allows us to recover D_j

by computing $D_j = \bigoplus_{i \neq j} D_i$. This allows us to recover D which then allows us to recover $d(\ell, x_j)$ by computing $d(\ell, x_j) = D \oplus \bigoplus_{i \neq j} d(\ell, x_i)$. $\square$

For a node v in $BF(k, d)$, let $|d(v)|$ denote the size of the data stored in node v. The following lemma is easy to check.

LEMMA 2.3. *For any k-block B with node sets $(\ell, x_1), \ldots, (\ell, x_k)$ and $(\ell+1, x_1), \ldots, (\ell+1, x_k)$, it holds $|d(\ell+1, x_i)| \leq (1 + 1/(k-1))|d(\ell, x_i)|$ up to an additive 1.*

For simplicity, we will ignore in the following the additive 1 due to the fact that $|d(\ell, x_i)|$ may not be perfectly divisible by $k-1$. This will only cause a constant factor deviation from the bounds below as long as the original data items have a size of z with $z \geq k$.

Given n servers, where $n = k^d$ for some $d \in \mathbb{N}$, and n data items $d_0, \ldots, d_{n-1}$, we apply our coding strategy in the following way: server s_i emulates the butterfly nodes $(0, i), \ldots, (d, i)$ and stores all the information stored in these nodes when applying the coding strategy above to $d_0, \ldots, d_{n-1}$. According to Lemma 2.3, node (ℓ, i) in $BF(k, d)$ has the property that $d(\ell, i) = d(\ell-1, i) \circ p_\ell(i)$ for some parity information $p_\ell(i)$ with $|p_\ell(i)| \leq |d(\ell-1, i)|/(k-1)$. Hence, it suffices for server s_i to store $d_i, p_1(i), \ldots, p_d(i)$ in order to be able to recover every $d(\ell, i)$.

Let $d(s_i) = d_i \circ p_1(i) \circ \ldots p_d(i)$. It is easy to prove by induction that $|p_\ell(i)| \leq (1 + 1/(k-1))^{\ell-1}|d_i|/(k-1)$ for all ℓ, which implies the following lemma under the assumption that $|d_i| = z$ for all i.

LEMMA 2.4. *For any $k > d$ and $z \geq k$ it holds that $|d(s_i)| \leq (1 + e)z$ for every server s_i.*

PROOF. Certainly, $\sum_{i=0}^{d-1}(1 + 1/(k-1))^i \leq \sum_{i=0}^{d-1} e^{i/(k-1)} \leq d \cdot e$. Since $k > d$ the lemma follows. $\square$

Notice that $d = \log_k n$. Hence, in order to ensure that $k > d$ we must choose $k > \log n / \log \log n$. For the rest of this section we will fix k to $\log n$. Then, for exactly n data items of size at least k, we have a storage strategy with a constant redundancy. If we have less than n data items, we may just add dummy data items (i.e., all bits are 0), and if we have more than n data items, we assume that we can use the following hashing strategy to distribute the data among the servers:

Let $\mathcal{K} \subseteq U$ be the set of all keys that have a data item in the system. We will use a hash function $f : U \to V$ to assign each data item to a server and a hash function $g : U \to \{0, \ldots, \gamma \cdot |\mathcal{K}|/n\}$ for some constant γ to assign each data item to a *layer*. The goal is to choose these two hash functions so that $h : U \to V \times \{0, \ldots, \gamma \cdot |\mathcal{K}|/n\}, x \mapsto (f(x), g(x))$ is injective, i.e., for every layer i at most one key is assigned to each server. Given that this is the case, each layer will define a set of n data items (when padded with dummies) with one per server, so we can apply the coding strategy above to each of these layers. If γ is constant, then Lemma 2.4 implies that the overall redundancy of our storage strategy is still constant.

The simplest way of realizing an injective h with low storage overhead for h (in fact, $\gamma = 2$ suffices) is to use cuckoo hashing [22]: each data item has two optional positions, and they are distributed among these optional positions so that there is no collision. Of course, in this case, a lookup request

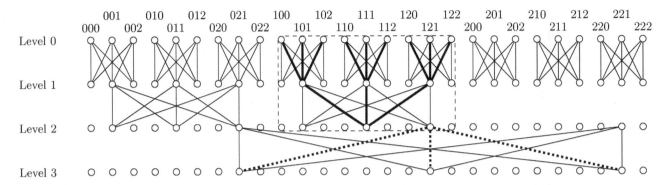

Figure 1: Visualization of a k-ary butterfly $BF(k,d)$ for $k = d = 3$. For a better readability most of the edges from level two and three are omitted. The edges shown between levels 1, 2, and 3 visualize three k-blocks at levels 1, 2, and 3. The dashed box denotes the sub-butterfly $BF((2,111))$. The thick solid lines in the dashed box denote the edges of $UT((2,111))$. The thick dotted lines denote the edges of $LT((2,121))$.

for some data item d would involve looking at both optional positions, but this would just double the work spent for the lookup operation described next, so in the following we just assume that h is an injective hash function that can be directly evaluated to determine the unique server and layer of a datum.

Choosing just a single hash function h for the data as described above is not yet enough for our lookup protocol to work. So for our IRIS system we will make use of $c = \Theta(\log m)$ hash functions $h_1, \ldots, h_c$ with the same properties as h that together satisfy certain expansion properties. That is, instead of just one, we will store c pieces of each data item in encoded form. To avoid the redundancy to go up to $\Theta(c)$, we will assume that z (the size of the data items) is at least $k \cdot c$. Then we can use Reed-Solomon codes [26] to encode each data item d via c pieces $d_1, \ldots, d_c$ so that $\sum_i |d_i| = O(|d|)$ and the recovery of any $c/4$ of these pieces is sufficient to recover d. In summary, we obtain the following result.

COROLLARY 2.5. *When using Reed-Solomon codes, the basic IRIS system has a constant redundancy.*

2.2 Lookup protocol

In the following let $B \subseteq V$ be the set of blocked servers. Only non-blocked servers participate in the lookup protocol, i.e., the blocked servers do not send or receive anything. Suppose that for every non-blocked server s_i the adversary issues a lookup request for datum d_i. The lookup protocol is divided into three stages: a *preprocessing stage*, a *probing stage*, and a *decoding stage*. In the preprocessing stage, the non-blocked servers determine a unique representative for each blocked server so that we can route in the k-ary butterfly as if all servers are still non-blocked (but, of course, the data in the blocked servers is lost). Also, information is collected that allows us to bound the work of decoding specific pieces of data items. In the probing stage, we issue read requests to the c pieces of each d_i and select $c/2$ of them to be decoded in the decoding stage.

2.2.1 Preprocessing stage

The first part of the preprocessing stage, the *butterfly completion stage*, is divided into four phases. In the first phase a tree of depth $O(\log n / \log \log n)$ is built over all non-blocked servers. Afterwards, in phase two, the constructed

tree is transformed into a doubly linked list L of n non-blocked servers. Phase three is dedicated to the rearrangement of L such that each non-blocked server with identifier i is at position i in L and for each blocked server with identifier j there is a non-blocked server at position j in L that is declared the *representative* of the blocked server. Finally, in phase four, the resulting list from phase three is transformed into a k-ary butterfly. In the following we assume that the adversary blocks exactly εn servers.

Phase 1.

A tree of depth $O(\log n / \log \log n)$ is built by using the so called *minimum rule* [9]: Initially each non-blocked server s holds its identifier in $\mathsf{val}(s)$ and sets $p(s) = NULL$. In each round each non-blocked server s contacts $\log n$ random non-blocked servers. If for one of these contacted servers s' it holds $\mathsf{val}(s') < \mathsf{val}(s)$, then s sets $\mathsf{val}(s) = \mathsf{val}(s')$ and $p(s) = \mathsf{id}(s')$. With this one can show:

LEMMA 2.6. *After $\log n / \log \log n + \alpha$ rounds, α constant, it holds, w.h.p.:*

(i) *The $p(s)$-values induce a tree T of depth $\log n / \log \log n + \alpha$ over all $(1 - \varepsilon)n$ non-blocked servers rooted at the server with minimum identifier.*

(ii) *The degree of each node in T is at most $O(\log^2 n / \log \log n)$.*

Phase 2.

Next we show how to transform T into a doubly linked list L of n non-blocked servers in which each non-blocked server is contained at most twice. First, using a bottom up approach, each non-blocked server s determines for each of its children s' in T the size $\mathsf{size}(s')$ of the subtree of T rooted at s' and the identifier of the rightmost server $\mathsf{rightmost}(s')$ in this subtree and reports it to its parent server. It is easy to show that this is possible in $O(depth(T))$ rounds. Using this information, in a top down approach, each non-blocked server then determines its position and its neighbors in a doubly linked list of n non-blocked servers as follows: First, the root r of T (i.e. the server r with $p(r) = NULL$) initiates a pre-order walk of T by performing Algorithm 1 with parameters $1, NULL$. Whenever a server receives a message, it also performs Algorithm 1. Clearly, after at most $depth(T)$ rounds each non-blocked server knows its position and its left neighbor in L (see Figure 2 for a visualization). In order to transform L into a *doubly* linked list each non-blocked server s sends its ID to its left neighbor and sets $\mathsf{right}(s)$ to the ID it receives, or to $NULL$ if it does not receive a message. In parallel to the transformation of T into a doubly linked list of the $(1-\varepsilon)n$ non-blocked servers, r initiates an additional pre-order traversal of T by additionally performing Algorithm 1 with parameters $(1-\varepsilon)n+1, \mathsf{rightmost}(r)$. In contrast to the first traversal of T the values $\mathsf{left}(s)$ and $\mathsf{pos}(s)$ in Algorithm 1 are now substituted by $\mathsf{left}_2(s)$ and $\mathsf{pos}_2(s)$. Also we use the modification that as soon as a non-blocked server sets its pos_2 value to n the algorithm terminates. Then, analogously to the right values each server sets its right_2 value. By this additional tree traversal the first εn servers of the traversal are appended to L. Notice that this pre-order traversal of T guarantees that the first εn servers visited form a connected subtree of T.

Algorithm 1 BuildListFromTree(x, l)

1: $\mathsf{left}(s) \leftarrow l$, $\mathsf{pos}(s) \leftarrow x$
2: **for all** children $\mathsf{child}_i(s)$ of s, $i \in \{1, \dots, c\}$ **do**
3:     **if** $i = 1$ **then**   ▷ $\mathsf{child}_i(s)$ is the left most child of s
4:         $\mathsf{left} \leftarrow s$
5:     **else**
6:         $\mathsf{left} \leftarrow \mathsf{rightmost}(\mathsf{child}_{i-1}(s))$
7:     **end if**
8:     $\mathsf{pos} \leftarrow \mathsf{pos}(s) + 1 + \sum_{j=1}^{i-1} \mathsf{size}(\mathsf{child}_j(s))$
9:     Send message $(\mathsf{pos}, \mathsf{left})$ to $\mathsf{child}_i(s)$
10: **end for**

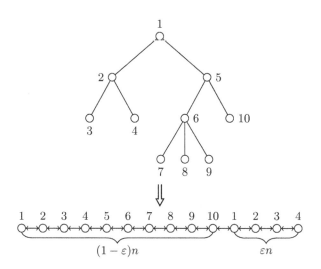

Figure 2: Transformation of T into a sorted list of n non-blocked servers. The numbers next to the tree nodes denote the order of their appearance in the tree traversal.

The following lemma can easily be shown.

LEMMA 2.7. *After* $2 \cdot depth(T)$ *rounds* T *is transformed into a doubly linked list* L *of size* n *over the* $(1-\varepsilon)n$ *non-blocked servers such that each non-blocked server is contained at most twice in* L.

Phase 3.

The goal of this phase is to rearrange L into a doubly linked list with the properties specified in Lemma 2.8.

LEMMA 2.8. *After* $O(1)$ *rounds it holds:*

(i) Each non-blocked server s_i *is at position* i *in* L.

(ii) For each blocked server s_j *the server* s' *with* $\mathsf{pos}(s') = j$ *or* $\mathsf{pos}_2(s') = j$ *is the unique representative of* s_j.

Initially, the *owner* of a position j in L is the server s' with $\mathsf{pos}(s') = j$ or $\mathsf{pos}_2(s') = j$.

First, each non-blocked server s' at position j contacts server s_j. If s_j is not blocked, then s' considers s_j as the new owner of j. s' then asks for the owners of the positions $j-1$ and $j+1$ and forwards that information to s_j, so that s_j can take over the position j in L.

If s_j is blocked, s' remains to be the owner of j and therefore becomes the representative of s_j.

Phase 4.

In this phase L is transformed into a k-ary butterfly using an extended k-ary butterfly.

DEFINITION 2.9 (EXTENDED k-ARY BUTTERFLY). *For any* $d, k \in \mathbb{N}$ *the* d-dimensional extended k-ary butterfly $EBF(k, d)$ *is a graph* (V, E) *with* $V = \bigcup_{\ell=0}^{d} V_\ell$ *and* $E = \bigcup_{\ell=1}^{d} E_\ell$ *where*

$$V_\ell = \{(\ell, i) \mid i \in \{1, \dots, n\}\} \text{ and}$$
$$E_\ell = \{\{(\ell-1, i), (\ell, j)\} \in V_{\ell-1} \times V_\ell \mid$$
$$\exists c \in [k] : |i-j| = c \cdot k^{\ell-1}\}.$$

Furthermore, we define $G(\ell) = (V_{\ell-1} \cup V_\ell, E_\ell)$, $\ell \in \{1, \dots, d\}$ *and denote a node* (ℓ, i) *as a level* ℓ *node.*

The idea of this phase is to introduce for each non-blocked server at position i in L exactly $\log_k n + 1$ virtual nodes $(0, i), \dots, (\log_k n, i)$ and to successively build the graphs $G(\ell)$, $\ell = 1, \dots, \log_k n$, beginning with $G(1)$.

The construction of $G(\ell)$, $\ell = 1, \dots, \log_k n$ proceeds in $\lceil \log k \rceil + 1$ rounds and assumes $G(\ell-1)$ has already been built. In the first round each non-blocked server s asks all non-blocked servers at distance $(k-1)k^{\ell-1}$ for their closest neighbors in $G(\ell-1)$. By this, s is introduced to all non-blocked servers at distance k^ℓ. In round $r \in \{2, \dots, \lceil \log k \rceil + 1\}$ each non-blocked server s asks all non-blocked servers at distance $2^{r-2} \cdot k^\ell$ for their neighbors in $G(\ell)$. See Figure 3 for a visualization. One can show that at the beginning of round r each non-blocked server knows all non-blocked servers at distance ck^ℓ, $c \in \{1, \dots, 2^{r-2}\}$. Thus, in round r each non-blocked server s is introduced to all non-blocked servers at distance $(2^{r-2} + c)k^\ell$, $c \in \{1, \dots, 2^{r-2}\}$. Hence, at the end of round r each non-blocked server knows all non-blocked servers at distance ck^ℓ, $c \in \{1, \dots, 2^{r-1}\}$.

LEMMA 2.10. *In the fourth phase of the butterfly completion stage a sorted list of* n *non-blocked servers is correctly transformed into an extended* k-ary butterfly in time $(2 + o(1)) \log n$ *and at any time the congestion at every non-blocked server is at most* $O(\log n)$.

PROOF. By induction on ℓ it is easy to show that $G(\ell)$, $\ell \in \{1, \dots, \log_k n\}$ is built correctly. Since the construction of each $G(\ell)$ takes $2(\lceil \log k \rceil + 1)$ rounds (each round described above actually consists of two rounds) the extended k-ary butterfly is built after $2(\lceil \log k \rceil + 1) \log_k n$ rounds. By Lemma 2.7 each non-blocked server is contained at most twice in L, implying that in each round each non-blocked server contacts (and is contacted by) at most four non-blocked servers and asks for their neighbors in $G(\ell - 1)$ and $G(\ell)$, respectively. Since each non-blocked server has at most $O(k)$ neighbors in $G(\ell-1)$ and $G(\ell)$, the congestion of each non-blocked server is at most $O(k)$ in each round. $\square$

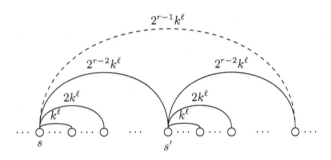

Figure 3: Visualization of the construction of $G(\ell)$ in round r where the non-blocked server s asks the non-blocked server s' at distance $2^{r-2}k^\ell$ for its neighbors. The dashed edge denotes a connection with maximum distance that s builds in round r.

It is easy to see that the d-dimensional k-ary butterfly is a subgraph of the d-dimensional extended k-ary butterfly. Thus, the following Lemma holds.

LEMMA 2.11. *In the butterfly completion stage a k-ary butterfly over n non-blocked servers is built in $(2+o(1)) \log n$ rounds. Furthermore, each blocked server is represented in the butterfly by one non-blocked server and the congestion at any non-blocked server is at most $O(\log n)$.*

Once the k-ary butterfly has been re-established, we can go ahead with collecting additional information. In particular, we are interested in the decoding work for specific data items. This is determined with the help of the following recursively defined function:

DEFINITION 2.12 (DECODING DEPTH). *For a node $u = (\ell, x)$ of $BF(k, d)$ the decoding depth $dd(u)$ is defined as:*

$$dd(u) = \begin{cases} 0 & \text{if } u \text{ is not blocked} \\ \infty & \text{if } \ell = d \text{ and } u \text{ is blocked} \\ \max_{v \in C(u)} \{dd(v)\} + 1 & \text{if } \ell < d \text{ and } u \text{ is blocked} \end{cases}$$

where $C(u)$ denotes the set of children of u in $LT(u)$ excluding one child with biggest decoding depth among these children. The decoding depth of a server s_i is defined as $dd(s_i) = dd((0,i))$, and the decoding depth of a sub-butterfly $BF(u)$ is defined as $dd(BF(u)) = \max_{(0,x) \in BF(u)} dd((0,x))$.

See Figure 4 for a visualization. The decoding depth of a node immediately implies an upper bound on the time needed for restoring the data of a blocked server.

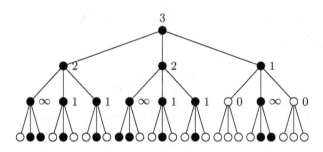

Figure 4: Visualization of decoding depth computation with some nodes and edges of the k-ary butterfly omitted. Black/white colored nodes represent blocked/non-blocked nodes. The labels next to the nodes denote their decoding depth at the corresponding level.

LEMMA 2.13. *If $dd(s_i) = \delta$ for a blocked server s_i, then any data item that has been assigned to s_i can be restored in time $O(\delta)$ by the nodes in $BF((\delta, i))$.*

The decoding depth is computed as follows: Starting from level $\log_k n$, the servers compute the $dd(u)$-values of the butterfly nodes level by level and disseminate them among their neighbors in the next lower level until the dd-values of all nodes have been computed. This can certainly be done in $O(\log_k n)$ communication rounds with congestion $O(k)$ in each round. At the end every server s_i knows $dd(s_i)$. Then the servers compute the $dd(BF(\cdot))$-values level by level in a way that, starting in level 0, each node u sends its $dd(BF(u))$-value to all of its neighbors v in the next higher level which will then be able to determine their $dd(BF(v))$-value by taking the maximum of the received values. Hence, at the end every node u (resp. the server owning it) knows $dd(BF(u))$. This process also takes $O(\log_k n)$ communication rounds with congestion $O(k)$ in each round. This ends the preprocessing stage.

LEMMA 2.14. *The preprocessing stage takes at most $(2 + o(1)) \log n$ communication rounds with at most $O(\log^2 n)$ congestion at every non-blocked server at each round.*

2.2.2 Probing Stage

Remember that the c pieces of each data item d are stored in the c servers responsible for $h_1(d), \ldots, h_c(d)$. At the beginning of the probing stage each non-blocked server s that received a lookup request for some data item d chooses c non-blocked servers $s_1(d), \ldots, s_c(d) \in V$ uniformly and independently at random. This can simply be realized by selecting c random servers in each round until c non-blocked servers have been found (which takes $O(1)$ communication rounds w.h.p.). s then asks each server $s_i(d)$ to send a probe(d, i) message from the butterfly node emulated by $s_i(d)$ in level $\log_k n$ to the butterfly node in level 0 responsible for $h_i(d)$ along the unique path of length $\log_k n$.

The probing takes place in synchronized rounds. The first $\log_k n + 1$ rounds work as follows. In round 0, all probe messages are active, and their *origin* is declared to be the server s that initiated that probe. In round r, all probe messages that remain to be active are currently in a node at level $\log_k n - r$. Consider any such node v. First of all, v checks the following rules:

- If the number of different (d, i)-pairs with a probe is more than $\alpha \cdot c$ (for a sufficiently large constant α),

124

then v deactivates all probes and informs their origins about the level in which that happened. Such a node v is called *congested*.

- If $dd(BF(v)) > \log_k n - r$, then v deactivates all probes and informs their origins about the level in which that happened. Such a node v is called *blocked*.

If none of the two rules apply, then v distinguishes between two cases. If $\log_k n - r > 0$, then v first combines, for those pairs (d, i) with multiple probes, all of these probes into a single probe and declares itself as the new origin of that probe. Then v forwards all probes to the next node on level $\log_k n - r - 1$ along their path. If $\log_k n - r = 0$, i.e., the probes have reached their destination, v delivers the requested data pieces of its probes to their origins. These probes have been successful.

Any origin of a probe that is informed about its probe, and which is not the initial origin of that probe, informs all origins of the probes that got merged into that probe so that within $O(\log_k n)$ communication rounds all servers get informed about which of their c probes were successful or got deactivated at a level. See Figure 5 for a visualization of the combining of probes and the splitting of their responses.

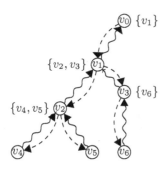

Figure 5: Visualization of combining and splitting of messages. The curved lines illustrate the combining of the probes, and the dashed lines illustrate the splitting of the responses.

If a server s that is responsible for a lookup request for d receives at least $c/2$ success messages, it can recover d from the collected pieces (or discovers that no data item exists in the system for the given search key in case there is a key mismatch) and is done, so it does not participate in the decoding stage any more. Otherwise, s declares d to *belong to level ℓ* where $\ell \in \{1, \ldots, \log_k n\}$ is the smallest level that contains at least $c/2$ active (d, i) probes (i.e., (d, i) probes that were not deactivated at level ℓ or earlier for d). It is easy to see that the probing stage satisfies the following property.

LEMMA 2.15. *The probing stage takes at most $O(\log_k n)$ communication rounds with at most $O(\log^2 n)$ congestion in every node at each round, w.h.p.*

By adapting the analysis in [2] (see Lemmas 4 and 5), one can show the following lemma.

LEMMA 2.16. *If the adversary can block at most $(1/25) \cdot 2^{\log_k n}$ servers, then for every $\ell \in \{1, \ldots, \log_k n\}$, the number of data items with requests belonging to level ℓ is at most n/k^ℓ.*

Before we prove Lemma 2.16 we point out the main differences to the analysis in [2] and introduce some required definitions.

The new aspect that we need to exploit in the analysis is the fact that if $dd(BF(v)) > \ell$ for a node v on level ℓ, then at least 2^ℓ nodes in $BF(v)$ must be blocked. This is because for every node (i, x) in $BF(k, d)$ with $dd((i, x)) > \ell$ for some $\ell \leq \log_k n - i$, $LT((i, x))$ must contain a complete binary tree of blocked nodes of depth ℓ rooted at (i, x) (Claim 2.17). This tree is also called a *witness tree* as it witnesses a high decoding depth of a node. Notice that due to the structure of the $BF(k, d)$, the leaves of such a witness tree must be distinct. Hence, if $dd(BF(v)) > \ell$ for a node v on level ℓ, then there must be a node $(0, x)$ in $BF(v)$ with a witness tree of depth ℓ, which implies the lower bound on 2^ℓ blocked nodes in $BF(v)$.

CLAIM 2.17. *Let $(i, x) \in BF(k, d)$ with $dd((i, x)) > \ell$ for $\ell \leq \log_k n - i$. Then, $LT((i, x))$ contains a witness tree of depth ℓ.*

PROOF. The proof is by induction on ℓ. For $\ell = 1$ let $u = (i, x) \in BF(k, d)$ with $dd(u) > 1$. Assume $LT(u)$ does not contain a complete binary tree of blocked nodes of depth 1. Then, at most one child of u in $LT(u)$ is blocked, and therefore by definition of $dd(u)$ it holds $dd(v) = 0$ for all $v \in C(u)$. Hence, $dd(u) = 1$ which contradicts $dd(u) > 1$. Suppose for each node $u = (i, x) \in BF(k, d)$ with $dd(u) > \ell$ for $\ell < \log_k n - i$, $LT(u)$ contains a complete binary tree of blocked nodes of depth ℓ. We show that the claim also holds for $\ell + 1$. Let $u = (i, x) \in BF(k, d)$ with $dd(u) > \ell + 1$. By definition of $dd(u)$ there exist at least two children v and w of u in $LT(u)$ with $dd(v), dd(w) \geq dd(u) - 1 > \ell$. Then, by the induction hypothesis, $LT(v)$ and $LT(w)$ contain a complete binary tree T_v and T_w of blocked nodes of depth ℓ. Notice that $LT(v)$ and $LT(w)$ are subtrees of $LT(u)$. Since $dd(u) \geq 1$, u is also blocked, and the tree induced by connecting u to the roots of T_v and T_w is a complete binary subtree in $LT(u)$ of blocked nodes of depth $\ell + 1$. $\square$

In the following we denote $BF(v)$ as *blocked* if the adversary blocks at least 2^ℓ servers from $BF(v)$. $BF(v)$ is denoted as *congested* if the servers from $BF(v)$ receive in total more than $k^\ell \alpha c/2$ probes for different (d, i) pairs in round ℓ. For a server s that received a lookup request for some data item d we define $s_i^{(\ell)}(d)$ as the node at level ℓ on the unique path of length $\log_k n$ from v to w, with v being the butterfly node on level $\log_k n$ emulated by $s_i(d)$ and w being the butterfly node in level 0 responsible for $h_i(d)$. A data item d is called *blocked/congested at level ℓ* if there are blocked/congested $BF(s_{i_i}^{(\ell_1)}(d)), \ldots, BF(s_{i_r}^{(\ell_r)}(d))$ with $\ell_i \geq \ell$, $r = c/4$, and $i_1, \ldots, i_r$ being pairwise different.

Proof of Lemma 2.16: The idea of this proof is as follows: First, we show that whenever a probe(d, i) is deactivated on a level ℓ, then $BF(s_i^{(\ell)}(d))$ is blocked or congested (Claim 2.18). Moreover, if a data item d is declared to belong to level ℓ, then at least $c/4$ of its (d, i)-probes have either been deactivated because of blocked sub-butterflies or because of congested sub-butterflies at level ℓ or higher. Many data items that belong to level ℓ therefore imply many blocked or congested sub-butterflies. But since only a limited fraction of them can be blocked or congested, we show that therefore only a limited fraction of the data items can belong to level ℓ. As a crucial ingredient for the proof, we require from the hash functions $h_1, \ldots, h_c$ that they satisfy a certain expansion property, which holds w.h.p. if the hash functions are chosen uniformly and independently at random (Claim 2.19).

CLAIM 2.18. *Whenever a (d, i) pair is deactivated in a level $\ell \geq 0$ by a node v, then $BF(v)$ is blocked or congested, w.h.p.*

PROOF. If (d, i) was deactivated due to $dd(BF(v)) > \ell$, then by Claim 2.17 $BF(v)$ contains at least 2^ℓ blocked servers. Now assume (d, i) was deactivated due to a too high congestion at v. Then, v received in round ℓ probe messages for more than αc different (d, i) pairs. Since the starting points for the lookup requests are chosen uniformly at random it holds $E\left[|\mathcal{M}_\ell(w)|\right] = E\left[|\mathcal{M}_\ell(w')|\right]$ for all w, w' at level ℓ in $BF(v)$ with $\mathcal{M}_\ell(w)$ being the set of (d, i)-pairs with probes received by node w. The Chernoff bounds [7] can be applied, implying

$$Pr\left[|\mathcal{M}_\ell(w)| \geq (1 + \delta) E\left[|\mathcal{M}_\ell(w)|\right]\right] \leq e^{-\min\{\delta, \delta^2\} E\left[|\mathcal{M}_\ell(w)|\right]/3}$$

for all $\delta \geq 0$ and all $w \in BF(v)$. Setting $\delta = 1/2$ gives $E\left[|\mathcal{M}_\ell(w)|\right] \geq 2\alpha c/3$ for all $w \in BF(v)$, w.h.p. Hence, the expected number of (d, i)-pairs with probes sent to $BF(v)$ is at least $2\alpha k^\ell c/3$, w.h.p. Furthermore, with M being the number of (d, i)-pairs with probes sent to $BF(v)$, the Chernoff bounds imply

$$Pr\left[M \leq \frac{2(1 - \delta)}{3} \alpha c k^\ell\right] \leq e^{-\delta^2 \alpha c k^\ell/3} \quad \text{for all } \delta \in [0, 1]$$

With $\delta = 1/4$ we get that there are more than $\alpha c k^\ell/2$ (d, i)-pairs with probes sent to $BF(v)$, w.h.p. $\square$

Claim 2.18 implies that if a lookup request for some data item d belongs to level ℓ, then d must be blocked or congested at level ℓ. In order to show that there cannot be too many of these data items, we introduce an expander property for collections of hash functions.

Recall that U is the key universe and $m = |U|$. For any sub-butterfly B let $V(B)$ be the set of servers emulating the nodes of B. Let $\mathcal{H}$ be the collection of hash functions $h_1, \ldots, h_c$. Given a set $S \subset U$ of keys and a $k \in \mathbb{N}$, we call $F \subseteq S \times \{1, \ldots, c\}$ a *b-bundle* of S if every $d \in S$ has exactly b many pairs (d, i) in F. Given $h_1, \ldots, h_c$ and a level $\ell \in \{0, \ldots, \log_k n\}$, let $\Gamma_{F, \ell}(S)$ be the union of the servers involved in these pairs at level ℓ, i.e., $\Gamma_{F, \ell}(S) = \bigcup_{(d,i) \in F} V(BF(s_i^{(\ell)}(d)))$. Given a $0 < \sigma < 1$, we call $\mathcal{H}$ a *(b, σ)-expander* if for any $\ell \leq \log_k n$, any $S \subseteq U$ with $|S| \leq \sigma n/k^\ell$, and any b-bundle F of S, it holds that $|\Gamma_{F, \ell}(S)| \geq k^\ell |S|$.

A proof of the following claim can be found in [2].

CLAIM 2.19. *If the hash functions $\mathcal{H} = \{h_1, \ldots, h_c\}$ are chosen uniformly and independently at random and $c \geq 12 \log m$, then $\mathcal{H}$ is a $(c/4, 1/24)$-expander, w.h.p.*

We remark that the hash functions have to form a $(c/4, \sigma)$-expander for some constant σ for our lookup protocol to work, but they do not have to be chosen at random. The proof above just illustrates that if they are chosen at random, they will form a $(c/4, \sigma)$-expander w.h.p.

We are now ready to upper bound the number of congested and blocked data items at level ℓ, which proves Lemma 2.16.

We start with the blocked data items. Let S be a set of data items that are blocked at level ℓ. For any data item d in S, at least $c/4$ of the sub-butterflies $BF(s_i^{(\ell_i)}(d))$ are blocked with $\ell_i \geq \ell$. Adding the corresponding pairs (d, i) to F, we obtain a $c/4$-bundle F of S. Due to Claim 2.17, the fraction of blocked servers in a blocked sub-butterfly of level ℓ' is at least $2^{\ell'}/k^{\ell'}$, which is least $2^{\log_k n}/n$ for any $\ell' \leq \log_k n$. Therefore, if the adversary can only block up to εn servers with $\varepsilon < \gamma \cdot 2^{\log_k n}/n$, then the number of servers covered by all $BF(s_i^{(\ell_i)}(d))$ with $(d, i) \in F$ must be less than $\gamma \cdot n$. Hence, also $|\Gamma_{F, \ell}(S)| < \gamma \cdot n$. On the other hand, we know from Claim 2.19 that for any $c/4$-bundle F of S with $|S| \leq (1/24)n/k^\ell$, $|\Gamma_{F, \ell}(S)| \geq k^\ell |S|$. Suppose now that $\gamma < 1/24$ and there is a set S of blocked data items of size $\gamma n/k^\ell$. Then, according to Claim 2.19, $|\Gamma_{F, \ell}(S)| \geq \gamma n$, which is not possible. Hence, the number of blocked data items at level ℓ is at most $\gamma n/k^\ell$.

Similarly, the number of congested data items can be upper bounded. Let S be a set of data items that are congested at level ℓ. Analogously to the case of blocked data items, we can construct a $c/4$ bundle F of S. Recall that a sub-butterfly on level ℓ is congested if it receives more than $\alpha c k^\ell/2$ probes for different (d, i) pairs. If α is sufficiently large, then we can have at most a γ-fraction of congested butterflies on level ℓ for all $\ell \in \{0, \ldots, \log_k n\}$. Hence, all of the congested sub-butterflies $BF(s_i^{(l_i)}(d))$ with $(d, i) \in F$ together contain at most a γ-fraction of the sub-butterflies on level ℓ. Again with Claim 2.19 we can deduce $|S| \leq \gamma n/k^\ell$ for $\gamma < 1/24$. Hence, all in all, at most $(2\gamma)n/k^\ell$ data items can be blocked or congested at level ℓ implying an upper bound of n/k^ℓ for the number of data items with lookup requests that belong to level ℓ. $\square$

2.2.3 Decoding Stage

The decoding stage proceeds in $\log_k n$ phases. Each phase $r \in \{1, \ldots, \log_k n\}$ is dedicated to decoding the requests belonging to level r and is divided into $O(\log_k n)$ rounds. In round 0 of phase r each server s that is responsible for a lookup request for some data item d that belongs to level r chooses a set $\mathcal{A}(s) \subseteq [c]$ of $c/2$ indices that were active at level r in the probing stage. For such a server s and $i \in \mathcal{A}(s)$ let w be the butterfly node in level 0 responsible for $h_i(d)$ and let v be the butterfly node in level $\log_k n$ emulated by $s_i(d)$. Each such server s then sends for each $i \in \mathcal{A}(s)$ a decode(d, i) message to $s_i(d)$ which will then be forwarded (and possibly combined with other decode(d, i) requests) from v to w until it reaches a node u on level r. From this point on, the request will be spread (and possibly combined with other requests to the same (d, i) item on the way) to all nodes in $UT(u)$, which takes r further rounds. In round i of the spreading, each node v at level $r - i$ determines whether it is congested. v is *congested* if one of the following conditions is satisfied:

- The number of different (d, i)-pairs for which v received a decode message at the beginning of this round is more than $\beta c \cdot k$ for a sufficiently large constant β.

- v received a decode(cong) message at the beginning of this round.

If v is congested and not at level 0, then v sends a

decode(cong) message to its children in $UT(v)$. If v is not congested and not at level 0, then v first combines, for the (remaining) pairs (d, i) with multiple decoding messages, all of those decoding messages to one message. Subsequently, v forwards for all remaining pairs (d, i) the message decode(d, i) to its children in $UT(v)$.

In the following we denote the sub-butterfly $BF(v)$ of a node v as *congested* if at least one node from $BF(v)$ receives more than βck decode massages for different (d, i)-pairs. Using the symmetry of k-ary sub-butterflies it is easy to show that if $BF(v)$ is congested for a node v, then all nodes on level 0 in $BF(v)$ receive a decode(cong) message. Congested sub-butterflies inform the origins of the decode(d, i) requests about that (by using splitting if needed). In non-congested sub-butterflies, the decoding is initiated which will recover the data pieces of all of the (at most βck) remaining requests within $O(r)$ communication rounds with a congestion of at most βck^2 per node (by using the distributed decoding described in Section 2.1). The recovered pieces are then delivered to their origins (by using splitting if needed).

At the end of phase r, every server s with a request belonging to level r has received responses for all $i \in \mathcal{A}(s)$, and if at least $c/4$ of these requests deliver decoded pieces, the server can recover its requested data item and is done. Otherwise, it changes its request to belong to level $r + 1$ so that it continues to be processed in the next phase. It is easy to see that the decoding stage satisfies the following property.

LEMMA 2.20. *The decoding stage takes at most $O(\log_k^2 n)$ communication rounds with at most $O(\log^3 n)$ congestion in every node at each round, w.h.p.*

Analogously to Lemma 2.16, in the decoding stage the following lemma holds:

LEMMA 2.21. *For every phase r, the number of data items with requests belonging to level r is at most $\varphi n / k^r$ with $\varphi = \Theta(k)$.*

PROOF. We show the lemma for $\varphi = k/24 + 1$ by induction on r. Let $\sigma = 1/24$. For $r = 1$ the claim obviously holds. The proof of the induction step is similar to the proof of Lemma 2.16. Recall that for each $r \geq 1$ at most $\sigma \cdot n / k^r$ lookup requests belong to level r. In phase r, a sub-butterfly is called *congested* if it receives more than $\varphi c/2\sigma$ decode messages for different (d, i)-pairs. Certainly, if β is a sufficiently large constant, then a sub-butterfly is congested whenever a node in it receives more than βck messages for different (d, i)-pairs.

By the induction hypothesis there are at most $\varphi n / k^r$ messages with requests for different data items in level r. For each lookup request that belongs to level r, $c/2$ decode messages are sent. Hence, there are less than $\varphi n / k^r \cdot c/2 \cdot 2\sigma/\varphi c = \sigma n / k^r$ congested sub-butterflies of dimension r. Let S be a set of congested data items at level r. Then, there exists a $c/4$-bundle F for S. By Claim 2.19 it holds $|\Gamma_{F,r}(S)| \geq k^r |S|$, if $|S| \leq (1/24)n/k^r$. Since there are less than $\sigma n / k^r$ congested sub-butterflies of dimension r, we have $|\Gamma_{F,r}(S)| < \sigma n$ and it follows $|S| < \sigma n / k^r$. Even if all requests for congested data items do not finish in round r, together with the number of requests belonging to level $r + 1$ from the probing stage, by Lemma 2.16 there are at most $n/k^{r+1} + \sigma n/k^r$ requests that participate in round $r+1$ of the decoding stage. Hence $\varphi \geq \sigma k + 1$, the number of requests participating in round $r + 1$ is at most $\varphi n / k^{r+1}$. $\square$

Hence, less than $\Theta(k)$ data items with lookup requests participate in the last phase of the decoding stage and therefore each node receives in this phase decoding requests for less than $\Theta(k)$ different data items. Thus, there cannot be a congested sub-butterfly any more and the decoding depth of $BF(k, d)$ must be less than $\log_k n$ when blocking at most $\gamma 2^{\log_k n} = \gamma n^{1/\log \log n}$ nodes with $\gamma < 1$, implying that all remaining data items can be decoded at the end.

3. ENHANCED IRIS

Next we present the enhanced IRIS system. Instead of using a simple parity coding strategy to recover from any blocked server within a k-block, it needs a more complex coding strategy that can recover from any two blocked servers within a k-block. Here, we can use the EVENODD scheme proposed in [6]. When using this scheme, we obtain the following results.

LEMMA 3.1. *For any k-block B with node sets $(\ell, x_1), \ldots, (\ell, x_k)$ and $(\ell+1, x_1), \ldots, (\ell+1, x_k)$ in which at most two $(\ell+1, x_j)$ are blocked, the information in the remaining nodes $(\ell+1, x_i)$ suffices to recover $d(\ell, x_1), \ldots, d(\ell, x_k)$.*

LEMMA 3.2. *For any k-block B with node sets $(\ell, x_1), \ldots, (\ell, x_k)$ and $(\ell+1, x_1), \ldots, (\ell+1, x_k)$ it holds: $|d(\ell+1, x_i)| \leq (1 + 2/(k-2))|d(\ell, x_i)|$ up to an additive 1.*

Another aspect in which the enhanced IRIS deviates from the basic IRIS is that the k-blocks are no longer organized in a k-ary butterfly. Instead, we make use of permutations with certain expansion properties.

Consider a set U of n' nodes that are organized into n'/k' groups of k' consecutive nodes. A permutation $\pi : U \to U$ is said to have an expansion of γ if for any subset S of at most $n'/[12(k')^5]$ groups and any subset W of nodes with exactly 3 nodes in each group in S it holds that $\pi(W)$ contains nodes from at least $\gamma|S|$ many groups.

LEMMA 3.3. *For any n' and k' with $n' \geq 12(k')^5$ there is a permutation on U with expansion at least $(1 + \delta)$ for a constant $\delta \geq 1/4$.*

PROOF. Let the permutation π be chosen uniformly at random from all permutations on U. Then the probability $p(s)$ that there exists a set S of groups with $|S| = s$ and a set of triples W from these groups so that $\pi(W)$ contains at most $(1 + \delta)|S|$ many groups satisfies

$$p(s) \leq \binom{n'/k'}{s}\binom{k'}{3}^s \binom{n'/k'}{(1+\delta)s}\left(\frac{(1+\delta)s}{n'/k'}\right)^{3s} \quad (1)$$

where $\binom{n'/k'}{s}$ is the number of possibilities for choosing s groups, $\binom{k'}{3}^s$ is the number of possibilities of choosing a triple in each of the selected groups, $\binom{n'/k'}{(1+\delta)s}$ is the number of possibilities for choosing $(1 + \delta)s$ groups that the triples have to map to, and $\left(\frac{(1+\delta)s}{n'/k'}\right)^{3s}$ is an upper bound on the probability that all of the triples are indeed mapped to the $(1 + \delta)$ groups. When choosing $s = \gamma n'/k'$, Equation (1) is at most

$$\left(\frac{e}{\gamma}\right)^s \left(\frac{(k')^3}{6}\right)^s \left(\frac{e}{(1+\delta)\gamma}\right)^{(1+\delta)s} ((1+\delta)\gamma)^{3s}$$
$$= \left(\frac{e^{2+\delta}(1+\delta)^{2-\delta}}{6}\right)^s ((k')^4\gamma)^{(1-\delta)s}$$

When choosing $\delta = 1/4$ and $\gamma \le 1/(12(k')^4)$, the first term is at most $4^{(1-\delta)s}$ and the second term is at most $(1/12)^{(1-\delta)s}$, so altogether, $p(s) \le (1/3)^{(1-\delta)s}$. When summing up over all $s \ge 1$, this gives an overall probability of less than 0.8 that the expansion of π is at most $(1 + \delta)$, which completes the proof. $\square$

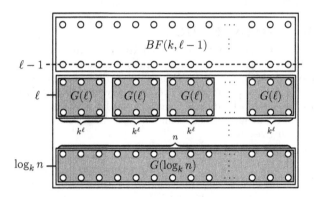

Figure 6: Visualization of the underlying topology used in enhanced IRIS where ℓ denotes the first level with $k^\ell \ge 12(\log k)^5$.

The encoding of the data now works as follows for each level ℓ (see Figure 6 for a visualization). For all levels ℓ with $k^\ell < 12(\log k)^5$ we just use the encoding via k-ary ℓ-dimensional sub-butterflies as in the basic IRIS, but for these levels k^ℓ is a constant, so these levels can tolerate a constant fraction of blocked nodes in each sub-butterfly while still being able to decode all data.

Next, suppose that ℓ satisfies $k^\ell \ge 12(\log k)^5$ and $\ell < 6$. Then we select a permutation π_ℓ that has an expansion of at least $5/4$ for $n' = k^\ell$ and $k' = \log k$. Consider the graph $G(\ell)$ that consists of $L = 20 \log k$ sublevels of k^ℓ nodes each that are partitioned into groups of k' consecutive nodes. Every node (i, x) in some group B in level i is connected to all nodes $(i + 1, \pi_\ell(y))$ with $(i, y) \in B$. This establishes complete bipartite graphs of k' nodes on each side, called k'-blocks. The encoding then works as follows for a set of data items $d_0, \ldots, d_{n'-1}$. Initially, d_i is placed in node $(0, i)$ for every $i \in \{0, \ldots, n' - 1\}$. Given that in level i we have already assigned data items $d(i, x)$ to the nodes (i, x), we compute, for each k'-block B, the data items for level $i + 1$ using the EVENODD coding strategy and assign them to the nodes of that k'-block in level $i+1$. We will use n' servers to emulate $G(\ell)$ with server s_i being responsible for the L nodes $(0, i)$, $(1, \pi_\ell(i))$, $(1, \pi_\ell(\pi_\ell(i)))$, and so on. In this way, each server just has to store $O(z + (z/(k'-2)) \sum_{i=0}^{3\ell k'}(1 + 2/(k'-2))^i) = O(z)$ information, where z is the size of the original data. The decoding depth of a node u at level i is now defined as follows:

$$dd(u) = \begin{cases} 0 & \text{if } u \text{ is not blocked} \\ \infty & \text{if } i = L \text{ and } u \text{ is blocked} \\ \max_{v \in C(u)} \{dd(v)\} + 1 & \text{if } i < L \text{ and } u \text{ is blocked} \end{cases}$$

where $C(u)$ denotes the neighbors of the k'-block of u in level $i+1$ excluding any two nodes of biggest decoding depth among these neighbors. It is not difficult to see that if the decoding depth of a node u at level i is more than d with $i+d \le$

L, then it must be possible to embed a complete *ternary* tree of blocked nodes with root u and depth d in $G(\ell)$. Unfortunately, the leaves of the tree are not guaranteed to be distinct any more like for the binary witness trees in the k-ary butterfly, but due to the expansion property of π_ℓ we know that this ternary tree must cover at least $3(5/4)^{d-1}$ blocked nodes at its leaves. Hence, suppose that there is a node $(0, x)$ in $G(\ell)$ with a decoding depth of more than L. Then there must be at least $\min\{3(5/4)^{L-1}, n'/[12(k')^5]\} \ge n'/[12(k')^5]$ blocked nodes at level L in $G(\ell)$, since $L = 20 \log k \ge 4\ell \log k$ and $(5/4)^{4\ell \log k} \ge k^\ell$. Therefore at least a $1/[12(k')^5]$-fraction of the n' servers must be blocked. Now, if $(k')^\ell \le 12(\log k')^5$, we are done since k' is a constant, so a constant fraction of the servers must be blocked. Otherwise, we add $L' = 20 \log k'$ additional layers to $G(\ell)$ using a permutation π'_ℓ with $n'' = k^\ell$ and $k'' = \log k'$ to increase the number of blocked servers further to at least $n''/[12(k'')^5]$ in case we cannot recover the data in some $(0, x)$ in $G(\ell)$. If $(k'')^\ell \ge 12(\log k'')^5$, we continue with the extension of $G(\ell)$ as for k' until after at most $\log^*(n')$ extensions [2] we finally end up with a constant fraction of blocked servers whenever the data of some $(0, x)$ cannot be recovered. Since $\ell < 6$ the final depth of $G(\ell)$ is at most $O(\log k)$ and the redundancy needed for $G(\ell)$ is bounded by $z \cdot 2^{O(\log^*(n'))}$.

If $k^\ell \ge 12(\log k)^5$ and $\ell \ge 6$, then we first choose a graph $G(\ell)$ using a permutation π_ℓ with $n' = k^\ell$ and $k' = k$ and $L = 4 \log n'$ levels to get the number of blocked servers up to $n'/(12k^5)$. Then we continue with the $\log^*$-construction as in the latter case (starting with $k' = \log k$ and $L = 20 \log k$), until we get the number of blocked servers up to a constant fraction before the decoding of a data item can fail. The final depth of $G(\ell)$ is at most $O(\log n')$ and the redundancy needed for $G(\ell)$ is bounded by $2^{O(\log^*(n'))}$.

Since we have $\log_k n$ many levels, where $k = \log n$, the overall redundancy needed is $\log_k n \cdot 2^{O(\log^*(n))} = O(\log n)$. Once the data has been encoded in this way, the lookup protocol proceeds as before, with the following differences. In the preprocessing stage, in addition to $BF(k, d)$ the permutations π_ℓ are recovered via permutation routing in $BF(k, d)$, for all $\ell \in \{1, \ldots, d\}$, such that the $G(\ell)$-graphs are also recovered. The decoding depth of a sub-butterfly $BF(u)$ is now ℓ if and only if the maximum level needed to decode all $(0, x)$ in $BF(u)$ is ℓ. The probing stage just uses $BF(k, d)$ as before while the decoding stage now uses the $G(\ell)$ graphs to serve the lookup requests belonging to level ℓ.

4. CONCLUSION AND FUTURE WORK

We presented the first scalable distributed information system that is provably robust against DoS-attacks by a current insider that can shutdown any ε-fraction of servers. An interesting challenge in this field of research is to enhance our system so that even write requests can be handled efficiently and correctly under a DoS-attack (as was shown for a past insider in [3]). Furthermore, notice that we did not try to optimize constants; from a practical perspective it would certainly be interesting how small (resp. large) they can be made.

---

[2]$\log^*(n)$ is the number of times the logarithm has to be applied to n until the result is at most 2.

5. REFERENCES

[1] B. Awerbuch and C. Scheideler. Towards a Scalable and Robust DHT. In *Proc. of SPAA*, pages 318–327, 2006.

[2] B. Awerbuch and C. Scheideler. A Denial-of-Service Resistant DHT. In *Proc. of DISC*, pages 33–47, 2007.

[3] M. Baumgart, C. Scheideler, and S. Schmid. A dos-resilient information system for dynamic data management. In *Proc. SPAA*, pages 300–309, 2009.

[4] D. Bernstein. SYN Cookies. In *http://cr.yp.to/syncookies.html*, 2008.

[5] A. Bhargava, K. Kothapalli, C. Riley, C. Scheideler, and M. Thober. Pagoda: A Dynamic Overlay Network for Routing, Data Management, and Multicasting. In *Proc. of SPAA*, pages 170–179, 2004.

[6] M. Blaum, J. Brady, J. Bruck, and J. Menon. Evenodd: an optimal scheme for tolerating double disk failures in raid architectures. *SIGARCH Comput. Archit. News*, 22(2):245–254, Apr. 1994.

[7] H. Chernoff. A measure of asymptotic efficiency for tests of a hypothesis based on the sums of observations. *Annals of Mathematical Statistics*, 23:409–507, 1952.

[8] D. Dittrich, J. Mirkovic, S. Dietrich, and P. Reiher. *Internet Denial of Service: Attack and Defense Mechanisms*. Prentice Hall PTR, 2005.

[9] B. Doerr, L. A. Goldberg, L. Minder, T. Sauerwald, and C. Scheideler. Stabilizing consensus with the power of two choices. In *Proc. of SPAA*, pages 149–158, 2011.

[10] P. Druschel and A. Rowstron. Pastry: Scalable, Distributed Object Location and Routing for Large-Scale Peer-to-Peer Systems. In *Proc. of Middleware*, pages 329–350, 2001.

[11] N. J. A. Harvey, M. B. Jones, S. Saroiu, M. Theimer, and A. Wolman. SkipNet: A Scalable Overlay Network with Practical Locality Properties. In *Proc. of USITS*, page 9, 2003.

[12] J. Ioannidis and S. M. Bellovin. Implementing Pushback: Router-Based Defense Against DDoS Attacks. In *Proc. of NDSS*, 2002.

[13] S. Kandula, D. Katabi, M. Jacob, and A. Berger. Botz-4-Sale: Surviving Organized DDoS Attacks that Mimic Flash Crowds. In *Proc. of NSDI*, pages 287–300, 2005.

[14] F. Kargl, J. Maier, and M. Weber. Protecting Web Servers from Distributed Denial of Service Attacks. In *Proc. of WWW*, pages 514–524, 2001.

[15] A. D. Keromytis, V. Misra, and D. Rubenstein. SOS: Secure Overlay Services. In *Proc. of SIGCOMM*, pages 61–72, 2002.

[16] Mazu Networks Inc. http://mazunetworks.com. 2008.

[17] J. Mirkovic and P. Reiher. A Taxonomy of DDoS Attacks and Defense Mechanisms. *Proc. of SIGCOMM*, 2004.

[18] W. G. Morein, A. Stavrou, D. L. Cook, A. D. Keromytis, V. Misra, and D. Rubenstein. Using Graphic Turing Tests to Counter Automated DDoS Attacks Against Web Servers. In *Proc. of CCS*, pages 8–19, 2003.

[19] M. Naor and U. Wieder. Novel Architectures for P2P Applications: the Continuous-Discrete Approach. In *Proc. of SPAA*, pages 50–59, 2003.

[20] G. Oikonomou, J. Mirkovic, P. Reiher, and M. Robinson. A Framework for Collaborative DDoS Defense. In *Proc. of ACSAC*, pages 33–42, 2006.

[21] V. N. Padmanabhan and K. Sripanidkulchai. The Case for Cooperative Networking. In *Proc. of IPTPS*, pages 178–190, 2002.

[22] R. Pagh and F. F. Rodler. Cuckoo hashing. In *Proc of ESA*, pages 121–133, 2001.

[23] D. Peleg. *Distributed Computing: A Locality-Sensitive Approach*. Society for Industrial and Applied Mathematics, 2000.

[24] E. Ratliff. The Zombie Hunters. In *The New Yorker*, 2005.

[25] S. Ratnasamy, P. Francis, M. Handley, R. Karp, and S. Shenker. A Scalable Content-Addressable Network. In *Proc. of SIGCOMM*, pages 161–172, 2001.

[26] I. Reed and G. Solomon. Polynomial codes over certain finite fields. *Journal of the Society of Industrial and Applied Mathematics*, 8(2):300–304, 1960.

[27] T. Stading, P. Maniatis, and M. Baker. Peer-to-Peer Caching Schemes to Address Flash Crowds. In *Proc. of IPTPS*, pages 203–213, 2002.

[28] A. Stavrou, D. Rubenstein, and S. Sahu. A Lightweight, Robust P2P System to Handle Flash Crowds. In *Proc. of ICNP*, pages 226–235, 2002.

[29] I. Stoica, D. Adkins, S. Zhuang, S. Shenker, and S. Surana. Internet Indirection Infrastructure. In *Proc. of SIGCOMM*, 2002.

[30] I. Stoica, R. Morris, D. Liben-Nowell, D. Karger, M. F. Kaashoek, F. Dabek, and H. Kalakrishnan. Chord: A Scalable Peer-to-Peer Lookup Service for Internet Applications. In *Technical Report MIT*, 2002.

[31] M. Walfish, H. Balakrishnan, D. Karger, and S. Shenker. DoS: Fighting Fire with Fire. In *Workshop on Hot Topics in Networks (HotNets)*, 2005.

[32] M. Walfish, M. Vutukuru, H. Balakrishnan, D. Karger, and S. Shenker. DDoS Defense By Offense. *Proc. of SIGCOMM*, 36(4):303–314, 2006.

[33] Wikipedia. Denial-of-service attack. http://en.wikipedia.org/wiki/Denial-of-service_attack, accessed 12-February-2013.

[34] X. Yang, D. Wetherall, and T. Anderson. A DoS-Limiting Network Architecture. In *Proc. of SIGCOMM*, pages 241–252, 2005.

SybilCast: Broadcast on the Open Airwaves

[Extended Abstract]

Seth Gilbert
National University of Singapore
Department of Computer Science
Singapore, 117417
seth.gilbert@comp.nus.edu.sg

Chaodong Zheng
National University of Singapore
Department of Computer Science
Singapore, 117417
chaodong.zheng@comp.nus.edu.sg

ABSTRACT

Consider a scenario where many wireless users are attempting to download data from a single base station. While most of the users are honest, some users may be malicious and attempt to obtain more than their fair share of the bandwidth. One possible strategy for attacking the system is to simulate multiple fake identities, each of which is given its own equal share of the bandwidth. Such an attack is often referred to as a *sybil attack*. To counter such behavior, we propose *SybilCast*, a protocol for multichannel wireless networks that limits the number of fake identities, and in doing so, ensures that each honest user gets at least a constant fraction of their fair share of the bandwidth. As a result, each honest user can complete his or her data download in asymptotically optimal time. A key aspect of this protocol is balancing the rate at which new identities are admitted and the maximum number of fake identities that can co-exist, while keeping the overhead low. Besides sybil attacks, our protocol can also tolerate spoofing and jamming.

Categories and Subject Descriptors

C.2.1 [**Computer Communications Networks**]: Network Architecture and Design—*Wireless communication*

Keywords

Wireless networks; sybil attack; fairness

1. INTRODUCTION

Consider the following scenario: 100 scientists sit in an auditorium, listening to a lecture. Most have a laptop open in front of them, and many are attempting to download data from the internet, perhaps a video of the preceding day's lecture[1]. Luckily, the wireless base station uses a *fair* version of 802.11, ensuring that each

registered user gets an equal share of the bandwidth[2]. Unfortunately, though, one clever attendee is upset with the slow download speed and finds a way to circumvent this fairness mechanism by simulating 200 distinct users. By doing so, he gets $2/3$ of the total available bandwidth. For the remaining users, their downloads now take three times as long as before. Such behavior is typically referred to as a *sybil attack* [4], where malicious users dishonestly generate large numbers of fake identities (also called *sybil identities*), injecting them into the system to gain some extra benefit or to conduct some other hostile activity.

In this paper, we develop a new protocol, *SybilCast*, that thwarts this type of malicious behavior in multichannel wireless networks. More specifically, our protocol can ensure that each honest participant will receive at least a constant fraction of its fair share of the bandwidth[3]. This implies that each download of data will complete in asymptotically optimal time, even in the presence of a sybil attack. In addition, our protocol is robust to message spoofing and wireless jamming.

Radio-resource testing. In order to thwart attacks, we leverage the ability of a radio to access multiple channels to solve two basic problems: the creation of too many sybil identities and the disruption caused by adversarial jamming.

Consider the following simple strategy: the base station chooses two clients (i.e., registered identities) that have requested data, and assigns each of them to listen to a randomly chosen channel. The base station then picks one of the two channels, and transmits a randomly chosen codeword. It then requests an acknowledgment. If both identities are controlled by a single real user (who is dishonest and only has one radio), then it cannot listen on both channels at once, and there is a 50% chance that it fails to receive the secret message and hence cannot send the acknowledgment. If this test is repeated sufficiently frequently, the dishonest identities will be detected. By contrast, if both clients represent honest (and distinct) users, they will listen as requested, receive the codeword, and hence be able to send the required acknowledgment.

What happens if the adversary jams the channels, preventing the honest nodes from receiving the codewords? If an honest node fails to receive the codeword, then it cannot send the required acknowledgment and will be treated as a dishonest user. However, since the channels are assigned at random, the honest users will receive the secret codeword with at least constant probability as long as

---

*The research in this paper has been supported by Singapore NUS FRC R-252-000-443-133.

[1]These are very diligent scientists, watching video lectures, rather than surfing Facebook, while ignoring the current speaker.

[2]Perhaps this is a computer science conference on experimental networking, as most existing 802.11 deployments are not fair; however there is much research related to fairness—see Section 2.

[3]Note that in this paper we focus on fairness in *downloading* data, assuming that data flows from the base station to the mobile devices tend to dominate the bandwidth usage. Similar techniques would also yield protocols for uploading data.

the malicious users cannot jam more than a constant fraction of all channels at any given time. This strategy combines *radio resource testing* [9, 12] with *uncoordinated frequency hopping* [18] to reliably detect sybil identities, and counter adversarial jamming.

Challenges. There are three key challenges when generalizing the above simple strategy: limiting the overhead, integrating newly arrived users (whether honest or malicious), and coping with message spoofing from malicious users.

First, the process of testing must be implemented efficiently with limited overhead: there is little benefit to eliminating sybil identities if the protocol for detecting these identities consumes all the available bandwidth. In general, the protocol must spend most of its time delivering data packets, not running tests. For example, it does not suffice to test one pair of processes at a time: if there are d active identities (many of which may be sybil identities), it will take $\Theta(d^2)$ time to test them all. Instead, the running time should depend on the number of real users, not the number of sybil identities. In addition, the malicious users may be colluding, and may be able to monitor multiple channels simultaneously; it will be insufficient to divide identities onto two channels.

The second challenge is coping with the continuous nature of the system. Clients continue to arrive over time, requesting data downloads. Malicious users continue to register new sybil identities. Thus it is insufficient to simply run a set of tests and then proceed with a standard data delivery protocol. A key aspect of our design is balancing the rate at which new users (and potentially new sybil identities) are admitted to the system and the rate at which sybil identities can be detected. For example, by reducing the admission rate, we can achieve a much tighter bound on the number of sybil identities; however, in doing so we risk reducing the throughput of the honest users.

A third challenge is coping with adversarial spoofing which, similar to adversarial jamming, can result in a denial-of-service attack. For example, the malicious users cam attempt to spoof messages from the honest clients to the base station, tricking the base station into thinking that the honest clients are dishonest. By careful use of uncoordinated frequency hopping, along with simple techniques like hash chains, we can overcome this attack.

Results. The SybilCast protocol provides the following guarantees. In a system with at most N real users, t dishonest users, and $c > 8t$ channels: if an honest user p requests a download m of size $|m| > c^2 \log^3 N$, and if there are at most $\texttt{contention}(p, m)$ concurrently active real users at any point during the request, then the download will complete in $O(|m| \cdot \texttt{contention}(p, m))$ time. This implies that the honest user has received an asymptotically fair share of the bandwidth. At the same time, we guarantee that there are at most $O(\texttt{contention}(p, m))$ sybil identities, i.e., $O(1)$ sybil identities for every real identity, on average.

Roadmap. In the reminder of the paper, Section 2 introduces related work. Section 3 models the network environment and the problem we want to solve. Section 4 describes the SybilCast protocol. Section 5 gives the analysis of the protocol. We conclude this paper with discussion and future work.

2. RELATED WORK

Our goal is to provide each user a *fair* share of the bandwidth. Fairness is a well-studied problem in network engineering, and is particularly challenging in wireless networks [14]. There exist many definitions of fairness in the literature, e.g., TCP fairness [15], index fairness [8], max-min fairness [7], proportional fairness [2], etc. In this paper, we focus on a simple notion of fairness: if

a set of n clients attempt to download data simultaneously, each should get approximately $1/n$ of the total available bandwidth.

In wired networks, scheduling and congestion control algorithms [5] are widely used to achieve fairness. In wireless networks, there is the additional problem of collisions and jamming. For example, in a single channel wireless network, Awerbuch et al. [1] propose an efficient MAC protocol which can tolerate an adaptive jammer and guarantee fairness. Later, Richa et al. [16] extend their work to cope with a more powerful reactive adversary. They also study how to achieve robustness and fairness when multiple networks coexist [17].

One implicit assumption that these proposals make is that clients can be reliably identified. Unfortunately, this is not always the case: a dishonest user can create an arbitrarily large number of fake identities. Douceur [4] observed this problem and coined the term "sybil attack" to describe such malicious behavior. Sybil attacks can do severe damage to many real-world systems, including reputation systems, peer-to-peer networks, and mobile/wireless networks. See James et al. [9] for a good summary of the potential dangers of sybil attacks, particularly to sensor networks.

Researchers have proposed various approaches to counter sybil attacks. The simplest solution is pre-distributing credentials. For example, James et al. [9] propose several schemes which bind pre-distributed keys with each node's identity. Another possibility is to use signed certificates to verify the identity of the clients. Unfortunately, distributing credentials in advance is difficult in a highly dynamic, rapidly changing wireless network.

The emergence of social networks has inspired new techniques for detecting sybil identities by relying on the relationships among users to detect fake identities [6, 20, 19].

The main approach that we adopt in this paper is known as "resource testing." The basic idea is to demand the client to prove it has a sufficient quantity of some resource; if the client wants to simulate two users, it must demonstrate twice as many resources. In this way, a resource constrained client cannot simulate too many users. The resource in question can be computation, storage, or a radio transceiver.

Several different radio resource testing techniques have been developed for wireless networks (again, see [9]), and are often classified in three categories [12]: *simultaneous sender testing*, *simultaneous receiver testing* and *forced collision testing*. (The strategy we use in this paper to detect sybil identities is one type of simultaneous receiver test.)

In one of the first papers to address sybil attacks in wireless networks, Mónica et al. combine radio resource testing with other (computational) resource testing techniques to construct sybil-free quorums in one-hop wireless ad-hoc network [11, 13]; these quorums can then be used to solve a variety of other problems.

The novelty of our approach lies in developing a protocol that can efficiently detect sybil identities with lower overhead than previous radio resource testing protocols. By balancing the admission rate and the detection rate, we achieve a good steady state constraint on the number of sybil identities. The other novel aspect of Sybil-Cast is coping with adversarial jamming and message spoofing. To the best of our knowledge, this is the first proposal that achieves both fairness and asymptotically optimal throughput in the presence of sybil identities and other malicious behavior.

3. MODEL AND PROBLEM STATEMENT

We consider a synchronous wireless network consisting of one base station and a dynamically changing set of clients. There are at most N clients, an unknown subset of which are active at any given time. We call these clients *wireless nodes*, or just nodes when there is no confusion. Each node may either be an honest node or a malicious node. Among these N nodes, up to t are malicious.

Notice that N is an upper bound on the system size, while the actual system size is unknown at any given time. In fact, the number of active nodes may change throughout an execution. We assume that a polynomial-factor estimation on N (i.e., a constant-factor approximation of $\log N$) is known.

Nodes communicate with the base station by using a multichannel wireless radio consisting of c independent channels. We assume $t < c/8$ and $N > c$. Fundamentally, we are assuming a reasonably large number of available channels, or a reasonably small number of colluding attackers. (Bluetooth [3], for example, specifies 79 channels, and there is every reason to believe that even more channels are possible.)

Every node (including the malicious nodes) and the base station has one radio transceiver. Time is divided into *rounds*, and each round is sufficiently long for two messages to be sent: a primary message and an acknowledgment. (Allowing for an acknowledgment in each round simplifies the presentation.) Each node and the base station can access only one channel in each round. The channels are collision-prone: if two or more nodes broadcast on the same channel concurrently, there is a collision and all information is lost. We do not assume collision detection.

A malicious node may: (a) jam channels (by broadcasting noise); (b) spoof messages (by claiming to be someone he is not); and (c) create sybil identities. Messages from the base station can be authenticated (by using signatures), but messages from wireless nodes are unauthenticated: a malicious node can claim to be any other active node or a new identity.

We assume that devices have access to certain cryptographic tools. The base station and the wireless nodes use a *pseudorandom number generator* (see, e.g., [10]) to generate sequences of "random" bits from small messages. (A pseudorandom number generator is a function which takes an input as a *key* and then generates a long sequence of pseudorandom bits. Moreover, obtaining the first i bits will not provide any information on the $(i+1)$st bit.) We also rely on hash functions, which we assume to be *irreversible* (i.e., the adversary cannot invert the hash function) and *collision-free* (i.e., different inputs to the hash function will yield different output). As can be seen, we assume "perfect" versions of these tools, as they are not the focus of this paper.

Problem statement. Nodes may attempt to enter the system at any time. When an honest node enters the system, it initiates a *request*, attempting to download data from the base station. No honest node will withdraw its request halfway. An honest node (and its request) is considered to be *active* from the point at which it enters the system. A request is considered complete (and the node becomes inactive) when the node has received all the requested data. We measure the performance in terms of the time it takes for a node to complete a request. For any requested data m from a particular honest node p, we define $\texttt{contention}(p, m)$ to be the maximum number of concurrently active nodes at any point during the request. (Note that this includes both honest nodes and malicious nodes, but not sybil identities.) In a perfectly fair system, it will take at least $|m| \cdot \texttt{contention}(p, m)$ time for p to fetch m, in the worst case, if each process is given a fair share of the total available bandwidth.

4. PROTOCOL

We now describe the SybilCast protocol, which consists of three parts: (a) registration, where new nodes (and potentially sybil identities) enter the system and request a download; (b) data delivery,

where the base station delivers data to the registered identities; and (c) verification, where the base station attempts to spot and eliminate sybil identities. The base station repeatedly executes these three phases, one iteration of which we call an *epoch*.

Registration. The goal of the registration phase is to deliver a unique and random binary string to each new request (and the node which sent it). We call this string a *final seed*. Each registered identity (which can be an honest node or a sybil identity) can use its final seed as the key for a pseudorandom number generator. The output of this pseudorandom number generator is a channel hopping sequence that the registered identity should follow during the ensuing data and verification phases. The length of the sequence is assumed to be sufficiently long so that for every request the corresponding node needs to register only once.

Data. The data phase is used to transmit data packets and deliver authentication messages from the base station to the registered identities. In each round of a data phase, the base station randomly chooses a registered identity, and sends it a packet on the channel specified by its final seed. The base station also includes a one-time random string, called a *nonce*, in each data packet. The base station will later use these nonces to verify whether the identities who should have been listening on that channel really were.

Verification. The verification phase allows the base station to detect and eliminate sybil identities. During the verification phase, each registered identity should transmit a verification message to the base station containing an encrypted list (using the final seed as the key) of the nonces received by the identity during the preceding data phase. The base station will receive and verify these messages and remove identities that fail to send verification messages or provide insufficient nonces[4].

The length of the three phases in each epoch is dynamically decided at the beginning of that epoch. Assume there are x registered identities at the beginning of an epoch, then each of the three phases has length $O\left((x + c) \log^2 N\right)$. This provides sufficient time for x new identities to be registered, while preventing the number of sybil identities from growing too fast. As we shall later see, this key design decision well balances the (new identities') admission rate and the (sybil identities') elimination rate. This schedule is illustrated in Figure 1.

In the remainder of this paper, we use $id(i)$ to denote the total number of registered identities at the beginning of epoch i; and $s(i)$ to denote the total number of sybil identities at the beginning of the data phase of epoch i. We now describe each phase in more detail.

4.1 Registration Phase

For an epoch i, the corresponding registration phase is subdivided into $\Theta((id(i) + c) \log N)$ sub-phases of length $\Theta(\log N)$. In each sub-phase, nodes compete to send their requests to the base station; the base station will deliver a *partial seed* to one winning node. A partial seed is a unique and random binary string, and if a node has collected $\Theta(\log N)$ partial seeds in one registration phase, then its registration is complete: it generates the final seed via a bitwise xor of the partial seeds. Each honest node will have at most one request and hence at most one identity at any time. However, malicious nodes may attempt to register multiple sybil identities to fulfill multiple requests simultaneously. The registration protocol is summarized in the pseudocode in Figure 2 which we now discuss in more detail.

As per our previous description, the length of each registration phase is determined by the number of registered identities that remain in the system at the beginning of the epoch. During the regis-

---

[4]We will give the precise meaning for "sufficient" and "insufficient" in Section 5.

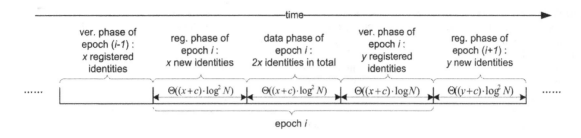

Figure 1: Dynamic phase length.

Base Station Registration:

1: $list \leftarrow \emptyset$ ▷ The requests that should have received at least one partial seed.
2: $q \leftarrow \Theta((sys\_size + c) \log N)$ ▷ Number of sub-phases; sys_size is the number of registered identities, i.e., $id(x)$ for epoch x.
3: **for** $(sp \leftarrow 1$ to $q)$ **do**
4:    $sent \leftarrow false$ ▷ Indicate whether a partial seed is already sent in this sub-phase.
5:    $ch \leftarrow \mathtt{random}(1, c)$ ▷ $\mathtt{random}(x, y)$ returns a uniformly chosen random value between x and y, both inclusive.
6:    $seq \leftarrow \mathtt{prng}(ch)$ ▷ $\mathtt{prng}(k)$ returns a pseudo random sequence with k as the key.
7:    $\mathtt{broadcast}(\langle REG\_START, seq, list, q, sp, sys\_size\rangle, ch)$ ▷ $\mathtt{broadcast}(m, c)$ broadcasts m on channel c.
8:    **for** $(r \leftarrow 1$ to $\Theta(\log N))$ **do**
9:      $msg \leftarrow \mathtt{listen}(seq[r])$ ▷ $\mathtt{listen}(c)$ returns the message obtained by listening on channel c.
10:      **if** $(msg.type = REG\_REQ)$ **then**
11:        **if** $(sent = true)$ **then continue**
12:        **if** $(sp < q/2$ **and** $|list| < sys\_size)$ **then**
13:          $req \leftarrow \mathtt{genReq}(msg.id)$ ▷ $\mathtt{genReq}(x)$ returns a new and empty request structure with x as the request's identity.
14:          $pseed \leftarrow \mathtt{randString}()$ ▷ $\mathtt{randString}()$ returns a random binary string; $pseed$ is the partial seed.
15:          $\mathtt{broadcast}(\langle REG\_RESP, pseed, msg.id, sp\rangle, seq[r])$
16:          $sent \leftarrow true, req.last\_hash = msg.hash$
17:          $list[msg.id] = req$ ▷ Adds the new request to $list$.
18:        **else if** $(sp \geq q/2$ **and** $msg.id \in list)$ **then**
19:          $req \leftarrow list[msg.id]$
20:          **if** $(\mathtt{hash}^{(sp-msg.lsp)}(msg.hash) = req.last\_hash)$ **then**
21:            $pseed \leftarrow \mathtt{randString}()$
22:            $\mathtt{broadcast}(\langle REG\_RESP, pseed, msg.id, sp\rangle, seq[r])$
23:            $sent \leftarrow true, req.pseed\_list \leftarrow req.pseed\_list \cup \{msg.last\_pseed\}, req.last\_hash = msg.hash$

Node Registration:

1: $k \leftarrow 0, secret \leftarrow \mathtt{randString}(), req \leftarrow \mathtt{genReq}(id)$ ▷ k counts the number of received partial seeds; id is the identity of the node
2: $req.lsp \leftarrow 0$ ▷ $req.lsp$ records the last sub-phase in which a partial seed is received, initially set to 0
3: $req.last\_pseed \leftarrow nil$ ▷ $req.lsp$ records the last partial seed the node received
4: **while** $(k < \Theta(\log N))$ **do**
5:    $ch \leftarrow \mathtt{random}(1, c)$
6:    **repeat**
7:      $msg \leftarrow \mathtt{listen}(ch)$
8:    **until** $msg.type = REG\_START$
9:    **if** $(msg.i < (msg.q)/2$ **and** $req.id \in msg.list)$ **then continue**   ▷ Only register once during the first half.
10:    **if** $(msg.i \geq (msg.q)/2$ **and** $req.id \notin msg.list)$ **then continue**   ▷ Only active during the second half if already on the list.
11:    **for** $(r \leftarrow 1$ to $\Theta(\log N))$ **do**
12:      **if** $(\mathtt{random}(1, 2^{r-1}) = 1)$ **then**   ▷ Broadcast with probability $1/2^{r-1}$
13:        $\mathtt{broadcast}(\langle REG\_REQ, id, \mathtt{hash}^{(msg.q-msg.sp)}(secret), req.lsp, req.last\_pseed\rangle, msg.seq[r])$
14:      $msg \leftarrow \mathtt{listen}(msg.seq[r])$
15:      **if** $(msg.type = REG\_RESP$ **and** $msg.id = id)$ **then**
16:        $req.pseed\_list \leftarrow req.pseed\_list \cup \{msg.pseed\}, req.lsp \leftarrow msg.sp, req.last\_pseed \leftarrow msg.pseed$
17:        $k \leftarrow k + 1$
18: $req.seed \leftarrow \mathtt{xor}(req.pseed\_list)$ ▷ Generate the final seed by bit-wise $\mathtt{xor}$ of partial seeds

Figure 2: Registration phase pseudocode (*top sub-figure for base station, bottom sub-figure for wireless nodes*).

tration phase, there can be significant contention among the nodes that are trying to register their requests. For example, if a large number of new nodes try to join the system during one registration phase, then each may only get a small number of partial seeds, with none completing the whole process. To avoid this, in the first round of each registration sub-phase in epoch i, the base station will send a *registration list* which includes requests that have already obtained at least one partial seed in the current registration phase. When the registration list is full, i.e., is of size $id(i)$, an honest node will only compete in this sub-phase if its request is already in the list.

Moreover, to simplify the analysis, we divide each registration phase into two parts of equal length. During the first half, each unregistered honest node is eligible to compete for its first partial seed. Once it receives its first partial seed (and hence gets into the registration list), it remains silent until the halfway point. During the second half, all honest nodes that have not been added to the registration list remain silent, while all honest nodes that are already in the registration list become eligible to compete for more partial seeds (so as to finish their registration process).

The base station will do the following in each sub-phase: (a) In the first round, the base station sends out a channel hopping sequence on a randomly chosen channel instructing each unregistered node that receives the message to use this sequence for the remainder of this sub-phase. (b) In each of the following $\Theta(\log N)$ rounds, the base station will listen to the channel specified by the previous sequence until a request is received. If multiple nodes send out requests simultaneously, a collision occurs and all requests are lost. If the base station successfully receives a request (i.e., if only one node broadcasts and there is no jamming) from a node that is eligible to receive partial seeds, then it sends back a response containing a partial seed. It also records which partial seeds are distributed to which request.

In each sub-phase, the base station keeps silent once a partial seed is sent; this implies the base station will send out at most one partial seed in each sub-phase.

Each honest node that wants to register an identity acts as follows: (a) Initially, it listens on a randomly chosen channel until a channel hopping sequence is received. (b) If it is eligible to compete for partial seeds in this sub-phase, then in each of the following $\Theta(\log N)$ rounds, it broadcasts its request with probability $1/2^{(r-1)}$ on the specified channel, where r is the round number. If the node receives a response which contains a partial seed for it, it records that partial seed. (c) It repeats (a) and (b) until $\Theta(\log N)$ partial seeds are collected or this registration phase is finished.

During the registration phase, the base station needs to determine which partial seeds are assigned to which requests. To ensure authenticity, each node uses a *hash chain* to prove that all of its requests come from the same node, i.e., itself. A hash chain is a technique which works as follows: before each node enters a registration phase, it generates a *secret* which is known only to itself. Each time a node sends out a request, it also includes $\mathtt{hash}^{(q-sp)}(secret)$, where q denotes the total number of sub-phases in this registration phase, and sp denotes the current sub-phase number[5]. Every time the base station receives a request from a node, it iterates the hash function for an appropriate number of times and verifies that the (recursive) hash of the last received value matches the current received value. If the result indeed matches, then the base station can be assured that it is talking to the same

node. Note, malicious nodes may still create multiple secrets and try to register multiple identities.

The second issue is coping with partial seeds that are lost. If the node does not receive a partial seed (due to jamming), then the base station learns of this when it receives the next request (which is authenticated by the hash chain). After receiving all the required partial seeds, the node participates in one additional registration sub-phase, ensuring that the base station knows it has received the last partial seed. (Note, for concision, the "one more sub-phase" needed to confirm the last partial seed is not implemented in the pseudocode in Figure 2.)

Since the malicious users can intercept a partial seed with at most constant probability in each registration sub-phase, by requiring $\Theta(\log N)$ partial seeds, we ensure that even if the malicious users overhear some of the partial seeds, they cannot learn the final seed of an honest node, with high probability. (If they did learn the final seed, they could jam all communication to this honest node during the data phase.) More precisely:

LEMMA 1. *For every request from an honest node that completes its registration, at least one of the partial seeds is not intercepted by any malicious user w.h.p.*[6]

PROOF. To obtain the partial seed sent out by the base station in any registration sub-phase, the malicious users must either: (a) know the channel hopping sequence of that sub-phase; or (b) listen on the channel on which the base station broadcasts the partial seed. By assumption, the malicious users can listen to at most $c/8$ channels in any one round, hence they can only obtain the hopping sequence and/or the partial seed with probability at most $1/8$ in each case. Since channels are chosen independently for each sub-phase, and since each node has to obtain $\Theta(\log N)$ partial seeds before it can be registered, the lemma follows. $\square$

4.2 Data Phase

For an epoch i, there are $\Theta((id(i) + c) \log^2 N)$ rounds in the corresponding data phase.

Data phases serve two purposes. The most important goal is to deliver data. In each round of a data phase, the base station will randomly choose a registered identity and send a data packet to it. Since the base station knows the channel hopping pattern (based on the final seed obtained during registration) and the malicious users do not (with high probability), we can ensure that each data packet for an honest node is delivered with constant probability. (The only way in which a packet is lost is if the malicious users successful include the channel in the $c/8$ channels that they can block.)

The second purpose is to transmit nonces to the registered identities. Each data packet contains a unique, randomly chosen nonce. All the identities listen on the channel specified by the sequence calculated from their final seed. Whether or not they are the intended recipient of the packet, they record the nonce[7]. At the end of the data phase, each honest node will have many nonces which can later be used for verification.

The above description is summarized in the pseudocode in Figure 3.

4.3 Verification Phase

The verification phase is the last key component of SybilCast. It is summarized in the pseudocode in Figure 4. The purpose of the verification phase is to let the base station eliminate sybil identities.

---

[5] $\mathtt{hash}^{(i)}(msg)$ means recursively apply $\mathtt{hash}(\ldots)$ for i times. E.g., $\mathtt{hash}^{(2)}(msg) = \mathtt{hash}(\mathtt{hash}(msg))$.

[6] We use "w.h.p." to abbreviate "with high probability."

[7] In fact, this is intended to allow for more rapid removal of sybil identities, in case—with very low probability—the system is accidentally flooded with sybil identities, exceeding the limit. This allows our protocol to *self-recover*.

Base Station Data Phase:

```
 1: for (r ← 1 to Θ((sys_size + c) log² N)) do          ▷ sys_size is the number of registered identities, i.e., id(x) for epoch x
 2:     req ← randomReq()                                 ▷ randomReq() returns a randomly chosen registered identity
 3:     seq ← prng(req.seed)
 4:     nonce ← randString()
 5:     broadcast(⟨DATA, req.id, data, nonce⟩, seq[r])    ▷ data is a portion of the data requested by the selected node
 6:     req.nonce_list = req.nonce_list ∪ {nonce}
 7:     for (each req' ≠ req that should listen to seq[r] in this round) do
 8:         req'.nonce_list = req'.nonce_list ∪ {nonce}
```

Node Data Phase:

```
 1: seq ← prng(req.seed)                                  ▷ req is the node's own request
 2: for (r ← 1 to Θ((sys_size + c) log² N)) do
 3:     msg ← listen(seq[r])
 4:     if (msg.type = DATA) then
 5:         req.nonce_list = req.nonce_list ∪ {msg.nonce}
 6:         if (msg.id = req.id) then deliver msg.data
```

Figure 3: Data phase pseudocode (*top sub-figure for base station, bottom sub-figure for registered nodes*).

For an epoch i, the verification phase consists of $\Theta(\log N)$ sub-phases each of length $\Theta(id(i) + c)$. Upon entering the verification phase, each honest node that has registered an identity randomly chooses $\Theta(c)$ rounds in each sub-phase, and sends out a verification packet in each of these selected rounds on the channel specified by the final seed. The verification packet contains all the nonces the node has collected during the preceding data phase in encrypted form, using the final seed as the key.

The base station's work during verification is simple. It randomly chooses a channel in each round and waits for verification packets. Upon receiving one such packet, it checks if the corresponding identity has provided enough nonces to prove it is not a sybil. If the base station receives no packets from an identity, or if all received packets sent from an identity provide insufficient nonces, then the base station will assume the identity is sybil and eliminate it. The precise meaning of "sufficient" will be defined in Section 5.

To ensure honest nodes cannot fail verification due to jamming or contention during the verification phase, SybilCast guarantees the following property:

LEMMA 2. *Each registered honest node will be successfully verified by the base station w.h.p. in every epoch, as long as it has collected sufficient nonces during the preceding data phase.*

PROOF. If an honest node p has enough nonces, the only possible reasons that can prevent it from being successfully verified are: (a) the honest node and the base station choose different channels; (b) collision among multiple nodes sending verification messages concurrently; or (c) malicious jamming. We now calculate the probability that the base station misses all verification messages from an honest node p during one verification phase.

In the following proof, we call every round in which node p sends a verification massage as a *slot*.

In any epoch i, during the verification phase, there are $\Theta(\log N)$ sub-phases each containing $\Theta(c)$ slots. Hence, p has $\Theta(c \log N)$ slots in total. In each slot, the base station chooses the same channel with p with probability $1/c$. On the other hand, in each slot, another node may collide with p with probability $\Theta\left(c/(id(i) + c)\right) \cdot (1/c) = \Theta\left(1/(id(i) + c)\right)$. Since there are at most $(id(i) - 1)$ other nodes, for every particular slot, the probability that there is no collision is $(1 - \Theta\left(1/(id(i) + c)\right))^{(id(i)-1)} = \Omega(1/e)$. Lastly,

the adversary may jam each slot with probability at most $1/8$, as we have shown in Lemma 1 that w.h.p. she doesn't know any node's final seed.

Combining these facts together, we can see that in each slot, the verification message from p will be missed by the base station with probability $1 - (\Omega(1/e) \cdot (7/8) \cdot (1/c)) = 1 - \Omega(1/c)$. Therefore, after one verification phase, the verification message from p will be missed by the base station with probability $(1 - \Omega(1/c))^{\Theta(c \log N)}$, i.e., $O(1/N^k)$ for any constant k. □

We also note here that our verification scheme is different from traditional radio resource testing in the sense that we do not use *immediate verification* but rather *deferred verification*. More specifically, instead of asking the nodes that received the nonce during a data round to send back an acknowledgment immediately, we *defer* this process to the verification phase. This design may allow sybil identities to remain in the system longer, but it brings two key benefits: (a) Immediate verification suffers from message spoofing and wireless jamming. Malicious nodes can spoof verification packets or jam the channels and hence force the base station remove honest nodes. This is not possible in SybilCast. (b) Deferred verification enables SybilCast to be *self-recoverable*. Imagine a scenario in which something unfortunate happens and one thousand sybil identities are injected into the system in one round. With immediate verification, these new sybil identities may persist for a very long time, as at most one identity can be verified in each round. In our system, however, they can only survive one epoch, at most.

5. ANALYSIS

In this section, we analyze the total time consumption for an honest node to complete a download request. We also show that SybilCast constrains the maximum number of sybil identities and provides asymptotically optimal transmission speed at the same time.

We assume an honest node p is requesting data m. We use $n^* = \text{contention}(p, m)$, for short, to denote the maximum number of *active nodes* during the entire request. An active node may be in one of two states: *joining* the network (i.e., the registration process), or *downloading* data. We use d^* to denote the maximum number of *registered identities* during the entire request. A registered identity can be either an honest node or a sybil identity.

Base Station Verification Phase:

```
1:  unver_list ← ∅                                              ▷ The list of unverified requests.
2:  for (every currently registered identity req) do
3:      unver_list ← unver_list ∪ {req.id}
4:  for (sp ← 1 to Θ(log N)) do
5:      for (r ← 1 to Θ(sys_size + c)) do                       ▷ sys_size is the number of registered identities, i.e., id(x) for epoch x
6:          msg ← listen(random(1, c))
7:          if (msg.type = VER_RESP and msg contains sufficient nonces) then
8:              unver_list ← unver_list \ {msg.id}
9:  for (every identity id in unver_list) do
10:     remove(id)                                               ▷ remove(x) removes identity x from the system
```

Node Verification Phase:

```
1:  seq ← prng(req.seed)                                        ▷ req is the node's own request
2:  enc_list ← encrypt(req.nonce_list, req.seed)                ▷ encrypt(x, k) returns the ciphertext of x with k as the key
3:  for (sp ← 1 to Θ(log N)) do
4:      rnd_list ← ∅
5:      while (|rnd_list| ≤ Θ(c)) do                            ▷ Choose Θ(c) random slots.
6:          rnd_list ← rnd_list ∪ {random(1, Θ(sys_size + c))}
7:      for (r ← 1 to Θ(sys_size + c)) do
8:          if (r ∈ rnd_list) then
9:              round_number ← sp · Θ(sys_size + c) + r
10:             broadcast(⟨VER_RESP, req.id, enc_list⟩, seq[round_number])
```

Figure 4: Verification phase pseudocode (*top sub-figure for base station, bottom sub-figure for registered nodes*).

5.1 Total Time Consumption

We first analyze how many rounds it will take for p to register with the base station.

LEMMA 3. *An honest node p can complete its registration process with the base station in $O((n^* + c)c \log^3 N + (d^* + c) \log^2 N)$ rounds w.h.p.*

PROOF (SKETCH). We begin by outlining two initial claims:

CLAIM 3.1. *In a registration sub-phase, assume there are exactly w honest nodes competing for the partial seed. Then, if $w < c$, each of these w nodes gets the partial seed with probability $\Omega(1/c)$. Otherwise, if $w \geq c$, each of these w nodes gets that partial seed with probability $\Omega(1/w)$.*

PROOF. We first consider the $w < c$ case. In this case, one can easily show that with at least some constant probability, these w honest nodes will spread themselves over at least $w/3$ channels. Hence, with probability $\Omega(w/c)$, the base station will broadcast the channel hopping sequence on a channel where there is at least one honest node. Meanwhile, since the malicious nodes can listen to or jam at most $1/8$ fraction of all channels at any time, thus with probability $7/8 \cdot \Omega(w/c) = \Omega(w/c)$, the channel hopping sequence will be successfully received by the honest nodes and will be unknown to the malicious nodes. Conditioned on these two events, assume $w' \leq w$ honest nodes receive the channel hopping sequence; then in one of the following $\Theta(\log N)$ rounds, there must exist a round in which each of these w' nodes sends out its request with probability p_s, where $1/2w' \leq p_s \leq 2/w'$. In that particular round, with probability at least $7/8$ there will be no malicious interference, hence each of these w' nodes can successfully obtain the partial seed with probability $7/8 \cdot p_s \cdot (1 - p_s)^{w'-1} \approx \Theta(1/w') = \Omega(1/w)$. By the argument of symmetry, we know each of these w honest nodes can

get the partial seed with probability $\Omega(1/w)$. Combine these results with the previous condition which happens with probability $\Omega(w/c)$ will immediately lead to the first part of our claim.

We now consider the $w \geq c$ case. We can again easily show with at least some constant probability, these w honest nodes will spread themselves over at least $c/3$ channels. Hence, with at least some constant probability, the base station will broadcast the channel hopping sequence on a channel where there is at least one honest node. Apply an argument similar to that above and we get the second part of our claim. □

CLAIM 3.2. *In any epoch i, if by the halfway point of the registration phase there are x requests from the honest nodes in the registration list, then w.h.p. these x requests will each obtain $\Theta(\log N)$ partial seeds by the end of that registration phase, and the honest nodes that sent them will be able to join the network.*

PROOF. Let $\mathcal{Y} = \{y_1, y_2, \cdots, y_x\}$ denotes the set of honest nodes that sent these x requests, and let Y_j be a random variable which denotes the number of partial seeds the jth honest node in $\mathcal{Y}$ received during the second half of the registration phase. According to Claim 3.1, during the second half of the registration phase, in each sub-phase, each of these x honest nodes gets a partial seed with probability at least $\min\{\Omega(1/c), \Omega(1/id(i))\} = \Omega(1/(id(i) + c))$. Since there are $\Theta((id(i) + c) \log N)$ independent sub-phases during the second half of the registration phase, we conclude that $\mathbb{E}(Y_j) = \Theta((id(i) + c) \log N) \cdot \Omega(1/(id(i) + c)) = \Omega(\log N)$. Apply a Chernoff Bound where $\mathbb{P}(Y_j \leq (1 - \delta)\mathbb{E}(Y_j)) \leq e^{-\mathbb{E}(Y_j)\delta^2/2}$ with $\delta = 1/2$, we conclude $\mathbb{P}(Y_j \leq \Omega(\log N)) \leq O(1/N^k)$ for any constant k. Hence, after the second half of the registration phase, each of these x requests will have $\Theta(\log N)$ partial seeds w.h.p. Moreover, the honest nodes that sent these requests will be able to join the network w.h.p. as well. □

We now prove the lemma. Claim 3.2 implies that in any epoch, if a request from an honest node is in the registration list by the

136

halfway point of the corresponding registration phase, then the honest node which sent the request will be registered, w.h.p., in that epoch (i.e., within $\Theta((id(i) + c) \log^2 N)$ rounds). Recall that d^* is the maximum number of registered identities while p is requesting m, which implies $id(i) \leq d^*$. We can thus conclude that once p's request is in the registration list by the halfway point of a registration phase, it will be registered after $O((d^* + c) \log^2 N)$ rounds w.h.p. In fact, the total number of rounds consumed since the beginning of this last epoch is $O((d^* + c) \log^2 N)$ as well.

We now calculate the number of rounds consumed before p is added to the registration list by the halfway point of some registration phase.

Assume that after some l epochs denoted as i_1 to i_l, at last in epoch i_{l+1}, node p successfully obtains its first partial seed during the first half of the registration phase. During the first half of any registration phase, we say a sub-phase is *open* if the registration list is not full at the beginning of this sub-phase.

By Claim 3.1, node p has a probability of $\Omega(1/c)$ to be added to the registration list if there are fewer than c honest nodes competing. If there are at least c honest nodes competing, then p has a probability of $\Omega(1/n^*)$ to be added to the registration list. Therefore, in expectation, $O(n^* + c)$ open sub-phases will elapse before p can successfully obtain its first partial seed. In fact, w.h.p., node p gets its first partial seed after $O((n^* + c) \log N)$ open sub-phases, as $(1 - \Omega(1/(n^* + c)))^{O((n^*+c)\log N)} \approx O(1/N^k)$ for any constant k.

Since each epoch i_j, where $1 \leq j \leq l$, contains at least $id(i_j)$ open sub-phases, we have $\sum_{j=1}^{l} id(i_j) = O((n^* + c) \log N)$. Therefore, w.h.p. after $\sum_{j=1}^{l} O((id(i_j) + c) \log^2 N) = \Theta(\log^2 N) \cdot \sum_{j=1}^{l} \Theta(id(i_j) + c) = \Theta(\log^2 N) \cdot O((n^*+c)c \log N) = O((n^*+c)c \log^3 N)$ rounds, p's request can get into the registration list during the first half of a registration phase. (Notice, we have ignored the data rounds and verification rounds in these l epochs, as for every epoch, the length of the data phase and verification phase is asymptotically equal to or less than the length of the corresponding registration phase.)

To sum up, w.h.p. the total number of rounds consumed before p is registered is: $O((n^* + c)c \log^3 N) + O((d^* + c) \log^2 N) = O((n^*+c)c \log^3 N + (d^*+c) \log^2 N)$. This proves the lemma. □

We now analyze the number of rounds consumed while p is downloading data.

LEMMA 4. *After registration, if $|m| = \Omega(\log N)$, p can finish downloading m in $O(d^*|m|)$ rounds w.h.p.*

PROOF. After p registers, it has to participate in another series of epochs before it can complete the reception of message m. During these epochs, there are at most d^* identities. Moreover, the malicious nodes may jam each data round with probability at most $1/8$. Hence, in each data round, node p receives a data packet with probability $\Omega(1/d^*)$. Since p needs to receive $|m|$ data packets in total, we expect $O(d^*|m|)$ data rounds will elapse before p's request can be completed. With the assumption $|m| = \Omega(\log N)$ and a standard Chernoff Bound, we conclude that p will get $|m|$ data packets within $O(d^*|m|)$ data rounds w.h.p.

On the other hand, since in any epoch the data phase is of the same length with the registration phase and is longer than the verification phase; and since the last epoch for downloading m is at most twice as long as the next-to-last epoch, we can conclude that w.h.p. the total number of rounds consumed while m is being delivered is $O(d^*|m|)$. □

5.2 Constraining Sybil Identities

Lemma 3 and Lemma 4 do not guarantee each honest node a fair share of the bandwidth, as d^* includes both real and sybil identities. In this subsection, we show that SybilCast guarantees an upper bound on the number of sybil identities and hence can provide asymptotically optimal transmission speed for each honest node. We first introduce the following definition, which describes the event where a sybil identity does not get a nonce that it should later report to the base station.

DEFINITION 5. *For any given sybil identity q, we say a data round is a **losing round** for q if in this round: (a) q is assigned to listen on channel b according to its final seed; (b) the base station broadcasts a data packet (with a nonce in it) on channel b; and (c) none of the t malicious users listen on channel b.*

We now argue that if there are more than $12t$ registered sybil identities, then all but $12t$ of them suffer a large number of losing rounds, with high probability. This lemma provide a lower bound on the length of the data phase (i.e., it has to be long enough to ensure that the sybil identities suffer enough losses), and it shows the threshold on the number of losses that indicate a sybil identity.

LEMMA 6. *In any epoch i, if $s(i) \geq 12t$ and $id(i) \leq N + 12t$, then after k data rounds where $k \geq \frac{20480}{27} \ln(1/\varepsilon)$, with probability at least $1 - 2N^{13t}\varepsilon$, at least $s(i) - 12t$ sybil identities will each suffer at least $81k/512c$ losing rounds[8].*

PROOF. We first show that in any data round, if there are more than $12t$ sybil identities, then with probability at least $25/32$, at least $4t$ channels will each be assigned at least one sybil identity.

Suppose W is the event that at most $4t$ channels each is assigned at least one sybil identity. With the assumption that $c > 8t$:

$$
\begin{aligned}
\mathbb{P}(W) &\leq \binom{c}{4t}\left(\frac{4t}{c}\right)^{12t} \leq \left(\frac{ec}{4t}\right)^{4t}\left(\frac{4t}{c}\right)^{12t} \\
&= e^{4t}\left(\frac{4t}{c}\right)^{8t} < e^{4t}\left(\frac{1}{2}\right)^{8t} \\
&= \left(\frac{e}{4}\right)^{4t} \leq \left(\frac{e}{4}\right)^4 < \frac{7}{32}
\end{aligned}
$$

Hence $\mathbb{P}(\overline{W}) > (1 - 7/32) = 25/32$.

We now prove the lemma. Fix a set $\mathcal{S}$ containing exactly $(12t + 1)$ sybil identities that have finished registration either in the current registration phase, or in some prior epoch. We will show, with probability at least $1 - 2\varepsilon$, at least one identity in $\mathcal{S}$ suffers $81k/512c$ losing rounds. We then take a union bound over the $O(N^{13t})$ possible sets $\mathcal{S}$ of size $12t+1$. From this we conclude, with probability at least $1 - 2N^{13t}\varepsilon$, the largest set of sybil identities that does not suffer $81k/512c$ losing rounds is of size at most $12t$.

As already shown, during the k data rounds, in expectation, sybil identities in $\mathcal{S}$ will be assigned to at least $4t$ channels in $25k/32$ rounds. Applying a standard Chernoff Bound, we see that when $k \geq \frac{64}{25\delta^2} \ln(1/\varepsilon)$, with probability at least $1 - \varepsilon$, sybil identities in $\mathcal{S}$ will be assigned to at least $4t$ channels in at least $(1 - \delta)25k/32$ rounds. We call this set of $(1 - \delta)25k/32$ rounds as $\mathcal{R}$.

For each round in $\mathcal{R}$, at least one sybil identity in $\mathcal{S}$ will receive a nonce from the base station with probability at least $4t/c$. Moreover, in case such event happens, the nonce will be missed by the corresponding sybil identities with probability at least $(1 - t/4t) =$

---

[8] We have made no effort to optimize the constants, focusing on ease of explanation.

3/4. Hence, in expectation, sybil identities in $\mathcal{S}$ lose at least $(1 - \delta)25k/32 \cdot (4t/c) \cdot (3/4) = (1 - \delta)75kt/32c$ nonces. Applying a Chernoff Bound, we see that, with probability at least $(1 - \varepsilon)^2$, sybil identities in $\mathcal{S}$ will in total lose at least $(1 - \delta)75kt/32c$ nonces when $k \geq \frac{512}{75(1-\delta)\delta^2} \ln(1/\varepsilon)$. Now, since each lost nonce affects at least one sybil identity in $\mathcal{S}$, we know that with probability at least $(1 - \varepsilon)^2$, at least one sybil identity in $\mathcal{S}$ will lose at least $(1-\delta)^2 75kt/32c \cdot (1/(12t+1)) \approx (1-\delta)^2 25k/128c$ nonces. With assignment $\delta = 1/10$, we can conclude when $k \geq \frac{20480}{27} \ln(1/\varepsilon)$, with probability at least $(1 - \varepsilon)^2 \geq (1 - 2\varepsilon)$, at least one sybil identity in $\mathcal{S}$ will suffer at least $81k/512c$ losing rounds.

Now, consider all possible sets $\mathcal{S}$ of size $12t + 1$. We have assumed that there are at most $N + 12t$ registered identities at the beginning of epoch i. Hence at the end of the registration phase for epoch i, there are at most $2(N + 12t)$ identities, and the number of possible sets $\mathcal{S}$ is bounded by $\binom{2N+24t}{12t+1} \leq (e(2N + 24t)/(12t + 1))^{12t+1} \leq N^{13t}$. Thus, by a union bound, the probability that every set $\mathcal{S}$ of size $12t + 1$ has at least one identity suffer at least $81k/512c$ losing rounds is at least $1 - 2N^{13t}\varepsilon$. □

Lemma 6 implies that if the malicious users register too many sybil identities, then over some period of time, most of these sybil identities will lose a significant fraction of the nonces they should receive. The base station can leverage this fact to eliminate most of the sybil identities during verification phases. We can also here identify precisely the threshold for rejecting an identity during the verification phase: *if the data phase in epoch i is of length $len(i)$, then reject an identity as a sybil if it loses at least $81len(i)/512c$ nonces that were sent to it.* This results in the following lemma:

LEMMA 7. *In every epoch, when the verification phase completes, there are at most $12t$ remaining sybil identities w.h.p.*

PROOF. We proceed by induction over epochs. The base case, epoch one, follows immediately from the fact that fewer than $12t$ identities are admitted in epoch one. Consider epoch i, and assume that there are at most $12t$ sybil identities remaining at the end of epoch $i-1$. Since there are at most N honest identities, this implies that $id(i) \leq N + 12t$.

Now, from Lemma 6 and our protocol description, we can show that the length of the data phase of epoch i, which is denoted as $len(i)$, is sufficiently long so that w.h.p. all but at most $12t$ sybil nodes are always rejected during the verification phase. Notably, for $2N^{13t}\varepsilon$ to be polynomially small in N, the number of data rounds we need is $\Omega(\ln(2N^{13t})) = \Omega(t \ln N)$. This always holds true as the length of the data phase is $\Theta((id(i) + c) \log^2 N)$. □

With Lemma 8, we can now bound the number of sybil identities:

LEMMA 8. *During the request of m, the number of sybil identities in the network is at most $O(n^*)$ w.h.p.*

PROOF. Lemma 7 states that at the end of any verification phase, w.h.p. there will be at most $12t$ sybil identities remain in the system. Hence, among the $id(i)$ identities at the beginning of any epoch i, at most $12t$ are sybil identities created by the t malicious nodes; and the remaining $id(i) - 12t$ identities are all honest identities each created by an honest node, i.e., $id(i) - 12t \leq n^*$. This further implies $id(i) \leq O(n^*)$ since $n^* \geq t$. On the other hand, SybilCast enforces at most $id(i)$ new identities can be registered in any epoch i. Combine these two facts together immediately yields the lemma. □

We now turn our attention to the honest nodes. In particular, we want to show no honest nodes will be incorrectly removed. To prove this, we first show that—even subject to lost messages due to jamming—an honest identity will not miss too many nonces.

LEMMA 9. *In any epoch i, after k data rounds where $k \geq \frac{8748c}{5} \ln(1/\varepsilon')$, with probability at least $(1 - \varepsilon')^2$, an honest node p will lose at most $25k/162c$ nonces.*

PROOF. According to our protocol, after k data rounds, in expectation, an honest node p will receive k/c nonces. Apply a Chernoff Bound and we can show, after $k \geq \frac{3c}{\delta^2} \ln(1/\varepsilon')$ data rounds, with probability at least $1 - \varepsilon'$, p will receive at most $(1 + \delta)k/c$ nonces.

We now take adversarial jamming into consideration. Recall the malicious users can only jam at most $c/8$ channels at any time. Therefore, if conditioned on the event that p *should* receive $(1 + \delta)k/c$ nonces, then in expectation, p will lose $\frac{(1+\delta)k}{8c}$ nonces due to adversarial jamming. Apply a Chernoff Bound again and we can show, after $k \geq \frac{24c}{\delta^2(1+\delta)} \ln(1/\varepsilon')$ data rounds, with probability at least $(1 - \varepsilon')^2$, p will lose at most $(1 + \delta)^2 \frac{k}{8c}$ nonces. With assignment $\delta = 1/9$, the lemma follows. □

Much as in the proof of Lemma 7, one can observe and show that the length of the data phase for any epoch i is sufficiently long so that w.h.p. each honest node, by Lemma 9, loses at most $25len(i)/162c$ nonces, which is smaller than the threshold for removing an identity. Combine this with Lemma 2, the following lemma immediately follows:

LEMMA 10. *No honest nodes will be (incorrectly) removed before its request is completed, w.h.p.*

Lastly, we state our main claim:

THEOREM 11. *If an honest node p requests data m where $|m| \geq c^2 \log^3 N$, and if there are at most $\mathtt{contention}(p, m)$ concurrently active nodes during the request; then p can get the data in $O(|m| \cdot \mathtt{contention}(p, m))$ time w.h.p.[9]*

PROOF. First, notice Lemma 10 guarantees honest nodes will not be incorrectly removed before their requests are completed. On the other hand, Lemma 8 shows that during the request of m, the number of sybil identities is bounded by $O(n^*)$. As a result, d^*, the maximum number of registered identities during the request of m, is also bounded by $O(n^*)$, or $O(\mathtt{contention}(p, m))$. Hence, Lemma 3 and Lemma 4 immediately imply the theorem. □

Theorem 11 implies SybilCast is asymptotically optimal in transmission speed: even in an environment where there are no malicious nodes, any fair-share protocol will in the worst case take $\Theta(|m| \cdot \mathtt{contention}(p, m))$ rounds to deliver $|m|$ packets to an honest node if there are $\mathtt{contention}(p, m)$ active nodes.

6. DISCUSSION AND FUTURE WORK

In this paper, we propose a new protocol called SybilCast that counters sybil attacks in multichannel wireless networks. It limits the maximum number of sybil identities and provides asymptotically optimal transmission speed for honest nodes. It can tolerate message spoofing and wireless jamming.

One natural question is whether we can achieve better performance if we limit the malicious users' capabilities. For example, what if the malicious users cannot spoof messages? Unfortunately,

---

[9]In fact, one can also easily show the following guarantee which is somewhat stronger: in any round where the base station is delivering packets, if there are at most $\mathtt{contention}_r(p, m)$ active real users in round r, then a given honest user receives a data packet with probability $\Theta(1/\mathtt{contention}_r(p, m))$; a constant fraction of the rounds are used to deliver data packets to honest users.

this constraint does not help as much as one might expect, as the most time consuming part is registration, which cannot be reduced (in either time or channels) if we want to prevent the malicious users from eavesdropping on the final seed. Nevertheless, this constraint does eliminate the need for a hash chain. If the adversary cannot jam communication *or* spoof messages, then it may be feasible to reduce the length of the registration phase and/or the number of channels. This change might lead to more sybil identities, but the faster registration process may make it cost-effective.

Another question concerns whether knowing an upper bound on the maximum system size, i.e., N, is necessary. Here, we assume that a polynomial estimate of N, i.e., a constant-factor estimate of $\log N$, is known (even though the actual number of active nodes is unknown). Knowledge of $\log N$ serves two purposes in SybilCast: (a) keeping the nodes and the base station tightly synchronized during an epoch; and (b) ensuring that necessary events happen with high probability. It seems likely that SybilCast can be modified to work without knowing N, as the base station is always aware of the *current* system size. In this case, probabilistic guarantees hold with high probability with respect to the *current* system size, not N.

Lastly, can we leverage the real motivations of malicious users to simplify the protocol? Here, we assume malicious users can be both *selfish* (e.g., hog bandwidth) and *adversarial* (e.g., disrupt communication). What if they are only selfish and conduct attacks only if such behavior can bring them more bandwidth? Is this an easier attack to prevent? To some extent, in the context of Sybil-Cast, the answer seems to be negative. Both jamming and spoofing can be used for selfish purposes: malicious users can jam honest users in data phases, and they can also spoof exit messages from honest users. Both behaviors result in honest users getting disconnected, and lead to more bandwidth allocated for the malicious users. On the other hand, it simplifies the problem: we need only limit the data sent to malicious users.

Future work. SybilCast relies on a central base station. We believe it may be possible to developed a decentralized version. The major challenge is to establish and propagate trust in a decentralized environment: we rely here on the base station as an authenticated transmitter. We also believe that the techniques developed here may be useful in constraining sybil identities in other types of problems (e.g., voting systems, spanning tree constructions, etc.). The SybilCast approach has relatively low overhead (when the parameters in the protocol are optimized for better performance), and hence can integrate well with other protocols.

Acknowledgments

We would like to thank Calvin Newport for many useful discussions and ideas that led to this paper.

7. REFERENCES

[1] B. Awerbuch, A. Richa, and C. Scheideler. A jamming-resistant mac protocol for single-hop wireless networks. In *Proceedings of the 27th ACM Symposium on Principles of Distributed Computing*, pages 45–54, 2008.

[2] S. K. Baruah, N. K. Cohen, C. G. Plaxton, and D. A. Varvel. Proportionate progress: A notion of fairness in resource allocation. *Algorithmica*, 15:600–625, 1996.

[3] Bluetooth Consortium. *Bluetooth Specification Version 2.1*, July 2007.

[4] J. Douceur. The sybil attack. In *Peer-to-Peer Systems*, volume 2429 of *Lecture Notes in Computer Science*, pages 251–260. Springer, 2002.

[5] C. T. Ee and R. Bajcsy. Congestion control and fairness for many-to-one routing in sensor networks. In *Proceedings of the 2nd International Conference on Embedded Networked Sensor Systems*, pages 148–161, 2004.

[6] K. Hoffman, D. Zage, and C. Nita-Rotaru. A survey of attack and defense techniques for reputation systems. *ACM Computing Surveys*, 42:1–31, December 2009.

[7] X. L. Huang and B. Bensaou. On max-min fairness and scheduling in wireless ad-hoc networks: Analytical framework and implementation. In *Proceedings of the 2nd ACM International Symposium on Mobile Ad-Hoc Networking & Computing*, pages 221–231, 2001.

[8] R. Jain, D. Chiu, and W. Hawe. A quantitative measure of fairness and discrimination for resource allocation in shared computer systems. 1984.

[9] N. James, E. Shi, D. Song, and A. Perrig. The sybil attack in sensor networks: Analysis & defenses. In *Proceedings of the 3rd International Symposium on Information Processing in Sensor Networks*, pages 259–268, 2004.

[10] M. G. Luby. *Pseudorandomness and Cryptographic Applications*. Princeton University Press, 1996.

[11] D. Mónica. Thwarting the sybil attack in wireless ad-hoc networks. Master's thesis, Instituto Superior Técnico, Universidade Técnica de Lisboa, July 2009.

[12] D. Mónica, J. Leitão, L. Rodrigues, and C. Ribeiro. On the use of radio resource tests in wireless ad-hoc networks. In *Proceedings of the 3rd Workshop on Recent Advances on Intrusion-Tolerant Systems*, pages F21–F26, June 2009.

[13] D. Mónica, J. Leitão, L. Rodrigues, and C. Ribeiro. Observable non-sybil quorums construction in one-hop wireless ad hoc networks. In *Proceedings of the 40th Annual IEEE/IFIP International Conference on Dependable Systems and Networks*, June 2010.

[14] T. Nandagopal, T. E. Kim, X. Gao, and V. Bharghavan. Achieving mac layer fairness in wireless packet networks. In *Proceedings of the 6th Annual International Conference on Mobile Computing and Networking*, pages 87–98. ACM, 2000.

[15] S. Pilosof, R. Ramjee, D. Raz, Y. Shavitt, and P. Sinha. Understanding tcp fairness over wireless lan. In *22nd Annual Joint Conference of the IEEE Computer and Communications*, volume 2, pages 863–872, 2003.

[16] A. Richa, C. Scheideler, S. Schmid, and J. Zhang. Competitive and fair medium access despite reactive jamming. In *Proceedings of the 31st International Conference on Distributed Computing Systems*, pages 507–516, 2011.

[17] A. Richa, C. Scheideler, S. Schmid, and J. Zhang. Competitive and fair throughput for co-existing networks under adversarial interference. In *Proceedings of the 2012 ACM Symposium on Principles of Distributed Computing*, pages 291–300, 2012.

[18] M. Strasser, S. Capkun, C. Popper, and M. Cagalj. Jamming-resistant key establishment using uncoordinated frequency hopping. In *Proceedings of the IEEE Symposium on Security and Privacy*, pages 64–78, May 2008.

[19] H. Yu, P. Gibbons, M. Kaminsky, and F. Xiao. Sybillimit: A near-optimal social network defense against sybil attacks. In *Proceedings of the IEEE Symposium on Security and Privacy*, pages 3–17, May 2008.

[20] P. R. Zimmermann. *The Official PGP User's Guide*. MIT Press, 1995.

On-the-Fly Pipeline Parallelism

I-Ting Angelina Lee*   Charles E. Leiserson*   Tao B. Schardl*   Jim Sukha†   Zhunping Zhang*

*MIT CSAIL
32 Vassar Street
Cambridge, MA 02139

*{angelee, cel, neboat, jzz}@mit.edu

†Intel Corporation
25 Manchester Street, Suite 200
Merrimack, NH 03054

†jim.sukha@intel.com

ABSTRACT

Pipeline parallelism organizes a parallel program as a linear sequence of s stages. Each stage processes elements of a data stream, passing each processed data element to the next stage, and then taking on a new element before the subsequent stages have necessarily completed their processing. Pipeline parallelism is used especially in streaming applications that perform video, audio, and digital signal processing. Three out of 13 benchmarks in PARSEC, a popular software benchmark suite designed for shared-memory multiprocessors, can be expressed as pipeline parallelism.

Whereas most concurrency platforms that support pipeline parallelism use a "construct-and-run" approach, this paper investigates "on-the-fly" pipeline parallelism, where the structure of the pipeline emerges as the program executes rather than being specified *a priori*. On-the-fly pipeline parallelism allows the number of stages to vary from iteration to iteration and dependencies to be data dependent. We propose simple linguistics for specifying on-the-fly pipeline parallelism and describe a provably efficient scheduling algorithm, the PIPER algorithm, which integrates pipeline parallelism into a work-stealing scheduler, allowing pipeline and fork-join parallelism to be arbitrarily nested. The PIPER algorithm automatically throttles the parallelism, precluding "runaway" pipelines. Given a pipeline computation with T_1 work and T_∞ span (critical-path length), PIPER executes the computation on P processors in $T_P \leq T_1/P + O(T_\infty + \lg P)$ expected time. PIPER also limits stack space, ensuring that it does not grow unboundedly with running time.

We have incorporated on-the-fly pipeline parallelism into a Cilk-based work-stealing runtime system. Our prototype Cilk-P implementation exploits optimizations such as lazy enabling and dependency folding. We have ported the three PARSEC benchmarks that exhibit pipeline parallelism to run on Cilk-P. One of these, *x264*, cannot readily be executed by systems that support only construct-and-run pipeline parallelism. Benchmark results indicate that Cilk-P has low serial overhead and good scalability. On *x264*, for example, Cilk-P exhibits a speedup of 13.87 over its respective serial counterpart when running on 16 processors.

Categories and Subject Descriptors

D.3.3 [**Language Constructs and Features**]: Concurrent programming structures; D.3.4 [**Programming Languages**]: Processors—*Run-time environments*.

General Terms

Algorithms, Languages, Theory.

Keywords

Cilk, multicore, multithreading, parallel programming, pipeline parallelism, on-the-fly pipelining, scheduling, work stealing.

1. INTRODUCTION

Pipeline parallelism[1] [6, 16, 17, 25, 27, 28, 31, 33, 35, 37] is a well-known parallel-programming pattern that can be used to parallelize a variety of applications, including streaming applications from the domains of video, audio, and digital signal processing. Many applications, including the *ferret*, *dedup*, and *x264* benchmarks from the PARSEC benchmark suite [4, 5], exhibit parallelism in the form of a *linear* pipeline, where a linear sequence $S = \langle S_0, \ldots, S_{s-1} \rangle$ of abstract functions, called *stages*, are executed on an input stream $I = \langle a_0, a_1, \ldots, a_{n-1} \rangle$. Conceptually, a linear pipeline can be thought of as a loop over the elements of I, where each loop *iteration* i processes an element a_i of the input stream. The loop body encodes the sequence S of stages through which each element is processed. Parallelism arises in linear pipelines because the execution of iterations can overlap in time, that is, iteration i may start after the preceding iteration $i-1$ has started, but before $i-1$ has necessarily completed.

Most systems that provide pipeline parallelism employ a *construct-and-run* model, as exemplified by the pipeline model in Intel Threading Building Blocks (TBB) [27], where the pipeline stages and their dependencies are defined *a priori* before execution. Systems that support construct-and-run pipeline parallelism include the following: [1, 11, 17, 25–27, 29–32, 35, 37, 38].

We have extended the Cilk parallel-programming model [15, 20, 24] to augment its native fork-join parallelism with *on-the-fly* pipeline parallelism, where the linear pipeline is constructed dynamically as the program executes. The Cilk-P system provides a flexible linguistic model for pipelining that allows the structure of the pipeline to be determined dynamically as a function of data in the input stream. Cilk-P also admits a variable number of stages across iterations, allowing the pipeline to take on shapes other than

This work was supported in part by the National Science Foundation under Grants CNS-1017058 and CCF-1162148. Tao B. Schardl is supported in part by an NSF Graduate Research Fellowship.

---

[1]Pipeline parallelism should not be confused with instruction pipelining in hardware [34] or software pipelining [22].

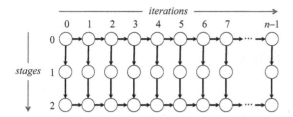

Figure 1: Modeling the execution of *ferret*'s linear pipeline as a pipeline dag. Each column contains nodes for a single iteration, and each row corresponds to a stage of the pipeline. Vertices in the dag correspond to nodes of the linear pipeline, and edges denote dependencies between the nodes. Throttling edges are not shown.

simple rectangular grids. The Cilk-P programming model is flexible, yet restrictive enough to allow provably efficient scheduling, as Sections 5 through 8 will show. In particular, Cilk-P's scheduler provides automatic "throttling" to ensure that the computation uses bounded space. As a testament to the flexibility provided by Cilk-P, we were able to parallelize the *x264* benchmark from PARSEC, an application that cannot be programmed easily using TBB [33].

Cilk-P's support for defining linear pipelines on the fly is more flexible than the ordered directive in OpenMP [29], which supports a limited form of on-the-fly pipelining, but it is less expressive than other approaches. Blelloch and Reid-Miller [6] describe a scheme for on-the-fly pipeline parallelism that employs futures [3, 14] to coordinate the stages of the pipeline, allowing even nonlinear pipelines to be defined on the fly. Although futures permit more complex, nonlinear pipelines to be expressed, this generality can lead to unbounded space requirements to attain even modest speedups [7].

To illustrate the ideas behind the Cilk-P model, consider a simple 3-stage linear pipeline such as in the *ferret* benchmark from PARSEC [4, 5]. Figure 1 shows a *pipeline dag* (directed acyclic graph) $G = (V, E)$ representing the execution of the pipeline. Each of the 3 horizontal rows corresponds to a stage of the pipeline, and each of the n vertical columns is an iteration. We define a pipeline *node* $(i, j) \in V$, where $i = 0, 1, \ldots, n-1$ and $j = 0, 1, 2$, to be the execution of $S_j(a_i)$, the jth stage in the ith iteration, represented as a vertex in the dag. The edges between nodes denote dependencies. A *stage edge* goes between two nodes (i, j) and (i, j'), where $j < j'$, and indicates that (i, j') cannot start until (i, j) completes. A *cross edge* between nodes $(i-1, j)$ and (i, j) indicates that (i, j) can start execution only after node $(i-1, j)$ completes. Cilk-P always executes nodes of the same iteration in increasing order by stage number, thereby creating a vertical chain of stage edges. Cross edges between corresponding stages of adjacent iterations are optional.

We can categorize the stages of a Cilk-P pipeline. A stage is a *serial stage* if all nodes belonging to the stage are connected by cross edges, it is a *parallel stage* if none of the nodes belonging to the stage are connected by cross edges, and it is a *hybrid stage* otherwise. The *ferret* pipeline, for example, exhibits a static structure often referred to as an "SPS" pipeline, since Stage 0 and Stage 2 are serial and Stage 1 is parallel. Cilk-P requires that pipelines be linear, since iterations are totally ordered and dependencies go between adjacent iterations, and in fact, Stage 0 of any Cilk-P pipeline is always a serial stage. Later stages may be serial, parallel, or hybrid, as we shall see in Sections 2 and 3.

To execute a linear pipeline, Cilk-P follows the lead of TBB and adopts a *bind-to-element* approach [25, 27], where *workers* (scheduling threads) execute pipeline iterations either to completion or until an unresolved dependency is encountered. In particular, Cilk-P and TBB both rely on "work-stealing" schedulers (see, for example, [2, 8, 10, 13, 15, 21]) for load balancing. In con-

trast, many systems that support pipeline parallelism, including typical Pthreaded implementations, execute linear pipelines using a *bind-to-stage* approach, where each worker executes a distinct stage and coordination between workers is handled using concurrent queues [17, 35, 38]. Some researchers report that the bind-to-element approach generally outperforms bind-to-stage [28, 33], since a work-stealing scheduler can do a better job of dynamically load-balancing the computation, but our own experiments show mixed results.

A natural theoretical question is, how much parallelism is inherent in the *ferret* pipeline (or in any pipeline)? How much speedup can one hope for? Since the computation is represented as a dag $G = (V, E)$, one can use a simple work/span analysis [12, Ch. 27] to answer this question. In this analytical model, we assume that each vertex $v \in V$ executes in some time $w(v)$. The **work** of the computation, denoted T_1, is essentially the serial execution time, that is, $T_1 = \sum_{v \in V} w(v)$. The **span** of the computation, denoted T_∞, is the length of a longest weighted path through G, which is essentially the time of an infinite-processor execution. The **parallelism** is the ratio T_1/T_∞, which is the maximum possible speedup attainable on any number of processors, using any scheduler.

Unlike in some applications, in the *ferret* pipeline, each node executes serially, that is, its work and span are the same. Let $w(i, j)$ be the execution time of node (i, j). Assume that the serial Stages 0 and 2 execute in unit time, that is, for all i, we have $w(i, 0) = w(i, 2) = 1$, and that the parallel Stage 1 executes in time $r \gg 1$, that is, for all i, we have $w(i, 1) = r$. Because the pipeline dag is grid-like, the span of this SPS pipeline can be realized by some staircase walk through the dag from node $(0, 0)$ to node $(n-1, 2)$. The work of this pipeline is therefore $T_1 = n(r+2)$, and the span is

$$T_\infty = \max_{0 \le x < n} \left\{ \sum_{i=0}^{x} w(i, 0) + w(x, 1) + \sum_{i=x}^{n-1} w(i, 2) \right\}$$
$$= n + r .$$

Consequently, the parallelism of this dag is $T_1/T_\infty = n(r+2)/(n+r)$, which for $1 \ll r \le n$ is at least $r/2 + 1$. Thus, if Stage 1 contains much more work than the other two stages, the pipeline exhibits good parallelism.

Cilk-P guarantees to execute the *ferret* pipeline efficiently. In particular, on an ideal shared-memory computer with up to $T_1/T_\infty = O(r)$ processors, Cilk-P guarantees linear speedup. Generally, Cilk-P executes a pipeline with linear speedup as long as the parallelism of the pipeline exceeds the number of processors on which the computation is scheduled. Moreover, as Section 3 will describe, Cilk-P allows stages of the pipeline themselves to be parallel using recursive pipelining or fork-join parallelism.

In practice, it is also important to limit the space used during an execution. Unbounded space can cause thrashing of the memory system, leading to slowdowns not predicted by simple execution models. In particular, a bind-to-element scheduler must avoid creating a *runaway* pipeline — a situation where the scheduler allows many new iterations to be started before finishing old ones. In Figure 1, a runaway pipeline might correspond to executing many nodes in Stage 0 (the top row) without finishing the other stages of the computation in the earlier iterations. Runaway pipelines can cause space utilization to grow unboundedly, since every started but incomplete iteration requires space to store local variables.

Cilk-P automatically *throttles* pipelines to avoid runaway pipelines. On a system with P workers, Cilk-P inhibits the start of iteration $i + K$ until iteration i has completed, where $K = \Theta(P)$ is the *throttling limit*. Throttling corresponds to putting *throttling edges* from the last node in each iteration i to the first node in iteration $i+K$. For the simple pipeline from Figure 1, throttling does not adversely affect asymptotic scalability if stages are uniform, but it can be a concern for more complex pipelines, as Section 11 will discuss. The Cilk-P scheduler guarantees efficient scheduling of pipelines as a function of the parallelism of the dag in which throttling edges are included in the calculation of span.

Contributions

Our prototype Cilk-P system adapts the Cilk-M [23] work-stealing scheduler to support on-the-fly pipeline parallelism using a bind-to-element approach. This paper makes the following contributions:

- We describe linguistics for Cilk-P that allow on-the-fly pipeline parallelism to be incorporated into the Cilk fork-join parallel programming model (Section 2).
- We illustrate how Cilk-P linguistics can be used to express the *x264* benchmark as a pipeline program (Section 3).
- We characterize the execution dag of a Cilk-P pipeline program as an extension of a fork-join program (Section 4).
- We introduce the PIPER scheduling algorithm, a theoretically sound randomized work-stealing scheduler (Section 5).
- We prove that PIPER is asymptotically efficient, executing Cilk-P programs on P processors in $T_P \leq T_1/P + O(T_\infty + \lg P)$ expected time (Sections 6 and 7).
- We bound space usage, proving that PIPER on P processors uses $S_P \leq P(S_1 + fDK)$ stack space for pipeline iterations, where S_1 is the serial stack space, f is the "frame size," D is the depth of nested pipelines, and K is the throttling limit (Section 8).
- We describe our implementation of PIPER in the Cilk-P runtime system, introducing two key optimizations: lazy enabling and dependency folding (Section 9).
- We demonstrate that the *ferret*, *dedup*, and *x264* benchmarks from PARSEC, when hand-compiled for the Cilk-P runtime system (we do not as yet have a compiler for the Cilk-P language), run competitively with existing Pthreaded implementations (Section 10).

We conclude in Section 11 with a discussion of the performance implications of throttling.

2. ON-THE-FLY PIPELINE PROGRAMS

Cilk-P's linguistic model supports both fork-join and pipeline parallelism, which can be nested arbitrarily. For convenience, we shall refer to programs containing nested fork-join and pipeline parallelism simply as *pipeline programs*. Cilk-P's on-the-fly pipelining model allows the programmer to specify a pipeline whose structure is determined during the pipeline's execution. This section reviews the basic Cilk model and shows how on-the-fly parallelism is supported in Cilk-P using a "pipe_while" construct.

We first outline the basic semantics of Cilk without the pipelining features of Cilk-P. We use the syntax of Cilk++ [24] and Cilk Plus [20] which augments serial C/C++ code with two principal keywords: cilk_spawn and cilk_sync.[2] When a function invocation is preceded by the keyword cilk_spawn, the function is *spawned* as a *child* subcomputation, but the runtime system may continue to execute the statement after the cilk_spawn, called the *continuation*, in parallel with the spawned subroutine without waiting for the child to return. The complementary keyword to cilk_spawn is cilk_sync, which acts as a local barrier and joins together all the parallelism forked by cilk_spawn within a function. Every function contains an implicit cilk_sync before the function returns.

---

[2]Cilk++ and Cilk Plus also include other features that are not relevant to the discussion here.

To support on-the-fly pipeline parallelism, Cilk-P provides a pipe_while keyword. A pipe_while loop is similar to a serial while loop, except that loop iterations can execute in parallel in a pipelined fashion. The body of the pipe_while can be subdivided into stages, with stages named by user-specified integer values that strictly increase as the iteration executes. Each stage can contain nested fork-join and pipeline parallelism.

The boundaries of stages are denoted in the body of a pipe_while using the special functions pipe_continue and pipe_wait. These functions accept an integer *stage argument*, which is the number of the next stage to execute and which must strictly increase during the execution of an iteration. Every iteration i begins executing Stage 0, represented by node $(i,0)$. While executing a node (i,j'), if control flow encounters a pipe_wait(j) or pipe_continue(j) statement, where $j > j'$, then node (i,j') ends, and control flow proceeds to node (i,j). A pipe_continue(j) statement indicates that node (i,j) can start executing immediately, whereas a pipe_wait(j) statement indicates that node (i,j) cannot start until node $(i-1,j)$ completes. The pipe_wait(j) in iteration i creates a cross edge from node $(i-1,j)$ to node (i,j) in the pipeline dag. Thus, by design choice, Cilk-P imposes the restriction that pipeline dependencies only go between adjacent iterations. As we shall see in Section 9, this design choice facilitates the "lazy enabling" and "dependency folding" runtime optimizations.

The pipe_continue and pipe_wait functions can be used without an explicit stage argument. Omitting the stage argument while executing stage j corresponds to an implicit stage argument of $j+1$, i.e., control moves onto the next stage.

Cilk-P's semantics for pipe_continue and pipe_wait statements allow for *stage skipping*, where execution in an iteration i can jump stages from node (i,j') to node (i,j), even if $j > j'+1$. If control flow in iteration $i+1$ enters node $(i+1,j'')$ after a pipe_wait, where $j' < j'' < j$, then we implicitly create a *null node* (i,j'') in the pipeline dag, which has no associated work and incurs no scheduling overhead, and insert stage edges from (i,j') to (i,j'') and from (i,j'') to (i,j), as well as a cross edge from (i,j'') to $(i+1,j'')$.

3. ON-THE-FLY PIPELINING OF *x264*

To illustrate the use of Cilk-P's pipe_while loop, this section describes how to parallelize the *x264* video encoder [39].

We begin with a simplified description of *x264*. Given a stream $\langle f_0, f_1, \ldots \rangle$ of video frames to encode, *x264* partitions the frame into a two dimensional array of "macroblocks" and encodes each macroblock. A macroblock in frame f_i is encoded as a function of the encodings of similar macroblocks within f_i and similar macroblocks in frames "near" f_i. A frame f_j is *near* a frame f_i if $i-b \leq j \leq i+b$ for some constant b. In addition, we define a macroblock (x',y') to be *near* a macroblock (x,y) if $x-w \leq x' \leq x+w$ and $y-w \leq y' \leq y+w$ for some constant w.

The type of a frame f_i determines how a macroblock (x,y) in f_i is encoded. If f_i is an *I-frame*, then macroblock (x,y) can be encoded using only *previous* macroblocks within f_i — macroblocks at positions (x',y') where $y' < y$ or $y' = y$ and $x' < x$. If f_i is a *P-frame*, then macroblock (x,y)'s encoding can also be based on nearby macroblocks in nearby preceding frames, up to the most recent preceding I-frame,[3] if one exists within the nearby range. If f_i is a *B-frame*, then macroblock (x,y)'s encoding can be based also on nearby macroblocks in nearby frames, likewise, up to the most recently preceding I-frame and up to the next succeeding I- or P-frame.

---

[3]To be precise, up to a particular type of I-frame called an *IDR-frame*.

```
1    // Symbolic names for important stages
2    const uint64_t PROCESS_IPFRAME = 1;
3    const uint64_t PROCESS_BFRAMES = 1 << 40;
4    const uint64_t END = PROCESS_BFRAMES + 1;
5    int i = 0;
6    int w = mv_range/pixel_per_row;
7
8    pipe_while(frame_t *f = next_frame()) {
9      vector<frame_t *> bframes;
10     f->type = decide_frame_type(f);
11     while(f->type == TYPE_B) {
12       bframes.push_back(f);
13       f = next_frame();
14       f->type = decide_frame_type(f);
15     }
16     int skip = w * i++;
17     pipe_wait(PROCESS_IPFRAME + skip);
18     while(mb_t *macroblocks = next_row(frame)) {
19       process_row(macroblocks);
20       if(f->type == TYPE_I) {
21         pipe_continue;
22       } else {
23         pipe_wait;
24       }
25     }
26     pipe_continue(PROCESS_BFRAMES);
27     cilk_for(int j=0; j<bframes.size(); ++j) {
28       process_bframe(bframes[j]);
29     }
30     pipe_wait(END);
31     write_out_frames(frame, bframes);
32   }
```

Figure 2: Example C++-like pseudocode for the *x264* linear pipeline. This pseudocode uses Cilk-P's linguistics to define hybrid pipeline stages on the fly, specifically with the `pipe_wait` on line 17, the input-data dependent `pipe_wait` or `pipe_continue` on lines 20–24, and the `pipe_continue` on line 26.

Based on these frame types, an *x264* encoder must ensure that frames are processed in a valid order such that dependencies between encoded macroblocks are satisfied. A parallel *x264* encoder can pipeline the encoding of I- and P-frames in the input stream, processing each set of intervening B-frames after encoding the latest I- or P-frame on which the B-frame may depend.

Figure 2 shows pseudocode for an *x264* linear pipeline. Conceptually, the *x264* pipeline begins with a serial stage (lines 8–17) that reads frames from the input stream and determines the type of each frame. This stage buffers all B-frames at the head of the input stream until it encounters an I- or P-frame. After this initial stage, s hybrid stages process this I- or P-frame row by row (lines 18–25), where s is the number of rows in the video frame. After all rows of this I- or P-frame have been processed, the PROCESS_BFRAMES stage processes all B-frames in parallel (lines 27–29), and then the END stage updates the output stream with the processed frames (line 31).

Two issues arise with this general pipelining strategy, both of which can be handled using on-the-fly pipeline parallelism. First, the encoding of a P-frame must wait for the encoding of rows in the previous frame to be completed, whereas the encoding of an I-frame need not. These conditional dependencies are implemented in lines 20–24 of Figure 2 by executing a `pipe_wait` or `pipe_continue` statement conditionally based on the frame's type. In contrast, many construct-and-run pipeline mechanisms assume that the dependencies on a stage are fixed for the entirety of a pipeline's execution, making such dynamic dependencies more difficult to handle. Second, the encoding of a macroblock in row x of P-frame f_i may depend on the encoding of a macroblock in a later row $x + w$ in the preceding I- or P-frame f_{i-1}. The code in Figure 2 handles such offset dependencies on line 17 by skipping w additional stages relative to the previous iteration. A similar stage-skipping trick is used on line 26 to ensure that the processing of a P-frame in iteration i depends only on the processing of the previous I- or P-frame, and not on the processing of preceding B-frames. Figure 3 illustrates the pipeline dag corresponding to the execution

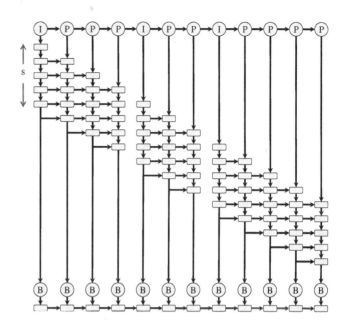

Figure 3: The pipeline dag generated for *x264*. Each iteration processes either an I- or P-frame, each consisting of s rows. As the iteration index i increases, the number of initial stages skipped in the iteration also increases. This stage skipping produces cross edges into an iteration i from null nodes in iteration $i - 1$. Null nodes are represented as the intersection between two edges.

of the code in Figure 2, assuming that $w = 1$. Skipping stages shifts the nodes of an iteration down, adding null nodes to the pipeline, which do not increase the work or span.

4. COMPUTATION-DAG MODEL

Although the pipeline-dag model provides intuition for programmers to understand the execution of a pipeline program, it is not as precise as we shall require. For example, a pipeline dag has no real way of representing nested fork-join or pipeline parallelism within a node. This section describes how to represent the execution of a pipeline program as a more refined "computation dag."

Let us first review the notion of a computation dag for ordinary fork-join Cilk programs [7, 8] without pipeline parallelism. A **fork-join computation dag** $G = (V, E)$ represents the execution of a Cilk program, where the vertices belonging to V are unit-cost instructions. Edges in E indicate ordering dependencies between instructions. The normal serial execution of one instruction after another creates a **serial edge** from the first instruction to the next. A `cilk_spawn` of a function creates two dependency edges emanating from the instruction immediately before the `cilk_spawn`: the **spawn edge** goes to the first instruction of the spawned function, and the **continue edge** goes to the first instruction after the spawned function. A `cilk_sync` creates a **return edge** from the final instruction of each spawned function to the instruction immediately after the `cilk_sync` (as well as an ordinary serial edge from the instruction that executed immediately before the `cilk_sync`).

To model an arbitrary pipeline-program execution as a **(pipeline) computation dag**, we follow a three-step process. First, we translate the code executed in each `pipe_while` loop into ordinary Cilk code augmented with special functions to handle cross and throttling dependencies. Second, we model the execution of this augmented Cilk program as a fork-join computation dag. Third, we show how to augment the fork-join computation dag with cross and throttling edges using the special functions.

The first step of this process does not reflect how a Cilk-P com-

```
1   int fd_out = open_output_file ();
2   bool done = false;
3   pipe_while (!done) {
4     chunk_t *chunk = get_next_chunk ();
5     if (chunk == NULL) {
6       done = true;
7     } else {
8       pipe_wait(1);
9       bool isDuplicate = deduplicate(chunk);
10      pipe_continue(2);
11      if (!isDuplicate)
12        compress(chunk);
13      pipe_wait(3);
14      write_to_file(fd_out, chunk);
15    }
16  }
```

Figure 4: Cilk-P pseudocode for the parallelization of the *dedup* compression program as an SSPS pipeline.

piler would actually compile a pipe_while loop. Indeed, such a code transformation is impossible for a compiler, because the boundaries of nodes are determined on the fly. Instead, this code-transformation step is simply a theoretical construct for the purpose of describing how the PIPER algorithm works in a way that can be analyzed.

We shall illustrate this three-step process on a Cilk-P implementation of the *dedup* compression program from PARSEC [4, 5]. The benchmark can be parallelized by using a pipe_while to implement an SSPS pipeline. Figure 4 shows Cilk-P pseudocode for *dedup*, which compresses the provided input file by removing duplicated "chunks," as follows. Stage 0 (lines 4–6) of the program reads data from the input file and breaks the data into chunks (line 4). As part of Stage 0, it also checks the loop-termination condition and sets the done flag to true (line 6) if the end of the input file is reached. If there is more input to be processed, the program begins Stage 1, which calculates the SHA1 signature of a given chunk and queries a hash table whether this chunk has been seen using the SHA1 signature as key (line 9). Stage 1 is a serial stage as dictated by the pipe_wait on line 8. Stage 2, which the pipe_continue on line 10 indicates is a parallel stage, compresses the chunk if it has not been seen before (line 12). The final stage, a serial stage, writes either the compressed chunk or its SHA1 signature to the output file depending on whether it is the first time the chunk has been seen (line 14).

As the first step in building the computation dag for an execution of this Cilk-P program, we transform the code executed from running the code in Figure 4 into the ordinary Cilk program shown in Figure 5. As shown in lines 3–32, a pipe_while is "lifted" using a C++ lambda function [36, Sec.11.4] and converted to an ordinary while loop using the variable i to index iterations. The loop body executes Stage 0 and spawns off a C++ lambda function that executes the remainder of the iteration (line 12). As one can see from this transformation, Stage 0 of a pipe_while loop is always a serial stage and the test condition of the pipe_while loop is considered part of Stage 0. These constraints guarantee that the repeated tests of the pipe_while loop-termination condition execute serially. Each stage ends with a cilk_sync (lines 10, 16, 21, and 25.) The last statement in the loop (line 29) is a call to a special function throttle, which implements the throttling dependency. The cilk_sync immediately after the end of the while loop (line 31) waits for completion of the spawned iterations.

The second step models the execution of this Cilk program as a fork-join computation dag $G = (V, E)$ as in [7, 8].

The third step is to produce the final pipeline computation dag by augmenting the fork-join computation dag with cross and throttling edges based on the special functions pipe_wait, pipe_continue, and throttle. For example, when iteration i executes the pipe_wait call in line 22, it specifies the start of

```
1   int fd_out = open_output_file ();
2   bool done = false;
3   [&]() {
4     int i = 0;  // iteration index
5     while (!done) { // pipe_while
6       chunk_t *chunk = get_next_chunk ();
7       if (chunk == NULL) {
8         done = true;
9       } else {
10        cilk_sync;
11        // Additional stages of iteration i
12        cilk_spawn [i, chunk, fd_out]() {
13          pipe_wait(1);
14          // node (i,1) begins
15          bool isDuplicate = deduplicate(chunk);
16          cilk_sync;
17          pipe_continue(2);
18          // node (i,2) begins
19          if (!isDuplicate)
20            compress(chunk);
21          cilk_sync;
22          pipe_wait(3);
23          // node (i,3) begins
24          write_to_file(fd_out, chunk);
25          cilk_sync;
26        }();
27      }
28      i++;
29      throttle(i - K);
30    }
31    cilk_sync;
32  }();
```

Figure 5: The Cilk Plus pseudocode that results from transforming the execution of the Cilk-P *dedup* implementation from Figure 4 into fork-join code augmented by dependencies indicated by the pipe_wait, pipe_continue, and throttle special functions. The unbound variable K is the throttling limit.

node $(i, 3)$ and adds a cross edge from the last instruction of node $(i-1, 3)$ to the first instruction of node $(i, 3)$. If node $(i-1, 3)$ is a null node, then the cross edge goes from the last instruction of the last real node in iteration $i-1$ before $(i-1, 3)$. This "collapsing" of null nodes may cause multiple cross edges to be generated from a single vertex in iteration $i-1$ to different vertices in iteration i. The pipe_continue call in line 17 simply indicates the start of node $(i, 2)$. The throttle call in line 29 changes the normal return edge from the last instruction in iteration $i-K$ (the return represented by the closing brace in line 26) into a throttling edge. Rather than going to the cilk_sync in line 31 as the return would, the edge is redirected to the invocation of throttle in iteration i.

5. THE PIPER SCHEDULER

PIPER executes a pipeline program on a set of P workers using work-stealing. For the most part, PIPER's execution model can be viewed as modification of the scheduler described by Arora, Blumofe, and Plaxton [2] (henceforth referred to as the ABP model) for computation dags arising from pipeline programs. PIPER deviates from the ABP model in one significant way, however, in that it performs a "tail-swap" operation.

We describe the operation of PIPER in terms of the pipeline computation dag $G = (V, E)$. Each worker p in PIPER maintains an *assigned vertex* corresponding to the instruction that p executes on the current time step. We say that a vertex x is *ready* if all its predecessors have been executed. Executing an assigned vertex v may *enable* a vertex x that is a direct successor of v in G by making x ready. Each worker maintains a *deque* of ready vertices. Normally, a worker pushes and pops vertices from the tail of its deque. A "thief," however, may try to steal a vertex from the head of another worker's deque. It is convenient to define the *extended deque* $\langle v_0, v_1, \ldots, v_r \rangle$ of a worker p, where $v_0 \in V$ is p's assigned vertex and $v_1, v_2, \ldots, v_r \in V$ are the vertices in p's deque in order from tail to head.

On each time step, each PIPER worker p follows a few simple rules for execution based on the type of p's assigned vertex v and how many direct successors are enabled by the execution of v, which is at most 2. (Although v may have multiple immediate successors in the next iteration due to the collapsing of null nodes, executing v can enable at most one such vertex, since the stages in the next iteration execute serially.) We assume that the rules are executed atomically.

If the assigned vertex v is not the last vertex of an iteration and its execution enables only one direct successor x, then p simply changes its assigned vertex from v to x. Executing a vertex v can enable two successors if v spawns a child x with continuation y or if v is the last vertex in a node in iteration i, which enables both the first vertex x of the next node in i and the first vertex y in a node in iteration $i+1$. In either case, p pushes y onto the tail of its deque and changes its assigned vertex from v to x. If executing v enables no successors, then p tries to pop an element z from the tail of its deque, changing its assigned vertex from v to z. If p's deque is empty, p becomes a **thief**. As a thief, p randomly picks another worker to be its **victim**, tries to steal the vertex z at the head of the victim's deque, and sets the assigned vertex of p to z if successful. These cases are consistent with the normal ABP model.

PIPER handles the end of an iteration differently, however, due to throttling edges. Suppose that a worker p has an assigned vertex v representing the last vertex in a given iteration in a given pipe_while loop, and suppose that the edge leaving v is a throttling edge to a vertex z. When p executes v, two cases are possible. In the first case, executing v does not enable z, in which case no new vertices are enabled, and p acts accordingly. In the second case, however, executing v does enable z, in which case p performs two actions. First, p changes its assigned vertex from v to z. Second, if p has a nonempty deque, then p performs a **tail swap**: it exchanges its assigned vertex z with the vertex at the tail of its deque.

This tail-swap operation is designed to reduce PIPER's space usage. Without the tail swap, in a normal ABP-style execution, when a worker p finishes an iteration i that enables a vertex via a throttling edge, p would conceptually choose to start a new iteration $i+K$, even if iteration $i+1$ were already suspended and on its deque. With the tail swap, p resumes iteration $i+1$, leaving $i+K$ available for stealing. The tail swap also enhances cache locality by encouraging p to execute consecutive iterations.

It may seem, at first glance, that a tail-swap operation might significantly reduce the parallelism, since the vertex z enabled by the throttling edge is pushed onto the bottom of the deque. Intuitively, if there were additional work above z in the deque, then a tail swap could significantly delay the start of iteration $i+K$. Lemma 4 will show, however, that a tail-swap operation only occurs on deques with exactly 1 element. Thus, whenever a tail swap occurs, z is at the top of the deque and is immediately available to be stolen.

6. STRUCTURAL INVARIANTS

During the execution of a pipeline program by PIPER, the worker deques satisfy two structural invariants, called the "contour" property and the "depth" property. This section states and proves these invariants.

Intuitively, we would like to describe the structure of the worker deques in terms of **frames** — activation records — of functions' local variables, since the deques implement a "cactus stack" [18, 23]. A pipe_while loop would correspond to a parent frame with a spawned child for each iteration. Although the actual Cilk-P implementation manages frames in this fashion, the control of a pipe_while really does follow the schema illustrated in Figure 5, where Stage 0 of an iteration i executes in the same lambda function as the parent, rather than in the child lambda function which

contains the rest of i. Consequently, we introduce "contours" to represent this structure.

Consider a computation dag $G = (V, E)$ that arises from the execution of a pipeline program. A **contour** is a path in G composed only of serial and continue edges. A contour must be a path, because there can be at most one serial or continue edge entering or leaving any vertex. We call the first vertex of a contour the **root** of the contour, which (except for the initial instruction of the entire computation) is the only vertex in the contour that has an incoming spawn edge. Consequently, contours can be organized into a tree hierarchy, where one contour is a parent of a second if the first contour contains a vertex that spawns the root of the second. Given a vertex $v \in V$, let $c(v)$ denote the contour to which v belongs.

The following two lemmas describe two important properties exhibited in the execution of a pipeline program.

LEMMA 1. *Only one vertex in a contour can belong to any extended deque at any time.*

PROOF. The vertices in a contour form a chain and are, therefore, enabled serially. □

The structure of a pipe_while guarantees that the "top-level" vertices of each iteration correspond to a contour, and that all iterations of the pipe_while share a common parent in the contour tree. These properties lead to the following lemma.

LEMMA 2. *If an edge (x, y) is a cross edge, then $c(x)$ and $c(y)$ are siblings in the contour tree and correspond to adjacent iterations in a pipe_while loop. If an edge (x, y) is a throttling edge, then $c(y)$ is the parent of $c(x)$ in contour tree.* □

As PIPER executes a pipeline program, the deques of workers are highly structured with respect to contours.

DEFINITION 3. *At any time during an execution of a pipeline program which produces a computation dag $G = (V, E)$, consider the extended deque $\langle v_0, v_1, \ldots, v_r \rangle$ of a worker p. This deque satisfies the **contour property** if for all $k = 0, 1, \ldots r - 1$, one of the following two conditions holds:*
1. *$c(v_{k+1})$ is the parent of $c(v_k)$.*
2. *The root of $c(v_k)$ is the start of some iteration i, the root of $c(v_{k+1})$ is the start of the next iteration $i+1$, and if $k+2 \leq r$, then $c(v_{k+2})$ is the common parent of both $c(v_k)$ and $c(v_{k+1})$.*

Contours allow us to prove an important property of the tail-swap operation.

LEMMA 4. *At any time during an execution of a pipeline program which produces a computation dag $G = (V, E)$, suppose that worker p enables a vertex x via a throttling edge as a result of executing its assigned vertex v_0. If p's deque satisfies the contour property (Definition 3), then either*
1. *p's deque is empty and x becomes p's new assigned vertex, or*
2. *p's deque contains a single vertex v_1 which becomes p's new assigned vertex and x is pushed onto p's deque.*

PROOF. Because x is enabled by a throttling edge, v_0 must be the last node of some iteration i, which by Lemma 2 means that $c(x)$ is the parent of $c(v_0)$. Because x is just being enabled, Lemma 1 implies that no other vertex in $c(x)$ can belong to p's deque. Suppose that p's extended deque $\langle v_0, v_1, \ldots, v_r \rangle$ contains $r \geq 2$ vertices. By Lemma 1, either v_1 or v_2 belongs to contour $c(x)$, neither of which is possible, and hence $r = 0$ or $r = 1$. If $r = 0$, then x is p's assigned vertex. If $r = 1$, then the root of $c(v_1)$ is the start of iteration $i+1$. Since x is enabled by a throttling edge, a tail swap occurs, making v_1 the assigned vertex of p and putting x onto p's deque. □

To analyze the time required for PIPER to execute a computation dag $G = (V, E)$, define the **enabling tree** $G_T = (V, E_T)$ as the tree containing an edge $(x, y) \in E_T$ if x is the last predecessor of y to execute. The **enabling depth** $d(x)$ of $x \in V$ is the depth of x in the enabling tree G_T.

DEFINITION 5. *At any time during an execution of a pipeline program which produces a computation dag $G = (V, E)$, consider the extended deque $\langle v_0, v_1, \ldots, v_r \rangle$ of a worker p. The deque satisfies the **depth property** if the following conditions hold:*

1. *For $k = 1, 2, \ldots, r-1$, we have $d(v_{k-1}) \geq d(v_k)$.*

2. *For $k = r$, we have $d(v_{k-1}) \geq d(v_k)$ or v_k has an incoming throttling edge.*

3. *The inequalities are strict for $k > 1$.*

THEOREM 6. *At all times during an execution of a pipeline program by PIPER, all deques satisfy the contour and depth properties (Definitions 3 and 5).*

PROOF. The proof is similar to the inductive proof of Lemma 3 from [2]. Intuitively, we replace the "designated parents" discussed in [2] with contours, which exhibit similar parent-child relationships. Although most of the proof follows from this substitution, we address the two most salient differences. The other minor cases are either straightforward or similar to these two cases.

First, we consider the consequences of the tail-swap operation, which may occur if the assigned vertex v_0 is the end of an iteration and executing v_0 enables a vertex z via a throttling edge. Lemma 4 describes the structure of a worker p's extended deque in this case, and in particular, states that the deque contains at most 1 vertex. If $r = 0$, the deque is empty and the properties hold vacuously. Otherwise, $r = 1$ and the deque contains one element v_1, in which case the tail-swap operation assigns v_1 to p and puts z into p's deque. The contour property holds, because $c(z)$ is the parent of $c(v_1)$. The depth property holds, because z is enabled by a throttling edge.

Second, we must show that the contour and depth properties hold when a worker p's assigned vertex v_0 belongs to some iteration i of a pipe_while, and executing v_0 enables a vertex y belonging to iteration $i+1$ via a cross edge (v_0, y). Assume that executing v_0 also enables x, where x also belongs to iteration i. (The case where x is not enabled is similar.) Since both v_0 and x belong to the same iteration, $c(v_0) = c(x)$, and by Lemma 2, $c(x)$ is a sibling of $c(y)$ in the contour tree. Suppose that before v_0 executes, p's extended deque is $\langle v_0, v_1, \ldots, v_r \rangle$, and thus after v_0 executes, p's extended deque is $\langle x, y, v_1, \ldots, v_r \rangle$. For vertices $v_2, v_3, \ldots, v_r$, if they exist, the conditions of the contour property continue to hold by induction. Since $c(x)$ and $c(y)$ are adjacent siblings in the contour tree, we need only show that $c(v_1)$, if it exists, is their parent. But if $c(v_1)$ is not the parent of $c(v_0) = c(x)$, then by induction it must be that $c(x)$ and $c(v_1)$ are adjacent siblings. In this case $c(v_1) = c(y)$, which is impossible by Lemma 1. The depth property holds because $d(x) = d(y) = d(v_0) + 1 \geq d(v_1) + 1 > d(v_1)$. $\square$

7. TIME ANALYSIS OF PIPER

This section bounds the completion time for PIPER, showing that PIPER executes pipeline program asymptotically efficiently. Specifically, suppose that a pipeline program produces a computation dag $G = (V, E)$ with work T_1 and span T_∞ when executed by PIPER on P processors. We show that for any $\varepsilon > 0$, the running time is $T_P \leq T_1/P + O(T_\infty + \lg P + \lg(1/\varepsilon))$ with probability at least $1 - \varepsilon$, which implies that the expected running time is $E[T_P] \leq T_1/P + O(T_\infty + \lg P)$. This bound is comparable to the work-stealing bound for fork-join dags originally proved in [8].

We adapt the potential-function argument of Arora, Blumofe, and Plaxton [2]. PIPER executes computation dags in a style similar to their work-stealing scheduler, except for tail swapping. Although Arora et al. ignore the issue of memory contention, we handle it using the "recycling game" analysis from [8], which contributes the additive $O(\lg P)$ term to the bounds.

As in [2], the crux of the proof is to bound the number of steal attempts performed during the execution of a computation dag G in terms of its span T_∞. We measure progress through the computation by defining a potential function for a vertex in the computation dag based on its depth in the enabling tree. Consider a particular execution of a computation dag $G = (V, E)$ by PIPER. For that execution, we define the **weight** of a vertex v as $w(v) = T_\infty - d(v)$, and we define the **potential** of vertex v at a given time as

$$\phi(v) = \begin{cases} 3^{2w(v)-1} & \text{if } v \text{ is assigned}, \\ 3^{2w(v)} & \text{otherwise}. \end{cases}$$

We define the potential of a worker p's extended deque $\langle v_0, v_1, \ldots, v_r \rangle$ as $\phi(p) = \sum_{k=0}^{r} \phi(v_k)$.

Given this potential function, the proof of the time bound follows the same overall structure as the proof in [2]. We sketch the proof.

First, we prove two properties of worker deques involving the potential function.

LEMMA 7. *At any time during an execution of a pipeline program which produces a computation dag $G = (V, E)$, the extended deque $\langle v_0, v_1, \ldots, v_r \rangle$ of every worker p satisfies the following:*

1. *$\phi(v_r) + \phi(v_{r-1}) \geq 3\phi(p)/4$.*

2. *Let ϕ' denote the potential after p executes v_0. Then we have $\phi(p) - \phi'(p) = 2(\phi(v_0) + \phi(v_1))/3$, if p performs a tail swap, and $\phi(p) - \phi'(p) \geq 5\phi(v_0)/9$ otherwise.*

PROOF. Property 1 follows from the depth property of Theorem 6. Property 2 follows from Lemma 4, if p performs a tail swap, and the analysis in [2] otherwise. $\square$

As in [2], we analyze the behavior of workers randomly stealing from each other using a balls-and-weighted-bins analog. We want to analyze the case where the top 2 elements are stolen out of any deque, however, not just the top element. To address this case, we modify Lemma 7 of [2] to consider the probability that 2 out of $2P$ balls land in the same bin.

LEMMA 8. *Consider P bins, where for $p = 1, 2, \ldots, P$, bin p has weight W_p. Suppose that $2P$ balls are thrown independently and uniformly at random into the P bins. For bin p, define the random variable X_p as*

$$X_p = \begin{cases} W_p & \text{if at least 2 balls land in bin } p, \\ 0 & \text{otherwise}. \end{cases}$$

Let $W = \sum_{p=1}^{P} W_p$ and $X = \sum_{p=1}^{P} X_p$. For any β in the range $0 < \beta < 1$, we have $\Pr\{X \geq \beta W\} > 1 - 3/(1-\beta)e^2$.

PROOF. For each bin p, consider the random variable $W_p - X_p$. It takes on the value W_p when 0 or 1 ball lands in bin p, and otherwise it is 0. Thus, we have

$$E[W_p - X_p] = W_p \left((1 - 1/P)^{2P} + 2P(1 - 1/P)^{2P-1}(1/P) \right)$$
$$= W_p (1 - 1/P)^{2P} (3P - 1)/(P - 1).$$

Since $(1 - 1/P)^P$ approaches $1/e$ and $(3P - 1)/(P - 1)$ approaches 3, we have $\lim_{P \to \infty} E[W_p - X_p] = 3W_p/e^2$. In fact, one can show that $E[W_p - X_p]$ is monotonically increasing, approaching the limit from below, and thus $E[W-X] \leq 3W/e^2$. By Markov's inequality, we have that $\Pr\{(W-X) > (1-\beta)W\} < E[W-X]/(1-\beta)W$, from which we conclude that $\Pr\{X < \beta W\} \leq 3/(1-\beta)e^2$. $\quad\square$

To use Lemma 8 to analyze PIPER, we divide the time steps of the execution of G into a sequence of **rounds**, where each round (except the first, which starts at time 0) starts at the time step after the previous round ends and continues until the first time step such that at least $2P$ steal attempts — and hence less than $3P$ steal attempts — occur within the round. The following lemma shows that a constant fraction of the total potential in all deques is lost in each round, thereby demonstrating progress.

LEMMA 9. *Consider a pipeline program executed by* PIPER *on P processors. Suppose that a round starts at time step t and finishes at time step t'. Let ϕ denote the potential at time t, let ϕ' denote the potential at time t', let $\Phi = \sum_{p=1}^{P} \phi(p)$, and let $\Phi' = \sum_{p=1}^{P} \phi'(p)$. Then we have* $\Pr\{\Phi - \Phi' \geq \Phi/4\} > 1 - 6/e^2$.

PROOF. We first show that stealing twice from a worker p's deque contributes a potential drop of at least $\phi(p)/2$. The proof follows a similar case analysis to that in the proof of Lemma 8 in [2] with two main differences. First, we use the two properties of ϕ in Lemma 7. Second, we must consider the case unique to PIPER, where p performs a tail swap after executing its assigned vertex v_0. In this case, p's deque contains a single ready vertex v_1 and p may perform a tail swap if executing v_0 enables a vertex via an outgoing throttling edge. If so, however, then by Lemma 7, the potential drops by at least $2(\phi(v_0)+\phi(v_1))/3 > \phi(p)/2$, since $\phi(p) = \phi(v_0) + \phi(v_1)$.

Now, suppose that we assign each worker p a weight of $W_p = \phi(p)/2$. These weights W_p sum to $W = \Phi/2$. If we think of steal attempts as ball tosses, then the random variable X from Lemma 8 bounds from below the potential decrease due to actions on p's deque. Specifically, if at least 2 steal attempts target p's deque in a round (which corresponds conceptually to at least 2 balls landing in bin p), then the potential drops by at least W_p. Moreover, X is a lower bound on the potential decrease within the round, i.e., $X \leq \Phi - \Phi'$. By Lemma 8, we have $\Pr\{X \geq W/2\} > 1 - 6/e^2$. Substituting for X and W, we conclude that $\Pr\{(\Phi - \Phi') \geq \Phi/4\} > 1 - 6/e^2$. $\quad\square$

We are now ready to prove the completion-time bound.

THEOREM 10. *Consider an execution of a pipeline program by* PIPER *on P processors which produces a computation dag with work T_1 and span T_∞. For any $\varepsilon > 0$, the running time is $T_P \leq T_1/P + O(T_\infty + \lg P + \lg(1/\varepsilon))$ with probability at least $1 - \varepsilon$.*

PROOF. On every time step, consider each worker as placing a token in a bucket depending on its action. If a worker p executes an assigned vertex, p places a token in the **work bucket**. Otherwise, p is a thief and places a token in the **steal bucket**. There are exactly T_1 tokens in the work bucket at the end of the computation. The interesting part is bounding the size of the steal bucket.

Divide the execution of G into rounds. Recall that each round contains at least $2P$ and less than $3P$ steal attempts. Call a round **successful** if after that round finishes, the potential drops by at least a $1/4$ fraction. From Lemma 9, a round is successful with probability at least $1 - 6/e^2 \geq 1/6$. Since the potential starts at $\Phi_0 = 3^{2T_\infty - 1}$, ends at 0, and is always an integer, the number of successful rounds is at most $(2T_\infty - 1)\log_{4/3}(3) < 8T_\infty$. Consequently, the expected number of rounds needed to obtain $8T_\infty$ successful rounds is at most $48T_\infty$, and the expected number of tokens in the steal bucket is therefore at most $3P \cdot 48T_\infty = 144PT_\infty$.

For the high-probability bound, suppose that the execution takes $n = 48T_\infty + m$ rounds. Because each round succeeds with probability at least $p = 1/6$, the expected number of successes is at least $np = 8T_\infty + m/6$. We now compute the probability that the number X of successes is less than $8T_\infty$. As in [2], we use the Chernoff bound $\Pr\{X < np - a\} < e^{-a^2/2np}$, with $a = m/6$. Choosing $m = 48T_\infty + 21\ln(1/\varepsilon)$, we have

$$\Pr\{X < 8T_\infty\} < e^{\frac{-(m/6)^2}{16T_\infty + m/3}} < e^{\frac{-(m/6)^2}{m/4 + m/3}} = e^{-m/21} \leq \varepsilon \,.$$

Hence, the probability that the execution takes $n = 96T_\infty + 21\ln(1/\varepsilon)$ rounds or more is less than ε, and the number of tokens in the steal bucket is at most $288T_\infty + 63\ln(1/\varepsilon)$.

The additional $\lg P$ term comes from the "recycling game" analysis described in [8], which bounds any delay that might be incurred when multiple processors try to access the same deque in the same time step in randomized work-stealing. $\quad\square$

8. SPACE ANALYSIS OF PIPER

This section derives bounds on the stack space required by PIPER by extending the bounds in [8] for fully strict fork-join parallelism to include pipeline parallelism. We show that PIPER on P processors uses $S_P \leq P(S_1 + fDK)$ stack space for pipeline iterations, where S_1 is the serial stack space, f is the "frame size," D is the depth of nested linear pipelines, and K is the throttling limit.

To model PIPER's usage of stack space, we partition the vertices of the computation dag G of the pipeline program into a tree of contours, as described in Section 6. Each contour in this partition is rooted at the start of a spawned subcomputation. The control for each `pipe_while` loop, which corresponds to a `while` loop as in line 5 of Figure 5, belongs to some contour in the contour tree with its iterations as children. Define the **pipe nesting depth** D of G as the maximum number of `pipe_while` contours on any path from leaf to root in the contour tree.

We assume that every contour c of G has an associated **frame size** representing the stack space consumed by c while it or any of its descendant contours are executing. The space used by PIPER on any time step is the sum of frame sizes of all contours c which are either (1) associated with a vertex in some worker's extended deque, or (2) **suspended**, meaning that the earliest unexecuted vertex in the contour is not ready. Let S_P denote the maximum over all time steps of the stack space used by PIPER during a P-worker execution of G. Thus, S_1 is the stack space used by PIPER for a serial execution. We now generalize the space bound $S_P \leq PS_1$ from [8], which deals only with fork-join parallelism, to pipeline programs.

THEOREM 11. *Consider a pipeline program with pipe nesting depth D executed on P processors by* PIPER *with throttling limit K. The execution requires $S_P \leq P(S_1 + fDK)$ stack space, where f is the maximum frame size of any contour of any* `pipe_while` *iteration and S_1 is the serial stack space.*

PROOF. We show that except for suspended contours that are `pipe_while` iterations, PIPER still satisfies the "busy-leaves property" [8]. More precisely, at any point during the execution, in the tree of active and suspended contours, each leaf contour either (1) is currently executing on some worker, or (2) is a suspended `pipe_while` iteration with a sibling iteration that is currently executing on some worker. In fact, one can show that for any `pipe_while` loop, the contour for the leftmost (smallest) iteration that has not completed is either active or has an active descendant in the contour tree. The bound of PS_1 covers the space used by all contours that fall into Case (1).

To bound the space used by contours from Case (2), observe that any pipe_while loop uses at most fK space for iteration contours, since the throttling edge from the leftmost active iteration precludes having more than K active or suspended iterations in any one pipe_while loop. Thus, each worker p has at most fDK iteration contours for any pipe_while loop that is an ancestor of the contour p's assigned vertex. Summing the space used over all workers gives $PfDK$ additional stack-space usage. $\square$

9. CILK-P RUNTIME DESIGN

This section describes the Cilk-P implementation of the PIPER scheduler. We first introduce the data structures Cilk-P uses to implement a pipe_while loop. Then we describe the two main optimizations that the Cilk-P runtime exploits: lazy enabling and dependency folding.

Data structures

Like the Cilk-M runtime [23] on which it is based, Cilk-P organizes runtime data into frames. Cilk-P executes a pipe_while loop in its own function, whose frame, called a *control frame*, handles the spawning and throttling of iterations. Furthermore, each iteration of a pipe_while loop executes as an independent child function, with its own *iteration frame*. This frame structure is similar to that of an ordinary while loop in Cilk-M, where each iteration spawns a function to execute the loop body. Cross and throttling edges, however, may cause the iteration and control frames to suspend.

Cilk-P's runtime employs a simple mechanism to track progress of an iteration i. The frame of iteration i maintains a *stage counter*, which stores the stage number of the current node in i, and a *status* field, which indicates whether i is suspended due to an unsatisfied cross edge. Because executed nodes in an iteration i have strictly increasing stage numbers, checking whether a cross edge into iteration i is satisfied amounts to comparing the stage counters of iterations i and $i-1$. Any iteration frame that is not suspended corresponds to either a currently executing or a completed iteration.

Cilk-P implements throttling using a *join counter* in the control frame. Normally in Cilk-M, a frame's join counter simply stores the number of active child frames. Cilk-P also uses the join counter to limit the number of active iteration frames in a pipe_while loop to the throttling limit K. Starting an iteration increments the join counter, while returning from an iteration decrements it. If a worker tries to start a new iteration when the control frame's join counter is K, the control frame suspends until a child iteration returns.

Using these data structures, one could implement PIPER directly, by pushing and popping the appropriate frames onto deques as specified by PIPER's execution model. In particular, the normal THE protocol [15] could be used for pushing and popping frames from a deque, and frame locks could be used to update fields in the frames atomically. Although this approach directly matches the model analyzed in Sections 7 and 8, it incurs unnecessary overhead for every node in an iteration. Cilk-P implements lazy enabling and dependency folding to reduce this overhead.

Lazy enabling

In the PIPER algorithm, when a worker p finishes executing a node in iteration i, it may enable an instruction in iteration $i+1$, in which case p pushes this instruction onto its deque. To implement this behavior, intuitively, p must **check right** — read the stage counter and status of iteration $i+1$ — whenever it finishes executing a node. The work to check right at the end of every node could amount to substantial overhead in a pipeline with fine-grained stages.

Lazy enabling allows p's execution of an iteration i to defer the check-right operation, as well as avoid any operations on its deque involving iteration $i+1$. Conceptually, when p enables work in iteration $i+1$, this work is kept on p's deque implicitly. When a thief p' tries to steal iteration i's frame from p's deque, p' first checks right on behalf of p to see whether any work from iteration $i+1$ is implicitly on the deque. If so, p' resumes iteration $i+1$ as if it had found it on p's deque. In a similar vein, the Cilk-P runtime system also uses lazy enabling to optimize the **check-parent** operation — the enabling of a control frame suspended due to throttling.

Lazy enabling requires p to behave differently when p completes an iteration. When p finishes iteration i, it first checks right, and if that fails (i.e., iteration $i+1$ need not be resumed), it checks its parent. It turns out that these checks find work only if p's deque is empty. Therefore, p can avoid performing these checks at the end of an iteration if its deque is not empty.

Lazy enabling is an application of the *work-first principle* [15]: minimize the scheduling overheads borne by the work of a computation, and amortize them against the span. Requiring a worker to check right every time it completes a node adds overhead proportional to the work of the pipe_while in the worst case. With lazy enabling, the overhead can be amortized against the span of the computation. For programs with sufficient parallelism, the work dominates the span, and the overhead becomes negligible.

Dependency folding

In *dependency folding*, the frame for iteration i stores a cached value of the stage counter of iteration $i-1$, hoping to avoid the checking of already satisfied cross edges. In a straightforward implementation of PIPER, before a worker p executes each node in iteration i with an incoming cross edge, it reads the stage counter of iteration $i-1$ to see if the cross edge is satisfied. Reading the stage counter of iteration $i-1$, however, can be expensive. Besides the work involved, the access may contend with whatever worker p' is executing iteration $i-1$, because p' may be constantly updating the stage counter of iteration $i-1$.

Dependency folding mitigates this overhead by exploiting the fact that an iteration's stage counter must strictly increase. By caching the most recently read stage-counter value from iteration $i-1$, worker p can sometimes avoid reading this stage counter before each node with an incoming cross edge. For instance, if p' finishes executing a node $(i-1, j)$, then all cross edges from nodes $(i-1, 0)$ through $(i-1, j)$ are necessarily satisfied. Thus, if p reads j from iteration $i-1$'s stage counter, p need not reread the stage counter of $i-1$ until it tries to execute a node with an incoming cross edge (i, j') where $j' > j$. This optimization is particularly useful for fine-grained stages that execute quickly.

10. EVALUATION

This section presents empirical studies of the Cilk-P prototype system. We investigated the performance and scalability of Cilk-P using the three PARSEC [4, 5] benchmarks that we ported, namely *ferret*, *dedup*, and *x264*. The results show that Cilk-P's implementation of pipeline parallelism has negligible overhead compared to its serial counterpart. We compared the Cilk-P implementations to TBB and Pthreaded implementations of these benchmarks. We found that the Cilk-P and TBB implementations perform comparably, as do the Cilk-P and Pthreaded implementations for *ferret* and *x264*. The Pthreaded version of *dedup* outperforms both Cilk-P and TBB, because the bind-to-element approaches of Cilk-P and TBB produce less parallelism than the Pthreaded bind-to-stage approach. Moreover, the Pthreading approach benefits more from "oversubscription." We study the effectiveness of dependency folding on a

P	Processing Time (T_P) Cilk-P	Pthreads	TBB	Speedup (T_S/T_P) Cilk-P	Pthreads	TBB	Scalability (T_1/T_P) Cilk-P	Pthreads	TBB
1	691.2	692.1	690.3	1.00	1.00	1.00	1.00	1.00	1.00
2	356.7	343.8	351.5	1.94	2.01	1.97	1.94	2.01	1.96
4	176.5	170.4	175.8	3.92	4.06	3.93	3.92	4.06	3.93
8	89.1	86.8	89.2	7.76	7.96	7.75	7.76	7.97	7.74
12	60.3	59.1	60.8	11.46	11.70	11.36	11.46	11.71	11.35
16	46.2	46.3	46.9	14.98	14.93	14.75	14.98	14.95	14.74

Figure 6: Performance comparison of the three *ferret* implementations. The experiments were conducted using *native*, the largest input data set that comes with the PARSEC benchmark suite.[4] The left-most column shows the number of cores used (P). Subsequent columns show the running time (T_P), speedup over serial running time (T_S/T_P), and scalability (T_1/T_P) for each system. The throttling limit was $K = 10P$.

P	Processing Time (T_P) Cilk-P	Pthreads	TBB	Speedup (T_S/T_P) Cilk-P	Pthreads	TBB	Scalability (T_1/T_P) Cilk-P	Pthreads	TBB
1	58.0	51.1	57.3	1.01	1.05	1.00	1.00	1.00	1.00
2	29.8	23.3	29.4	1.96	2.51	1.99	1.94	2.19	1.95
4	16.0	12.2	16.2	3.66	4.78	3.61	3.63	4.18	3.54
8	10.4	8.2	10.3	5.62	7.08	5.70	5.57	6.20	5.58
12	9.0	6.6	9.0	6.53	8.83	6.57	6.47	7.72	6.44
16	8.6	6.0	8.6	6.77	9.72	6.78	6.71	8.50	6.65

Figure 7: Performance comparison of the three *dedup* implementations. The experiments were conducted using *native*, the largest input data set that comes with the PARSEC benchmark suite. The column headers are the same as in Figure 6. The throttling limit was $K = 4P$.

P	Encoding Time (T_P) Cilk-P	Pthreads	Speedup (T_S/T_P) Cilk-P	Pthreads	Scalability (T_1/T_P) Cilk-P	Pthreads
1	217.1	223.0	1.02	0.99	1.00	1.00
2	97.0	105.3	2.27	2.09	2.24	2.12
4	47.7	53.3	4.63	4.14	4.55	4.19
8	25.9	26.7	8.53	8.27	8.40	8.36
12	18.6	19.3	11.84	11.44	11.66	11.57
16	16.0	16.2	13.87	13.63	13.66	13.76

Figure 8: Performance comparison between the Cilk-P implementation and the Pthreaded implementation of *x264* (encoding only). The experiments were conducted using *native*, the largest input data set that comes with the PARSEC benchmark suite. The column headers are the same as in Figure 6. The throttling limit was $K = 4P$.

synthetic benchmark called *pipe-fib*, demonstrating that this optimization can be effective for applications with fine-grained stages.

We ran all experiments on an AMD Opteron system with 4 2 GHz quad-core CPU's having a total of 8 GBytes of memory. Each processor core has a 64-KByte private L1-data-cache and a 512-KByte private L2-cache. The 4 cores on each chip share the same 2-MByte L3-cache. The benchmarks were compiled with GCC (or G++ for TBB) 4.4.5 using -O3 optimization, except for *x264*, which by default comes with -O4.

Performance evaluation on PARSEC benchmarks

We implemented the Cilk-P versions of the three PARSEC benchmarks by hand-compiling the relevant `pipe_while` loops using techniques similar to those described in [23]. We then compiled the hand-compiled benchmarks with GCC. The *ferret* and *dedup* applications can be parallelized as simple pipelines with a fixed number of stages and a static dependency structure. In particular, *ferret* uses the 3-stage SPS pipeline shown in Figure 1, while *dedup* uses a 4-stage SSPS pipeline as described in Figure 4.

For the Pthreaded versions, we used the code distributed with PARSEC. The PARSEC Pthreaded implementations of *ferret* and *dedup* employ the **oversubscription method** [33], a bind-to-stage approach that creates more than one thread per pipeline stage and utilizes the operating system for load balancing. For the Pthreaded

---

[4]We dropped four out of the 3500 input images from the original *native* data set, because those images are black-and-white, which trigger an array index out of bound error in the image library provided.

implementations, when the user specifies an input parameter of Q, the code creates Q threads per stage, except for the first (input) and last (output) stages which are serial and use only one thread each. To ensure a fair comparison, for all applications, we ran the Pthreaded implementation using `taskset` to limit the process to P cores (which corresponds to the number of workers used in Cilk-P and TBB), but experimented to find the best setting for Q.

We used the TBB version of *ferret* that came with the PARSEC benchmark, and implemented the TBB version of *dedup*, both using the same strategies as for Cilk-P. TBB's construct-and-run approach proved inadequate for the on-the-fly nature of *x264*, however, and indeed, in their study of these three applications, Reed, Chen, and Johnson [33] say, "Implementing *x264* in TBB is not impossible, but the TBB pipeline structure is not suitable." Thus, we had no TBB benchmark for *x264* to include in our comparisons.

For each benchmark, we throttled all versions similarly. For Cilk-P, a throttling limit of $4P$, where P is the number of cores, seems to work well in general, although since *ferret* scales slightly better with less throttling, we used a throttling limit of $10P$ for our experiments. TBB supports a settable parameter that serves the same purpose as Cilk-P's throttling limit. For the Pthreaded implementations, we throttled the computation by setting a size limit on the queues between stages, although we did not impose a queue size limit on the last stage of *dedup* (the default limit is 2^{20}), since the program deadlocks otherwise.

Figures 6–8 show the performance results for the different implementations of the three benchmarks. Each data point in the study was computed by averaging the results of 10 runs. The standard deviation of the numbers was typically just a few percent, indicating that the numbers should be accurate to within better than 10 percent with high confidence (2 or 3 standard deviations). We suspect that the superlinear scalability obtained for some measurements is due to the fact that more L1- and L2-cache is available when running on multiple cores.

The three tables from Figures 6–8 show that the Cilk-P and TBB implementations of *ferret* and *dedup* are comparable, indicating that there is no performance penalty incurred by these applications for using the more general on-the-fly pipeline instead of a construct-and-run pipeline. Both Cilk-P and TBB execute using a bind-to-element approach.

The *dedup* performance results for Cilk-P and TBB are inferior to those for Pthreads, however. The Pthreaded implementation scales to about 8.5 on 16 cores, whereas Cilk-P and TBB seem to plateau at around 6.7. There appear to be two reasons for this discrepancy.

First, the *dedup* benchmark on the test input has limited parallelism. We modified the Cilkview scalability analyzer [19] to measure the work and span of our hand-compiled Cilk-P *dedup* programs, observing a parallelism of merely 7.4. The bind-to-stage Pthreaded implementation creates a pipeline with a different structure from the bind-to-element Cilk-P and TBB versions, which enjoys slightly more parallelism.

Second, since file I/O is the main performance bottleneck for *dedup*, the Pthreaded implementation effectively benefits from **oversubscription** — using more threads than processing cores — and its strategic allocation of threads to stages. Specifically, since the first and last stages perform file I/O, which is inherently serial, the Pthreaded implementation dedicates one thread to each of these stages, but dedicates multiple threads to the other compute-intensive stages. While the writing thread is performing file I/O (i.e., writing data out to the disk), the OS may deschedule it, allowing the compute-intensive threads to be scheduled. This behavior explains how the Pthreaded implementation scales by more than a

Program	Dependency Folding	T_S	T_1	T_{16}	Serial Overhead	Speedup T_S/T_{16}	Scalability T_1/T_{16}
pipe-fib	no	20.8	22.3	3.8	1.07	5.15	5.82
pipe-fib-256	no	20.8	20.9	1.7	1.01	12.26	12.31
pipe-fib	yes	20.8	21.7	1.8	1.05	11.85	12.40
pipe-fib-256	yes	20.8	20.9	1.7	1.01	12.56	12.62

Figure 9: Performance evaluation using the *pipe-fib* benchmark. We tested the system with two different programs, the ordinary *pipe-fib*, and the *pipe-fib-256*, which is coarsened. Each program is tested with and without the dependency folding optimization. For each program for a given setting, we show the running time of its serial counter part (T_S), running time executing on a single worker (T_1), on 16 workers (T_{16}), its serial overhead, scalability, and speedup obtained running on 16 workers.

factor of P for $P = 2$ and 4, even though the computation is restricted to only P cores using `taskset`. Moreover, when we ran the Pthreaded implementation without throttling on a single core, the computation ran about 20% faster than the serial implementation, which makes sense if computation and file I/O are effectively overlapped. With multiple threads per stage, throttling appears to inhibit threads working on stages that are further ahead, allowing threads working on heavier stages to obtain more processing resources, and thereby balancing the load.

In summary, Cilk-P performs comparably to TBB while admitting more expressive semantics for pipelines. Cilk-P also performs comparably to the Pthreaded implementations of *ferret* and *x264*, although its bind-to-element strategy seems to suffer on *dedup* compared to the bind-to-stage strategy of the Pthreaded implementation. Despite losing the *dedup* "bake-off," Cilk-P's strategy has the significant advantage that it allows pipelines to be expressed as deterministic programs. Determinism greatly reduces the effort for debugging, release engineering, and maintenance (see, for example, [9]) compared with the inherently nondeterministic code required to set up Pthreaded pipelines.

Evaluation of dependency folding

We also studied the effectiveness of dependency folding. Since the PARSEC benchmarks are too coarse grained to permit such a study, we implemented a synthetic benchmark, called *pipe-fib*, to study this optimization technique. The *pipe-fib* benchmark computes the nth Fibonacci number F_n in binary. It uses a pipeline algorithm that operates in $\Theta(n^2)$ work and $\Theta(n)$ span. To construct the base case, *pipe-fib* allocates three arrays of size $\Theta(n)$ and initializes the first two arrays with the binary representations of F_1 and F_2, both of which are 1. To compute F_3, *pipe-fib* performs a ripple-carry addition on the two input arrays and stores the sum into the third output array. To compute F_n, *pipe-fib* repeats the addition by rotating through the arrays for inputs and output until it reaches F_n. In the pipeline for this computation, each iteration i computes F_{i+2}, and a stage j within the iteration computes the jth bit of F_{i+2}. Since the benchmark stops propagating the carry bit as soon as possible, it generates a triangular pipeline dag in which the number of stages increases with iteration number.

Figure 9 shows the performance results[5] obtained by running the ordinary *pipe-fib* with fine-grained stages, as well as *pipe-fib-256*, a coarsened version of *pipe-fib* in which each stage computes 256 bits instead of 1. As the data in the first row show, even though the serial overhead for *pipe-fib* without coarsening is merely 7%, it fails to scale and exhibits poor speedup. The reason is that checking for dependencies due to cross edges has a relatively high overhead compared to the little work in each fine-grained stage. As the data for *pipe-fib-256* in the second row show, coarsening the stages improves both serial overhead and scalability. Ideally, one would

---

[5]Figure 9 shows the results from a single run, but these data are representative of other runs with different input sizes.

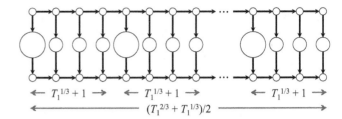

Figure 10: Sketch of the pathological unthrottled linear pipeline dag, which can be used to prove Theorem 13. Small circles represent nodes with unit work, medium circles represent nodes with $T_1^{1/3} - 2$ work, and large circles represent nodes with $T_1^{2/3} - 2$ work. The number of iterations per cluster is $T_1^{1/3} + 1$, and the total number of iterations is $(T_1^{2/3} + T_1^{1/3})/2$.

like the system to coarsen automatically, which is what dependency folding effectively does.

Further investigation revealed that the time spent checking for cross edges increases noticeably when the number of workers increases from 1 to 2. It turns out that when iterations are run in parallel, each check for a cross-edge dependency necessarily incurs a true-sharing conflict between the two adjacent active iterations, an overhead that occurs only during parallel execution. Dependency folding eliminated much of this overhead for *pipe-fib*, as shown in the third row of Figure 9, leading to scalability that exceeds the coarsened version without the optimization, although a slight price is still paid in speedup. Employing both optimizations, as shown in the last row of the table, produces the best numbers for both speedup and scalability.

11. CONCLUSION

What impact does throttling have on theoretical performance? PIPER relies on throttling to achieve its provable space bound and avoid runaway pipelines. Ideally, the user should not worry about throttling, and the system should perform well automatically, and indeed, PIPER's throttling of a pipeline computation is encapsulated in Cilk-P's runtime system. But what price is paid?

We can pose this question theoretically in terms of a pipeline computation G's ***unthrottled dag***: the dag $\widehat{G} = (V, \widehat{E})$ with the same vertices and edges as G, except without throttling edges. How does adding throttling edges to an unthrottled dag affect span and parallelism?

The following two theorems provide two partial answers to this question. First, for ***uniform*** pipelines, where the cost of a node (i, j) is identical across all iterations i — all stages have the same cost — throttling does not affect the asymptotic performance of PIPER executing $\widehat{G}$.

THEOREM 12. *Consider a uniform unthrottled linear pipeline* $\widehat{G} = (V, \widehat{E})$ *having n iterations and s stages. Suppose that* PIPER *throttles the execution of $\widehat{G}$ on P processors using a window size of $K = aP$, for some constant $a > 1$. Then* PIPER *executes $\widehat{G}$ in time* $T_P \leq (1 + c/a)T_1/P + cT_\infty$ *for some sufficiently large constant c, where T_1 is the total work in $\widehat{G}$ and T_∞ is the span of $\widehat{G}$.* $\square$

Second, we consider ***nonuniform*** pipelines, where the cost of a node (i, j) may vary across iterations. It turns out that nonuniform pipelines can pose performance problems, not only for PIPER, but for any scheduler that throttles the computation. Figure 10 illustrates a pathological nonuniform pipeline for any scheduler that uses throttling. In this dag, T_1 work is distributed across $(T_1^{1/3} + T_1^{2/3})/2$ iterations such that any $T_1^{1/3} + 1$ consecutive iterations consist of 1 ***heavy*** iteration with $T_1^{2/3}$ work and $T_1^{1/3}$ ***light*** iterations of $T_1^{1/3}$ work each. Intuitively, achieving a speedup of 3 on this dag requires having at least 1 heavy iteration and $\Theta(T_1^{1/3})$

light iterations active simultaneously, which is impossible for any scheduler that uses a throttling limit of $K = o(T_1^{1/3})$. The following theorem formalizes this intuition.

THEOREM 13. *Let $\widehat{G} = (V, \widehat{E})$ denote the nonuniform unthrottled linear pipeline shown in Figure 10, with work T_1 and span $T_\infty \leq 2T_1^{2/3}$. Let S_1 denote the optimal stack-space usage when $\widehat{G}$ is executed on 1 processor. Any P-processor execution of $\widehat{G}$ that achieves $T_P \leq T_1/\rho$, where ρ satisfies $3 \leq \rho \leq O(T_1/T_\infty)$, uses space $S_P \geq S_1 + (\rho-3)T_1^{1/3}/2 - 1$.* □

Intuitively, these two theorems present two extremes of the effect of throttling on pipeline dags. One interesting avenue for research is to determine what are the minimum restrictions on the structure of an unthrottled linear pipeline G that would allow a scheduler to achieve parallel speedup on P processors using a throttling limit of only $\Theta(P)$.

12. ACKNOWLEDGMENTS

Thanks to Loren Merritt of x264 LLC and Hank Hoffman of University of Chicago (formerly of MIT CSAIL) for answering questions about *x264*. Thanks to Yungang Bao of Institute of Computing Technology, Chinese Academy of Sciences (formerly of Princeton) for answering questions about the PARSEC benchmark suite. Thanks to Bradley Kuszmaul of MIT CSAIL for tips and insights on file I/O related performance issues. Thanks to Arch Robison of Intel for providing constructive feedback on an early draft of this paper. Thanks to Will Hasenplaugh of MIT CSAIL and Nasro Min-Allah of COMSATS Institute of Information Technology in Pakistan for helpful discussions. We especially thank the reviewers for their thoughtful comments.

13. REFERENCES

[1] K. Agrawal, C. E. Leiserson, and J. Sukha. Executing task graphs using work-stealing. In *IPDPS*, pp. 1–12. IEEE, 2010.

[2] N. S. Arora, R. D. Blumofe, and C. G. Plaxton. Thread scheduling for multiprogrammed multiprocessors. *Theory of Computing Systems*, pp. 115–144, 2001.

[3] H. C. Baker, Jr. and C. Hewitt. The incremental garbage collection of processes. *SIGPLAN Notices*, 12(8):55–59, 1977.

[4] C. Bienia, S. Kumar, J. P. Singh, and K. Li. The PARSEC benchmark suite: Characterization and architectural implications. In *PACT*, pp. 72–81. ACM, 2008.

[5] C. Bienia and K. Li. Characteristics of workloads using the pipeline programming model. In *ISCA*, pp. 161–171. Springer-Verlag, 2010.

[6] G. E. Blelloch and M. Reid-Miller. Pipelining with futures. In *SPAA*, pp. 249–259. ACM, 1997.

[7] R. D. Blumofe and C. E. Leiserson. Space-efficient scheduling of multithreaded computations. *SIAM Journal on Computing*, 27(1):202–229, Feb. 1998.

[8] R. D. Blumofe and C. E. Leiserson. Scheduling multithreaded computations by work stealing. *JACM*, 46(5):720–748, 1999.

[9] R. L. Bocchino, Jr., V. S. Adve, S. V. Adve, and M. Snir. Parallel programming must be deterministic by default. In *First USENIX Conference on Hot Topics in Parallelism*, 2009.

[10] F. W. Burton and M. R. Sleep. Executing functional programs on a virtual tree of processors. In *FPCA*, pp. 187–194. ACM, 1981.

[11] C. Consel, H. Hamdi, L. Réveillère, L. Singaravelu, H. Yu, and C. Pu. Spidle: a DSL approach to specifying streaming applications. In *GPCE*, pp. 1–17. Springer-Verlag, 2003.

[12] T. H. Cormen, C. E. Leiserson, R. L. Rivest, and C. Stein. *Introduction to Algorithms*. The MIT Press, third edition, 2009.

[13] R. Finkel and U. Manber. DIB — A distributed implementation of backtracking. *ACM TOPLAS*, 9(2):235–256, 1987.

[14] D. Friedman and D. Wise. Aspects of applicative programming for parallel processing. *IEEE Transactions on Computers*, C-27(4):289–296, 1978.

[15] M. Frigo, C. E. Leiserson, and K. H. Randall. The implementation of the Cilk-5 multithreaded language. In *PLDI*, pp. 212–223. ACM, 1998.

[16] J. Giacomoni, T. Moseley, and M. Vachharajani. FastForward for efficient pipeline parallelism: A cache-optimized concurrent lock-free queue. In *PPoPP*, pp. 43–52. ACM, 2008.

[17] M. I. Gordon, W. Thies, and S. Amarasinghe. Exploiting coarse-grained task, data, and pipeline parallelism in stream programs. In *ASPLOS*, pp. 151–162. ACM, 2006.

[18] E. A. Hauck and B. A. Dent. Burroughs' B6500/B7500 stack mechanism. *Proceedings of the AFIPS Spring Joint Computer Conference*, pp. 245–251, 1968.

[19] Y. He, C. E. Leiserson, and W. M. Leiserson. The Cilkview scalability analyzer. In *SPAA*, pp. 145–156, 2010.

[20] Intel Corporation. *Intel® Cilk™ Plus Language Extension Specification, Version 1.1*, 2013. Document 324396-002US. Available from http://cilkplus.org/sites/default/files/open_specifications/Intel_Cilk_plus_lang_spec_2.htm.

[21] D. A. Kranz, R. H. Halstead, Jr., and E. Mohr. Mul-T: A high-performance parallel Lisp. In *PLDI*, pp. 81–90. ACM, 1989.

[22] M. Lam. Software pipelining: an effective scheduling technique for VLIW machines. In *PLDI*, pp. 318–328. ACM, 1988.

[23] I.-T. A. Lee, S. Boyd-Wickizer, Z. Huang, and C. E. Leiserson. Using memory mapping to support cactus stacks in work-stealing runtime systems. In *PACT*, pp. 411–420. ACM, 2010.

[24] C. E. Leiserson. The Cilk++ concurrency platform. *J. Supercomputing*, 51(3):244–257, 2010.

[25] S. MacDonald, D. Szafron, and J. Schaeffer. Rethinking the pipeline as object-oriented states with transformations. In *HIPS*, pp. 12 – 21. IEEE, 2004.

[26] W. R. Mark, R. S. Glanville, K. Akeley, and M. J. Kilgard. Cg: a system for programming graphics hardware in a C-like language. In *SIGGRAPH*, pp. 896–907. ACM, 2003.

[27] M. McCool, A. D. Robison, and J. Reinders. *Structured Parallel Programming: Patterns for Efficient Computation*. Elsevier, 2012.

[28] A. Navarro, R. Asenjo, S. Tabik, and C. Caşcaval. Analytical modeling of pipeline parallelism. In *PACT*, pp. 281–290. IEEE, 2009.

[29] *OpenMP Application Program Interface, Version 3.0*, 2008. Available from http://www.openmp.org/mp-documents/spec30.pdf.

[30] G. Ottoni, R. Rangan, A. Stoler, and D. I. August. Automatic thread extraction with decoupled software pipelining. In *MICRO*, pp. 105–118. IEEE, 2005.

[31] A. Pop and A. Cohen. A stream-computing extension to OpenMP. In *HiPEAC*, pp. 5–14. ACM, 2011.

[32] R. Rangan, N. Vachharajani, M. Vachharajani, and D. I. August. Decoupled software pipelining with the synchronization array. In *PACT*, pp. 177–188. ACM, 2004.

[33] E. C. Reed, N. Chen, and R. E. Johnson. Expressing pipeline parallelism using TBB constructs: a case study on what works and what doesn't. In *SPLASH*, pp. 133–138. ACM, 2011.

[34] R. Rojas. Konrad Zuse's legacy: The architecture of the Z1 and Z3. *IEEE Annals of the History of Computing*, 19(2):5–16, Apr. 1997.

[35] D. Sanchez, D. Lo, R. M. Yoo, J. Sugerman, and C. Kozyrakis. Dynamic fine-grain scheduling of pipeline parallelism. In *PACT*, pp. 22–32. IEEE, 2011.

[36] B. Stroustrup. *The C++ Programming Language*. Addison-Wesley, fourth edition, 2013.

[37] M. A. Suleman, M. K. Qureshi, Khubaib, and Y. N. Patt. Feedback-directed pipeline parallelism. In *PACT*, pp. 147–156. ACM, 2010.

[38] W. Thies, V. Chandrasekhar, and S. Amarasinghe. A practical approach to exploiting coarse-grained pipeline parallelism in C programs. In *MICRO*, pp. 356–369. IEEE, 2007.

[39] T. Wiegand, G. J. Sullivan, G. Bjøntegaard, and A. Luthra. Overview of the H.264/AVC video coding standard. *IEEE Transactions on Circuits and Systems for Video Technology*, 13(7):560–576, 2003.

Reducing Contention Through Priority Updates

Julian Shun
Carnegie Mellon University
jshun@cs.cmu.edu

Guy E. Blelloch
Carnegie Mellon University
guyb@cs.cmu.edu

Jeremy T. Fineman
Georgetown University
jfineman@cs.georgetown.edu

Phillip B. Gibbons
Intel Labs, Pittsburgh
phillip.b.gibbons@intel.com

ABSTRACT

Memory contention can be a serious performance bottleneck in concurrent programs on shared-memory multicore architectures. Having all threads write to a small set of shared locations, for example, can lead to orders of magnitude loss in performance relative to all threads writing to distinct locations, or even relative to a single thread doing all the writes. Shared write access, however, can be very useful in parallel algorithms, concurrent data structures, and protocols for communicating among threads.

We study the "priority update" operation as a useful primitive for limiting write contention in parallel and concurrent programs. A *priority update* takes as arguments a memory location, a new value, and a comparison function $>_p$ that enforces a partial order over values. The operation atomically compares the new value with the current value in the memory location, and writes the new value only if it has *higher priority* according to $>_p$. On the implementation side, we show that if implemented appropriately, priority updates greatly reduce memory contention over standard writes or other atomic operations when locations have a high degree of sharing. This is shown both experimentally and theoretically. On the application side, we describe several uses of priority updates for implementing parallel algorithms and concurrent data structures, often in a way that is deterministic, guarantees progress, and avoids serial bottlenecks. We present experiments showing that a variety of such algorithms and data structures perform well under high degrees of sharing. Given the results, we believe that the priority update operation serves as a useful parallel primitive and good programming abstraction as (1) the user largely need not worry about the degree of sharing, (2) it can be used to avoid non-determinism since, in the common case when $>_p$ is a total order, priority updates commute, and (3) it has many applications to programs using shared data.

Categories and Subject Descriptors: D.1.3 [Programming Techniques]: Concurrent Programming—*Parallel programming*

Keywords: Memory Contention, Parallel Programming

1. INTRODUCTION

When programming algorithms and applications on shared memory machines, contention in accessing shared data structures is often a major source of performance problems. The problems can be particularly severe when there is a high degree of sharing of data among threads. With naive data structures the performance issues are typically due to contention over locks. Lock-free data structures alleviate the contention, but such solutions only partially solve issues of contention because even the simplest lock free shared write access to a single memory location can create severe performance problems. For example, simply having all threads write to a small set of shared locations can lead to orders of magnitude loss in performance relative to writing to distinct locations. The problem is caused by coherence protocols that require each thread to acquire the cache line in exclusive mode to update a location; this cycling of the cache line through the caches incurs significant overhead—far greater than even the cost of having a single thread perform all of the writes. The performance is even worse when using operations such as a compare-and-swap to atomically update shared locations.

To avoid these issues, researchers have suggested a variety of approaches to reduce the cost of memory contention. One approach is to use *contention-aware schedulers* [26, 11] that seek to avoid co-scheduling threads likely to contend for resources. For many algorithms, however, high degrees of sharing cannot be avoided via scheduling choices. A second approach is to use *hardware combining*, in which concurrent associative operations on the same memory location can be "combined" on their way through the memory system [13, 12, 9, 3]. Multiple writes to a location, for example, can be combined by dropping all but one write. No current machines, however, support hardware combining. A third approach is to use *software combining* based on techniques such as combining funnels [22] or diffracting trees [21, 8]. These approaches tend to be complicated and have significant overhead, because a single operation is implemented by multiple accesses that traverse the shared combining structure. In cases where the contending operations are (atomic) updates to a shared data structure, more recent work has shown that having a single combiner thread perform the updates greatly reduces the overheads [14, 10]. This approach, however, does not scale in general. A fourth approach *partitions* the memory among the threads such that each location (more specifically, each cache line) can be written by only a single thread. This avoids the cycling-of-cachelines problem: Each cache line alternates between the designated writer and a set of parallel readers. Such partitioning, however, severely limits the sorts of algorithms that can be used. Finally, the *test and test-and-set* operation can be used to significantly reduce contention in some settings [20, 16, 18, 17]. While contention can still arise from multiple threads attempting to initially set the location, any subsequent thread will see the location set during its "test" and drop out without performing a test-and-set. This operation has limited applicability, however, so our aim is to identify a more generally applicable operation with the same contention-reducing benefits.

Throughout the paper we will use the term *sharing* to indicate that a location is shared among many parallel operations, and *contention* to indicate a performance problem due to such sharing.

Priority Update. In this paper we study a generalization of the test-and-set operation, which we call *priority update*. A *priority update* takes as arguments a memory location, a new value, and a $>_p$ function that enforces a partial order over values. The operation atomically compares the new value with the current value in the memory location, and writes the new value only if it has *higher priority* according to $>_p$. At any (quiescent) time a location will contain the highest priority value written to it so far. A test-and-set is a special case of priority update over two values—the location initially holds 0, the new value to be written is 1, and 1 has a higher priority than 0. Another special case is the *write-with-min* over integers, where the minimum value written has priority. The priority update, however, can also be used when values do not fit in a hardware "word". For example the values could be character strings represented as pointers to the string stored in a memory word, or complex structures where a subfield is compared. The operation is therefore more general than what could be reasonably expected to be implemented in hardware.

We provide evidence that the priority update operation serves as a good abstraction for programmers of shared memory machines because it is useful in many applications on shared data (often in a way that is deterministic, guarantees progress, and avoids serial bottlenecks), and when implemented appropriately (see below) performs reasonably well under any degree of sharing. This latter point is illustrated in Figure 1. Each data point represents the time for 5 runs of 10^8 operations each on a 40-core machine. The x-axis gives the number of distinct locations being operated on—hence the leftmost point is when all operations are on the same location and at the right the graph approaches no sharing. (More details on the setup and further experimental comparisons are described in Section 3.1.) As can be seen, when there is a high degree of sharing (e.g., only 8 locations) the read, the test-and-set, and the priority update (with random values) are all over two orders of magnitude faster than the other operations. One would expect the read to do well because the cache lines can be shared. Similarly the test-and-set does well because it can be implemented using a test and test-and-set (as described above) so that under a high degree of sharing only the early operations will attempt to set a location, and the rest will access the already set location in shared mode.

The priority update can be implemented in software with a read, a local comparison, and a compare-and-swap. The compare-and-swap is needed only when the value being written is smaller than the existing value. Thus, when applied

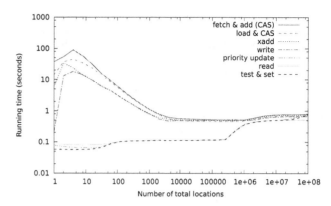

Figure 1. Impact of sharing on a variety of operations. Times are for 5 runs of 100 million operations to varying number of memory locations on a 40-core Intel Nehalem (log-log scale). Since the number of operations is fixed, fewer locations implies more operations sharing those locations.

with random values (or in a random order) most invocations of priority update only *read* shared data, which is why the running time nearly matches the read curve, and is effectively the same as the test-and-set curve. The curve shows that the high sharing case is actually the best case for a priority update. This implies the user need not worry about contention, although, as with reads, the user might still need to worry about the memory footprint and whether it fits in cache—the steps in the curve arise each time the number of locations no longer fits within a cache at a particular level.

Applications of Priority Updates. Priority updates have many applications. Here we outline several such applications and go into significantly more detail in Sections 4 and 5. The operation can be used directly within an algorithm to take the minimum or maximum of a set of values, but it also has several other important properties. Due to the fact that the operation is commutative [25, 24] (order does not matter) in the common case when $>_p$ is a total order, it can often be used to avoid non-determinism when sharing data. By assigning threads unique priorities it can also be used to guarantee (good) progress by making sure at least the highest priority thread for each location succeeds in a protocol.

Priority updates are used in a recently introduced technique called *deterministic reservations* to implement a speculative for-loop [1]. The idea is to give each iteration of the loop a priority based on its iteration number (earlier iterates have higher priority). Then any prefix of the iteration space can be executed in parallel such that when accessing any data that might be shared by other iterations, the iteration "reserves" the shared data using a priority update. A second "commit" phase is used to check whether the iteration has "won" on all the data it shares and if so proceeds with any updates to the global shared state. The approach has the advantage that it guarantees the same order of execution of the iterates as in the sequential order. Furthermore, it guarantees progress since at least the earliest iterate will always succeed (and often many iterates succeed in parallel, if different locations are used).

Priority updates have applications in many graph algorithms. They can be used in parallel versions of both Boruvka's and Kruskal's minimum spanning forest algorithms to select minimum-weight edges. They can be used in single-source shortest paths to update the neighbors of a vertex with the potentially shorter path. They can also be used in certain graph algorithms to guarantee determinism. In particular any conflicts can be broken using priorities so that they are always broken in the same way. For example, in breadth-first search (BFS), it can be used to deterministically generate a BFS tree.

Priority updates on locations can also be used to efficiently implement a more general dictionary-based priority update where the "locations" are based on keys. Each insert consists of a key-value pair, and updates the data associated with the key if either the key does not appear in the dictionary or the new value has higher priority.

In this paper we describe these algorithms and present experimental results. We study the performance of several of these algorithms including BFS, Kruskal's minimum spanning forest algorithm, a maximal matching algorithm and a dictionary-based remove duplicates algorithm. We present timing results for inputs with high sharing, and for BFS and remove duplicates, we compare timings with versions that use writes instead of priority updates.

Contributions. In summary, the main contributions of this paper are as follows. First, this paper generalizes and unifies special cases of priority update operations from the literature, and is the first to call out priority update as a key primitive in ensuring that having many threads updating a few locations does not result in cache/memory system performance problems. Second, we provide the first comprehensive experimental study of priority update vs. other widely-used operations under varying degrees of sharing, demonstrating up to orders of magnitude differences on modern multicores from both Intel and AMD. We also present the first analytic justification for priority update's good performance. Third, we present several examples of algorithms for a number of important problems that demonstrate a variety of ways to benefit from priority updates. Finally, we present the first experimental study demonstrating the (good) performance of priority update algorithms on inputs that result in a high degree of write sharing, extending the study in [1] by considering a wider range of degrees of sharing, running on more cores, and providing a comparison to implementations using alternative primitives.

2. PRIORITY UPDATES

A *priority update* takes as arguments a memory location containing a value of type T, a new value of type T to write, and a binary comparison function $>_p : T \times T \to bool$ that enforces a partial order over values. The priority update atomically compares the two values and replaces the current value with the new value if the new value has higher priority according to $>_p$. It does not return a value. In the simplest form, called a *write-with-min* (or write-with-max), T is a number type, and the comparison function is standard numeric less-than (or greater-than). Our implementation below, however, allows T to be an arbitrary type with an arbitrary comparison function. When $>_p$ defines a total order over T, priority updates commute—i.e., the value ending up in the location will be the same independent of the ordering of the updates.

A priority update can be implemented as shown in Figure 2 using a compare-and-swap (CAS). Because CAS (on

---

procedure PRIORITYUPDATE($addr, newval, >_p$)
    $oldval \leftarrow *addr$
    while ($newval >_p oldval$) **do**
      if CAS($addr, oldval, newval$) **then**
        return
      else
        $oldval \leftarrow *addr$

Figure 2. Priority Update Implementation.

---

a single word, or sometimes a double length word) is provided as a hardware atomic on modern machines, no new hardware primitives are required. If the value does not "fit" in a word, one can use a pointer to the actual data being compared (pointers certainly fit in a word), so the implementation can easily be applied to a variety of types (e.g., structures with one of the fields being compared, variable-length character strings with lexicographic comparison, or even more complex structures). One should distinguish the comparison function $>_p$ defining the partial order over the values from the "compare" in compare-and-swap, which is a comparison for equality and is applied to the indirect representation of the value (e.g., the bits in the pointer) and not the abstract type. We assume the object is not mutated during the operation so that equality of the indirect representation (pointer) implies equality of the abstract value.

In the best case, the given implementation of priority update completes immediately after a single application of the comparison function, determining that the value already stored in the location has higher priority than the new value. Otherwise an *update attempt* occurs with the compare-and-swap operation. (Because our implementation uses CAS to attempt an update, we will also refer to this as a **CAS attempt**.) If successful, we say that an **update** occurs. If not, the priority update retries, completing only when the value currently stored has an equal or higher priority than the new value, or when a successful update occurs.

As noted earlier, a test-and-set is a special case of priority update over two values. A **write-once** operation is another special case of a priority update where the contents of a location starts in an "empty" state and once one value is written to the location, making it "full", no future values will overwrite it. As with test-and-set there are just two priorities—empty and full. A third special case is the priority write from the PRAM literature [15]—a synchronous concurrent write from the processors that resolves writes to a common location by taking the value from the highest (or lowest) numbered processor. This can be implemented by using pointers to (processor number, value) pairs: *addr* contains a pointer to the current pair, *newval* is a pointer to a new pair, and $>_p$ chases the two pointers and compares the processor numbers. We note that both test-and-sets and PRAM-style priority writes commute because the values form a total order, but that write-once operations do not because there are many values with equal priority and the first one that arrives is written.

Although the version of priority update we described does not return a value, it is easy to extend it to return the old value stored in the location. Indeed in one of our applications we can make use of this feature.

3. CONTENTION IN SHARED MEMORY OPERATIONS

In this paper we distinguish between sharing and contention. By *sharing* we mean operations that share the same memory location (or possibly other resource)—for example, a set of instructions reading a single location. By *contention* we mean some form of sequential access to a resource that causes a bottleneck. Contention can be a major source of performance problems on parallel systems while sharing need not be. A key motivation for the priority update operation is to reduce contention under a high degree of sharing.

Although contention can be a problem in any system with sequential access to a shared resource, the problem is amplified for memory updates on cache coherent shared memory machines because of the need to acquire a cache line in exclusive mode. In the widely used MESI (Modified, Exclusive, Shared, Invalid) protocol [19] and its variants, a read can acquire a cache line in shared mode and any number of other caches can simultaneously acquire the line. Concurrent reads to shared locations therefore tend to be reasonably efficient. In fact since most machines support some form of snooping, reading a value that is in another cache can be faster than reading from memory.

On the other hand, in the MESI protocol (and other similar protocols implemented on current multicores) concurrent writes can be very inefficient. In particular the protocol requires that a cache line be acquired in exclusive mode before making an update to a memory location. This involves invalidating all copies in other caches and waiting for the invalidates to complete. If a set of caches simultaneously make an update request for a location (or even different locations within a line) then the cache line will need to be acquired in exclusive mode by the caches one at a time, doing a dance around the machine. The cost of each acquisition is high because it involves communicating with the cache that has the line in exclusive or modified state, waiting for it to complete its operation, getting a copy of the newly updated line, and updating any tables that keep track of ownership. If the cores make a sequence of requests to a small set of locations then all requests could be rotating through the caches. Because of the cost of the protocol, this can be much more expensive than simply having one core do all the writes. On a system with just 8 cores this can be a serious performance bottleneck, and on one with 40 cores it can be crippling, as the experiments later in this section demonstrate.

If there are a mix of read and write requests to a shared location then the efficiency will fall between the all-read and all-write cases, depending on the ratio of reads to writes as well as more specifics about how the protocol is implemented. Our experiments show that for this case there is actually a significant difference in performance between the protocols implemented on the AMD Opteron and the Intel Nehalem multicores.

In this section we study the cost of write sharing among caches (cores) on modern multicores. Along with other operations, we study the cost of a priority update and give both experimental evidence (Section 3.1) and theoretical justification (Section 3.2) of its efficiency.

3.1 Experimental Measurements of Contention

We study the cost of contention under varying degrees of sharing on two contemporary shared memory multicores (from Intel and AMD) for a variety of memory operations—priority update (using write-with-min), test-and-set, fetch-and-add using CAS, fetch-and-add using the x86 assembly instruction `xadd`, load-and-CAS, (plain) write, and read[1]. We compare the performance of priority update (write-with-min) when values are random versus when values arrive in a decreasing order (the worst case). We also study the performance of priority update where the comparison is on character strings.

The Intel machine that we use is a 40-core (with hyperthreading) Nehalem-EX machine with 4×2.4GHz Intel 10-core E7-8870 Xeon processors and 256GB of main memory. The AMD machine that we use is a 64-core machine with 4×2.4GHz AMD 16-core Opteron 6278 processors and 188GB of main memory. The programs on the Intel machine were compiled with Intel's `icpc` compiler (version 12.1.0, which supports Cilk Plus) with the `-O3` flag. The programs on the AMD machine were compiled using the `g++` compiler (version 4.8.0 which supports Cilk Plus) with the `-O2` flag.

In the experiments, we perform 10^8 operations on a varying number of random locations. On each machine we performed two sets of experiments. The first set of experiments choose the locations randomly in $[0, x)$ where x is the total number of locations written to and locations 0 through x appear contiguously in memory. The second set of experiments choose the locations randomly from $\{h(i) : i \in [0, x)\}$ where $h(i)$ is a hash function that maps i to an integer in $[0, 10^8)$. In the first set of experiments, there will be high false sharing due to concurrent writing to locations on the same cache line. The second set is supposed to represent what we view as a more common usage of priority update, which is a set of writes to a potentially large set of locations but for which there is heavy load at a few locations. There is significantly less effect of false sharing in the second set since the heavily loaded locations are unlikely to be on the same cache line.

Figure 3(a) shows that with high sharing (low number of total locations) and high false sharing, priority update outperforms plain write, both versions of fetch-and-add, and load-and-CAS by orders of magnitude. Due to an Intel anomaly (see the Appendix), there is a spike in the running time for priority update between 256 and 8192 locations, but even with this anomaly, priority update still outperforms plain write, fetch-and-add and load-and-CAS by an order of magnitude. This anomaly disappears when we reduce the false sharing effect, as shown in Figure 3(b). Figure 3(b), which is a repeat of Figure 1, also shows that the performance of priority update is very close to the performance of both test-and-set and read. For writing to 10^8 locations (the lowest degree of sharing), priority update is slightly slower than fetch-and-add, and test-and-set is slightly slower than write (even though intuitively fetch-and-add does more work than priority update and write does more work than test-and-set). We conjecture this behavior to be due to the branch in both priority update and test-and-set obstructing speculation on the hardware compare-and-swap instruction. We note that `xadd` is consistently faster than implementing a fetch-and-add with a CAS, because the CAS could fail. Also, we noticed that `xadd` performs about the same as a CAS without a load. Preliminary experiments on a new 32-core Intel Sandy Bridge machine yielded results that were qualitatively similar to Figures 3(a) and 3(b).

---

[1]The read includes a write to local memory to get around compiler optimizations.

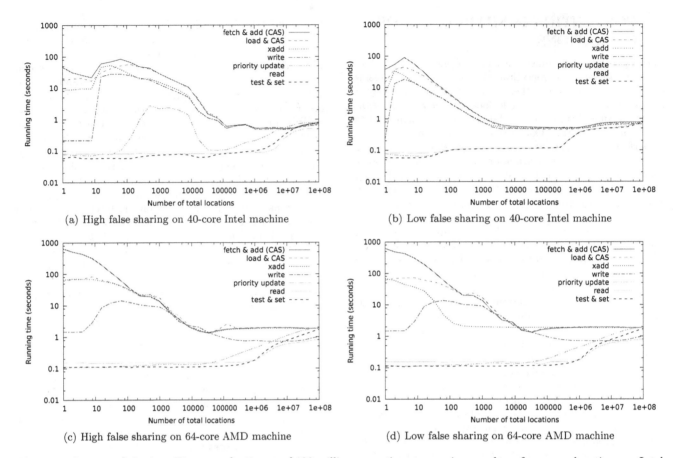

(a) High false sharing on 40-core Intel machine

(b) Low false sharing on 40-core Intel machine

(c) High false sharing on 64-core AMD machine

(d) Low false sharing on 64-core AMD machine

Figure 3. Impact of sharing. Times are for 5 runs of 100 million operations to varying number of memory locations on Intel and AMD machines. under high and low degrees of false sharing (log-log scale). Since the number of operations is fixed, fewer locations implies more operations sharing those locations.

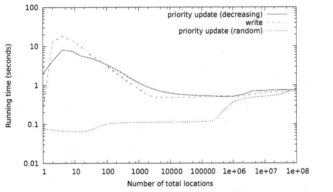

Figure 4. Comparing priority update (write-with-min) on random values vs. decreasing values. Times are for 5 runs of 100 million operations to varying number of memory locations with low false sharing on the 40-core Intel machine (log-log scale).

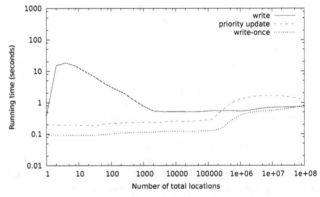

Figure 5. Priority update on character strings based on trigram distribution of the English language. Times are for 5 runs of 100 million operations to varying number of memory locations with low false sharing on the 40-core Intel machine (log-log scale).

Figures 3(c) and 3(d) show the same two experiments on the AMD machine. Note that even with high false sharing, the anomaly for the priority update operation observed for the Intel machine does not appear for the AMD machine. Except for this anomaly, the performance on the Intel machine is better than the performance on the AMD machine.

Note that for priority update, the relative order of values over time greatly impacts the number of update attempts

and hence the cost. In the above experiments, the priority update uses random values, which is also the setting studied in our theoretical analysis. The worst case is when the values have increasing priorities over time, as this incurs the most update attempts. With write-with-min, for example, this case arises when values occur in decreasing order. Figure 4 shows that the performance of this case (labeled "priority update (decreasing)") is much worse than the random case.

Figure 5 shows the performance of priority update, where the comparison is on character strings based on the trigram distribution of the English language (the *trigrams* input in Section 5). This uses the more general form of priority update as the comparison function requires dereferencing the pointers to the strings. We also compare the performance to using plain writes and write-once to update the values at the shared locations. Note that no pointer dereferencing needs to be done in these versions—plain write just overwrites the pointer at the location, and write-once writes the pointer to the location only if it is empty. Similar to the performance on integer values shown in Figure 3, the performance of the version using plain writes is an order of magnitude worse than the priority update and write-once versions. The write-once version is faster than the priority update version, and the gap is more significant here (compared to priority update vs. test-and-set in Figure 3) due to the cost of pointer dereferencing in the priority update.

3.2 Priority Update Performance Guarantees

As discussed in Section 2, priority update is a further generalization of the test-and-set and write-once operations. Unlike those operations, in a priority update a value can change multiple times instead of just once. However, if the ordering of operations is randomized, then our analysis shows that the number of updates is small, with most invocations only reading the shared data. We begin with a straightforward analysis of sequential updates and then extend the analysis to a collection of parallel priority updates. There are two main challenges in the parallel analysis: developing a cost model that reasonably captures the read/write asymmetry in the coherence protocol, and coping with the fact that different access delays cause operations to fall out of sync.

In this section we consider priority update operations where $>_p$ defines a total order over the value domain T. Values can be repeated, so that the number of operations n can be much larger than the number of priorities or the size of T. We say that a collection of priority update operations has ϕ **occurring priorities** if the values in those operations fall into exactly ϕ distinct priorities according to $>_p$.

We begin with the simplest case of a sequence of priority updates, performed in random order. Here, all update attempts succeed as there are no concurrent CAS operations. This simple lemma shows that the value stored in the location is updated very few times.

LEMMA 1. *Consider a random sequential ordering on a collection of priority update operations to a single location, with ϕ occurring priorities. Then H_ϕ updates occur in expectation and $O(\ln \phi)$ updates occur with high probability (in ϕ), where $H_i \approx \ln i$ is the ith harmonic number.*

PROOF. Let S be the subsequence of priority updates that are the first occurrences in the original sequence of a distinct priority—these are the only operations that could possibly perform an update. Let X_k be an indicator for the event that the kth operation in S performs an update. Then $X_k = 1$ with probability $\frac{1}{k}$, as it updates only if its priority is the highest among the first k operations in S. The expected number of updates is then given by $E[X_1 + \cdots + X_\phi] = E[X_1] + \cdots + E[X_\phi] = \frac{1}{1} + \frac{1}{2} + \frac{1}{3} + \cdots + \frac{1}{\phi} = H_\phi$. Applying a Chernoff bound gives a high probability result. □

We generalize Lemma 1 to provide bounds on the runtime when performing priority updates in parallel under two models. In either model, we assume that if multiple concurrent CAS'es are executing an update attempt, the one that "wins" and successfully updates the value is independent of the data being written. We also assume that the comparison function $>_p$ takes constant time, although our analysis can be easily extended to non-constant time comparison functions.

We assume that a collection of n priority updates are ordered[2] and have values corresponding to a random permutation of the set $\{1, \ldots, n\}$, with 1 being the highest priority and each location initialized to a special lowest-priority value ∞. This is equivalent to randomly ordering the priority updates and then assigning each value to its relative rank in the total order. While we assume the values are distinct, the bounds can be readily sharpened to take into account the actual number of occurring priorities, as in Lemma 1. Note that the actual values of the priority updates do not matter, as long as the order of the priority updates is randomized.

Our models are based around a simplified cache-coherence protocol, where a cache line can be in invalid, shared, or exclusive mode. A core performing a CAS requests the relevant cache line in exclusive mode, thereby invalidating the line in all other caches, and performs the CAS.[3] When reading a cache line that is invalid in the local cache, the core first requests the line in shared mode then performs the read. We charge a constant time of c for acquiring the line in either mode, but some acquisitions may serialize due to conflicts depending on which model we adopt.

In the **fair model**, we view outstanding cache-line requests to a particular memory location as ordered in a queue. New requests are added to the end of the queue. When a CAS (exclusive request) is serviced, no other operations may proceed. When a read is processed, all other reads before the next CAS in the queue may be serviced in parallel, and if the cache line is modified, c time is charged for acquiring the line (the first reader puts the line in shared mode).

In the **adversarial model**, operations are not queued. Instead, an adversary may arbitrarily order any outstanding CAS and read operations (e.g., based on the locations being written), but without considering the values being written.

3.2.1 Bounds for the Fair Model

To analyze priority updates to a single location in the fair model, we view operations as being processed in rounds induced by the queue ordering. Each round processes p operations, one per core, which may be either of the two steps of a priority update: a read or a CAS.[4] More precisely, let v_j denote the value stored at the start of round j. For any core performing the read step, we pessimistically assume that it observes the value v_j. The core then compares its value to v_j, and commits to either performing a CAS in round $j + 1$ or skipping the CAS attempt step and proceeding to the

---

[2] Cores have disjoint subsequences of this ordering, determined at runtime by the scheduler.

[3] To clarify, once a core is granted exclusive mode, our model assumes that the CAS completes immediately. A priority update, however, consists of two steps—a read and a CAS—and while the line could be invalidated in between those two steps, our experiments on both Intel Nehalem and AMD Opteron multicores support assuming it is not.

[4] Here, we assume the type fits in a word. The analysis readily extends to the more general case where $>_p$ must chase pointers.

next operation (i.e., issuing another read). Since a CAS in round $j + 1$ is based on the value observed in round j, there is at most 1 successful CAS per round. All reads between consecutive CAS attempts complete in c time, so we can charge those reads against the preceding CAS attempt. The goal is to bound the number of unsuccessful CAS attempts.

We have $v_1 = \infty$ initially. Every core issues a read in round 1, compares its value against ∞, and then issues a CAS in round 2 comparing against $v_1 = \infty$. Because the CAS attempts are serialized, the time to complete round 2 is $\Theta(cp)$. Exactly one core (the first one in the queue) succeeds in round 2, so the value v_3 observed at the start of round 3 is one drawn uniformly at random from $\{1, \ldots, n\}$.

LEMMA 2. *The expected total time for performing n randomly ordered priority updates to a single location using p cores under the fair model is $O(\frac{n}{p} + c \ln n + cp)$.*

PROOF. By Lemma 1, there are $O(\ln n)$ successful updates, so the goal is to bound the number of unsuccessful CAS attempts. We start by bounding the number of priority updates that include at least one failed CAS.

An unsuccessful CAS occurs only if a successful CAS is made in the same or preceding round (which is bounded by $O(\ln n)$ in Lemma 1). We call **phase i** the set of rounds during which a) the value stored in the location falls between $\frac{n}{2^{i-1}}$ and $\frac{n}{2^i}$ (recall that we are assuming values are the relative ranks), and b) a successful CAS occurs. We want to bound the number of new priority updates during these rounds that perform a (failed) CAS attempt. First, observe that phase i consists of $O(1)$ rounds in expectation, as each successful update has probability $\frac{1}{2}$ of reducing the value below the threshold of $\frac{n}{2^i}$. Moreover, in each of these rounds, each core has probability at most $\frac{1}{2^{i-1}}$ of performing a priority update of a value below $\frac{n}{2^{i-1}}$. Summing across all cores and all rounds in the phase, the expected number of (failed) priority updates during phase i is at most $O(\frac{p}{2^{i-1}})$. Summing across all phases, the total number of such failed priority updates is $O(p)$.

A failed priority update may retry several times, but a random failed update has probability $\frac{1}{2}$ of retrying through each subsequent phase because the value stored at the location is halved. Thus, there are an expected $O(1)$ retries per priority update that make any CAS attempt. Combining with the above, we get $O(p)$ unsuccessful CAS attempts.

We charge c for each of the $O(\ln n)$ successful and $O(p)$ unsuccessful CAS's. As for the reads, any of the reads that must reacquire a cache line (taking c time) can be charged to the preceding CAS attempt, only doubling the time. The first read takes c time, and the remaining reads and all local computation take $O(\frac{n}{p})$ time, completing the proof. $\square$

The above results are for performing priority updates to a single location. Now we analyze the time for *multiple locations* where cores apply operations to locations chosen uniformly at random from $\{1, \ldots, m\}$, where m is the number of locations. Let n_i be the number of operations at the ith location. Here, we assume that all locations can fit simultaneously in cache and that there are no false-sharing effects. The difficulty here is that the round analysis only applies to each individual location—the model has a separate queue for each location, and simply multiplying the CAS-components of the bound by m is too pessimistic.

THEOREM 3. *The expected total time for performing n randomly ordered priority updates to m randomly chosen locations under the fair model is $O(\frac{n}{p} + cm \ln(\frac{n}{m}) + (cp)^2)$.*

PROOF. According to the analysis of Lemma 2, there are at most $O(\ln(n_i) + p)$ CAS attempts when p cores perform $O(n_i)$ updates to location i. Increasing the number of locations only decreases the number of CAS failures, since not all cores choose the same location. So a bound of $O(\frac{n}{p} + cm \ln(\frac{n}{m}) + cpm)$ follows by maximizing the logarithmic term (setting $n_i = \frac{n}{m}$ for all i) and multiplying by m locations. This bound is pessimistic, so we will improve it for $m > p$. The $O(cm \ln(\frac{n}{m}))$ term seems inherent because each update invalidates the line in all other caches, so the time to reload those lines later is $O(cpm \ln(\frac{n}{m}))$ (which is divided across p cores). Our goal is to reduce the $O(cpm)$ term.

Consider the round analysis as in Lemma 2 applied to a single location. The main question is how many (unsuccessful) CAS'es are launched on this location during a round containing a successful CAS. The maximum duration of a round is $O(cp)$ if every core performs a CAS attempt. Each core may thus sample up to $O(cp)$ locations within a round (each sample is independent from the rest), giving a probability of $O(\frac{cp}{m})$ of choosing this location in any of those attempts. Summing across all cores, the expected number of priority updates to this location per round is $O(\frac{cp^2}{m})$, only some of which may actually perform a CAS attempt. As in Lemma 2, the likelihood of performing a CAS attempt decreases geometrically per phase, so the total number of failed CAS'es on this location is $O(\frac{cp^2}{m})$. Summing across all locations gives $O(cp^2)$ failed attempts, each taking c time. $\square$

3.2.2 Bounds for the Adversarial Model

We now analyze priority updates under the adversarial model. Recall that in the adversarial model, an adversary may order any outstanding CAS and read operations arbitrarily (e.g., based on the locations being written), but without considering the actual values being written.

LEMMA 4. *The total time for performing n randomly ordered priority updates to a single location using p cores under the adversarial model is $O(\frac{n}{p} + cp \ln n)$ with high probability.*

PROOF. By Lemma 1, the number of random updates is $O(\ln n)$ with high probability. We now prove the number of attempts is at most $O(p \ln n)$, which implies the lemma. We say that a CAS fails due to the ith update if the old value conditioned on in the CAS is that of the $(i-1)$th update. There can be at most 1 CAS failure due to the ith update on each core, as any subsequent priority update on the same core would read the ith update and hence only fail due to a later update. There can thus be at most $p - 1$ CAS failures per update, for a total of $O(p \ln n)$ CAS attempts. $\square$

In the adversarial model, the bound of Lemma 4 generalizes to $O(\frac{n}{p} + cpm \ln(\frac{n}{m}))$—for n operations the time for reads is still $O(\frac{n}{p})$; now each location i can take $O(cp \ln(n_i))$ time, leading to a total contribution of $O(\sum_{i=1}^{m} cp \ln(n_i))$ which is maximized when $n_i = \frac{n}{m}$ for all i.

THEOREM 5. *The total time for performing n randomly ordered priority updates to m randomly chosen locations under the adversarial model is $O(\frac{n}{p} + cpm \ln(\frac{n}{m}))$ with high probability.*

For reasonably sized n, the bounds in this section (under both models) are much better than the bounds for operations that always have to access a cache line in exclusive mode. Such operations will run in $O(cn)$ at best assuming either the fair or adversarial model—all accesses will be sequentialized and will involve a cache miss.

4. APPLICATIONS OF PRIORITY UPDATE

Priority updates are well-suited to a widely applicable two-phase programming style, which we call *update-and-read* in its general form, and *reserve-and-commit* in a special case. An **update-and-read** program alternates two types of phases. During an *update* phase, multiple update attempts occur on some collection of objects, using either a priority update, a plain write, or another write primitive. During the subsequent *read* phase, the value that was successfully recorded is read. Using priority updates or write-once operations during the update phase is desirable to achieve better performance (see Section 5). Moreover, the commutative nature of priority updates implies that the values stored at completion of the read phase are deterministic.

When operating on a collection of interacting objects (e.g., vertices of a graph), where each object seeks to update a "neighborhood" of objects, a **reserve-and-commit** style is more appropriate. In the *reserve* (update) phase, each object in parallel attempts to reserve the neighborhood of objects that it would read from or write to. In the *commit* (read) phase, each object in parallel checks whether it holds a reservation on its neighborhood, and if so, performs the desired operations. There should be a synchronization point between the reserve and commit phases, guaranteeing that commits and reserves cannot occur concurrently with each other. Since reservations are exclusive (indeed reservations are acting as mutual-exclusion locks), this approach guarantees that each commit behaves atomically. As with the generic update-and-read, the reservations can be implemented using either a priority update, write-once or plain write. The priority update is more desirable both for performance and to guarantee forward progress when multiple objects are reserved.

If used correctly and employing a priority update, this reserve-and-commit style can be thought of as a special case of transactional programming, but one in which forward progress guarantees are possible. The reserve phase essentially speculatively attempts a "transaction," and the commit phase commits transactions that do not interfere. By using priority updates, there is a total order over reservations, guaranteeing that at least one reserver (i.e., the one with the highest priority) is able to commit. This forward-progress guarantee does not apply when using a plain write or a write-once, as it is possible that no reserver "wins" on all of its neighbors.

The technique of **deterministic reservations** [1] extends this reserve-and-commit abstraction to an entire parallel loop. In this technique, a sequence of iterates are considered in parallel, and the reservations are made using priority updates according to the iterates' ranks in the sequence. In the commit phase, iterates that successfully reserved their neighborhoods perform their commit operation. All uncommitted iterates are gathered, and this process repeats until no iterates remain. Deterministic reservations has several appealing features [1]. First, the behavior is consistent with a sequential execution of the loop, so the results are deterministic. Second, the performance can be tuned by operating on a prefix of the sequence: a smaller prefix decreases data sharing thereby decreasing total work, whereas a larger prefix may allow more parallelism [2]. Third, since the reservations themselves are based on iterate priorities, some forward progress is guaranteed in each round.

Note that because the highest priority update succeeds for *each* location, priority updates often enable considerable *parallel* progress in each update-and-read phase, yielding good parallel speed-ups (see Section 5). For example, with deterministic reservations, often $\Omega(p)$ iterates succeed in parallel.

The remainder of this section describes several algorithms that use priority update, most of which employ some form of update-and-read. The exception is connected components, where a priority update is used to asynchronously update values. In some of these cases (e.g., breadth-first-search and maximal matching), several write primitives maintain correctness of the algorithms and priority updates are just desirable for performance. In others (e.g., connected components, minimum spanning forest, and single-source shortest paths), the priority update is necessary for correctness of the given algorithm.

Breadth-First Search. The **breadth-first search** (BFS) problem takes as input an undirected graph G and a source vertex r and returns a breadth-first-search tree represented by an array of parent pointers. The BFS algorithm proceeds in rounds, during which all vertices on the frontier (initialized to contain only the source vertex) attempt to place all of their neighbors on the next frontier. Our experiments use modifications of the BFS implementations from the publicly available problem-based benchmark suite (PBBS) [23]. To guarantee that each vertex is added only once, each round is implemented with an update-and-read style. During the update phase, a frontier vertex writes its ID to its neighbors. During the read phase, each frontier vertex checks to see if successfully reserved its neighbor, and if so it adds the neighbor to the next frontier. Since only one frontier vertex will successfully reserve a neighbor, there will be no duplicates on the next frontier.

This BFS algorithm may be correctly implemented by using priority updates (write-with-min), write-once, or plain writes, with plain writes being less efficient (see Section 5) and priority updates guaranteeing a deterministic BFS-tree output [1].

We also use a version of deterministic BFS that has only one phase per round and returns the same BFS tree as a sequential implementation. This version uses a priority update on pairs $(index, parent)$, where $index$ is a vertex's parent's order in a sequential BFS traversal, and $parent$ is the vertex's parent's ID. The priority update does a min-comparison only on the $index$ field of the pair. All frontier vertices perform priority updates to neighbors and if it successfully updates the neighbor's location, it adds the neighbor to the next frontier in the same phase. Since this implementation only has a single phase, it allows for duplicate vertices on the frontier (multiple priority updates may succeed on the same neighbor). The form of priority update used here is more general than write-with-min.

Maximal Matching. The **maximal matching** (MM) problem takes an undirected graph $G = (V, E)$ and returns a subset $E' \subseteq E$ such that no two edges in E' have an endpoint in common (matching) and all edges in $E \setminus E'$ share at least one endpoint with an edge in E' (maximal). The reserve-and-commit style can be used to solve the MM problem [2]. During the reserve phase, each edge checks if either of its endpoints have been matched; if so the edge removes itself from the graph and otherwise it reserves both endpoints by using a priority update (write-with-min) with the edge's unique ID. During the commit phase, every remaining edge checks if both of its endpoints contain its reservation; if so, it joins the matching and removes itself from the graph. The algorithm can also be implemented using write-once or plain writes, but forward progress is not guaranteed because it is possible that no edge succeeds in reserving both of its endpoints in an iteration.

Connected Components. For an undirected graph $G = (V, E)$, a connected component $C \subseteq V$ is one in which all vertices in C can reach one another. The **connected components** problem is to find $C_1, \ldots, C_k$ such that each C_i is a connected component, there is no path between vertices belonging to different components, and $C_1 \cup \cdots \cup C_k = V$. A simple vertex-based algorithm assigns each vertex a unique ID at the start, and in each iteration every vertex sets its ID to the minimum ID of all its neighbors. The algorithm terminates when no vertex's ID changes in an iteration. In each iteration, each vertex performs a priority update (write-with-min) to all of its neighbors' IDs. This is an example of using priority update to guarantee the correctness of an algorithm, and where the priority update yields a remarkably simple solution.

Minimum Spanning Forest. For an undirected graph $G = (V, E)$, the **spanning forest** problem returns a set of edges $F \subseteq E$ such that for each connected component $C_i = (V_i, E_i)$ of G, a spanning tree of C_i is contained in F and F contains no cycles. The **minimum spanning forest** (MSF) problem takes as input an undirected graph $G = (V, E)$ with weights $w : E \to \mathbb{R}$ and returns a spanning forest with minimum total weight.

Most MSF algorithms begin with an empty spanning forest and grow the spanning forest incrementally by adding "safe" edges (those with minimum weight crossing a cut) [6]. Kruskal's algorithm considers edges in sorted order by weight and iteratively adds edges that connect two different components, using a union-find data structure to query the components. This algorithm can be parallelized by accepting an edge into the MSF if no earlier edge in the sorted order is connected to the same component. Boruvka's algorithm is similar to Kruskal's except that Kruskal's sorts all edges initially and employs a union-find data structure over connected components, whereas Boruvka's algorithm uses contraction to reduce connected components.

In either case, a reserve-and-commit style is applicable: During the reserve phase each edge that has endpoints in separate components writes its weight/ID to the component containing each endpoint, and during the commit phase each edge checks whether its ID was written to at least one component—if so, it joins the MSF. As with connected components, the priority update (write-with-min) is required for correctness here, otherwise, the edge added may not be a safe edge. For our experiments, we use the parallel implementation of Kruskal's algorithm from PBBS [23].

Hash-based Dictionary. Using priority updates to a

Input	Num. Vertices	Num. Directed Edges	Sharing Level
3D-grid	10^7	6×10^7	Low
random-local	10^7	10^8	Low
rMat	2^{24}	10^8	Medium
4-comb	2.5×10^7	10^8	High
exponential	5×10^6	1.1×10^8	High
4-star	5×10^7	10^8	High

Table 1. Inputs for graph applications.

single location it is possible to implement a dictionary that supports insertions of $(key, value)$-pairs such that the values of multiple insertions of the same key will be combined with a priority update. This can be thought of as a generalization of priority updates in which the "locations" are not memory addresses or positions in an array, but instead are indexed by arbitrary (hashable) keys. Applications of such key-based priority updates include making reservations on entries in a dictionary instead of locations in memory. Another application is to remove duplicates in a prioritized and/or deterministic way. For example we might have a large set of documents and want to keep only one copy of each word, but want it to be the first occurrence of the word (we assume the work is tagged with some other information that distinguishes occurrences, such as their location).

Our experiments use modifications of the hash table-based dictionary from PBBS [23] that supports priority inserts. The table is based on linear probing and once a location containing the same key or an empty location has been found, a priority update is used on the location with the priorities being based on the value associated with the key.

Other Applications. Priority updates are applicable to other problems whose solutions are implemented using deterministic reservations [1]. These problems include Delaunay triangulation and refinement [7], maximal independent set and randomly permuting an array. In most of these cases (as with maximal matching), write-once and plain write implementations are correct, but because multiple reservations are required to commit, priority updates are necessary to guarantee forward progress. Moreover, the priority update version guarantees a consistent, deterministic output once the random numbers are fixed. A priority update (write-with-min) can be naturally applied to a single-source shortest paths implementation to asynchronously update potentially shorter paths to vertices. A write-once or plain write implementation would not be correct here, since we must store the shortest path to each vertex. Priority updates are also useful in other parallel algorithms that, like deterministic reservations, impose a random priority order among elements [4].

5. EXPERIMENT STUDY: APPLICATIONS

We used the Intel Nehalem machine set-up described in Section 3.1. For sequential programs, we used the g++ 4.4.1 compiler with the -O2 flag. For the breadth-first search, maximal matching, minimum spanning forest, and remove duplicates applications, we ran experiments on inputs that exhibit varying degrees of sharing. We describe the experimental setup for each of applications in more detail below. All times reported are based on the median of three trials.

The inputs used for the graph algorithms are shown in Table 1. Because in our algorithms a vertex can only be simultaneously processed by its neighbors, graphs with low degree

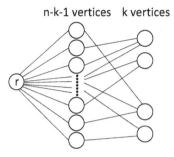

Figure 6. k-comb graph (used for BFS experiments).

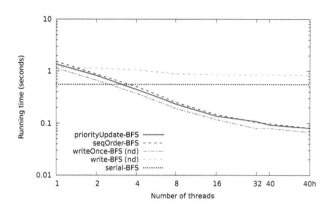

Figure 7. BFS times vs. number of cores on the 4-comb graph (log-log scale). (nd) indicates a non-deterministic implementation.

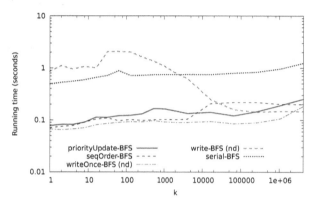

Figure 8. BFS times on different k-comb graphs with $n = 2.5 \times 10^7$ on 40 cores (log-log scale). Lower k means higher sharing. (nd) indicates a non-deterministic implementation.

overall exhibit low sharing while graphs containing some vertices of high degree can exhibit high sharing (depending on the application). *3D-grid* is a grid graph in 3-dimensional space. Every vertex has six edges, each connecting it to its two neighbors in each dimension, and thus is a low-sharing graph. *random-local* is another low-sharing graph in which every vertex has five undirected edges to neighbors chosen randomly where the probability of an edge between two vertices is inversely correlated with their distance in the vertex array (vertices tend to have edges to other vertices that are close in memory). The *rMat* graph is a graph with a power-law distribution of degrees. We used the algorithm described in [5] with parameters $a = 0.5, b = c = 0.1, d = 0.3$ to generate the rMat graph. The *k-comb* graph is a three layered graph (see Figure 6) with the first layer containing only the source vertex r, second layer containing $n - k - 1$ vertices and third layer containing k vertices. The source vertex has an edge to all vertices in the second layer, and each vertex in the second layer has an edge to a randomly chosen vertex in the third layer. There are a total of $4(n - k - 1)$ directed edges in this graph. For our experiments we used varying k to model concurrent operations to k random locations. The *exponential* graph has an exponential distribution in vertex degrees, and given a degree, incident edges from each vertex are chosen uniformly at random. The *4-star* graph is a graph with four "center" vertices and each of the $n - 4$ remaining vertices is connected to a randomly chosen center vertex (total of $2(n - 4)$ directed edges).

In BFS, because many vertices may compete to become the parent of the same neighbor, there can be high sharing. The k-comb graph illustrates this: In the first round the source vertex r explores the $n - k - 1$ vertices in the second level, without sharing; in the second round all of the second level vertices contend on vertices in the third level (see Figure 6). We chose to model sharing on k-comb graphs with different k values in order to observe the effect of write sharing that we discussed in Section 3, where a lower k value corresponds to higher sharing. We show four versions of parallel BFS which deal with reserving neighbors and placing them onto the frontier differently. The first version uses a priority update with the minimum function (*priorityUpdate-BFS*) in a two-phase update-and-read style; the second uses a priority update in a single phase, produces the sequential BFS tree but allows for duplicate vertices on the frontier (*seqOrder-BFS*); the third uses a test-and-set (*testSet-BFS*); and the fourth uses a plain write (*write-BFS*) (see Section 4 for details). Figure 7 compares the four BFS implementations and the sequential BFS implementation (*serial-BFS*) as a function of number of cores on the 4-comb graph. Table 2(a) shows the running times for each of the BFS im-

plementations on all of our graphs. The (nondeterministic) test-and-set implementation is the fastest because only one actual write is done per vertex. However the priority update implementations do not do much worse even on the high-sharing comb graph while the plain-write implementation does poorly on it (even worse than serial-BFS). The two-phase and one-phase priority update implementations are comparable in performance. Using a family of k-comb graphs with varying k, we model the effect of write sharing on k locations for BFS when utilizing all 40 cores. A lower value of k corresponds to higher sharing. Figure 8 shows that for values of k up to around 10000, priorityUpdate-BFS and seqOrder-BFS outperform write-BFS, by nearly an order of magnitude for small k, and is almost as fast as testSet-BFS. For higher values of k where there is little sharing, priorityUpdate-BFS and seqOrder-BFS are slower than writeBFS due to the overhead of the test and compare-and-swap, however they are deterministic. For values of k less than 2000 (high sharing), write-BFS is worse than even the sequential implementation.

For maximal matching and minimum spanning forest, the 4-star and exponential graphs exhibit high sharing. We show the times for implementations using priority updates and also serial implementations on the various graphs in Tables 2(b) and 2(c). We see that even for the high-sharing graphs the implementations performs well (less than 3 times worse than the lower-sharing inputs on 80 hyper-threads).

<table>
<tr><td>(a)</td><td>Breadth-First Search</td><td colspan="2">3D-grid</td><td colspan="2">random-local</td><td colspan="2">rMat</td><td colspan="2">4-comb</td><td colspan="2">exponential</td><td colspan="2">4-star</td></tr>
<tr><td></td><td></td><td>(1)</td><td>(40h)</td><td>(1)</td><td>(40h)</td><td>(1)</td><td>(40h)</td><td>(1)</td><td>(40h)</td><td>(1)</td><td>(40h)</td><td>(1)</td><td>(40h)</td></tr>
<tr><td></td><td>serial-BFS</td><td>2.03</td><td>–</td><td>2.77</td><td>–</td><td>3.13</td><td>–</td><td>0.555</td><td>–</td><td>1.19</td><td>–</td><td>0.317</td><td>–</td></tr>
<tr><td></td><td>priorityUpdate-BFS</td><td>4.03</td><td>0.307</td><td>7.02</td><td>0.247</td><td>8.37</td><td>0.306</td><td>1.38</td><td>0.08</td><td>3.18</td><td>0.199</td><td>0.885</td><td>0.066</td></tr>
<tr><td></td><td>seqOrder-BFS</td><td>3.12</td><td>0.339</td><td>5.42</td><td>0.258</td><td>6.28</td><td>0.365</td><td>1.54</td><td>0.081</td><td>3.05</td><td>0.285</td><td>0.849</td><td>0.064</td></tr>
<tr><td></td><td>testSet-BFS (nd)</td><td>2.66</td><td>0.25</td><td>4.8</td><td>0.16</td><td>5.45</td><td>0.211</td><td>1.14</td><td>0.066</td><td>2.17</td><td>0.097</td><td>0.664</td><td>0.055</td></tr>
<tr><td></td><td>write-BFS (nd)</td><td>4.3</td><td>0.28</td><td>6.13</td><td>0.246</td><td>7.74</td><td>0.298</td><td>1.2</td><td>0.954</td><td>3.18</td><td>0.224</td><td>0.888</td><td>0.063</td></tr>
</table>

<table>
<tr><td>(b)</td><td>Maximal Matching</td><td colspan="2">3D-grid</td><td colspan="2">random-local</td><td colspan="2">rMat</td><td colspan="2">exponential</td><td colspan="2">4-star</td></tr>
<tr><td></td><td></td><td>(1)</td><td>(40h)</td><td>(1)</td><td>(40h)</td><td>(1)</td><td>(40h)</td><td>(1)</td><td>(40h)</td><td>(1)</td><td>(40h)</td></tr>
<tr><td></td><td>serial-Matching</td><td>0.527</td><td>–</td><td>0.764</td><td>–</td><td>1.0</td><td>–</td><td>0.674</td><td>–</td><td>0.823</td><td>–</td></tr>
<tr><td></td><td>priorityUpdate-Matching</td><td>1.41</td><td>0.091</td><td>1.8</td><td>0.113</td><td>2.82</td><td>0.142</td><td>1.27</td><td>0.082</td><td>0.641</td><td>0.062</td></tr>
</table>

<table>
<tr><td>(c)</td><td>Minimum Spanning Forest</td><td colspan="2">3D-grid</td><td colspan="2">random-local</td><td colspan="2">rMat</td><td colspan="2">exponential</td><td colspan="2">4-star</td></tr>
<tr><td></td><td></td><td>(1)</td><td>(40h)</td><td>(1)</td><td>(40h)</td><td>(1)</td><td>(40h)</td><td>(1)</td><td>(40h)</td><td>(1)</td><td>(40h)</td></tr>
<tr><td></td><td>serial-MSF</td><td>5.3</td><td>–</td><td>7.29</td><td>–</td><td>9.54</td><td>–</td><td>7.45</td><td>–</td><td>13.3</td><td>–</td></tr>
<tr><td></td><td>priorityUpdate-MSF</td><td>10.7</td><td>0.455</td><td>14.1</td><td>0.614</td><td>19.0</td><td>0.816</td><td>12.2</td><td>0.53</td><td>29.4</td><td>1.04</td></tr>
</table>

<table>
<tr><td>(d)</td><td>Remove Duplicates Algorithm</td><td colspan="2">allDiff</td><td colspan="2">$\sqrt{n}$-unique</td><td colspan="2">trigrams</td><td colspan="2">allEqual</td></tr>
<tr><td></td><td></td><td>(1)</td><td>(40h)</td><td>(1)</td><td>(40h)</td><td>(1)</td><td>(40h)</td><td>(1)</td><td>(40h)</td></tr>
<tr><td></td><td>serial-RemDups</td><td>3.25</td><td>–</td><td>0.364</td><td>–</td><td>0.975</td><td>–</td><td>0.255</td><td>—</td></tr>
<tr><td></td><td>priority-UpdateRemDups</td><td>3.31</td><td>0.078</td><td>0.442</td><td>0.021</td><td>1.07</td><td>0.033</td><td>0.318</td><td>0.02</td></tr>
<tr><td></td><td>writeOnce-RemDups (nd)</td><td>2.16</td><td>0.072</td><td>0.433</td><td>0.021</td><td>1.03</td><td>0.035</td><td>0.312</td><td>0.021</td></tr>
<tr><td></td><td>write-RemDups (nd)</td><td>3.3</td><td>0.083</td><td>0.471</td><td>0.028</td><td>1.05</td><td>0.291</td><td>0.386</td><td>3.19</td></tr>
</table>

Table 2. Running times (seconds) of algorithms over various inputs. (40h) indicates the running time on 40 cores with hyper-threading and (1) indicates the running time on 1 thread. (nd) indicates a non-deterministic implementation.

Input	Size	Sharing Level
allDiff	10^7	Low
$\sqrt{n}$-unique	10^7	Medium
trigrams	10^7	Medium
allEqual	10^7	High

Table 3. Inputs for Remove Duplicates.

The input to the **remove duplicates** problem is a sequence of $(key, value)$ pairs, and the return value is a sequence containing a subset of the input pairs that contains only one element of any given *key* from the input. We use the hash-based dictionary described in Section 4 to solve this problem. For pairs with equal keys, the pair that is kept is determined based on the *value* of the keys. We use the sequence inputs from Table 3. The **allDiff** sequence contains pairs all with different keys. The $\sqrt{n}$-**unique** sequence contains $\sqrt{n}$ copies of each of $\sqrt{n}$ unique keys. The **allEqual** sequence contains pairs with all the same key. Finally, the **trigrams** sequence contains string keys based on the tri-gram distribution of the English language. The values of the pairs are random integers. The level of sharing at a location in the hash table is a function of the number of equal keys inserted at the location. Hence sequences with many equal keys will exhibit high sharing, whereas sequences with few equal keys will have low sharing. We show experiments for three versions of the parallel hash table which deal with insertions of duplicate keys differently. The first version, **write-RemDups**, always performs a write of the value to the location when encountering a key that has already been inserted; the second version, **writeOnce-RemDups**, does not do anything when encountering an already inserted key; and the last version, **priorityUpdate-RemDups**, uses a priority update with the minimum function on the values associated with the keys when encountering duplicate keys.

In Figure 9, we compare the performance of the various parallel implementations, along with a serial implementation (**serial-RemDups**) on the sequence of all equal keys, which exhibits the highest sharing. The priority update and

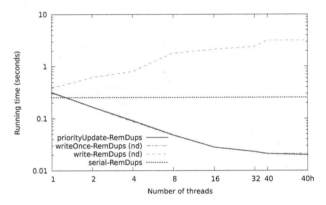

Figure 9. Remove Duplicates times on the allEqual sequence (log-log scale). (nd) indicates a non-deterministic implementation.

write-once implementations scale gracefully with an increasing number of threads, while on a large number of threads, the plain write implementation performs an order of magnitude worse. The priority update and write-once implementations of remove duplicates have similar performance, but the former also has the advantage that it is deterministic. The timings for all of the inputs are shown in Table 2(d).

6. CONCLUSION

We have compared the performance of several operations that are used when threads concurrently write to a small number of shared memory locations. Operations such as plain writes, compare-and-swap and fetch-and-add perform poorly under such high sharing, whereas priority update performs much better and close to the performance of reads. Using priority updates also has other benefits such as determinism, progress guarantees and correctness guarantees for certain algorithms. We show experiments for several applications that use priority update and demonstrate that even for high-sharing inputs, these applications are efficient and get good speedup. Given these results, we believe the priority update operation serves as a useful parallel primitive and good programming abstraction, and deserves further study.

Acknowledgments. This work is partially supported by the National Science Foundation under grants CCF-1018188 and CCF-1218188, by Intel Labs Academic Research Office for the Parallel Algorithms for Non-Numeric Computing Program, and by the Intel Science and Technology Center for Cloud Computing.

References

[1] G. E. Blelloch, J. T. Fineman, P. B. Gibbons, and J. Shun. Internally deterministic algorithms can be fast. In *PPoPP*, 2012.

[2] G. E. Blelloch, J. T. Fineman, and J. Shun. Greedy sequential maximal independent set and matching are parallel on average. In *SPAA*, 2012.

[3] G. E. Blelloch, P. B. Gibbons, and H. V. Simhadri. Combinable memory-block transactions. In *SPAA*, 2008.

[4] G. E. Blelloch, H. V. Simhadri, and K. Tangwongsan. Parallel and I/O efficient set covering algorithms. In *SPAA*, 2012.

[5] D. Chakrabarti, Y. Zhan, and C. Faloutsos. R-mat: A recursive model for graph mining. In *SDM*, 2004.

[6] T. H. Cormen, C. E. Leiserson, R. L. Rivest, and C. Stein. *Introduction to Algorithms (3rd ed.)*. MIT Press, 2009.

[7] M. de Berg, O. Cheong, M. van Kreveld, and M. Overmars. *Computational Geometry: Algorithms and Applications*. Springer-Verlag, 2008.

[8] G. Della-Libera and N. Shavit. Reactive diffracting trees. *J. Parallel Distrib. Comput.*, 2000.

[9] Z. Fang, L. Zhang, J. B. Carter, A. Ibrahim, and M. A. Parker. Active memory operations. In *SC*, 2007.

[10] P. Fatourou and N. D. Kallimanis. Revisiting the combining synchronization technique. In *PPoPP*, 2012.

[11] A. Fedorova, S. Blagodurov, and S. Zhuravlev. Managing contention for shared resources on multicore processors. *Commun. ACM*, 2010.

[12] A. Gottlieb, R. Grishman, C. P. Kruskal, C. P. Mcauliffe, L. Rudolph, and M. Snir. The NYU Ultracomputer—designing an MIMD parallel computer. *IEEE Trans. Comput.*, 1983.

[13] A. Gottlieb, B. D. Lubachevsky, and L. Rudolph. Basic techniques for the efficient coordination of very large numbers of cooperating sequential processors. *ACM Trans. Program. Lang. Syst.*, 1983.

[14] D. Hendler, I. Incze, N. Shavit, and M. Tzafrir. Flat combining and the synchronization-parallelism tradeoff. In *SPAA*, 2010.

[15] J. JaJa. *Introduction to Parallel Algorithms*. Addison-Wesley Professional, 1992.

[16] J. M. Mellor-Crummey and M. L. Scott. Algorithms for scalable synchronization on shared-memory multiprocessors. *ACM Trans. Comput. Syst.*, 1991.

[17] J. M. Mellor-Crummey and M. L. Scott. Scalable reader-writer synchronization for shared-memory multiprocessors. In *PPOPP*, 1991.

[18] J. M. Mellor-Crummey and M. L. Scott. Synchronization without contention. *SIGPLAN Not.*, 1991.

[19] M. S. Papamarcos and J. H. Patel. A low-overhead coherence solution for multiprocessors with private cache memories. In *ISCA*, 1984.

[20] L. Rudolph and Z. Segall. Dynamic decentralized cache schemes for mimd parallel processors. In *ISCA*, 1984.

[21] N. Shavit and A. Zemach. Diffracting trees. *ACM Trans. Comput. Syst.*, 1996.

[22] N. Shavit and A. Zemach. Combining funnels: a dynamic approach to software combining. *J. Parallel Distrib. Comput.*, 2000.

[23] J. Shun, G. E. Blelloch, J. T. Fineman, P. B. Gibbons, A. Kyrola, H. V. Simhadri, and K. Tangwongsan. Brief announcement: the Problem Based Benchmark Suite. In *SPAA*, 2012.

[24] G. L. Steele Jr. Making asynchronous parallelism safe for the world. In *POPL*, 1990.

[25] W. E. Weihl. Commutativity-based concurrency control for abstract data types. *IEEE Trans. Computers*, 1988.

[26] S. Zhuravlev, S. Blagodurov, and A. Fedorova. Addressing shared resource contention in multicore processors via scheduling. In *ASPLOS*, 2010.

APPENDIX

Studying a False Sharing Anomaly. As seen in Figure 3(a), under false sharing priority update (write-with-min) performs very poorly at 1024 locations. To hone in on this problem we studied the two machines under varying ratios of reads to writes to a small set of locations. Figure 10 shows the times for concurrently performing $10^8 - x$ reads and x writes on 1024 randomly chosen (adjacent) memory locations on each of the two architectures for varying x. Note that even for low fractions of writes (0.0001), the Intel Nehalem performs an order of magnitude worse than the AMD Opteron (which is a slower machine). This suggests that on the Intel Nehalem even when the vast majority of operations on a location are reads, there is still a big performance penalty from the cache coherence protocol of the very few writes. This effect is the cause of the hump in Figure 3(a) around the 1000 location point.

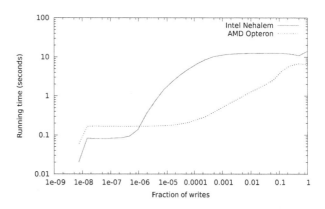

Figure 10. Studying a false sharing anomaly. Times are for 5 runs of 100 million concurrent reads/writes to 1024 random locations (with the fraction of writes varying) on the 40-core Intel Nehalem and the 64-core AMD Opteron machines (log-log scale).

HEX: Scaling Honeycombs
is Easier than Scaling Clock Trees*

Danny Dolev
Hebrew University of Jerusalem
Edmond Safra Campus, 91904 Jerusalem, Israel
dolev@cs.huji.ac.il

Christoph Lenzen
Massachusetts Institute of Technology
32 Vassar Street, 02139 Cambridge, USA
clenzen@csail.mit.edu

Matthias Függer, Martin Perner, and Ulrich Schmid
Vienna University of Technology
Treitlstrasse 3, 1040 Vienna, Austria
{fuegger,mperner,s}@ecs.tuwien.ac.at

ABSTRACT

We argue that grid structures are a very promising alternative to the standard approach for distributing a clock signal throughout VLSI circuits and other hardware devices. Traditionally, this is accomplished by a delay-balanced clock tree, which distributes the signal supplied by a single clock source via carefully engineered and buffered signal paths.

Our approach, termed HEX, is based on a hexagonal grid with simple intermediate nodes, which both control the forwarding of clock ticks in the grid and supply them to nearby functional units. HEX is Byzantine fault-tolerant, in a way that scales with the grid size, self-stabilizing, and seamlessly integrates with multiple synchronized clock sources, as used in multi-synchronous Globally Synchronous Locally Asynchronous (GALS) architectures. Moreover, HEX guarantees a small clock skew between neighbors even for wire delays that are only moderately balanced. We provide both a theoretical analysis of the worst-case skew and simulation results that demonstrate very small typical skew in realistic runs.

Categories and Subject Descriptors

B.8.1 [**Performance and Reliability**]: Reliability, Testing, and Fault-Tolerance; F.2.2 [**Analysis of Algorithms and Problem Complexity**]: Nonnumerical Algorithms and Problems

Keywords

fault-tolerant distributed algorithms; time distribution in grids; Byzantine fault-tolerance; self-stabilization

1. INTRODUCTION

Being able to distribute a synchronized clock signal to a large number of spatially distributed functional units is crucial for the synchronous design paradigm. In *Very Large Scale Integration* (VLSI) circuits and other hardware devices (as well as in master-slave-type network clock synchronization approaches like IEEE1588 [12]), this is accomplished by means of a *clock tree*, which distributes the clock signal supplied by a single clock source to all functional units attached as leaf nodes. Topologies that guarantee equal wire lengths from the root to the leaves, like H-trees (recursively constructed from a H-shaped wiring topology by attaching four smaller H-shapes to the four open ends), combined with carefully engineered wire geometries, clock signal regeneration buffers, etc. are used to ensure that clock pulses arrive at all functional units (that is, those making up a synchronous sub-system) simultaneously. This must be achieved with a *clock skew*, i.e., the maximum difference of the occurrence real-times of corresponding clock pulses at different functional units, well below half the clock cycle time: When a functional unit sends some data, say, on local clock count 1000, the receiver is expected to receive and process the data when pulse 1001 occurs according to its clock count.

Clock trees are attractive for several reasons. Besides conceptual simplicity, their height is only logarithmic in the number of the leaves (which is proportional to the die area), and the number of internal clock wires is linear in this number. As trees are planar graphs, it would (in principle) even be possible to route these links on a single interconnect layer.

These advantages come at a price, though: Spatially close functional units may be clocked via root-leaf paths that share few nodes, possibly only the root. The worst-case skew perceived between such functional units is the maximal difference of the signal propagation delay on these disjoint paths, which prohibits deep clock trees. Moreover, clock tree engineering must ensure that the maximum delay discrepancy remains below the acceptable clock skew, which is very

*This work has been supported by the Swiss National Science Foundation (SNSF), by the German Research Foundation (DFG, reference number Le 3107/1-1), by the Austrian Science Foundation (FWF) project FATAL (P21694), by The Israeli Centers of Research Excellence (I-CORE) program, (Center No. 4/11), by the ISG (Israeli Smart Grid) Consortium, administered by the office of the Chief Scientist of the Israeli Ministry of Industry and Trade and Labor, and by grant 3/9778 of the Israeli Ministry of Science and Technology. Danny Dolev is Incumbent of the Berthold Badler Chair.

difficult for clock speeds in the GHz range [1, 8, 19, 23, 27, 29]. In particular, given that a clock tree typically supplies a significant part of the chip (possibly even the entire die), the logarithmic height of a clock tree inevitably results in long wires. Making the resulting signal propagation delays as equal as possible, despite non-negligible wire resistances and coupling capacitances etc., is an engineering challenge that requires considerable efforts and costs. The resulting clock trees incorporate complex wire geometries and strong clock buffers, and thus suffer from large area and power consumption [15]. Moreover, further skew reduction typically requires extended clock tree topologies, such as trees with cross-links, meshes and multi-level trees [16, 29].

An even more serious issue with clock trees, which also arises in applications where there are no severe skew requirements, is lacking robustness. First of all, at the top level, a single clock source obviously constitutes a single point of failure. This is avoided by *Globally Asynchronous Locally Synchronous* (GALS) [2] architectures, where different parts of a chip are clocked by different clock sources & clock trees. However, using independent and hence unsynchronized clock domains gives away the advantages of global synchrony and thus requires non-synchronous cross-domain communication mechanisms or synchronizers [4, 13, 21]. Multi-synchronous clocking [25, 28] (also called *mesochronous* clocking [18]), which guarantees some upper bound on the skew between clock domains, has been invented to avoid this. The resulting multi-synchronous GALS architectures can rely on a common time base, which is attractive not only for applications programmers but also for metastability-free high-speed communication between different clock domains [20].

Still, the problem of limited robustness of clock trees persists even in GALS architectures: If just one internal wire or clock buffer in a clock tree breaks, e.g., due to some manufacturing defect or electromigration, *all* the functional units supplied via the affected subtree will stop working correctly. Therefore, it is desirable to have fairly small clock trees in a GALS system, necessitating a large number of synchronized clock domains. Overcoming the fundamental scalability and robustness issues of clock trees hence introduces the new challenge of robustly establishing a tight synchronization among a large number of clock domains.

Contribution: In this paper, we tackle this problem by proposing an alternative way for distributing a synchronized clock signal throughout an integrated circuit. Our approach, termed HEX, is based on a sufficiently connected wiring topology, namely, a *hexagonal grid*.[1] At each grid point, we place an (intermediate) node that controls when the clock pulses are forwarded to adjacent nodes and supplies the clock to nearby functional units, typically using a *small* local clock tree. It will turn out that HEX compares favorably to clock trees in most aspects.

In particular, with respect to robustness, our approach supports multiple synchronized clock sources and tolerates Byzantine failures of both clock sources and nodes. Its resilience to failures even scales with the size of the grid, in the sense that it supports a constant density of isolated Byzantine nodes, and it can handle a larger number of more benign failures like broken wires and mute clock sources and nodes.

It is also self-stabilizing [3], in the sense that it can recover from an arbitrary number of transient failures.[2]

Furthermore, HEX has enticing properties with respect to the achievable skew between neighbors in the grid, which are typically the ones who need to communicate synchronously with each other. First of all, given that length and width of the grid grow as $\sqrt{n}$ and the density of HEX nodes should be roughly constant (with respect to n), wires are much shorter than in a clock tree. HEX hence neither requires strong clock buffers nor special wires, such that the maximal difference ε of the end-to-end delays between neighbors in the grid should be easily brought down to small values even by moderate engineering efforts. Second, for a proper embedding of the HEX topology, physically close nodes are also well-synchronized: In the fault-free case, HEX guarantees a worst-case skew between neighbors that is quadratic in ε. Depending on the number and severity of faults, this bound gracefully degrades. Moreover, it obeys a locality property: The adverse effect of faults on the neighbor skew decreases with the distance from the fault in the grid.

Related Work: Apart from the rich literature on clock tree engineering and extended topologies for skew reduction, see e.g. [1, 8, 15, 16, 19, 22, 23, 26, 29], we are not aware of much research on alternative clock distribution techniques. An exception is the work on distributed clock generation without local oscillators, which inherently also solves the problem of clock distribution. These approaches are essentially based on (distributed) ring oscillators, which are formed by gates arranged in a feedback loop. In [17], a regular structure of closed loops of an odd number of inverters is used for distributed clock generation. Similarly, [6, 7] employ local pulse generation cells, arranged in a two-dimensional grid, with each cell inverting its output signal when its four inputs (from the up, down, left and right neighbor) match the current clock output value. A more elaborate approach along the same lines uses an array of PLLs that are mutually synchronized among each other, using digital feedback exchanged across some (sparse) communication topology [11, 14, 24] like a grid. However, to the best of our knowledge, none of these approaches has been analyzed for its fault-tolerance properties, not to speak of self-stabilization.

The only fault-tolerant clock generation approaches for multi-synchronous GALS systems known to us are the Byzantine fault-tolerant DARTS approach [9, 10] and our self-stabilizing Byzantine fault-tolerant FATAL algorithm proposed in [5]. However, both approaches are complex and require a fully-connected interconnect topology. Consequently, they are not useful for distributing a synchronized clock to a large number of functional units, but are of course suitable candidates for the clock sources required by our HEX grid.

2. ALGORITHM & TOPOLOGY

We consider a set of nodes executing a pulse generation and forwarding algorithm, which communicate by message passing over a communication network whose underlying undirected communication graph is a cylindric hexagonal grid. Formally, the directed communication graph $G = (V, E)$ of our HEX grid is defined as follows (see Figure 1):

---

[1] Note that clock distribution by means of our HEX grid is fundamentally different from using a clock mesh [29] for averaging out large clock skews among near-by leaf nodes.

[2] Note, however, that our very simple algorithm is *not* self-stabilizing in the presence of ongoing Byzantine failures. There are non-stabilizing executions with Byzantine faults, although they seem unlikely to occur in practice.

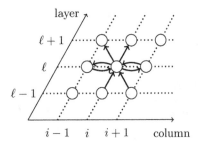

Figure 1: Node (ℓ, i) **and its incident links in the cylindric hexagonal grid topology. Column coordinates are modulo** W **and layer coordinates (rows) are between** 0 **and** L.

Letting $L \in \mathbb{N}$ denote its length and $W \in \mathbb{N}$ its width, the set of nodes V is the set of tuples $(\ell, i) \in [L + 1] \times [W]$. Herein, $[L + 1] := \{0, \ldots, L\}$ denotes the row index set, referred to as *layers*, and $[W] = \{0, \ldots, W - 1\}$ the column index set of the nodes in the grid. For each node $(\ell, i) \in V$, $\ell \in [L + 1]$, $i \in [W]$, the following links are in E: Incoming and outgoing links to neighboring nodes of the same layer, namely from (ℓ, i) to $(\ell, i - 1 \bmod W)$, called the left neighbor of (ℓ, i), and to $(\ell, i + 1 \bmod W)$, called the right neighbor, and vice versa from the left and the right neighbor to (ℓ, i); if (ℓ, i) is in a layer greater than 0, then it has incoming links from $(\ell - 1, i)$, called its lower left neighbor, and $(\ell - 1, i + 1 \bmod W)$, called its lower right neighbor; if (ℓ, i) is in a layer smaller than L, then it has outgoing links to $(\ell + 1, i - 1 \bmod W)$, its upper left neighbor, and $(\ell + 1, i)$, its upper right neighbor. Figure 1 depicts the structure of the resulting HEX grid and shows a node's communication channels within the grid. The neighboring nodes of node (ℓ, i) form a hexagon, hence the name HEX grid. Due to the fact that column coordinates are modulo W, the HEX grid has a cylindric shape; we will briefly discuss the issue of embedding a HEX grid on a chip in Section 5.

Each node of the grid runs an algorithm that can broadcast *trigger messages* (representing clock pulses) over its outgoing links, as well as receive trigger messages over its incoming links. Each (fault-free) link guarantees an end-to-end communication delay (i.e., the time between sending and processing a trigger message) within $[d^-, d^+] \subset (0, \infty)$, where $\varepsilon := d^+ - d^- \le d^+/2$. Each node further has access to a (possibly inaccurate) clock to measure timeouts.

Nodes at layer 0 are special in that they execute a pulse generation algorithm like the one of [5, 10], whose purpose is to generate synchronized and well-separated consecutive initial trigger messages. For each pulse number $k \in \mathbb{N}$, the time between any (non-faulty) node in layer 0 generating its kth trigger message and another node in layer 0 generating its $(k + 1)^{\text{th}}$ trigger message is sufficiently large. The precise meaning of "sufficiently large" depends on the desired fault-tolerance properties; we will elaborate on this in Section 3.2. Note that it is desirable to keep the maximal time between pulses small in order to guarantee a high operating frequency.

Nodes at layers larger than 0 run the simple pulse forwarding algorithm specified in Algorithm 1. Basically, nodes forward pulse k once they received trigger messages for pulse k from two adjacent neighbors. Since clock pulses and trig-

ger messages are anonymous, i.e., can carry no information except their sole occurrence, care must be taken in order not to generate multiple trigger messages for a single pulse. The simple solution we use here relies on a sufficiently large separation between pulses, which relieves us from locally keeping track of pulse counts. Nodes can simply go to sleep for a while after forwarding a pulse and clear their history upon waking up again. In order to support practical (hence inaccurate) ways of implementing local timeouts, we allow the sleeping time to vary within the interval $[T^-, T^+]$. In the fault-free case, comparing the minimal and maximal possible speeds of pulse propagation shows that $T^- \in \mathcal{O}(\varepsilon L)$ is sufficient; with faults and in particular for self-stabilization, more care is required. The respective constraints on T^- and T^+ will be discussed in Section 3.2. Due to its simplicity, the forwarding algorithm can easily be implemented by means of an asynchronous state machine.

Algorithm 1: Pulse forwarding algorithm for nodes in layer $\ell > 0$.

---

once *received trigger messages from (left and lower left) or (lower left and lower right) or (lower right and right) neighbors* **do**

   | broadcast trigger message; // local clock pulse
   | sleep for some time within $[T^-, T^+]$;
   | forget previously received trigger messages

While the purpose of the nodes in layer 0 is to generate pulses in a synchronized way, which typically necessitates full interconnection between all these nodes, the purpose of the nodes at higher layers is to propagate these pulses throughout the entire system via a low-connectivity network. Synchronized pulses generated by layer 0 propagate as "waves" through the HEX grid up to the very last layer. In the fault-free case, the propagation of every pulse can hence be analyzed independently.

3. SKEW & RESILIENCE

We are now going to analyze the skew and fault-tolerance properties of the algorithm and topology presented in the previous section. By $t_{\ell,i}^{(k)}$, we denote the *triggering time* of node (ℓ, i), i.e., the time when it forwards the kth pulse. Generally, we will use superscript $^{(k)}$ to denote variables associated with the kth pulse. When indexing nodes and trigger times, we will usually omit "mod W" to simplify the notation.

3.1 The Fault-free Case

As discussed earlier, in the fault-free case, we can restrict our attention to a single pulse and hence omit all pulse indices. We just assume that, initially, all nodes have cleared their memory and are waiting for the next pulse generated by the nodes in layer 0.

DEFINITION 3.1 (CAUSAL LINKS AND PATHS). *We say that a node is* left-triggered / centrally triggered / right-triggered, *if the satisfied guard from Algorithm 1 causing the node to trigger has received trigger messages from the* left and lower left / lower left and lower right / lower right and right neighbors, *respectively. In each case both of the respective links are* causal. *A causal path consists of causal links only.*

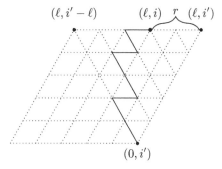

$(\ell, i'-\ell)$ $\quad (\ell, i)$ r (ℓ, i')

$(0, i')$

Figure 2: Illustration of the situation in Lemma 3.3.

Note that a link being causal implies that its endpoint is triggered at least d^- time after its origin. For instance, if (ℓ, i) is left-triggered, the links $((\ell, i-1), (\ell, i))$ and $((\ell-1, i), (\ell, i))$ are causal, while $((\ell, i+1), (\ell, i))$, $((\ell-1, i+1), (\ell, i))$ are not.

The following definition backtraces a sequence of causal links, either to the node in layer 0 starting the causal chain or to some specific column of interest.

DEFINITION 3.2 (LEFT ZIG-ZAG PATHS). *Given are a layer $0 < \ell \in [L+1]$ and column indices $i, i' \in [W]$, $i < i'$. The causal left zig-zag path $p_{\text{left}}^{i' \to (\ell, i)}$ is composed of rightward links $((\ell', j-1), (\ell', j))$ and up-left links $((\ell'-1, j+1), (\ell', j))$. It is inductively defined as follows. We start with the 0-length path $((\ell, i))$. Suppose that in some step of the construction the current path originates at node (ℓ', j) with $\ell' > 0$. If (ℓ', j) is left-triggered, we extend the path by adding the rightward link $((\ell', j-1), (\ell', j))$ as first link (and $(\ell', j-1)$ as its origin). Otherwise, the up-left link $((\ell'-1, j+1), (\ell', j))$ is causal and can be added as prefix to the path (and $(\ell'-1, j+1)$ as its origin). In the case of adding an up-left link the construction terminates if $\ell' - 1 = 0$ or if both $j + 1 = i'$ and the path now contains more up-left than rightward links.*

Since causal paths are acyclic, there must be fewer than W left-links before we go from ℓ' to $\ell'-1$, implying that the construction terminates after a finite number of steps. We now prove a useful technical lemma, which reveals a connection between the triggering times of two nodes at the same layer and left zig-zag paths, and thereby gives a bound on the maximum difference of their skew.

LEMMA 3.3. *Suppose that path π is a prefix of some left zig-zag path $p_{\text{left}}^{i' \to (\ell'', i'')}$ and that π starts at node (ℓ', i') and ends at node (ℓ, i). Let r be the number of up-left links minus the number of rightward links along π. Then*

$$t_{\ell, i'} \le t_{\ell, i} + rd^- + (\ell - \ell')\varepsilon.$$

PROOF. From Definition 3.2, it follows that left zig-zag paths contain more up-left than rightward links or start at layer 0; hence, $\ell' < \ell$. W.l.o.g., we set $\ell' = 0$, i.e., we shift all layer indices by ℓ' and the new value of ℓ now represents $\ell - \ell'$. Moreover, since the path $p_{\text{left}}^{i' \to (\ell'', i'')}$ starts at node (ℓ', i'), we must have $r > 0$, since otherwise the construction of the left zig-zag path would have terminated before reaching (ℓ', i'), cf. Figure 2.

Consider the set S of nodes in the triangle with corners $(0, i')$, $(\ell, i' - \ell)$, and (ℓ, i') in Figure 2.[3] Observe that $p_{\text{left}}^{i' \to (\ell'', i'')}$ starts at the lower corner of the triangle and the prefix π never leaves it. By induction on the kth diagonal of the triangle $(k, i'), \ldots, (\ell, i' - (\ell - k))$ (for $k \in [\ell + 1]$), we will prove that each node p that is both on the diagonal k and either on π or to the right of π is triggered at the latest at time $t_p \le t_{\ell, i} - (\ell - r)d^- + kd^+$. Since this implies that $t_{\ell, i'} \le t_{\ell, i} + rd^- + \ell\varepsilon$, this will establish the claim of the lemma.

To this end, let us show the induction hypothesis first for each node on π. Observe that node (ℓ, i) is on diagonal $(\ell - r)$. Hence, a node p that is h hops from (ℓ, i) on π must be on a diagonal $k \ge (\ell - r) - h$. Since $p_{\text{left}}^{i' \to (\ell'', i'')}$ is causal, it follows that $t_p \le t_{\ell, i} - hd^- \le t_{\ell, i} - (\ell - r)d^- + kd^+$, showing the statement for nodes on π.

Note that all nodes on diagonal 0 are either on or to the left of π, hence we already covered the induction anchor at $k = 0$. For the induction step from k to $k+1$, observe that any node will be left-triggered within at most d^+ time once both its left and lower-left neighbors are triggered. For any node p on the $(k+1)^{th}$ diagonal that is strictly right of π, its left and lower-left neighbor are on the diagonal k of S and either on π or to the right of π. The statement for diagonal k thus implies $t_p \le t_{\ell, i} - (\ell - r)d^- + kd^+ + d^+$. Since we already covered nodes on π, the induction step succeeds. $\square$

Based on the following definition, we will now develop bounds on the maximal skew in a given layer.

DEFINITION 3.4 (DISTANCE AND SKEW POTENTIAL). *For $i, j \in \mathbb{Z}$, let $d := i - j \bmod W$ and define $|i - j|_W := \min\{d, W - d\}$. For $\ell \in [L+1]$, the skew potential on layer ℓ is Δ_ℓ, where $\Delta_\ell := \max_{i, j \in [W]}\{t_{\ell, i} - t_{\ell, j} - |i - j|_W d^-\}$.*

We first prove a weak bound on the maximal skew at the upper layers that holds *independently* of the initial potential Δ_0. Notice that this result implies tolerance of HEX against arbitrary layer 0 skews.

LEMMA 3.5. *For all $\ell \in \{W - 2, \ldots, L\}$ we have that $\Delta_\ell \le 2(W - 2)\varepsilon$.*

PROOF. W.l.o.g. assume that $\ell = W - 2$ and fix $i, i' \in [W]$, $i < i'$ (wrap-around cases are symmetrical). We distinguish two cases.

Case 1: $p_{\text{left}}^{i' \to (\ell, i)}$ starts at node (ℓ', i') for some $\ell' \in \{1, \ldots, \ell - 1\}$. Then, by Lemma 3.3,

$$t_{\ell, i'} \le t_{\ell, i} + (i' - i)d^- + (\ell - \ell')\varepsilon \le t_{\ell, i} + (i' - i)d^- + \ell\varepsilon.$$

Case 2: $p_{\text{left}}^{i' \to (\ell, i)}$ starts at node $(0, j)$, $j \in [W]$. Then the path has length at least $2\ell - (i' - i)$, since at least ℓ up-left and $\ell - (i' - i)$ right links are required for the path to originate at layer 0. Denote by t_0 the earliest time when a pair of two adjacent nodes in layer 0 are both triggered. Clearly, the second node on $p_{\text{left}}^{i' \to (\ell, i)}$ cannot be triggered before time $t_0 + d^-$ because it is in layer 1. Hence, $t_{\ell, i} \ge t_0 + (2\ell - (i' - i))d^-$ and thus

$$t_{\ell, i} \ge t_0 + (2(W - 2) - (i' - i))d^-. \tag{1}$$

---

[3]Here we assume w.l.o.g. that $i' - \ell \ge 0$, i.e., no wrap-around within the triangle. The general case is treated analogously, ignoring that some of the index pairs may actually refer to the same node.

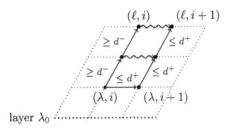

Figure 3: Illustration of Case 1 of Lemma 3.6.

Denote by $(0, j_0)$ a node with $\max\{t_{0,j_0}, t_{0,j_0+1}\} = t_0$; by definition of t_0 such a node exists. We claim that all nodes in layer $W-2$ are triggered no later than time $t_0 + 2(W-2)d^+$. This follows by induction on the layers $\lambda \in [W-1]$, where the hypothesis is that all nodes $(\lambda, j-\lambda), (\lambda, j-\lambda+1), \ldots, (\lambda, j+1)$ are triggered until time $t_0 + 2\lambda d^+$. Since in layer λ these are $2+\lambda$ nodes, i.e., all W nodes in layer $W-2$, this will prove the claim. By the definition of t_0, the induction hypothesis holds for $\lambda = 0$. To perform the step from λ to $\lambda+1$, observe that all nodes $(\lambda+1, j-\lambda), (\lambda+1, j-\lambda+1), \ldots, (\lambda+1, j)$ are triggered no later than time $t_0 + (2\lambda+1)d^+$, since by the hypothesis their lower left and lower right neighbors are triggered at least d^+ before that time. Until time $t_0 + 2(\lambda+1)d^+$, nodes $(\lambda+1, j-(\lambda+1))$ and $(\lambda+1, j+1)$ then must follow, completing the induction. In particular, this shows that $t_{\ell,i'} \leq t_0 + 2(W-2)d^+$ and hence, by using (1),

$$t_{\ell,i'} - t_{\ell,i} \leq (i'-i)d^- + 2(W-2)\varepsilon.$$

Overall, since i and $i' > i$ were arbitrary, from the two cases and symmetry for $i' < i$, we conclude that

$$\Delta_\ell = \max_{i,i' \in [W]} \{t_{\ell,i'} - t_{\ell,i} - |i'-i|_W d^-\} \leq 2(W-2)\varepsilon,$$

as claimed. $\square$

Next, we derive more refined bounds on the skew between two neighboring nodes in the same layer $\ell > 0$. In contrast to Lemma 3.5, the next lemma takes the maximal skew in previous layers into account.

Lemma 3.6. *For all $\ell_0 \in [L]$ and $\ell \in \{\ell_0 + 1, \ldots, L\}$, it holds for each $i \in [W]$ that*

$$|t_{\ell,i} - t_{\ell,i+1}| \leq d^+ + \left\lceil \frac{(\ell - \ell_0)\varepsilon}{d^+} \right\rceil \varepsilon + \Delta_{\ell_0}.$$

Proof. Fix some value of $\ell \geq 1$, set $i+1 = W-1$, and assume that $\ell_0 = 0$ and $t_{\ell,i} < t_{\ell,i+1}$ (all wrap-around cases are symmetrical). Define $\lambda_0 := \lfloor \ell d^- / d^+ \rfloor$, such that

$$\ell - \lambda_0 = \ell - \left\lfloor \frac{\ell d^-}{d^+} \right\rfloor = \left\lceil \frac{\ell \varepsilon}{d^+} \right\rceil. \tag{2}$$

We distinguish three cases.

Case 1: $t_{\lambda,i+1} \leq t_{\lambda,i} + d^+$ for some $\lambda \geq \lambda_0$ (Figure 3). W.l.o.g. let λ be maximal with this property. Hence, for all $\lambda' \in \{\lambda+1, \ldots, \ell\}$, it follows that $t_{\lambda',i+1} > t_{\lambda',i} + d^+$. Notice that the choice of λ implies that for all such λ', node (λ', i) cannot be right-triggered, as the links $((\lambda', i+1), (\lambda', i))$ cannot be causal. Hence, all links $((\lambda'-1, i), (\lambda', i))$ must be causal. By induction on λ', we infer $t_{\ell,i} \geq t_{\lambda,i} + (\ell - \lambda)d^-$.

Furthermore, since the condition ensures that the trigger message from (λ', i) to $(\lambda', i+1)$ arrives well before time

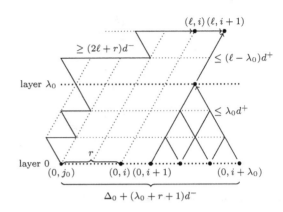

Figure 4: Illustration of Case 2 of Lemma 3.6.

$t_{\lambda',i+1}$, node $(\lambda', i+1)$ will be triggered at the latest when the trigger message from its lower left neighbor $(\lambda'-1, i+1)$ arrives. Again by induction on λ', we infer that $t_{\ell,i+1} \leq t_{\lambda,i+1} + (\ell - \lambda)d^+$, and hence

$$t_{\ell,i+1} \leq t_{\lambda,i} + (\ell - \lambda + 1)d^+. \tag{3}$$

By (2), thus $t_{\ell,i} - t_{\ell,i+1} \leq (\ell - \lambda)\varepsilon + d^+ \leq d^+ + \lceil \ell\varepsilon/d^+ \rceil \varepsilon$.

Case 2: Case 1 does not apply and $p_{\text{left}}^{i+1 \to (\ell,i)}$ **starts at some node** $(0, j_0)$, **for** $j_0 \neq i+1$ (Figure 4).

If $p_{\text{left}}^{i+1 \to (\ell,i)}$ contained more left-up links than rightward links, it would contain a subpath originating at a node in column $i+1$ that also would have more left-up than rightward links. This is not possible, since then the construction would have terminated at this node, either resulting in the path originating at a layer $\ell' > 0$ or at node $(0, i+1)$. Hence $p_{\text{left}}^{i+1 \to (\ell,i)}$ is of length $2\ell + r$ for some $r \geq 0$ and $j_0 = i - r \mod W$.

For all indices $j \in \{i+1, i+2, \ldots, i+1+\lambda_0\}$ we have that $|j - j_0|_W \leq j - i + r$. We obtain that

$$\begin{aligned}
t_{\ell,i} &\geq t_{0,j_0} + (2\ell + r)d^- \\
&= t_{0,j} - (t_{0,j} - t_{0,j_0} - |j - j_0|_W d^-) \\
&\quad - |j - j_0|_W d^- + (2\ell + r)d^- \\
&\geq t_{0,j} - \Delta_0 - (j-i)d^- + 2\ell d^- \\
&\geq t_{0,j} - \Delta_0 + (2\ell - \lambda_0 - 1)d^-.
\end{aligned}$$

Moreover, by induction on $\lambda \in \{0, \ldots, \lambda_0\}$, it follows that all nodes $(\lambda, i+1), \ldots, (\lambda, (i+1+\lambda_0 - \lambda) \mod W)$ are triggered by time

$$\max_{j \in [i+\lambda_0+2] \setminus [i+1]} \{t_{0,j}\} + \lambda d^+ \leq t_{\ell,i} + \Delta_0 - (2\ell - \lambda_0 - 1)d^- + \lambda d^+.$$

In particular, by the definition of λ_0, $t_{\lambda_0,i+1} \leq t_{\ell,i} + \Delta_0 - (\ell - \lambda_0 - 1)d^-$. Since Case 1 does not hold, we can use similar arguments as for deriving (3) to obtain that $t_{\ell,i+1} \leq t_{\lambda_0,i+1} + (\ell - \lambda_0)d^+$. It follows that

$$t_{\ell,i+1} \leq t_{\ell,i} + d^- + (\ell - \lambda_0)\varepsilon + \Delta_0 = t_{\ell,i} + d^- + \left\lceil \frac{\ell\varepsilon}{d^+} \right\rceil \varepsilon + \Delta_0.$$

Case 3: Neither Case 1 nor Case 2 apply (Figure 5). In other words, $p_{\text{left}}^{i+1 \to (\ell,i)}$ starts at node $(\ell', i+1)$ for some $\ell' < \ell$, and $t_{\lambda,i+1} > t_{\lambda,i} + d^+$ for all $\lambda \in \{\lambda_0, \ldots, \ell\}$. Note that by construction the first link of $p_{\text{left}}^{i+1 \to (\ell,i)}$ is $((\ell', i+1), (\ell'+1, i))$. Hence, we have that $\ell' < \lambda_0 - 1$, as otherwise node $(\ell'+1, i+1)$ would be triggered no later than time

168

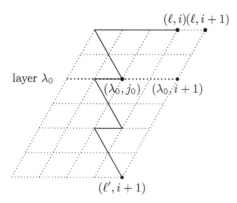

Figure 5: Illustration of Case 3 of Lemma 3.6.

$\max\{t_{\ell',i+1} + d^+, t_{\ell'+1,i} + d^+\} = t_{\ell'+1,i} + d^+$, contradicting the fact that Case 1 does not apply.

Let (λ_0, j_0) be the last node on the causal path $p_{\text{left}}^{i+1 \to (\ell,i)}$ in layer λ_0. Observe that $j_0 + r - l = i$, where r (resp. l) is the number of rightward (resp. up-left) hops of $p_{\text{left}}^{i+1 \to (\ell,i)}$ after (λ_0, j_0). The prefix of $p_{\text{left}}^{i+1 \to (\ell,i)}$ ending at (λ_0, j_0) satisfies the precondition of Lemma 3.3, yielding $t_{\lambda_0,i+1} \leq t_{\lambda_0,j_0} + (i + 1 - j_0)d^- + (\lambda_0 - \ell')\varepsilon$. Recall that since Case 1 does not apply, we have by (3) that $t_{\ell,i+1} \leq t_{\lambda_0,i+1} + (\ell - \lambda_0)d^+$. Using that $d^+ = d^- + \varepsilon$, we obtain

$$t_{\ell,i+1} \leq t_{\lambda_0,j_0} + (\ell - \lambda_0 + i + 1 - j_0)d^- + (\ell - \ell')\varepsilon.$$

By construction, $p_{\text{left}}^{i+1 \to (\ell,i)}$ is of length $2(\ell - \ell') - 1$ and its prefix ending at node (λ_0, j_0) is of length $2(\lambda_0 - \ell') - (i + 1 - j_0)$. Therefore, the length of the suffix of $p_{\text{left}}^{i+1 \to (\ell,i)}$ starting at (λ_0, j_0) is $2(\ell - \lambda_0) + (i - j_0)$. Because this suffix is a causal path, we may infer that

$$t_{\ell,i} \geq t_{\lambda_0,j_0} + (2(\ell - \lambda_0) + (i - j_0))d^-.$$

Altogether, we arrive at

$$
\begin{aligned}
t_{\ell,i+1} - t_{\ell,i} &\leq (\ell - \ell')\varepsilon - (\ell - \lambda_0 - 1)d^- \\
&\leq \ell\varepsilon - \left(\frac{\ell\varepsilon}{d^+} - 1\right)d^- = d^- + \frac{\ell\varepsilon^2}{d^+}.
\end{aligned}
$$

Since these cases are exhaustive and for each the claimed bound holds, this concludes the proof. $\square$

Finally, by some slightly modified reasoning, it is also possible to derive a skew bound in W.

COROLLARY 3.7. Set $\delta := d^-/2 - \varepsilon$. For each layer $\ell \in \{W, \ldots, L\}$ and all $i \in [W]$ it holds that

$$|t_{\ell,i} - t_{\ell,i+1}| \leq \max\left\{d^+ + \left\lceil\frac{W\varepsilon}{d^+}\right\rceil\varepsilon, \Delta_{\ell-W} + d^+ - W\delta\right\}.$$

PROOF SKETCH. The proof is analogous to the one of Lemma 3.6, where Case 2 is treated slightly differently. Assuming w.l.o.g. that $\ell = W$, in Case 2 we bound for all indices $j \in \{i+1, i+2, \ldots, i + \lambda_0 + 1\}$

$$t_{\ell,i} \geq t_{0,j} - \Delta_0 - |j - j_0|_W d^- + 2\ell d^- \geq t_{0,j} - \Delta_0 + \frac{3\ell d^-}{2},$$

where in the second step we exploit that $|j - j_0|_W$ is upper bounded by $W/2 = \ell/2$. Proceeding as in the proof of Lemma 3.6, the claimed bound follows. $\square$

We are now ready to derive our main result, namely, bounds on the worst-case skews between neighbors.

THEOREM 3.8 (SKEW BOUNDS—FAULT-FREE CASE). *Suppose that $\varepsilon \leq d^+/7$. Then the following upper bounds hold on the intra-layer skew $\sigma_\ell := \max_{i \in [W]}\{|t_{\ell,i} - t_{\ell,i+1}|\}$ in layer ℓ. If $\Delta_0 = 0$, then σ_ℓ is uniformly bounded by $d^+ + \lceil W\varepsilon/d^+\rceil\varepsilon$ for any $\ell \in [L+1]$. In the general case,*

$$\forall \ell \in \{1, \ldots, 2W - 3\} : \sigma_\ell \leq d^+ + 2W\varepsilon^2/d^+ + \Delta_0.$$
$$\forall \ell \in \{2W - 2, \ldots, L\} : \sigma_\ell \leq d^+ + \lceil W\varepsilon/d^+\rceil\varepsilon.$$

Moreover, regarding the inter-layer skew of layer $\ell \in [L]$, for all $i \in [W]$ that

$$t_{\ell,i} - \sigma_\ell + d^- \leq t_{\ell+1,i} \leq t_{\ell,i} + \sigma_\ell + d^+ \text{ and}$$
$$t_{\ell,i+1} - \sigma_\ell + d^- \leq t_{\ell+1,i} \leq t_{\ell,i+1} + \sigma_\ell + d^+.$$

PROOF. Assume first that $\Delta_0 = 0$. For the sake of the argument, imagine that the HEX grid would start at layer $-(W-1)$, where for all $i \in [W]$ and all $\ell \in \{-(W-1), \ldots, 0\}$ we would have that $t_{\ell,i} = \ell d^+$. Clearly, starting from any execution on the actual grid, this would result in a feasible execution on the extended grid if we choose all link delays on the imagined links to be d^+. It follows that $\Delta_\ell = 0$ for all $\ell \in \{-(W-1), \ldots, 0\}$. From Lemma 3.5, we obtain that $\Delta_\ell < (2W-1)\varepsilon$ for all $\ell \in \{1, \ldots, L\}$ (since we have negative layer indices until $-(W-1)$, the lemma also applies to layers $1, \ldots, W - 3$). Now we apply Corollary 3.7 to all layers $\{1, \ldots, L\}$, yielding that

$$\sigma_\ell \leq \max\left\{d^+ + \left\lceil\frac{W\varepsilon}{d^+}\right\rceil\varepsilon, W(2\varepsilon - \delta) + d^-\right\}.$$

Since $\varepsilon \leq d^+/7$, we have that $2\varepsilon - \delta \leq 0$, showing the first statement.

Now consider the case where Δ_0 is arbitrary. The bound on σ_ℓ for $\ell \in \{1, \ldots, 2W - 3\}$ follows from Lemma 3.6. For $\ell \geq 2W - 2$, observe first that we can apply Lemma 3.5 to all layers $\ell \in \{W - 2, \ldots, L\}$. Hence the same bound as in the previous case holds due to Corollary 3.7 applied to layers $\ell \in \{2W - 2, \ldots, L\}$.

The third inequality of the theorem holds since

$$
\begin{aligned}
t_{\ell,i} - \sigma_\ell + d^- &\leq \min\{t_{\ell,i}, t_{\ell,i+1}\} + d^- \\
&\leq t_{\ell+1,i} \\
&\leq \max\{t_{\ell,i}, t_{\ell,i+1}\} + d^+ \\
&\leq t_{\ell,i} + \sigma_\ell + d^+;
\end{aligned}
$$

the final inequality is proved analogously. $\square$

We remark that it is fairly straightforward to construct worst-case executions that almost match these bounds (cf. Figure 6), i.e., they are essentially tight.

3.2 Fault-Tolerance Properties

We will now shed light on the fault-tolerance properties of our approach. We will consider transient and permanent faults, and for permanent faults we distinguish between *crash faults*, where a node simply ceases to operate, and *Byzantine faults*, where a node behaves arbitrarily. For the sake of simplicity, we will not discuss link failures, which can be understood by essentially the same arguments and insights we present for node failures.

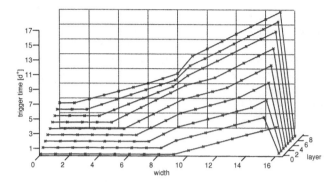

Figure 6: A worst-case pulse wave, with maximal intra-layer skew between the top-layer nodes in columns 8 and 9. Nodes in and left of column 8 are left-triggered (except for the "flat" region) with minimal delays of d^-. Nodes in and right of column 9 are slow due to large delays of d^+ and large initial skews in the respective region of layer 0. To focus on the essential central part of the grid, we introduced a barrier of "dead" nodes in column 16.

Due to the large number of possible fault patterns, we cannot hope for a comprehensive and exhaustive formal analysis of all cases within the scope of this paper. Thus, we will mostly confine ourselves to a qualitative discussion of the effects of faults; in Section 4, we will elaborate on some concrete scenarios by means of simulations.

Byzantine Faults. Since the communication structure of our algorithm is extremely simple, it is not difficult to understand the "options" of Byzantine nodes for disrupting the system's operation. If they have the possibility to generate "false" pulses, i.e., trigger non-faulty nodes without the support of other non-faulty nodes, this will clearly break our protocol: Once this happens, this will cause a chain reaction distributing the false pulse just like a correct one.

A similar problem arises if a node has a second faulty neighbor (even if it is just a crash fault) and the two faults are not just the left and right neighbor. If both faulty neighbors are not sending trigger messages, the node is not going to be triggered. However, if a Byzantine neighbor *does* send a trigger message, the node can be triggered. Hence, a Byzantine node can essentially trigger the node at an arbitrary time between pulses, which again enables it to create a false pulse. We therefore require the following.

CONDITION 3.9 (FAULT SEPARATION). *No node can be triggered by Byzantine nodes only. (This is equivalent to no two neighbors being Byzantine unless they are both in layer L.) Every node with a Byzantine neighbor can be triggered by a pair of non-faulty nodes.*

With Condition 3.9 in place, the power of a Byzantine node is reduced to (i) locally accelerating the progress of a pulse by sending messages prematurely, (ii) delaying or halting the progress of a pulse by sending a message late or not at all, or (iii) asymmetrically combining (i) and (ii) by speeding up the progress of a pulse on one side and delaying it on the other side. For a single faulty node, the respective effects are always limited to increasing skews by at most a few d^+, since we can "work around" the defective node in our reasoning. In particular, when inductively constructing a zig-zag path (which will imply a skew bound), we can switch to the other causal link of the current node if we run into a Byzantine node. Note that such a node could increase the skew caused along the original (shortest) zig-zag path, since it may trigger the next node along the path (and hence the fast node among the two suffering from the worst-case skew) d^- time earlier than a correct node. Similarly, since a Byzantine node could impair our reasoning why the slow node is triggered in a timely fashion, we can just avoid reasoning about the faulty node's behavior and make a short "detour". In both cases, the alternative paths considered have lengths almost identical to the ones constructed for the fault-free case, which results in a small increase of the corresponding skew bounds only.

Crash Faults and Fault Containment. For multiple faults, such arguments do not apply in all cases. For example, if every other node in a layer is crash-faulty, Condition 3.9 is not violated. Yet, no node in the layers above is triggered at all.

It is easy to see, however, that such problematic fault patterns entail faults in close vicinity to each other. If it is not the case that an entire layer "blocks" pulses and sufficiently many layers above it are fault-free the caused damage to the synchronization quality will "heal". An extreme case of this kind of resilience is illustrated by Theorem 3.8, which shows that within $2W - 2$ layers the strong skew bounds of the fault-free case are established for *arbitrary* initial skews, provided that there are sufficiently many consecutive fault-free layers (and the pulse arrives at the lowest of them at all). Less severe problems will cause less hassle (cf. Section 4).

Pulse Separation. As discussed in Section 2, we require that pulses arrive at each node sufficiently well-separated so that the nodes do not need to keep track of the pulse number and can rely on the proposed simple sleeping mechanism instead. This amounts to ensuring that, for each node, the sleep period of at most T^+ after triggering pulse k is over before any signal of pulse $k + 1$ arrives, i.e.,

$$t_{\ell,i}^{(k)} + T^+ \le \max\{t_{\ell,i-1}^{(k+1)}, t_{\ell-1,i}^{(k+1)}, t_{\ell-1,i+1}^{(k+1)}, t_{\ell,i+1}^{(k+1)}\} + d^-.$$

In the fault-free case, the following condition is sufficient:

CONDITION 3.10 (FAULT-FREE SEPARATION TIME). *For all $k \in \mathbb{N}$, we require that*

$$\min_{i \in [W]}\{t_{0,i}^{(k+1)}\} \ge \max_{i \in [W]}\{t_{0,i}^{(k)}\} + L\varepsilon + T^+.$$

If there are no faults, $t_{\ell,i}^{(k)} \le \max_{i \in [W]}\{t_{0,i}^{(k)}\} + \ell d^+$ and any node in layer $\ell - 1$ or ℓ will not trigger pulse $k + 1$ before time $\min_{i \in [W]}\{t_{0,i}^{(k+1)}\} + (\ell - 1)d^-$. Since $\ell \le L$, we see that Condition 3.10 is sufficient in the fault-free case.

In the presence of faults, a conservative bound would argue that the longest feasible time for a pulse to reach all nodes is bounded by WLd^+,[4] however, such a worst-case bound will be of little significance in practice. For the system to be operational, the number of faults must be sufficiently small to maintain reasonable skews. Moreover, faults significantly affecting the time to complete pulses, yet at the same time not causing large skews, appear extremely unlikely. Hence adding a slack of a few d^+ to Condition 3.10

---

[4]This follows since acceptable fault patterns disallow that non-faulty nodes are triggered by faulty ones, implying that the pulse must be complete if for more than d^+ time no node is triggered.

should suffice in all relevant cases. This view is supported by our simulations, see Section 4.

Self-stabilization. *Self-stabilization* is the ability of the system to recover from an unbounded number of arbitrary transient faults [3]. That is, once transient faults cease, the system will resume normal operation within a bounded *stabilization time*. This is equivalent to demanding that a system where the individual components behave according to their specification will resume normal operation from an arbitrary initial state, since arbitrary faults may result in arbitrary states. Recall that the pulse generation at layer 0 is outside the scope of this paper; to make the system as a whole self-stabilizing, clearly a self-stabilizing algorithm is to be employed for that purpose.

THEOREM 3.11. *Suppose* $\max_{k \in \mathbb{N}}\{\Delta_0^{(k)}\} \leq \Delta$ *and denote* $\sigma_0 := \Delta + d^-$. *Assume that*[5]

$$\min_{i \in [W]}\{t_{0,i}^{(k+1)}\} \geq \max_{i \in [W]}\{t_{0,i}^{(k)}\} + Wd^+ + L\varepsilon + T^+,$$

that $T^- > \sigma_\ell + d^+ + \varepsilon + t_{pulse}$ *for all* $\ell \in [L+1]$, *where* σ_ℓ *is as in Theorem 3.8 with* $\Delta_0 = \Delta$, *and that the pulse generation algorithm employed at layer 0 is self-stabilizing. Then, HEX self-stabilizes within L pulses once layer 0 stabilized, in the sense that each node triggers exactly once per pulse, and for each pulse the bounds from Theorem 3.8 apply.*

PROOF. For simplicity, we denote the first correctly generated pulse as pulse 0. Hence the induction hypothesis is that layer ℓ executes pulses $k \geq \ell$ correctly. Denote for $k \in \mathbb{N}_0$ by $t_-^{(k)}$ and $t_+^{(k)}$ the times when the first and last nodes in layer 0 trigger their k^{th} pulse, respectively. To perform the induction step from $\ell \in \mathbb{N}_0$ to $\ell + 1$, observe that the induction hypothesis applied to layer ℓ implies that, for all $k \geq \ell$, no nodes in layer ℓ are triggered during

$$\left[t_+^{(k)} + \ell d^+, t_-^{(k+1)} + \ell d^-\right].$$

Consequently, no trigger messages from layer ℓ are received by nodes in layer $\ell + 1$ during

$$\left[t_+^{(k)} + (\ell+1)d^+, t_-^{(k+1)} + (\ell+1)d^-\right].$$

Hence no node in layer $\ell + 1$ can be triggered twice during this period. If for d^+ additional time no node in layer $\ell+1$ is triggered within this interval, this implies that all messages have been received and therefore no further nodes may trigger. Overall, it follows that no node on layer $\ell + 1$ may be triggered during the interval

$$[t_+^{(k)} + (\ell+1)d^+ + Wd^+, t_-^{(k+1)} + (\ell+1)d^-],$$

implying that none of these nodes is sleeping during

$$[t_+^{(k)} + (\ell+1)d^+ + Wd^+ + T^+, t_-^{(k+1)} + (\ell+1)d^-].$$

By the prerequisites of the theorem, this time interval is non-empty. Hence, all nodes in layer $\ell + 1$ will be ready to participate in pulse $k + 1$.

It remains to show that each node will trigger exactly once per pulse and that the skew bounds hold. To see this, we show by induction on the layers $\ell \in \{1, \ldots, L\}$ that (i) for pulses $k > \ell$, no node in layer $1, \ldots, \ell$ will trigger due to a "falsely" memorized trigger message from a neighbor from

---

[5]We assume that messages are zero-length signal pulses here.

which the trigger message for pulse k has not been received yet and (ii) that the skew bounds from Theorem 3.8 apply to layers $1, \ldots, \ell$ for pulses $k > \ell$. Note that (ii) follows from (i) and the fact that we just showed that no node on layer $\ell' \in \{1, \ldots, \ell\}$ is sleeping when pulse k arrives, since this implies that the assumptions on the behaviour of the nodes made in Section 3.1 hold and Theorem 3.8 applies.

To anchor the induction at $\ell = 0$, we just observe that the skew bounds are satisfied with respect to σ_0, as we will not require more than that for the induction step. For the step from ℓ to $\ell+1 \in \mathbb{N}$, recall that we already know that all nodes on layer $\ell + 1$ will be triggered at least once for each pulse $k \geq \ell+1$. Hence, for node $(\ell+1, i)$, $i \in \{1, \ldots, W\}$, we can define $t_{\ell+1,i}^{(k)}$ as the first such triggering time (uniqueness will follow later). For each i, one of the links $((\ell, i), (\ell+1, i))$ or $((\ell, i+1), (\ell+1, i))$ is causal. W.l.o.g. let it be $((\ell, i), (\ell+1, i))$ (the other case is symmetrical). Then $t_{\ell+1,i}^{(k)} \geq t_{\ell,i}^{(k)} + d^-$. It follows that $t_{\ell,i+1}^{(k)} \leq t_{\ell,i}^{(k)} + \sigma_\ell \leq t_{\ell+1,i}^{(k)} + \sigma_\ell - d^-$. Hence, since nodes $(\ell+1, i-1)$ and $(\ell+1, i+1)$ follow at most d^+ after $t_{\ell,i+1}^{(k)}$, we observe

$$\max\left\{t_{\ell+1,i-1}^{(k)}, t_{\ell,i}^{(k)}, t_{\ell,i+1}^{(k)}, t_{\ell+1,i+1}^{(k)}\right\} \leq t_{\ell+1,i}^{(k)} + \sigma_\ell + \varepsilon,$$

implying that node $(\ell+1, i)$ will not receive any message from pulses $\leq k$ after time $t_{\ell+1,i}^{(k)} + \sigma_\ell + d^+ + \varepsilon \leq t_{\ell+1,i}^{(k)} + T^-$, showing (i) for $\ell + 1$. As (ii) follows by Theorem 3.8, this completes the induction and also the proof. □

Note that the same reasoning applies in the presence of crashed nodes, provided the skew bounds (and thus also T^-) are adapted accordingly. For Byzantine faults, stabilization is more involved and requires to modify the algorithm: If a node has e.g. a Byzantine lower-left neighbor and misses the trigger signal of pulse k from its right neighbor due to sleeping, but just wakes up before the signal from its lower right neighbor arrives, the Byzantine neighbor can trigger the node at any later point in time. In particular, it can send the node to sleep such that the same situation occurs in pulses $k + 1, k + 2, \ldots$ Slightly more complex triggering rules that take into account the timing of the received signals may circumvent this issue.

It should also be noted that the required pulse separation time of Theorem 3.11 can be reduced, since a more involved analysis can be used to prove stabilization without a linear additive term of Wd^+. The detailed exploration of these issues, which determine the maximum sustainable clock frequency, is an important part of our future work.

4. SIMULATION EXPERIMENTS

In order to get an idea of the behavior of HEX in realistic scenarios, we developed a framework for simulation experiments. Rather than simulating the simple VHDL implementation[6] of Algorithm 1 in Modelsim directly, we used Matlab due to its greater flexibility and controllability.

---

[6]Algorithm 1 just consists of a 3-state asynchronous state machine in conjunction with memory flags (flip-flops) for memorizing the reception of trigger signals from neighbors. State *fire*, entered when the node is triggered, signals a clock pulse to its neighbors and is immediately left for state *sleep*, where the clock pulse is reverted and the sleep timeout is started. When it expires, the state machine clears all memory flags and enters the state *wait*, where it remains until one of the triggering conditions becomes true.

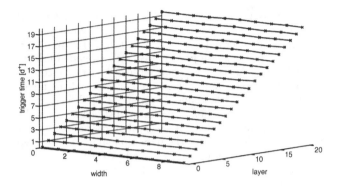

Figure 7: Pulse wave propagation for uniformly chosen link delays in $[50, 55]$ and $\sigma_0 = \Delta_0 = 0$.

	intra-layer		inter-layer		
init. layer 0	avg	max	min	avg	max
0	2.19	13	50	53.95	67
rand. $[0, d^-]$	3.31	44	50	54.84	103
rand. $[0, d^+]$	3.42	49	50	54.94	108
ramp d^+	12.99	55	34	60.08	110

Table 1: Intra- and inter-layer skews of all nodes in the grid from 100 simulation runs, for uniformly random link delays in $[50, 55]$.

	intra-layer		inter-layer		
init. layer 0	avg	max	min	avg	max
0	9.66	56	50	68.89	124
rand. $[0, d^-]$	10.37	62	50	69.43	131
rand. $[0, d^+]$	10.94	66	46	69.86	146
ramp d^+	23.4	79	-15	74.51	150

Table 2: Intra- and inter-layer skews of all nodes in the grid from 100 simulation runs, for uniformly random link delays in $[50, 75]$.

To complement the analytic results provided in the previous section, this section provides a glimpse of our simulation results. Their primary purpose is the following:

(1) *Demonstrating small typical skew in the fault-free case.* The quite fancy scenarios required for establishing the worst-case skews in Theorem 3.8 suggest that they are very unlikely to occur in practice. Our simulation studies support this view.

(2) *Demonstrating fault locality.* As argued in Section 3.2, HEX implicitly confines the effects of faulty nodes. Our simulation results show that this is indeed true, even for clustered crash faults and multiple (but separated) Byzantine nodes.

For our simulations, we developed a Matlab implementation of Algorithm 1 that can be plugged into arbitrarily sized grids with configurable topologies. We implemented different choices for the individual link delays, including uniformly at random from $[d^-, d^+]$ and fixed values. Different choices for the triggering times of the nodes in layer 0 are also provided.

The primary quantities of interest observed in our simulation runs are the intra-layer neighbor skews $\max\{|t_{\ell,i} - t_{\ell,i+1}|, |t_{\ell,i} - t_{\ell,i-1}|\}$ of every node (ℓ, i) in layer ℓ, as well as the inter-layer neighbor skews, i.e., $t_{\ell+1,i-1} - t_{\ell,i}$ and $t_{\ell+1,i} - t_{\ell,i}$ of every node (ℓ, i) relative to its direct layer $\ell+1$ neighbors $(\ell+1, i-1)$ and $(\ell+1, i)$, respectively. Note that the former is defined in terms of the absolute values due to the symmetry of the topology (and thus skews) within a layer, whereas the latter respects the sign of the difference in trigger times. This is of interest, since the (non-zero) *expected* clock skew between adjacent layers can be compensated at the level of the (final) local clocks (to be synchronized by means of the HEX pulses), thereby providing clocks that are also well-synchronized between different layers.

We compute the skews from the matrix of all triggering times $t_{\ell,i}$ obtained in a simulation run; this data also allows us to visualize the detailed propagation of a pulse throughout the grid.

The Fault-free Case. We conducted a suite of simulations that complement the analytic intra- and inter-layer worst-case skew bounds given in Theorem 3.8. As an appetizer, Figure 7 shows a 3D plot of a typical pulse propagation wave in a grid with $W = 10$ and $L = 20$. The entire grid (sliced between width $W - 1$ and $0 \equiv W$) lies in the $(\ell \in [L + 1], i \in [W])$ plane, the z-axis gives the triggering time $t_{\ell,w}$ of the corresponding node (ℓ, i). To improve

the readability of intra-layer skews, we connected all points $(\ell, i, t_{\ell,w})$ and $(\ell, i + 1, t_{\ell,i+1})$, $i \in [W - 1]$. It is apparent that the wave propagates evenly throughout the grid, nicely smoothing out differences in link delays. We note, though, that by choosing the delays accordingly, we were able to produce pulse propagation waves exhibiting the worst-case skew of Lemma 3.6 (see Figure 6).

Table 1 and Table 2 show, for four different choices of the layer 0 skews between neighbors, the average and maximal intra-layer skews and the minimal, average, and maximal inter-layer skews, respectively. These values where computed over all nodes and 100 simulation runs.

Table 1 shows the skews for link delays chosen uniformly at random from $[50, 55]$ (such that $d^+ = 1.1d^-$ and $\varepsilon/d^+ = 1/11$) in all settings. The triggering times of the layer 0 nodes $t_{0,i}$ are (i) all 0 (resulting in $\sigma_0 = 0$ and skew potential $\Delta_0 = 0$), (ii) uniformly in $[0, d^-]$ (i.e., $\sigma_0 \approx d^-$ and $\Delta_0 = 0$), (iii) uniformly in $[0, d^+]$ (i.e., $\sigma_0 \approx d^+$ and $\Delta_0 \approx \varepsilon$), and (iv) ramping-up/down by d^+, i.e., $t_{0,i+1} = t_{0,i} + d^+$ for $0 \leq i < W/2$ and $t_{0,i+1} = t_{0,i} - d^+$ for $W/2 \leq i < W - 1$ (i.e., $\sigma_0 = d^+$ and $\Delta_0 = W\varepsilon/2 = 25$). Note that (iii) resp. (iv) reasonably model the average case and worst-case input provided by a layer 0 clock generation scheme with neighbor skew bound d^+, respectively.

Figure 8 shows the histogram of the skew distribution of (i). For (ii) and (iii) the distributions look very similar, whereas for the extreme case of (iv) the large initial skews result in noticeably worse bounds for the first few layers. Due to lack of space, we summarize the results in Table 2.

Our simulation results show that the typical skews are considerably smaller than our analytic worst-case bounds: For example, plugging the above parameters and $\Delta_0 = 0$ into Theorem 3.8 yields an intra-layer skew bound of $d^+ + \lceil W\varepsilon/d^+ \rceil \varepsilon \approx 80$ and an inter-layer skew in the range of $\approx [-30, 135]$. By contrast, even for setting (iii) with $\Delta_0 \approx \varepsilon$, the average of the observed intra-layer skew is below 4, with a maximum of 49, and the range of inter-layer skews is $[50, 108]$. It should be particularly noted that for settings (i)-(iii) the minimal inter-layer skew is always 50, showing

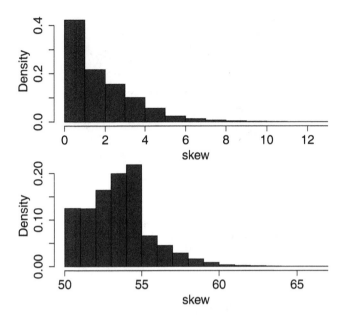

Figure 8: Cumulated histograms for intra-layer (top) and inter-layer (bottom) skew for uniformly chosen link delays in $[50, 55]$ and $\sigma_0 = \Delta_0 = 0$.

that all nodes were centrally triggered and no "intervention" by neighbors within a layer was ever necessary.

Table 2 gives the skews for link delays chosen uniformly in $[50, 75]$ (such that $d^+ = 1.5d^-$ and $\varepsilon/d^+ = 1/3$). Note that the latter choice of d^+ and d^- violates the constraint $\varepsilon \leq d^+/7$ of Theorem 3.8; we included this scenario to also shed some light on the behavior of HEX in extreme situations, however. Qualitatively, the situation is very similar to the previous one, except that the grid does not recover as well from the large initial skews of (iv). Small values of ε hence provide excellent skew bounds and fast recovery from initial skews in the fault-free setting, which has been supported by preliminary simulation runs as well.

Failures. To back up our considerations related to failures in Section 3.2, we provide two 3D plots of wave propagation in the presence of crashed and Byzantine faulty nodes, respectively, which clearly demonstrate the claimed failure locality property. Figure 9 shows a setup where a whole cluster of nodes $((3,7), (3,8), (4,6), (4,7), (4,8), (5,6)$ and $(5,7))$ has crashed.[7] Observe that the disturbances (= increase) of the skew emanating from the faulty nodes fade with the distance from the fault location, and how nodes above establish synchrony via left- and right-triggering.

Figure 10 shows a scenario with a single Byzantine node $(2,8)$ that sends a zero-delay trigger message to its right and up-right neighbors when triggered itself and delays the messages to its other neighbors for $3d^+$. It is evident from the figure that the disruptive power of this fault is not much worse than that of a crash fault. This is also confirmed by Table 3, which provides the analog to the fault-free results given in Table 1. Further simulations, shown in Figure 11 and Figure 12, confirmed that this also holds in the presence of multiple (separated) Byzantine faults.

---

[7] Note that the Node $(6,6)$ cannot make progress as both neighbors in layer 5 have crashed.

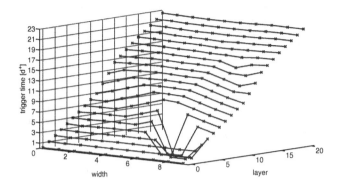

Figure 9: Pulse wave propagation for uniformly chosen link delays in $[50, 55]$ and $\sigma_0 = 0$, with a cluster of crashed nodes ("fake" trigger time -1).

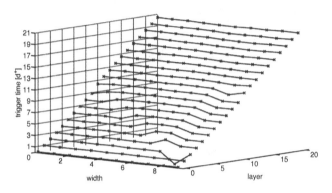

Figure 10: Pulse wave propagation for uniformly chosen link delays in $[50, 55]$ and $\sigma_0 = 0$, with one Byzantine node ("fake" trigger time of -1).

5. CONCLUSIONS & FUTURE WORK

In this work, we proposed a candidate for a scalable and fault-tolerant alternative for clock distribution in VLSI circuits. Whereas our analysis proved that HEX has excellent features, several important issues still need to be addressed for making the approach feasible in practice. An important part of our future work is devoted to the following topics:

Clock Frequency. Due to the tick separation requirement required for self-stabilization (cf. Theorem 3.11) of Algorithm 1, HEX cannot be used for distributing very high-frequency clock pulses. Several solutions are conceivable to eventually achieve this: Local clock multipliers, e.g. (i) Phase-Locked Loops (PLL) that lock on the low-frequency pulses, or (ii) pausible high-frequency local clocks started upon a tick that generate a fixed number of fast clock pulses. Note that (i) provides smoother clocks but requires low-jitter input clocks (guaranteed by HEX at least for static crash failures). Alternatively, (iii) pipelining of ticks as in [9] could be used. This would avoid the need for sleeping times and tick separation, but requires additional hardware for locally counting ticks and a considerably more involved self-stabilization analysis.

Embedding. The presented topology can be embedded into a VLSI circuit using two interconnect layers: One simply "squeezes" the cylindric shape of the HEX grid flat. However, this simplistic solution has two substantial drawbacks. First, the now physically close nodes from opposite "sides"

init. layer 0	intra-layer		inter-layer		
	avg	max	min	avg	max
0	6.51	64	41	56.15	113
rand. $[0, d^-]$	7.16	82	27	56.79	140
rand. $[0, d^+]$	7.24	85	24	56.87	143
ramp d^+	13.05	165	-18	59.85	162

Table 3: Skews of all nodes in the grid from 100 simulation runs with a single Byzantine node, for uniformly chosen link delays in $[50, 55]$.

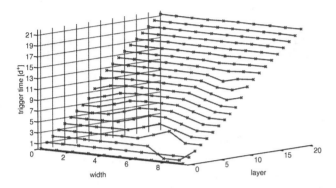

Figure 11: Pulse wave propagation for uniformly chosen link delays in $[50, 55]$ and $\sigma_0 = \Delta_0 = 0$, with two byzantine nodes ("fake" trigger time -1).

of the original cylinder are distant in the grid and therefore may suffer from larger skews. This might entail that actually half of the nodes cannot be used for clocking. Second, it might be difficult to synchronize the nodes at layer 0 unless they are physically close. This requires that either $W \ll L$ and the chip is rectangular with a large discrepancy in side lengths, or a way of (reliably and accurately) distributing a clock signal to nodes arranged in a line.

As a remedy, we propose the use of a slightly modified topology that arranges the nodes of each layer in a circular pattern. To avoid large variations in link lengths, we include "doubling layers" where we "duplicate" the nodes of a standard layer to quickly increase the number of nodes (see Figure 13). This topology has several advantages over a cylindric HEX grid: (i) only a few links require an addi-

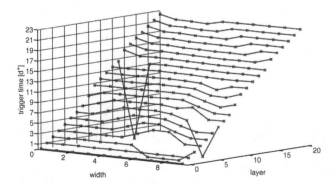

Figure 12: Pulse wave propagation for uniformly chosen link delays in $[50, 55]$ and $\sigma_0 = \Delta_0 = 0$, with multiple byzantine nodes ("fake" trigger time -1).

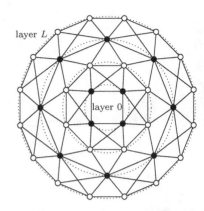

Figure 13: Alternative Topology. White nodes are in doubling layers. Doubling layers become less frequent with increasing distance from the center.

tional interconnect layer, (ii) doubling layers will help disperse skews and thus may only improve the bounds,[8] and (iii) since the "initial" width W close to the clock source is very small and most doubling layers are close to the source as well, any initial skew will be mitigated very quickly.

Fault-tolerance Properties. A more detailed theoretical analysis as well as measurements that determine realistic fault patterns are in order to make best use of the potential for resilience of the HEX topology. In particular, a simple solution for self-stabilization despite ongoing Byzantine faults seems both possible and highly desirable, and a quantitative analysis of the skews in the presence of a larger number of faults is of interest. Concerning the latter, suitable probabilistic fault models are to be established and analyzed.

Skews in Realistic Executions. Regarding the skew bounds from Theorem 3.8, even for a fairly large value of ε, say $0.1d^+$, it appears reasonable to assume that $\min\{L, W\} \cdot \varepsilon^2/d^+ \leq d^+$, since otherwise the chip would comprise at least 10,000 HEX nodes. Moreover, since link lengths are near-identical (or vary within a small constant factor for the alternative topology proposed above), smaller ε should be affordable at reasonable costs. The skew bound is thus essentially $\mathcal{O}(d^+)$, where the constant depends on the fault patterns and the fault locality properties of HEX. This should be contrasted with the skew on a clock tree, where the dominating term is the maximal difference of signal propagation times to the leaves. While the latter may be small compared to the total delays in a tree, one needs to take into account that the total distance bridged by the signal is (for an H-tree) close to half of the circumference of the (rectangular) chip. In particular for large chips, HEX may thus be competitive in terms of the skew between physically close functional units, despite its excellent resilience to faults! Improving our understanding of the skew incurred by HEX in realistic executions with multiple faults is thus a pivotal part of our future work.

Static Systems. An important special case occurs when the delay of each individual link is the same in each pulse (up to negligible fluctuations) and faults are *static* in the sense that the respective nodes respond identically in each

---

[8]This follows from the proofs in Section 3.1; the rightward/leftward links vital for the slower node catching up are in smaller layers than those required to trigger a fast node early.

pulse. Then the system will stabilize to a fixed triggering pattern that is identically reproduced for each pulse. Note that this covers an important class of realistic fault patterns, in particular, manufacturing defects and electric wear-out as well as the result of some dynamic grid reconfiguration in case of failures. Understanding this setting is thus of high interest for potential applications of our scheme.

6. REFERENCES

[1] R. Bhamidipati, A. Zaidi, S. Makineni, K. Low, R. Chen, K.-Y. Liu, and J. Dalgrehn. Challenges and Methodologies for Implementing High-Performance Network Processors. *Intel Technology Journal*, 6(3):83–92, 2002.

[2] D. M. Chapiro. *Globally-Asynchronous Locally-Synchronous Systems*. PhD thesis, Stanford University, 1984.

[3] E. W. Dijkstra. Self-Stabilizing Systems in Spite of Distributed Control. *Communications of the ACM*, 17(11):643–644, 1974.

[4] C. Dike and E. Burton. Miller and Noise Effects in a Synchronizing Flip-Flop. *IEEE Journal of Solid-State Circuits*, SC-34(6):849–855, 1999.

[5] D. Dolev, M. Függer, C. Lenzen, and U. Schmid. Fault-Tolerant Algorithms for Tick-Generation in Asynchronous Logic: Robust Pulse Generation - [Extended Abstract]. In *Proc. 13th Symposium on Stabilization, Safety, and Security of Distributed Systems (SSS)*, pages 163–177, 2011.

[6] S. Fairbanks. Method and Apparatus for a Distributed Clock Generator, 2004. US patent no. US2004108876.

[7] S. Fairbanks and S. Moore. Self-Timed Circuitry for Global Clocking. In *Proc. 11th Symposium on Advanced Research in Asynchronous Circuits and Systems (ASYNC)*, pages 86–96, 2005.

[8] E. G. Friedman. Clock Distribution Networks in Synchronous Digital Integrated Circuits. *Proceedings of the IEEE*, 89(5):665–692, 2001.

[9] M. Függer, A. Dielacher, and U. Schmid. How to Speed-Up Fault-Tolerant Clock Generation in VLSI Systems-on-Chip via Pipelining. In *Proc. 8th European Dependable Computing Conference (EDCC)*, pages 230–239, 2010.

[10] M. Függer and U. Schmid. Reconciling Fault-Tolerant Distributed Computing and Systems-on-Chip. *Distributed Computing*, 24(6):323–355, 2012.

[11] V. Gutnik and A. Chandrakasan. Active GHz Clock Network Using Distributed PLLs. *IEEE Journal of Solid-State Circuits*, 35(11):1553–1560, 2000.

[12] IEEE-SA Standards Board. IEEE Standard for a Precision Clock Synchronization Protocol for Networked Measurement and Control Systems. *IEEE Std 1588-2008 (Revision of IEEE Std 1588-2002)*, pages c1–269, 2008.

[13] D. J. Kinniment, A. Bystrov, and A. V. Yakovlev. Synchronization Circuit Performance. *IEEE Journal of Solid-State Circuits*, SC-37(2):202–209, 2002.

[14] A. Korniienko, E. Colinet, G. Scorletti, E. Blanco, D. Galayko, and J. Juillard. A Clock Network of Distributed ADPLLs Using an Asymmetric Comparison Strategy. In *Proc. 2010 Symposium on Circuits and Systems (ISCAS)*, pages 3212–3215, 2010.

[15] D.-J. Lee, M.-C. Kim, and I. Markov. Low-power Clock Trees for CPUs. In *Proc. 2010 Conference on Computer-Aided Design (ICCAD)*, pages 444–451, 2010.

[16] D.-J. Lee and I. Markov. Multilevel Tree Fusion for Robust Clock Networks. In *2011 Conference on Computer-Aided Design (ICCAD)*, pages 632–639, 2011.

[17] M. S. Maza and M. L. Aranda. Interconnected Rings and Oscillators as Gigahertz Clock Distribution Nets. In *Proc. 13th Great Lakes Symposium on VLSI (GLSVLSI)*, pages 41–44, 2003.

[18] D. G. Messerschmitt. Synchronization in Digital System Design. *IEEE Journal on Selected Areas in Communications*, 8(8):1404–1419, 1990.

[19] C. Metra, S. Francescantonio, and T. Mak. Implications of Clock Distribution Faults and Issues with Screening them During Manufacturing Testing. *IEEE Transactions on Computers*, 53(5):531–546, 2004.

[20] T. Polzer, T. Handl, and A. Steininger. A Metastability-Free Multi-synchronous Communication Scheme for SoCs. In *Proc. 11th Symposium on Stabilization, Safety, and Security of Distributed Systems (SSS)*, pages 578–592, 2009.

[21] C. L. Portmann and T. H. Y. Meng. Supply Noise and CMOS Synchronization Errors. *IEEE Journal of Solid-State Circuits*, SC-30(9):1015–1017, 1995.

[22] S. Reddy, G. Wilke, and R. Murgai. Analyzing Timing Uncertainty in Mesh-based Clock Architectures. In *Proc. Design, Automation and Test in Europe (DATE)*, volume 1, pages 1–6, 2006.

[23] P. Restle, T. McNamara, D. Webber, P. Camporese, K. Eng, K. Jenkins, D. Allen, M. Rohn, M. Quaranta, D. Boerstler, C. Alpert, C. Carter, R. Bailey, J. Petrovick, B. Krauter, and B. McCredie. A Clock Distribution Network for Microprocessors. *IEEE Journal of Solid-State Circuits*, 36(5):792–799, 2001.

[24] M. Saint-Laurent and M. Swaminathan. A Multi-PLL Clock Distribution Architecture for Gigascale Integration. In *Proc. 2001 IEEE Computer Society Workshop on VLSI (WVLSI)*, pages 30–35, 2001.

[25] Y. Semiat and R. Ginosar. Timing Measurements of Synchronization Circuits. In *Proc. 9th Symposium on Asynchronous Circuits and Systems (ASYNC)*, 2003.

[26] R. Shelar. Routing with Constraints for Post-Grid Clock Distribution in Microprocessors. *IEEE Transactions on Computer-Aided Design of Integrated Circuits and Systems*, 29(2):245–249, 2010.

[27] C. N. Sze. ISPD 2010 High Performance Clock Network Synthesis Contest: Benchmark Suite and Results. In *Proc. 19th Symposium on Physical Design (ISPD)*, pages 143–143, 2010.

[28] P. Teehan, M. Greenstreet, and G. Lemieux. A Survey and Taxonomy of GALS Design Styles. *IEEE Design and Test of Computers*, 24(5):418–428, 2007.

[29] C. Yeh, G. Wilke, H. Chen, S. Reddy, H. Nguyen, T. Miyoshi, W. Walker, and R. Murgai. Clock Distribution Architectures: a Comparative Study. In *Proc. 7th Symposium on Quality Electronic Design (ISQED)*, pages 85–91, 2006.

Coalescing-Branching Random Walks on Graphs

Chinmoy Dutta [*]
Twitter
chinmoy@twitter.com

Gopal Pandurangan [†]
Nanyang Technological
University
Brown University
gopalpandurangan@gmail.com

Rajmohan Rajaraman [‡]
Northeastern University
rraj@ccs.neu.edu

Scott Roche [§]
Northeastern University
str@ccs.neu.edu

ABSTRACT

We study a distributed randomized information propagation mechanism in networks we call the *coalescing-branching random walk* (cobra walk, for short). A cobra walk is a generalization of the well-studied "standard" random walk, and is useful in modeling and understanding the Susceptible-Infected-Susceptible (SIS)-type of epidemic processes in networks. It can also be helpful in performing light-weight information dissemination in resource-constrained networks. A cobra walk is parameterized by a *branching factor* k. The process starts from an arbitrary node, which is labeled *active* for step 1. (For instance, this could be a node that has a piece of data, rumor, or a virus.) In each step of a cobra walk, each active node chooses k random neighbors to become active for the next step ("branching"). A node is active for step $t + 1$ only if it is chosen by an active node in step t ("coalescing"). This results in a stochastic process in the underlying network with properties that are quite different from both the standard random walk (which is equivalent to the cobra walk with branching factor 1) as well as other gossip-based rumor spreading mechanisms.

We focus on the *cover time* of the cobra walk, which is the number of steps for the walk to reach all the nodes, and derive almost-tight bounds for various graph classes. Our main technical result is an $O(\log^2 n)$ high probability bound for the cover time of cobra walks on expanders, if either the expansion factor or the branching factor is sufficiently large; we also obtain an $O(\log n)$ high probability bound for the *partial cover time*, which is the number of steps needed for the walk to reach at least a constant fraction of the nodes. We show that the cobra walk takes $O(n \log n)$ steps on any n-node tree for $k \geq 2$, and $\tilde{O}(n^{1/d})$ steps on a d-dimensional grid for $k \geq 2$, with high probability.

Categories and Subject Descriptors

G.3 [**Probability and Statistics**]: Stochastic processes; Probabilistic Algorithms; G.2.2 [**Discrete Mathematics: Graph Theory**]: Graph algorithms

General Terms

Algorithms, Theory

Keywords

Random Walks, Networks, Information Spreading, Cover Time, Epidemic Processes

[*]Chinmoy Dutta was at Northeastern University when this work was done, and supported by NSF grant CCF-0845003 and a Microsoft grant to Ravi Sundaram.

[†]Supported in part by Nanyang Technological University grant M58110000, Singapore Ministry of Education (MOE) Academic Research Fund (AcRF) Tier 2 grant MOE2010-T2-2-082, and MOE AcRF Tier 1 grant MOE2012-T1-001-094, and by a grant from the United States-Israel Binational Science Foundation (BSF).

[‡]Partially supported by NSF grants CCF-1216038 and CSR-1217812. Part of this work was done when Rajmohan Rajaraman was a Visiting Scientist at Google Research.

[§]Partially supported by NSF grant CSR-1217812 and by a grant from the United States-Israel Binational Science Foundation (BSF).

1. INTRODUCTION

We study a distributed propagation mechanism in networks, called the *coalescing-branching random walk* (*cobra walk*, for short). A cobra walk is a variant of the standard random walk, and is parameterized by a *branching factor*, k. The process starts from an arbitrary node, which is initially labeled *active*. For instance, this could be a node that has a piece of data, rumor, or a virus. In a cobra walk, for each discrete time step, each active node chooses k random neighbors (sampled independently with replacement) to become active for the next step; this is the "branching" property, in which each node spawns multiple independent random walks. A node is active for step t if and only if it is chosen by an active node in step $t - 1$; this is the "coalescing" property, i.e., if multiple walks meet at a node, they coalesce into one walk.

A cobra walk generalizes the standard random walk [35, 39], which is equivalent to a cobra walk with $k = 1$. Random walks on graphs have a wide variety of applications, including being fundamental primitives in distributed network algorithms for load balancing, routing, information propagation, gossip, and search [16, 17, 8, 44]. Being local and requiring little state information, random walks and their variants are especially well-suited for self-organizing dynamic networks such as Internet overlay, ad hoc wireless, and sensor networks [44]. As a propagation mechanism, one parameter of interest is the *cover time*, the expected time it takes to cover all the nodes in a network. Since the cover time of the standard random walk can be large — $\Theta(n^3)$ in the worst case, $\Theta(n \log n)$ even for expanders [35] — some recent studies have studied simple adaptations of random walks that can speed up cover time [1, 5, 18]. Our analysis of cobra walks continues this line of research, with the aim of studying a lightweight information dissemination process that has the potential to improve cover time significantly.

Our primary motivation for studying cobra walks is their close connection to SIS-type epidemic processes in networks. The SIS (standing for Susceptible Infected Susceptible) model (e.g., [20]) is widely used for capturing the spread of diseases in human contact networks or propagation of viruses in computer networks. Three basic properties of an SIS process are: (a) a node can infect one or more of its neighbors ("branching" property); (b) a node can be infected by one or more of its neighbors ("coalescence" property) and (c) an infected node can be cured and then become susceptible to infection at a later stage. Cobra walks satisfy all these properties, while standard random walks and other gossip-based propagation mechanisms violate one or more. Also, while there has been considerable work on the SIS model ([28, 43, 31, 20, 40, 19, 6]), it has been analytically hard to tackle basic *coverage* questions: (1) How long will it take for the epidemic to infect, say, a constant fraction of network? (2) Will every node be infected at some point, and how long will this take? Our analysis of cobra walks in certain special graph classes is a step toward a better understanding of such questions for SIS-type processes.

1.1 Our results and techniques

We derive near-tight bounds on the cover time of cobra walks on trees, grids, and expanders. These special graph classes arise in many distributed network applications, especially in the modeling and construction of peer-to-peer (P2P), overlay, ad hoc, and sensor networks. For example, expanders have been used for modeling and construction of P2P and overlay networks, grids and related graphs have been used as models for ad hoc and sensor networks, and spanning trees are often used as backbones for various information propagation tasks.

We begin with an observation that Matthew's Theorem [37, 35] for random walks extends to cobra walks; that is, the cover time of a cobra walk on an n-node graph is at most $\ln n$ times the maximum hitting time of a node. Hitting time is the expected time until a walk originating at $u \in V$ reaches $v \in V$ for the first time. For many graphs, this bound is also a tight bound. This enables us to focus on deriving bounds for the hitting time.

We face two technical challenges in our analysis. First, unlike in a standard random walk, cobra walks have multiple "active" nodes at any step, and in almost all graphs,

it is difficult to characterize the distribution of the active nodes at any point of time. Second, the combination of the branching and coalescing properties introduces a non-trivial dependence among the active nodes, making it challenging to quantify the probability that a given node is made active during a given time period. Surprisingly, these challenges manifest even in tree networks. We present a result that gives tight bound on the cover time for trees, which we obtain by establishing a recurrence relation for the expected time taken for the cobra walk to cross an edge along a given path of the tree.

- For an arbitrary n-node tree, a cobra walk with $k \geq 2$ covers all nodes in $O(n \log n)$ steps with high probability (w.h.p., for short)[1] (Theorem 5 of Section 3.1).

For a matching lower bound, we note that the cover time of a cobra walk in a star graph is $\Omega(n \log n)$ w.h.p. We conjecture that the cover time for *any n-node graph* is $O(n \log n)$. By exploiting the regular structure of a grid, we establish improved and near-tight bounds for the cover time on d-dimensional grids.

- For a d-dimensional grid, we show that a cobra walk with $k \geq 2$ takes $\tilde{O}(n^{1/d})$ steps, w.h.p. (cf. Theorem 8 of Section 3.2).

Our main technical result is an analysis of cobra walks on expanders, which are graphs in which every set S of nodes of size at most half the number of vertices has at least $\alpha|S|$ neighbors for a constant α, which is referred to as the expansion factor.

- We show that for an n-node constant-degree expander, a cobra walk covers a constant fraction of nodes in $O(\log n)$ steps and all the nodes in $O(\log^2 n)$ steps w.h.p. assuming that either the branching factor or the expansion factor is sufficiently large (cf. Theorems 9 and 10 of Section 4).

Our analysis for expanders proceeds in two phases. We show that in the first phase, which consists of $O(\log n)$ steps, the branching process dominates resulting in an exponential growth in the number of active nodes until a constant fraction of nodes become active, with high probability. In the second phase, though a large fraction of the nodes continues to be active, dependencies caused by the coalescing property prevent us from treating the process as multiple independent random walks, analyzed in [2] (or even d-wise independent walks for a suitably large d). We overcome this hurdle by carefully analyzing these dependencies and bounding relevant conditional probabilities, and define a time-inhomogeneous Markov process that is stochastically dominated by the cobra walk in terms of coverage. We then use the notion of merging conductance and the machinery introduced in [38] to analyze time-inhomogeneous Markov chains, and establish an $O(\log n)$ bound w.h.p. on the maximum hitting time, leading to an $O(\log^2 n)$ bound on the cover time.

1.2 Related work and comparison

Branching and coalescing processes. There is a large body of work on branching processes (without coalescence)

---

[1] By the term "with high probability" (w.h.p., for short) we mean with probability $1 - 1/n^c$, for some constant $c > 0$.

on various discrete and non-discrete structures [33, 36, 4]. A study of coalescing random walks (without branching) was performed in [15] with applications to voter models. Others have looked at processes that incorporate branching and coalescing particle systems [3, 41]. However, these studies treat the particle systems as continuous-time systems, with branching, coalescing, and death rates on restricted-topology structures such as integer lattices. To the best of our knowledge, ours is the first work that studies random walks that branch and coalesce in discrete time and on various classes of non-regular finite graphs.

Random walks and parallel random walks. Feige [24, 23] showed that the cover time of a random walk on any undirected n-node connected graph is between $\Theta(n \log n)$ and $\Theta(n^3)$ with both the lower and upper bounds being achieved in certain graphs. With the rapidly increasing interest in information (rumor) spreading processes in large-scale networks and the gossiping paradigm (e.g., see [9] and the references therein), there have been a number of studies on speeding up the cover time of random walks on graphs. One of the earliest studies is due to Adler et al [1], who studied a process on the hypercube in which in each round a node is chosen uniformly at random and covered; if the chosen node was already covered, then an uncovered neighbor of the node is chosen uniformly at random and covered. For any d-regular graph, Dimitrov and Plaxton showed that a similar process achieves a cover time of $O(n + (n \log n)/d)$ [18]. For expander graphs, Berenbrink et al showed a simple variant of the standard random walk that achieves a linear (i.e., $O(n)$) cover time [5].

It is instructive to compare cobra walks with other mechanisms to speed up random walks as well as with gossip-based rumor spreading mechanisms. Perhaps the most related mechanism is that of parallel random walks which was first studied in [7] for the special case where the starting nodes are drawn from the stationary distribution, and in [2] for arbitrary starting nodes. Nearly-tight results on the speedup of cover time as a function of the number of parallel walks have been obtained by [22] for several graph classes including the cycle, d-dimensional meshes, hypercube, and expanders. (Also see [21] for results on mixing time.) Though cobra walks are similar to parallel random walks in the sense that at any step multiple nodes may be selecting random neighbors, there are significant differences between the two mechanisms. First the cover times of these walks are not comparable. For instance, while k parallel random walks may have a cover time of $\Omega(n^2/\log k)$ for any $k \in [1, n]$ [22], a 2-branching cobra walk on a line has a cover time of $O(n)$. Second, while the number of active nodes in k parallel random walks is always k, the number of active nodes in any k-branching cobra walk is continually changing and *may not even be monotonic*. Most importantly, the analysis of cover time of cobra walks needs to address several dependencies in the process by which the set of active nodes evolve; we use the machinery of time-inhomogenous Markov chains to obtain the cover time bound for bounded-degree expanders (see Section 4).

The works of [16, 17] presented distributed algorithms for performing a standard random walk in sublinear time, i.e., in time sublinear in the length of the walk. In particular, the algorithm of [17] performs a random walk of length ℓ in $\tilde{O}(\sqrt{\ell D})$ rounds w.h.p. on an undirected network, where D is the diameter of the network. However, this speed up comes with a drawback: the message complexity of the above faster algorithm is much worse compared to the naive sequential walk which takes only ℓ messages. In contrast, we note that the speedup in cover time given by a cobra walk over the standard random walk comes only at the cost of a slightly worse message complexity.

Gossip-based mechanisms. Gossip-based information propagation mechanisms have also been used for information (rumor) spreading in distributed networks. In the most typical rumor spreading models, gossip involves either a push step, in which nodes that are aware of a piece of information (being disseminated) pass it to random neighbors, or a pull step, in which nodes that are unaware of the information attempt to extract the information from one of their randomly chosen neighbors, or some combination of the two. In such models, the knowledgeable nodes or the ignorant nodes participate in the dissemination problem in *every* round (step) of the algorithm. The main parameter of interest in many of these analyses is the number of rounds needed till all the nodes in the network get to know the information.

The rumor spreading mechanism that is most closely related to cobra walks is the basic push protocol, in which in every step every informed node selects a random neighbor and pushes the information to the neighbor, thus making it informed. Feige et al. [25] show that the push process completes in every undirected graph in $O(n \log n)$ steps, with high probability. Since then, the push protocol and its variants have been extensively analyzed both for special graphs, as well as for general graphs in terms of their expansion properties (see e.g., [10, 11, 12, 30, 29, 27, 26]). Again, though cobra walks and push-based rumor spreading share the property that multiple nodes are active in a given step, the two mechanisms differ significantly. While the set of active nodes in rumor spreading is monotonically nondecreasing, this is not so in cobra walks, an aspect that makes the analysis challenging especially with regard to full coverage. Furthermore, the message complexity of the push protocol can be substantially different than that of cobra. A simple example is the star network, which the push protocol covers in $\Theta(n \log n)$ steps with a message complexity of $\Theta(n^2 \log n)$, while the 2-branching cobra walk has both cover time and message complexity $\Theta(n \log n)$. This can be extended to show similar results for star-based networks that have been proposed as models for Internet-scale networks [14].

1.3 Applications

As mentioned at the outset, cobra walks are closely related to the SIS model in epidemics, but they may be easier to analyze using tools from random walk and Markov chain analyses. While the persistence time and epidemic density of SIS-type epidemic models are well studied [28, 34, 43], to the best of our knowledge the time needed for a SIS-type process to affect a large fraction (or the whole) of the network has not been well-studied. Our results and analyses of cobra walks on more general networks can be useful in predicting the time taken for a real epidemic process following an SIS-type model to spread in a network.

Cobra walks can also serve as a lightweight information dissemination protocol in networks, similar to the push protocol. As pointed out earlier, in certain types of networks, the message complexity incurred by a cobra walk to cover a network can be smaller than that for the push protocol. This can be useful, especially in infrastructure-less anonymous networks, where nodes don't have unique identities and and may not even know the number of neighbors. In such networks, it is difficult to detect locally when coverage is completed[2]. If nodes have a good upper bound on n (the network size), however, then nodes can terminate the protocol after a number of steps equal to the estimated cover time. In such a scenario, message complexity is also an important performance criterion.

2. PRELIMINARIES

Let G be a connected graph with vertex set V and edge set E, and let $|V| = n$. We define a coalescing-branching (cobra) random walk on G with branching factor k starting at some arbitrary $v \in V$ as follows: At time $t = 0$ we place a pebble at v. Then in the next and every subsequent time step, every pebble in G clones itself $k - 1$ times (so that there are now k pebbles at each vertex that originally had a pebble). Each pebble independently selects a neighbor of its current vertex uniformly at random and moves to it. Once all pebbles make their one-hop moves, if two pebbles are at the same vertex they coalesce into a single pebble, and the next round begins. In a cobra-walk, a vertex receive a pebble an arbitrary number of times.

For a time step t of the process, let S_t be the **active set**, the set of all vertices of G that have a pebble. We will use two different definitions of the neighborhood of S_t: Let $N(S_t)$ be the **inclusive** neighborhood, the union of the set of neighbors of all vertices in S_t (which can include members of S_t itself). Let $\Gamma(S_t)$ be the **non-inclusive neighborhood**, which is the union of the set of neighbors of all vertices of S_t such that $S_t \cap \Gamma(S_t) = \emptyset$.

Let the expected **maximum hitting time** h_{max} of a cobra-walk on G be defined as the $\max_{u,v \in V} \mathbb{E}[h_{u,v}]$ where $h_{u,v}$ is the time it takes a cobra-walk starting at vertex u to first reach v with at least one pebble.

We are interested in two different notions of cover time, the time until all vertices of G have been visited by a cobra-walk at least once. Let τ_v be the minimum time t such that, for a cobra-walk starting from v, $\forall u \in V - v$, $u \in S_t$ for some $t \leq \tau_v$ which may depend on u. Then we define the **cover time** of a cobra-walk on G to be $\max_{v \in V} \tau_v$. We define the **expected cover time** to be $\max_{v \in V} \mathbb{E}[\tau_v]$. Note that in the literature for simple random walks, cover time usually refers to the expected cover times. In this paper we will show high-probability bounds on the cover time.

In Section 6 we will be proving results for cobra-walks on expanders. In this paper, we will use a spectral definition for expanders and then use Tanner's theorem to translate that to neighborhood and cut-based notions of expanders.

DEFINITION 1. An ϵ-**expander** graph is a d-regular graph whose adjacency matrix has eigenvalues α_i such that $|\alpha_i| \leq \epsilon d$ for $i \geq 2$.

We also want to define the notion of an ϵ-approximation:

DEFINITION 2. G is an ϵ-**approximation** for a graph H if $(1 - \epsilon)H \preccurlyeq G \preccurlyeq (1 + \epsilon)H$, where $H \preccurlyeq G$ if for all x, $x^T L_H x \leq x^T L_G x$, where L_G and L_H are the Laplacians of G and H, respectively.

---

[2]In networks with identities and knowledge of neighbors, a node can locally stop sending messages when all neighbors have the rumor. This reduces the overall message complexity until cover time.

Finally, we will rely on the neighborhood expansion of a set S on G, where we define $N(S)$ as the inclusive neighborhood. For this we will use Tanner's theorem [42], which gives us a lower bound on the size of the neighborhood of S for sufficiently strong expanders.

THEOREM 3. *Let G be a d-regular graph that ϵ- approximates $\frac{d}{n}K_n$. Then for all $S \subseteq V$ with $|S| = \delta n$, $|N(S)| \geq \frac{|S|}{\epsilon^2(1-\delta)+\delta}$.*

3. COVER TIME FOR TREES AND GRIDS

A useful tool in bounding the cover time for simple random walks is Matthew's Theorem [37, 35], which bounds the expected cover time of a graph by the maximum expected hitting time $h_{u,v}$ between any two nodes u and v times the harmonic number H_n. Here we show that this result can be extended to cobra walks. The full proof can be found in the full version of the paper, but the key idea is that we map the cobra walk on G to a simple walk on much larger graph derived from G and then show that this satisfies the conditions for the proof of Matthew's Theorem on simple walks.

THEOREM 4. **Matthew's Theorem for Cobra Walks** *Let G be a connected graph on n nodes. Let w be a cobra walk on G starting at an arbitrary node. Then the cover-time of w on G, $C(G)$, is bounded from above by $h_{max} \ln n$ in expectation and by $O(h_{max} \ln n)$ with high probability.*

Matthew's theorem for cobra walks is used in proving the cover time for trees and grids.

3.1 Trees

THEOREM 5. *For any tree, the cover time of a cobra walk starting from any node is $O(n \ln n)$ w.h.p.*

We will prove our main result by calculating the maximum hitting time of a cobra walk on a tree T and then applying Matthew's theorem. Cobra walks on trees are especially tractable because they follow two nice properties. Since a tree has a unique path between any two nodes, we only need keep track of the pebble closes to the target. In addition, the fact that there is one simple path between any two nodes limits the number of collisions we need to keep track of, a property which is not true for general graphs and makes cobra walk harder to analyze on them. For this section, we fix the branching factor $k = 2$. For $k > 2$ but still constant, the cover time would not be asymptotically better.

The general idea behind the proof is as follows. We take the longest path w.r.t. hitting time in the tree. Along each node in this path, except for the first and last, there will be a subtree rooted at that node. If a cobra walk's closest pebble to the endpoint is at node l, the walk from this point can either advance with at least one pebble, or it can not advance by either backtracking along the path, going down the subtree rooted at l, or both. We show via a stochastic dominance argument that a biased random walk from l, whose transition probabilities are tuned to be identical to cobra walk's, will next advance to $l + 1$ in a time that is dominated primarily by the size of the subtree at l. This is done by analyzing the return times in the non-advancement scenarios listed above. Thus summing up over the entire walk, the hitting time is dominated by a linear function of the size of the entire tree.

In Lemma 6 we bound the return time of a cobra walk to a root of the tree.

LEMMA 6. *Let T be a tree of size M. Pick a root, r, and let r have d children. Then a cobra walk on T starting at r will have a return time to r of $O(4M/d)$.*

PROOF. To show that the Lemma holds for a cobra walk, we will actually show that it holds for a simple random walk with transition probabilities modified to resemble those of a cobra walk. For this simple random walk, we start at r and in the first step pick one of the children of r, r'. Let $(d'+1)$ be the degree of r'. Then we define transition probabilities as follows: p is the probability of returning to r in the next step, and q is the probability of continuing down the tree. They are given as: $p = \left(1 - \left(\frac{d'}{(d'+1)}\right)^2\right)$, $q = \left(\frac{d'}{(d'+1)}\right)^2$, $\frac{p}{q} = \frac{(d')^2}{(2d'+1)}$. Note that these are the exact same probabilities that a cobra walk at node r' would have for sending (not sending) at least one (any) pebbles back to the root.

The rest of the proof follows by mathematical induction. Consider a tree T that has only two levels. Starting from r, the return time, 2, is constant, the relationship holds. For the inductive case, assume that the hypothesis holds. Then:

$$
\begin{aligned}
r(T) &\leq 1 + \sum_{r' \in N(r)} p(r')h_{r',r} \leq 1 + \frac{1}{d}\sum_{r' \in N(r)} h_{r',r} \\
&\leq 1 + \frac{1}{d}\sum_{r' \in N(r)}\left(1 + \frac{d'^2}{2d'+1}c\frac{|T'|}{d'}\right) \\
&\leq 2 + \frac{c|T|}{2d}
\end{aligned}
$$

Setting $c = 4$ gives us the result of the lemma for the biased random walk, and it is easy to see that by stochastic dominance this holds also for the cobra walk. $\square$

Finally, we show a key lemma for the hitting time of a single step of a path along a tree.

LEMMA 7. *Fix a path in a tree T made up of nodes $1, \dots, l, (l+1), \dots, t$. Then, the expected time it takes for a cobra walk starting at node l to get to $l+1$ with at least one pebble is given by:*

$$
h_{l,(l+1)} = \frac{5}{4} + \frac{12}{5}\sum_{i=l}^{2}\left(\frac{1}{5}\right)^{l-i}|T_i| \tag{1}
$$

where T_l is the induced subtree formed by taking node l, its neighbors not on the path being traversed, and all of their descendants.

Informally, we prove that the one-step hitting time is bounded by above by the worst case scenario that either both pebbles go back along the path or down the subtree rooted at l and establish a simple recurrence relation.

PROOF. Vertex l is viewed through the context of having one edge to the node $l-1$, one edge to node l, and d edges to some other nodes. Thus it can be viewed as the root of a tree, and T_l as the induced subgraph of l and all nodes reached through its d_l not-on-path children. We will need the following probabilities:

- Probability of a pebble going from l to $l+1 = p = \left(1 - \left(\frac{(d_l + 1)}{(d_l + 2)}\right)^2\right)$

- Probability of a pebble not going from l to $l+1 = 1 - p = q$.

- Probability of a cobra walk sending both pebbles from l to $l-1$ conditioned on it *not* sending any pebbles from l to $l+1 = q_l' = \left(\frac{1}{(d_l + 1)^2}\right)$

- Probability of a cobra walk sending at least one pebble to the subtree T_l conditioned on its not sending any pebbles to $l+1 = q_l'' = \left(\frac{(d_l)}{(d_l + 1)}\right)^2 + 2\left(\frac{d_l}{(d_l + 1)^2}\right) = \frac{d_l^2 + 2d_l}{(d_l + 1)^2}$

Note that, conditioned on a pebble not advancing to node $l+1$, we actually have three disjoint events: (A) Both pebbles go to $l-1$, (B) one pebble goes to $l-1$ and one pebble goes into subtree T_l, and (C) both pebbles go into T_l. We define an alternate event B', which is the event that one pebble goes down T_l and nothing else happens (thus, it is not technically in the space of cobra walk actions). If we let R be the time until first return of the cobra walk to l conditioned on no pebble going to $l+1$, we wish to show that $E[R|B] \leq E[R|B']$ and that $E[R|C] \leq E[R|B']$. What is the relationship between B and B'? Consider two random variables, X and Y, and let X be the time until first return of a pebble that travels from l to $l-1$, Y be the time until first return of a pebble that travels into T_l. Then $R|B$ is just another random variable, $U = \min(X, Y)$. Since $U \leq Y$ over the entire space, $E[U] \leq E[Y]$, and clearly $R|B'$ is equivalent to Y. Thus $E[R|B] \leq E[R|B']$ It is also easy to see that $E[R|B'] \geq E[R|C]$. Thus by the law of total expectation we have:

$$
\begin{aligned}
E[R] &= E[R|A]\Pr(A) + E[R|B]\Pr(B) + E[R|C]\Pr(C) \\
&\leq E[R|A]\Pr(A) + (\Pr(B) + \Pr(C))E[R|B'] \\
&= E[R|A]\Pr(A) + E[R|B'](1 - \Pr(A))
\end{aligned}
$$

Then the hitting time can be expressed as:

$$
\begin{aligned}
h_{l,l+1} &\leq p + q(E[R] + h_{l,l+1}) \\
\Rightarrow (1-q)h_{l,l+1} &\leq p + q(E[R]) \\
\Rightarrow h_{l,l+1} &\leq 1 + \frac{q}{p}(q_l'(1 + h_{l-1,l}) + q_l'' r(T_l))
\end{aligned}
$$

Note that $q/p = \frac{(d_l+1)^2}{(2d_l+3)}$. Since $r(T_l) \leq 4|T_l|/d_l$ by Lemma 6, we continue with: $h_{l,l+1} \leq 1 + \frac{(d_l+1)^2}{(2d_l+3)}\frac{1}{(d_l+1)^2}(1+h_{l-1,l}) + \frac{(d_l+1)^2}{(2d_l+3)}\frac{(d_l^2+2d_l)}{(d_l+1)^2}\frac{4|T_l|}{d_l} \leq 1 + \frac{1}{5}(1+h_{l-1,l}) + \frac{12}{5}|T_l|$ w.h.p.

If we expand the relation, we get: $h_{l,l+1} \leq \sum_{i=0}^{l}\left(\frac{1}{5}\right)^i + \frac{12}{5}\left(|T_l| + \left(\frac{1}{5}\right)|T_{l-1}| + \left(\frac{1}{5}\right)^2|T_{l-2}| + \dots + \left(\frac{1}{5}\right)^{l-2}|T_2|\right)$, and thus $h_{l,l+1} \leq \frac{5}{4} + \frac{12}{5}\sum_{i=l}^{2}\left(\frac{1}{5}\right)^{l-i}|T_i|$ $\square$

We are finally ready to prove our main results for the tree, Theorem 5, that the cobra walk cover time of an arbitrary tree occurs in $O(n \ln n)$ steps.

PROOF. By Matthew's Theorem for cobra walks, $C(G) \leq (\ln n + o(1))h_{max}$. We just need to prove that h_{max} occurs in linear time.

Let P be the path for which $h_{u,v}$ is maximized, and let the path consist of the sequence of nodes $1, 2, \ldots, t$. As in the proof of the single-step hitting time, we note that for all but the first and last nodes on P, there is a subtree T_l of size $|T_l|$ rooted at each nodes. Because $h_{1,t} \leq h_{1,2} + h_{2,3} + \ldots h_{t-1,t}$ we obtain the desired result from Lemma 7 as follows:

$$
\begin{aligned}
h_{1,t} &\leq \frac{5}{4}t + \frac{12}{5} \sum_{j=2}^{t-1} \left[|T_j| \sum_{i=0}^{\infty} \left(\frac{1}{5} \right)^i \right] \\
&\leq \frac{5}{4}t + \frac{12}{5} \frac{5}{4} \sum_{j=2}^{t-1} |T_j| \leq 4n.
\end{aligned}
$$

$\square$

We note that for the line network, we can improve the bound we obtain for trees and show that the cover time of a cobra walk is $O(n)$ w.h.p.

3.2 Grids

For a d-dimensional grid, we show the following theorem whose proof is in the full version.

THEOREM 8. *Let G be a finite d-dimensional grid for some constant d, without wrap-around edges. Then the cover time of a cobra walk on G is $\tilde{O}(n^{1/d})$ w.h.p for branching factor $k = 2$.*

Here we present a sketch of the proof, which can be found in the long version of the paper.

Consider a cobra-walk which starts at the origin of the lattice $(0, \ldots, 0)$. In each step of the cobra-walk, we define the following process to determine which pebble we are tracking as we move towards the target vertex $(n^{1/d}, \ldots, n^{1/d})$. We focus on one dimension at a time. W.l.o.g. consider the first dimension. We refer to a $+1$ motion as movement in the "right" direction (towards the first coordinate of the target) and -1 as a movement away from the target in the first dimension. From the current node, two pebbles pick neighbors uniformly at random. We follow a pebble that makes most progress in the direction of the target along the first dimension. That is, if one of the pebbles goes to the neighbor in the $+1$ direction, we track that pebble and move to the node it selected. If both pebbles pick the -1 neighbor, we move to that neighbor. Otherwise, we randomly pick one of the nodes that were selected by the pebbles and note there was a movement of 0 in the first dimension. Projecting this process onto the first dimension, we have a biased random walk (towards the target) in that dimension. After $O(n^{1/d})$ steps, we can use a large deviation bound (e.g. Theorems 2.8 and 2.8 in [13]) to show that with constant probability, we reach the target's first coordinate value to within $n^{1/2d}$ distance.

What is happening in the other coordinates? It is easy to see that projecting our walk described above on any other dimension creates an unbiased random walk over that dimension. Hence, after $O(n^{1/d})$ steps, with constant probability, we are within $n^{1/2d}$ steps of the position we started in.

After approaching the target in the first dimension, we repeat the process in the other dimensions. Each dimension requires $O(n^{1/d})$ steps. At the end of the first phase, with constant probability, for each coordinate, we are at most $n^{1/2d}$ steps away from the target. We keep doing this for $\log \log n$ phases. At the end of phase i we are a distance at most $n^{\frac{1}{d2^{i+1}}}$ from the target with probability p^i for some constant $0 < p < 1$. After $\log \log n$ phases the walk will be within $O(1)$ distance (in each dimension) from the target with probability $1/\text{polylog}(n)$.

The last $O(1)$ steps to the target can be made by the walk by taking $O(1)$ "advance" steps, which will happen with at least a constant probability. Thus, in $O(n^{1/d})$ steps we reach the target with probability $1/\text{polylog}(n)$.

In expectation, we will reach the target after $O(n^{1/d}\text{polylog}(n))$ steps. Applying Matthew's bound yields the result of the lemma.

4. ANALYSIS FOR EXPANDERS

For expander graphs, we are able to prove a high probability cover time result of $O(\log^2 n)$. We break the proof up into two phases. In the first phase we show that a cobra walk starting from any node will reach a constant fraction of the nodes in logarithmic time w.h.p. In the second phase, we create a process which stochastically dominates the cobra walk and show that this new process, will cover the entire rest of the graph again in polylogarithmic time w.h.p.

The main result of this section can be stated in the following two theorems, which when taken together imply that w.h.p. ϵ-expander G will be covered in $O(\log^2 n)$ time.

THEOREM 9. *Let G be any ϵ-expander with ϵ, δ not depending on n (number of nodes in G), with $\delta < \frac{16}{30d^2}$, and ϵ, a sufficiently small constant such that*

$$
\frac{1}{\epsilon^2(1-\delta)+\delta} > \frac{d(de^{-k} + (k-1)) - \frac{k^2}{2}}{d(e^{-k} + (k-1)) - \frac{k^2}{2}}, \tag{2}
$$

then in time $O(\log n)$, w.h.p. a cobra walk on G with branching factor k, will attain an active set of size δn.

We note that the condition in the above theorem is satisfied if either ϵ is sufficiently small, or k is sufficiently large. For instance when $k = 2$, the above condition holds for strong expanders, such as the Ramanujan graphs, which have $\epsilon \leq 2\sqrt{d-1}/d$, and random d-regular graphs, for d sufficiently large.

THEOREM 10. *Let G be as above, and let W be a cobra walk on G that at time T has reached an active set of size δn. Then w.h.p in an additional $O(\log^2 n)$ steps every node of G will have visited by W at least once.*

To prove Theorem 9 we prove that active sets up to a constant fraction of V are growing at each step by a factor greater than one. The proof can be found in the full version.

LEMMA 11. *Let G be any ϵ-expander with ϵ, δ satisfying the conditions of Theorem 9. Then for any time $t \geq 0$, the cobra walk on G with active set S_t such that $|S_t| \leq \delta n$ satisfies $\mathbb{E}[|S_{t+1}|] \geq (1+\nu)|S_t|$ for some constant $\nu > 0$.*

Next, we use a standard martingale argument to show that the number of nodes in S_t is concentrated around its expectation. The proof of Lemma 12 can also be found in the full version of the paper.

LEMMA 12. *For a cobra walk on a d-regular ϵ-expander that satisfies the conditions in Lemma 11, at any time t*

$$\Pr\left[|S_{t+1}| - \mathbb{E}[|S_{t+1}|] \leq -\tau|S_t|\right] \leq e^{-\frac{\tau^2|S_t|}{2k}} \quad (3)$$

Finally, using the bound of Lemma 12 we show that with high probability we will cover at least δn of the nodes of G with a cobra walk in logarithmic time by showing that the active set for some $t = O(\log n)$ is of size at least δn.

LEMMA 13. *For a cobra walk on d-regular, ϵ-expander G, there exists a time T such that $T = O(\log n)$ and $|S_T| \geq \delta n$.*

The key to proving Lemma 13 is to view a cobra-walk on G as a Markov process over a different state space consisting of all of the possible sizes of the active set. In this interpretation, all configurations of pebbles in a cobra-walk in which i nodes are active are equivalent. The goal is to show that this new Markov process will reach a state corresponding to an active set of size δn quickly w.h.p. To prove this, we first show that it is dominated by a restricted Markov chain over the same state space in which any negative growth in the size of the active set is replaced with a transition to the initial state (in which only one node is active). We then in turn show that the restricted walk is dominated by an even more restricted walk in which the probability of negative growth is higher than in the first restricted walk, bounded from below from a constant, and no longer dependent on the size of the current state. We then show that the goal of the lemma is achieved even in this walk by relating the process to a negative binomial random variable.

PROOF. We view a cobra-walk on G as a random walk W over the state space consisting of all of the possible sizes of the active set: $S(W) = \{1, \ldots, n\}$. We then define a Markov process M_1 that stochastically dominates W: Let $\tau = \nu/2$, where ν is the expected growth factor of the active set as shown in Lemma 11. The states of M_1, $S(M_1)$ are the same as W's, but the transitions between states differ. Each $i \in S(W)$ can have out-arcs to many different states, but the corresponding $i \in S(M_1)$ has only two transitions. With probability $p_i = 1 - e^{-\frac{\nu^2 i}{8k}}$ transition to state $(1+\nu/2)i$, and with probability $1 - p_i$ transition to state 1. Note that p_i is derived from Lemma 12.

In M_1, each transition probability is still a function of the current state i, and as mentioned above we would like to eliminate this dependence. Thus, define M_2 as a random walk over the same state space. However, we will deal only with a subset of $S(M_2)$: the states: $(1 + \nu/2)^i C$ for $i \in \mathbb{Z}$ and a suitably large constant C. We then have the following transitions for each state in the chain (which will begin once it hits C). Setting $r = \nu^2/8k$, at state $(1 + \nu/2)^i C : 1)$ Transition to state $(1 + \nu/2)^{i+1}C$ with probability $p_i' = 1 - e^{-rC(1+\frac{i\nu}{2})}$ 2) Transition to state C with probability $1 - p_i'$. This Markov chain oscillates between failure (going to C) and growing by a factor of $1 + \nu/2$. Note that to get success (i.e., reaching a state of at least δn), we need $\Omega(\log n)$ growing transitions.

The probability that in a walk on this state space that we "fail" and go back to C before hitting δn is bounded by $1/2$, since $\sum_{i=0}^{\infty} e^{-rC(1+i\frac{\nu}{2})} \leq e^{-rC} \sum_{i=0}^{\infty} e^{irC\frac{\nu}{2}} = \frac{e^{-rC}}{1-e^{-rC\frac{\nu}{2}}} \leq \frac{1}{2}$, provided that C is sufficiently large as a function of r

(which is itself only a function of the branching factor and the constant ν).

Consider each block of steps that end in a failure (meaning we return to C). Then clearly w.h.p. after $b \log n$ trials, for some constant b, we will have a trial that ends in success (i.e., reaching an active set of size δn nodes). In these $b \log n$ trials, there are exactly that many returns to C. However, looking across all trials that end in failure, there are also only a total of $O(\log n)$ steps that are successful (i.e., involve a growth rather than shrinkage). To see why this is true, note that the probability of a failure after a string of growth steps goes down supralinearly with each step, so that if we know we are in a failing trial it is very likely that we fail after only a few steps. Thus, there cannot be too many successes before each failure. Indeed, the probability that we fail at step i within a trial can be bounded. Thus $\Pr[\text{Failure at step i} \mid \text{eventual failure}]$

$$= \frac{\Pr[\text{Failure at step i}]}{\Pr[\text{Eventual failure}]}$$

$$= \frac{e^{-rC(1+i\nu/2)}}{\sum_{i=1}^{\infty}\left(\prod_{j=1}^{l-1}(1 - e^{-rC(1+j\nu/2)})\right)e^{-rC(1+l\nu/2)}}$$

$$\geq \frac{1}{\sum_{i=1}^{\infty} e^{-irC\nu/2}} \geq 1 - e^{-rC\nu/2}$$

and thus the probability of advancing is no more than $e^{-rC\nu/2}$, also a quantity that does not depend on i. This is a negative binomial random variable with distribution $w(k, p)$, the number of coin flips needed to obtain k heads with heads probability p. Identifying heads with a failure (i.e. returning to C) and tails with making a growth transition, we have a random variable $w(k, p)$, the number of coin flips needed for k failures with probability of failure $p = 1 - e^{-rC\nu/2}$. It is well known that $\Pr[w(k, p) \leq m] = \Pr[B(m, p) \geq k]$, where $B(m, p)$ is the binomial random variable counting the number of heads within m p-biased coin flips. Thus, $\Pr[w(k, p) > m] = \Pr[B(m, p) < k]$. Setting $k = a\log n$ and $m = b\log n$, we have, $\Pr[B(m, p) \leq \mathbb{E}[B(m, p)] - t] = \Pr[B(m, p) < pm - t] \leq e^{\frac{-2t^2}{m}}$. We let $k = pm - t$, and solving for t we get $t = (pb - a)\log n$. This gives us

$$\Pr[B(m, p) < k)] \leq \frac{1}{n^{\frac{(pb-a)^2}{b}}},$$

establishing there are at most $O(\log n)$ success within $O(\log n)$ trials ending in failure. Via stochastic dominance this bound holds for our original cobra walk process.

$\square$

Once the active set has reached size $\Omega(n)$, we need a different method to show that the cobra-walk achieves full coverage in $O(\log^2 n)$ time. We can not simply pick a random pebble and restart the cobra-walk from this point $O(\log n)$ times because we know nothing about the distribution of the δn pebbles after restart, and the restarting method would require the pebbles to be i.i.d. uniform across the nodes of G. As a result, we are unable to establish a straightforward bound on h_{max} and invoke Matthew's Theorem.

Hence, we develop a different process, which we will call W_{alt}, that is stochastically dominated by the cobra walk. In W_{alt}, no more branching or coalescing occurs, and we also modify the transition probabilities of the pebbles on a node-by-node basis, depending on the number of pebbles at a node.

DEFINITION 14. *For any time t and any collection of S pebbles on V (there can be more than 1 pebble at a node), define $W_{alt}(t+1)$ as follows. Let $A \subseteq V$ be the set of all nodes with 1 pebble at time t. Let $B \subseteq V$ be the set of all nodes with exactly 2 pebbles, and let C be the set of all nodes with more than 2 pebbles. Then, (a) for every $v \in A$, the pebble at v uniformly at random selects a node in $N(v)$ and moves to it; (b) for every $v \in B$, each pebble at v uniformly at random selects its own node in $N(v)$ and moves to it; (c) for every $v \in C$, arbitrarily order the pebbles at v, the first two pebbles then pick a neighbor to hop to uniformly at random. The remaining pebbles then pick with probability $1/2$ one of the two neighbors already selected and move to that node.*

If at time t a node during process W_{alt} has two or more pebbles, at each time step it behaves identically to a node running a cobra walk. On the other hand, if there is only one pebble at node running W_{alt} it acts like a simple random walk. Thus the number of active nodes at the next time step in W_{alt} is a (possibly proper) subset of the nodes with pebbles if the graph were running the cobra walk instead. Since this will be true at every time step, W_{alt} stochastically dominates the cobra walk w.r.t cover time τ of G, and it will be enough to prove the following:

THEOREM 15. *Let G be a bounded-degree d-regular ϵ-expander graph, with ϵ sufficiently high to satisfy the conditions in Lemma 11. Let there be δn pebbles distributed arbitrarily over V, with at most one pebble per node. Let $\delta < \frac{16}{30d^2}$. Let λ be the second-largest eigenvalue of the adjacency matrix of G. From our ϵ-expander definition, $\lambda \leq \epsilon d$. For every ϵ, there is a constant ϵ' that is the node expansion constant of G. Furthermore, let constant $\gamma = \frac{\epsilon'}{\epsilon^2(1-\delta)+\delta}$, and let $s = \frac{5\log n + 6\log d + \log 9}{-\log\left(1-\frac{1}{2}\left(\frac{\gamma}{64d^{10}}\right)^2\right)}$. Starting from this configuration, the cover time of W_{alt} on G is $O(\log^2 n)$, with high probability.*

PROOF. Our proof relies on showing that each node in G has a constant probability of being visited by at least one pebble during an epoch of W_{alt} lasting $\Theta(\log n)$ time. Once this has been established, all nodes of G will be covered w.h.p. after $O(\log n)$ epochs lasting $\Theta(\log n)$ steps each.

Define E_i to be the event that pebble i covers an arbitrary node v in s steps. We want to prove that the probability that v is covered by at least one pebble, $\Pr\left[\bigcup_i E_i\right]$, is constant. Using a second-order inclusion-exclusion approximation:

$$\Pr\left[\bigcup_i E_i\right] \geq \sum_i \Pr[E_i] - \sum_{i \neq j} \Pr[E_i \cap E_j]$$
$$= \sum_i \Pr[E_i] - \sum_{i \neq j} \Pr[E_i] \Pr[E_j|E_i].$$

As a marginal probability, $\Pr[E_i]$ can be viewed as the probability that the random walk of pebble i hits v at time s. Thus, we only need to look at the elements of zA^i, where A is the stochastic matrix of the simple random walk on G and z is a vector with $z(l) = 1$ for the l, the position of pebble i

at the beginning of the epoch and 0 in all other positions. In [2] it is proved in Lemma 4.8 that each coordinate of $A^{s'}z$ differs from $1/n$ by at most $\frac{1}{2n}$ for $s' = \frac{\ln 2n}{\ln \epsilon}$. Since $s > s'$, this hold for our case as well. Thus $\Pr[E_i = 1] \geq \frac{1}{2n}$.

Next we establish an upper bound for $\Pr[E_j|E_i]$. Due to the conditioning on the walk of pebble i, we can't use the transition matrix A^i, but we would like to do something similar. The transition matrix governing the walk of pebble j conditioned on a fixed walk of pebble i can be characterized at each step by transition matrix $P_{l(i,t)}$, where $l(i,t)$ is the location of pebble i at time t, can be described as follows. For every row k of $P_{l(i,t)}$ s.t. $k \neq l(i,t)$ we have an exactly copy of the kth row of A, the transition matrix of an independent random walk on G. When $k = l(i,t)$ this represents the walk of j when pebbles i and j are co-located at node k. To establish an upper bound, we assume the worst case, that j is ordered as the 3rd or higher pebble at k. Let τ be the neighbor of node k chosen by pebble i. Then $P[k,\tau] = 1/2 + 1/2d$, and for all other positions of row k where A is non-zero, the corresponding position in $P = 1/2d$. These represent the transition probabilities according to W_{alt} as described earlier.

From an initial probability distribution z chosen over $V(G)$, the probability of pebble j being at node v conditioned on the walk of pebble i is the vth component of $z\prod_{t=1}^{s} P_{l(i,t)}$. In Lemma 16 we show that the largest component of $z\prod_{t=1}^{s} P_{l(i,t)}$ is no more than $\frac{5d^2}{2n}$. With this result, we then have:

$$\Pr\left[\bigcup E_i\right] \geq \sum_i \Pr[E_i] - \frac{1}{2}\sum_{i \neq j} \Pr[E_i]\Pr[E_j|E_i]$$
$$\geq \delta n \frac{1}{2n} - \frac{1}{2}\binom{\delta n}{2}\frac{3}{2n}\frac{5d^2}{2n}$$
$$\geq \frac{\delta}{2} - \frac{15}{16}\delta^2 d^2$$

which will be a constant for the sufficiently small δ (depending only on d) given in the statement of the Theorem. $\square$

LEMMA 16. *Let G, γ, ϵ', and s be as stated in Theorem 15. Let i and j be two pebbles walking according to the rules of W_{alt} on G. Fix the walk of i, and let $\{P_{l(i,t)}\}$ be the sequence of perturbed transition matrices for the walk of pebble j depending on i. Then starting i from an arbitrary node, after s steps, the probability that j is at any node is at most $5d^2/2n$.*

PROOF. The proof of this lemma relies heavily on Theorem 3.2 in [32], which we review and state here. Let P be an irreducible, ergodic Markov process for which reversibility and strong aperiodicity are not required. Consider the weighted transition from state i to j, $w_{ij} = \pi_i p_{ij}$, where π_i is the stationary distribution of i and p_{ij} is the transition probability from i to j of P. For $A \subset V$, we define the **merging conductance** of set A as

$$\Phi_P^*(A) = \frac{\sum_{j_1 \in A}\sum_{j_2 \in V-A}\sum_i \frac{w_{j_1 i} w_{j_2 i}}{\pi_i}}{\sum_{i \in A}\pi_i} \quad (4)$$

The merging conductance of graph G is thus

$$\Phi_P^*(G) = \min_{A \subset S: \sum_{i \in A}\pi_i \leq \frac{1}{2}} \Phi_P^*(A)$$

Intuitively, the merging conductance can be viewed as a measure of the flow coming into all nodes from both A and

$V - A$ for some set A. The higher the merging conductance of a graph, the more well connected it is and evenly distributed the flow is. If we define $\|\vec{x}(t)\| = \sum \frac{(p_i(t) - \pi_i)^2}{\pi_i}$ to be a measure of the distance of a distribution $\vec{p}$ over V from the stationary distribution of P, then [38] gives us the following theorem, which indicates that for a graph ǧwith merging conductance bounded away from zero, convergence to the stationary distribution occurs in logarithmic time.

THEOREM 17 ([38, THEOREM 3.2]). *For an arbitrary initial distribution* $\vec{x}(0)$ *over* V

$$\|\vec{x}(t)\| \leq (1 - \frac{1}{2}(\Phi_P^*)^2)^t \|\vec{x}(0)\|$$

We also need the following lemma for bounds on the maximum and minimum of the stationary distribution of the conditional walk of pebble j.

LEMMA 18. *For the walk of pebble* j *as described on* W_{alt} *for a suitable d-regular ϵ-expander* G*, conditioned on the walk of pebble* i*. the stationary distribution of the walk of* j *has bounds* $\pi_{min} \geq \frac{1}{2nd^2}$ *and* $\pi_{max} \leq \frac{2d^2}{n}$*.*

Next we establish a lower bound for the number of terms in the sum in the numerator of Equation 4. Let A be the set for which $\Phi_P^*(G)$ is minimized. Furthermore, since G is an ϵ-expander, we also know that its cobra walk expansion is a constant ϵ' and depends only on ϵ. We would like to calculate the number of nodes in G that have at least one neighbor in A and at least one neighbor in $V - A$. First, we lower-bound the size of the set of nodes with at least one edge to A. This set is just $N(A)$, the inclusive neighborhood of A, which from Tanner's theorem can be bounded from below by $\frac{|A|}{\epsilon^2(1-\delta)+\delta}$. Of the node in $N(A)$, we also need to bound the number that also have at least one edge to $V - A$. However, this is just the non-inclusive neighborhood of $N(A)$, $\Gamma(N(A))$, and we can use the node expansion of G to show that $|\Gamma(N(A))| \geq \frac{\epsilon'|A|}{\epsilon^2(1-\delta)+\delta}$. Thus we get:

$$
\begin{aligned}
\Phi_P^*(G) &\leq \frac{\epsilon'|A|}{\epsilon^2(1-\delta)+\delta} \frac{\frac{\pi_{min}^2(1/2d)^2}{\pi_{max}}}{|A|\pi_{max}} \\
&\leq \frac{\epsilon'}{\epsilon^2(1-\delta)+\delta} \left(\frac{1}{2d^2}\right)^2 \left(\frac{1}{2d}\right)^2 \frac{1}{n^2} \left(\frac{n}{2d^2}\right)^2 \\
&\leq \frac{\epsilon'}{\epsilon^2(1-\delta)+\delta} \frac{1}{64d^{10}}
\end{aligned}
$$

Letting $\gamma = \frac{\epsilon'}{\epsilon^2(1-\delta)+\delta}$, we note that the expression above is a constant as long as $d, \epsilon, \delta, \epsilon'$ are constants, which will be true in a d-regular ϵ-expander.

Starting from a distribution $\vec{x}(0)$ whose norm $\|\vec{x}(0)\|$ will be maximized when the walk is started from node s.t. $\pi_i = \pi_{min}$, we have:

$$
\begin{aligned}
\|\vec{x}(0)\| &\leq \frac{(1 - \pi_{min})^2}{\pi_{min}} + (n-1)\frac{(\pi_{max})^2}{\pi_{min}} \\
&\leq 2d^2 n + (n-1)\left(\frac{2d^2}{n}\right)^2 (2d^2 n) \\
&\leq 2d^2 n + 8d^6 < 9d^6 n
\end{aligned}
$$

for $d > 1$. Finally, we want to show that $\|\vec{x}(s)\| < \frac{1}{n^4}$. With this, it is clear to see that the maximum difference

$|p_i(t) - \pi_i| < \frac{1}{n^2}$ which implies that the maximum probability $\Pr[E_j|E_i] < \frac{2d^2}{n} + \frac{1}{n^2} < \frac{5d^2}{2n}$ as required in Theorem 15. To do this we need to show that $\left(1 - \frac{1}{2}\left(\frac{\gamma}{64d^{10}}\right)^2\right)^s \leq \frac{1}{9d^9n^5}$, which will be true for the set value of s in the definition of the Theorem.

A final note: because $\Phi_P^*(G) \leq \frac{\gamma}{64d^{10}}$ for every matrix $P_{l(i,t)}$, we can apply Theorem 17 in the exponentiation even though each matrix is different. $\square$

5. CONCLUSION

We studied a generalization of the random walk, namely the cobra walk, and analyzed its cover time for trees, grids, and expander graphs. The cobra walk is a natural random process, with potential applications to epidemics and gossip-based information spreading. We plan to explore further the connections between cobra walks and the SIS model, and pursue their practical implications. From a theoretical standpoint, there are several interesting open problems regarding cobra walks that remain to be solved. First is to obtain a tight bound for the cover time of cobra walks on expanders. Our upper bound is $O(\log^2 n)$, while the diameter $\Omega(\log n)$ is a basic lower bound. Another pressing open problem is to determine the worst-case bound on the cover time of cobra walks on general graphs. It will also be interesting to establish and compare the message complexity of cobra walk with the standard random walk and other gossip-based rumor spreading processes.

Acknowledgments

The authors would like to thank the reviewers and are especially grateful to the reviewer who suggested an improved result and proof for the cover time of grids.

6. REFERENCES

[1] M. Adler, E. Halperin, R. M. Karp, and V. V. Vazirani. A stochastic process on the hypercube with applications to peer-to-peer networks. In *STOC*, pages 575–584, 2003.

[2] N. Alon, C. Avin, M. Koucký, G. Kozma, Z. Lotker, and M. R. Tuttle. Many random walks are faster than one. In *SPAA*, pages 119–128, 2008.

[3] S. R. Arthreya and J. M. Swart. Branching-coalescing particle systems. *Probability theory and related fields*, 131(3):376–414, 2005.

[4] I. Benjamini and S. Müller. On the trace of branching random walks. *arXiv preprint arXiv:1002.2781*, 2010.

[5] P. Berenbrink, C. Cooper, R. Elsässer, T. Radzik, and T. Sauerwald. Speeding up random walks with neighborhood exploration. In *SODA*, pages 1422–1435, 2010.

[6] N. Berger, C. Borgs, J. T. Chayes, and A. Saberi. On the spread of viruses on the internet. In *Proceedings of the sixteenth annual ACM-SIAM symposium on Discrete algorithms*, pages 301–310. Society for Industrial and Applied Mathematics, 2005.

[7] A. Broder. Generating random spanning trees. In *FOCS*, 1989.

[8] M. Bui, T. Bernard, D. Sohier, and A. Bui. Random walks in distributed computing: A survey. In *IICS*, pages 1–14, 2004.

[9] J.-Y. Chen and G. Pandurangan. Almost-optimal gossip-based aggregate computation. *SIAM J. Comput.*, 41(3):455–483, 2012.

[10] F. Chierichetti and S. L. andAlessandro Panconesi. Almost tight bounds for rumour spreading with conductance. In *STOC*, pages 399–408, 2010.

[11] F. Chierichetti, S. Lattanzi, and A. Panconesi. Rumour spreading and graph conductance. In *SODA*, pages 1657–1663, 2010.

[12] F. Chierichetti, S. Lattanzi, and A. Panconesi. Rumor spreading in social networks. *Theoretical Computer Science*, 412(24):2602–2610, 2011.

[13] F. Chung, L. Lu, C. B. of the Mathematical Sciences, and N. S. F. (U.S.). *Complex graphs and networks*. Number no. 107 in CBMS Regional Conference Ser. in Mathematics Series. American Mathematical Society, 2006.

[14] F. Comellas and S. Gago. A star based model for the eigenvalue power law of internet graphs. *Phys. A*, 351:680–686, 2005.

[15] C. Cooper, R. Elsässer, H. Ono, and T. Radzik. Coalescing random walks and voting on graphs. In *Proceedings of the 2012 ACM symposium on Principles of distributed computing*, pages 47–56. ACM, 2012.

[16] A. Das Sarma, D. Nanongkai, and G. Pandurangan. Fast distributed random walks. In *PODC*, pages 161–170, 2009.

[17] A. Das Sarma, D. Nanongkai, G. Pandurangan, and P. Tetali. Efficient distributed random walks with applications. In *PODC*, 2010.

[18] N. B. Dimitrov and C. G. Plaxton. Optimal cover time for a graph-based coupon collector process. In *ICALP*, pages 702–716, 2005.

[19] M. Draief and A. Ganesh. A random walk model for infection on graphs: spread of epidemics & rumours with mobile agents. *Discrete Event Dynamic Systems*, 21(1):41–61, 2011.

[20] R. Durrett. Some features of the spread of epidemics and information on a random graph. *Proceedings of the National Academy of Sciences*, 107(10):4491–4498, 2010.

[21] K. Efremenko and O. Reingold. How well do random walks parallelize? In *APPROX-RANDOM*, pages 476–489, 2009.

[22] R. Elsässer and T. Sauerwald. Tight bounds for the cover time of multiple random walks. In *ICALP (1)*, pages 415–426, 2009.

[23] U. Feige. A tight lower bound on the cover time for random walks on graphs. *Random Struct. Algorithms*, 6(4):433–438, 1995.

[24] U. Feige. A tight upper bound on the cover time for random walks on graphs. *Random Struct. Algorithms*, 6(1):51–54, 1995.

[25] U. Feige, D. Peleg, P. Raghavan, and E. Upfal. Randomized broadcast in networks. *Random Structures an Algorithms*, 1(4):447–460, 1990.

[26] N. Fountoulakis and K. Panagiotou. Rumor spreading on random regular graphs and expanders. In *APPROX-RANDOM*, pages 560–573, 2010.

[27] N. Fountoulakis, K. Panagiotou, and T. Sauerwald. Ultra-fast rumor spreading in social networks. In *SODA*, pages 1642–1660, 2012.

[28] A. Ganesh, L. Massoulie, and D. Towsley. The effect of network topology on the spread of epidemics. In *INFOCOM*, volume 2, pages 1455 – 1466, march 2005.

[29] Giakkoupis. Tight bounds for rumor spreading in graphs of a given conductance. In *STACS*, pages 57–68, 2011.

[30] G. Giakkoupis and T. Sauerwald. Rumor spreading and vertex expansion. In *SODA*, pages 1623–1641, 2012.

[31] O. Givan, N. Schwartz, A. Cygelberg, and L. Stone. Predicting epidemic thresholds on complex networks: Limitations of mean-field approaches. *Journal of Theoretical Biology*, 288:21–28, 2011.

[32] C. Gkantsidis, M. Mihail, and A. Saberi. Throughput and congestion in power-law graphs. In *SIGMETRICS*, pages 148–159, 2003.

[33] T. E. Harris. *The theory of branching processes*. Die Grundlehren der Mathematischen Wissenschaften, Bd. 119. Springer-Verlag, Berlin, 1963.

[34] D. A. Kessler. Epidemic Size in the SIS Model of Endemic Infec- Tions. *ArXiv e-prints*, Sept. 2007.

[35] L. Lovász. Random walks on graphs: a survey. In *Combinatorics, Paul Erdös is Eighty*, pages 1–46. 1993.

[36] N. Madras and R. Schinazi. Branching random walks on trees. *Stochastic Processes and their Applications*, 42(2):255 – 267, 1992.

[37] P. Matthews. Covering problems for brownian motion on spheres. *The Annals of Probability*, pages 189–199, 1988.

[38] M. Mihail. Conductance and convergence of markov chains-a combinatorial treatment of expanders. In *Foundations of Computer Science, 1989., 30th Annual Symposium on*, pages 526–531. IEEE, 1989.

[39] M. Mitzenmacher and E. Upfal. *Probability and Computing: Randomized Algorithms and Probabilistic Analysis*. Cambridge University Press, 2004.

[40] R. Parshani, S. Carmi, and S. Havlin. Epidemic threshold for the susceptible-infectious-susceptible model on random networks. *Physical review letters*, 104(25):258701, 2010.

[41] R. Sun and J. M. Swart. The brownian net. *The Annals of Probability*, 36(3):1153–1208, 2008.

[42] R. M. Tanner. Explicit concentrators from generalized n-gons. *SIAM Journal on Algebraic Discrete Methods*, 5(3):287–293, 1984.

[43] P. Van Mieghem. The n-intertwined SIS epidemic network model. *Computing*, 93:147–169, 2011.

[44] M. Zhong and K. Shen. Random walk based node sampling in self-organizing networks. *Operating Systems Review*, 40(3):49–55, 2006.

Parallel Rotor Walks on Finite Graphs and Applications in Discrete Load Balancing[*]

Hoda Akbari and Petra Berenbrink
Simon Fraser University
Burnaby, BC, Canada
hodaa@sfu.ca, petra@sfu.ca

ABSTRACT

We study the parallel *rotor walk* process, which works as follows: Consider a graph along with an arbitrary distribution of *tokens* over its nodes. Every node is equipped with a rotor that points to its neighbours in a fixed circular order. In each *round*, every node distributes all of its tokens using the rotor. One token is allocated to the neighbour pointed at by the rotor, then the rotor moves to the subsequent neighbour, and so on, until no token remains.

The process can be considered as a deterministic analogue of a process in which tokens perform one independent random walk step in each round. We compare the distribution of tokens in the rotor walk process with expected distribution in the random walk model. The similarity between the two processes is measured by their *discrepancy*, which is the maximum difference between the corresponding distribution entries over all rounds and nodes. We analyze a lazy variation of rotor walks that simulates a random walk with loop probability of $1/2$ on each node, and each node sends not all its tokens, but every other token in each round.

Viewing the rotor walk as a load balancing process, we prove that the rotor walk falls in the class of *bounded-error diffusion processes* introduced in [11]. This gives us discrepancy bounds of $\mathcal{O}(\log^{3/2} n)$ and $\mathcal{O}(1)$ for hypercube and r-dimensional torus with $r = \mathcal{O}(1)$, respectively, which improve over the best existing bounds of $\mathcal{O}(\log^2 n)$ and $\mathcal{O}(n^{1/r})$. Also, as a result of switching to the load balancing view, we observe that the existing load balancing results can be translated to rotor walk discrepancy bounds not previously noticed in the rotor walk literature.

We also use the idea of rotor walks to propose and analyze a randomized rounding discrete load balancing process that achieves the same balancing quality as similar protocols [11, 3], but uses fewer number of random bits compared to [3], and avoids the *negative load* problem of [11].

Categories and Subject Descriptors

G.2.2 [**Graph Theory**]: Network Problems

[*]This material is based upon work supported by the NSERC discovery grant "Randomized Algorithms for Distributed Systems".

General Terms

Algorithms, Performance

Keywords

rotor walks, random walks, deterministic graph walks, Propp machines, discrete diffusion

1. INTRODUCTION

In this paper we consider the *rotor walk* model, which works as follows: A regular graph of order n and degree d is given, along with an arbitrary distribution of *tokens* over its nodes. The process works in rounds and in every *round* each node distributes all of its tokens to its neighbours. We assume that every node is equipped with a rotor and its neighbours are arranged in a fixed circular list. At the beginning of a round, the rotor is directed toward one of the neighbours (the neighbour might be chosen randomly or depending on the neighbour that got the last token in the previous round). Then one token is allocated to that neighbour, the rotor is directed to the next neighbour in the circular list, and so on, until no token remains.

Rotor walks were first proposed as deterministic analogues of a *random walk* model. A standard random walk is defined as follows. Suppose the same graph and token distribution is given, but instead of allocating tokens using rotors, in each round every token independently performs one random walk step by moving to a randomly chosen neighbour. Note that, if we assume that the initial rotor position is chosen randomly at the beginning of a round, then the number of tokens that a node sends to any of its neighbours is expectedly the same as that of the random walk model. Hence, the idea of the rotor walks is to get a token distribution similar to that of the random walk model, while avoiding the high variance of the random walk. Several publications (see Section 1.1) address the question of how closely rotor walks approximate the expected token distributions of random walk models. The closeness of the two models is usually measured as the maximum, over every round and every node, difference in the number of tokens between the two models. This is called the *discrepancy* between the two models.

Note that the concept of rotor walks can be generalized to a wide class of non-standard random walks (where the neighbours are not chosen uniformly at random and tokens is also allowed to remain at the same node), resulting in deterministic versions of time-homogeneous Markov chains [15].

Another closely related model is *diffusion load balancing*. Again, we have network of processors along with an initial token (task) distribution. Now every node is allowed to balance its load with its neighbours. For instance, one can think of a process that distributes the tokens using a rotor on every node, or another process in which tokens can move to randomly chosen neighbours (the latter process is motivated by game theoretic considerations). Nodes can also calculate the load difference to each of their neighbours. Over each edge, the node with higher load sends the load difference divided by $d + 1$ tokens to the other node. We call this process *standard diffusion*. The goal of these processes is to distribute the load as evenly as possible. In this context, the discrepancy is usually defined as the maximum difference in the number of tokens on any pair of nodes. In this paper, we will use the term *imbalance* to refer to this definition. The *convergence time* of a process is defined as the number of rounds required to reach constant imbalance.

In load balancing one distinguishes between *continuous* processes where tasks can be split arbitrarily and the more realistic *discrete* case where tasks cannot be split. The standard continuous diffusion mentioned above is closely related to that of random walks with self-loop probability $1/(d + 1)$. In other words, the token distribution of the continuous diffusion process is the same as the expected token distribution of the random walk process. Hence, continuous diffusion is essentially equivalent to the random walks with uniform stationary distribution. It is therefore well studied with tight convergence time bounds [20].

In discrete load balancing, the processes usually try to stay as close as possible to the ideal continuous case by applying rounding techniques. For example, if the continuous process would forward 3.7 tokens to a neighbour, the node could (deterministically) simply round up or down, or it could send 3 tokens with a probability of 0.3 and 4 tokens with a probability of 0.7 (*randomized rounding*; for more information we refer the reader to Section 1.1). Another possibility would be to distribute the tokens using a rotor. All these rounding schemes generate *rounding errors* which propagate through the network over rounds. As a result, discrete processes are not able to balance the load perfectly. In analyzing a discrete process, one usually obtains a bound on the discrepancy between the continuous and the discrete process. At the convergence time of the continuous process, the imbalance of the discrete process is at most twice this discrepancy.

In this paper, we consider a deterministic rotor walk as a model of discrete diffusion or deterministic random walks. We also consider a random rotor walk model which translates into a model for a discrete diffusion or a partially derandomized random walk model. For hypercubes and tori, the deterministic walk has a discrepancy of $\mathcal{O}(\log^{3/2} n)$ and d, respectively. For the randomized rotor walks, we obtain discrepancy bounds of $\mathcal{O}(d \log \log n/(1 - \lambda))$ for regular graphs (λ is the second largest eigenvalue in absolute value of the random walk transition matrix), $\Theta(\log n)$ for hypercubes, and $\mathcal{O}(\sqrt{\log n})$ for tori. See Section 1.2 for a more detailed description of our results.

1.1 Related Work

In this section we review the literature for all three areas mentioned in the introduction, rotor walks, random walks, and diffusion load balancing.

Rotor Walks. Originally introduced in [21], the rotor walk model was employed by Jim Propp for derandomizing the random walk, thereby frequently appearing under the names of *Propp machines* and *deterministic random walks* [4, 5, 8, 13, 16]. It has been shown that the rotor walks capture the average behaviour of random walks in a variety of respects such as hitting probabilities and hitting times [15].

Cooper and Spencer [6] consider rotor walks on infinite grids with constant dimensions; they bound the discrepancy by a constant

which depends on the dimension of the grid. The constants are known for one [4] and two [8] dimensions.

Cooper et al. [5] show for infinite d-regular trees that there exists an initial token distribution and direction of the rotors that results in a discrepancy of $\Omega(\sqrt{dt})$ for an arbitrary round t. Note that the initial token distribution and rotor directions depend on t. Kijima et al. [16] obtain discrepancy bounds of $\mathcal{O}(n|E|)$ for arbitrary graphs and $1.5 \log^3 n + \mathcal{O}(\log^2 n)$ for hypercubes. The latter hypercube bound holds both in case of lazy and non-lazy random walks. For expanders and constant-degree tori, the discrepancy bound implied by their general bound is not better than $\mathcal{O}(n^2)$.

Diffusion Load Balancing. Rabani et al. [22] present an analysis technique that compares the load distribution of a discrete algorithm with that of a continuous counterpart. The technique works for most discrete diffusion algorithms, including rotor walks. The authors show an imbalance bound of $\mathcal{O}(d \log n/(1 - \lambda))$ for arbitrary graphs, where λ is the second largest eigenvalue in absolute value of the transition matrix of the underlying Markov Chain [22]. This yields an imbalance bound of $\mathcal{O}(n^{1/2d})$ for tori, and $\mathcal{O}(d \log n)$ for expanders. For hypercubes, the same technique with a tighter analysis gives a bound of $\Theta(\log^2 n)$ [3]. In fact, due to the technique used, these results are not only imbalance bounds, but also discrepancy bounds. Note that for graph classes such as hypercubes, tori, and expanders, the discrepancy bounds obtained from [22] are better than those of [16].

Friedrich et al. [11] propose a deterministic load balancing process in which the scheduled continuous load transfer on each edge is rounded up or down deterministically, such that the sum of the rounding errors on each edge up to an arbitrary round t is bounded by a constant. This property (formally defined in Section 2) is called the *bounded-error property*. The authors first show that their process has the bounded error property on any graph. Then they show that any process with bounded-error property achieves a discrepancy of $\mathcal{O}(\log^{3/2} n)$ for hypercubes and $\mathcal{O}(1)$ for constant-degree tori. There are no similar results for other graph classes. Note that the downside of the algorithm in [11] is that the outgoing demand of a node might exceed its available load, leading to so-called *negative load*, which makes the process infeasible. Though in [11] the authors propose a solution to the problem, it comes at the cost of requiring additional information on nodes and degrading the double-sided imbalance bound to a one-sided maximum load bound.

In [2], the authors propose an algorithm that achieves discrepancy of $\mathcal{O}(d)$ for any graph. The algorithm is surprisingly simple. It tries for every edge e and round t to calculate the number of tokens that should be sent over e in t such that the total number of tokens forwarded over e (over the first t steps) stays as close as possible to the amount of load that is sent by the continuous algorithm over e during the t steps. However, their algorithm can also have negative load when the initial load of any node is not sufficiently large.

Many papers suggest randomized rounding processes [2, 3, 11] to convert the continuous load that is transferred over an edge into discrete load. The algorithms in [2, 11] round the continuous load on each edge independently from all other edges. If a node rounds up on too many edges it cannot have a sufficient number of tokens. This can lead to negative load on some of the nodes. In contrast, the algorithm of [3] avoids this problem. It calculates a the total number of *extra* tokens (difference between the total continuous flow forwarded over all edges minus the number of tokens forwarded by the discrete algorithm after rounding *down*) a nodes should forward to its neighbours and sends these tokens to randomly chosen neighbours (without replacement).

The randomized algorithm of [11] achieves imbalance bound of $\mathcal{O}(d \log \log n/(1 - \lambda))$ for regular graphs, $\mathcal{O}(d \log \log n)$ for expanders, $\mathcal{O}(\log^2 n \log \log n)$ for hypercubes, and $\mathcal{O}(n^{1/2d} \log \log n)$ for tori. For the algorithm in [3], the bounds are $\mathcal{O}(d \log \log n/(1 - \lambda))$ and $d\sqrt{\log n} + \sqrt{d \log n \log d/(1-\lambda)}$ for regular graphs, $\mathcal{O}(d \log \log n)$ for expanders, $\mathcal{O}(\log n)$ for hypercubes, and $\mathcal{O}(\sqrt{\log n})$ for tori. In [2], the imbalance is of $\mathcal{O}(\sqrt{d \log n})$ for arbitrary graphs.

Note that a close look at the analysis techniques in all the papers mentioned here shows that the authors do not only bound the imbalance but also the discrepancy.

Random Walks. Due to their vast applications, random walks and Markov chains have been well studied. In close relation to the convergence time of a continuous diffusion process is the notion of mixing time of a Markov chain which determines how fast the Markov chain approaches its stationary distribution. For more details on the topic, we refer the reader to [18].

Our model also has similarities to the *balancing* or *smoothing networks* [1, 14, 17, 19] and quasirandom rumour spreading [9].

1.2 Our Contribution

In this paper we consider two rotor walk models, a deterministic model called *D_Propp* and a randomized model called *R_Propp*.

D_Propp. Similar to [11], *D_Propp* follows a *lazy* continuous process where every node keeps half of the tokens and distributes the other half using a rotor. The rotor points to neighbour $i + 1$ at the beginning of a round when the rotor stopped at i in the previous round. Our analysis relies on the result by Friedrich et al. [11], which is based on the unimodality of transition probabilities, a property that requires loop probabilities of at least $1/2$.

Our main contribution in analyzing *D_Propp* is proving that it exhibits the *bounded-error property* on any graph (Theorem 3.1). Hence, similar to the process of [11], we get discrepancy bounds of the order of $\mathcal{O}(\log^{3/2} n)$ for hypercubes and $\mathcal{O}(1)$ for constant-degree tori. Compared to the process of [11], our algorithm is much simpler and avoids negative loads, thus achieving double-sided bounds. Compared to [2] the algorithm has the same discrepancy bounds for tori but avoids negative load. Note that for hypercubes, the $\mathcal{O}(\log n)$ imbalance bound of [2] is better than ours.

There are not many discrepancy results for rotor walks or diffusion balancing with rotors for finite graphs. We are only aware of [16] which shows results for arbitrary graphs but gives weaker bounds than [22] for graph classes such as tori, expanders, and hypercubes. Compared to [22] our bound of $\mathcal{O}(\log^{3/2} n)$ improves their bound of $\mathcal{O}(\log^2 n)$ for hypercubes. For finite constant-degree tori, our discrepancy bound of $\Theta(1)$ extends the constant discrepancy results for infinite grids [6] and significantly improves the existing bound of $\mathcal{O}(n^{1/2d})$ in [22].

The immediate question is, whether the bounded-error property results in discrepancy bounds independent of n for finite graphs other than hypercubes and tori. As we observe in Remark 3.3, this does not hold for finite trees where discrepancies of $\Omega(\sqrt{d \log_d n})$ can arise. This follows from the result of [5] on infinite regular trees (see Section 1.1).

R_Propp. In Section 4, we analyze a randomized rotor walks as a discrete load balancing scheme with randomized rounding. *R_Propp* distributes all but a $1/(d + 1)$ fraction of tokens to the neighbours using a rotor that chooses its initial position randomly at the beginning of every round.

We obtain discrepancy bounds of $\mathcal{O}(d \log \log n/(1 - \lambda))$ for regular graphs, $\Theta(\log n)$ for hypercubes, and $\mathcal{O}(\sqrt{\log n})$ for tori. All the bounds hold *with high probability* (with probability least $1 - \mathcal{O}(n^{-\alpha})$ for some constant $\alpha > 0$). *R_Propp* achieves the same imbalance bounds as the process of [3] where the extra tokens are sent to randomly chosen neighbours *without* replacement. We can also show (in the full version of this paper) that the same discrepancy bounds as the ones in [3] hold when the extra tokens are forwarded *with* replacement. Hence, our algorithm achieves the same results as both processes (with and without replacement), but with a smaller amount of randomization. It would be interesting to see if it is sufficient to choose a random rotor position only once in the very beginning of the process, too. Compared to [2, 11], our algorithm does not create negative load. Our results for hypercubes and tori improve the results of [11]. Note that the discrepancy bounds of [2] are better for large d or large λ.

2. MODEL AND NOTATION

We model the network by an undirected loop-free d-regular graph $G = (V, E)$, where $V = \{1, \cdots, n\}$ is the set of nodes. For $i \in V$, $N(i)$ is the set of nodes adjacent to i. $r_i^{\mathcal{P}}(t)$ represents the state of i's rotor (its position in the circular list) in the beginning of round t of process $\mathcal{P}$.

Initially m tokens are arbitrarily distributed over the network. For a fixed process $\mathcal{P}$, $x_i(t)$ is *load* of node i in round t, which is defined as the number of tokens assigned to it in that round. The average load is $\bar{x} := m/n$. The vector $x^{\mathcal{P}}(t) = (x_1^{\mathcal{P}}(t), \ldots, x_n^{\mathcal{P}}(t))$ denotes the load of nodes in round t. $y_{i,j}^{\mathcal{P}}(t)$ is defined as the load transferred from node i to node j in round t, so that

$$x_i^{\mathcal{P}}(t+1) = x_i^{\mathcal{P}}(t) - \sum_{(i,j) \in E} (y_{i,j}^{\mathcal{P}}(t) - y_{j,i}^{\mathcal{P}}(t)).$$

We say the continuous diffusion process $\mathcal{P}$ is *governed* by *diffusion matrix* $\mathbf{P}$, when for all $t \geq 0$ we have

$$x^{\mathcal{P}}(t+1) = x^{\mathcal{P}}(t) \mathbf{P}.$$

The second largest eigenvalue in absolute value of the diffusion matrix is denoted by λ. For a discrete process $\mathcal{P}$ and the continuous process with diffusion matrix $\mathbf{P}$, the *directional rounding error* on edge (i, j) in round t is defined as:

$$e_{i \to j}^{\mathcal{P}}(t) := x_i^{\mathcal{P}}(t) \cdot \mathbf{P}_{i,j} - y_{i,j}^{\mathcal{P}}(t).$$

We define the rounding error on edge (i, j) in round t as

$$e_{i,j}^{\mathcal{P}}(t) := e_{i \to j}^{\mathcal{P}}(t) - e_{j \to i}^{\mathcal{P}}(t).$$

We also define

$$\Lambda_{i,j}^{\mathcal{P}}(t) := \sum_{\tau=1}^{t} e_{i,j}^{\mathcal{P}}(\tau),$$

as the *accumulated rounding error* on edge (i, j) in round t, which is the sum of all the rounding errors on (i, j) up to the end of round t. A process $\mathcal{P}$ is said to have the *bounded-error property* if for some constant α, and all $(i, j) \in E$ and $t \geq 0$, the inequality $\left| \Lambda_{i,j}^{\mathcal{P}}(t) \right| \leq \alpha$ holds regardless of the network topology and initial load distribution.

In randomized settings, we say an event occurs *with high probability (w.h.p)* if it has probability at least $1 - \mathcal{O}(n^{-\alpha})$ for some constant $\alpha > 0$. For arbitrary real a, we use $\{a\}$ to denote $a - \lfloor a \rfloor$.

3. THE DETERMINISTIC PROPP PROCESS

In this section, we introduce and analyze the D_Propp process. D_Propp mimics the $RW(2)$ diffusion process. $RW(2)$ is similar to a random walk with self-loop probability of $1/2$ governed by the matrix $\mathbf{P}^{\mathcal{L}}$, where $\mathbf{P}^{\mathcal{L}}_{i,i} = 1/2$, and for all adjacent nodes i, j we have $\mathbf{P}^{\mathcal{L}}_{i,j} = 1/(2d)$. We follow the notation defined in Section 2, using the superscripts $\mathcal{D}$ for D_Propp and $\mathcal{L}$ for $RW(2)$. When clear from context, we omit the superscript $\mathcal{D}$.

Algorithm D_Propp. Our algorithm works in rounds, in every round every node i distributes all its tokens among itself and its neighbours. A round, in turn, consists of steps. In each step i assigns one token to itself or a neighbour. Hence, if a node i has load $x_i(t)$ at the beginning of round t, from the viewpoint of i the round consists of $x_i(t)$ steps.

The rotor of each node i has $2d$ states $0, \ldots, 2d - 1$. The states $0, \ldots, d - 1$ point to the neighbours of i in an arbitrary fixed order, and the rest of the states point to i itself. $r_i(t)$ is the state of i's rotor in the beginning of round t. Let $r_i(t, s)$ and $\hat{r}_i(t, s)$ denote the state of i's rotor in the beginning of step s of round t, and its target node, respectively. In each step, a rotor assigns one token to the node it is pointing to, and then it moves the pointer to the subsequent state (Equations (3.2) and (3.3)). Once every token is assigned, the actual load transfer is performed at the end of the round synchronously (Equation (3.5)).

After feeding $2d \lfloor x_i(t)/2d \rfloor$ tokens to the rotor, each state is visited $\lfloor x_i(t)/2d \rfloor$ times and the rotor reaches the same state $r_i(t)$ as it was in the beginning of the round. At this point, $(x_i(t) \bmod 2d)$ tokens are still left. Let us call these tokens *extra tokens*. A node $j \in N(i)$ receives an extra token if and only if one of the $(x_i(t) \bmod 2d)$ rotor states starting from $r_i(t)$ points to j (Equation (3.4)).

$$r_i^{\mathcal{D}}(t) = (r_i^{\mathcal{D}}(t-1) + x_i^{\mathcal{D}}(t-1)) \bmod 2d \quad (3.1)$$

$$r_i^{\mathcal{D}}(t, 1) = r_i^{\mathcal{D}}(t) \quad (3.2)$$

$$r_i^{\mathcal{D}}(t, s+1) = (r_i^{\mathcal{D}}(t, s) + 1) \bmod 2d \quad (3.3)$$

$$y_{i,j}^{\mathcal{D}}(t) = \begin{cases} \left\lfloor \dfrac{x_i^{\mathcal{D}}(t)}{2d} \right\rfloor + 1 & \text{if } \hat{r}_i^{\mathcal{D}}(t, s) = j, \text{ for} \\ & \text{some } s \text{ between 1 and} \\ & (x_i^{\mathcal{D}}(t) \bmod 2d) \\ \left\lfloor \dfrac{x_i^{\mathcal{D}}(t)}{2d} \right\rfloor & \text{otherwise.} \end{cases} \quad (3.4)$$

$$x_i^{\mathcal{D}}(t+1) = x_i^{\mathcal{D}}(t) - \sum_{(i,j) \in E} (y_{i,j}^{\mathcal{D}}(t) - y_{j,i}^{\mathcal{D}}(t)) \quad (3.5)$$

Figure 1: The D_Propp diffusion process: Equations of round t.

Our analysis of the D_Propp process in Section 3.1 shows the following results:

THEOREM 3.1. *The D_Propp diffusion scheme exhibits the bounded-error property.*

Let the variable T denote the convergence time of $RW(2)$, and r be a constant. Then Theorem 3.1 yields:

COROLLARY 3.2. *The discrepancy between D_Propp and $RW(2)$ (hence, the imbalance at every round $t \geqslant T$) is $\mathcal{O}(\log^{3/2} n)$ for hypercubes and $\mathcal{O}(1)$ for r-dimensional tori.*

According to Theorem 3.1, rotor walks have bounded-error property on *any* graph, while Corollary 3.2 gives discrepancy results only for torus and hypercube. This raises the question whether the bounded-error property results in discrepancy bounds independent of n for finite graphs other than hypercubes and tori. For finite trees, Remark 3.3 answers this question negatively:

REMARK 3.3. *[5] shows that for an arbitrary parameter t there exists an initial token distribution and rotor direction such that in round t a high discrepancy is enforced at the root (see Section 1.1 for more details). We note that the construction of [5] truncated at depth t still causes the same discrepancy at the root. This yields a discrepancy lower bound of $\Omega(\sqrt{d \log_d n})$ which depends on the order of the graph.*

3.1 Analysis

To prove the bounded-error property for D_Propp, we first derive a formula for the edge errors in the observation below (recall that $\{a\} := a - \lfloor a \rfloor$).

OBSERVATION 3.4. *For arbitrary $(i, j) \in E$ and $t \geqslant 0$ we have:*

$$e_{i \to j}(t) = \begin{cases} \left\{ \dfrac{x_i(t)}{2d} \right\} - 1 & \text{if } \hat{r}_i(t, s) = j, \text{ for} \\ & \text{some } s \text{ between 1 and} \\ & (x_i^{\mathcal{D}}(t) \bmod 2d) \\ \left\{ \dfrac{x_i(t)}{2d} \right\} & \text{otherwise.} \end{cases}$$

PROOF. Recall $e_{i \to j}(t)$ is defined as $x_i(t) \cdot \mathbf{P}_{i,j} - y_{i,j}(t)$, which yields: $e_{i \to j}(t) = x_i(t)/2d - y_{i,j}(t)$. The proof now follows from Equation (3.4). $\square$

We define the *directional* accumulated error on edge (i, j) in round t as $\Lambda_{i \to j}(t) := \sum_{\tau=1}^{t} e_{i \to j}(\tau)$. The key ingredient of our analysis is switching from the global round-oriented view of the process to a local view from an arbitrarily fixed node. Let $S_i(t) := \sum_{\tau=1}^{t} x_i(\tau)$ with $S_i(0) := 0$. For every edge (i, j), we define $\lambda_{i,j}(t)$ inductively as follows. Define $\lambda_{i,j}(0) := 0$ and for k, $S_i(t) < k \leqslant S_i(t+1)$ we define:

$$\lambda_{i,j}(k) := \begin{cases} \lambda_{i,j}(k-1) + \frac{1}{2d} - 1 & \text{if } \hat{r}_i(t, k - S_i(t)) = j, \\ \lambda_{i,j}(k-1) + \frac{1}{2d} & \text{otherwise.} \end{cases} \quad (3.6)$$

OBSERVATION 3.5. *For arbitrary $(i, j) \in E$ and arbitrary t, we have $|\lambda_{i,j}(t)| < 1$.*

PROOF. From the definition of $\lambda_{i,j}(t)$, it follows that for arbitrary $(i, j) \in E$, $\lambda_{i,j}(.)$ is a periodic function with period $2d$ and amplitude $1 - 1/2d$, with $\lambda_{i,j}(0) = 0$. Thus $\max_t \lambda_{i,j}(t) - \min_t \lambda_{i,j}(t) = 1 - 1/2d < 1$, where $\max_t \lambda_{i,j}(t) \geqslant 0$ and $\min_t \lambda_{i,j}(t) \leqslant 0$. Therefore we must have $\min_t \lambda_{i,j}(t) > -1$ and $\max_t \lambda_{i,j}(t) < 1$, which yields $|\lambda_{i,j}(t)| < 1$. $\square$

The following lemma provides a method for translating $\Lambda_{i \to j}(.)$ to $\lambda_{i,j}(.)$:

LEMMA 3.6. *For arbitrary edge (i, j) and $t \geqslant 0$ we have:*

$$\Lambda_{i \to j}(t) = \lambda_{i,j}(S_i(t)).$$

PROOF. The proof is by induction on t. The base case $\Lambda_{i\to j}(0) = \lambda_{i,j}(0) = 0$ is trivial. It suffices to prove that $\lambda_{i,j}(S_i(k)) - \Lambda_{i\to j}(k) = 0$ holds, assuming $\Lambda_{i\to j}(k-1) = \lambda_{i,j}(S_i(k-1))$. The assumption yields:

$$\lambda_{i,j}(S_i(k)) - \Lambda_{i\to j}(k) \qquad (3.7)$$

$$= \lambda_{i,j}(S_i(k)) - \lambda_{i,j}(S_i(k-1)) - e_{i\to j}(k). \qquad (3.8)$$

We express $\lambda_{i,j}(S_i(k)) - \lambda_{i,j}(S_i(k-1))$ in Equation (3.8) as a telescoping sum. Observe that $\lambda_{i,j}(.)$ is a periodic sequence with period $2d$. Hence, for arbitrary integers $q, \ell \geqslant 0$ we have:

$$\sum_{s=q+1}^{q+2d\ell} (\lambda_{i,j}(s) - \lambda_{i,j}(s-1)) = \lambda_{i,j}(q + 2d\ell) - \lambda_{i,j}(q) = 0.$$

This is used to simplify the summation below by separating a multiple of $2d$ terms (the second sum) from it:

$$\lambda_{i,j}(S_i(k)) - \lambda_{i,j}(S_i(k-1))$$

$$= \sum_{s=S_i(k-1)+1}^{S_i(k)} (\lambda_{i,j}(s) - \lambda_{i,j}(s-1))$$

$$= \sum_{s=S_i(k-1)+1}^{S_i(k)-2d\lfloor x_i(k)/(2d)\rfloor} (\lambda_{i,j}(s) - \lambda_{i,j}(s-1)) +$$

$$\sum_{s=S_i(k)-2d\cdot\lfloor x_i(k)/(2d)\rfloor+1}^{S_i(k)} (\lambda_{i,j}(s) - \lambda_{i,j}(s-1)), \qquad (3.9)$$

Note that the second sum is 0. We now consider two cases:
(I) For some $1 \leqslant s \leqslant (x_i(k) \bmod 2d)$, we have $\hat{r}_i(k,s) = j$.
(II) Case (I) does not happen.
In case (I), we use Equation (3.6) and Observation 3.4 to write:

$$\lambda_{i,j}(S_i(k)) - \lambda_{i,j}(S_i(k-1))$$

$$= \sum_{s=S_i(k-1)+1}^{S_i(k-1)+(x_i(k)\bmod 2d)} (\lambda_{i,j}(s) - \lambda_{i,j}(s-1))$$

$$= \frac{1}{2d}\cdot((x_i(k)\bmod 2d) - 1) + \left(\frac{1}{2d} - 1\right)$$

$$= \left\{\frac{x_i(k)}{2d}\right\} - 1 \quad = e_{i\to j}(k), \qquad (3.10)$$

Similarly, in case (II) as well, we get

$$\lambda_{i,j}(S_i(k)) - \lambda_{i,j}(S_i(k-1)) = e_{i\to j}(k).$$

Combined with Equations (3.8) and (3.10), this finishes the proof. $\square$

PROOF OF THEOREM 3.1. We show that $|\Lambda_{i,j}(t)| < 2$ for all $t \geqslant 0$ and $(i,j) \in E$. Recall that $\Lambda_{i,j}(t) := \sum_{\tau=1}^{t} e_{i,j}(\tau)$, where $e_{i,j}(\tau) = e_{i\to j}(\tau) - e_{j\to i}(\tau)$. Thus we have $\Lambda_{i,j}(t) = \Lambda_{i\to j}(t) - \Lambda_{j\to i}(t)$. Hence, to prove $|\Lambda_{i,j}(t)| < 2$, it suffices to show $|\Lambda_{i\to j}(t)| < 1$. For the sake of contradiction, suppose for some $t_1 \geqslant 0$ and $(i_1, j_1) \in E$, we have $|\Lambda_{i_1\to j_1}(t_1)| \geqslant 1$. By Lemma 3.6, it holds that $\Lambda_{i_1\to j_1}(t_1) = \lambda_{i_1,j_1}(S_{i_1}(t_1))$; therefore $|\lambda_{i_1,j_1}(S_{i_1}(t_1))| \geqslant 1$. This contradicts Observation 3.5, and the proof follows. $\square$

PROOF OF COROLLARY 3.2. We apply Theorems A.9 and A.10 by Friedrich et al. [11] to the Theorem 3.1. This shows that the discrepancy between D_Propp and $RW(2)$ is $\mathcal{O}(\log^{3/2} n)$ for hypercube, and $\mathcal{O}(1)$ for r-dimensional torus with $r = \mathcal{O}(1)$, as required. $\square$

4. THE RANDOMIZED PROPP PROCESS

In this section, we analyze a randomized rotor walk, called R_Propp, which randomly repositions the rotors at the beginning of each round. We view R_Propp as a randomized rounding diffusion process. R_Propp mimics the standard diffusion process $RW(d+1)$, which similar to a random walk with self-loop probability of $1/(d+1)$, is governed by the diffusion matrix $\mathbf{P}^\mathcal{S}$, where for all neighbouring nodes i, j, $\mathbf{P}^\mathcal{S}_{i,j} = \frac{1}{d+1}$.

We follow the notation defined in Section 2, using $\mathcal{R}$ for R_Propp, $\mathcal{S}$ for standard diffusion and capitalized letters for loads and flows, to emphasize these variables are now random. When clear from context, we omit the superscripts.

Algorithm R_Propp. The algorithm works, similar to D_Propp, in rounds consisting of one step for each token. Each rotor has $d+1$ states, corresponding to the nodes in $N(i) \cup \{i\}$. In the beginning of each round, each rotor is directed to a random state (Equation (4.1)). Again, $r_i(t)$ is the state of i's rotor in the beginning of round t. Let $r_i(t,s)$ denote the state of i's rotor in the beginning of step s of round t, and and let $\hat{r}_i(t,s)$ be the target node. Upon feeding it a token, a rotor assigns the token to the node it is pointing to, and moves to the subsequent state (Equations (4.2) and (4.3)). A node j receives an extra token if and only if one of the $(X_i(t) \bmod (d+1))$ rotor states starting from $r_i(t)$ points to j (Equation (4.4)). Once every token is assigned, the actual load transfer is performed at the end of each round synchronously (Equation (4.5)).

$$r_i^\mathcal{R}(t) = \text{an integer in } [0,d] \text{ chosen independently}$$
$$\text{and uniformly at random;} \qquad (4.1)$$

$$r_i^\mathcal{R}(t,1) = r_i^\mathcal{R}(t) \qquad (4.2)$$

$$r_i^\mathcal{R}(t,s+1) = (r_i^\mathcal{R}(t,s) + 1) \bmod (d+1) \qquad (4.3)$$

$$Y_{i,j}^\mathcal{R}(t) = \begin{cases} \left\lfloor \frac{X_i^\mathcal{R}(t)}{(d+1)} \right\rfloor + 1 & \text{if } \hat{r}_i^\mathcal{R}(t,s) = j, \text{ for} \\ & \text{some } s \text{ between 1 and} \\ & (X_i^\mathcal{R}(t) \bmod (d+1)) \\ \left\lfloor \frac{X_i^\mathcal{R}(t)}{(d+1)} \right\rfloor & \text{otherwise.} \end{cases}$$
$$\qquad (4.4)$$

$$X_i^\mathcal{R}(t+1) = X_i^\mathcal{R}(t) - \sum_{(i,j)\in E} (Y_{i,j}^\mathcal{R}(t) - Y_{j,i}^\mathcal{R}(t)) \qquad (4.5)$$

Figure 2: The R_Propp diffusion process: Equations of round t.

Note that, similar to D_Propp, R_Propp avoids the negative load which can occur in the randomized rounding algorithms in [11, 12], while achieving the same bounds on the imbalance (double-sided).

To analyze R_Propp, we first consider general graphs (Theorem 4.1), and then we show improved bounds for hypercubes and tori (Theorem 4.2). In both theorems, the variable T denotes the convergence time of $RW(d+1)$. We assume that the imbalance of the initial distribution is of $\mathcal{O}(\exp(n^\kappa))$ for some constant κ.

THEOREM 4.1. *The discrepancy between R_Propp and $RW(d+1)$ (hence, the imbalance at $t = T$) is $\mathcal{O}(d \log\log n/(1-\lambda))$ w.h.p.*

Note that for d-regular expander, the discrepancy between R_Propp and $RW(d+1)$ is $\mathcal{O}(d \log\log n)$.

THEOREM 4.2. *The discrepancy between R_Propp and RW(d + 1) (hence, the imbalance at time $t = T$) is w.h.p., $\mathcal{O}(\sqrt{\log n})$ if G is an r-dimensional torus with $r = \mathcal{O}(1)$ and $\Theta(\log n)$ if G is a hypercube.*

4.1 Definitions and Basic Facts

For arbitrary node k at round t, let

$$E_k(t) := X_k^{\mathcal{R}}(t) - x_k^{\mathcal{S}}(t)$$

denote the difference between the loads of *R_Propp* and *RW(d+1)*. It is known [22] that

$$E_k(t+1) = \sum_{s=0}^{t} \sum_{(i,j)\in E} E_{i,j}(t-s)\left(\mathbf{P}_{i,k}^s - \mathbf{P}_{j,k}^s\right).$$

For our proofs, we slightly reformulate this expression:

$$E_k(t+1) = \sum_{s=0}^{t} \sum_{i\in V} \sum_{j\in N(i)} E_{i\to j}(t-s)\left(\mathbf{P}_{i,k}^s - \mathbf{P}_{j,k}^s\right).$$

For each edge (i,j) we define the Bernoulli random variable $Z_{i,j}^{(t)}$ which is one if an extra token is sent from i to j in round t and zero otherwise. More formally,

$$Z_{i,j}(t) := \begin{cases} 1 & \text{if } \hat{r}_i^{\mathcal{R}}(t,s) = j, \text{ for some } s \\ & \text{between 1 and } (X_i^{\mathcal{R}}(t) \bmod (d+1)) \\ 0 & \text{otherwise.} \end{cases} \quad (4.6)$$

The rounding error on edge (i,j) in round t, denoted by $E_{i\to j}(t)$ is obtained by the following formula (recall that $\{a\} := a - \lfloor a \rfloor$):

$$E_{i\to j}(t) := \left\{\frac{X_i(t)}{d+1}\right\} - Z_{i,j}^{(t)} \quad (4.7)$$

Thus we have:

$$\begin{aligned} &X_i(t+1) \\ &= X_i(t) + \sum_{j\in N(i)} \left(\frac{X_j(t) - X_i(t)}{d+1} + E_{i\to j}(t) - E_{j\to i}(t)\right). \end{aligned} \quad (4.8)$$

We now observe the following facts:

OBSERVATION 4.3. *For every edge (i,j) and round t,*

1. $\mathbf{Ex}\left[Z_{i,j}^{(t)} \mid X(t)\right] = \left\{\frac{X_i(t)}{d+1}\right\}$;
2. $\mathbf{Ex}\left[E_{i\to j}(t) \mid X(t)\right] = 0.$

4.2 A General Bound for Arbitrary Graphs

In this section we provide an analysis of *R_Propp* for general graphs, proving the Theorem 4.1.

The Proof Outline. To bound $E_k(t+1)$, we first find a probabilistic bound on the error on arbitrary node k and round t. Fix a node k and round t. Define

$$\mathcal{S}_k(s) := \sum_{i\in V} \sum_{j\in N(i)} E_{i\to j}(t-s)\left(\mathbf{P}_{i,k}^s - \mathbf{P}_{j,k}^s\right). \quad (4.9)$$

We break the summation at $t_0 := \min\left\{\frac{C\log\log n}{1-\lambda}, t\right\}$, where $C \geqslant 1$ is an arbitrary constant:

$$|E_k(t+1)| \leqslant \left|\sum_{s=0}^{t_0-1} \mathcal{S}_k(s)\right| + \left|\sum_{s=t_0}^{t} \mathcal{S}_k(s)\right| \quad (4.10)$$

It is easy to bound the first sum deterministically (Observation 4.4). To bound the second sum, we first use the method of averaged bounded differences (Lemma A.11) to obtain a concentration result for $\mathcal{S}_k(s)$ for arbitrary s. We consider the Doob sequence of the function $\mathcal{S}_k(s)$ with respect to the sequence of randomly chosen rotor states in round s (Lemma 4.5). A similar technique is used in [3], but their function and random variables span several rounds and the Lipschitz constants are estimated quite differently.

In Lemma 4.6 we bound each $\mathcal{S}_k(s)$ by a properly chosen δ_s. Then we argue that the whole sum is bounded by the sum of δ_s values w.h.p.

It is not hard to verify that the following bound holds on the first summation of Equation (4.10):

OBSERVATION 4.4. *For arbitrary node k we have*

$$\left|\sum_{s=0}^{t_0-1} \mathcal{S}_k(s)\right| \leqslant 2\,Cd\log\log n/(1-\lambda).$$

Now we give the bound for a fixed round:

LEMMA 4.5. *For fixed node k, round s, and $\delta > 0$,*

$$\mathbf{Pr}\left[\mathcal{S}_k(s) \geqslant \delta\right] \leqslant 2\exp\left(-\delta^2/16\,d^2\lambda^{2s}\right).$$

PROOF. Note that by the definition of $\mathcal{S}_k(s)$ (Equation (4.9)), for a fixed $X(t-s)$, the function $\mathcal{S}_k(s)$ depends only on the randomly chosen rotor states $r_i(t-s)$, for $1 \leqslant i \leqslant n$. We represent these random variables as a sequence $Y_1, Y_2, \ldots, Y_n$, such that for any $\ell \geqslant 1$, we have $Y_\ell = r_\ell(t-s)$. Let $\mathbf{Y}_\ell$ denote $Y_1, Y_2, \ldots, Y_\ell$. Consider the martingale sequence $\mathbf{Ex}\left[\mathcal{S}_k(s) \mid X(t-s), \mathbf{Y}_\ell\right], 1 \leqslant \ell \leqslant n$. To apply the method of averaged bounded differences (Lemma A.11), we first provide a bound on the following expression:

$$c_\ell := \Big| \mathbf{Ex}\left[\mathcal{S}_k(s) \mid X(t-s), \mathbf{Y}_\ell\right] - $$
$$\mathbf{Ex}\left[\mathcal{S}_k(s) \mid X(t-s), \mathbf{Y}_{\ell-1}\right] \Big| \quad (4.11)$$

We have:

$$\mathbf{Ex}\left[\mathcal{S}_k(s) \mid X(t-s), \mathbf{Y}_\ell\right] - \mathbf{Ex}\left[\mathcal{S}_k(s) \mid X(t-s), \mathbf{Y}_{\ell-1}\right]$$
$$\leqslant \sum_{i\in V} \sum_{j\in N(i)} \Big(\mathbf{Ex}\left[E_{i\to j}(t-s) \mid X(t-s), \mathbf{Y}_\ell\right]$$
$$- \mathbf{Ex}\left[E_{i\to j}(t-s) \mid X(t-s), \mathbf{Y}_{\ell-1}\right] \Big) \cdot \left(\mathbf{P}_{i,k}^s - \mathbf{P}_{j,k}^s\right)$$
$$\leqslant \sum_{i\in V} \sum_{j\in N(i)} \left(\mathbf{P}_{i,k}^s - \mathbf{P}_{j,k}^s\right) \cdot$$
$$\left(\mathbf{Ex}\left[\left\{\frac{X_i(t-s)}{d+1}\right\} - Z_{i,j}(t-s) \mid X(t-s), \mathbf{Y}_\ell\right] - \right.$$
$$\left. \mathbf{Ex}\left[\left\{\frac{X_i(t-s)}{d+1}\right\} - Z_{i,j}(t-s) \mid X(t-s), \mathbf{Y}_{\ell-1}\right] \right)$$
$$\leqslant \sum_{i\in V} \sum_{j\in N(i)} \Big(\mathbf{Ex}\left[Z_{i,j}(t-s) \mid X(t-s), \mathbf{Y}_\ell\right]$$
$$- \mathbf{Ex}\left[Z_{i,j}(t-s) \mid X(t-s), \mathbf{Y}_{\ell-1}\right] \Big) \cdot \left(\mathbf{P}_{i,k}^s - \mathbf{P}_{j,k}^s\right) \quad (4.12)$$
$$= \sum_{i\in V} \sum_{j\in N(i)} \Delta_{i,j}(t-s) \cdot \left(\mathbf{P}_{i,k}^s - \mathbf{P}_{j,k}^s\right), \quad (4.13)$$

where $\Delta_{i,j}(t-s) := \mathbf{Ex}\left[Z_{i,j}(t-s) \mid X(t-s), \mathbf{Y}_\ell\right] - \mathbf{Ex}\left[Z_{i,j}(t-s) \mid X(t-s), \mathbf{Y}_{\ell-1}\right]$, and Equation (4.12) holds since conditioned on $X(t-s)$, the variables $X_i(t-s)$ are obtained deterministically.

To bound Equation (4.13) we consider $\sum_{j \in N(i)} |\Delta_{i,j}(t-s)|$ for $i = \ell$ and $i \neq \ell$ separately:

Case $i = \ell$. Let $b := (X_\ell(t-s) \bmod (d+1))$ be the number of extra tokens of ℓ in round $t-s$. Knowing Y_ℓ determines the b destinations of the extra tokens, namely $j_1, \ldots, j_b \in N(i) \cup \{i\}$. Prior to this, for all $j \in N(i)$ we had

$$\mathbf{Ex}\left[Z_{i,j}(t-s) \mid X(t-s), \mathbf{Y}_{\ell-1}\right] = b/(d+1).$$

After Y_ℓ is determined, we have $\mathbf{Ex}\left[Z_{i,j}(t-s) \mid X(t-s), \mathbf{Y}_\ell\right] = 1$ if $j \in \{j_1, \cdots, j_b\}$, and $\mathbf{Ex}\left[Z_{i,j}(t-s) \mid X(t-s), \mathbf{Y}_\ell\right] = 0$ otherwise. Thus, $\Delta_{i,j}(t-s) = 1 - b/(d+1)$ if $j \in \{j_1, \ldots, j_b\} - \{i\}$ and $\Delta_{i,j}(t-s) = -b/(d+1)$ otherwise.

Case $i \neq \ell$. In this case Y_ℓ corresponds to $r_\ell(t-s)$, which is the randomly chosen rotor state on node ℓ in round $t-s$. Given $X(t-s)$, the random variable $Z_{i,j}(t-s)$ is independent of Y_ℓ. Hence,

$$\sum_{j \in N(i)} |\Delta_{i,j}(t-s)| = \sum_{j \in N(i)} \left| \mathbf{Ex}\left[Z_{i,j}(s) \mid X(t-s), \mathbf{Y}_\ell \right] \right.$$
$$\left. - \mathbf{Ex}\left[Z_{i,j}(s) \mid X(t-s), \mathbf{Y}_{\ell-1} \right] \right|$$
$$= 0.$$

Combining the two cases, we obtain:

$$\sum_{i \in V} \sum_{j \in N(i)} \Delta_{i,j}(t-s) \cdot \left(\mathbf{P}_{i,k}^s - \mathbf{P}_{j,k}^s \right)$$
$$= \sum_{j \in N(\ell)} \Delta_{\ell,j}(t-s) \cdot \left(\mathbf{P}_{\ell,k}^s - \mathbf{P}_{j,k}^s \right)$$
$$= \sum_{j \in \{j_1,\ldots,j_b\}} \Delta_{\ell,j}(t-s) \cdot \left(\mathbf{P}_{\ell,k}^s - \mathbf{P}_{j,k}^s \right)$$
$$+ \sum_{j \in N(\ell)-\{j_1,\ldots,j_b\}} \Delta_{\ell,j}(t-s) \cdot \left(\mathbf{P}_{\ell,k}^s - \mathbf{P}_{j,k}^s \right)$$
$$= \sum_{j \in \{j_1,\ldots,j_b\}} (1 - b/(d+1)) \cdot \left(\mathbf{P}_{\ell,k}^s - \mathbf{P}_{j,k}^s \right)$$
$$+ \sum_{j \in N(\ell)-\{j_1,\ldots,j_b\}} (-b/(d+1)) \cdot \left(\mathbf{P}_{\ell,k}^s - \mathbf{P}_{j,k}^s \right). \quad (4.14)$$

Combining Equations (4.11), (4.13), and (4.14), and using the Cauchy–Schwarz inequality, we have:

$$c_\ell^2 \leqslant d \cdot \max \left\{ (1 - b/(d+1))^2, (-b/(d+1))^2 \right\}$$
$$\cdot \sum_{j \in N(\ell)} \left(\mathbf{P}_{\ell,k}^s - \mathbf{P}_{j,k}^s \right)^2$$
$$\leqslant d \sum_{j \in N(\ell)} \left(\mathbf{P}_{\ell,k}^s - \mathbf{P}_{j,k}^s \right)^2.$$

To apply Lemma A.11, we consider $\sum_{1 \leqslant \ell \leqslant n} c_\ell^2$:

$$\sum_{1 \leqslant \ell \leqslant n} c_\ell^2 \leqslant d \sum_{1 \leqslant \ell \leqslant n} \sum_{j \in N(\ell)} \left(\mathbf{P}_{\ell,k}^s - \mathbf{P}_{j,k}^s \right)^2$$
$$\leqslant 4d \sum_{1 \leqslant \ell \leqslant n} \sum_{j \in N(\ell)} \left(\mathbf{P}_{\ell,k}^s - \frac{1}{n} \right)^2$$
$$\leqslant 8 d^2 \lambda^{2s}. \quad \text{(Lemma A.12)} \quad (4.15)$$

Using Equation (4.9), Observation 4.3 and linearity of expectation, we get $\mathbf{Ex}[\mathcal{S}_k(s) \mid X(t-s)] = 0$. By Lemma A.11, for any $\delta \geqslant 0$ we have:

$$\mathbf{Pr}\left[|\mathcal{S}_k(s)| \geqslant \delta \mid X(t-s) \right] \leqslant 2 \exp\left(-\delta^2/16 \, d^2 \lambda^{2s} \right). \quad (4.16)$$

Applying the law of total probability to Equation (4.16), completes the proof. □

LEMMA 4.6. *For arbitrary node k we have:*

$$\mathbf{Pr}\left[\left| \sum_{s=t_0}^{t} \mathcal{S}_k(s) \right| \geqslant \frac{8 \, d \, \sqrt{7C}}{1-\lambda} \right] = \mathcal{O}(n^{-2C}).$$

PROOF. We prove the bound by providing different bounds for different elements of the sum, bounding each $\mathcal{S}_k(s)$ by a properly chosen δ_s. Define $\delta_s := 4 \, d \, \sqrt{7C \log n} \lambda^s$. We have:

$$\sum_{s=\frac{\log\log n}{1-\lambda}}^{t} \delta_s = \sum_{s=\frac{\log\log n}{1-\lambda}}^{t} 4d \, \sqrt{7C \log n} \, \lambda^{s/2}$$
$$\leqslant 4 \, d \, \sqrt{7C \log n} \, \frac{\lambda^{\log\log n/(2(1-\lambda))}}{1-\sqrt{\lambda}}$$
$$\leqslant \frac{8 \, d \, \sqrt{7C}}{1-\lambda} \quad \text{(Since $\lambda \leqslant 1$).} \quad (4.17)$$

Therefore, we have:

$$\mathbf{Pr}\left[\left| \sum_{s=t_0}^{t} \mathcal{S}_k(s) \right| \geqslant \frac{8d \, \sqrt{7C}}{1-\lambda} \right] \leqslant \sum_{s=\frac{\log\log n}{1-\lambda}}^{t} \mathbf{Pr}\left[|\mathcal{S}_k(s)| \geqslant \delta_s \right]$$
$$\leqslant 2 \, n^{-6C} \sum_{s=1}^{\infty} \frac{\lambda^s}{\log n}$$
$$= \mathcal{O}(n^{-2C}),$$

where we use $\frac{1}{1-\lambda} = \mathcal{O}(n^4)$ [3, Lemma 2.1]. □

PROOF OF THEOREM 4.1. Now, using Equation (4.10), Observation 4.4 and Lemma 4.6 we get for arbitrary $1 \leqslant k \leqslant n$ and arbitrary constant $C \geqslant 1$, with probability at least $1 - \mathcal{O}(n^{-2C})$,

$$|E_k(t+1)| \leqslant \frac{Cd \log\log n}{1-\lambda} + \frac{8 \, d \, \sqrt{7C}}{1-\lambda}$$
$$= \mathcal{O}\left(\frac{d \log\log n}{1-\lambda} \right). \quad (4.18)$$

Using the results in [22], we have $T = \mathcal{O}(\log(Kn)/1-\lambda) = \mathcal{O}(n^{\kappa+5})$. We choose $C \geqslant \kappa + 6$. By the union bound we have for all k and $t \leqslant T$

$$|E_k(t+1)| = \mathcal{O}(d \log\log n/(1-\lambda))$$

with probability at least $1 - \mathcal{O}(n^{-C})$. □

4.3 Graph-specific Bounds

In this section we prove Theorem 4.2 which for hypercubes and tori improves the bounds of Theorem 4.1.

The Proof Outline. We provide a probabilistic bound on $E_k(t+1)$ for arbitrarily fixed round t and node k. We follow the martingale argument of [3] (with slight changes) up to deriving the expression for the sum of squared Lipschitz constants, which in our case has an additional factor of d compared to that of [3]. Though this is not an issue for when $d = \mathcal{O}(1)$ (e.g. constant degree tori (Lemma 4.7)), for hypercubes we have to reformulate the sum to a new expression (Equation (4.19)) and estimate it in a different way compared to [3], so that we obtain the same imbalance bound of $\mathcal{O}(\log n)$ for hypercube (Lemma 4.8).

PROOF OF THEOREM 4.2 . Fix arbitrary round t and node k. The variable $E_k(t+1)$ depends on the random rotor states in the first t rounds. We denote these variables by $Y_1, Y_2, \ldots, Y_{tn}$, such that for any $\ell \geqslant 1$, we have $Y_\ell = r_i(s)$ iff $\ell = (s-1)n + i$. We apply the method of averaged bounded differences (Lemma A.11) on the martingale $\mathbf{Ex}\left[E_k(t+1) \mid \boldsymbol{Y}_\ell\right], (1 \leqslant \ell \leqslant tn)$. Define

$$c_\ell := \left| \mathbf{Ex}\left[E_k(t+1) \mid \boldsymbol{Y}_\ell\right] - \mathbf{Ex}\left[E_k(t+1) \mid \boldsymbol{Y}_{\ell-1}\right] \right|.$$

Following steps generally similar to [3], we write:

$$\sum_{\ell=1}^{tn} c_\ell^2 = \sum_{s=0}^{t} \sum_{i=1}^{n} \left(\sum_{j \in N(i)} \Delta_{i,j}(t-s) \cdot \left(\mathbf{P}_{i,k}^s - \mathbf{P}_{j,k}^s\right) \right)^2, \tag{4.19}$$

where we used

$$\Delta_{i,j}(s) := \mathbf{Ex}\left[Z_{i,j}(s) \mid \boldsymbol{Y}_\ell\right] - \mathbf{Ex}\left[Z_{i,j}(s) \mid \boldsymbol{Y}_{\ell-1}\right]$$

where $\ell = (s-1) \cdot n + i$. By Observation 4.3, linearity of expectation, and the law of total probability, we get

$$\mathbf{Ex}\left[E_k(t+1)\right] = 0.$$

By Lemma A.11, if we choose $\delta^2 = (\alpha + \kappa + 6)\log n \cdot \sum_{\ell=1}^{tn} c_\ell^2$ for arbitrary $\alpha > 0$, then for every node k and round $t \leqslant T$ with probability $1 - \mathcal{O}(n^{-(\alpha+\kappa+6)})$ we have $|E_k(t+1)| \leqslant \delta$. Since $T = \mathcal{O}(n^{\kappa+5})$, with probability $1 - \mathcal{O}(n^{-\alpha})$, for every $k \in V$ and round $t \leqslant T$, we have $|E_k(t+1)| \leqslant \delta$. As $\sum_{\ell=1}^{tn} c_\ell^2$ is of $\mathcal{O}(1)$ for torus and $\mathcal{O}(\log n)$ for hypercube (Lemmas 4.8 and 4.7), the proof holds.

We now provide the tightness of the bound for hypercubes. To do this, we show that there is an initial load vector for the hypercube with $d = 2^\kappa - 1$ dimensions ($\kappa \geqslant 1$), such that the discrepancy between R_Propp and $RW(d+1)$ is $\Omega(\log n)$ with probability $1 - n^{\Omega(1)}$.

The construction relies on *2-vertex colouring (2-VC)* of graphs. In a 2-VC, no two nodes with distance of at most two have the same colour. The minimum number of colours required by any 2-VC of G is denoted by $\chi_{\bar{2}}(G)$. It is known [23] that for d-dimensional hypercube, $d + 1 \leqslant \chi_{\bar{2}}(G) \leqslant 2^{\lceil \log_2(d+1) \rceil}$. Hence, if $d = 2^\kappa - 1$, we have $\chi_{\bar{2}}(G) = d + 1$. Let $\{C_1, \ldots, C_{d+1}\}$ denote the partitioning of V induced by the colour assignment, and $V_1 := C_1 \cup \ldots \cup C_{(d+1)/2}$. We choose $X(0)$ such that $X_i(0) = (d+1)/2$ if $i \in V_1$ and $X_i(0) = 0$ otherwise. $RW(d+1)$ sends a load of $1/2$ from every node in V_1 to its neighbours in the first round. For arbitrary node i, the set $\{i\} \cup N(i)$ contains exactly $(d+1)/2$ such nodes. Hence, $RW(d+1)$ balances the load in one round. In R_Propp, an arbitrary node i receives a token on the edge $(i, j)(j \in V_1)$ with probability $1/2$. For fixed i these events are independent, thus we have:

$$\mathbf{Pr}\left[X_i(1) \geqslant \frac{3}{8}(d+1)\right] \geqslant \binom{(d+1)/2}{3(d+1)/8} 2^{-(d+1)/2}$$

$$\geqslant \left(\frac{4}{3}\right)^{3(d+1)/8} \cdot 2^{-(d+1)/2}$$

$$\geqslant n^{-1+\alpha},$$

for some constant $\alpha > 0$. To achieve independence, we consider only a subset of V with pairwise distance of at least 3. Since all nodes have degree $\log n$, there exists $S \subset V$ of size at least $n/\log^3 n$ with this property. This yields:

$$\mathbf{Pr}\left[\exists u \in S : X_u(1) \geqslant \frac{3}{8}(d+1)\right] \geqslant 1 - (1 - n^{-1+\alpha})^{|S|}$$

$$\geqslant 1 - n^{-\beta},$$

for some constant β. Also, in $RW(d+1)$ for arbitrary node u we have $x_u(2) = (d+1)/4$. Hence, with probability at least $1 - n^{-\beta}$, R_Propp has discrepancy of $(d+1)/8 = \Omega(\log n)$ from $RW(d+1)$. $\square$

LEMMA 4.7. *For an r-dimensional torus with $r = \mathcal{O}(1)$, we have $\sum_{\ell=1}^{tn} c_\ell^2 = \mathcal{O}(1)$.*

PROOF.

$$\sum_{\ell=1}^{tn} c_\ell^2 = \sum_{s=0}^{t} \sum_{i=1}^{n} \left(\sum_{j \in N(i)} \Delta_{i,j}(t-s) \cdot \left(\mathbf{P}_{i,k}^s - \mathbf{P}_{j,k}^s\right) \right)^2$$

$$\leqslant \sum_{s=0}^{t} \sum_{i=1}^{n} \left(\max_{j \in N(i)} \left|\mathbf{P}_{i,k}^s - \mathbf{P}_{j,k}^s\right| \cdot \sum_{j \in N(i)} \left|\Delta_{i,j}(t-s)\right| \right)^2. \tag{4.20}$$

Consider an arbitrary round s and node i. Let $b = (X_\ell(s) \bmod (d+1))$ be the number of extra tokens of i in round s and Y_ℓ with $\ell = (s-1)n + i$ be the randomly chosen rotor state of node i in round s. Knowing Y_ℓ determines the b destinations of the extra tokens, namely $j_1, \ldots, j_b \in N(i) \cup \{i\}$. Prior to knowing Y_ℓ, for all $j \in N(i)$, we had $\mathbf{Ex}\left[Z_{i,j}(s) \mid X^\cdot(s) \boldsymbol{Y}_{\ell-1}\right] = b/(d+1)$. After Y_ℓ is determined, we have $\mathbf{Ex}\left[Z_{i,j}(s) \mid X^\cdot(s) \boldsymbol{Y}_\ell\right] = 1$ if $j \in \{j_1, \ldots, j_b\} - \{i\}$, and $\mathbf{Ex}\left[Z_{i,j}(s) \mid X(t-s), \boldsymbol{Y}_\ell\right] = 0$ otherwise. Hence, we get

$$\sum_{j \in N(i)} \left|\Delta_{i,j}(t-s)\right| = \mathcal{O}(d).$$

Therefore, it follows from Equation (4.20) that:

$$\sum_{\ell=1}^{tn} c_\ell^2 \leqslant \mathcal{O}(d^2) \sum_{s=0}^{t} \sum_{i=1}^{n} \left(\max_{j \in N(i)} \left|\mathbf{P}_{i,k}^s - \mathbf{P}_{j,k}^s\right| \right)^2$$

$$= \mathcal{O}((\Upsilon_2(G))^2)$$

$$= \mathcal{O}(1), \quad \text{(By [3, Theorem 4.2])}$$

where

$$\Upsilon_2(G) := \max_{k \in V} \left(\frac{1}{2} \sum_{t=0}^{\infty} \sum_{i=1}^{n} \max_{j \in N(i)} \left|\mathbf{P}_{i,k}^t - \mathbf{P}_{j,k}^t\right|^2 \right)^{1/2}$$

is the refined local divergence measure as defined in [3]. $\square$

LEMMA 4.8. *For a hypercube, $\sum_{\ell=1}^{tn} c_\ell^2 = \mathcal{O}(d)$.*

PROOF. Without loss of generality, let $k = 0^d$ (for simplicity, we denote 0^d by 0). It suffices to prove that the following three statements hold for a properly chosen $t' = \mathcal{O}\left(\frac{\log d}{1-\lambda_2}\right) = \mathcal{O}(d \log d)$:

$$\sum_{s=t'}^{\infty} \sum_{i=1}^{n} \left(\sum_{j \in N(i)} \Delta_{i,j}(t-s) \cdot \left(\mathbf{P}_{i,0}^s - \mathbf{P}_{j,0}^s\right) \right)^2 = \mathcal{O}(1);$$

$$\sum_{s=0}^{t'-1} \sum_{\|i\| \geqslant 5} \left(\sum_{j \in N(i)} \Delta_{i,j}(t-s) \cdot \left(\mathbf{P}_{i,0}^s - \mathbf{P}_{j,0}^s\right) \right)^2 = \mathcal{O}(d);$$

$$\sum_{s=0}^{t'-1} \sum_{\|i\|\leqslant 4} \left(\sum_{j\in N(i)} \Delta_{i,j}(t-s) \cdot \left(\mathbf{P}_{i,0}^s - \mathbf{P}_{j,0}^s \right) \right)^2 = \mathcal{O}(d),$$

where $\|i\|$ denotes the distance of node i from node 0^d.

By symmetry of the hypercube, for any two nodes i, j with $\|i\|_1 = \|j\|_1$ and any round s, we have $\mathbf{P}_{i,0}^s = \mathbf{P}_{j,0}^s$. Thus, we can define $\mathbf{P}_h^s$ to denote $\mathbf{P}_{i,0}^s$ for arbitrary node i with $\|i\| = h$.

In the following, we only prove the third statement. The proofs of the first two statements are much simpler. We have:

$$\sum_{s=0}^{t'-1} \sum_{\|i\|\leqslant 4} \left(\sum_{j\in N(i)} \Delta_{i,j}(t-s) \cdot \left(\mathbf{P}_{i,0}^s - \mathbf{P}_{j,0}^s \right) \right)^2$$

$$\leqslant 2 \sum_{s=0}^{t'-1} \sum_{\|i\|\leqslant 4} \left(\mathbf{P}_{\|i\|}^s - \mathbf{P}_{\|i\|+1}^s \right)^2 \left(\sum_{\substack{j\in N(i),\\ \|j\|=\|i\|+1}} \Delta_{i,j}(t-s) \right)^2$$

$$+ 2 \sum_{s=0}^{t'-1} \sum_{1\leqslant\|i\|\leqslant 4} \left(\mathbf{P}_{\|i\|}^s - \mathbf{P}_{\|i\|-1}^s \right)^2 \left(\sum_{\substack{j\in N(i),\\ \|j\|=\|i\|-1}} \Delta_{i,j}(t-s) \right)^2 \tag{4.21}$$

Consider an arbitrary round s and node i. Let $b = \left(X_\ell^{\mathrm{mod}}\ (s)(d+1) \right)$ be the number of extra tokens of i in round s and Y_ℓ with $\ell = (s-1)\,n + i$ be the randomly chosen rotor state of node i in round s. Observe that $\Delta_{i,j}(s) = 1 - b/(d+1)$ if j receives an extra token and $\Delta_{i,j}(s) = -b/(d+1)$ otherwise. On the other hand, since $\|i\| \leqslant 4$, the set $\{\Delta_{i,j}(s) : j \in N(i), \|j\| = \|i\| - 1\}$ has size at most 4. With each $\Delta_{i,j}(s)$ lying in $(-1, 1)$, we have:

$$\left| \sum_{\substack{j\in N(i),\\ \|j\|=\|i\|-1}} \Delta_{i,j}(s) \right| \leqslant \sum_{\substack{j\in N(i),\\ \|j\|=\|i\|-1}} |\Delta_{i,j}(s)| \leqslant 4.$$

We also observe that $\sum_{j\in N(i)\cup\{i\}} \Delta_{i,j}(s) = 0$, hence:

$$\left| \sum_{\substack{j\in N(i),\\ \|j\|=\|i\|+1}} \Delta_{i,j}(s) \right| = \left| \sum_{\substack{j\in N(i),\\ \|j\|=\|i\|-1}} \Delta_{i,j}(s) + \Delta_{i,i}(s) \right|$$

$$\leqslant \left| \sum_{\substack{j\in N(i),\\ \|j\|=\|i\|-1}} \Delta_{i,j}(s) \right| + |\Delta_{i,i}(s)|$$

$$\leqslant 5.$$

Therefore it follows from Equation (4.21) that:

$$\sum_{s=0}^{t'-1} \sum_{\|i\|\leqslant 4} \left(\sum_{j\in N(i)} \Delta_{i,j}(t-s) \cdot \left(\mathbf{P}_{i,0}^s - \mathbf{P}_{j,0}^s \right) \right)^2$$

$$\leqslant 5 \sum_{s=0}^{t'-1} \sum_{\|i\|\leqslant 4} \left(\mathbf{P}_{\|i\|}^s - \mathbf{P}_{\|i\|+1}^s \right)^2$$

$$+ 4 \sum_{s=0}^{t'-1} \sum_{1\leqslant\|i\|\leqslant 4} \left(\mathbf{P}_{\|i\|}^s - \mathbf{P}_{\|i\|-1}^s \right)^2$$

$$\leqslant 5 \sum_{h=0}^{4} \left(\binom{d}{h} + \binom{d}{h+1} \right) \cdot \sum_{s=0}^{t'-1} (\mathbf{P}_h^s)^2 \quad \text{(Lemma A.13)}$$

$$= 5 \sum_{h=0}^{4} \binom{d+1}{h+1} \cdot \sum_{s=0}^{t'-1} (\mathbf{P}_h^s)^2 . \tag{4.22}$$

Observe that,

$$\sum_{h=0}^{4} \binom{d+1}{h+1} \cdot \sum_{s=0}^{t'-1} (\mathbf{P}_h^s)^2$$

$$= d+1 + \binom{d+1}{1} \cdot \sum_{s=1}^{t'-1} (\mathbf{P}_0^s)^2 + \binom{d+1}{2} \cdot \sum_{s=1}^{t'-1} (\mathbf{P}_1^s)^2$$

$$+ \sum_{h=2}^{4} \binom{d+1}{h+1} \cdot \sum_{s=0}^{t'-1} (\mathbf{P}_h^s)^2$$

$$\leqslant d+1+t'/d + (d+1)^2 \cdot \left(\sum_{s=1}^{6} (\mathbf{P}_1^s)^2 + \left(\sum_{s=7}^{t'-1} \mathbf{P}_1^s \right)^2 \right)$$

$$+ \sum_{h=2}^{4} \binom{d+1}{h+1} \cdot \sum_{s=0}^{t'-1} \frac{1}{\binom{d}{h}^2} \quad \text{(By Lemma A.14)}$$

$$\leqslant d+1+t'/d + (d+1)^2 \cdot \left(\sum_{s=1}^{6} \frac{1}{(d+1)^2} + \left(\sum_{s=7}^{t'-1} \mathbf{P}_1^s \right)^2 \right)$$

$$+ 2\,t'/d$$

$$= \mathcal{O}\left(d + d^2 \cdot \left(\sum_{s=7}^{t'-1} \mathbf{P}_1^s \right)^2 \right). \tag{4.23}$$

Now, it suffices to prove $\sum_{s=7}^{t'-1} \mathbf{P}_1^s = \mathcal{O}(d^{-1})$. Observe that in the step t of a random walk starting from i, the probability that the distance from 0^d does not increase is at most $(t+\|i\|)/(d+1)$. Consider a random walk of length 7 starting from an arbitrary node i with $\|i\| = 1$. To arrive at a node j with $\|j\| \leqslant 2$ at step 7, the random walk can at most 4 times increase its distance to $0^{\log n}$, hence there must be at least 3 steps in which the distance does not increase: This implies for all j with $\|j\| \leqslant 2$,

$$\sum_{j:\|j\|\leqslant 2} \mathbf{P}_{i,j}^7 \leqslant \binom{7}{3} \cdot \left(\frac{8}{d+1} \right)^3 = \mathcal{O}(d^{-3}). \tag{4.24}$$

We have:

$$\sum_{s=7}^{t'-1} \mathbf{P}_1^s = \sum_{s=7}^{t'-1} \mathbf{P}_{i,0}^s$$

$$\leqslant \sum_{s=7}^{t'-1} \left(\sum_{\substack{j\\ \|j\|\leqslant 2}} \mathbf{P}_{i,j}^7 \cdot \mathbf{P}_{j,0}^{s-7} + \sum_{\substack{j\\ 3\leqslant\|j\|\leqslant d}} \mathbf{P}_{i,j}^7 \cdot \mathbf{P}_{j,0}^{s-7} \right)$$

$$\leqslant \sum_{s=7}^{t'-1} \left(\sum_{\substack{j\\ \|j\|\leqslant 2}} \mathbf{P}_{i,j}^7 \cdot \mathbf{P}_{j,0}^{s-7} + \left(\frac{1}{\binom{d}{3}} \cdot \sum_{\substack{j\\ 3\leqslant\|j\|\leqslant d/2}} \mathbf{P}_{i,j}^7 \right) \right.$$

$$\left. + \left(\frac{1}{\binom{d}{d/2}} \cdot \sum_{\substack{j\\ d/2\leqslant\|j\|\leqslant d}} \mathbf{P}_{i,j}^7 \right) \right)$$

$$\leqslant t' \cdot \left(\mathcal{O}(d^{-3}) \cdot \left(\sum_{\substack{j\\ \|j\|\leqslant 2}} \mathbf{P}_{0,j}^{s-7} \right) + \frac{1}{\binom{d}{3}} \cdot 1 + \frac{1}{\binom{d}{d/2}} \right)$$

$$= \mathcal{O}(d^{-1}). \quad \text{(Using Equation (4.24))} \tag{4.25}$$

where we have used Lemmas A.14 and A.13 to simplify the expressions. Applying Equation (4.25) to Equation (4.23) and subsequently Equation (4.22) finishes the proof. $\square$

References

[1] W. Aiello, R. Venkatesan, and M. Yung. Coins, weights and contention in balancing networks. In *PODC*, pages 193–205. ACM, 1994.

[2] H. Akbari, P. Berenbrink, and T. Sauerwald. A simple approach for adapting continuous load balancing processes to discrete settings. In *PODC*, pages 271–280, 2012.

[3] P. Berenbrink, C. Cooper, T. Friedetzky, T. Friedrich, and T. Sauerwald. Randomized diffusion for indivisible loads. In *SODA*, pages 429–439. SIAM, 2011.

[4] J. Cooper, B. Doerr, J. Spencer, and G. Tardos. Deterministic random walks on the integers. volume 28, pages 2072–2090. Academic Press Ltd., 2007.

[5] J. N. Cooper, B. Doerr, T. Friedrich, and J. Spencer. Deterministic random walks on regular trees. In *SODA*, pages 766–772, 2008.

[6] J. N. Cooper and J. Spencer. Simulating a random walk with constant error. *Comb. Probab. Comput.*, 15:815–822, 2006.

[7] P. Diaconis, R. L. Graham, and J. A. Morrison. Asymptotic analysis of a random walk on a hypercube with many dimensions. *Random Structures Algorithms*, 1(1):51–72, 1990.

[8] B. Doerr and T. Friedrich. Deterministic random walks on the two-dimensional grid. *Comb. Probab. Comput.*, 18(1-2):123–144, 2009.

[9] B. Doerr, T. Friedrich, and T. Sauerwald. Quasirandom rumor spreading. In *SODA*, pages 773–781. SIAM, 2008.

[10] D. P. Dubhashi and A. Panconesi. *Concentration of Measure for the Analysis of Randomized Algorithms*. Cambridge University Press, 2009.

[11] T. Friedrich, M. Gairing, and T. Sauerwald. Quasirandom load balancing. *SIAM J. Comput.*, 41(4):747–771, 2012.

[12] T. Friedrich and T. Sauerwald. Near-perfect load balancing by randomized rounding. In *STOC*, pages 121–130, 2009.

[13] T. Friedrich and T. Sauerwald. The cover time of deterministic random walks. In *COCOON*, pages 130–139, 2010.

[14] M. Herlihy and S. Tirthapura. Randomized smoothing networks. *J. Parallel Distrib. Comput.*, 66(5):626–632, 2006.

[15] A. E. Holroyd and J. Propp. Rotor walks and markov chains. *Algorithmic Probability and Combinatorics*, pages 105–126, 2010.

[16] S. Kijima, K. Koga, and K. Makino. Deterministic random walks on finite graphs. In *ANALCO*, pages 16–25, 2012.

[17] M. Klugerman and C. G. Plaxton. Small-depth counting networks. In *STOC*, pages 417–428. ACM, 1992.

[18] D. A. Levin, Y. Peres, and E. L. Wilmer. *Markov chains and mixing times*. American Mathematical Society, 2006.

[19] M. Mavronicolas and T. Sauerwald. The impact of randomization in smoothing networks. *Distributed Computing*, 22:381–411, 2010.

[20] S. Muthukrishnan, B. Ghosh, and M. H. Schultz. First- and second-order diffusive methods for rapid, coarse, distributed load balancing. *Theory Comput. Syst.*, 31(4):331–354, 1998.

[21] V. B. Priezzhev, D. Dhar, A. Dhar, and S. Krishnamurthy. Eulerian walkers as a model of self-organised criticality. Technical Report cond-mat/9611019. TIFR-TH-96-43, Tata Inst. Fundam. Res., 1996.

[22] Y. Rabani, A. Sinclair, and R. Wanka. Local divergence of markov chains and the analysis of iterative load-balancing schemes. In *FOCS*, pages 694–703. IEEE Computer Society, 1998.

[23] P. Wan. Near-optimal conflict-free channel set assignments for an optical cluster-based hypercube network. *J. Comb. Optim.*, 1(2):179–186, 1997.

APPENDIX

THEOREM A.9 ([11, THEOREM 4.2]). *For all initial load vectors on the d-dimensional hypercube with n nodes, the deviation between the idealized process and a discrete process with accumulated rounding errors at most ξ is $O(\xi \log^{3/2} n)$ at all times.*

THEOREM A.10 ([11, THEOREM 5.4]). *For all initial load vectors on the d-dimensional torus with n nodes, the deviation between the idealized process and a discrete process with accumulated rounding errors at most ξ is $O(\xi)$ at all times.*

LEMMA A.11 ([10, P. 68]). *Let $Y_1, \ldots, Y_n$ be an arbitrary set of random variables and let f be a function of these random variables satisfying the property that for each $1 \leqslant \ell \leqslant n$, there is a non-negative c_ℓ such that*

$$\left| \mathbf{Ex}\left[f \mid Y_\ell, Y_{\ell-1}, \ldots, Y_1\right] - \mathbf{Ex}\left[f \mid Y_{\ell-1}, \ldots, Y_1\right] \right| \leqslant c_\ell.$$

Then for any $\delta > 0$,

$$\mathbf{Pr}\left[|f - \mathbf{Ex}\left[f\right]| > \delta\right] \leqslant 2 \exp\left(-\frac{\delta^2}{2c} \right),$$

where $c := \sum_{\ell=1}^{n} c_\ell^2$.

LEMMA A.12 ([20, LEMMA 1]). *Consider $\mathbf{w}^{t+1} = M\mathbf{w}^t$ where M is a diffusion matrix. We have $\Phi_t \leqslant \lambda^{2t}\Phi_0$ (where λ is the second largest eigenvalue in absolute value of M and $\Phi_t := \sum_i (\mathbf{w}_i^t - \bar{w})^2$, where $\bar{w} = \sum_i \mathbf{w}_i^t/n$)*

The following results hold for a hypercube of order n:

LEMMA A.13 ([7, LEMMA 6]). *For any fixed t, $\mathbf{P}_{p,0}^t$ is decreasing for $0 \leqslant p \leqslant \log n$.*

LEMMA A.14 ([3, LEMMA D.3]). *For any $t \in \mathbb{N}_{>0}$, $\mathbf{P}_{0,0}^t \leqslant \frac{1}{\log n+1}$. Moreover, for any $1 \leqslant p \leqslant \frac{\log n}{2}$ and $t \in \mathbb{N}$,*

$$\mathbf{P}_{p,0}^t \leqslant \frac{1}{\binom{\log n}{p}},$$

and for any $\log n/2 \leqslant p \leqslant \log n$,

$$\mathbf{P}_{p,0}^t \leqslant \frac{1}{\binom{\log n}{\log n/2}}.$$

Parallel Graph Decompositions Using Random Shifts *

Gary L. Miller
CMU
glmiller@cs.cmu.edu

Richard Peng †
CMU
yangp@cs.cmu.edu

Shen Chen Xu
CMU
shenchex@cs.cmu.edu

ABSTRACT

We show an improved parallel algorithm for decomposing an undirected unweighted graph into small diameter pieces with a small fraction of the edges in between. These decompositions form critical subroutines in a number of graph algorithms. Our algorithm builds upon the shifted shortest path approach introduced in [Blelloch,Gupta,Koutis,Miller,Peng, Tangwongsan, SPAA 2011]. By combining various stages of the previous algorithm, we obtain a significantly simpler algorithm with the same asymptotic guarantees as the best sequential algorithm.

Categories and Subject Descriptors

F.2 [**Theory of Computation**]: Analysis of Algorithms and Problem Complexity

Keywords

Parallel algorithms; Low-diameter decompositions; Graph partitioning

1. INTRODUCTION

Graph decomposition aims to partition the vertices of a graph into well connected pieces so that few edges are between pieces. A variety of measures of the connectivity within a piece, such as diameter, conductance, and spectral properties have been studied. The more intricate measures such as conductance have proven to be particularly useful in applications [25], and have been well studied [20, 24]. However, these algorithms, as well as many others, use simpler low diameter decompositions as a subroutine. This variant takes a much more simplistic view of the connectivity within each piece, and measures it using only the diameter.

---

*Partially supported by the National Science Foundation under grant number CCF-1018463 and CCF-1065106
†Supported by a Microsoft Fellowship

The various shortcomings of such decompositions as a stand-alone routine are offset by its potential as an algorithmic tool. Low diameter decompositions/clusterings were first introduced in [4, 6], and have been used as core subroutine for a number of algorithms such as: approximations to sparsest cut [20, 24]; construction of spanners [12]; parallel approximations of shortest path in undirected graphs [13]; and generating low-stretch embedding of graphs into trees [3, 16, 15, 2].

More recently, the connection of low diameter decomposition with generating low stretch spanning trees was used in [9] to give nearly-linear work parallel solvers for SDD linear systems. These solvers can in turn be used as a black-box in algorithms for computing maximum flow and negative-length shortest path [11, 14]. This led to parallel algorithms whose work is within polylog factors of the best known sequential algorithms. As these are problems for which work-efficient parallelizations have proven to be elusive, parallel solvers for SDD linear systems represent a promising new direction for designing parallel algorithms.

The parallel SDD linear system solver algorithm from [9] is of mostly theoretical interest due to a large polylog factor in work. Much of this is due to the nearly-linear work, parallel low diameter decomposition algorithm introduced in the same paper, which was in turn used as a subroutine to generate tree embeddings. Therefore, finding improved parallel graph decomposition routines represent a natural direction for finding faster parallel solver algorithms.

In order to formally specify the diameter of a piece, it is crucial to emphasize the distinction between weak and strong diameter. The diameter of a piece $S \subseteq V$ can be defined in two ways, weak and strong diameter. Both of them define diameter to the maximum length of a shortest path between two vertices in S, while the difference is in the set of allowed paths. **Strong diameter** restricts the shortest path between two vertices in S to only use vertices in S, while **weak diameter** allows for shortcuts through vertices in $V \setminus S$. The optimal tree metric embedding algorithm [16] relies on weak diameter. It has been parallelized with polylog work overhead [10], but takes quadratic work.

A trend in algorithms that use weak diameter is that their running time tends to be quadratic. This is also the case with parallel algorithms for computing low diameter decompositions [5]. To date, nearly-linear work algorithms for finding tree embedding use strong diameter instead. While this leads to more difficulties in bounding diameters, the overall work is easier to bound since each piece certifies its own diameter, and therefore does not need to examine other pieces.

For SDD linear system solvers [10], strong diameter is also crucial because the final tree (which the graph embeds into) is formed by combining the shortest path tree in each of the pieces. As a result, we will use diameter of a piece to denote **strong diameter** for the rest of this paper, and define a low diameter decomposition as follows:

DEFINITION 1.1. *Given an undirected, unweighted graph $G = (V, E)$, a (β, d) decomposition is a partition of V into subsets $S_1 \ldots S_k$ such that:*

- *The (strong) diameter of each S_i is at most d.*

- *The number of edges with endpoints belonging to different pieces is at most βm.*

A standard choice of parameters for such decompositions is $(\beta, O(\frac{\log n}{\beta}))$, which are in some sense optimal. Furthermore, when computing tree embedding, β is often set to $\log^{-c} n$ for some constant c. As a result, the algorithm given in [9], as well as our algorithm are geared towards small diameters. This makes the running time of these algorithms more than the $\mathcal{NC}$ algorithms such as [5] for large values of β. However, they suffice for the purpose of generating tree/subgraph embedding in polylog depth, as well as low work parallel graph algorithms.

Obtaining these decompositions in the sequential setting can be done via a process known as ball growing. This process starts with a single vertex, and repeatedly adds the neighbors of the current set into the set. It terminates when the number of edges on the boundary is less than a β fraction of the edges within, which is equivalent to the piece having small conductance. Once the first piece is found, the algorithm discards its vertices and repeats on the remaining graph. The final bound of βm edges between the pieces can in turn be obtained by summing this bound over all the pieces. Using a consumption argument, one could prove that the diameter of a piece does not exceed $O(\frac{\log n}{\beta})$. Because we are okay with a depth that depends on $1/\beta$, and the piece's diameters can be bounded by $O(\frac{\log n}{\beta})$, finding a single piece is easy to parallelize. However, the strong diameter requirement means that we cannot start finding the second ball until we are done finding the first. This leads to a chain of sequential dependencies that may be as long as $\Omega(n)$, and is the main challenge in obtaining a parallel decomposition algorithm.

The parallel SDD linear system solver algorithm given in [9] relied on a parallel algorithm that computes a $O(\beta, \frac{\log^4 n}{\beta})$ decomposition in $O(\frac{\log^3 n}{\beta})$ depth and $O(m \log^2 n)$ work. This algorithm showed that some of the ball growing steps can be performed simultaneously in parallel, leading to balls which have small overlap. Then a randomly shifted shortest path routine is used to resolve these overlaps. In this paper we show that these two steps can be combined in a simple, global routine. This leads to a simple algorithm that picks random shifts in a more intricate way and assigns vertices to pieces using one shortest path invocation. In the PRAM model, our result can be described by the following theorem:

THEOREM 1.2. *There is an algorithm* PARTITION *that takes an unweighted graph with n vertices, m edges, a parameter $\beta \leq 1/2$ and produces a $(\beta, O(\frac{\log n}{\beta}))$ decomposition in expected $O(\frac{\log^2 n}{\beta})$ depth and $O(m)$ work.*

We will give an overview of our algorithm in Section 2 and define our notations and give relevant background in Section 3. Section 4 contains the analysis of our partition routine, and modifications to make it more suitable for implementation and parallelization are given in Section 5. In Section 6 we discuss some possible extensions to our algorithm.

2. OVERVIEW AND RELATED WORKS

In this section we give an intuitive view of our partition routine and discuss how it relates to various other graph decomposition algorithms that have been studied in the past. We will defer the implementation details to Section 5. A simple interpretation of our algorithm executing in parallel is outlined in Algorithm 1.

Algorithm 1 Parallel Partition Algorithm

PARALLEL PARTITION

Input: Undirected, unweighted graph $G = (V, E)$, parameter $0 < \beta < 1$ and parameter d indicating failure probability.
Output: $(\beta, O(\log n/\beta))$ decomposition of G with probability at least $1 - n^{-d}$.

1: *IN PARALLEL* each vertex u picks δ_u independently from an exponential distribution with mean $1/\beta$.
2: *IN PARALLEL* compute $\delta_{\max} = \max\{\delta_u \mid u \in V\}$
3: Perform *PARALLEL BFS*, with vertex u starting when the vertex at the head of the queue has distance more than $\delta_{\max} - \delta_u$.
4: *IN PARALLEL* Assign each vertex u to point of origin of the shortest path that reached it in the BFS.

Steps 1, 2, and 4 of our algorithm are done independently at each vertex and are clearly parallelizable. So the main algorithmic aspects of our algorithm is in step 3, which is performing a breadth first search while recording the point of origin. Such processes have been well-studied [21, 8], and we will discuss how to use such routines in a black-box manner in Section 5. More intuitively, our algorithm can also be viewed as performing parallel ball growing with random delays. Each vertex u picks a start time according to some distribution, and if u is not already part of some other cluster at that time, u starts a cluster of its own and performs a breadth first search. The search takes one unit of time to propagate across an edge, and each such time steps can be performed in parallel over all vertices. If a vertex v visited during the search is not yet part of any other cluster, it joins the cluster of the vertex that first reached it, and its neighbors are added to the BFS queue. The randomized start times leads to both required properties of the decompositions, as well as small bound on the depth of the BFS trees. Figure 1 shows the resulting partitions of our algorithm with a 1000×1000 square grid as input and different values of β used to generate the delays. Lower β leads to larger diameter and fewer edges on the boundaries, which matches our more detailed analysis in Section 4.

To our knowledge, low diameter decompositions as stated in Definition 1.1 were first used for distributed algorithms in [4]. Subsequently it has been used as a key subroutine in the construction of low-stretch spanning trees algorithms [3], or more generally embeddings of graphs into trees [7]. Another application of unweighted decompositions is for efficiently computing separators in minor-free graphs [23, 28].

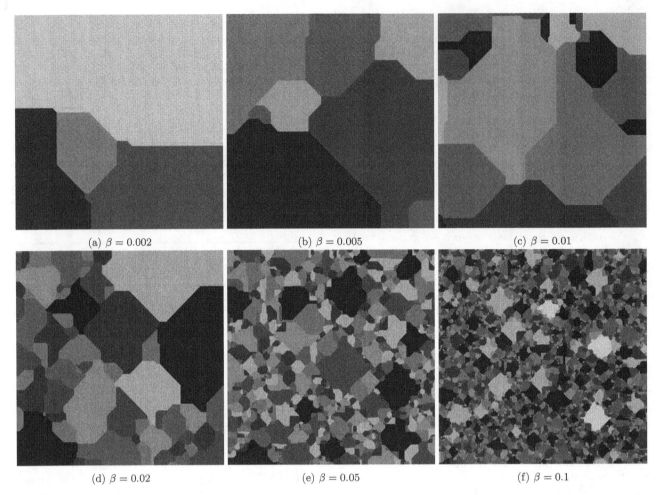

| (a) $\beta = 0.002$ | (b) $\beta = 0.005$ | (c) $\beta = 0.01$ |

| (d) $\beta = 0.02$ | (e) $\beta = 0.05$ | (f) $\beta = 0.1$ |

Figure 1: Decompositions generated by our algorithm on a 1000×1000 grid under varying values of β. Different colors represent different clusters

Our algorithm can be directly substituted into these algorithms, although the main improvements that we obtain are for generating low stretch spanning trees using the framework of [9].

A definition related to low diameter decomposition is block decompositions from [22]. One of their main algorithmic routines is to partition a graph into $O(\log n)$ blocks such that each connected piece in a block has diameter $O(\log n)$. This decomposition can also be obtained by iteratively running a $(\frac{1}{2}, O(\log n))$ low diameter decomposition $O(\log n)$ times. This is because the number of edges not in a block decreases by a factor of 2 per iteration.

The main scheme of our algorithm is to pick radii of the balls independently from some distribution. Similar approaches have been used in computing block decompositions in [22], as well as finding (r, ρ, γ)-probabilistic partitions needed for the Bartal trees [7]. Our partition scheme differs from these in that the process behaves identically on all vertices, and our guarantees are in terms of strong diameter. The first difference means that the formation of clusters in our algorithm does not have sequential dependencies; while the later actually leads to a lower work term. A typical method for meeting weak diameter requirements is to broadcast to all vertices within a certain distance [4, 22]. As the graph may have small diameter, this can lead to work

that is quadratic in the number of vertices. By broadcasting only along shortest paths in a way that is akin to breadth first search, we are able to reduce this to $O(m)$ work.

Aside from being directly related to decomposition schemes for unweighted undirected graphs, our algorithm can also be adapted to give guarantees similar to other improved decomposition schemes. When viewed as a sequential algorithm, it can also lead to similar guarantees on weighted graphs to the decomposition scheme from [7] as well as generalizations needed for improved low stretch spanning tree algorithms [7, 15]. However, the parallel performance of our algorithm in the weighted setting is less clear, and we will describe this question in more detail in Section 6.

3. BACKGROUND AND NOTATIONS

In this section we state some standard notations, and review some key ideas introduced in the Blelloch et al. algorithm [9]. Given a graph G, we use $\text{dist}(u, v)$ to denote the length of the shortest path from u to v. As with earlier works on tree embedding, we will pick a special vertex in each piece, and use the distance to the farthest vertex from it as an estimate for the diameter. This simplification can be made since the graph is undirected and the final bound allows for constant factors (specifically 2). We will denote this special vertex the center of the piece, and denote the piece centered at u using S_u.

As the number of pieces in the final decomposition may be large (e.g. the line graph), a parallel algorithm needs to construct a number of pieces simultaneously. On the other hand, for closely connected graphs such as the complete graph, a single piece may contain the entire graph. As a result, if too many pieces are grown independently, the total work may become quadratic. The decomposition algorithm by Blelloch et al. [9] addressed this tradeoff by gradually increasing the number of centers picked iteratively. It was motivated by the (β, W) decompositions used in an algorithm by Cohen for approximating shortest paths in undirected graphs [13]. By running iterations with gradually more centers, it can be shown that the resulting pieces at each iteration have small overlap. This overlap is in turn resolved using a shifted shortest path algorithm, which introduces shifts (denoted by δ) at the centers and assigns vertex v to S_u that minimizes the shifted distance:

$$\text{dist}_{-\delta}(u,v) = \text{dist}(u,v) - \delta_u. \qquad (1)$$

It was shown that by picking shifts uniformly from a sufficiently large range, a $(\beta, O(\frac{\log^c n}{\beta}))$ decomposition can be obtained.

Our algorithm can be viewed as a more streamlined algorithm that combines these two components. Note that sampling vertices with exponentially increasing density can be emulated by adding a large, step-like increase to the shifts of centers picked in earlier iterations. Furthermore, the need to have exponentially decreasing number of centers in the iterations suggests that the exponential distribution can be used in place of the (locally) uniform distribution. This distribution has been well-studied, and the properties of it that we will need have been used to study its order statistics in fault tolerance [27]. For a parameter γ, this distribution is defined by the density function:

$$f_{Exp}(x,\gamma) = \begin{cases} \gamma \exp(-\gamma x) & \text{if } x \geq 0, \\ 0 & \text{otherwise.} \end{cases}$$

We will denote it using $Exp(\gamma)$ and will also make use of its cumulative density function:

$$F_{Exp}(x,\gamma) = \mathbf{Pr}\left[Exp(\gamma) \leq x\right] = \begin{cases} 1 - \exp(-\gamma x) & \text{if } x \geq 0, \\ 0 & \text{otherwise.} \end{cases}$$

A crucial fact about the exponential distribution is that it is memoryless. That is, if we condition on $Exp(\gamma) \geq t$, then $Exp(\gamma) - t$ will follow the same distribution. We will also use order statistic of random independent variables following the exponential distribution. Given n random variables $X_1 \ldots X_n$, the ith order statistic of them is the value of the ith smallest random variable. Another property of exponential distributions is that the difference between its order statistics also follow exponential distributions. The following fact as stated on page 19 of [17] has been used in a variety of settings.

FACT 3.1. *The n variables $X_{(1)}, X_{(2)} - X_{(1)}, \cdots, X_{(n)} - X_{(n-1)}$ are independent and the density of $X_{(k+1)} - X_{(k)}$ is given by $f_{Exp}(x,\gamma)$ where $\gamma = (n - k)$.*

Let $X_{(i)}^n$ denote the ith order statistic of n i.i.d. exponential random variables. An intuitive way to prove the above

fact is that by the i.i.d assumption, the cumulative density distribution of $X_{(1)}^n$ is given by

$$F_{X_{(1)}^n}(x) = 1 - (1 - F(x))^n$$
$$= 1 - \exp(-n\beta x)$$

where $F(x) = 1 - \exp(-\beta x)$ is the cumulative distribution of $Exp(\beta)$. This shows that $X_{(1)}^n$ is has an exponential distribution with mean $1/(n\beta)$. Conditioning on $X_{(1)}^n$, we get that $X_{(2)}^n - X_{(1)}^n$ is again an exponential distribution equal to $X_{(1)}^{n-1}$ because of the memoryless property of exponential distributions. We can repeat this argument to get the density of $X_{(k+1)}^n - X_{(k)}^n$ for all k up to $n - 1$ [17].

4. ANALYSIS

In this section, we will show that our partition routine indeed constructs a $(\beta, O(\frac{\log n}{\beta}))$ decomposition. For the purpose of this proof, we use a slightly different formulation of our algorithm given in Algorithm 2. In this view, our algorithm picks shifts δ_u for all vertices from independent exponential distributions with parameter β, and then assigns each vertex to a piece so that the shifted distances defined in (1) to the center of that piece is minimized.

Algorithm 2 Partition Algorithm Using Exponentially Shifted Shortest Paths

PARTITION

Input: Undirected, unweighted graph $G = (V, E)$, parameter β and parameter d indicating failure probability.
Output: $(\beta, O(\log n/\beta))$ decomposition of G with probability at least $1 - n^{-d}$.

1: For each vertex u, pick δ_u independently from $Exp(\beta)$
2: Compute S_u by assigning each vertex v to the vertex that minimizes $\text{dist}_{-\delta}(u,v)$, breaking ties lexicographically
3: **return** $\{S_u\}$

We start by showing that the assignment process readily leads to bounds on strong diameter. Specifically, the strong diameter of S_u can be measured using distances from u in the original graph.

LEMMA 4.1. *If $v \in S_u$ and v' is the last vertex on the shortest path from u to v, then $v' \in S_u$ as well.*

Proof The proof is by contradiction, suppose v' belongs to $S_{u'}$ for some $u' \neq u$. The fact that v' is the vertex before v on the shortest path from u implies $\text{dist}_{-\delta}(u,v) = \text{dist}_{-\delta}(u,v') + 1$. Also, as v' is adjacent to v, we also have $\text{dist}_{-\delta}(u',v) \leq \text{dist}_{-\delta}(u',v') + 1$. Since v' belongs to $S_{u'}$ instead of S_u, we must have one of the following two cases:

1. v' is strictly closer to u' than u in terms of shifted distance. In this case we have $\text{dist}_{-\delta}(u',v') < \text{dist}_{-\delta}(u,v')$, which when combined with the conditions above gives:

$$\text{dist}_{-\delta}(u',v) \leq \text{dist}_{-\delta}(u',v') + 1$$
$$< \text{dist}_{-\delta}(u,v') + 1$$
$$= \text{dist}_{-\delta}(u,v).$$

So v is strictly closer to u' than u as well, which implies that v should not be assigned to S_u.

2. The shifted distances are the same, and u' is lexicographically earlier than u. Here a similar calculation gives $\text{dist}_{-\delta}(u', v) \leq \text{dist}_{-\delta}(u, v)$. If the inequality holds strictly, we are back to the case above. In case of equality, the assumption that u' is lexicographically earlier than u means v should not be in S_u as well.

∎

Note that the second case is a zero probability event, and its proof is included to account for roundings in implementations that we will describe in Section 5.

To bound the strong diameter of the pieces, it suffices to bound the distance from a vertex to the center of the piece that it is assigned to. Since any vertex $v \in S_u$ could have been potentially included in S_v, the shift value of the center δ_u serves as an upper bound on the distance to any vertex in S_u. Therefore, $\delta_{\max} = \max_u \delta_u$ serves as an upper bound for the diameter of each piece. Its expected value and concentration can be bounded as follows.

LEMMA 4.2. *The expected value of the maximum shift value is given by H_n/β where H_n is the nth harmonic number. Furthermore, with high probability, $\delta_u \leq O(\frac{\log n}{\beta})$ for all vertices u.*

Our proof below proof closely following the presentation in Chapter 1.6. of [17].

Proof The expected value can be found by summing over the differences in order statistics given in Fact 3.1.

$$
\begin{aligned}
\mathbf{E}\left[\max_{u \in V} \delta_u\right] &= \mathbf{E}\left[X_{(n)}^n\right] \\
&= \frac{1}{\beta} \sum_{i=1}^{n} \frac{1}{n} \\
&= \frac{H_n}{\beta}.
\end{aligned}
$$

For the concentration bound, by the cumulative distribution function of the exponential distribution the probability of $\delta_u \geq (d+1) \cdot \frac{\ln n}{\beta}$ is:

$$
\exp\left(-(d+1) \cdot \beta \frac{\ln n}{\beta}\right) = \exp(-(d+1) \ln n) \\
\leq n^{-(d+1)}.
$$

Applying union bound over the n vertices then gives the bound. ∎

The other property that we need to show is that few edges are between the pieces. We do so by bounding the probability of two endpoints of an edge being assigned to two different pieces. In order to keep symmetry in this argument, it is helpful to consider shifted distances from a vertex to the midpoint of an edge. This slight generalization can be formalized by replacing an edge uv with two length $1/2$ edges, uw and wv. We first show that an edge's end points can be in different pieces only if there are two different vertices whose shifted shortest path to its midpoint are within 1 of the minimum.

LEMMA 4.3. *Let uv be an edge with midpoint w such that when partitioned using shift values δ, $u \in S_{u'}$ and $v \in S_{v'}$. Then both $\text{dist}_{-\delta}(u', w)$ and $\text{dist}_{-\delta}(v', w)$ are within 1 of the minimum shifted distance to w.*

Proof Let the pieces that contain u and v be $S_{u'}$ and $S_{v'}$ respectively ($u' \neq v'$). Let the minimizer of $\text{dist}_{-\delta}(x, w)$ be w'. Since w is distance $1/2$ from both u and v, we have

$$
\text{dist}_{-\delta}(w', u), \text{dist}_{-\delta}(w', v) \leq \text{dist}_{-\delta}(w', w) + 1/2.
$$

Suppose $\text{dist}_{-\delta}(u', w) > \text{dist}_{-\delta}(w', w) + 1$, then we have:

$$
\begin{aligned}
\text{dist}_{-\delta}(u', u) &\geq \text{dist}_{-\delta}(u', w) - 1/2 \\
&> \text{dist}_{-\delta}(w', w) + 1/2 \\
&\geq \text{dist}_{-\delta}(w', u),
\end{aligned}
$$

a contradiction with u' being the minimizer of $\text{dist}_{-\delta}(x, u)$. The case with v follows similarly. ∎

An even more accurate characterization of this situation can be obtained using the additional constraint that the shortest path from w' to w must go through one of u or v. However, this lemma suffices for abstracting the situation further to applying random decreases $\delta_1, \delta_2 \ldots \delta_n$ to a set of numbers $d_1 \ldots d_n$ corresponding to $\text{dist}(x, w)$. We now turn our attention to analyzing the probability of another shifted value being close to the minimum when shifts are picked from the exponential distribution.

The memoryless property of the exponential distribution gives an intuitive way to bound this probability. Instead of considering the vertices picking their shift values independently, consider them as light bulbs with lifetime distributed according to $Exp(\beta)$, and the d_is indicate the time each light bulb is turned on. Then $\min_i d_i - \delta_i$ corresponds to the time when the last light bulb burns out, and we want to bound the time between that and the second last. In this setting, the memoryless property of exponentials gives that when the second to last light bulb fails, the behavior of the last light bulb does not change and its lifetime after that point still follows the same distribution. Therefore, the probability that the difference between these two is less than c can be bounded using the cumulative distribution function:

$$
\begin{aligned}
1 - \exp(-c\beta) &\approx 1 - (1 - c\beta) \qquad \text{(When $c\beta$ is small)} \\
&= c\beta.
\end{aligned}
$$

The only case that is not covered here is when the last light bulb has not been turned on yet when the second last failed. However, in that case this probability can only be less. We give a rigorous version of this intuitive proof below. An algebraic proof using the definition of the exponential distribution can be found in Appendix A.

LEMMA 4.4. *Let $d_1 \leq \ldots \leq d_n$ be arbitrary values and $\delta_1 \ldots \delta_n$ be independent random variables picked from $Exp(\beta)$. Then the probability that between the smallest and the second smallest values of $d_i - \delta_i$ are within c of each other is at most $O(\beta c)$.*

Proof It is more convenient to consider the differences between the largest and second largest of the negations of the shifted values, $-(d_i - \delta_i)$. Let d_i' denote $-d_i$, by the assumption of $d_1 \leq \ldots \leq d_n$ we have $d_1' \geq \ldots \geq d_n'$. Define $X_i = d_i' + \delta_i - d_1'$ and let $X_{(i)}$ denote the ith order statistic of $X_1, \ldots, X_n$, we would like to show that

$$
\mathbf{Pr}\left[X_{(n)} - X_{(n-1)} > c\right] \geq \exp(\beta c).
$$

Since X_is are independent, the memoryless property of exponential distributions gives that when conditioned on

$X_i \geq 0$, X_i still follows an exponential distribution with mean $1/\beta$. For all subsets $S \subseteq \{1 \ldots n\}$, let $\mathcal{E}_S$ denote the event that for all $i \in S$, $X_i \geq 0$, and for all $i \notin S$, $X_i < 0$. By the law of total probability, we have

$$\mathbf{Pr}\left[X_{(n)} - X_{(n-1)} > c\right]$$
$$= \sum_S \mathbf{Pr}\left[X_{(n)} - X_{(n-1)} > c \mid \mathcal{E}_S\right] \mathbf{Pr}\left[\mathcal{E}_S\right].$$

Since $X_n = \delta_n \geq 0$, $\mathbf{Pr}\left[\mathcal{E}_S\right] = 0$ when $S = \emptyset$ or $S \not\ni n$. The only other case with $|S| = 1$ is when $S = \{n\}$. Here we have $\mathbf{Pr}\left[X_1 > c\right] \geq 1 - \exp(\beta c)$. Combining this with $X_{(n)} \geq X_1$ and $X_{(n-1)} < 0$ gives a probability of at least $\exp(\beta c)$.

It remains to consider the case where $|S| \geq 2$. In this case both $X_{(n)}$ and $X_{(n-1)}$ are from elements in S, so it suffices to consider the X_is given by $i \in S$. These $|S|$ variables are distributed the same as $|S|$ independent random variables following $Exp(\beta)$. Therefore by the distribution of order statistics given in Fact 3.1 we have:

$$\mathbf{Pr}\left[X_{(n)} - X_{(n-1)} > c \mid \mathcal{E}_S, |S| \geq 2\right] = \exp(-\beta c).$$

This means for any S, we have

$$\mathbf{Pr}\left[X_{(n)} - X_{(n-1)} > c \mid \mathcal{E}_S\right] \mathbf{Pr}\left[\mathcal{E}_S\right] \geq \exp\left(-\beta c\right) \mathbf{Pr}\left[\mathcal{E}_S\right].$$

Summing over all S and using the fact that $\sum_S \mathbf{Pr}\left[\mathcal{E}_S\right] = 1$ gives that

$$\mathbf{Pr}\left[X_{(n)} - X_{(n-1)} > c\right] \geq \exp\left(-\beta c\right),$$

or equivalently

$$\mathbf{Pr}\left[X_{(n)} - X_{(n-1)} \leq c\right] \leq 1 - \exp\left(-\beta c\right) < \beta c.$$

∎

Using this Lemma with $c = 1$ and applying linearity of expectation gives the bound on the number of edges between pieces.

COROLLARY 4.5. *The probability of an edge $e = uv$ having u and v in different pieces is bounded by $O(\beta)$, and the expected number of edges between pieces is $O(\beta m)$.*

5. IMPLEMENTATION AND PARALLELIZATION

Our partition routine as described in Algorithm 2 requires computing $\mathrm{dist}_{-\delta}(u, v)$ for all pairs of vertices u and v. Standard modifications allow us to simplify it to the form shown in Algorithm 1, which computes BFS involving small integer distances.

The first observation is that the $-\delta_u$ shift at vertex u can be simulated by introducing a super source s with distance $-\delta_u$ to each vertex u. Then if we compute single source shortest path from s to all vertices, the component that v belongs to is given by the first vertex on the shortest path from s to it. Two more observations are needed to transform this shortest path setup to a BFS. First, the negative lengths on edges leaving s can be fixed by adding $\delta_{\max} = \max_u \delta_u$ to all these weights. Second, note that the only edges with non-integral lengths are the ones leaving s. In this shortest path algorithm, the only time that we need to examine the non-integer parts of lengths is when we compare two distances whose integer parts are tied. So the fractional parts can be viewed as tie-breakers for equal integer distances, and all

distances with the same integer part can be processed in parallel. We'll show below that these tie breakers can also be replaced by a random permutation of integers.

Therefore, the algorithm is equivalent to computing shortest path when all edge lengths are integer, with an extra tie breaking rule for comparing distances. In order to use unweighted BFS, it remains to handle the edges with non-unit lengths leaving s, and we do so by processing the those edges in a delayed manner. An edge from s to v only causes v to be added to the BFS queue when the frontier of the search has reached a distance larger than the length of that edge and v has not been visited yet. So it suffices to check all vertices v with a length L edge to s when the BFS frontier moves to distance L, and add the unvisited ones to that level.

The exact cost of running a parallel breadth first search depends on the model of parallelism. There has been much practical work on such routines when the graph has small diameter [21, 8, 26]. For simplicity we will use the $O(\Delta \log n)$ depth and $O(m)$ work bound in the PRAM model given in [18]. Here Δ is the maximum distance that we run the BFS to, and can be bounded by $O(\frac{\log n}{\beta})$. This allows us to prove our main claim about the performance of PARTITION.

Proof of Theorem 1.2: Consider running PARTITION using the BFS based implementation described above, and repeating until we have an $(\beta, O(\frac{\log n}{\beta}))$ partition. Since the δ_us are generated independently, they can be computed in $O(n)$ work and $O(1)$ depth in parallel. The rest of the running time comes from assigning vertices to pieces using shifted shortest path. As the maximum distance from a vertex to the center of its piece is $O(\frac{\log n}{\beta})$ (or we could stop the algorithm at this point), this BFS can be done in $O(m)$ work and $O(\frac{\log^2 n}{\beta})$ depth using parallel BFS algorithms. The resulting decomposition can also be verified in $O(\log n)$ depth and $O(m)$ time.

It remains to bound the success probability of each iteration. Lemma 4.1 gives that the shortest path from u to any $v \in S_u$ is contained in S_u, so $\max_{v \in S_u} \mathrm{dist}(u, v)$ is an upper bound for the strong diameter of each subset. For each vertex $v \in S_u$, since $\mathrm{dist}_{-\delta}(v, v) = d(v, v) - \delta_v \leq 0$ is a candidate, $\mathrm{dist}_{-\delta}(u, v) \leq -\delta_v$. Lemma 4.2 then allows us to bound this value by $O(\log n/\beta)$ with high probability. The expected number of edges between pieces follows from Corollary 4.5, so with constant probability we meet both requirements of a $(\beta, O(\frac{\log n}{\beta}))$ partition. Therefore, we are expected to iterate a constant number of times, giving the expected depth and work bounds. ∎

One practical aspect worth noting is that the fractional parts of the δ values can be viewed as a lexicographical ordering upon all vertices which are used for tie breaking. This is where the tie breaking rule specified in Section 4 may be of use. As the exponential distribution is memoryless and the shifts are generated independently, the fractional parts can also be emulated by directly generating a random permutation of the vertices. This view is perhaps closer to the use of random permutations in the optimal tree-metric embedding algorithm [16].

Similar ideas may also be used in practice instead of computing δ_u. Although generating random variables from such distributions have been studied extensively [19], avoiding these routines might further reduce the cost of this stage of the algorithm. One possibility is to generate a random permutation of the vertices, and assign the shift values based on positions in the permutation. We believe that the slight changes in distributions could be accounted for using a more intricate analysis, but might be more easily studied empirically.

6. CONCLUSION / REMARKS

We showed a simple parallel algorithm for computing low diameter decompositions of undirected unweighted graphs. Given a graph G with n vertices and m edges along with any parameter β, it returns a $(\beta, O(\frac{\log n}{\beta}))$ decomposition in $O(\frac{\log^2 n}{\beta})$ depth and $O(m)$ work. This routine can be used in place of PARTITION from [9] to give a faster algorithm for solving SDD linear systems. It also represents a different view of ball growing, which is at the core of the best sequential low stretch spanning tree algorithms [15, 1, 2].

We believe that our approach may lead to a variety of improvements in algorithms that use ball growing or low diameter decompositions. Many of these applications take place in the weighted setting, and rely on additional clustering-based properties. As a result, many of them are perhaps better examined on a per-application basis. The analysis of the partition routine from Section 4 can be readily extended to the weighted case. However, the depth of the algorithm is harder to control since hop count is no longer closely related to diameter. We believe obtaining similar parallel guarantees in the weighted setting, as well as showing clustering-based properties are interesting directions for future work.

7. REFERENCES

[1] I. Abraham, Y. Bartal, and O. Neiman. Nearly tight low stretch spanning trees. pages 781–790, 2008.

[2] I. Abraham and O. Neiman. Using petal-decompositions to build a low stretch spanning tree. In *Proceedings of the 44th symposium on Theory of Computing*, STOC '12, pages 395–406, New York, NY, USA, 2012. ACM.

[3] N. Alon, R. Karp, D. Peleg, and D. West. A graph-theoretic game and its application to the k-server problem. *SIAM J. Comput.*, 24(1):78–100, 1995.

[4] B. Awerbuch. Complexity of network synchronization. *J. Assoc. Comput. Mach.*, 32(4):804–823, 1985.

[5] B. Awerbuch, B. Berger, L. Cowen, and D. Peleg. Low-diameter graph decomposition is in NC. In *Proceedings of the Third Scandinavian Workshop on Algorithm Theory*, SWAT '92, pages 83–93, London, UK, UK, 1992. Springer-Verlag.

[6] B. Awerbuch, A. V. Goldberg, M. Luby, and S. A. Plotkin. Network decomposition and locality in distributed computation (extended abstract). pages 364–369, 1989.

[7] Y. Bartal. Probabilistic approximation of metric spaces and its algorithmic applications. In *Foundations of Computer Science, 1996. Proceedings., 37th Annual Symposium on*, pages 184–193, 1996.

[8] S. Beamer, K. Asanović, and D. Patterson. Direction-optimizing breadth-first search. In *Proceedings of the International Conference on High Performance Computing, Networking, Storage and Analysis*, SC '12, pages 12:1–12:10, Los Alamitos, CA, USA, 2012. IEEE Computer Society Press.

[9] G. Blelloch, A. Gupta, I. Koutis, G. Miller, R. Peng, and K. Tangwongsan. Nearly-linear work parallel sdd solvers, low-diameter decomposition, and low-stretch subgraphs. *Theory of Computing Systems*, pages 1–34, March 2013.

[10] G. E. Blelloch, A. Gupta, and K. Tangwongsan. Parallel probabilistic tree embeddings, k-median, and buy-at-bulk network design. In *Proceedinbgs of the 24th ACM symposium on Parallelism in algorithms and architectures*, SPAA '12, pages 205–213, New York, NY, USA, 2012. ACM.

[11] P. Christiano, J. A. Kelner, A. Mądry, D. Spielman, and S.-H. Teng. Electrical Flows, Laplacian Systems, and Faster Approximation of Maximum Flow in Undirected Graphs. In *Proceedings of the 43rd ACM Symposium on Theory of Computing (STOC)*, 2011.

[12] E. Cohen. Fast algorithms for constructing t-spanners and paths with stretch t. *SIAM J. Comput.*, 28(1):210–236, 1998.

[13] E. Cohen. Polylog-time and near-linear work approximation scheme for undirected shortest paths. *J. ACM*, 47(1):132–166, 2000.

[14] S. I. Daitch and D. A. Spielman. Faster approximate lossy generalized flow via interior point algorithms. In *Proceedings of the 40th annual ACM symposium on Theory of computing*, STOC '08, pages 451–460, New York, NY, USA, 2008. ACM.

[15] M. Elkin, Y. Emek, D. A. Spielman, and S.-H. Teng. Lower-stretch spanning trees. *SIAM Journal on Computing*, 38(2):608–628, 2008.

[16] J. Fakcharoenphol, S. Rao, and K. Talwar. A tight bound on approximating arbitrary metrics by tree metrics. *J. Comput. System Sci.*, 69(3):485–497, 2004.

[17] W. Feller. *An introduction to probability theory and its applications. Vol. II.* Second edition. John Wiley & Sons Inc., New York, 1971.

[18] P. N. Klein and S. Subramanian. A randomized parallel algorithm for single-source shortest paths. *Journal of Algorithms*, 25:205–220, 1997.

[19] D. E. Knuth. *The art of computer programming, volume 2 (3rd ed.): seminumerical algorithms.* Addison-Wesley Longman Publishing Co., Inc., Boston, MA, USA, 1997.

[20] T. Leighton and S. Rao. Multicommodity max-flow min-cut theorems and their use in designing approximation algorithms. *Journal of the ACM*, 1999.

[21] C. E. Leiserson and T. B. Schardl. A work-efficient parallel breadth-first search algorithm (or how to cope with the nondeterminism of reducers). In *Proceedings of the 22nd ACM symposium on Parallelism in algorithms and architectures*, SPAA '10, pages 303–314, New York, NY, USA, 2010. ACM.

[22] N. Linial and M. Saks. Decomposing graphs into regions of small diameter. In *Proceedings of the second annual ACM-SIAM symposium on Discrete algorithms*, SODA '91, pages 320–330, Philadelphia, PA, USA, 1991. Society for Industrial and Applied Mathematics.

[23] S. Plotkin, S. Rao, and W. D. Smith. Shallow excluded minors and improved graph decompositions. In *Proceedings of the fifth annual ACM-SIAM symposium on Discrete algorithms*, SODA '94, pages

462–470, Philadelphia, PA, USA, 1994. Society for Industrial and Applied Mathematics.

[24] J. Sherman. Breaking the multicommodity flow barrier for $O(\sqrt{logn})$-approximations to sparsest cut. In *Proceedings of the 2009 50th Annual IEEE Symposium on Foundations of Computer Science*, FOCS '09, pages 363–372, Washington, DC, USA, 2009. IEEE Computer Society.

[25] J. Shi and J. Malik. Normalized cuts and image segmentation. *IEEE Transactions on Pattern Analysis and Machine Intelligence*, 22:888–905, 1997.

[26] J. Shun and G. E. Blelloch. Ligra: A lightweight graph processing framework for shared memory. 2013.

[27] K. S. Trivedi. *Probability and statistics with reliability, queuing and computer science applications.* John Wiley and Sons Ltd., Chichester, UK, 2nd edition edition, 2002.

[28] C. Wulff-Nilsen. Separator theorems for minor-free and shallow minor-free graphs with applications. In *Proceedings of the 2011 IEEE 52nd Annual Symposium on Foundations of Computer Science*, FOCS '11, pages 37–46, Washington, DC, USA, 2011. IEEE Computer Society.

APPENDIX

A. ALTERNATE PROOF OF KEY PARTITION LEMMA

We give alternate, more formulaic proofs of Lemma 4.2, which bounds the difference between the shortest and second shortest shifted distance to any point in the graph.

Proof of Lemma 4.4:

Let $\mathcal{E}$ denote the number of indices i such that:

$$d_i - \delta_i \leq d_j - \delta_j + c \ \forall j.$$

For each vertex i, let $\mathcal{E}_i$ be an indicator variable for the event that:

$$d_i - \delta_i \leq d_j - \delta_j + c \ \forall j.$$

We will integrate over the value of $t = d_i - \delta_i$. For a fixed value of t, $\mathcal{E}_i$ occurs if and only if $\delta_j \leq d_j - t + c$ for each j. As the shift values are picked independently, we can multiply the cumulative distribution functions for $Exp(\beta)$ and get:

$$\mathbf{Pr}\left[\mathcal{E}_i\right]$$
$$= \int_{t=-\infty}^{\infty} f_{Exp}(d_i - t, \beta) \prod_{j \neq i} F_{Exp}(d_j - t + c, \beta).$$

When $t > d_1 + c$, $d_1 - t + c < 0$ and $f_{Exp}(d_1 - t, \beta) = F_{Exp}(d_1 - t + c, \beta) = 0$. So it suffices to evaluate this integral up to $t = d_1 + c$. Also, we may use $\exp(-\beta x)$ as an upper bound as $f_{Exp}(x, \beta)$, and arrive at:

$$\mathbf{Pr}\left[\mathcal{E}_i\right]$$

$$\leq \int_{t=-\infty}^{d_1+c} \beta \exp(-\beta(d_i - t)) \prod_{j \neq i} F_{Exp}(d_j - t + c)$$

$$\leq \int_{t=-\infty}^{d_1+c} \beta \exp(-\beta(d_i - t)) \prod_{j \neq i} (1 - \exp(-\beta(d_j - t + c))).$$

We now bound $\mathbf{E}\left[\mathcal{E}\right] = \mathbf{E}\left[\sum_i \mathcal{E}_i\right]$. By linearity of expectation we have:

$$\mathbf{E}\left[\sum_i \mathcal{E}_i\right] \leq \sum_i \int_{t=-\infty}^{d_1+c} \beta \exp\left(-\beta(d_i - t)\right)$$
$$\prod_{j \neq i} (1 - \exp(-\beta(d_j - (t - c))))$$
$$= \exp(\beta c) \int_{t=-\infty}^{d_1+c} \beta \sum_i \exp\left(-\beta(d_i - t + c)\right)$$
$$\prod_{j \neq i} (1 - \exp(-\beta(d_j - t + c))).$$

Observe that the expression being integrated is the derivative w.r.t. t of:

$$-\prod_i \left(1 - \exp(-\beta(d_i - t + c))\right).$$

Therefore we get:

$$\mathbf{E}\left[\mathcal{E}\right] \leq -\exp(\beta c) \prod_i (1 - \exp(-\beta(d_i - t + c))) \Big|_{t=-\infty}^{t=d_1+c}$$

When $t \to -\infty$, $-\beta(d_i - t + c) \to -\infty$. Therefore $\exp(-\beta(d_i - t + c)) \to 0$, and the overall product tends to $-\exp(\beta c)$.

When $t = d_1 + c$, we have:

$$-\exp(\beta c) \prod_i (1 - \exp(-\beta(d_i - (d_1 + c) + c)))$$
$$= -\exp(\beta c) \prod_i (1 - \exp(-\beta(d_i - d_1)))$$
$$\leq -\exp(\beta c) \prod_i (1 - \exp(0)) = 0 \qquad (\text{Since } d_i \geq d_1)$$

Combining these two gives $\mathbf{E}\left[\mathcal{E}\right] \leq \exp(\beta c)$.

By Markov's inequality the probability of there being another vertex being within c of the minimum is at most $\exp(\beta c) - 1 \leq O(\beta c)$ for $c = 1$. ∎

A Constant Factor Approximation Algorithm for the Storage Allocation Problem

[Extended Abstract]

Reuven Bar-Yehuda
Department of Computer
Science, Technion
Haifa 32000, Israel
reuven@cs.technion.ac.il

Michael Beder
Department of Computer
Science, Technion
Haifa 32000, Israel
bederml@cs.technion.ac.il

Dror Rawitz
School of Electrical
Engineering, Tel-Aviv Univ.
Tel-Aviv 69978, Israel
rawitz@eng.tau.ac.il

ABSTRACT

We study the STORAGE ALLOCATION PROBLEM (SAP) which is a variant of the UNSPLITTABLE FLOW PROBLEM ON PATHS (UFPP). A SAP instance consists of a path $P = (V, E)$ and a set J of tasks. Each edge $e \in E$ has a capacity c_e and each task $j \in J$ is associated with a path I_j in P, a demand d_j and a weight w_j. The goal is to find a maximum weight subset $S \subseteq J$ of tasks and a height function $h : S \to \mathbb{R}^+$ such that (i) $h(j) + d_j \leq c_e$, for every $e \in I_j$; and (ii) if $j, i \in S$ such that $I_j \cap I_i \neq \emptyset$ and $h(j) \geq h(i)$, then $h(j) \geq h(i) + d_i$. SAP can be seen as a rectangle packing problem in which rectangles can be moved vertically, but not horizontally.

We present a polynomial time $(9 + \varepsilon)$-approximation algorithm for SAP. Our algorithm is based on a variation of the framework for approximating UFPP by Bonsma et al. [FOCS 2011] and on a $(4 + \varepsilon)$-approximation algorithm for δ-small SAP instances (in which $d_j \leq \delta \cdot c_e$, for every $e \in I_j$, for a sufficiently small constant $\delta > 0$). In our algorithm for δ-small instances, tasks are packed carefully in strips in a UFPP manner, and then a $(1 + \varepsilon)$ factor is incurred by a reduction from SAP to UFPP in strips. The strips are stacked to form a SAP solution. Finally, we show that SAP is strongly NP-hard, even with uniform weights and even if assuming the *no bottleneck assumption*.

Categories and Subject Descriptors

F.2.2 [**Analysis of Algorithms and Problem Complexity**]: Nonnumerical Algorithms and Problems—*Sequencing and scheduling*; G.2.1 [**Discrete Mathematics**]: Combinatorics—*Combinatorial algorithms*

Keywords

approximation algorithms; bandwidth allocation; rectangle packing; storage allocation; unsplittable flow

SPAA'13, July 23–25 2013, Montréal, Québec, Canada.
Copyright is held by the owner/author(s). Publication rights licensed to ACM.
Copyright 2013 ACM 978-1-4503-1572-2/13/07 ...$15.00.

1. INTRODUCTION

1.1 The Problems

In the UNSPLITTABLE FLOW PROBLEM ON PATHS (UFPP) an instance consists of a path $P = (V, E)$ with m edges and a set J of n tasks. Each edge $e \in E$ has a capacity c_e. Each task $j \in J$ has a starting vertex $s_j \in V$, ending vertex $t_j \in V$, a demand d_j and a weight w_j. We denote the path from s_j to t_j by I_j, and we say that $j \in J$ *uses* an edge $e \in E$ if $e \in I_j$. Given a set S of tasks and an edge $e \in E$, define $S(e) = \{j \in J : e \in I_j\}$ to be the set of tasks in S that use e. A feasible UFPP solution is a set of tasks $S \subseteq J$ such that $\sum_{j \in S(e)} d_j \leq c_e$, for every $e \in E$. The goal in UFPP is to find a feasible solution of maximum weight.

We study a variant of UFPP called the STORAGE ALLOCATION PROBLEM (SAP). In SAP we have an additional constraint: it is also required that every task in the solution is given the same contiguous portion of the resource in every edge along its path. More formally, a feasible SAP solution is a subset $S \subseteq J$ and a height function $h : S \to \mathbb{R}^+$ such that (i) $h(j) + d_j \leq c_e$, for every $j \in S$ and $e \in I_j$, and (ii) if $j, i \in S$ such that $I_j \cap I_i \neq \emptyset$ and $h(j) \geq h(i)$, then $h(j) \geq h(i) + d_i$. It follows that SAP is a rectangle packing problem in which each rectangle of height d_j can be moved vertically, but not horizontally. We note that while any SAP solution induces a UFPP solution, the converse is not always true, as shown in Figure 1.

SAP naturally arises in scenarios where tasks require contiguous static portions of a resource. An object may require a contiguous range of storage space (e.g., memory allocation) for a specific time interval ($[s_j, t_j)$ for task j). A task may require bandwidth, but will only accept a contiguous set of frequencies or wavelengths. The resource may be a banner, where each task is an advertisement that requires a contiguous portion of the banner.

Given a SAP or a UFPP instance, an edge $e \in E$ is called a *bottleneck edge* of a task j, if $c_e = \min_{f \in I_j} c_f$. Define $b(j) \triangleq \min_{f \in I_j} c_f$, namely $b(j)$ is the capacity of a bottleneck edge of j. Given $\delta > 0$, a task j is called δ-*small* if $d_j \leq \delta b(j)$, otherwise it is called δ-*large*. A SAP or a UFPP instance is called δ-*small* (δ-*large*) if $d_j \leq \delta b(j)$ ($d_j > \delta b(j)$), for every $j \in J$. In the special case of SAP with uniform capacities (SAP-U), all edges in I_j are bottleneck edges, for every task j. The same goes for UFPP with uniform capacities (UFPP-U). An instance in which the maximum demand is bounded by the minimum edge

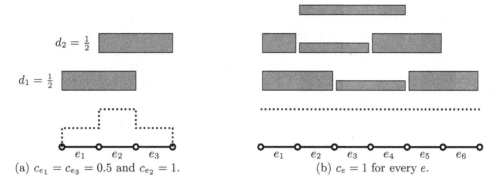

(a) $c_{e_1} = c_{e_3} = 0.5$ and $c_{e_2} = 1$.   (b) $c_e = 1$ for every e.

Figure 1: The dotted line represents the capacity of the edges, and the strips correspond to tasks. Thick strips have demand $\frac{1}{2}$, while thin strips have demand $\frac{1}{4}$. The task sets in both instances form UFPP solutions. However, in both instances there is no SAP solution that contains all tasks. (The instance on the right was given in [12].)

capacity, i.e., $\max_j d_j \leq \min_e c_e$, is said to satisfy the *no-bottleneck assumption* (NBA).

1.2 Our Contribution

We present a polynomial time $(9 + \varepsilon)$-approximation algorithm for SAP, for every constant $\varepsilon > 0$. Our algorithm is based on the recent constant factor approximation algorithm for UFPP by Bonsma et al. [6]. As done in [6] we partition the task set into three sets: *small* tasks, *medium* tasks, and *large* tasks.[1] Small tasks are δ-small for some $\delta > 0$, large tasks are δ'-large for some $\delta' > \delta$, and medium tasks are δ-large and δ'-small.

The algorithms for small and medium tasks by Bonsma et al. [6] are based on an approximation framework that provides $(1 + \varepsilon)\alpha$-approximate solutions given a certain type of α-approximation algorithm for UFPP with "almost uniform" capacities ($c_e \in [2^k, 2^{k+\ell})$, for some k and a constant ℓ). Our algorithm for medium tasks uses a variation of this framework for SAP. The main difference is that in SAP we also need to worry about the height assignments. Additionally, we provide a 2-approximation algorithm for "almost uniform" instances. We do this by extending the dynamic programming algorithm for SAP with uniform capacities from [4] to "almost uniform" capacities. A factor 2 is lost due to the framework's requirement from the α-approximation algorithm for "almost uniform" instances. Hence, combined with the above framework we obtain a $(2+\varepsilon)$-approximation algorithm for medium tasks.

Our $(4 + \varepsilon)$-approximation algorithm for small tasks is based on partitioning the instance into instances in which bottlenecks are within factor 2 of each other. We show how to compute an approximate solution for each instance and then explain how to adjust the heights in order to combine them. This can be seen as a variant of the framework for medium tasks, in which the α-approximation algorithm should satisfy an additional requirement: the tasks must be packed in a strip. We use an LP-rounding $(4 + \varepsilon)$-approximation algorithm for the UFPP version of each such instance that computes approximate solutions in which tasks are packed in strips. (We also provide an alternative local

ratio $(5 + \varepsilon)$-approximation algorithm.) A $(1 + \varepsilon)$ factor is incurred by a reduction from SAP to UFPP in strips [4]. Finally a SAP solution is obtained by stacking the strips.

As for large tasks, Bonsma et al. [6] presented an approximation algorithm for large instances of UFPP that is based on (i) a reduction from UFPP to a special case of the RECTANGLE PACKING problem, and (ii) an algorithm that solves this special case that correspond to instances that are obtained by the reduction. Their algorithm provides a schedule that is induced by a subset of pairwise non-intersecting rectangles, and therefore it is also a SAP schedule. It follows that this algorithm is also an approximation algorithm for large instances of SAP. In this paper, we give a tighter analysis and provide a better upper bound on the approximation ratio for large instances of SAP.

Finally, using a reduction from BIN PACKING, we show that SAP is strongly NP-hard, even with uniform weights and even under the NBA. We note that it can be shown that even SAP-U is strongly NP-hard using the similar, but more complicated construction, that was used to show that CALL SCHEDULING with unit bandwidth and arbitrary duration is strongly NP-hard [14].

1.3 Related Work

The special case of SAP-U (or UFPP-U) with unit capacities and demands is the MAXIMUM INDEPENDENT SET problem in interval graphs which is solvable in polynomial time (see, e.g., [17]). Both SAP-U and UFPP-U are NP-hard, since they contain KNAPSACK as the special case in which the paths of all requests share an edge. When the number of edges in P is constant, UFPP is a special case of MUTLI-DIMENSIONAL KNAPSACK and hence admits a PTAS [15].

Bar-Noy et al. [3] designed local ratio algorithms for UFPP-U and SAP-U with ratio 3 and 7, respectively. The latter was obtained using a reduction from SAP-U to UFPP-U that was based on an algorithm for the DYNAMIC STORAGE ALLOCATION PROBLEM (DSA) by Gergov [16]. In DSA the goal is to find the minimum capacity c for all edges along with a SAP solution that contains all tasks. An extension of SAP-U in which each task j has a time window was studied in [3, 18]. Calinescu et al. [8] developed a randomized approximation algorithm for UFPP-U with expected performance ratio of $2 + \varepsilon$, for every $\varepsilon > 0$. They obtained

---

[1]We note that Bonsma et al. [6] use tiny, medium, and large, since they consider both medium and tiny tasks as small tasks.

this result by dividing the given instance into an instance with large tasks and an instance with small tasks. They use dynamic programming to compute an optimal solution for the large instance, and a randomized LP-based algorithm to obtain a $(1+\varepsilon)$-approximate solution for the small instance. They also present a 3-approximation algorithm for UFPP-U that is different from the one given in [3].

Chen et al. [12] studied the special case of SAP-U where all demands are multiples of $1/K$, for some integer K. They developed an $O(n(nK)^K)$ time dynamic programming algorithm to solve this special case of SAP-U, and also gave an approximation algorithm with ratio $\frac{e}{e-1}+\varepsilon$, for any $\varepsilon > 0$, assuming that $d_j = O(1)/K$ for every j. Bar-Yehuda et al. [4] presented approximation algorithms for SAP-U that is based on a reduction from SAP-U to UFPP-U that works on very small instances, namely on instances in which $d_j \leq \delta$, for a constant $\delta > 0$. (Here we assume that the uniform capacity is 1). The reduction is based on an algorithm for DSA by Buchsbaum et al. [7]. Bar-Yehuda et al. also presented a dynamic programming algorithm for large instances of SAP-U, and this lead to two approximation algorithms for SAP-U, a randomized algorithm with ratio $2+\varepsilon$ and a deterministic algorithm with ratio $\frac{2e-1}{e-1}+\varepsilon < 2.582$.

Bansal et al. [1] gave a deterministic quasi-polynomial time approximation scheme for instances of UFPP, where all capacities and demands are quasi-polynomial, thereby ruling out an APX-hardness result for such instances of UFPP, unless NP $\subseteq$ DTIME$(2^{\text{polylog}(n)})$. Chakrabarti et al. [9] presented a constant factor approximation algorithm for UFPP under the NBA and an $O(\log(d_{\max}/d_{\min}))$-approximation algorithm for UFPP by extending the approach of [8]. Chekuri et al. [11] used an LP-based deterministic algorithm to obtain a $(2+\varepsilon)$-approximation algorithm for UFPP under the NBA. Bansal et al. [2] developed an $O(\log n)$-approximation algorithm for UFPP, beating the integrality gap of the natural LP-relaxation, which was shown to be $\Omega(n)$ [9]. This result has been generalized to trees and uniform weights by Chekuri et al. [10] who also provided an $O(\log^2 n)$-approximation algorithm for the weighted case. They also developed an LP formulation for UNSPLITTABLE FLOW in trees with general weights with an $O(\log^2 n)$ integrality gap.

Bonsma et al. [6] developed a $(7+\varepsilon)$ approximation algorithm for UFPP, being the first constant-factor approximation algorithm for the problem. They also showed that UFPP is strongly NP-hard even for instances with demands in $\{1,2,3\}$. Chrobak et al. [13] showed that UFPP-U is strongly NP-hard even for the case of uniform weights.

1.4 Paper Organization

The remainder of the paper is organized as follows. Section 2 contains definitions and a few preliminary observations. A formal description of our results is given in Section 3. Our algorithms for medium, small, and large SAP instances are given in Sections 4, 5, and 6, respectively. We show that SAP is strongly NP-hard in Section 7. We conclude in Section 8.

2. PRELIMINARIES

Given a task set $S \subseteq J$, the demand of S is denoted by $d(S)$, namely $d(S) \triangleq \sum_{j \in S} d_j$. The load of S on an edge e is defined as $d(S(e)) = \sum_{j \in S(e)} d_j$. A feasible UFPP solution

is a set of tasks $S \subseteq J$ such that $d(S(e)) \leq c_e$, for every $e \in E$. A UFPP solution S is called B-packable if $d(S(e)) \leq B$, for every $e \in E$. Given a SAP solution (S, h), the makespan of an edge e is defined as $\mu_h(S(e)) \triangleq \max_{j \in S(e)}(h(j) + d_j)$. Observe that $d(S(e)) \leq \mu_h(S(e))$, for every $e \in E$. A SAP solution (S, h) is called B-packable if $\mu_h(S(e)) \leq B$, for every $e \in E$.

The following observation bounds the load of a UFPP solution on the edges in term of the maximum bottleneck. A similar observation was made in [6].

OBSERVATION 1. *Let S be a feasible UFPP solution. Then $d(S(e)) \leq 2 \max_{j \in S} b(j)$, for every $e \in E$.*

PROOF. Let e be an edge. Any task $j \in S(e)$ must use an edge with capacity at most $B = \max_{j \in S} b(j)$. Let e_L and e_R be the closest such edges to the left and to the right, respectively. (It may be that $e_L = E_R = e$.) Hence, $d(S(e)) \leq d(S(e_L)) + d(S(e_R)) \leq 2B$. □

The next observation is the analogous observation for SAP.

OBSERVATION 2. *Let (S, h) be a feasible SAP solution. Then $\mu_h(S(e)) \leq \max_{j \in S} b(j)$, for every $e \in E$.*

PROOF. Let $e \in E$ be an edge and let $S(e) = \{j_1, \ldots, j_p\}$ such that $h(j_i) + d_{j_i} \leq h(j_{i+1})$, for every i. The observation follows, since $\mu_h(S(e)) = h(j_p) + d_{j_p} \leq b(j_p) \leq \max_{j \in S} b(j)$. □

Finally, we need the following standard result that is used when one partitions the input into small and large instances. Given a SAP instance, let J_S and J_L be the subset of δ-small tasks and the subset of δ-large tasks, respectively.

LEMMA 3. *Let S_1 and S_2 be an r_1-approximate solution with respect to J_S and an r_2-approximate solution with respect to J_L, respectively. Then, the solution of greater weight is an $(r_1 + r_2)$-approximation for the original instance.*

PROOF. Let S^* be an optimal solution for the original instance. Either $w(S^* \cap J_S) \geq \frac{r_1}{r_1+r_2} w(S^*)$ or $w(S^* \cap J_L) \geq \frac{r_2}{r_1+r_2} \cdot w(S^*)$. Hence, either

$$w(S_1) \geq \frac{1}{r_1} \cdot \frac{r_1}{r_1+r_2} \cdot w(S^*) = \frac{1}{r_1+r_2} \cdot w(S^*)$$

or

$$w(S_2) \geq \frac{1}{r_2} \cdot \frac{r_2}{r_1+r_2} \cdot w(S^*) = \frac{1}{r_1+r_2} \cdot w(S^*) .$$

The lemma follows. □

3. STATEMENT OF RESULTS

In this section we provide a formal statement of our results. We start with our results regarding small, medium, and large instances.

THEOREM 1. *There exists a polynomial time algorithm such that for every constant $\varepsilon > 0$, there exists a constant $\delta > 0$, such that the algorithm computes $(4+\varepsilon)$-approximate solutions for δ-small SAP instances.*

THEOREM 2. *There exists a polynomial time $(2+\varepsilon)$-approximation algorithm for δ-large and $(1-2\beta)$-small SAP instances for every constants $\varepsilon > 0$, $\beta \in (0, \frac{1}{2})$, and $\delta \in (0, 1-2\beta)$.*

THEOREM 3. *There exists a polynomial time* $(2k - 1)$-*approximation algorithm for* $\frac{1}{k}$-*large SAP instances for every integer* $k \geq 1$.

The proofs of Theorems 1, 2, and 3 are given in Sections 5, 4, and 6, respectively. Our result for general SAP instances follows.

THEOREM 4. *There exists a polynomial time* $(9 + \varepsilon)$-*approximation algorithm for* SAP.

PROOF. Set $k = 2$ and $\beta = \frac{1}{4}$. By Theorem 1 there exists a constant $\delta > 0$ for which there is a polynomial time $(4 + \varepsilon)$-approximation algorithm for δ-small SAP instances. By Theorem 2 there is a $(2+\varepsilon)$-approximation algorithm for δ-large and $\frac{1}{2}$-small SAP instances. Also, there a polynomial time 3-approximation algorithm for $\frac{1}{2}$-large SAP instances by Theorem 3. The theorem follows from Lemma 3. $\square$

We also provide a hardness result.

THEOREM 5. SAP *is strongly NP-hard, even with uniform weights and even if assuming the NBA.*

4. MEDIUM TASKS

In this section we prove Theorem 2. We present a polynomial time algorithm that computes $(2 + \varepsilon)$-approximate solutions for δ-large and $(1 - 2\beta)$-small instance of SAP, for any constants $\varepsilon > 0$, $\beta \in (0, \frac{1}{2})$, and $\delta \in (0, 1 - 2\beta)$.

4.1 Approximation Framework for SAP

Following [6], we present a framework that acts as a reduction from a SAP instance to multiple "almost uniform" SAP instances. Given an α-approximation algorithm for almost uniform instances, the framework provides a $(1 + \varepsilon)\alpha$-approximation algorithm. As opposed to the framework from [6] that was designed for UFPP, our framework has an additional difficulty which is taking care of height assignments.

Let $k \in \mathbb{Z}$ and $\ell \in \mathbb{N}$. Given a SAP instance, let $J^{k,\ell} = \left\{ j \in J : 2^k \leq b(j) < 2^{k+\ell} \right\}$ and let $E^{k,\ell} = \cup_{j \in J^{k,\ell}} I_j$. We observe that without loss of generality, we may assume that for each $J^{k,\ell}$, edge capacities are between 2^k and $2^{k+\ell}$.

OBSERVATION 4. $c_e \geq 2^k$, *for every* $e \in E^{k,\ell}$.

PROOF. If $j \in J^{k,\ell}$, then $c_e \geq b(j) \geq 2^k$, for every $e \in I_j$. $\square$

OBSERVATION 5. *Let* (S, h) *be a feasible SAP solution such that* $S \subseteq J^{k,\ell}$. *Then* $\mu_h(S(e)) \leq \min(c_e, 2^{k+\ell})$, *for every edge* $e \in E$.

PROOF. Observation 2 implies that any feasible SAP solution $S \subseteq J^{k,\ell}$ is $2^{k+\ell}$-packable. $\square$

Thus, from the view point of tasks in $J^{k,\ell}$, the capacity of $e \in E^{k,\ell}$ is $\min(c_e, 2^{k+\ell})$.

Let $q = \log \lceil 1/\beta \rceil$ and let ℓ be a constant that will be determined later. Algorithm **AlmostUniform** is our framework for computing SAP solutions, and it is based on the framework for UFPP that was given in [6]. The main difference is that with SAP one cannot simply combine subsolutions. A height function for the tasks should also be computed. This motivates the following definition.

DEFINITION 1. *Let* $\beta > 0$. *A feasible SAP solution* (S, h) *where* $S \subseteq J^{k,\ell}$ *is called* β-*elevated if* $h(j) \geq \beta 2^k$, *for every* $j \in S$.

Algorithm **AlmostUniform** uses an algorithm called **Elevator** that computes an α-approximate β-elevated SAP solution for $J^{k,\ell}$. Notice that a necessary condition for the existence of such nonempty SAP solution is that there are $(1 - \beta)$-small tasks in $J^{k,\ell}$.

Algorithm 1 : AlmostUniform (J, ℓ)

1: $\mathcal{K} \leftarrow \left\{ k \in \mathbb{Z} : J^{k,\ell} \neq \emptyset \right\}$
2: **for each** $k \in \mathcal{K}$ **do**
3: $\quad (S^{k,\ell}, h^{k,\ell}) \leftarrow$ **Elevator**$(J^{k,\ell}, \beta)$
4: **end for**
5: **for each** $r \in \{0, \ldots, \ell + q - 1\}$ **do**
6: $\quad$ Let $\mathcal{K}(r) = \mathcal{K} \cap \{r + i \cdot (\ell + q) : i \in \mathbb{Z}\}$
7: $\quad S_r \leftarrow \bigcup_{k \in \mathcal{K}(r)} S^{k,\ell}$, $h_r \leftarrow \bigcup_{k \in \mathcal{K}(r)} h^{k,\ell}$
8: **end for**
9: $r^* \leftarrow \operatorname{argmax}_{r \in \{0, \ldots, \ell+q-1\}} w(S_r)$
10: Return (S_{r^*}, h_{r^*})

Since ℓ is a constant there is a linear number of subsets $J^{k,\ell}$. Hence, if the running time of Algorithm **Elevator** is polynomial, then the running time of Algorithm **AlmostUniform** is also polynomial. It remains to show that the computed solution is indeed $(1 + \varepsilon)\alpha$-approximate, for an appropriate choice of ℓ.

LEMMA 6. *The solution* (S_r, h_r) *computed by Algorithm* **AlmostUniform** *is a feasible SAP solution, for every* $r \in \{0, \ldots, \ell + q - 1\}$.

PROOF. Given r, let $k_0 = \min K(r)$. Also given $i \in K(r)$, let $i^+ = \min \{k \in K(r) : k > i\}$. For $i \in K(r)$, let $S_i = \bigcup_{k \in K(r), k \leq i} S^{k,\ell}$ and let $h_i = \bigcup_{k \in K(r), k \leq i} h^{k,\ell}$. We prove that (S_i, h_i) is feasible by induction on i. In the base case we have $i = k_0$, and we have that $(S_i, h_i) = (S^{k_0,\ell}, h^{k_0,\ell})$ is feasible due to our assumption on Algorithm **Elevator**. For the inductive step, we assume that the claim holds for i and prove that it holds for i^+. We know that (S_i, h_i) is feasible due to the inductive hypothesis, and by Observation 5 we know that $\mu_{h_i}(S_i(e)) \leq \min(c_e, 2^{i+\ell})$, for every edge $e \in E$. Since **Elevator** computes a β-elevated SAP solution for $J^{i^+,\ell}$, it follows that

$$h_{i^+}(j) \geq \beta \cdot 2^{i^+} \geq 2^{-q} \cdot 2^{i^+} = 2^{i^+ - q} \geq 2^{i+\ell},$$

for every $j \in S_{i^+}$. Hence (S_{i^+}, h_{i^+}) is a feasible SAP schedule. $\square$

The UFPP version of the following lemma appeared in [6] and applies here as well. We provide a proof for completeness.

LEMMA 7. *If* **Elevator** *computes* α-*approximate solutions, then* $w(S_{r^*}) \geq \frac{\ell}{\ell+q} \cdot \frac{1}{\alpha} \text{OPT}_{SAP}(J)$.

PROOF. Let (S, h) be an optimal SAP solution for J. Since each $S^{k,\ell}$ is a β-elevated α-approximation for $J^{k,\ell}$ and every task $j \in J$ belongs to exactly ℓ sets $J^{k,\ell}$, it follows that

$$\sum_{r=0}^{\ell+q-1} w(S_r) = \sum_{r=0}^{\ell+q-1} \sum_{k\in\mathcal{K}(r)} w(S^{k,\ell})$$

$$\geq \sum_{r=0}^{\ell+q-1} \sum_{k\in\mathcal{K}(r)} \frac{1}{\alpha}\cdot\mathrm{OPT_{SAP}}(J^{k,\ell})$$

$$= \frac{1}{\alpha}\cdot\sum_{k\in\mathcal{K}} \mathrm{OPT_{SAP}}(J^{k,\ell})$$

$$\geq \frac{1}{\alpha}\cdot\sum_{k\in\mathcal{K}} w(S\cap J^{k,\ell})$$

$$= \frac{\ell}{\alpha}\cdot\mathrm{OPT_{SAP}}(J)\ .$$

Therefore, $w(S_{r^*}) \geq \frac{1}{\alpha}\cdot\frac{\ell}{\ell+q}\cdot\mathrm{OPT_{SAP}}(J)$. $\square$

By choosing the right value of ℓ we obtain a $(1+\varepsilon)\alpha$-approximation algorithm.

LEMMA 8. *Suppose we are given a polynomial time algorithm that computes an α-approximate β-elevated SAP solution for $J^{k,\ell}$, for every k and ℓ. Then, if $\ell = \frac{1}{\varepsilon}\log\lceil 1/\beta\rceil$, Algorithm AlmostUniform computes a $(1+\varepsilon)\alpha$-approximate solution in polynomial time.*

PROOF. We know that the computed solution is feasible due to Lemma 6, and by Lemma 7 we have that

$$w(S_{r^*}) \geq \frac{1}{\alpha}\cdot\frac{\ell}{\ell+\log\lceil 1/\beta\rceil}\cdot\mathrm{OPT_{SAP}}(J) = \frac{1}{\alpha}\cdot\frac{1}{1+\varepsilon}\cdot\mathrm{OPT_{SAP}}(J)\ ,$$

as required. $\square$

4.2 Computing β-elevated 2-approximations

In this section we present an algorithm that computes a β-elevated solution for $J^{k,\ell}$, for any k and ℓ. Throughout the section we consider medium tasks, namely we assume that every task $j \in J^{k,\ell}$ is δ-large and $(1-2\beta)$-small, for constants $\varepsilon > 0$, $\beta \in (0,\frac{1}{2})$, and $\delta \in (0, 1-2\beta)$.

Our algorithm is based on the following simple observation that was given in [4] for SAP-U.

OBSERVATION 9. *Given a SAP instance, there exists an optimal solution (S,h) such that, for every task j, either $h(j) = 0$ or there exists a task $j' \neq j$ such that $I_j \cap I_{j'} \neq \emptyset$ and $h(j) = h(j') + d_{j'}$.*

The proof of the observation uses a "gravity" argument, namely given a solution (S,h), apply gravity on the tasks in S, until all tasks cannot fall any further. (See example in Figure 2.)

Using Observation 9 we are able to consider a specific type of optimal solutions.

LEMMA 10. *Suppose we are given a δ-large SAP instance, where $c_e \in [B, B2^\ell)$, for every $e \in E$, for some B. Then there exists an optimal solution (S^*, h^*) such that:*

(i) $|S^*(e)| < 2^\ell/\delta$, for every e, and

(ii) there exists a subset $H_j \subseteq S^* \setminus \{j\}$ of size at most $2^\ell/\delta$ such that $h^*(j) = d_{S^*}(H_j)$, for every task $j \in S^*$.

PROOF. Let (S^*, h^*) be an optimal SAP solution whose existence is implied in Observation 9. To prove (i) observe that $d_j \geq \delta b(j) \geq \delta B$, for every $j \in S^*$ and that $c_e < B2^\ell$, for every $e \in E$. Thus from the feasibility of S^*, if follows that each edge $e \in E$ is used by less than $B2^\ell/(\delta B) = 2^\ell/\delta$ tasks. (ii) follows from Observation 9 and (i). $\square$

Lemma 10 implies an upper bound on the number of possibilities for the height of a task $j \in J$, given a δ-large SAP instance, where $c_e \in [B, B2^\ell)$, for every $e \in E$, for some B. Since the maximal number of tasks assigned to an edge is at most $L = 2^\ell/\delta$, the number of possible heights is bounded by $\sum_{i=0}^{L}\binom{n}{i} = O(n^L)$. It follows that there are at most $O(n^{O(L^2)})$ possibilities for assigning a task set and its corresponding heights to a given edge $e \in E$. Therefore, an optimal SAP solution for J can be computed using a dynamic programming algorithm similar to the one described in [4].

LEMMA 11. *There is a polynomial time algorithm that computes an optimal solution for a δ-large SAP instance, where $c_e \in [B, B2^\ell)$, for every $e \in E$, for some B.*

PROOF. Let $V = \{v_0, \ldots, v_m\}$ and $E = \{e_1, \ldots, e_m\}$. Given a vertex $v_i \in V$, let P_i be the path that is induced by $V_i = \{v_i, \ldots, v_m\}$. Let J_i be the tasks that are fully contained in P_i. A feasible solution (S_i, h_i) is called *proper* with respect to e_i if $e_i \in I_j$, for every $j \in S_i$. Recall that there are $O(n^L)$ possibilities for choosing S_i, and that given S_i there are $O(n^{L^2})$ possibilities for choosing h_i. A solution (S_{i+1}, h_{i+1}) is *compatible* with the proper pair (S_i, h_i) if (i) it is proper with respect to e_{i+1}, (ii) Either $j \in S_i \cap S_{i+1}$ or $j \notin S_i \cap S_{i+1}$ for every j such that $e_i, e_{i+1} \in I_j$, and (iii) $h_i(j) = h_{i+1}(j)$ for every $j \in S_i \cap, S_{i+1}$.

We define a dynamic programming table of size $O(n^{L+L^2})$ as follows. For an edge e_i and a pair (S_i, h_i) that is proper with respect to e_i the state $\Pi(e_i, S_i, h_i)$ stands for the maximum weight of a pair (S', h') such that $S' \subseteq J_i$ and $(S_i \cup S', h_i \cup h')$ is feasible. We initialize the table Π by setting $\Pi(e_m, S_m, h_m) = 0$ for every proper pair (S_m, h_m) with respect to e_m. We compute the rest of the entries by using:

$$\Pi(e_i, S_i, h_i) = \max_{\substack{(S_{i+1}, h_{i+1}) \\ \text{is compatible with} \\ (S_i, h_i)}} \{w(S_{i+1}\setminus S_i) + \Pi(e_{i+1}, S_{i+1}, h_{i+1})\}$$

The weight of an optimal solution is $\Pi(e_0, \emptyset, h_\emptyset)$, where e_0 is a dummy edge and $h_\emptyset$ is a function whose domain is the empty set.

To compute each entry $\Pi(e_i, S_i, h_i)$ we need to go through all the possibilities for a solution (S_{i+1}, h_{i+1}) that is compatible with (S_i, h_i). There are no more than $O(n^{L+L^2})$ such possibilities. Hence, the total running time is $O(m \cdot n^{L+L^2}\cdot n^{(L+L^2)}) = O(m\cdot n^{O(L^2)})$. In order to compute a corresponding solution, one needs to keep track of which option was taken in the recursive computation. An optimal solution can be reconstructed in a top down manner. $\square$

Lemma 11 implies that solving SAP on $J^{k,\ell}$ can be done in polynomial time. It remains to obtain a β-elevated solution.

LEMMA 12. *Suppose we are given a $(1-2\beta)$-small SAP instance. A SAP solution (S, h) for $J^{k,\ell}$ can be partitioned into two β-elevated SAP solutions (S_1, h_1) and (S_2, h_2) in linear time.*

PROOF. Consider a task $j \in S$ such that $h(j) < \beta 2^k$. Since j is $(1-2\beta)$-small and $c_e \geq 2^k$ due to Observation 4,

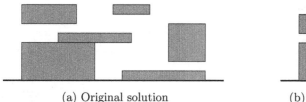
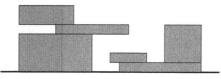

(a) Original solution   (b) Solution after application of gravity

Figure 2: Solution (b) is obtained by applying gravity on Solution (a).

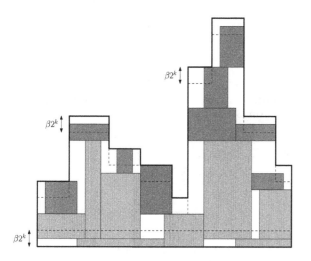

Figure 3: An example of partition of optimal solution into two β-elevated solutions. The light tasks belong to S_1, while the dark tasks belong to S_2.

we have that

$$
\begin{aligned}
h(j) + d(j) &< \beta 2^k + (1 - 2\beta) b(j) \\
&\leq \beta 2^k + (1 - 2\beta) c_e \\
&= c_e + \beta 2^k - 2\beta c_e \\
&\leq c_e - \beta 2^k , \qquad\qquad (1)
\end{aligned}
$$

for every $e \in I_j$. Define $S_1 = \left\{ j \in S : h(j) < \beta 2^k \right\}$ and $S_2 = S \setminus S_1$. Also, define $h_1(j) = h(j) + \beta 2^k$, for all $j \in S_1$, and $h_2(j) = h(j)$, for all $j \in S_2$. (See example in Figure 3.) (S_1, h_1) is β-elevated due to (1), while (S_2, h_2) is β-elevated by definition. Finally, it is not hard to verify that the described partition can be done in linear time. $\square$

The 2-approximation algorithm follows due to Lemmas 11 and 12.

LEMMA 13. *There is a polynomial time algorithm that computes β-elevated 2-approximations for $J^{k,\ell}$, given a δ-large and $(1 - 2\beta)$-small SAP instance.*

PROOF. An optimal solution (S^*, h^*) for $J^{k,\ell}$ can be computed in polynomial time due to Lemma 11. (S^*, h^*) can be partitioned into two β-elevated solutions (S_1, h_1) and (S_2, h_2) due to Lemma 12. Since $w(S^*) = w(S_1) + w(S_2)$, one of the two solutions is 2-approximate. $\square$

We conclude this section with the proof of Theorem 2.

PROOF OF THEOREM 2. By Lemma 13 there exists a polynomial time algorithm that computes β-elevated 2-approximate solutions for $J^{k,\ell}$, for every k and ℓ. Therefore, by Lemma 8, Algorithm **AlmostUniform** is a $(2 + \varepsilon)$-approximation algorithm for δ-large and $(1 - 2\beta)$-small SAP instances. $\square$

5. SMALL TASKS

In this section we prove Theorem 1, namely we present a polynomial time algorithm that, for every $\varepsilon > 0$, computes $(4 + \varepsilon)$-approximate solutions for δ-small instance of SAP, for some constant $\delta > 0$ (depending on ε).

We first present an LP-rounding algorithm for UFPP instances in which bottlenecks are within factor 2 of each other. A $(1 + \varepsilon)$ factor is incurred by a reduction from SAP to UFPP in strips [4]. Then, we show how to use this algorithm to design an algorithm for small instances. We partition the instance into instances in which tasks have similar bottleneck, and then use the above algorithm to compute an approximate solution that resides in a strip. A SAP solution is obtained by stacking the strips.

5.1 Packing Small Tasks in Strips

As a first step we consider the following special case of SAP. Let $B > 0$, and assume we are given a δ-small SAP instance in which $b(j) \in [B, 2B]$, for every $j \in J$. Note that due to Observation 2, without loss of generality we may assume that all edge capacities are between B and $2B$. We present a LP-rounding algorithm that computes a $\frac{1}{2}B$-packable $(4 + \varepsilon)$-approximate SAP solution. An alternative local ratio $(5 + \varepsilon)$-approximation algorithm is also provided in Appendix A.

The first step is an LP-rounding algorithm that computes $\frac{1}{2}B$-packable UFPP solutions. The algorithm is based on the following integer linear formulation of UFPP:

$$
\max \sum_{j \in J} w_j \cdot x_j \qquad\qquad (2)
$$

$$
\text{s.t.} \sum_{j \in S(e)} d_j x_j \leq c_e \qquad \forall e \in E
$$

$$
x_j \in \{0, 1\} \qquad \forall j \in J
$$

where $x_j = 1$ represents that j is in the solution. An LP-relaxation is obtained by replacing the integrality constraints with $x_j \in [0, 1]$, for every $j \in J$.

Let x^* be an optimal fractional solution of (2) and define $x' = \frac{1}{4} x^*$. The solution x' satisfies $\sum_{j \in S(e)} d_j x_j \leq \frac{1}{2} B$, and therefore it is feasible with respect to (2) with $c_e = \frac{1}{2} B$, for every e. Since this is a uniform capacity instance we may use the following result of Chekuri, Mydlarz, and Shepherd [11] to obtain an integral solution.

THEOREM 6 ([11]). *For every constant $\varepsilon > 0$, there exists a constant $\delta > 0$, such that given a δ-small instance of UFPP-U, an integral solution x such that $wx \geq \frac{1}{1+\varepsilon}wx^*$ can be found in polynomial time.*

We now transform our UFPP-U solution into a SAP solution using the following result:

LEMMA 14 ([4]). *There exists a constant $\delta_0 > 0$, such that if S is a B-packable UFPP solution to some δ-small instance, where $\delta \in (0, \delta_0)$, then S can be transformed into a B-packable SAP solution (S', h') such that $w(S') \geq (1 - 4\delta)w(S)$ in polynomial time.*

Using Lemma 14 we obtain an approximate SAP solution.

LEMMA 15. *There exists a polynomial time algorithm such that for every constant $\varepsilon > 0$, there exists a constant $\delta > 0$, such that the algorithm computes $\frac{1}{2}B$-packable $(4+\varepsilon)$-approximate solutions for δ-small SAP instances in which $b(j) \in [B, 2B)$, for every $j \in J$.*

PROOF. Let $\delta_1 = \delta(\frac{\varepsilon}{5})$ be the constant required by Theorem 6. Set $\delta = \delta(\varepsilon)$ such that $\delta < \min\{\delta_1, \delta_0\}$ and $1 - 4\delta > (4 + \frac{4}{5}\varepsilon)/(4 + \varepsilon)$. Apply the algorithm from [11] to compute a $\frac{1}{2}B$-packable $4 \cdot (1 + \frac{\varepsilon}{5})$-approximate UFPP solution S. By Lemma 14, S can be transformed into a $\frac{1}{2}B$-packable SAP solution (S', h') such that $w(S') \geq (1 - 4\delta)w(S)$ in polynomial time. It follows that

$$w(S') \geq \frac{1-4\delta}{4 \cdot (1+\varepsilon/5)} \cdot \text{OPT}_{\text{UFPP}}(J) \geq \frac{1}{4+\varepsilon} \cdot \text{OPT}_{\text{SAP}}(J) \,,$$

as required. □

5.2 Stacking Strips

The next step is to partition the instance. Let $J_t = \{j \in J : 2^t \leq b(j) < 2^{t+1}\}$, for every t. Algorithm **Strip-Pack** computes an approximate solution for J_t, for each t, and them combines the solutions. An example of a solution produced by Algorithm **Strip-Pack** is shown in Figure 4.

Algorithm 2 : Strip-Pack (J,w)

1: **for** each t **do**
2:     Compute a 2^{t-1}-packable SAP solution (S_t, h_t) for J_t
3:     $h'_t(j) = h_t(j) + 2^{t-1}$, for every $j \in J_t$
4: **end for**
5: $S \leftarrow \bigcup_t S_t$, $h \leftarrow \bigcup_t h'_t$
6: Return (S, h)

We conclude the section by showing that Algorithm **Strip-Pack** computes $(4+\varepsilon)$-approximate solutions.

PROOF OF THEOREM 1. First, the running time of Algorithm **Strip-Pack** is polynomial, since there are at most $O(n)$ nonempty subsets J_t, and for each such subset we call Algorithm **Strip-Pack** and the algorithm from Lemma 14, both of which run in polynomial time.

By Lemma 15 we have that Algorithm **Strip-Pack** computes a 2^{t-1}-packable $(4+\varepsilon)$-approximate solution (S_t, h_t) for J_t, for every t. By lifting the solution (S_t, h_t) by 2^{t-1}, Algorithm **Strip-Pack** ensures that a feasible SAP solution is obtained. Also, let (S^*, h^*) be an optimal solution for J.

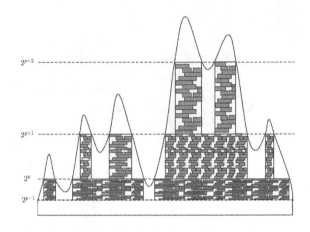

Figure 4: An example of a solution produced by Algorithm Strip-Pack.

Then,

$$\begin{aligned}
w(S) &= \sum_t w(S_t) \\
&\geq \frac{1}{4+\varepsilon} \sum_t \text{OPT}_{\text{SAP}}(J_t) \\
&\geq \frac{1}{4+\varepsilon} \sum_t w(S^* \cap J_t) \\
&= \frac{1}{4+\varepsilon} \cdot w(S^*) \,,
\end{aligned}$$

as required. □

6. LARGE TASKS

In this section we consider $\frac{1}{k}$-large instances of SAP, for an integer $k \geq 1$. Recall that in such instances $d_j > \frac{1}{k}b(j)$, for every j. We present a $(2k-1)$-approximation algorithm for $\frac{1}{k}$-large instances of SAP.

Bonsma et al. [6] presented a $2k$-approximation algorithm for $\frac{1}{k}$-large UFPP instances, for any $k \geq 2$, that is based on a reduction from UFPP to a special case of RECTANGLE PACKING (or MAXIMUM INDEPENDENT SET in rectangle intersection graphs). The reduction is as follows. Let $j \in J$ be a task. The *residual capacity* of j is defined as $\ell(j) \triangleq b(j) - d_j$. Task j is *associated* with the rectangle $R(j) = [s_j, t_j] \times [\ell(j), b(j))$. In SAP terms, it is the rectangle that is induced by assigning height $\ell(j)$ to j. See example in Figure 5.

Let $\mathcal{R}(S) = \{R(j) : j \in S\}$ be the family of rectangles that is obtained from a subset $S \subseteq J$. Bonsma et al. [6] showed that the set of rectangles $\mathcal{R}(S)$ that correspond to a feasible UFPP schedule S, can be colored using $2k$ colors such that any color induces a pairwise non-intersecting subset of rectangles. Hence the total weight of the tasks that correspond to one of these subsets is at least $\frac{1}{2k}w(S)$. Bonsma et al. presented a polynomial time algorithm that solves the special case of RECTANGLE PACKING that correspond to instances that are obtained by the above reduction.

THEOREM 7 ([6]). *There is an $O(n^4)$ algorithm that computes an optimal rectangle packing of $\mathcal{R}(J)$, for every UFPP instance J.*

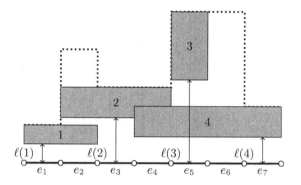

Figure 5: An example of four tasks that are placed at height $\ell(j) = b(j) - d_j$, for every j.

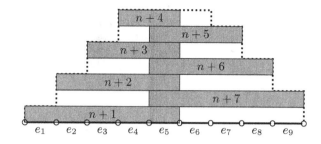

Figure 7: An example of a SAP instance with $k = 4$. The dotted line represents the capacity of the edges, and the dark strips correspond to tasks $n+1, \ldots, n+2k-1$. Tasks $1, \ldots, n$ correspond to e_6.

We note that the algorithm from [6] provides a UFPP schedule which is induced by a subset of pairwise non-intersecting rectangles, and therefore it is also a SAP schedule. It follows that this algorithm is also a $2k$-approximation algorithm for $\frac{1}{k}$-large instances of SAP. In what follows we use the geometric properties of SAP to show that $\mathcal{R}(S)$ can be colored using only $2k-1$ colors for any $\frac{1}{k}$-large SAP solution (S, h). This implies a $(2k-1)$-approximation algorithm for $\frac{1}{k}$-large instances of SAP, for any integer $k \geq 1$.

Given a feasible SAP solution (S, h), let

$$N_S(j) = \left\{ j' \in S \setminus \{j\} : R(j') \cap R(j) \neq \emptyset \right\} ,$$

and let $\deg_S(R(j))$ be the number of rectangles in $\mathcal{R}(S)$ that intersect $R(j)$, namely $\deg_S(R(j)) = |N_S(j)|$. We show that there exists a rectangle $R(j)$ whose degree is at most $2k-2$. This implies that a $(2k-1)$-coloring can be obtained in a greedy manner.

LEMMA 16. *Let (Q, h) be a $\frac{1}{k}$-large SAP solution that contains a task j' such that $\ell(j') < b(j) \leq b(j')$, for every $j \in Q$. If there exists an edge e such that $e \in I_j$, for every $j \in Q$, then $|Q| \leq k$.*

PROOF. Suppose that $|Q| > k$. Since $\ell(j') < b(j) \leq b(j')$, for every $j \in Q$ we have that

$$\sum_{j \in Q \setminus \{j'\}} d_j > \frac{1}{k} \sum_{j \in Q \setminus \{j'\}} b(j)$$
$$> \frac{1}{k} \sum_{j \in Q \setminus \{j'\}} \ell(j')$$
$$= \frac{1}{k} (|Q| - 1) \cdot \ell(j') \geq \ell(j') .$$

Therefore, $\sum_{j \in Q} d_j > \ell(j') + d_{j'} = b(j')$, in contradiction to Observation 2 since there exists an edge e such that $e \in I_j$, for every $j \in Q$. $\square$

We are now ready to show that there exists a task whose rectangle has at most $2k-2$ neighbors.

LEMMA 17. *Let (S, h) be a $\frac{1}{k}$-large solution. Then there exists a task $j \in S$ such that $\deg_S(R(j)) \leq 2k-2$.*

PROOF. Let j_0 be the task with minimal right endpoint, and let e_0 be the right most edge in I_{j_0}. Define

$$Q^- = \{j \in S : b(j) \leq b(j_0)\} \cap N(j_0) ,$$
$$Q^+ = \{j \in S : b(j) \geq b(j_0)\} \cap N(j_0) .$$

Observe that $j_0 \in Q^- \cap Q^+$. Consider $j \in Q^-$. Since $R(j) \cap R(j_0) \neq \emptyset$, it follows that $b(j) > \ell(j_0)$. Hence Q^- satisfies the conditions of Lemma 16 with $j' = j_0$ and $e = e_0$, and we have that $|Q^-| \leq k$. Furthermore, observe that $\ell(j) < b(j_0)$, for every $j \in Q^+$, and thus $\cap_{j \in Q^+} R(j) \neq \emptyset$. It follows that $\ell(j') < b(j_0) \leq b(j) \leq b(j')$, for every $j \in Q^+$, for a task j' such that $b(j') = \max_{i \in Q^+} b(i)$. Hence Q^+ satisfies the conditions of Lemma 16 with $e = e_0$. The lemma follows since $\deg_S(R(j)) \leq |Q^-| + |Q^+| - 2 = 2k-2$. $\square$

We are now ready to prove Theorem 3.

PROOF OF THEOREM 3. Lemma 17 implies that a coloring using $2k-1$ colors can be obtained in a greedy manner. The theorem follows due to Theorem 7. $\square$

We note that Lemma 17 is tight for the case of $k = 2$. Figure 6 shows a $\frac{1}{2}$-large SAP solution and the resulting RECTANGLE PACKING instance. Since the instance is a 5-cycle, it is not 2-colorable.

7. HARDNESS RESULT

In this section we prove that SAP is strongly NP-hard using a reduction from BIN PACKING.

Given a BIN PACKING instance containing n items of sizes $s_1, \ldots, s_n$, a bin of size 1, and an integer k, we construct the following SAP instance. First the path P contains $2k+1$ edges, with capacities:

$$c_{e_i} = \begin{cases} 2i - 1 & i \leq k, \\ 2k - 1 & i \in \{k+1, k+2\}, \\ 2(2k+2-i) & i \geq k+3. \end{cases}$$

Also, there are $n + 2k - 1$ unit weight tasks with demands:

$$d_j = \begin{cases} s_j & j \leq n, \\ 1 & j > n. \end{cases}$$

and intervals:

$$I_j = \begin{cases} \{e_{k+2}\} & j \leq n, \\ \{e_{j-n}, \ldots, e_{k+1}\} & n < j \leq n+k \\ \{e_{k+1}, \ldots, e_{j-n+2}\} & j > n+k \end{cases}$$

The first n tasks represent the items and the remaining $2k-1$ tasks are used to construct a schedule that induces k bins. Such a solution containing tasks $\{n+1, \ldots, n+2k-1\}$ is given in Figure 7.

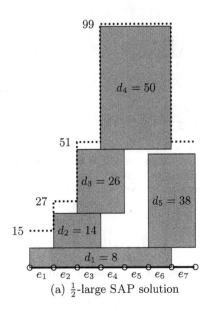

(a) $\frac{1}{2}$-large SAP solution

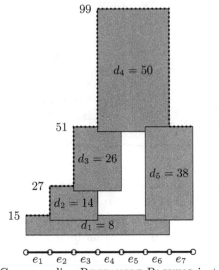

(b) Corresponding RECTANGLE PACKING instance.

Figure 6: An example of a SAP solution with five tasks whose corresponding rectangles form a cycle.

LEMMA 18. *There exists a solution to the* BIN PACKING *instance with k bins if and only if there exists a solution to the* SAP *instance with weight $n + 2k - 1$.*

PROOF. First, observe that since $e_{k+1} \in I_j$ for every $j \in \{n+1, \ldots, n+2k-1\}$, there is only one possible configuration to schedule the tasks $\{n+1, \ldots, n+2k-1\}$ together (see example in Figure 7 for $k = 4$). Hence, in a SAP solution with weight $n + 2k - 1$, the first n tasks are placed in k bins that are formed by the remaining $2k-1$ tasks. The lemma follows. $\square$

Theorem 5 follows from Lemma 18 since BIN PACKING is strongly NP-hard. Note that the reduction constructs instances with uniform weights that satisfy the NBA.

8. CONCLUSION

We presented a $(9+\varepsilon)$-approximation algorithm for SAP. Our approximation ratios for medium and large instances match the ratios for UFPP from [6]. In fact our ratio for large tasks is even better (3 instead of 4). However, our approximation ratio for small instances is larger ($4 + \varepsilon$ vs. $1 + \varepsilon$). This larger ratio stem from our need to pack small tasks in strips in order to use the transformation from a UFPP solution to a SAP solution. The ratio for small instances may have been smaller, if we had such a transformation that works on non-uniform instances. Hence, it would be interesting to come up with algorithms for an extended version of DSA in which one is given a path $P = (V, E)$ with a non-uniform capacity vector $c \in \mathbb{R}_+^{|E|}$ and a set of (small) tasks, and the goal is to find the minimum coefficient ρ such that all tasks can be packed within the capacity vector $\rho \cdot c$.

Acknowledgment

We thank an anonymous referee for pointing out that we can use LP-rounding instead of local ratio for computing a $\frac{1}{2}B$-packable SAP solution in Section 5.1.

9. REFERENCES

[1] N. Bansal, A. Chakrabarti, A. Epstein, and B. Schieber. A quasi-ptas for unsplittable flow on line graphs. In *38th Annual ACM Symposium on the Theory of Computing*, pages 721–729, 2006.

[2] N. Bansal, Z. Friggstad, R. Khandekar, and M. R. Salavatipour. A logarithmic approximation for unsplittable flow on line graphs. In *20th Annual ACM-SIAM Symposium on Discrete Algorithms*, pages 702–709, 2009.

[3] A. Bar-Noy, R. Bar-Yehuda, A. Freund, J. Naor, and B. Shieber. A unified approach to approximating resource allocation and schedualing. *Journal of the ACM*, 48(5):1069–1090, 2001.

[4] R. Bar-Yehuda, M. Beder, Y. Cohen, and D. Rawitz. Resource allocation in bounded degree trees. *Algorithmica*, 54(1):89–106, 2009.

[5] R. Bar-Yehuda and S. Even. A local-ratio theorem for approximating the weighted vertex cover problem. *Annals of Discrete Mathematics*, 25:27–46, 1985.

[6] P. Bonsma, J. Schulz, and A. Wiese. A constant factor approximation algorithm for unsplittable flow on paths. In *52nd Annual IEEE Symposium on Foundations of Computer Science*, pages 47–56, 2011.

[7] A. L. Buchsbaum, H. Karloff, C. Kenyon, N. Reingold, and M. Thorup. OPT versus LOAD in dynamic storage allocation. *SIAM Journal on Computing*, 33(3):632–646, 2004.

[8] G. Calinescu, A. Chakrabarti, H. J. Karloff, and Y. Rabani. Improved approximation algorithms for resource allocation. In *9th International Integer Programming and Combinatorial Optimization Conference*, volume 2337 of *LNCS*, pages 401–414, 2002.

[9] A. Chakrabarti, C. Chekuri, A. Gupta, and A. Kumar. Approximation algorithms for the unsplittable flow problem. *Algorithmica*, 47(1):53–78, 2007.

[10] C. Chekuri, A. Ene, and N. Korula. Unsplittable flow in paths and trees and column-restricted packing integer programs. In *12th International Workshop on Approximation Algorithms for Combinatorial Optimization Problems*, volume 5687 of *LNCS*, pages 42–55, 2009.

[11] C. Chekuri, M. Mydlarz, and F. B. Shepherd. Multicommodity demand flow in a tree and packing integer programs. *ACM Transactions on Algorithms*, 3(3), 2007.

[12] B. Chen, R. Hassin, and M. Tzur. Allocation of bandwidth and storage. *IIE Transactions*, 34:501–507, 2002.

[13] M. Chrobak, G. J. Woeginger, K. Makino, and H. Xu. Caching is hard - even in the fault model. *Algorithmica*, 63(4):781–794, 2012.

[14] T. Erlebach and K. Jansen. The complexity of path coloring and call scheduling. *Theoretical Computer Science*, 255(1–2):33–50, 2001.

[15] A. M. Frieze and M. R. B. Clarke. Approximation algorithms for the m-dimensional $0 - 1$ knapsack problem: worst-case and probabilistic analyses. *European Journal of Operational Research*, 15:100–109, 1984.

[16] J. Gergov. Algorithms for compile-time memory optimization. In *10th Annual ACM-SIAM Symposium on Discrete Algorithms*, pages 907–908, 1999.

[17] M. C. Golumbic. *Algorithmic Graph Theory and Perfect Graphs*. Academic Press, 1980.

[18] S. Leonardi, A. Marchetti-Spaccamela, and A. Vitaletti. Approximation algorithms for bandwidth and storage allocation problems under real time constraints. In *20th Conference on Foundations of Software Technology and Theoretical Computer Science*, volume 1974 of *LNCS*, pages 409–420, 2000.

APPENDIX

A. A LOCAL RATIO ALGORITHM FOR PACKING SMALL TASKS IN A STRIP

In this section we provide a local ratio algorithm that computes $\frac{1}{2}B$-packable $(5 + \varepsilon)$-approximate solutions for δ-small SAP instances in which edge capacities are between B and $2B$, for some constant $\delta > 0$ (depending on ε).

Algorithm 3 : Strip(J, w)

1: **if** $J = \emptyset$ **then** return $\emptyset$
2: Let $j^* \in J$ be a task such that $t^* = \min_{j \in J} t_j$
3: Define $w_1(j) = w(j^*) \cdot \begin{cases} 1 & j = j^*, \\ 2d_j/B & j \neq j^*, I_j \cap I_{j^*} \neq \emptyset \\ 0 & \text{otherwise,} \end{cases}$
  and $w_2 = w - w_1$
4: Let J^+ be the set of positive weighted tasks
5: $S' \leftarrow$ **Strip**(J^+, w_2)
6: Let e^* be the right-most edge of j^*
7: **if** $d(S'(e^*)) \leq \frac{1}{2}B - d_{j^*}$ **then** $S \leftarrow S' \cup \{j^*\}$
  else $S \leftarrow S'$
8: Return S

Sorting the tasks according to their right end-point can be done in $O(n \log n)$. There are $O(n)$ recursive calls, each

requiring linear time. Hence the running time of Algorithm **Strip** is polynomial.

We show that Algorithm **Strip** computes approximate solutions whose load on any edge is at most $\frac{1}{2}B$.

LEMMA 19. *Given a δ-small SAP instance in which $b(j) \in [B, 2B]$, for every $j \in J$, Algorithm Strip computes a $\frac{1}{2}B$-packable UFPP solution S. Furthermore, $w(S) \geq \frac{5}{1-4\delta} \cdot \text{OPT}_{\text{SAP}}(J)$.*

PROOF. We first prove that S is $\frac{1}{2}B$-packable, for every e, by induction on the number of recursive calls. In the base case $S = \emptyset$ and we are done. For the inductive step, assume that $d(S'(e)) \leq \frac{1}{2}B$, for every $e \in E$. First, $d(S(e)) = d(S'(e)) \leq \frac{1}{2}B$, for every $e \notin I_{j^*}$. For $e \in I_{j^*}$, observe that $d(S(e)) \leq d(S(e^*)) \leq \frac{1}{2}B$.

We prove that S is $\frac{5}{1-4\delta}$-approximate also by induction on the number of recursive calls. In the base case $S = \emptyset$ is optimal. For the inductive step, assume that S' is $\frac{5}{1-4\delta}$-approximate with respect to J^+ and w_2. Since $w_2(j^*) = 0$, S is also $\frac{5}{1-4\delta}$-approximate with respect to J and w_2, We show that S is also $\frac{5}{1-4\delta}$-approximate with respect to J and w_1. This completes the proof since by the Local Ratio Theorem [5, 3] we get that S is $\frac{5}{1-4\delta}$-approximate with respect to J and $= w$ as well.

It remains to show that S is $\frac{5}{1-4\delta}$-approximate with respect to J and w_1. Notice that either $j^* \in S$ or $d(S(e^*)) + d_{j^*} > \frac{1}{2}B$. If $j^* \in S$, then $w_1(S) \geq w(j^*)$. Otherwise,

$$w_1(S) > w(j^*) \cdot 2 \cdot \frac{B/2 - d_{j^*}}{B}$$
$$\geq w(j^*) \cdot 2 \cdot \frac{B/2 - 2\delta B}{B}$$
$$= w(j^*) \cdot (1 - 4\delta) .$$

On the other hand, for a feasible SAP solution T we have that

$$w_1(T) = w_1(T(e^*)) \leq w(j^*) + w(j^*) \cdot 2 \cdot 2B/B = 5w(j^*),$$

due to Observation 1. Therefore $w(S)$ is $\frac{5}{1-4\delta}$-approximate with respect to J and w_1. □

The following lemma replaces Lemma 15.

LEMMA 20. *There exists a polynomial time algorithm such that for every constant $\varepsilon > 0$, there exists a constant $\delta > 0$, such that the algorithm computes $\frac{1}{2}B$-packable $(5+\varepsilon)$-approximate solutions for δ-small SAP instances in which $b(j) \in [B, 2B]$, for every $j \in J$.*

PROOF. First, execute Algorithm **Strip** to compute a $\frac{1}{2}B$-packable $\frac{5}{1-4\delta}$-approximate UFPP solution S. By Lemma 14, S can be transformed into a $\frac{1}{2}B$-packable SAP solution (S', h') such that $w(S') \geq (1 - 4\delta)w(S)$ in polynomial time. It follows that

$$w(S') \geq \frac{(1-4\delta)^2}{5} \cdot \text{OPT}_{\text{SAP}}(J) \geq \frac{1-8\delta}{5} \cdot \text{OPT}_{\text{SAP}}(J) .$$

The lemma follows by setting δ such that $\delta < \delta_0$ and $\frac{5}{1-8\delta} \leq 5 + \varepsilon$. □

Work-Efficient Matrix Inversion in Polylogarithmic Time

Peter Sanders
Institute for Theoretical
Informatics
Karlsruhe Institute of
Technology
Karlsruhe, Germany
sanders@kit.edu

Jochen Speck
Institute for Theoretical
Informatics
Karlsruhe Institute of
Technology
Karlsruhe, Germany
speck@kit.edu

Raoul Steffen
Institute for Theoretical
Informatics
Karlsruhe Institute of
Technology
Karlsruhe, Germany

ABSTRACT

We present an algorithm for matrix inversion that combines the practical requirement of an optimal number of arithmetic operations and the theoretical goal of a polylogarithmic critical path length. The algorithm reduces inversion to matrix multiplication. It uses Strassen's recursion scheme but on the critical path, it breaks the recursion early switching to an asymptotically inefficient yet fast use of Newton's method. We also show that the algorithm is numerically stable. Overall, we get a candidate for a massively parallel algorithm that scales to exascale systems even on relatively small inputs. Preliminary experiments on multicore machines give the surprising result that even on such moderately parallel machines the algorithm outperforms Intel's Math Kernel Library and that Strassen's algorithm seems to be numerically more stable than one might expect.

Categories and Subject Descriptors

F.2.1 [Numerical Algorithms and Problems]: Computations on matrices

G.1.0 [Numerical Analysis]: Parallel algorithms

G.1.3 [Numerical Linear Algebra]:Matrix Inversion

Keywords: parallel algorithms; polylogarithmic time; linear algebra; matrix inversion; numerics; Strassen's inversion algorithm; Newton approximation;

1. INTRODUCTION

Besides matrix multiplication, matrix inversion is perhaps the most fundamental operation in linear algebra. Hence, there has been intensive research on parallel matrix inversion and related operations. Indeed, the most widely used benchmark for supercomputers – LINPACK, basically measures the performance of LU decomposition which is often used to replace inversion. We stick to inversion here since it is simpler and more fundamental. More generally speaking, some of the observations made here may also be relevant for making parallel computations more scalable for applications completely unrelated to linear algebra.

Our starting point was the puzzling observation that there is a significant gap between theoretical and practical research on parallel matrix inversion. Theoretical work beginning already in the

1970s has focused on the question whether matrix inversion can be done in polylogarithmic time on a PRAM. Although the answer is positive [8, 18–20], this had no impact on practical implementations since all these algorithms are inefficient – they perform at least a logarithmic factor more work than the sequential algorithm. In contrast, practical algorithms perform the same amount of work up to a lower order term or at most invest a small constant factor more work. However, all these algorithms have a critical path length of $\Omega(n)$, i.e., even with an arbitrary number of processing elements we cannot get faster than this bound. In the past, this limitation seemed rather academic since parallel machines had a fairly small number of processors. However, with the advent of petascale machines and intensive research on exascale machines, this situation has changed. Since clock frequencies stagnate and since more and more parallelism is needed to hide memory access latencies, the amount of parallelism needed in the largest machines is exploding – we may be looking at 10^{10} logical threads for the largest machines of the near future [13, page 198]. With $\Omega(n)$-algorithms, such systems will only work efficiently for huge inputs – thus severely limiting the range of possible applications.

Already now, the fastest machine in the LINPACK benchmark needs petabytes of memory for achieving its maximum performance and needs more than 23 hours to complete the benchmark at $n = N_{\max}$.[1] Note that in November 1995 the same experiment took less than 5 min.[2] Since typically, a not much smaller input is required to achieve half the peak performance ($n = N_{1/2}$), this might indicate that it gets more and more difficult to use the largest supercomputers for applications that need user interactions.

Reconsidering the old virtue of polylogarithmic execution time might therefore become practically relevant. The subject of this paper is to show that this is at least true for matrix inversion. After introducing basic results and notation in Section 2, we introduce our algorithm NeSt (**Ne**wton-**St**rassen inversion) in Section 3. The algorithm uses Strassen's recursion scheme [24] which expresses inversion in terms of matrix multiplication and smaller matrix inversions. Using the scheme all the way down to constant size matrices would lead to yet another algorithm with critical path length of $\Omega(n)$. Therefore, we switch to Pan's adaptation of Newton's algorithm [18, 19] at a recursion depth of $O(\log \log n)$. At this level of recursion, the work inherent in the inversions becomes a sufficiently small lower order term to allow for such a fast yet inefficient algorithm. Overall, NeSt has a polylogarithmic critical path length and requires at most a small constant factor times the work of any other inversion algorithm. Additionally, in section 3.5, we present

---

[1] www.top500.org, June 2012: $N_{\max} = 12\,681\,215$, $R_{\max} = 16.3$ petaFLOPS.

[2] $N_{\max} = 42\,000$, $R_{\max} = 170.4$ gigaFLOPS.

a variant of NeSt for which we can prove numerical stability in a certain sense.

Section 4 reports on a multicore implementation whose original purpose was to demonstrate that the algorithm is practical both with respect to efficiency and numerical stability. Surprisingly, it turned out that even on such small scale machines NeSt outperforms Intel's Math Kernel Library, i.e., a library that is supposed to supply highly tuned implementations. The errors produced by NeSt compare with those of the MKL algorithm. The conclusion (Section 5) summarizes results and discusses future research direction.

More Related Work

This paper draws on the result of Raoul Steffen's diploma thesis [23].

Practical work in parallel linear algebra including matrix inversion focuses on blocked versions[3] of sequential algorithms, e.g., Gaussian elimination and similar algorithms for inversion, LU decomposition and Cholesky decomposition (e.g. [3]). By interpreting the block operations as tasks in a directed acyclic graph, flexible scheduling techniques can be applied to achieve good parallelization [14,22]. These techniques are being used in widely used libraries such as ATLAS [16], LAPACK [17], and MKL [7].

Bailey and Ferguson [1] propose to use Newton iteration to postprocess the result of Strassen's algorithm in order to improve numerical stability. Our main result uses Newton iterations very differently and for a different purpose – run Newton on small subinstances to increase parallelism. In Section 3.5 we also show that a variant of their algorithm is numerically stable under certain assumptions. The experiments in [1] show that Strassen's inversion with his multiplication algorithm may indeed be unstable on general matrices. However our experiments indicate that this problem may not apply to the inversion alone on symmetric positive definite matrices even when they have fairly large condition number.

2. PRELIMINARIES

When not otherwise mentioned, we deal with $n \times n$ matrices. While the algorithms work with arbitrary n without special handling, for the analysis we assume n to be a power of two. For an algorithm A, $W_A(n)$ denotes the work done by A measured as number of floating point operations performed and T_A denotes its critical path length, i.e., the longest path through the computation DAG (the nodes are the arithmetical operations and the edges denote the data flow). Since the computations are very regular, this will be asymptotically the same as the execution time on sufficiently powerful models of parallel computation such as a PRAM. The subscript M stands for matrix multiplication, S for Strassen's matrix inversion algorithm, N for matrix inversion by Newton approximation, and O for our algorithm NeSt. We call cond $M = \|M\| \cdot \|M^{-1}\|$ the *condition* of M. All norms in this paper are 2-norms, i.e.:

$$\|\mathbf{x}\| = \sqrt{x_1^2 + .. + x_n^2} \qquad \|M\| = \max_{\|\mathbf{x}\|=1} \|M\mathbf{x}\| \qquad (1)$$

We focus on inversion of symmetric positive definite inputs since these are directly relevant for many applications [12, p.260] and since we can reduce to this case as follows: For any non-singular matrix $\bar{M}$, $M = \bar{M}^T \bar{M}$ is always symmetric positive definite and we can invert $\bar{M}$ [6] using

$$\bar{M}^{-1} = (\bar{M}^T \bar{M})^{-1} \bar{M}^T = M^{-1} \bar{M}^T . \qquad (2)$$

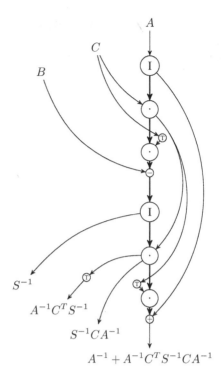

Figure 1: DAG of Strassen's matrix inversion algorithm. The operations **I** and **T** stand for recursive inversion and for transposition, respectively.

The two additional matrix multiplications increase the required work by a constant factor depending on the work-complexity of the multiplication. Our algorithm can also directly be applied to "well-conditioned" nonsymmetric matrices. However this may fail in cases where a traditional algorithm needs pivoting. Since we are not aware of pivoting algorithms leading to polylogarithmic time, the above symmetrization approach seems without an alternative here.

2.1 Matrix Multiplication

Matrix multiplication needs between $2n^3$ operations for the naive approach and $O(n^\beta)$ for more sophisticated algorithms with the best known result having $\beta = 2.3727$ [25]. Some of these algorithms can be expressed recursively using independent subproblems leading to a critical path length of $T_M = O(\log n)$.[4] For the analysis we assume $W_M(n) \sim n^\beta$ and $\beta \geq 2$.

Often we use matrix multiplication and already know that the result will be symmetric. We call this case *symmetric multiplication*. Algorithms can take advantage of symmetric multiplication. For example, standard multiplication can simply calculate the lower triangle and then transpose the result to get the full matrix, saving almost half of the effort. $W_M^{symm}(n) \leq W_M(n)$ shall denote the work necessary for symmetric multiplication and $\bar{W}_M(n) = \frac{1}{2}(W_M(n) + W_M^{symm}(n))$ the average of symmetric and full multiplication.

NeSt is based on two other algorithms for matrix inversion, Strassen's algorithm and Newton Approximation:

---

[3]Blocked algorithms are often also called "tiled".

[4]Usually, parallelization is not discussed in papers on fast matrix multiplication so that we are not sure whether this applies to all these algorithms.

2.2 Strassen's Inversion Algorithm

Strassen's matrix inversion algorithm recursively breaks down the inversion into smaller inversions and matrix multiplications by the following formula that can be viewed as applying Gaussian elimination to a 2×2 matrix of matrices[5] [24]:

$$M = \begin{pmatrix} A & C^T \\ C & B \end{pmatrix} \text{ where } A \text{ is an } n' \times n' \text{ matrix.}$$

$$M^{-1} = \begin{pmatrix} A^{-1} + A^{-1}C^T S^{-1} C A^{-1} & -A^{-1}C^T S^{-1} \\ -S^{-1}CA^{-1} & S^{-1} \end{pmatrix}$$

$$\text{with } S = B - CA^{-1}C^T$$

Usually, the size n' of A is set to $\frac{n}{2}$, but it can be chosen arbitrarily for the formula to work. This allows to process odd n without adaptations. Indeed, the special case with $n' = 1$ is Gaussian elimination.

Strassen's inversion algorithm is not to be confused with his *matrix multiplication* algorithm, which appeared in the same paper. The variant for symmetric matrices requires four multiplications and two recursive inversions, all of size $\frac{n}{2}$, see Fig. 1. Since all the key operations of Strassen's algorithm have to be executed serially, we get the following recurrence for the critical path length:

$$T_S(n) \geq 4T_M(n/2) + 2T_S(n/2)$$

Solving this recurrence yields

$$T_S(n) = \Omega(n).$$

With respect to work, Strassen's algorithm and an observation that matrix inversion can also emulate matrix multiplication [6] show that

$$W_S(n) = \Theta(W_M(n))$$

and that

$$\Theta(W_{M'}(n)) = \Theta(W_I(n)) \tag{3}$$

for any work-optimal multiplication and inversion algorithms M' and I. Refer to Section 3 for an analysis of a generalized algorithm that also yields constant factors.

2.3 Newton Approximation

Newton approximation can be used to invert matrices. Following the formula

$$X_{i+1} = (2I - X_i M)X_i$$

X_i converges quadratically towards the inverse of M. Pan and Reif found and improved a suitable initial approximation that is easy to compute [18, 19]. For symmetric positive definite matrices they suggest:

$$X_0 = tI \quad \text{with } t = \frac{1}{\|M\|_\infty} = 1 \Big/ \max_i \sum_j |m_{ij}| \tag{4}$$

They showed that, when the condition of the input matrix is polynomial in n, $\mathrm{O}(\log n)$ iterations suffice to reach a fixed error bound. Therefore, with a multiplication subroutine with logarithmic critical path length, Newton approximation has critical path length

$$T_N(n) = \mathrm{O}(\log^2 n).$$

Since each of the iterations needs as much work as an inversion, by Equation (3), Newton approximation has an additional $\log n$ factor on the work-complexity compared to a work-optimal algorithm.

[5]We use the variant for symmetric M.

3. THE ALGORITHM

In this section we define the combined algorithm NeSt. It takes a parameter $h \in \{0, .., \log n\}$ for the recursion depth. Afterwards, we present a theoretical analysis of NeSt's work- and time-complexity. Finally, we present a way to bound the forward error in Strassen's inversion algorithm.

3.1 Algorithm NeSt

To invert a matrix M, perform h levels of Strassen's inversion algorithm. For the remaining recursive inversions use Newton approximation.

3.2 Work-Complexity

Newton approximation requires $\mathrm{O}(\log n)$ iterations, each of which does two multiplications of which one is symmetric. We neglect the cheap initialization step and assume

$$W_N(n) = \alpha \log n \bar{W}_M(n)$$

where α will depend on the condition of the input.

Strassen's inversion algorithm requires two recursive inversions and four multiplications of which two are symmetric. We assume that transpositions and additions are done together with the multiplications at negligible cost. Using

$$W_S(n) = 2\left(W_S\left(\frac{n}{2}\right) + 2\bar{W}_M\left(\frac{n}{2}\right)\right)$$

we get

$$W_O(n,h) = \begin{cases} 2\left(W_O\left(\frac{n}{2}, h-1\right) + 2\bar{W}_M\left(\frac{n}{2}\right)\right) & \text{if } h > 0 \\ W_N(n) & \text{if } h = 0 \end{cases}$$

$$= \underbrace{2^h W_N\left(\frac{n}{2^h}\right)}_{g} + \underbrace{\sum_{i=1}^{h} 2^i \cdot 2\bar{W}_M\left(\frac{n}{2^i}\right)}_{f}$$

Since $\bar{W}_M(n) \sim n^\beta$, we have $\bar{W}_M(n/2^i) = \bar{W}_M(n)/2^{i\beta}$. This yields

$$f = 2\bar{W}_M(n)\sum_{i=1}^{h}\frac{2^i}{2^{i\beta}} = 2\bar{W}_M(n)\sum_{i=1}^{h} 2^{i(1-\beta)}$$

$$\leq \frac{4}{2^\beta - 2}\bar{W}_M(n) \tag{5}$$

using the geometric series. For g we get

$$g = 2^h \frac{\alpha(\log n - \log 2^h)}{2^{h\beta}}\bar{W}_M(n) \leq \frac{\alpha \log n}{2^{h(\beta-1)}}\bar{W}_M(n)$$

Overall this is

$$W_O(n,h) \leq \left(\underbrace{\frac{4}{2^\beta - 2}}_{(6a)} + \underbrace{\frac{\alpha \log n}{2^{h(\beta-1)}}}_{(6b)}\right)\bar{W}_M(n) \tag{6}$$

Note that for not too small h, inequality (5) is rather sharp. Hence, for small h (6a) is overestimated, but then (6b) dominates the sum anyway.

3.3 Time-Complexity

All $\alpha \log n$ multiplications done by Newton approximation have do be done one after another. We neglect the cheap initialization step that can be done in time $\mathrm{O}(\log n)$. Thus

$$T_N(n) = \alpha \log n T_M(n).$$

Strassen's inversion algorithm requires both recursive inversions and all four multiplications to be done one after another. Thus

$$T_S(n) = 2\left(T_S\left(\frac{n}{2}\right) + 2T_M\left(\frac{n}{2}\right)\right) .$$

For NeSt we get

$$T_O(n,h) = \begin{cases} 2\left(T_O\left(\frac{n}{2}, h-1\right) + 2T_M\left(\frac{n}{2}\right)\right) & \text{if } h > 0 \\ T_N(n) & \text{if } h = 0 \end{cases}$$

$$= 2^h T_N\left(\frac{n}{2^h}\right) + \sum_{i=1}^{h} 2^i \cdot 2T_M\left(\frac{n}{2^i}\right)$$

$$\leq 2^h T_N(n) + \sum_{i=1}^{h} 2^i \cdot 2T_M(n)$$

$$\leq 2^h(\alpha \log n + 4)T_M(n) \tag{7}$$

3.4 Choosing Recursion Depth

Now we want to take a closer look at the complexities.

The factor in Equation (6) multiplied with $\bar{W}_M(n)$ has two summands. The first, (6a), does not depend on the recursion depth and accounts for the cost of Strassen's algorithm (or NeSt with $h = \log n$). It ranges from $(6a) = \frac{2}{3}$ for standard multiplication to $(6a) = 2$ for the theoretical limit of $\beta = 2$. The second summand, (6b), is the additional work due to the use of Newton approximation. The deeper the recursion (i.e. the larger h), the smaller it gets. In contrast, the factor 2^h on the critical path (7) grows with the recursion depth. At full recursion depth, it becomes n. As we see, h allows us to trade parallelizability for additional work. The two extremes correspond to pure Newton approximation and Strassen's inversion algorithm, respectively.

We now look for a choice of h which at the same time makes the work associated with Newton's method a lower order term and minimizes the asymptotic critical path length. This is the case when Equation (6b) becomes $o(1)$, i.e., $\log n / 2^{h(\beta-1)} = o(1)$ or

$$h = \frac{\log \log n}{\beta - 1} + \omega(1).$$

For simplicity, we set $h = \frac{(1+\epsilon) \log \log n}{\beta - 1}$ for some small constant ϵ. Plugging this into Equation 7 yields critical path length

$$2^{\frac{(1+\epsilon) \log \log n}{\beta - 1}} (\alpha \log n + 4)T_M(n) = O(\log^{\frac{\beta+\epsilon}{\beta-1}}(n)T_M(n))$$

These arguments imply our main theoretical result:

THEOREM 3.1. *NeSt with* $h = (1 + \epsilon)\frac{\log \log n}{\beta - 1}$ *is an inversion algorithm for symmetric positive definite matrices with*

$$W_O(n) = \left(\frac{4}{2^\beta - 2} + o(1)\right)\bar{W}_M(n)$$

and

$$T_O(n) = O(\log^{\frac{\beta+\epsilon}{\beta-1}}(n)T_M(n))$$

for any constant $\epsilon > 0$. $\square$

Using standard multiplication or some blocked version thereof where $\bar{W}_M(n) \approx \frac{3}{2}n^3$ and $T_M(n) = O(\log n)$ this yields

$$W_O(n) = \left(\frac{2}{3} + o(1)\right)\frac{3}{2}n^3 = (1 + o(1))n^3$$

and

$$T_O(n) = O(\log^{2.5+\epsilon} n)$$

for any $\epsilon > 0$. For reference, this is about the same amount of arithmetic operations as by conventional inversion codes for symmetric matrices such as the one used in Intel's MKL library. For an "ultimate" matrix multiplication algorithm with $\beta = 2$ and $T_M = O(\log n)$ we get $T_O(n) = O(\log^{3+\epsilon} n)$.

3.5 Numerical Stability

Numerical stability is a main concern when using alternative inversion methods, including Strassen's algorithm. In the following we present a first order error analysis for a variant of NeSt – NeStS which adapts an idea proposed by Bailey and Ferguson to NeSt [1]: On each level of recursion, the result returned by Strassen's formula is postprocessed by one Newton iteration. The two additional multiplications for each recursive call do asymptotically neither cost more nor take longer than the inversion, thus increasing the work and running time only by a constant factor.

For this analysis we adapt the approach of error analysis from [5, 10] to support Newton iterations. Consider a matrix A and a vector $\bar{\mathbf{x}}$ with defective representation $\mathbf{x} = \bar{\mathbf{x}} + \delta_{\mathbf{x}}$ and absolute error $\delta(\mathbf{x}) = \|\delta_{\mathbf{x}}\|$. Then the error of $A\mathbf{x}$ is

$$\delta(A\mathbf{x}) = \|A\bar{\mathbf{x}} - A\mathbf{x}\| \leq \|A\| \cdot \delta(\mathbf{x}) .$$

We see, that the error is *magnified* at most by the norm of A. For matrices, the same holds for the operator norm (1):

$$B = \bar{B} + \delta_B \qquad \delta(B) = \|\delta_B\|$$

$$\delta(AB) = \|A\bar{B} - AB\| \leq \|A\| \cdot \delta(B)$$

Strassen's algorithm uses multiple subsequent matrix multiplications. The concern is, that the error of underlying recursive inversions is magnified by each level of recursion, resulting in useless data when the outermost recursion finally returns. However for NeStS we can show, that the single Newton iteration suffices to decrease the so magnified error in every recursion. Thereby, it returns below a fixed bound at the end of every (recursive) call including the initial outermost one. Still, this is a rather theoretical evaluation and the proven stability is far from what can be found in practical experiments. Unfortunately, no better technique that gives results close to practical observations seems to be known.

THEOREM 3.2. *If the error of the base inversions is at most* $\xi = p(\kappa)^{-2}(\kappa\Lambda)^{-1}$ *with* $p(x) = 2 + 4x + 4x^2 + 2x^3 + x^4$, $\kappa = \text{cond } M$ *and* $\Lambda = \|M\|$, *then the error of NeStS is at most* ξ.

For the proof see appendix B.

4. EXPERIMENTS

The goal of our experiments was to verify the practical usability of NeSt concerning two criteria. First, the work should not exceed that of existing algorithms by too much. Experiments help to test for effects that are not covered by the theoretical analysis, e.g. caching. Also, we examine the runtime on different numbers of cores to test for scalability. Second, the numerical errors must be small enough for the results to be useful. We concentrate on a shared memory implementation that yields quite good and predictable results. In Appendix A we report on first results of a distributed memory implementation on a cluster.

4.1 Test Setup

For the main running time tests we used a 32-core NUMA machine with four Intel Xeon X7560 processors with eight cores each, running at 2.266 GHz. Each core can finish two FMAC-operations (i.e. multiplication and addition) in one step, so the theoretical limit

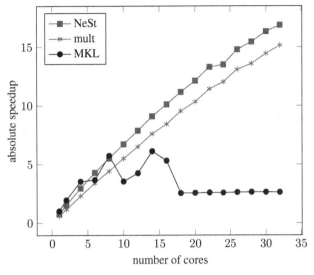
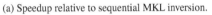

(a) Speedup relative to sequential MKL inversion.

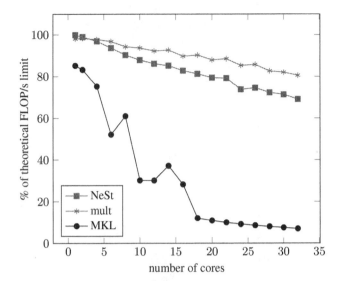

(b) Percentage of the theoretical FLOP/s limit reached. The theoretical limit of the computer is 9.064 GFLOP/s per core.

Figure 2: Results from timing different inversion methods and multiplication. Matrix size is 2^{14}.

on the floating point operations is 9.064 GFLOP/s per core. Our code is written in C++ and we use the GNU compiler collection (gcc) version 4.4.3 with maximum optimization (-O3) and static linking. To do tests on fewer cores we instructed the OpenMP library responsible for parallelization to use only the desired subset of cores. The subset was chosen to be as close together as possible, i.e. first activate all cores on one socket.

Because the availability of the large machine was limited, the numeric and recursion depth experiments were run on an 8-core UMA machine with two Intel Xeon 5345.

Tests with $n < 2^{13}$ have been repeated 30 times, tests with $n \geq 2^{13}$ three times. The plots show the medians. Because the individual results are so close together, the standard deviations would not be readable in the plot. All tests use double precision (64-bit) floating point arithmetics. To quantify the numerical error of a supposed inverse $\tilde{M}$ we do not use the very expensive to compute operator norm (1), but instead compute the error as

$$\text{error}(\tilde{M}) = \max_{ij} |r_{ij}| \text{ with } (r_{ij}) = I - \tilde{M}M . \quad (8)$$

We base our experiments on the Intel Math Kernel Library (MKL), a highly optimized vendor library advertised for use with our machines. We use version 10.3 Update 6 which came as part of Intel Composer XE 2011. The linked OpenMP library is also part of this package. We use MKL both for its matrix multiplication routine and to compare to its inversion code. We call the MKL routines that specifically invert symmetric positive definite matrices (dpotrf/dpotri) and refer to them as *MKL inversion* from here on.

Parallelization and low level tuning mainly comes from the MKL multiplication subroutines. Most of the additions and transpositions are done on-the-fly by these multiplication subroutines as defined in the BLAS standard. We did implement the possibility to parallelize addition, transposition, initialisation, and the evaluation of the error measure. However, later tuning showed that this was only beneficial for very large matrices and was not used for smaller calls for that reason. Since it is not supported by the BLAS interface of the MKL, we do not exploit symmetric multiplication. We use recursion depth $h = \lceil \log \log n \rceil$. Our implementation of New-

ton approximation does not use a precalculated number of iterations, but calculates the remaining error (according to Equation (8)) in each step. Normally the error should be squared in every iteration, i.e. $e_{new} = e_{old}^2$. When the border of representability is reached, this no longer happens and the iterations should stop. Our implementation detects this by comparing if $e_{new} > e_{old}^{1.2}$.

In order to generate symmetric positive definite matrices M with tunable condition, we exploit that they can be written as

$$M = QDQ^T$$

where Q is an orthogonal matrix and D is a diagonal matrix. D holds the eigenvalues of M which determine the condition. In order to generate "interesting" instances with a bound κ on the condition, we choose the eigenvalues as 2^X with X uniformly distributed in $[-\frac{1}{2} \log \kappa, \frac{1}{2} \log \kappa]$. This exponential distribution is chosen since the numerical difficulty is driven by the ratios between eigenvalues and not by their difference. We choose $\kappa = 2^{10}$ where not stated otherwise. The orthogonal matrix Q is selected in some sense uniformly by first filling it with n-dimensional vectors pointing in uniformly distributed directions. This is achieved by using the normal distribution for each coordinate value [15]. Q is then orthogonalized using MKL's LAPACK functions geqrf and orgqr.

4.2 Results

The first experiment (Fig. 2a) examines how the running time improves if we use MKL inversion or NeSt on one or multiple cores compared to MKL on a single core. The running times on a single core (MKL: 569.4sec., NeSt: 747.8sec., multiplication: 989.9sec.) show that the constant factor of NeSt in practice is only 1.31 times as high as that of the MKL implementation. MKL's performance breaks down, as soon as it is confronted with more than one processor socket (8 cores). This indicates the high dependence of the algorithm on fast inter-core communication. NeSt, on the other hand, scales equally well on one socket but continues this trend on more cores.

The second experiment (Fig. 2b) examines how well the algorithms make use of the available floating point units. It is actually based on the same timings as the experiment before, but in-

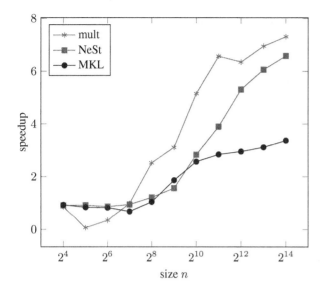

Figure 3: Speedup of inversion methods and multiplication with 8 cores compared to the same algorithm on 1 core.

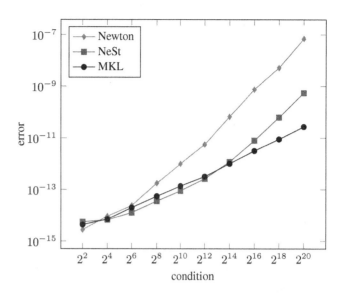

Figure 4: Error (by Equation (8)) of different inversion methods by matrix condition for matrices of size 2^{13}.

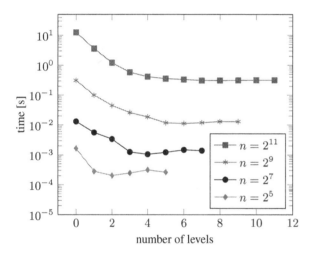

Figure 5: Running time of NeSt on 8 cores for different recursion depths (0 = pure Newton, 3 = NeSt for $n \leq 2^8$, 4 = NeSt for $n > 2^8$, max.= pure Strassen) and matrix sizes.

corporates the count of floating point instructions of the respective algorithm. The operation counts for NeSt and multiplication are computed with formulas that neglect at most linear terms. The operation count for the MKL inversion is taken from the MKL manual [7], where it is given as "approximately" n^3. Again, the performance of the MKL inversion breaks down at more than one socket, and even before it drops rather rapidly, while the performance of NeSt and multiplication degrades only slowly.

The next experiment (Fig. 3) investigates scalability as a function of input size. MKL's inversion routine starts to see some speedups from $n = 2^9$ to $n = 2^{10}$ but cannot really profit from larger inputs. This is an indication that it uses very fine grained parallelism which may be a good idea for few processors and small inputs but does not exploit the coarse grained parallelism available in large inputs. MKL's multiplication routine shows speedup from $n = 2^8$ on and then quickly gains for larger n. NeSt lags behind MKL's multiplication routine by a factor of two to four in the matrix dimension

since it is based on matrix multiplications of size $n/2$ to $n/8$, but profits from the multiplications' continued gain.

Now we want to take a look at the numerical errors (Fig. 4) for different matrix conditions. Surprisingly, Newtons method produces the largest errors. For matrices of not very high condition, NeSt and the MKL inversion produce about the same error, confirming that NeSt is indeed a suitable choice. Only for high conditions above 2^{14} we get larger errors from NeSt.

With the last experiment (Fig. 5), we want to examine the effect of different recursion depths on the running time. For small input sizes ($n \leq 2^7$) we can see a local minimum around a recursion depth of three, confirming that indeed it makes sense to break the recursion early and switch to an inefficient algorithm in order to use the available parallelism. We expect that on large scale machines the same applies for realistic input sizes.

5. CONCLUSION

With NeSt we created an algorithm for matrix inversion that retains the work-efficiency of Strassen's inversion algorithm while incorporating the polylog time-complexity of Newton approximation. Reducing the input size for Newton approximation not only compensates for its $\log n$ factor on the work complexity, it even makes it a lower order term. Our theoretical analysis proves low constant factors on the work-complexity of NeSt. Experiments confirm that NeSt has low overheads even for sequential execution and that it is easy to parallelize. Surprisingly it outperforms a vendor library even on multicore machines. Another surprise is that NeSt shows better numerical stability on symmetric positive definite matrices than expected from theory.

5.1 Future Work

The next step from the practical side are experiments with a massively parallel distributed memory implementation of NeSt, which we have recently started working on (see app. A). This should in principle be easy since we basically need a good implementation of matrix multiplication and there has been significant previous work on this, e.g. [2, 21].

On the theoretical side, we could look for faster efficient inversion algorithms and for efficient polylogarithmic time algorithms for other linear algebra problems such as LU decomposition, Cholesky decomposition and solving linear systems. Reif gives recursive algorithms for LU and Cholesky decompositions [20] yet does not discuss work efficiency.

With respect to numerical stability it would be interesting to better understand why (or when) Strassen's algorithm is stable for symmetric positive definite matrices. One approach might be to build on the following observations: Partial pivoting does nothing on symmetric positive definite matrices [11] and it is considered to be stable in practice. Furthermore, blocked versions of Gaussian elimination have been shown to be not significantly more unstable than standard ones [12] and Strassen's inversion algorithm can be viewed as blocked Gaussian elimination with maximal block size.

Acknowledgment.

This work was partly supported by the German Research Foundation (DFG) as part of the Transregional Collaborative Research Center "Invasive Computing" (SFB/TR 89).

6. REFERENCES

[1] D. H. Bailey and H. R. P. Ferguson. A Strassen-Newton algorithm for high-speed parallelizable matrix inversion. In *Proc. 1988 ACM/IEEE conference on Supercomputing*, Supercomputing '88, pages 419–424, Los Alamitos, CA, USA, 1988. IEEE Computer Society Press.

[2] Grey Ballard, James Demmel, Olga Holtz, Benjamin Lipshitz, and Oded Schwartz. Communication-optimal parallel algorithm for strassen's matrix multiplication. In *24th ACM Symposium on Parallelism in Algorithms and Architectures*, pages 193–204, New York, NY, USA, 2012. ACM.

[3] Alfredo Buttari, Julien Langou, Jakub Kurzak, and Jack Dongarra. A class of parallel tiled linear algebra algorithms for multicore architectures. *Parallel Computing*, 35(1):38 – 53, 2009.

[4] Lynn E. Cannon. *A Cellular Computer to Implement the Kalman Filter Algorithm*. PhD thesis, Montana State University, Bozeman, MN, 1969.

[5] B. Codenotti, M. Leoncini, and F. P. Preparata. The role of arithmetic in fast parallel matrix inversion. *Algorithmica*, 30:685–707, 2001. 10.1007/s00453-001-0033-7.

[6] Thomas H. Cormen, Clifford Stein, Ronald L. Rivest, and Charles E. Leiserson. *Introduction to Algorithms*. McGraw-Hill Higher Education, 2nd edition, 2001.

[7] Intel Corporation. Intel math kernel library reference manual, 2011. Document Number 630813-043US.

[8] L. Csanky. Fast parallel matrix inversion algorithms. *SIAM Journal on Computing*, 5(4):618–623, 1976.

[9] Eliezer Dekel, David Nassimi, and Sartaj Sahni. Parallel matrix and graph algorithms. *SIAM Journal on computing*, 10(4):657–675, 1981.

[10] James Demmel, Ioana Dumitriu, and Olga Holtz. Fast linear algebra is stable. *Numerische Mathematik*, 108:59–91, 2007. 10.1007/s00211-007-0114-x.

[11] Gene H. Golub and Charles F. Van Loan. *Matrix Computations*. Johns Hopkins University Press, Baltimore, MD, USA, 3rd edition, 1996.

[12] Nicholas J. Higham. *Accuracy and Stability of Numerical Algorithms*. Society for Industrial and Applied Mathematics, Philadelphia, PA, USA, 2nd edition, 2002.

[13] P. Kogge, K. Bergman, S. Borkar, D. Campbell, W. Carson, W. Dally, M. Denneau, P. Franzon, W. Harrod, K. Hill, et al. Exascale computing study: Technology challenges in achieving exascale systems. Technical report, DARPA, September 2008.

[14] Jakub Kurzak, Hatem Ltaief, Jack Dongarra, and Rosa M. Badia. Scheduling dense linear algebra operations on multicore processors. *Concurrency and Computation: Practice and Experience*, 22(1):15–44, 2010.

[15] Mervin E. Muller. A note on a method for generating points uniformly on n-dimensional spheres. *Commun. ACM*, 2(4):19–20, April 1959.

[16] Netlib. Automatically Tuned Linear Algebra Software.

[17] Netlib. Linear Algebra PACKage.

[18] Victor Pan and John Reif. Efficient parallel solution of linear systems. In *Proc. 17th Annual ACM Symposium on Theory of Computing*, STOC '85, pages 143–152, New York, NY, USA, 1985. ACM.

[19] Victor Pan and John Reif. Fast and efficient parallel solution of dense linear systems. *Computers & Mathematics with Applications*, 17(11):1481 – 1491, 1989.

[20] John H. Reif. $O(\log^2 n)$ time efficient parallel factorization of dense, sparse separable, and banded matrices. In *Proc. 6th Annual ACM Symposium on Parallel Algorithms and Architectures*, SPAA '94, pages 278–289, New York, NY, USA, 1994. ACM.

[21] Edgar Solomonik and James Demmel. Communication-optimal parallel 2.5d matrix multiplication and lu factorization algorithms. *Euro-Par 2011 Parallel Processing*, pages 90–109, 2011.

[22] Fengguang Song, Asim YarKhan, and Jack Dongarra. Dynamic task scheduling for linear algebra algorithms on distributed-memory multicore systems. In *Proc. Conference on High Performance Computing Networking, Storage and Analysis*, SC '09, pages 19:1–19:11, New York, NY, USA, 2009. ACM.

[23] Raoul Steffen. Exascale ready work-optimal matrix inversion. Diploma thesis, Karlsruhe Institute of Technology, Karlsruhe, Germany, Aug 2012.

[24] Volker Strassen. Gaussian elimination is not optimal. *Numerische Mathematik*, 13:354–356, 1969. 10.1007/BF02165411.

[25] Virginia Vassilevska Williams. Multiplying matrices faster than Coppersmith-Winograd. In *Proc. 44th Symposium on Theory of Computing*, STOC '12, pages 887–898, New York, NY, USA, 2012. ACM.

APPENDIX

A. DISTRIBUTED MEMORY IMPLEMENTATION

We have access to a 400 node cluster at our computing center (IC2) where each node has two Intel Xeon E5-2670 8-core processors clocked at 2.6 GHz and 64 GB of main memory. The interconnection network is InfiniBand 4x QDR.

The good news is that we "only" need a distributed memory matrix multiplication algorithm to implement our inversion. However, we did not find a highly tuned ready-to-use implementation and thus tried to implement one ourselves.

We first considered a memory aware generalization of the DNS algorithm [9, 21] since this asymptotically yields logarithmic critical path length at low communication volume. However, on our moderately sized machine the constant factors involved in the broad-

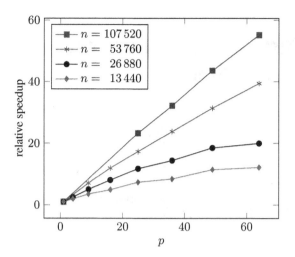

Figure 6: Speedup of NeSt with recursion depth $h = 4$ when run on p 16-core nodes relative to NeSt on a single 16-core node.

cast and reduction operations of this algorithm are prohibitive compared to the much simpler Cannon algorithm [4]. This algorithm is based on splitting the matrices into pieces of size $n/\sqrt{p} \times n/\sqrt{p}$ using only cyclic shift communication in $\sqrt{p}$ steps. Our implementation uses one MPI process per node and calls the MKL locally using all 16 cores. By using asynchronous send-receive operations our code should in principle be able to overlap calculation and communication.

Figure 6 shows the resulting (relative) speedup for our inversion algorithm (for larger inputs not fitting into a single node, the underlying single node execution times are extrapolated). As to be expected, the results are very good for large inputs. However, for those inputs, also algorithms with critical path length n could work well. For smaller inputs, the scalability is quite limited. Closer consideration shows that the node-local matrix multiplications are (reproducibly) very slow for certain input sizes although they are fast for larger and smaller inputs. Hence, using a more robust library and further tuning there is hope that one can get good speedups also for siginificantly smaller inputs.

B. PROOF OF THEOREM 3.2

The basic inequalities are as follows. If X, Y and Z are matrices of which X and Y carry errors $\delta(X)$, $\delta(Y)$, then upon multiplication the error is magnified at most by the norm of the other matrix:

$$\delta(XZ) \le \delta(X) \cdot \|Z\|$$
$$\delta(XY) \le \delta(X) \cdot \|Y\| + \delta(Y) \cdot \|X\|$$

Upon addition, the error is added, too:

$$\delta(X + Y) \le \delta(X) + \delta(Y)$$

The norm of a submatrix X' of X is bounded by the norm of its supermatrix:

$$\|X'\| \le \|X\|$$

The error of a partitioned matrix $U = \left(\begin{smallmatrix} V & W \\ X & Y \end{smallmatrix} \right)$ is bounded by the sum of errors of its partitions:

$$\delta(U) \le \delta(V) + \delta(W) + \delta(X) + \delta(Y)$$

PROOF. by induction over the recursion depth. It suffices to show, that the error bound holds for the output of one level of NeStS. The following pseudocode defines the variable names.

$$
\begin{aligned}
\text{input: } M &= \begin{pmatrix} A & C^T \\ C & B \end{pmatrix} \\
\tilde{A} &= \text{Inv}(A) \\
C\tilde{A} &= C \cdot \tilde{A} \\
S &= B - C\tilde{A} \cdot C^T \\
\tilde{S} &= \text{Inv}(S) \\
P &= -\tilde{S} \cdot C\tilde{A} \\
R &= \tilde{A} - (C\tilde{A})^T \cdot P \\
M' &= \begin{pmatrix} R & P^T \\ P & \tilde{S} \end{pmatrix} \\
\tilde{M} &= (2I - M'M)M' \\
\text{output: } \tilde{M} &
\end{aligned}
$$

Let
$$\chi_X = \|\tilde{X} - X^{-1}\| \text{ for } X \in \{A, S, M\}$$
$\bar{f}$ be the exact (arithmetic) value of f
$$\delta(f) = \|f - \bar{f}\|$$
$$\Lambda = \|M\|$$
$$\lambda = \|M^{-1}\|$$
$$\kappa = \text{cond } M = \Lambda \lambda$$

Then
$$\delta(\tilde{A}) = \chi_A \le \xi$$
$$\delta(C\tilde{A}) \le \|C\|\delta(\tilde{A}) \le \xi\Lambda$$
$$\delta(S) \le \delta(C\tilde{A})\|C^T\| \le \xi\Lambda^2$$
$$
\begin{aligned}
\delta(\tilde{S}) &= \|\tilde{S} - \bar{S}^{-1}\| \\
&\le \|\tilde{S} - S^{-1}\| + \|S^{-1} - \bar{S}^{-1}\| \\
&\le \chi_S + \|S^{-1}\|\|\bar{S} - S\|\|\bar{S}^{-1}\| \\
&\le \xi + \delta(S)\lambda^2 \\
&\le \xi + \xi\kappa^2
\end{aligned}
$$
$$\delta(P) \le \delta(\tilde{S})\|C\tilde{A}\| + \|\tilde{S}\|\delta(C\tilde{A}) \le 2\xi\kappa + \xi\kappa^3$$
$$
\begin{aligned}
\delta(R) &\le \delta(\tilde{A}) + \delta(C\tilde{A})\|P\| + \|C\tilde{A}\|\delta(P) \\
&\le \xi + 3\xi\kappa^2 + \xi\kappa^4
\end{aligned}
$$
$$
\begin{aligned}
\delta(M') &\le \delta(R) + 2\delta(P) + \delta(\tilde{S}) \\
&\le 2\xi + 4\xi\kappa + 4\xi\kappa^2 + 2\xi\kappa^3 + \xi\kappa^4 \\
&= \xi \cdot p(\kappa)
\end{aligned}
$$

One level of Newton approximation squares the error:
$$\|I - \tilde{M}M\| \le \|I - M'M\|^2$$
$$\Rightarrow \quad \|M^{-1} - \tilde{M}\|\frac{1}{\|M^{-1}\|} \le \|M^{-1} - M'\|^2\|M\|^2$$
$$\Leftrightarrow \quad \|M^{-1} - \tilde{M}\| \le \|M^{-1} - M'\|^2\|M\|^2\|M^{-1}\|$$
$$= \|M^{-1} - M'\|^2\Lambda^2\lambda$$

Thus
$$
\begin{aligned}
\chi_M = \delta(\tilde{M}) &\le \delta(M')^2\kappa\Lambda \\
&\le \xi^2 \cdot p(\kappa)^2\kappa\Lambda \\
&\le \xi
\end{aligned}
$$

$\square$

221

Communication Optimal Parallel Multiplication
of Sparse Random Matrices*

Grey Ballard
UC Berkeley
ballard@eecs.berkeley.edu

Aydın Buluç
Lawrence Berkeley Natl. Lab.
abuluc@lbl.gov

James Demmel
UC Berkeley
demmel@cs.berkeley.edu

Laura Grigori
INRIA Paris - Rocquencourt
laura.grigori@inria.fr

Benjamin Lipshitz
UC Berkeley
lipshitz@cs.berkeley.edu

Oded Schwartz
UC Berkeley
odedsc@eecs.berkeley.edu

Sivan Toledo
Tel-Aviv University
stoledo@tau.ac.il

ABSTRACT

Parallel algorithms for sparse matrix-matrix multiplication typically spend most of their time on inter-processor communication rather than on computation, and hardware trends predict the relative cost of communication will only increase. Thus, sparse matrix multiplication algorithms must minimize communication costs in order to scale to large processor counts.

In this paper, we consider multiplying sparse matrices corresponding to Erdős-Rényi random graphs on distributed-memory parallel machines. We prove a new lower bound on the expected communication cost for a wide class of algorithms. Our analysis of existing algorithms shows that, while some are optimal for a limited range of matrix density and number of processors, none is optimal in general. We obtain two new parallel algorithms and prove that they match the expected communication cost lower bound, and hence they are optimal.

---

*We acknowledge funding from Microsoft (Award #024263) and Intel (Award #024894), and matching funding by U.C. Discovery (Award #DIG07-10227). Additional support comes from ParLab affiliates National Instruments, Nokia, NVIDIA, Oracle and Samsung, as well as MathWorks. Research is also supported by DOE grants DE-SC0004938, DE-SC0005136, DE-SC0003959, DE-SC0008700, and AC02-05CH11231, and DARPA grant HR0011-12-2-0016, and grant 1045/09 from the Israel Science Foundation (founded by the Israel Academy of Sciences and Humanities), and grant 2010231 from the US-Israel Bi-National Science Foundation. Authors from Lawrence Berkeley National Laboratory were supported by the DOE Office of Advanced Scientific Computing Research under contract number DE-AC02-05-CH-11231.

Categories and Subject Descriptors

F.2.1 [**Analysis of Algorithms and Problem Complexity**]: Numerical Algorithms and Problems—*Computations on matrices*

Keywords

communication-avoiding algorithms; communication-cost lower bounds; sparse matrix multiplication; random graphs

1. INTRODUCTION

Computing the product of two sparse matrices is a fundamental problem in combinatorial and scientific computing. Generalized sparse matrix-matrix multiplication is used as a subroutine in algebraic multigrid [5], graph clustering [29] and contraction [16], quantum chemistry [30], and parsing context-free languages [23]. Large-scale data and computation necessitates the use of parallel computing where communication costs quickly become the bottleneck. Existing parallel algorithms for multiplying sparse matrices perform reasonably well in practice for limited processor counts, but their scaling is impaired by increased communication costs at high concurrency.

Achieving scalability for parallel algorithms for sparse matrix problems is challenging because the computations tend not to have the surface to volume ratio (or potential for data re-use) that is common in dense matrix problems. Further, the performance of sparse algorithms is often highly dependent on the sparsity structure of the input matrices. We show in this paper that existing algorithms for sparse matrix-matrix multiplication are not optimal in their communication costs, and we obtain new algorithms which are communication optimal, communicating less than the previous algorithms and matching new lower bounds.

Our lower bounds require two important assumptions: (1) the sparsity of the input matrices is random, corresponding to Erdős-Rényi random graphs [14] (see Definition 2.1) and they are sparse enough that the output is also sparse, and (2) the algorithm is *sparsity-independent*; namely, the computation is partitioned to processors independent of the sparsity structure of the input matrices (see Definition 2.5). The second assumption applies to nearly all existing algorithms for general sparse matrix-matrix multiplication. While *a priori* knowledge of sparsity structure can certainly reduce communication for many important classes of inputs, we are not aware of any algorithms that dynamically determine and efficiently exploit the structure of general input matrices. In fact, a common technique of current library implementations is to randomly permute rows and columns of the input matrices in an attempt to destroy their structure and improve computational load balance [8, 9]. Because the input matrices are random, our analyses are in terms of expected communication costs.

We make three main contributions in this paper.

1. **We prove new communication lower bounds.** While there is a previous lower bound which applies to sparse matrix-matrix multiplication [4], it is too low to be attainable. We use a similar proof technique but devise a tighter lower bound on the communication costs in expectation for random input matrices which is independent of the local memory size of each processor. See Section 3 for details.

2. **We obtain two new communication-optimal algorithms.** Our 3D iterative and recursive algorithms (see Sections 4.3 and 4.4) are adaptations of dense ones [13, 26], though an important distinction is that the sparse algorithms do not require extra local memory to minimize communication. We also improve an existing algorithm, Sparse SUMMA, to be communication-optimal in some cases.

3. **We provide a unified communication analysis of existing and new algorithms.** See Table 1 for a summary of the expected communication costs of the algorithms applied to random input matrices. See Section 4 for a description of the algorithms and their communication analysis.

2. PRELIMINARIES

Throughout the paper, we use $\mathbf{A}$, $\mathbf{B}$ and $\mathbf{C}$ to denote the input and output matrices of the computation $\mathbf{C} = \mathbf{A} \cdot \mathbf{B}$ over an arbitrary semiring. For sparse matrix indexing, we use the colon notation, where $\mathbf{A}(:, i)$ denotes the ith column, $\mathbf{A}(i, :)$ denotes the ith row, and $\mathbf{A}(i, j)$ denotes the element at the (i, j)th position of matrix $\mathbf{A}$. We use flops to denote the number of nonzero arithmetic operations required when computing the product of matrices $\mathbf{A}$ and $\mathbf{B}$ and $nnz(\cdot)$ to denote the number of nonzeros in a matrix or submatrix.

We consider the case where $\mathbf{A}$ and $\mathbf{B}$ are $n \times n$ ER(d) matrices:

DEFINITION 2.1. *An $n \times n$ ER(d) matrix is an adjacency matrix of an Erdős-Rényi graph [14] with parameters n and d/n, that is, a square matrix of dimension n where each entry is nonzero with probability d/n. We assume $d \ll \sqrt{n}$.*

It is not important for our analysis to which semiring the matrix entries belong, though we assume algorithms do not exploit cancellation in the intermediate values or output entries.

The following facts will be useful for our analysis.

LEMMA 2.2. *Let $\mathbf{A}$ and $\mathbf{B}$ be $n \times n$ ER(d) matrices. Then*

(a) the expected number of nonzeros in $\mathbf{A}$ and in $\mathbf{B}$ is dn,

(b) the expected number of scalar multiplications in $\mathbf{A} \cdot \mathbf{B}$ is $d^2 n$, and

(c) the expected number of nonzeros in $\mathbf{C}$ is $d^2 n(1 - o(1))$.

PROOF. Since each entry of $\mathbf{A}$ and $\mathbf{B}$ is nonzero with probability d/n, the expected number of nonzeros in each matrix is $n^2(d/n) = dn$. For each of the possible n^3 scalar multiplications in $\mathbf{A} \cdot \mathbf{B}$, the computation is required only if both corresponding entries of $\mathbf{A}$ and $\mathbf{B}$ are nonzero, which are independent events. Thus the probability that any multiplication is required is d^2/n^2, and the expected number of scalar multiplications is $d^2 n$. Finally, an entry of $\mathbf{C} = \mathbf{A} \cdot \mathbf{B}$ is zero only if all n possible scalar multiplications corresponding to it are zero. Since the probability that a given scalar multiplication is zero is $(1 - d^2/n^2)$ and the n possible scalar multiplications corresponding to a single output entry are independent, the probability that an entry of $\mathbf{C}$ is zero is $(1 - d^2/n^2)^n = 1 - d^2/n + O(d^4/n^2)$. Thus the expected number of nonzeros of $\mathbf{C}$ is $n^2(d^2/n - O(d^4/n^2)) = d^2 n(1 - o(1))$, since we assume $d \ll \sqrt{n}$. $\square$

DEFINITION 2.3. *The computation cube of square $n \times n$ matrix multiplication is an $n \times n \times n$ lattice $\mathcal{V}$ where the voxel at location (i, j, k) corresponds to the scalar multiplication $\mathbf{A}(i, k) \cdot \mathbf{B}(k, j)$. We say a voxel (i, j, k) is nonzero if, for given input matrices $\mathbf{A}$ and $\mathbf{B}$, both $\mathbf{A}(i, k)$ and $\mathbf{B}(k, j)$ are nonzero.*

Given a set of voxels $V \subset \mathcal{V}$, the projections of the set onto three orthogonal faces corresponds to the input entries of $\mathbf{A}$ and $\mathbf{B}$ that are necessary to perform the multiplications and the output entries of $\mathbf{C}$ which the products must update. The computation cube and this relationship of voxels to input and output matrix entries is shown in Figure 1. The following lemma due to Loomis and Whitney relates the volume of V to its projections:

LEMMA 2.4. *[21] Let V be a finite set of lattice points in $\mathbf{R}^3$, i.e., points (x, y, z) with integer coordinates. Let V_x be the projection of V in the x-direction, i.e., all points (y, z) such that there exists an x so that $(x, y, z) \in V$. Define V_y and V_z similarly. Let $|\cdot|$ denote the cardinality of a set. Then $|V| \le \sqrt{|V_x| \cdot |V_y| \cdot |V_z|}$.*

DEFINITION 2.5. *A sparsity-independent parallel algorithm for sparse matrix-matrix multiplication is one in which the assignment of entries of the input and output matrices to processors and the assignment of computation voxels to processors is independent of the sparsity structure of the input (or output) matrices. If an assigned matrix entry is zero, the processor need not store it; if an assigned voxel is zero, the processor need not perform any of the computations that depend on it.*

Our lower bound argument in Section 3 applies to all sparsity-independent algorithms. However, we analyze a more restricted class of algorithms in Section 4, those that assign contiguous brick-shaped sets of voxels to each processor.

	Algorithm	Bandwidth cost	Latency cost
	Previous Lower Bound [4]	$\frac{d^2 n}{P\sqrt{M}}$	0
	Lower Bound [here]	$\min\left\{\frac{dn}{\sqrt{P}}, \frac{d^2 n}{P}\right\}$	1
1D	Naïve Block Row [7]	dn	P
	Improved Block Row* [12]	$\frac{d^2 n}{P}\log P$	$\min\{\log P, \frac{dn}{P}\}$
	Outer Product* [20]	$\frac{d^2 n}{P}\log P$	$\log P$
2D	Sparse SUMMA [7]	$\frac{dn}{\sqrt{P}}$	$\sqrt{P}$
	Improved Sparse SUMMA [here]	$\frac{dn}{\sqrt{P}}$	$\log P\frac{dn}{M\sqrt{P}}$
3D	Iterative* [here]	$\min\left\{\frac{dn}{\sqrt{P}}, \frac{d^2 n}{P}\left\lceil\log\frac{P}{d^2}\right\rceil\right\}$	$\log P$
	Recursive [here]	$\min\left\{\frac{dn}{\sqrt{P}}, \frac{d^2 n}{P}\left\lceil\log\frac{P}{d^2}\right\rceil\right\}$	$\log P$

Table 1: Asymptotic expected communication costs of sparsity-independent algorithms. Algorithms marked with an asterisk make use of all-to-all communication; the logarithmic factors in the bandwidth costs can be removed at the expense of higher latency costs, see Section 2.2.

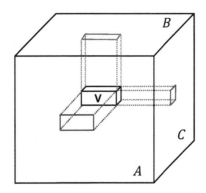

Figure 1: The computation cube for matrix multiplication, with a specified subset of voxels V along with its three projections. Each voxel corresponds to the multiplication of its projection onto A and B, and contributes to its projection onto C.

2.1 Communication Model

We use the parallel distributed-memory communication model of [4]. In this model, every processor has a local memory of size M words which is large enough to store one copy of the output matrix **C** distributed across the processors: $M = \Omega(d^2 n/P)$. To estimate the running time of a parallel algorithm with random inputs, we count the expected cost of communication in terms of number of words W (*bandwidth cost*) and number of messages S (*latency cost*) along the critical path of the algorithm. To be precise, W and S are the maxima over all paths through the algorithm of the expected bandwidth and latency costs, respectively. If two pairs of processors communicate messages of the same size simultaneously, we count that as the cost of one message. We assume a single processor can communicate only one message to one processor at a time. In this model, we do not consider contention or the number of hops a message travels; we assume the network has all-to-all connectivity.

2.2 All-to-all Communication

Several of the algorithms we discuss make use of all-to-all communication. If each processor needs to send b different words to every other processor (so each processor

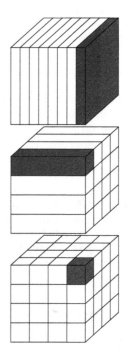

Figure 2: How the cube is partitioned in 1D (top), 2D (middle), and 3D (bottom) algorithms.

needs to send a total of $b(P - 1)$ words), the bandwidth lower bound is $W = \Omega(bP)$ and the latency lower bound is $S = \Omega(\log P)$. These bounds are separately attainable, but it has been shown that they are not simultaneously attainable [6]. Depending on the relative costs of bandwidth and latency, one may wish to use the *point-to-point* algorithm (each processor sends data directly to each other processor), which incurs costs of $W = O(bP)$, $S = O(P)$ or the *bit-fixing* algorithm (each message of b words is sent by the bit-fixing routing algorithm), which incurs costs of $W = O(bP\log P)$, $S = O(\log P)$. Both of these are optimal, in the sense that neither the bandwidth cost nor the latency cost can be asymptotically improved without asymptotically increasing the other one [6, Theorem 2.9].

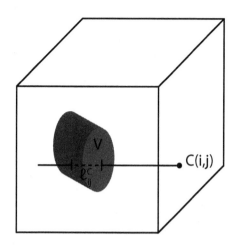

Figure 3: Graphical representation of V and ℓ_{ij}^C.

3. LOWER BOUNDS

The general lower bounds for direct linear algebra of $W = \Omega(\text{flops}/(P\sqrt{M}))$ [4] apply to our case and give

$$W = \Omega\left(\frac{d^2n}{P\sqrt{M}}\right). \qquad (1)$$

This bound is highest when M takes its minimum value d^2n/P, in which case it becomes $W = \Omega(\sqrt{d^2n/P})$. In this section we improve (increase) this lower bound by a factor of $\sqrt{n} \cdot \min\{1, d/\sqrt{P}\}$. For larger values of M, the lower bound in Equation 1 becomes weaker, whereas our new bound does not, and the improvement factor increases to $\sqrt{M} \cdot \min\{1, \sqrt{P}/d\}$. The previous memory-independent lower bound of $W = \Omega((\text{flops}/P)^{2/3} - nnz/P)$ [2] reduces to the trivial bound $W = \Omega(0)$.

THEOREM 3.1. *A sparsity-independent sparse matrix multiplication algorithm with load-balanced input and output applied to $ER(d)$ input matrices on P processors has an expected communication cost lower bound of*

$$W = \Omega\left(\min\left\{\frac{dn}{\sqrt{P}}, \frac{d^2n}{P}\right\}\right).$$

PROOF. Consider the n^3 voxels that correspond to potential scalar multiplications $\mathbf{A}(i,k) \cdot \mathbf{B}(k,j)$. A sparsity-independent algorithm gives a partitioning of these multiplications among the P processors. Let V be the largest set of voxels assigned to a processor, so $|V| \geq \frac{n^3}{P}$. For each i,j, let ℓ_{ij}^C be the number of values of k such that $(i,j,k) \in V$, see Figure 3. We count how many of the voxels in V correspond to $\ell_{ij}^C < \frac{n}{4}$ and divide into two cases.

Case 1: At least $\frac{n^3}{2P}$ voxels of V correspond to $\ell_{ij}^C < \frac{n}{4}$. Let V' be these voxels, so $|V'| \geq \frac{n^3}{2P}$. We will analyze the communication cost corresponding to the computation of V' and get a bound on the number of products computed by this processor that must be sent to other processors. Since the output is load balanced and the algorithm is sparsity-independent, the processor that computes V' is allowed to store only a particular set of $\frac{n^2}{P}$ entries of $\mathbf{C}$ in the output data layout. Since every voxel in V' corresponds to an $\ell_{ij}^C < \frac{n}{4}$, the $\frac{n^2}{P}$ output entries stored by the processor correspond to at most $\frac{n^3}{4P}$ voxels in V', which is at most half

of $|V'|$. All of the nonzero voxels in the remainder of V' contribute to entries of $\mathbf{C}$ that must be sent to another processor. In expectation, this is at least $\frac{d^2n}{4P}$ nonzero voxels, since each voxel is nonzero with probability $\frac{d^2}{n^2}$. Moreover, from the proof of Lemma 2.2, only a small number of the nonzero entries of $\mathbf{C}$ have contributions from more than one voxel, so very few of the values can be summed before being communicated. The expected bandwidth cost is then bounded by

$$W = \Omega(d^2n/P).$$

Case 2: Fewer than $\frac{n^3}{2P}$ voxels of V correspond to $\ell_{ij}^C < \frac{n}{4}$. This means that at least $\frac{n^3}{2P}$ voxels of V correspond to $\ell_{ij}^C \geq \frac{n}{4}$. Let V'' be these voxels, so $|V''| \geq \frac{n^3}{2P}$. We will analyze the communication cost corresponding to the computation of V'' and get a lower bound on the amount of input data needed by this processor. For each i,k, let ℓ_{ik}^A be the number of values of j such that $(i,j,k) \in V''$. Similarly, for each j,k, let ℓ_{jk}^B be the number of values of i such that $(i,j,k) \in V''$. Partition V'' into three sets: V_0 is the set of voxels that correspond to $\ell_{ik}^A > \frac{n}{d}$ and $\ell_{jk}^B > \frac{n}{d}$; V_A is the set of voxels that correspond to $\ell_{ik}^A \leq \frac{n}{d}$; and V_B is the set of voxels that correspond to $\ell_{jk}^B \leq \frac{n}{d}$ and $\ell_{ik}^A > \frac{n}{d}$. At least one of these sets has at least $\frac{n^3}{6P}$ voxels, and we divide into three subcases.

Case 2a: $|V_0| \geq \frac{n^3}{6P}$. Let p_A, p_B, and p_C be the sizes of the projections of V_0 onto $\mathbf{A}$, $\mathbf{B}$, and $\mathbf{C}$, respectively. Lemma 2.4 implies that $p_A p_B p_C \geq |V_0|^2 = \frac{n^6}{36P^2}$. The assumptions of Case 2 implies $p_C \leq \frac{|V_0|}{n/4} \leq \frac{n^4}{24P}$. Thus $p_A p_B \geq \frac{n^4}{24P}$, or

$$\max\{p_A, p_B\} \geq \frac{n^2}{\sqrt{24P}}.$$

Since the situation is symmetric with respect to $\mathbf{A}$ and $\mathbf{B}$, assume without loss of generality that $\mathbf{A}$ has the larger projection, so $p_A \geq \frac{n^2}{\sqrt{24P}}$. Since the density of $\mathbf{A}$ is $\frac{d}{n}$, this means that the expected number of nonzeros in the projection of V_0 onto $\mathbf{A}$ is at least $\frac{dn}{\sqrt{24P}}$. Since each of these nonzeros in $\mathbf{A}$ corresponds to a $\ell_{ik}^A > \frac{n}{d}$, it is needed to compute V_0 with probability at least

$$1 - \left(1 - \frac{d}{n}\right)^{n/d} > 1 - \frac{1}{e}.$$

Thus in expectation a constant fraction of the nonzeros of $\mathbf{A}$ in the projection of V_0 are needed. The number of nonzeros the processor holds in the initial data layout is $\frac{dn}{P}$ in expectation, which is asymptotically less than the number needed for the computation. Thus we get a bandwidth lower bound of

$$W = \Omega(dn/\sqrt{P}).$$

Case 2b: $|V_A| \geq \frac{n^3}{6P}$. Each voxel in V_A corresponds to $\ell_{ik}^A \leq \frac{n}{d}$. In this case we are able to bound the re-use of entries of $\mathbf{A}$ to get a lower bound. Count how many entries of $\mathbf{A}$ correspond to each possible value of ℓ_{ik}^A, $1 \leq r \leq \frac{n}{d}$, and call this number N_r. Note that $\sum_{r=1}^{n/d} r \cdot N_r = |V_A|$. Suppose a given entry $\mathbf{A}(i,k)$ corresponds to $\ell_{ik}^A = r$. We can bound the probability that $\mathbf{A}(i,k)$ is needed by the processor to compute V_A as a function $f(r)$. The probability that $\mathbf{A}(i,k)$ is needed is the probability that both $\mathbf{A}(i,k)$ is nonzero and one of the r voxels corresponding to $\mathbf{A}(i,k)$ in V_A is nonzero, so

$$f(r) = \frac{d}{n}\left(1 - \left(1 - \frac{d}{n}\right)^r\right) \geq \frac{rd^2}{2n^2},$$

since $r \leq \frac{n}{d}$. Thus the expected number of nonzeros of $\mathbf{A}$ that are needed by the processor is

$$\sum_{r=1}^{n/d} N_r f(r) \geq \frac{d^2}{2n^2} \sum_{r=1}^{n/d} r \cdot N_r \geq \frac{d^2 n}{12P}.$$

This is asymptotically larger than the number of nonzeros the processor holds at the beginning of the computation, so we get a bandwidth lower bound of

$$W = \Omega(d^2 n/P).$$

Case 2c: $|V_B| \geq \frac{n^3}{6P}$. The analysis is identical to the previous case, except we look at the number of nonzeros of $\mathbf{B}$ that are required.

Since an algorithm may be in any of these cases, the overall lower bound is the minimum:

$$W = \Omega\left(\min\left\{\frac{dn}{\sqrt{P}}, \frac{d^2 n}{P}\right\}\right).$$

□

4. ALGORITHMS

In this section we consider algorithms which assign contiguous bricks of voxels to processors. We categorize these algorithms into 1D, 2D, and 3D algorithms, as shown in Figure 2, depending on the dimensions of the brick of voxels assigned to each processor: 1D algorithms correspond to bricks with two dimensions of length n (and 1 shorter), 2D algorithms correspond to bricks with one dimension of length n (and 2 shorter), and 3D algorithms correspond to bricks with all 3 dimensions shorter than n. Table 1 provides a summary of the communication costs of the sparsity-independent algorithms we consider.

4.1 1D Algorithms

4.1.1 Naïve Block Row Algorithm

The naïve block row algorithm [7] distributes the input and output matrices to processors in a block row fashion. Then in order for processor i to compute the ith block row, it needs access to the ith block row of $\mathbf{A}$ (which it already owns), and potentially all of $\mathbf{B}$. Thus, we can allow each processor to compute its block row of $\mathbf{C}$ by leaving $\mathbf{A}$ and $\mathbf{C}$ stationary and cyclically shifting block rows of $\mathbf{B}$ around a ring of the processors. This algorithm requires P stages, with each processor communicating with its two neighbors in the communication ring. The size of each message is the number of nonzeros in a block row of $\mathbf{B}$, which is expected to be dn/P words. Thus, the expected bandwidth cost of the block row algorithm is dn and the latency cost is P. An analogous block column algorithm works by cyclically shifting block columns of $\mathbf{A}$ with identical communication costs.

4.1.2 Improved Block Row Algorithm

The communication costs of the block row algorithm can be reduced without changing the assignment of matrix entries or voxels to processors [12]. The key idea is for each processor to determine exactly which rows of $\mathbf{B}$ it needs to access in order to perform its computations. For example, if processor i owns the ith block row of $\mathbf{A}$, $\mathbf{A}_i$, and the jth subcolumn of $\mathbf{A}_i$ contains no nonzeros, then processor i doesn't need to access the jth row of $\mathbf{B}$. Further, since the height of a subcolumn is n/P, the probability that the subcolumn is completely empty is

$$Pr\left[nnz(\mathbf{A}_i(:,j)) = 0\right] = \left(1 - \frac{d}{n}\right)^{n/P} \approx 1 - \frac{d}{P},$$

assuming $d < P$. In this case, the expected number of subcolumns of $\mathbf{A}_i$ which have at least one nonzero is dn/P. Since processor i needs to access only those rows of $\mathbf{B}$ which correspond to nonzero subcolumns of $\mathbf{A}_i$, and because the expected number of nonzeros in each row of $\mathbf{B}$ is d, the expected number of nonzeros of $\mathbf{B}$ that processor i needs to access is $d^2 n/P$.

Note that the local memory of each processor must be of size $\Omega\left(d^2 n/P\right)$ in order to store the output matrix $\mathbf{C}$. Thus, it is possible for a processor to gather all of their required rows of $\mathbf{B}$ at once. The improved algorithm consists of each processor determining which rows it needs, requesting those rows from the appropriate processors, and then sending and receiving approximately d rows. While this can be implemented in various ways, the bandwidth cost of the algorithm is at least $\Omega\left(d^2 n/P\right)$ and if point-to-point communication is used, the latency cost is at least $\Omega(\min\{P, dn/P\})$. The block column algorithm can be improved in the same manner.

4.1.3 Outer Product Algorithm

Another possible 1D algorithm is to partition $\mathbf{A}$ in block columns, and $\mathbf{B}$ in block rows [20]. Without communication, each processor locally generates an $n \times n$ sparse matrix of rank n/P, and processors combine their results to produce the output $\mathbf{C}$. Because each column of $\mathbf{A}$ and row of $\mathbf{B}$ have about d nonzeros, the expected number of nonzeros in the locally computed output is $d^2 n/P$. By deciding the distribution of $\mathbf{C}$ to processors up front, each processor can determine where to send each of its computed nonzeros. The final communication pattern is realized with an all-to-all collective in which each processer sends and receives $O(d^2 n/P)$ words. Note that assuming $\mathbf{A}$ and $\mathbf{B}$ are initially distributed to processors in different ways may be unrealistic; however, no matter how they are initially distributed, $\mathbf{A}$ and $\mathbf{B}$ can be transformed to block column and row layouts with all-to-all collectives for a communication cost which is dominated by the final communication phase.

To avoid the all-to-all, it is possible to compute the expected number of blocks of the output which actually contain nonzeros; the best distribution of $\mathbf{C}$ is 2D, in which case the expected number of blocks of $\mathbf{C}$ you need to communicate is $\min\{P, dn/\sqrt{P}\}$. Thus for $P > (dn)^{2/3}$, the outer product algorithm can have $W = O(d^2 n/P)$ and $S = O(dn/\sqrt{P})$.

4.2 2D Algorithms

4.2.1 Sparse SUMMA

In the Sparse SUMMA algorithm [7], the brick of voxels assigned to a processor has its longest dimension (of length n) in the k dimension. For each output entry of $\mathbf{C}$ to which it is assigned, the processor computes all the nonzero voxels which contribute to that output entry. The algorithm has a bandwidth cost of $O(dn/\sqrt{P})$ and a latency cost of $O(\sqrt{P})$ [7].

4.2.2 Improved Sparse SUMMA

In order to reduce the latency cost of Sparse SUMMA, each processor can gather all the necessary input data up front. That is, each processor is computing a product of a block row of $\mathbf{A}$ with a block column of $\mathbf{B}$, so if it gathers all the nonzeros in those regions of the input matrices, it can compute its block of $\mathbf{C}$ with no more communication. Since every row of $\mathbf{A}$ and column of $\mathbf{B}$ contain about d nonzeros, and the number of rows of $\mathbf{A}$ and columns of $\mathbf{B}$ in a block is $n/\sqrt{P}$, the number of nonzeros a processor must gather is $O(dn/\sqrt{P})$. If $d > \sqrt{P}$, then the memory requirements for this gather operation do not exceed the memory requirements for storing the block of the output matrix $\mathbf{C}$, which is $\Omega(d^2 n/P)$.

The global communication pattern for each processor to gather its necessary data consists of allgather collectives along processor columns and along processor grids. The bandwidth cost of these collectives is $O(dn/\sqrt{P})$, which is the same as the standard algorithm, and the latency cost is reduced to $O(\log P)$. To our knowledge, this improvement has not appeared in the literature before.

We might also consider applying the optimization that improved the 1D block row (or column) algorithm. Processor (i, j) would need to gather the indices of the nonzero subcolumns of $\mathbf{A}_i$ and the nonzero subrows of $\mathbf{B}_j$. This requires receiving $\Omega(dn/\sqrt{P})$ words, and so it cannot reduce the communication cost of Sparse SUMMA.

As in the dense case, there are variants on the Sparse SUMMA algorithm that leave one of the input matrices stationary, rather than leaving the output matrix $\mathbf{C}$ stationary [18]. When multiplying $ER(d)$ matrices, stationary input matrix algorithms require more communication than the standard approach because the global data involved in communicating $\mathbf{C}$ is about $d^2 n$, while the global data involved in communicating $\mathbf{A}$ and $\mathbf{B}$ is only dn.

4.3 3D Iterative Algorithm

In this section we present a new 3D iterative algorithm. We start with a dense version of the algorithm and apply a series of improvements in order to match the lower bound.

4.3.1 3D Algorithms for Dense Matrix Multiplication

The term "3D" originates from dense matrix multiplication algorithms [1], where the processors are organized in a 3-dimensional grid, and the computational cube is mapped directly onto the cube of processors. In the simplest case, the processors are arranged in a $\sqrt[3]{P} \times \sqrt[3]{P} \times \sqrt[3]{P}$ grid. Let $\mathbf{A}$ be distributed across the $P^{2/3}$ processors along one face of the cube and $\mathbf{B}$ be distributed across the $P^{2/3}$ processors along a second face of the cube. Then each input matrix can be broadcast through the cube in the respective dimensions so that every processor in the cube owns the block of $\mathbf{A}$ and the block of $\mathbf{B}$ it needs to compute its local multiplication. After the computation, the matrix $\mathbf{C}$ can be computed via a reduction in the third dimension of the cube, resulting in the output matrix being distributed across a third face of the cube.

The communication cost of this algorithm is the cost of the two broadcasts and one reduction. The size of the local data in each of these operations is $n^2/P^{2/3}$, and the number of processors involved is $P^{1/3}$, so the total bandwidth cost is $O(n^2/P^{2/3})$ and the total latency cost is $O(\log P)$. These communication costs are less than the costs of 2D algorithms for dense multiplication [1, 11, 28]. However, because the local computation involves matrices of size $n^2/P^{2/3}$, the 3D algorithm requires more local memory than is necessary to store the input and output matrices.

This tradeoff between memory requirements and communication costs can be managed in a continuous way by varying the dimensions of the processor grid (or, equivalently, the dimensions of the bricks of voxels assigned to processors) [22, 25, 27]. Instead of using a cubic $\sqrt[3]{P} \times \sqrt[3]{P} \times \sqrt[3]{P}$ processor grid, we can use a $c \times \sqrt{P/c} \times \sqrt{P/c}$ grid, where $1 \leq c \leq \sqrt[3]{P}$ and $c = 1$ reproduces a 2D algorithm. The approach that generalizes Cannon's algorithm [11] is presented as "2.5D-matrix-multiply"[1] as Algorithm 2 by Solomonik and Demmel [27] and the approach that generalizes SUMMA is presented as "2.5D-SUMMA" in Algorithm 1 by Solomonik et al. [26]. Both approaches yields a bandwidth cost of $O(n^2/\sqrt{Pc})$, a latency cost of $O(\sqrt{P/c^3} + \log c)$, and local memory requirements of $O(cn^2/P)$.

4.3.2 Converting to Sparse Case

Naïve 3D algorithms for sparse matrix multiplication can be devised directly from the dense versions. As in [27, 26], we assume the data initially resides only on the one of the c layers and gets replicated along the third dimension before the multiplications start. Then, each of those layers executes a partial 2D algorithm (with the partial contribution to $\mathbf{C}$ remaining stationary), in the sense that each layer is responsible for computing $1/c$ of the total computation. Consequently, the number of steps in the main stage of the algorithm becomes $\sqrt{P/c^3}$. The final stage of the algorithm is a reduction step among groups of c processors, executed concurrently by all groups of processors representing a fiber along the third processor dimension.

The latency cost is identical to the dense algorithm: $O(\sqrt{P/c^3} + \log c)$. The first term comes from the main stage and the second term comes from the initial replication and final reduction phases. The bandwidth cost can be computed based on the number of nonzeros in each block of $\mathbf{A}$, $\mathbf{B}$, or $\mathbf{C}$ communicated. In the initial replication phase, blocks of $\mathbf{A}$ and $\mathbf{B}$ of dimension $n/\sqrt{P/c} \times n/\sqrt{P/c}$ are broadcast to c different processors for a bandwidth cost of $O(cdn/P)$. In the main stage of the algorithm, the same size blocks are communicated during each of the $\sqrt{P/c^3}$ steps for a total bandwidth cost of $O(dn/\sqrt{Pc})$. The final reduction is significantly different from a dense reduction, resembling more closely a gather operation since the expected number of collisions in partial contributions of $\mathbf{C}$ is very small for $d \ll \sqrt{n}$. Thus, we expect the size of the output to be almost as large as the sum of the sizes of the inputs. The bandwidth cost of the final phase is then $O(cd^2 n/P)$.

Thus, the straightforward conversion of the dense 3D algorithm to the sparse case results in the same latency cost

---

[1]The origin of the name "2.5D" comes from the fact that the algorithm interpolates between existing 2D and 3D algorithms. We use the term 3D to describe both 3D and 2.5D dense algorithms.

and a total bandwidth cost of $O(dn/\sqrt{Pc} + cd^2n/P)$. Further, this algorithm will require extra local memory, because gathering the output matrix onto one layer of processors requires $\Omega(cd^2n/P)$ words of memory, a factor of $\Omega(c)$ times as much as required to store $\mathbf{C}$ across all processors. The extra space required for $\mathbf{C}$ dominates the space required for replication of $\mathbf{A}$ and $\mathbf{B}$.

4.3.3 Removing Input Replication and Assumption on Initial Data Distribution

In developing a more efficient 3D algorithm for the sparse case, our first observation is that we can avoid the first phase of input replication. This replication can also be avoided in the dense case, but it will not affect the asymptotic communication costs.

The dense 2.5D algorithms assume that the input matrices initially reside on one $\sqrt{P/c} \times \sqrt{P/c}$ face of the processor grid, and the first phase of the algorithm involves replicating $\mathbf{A}$ and $\mathbf{B}$ to each of the c layers. One can view the distribution of computation as assigning $1/c^{\text{th}}$ of the outer products of columns of $\mathbf{A}$ with corresponding rows of $\mathbf{B}$ to each of the c layers. In this way, each layer of processors needs only $1/c^{\text{th}}$ of the columns of $\mathbf{A}$ and rows of $\mathbf{B}$ rather than the entire matrices.

In order to redistribute the matrices across c sets of processors in a 2D blocked layout with block size $n/\sqrt{P/c} \times n/\sqrt{P/c}$, blocks of $\sqrt{c} \times \sqrt{c}$ processors can perform all-to-all operations, as shown in Figure 4. The cost of this operation is $W = O(dn/P \log c)$ and $S = O(\log c)$ if the bit-fixing algorithm is used, removing the initial replication cost from Section 4.3.2. This optimization also removes the extra memory requirement for storing copies of $\mathbf{A}$ and $\mathbf{B}$.

We will see in Section 4.3.4 that the output matrix can be returned in the same 2D blocked layout as the input matrices were initially distributed.

4.3.4 Improving Communication of $\mathbf{C}$

Our next observation for the sparse case is that the final reduction phase to compute the output matrix becomes a gather rather than a reduction. This gather operation collects $\mathbf{C}$ onto one layer of processors; in order to balance the output across all processors, we would like to scatter $\mathbf{C}$ back along the third processor dimension. However, performing a gather followed by a scatter is just an inefficient means of performing an all-to-all collective. Thus we should replace the final reduction phase with a final all-to-all phase. This optimization reduces the bandwidth cost of the 3D algorithm to $O(dn/\sqrt{Pc} + d^2n/P)$. Note that the cost of replicating $\mathbf{A}$ and $\mathbf{B}$ in the first phase of the algorithm would no longer always be dominated by the reduction cost of $\mathbf{C}$, as in Section 4.3.2, but the cost of the input all-to-all from Section 4.3.3 is dominated by the output all-to-all. By replacing the reduction phase with an all-to-all, we also remove the memory requirement of $\Omega(cd^2n/P)$.

4.3.5 Improving Communication of $\mathbf{A}$ and $\mathbf{B}$

Furthermore, we can apply the optimization described in Section 4.2.2: to reduce latency costs in the main phase of the 3D algorithm (which itself is a 2D algorithm), processors can collect all the entries of $\mathbf{A}$ and $\mathbf{B}$ they need upfront rather than over several steps. This collective operation consists of groups of $\sqrt{P/c^3}$ processors performing allgather operations (after the initial circular shifts of Can-

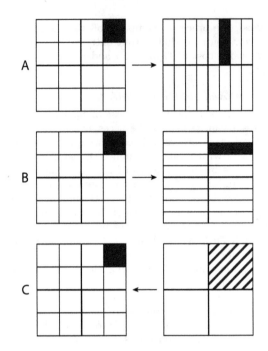

Figure 4: Possible redistribution scheme for input and output matrices for the 3D algorithm with $4 \times 2 \times 2$ processor grid ($c = 4$). The colored regions denote submatrices owned by a particular processor. The input matrices are initially in a 2D block distribution, and redistribution occurs in all-to-all collectives among disjoint sets of 4 processors. Since each of the c layers are 2×2 grids, the intermediate phase consists of allgather collectives among pairs of processors. After local computation, the output matrix is redistributed (and nonzeros combined if necessary) via all-to-all collectives among the same disjoint sets of 4 processors, returning the output matrix also in a 2D block distribution.

non's algorithm, for example). Since the data per processor in the allgather operation is $O(cdn/P)$, the bandwidth cost of the main phase remains $O(dn/\sqrt{Pc})$. The latency cost is reduced from $O(\sqrt{P/c^3})$ to $O(\log(\sqrt{P/c^3}))$, yielding a total latency cost (assuming the bit-fixing algorithm is used for the all-to-all) of $O(\log P)$. The local memory requirements increase to $\Omega(dn/\sqrt{Pc})$; when $c \geq P/d^2$, this requirement is no more than the space required to store $\mathbf{C}$.

4.3.6 Optimizing c

If $d > \sqrt{P}$, then $d^2n/P > dn/\sqrt{P}$, and the communication lower bound from Section 3 is $\Omega(dn/\sqrt{P})$. Thus, choosing $c = 1$ eliminates the $d^2n/P \log c$ term, and the 3D algorithm reduces to a 2D algorithm which is communication optimal.

However, in the case $d < \sqrt{P}$, which will become the case in a strong-scaling regime, increasing c can reduce communication. In this case, the lower bound from Section 3 is $\Omega(d^2n/P)$. Depending on the all-to-all algorithm used, increasing c causes slow increases on latency costs and on the $d^2n/P \log c$ bandwidth cost term, but it causes more rapid decrease in the $dn/\sqrt{Pc}$ term. Choosing $c = \Theta(P/d^2)$ balances the two terms in the bandwidth cost, yielding a total bandwidth cost of $O(d^2 n/P)$, which attains the lower bound in this case.

In summary, choosing $c = \min\left\{1, P/d^2\right\}$ allows for a communication optimal 3D sparse matrix multiplication algorithm, with a slight tradeoff between bandwidth and latency costs based on the all-to-all algorithm used. Additionally, making this choice of c means that asymptotically no extra memory is needed over the space required to store $\mathbf{C}$.

4.4 3D Recursive Algorithm

We also present a new 3D recursive algorithm which is a parallelization of a sequential recursive algorithm using the techniques of [3, 13]. Although we have assumed that the input matrices are square, the recursive algorithm will use rectangular matrices for subproblems. Assume that P processors are solving a subproblem of size $m \times k \times m$, that is $\mathbf{A}$ is $m \times k$, and $\mathbf{B}$ is $k \times m$, and $\mathbf{C}$ is $m \times m$. We will split into four subproblems, and then solve each subproblem independently on a quarter of the processor. There are two natural ways to split the problem into four equal subproblems that respect the density similarity between $\mathbf{A}$ and $\mathbf{B}$, see Figure 5.

1. Split m in half, creating four subproblems of shape $(m/2) \times k \times (m/2)$. In this case each of the four subproblems needs access to a different part of $\mathbf{C}$, so no communication of $\mathbf{C}$ is needed. However one half of $\mathbf{A}$ and $\mathbf{B}$ is needed for each subproblem, and since each quarter of the processors holds only one quarter of each matrix, it will be necessary to replicate $\mathbf{A}$ and $\mathbf{B}$. This can be done via allgather collectives among disjoint pairs of processors at the cost of $O\left(dmk/(nP)\right)$ words and $O(1)$ messages.

2. Split k in quarters, creating four subproblems of shape $m \times (k/4) \times m$. In this case each of the four subproblems needs access to a different part of $\mathbf{A}$ and $\mathbf{B}$, so with the right data layout, no communication of $\mathbf{A}$ or $\mathbf{B}$ is needed. However each subproblem will compute nonzeros across all of $\mathbf{C}$, so those entries need to be redistributed and combined if necessary. This can be done via all-to-all collective among disjoint sets of 4 processors at a cost of $O(d^2 m^2/(nP))$ words and $O(1)$ messages.

At each recursive step, the algorithm chooses whichever split is cheapest in terms of communication cost. Initially, $m = k = n$ so split 1 costs $O(dn/P)$ words and is cheaper than split 2, which costs $O(d^2 n/P)$ words. There are two cases to consider.

Case 1: If $P \leq d^2$, the algorithm reaches a single processor before split 1 becomes more expensive than split 2, so only split 1 is used. This case corresponds to a 2D algorithm, and the communication costs are

$$W = \sum_{i=0}^{\log_4 P - 1} O\left(\frac{d(n/2^i)n}{P/4^i}\right)$$
$$= O\left(\frac{dn}{\sqrt{P}}\right)$$

and

$$S = O(\log P).$$

Case 2: If $P > d^2$, split 1 becomes more expensive than split 2 after $\log_2 d$ steps. After $\log_2 d$ steps, the subproblems

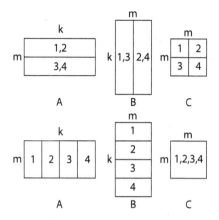

Figure 5: Two ways to split the matrix multiplication into four subproblems, with the parts of each matrix required by each subproblem labelled. On the left is split 1 and on the right is split 2.

have dimensions $(n/d) \times n \times (n/d)$ and there are P/d^2 processors working on each subproblem. The first $\log_2 d$ steps are split 1, and the rest are split 2, giving communication costs of

$$W = \sum_{i=0}^{\log_2 d - 1} O\left(\frac{d(n/2^i)n}{P/4^i}\right) + \sum_{i=\log_2 d}^{\log_4 P} O\left(\frac{d^2 n}{P}\right)$$
$$= O\left(\frac{d^2 n}{P}\left\lceil \log \frac{P}{d^2}\right\rceil\right),$$

and

$$S = O(\log P).$$

This case corresponds to a 3D algorithm.

In both cases, the communication costs match the lower bound from Section 3 up to factors of at most $\log P$. Only layouts that are compatible with the recursive structure of the algorithm will allow these communication costs. One simple layout is to have $\mathbf{A}$ is block-column layout, $\mathbf{B}$ in block-row layout. Then $\mathbf{C}$ should have blocks of size $n/d \times n/d$, each distributed on a different $\lceil P/d^2 \rceil$ of the processors.

5. RELATED WORK

The classical serial algorithm of Gustavson [19], which is the algorithm currently implemented in MATLAB [15], does optimal work for the case of flops $\ll nnz, n$. Yuster and Zwick [31] gave a $O(nnz^{0.7}n^{1.2} + n^{2+o(1)})$ time serial algorithm for multiplying matrices over a ring, which uses Strassen-like fast dense rectangular matrix multiplication as a subroutine. Their algorithm is theoretically close to optimal for the case of $nnz(\mathbf{C}) = \Theta(n^2)$, an assumption that does not always hold and in particular is not true when $d \ll \sqrt{n}$. They did not analyze communication cost.

The 1D improved block-row algorithm is due to Challacombe [12], who calls the calculation of required indices of $\mathbf{B}$ the "symbolic" phase. His algorithm uses the allgather collective for the symbolic phase and point-to-point communication for the subsequent numerical phase. Challacombe, however, did not analyze his algorithm's communication costs. Kruskal et al. [20] gave a parallel algorithm based on outer products, which has

$$O((\text{flops}/P) \log n / \log(\text{flops}/P))$$

cost in the EREW PRAM model, which does not include communication costs.

Sparse SUMMA and its analysis is due to Buluç and Gilbert [7], who also analyzed the 1D naïve block-row algorithm. Their follow-up work showed that Sparse SUMMA provides good speedup to thousands of cores on various different input types, but its scaling is limited by the communication costs that consume the majority of the time [9]. Recent work by Campagna et al. [10] sketches a parallel algorithm that replicates the inputs (but not the output) to all the processors to avoid later communication. In our model, their algorithm has bandwidth cost $W = O(dn)$.

Grigori et al. [17] gave tight communication lower and upper bounds for Cholesky factorization of sparse matrices corresponding to certain grids. Pietracaprina et al. [24] gave lower bounds on the number of rounds it takes to compute the sparse matrix product in MapReduce. Their lower bound analysis, however, is not parametrized to the density of the inputs and uses the inequality flops $\leq nnz \cdot \min(nnz, n)$. While it is true that there exist assignment of input matrices for which the inequality is tight, the lower bound does not hold for input matrix pairs for which the inequality is not tight. By parametrizing the density of inputs, we show that our algorithms are communication optimal over all ER(d) matrices.

6. DISCUSSION

While many ideas from dense matrix multiplication translate directly to sparse input matrices, there are two key differences in the sparse case. First, for the nonzero density we consider in this paper (i.e., $d \ll \sqrt{n}$), the possible data re-use is much more limited than in the dense case. Second, because $\mathbf{C}$ is denser than $\mathbf{A}$ and $\mathbf{B}$, the communication costs of sparse algorithms are skewed towards $\mathbf{C}$; dense multiplication of square matrices enjoys a symmetry among the three matrices.

The first difference leads to new, tighter lower bounds. In the dense case, there is (in principle) an opportunity for $O(n)$ re-use since each entry of $\mathbf{A}$, $\mathbf{B}$, and $\mathbf{C}$ is involved in n scalar multiplications. The general lower bound of [4] implies that the best possible data re-use for matrix computations is only $O(\sqrt{M})$. In the sparse case, for $d \ll \sqrt{n}$, we cannot hope to attain that amount of re-use. Given that there are $\Theta(d^2 n/P)$ flops performed on each processor, is it possible to get better than constant re-use? Because the size of the output is $\Theta(d^2 n/P)$, we cannot hope to get better than constant re-use of output entries; thus, to communicate fewer than $\Theta(d^2 n/P)$ words, we should try to avoid communicating output entries. There is (in principle) an opportunity for $O(d)$ re-use of input entries since each is involved in that many scalar multiplications. The lower bound proved in Section 3 shows that if we avoid communicating output entries, the best possible re-use of input entries is only $O(d/\sqrt{P})$, requiring reading $\Omega(dn/\sqrt{P})$ words. This amount of communication is less than $\Theta(d^2 n/P)$ if $d > \sqrt{P}$; otherwise, communicating $\Omega(d^2 n/P)$ words is the best an algorithm can do. Thus, the lower bound becomes a minimum of the two quantities $\Omega(dn/\sqrt{P})$ and $\Omega(d^2 n/P)$.

Table 1 summarizes the communication costs of the various algorithms analyzed in Section 4. It shows that ignoring

logarithmic factors, there exist 1D algorithms that attain the lower bound when $O(d^2 n/P)$ is the smaller of the two expressions, and there exists a 2D algorithm that attains the lower bound when $O(dn/\sqrt{P})$ is the smaller of the two. The 2D algorithm, which attains better than constant re-use, does so by not communicating $\mathbf{C}$ and attaining $O(d/\sqrt{P})$ re-use of $\mathbf{A}$ and $\mathbf{B}$ entries. Both of the 3D algorithms provide a unified approach to matching either bound and attaining communication optimality.

There are many possible extensions of the algorithms and analysis presented in this paper. The new algorithms have not yet been benchmarked and compared against previous algorithms. We plan to extend recent performance studies [9] to include all of the algorithms considered here. Additionally, we hope that our analysis can be extended to many more types of input matrices, including those with rectangular dimensions, different nonzero densities (e.g., multiplying an ER(d_A) matrix by an ER(d_B) matrix with $d_A \neq d_B$, or considering $d \geq \sqrt{n}$), and different sparsity structures (e.g., corresponding to grids, planar graphs, or expanders). We are especially interested in sparsity structures corresponding to applications which are currently bottlenecked by sparse matrix-matrix multiplication, such as the triple product computation within algebraic multigrid. In the case of matrix multiplication, we have shown how to apply ideas from dense algorithms to obtain communication-optimal sparse algorithms. Perhaps similar adaptions can be made for other matrix computations such as direct factorizations.

7. REFERENCES

[1] R. Agarwal, S. Balle, F. Gustavson, M. Joshi, and P. Palkar. A three-dimensional approach to parallel matrix multiplication. *IBM Journal of Research and Development*, 39(5):575 –582, September 1995.

[2] G. Ballard, J. Demmel, O. Holtz, B. Lipshitz, and O. Schwartz. Brief announcement: Strong scaling of matrix multiplication algorithms and memory-independent communication lower bounds. In *Proceedings of the 24th ACM Symposium on Parallelism in Algorithms and Architectures*, SPAA '12, pages 77–79, New York, NY, USA, 2012. ACM.

[3] G. Ballard, J. Demmel, O. Holtz, B. Lipshitz, and O. Schwartz. Communication-optimal parallel algorithm for Strassen's matrix multiplication. In *Proceedings of the 24th ACM Symposium on Parallelism in Algorithms and Architectures*, SPAA '12, pages 193–204, New York, NY, USA, 2012. ACM.

[4] G. Ballard, J. Demmel, O. Holtz, and O. Schwartz. Minimizing communication in numerical linear algebra. *SIAM. J. Matrix Anal. & Appl*, 32:pp. 866–901, 2011.

[5] W. Briggs, V. Henson, and S. McCormick. *A Multigrid Tutorial: Second Edition*. Society for Industrial and Applied Mathematics, Philadelphia, PA, USA, 2000.

[6] J. Bruck, C.-T. Ho, S. Kipnis, and D. Weathersby. Efficient algorithms for all-to-all communications in multi-port message-passing systems. In *Proceedings of the sixth annual ACM symposium on Parallel algorithms and architectures*, SPAA '94, pages 298–309, New York, NY, USA, 1994. ACM.

[7] A. Buluç and J. Gilbert. Challenges and advances in parallel sparse matrix-matrix multiplication. In

ICPP'08: Proc. of the Intl. Conf. on Parallel Processing, pages 503–510, Portland, Oregon, USA, 2008. IEEE Computer Society.

[8] A. Buluç and J. Gilbert. The Combinatorial BLAS: Design, implementation, and applications. *Int. J. High Perform. Comput. Appl.*, 25(4):496–509, November 2011.

[9] A. Buluç and J. Gilbert. Parallel sparse matrix-matrix multiplication and indexing: Implementation and experiments. *SIAM Journal of Scientific Computing (SISC)*, 34(4):170 – 191, 2012.

[10] A. Campagna, K. Kutzkov, and R. Pagh. On parallelizing matrix multiplication by the column-row method. *arXiv preprint arXiv:1210.0461*, 2012.

[11] L. Cannon. *A cellular computer to implement the Kalman filter algorithm*. PhD thesis, Montana State University, Bozeman, MN, 1969.

[12] M. Challacombe. A general parallel sparse-blocked matrix multiply for linear scaling SCF theory. *Computer physics communications*, 128(1-2):93–107, 2000.

[13] J. Demmel, D. Eliahu, A. Fox, S. Kamil, B. Lipshitz, O. Schwartz, and O. Spillinger. Communication-optimal parallel recursive rectangular matrix multiplication. In *International Parallel & Distributed Processing Symposium (IPDPS)*. IEEE, 2013.

[14] Paul Erdős and Alfréd Rényi. On random graphs. *Publicationes Mathematicae Debrecen*, 6:290–297, 1959.

[15] J. Gilbert, C. Moler, and R. Schreiber. Sparse matrices in Matlab: Design and implementation. *SIAM Journal of Matrix Analysis and Applications*, 13(1):333–356, 1992.

[16] J. Gilbert, S. Reinhardt, and V. Shah. A unified framework for numerical and combinatorial computing. *Computing in Science and Engineering*, 10(2):20–25, 2008.

[17] L. Grigori, P.-Y. David, J. Demmel, and S. Peyronnet. Brief announcement: Lower bounds on communication for sparse Cholesky factorization of a model problem. In *Proceedings of the 22nd ACM Symposium on Parallelism in Algorithms and Architectures*, SPAA '10, pages 79–81, New York, NY, USA, 2010. ACM.

[18] J. Gunnels, C. Lin, G. Morrow, and R. van de Geijn. A flexible class of parallel matrix multiplication algorithms. In *Proceedings of the First Merged International Parallel Processing Symposium and Symposium on Parallel and Distributed Processing 1998*, pages 110–116. IEEE, 1998.

[19] F. Gustavson. Two fast algorithms for sparse matrices: Multiplication and permuted transposition. *ACM Transactions on Mathematical Software*, 4(3):250–269, 1978.

[20] C. Kruskal, L. Rudolph, and M. Snir. Techniques for parallel manipulation of sparse matrices. *Theor. Comput. Sci.*, 64(2):135–157, 1989.

[21] L. Loomis and H. Whitney. An inequality related to the isoperimetric inequality. *Bulletin of the AMS*, 55:961–962, 1949.

[22] W. McColl and A. Tiskin. Memory-efficient matrix multiplication in the BSP model. *Algorithmica*, 24:287–297, 1999.

[23] G. Penn. Efficient transitive closure of sparse matrices over closed semirings. *Theoretical Computer Science*, 354(1):72–81, 2006.

[24] A. Pietracaprina, G. Pucci, M. Riondato, F. Silvestri, and E. Upfal. Space-round tradeoffs for mapreduce computations. In *Proceedings of the 26th ACM International Conference on Supercomputing*, pages 235–244. ACM, 2012.

[25] M. Schatz, J. Poulson, and R. van de Geijn. Parallel matrix multiplication: 2d and 3d, FLAME Working Note #62. Technical Report TR-12-13, The University of Texas at Austin, Department of Computer Sciences, June 2012.

[26] E. Solomonik, A. Bhatele, and J. Demmel. Improving communication performance in dense linear algebra via topology aware collectives. In *Proceedings of 2011 International Conference for High Performance Computing, Networking, Storage and Analysis*, page 77. ACM, 2011.

[27] E. Solomonik and J. Demmel. Communication-optimal parallel 2.5D matrix multiplication and LU factorization algorithms. In *Euro-Par'11: Proceedings of the 17th International European Conference on Parallel and Distributed Computing*. Springer, 2011.

[28] R. van de Geijn and J. Watts. SUMMA: Scalable universal matrix multiplication algorithm. *Concurrency - Practice and Experience*, 9(4):255–274, 1997.

[29] S. Van Dongen. Graph clustering via a discrete uncoupling process. *SIAM Journal on Matrix Analysis and Applications*, 30(1):121–141, 2008.

[30] J. VandeVondele, U. Borštnik, and J. Hutter. Linear scaling self-consistent field calculations with millions of atoms in the condensed phase. *Journal of Chemical Theory and Computation*, 8(10):3565–3573, 2012.

[31] R. Yuster and U. Zwick. Fast sparse matrix multiplication. *ACM Transactions on Algorithms*, 1(1):2–13, 2005.

Communication Efficient Gaussian Elimination with Partial Pivoting using a Shape Morphing Data Layout[*]

Grey Ballard
UC Berkeley
ballard@cs.berkeley.edu

James Demmel
UC Berkeley
demmel@cs.berkeley.edu

Benjamin Lipshitz
UC Berkeley
lipshitz@cs.berkeley.edu

Oded Schwartz
UC Berkeley
odedsc@cs.berkeley.edu

Sivan Toledo
Tel-Aviv University
stoledo@tau.ac.il

ABSTRACT

High performance for numerical linear algebra often comes at the expense of stability. Computing the LU decomposition of a matrix via Gaussian Elimination can be organized so that the computation involves regular and efficient data access. However, maintaining numerical stability via partial pivoting involves row interchanges that lead to inefficient data access patterns. To optimize communication efficiency throughout the memory hierarchy we confront two seemingly contradictory requirements: partial pivoting is efficient with column-major layout, whereas a block-recursive layout is optimal for the rest of the computation. We resolve this by introducing a shape morphing procedure that dynamically matches the layout to the computation throughout the algorithm, and show that Gaussian Elimination with partial pivoting can be performed in a communication efficient and cache-oblivious way. Our technique extends to QR decomposition, where computing Householder vectors prefers a different data layout than the rest of the computation.

Categories and Subject Descriptors

F.2.1 [**Analysis of Algorithms and Problem Complexity**]: Numerical Algorithms and Problems—*Computations on matrices*

Keywords

communication-avoiding algorithms; matrix factorization; matrix data layouts; cache oblivious algorithms

[*]We acknowledge funding from Microsoft (Award #024263) and Intel (Award #024894), and matching funding by U.C. Discovery (Award #DIG07-10227). Additional support comes from ParLab affiliates National Instruments, Nokia, NVIDIA, Oracle and Samsung, as well as MathWorks. Research is also supported by DOE grants DE-SC0004938, DE-SC0005136, DE-SC0003959, DE-SC0008700, and AC02-05CH11231, and DARPA grant HR0011-12-2-0016, and grant 1045/09 from the Israel Science Foundation (founded by the Israel Academy of Sciences and Humanities), and grant 2010231 from the US-Israel Bi-National Science Foundation.

1. INTRODUCTION

Do we need to trade off numerical stability for high performance? This has been the most important question in numerical linear algebra for at least 20 years. It has motivated an enormous body of deep research. In this paper we show that for one very famous computation in numerical linear algebra, the answer is no: Gaussian Elimination with partial pivoting can be performed in a communication avoiding way.

High performance computers do not resemble simple computational models like the RAM model. They rely on parallelism and complex memory hierarchies to deliver high performance. In the past, such architectures were confined to supercomputers, but today they are ubiquitous. To run fast, an algorithm must be able to utilize many processors concurrently and to avoid communication as much as possible.

Out of all the effective algorithms for a given problem, only a subset exhibits high levels of parallelism and requires little communication between processors and/or between levels of the memory hierarchy. Does this subset always contain algorithms that are as stable as the best performing ones for the problem, or do we need to trade off stability for high performance? Consider Csanky's algorithm for matrix inversion: it has long been a classic example of a highly parallel but highly unstable algorithm; no known stable algorithm is as parallel. Twenty years ago, one of the authors suggested in an influential paper that even in practice, we must trade off stability in return for useful amounts of parallelism [6]. That paper has motivated a huge amount of research, with two main focal points. One has been the stability of so-called fast (Strassen-like) algorithms; this research has so far culminated in algorithms that are stable and fast in theory, but it remains to be seen whether they are also fast in practice [7]. The other focal point has been in algorithms that perform as little communication as possible, culminating in the definition of communication avoidance [5] and in a class of algorithms with that property.

An algorithm is called *communication avoiding* if it performs asymptotically as little communication as possible in two metrics: the total amount of data measured in words transferred between processors or levels of the memory hierarchy (the *bandwidth* it consumes), and the number of messages or block-transfers that carry this data (and therefore the number of times the message or cache-miss *latency* impacts the execution). To show that an algorithm is communication avoiding, one must exhibit a communication lower bound. For many matrix algorithms, lower bounds of the form $\Omega(f/M^{1/2})$ have been established on the number of words and $\Omega(f/(LM^{1/2}))$ on the number of messages, where f is the number of arithmetic operations performed by the algorithm, L is the maximum block-transfer size, and M is the size of the fast memory in a hierarchy or the local memory in a distributed memory parallel computer [5, 16, 17].

Minimizing the number of words communicated while preserving numerical stability has proved relatively easy for many problems. For Gaussian Elimination with partial pivoting (using the largest-magnitude element in a column to eliminate the rest of the column), a 1997 algorithm with a recursive schedule did the trick [14, 21] for the sequential (memory-hierarchy) case; this algorithm is also cache oblivious, in the sense that its schedule does not depend on M.

Minimizing the number of block-transfers while maintaining stability has proved much harder. The first communication avoiding algorithm for Gaussian Elimination [13] used a pivoting rule called tournament pivoting that was both more complicated and theoretically less stable than partial pivoting. A second-generation communication avoiding Gaussian Elimination algorithm [18] was even more complicated, but also more stable. The fundamental challenge that required the new pivoting rules is that partial pivoting steps works well when the matrix is stored by column, whereas updating the reduced matrix works well when the matrix is stored with contiguous blocks. The question of whether the simple, elegant, and stable partial pivoting rule can be used in a communication avoiding algorithm remained open.

In this paper we answer this question in the affirmative for the sequential case using a technique we call *shape morphing*: switching the data layout of parts of the matrix back and forth between column-major layout and recursive block-contiguous layout. Doing so allows Gaussian Elimination to access contiguous memory locations both when searching for a pivot down a column and applying row interchanges, and when computing the U factor and updating the reduced matrix (Schur complement). The shape morphing steps add data movement overhead to the algorithm, but we show that the overall algorithm remains asymptotically optimal. The algorithm is recursive and also cache-oblivious.

The same technique also produces communication avoiding algorithms for the related problem of QR factorization. In addition, we present a communication efficient algorithm for solving a triangular system where the right sides form a rectangular matrix. This subroutine is necessary inside SMLU but is also useful in several other contexts [2].

In the next section, we describe our communication cost model, and in Section 3 we describe the relevant matrix data layouts. We present the original recursive algorithms for LU and QR factorizations in Section 4 and discuss the new algorithms associated with shape-morphing and their analysis in Section 5. In Section 6 we discuss our main conclusions and the implications of the shape-morphing technique.

Algorithm 1 SMLU, in words. See Figure 3 and Algorithm 8 for further details.

> **if** one column **then**
> > solve the problem for a column
> **end if**
> recursively factor the left half
> forward permute
> reshape everything to recursive format
> update right half with triangular solve and Schur update
> reshape everything back to column format
> recursively factor the right half
> back permute
> combine pivots

Algorithm 2 SMQR, in words. See Figure 4 for further details.

> **if** one column **then**
> > solve the problem for a column
> **end if**
> recursively factor the left half
> reshape everything to recursive format
> update right half with triangular and general matrix multiplies
> reshape right half back to column format
> recursively factor the right half
> reshape right half to recursive format
> compute auxiliary triangular matrix T with triangular and general matrix multiplies
> reshape everything back to column format

---

2. MACHINE MODEL

We model a sequential computer as having an infinite slow memory and a finite fast memory of size M. All computation takes place in the fast memory, and we consider communication between the fast and slow memory. We count both the number of words of data W (or *bandwidth cost*) and the number of messages S (*latency cost*) transferred, and model the communication time as

$$\alpha \cdot S + \beta \cdot W,$$

where α and β are machine-dependent parameters. There is one more parameter, L, which is the size in words of the maximum allowed message (or block-transfer size). We make no assumptions on the size of L beyond the trivial requirements $1 \leq L \leq M$.

It is instructive to contrast our model to the ideal-cache model of [12]. There, the authors make a "tall cache" assumption that $M = \Omega(L^2)$. We do not make this assumption, so latency optimality is a stricter requirement in our model. Additionally, their model only allows messages of size L, which is equivalent to setting $\beta = 0$ in our model.

One may also consider models where there is a hierarchy of memories, each faster and smaller than the previous one, where the largest/slowest memory is infinite and the computation occurs only in the smallest/fastest memory, and one wishes to minimize the communication costs across every level of the hierarchy. A *cache-oblivious* algorithm is one that requires no tuning based on the machine parameters M and L. An algorithm that is cache-oblivious and communication-optimal in the two-level model, such as the SMLU algorithm that is the subject of this paper, is also communication-optimal with respect to every level of any hierarchical model.

3. DATA LAYOUTS

We consider two main data layouts: *column-major* and *rectangular-recursive*. The column-major layout is the layout used by standard libraries like LAPACK and stores each column contiguously with elements in a column ordered from top to bottom and columns themselves ordered from left to right. The rectangular-recursive layout is a generalization of block-recursive or Morton ordering [19], which is well-defined for square matrices with dimension a power of two. We also briefly mention *block-contiguous* layout, a cache-aware data layout in which blocks of the matrix are stored contiguously, in column-major order. The block-contiguous layout is used, for example, by the CALU algorithm [13].

The main motivation for recursive layouts like rectangular-recursive is that they map well to recursive algorithms: at every node in the recursion tree, the computation involves submatrices which are stored contiguously in memory. The rectangular-recursive layout, illustrated in Figure 2, corresponds to recursively splitting the largest dimension of the matrix and storing each of the two submatrices contiguously in memory. Choosing how to break ties for a square matrix (choosing whether to split horizontally or vertically) and deciding how to split odd dimensions leads to several variations of the rectangular-recursive layout. Here, we choose to split square matrices into left and right halves because that corresponds most closely to the column-major layout, and for odd dimensions, we choose to assign the extra row to top halves and the extra column to left halves. The latter decision is arbitrary but the same choice must be made throughout the algorithm. When applied to square power-of-two matrices, our choices lead to a standard И-Morton ordering.

There are several alternatives for generalizing Morton ordering [9, 10, 11, 15]. The simplest approach is to pad both rows and columns with zeros to obtain a square power-of-two matrix. However this can increase the number of matrix elements by a factor of 4 times the ratio of large dimension to small dimension. This approach is explored in [11], where the authors avoid the extra space and computation on padded rows and columns using "decorations" which denote full, partial, and zero submatrices. Hybrid layouts are also often used, storing small blocks in column or row-major layout and ordering the blocks using a Morton ordering. One can view our rectangular-recursive layout as the "recursive block column layout" from [9] with 1×1 block sizes.

We consider another alternative for generalizing Morton ordering to a specific class of rectangular matrices. If the smaller dimension of a rectangular matrix is a power of two and the larger dimension is a multiple of the smaller dimension, then the matrix can be divided up into several square power-of-two matrices. In this case, the elements within the square submatrices can be stored in standard Morton ordering, and the squares themselves can be ordered from top to bottom or left to right. This layout is illustrated in Figure 1. For the purposes of LU and QR factorizations, if the original matrix is square with power of two dimension, then all submatrices encountered can be stored in this layout. To preserve generality and avoid padding the original matrix, we describe our algorithms with the rectangular-recursive layout instead of this "stack of squares" layout.

4. RECTANGULAR RECURSIVE ALGORITHMS FOR LU AND QR

Many recursive algorithms for linear algebra computations are cache-oblivious, but in order to minimize latency costs the data layout must be chosen carefully. Morton ordering works very well for the recursive matrix multiplication algorithm, where the eight recursive subproblems involve matrix quadrants. The natural extension of Morton ordering to symmetric matrices also maps nicely to the square recursive algorithm for Cholesky decomposition [1, 3, 14]. In this algorithm, subroutines and recursive subproblems involve matrix quadrants (which may be symmetric, triangular, or dense).

For LU decomposition, the analogous square recursive algorithm (and standard Morton ordering) is not sufficient: in order to maintain numerical stability, row (and possibly column) interchanges are necessary. Partial pivoting, the most common scheme, involves at each step of the algorithm selecting the maximum element in absolute value in a column and interchanging the corresponding row with the diagonal element's row. For this reason, the square recursive algorithm for Cholesky does not generalize to nonsymmetric matrices: the top left quadrant of the matrix cannot be factored without accessing (and possibly interchanging) rows from the bottom left quadrant of the matrix.

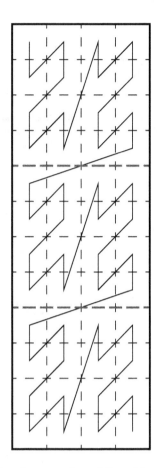

Figure 1: Stacks of squares layout for a 12×4 matrix. The 3 square 4×4 blocks are stored contiguously, each in Morton order.

In order to respect the column-access requirement of partial pivoting, Toledo [21] and Gustavson [14] developed a "rectangular recursive" algorithm (RLU) which recursively splits the matrix into left and right halves instead of quadrants. The steps of the computation are shown in Figure 3. Given an $m \times n$ input matrix, recursive subproblems are of size $m \times \frac{n}{2}$ and $\left(m - \frac{n}{2}\right) \times \frac{n}{2}$, and algorithms for triangular solve with multiple right hand sides (TRSM) and matrix multiplication are used as subroutines. Because the recursion splits the matrix into left and right halves, the base of the recursion consists of factoring single columns with partial pivoting: finding the maximum element, swapping it with the diagonal, and scaling the column with its reciprocal.

A similar algorithm for QR decomposition was developed by Elmroth and Gustavson [8]. The standard Householder QR algorithm works column-by-column, computing a Householder vector that annihilates all subdiagonal entries in the column and applying the orthogonal transformation to the trailing matrix. In order to compute one Householder vector per column, a rectangular recursive algorithm is necessary so that the base of the recursion consists of computing a single Householder vector to annihilate the entire column below the diagonal. The basic steps of the computation are shown in Figure 4. In the rectangular recursive QR algorithm, an auxiliary triangular matrix T is computed so that the update of the trailing matrix can be done with matrix multiplication.

Abandoning the requirement that the orthogonal factor Q be computed with one Householder vector per column allows for a square recursive algorithm for QR [11]. The square recursive algorithm

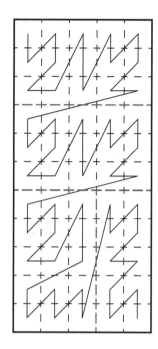

Figure 2: Rectangular-recursive order for a 11×5 matrix. At the first level, the top 6 rows are split from the bottom 5. At the second level, the top 6×5 block is split into two 3×5 blocks, whereas the bottom 5×5 block is split into a 5×3 block and a 5×2 block.

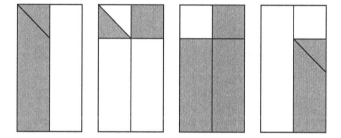

Figure 3: Cartoon of rectangular recursive algorithm for LU [14, 21]. Shaded areas correspond to computation. In SMLU, the first and fourth steps assume column-major ordering, and the second and third steps assume rectangular recursive ordering.

maps nicely onto standard Morton ordering, as each computation involves matrix quadrants. However, because the orthogonalization is based on many Givens rotations per column instead of one Householder vector per column, the standard trailing matrix update techniques do not apply. The approach from [11] is to explicitly construct the orthogonal factor Q, using matrix multiplication to update the trailing matrix. This technique leads to an increase in the total flop count of the decomposition compared to the standard algorithm, by a factor of approximately $3\times$.

By using shape morphing, we show that the rectangular recursive algorithm of Elmroth and Gustavson [8] can maintain the standard format of representing the orthogonal factor by its Householder vectors (one per column) and still achieve cache-obliviousness, minimizing both words and messages. The rectangular recursive algorithm also increases the flop count with respect to the standard algorithm, by about 17% for tall skinny matrices and about 30% for

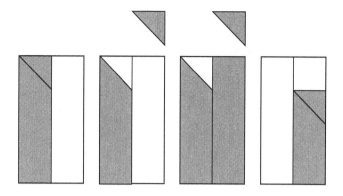

Figure 4: Cartoon of rectangular recursive algorithm for QR [8]. Shaded areas correspond to computation. The triangles correspond to the intermediate T factor. In SMQR, the first and fourth steps assume column-major ordering, and the second and third steps assume rectangular recursive ordering.

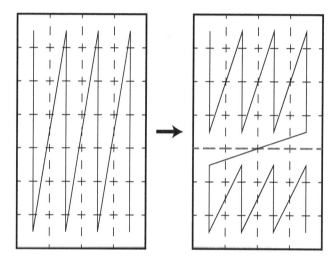

Figure 5: One recursive step in converting from column-major to rectangular recursive order.

square matrices. To limit the increase in computation, one can use a hybrid algorithm, using the rectangular recursive algorithm on panels of sufficiently small width. Since this tuning parameter prevents the algorithm from begin cache-oblivious, we do not consider the hybrid algorithm here.

5. ALGORITHMS AND ANALYSIS

5.1 Converting Rectangular Recursive to Column Major and Back

The algorithm for reshaping a rectangular $m \times n$ matrix from column-major order to rectangular recursive order is provided in Algorithm 4. The algorithm is recursive; at each step it splits the matrix along its largest dimension and is then recursively called on both submatrices. When the input is short and fat ($m \leq n$), splitting the matrix does not require any data movement, since in column-major order the left and right halves of the matrix are already contiguous. When the input is tall and skinny ($m > n$), splitting the matrix requires "separating" each column into its top and bottom halves. We perform this operation with the SEPARATE function: since it involves contiguously streaming through the input and contiguously writing to two output locations, as illustrated in Figure 5, the communication cost is $O(mn)$ words and $O(mn/L)$ messages. The recurrence for the communication cost is therefore

$$\text{RSH}(m,n) = \begin{cases} 2\text{RSH}(m/2,n) + O\left(\frac{mn}{L}\alpha + mn\beta\right) \\ \qquad \text{if } m > n \text{ and } mn > M \\ 2\text{RSH}(m,n/2) \\ \qquad \text{if } m \leq n \text{ and } mn > M \\ O\left(\left(\frac{mn}{L}+1\right)\alpha + mn\beta\right) \\ \qquad \text{if } mn \leq M. \end{cases}$$

There are at most $\log_2 \frac{mn}{M}$ recursive steps, and each has communication cost bounded by $O(\frac{mn}{L}\alpha + mn\beta)$, so the solution is

$$\text{RSH}(m,n) = O\left(\frac{mn}{L}\log\frac{mn}{M} + 1\right)\alpha$$
$$+ O\left(mn\left(\log\frac{mn}{M}+1\right)\right)\beta.$$

Reshaping from rectangular recursive order to column-major order is described in Algorithm 10, and has identical costs.

Algorithm 3 $\begin{pmatrix} A_1 \\ A_2 \end{pmatrix} = \text{SEPARATE}(A,m,n,m_1)$

Input: A is $m \times n$ in column-major order
Output: A_1 is the first m_1 rows of A in column-major order, A_2 is the remaining $m - m_1$ rows of A in column-major order
  for j in 1:n **do**
    $A_1(1:m_1,j) = A(1:m_1,j)$
    $A_2(1:m-m_1,j) = A(m_1+1:m,j)$
  end for

Algorithm 4 $B = \text{RESHAPETORECURSIVE}(A,m,n)$

Input: A is $m \times n$ with $m \geq n$ in column-major order
Output: B is the same matrix in rectangular recursive order
  if $m = n = 1$ **then**
    $B(1,1) = A(1,1)$
    return
  end if
  if $m > n$ **then**
    $m_1 = \lceil m/2 \rceil$, $m_2 = \lfloor m/2 \rfloor$
    $\begin{pmatrix} B_1 \\ B_2 \end{pmatrix} = \text{SEPARATE}(A,m,n,m_1)$
    $B_1 = \text{RESHAPETORECURSIVE}(B_1,m_1,n)$
    $B_2 = \text{RESHAPETORECURSIVE}(B_2,m_2,n)$
    $B = \begin{pmatrix} B_1 \\ B_2 \end{pmatrix}$
  else
    $n_1 = \lceil n/2 \rceil$, $n_2 = \lfloor n/2 \rfloor$
    $\begin{pmatrix} B_1 & B_2 \end{pmatrix} = A$
    $B_1 = \text{RESHAPETORECURSIVE}(B_1,m,n_1)$
    $B_2 = \text{RESHAPETORECURSIVE}(B_2,m,n_2)$
    $B = \begin{pmatrix} B_1 & B_2 \end{pmatrix}$
  end if

5.2 Rectangular Matrix Multiplication

The SMLU algorithm requires a recursive matrix multiplication algorithm for square matrices stored in rectangular recursive order. The rectangular recursive matrix multiplication algorithm and its communication cost analysis are in [12]. In our model the commu-

nication costs are worked out in [3] and are

$$\text{GEMM}(m,n,k) = O\left(\frac{mnk}{\sqrt{M}L} + \frac{mn+mk+nk}{L} + 1\right)\alpha$$
$$+ O\left(\frac{mnk}{\sqrt{M}} + mn + mk + nk\right)\beta,$$

where m, n, k are the three matrix dimensions.

5.3 Rectangular Triangular Solve

The SMLU algorithm requires a recursive triangular solve on matrices stored in rectangular-recursive layout. An algorithm for square matrices with optimal communication costs is given in [3]. In Algorithm 5 we generalize to the case of rectangular matrices. Let A be an $m \times n$ matrix, and L be an $m \times m$ unit lower triangular matrix.[1] At each recursive step, split the larger of m and n. Splitting m gives two recursive calls to RECTRSM and one call to matrix multiplication. Splitting n gives two recursive calls to RECTRSM. Thus the communication cost recurrence is:

$$\text{TRSM}(m,n) = \begin{cases} 2\text{TRSM}(m/2,n) + \text{GEMM}(m,m,n) \\ \qquad \text{if } m > n \text{ and } 2mn + m^2 > M \\ 2\text{TRSM}(m,n/2) \\ \qquad \text{if } n \geq m \text{ and } 2mn + m^2 > M \\ O\left(\left(\frac{mn+m^2}{L}+1\right)\alpha + (mn+m^2)\beta\right) \\ \qquad \text{if } 2mn + m^2 \leq M \end{cases}$$

with solution

$$\text{TRSM}(m,n) = O\left(\frac{m^2n}{L\sqrt{M}} + \frac{mn+m^2}{L} + 1\right)\alpha$$
$$+ \left(\frac{m^2n}{\sqrt{M}} + mn + m^2\right)\beta.$$

Algorithm 5 $U = \text{RECTRSM}(A,L,m,n)$

Input: A is $m \times n$, L is $m \times m$ and unit lower triangular, both in rectangular recursive layout
Output: $U = L^{-1}A$ in rectangular recursive layout
  if $m = n = 1$ **then**
    $U(1,1) = A(1,1)$
    return
  end if
  if $m > n$ **then**
    $m_1 = \lceil m/2 \rceil$, $m_2 = \lfloor m/2 \rfloor$
    $\begin{pmatrix} L_{11} & \\ L_{21} & L_{22} \end{pmatrix} = L$
    $\begin{pmatrix} U_1 \\ U_2 \end{pmatrix} = U$
    $U_1 = \text{RECTRSM}(U_1,L_{11},m_1,n)$
    $U_2 = \text{RECGEMM}(L_{21},U_1,U_2,m_2,m_1,n)$
    $U_2 = \text{RECTRSM}(U_2,L_{22},m_2,n)$
    $U = \begin{pmatrix} U_1 \\ U_2 \end{pmatrix}$
  else
    $n_1 = \lceil n/2 \rceil$, $n_2 = \lfloor n/2 \rfloor$
    $\begin{pmatrix} U_1 & U_2 \end{pmatrix} = U$
    $U_1 = \text{RECTRSM}(U_1,L,m,n_1)$
    $U_2 = \text{RECTRSM}(U_2,L,m,n_2)$
    $U = \begin{pmatrix} U_1 & U_2 \end{pmatrix}$
  end if

---

[1] A non-unit lower triangular matrix changes only the base case computation.

5.4 Pivoting

The SMLU algorithm returns a pivot vector p of length m, where $p(i) = j$ indicates that row j in the original matrix has been pivoted to row i in the output. Two subroutines are required to manage the pivoting.

First, APPLYPIVOTS, presented as Algorithm 6, applies a pivot vector to a matrix. It applies the pivot vector to each column of the matrix in sequence. For each column, it applies the pivot vector recursively by streaming through the entire column to separate entries between those that belong in the top half from those that belong in the bottom half of the permuted column, the calling itself on both the top and bottom halves. If $m < M$, at least one column fits into memory and APPLYPIVOTS needs to read the matrix only once. If $m > M$, it reads and writes each column $\log(m/M)$ times. The communication costs are

$$\text{APPLYPIVOTS}(m, n) = O\left(\frac{mn}{L}\left(1 + \log\frac{m}{M}\right) + 1\right)\alpha$$
$$+ O\left(mn\left(1 + \log\frac{m}{M}\right)\right)\beta.$$

It is also necessary to combine two pivot vectors into one, which is done by COMBINEPIVOTS, presented in Algorithm 7. This is accomplished by two calls to APPLYPIVOTS with $n = 1$, so the communication costs are

$$\text{COMBINEPIVOTS}(m) = O\left(\frac{m}{L}\left(1 + \log\frac{m}{M}\right) + 1\right)\alpha$$
$$+ O\left(m\left(1 + \log\frac{m}{M}\right)\right)\beta.$$

Algorithm 6 APPLYPIVOTS(A,P,m,n)

Input: A is $m \times n$ in column-major order, P is a pivot vector
Output: The rows of A are pivoted according to P

  if $m = n = 1$ **then**
    return
  end if
  if $n - 1$ **then**
    $m_1 = \lceil m/2 \rceil, m_2 = \lfloor m/2 \rfloor$
    $c_1 =$ new array of length m_1
    $c_2 =$ new array of length m_2
    $P_1 =$ new array of length m_1
    $P_2 =$ new array of length m_2
    $j = 1; k = 1$
    for i in $1 : n$ **do**
      if $P(i) \leq m_1$ **then**
        $c_1(j) = A(i)$
        $P_1(j) = P(i)$
        $j = j + 1$
      else
        $c_2(j) = A(i)$
        $P_2(j) = P(i) - m_1$
        $k = k + 1$
      end if
    end for
    APPLYPIVOTS($c_1,P_1,m_1,1$)
    APPLYPIVOTS($c_2,P_2,m_2,1$)
  else
    $n_1 = \lceil n/2 \rceil, n_2 = \lfloor n/2 \rfloor$
    $\begin{pmatrix} A_1 & A_2 \end{pmatrix} = A$
    APPLYPIVOTS(A_1,P,m,n_1)
    APPLYPIVOTS(A_2,P,m,n_2)
  end if

Algorithm 7 $P = $ COMBINEPIVOTS(P_L,P_R,m_L,m_R)

Input: P_L, P_R are left and right pivot vectors
Output: P is the combined pivot vector

  // Convert the size of the right pivot vector
  $k = m_L - m_R$
  $P'_R =$ new vector of length m_L
  $P'_R(1 : k) = 1 : k$
  $P'_R(k + 1 : m_L) = P_R + k$

  // Combine pivots
  $P_I = $ APPLYPIVOTS($1 : m_L,P_L,m_L,1$)
  $P = $ APPLYPIVOTS($P'_R,P_I,m_L,1$)

5.5 Analysis of SMLU

Detailed pseudocode for SMLU appears in Algorithm 8. Each call to SMLU has two recursive calls to itself, two calls to APPLYPIVOTS, four calls each to RESHAPETORECURSIVE and RESHAPETOCOLMAJOR, one call to RECTRSM, one to RECGEMM, and one call to COMBINEPIVOTS. The recursive communication costs are thus

$$\text{SMLU}(m, n) \leq 2\text{SMLU}\left(m, \frac{n}{2}\right) + 2\text{APPLYPIVOTS}\left(m, \frac{n}{2}\right)$$
$$+ 8\text{RSH}\left(m, \frac{n}{2}\right) + \text{TRSM}\left(\frac{n}{2}, \frac{n}{2}\right)$$
$$+ \text{GEMM}\left(m, \frac{n}{2}, \frac{n}{2}\right) + \text{COMBINEPIVOTS}(m)$$

which simplifies to

$$\text{SMLU}(m, n) \leq 2\text{SMLU}\left(m, \frac{n}{2}\right)$$
$$+ O\left(\frac{mn^2}{L\sqrt{M}} + \frac{mn}{L}\log\frac{mn}{M} + \frac{mn}{L}\right)\alpha$$
$$+ O\left(\frac{mn^2}{\sqrt{M}} + mn\log\frac{mn}{M} + mn\right)\beta.$$

If $M < m$, one column of the matrix does not fit in fast memory, so the base case costs are $\text{SMLU}(1, m) = m\left(\beta + \frac{\alpha}{L}\right)$. If $M \geq m$, then M/m columns fit into fast memory at once, so the base case costs are $\text{SMLU}(\frac{M}{m}, m) = M\left(\beta + \frac{\alpha}{L}\right)$. The solution to the recurrence is

$$\text{SMLU}(m, n) = \begin{cases} O\left(\left(\frac{mn^2}{\sqrt{M}} + mn\log\frac{mn}{M}\log n\right)\left(\beta + \frac{\alpha}{L}\right) + \alpha\right) \\ \qquad\qquad\qquad\qquad\qquad\qquad\qquad \text{if } M < m \\ O\left(\left(\frac{mn^2}{\sqrt{M}} + mn\left(\log\frac{mn}{M}\right)^2 + mn\right)\left(\beta + \frac{\alpha}{L}\right) + \alpha\right) \\ \qquad\qquad\qquad\qquad\qquad\qquad\qquad \text{if } M \geq m \end{cases}$$

Recall that the communication lower bound for LU [5] is

$$\text{LU}(m, n) = \Omega\left(\left(\frac{mn^2}{\sqrt{M}} + mn\right)\left(\beta + \frac{\alpha}{L}\right) + \alpha\right).$$

Compared to this lower bound, SMLU has an extra polylogarithmic factor on the mn term. In the square case, $m = n$, SMLU asymptotically matches the lower bound except in the tiny range

$$\frac{n^2}{(\log(n))^4} \ll M \ll n^2.$$

In the rectangular case, SMLU may be larger than the lower bound by a logarithmic factor in a larger range

$$\frac{n^2}{(\log(mn))^4} \ll M \ll mn.$$

Compared to the original rectangular recursive algorithm for LU [14, 21], with partial pivoting but without shape morphing, SMLU has a bandwidth cost with an extra $\log(mn/M)$ on the mn term. Thus, outside the ranges given above, shape morphing does not increase the bandwidth costs asymptotically. In all cases, shape morphing does reduce latency costs relative to the original rectangular recursive algorithm.

Algorithm 8 $P = \text{SMLU}(A, m, n)$

---

if n = 1 **then**
    $P = 1 : m$
    $i = \text{ArgMax}(|A|)$
    $\text{Swap}(A(1), A(i))$
    $\text{Swap}(P(1), P(i))$
    $\text{Scale}(A(2 : m), 1/A(1))$
else

    // set submatrix dimensions
    $n_1 = \lceil \frac{n}{2} \rceil$
    $n_2 = n - n_1$
    $m_1 = n_1$
    $m_2 = m - m_1$

    // recurse on left half
    $\begin{pmatrix} A_1 & A_2 \end{pmatrix} = A$
    $P_{\text{L}} = \text{SMLU}(A_1, m, n_1)$

    // forward pivot
    $\text{APPLYPIVOTS}(A_2, P_{\text{L}}, m, n_2)$

    // separate top m_1 rows from bottom m_2 rows
    $\begin{pmatrix} A_{11} \\ A_{21} \end{pmatrix} = \text{SEPARATE}(A_1, m, n_1, m_1)$
    $\begin{pmatrix} A_{12} \\ A_{22} \end{pmatrix} = \text{SEPARATE}(A_2, m, n_2, m_1)$

    // convert each quadrant to Morton ordering
    $\text{RESHAPETORECURSIVE}(A_{11}, m_1, n_1)$
    $\text{RESHAPETORECURSIVE}(A_{12}, m_1, n_2)$
    $\text{RESHAPETORECURSIVE}(A_{21}, m_2, n_1)$
    $\text{RESHAPETORECURSIVE}(A_{22}, m_2, n_2)$

    // triangular solve with Morton ordered arrays
    $A_{12} = \text{RECTRSM}(A_{12}, A_{11}, n_1, n_2)$

    // Schur update with Morton ordered arrays
    $A_{22} = \text{RECGEMM}(A_{21}, A_{12}, A_{22}, m_2, n_1, n_2)$

    // convert quadrants back to column major
    $A_{11} = \text{RESHAPETOCOLMAJOR}(A_{11}, m_1, n_1)$
    $A_{12} = \text{RESHAPETOCOLMAJOR}(A_{12}, m_1, n_2)$
    $A_{21} = \text{RESHAPETOCOLMAJOR}(A_{21}, m_2, n_1)$
    $A_{22} = \text{RESHAPETOCOLMAJOR}(A_{22}, m_2, n_2)$

    // recurse on (bottom of) right half
    $P_{\text{R}} = \text{SMLU}(A_{22}, m_2, n_2)$

    // back pivot
    $\text{APPLYPIVOTS}(A_{21}, P_{\text{R}}, m_2, n_1)$

    // combine pivots
    $P = \text{COMBINEPIVOTS}(P_{\text{L}}, P_{\text{R}}, m, m_2)$
    $A = \text{COMBINE}(\begin{pmatrix} A_{11} & A_{12} \end{pmatrix}, \begin{pmatrix} A_{21} & A_{22} \end{pmatrix}, m, n, m_1)$
end if

---

6. DISCUSSION

Because of the impact of communication costs on performance, there is a long history of algorithmic innovation to reduce communication costs for LU factorizations. Table 1 highlights several of the innovations, including SMLU presented here, and compares the asymptotic communication costs and other characteristics for a particular scenario: the table assumes a square matrix ($m = n$), very long cache lines ($L = \Theta(M)$), and reasonably sized matrices ($\sqrt{M} < n < M$).

The LAPACK library [2] was developed in the early 1990s to provide a standard for high performance implementations for fundamental computations in linear algebra. The algorithms are based on "blocking" in order to cast much of the work in terms of matrix-matrix multiplication which can attain high data re-use, rather than working column-by-column and performing most of the work as matrix-vector operations. The LU factorization algorithm in LAPACK is a right-looking, blocked algorithm, and by choosing the right block size, the algorithm asymptotically reduces the communication costs compared to the column-by-column algorithm. In fact, for very large matrices ($m, n > M$) it can attain the communication lower bounds for LU proved recently in [5, 13]. However, for reasonably sized matrices ($m, n < M$) the blocked algorithm is sub-optimal with respect to its communication costs.

In the late 1990s, both Toledo [21] and Gustavson [14] independently showed that using recursive algorithms can reduce communication costs. The analysis in [21] shows that the RLU algorithm moves asymptotically fewer words than the LAPACK algorithm when $m < M$ (though latency cost is not considered in that work). In fact, the RLU algorithm attains the bandwidth cost lower bounds. Furthermore, RLU is cache-oblivious, as later defined in [12], so it minimizes bandwidth cost for any fast memory size and between any pair of successive levels of a memory hierarchy.

Motivated by the growing latency cost on both sequential and parallel machines, Grigori, Demmel, and Xiang [13] considered bandwidth and latency cost metrics and presented an algorithm that minimizes both. In the sequential case, cache lines are often short, but in some cases, such as out-of-core computation, the long cache line model with latency costs is appropriate. In order to attain the lower bound for latency cost (proved in that paper via reduction from matrix multiplication), the authors used the block-contiguous layout and introduced tournament pivoting as a new and different scheme than partial pivoting. Tournament pivoting scheme makes different pivoting choices than partial pivoting and is theoretically less stable (though the two schemes are equivalent in a weak sense and have similar characteristics in practice [13]). The drawbacks to CALU are that it requires knowledge of the fast memory size for both algorithm and data layout (*i.e.*, it is not cache-oblivious), and that, because of its youth, tournament pivoting does not enjoy the same confidence from the numerical community as partial pivoting.

Making the RLU algorithm latency optimal has been an open problem for a few years. For example, arguments are made in [4] and [13] that RLU is not latency optimal for several different fixed data layouts. Through shape morphing, we show that attaining communication optimality, being cache oblivious, and using partial pivoting are all simultaneously achievable. The technique generalizes to QR decomposition, for which a similar history of algorithmic innovation exists. SMLU is not optimal only in a small range and only by a polylogarithmic factor. It remains open whether one can close or reduce this gap.

Unfortunately, the idea of shape-morphing is unlikely to yield the same benefits in the parallel case (*i.e.*, attaining the latency lower bound while using partial pivoting). Choosing pivots for each of n columns lies on the critical path of the algorithm and therefore

Algorithm	Bandwidth Cost	Latency Cost	Pivoting	Data Layout	Cache Oblivious
Lower Bound [5, 13]	$\Omega\left(\frac{n^3}{\sqrt{M}}\right)$	$\Omega\left(\frac{n^3}{M^{3/2}}\right)$	any	any	-
Naïve	$O(n^3)$	$O\left(\frac{n^3}{M}\right)$	partial	CM	✓
LAPACK [2]	$O\left(\frac{n^4}{M}\right)$	$O\left(\frac{n^3}{M}\right)$	partial	CM	✗
RLU [21]	$O\left(\frac{n^3}{\sqrt{M}} + n^2\log\frac{n^2}{M}\right)$	$O\left(\frac{n^3}{M}\right)$	partial	CM	✓
CALU [13]	$O\left(\frac{n^3}{\sqrt{M}}\right)$	$O\left(\frac{n^3}{M^{3/2}}\right)$	tournament	BC	✗
SMLU	$O\left(\frac{n^3}{\sqrt{M}} + n^2\log^2\frac{n^2}{M}\right)$	$O\left(\frac{n^3}{M^{3/2}} + \frac{n^2}{M}\log^2\frac{n^2}{M}\right)$	partial	CM or RR	✓

Table 1: Asymptotic communication costs and characteristics of LU factorization algorithms. This table assumes a square matrix ($m = n$), very long cache lines ($L = \Theta(M)$), and reasonably sized matrices ($\sqrt{M} \le n \le M$). We use the acronyms CM, BC, and RR for column-major, block-contiguous, and rectangular-recursive data layouts, respectively, as defined in Section 3.

must be done in sequence. Each pivot choice either requires at least one message or for the whole column to reside on a single processor. This seems to require either $\Omega(n)$ messages or $\Omega(n^2)$ words moved. Tournament pivoting in the parallel case achieves substantially lower communication costs [13, 20].

7. REFERENCES

[1] N. Ahmed and K. Pingali. Automatic generation of block-recursive codes. In *Euro-Par '00: Proceedings from the 6th International Euro-Par Conference on Parallel Processing*, pages 368–378, London, UK, 2000. Springer-Verlag.

[2] E. Anderson, Z. Bai, C. Bischof, J. Demmel, J. Dongarra, J. Du Croz, A. Greenbaum, S. Hammarling, A. McKenney, S. Ostrouchov, and D. Sorensen. *LAPACK's user's guide*. Society for Industrial and Applied Mathematics, Philadelphia, PA, USA, 1992. Also available from http://www.netlib.org/lapack/.

[3] G. Ballard, J. Demmel, O. Holtz, and O. Schwartz. Communication-optimal parallel and sequential Cholesky decomposition. In *SPAA '09: Proceedings of the Twenty-First Annual Symposium on Parallelism in Algorithms and Architectures*, pages 245–252, New York, NY, USA, 2009. ACM.

[4] G. Ballard, J. Demmel, O. Holtz, and O. Schwartz. Communication-optimal parallel and sequential Cholesky decomposition. *SIAM Journal on Scientific Computing*, 32(6):3495–3523, 2010.

[5] G. Ballard, J. Demmel, O. Holtz, and O. Schwartz. Minimizing communication in numerical linear algebra. *SIAM J. Matrix Analysis Applications*, 32(3):866–901, 2011.

[6] J. Demmel. LAPACK Working Note 53: Trading off parallelism and numerical stability. Technical report, University of Tennessee, Knoxville, TN, USA, 1992.

[7] J. Demmel, I. Dumitriu, and O. Holtz. Fast linear algebra is stable. *Numerische Mathematik*, 108(1):59–91, 2007.

[8] E. Elmroth and F. Gustavson. New serial and parallel recursive QR factorization algorithms for SMP systems. *Applied Parallel Computing Large Scale Scientific and Industrial Problems*, pages 120–128, 1998.

[9] E. Elmroth, F. Gustavson, I. Jonsson, and B. Kågström. Recursive blocked algorithms and hybrid data structures for dense matrix library software. *SIAM Review*, 46(1):3–45, 2004.

[10] J. Frens and D. Wise. Auto-blocking matrix-multiplication or tracking BLAS3 performance from source code. In *In Proceedings of the Sixth ACM SIGPLAN Symposium on Principles and Practice of Parallel Programming*, pages 206–216, 1997.

[11] J. Frens and D. Wise. QR factorization with Morton-ordered quadtree matrices for memory re-use and parallelism. *SIGPLAN Not.*, 38(10):144–154, 2003.

[12] M. Frigo, C. Leiserson, H. Prokop, and S. Ramachandran. Cache-oblivious algorithms. In *FOCS '99: Proceedings of the 40th Annual Symposium on Foundations of Computer Science*, pages 285–297, Washington, DC, USA, 1999. IEEE Computer Society.

[13] L. Grigori, J. Demmel, and H. Xiang. CALU: A communication optimal LU factorization algorithm. *SIAM Journal on Matrix Analysis and Applications*, 32(4):1317–1350, 2011.

[14] F. Gustavson. Recursion leads to automatic variable blocking for dense linear-algebra algorithms. *IBM J. Res. Dev.*, 41(6):737–756, 1997.

[15] F. Gustavson, A. Henriksson, I. Jonsson, B. Kågström, and P. Ling. Recursive blocked data formats and BLAS's for dense linear algebra algorithms. *Applied Parallel Computing Large Scale Scientific and Industrial Problems*, pages 195–206, 1998.

[16] J. W. Hong and H. T. Kung. I/O complexity: The red-blue pebble game. In *STOC '81: Proceedings of the thirteenth annual ACM symposium on theory of computing*, pages 326–333. ACM, 1981.

[17] D. Irony, S. Toledo, and A. Tiskin. Communication lower bounds for distributed-memory matrix multiplication. *J. Parallel Distrib. Comput.*, 64(9):1017–1026, 2004.

[18] A. Khabou, J. Demmel, L. Grigori, and M. Gu. LU factorization with panel rank revealing pivoting and its communication avoiding version. Technical Report UCB/EECS-2012-15, EECS Department, University of California, Berkeley, Jan 2012.

[19] G. Morton. *A Computer Oriented Geodetic Data Base and a New Technique in File Sequencing*. International Business Machines Company, 1966.

[20] E. Solomonik and J. Demmel. Communication-optimal parallel 2.5D matrix multiplication and LU factorization algorithms. In *Euro-Par'11: Proceedings of the 17th*

International European Conference on Parallel and Distributed Computing. Springer, 2011.

[21] S. Toledo. Locality of reference in LU decomposition with partial pivoting. *SIAM J. Matrix Anal. Appl.*, 18(4):1065–1081, 1997.

APPENDIX

We include supplementary algorithms here. Algorithm 9 is the reverse of Algorithm 3, and Algorithm 10 is the reverse of Algorithm 4.

Algorithm 9 $A = \text{COMBINE}(A_1, A_2, m, n, m_1)$

Input: A_1 is $m_1 \times n$ and A_2 is $m - m_1 \times n$ both in column-major order

Output: A is $m \times n$, the first m_1 rows are from A_1 and the remaining rows are from A_2

    for j in 1:n **do**

        $A(1 : m_1, j) = A_1(1 : m_1, j)$

        $A(m_1 + 1 : m, j) = A_2(1 : m - m_1, j)$

    end for

Algorithm 10 $B = \text{RESHAPETOCOLMAJOR}(A, n, m)$

Input: A is $m \times n$ with $m \geq n$ in rectangular recursive order

Output: B is the same matrix in column-major order

    if $m = n = 1$ **then**

        $B(1, 1) = A(1, 1)$

        return

    end if

    if $m > n$ **then**

        $m_1 = \lceil m/2 \rceil, m_2 = \lfloor m/2 \rfloor$

        $\begin{pmatrix} B_1 \\ B_2 \end{pmatrix} = A$

        $B_1 = \text{RESHAPETOCOLMAJOR}(B_1, m_1, n)$

        $B_2 = \text{RESHAPETOCOLMAJOR}(B_2, m_2, n)$

        $B = \text{COMBINE}(B_1, B_2, m, n, m_1)$

    else

        $n_1 = \lceil n/2 \rceil, n_2 = \lfloor n/2 \rfloor$

        $\begin{pmatrix} B_1 & B_2 \end{pmatrix} = A$

        $B_1 = \text{RESHAPETOCOLMAJOR}(B_1, m, n_1)$

        $B_2 = \text{RESHAPETOCOLMAJOR}(B_2, m, n_2)$

        $B = \begin{pmatrix} B_1 & B_2 \end{pmatrix}$

    end if

Optimal Patrolling of Fragmented Boundaries*

Andrew Collins
University of Liverpool
acollins@liverpool.ac.uk

Jurek Czyzowicz
Université du Québec en
Outaouais
Jurek.Czyzowicz@uqo.ca

Leszek Gąsieniec
University of Liverpool
L.A.Gasieniec@liverpool.ac.uk

Adrian Kosowski
Inria Bordeaux Sud-Ouest
kosowski@labri.fr

Evangelos Kranakis
Carleton University
kranakis@scs.carleton.ca

Danny Krizanc
Wesleyan University
dkrizanc@wesleyan.edu

Russell Martin
University of Liverpool
Russell.Martin@liverpool.ac.uk

Oscar Morales Ponce
Chalmers University of
Technology
oscarmponce@gmail.com

ABSTRACT

A set of mobile robots is deployed on a simple curve of finite length, composed of a finite set of *vital segments* separated by *neutral segments*. The robots have to patrol the vital segments by perpetually moving on the curve, without exceeding their uniform maximum speeds. The quality of patrolling is measured by the *idleness*, i.e., the longest time period during which any vital point on the curve is not visited by any robot. Given a configuration of vital segments, our goal is to provide algorithms describing the movement of the robots along the curve so as to minimize the idleness.

Our main contribution is a proof that the optimal solution to the patrolling problem is attained either by the *cyclic strategy*, in which all the robots move in one direction around the curve, or by the *partition strategy*, in which the curve is partitioned into sections which are patrolled separately by individual robots. These two fundamental types of strategies were studied in the past in the robotics community in different theoretical and experimental settings. However, to our knowledge, this is the first theoretical analysis proving optimality in such a general scenario. Throughout the paper we assume that all robots have the same maximum speed. In fact, the claim is known to be invalid when this assumption does not hold, cf. [Czyzowicz et al., *Proc.* ESA 2011].

Categories and Subject Descriptors

C.2.4 [**Computer-Communication Networks**]:
Distributed Systems

*Supported by ANR project DISPLEXITY and by NCN under contract DEC-2011/02/A/ST6/00201. The full version of this paper is available online at: http://hal.inria.fr/hal-00686270.

Keywords

Algorithms; Mobile robots; Boundary patrolling; Idleness

1. INTRODUCTION

Protecting an environment by a set of stationary or mobile point-guards has been studied before in various scenarios. The problem of patrolling a one-dimensional boundary using mobile robots has many real-world applications, and is extensively studied under the names of *boundary patrolling* and *fence patrolling* in the robotics literature [11]. In order to prevent an intruder from penetrating into a protected region, the boundary of the region must be patrolled. Some parts of the boundary may be monitored with stationary devices like sensors or cameras (or they do not need to be monitored at all), while other portions require the aid of moving robots such as walking guards, illumination rays, mobile robotic devices, etc. Since the feasibility of an intrusion likely depends on the time during which the intruder remains undiscovered, it is important to design patrolling protocols which minimize the time during which boundary points are unprotected.

Some portions of the boundary may be impenetrable at all, or they may be monitored with stationary devices like sensors or cameras. This paper is devoted to the scenario in which only a finite number n of boundary segments, referred to as *vital regions*, need to be patrolled by a set of k mobile robots. The remaining part of the boundary, called *neutral regions*, do not have to be monitored by the mobile robots, but may nevertheless be traversed by a robot since this may be the way to reach one vital region from another. We study the problem of patrolling with the goal of minimizing the idleness of points located in the vital regions, i.e., the longest time during which such a point remains unvisited by a robot. We assume that at any time during the traversal the speed of each robot cannot exceed a certain maximum value, identical for all robots. Our goal is to define a set of functions describing the trajectories of all the robots in time.

The most common heuristics adopted in the past to solve a variety of patrolling problems include the *cyclic strategy*, where robots move in one direction around the cycle covering the environment, and the *partition strategy*, in which the environment is partitioned into sections patrolled separately by individual robots (or subsets of robots), using the terminology introduced in [6]. However, to the best of our knowledge, no theoretical studies formally proving the optimality of such approaches in this setting were done in the past.

It is worth noting, that in the more heterogeneous scenario where robots have different maximum speeds, neither the cyclic strategy nor the partition strategy leads to the optimal performance. In fact, it has been shown in [11] that for the case of 3 mobile robots with different maximal speeds patrolling a cycle (forming a single vital region), neither a partition strategy nor a cyclic strategy is optimal. It turns out that a specific hybrid strategy is better than each of these two fundamental approaches. See also [24].

1.1 Model, Preliminaries, and Notation

We consider $k \geq 1$ mobile robots. Each robot moves along a continuous rectifiable curve C, i.e., a curve of finite length.

DEFINITION 1.1 (TRAVERSAL STRATEGY). *A traversal strategy for a single mobile robot is a continuous function $f : [0, +\infty) \to C$ such that $t \mapsto f(t)$, whereby $f(t)$ is the position of the robot on the rectifiable curve at time $t \geq 0$. A traversal strategy for k mobile robots consists of k such continuous functions, one f_i for each mobile robot $1 \leq i \leq k$.*

Without loss of generality, we assume that the curve C is either a segment of unit length (when C is an open curve), or a cycle of unit perimeter (when C is a closed curve). In both cases, we will adopt the unit segment $[0, 1]$ to represent uniquely all points on the curve, noting that in the case of the cycle, points 0 and 1 are identified with each other. All robots move along C at speeds not exceeding the unit maximum value understood to be 1.

DEFINITION 1.2 (UNIT MAXIMUM SPEED). *Let $dist(p, q)$ denote the distance between any points $p, q \in C$ along the curve C. We say that the traversal strategy for k robots respects the robots' unit maximum speed if for any $1 \leq i \leq k$ and any $t_1, t_2 \in [0, +\infty)$ we have $\frac{dist(f_i(t_1), f_i(t_2))}{|t_1 - t_2|} \leq 1$.*

In what follows, we will always consider traversal strategies that respect the maximum speed of each robot. The task of the k robots is to patrol so-called vital regions, located in the unit-length curve C (along which the robots move), so as to minimize the idleness of the points in the vital regions.

DEFINITION 1.3 (VITAL AND NEUTRAL REGIONS). *Each considered curve C contains n disjoint vital regions represented by closed intervals $V_1, V_2, \ldots, V_n$, where $V_i = [b_i, e_i]$ and $e_i < b_{i+1}$ for $1 \leq i \leq n-1$, with $b_1 = 0$ and $e_n \leq 1$. The vital regions are separated by open intervals from N called neutral regions. In other word the curve $C = (V, N)$, where $[0, 1] \supseteq V = \bigcup_{i=1}^{n} V_i$, and $N = [0, 1] \setminus V$.*

DEFINITION 1.4 (IDLENESS). *Let $\mathcal{A}$ be a traversal strategy consisting of k continuous functions f_i for a system of k mobile robots, respectively, and traversing the given curve.*

1. *The idleness induced by $\mathcal{A}$ at a point x of the curve, denoted by $I_x(\mathcal{A})$, is the supremum of the length of time intervals during which point x remains unvisited by any agent:*

$$I_x(\mathcal{A}) = \sup_{\{0 \leq T_1 < T_2 \,:\, \forall i \forall t \in [T_1, T_2] \ f_i(t) \neq x\}} (T_2 - T_1).$$

2. *The idleness of the system of k mobile robots induced by $\mathcal{A}$ is defined by $I(\mathcal{A}) = \sup_{x \in V} I_x(\mathcal{A})$, the supremum taken over all vital points of the curve.*

3. *Finally, the idleness of the system of k mobile robots is defined by $I_{opt} = \inf_{\mathcal{A}} I(\mathcal{A})$, the infimum taken over all traversal strategies $\mathcal{A}$.*

We can now formulate the main question we will address in this paper.

Question. Suppose that we have k mobile robots traversing a given rectifiable open curve (resp., closed curve) $C = (V, N)$, represented w.l.o.g. as the unit-length segment (resp., the unit-perimeter cycle). What traversal strategy should the mobile robots follow so as to minimize the idleness of the system?

1.2 Related work

The act of *patrolling* is defined as the perpetual process of surveillance consisting of walking around a terrain in order to protect or supervise it; it is performed either in a static or in a dynamically changing environment. It has been studied extensively in robotics literature (cf. [3, 6, 14, 16, 17, 23, 26, 37]) and it is sometimes viewed as a variant of *coverage* - a central task in robotics. Patrolling can be useful in settings where objects or humans need to be rescued from a disaster environment, but also network administrators may use mobile robot patrols to detect network failures or to discover web pages which need to be indexed by search engines, cf. [26].

Similarly, *boundary patrolling* may be motivated by the task of detecting intruders (from the exterior) in a two dimensional terrain by patrolling its boundary. There exist several studies on boundary patrolling (cf. [2, 16, 17, 34]); often the approach followed is ad hoc, emphasizing either experimental results (e.g. [26]), or uncertainty of the model and robustness of the solutions when failures are possible (e.g., [16, 17, 23]), or non-deterministic solutions (e.g. [2]).

The fundamental measure for evaluating the efficiency of patrolling is the criterion of *idleness*, first introduced in [26]. The general idea is to measure frequency of visits of the points of the environment by incoming robots (cf. [3, 6, 16, 17, 26]). As such the idleness is sometimes viewed as the average (cf. [16]), worst-case (cf. [37]), probabilistic (cf. [2]) or experimentally verified (cf. [26]) time elapsed since the last visit of a node (cf. [3, 6]). Also, in some papers the terms of *blanket time* (cf. [37]) or *refresh time* (cf. [34]) are being used instead, so as to indicate a similar measure of algorithm efficiency. Several approaches to patrolling based on idleness criteria were surveyed in [3], including machine learning, negotiation mechanisms for generating paths, heuristics based on local idleness, as well as approximation to the Traveling Salesmen Problem (TSP). Some papers study patrolling based on swarm or ant-based algorithms (cf. [18, 27, 37]) and explore various robot capabilities (sensing, memory, locomotion, etc). The *skeletonization technique*, where a terrain is first partitioned into cells is often applied in geometric environments prior to employing graph-theoretic methods in discrete time. In graph environments, cyclic strategies often rely on either TSP-related solutions or spanning tree-based approaches ([21, 34]). For the case of boundary patrolling where the robots maintain distinct maximal speeds partial solutions for small numbers of robots were proposed (cf. [11]).

One may also consider as a variant of patrolling the problem of searching a graph or polygon by teams of mobile robots (cf., e.g. [19, 36]), which are looking for a stationary or mobile intruder. This falls into the vastly investigated domain of cops and robbers (see [20]).

The patrolling problem may be viewed as a version of an *art gallery* question, in which a set of stationary or mobile guards have to protect a given geometric environment (see [28, 32, 35]). In the setting with stationary guards, in most research papers the number of guards, needed to view the entire environment, has to be minimized. The problem is NP-hard and many approximation and inapproximability results were obtained (cf. [15, 22]). For the case of mobile guards, often known as the *watchman route problem*, the question of a single watchman was most often addressed. The optimization criterion is the path length traversed by the watchman, so that every point of the environment is seen from some position on the path. This is closely related to the traveling salesman problem. Unsurprisingly, many general watchman route problems are NP-hard (e.g. watchman tours of simple polygon with holes, suggested in [7] and corrected in [13]), touring a sequence of non-convex polygons [12], or link-distance watchman tours of simple polygon with holes [4]). However, for many specific cases polynomial-time algorithmic solutions are available. The solution for simple polygons was proposed by [8], while [9], [31] and [10] solve, respectively, the "zookeeper route", "safari route" and "aquarium keeper" problems.

In the *m-watchmen routes* problem, the sum S of m path-lengths must be minimized, so that each point of the environment must be seen from some position of one of the watchmen (cf., e.g. [29, 33]). Clearly, S decreases with increasing m. Hence at one extremity, we obtain the case when m is large enough to have $S = 0$ (m stationary guards for art gallery are sufficient), and on the other extremity the single watchman question arises. As the m-watchmen routes problem is NP-hard for simple polygons (cf. [1]), some restricted classes of polygons were considered in [5, 30].

Central to the watchman route problem is the notion of *visibility*. Some papers (e.g. [25, 31]) considered limited visibility of the mobile (e.g. [31]) or stationary (e.g. [25]) guards. Our work corresponds to a patrolling problem in the case of *zero visibility*, in which the robot sees only the point of the environment at which it is currently present.

1.3 Outline and results of the paper

We start by recalling the *partition strategy* of patrolling in Section 2, in which each robot traverses some sub-interval of the curve back and forth. This strategy is always optimal on open curves (i.e., on the unit segment), but it need not be optimal for closed curves (i.e., for the unit cycle).

Our main results concern closed curves, and are given in Section 3. We prove that the optimal idleness for patrolling the boundary is always attained by the better of two strategies: the before-mentioned partition strategy, and the *cyclic strategy*, in which equally-spaced robots patrol the cycle, moving in the same direction. The choice of the strategy and the robots' responsibilities depends on the arrangement of the vital regions around the boundary. Our approach consists in showing that finding the optimal idleness for k robots and for any set of n vital intervals may be reduced to finding the idleness for some *critical* set of $2k + 1$ vital points (always resulting in the cyclic strategy) or of a critical set of $k + 1$ vital points (resulting in either the cyclic or the partition strategy).

Finally, in Section 4, we propose an $O(kn \log n)$ algorithm for designing traversal strategies with optimal idleness for robots on both open and closed curves.

2. OPTIMAL PATROLLING STRATEGY FOR THE SEGMENT

We study first patrolling with k mobile robots of a terrain modelled by a curve $C = (V, N)$ consisting of n vital regions in $V \subseteq [0, 1]$, recall Definition 1.3.

In order to describe the region patrolled by a single robot in the partition strategies we propose, we will frequently refer to the concept of a lid.

DEFINITION 2.1 ((d, k)-LID COVER). *A d-lid is a contiguous interval on the curve of length d. We say that a curve $C = (V, E)$ has a (d, k)-lid cover if all of its vital regions can be covered by some set of k (not necessarily disjoint) d-lids.*

A natural approach to patrolling the segment is based on the partition strategy, in which each of the robots patrols exactly one of the k lids of the lid cover of minimum lid size L. The robot moves back and forth between its endpoints at maximum speed.

Partition strategy (on the segment)

1. Compute a (L, k)-lid cover of C, where L is chosen as the minimum lid length for which C admits such a lid cover. Let the i-th lid, $1 \le i \le k$, be a segment of the form $[c_i, c_i + L]$.

2. Deploy the i-th mobile robot so that at time $t = 2Lj + \tau$, where j is a non-negative integer and $-L \le \tau < L$, the position $f_i(t)$ of this robot on the lid is $f_i(t) = c_i + |\tau|$.

We observe that each of the points of every lid, and consequently every vital point of the segment, is visited at least once during each time interval of size $2L$. So, for this strategy we have an idleness of $I \le 2L$. The idleness of the partition strategy is, in fact, optimal on the segment.

THEOREM 2.1 (k ROBOTS). *The optimal idleness for k mobile robots moving at speed at most 1 on a unit segment is given by $I = 2L$, where L is the minimum value such that the terrain admits a (L, k)-lid cover.*

To prove the theorem, we start by showing a property of a greedy cover of the segment with lids.

LEMMA 2.2. *Suppose that L is the minimum value, s.t., a given terrain C admits a (L, k)-lid cover, and let $L' < L$. Then, $C \setminus [0, L']$ does not admit a $(L', k-1)$-lid cover.*

PROOF. Indeed, if the region $C \setminus [0, L']$ admitted a $(L', k-1)$-lid cover, then one could obtain a (L', k)-lid cover of C simply by adding lid $[0, L']$ to the lid cover obtained for the region $C \setminus [0, L']$. This contradicts the minimality of L. □

LEMMA 2.3. *Any patrolling strategy may be converted to a strategy, achieving the same idleness, for which the relative order of the mobile robots on the segment is maintained throughout the traversal.*

PROOF. The proof is based on the simple observation that when two mobile robots meet while moving in opposite directions they can "exchange" roles, so that the coverage of the points on the segment by one robot is the same as coverage by the other. Since after this change of roles the set of visited nodes at any time remains the same, this does not affect the idleness of visited nodes. □

The proof of the claim $I \geq 2L$ now proceeds by induction on the number of robots. It is clearly true for $k = 1$, since the idleness of the strategy cannot be smaller than twice the distance between the extremal vital points C, which corresponds precisely to the size of the smallest lid cover.

Suppose, by contradiction, that there exists a value of k and some terrain C such that the idleness of some patrolling strategy $\mathcal{A}$ is $I = 2L' < 2L$. By Lemma 2.3, w.l.o.g. we can assume that the robots never change places along the segment. Consider the trajectory of the leftmost robot r_1 following strategy $\mathcal{A}$. Let c be the supremum of all points along the segment reached by robot r_1. If point c is reached by robot r_1 at some time t, its last visit to point 0 must have been no later than at time $t - c$, and the next visit to point 0 will take place at time not earlier than $t + c$. From Lemma 2.3, we have that point 0 is never visited by any robot when it is not visited by r_1. Consequently, we must have $2c \leq 2L'$, and so $c \leq L'$. It follows that the region $C \setminus [0, L']$ must be patrolled solely by the set of $k - 1$ robots, without the help of r_1, with idleness at most $2L'$. From the inductive assumption, we have that $C \setminus [0, L']$ admits a L'-lid cover. This is a contradiction, by Lemma 2.2. This completes the proof of Theorem 2.1.

The complexity of computing the optimal lid cover for the partition strategy is discussed in detail in Section 4.

3. OPTIMAL PATROLLING STRATEGY FOR THE CYCLE

In this section we are interested in computing the optimal idleness for k mobile robots traversing terrains represented as a unit-perimeter cycle $C = (V, N)$ with vital and neutral regions in V and N respectively. The class of strategies under consideration in a cycle is larger than in the case of a segment due to the ability of the robots to traverse the perimeter of the cycle. In particular, the robots on the cycle can also apply a *cyclic strategy*, performing *clockwise* (direction aligned with increasing indices of intervals in $V \subseteq [0, 1]$) rotations around the cycle with even time spacing.

Cyclic strategy (on the cycle)

1. Deploy the i-th mobile robot at time 0 at position i/k along the circumference of the cycle.

2. Release all robots at their maximum speed to perform a clockwise traversal of the cycle.

OBSERVATION 3.1. *The idleness of the cyclic strategy on the cycle is $I = 1/k$, for any (non-empty) set of vital regions.*

At the same time, we observe that the partition strategy introduced in the previous section is also applicable in the cycle, achieving an idleness of $I = 2L$, where L is the size of the minimum lid cover of the vital regions of the cycle with k lids. Depending on the configuration of the vital regions, one

or the other of these two strategies may prove superior. In one extremal case when the cycle has no neutral regions, the cyclic strategy achieves an idleness of $1/k$, while the partition strategy has an idleness of $2/k$. At the other extreme, for vital regions consisting of k discrete points, the idleness of the cyclic strategy is still $1/k$, but the partition strategy has an idleness of 0. This leads us naturally to a strategy which selects the better of the two approaches.

Combined strategy (on the cycle)

1. Let L be the lid size of the minimum (with respect to lid size) lid cover of the vital regions of the cycle with k lids.

2. If $2L < 1/k$, apply *Partition strategy*.

3. Else, apply *Cyclic strategy*.

OBSERVATION 3.2. *The idleness of the combined strategy on the cycle is $I = \min\{1/k, 2L\}$, where L is the minimum possible lid size of a (L, k)-lid cover of the cycle.*

This claim gives rise to the following natural question. Does there exist any other strategy which can achieve better idleness than both the partition and cyclic approaches? Such a question admits a positive answer for the cycle in the scenario where robots have different speeds [11], even when neutral regions are not present. In our scenario, with neutral regions but for robots with equal maximal speeds, the combined strategy turns out to be optimal. The proof of this fact is surprisingly involved.

THEOREM 3.3. *The idleness $I(\mathcal{A})$ of any traversal strategy $\mathcal{A}$ in a cycle with neutral regions satisfies $I \geq \min\{1/k, 2L\}$, where L is the minimum possible lid size of a (L, k)-lid cover of the cycle.*

The rest of this section is devoted to the proof of Theorem 3.3, which proceeds in three technical lemmas. First, we show that for any cycle with neutral regions we can find a subset of either exactly $k + 1$ or exactly $2k + 1$ (discrete) vital points that satisfy specific properties. Then, we show that the lower bound can be proved simply by considering the patrolling problem on the selected subset of points.

LEMMA 3.4 (CRITICAL POINT). *Let $C = (V, N)$ be a cycle with set of vital regions V. Let L be the minimum size of the lid cover of the vital regions of C with k lids, and let $B = \sup\{dist(e, b) : b, e \in [0, 1], [b, e] \subseteq N\}$. Then:*

(1) If $B \geq 1/(2k)$, then there exists a set of $k + 1$ vital points $\{v_0, \ldots, v_k\} \subseteq V$, ordered clockwise, such that $\min_{0 \leq i \leq k} dist(v_i, v_{(i+1) \bmod (k+1)}) \geq \min\{1/(2k), L\}$.

(2) If $B < 1/(2k)$, then there exists a set of $2k + 1$ vital points $\{v_0, \ldots, v_{2k}\} \subseteq V$, ordered clockwise, s.t. $\min_{0 \leq i \leq 2k} dist(v_i, v_{(i+2) \bmod (2k+1)}) > 1/(2k)$.

PROOF. To prove clause (1), let v_0 be the first vital point located at the clockwise endpoint of a neutral region of length B. Fix $\epsilon > 0$ and consider the set of points chosen iteratively as follows: let v_{i+1} be the first vital point located at arc distance not less than $L - \epsilon$ from v_i, moving in the clockwise direction. We claim that point v_k is reached before completing one full rotation around the cycle, starting from

v_0. Indeed, if this were not the case, then there would exist a set of k lids: $[v_0, v_0 + L - \epsilon], \ldots, [v_{k-1}, v_{k-1} + L - \epsilon]$, covering the whole of V, a contradiction with the minimality of lid cover size L. Finally, note that the distance between points v_0 and v_k is at least $B \geq 1/(2k)$. Parametrizing each of the points v_i as $v_i(\epsilon)$, it follows that for any $\epsilon > 0$, we can find a set of $k + 1$ points $(v_0(\epsilon), v_1(\epsilon), \ldots, v_k(\epsilon))$ such that $\min_{0 \leq i \leq k} dist(v_i(\epsilon), v_{(i+1) \mod (k+1)}(\epsilon)) \geq \min\{1/(2k), L\} - \epsilon$. By taking into account that the set of vital points V is a closed set and $v_i(\epsilon)$ is non-decreasing and bounded (w.r.t. shifts in the clockwise direction) for any sequence $\epsilon \searrow 0$, we converge to a sequence of vital points $(v_0(0), \ldots, v_k(0))$ satisfying clause (1).

To prove clause (2), we will show a slightly stronger version "(2')" of this clause in which we replace the assumption "$B < 1/(2k)$" by "$B \leq 1/(2k)$". Suppose that terrain (V, N) is a counterexample to the claim of (2'), such that for any other terrain (V', N') which violates clause (2') it holds that $V' \subsetneq V$. (Such an inclusion-wise minimal counterexample always exists, since the set of vital points is by assumption a closed set.) By the minimality of V, the set of its vital points must be discrete, say, $V = \{u_0, \ldots, u_{n-1}\}$.

Assume that for some $0 \leq i \leq n$, $dist(u_i, u_{(i+2) \mod (n)}) \leq 1/(2k)$. The terrain $(V \setminus \{u_{i+1}\}, N \cup \{u_{i+1}\})$ has no neutral intervals of length greater than $1/(2k)$, and thus is a smaller counterexample to our claim, a contradiction. It follows that $\min_{0 \leq i < n} dist(u_i, u_{(i+2) \mod (n)}) > 1/(2k)$. Since for all $0 \leq i < n$, $dist(u_i, u_{(i+1) \mod (n)}) < 1/(2k)$, we must have $n \geq 2k + 1$. So, choosing points $\{v_0, \ldots, v_{2k}\}$ as $v_i = u_i$, for all $0 \leq i \leq 2k$, we find in V the subset of vital points satisfying clause (2'). So, V cannot be a counter-example to the claim. $\square$

LEMMA 3.5 ($\boldsymbol{k+1}$ **POINTS**). *Let $(v_0, v_1, \ldots, v_k)$ be a set of $k + 1$ points chosen from vital regions of the terrain, arranged in the clockwise order. The idleness $I(\mathcal{A})$ of any traversal strategy $\mathcal{A}$ for k mobile robots in this terrain satisfies $I(\mathcal{A}) \geq \min\left\{\frac{1}{k}, 2s\right\}$, where: $s = \min_{0 \leq i \neq j \leq k} dist(v_i, v_j)$.*

PROOF. Let $(v_0, v_1, \ldots, v_k)$ be $k+1$ vital points chosen so that $dist(v_i, v_{(i+1)}) \geq s$, for all $0 \leq i \leq k$. Throughout the proof, indices of points and robots are understood modulo $k + 1$, i.e. for all integers i, j we assume $v_i \equiv v_{i \mod (k+1)}$ and $r_j \equiv r_{j \mod (k+1)}$. We will show that the claim holds even if $\{v_0, v_1, \ldots, v_k\}$ are the only vital points of the cycle.

If the idle time of any strategy is at least equal to $2s$, the claim holds. Now, consider any (sufficiently small) $\epsilon > 0$ such that there exists a strategy $\mathcal{A}$ with $I(\mathcal{A}) < 2s - \frac{\epsilon}{2}$. We will show that there exists a point v_i, $0 \leq i \leq k$, such that the time between some two consecutive visits of a robot to point v_i is greater than $\tau = \frac{1}{k} - \epsilon$ when following strategy $\mathcal{A}$. (This completes the proof of the Lemma, since we then have that for any $\epsilon > 0$, $I(\mathcal{A}) < 2s - \frac{\epsilon}{2} \longrightarrow I(\mathcal{A}) > \frac{1}{k} - \epsilon$.)

Without loss of generality, by modifying the trajectories of the robots, we can convert a strategy $\mathcal{A}$ into another strategy $\mathcal{A}'$ so that the following properties are satisfied by $\mathcal{A}'$:

(i) if a robot following $\mathcal{A}'$ leaves some vital point v_i, then it does not reenter this vital point before reaching some other vital point first (namely, v_{i-1} or v_{i+1}),

(ii) no two robots following $\mathcal{A}'$ ever meet,

(iii) if a vital point is visited by a robot following strategy $\mathcal{A}$ at time t, then it is visited by a robot following strategy $\mathcal{A}'$ within the interval $[t - \frac{\epsilon}{4}, t + \frac{\epsilon}{4}]$.

For completeness, we outline the technical steps which are required to perform the above conversion. First, property (i) is achieved by modifying the trajectories of the robots in neutral regions, only. Next, properties (ii) and (iii) can be ensured by first converting the strategy to one which preserves the ordering of the robots as in Lemma 2.2, and then delaying the movements of some of the robots to avoid meetings, without changing the time intervals during which a vital point is occupied by more than $\frac{\epsilon}{4}$.

By property (iii), if a point is unvisited by $\mathcal{A}'$ in time interval $[t_1, t_2]$, then it is unvisited by $\mathcal{A}$ in the time interval $[t_1 + \frac{\epsilon}{4}, t_2 - \frac{\epsilon}{4}]$. It now suffices to show that the time between some two consecutive visits of a robot following strategy $\mathcal{A}'$ to point v_i is greater than $\tau + \frac{\epsilon}{2} = \frac{1}{k} - \frac{\epsilon}{2}$. Moreover, $I(\mathcal{A}') \leq I(\mathcal{A}) + \frac{\epsilon}{2} < 2s$. From now on we consider robots following $\mathcal{A}'$, only.

Since no two robots following $\mathcal{A}'$ ever meet by (ii), we can denote an arbitrarily chosen robots by r_1, and the other robots by $r_2, \ldots, r_k$ in clockwise order; this order never changes throughout the traversal.

Suppose that at some time t, some robot r_j leaves point v_i on the arc towards point v_{i+1}. By (i), the next vital point it reaches has to be point v_{i+1}. Therefore, robot r_j cannot reenter point v_i before time $t + 2dist(v_i, v_{i+1}) \geq t + 2s > t + I(\mathcal{A}')$. So, some other robot must visit point v_i in between the two visits by robot r_j. Since the robots never meet, it follows that within the time interval $[t, t + I(\mathcal{A}')]$, robot r_{j-1} entered node v_i. Before this visit, the previous vital point visited by r_{j-1} must have been v_{i-1}. It follows that to each traversal of the arc (v_i, v_{i+1}) by robot r_j that starts at some time t, we can assign a distinct traversal of the arc (v_{i-1}, v_i) by robot r_{j-1} that ends within the time interval $[t, t + I(\mathcal{A}')]$. Fix two values of time T_1 and T_2, $0 \leq T_1 < T_2$. From now on, we will apply certain counting arguments within the time interval $[T_1, T_2]$. Let us denote by $C_j(i, i+1)$ the number of traversals of arc (v_i, v_{i+1}) by robot r_j starting in the time interval $[T_1, T_2]$. Since only the first and last traversals of (v_i, v_{i+1}) by robot r_j within this time interval may be unmatched by corresponding traversals of (v_{i-1}, v_i) by robot r_{j-1} within the same time interval, we have:

$$C_j(i, i+1) - C_{j-1}(i-1, i) \leq 2.$$

Let $C(i, i+1) = \sum_{j=1}^{k} C_j(i, i+1)$ be the total number of traversals of the arc (v_i, v_{i+1}) by all robots starting within the time interval $[T_1, T_2]$. Summing the above inequalities, we have:

$$C(i, i+1) - C(i-1, i) \leq 2k.$$

An analogous analysis can be performed for the counter-clockwise direction, i.e., considering values of the form $C(i+1, i)$, corresponding to traversal of the arc from v_{i+1} to v_i. We obtain:

$$C(i, i-1) - C(i+1, i) \leq 2k.$$

In general, by iterating the above around the cycle, for any two vital points v_{i_1} and v_{i_2} we obtain:

$$C(i_1, i_1 + 1) - C(i_2, i_2 + 1) \leq 2k^2.$$

Denoting by $C^{cw} = \min_{0 \leq i \leq k} C(i, i+1)$, we have for any i:

$$C(i, i+1) \leq C^{cw} + 2k^2.$$

An analogous analysis can be performed for the counter-clockwise direction, i.e., considering values of the form $C(i +$

$1, i)$, corresponding to traversal of the arc from v_{i+1} to v_i. Consequently, denoting $C^{cc} = \min_{0 \leq i \leq k} C(i+1, i)$, we have for any i:

$$C(i+1, i) \leq C^{cc} + 2k^2.$$

Now, denote by $W_j(i) \geq 0$ the total time spent by robot r_j at point v_i within the time interval $[T_1, T_2]$, and let $W(i) = \sum_{j=1}^{k} W_j(i)$. Without loss of generality, let v_0 be a vital point with the minimal total waiting time, i.e., $W(0) = \min_{0 \leq i \leq k} W(i)$.

With respect to point v_0, the trajectory of each robot r_j within the time interval $[T_1, T_2]$ can be described by an ordered sequence of time moments $(e_j^1, l_j^1, e_j^2, l_j^2, \ldots, l_j^{n_j})$, where e_j^p is the time at which robot r_j enters point v_0 for the p-th time, whereas l_j^p is the time at which robot r_j leaves point v_0 for the p-th time. We assume that $T_1 \leq e_j^1 \leq l_j^1 < e_j^2 \leq l_j^2 < \ldots < e_j^{n_j} \leq l_j^{n_j} \leq T_2$, where we put $e_j^1 = T_1$ if robot r_j was located at node v_0 at time T_1, and $l_j^{n_j} = T_2$ if robot r_j was located at node v_0 at time T_2. For the sake of notation, let $l_j^0 = T_1$ and $e_j^{n_j+1} = T_2$.

During the time interval $[T_1, T_2]$, point v_0 is covered by a robot during the set of moments X given as:

$$X = \bigcup_{j=1}^{k} \bigcup_{p=1}^{n_j} [e_j^p, l_j^p],$$

such that $|X| = W(0)$. (Here, $|X|$ denotes the measure of X, i.e., the sum of lengths of time intervals contained in X. Note that all of the time intervals $[e_j^p, l_j^p]$ in the above union are disjoint, since no two robots following strategy $\mathcal{A}'$ ever meet by the definition of the strategy.) During the remaining time, i.e. $\overline{X} = [T_1, T_2] \setminus X$, no robot is located at v_0. We observe that $\overline{X}$ is a union of at most $1 + \sum_{j=1}^{k} n_j$ intervals. Hence, there exists some time interval of length τ:

$$\tau \geq \frac{|\overline{X}|}{1 + \sum_{j=1}^{k} n_j} = \frac{(T_2 - T_1) - |X|}{1 + \sum_{j=1}^{k} n_j} = \frac{(T_2 - T_1) - W(0)}{1 + \sum_{j=1}^{k} n_j} \tag{1}$$

during which v_0 remains unvisited.

Notice that each robot r_j leaves point v_0 at least $n_j - 1$ times in the time interval $[T_1, T_2]$, going towards either point v_1 or point v_k. Thus, we have:

$$C(0, 1) + C(0, k) \geq \sum_{j=1}^{k} (n_j - 1) = \sum_{j=1}^{k} n_j - k.$$

Taking into account that $C(0, 1) \leq C^{cw} + 2k^2$ and $C(0, k) \leq C^{cc} + 2k^2$, we have:

$$\sum_{j=1}^{k} n_j \leq C^{cw} + C^{cc} + 4k^2 + k. \tag{2}$$

Moreover, since each arc of the cycle is traversed in either direction a total of at least $C^{cw} + C^{cc}$ times, the total distance covered by all the robots is at least $C^{cw} + C^{cc}$. Thus, the total time of movement of all k robots within the time interval $[T_1, T_2]$ is at least $C^{cw} + C^{cc}$, and we obtain the inequality:

$$C^{cw} + C^{cc} + \sum_{i=0}^{k} W(i) \leq k(T_2 - T_1)$$

$$C^{cw} + C^{cc} \leq k(T_2 - T_1) - (k+1)W(0). \tag{3}$$

Combining inequalities (1), (2), and (3), we obtain:

$$\tau \geq \frac{(T_2 - T_1) - W(0)}{k(T_2 - T_1) - (k+1)W(0) + 4k^2 + k + 1} \geq$$

$$\geq \frac{1}{k + \frac{4k^2 + k + 1 - W(0)}{(T_2 - T_1) - W(0)}} \geq \frac{1}{k + \frac{4k^2 + k + 1}{(T_2 - T_1) - (4k^2 + k + 1)}} >$$

$$> \frac{1}{k} - \frac{4k^2 + k + 1}{(T_2 - T_1) - (4k^2 + k + 1)}.$$

In the above, we assumed that $(T_2 - T_1) - W(0) > 0$, i.e., there cannot be a robot covering v_0 throughout the time interval $[T_1, T_2]$. This is true, since otherwise, taking into account that $W(i) \geq W(0)$ for all $1 \leq i \leq k$, all $k+1$ points would have to be covered by a robot throughout $[T_1, T_2]$, and there are only k robots, a contradiction.

Now, suppose that T_2 is chosen to be sufficiently large so that $\frac{4k^2 + k + 1}{(T_2 - T_1) - (4k^2 + k + 1)} < \frac{\epsilon}{2}$. We then have $\tau \geq \frac{1}{k} - \frac{\epsilon}{2}$, and so there exists a vital point on the cycle such that the time between some two successive visits of robots following $\mathcal{A}'$ to this point is greater than $\frac{1}{k} - \frac{\epsilon}{2}$. This completes the proof of Lemma 3.5. $\square$

LEMMA 3.6 ($2k + 1$ POINTS). Let $(v_0, v_1, \ldots, v_{2k})$ be a set of $2k + 1$ points chosen from vital regions of the terrain, listed in the clockwise order, s.t., $dist(v_i, v_{(i+2) \mod (2k+1)}) > \frac{1}{2k}$. The idleness $I(\mathcal{A})$ of any traversal strategy $\mathcal{A}$ for k mobile robots in this terrain satisfies $I(\mathcal{A}) \geq \frac{1}{k}$.

PROOF. Let $(v_0, v_1, \ldots, v_{2k})$ be $2k + 1$ vital points chosen in accordance with the assumptions of the lemma. For the proof of the lower bound, we introduce the concept of a *shadow robot*, which can be seen as an auxiliary robot which temporarily appears in the system and assists robots in their patrolling task. More precisely, given a strategy $\mathcal{A}$, consider the trajectory of a robot r_j. Suppose that the robot leaves a vital point v_i at some time t_a, moves to an adjacent vital point $v_{i_1} \in \{v_{i-1}, v_{i+1}\}$ and then returns to point v_i at time t_b, without encountering any other vital points within the interval $[t_a, t_b]$. We say that a shadow robot r_j^{i*} is created at time t_a at point v_i, waits at v_i protecting it until time t_b, and then disappears. The addition of such a shadow robot, obviously, cannot increase the idleness of the strategy.

Observe that one robot can create at most two shadow robots at a time: when r_j is located anywhere within a closed arc $[v_i, v_{i+1}]$, then it may only have the shadow robots r_j^{i*} and $r_j^{(i+1)*}$. Robot r_j and its shadow robots can wait at not more than two vital points simultaneously.

Will show that the claim holds even if $\{v_0, v_1, \ldots, v_{2k}\}$ are the only vital points of the cycle. The rest of the proof proceeds analogously to the proof of Lemma 3.5, subject to the inclusion of shadow robots in the team of robots patrolling the terrain. Once again, for a fixed $\epsilon > 0$, we modify the trajectories of the robots, converting any strategy $\mathcal{A}$ into another strategy $\mathcal{A}'$ fulfilling the following properties:

(i) if a robot following $\mathcal{A}'$ leaves some vital point v_i, then it does not reenter this vital point before reaching some other vital point first (namely, v_{i-1} or v_{i+1}),

(ii) no two robots following $\mathcal{A}'$ ever meet each other or the shadow robots of other robots,

(iii) if a point P is visited by a robot following strategy $\mathcal{A}$ at time t, then it is visited by a robot or shadow robot following strategy $\mathcal{A}'$ within the interval $[t - \frac{\epsilon}{4}, t + \frac{\epsilon}{4}]$.

From now on we consider robots $(r_1, r_2, \ldots, r_k)$ and their shadow robots following $\mathcal{A}'$, only, and proceed to perform a modification of the proof of Lemma 3.5 which takes shadow robots into account.

Suppose that $I(\mathcal{A}') < 1/k - \epsilon$. We will call a traversal of the directed arc (v_i, v_{i+1}) by robot r_j *shadowless* if after arriving at v_{i+1}, the next vital point visited by robot r_j is v_{i+2} (not v_i). Equivalently, a traversal of arc (v_i, v_{i+1}) is shadowless if r_j does not leave its shadow robot r_j^{i*} at v_i during this traversal.

Fix a time interval $[T_1, T_2]$. For all $0 \leq i \leq 2k$, we will denote by $C_j(i, i+2)$ the number of shadowless traversals of the directed arc (v_i, v_{i+1}) by robot r_j starting in this time interval. Suppose that robot r_j initiates a shadowless traversal at some time t. Since $dist(v_i, v_{i+2}) > \frac{1}{2k}$ by assumption, we have that the next visit of this robot to v_i takes place after time $t + 1/k > t + I(\mathcal{A}')$. Since v_i is not occupied by a shadow robot, the robot r_{j-1} must arrive at point v_i at some time $t' \in (t, t + 1/k)$. The previous vital point occupied by robot r_{j-1} before t' must have been v_{i-1}. Before that, the robot cannot have occupied vital point v_i, since then, during its traversal from v_i to v_{i-1} and back to v_i, the shadow robot r_{j-1}^{i*} would have existed at v_i. This shadow robot must have met robot r_i at point v_i at time t, which contradicts the assumption that robots and shadow robots do not meet. It follows that before arriving at v_{i-1} robot r_{j-1} must have been located at v_{i-2}. Thus, robot r_{j-1} was performing a shadowless traversal of (v_{i-2}, v_{i-1}). This traversal counts towards $C_{j-1}(i-2, i)$ if robot r_j left v_{i-2} within the interval $[T_1, T_2]$. Following the reasoning from Lemma 3.5, we obtain the following bound:

$$C_j(i, i+2) - C_{j-1}(i-2, i) \leq 2.$$

Summing the above inequalities over all robots, and performing analysis for the counter-clockwise direction we get:

$$C(i, i+2) - C(i-2, i) \leq 2k.$$

$$C(i, i-2) - C(i+2, i) \leq 2k.$$

Since the number of points $2k + 1$ is odd, by iterating the above around the cycle at most $2k$ times in one direction, for any two vital points v_{i_1} and v_{i_2} we obtain:

$$C(i_1, i_1 + 2) - C(i_2, i_2 + 2) \leq 2k^2.$$

$$C(i_1, i_1 - 2) - C(i_2, i_2 - 2) \leq 2k^2.$$

Denoting $C^{cw} = \min_{0 \leq i \leq 2k} C(i, i+2)$ and similarly $C^{cc} = \min_{0 \leq i \leq 2k} C(i+2, i)$, we have for any i:

$$C(i, i+2) \leq C^{cw} + 2k^2.$$

$$C(i+2, i) \leq C^{cc} + 2k^2.$$

Now, denote by $W_j(i) \geq 0$ the total time spent by robot r_j at point v_i and by its shadow r_j^{i*} within the time interval $[T_1, T_2]$, and let $W(i) = \sum_{j=1}^{k} W_j(i)$. Without loss of generality, let v_0 be a vital point with the minimal total waiting time, i.e., $W(0) = \min_{0 \leq i \leq 2k} W(i)$.

With respect to point v_0, the trajectory of each robot r_j within the time interval $[T_1, T_2]$ can be described by an ordered sequence of time moments $(e_j^1, l_j^1, e_j^2, l_j^2, \ldots, l_j^{n_j})$, where

e_j^p is the time at which robot r_j enters point v_0 for the p-th time after a shadowless traversal (of arc (v_{2k-1}, v_2k) or (v_2, v_1)), whereas l_j^p is the time at which robot r_j leaves point v_0 starting its p-th shadowless traversal (of arc (v_0, v_1) or (v_0, v_{2k})). We assume that $T_1 \leq e_j^1 \leq l_j^1 < e_j^2 \leq l_j^2 < \ldots < e_j^{n_j} \leq l_j^{n_j} \leq T_2$, and make the same boundary assumptions as in the proof of Lemma 3.5.

During the time interval $[T_1, T_2]$, point v_0 is covered by some robot or some shadow robot during the set of moments X given as:

$$X = \bigcup_{j=1}^{k} \bigcup_{p=1}^{n_j} [e_j^p, l_j^p],$$

such that $|X| = W(0)$. During the remaining time, i.e. $\overline{X} = [T_1, T_2] \setminus X$, no robot and no shadow robot is located at v_0. We observe that $\overline{X}$ is a union of at most $1 + \sum_{j=1}^{k} n_j$ intervals. Hence, there exists some time interval of length τ during which point v_0 remains unvisited, lower-bounded by an inequality of the same form as (1):

$$\tau \geq \frac{|\overline{X}|}{1 + \sum_{j=1}^{k} n_j} = \frac{(T_2 - T_1) - |X|}{1 + \sum_{j=1}^{k} n_j} = \frac{(T_2 - T_1) - W(0)}{1 + \sum_{j=1}^{k} n_j} \tag{4}$$

Notice that each robot r_j leaves point v_0 at least $n_j - 1$ times in the time interval $[T_1, T_2]$, embarking on a shadowless traversal of the arc either to point v_1 (and then to v_2) or to point v_{2k} (and then to v_{2k-1}). Thus, we have:

$$C(0, 2) + C(0, 2k-1) \geq \sum_{j=1}^{k} (n_j - 1) = \sum_{j=1}^{k} n_j - k.$$

Taking into account that $C(0, 2) \leq C^{cw} + 2k^2$ and $C(0, 2k-1) \leq C^{cc} + 2k^2$, we have:

$$\sum_{j=1}^{k} n_j \leq C^{cw} + C^{cc} + 4k^2 + k. \tag{5}$$

For any robot r_j, we trace its trajectory within the time interval $[T_1, T_2]$, looking at the number of shadow robots in time. At any time, r_j and its shadow robots may be waiting at at most two vital points in total. Moreover, suppose that r_j embarks on a shadowless traversal of some arc (v_i, v_{i+1}), leaving v_i at some moment of time t, arriving at v_{i+1} not earlier than at time $t + dist(v_i, v_{i+1})$. Then, throughout the time interval $[t, t + dist(v_i, v_{i+1})]$, robot r_j can have at most one shadow located at v_{i+1}. Suppose this shadow robot $r_j^{(i+1)*}$ exists. Then, the last traversal of r_j preceding time t must have been one of the arc (v_{i+1}, v_i), and not shadowless. Tracing back in time the zig-zags of robot r_j between points v_i, v_{i+1}, during which it had shadows at both v_i and v_{i+1}, we come back to the earliest traversal of arc (v_i, v_{i+1}) (or possibly arc (v_{i+1}, v_i), directly after the robot's arrival from v_{i-1} (respectively, from v_{i+2}). During this traversal, of duration at least $dist(v_i, v_{i+1})$, robot r_j had precisely one shadow located at v_i (respectively, at v_{i+1}). In summary, we have shown that during every shadowless traversal of arc (v_i, v_{i+1}), robot r_j either has no shadow, or it has exactly 1 shadow and we can associate with this traversal another time period of length $dist(v_i, v_{i+1})$ during which it has exactly 1 shadow (with no overlap of time periods). The same argument applies for the counter-clockwise direction. Thus, we obtain a bound on the total waiting time of robot

r_j and its shadows:

$$\sum_{i=0}^{2k} W_j(i) \leq 2(T_2 - T_1)$$

$$-2\sum_{i=0}^{2k}(C_j(i, i+2) + C_j(i+1, i-1) - 2)dist(v_i, v_{i+1}),$$

where the constant is subtracted from C_j to account for boundary conditions around times T_1 and T_2. Summing over all k robots we obtain:

$$\sum_{i=0}^{2k} W(i) \leq 2k(T_2 - T_1)$$

$$-2\sum_{i=0}^{2k}(C(i, i+2) + C(i+1, i-1) - 2)dist(v_i, v_{i+1}).$$

Taking into account that the circumference of the cycle is 1 and that $W(0)$ is the minimum of all $W(i)$, we have:

$$W(0) \leq \frac{1}{2k+1}\sum_{i=0}^{2k} W(i) \leq$$

$$\leq \frac{2k(T_2 - T_1) - 2(C^{cc} + C^{cw}) + 4}{2k+1}.$$

and finally:

$$C^{cc} + C^{cw} < k(T_2 - T_1) - (k + \tfrac{1}{2})W(0) + 2. \qquad (6)$$

Combining inequalities (4), (5), and (6), we obtain:

$$\tau \geq \frac{(T_2 - T_1) - W(0)}{k(T_2 - T_1) - (k + \frac{1}{2})W(0) + 4k^2 + k + 3} \geq$$

$$\geq \frac{1}{k + \frac{1}{2}\frac{2(4k^2+k+3) - W(0)}{(T_2-T_1) - W(0)}} \geq \frac{1}{k + \frac{4k^2+k+3}{(T_2-T_1) - 2(4k^2+k+3)}} >$$

$$> \frac{1}{k} - \frac{4k^2 + k + 3}{(T_2 - T_1) - 2(4k^2 + k + 3)}.$$

In the above, we assumed that $(T_2 - T_1) - W(0) > 0$, i.e., there cannot be a robot covering v_0 throughout the time interval $[T_1, T_2]$. This is true, since otherwise, taking into account that $W(i) \geq W(0)$ for all $1 \leq i \leq k$, all $2k+1$ points would have to be covered by a robot or its shadow robot throughout $[T_1, T_2]$, and there are at most $2k$ robots and shadow robots in total at any time, a contradiction.

Now, suppose that T_2 is chosen to be sufficiently large so that $\frac{4k^2+k+3}{(T_2-T_1) - 2(4k^2+k+3)} < \frac{\epsilon}{2}$. We then have $\tau \geq \frac{1}{k} - \frac{\epsilon}{2}$, and so there exists a vital point on the cycle such that the time between some two successive visits of robots following $\mathcal{A}'$ to this point is greater than $\frac{1}{k} - \frac{\epsilon}{2}$. This completes the proof of the lemma. $\square$

To complete the proof of Theorem 3.3, we consider an arbitrary terrain $C = (V, N)$. Let B be the length of the longest neutral interval of C, as defined in Lemma 3.3. We have two cases to consider.

- If $B \geq 1/(2k)$, then by clause (1) of Lemma 3.4, there exists a subset of $k+1$ vital points $\{v_0, \ldots, v_k\} \subseteq V$ such that for these points, in Lemma 3.5 we have $s =$

$\min\{1/(2k), L\}$. Now, by Lemma 3.5 we obtain that for any strategy $\mathcal{A}$, the idleness is lower bounded by $I(\mathcal{A}) \geq \min\{1/k, 2s\} = \min\{1/k, 2L\}$.

- If $B < 1/(2k)$, then by clause (2) of Lemma 3.4, there exists a subset of $2k+1$ vital points $\{v_0, \ldots, v_{2k}\} \subseteq V$ that satisfies the assumptions of Lemma 3.6. Thus, by Lemma 3.6 we obtain that for any strategy $\mathcal{A}$, the idleness is lower bounded by $I(\mathcal{A}) \geq 1/k$.

In either case, we obtain that the idleness of any strategy patrolling C is at least $\min\{1/k, 2L\}$, which proves the claim of the Theorem.

4. COMPUTING OPTIMAL ROBOT TRAJECTORIES

Let $C = (V, N)$ be the unit segment $[0, 1]$ with vital and neutral regions. Assume w.l.o.g. that the vital intervals in C are arranged in a data structure from left to right as $V_i = [b_i, e_i]$, for $i = 1, 2, \ldots, n$ where $b_1 = 0$, $b_i \leq e_i < b_{i+1}$. We assume that arithmetic operations involving these values can be performed in unit time.

Recall that in this case the solution is based on the use of lids, where with each lid we associate a different robot. We show first that one can test in time $O(\min\{n, k \log n\})$ whether for a collection of k lids each of length d can cover all vital points in $[0, 1]$.

We propose a recursive procedure $TestLidSize(k, d, p)$ that operates on sub-intervals of the form $[p, 1]$ of C, where k stands for the number of available lids and $d \leq 1$ refers to the uniform length of the lids. The procedure returns value $true$ if all vital points in C can be covered with the collection of k lids. Otherwise the returned value is $false$.

Procedure $TestLidSize(k, d, p)$: {true,false};

1. Use the next lid to cover segment $[p, p+d]$;

2. **if** $(p + d) \geq e_n$ **then** return($true$);
   /* all vital points are covered */

3. $p^* = \inf\{p' \in V : p' > p + d\}$;
   /* p^* exists since $p + d < e_n$. */

4. **if** $(k > 1)$ **then** $return(TestLidSize(k-1, d, p^*))$
   else return($false$);

LEMMA 4.1. *For any positive integer k, $d > 0$, and $p \in C = (V, N)$, such that p is vital, procedure $TestLidSize(k, d, p)$ verifies in time $O(\min\{n, k \log n\})$ whether all vital points in $[p, e_n]$ can be covered by k lids of length d.*

PROOF. We first show that our recursive procedure performs verification correctly. In the proof we use induction on k. More precisely, we assume inductively that for any $1 \leq l < k$ and $q \in C$ the call $TestLidSize(l, d, q)$ verifies whether one can cover all valid points in the interval $[q, e_n]$ using l lids of length d.

Consider the call $TestLidSize(k, d, p)$ in which the first lid is chosen to cover all vital points in $[p, p+d]$. A further recursive call $TestLidSize(k-1, d, p^*)$ verifies whether the remaining $k-1$ lids suffice to cover all valid points in $[p^*, e_n]$, where $p^* = \inf\{$vital $p' \in C = [p+d, e_n] : p' > p+d\}$. By the inductive assumption on k, we know that this call provides the correct answer. And if this answer is positive, i.e., the vital points in $[p^*, e_n]$ can be covered by $k - 1$ lids we conclude that all vital points in $[p, e_n]$ (formed of vital points in $[p, p + d]$ and $[p^*, e_n]$) can be covered by k lids. Alternatively, if $k - 1$ lids are insufficient to cover vital points $[p^*, e_n]$ the extra lid that covers vital points in $[p, p + d]$ is of no use for valid points in $[p^*, e_n]$ since the left endpoint of this lid must be aligned with p. Thus in this case, as expected, the answer computed by $TestLidSize(k, d, p)$ is also negative.

The time complexity $O(\min\{n, k \log n\})$ is dominated by computation of p^* at most k times, see line 3. If $p + d$ is vital and $(p + d) \neq e_j$, for any $1 \leq j < n$, p^* can be computed in constant time. Otherwise, we either use binary search on points $b_1, \ldots, b_n$ to find p^* imposing complexity $O(k \log n)$ or we search through this list of points in time $O(n)$. $\square$

We now show how to efficiently compute the optimal (minimal) size of the lid. We will need the following lemma.

LEMMA 4.2. *If L is the optimal (minimal) size of lids, there must be some integer $1 \leq l \leq k$, s.t, $L = \frac{e_j - b_i}{l}$, for some $1 \leq i \leq j \leq n$.*

PROOF. Consider any cover based on lids with the minimal size. In such a cover one can arrange the lids so that they touch but do not overlap with each other. If such an arrangement is not possible, one could decrease the length of the lids, contradicting the minimality of their length. Thus, we can assume that in the cover all the lids are partitioned into maximal sequences, such that in each sequence the lids are placed tightly one after another, but different sequences do not share their endpoints. Consider any such sequence based on m lids. The left endpoint of the leftmost lid in this sequence must coincide with some b_i. Otherwise, this would not be the leftmost lid in the sequence. If the right endpoint of the rightmost (m-th) lid in this sequence coincides with some e_j, the claim of the lemma follows. Assume, to the contrary, that this is not the case for any maximal sequence of lids. This means that the last lid in each maximal sequence overlaps with some neutral region, and consequently, that the length of the lids could be decreased. $\square$

4.1 Optimal lids

We now present the algorithm that computes the optimal size of lids. Using Lemma 4.2, one can observe that we need to test at most $O(kn^2)$ values We can sort these values in time $O(kn^2 \log n)$ and later use binary search to find the optimal value. The number of tests during the binary search is $O(\log n)$ and the cost of each test is $O(\min\{n, k \log n\})$, see Lemma 4.1. Thus the total complexity is dominated by sorting performed in time $O(kn^2 \log n)$.

OBSERVATION 4.3. *The optimal size of lids can be computed in time $O(kn^2 \log n)$.*

The complexity of this algorithm can be further improved if we use an implicit representation of $O(kn^2)$ candidates based on values $\frac{e_j - b_i}{l}$, for $1 \leq i \leq j \leq n$ and $1 \leq l \leq k$, and perform search for the optimal size of lids in a more sophisticated fashion. We perform search among values based on each l separately.

Let M_i^l represent implicitly the list of values $(\frac{e_i - b_i}{l}, \frac{e_{i+1} - b_i}{l}, \ldots, \frac{e_n - b_i}{l})$, for $1 \leq i \leq n$. Each list M_i^l contains at most n values. Any value from this list can be calculated on the

basis of the sequence $e_i, \ldots, e_n$, where values e_1 through e_n are stored in an array of length n. In particular, using this representation one can calculate the value of any requested element in M_i^l in constant time.

The search algorithm operates in rounds on all M_i^ls simultaneously. At the beginning all entries in M_i^l are potential candidates for being the optimal length of the lids. During each round the list of candidates in half of the M_i^ls is reduced by half but the remaining candidates in M_i^l always form a sublist of consecutive elements in M_i^l. The reduction process in each round is performed as follows.

Procedure FastLidSearch(l, C): $\{true, false\}$;.
repeat in consecutive rounds
1. Find the medians m_i^l among the remaining candidates in each M_i^l.
2. Find the median m^* among m_i^l, for all $1 \leq i \leq n$.
3. Use procedure $TestLidSize$ to test whether m^* is long enough.
4. And if yes, reduce by half the content of lists M_i^l with $m_i^l > m^*$.
5. Otherwise, reduce by half the content of lists M_i^l with $m_i^l < m^*$.

until only one candidate value is left.

Note that the cost of each round, in which there are $a \leq kn$ non-empty lists M_i^l, can be bounded by $O(a + \min\{n, k \log n\})$. We will now compute the bound on the total number of rounds. At the start we associate with each list M_i^l a potential of $\log n$. This means that the combined potential of all lists is $kn \log n$. During each round the potential of half of the lists is reduced by 1. Eventually some lists M_i^l become empty which is reflected in the null potential. Note that until at least $\frac{kn}{2}$ lists are non-empty the combined potential is reduced by $\frac{kn}{4}$ during each round. Thus the number of rounds with at least $\frac{kn}{2}$ non-empty lists is limited by $(kn \log n)/(\frac{kn}{4}) = 4 \log n$, and the total duration of these rounds is $O(\log n \cdot (kn + \min\{n, k \log n\}))$. Furthermore, we reduce the number of non-empty lists from $\frac{kn}{2}$ to $\frac{nk}{4}$ also in at most $(\frac{kn}{2} \log n)/(\frac{kn}{8}) = 4 \log n$ rounds, and the total duration of these rounds is $O(\log n \cdot (\frac{kn}{2} + \min\{n, k \log n\}))$. Thus, if we continue this process until only one element in one list is left, the total time of execution is bounded by:

$$O\left(\sum_{j=0}^{\log(kn)} \left(\log n \cdot (\frac{kn}{2^j} + \min\{n, k \log n\})\right)\right) =$$

$$= O(kn \log n + \log n (\log n + \log k) \min\{n, k \log n\}) =$$

$$= O(kn \log n + k \log^3 n + n \log k \log n) = O(kn \log n).$$

COROLLARY 4.4. *The optimal size of lids can be computed in time $O(kn \log n)$.* $\square$

This approach is also applicable to the combined strategy on the cycle, since, in fact, the optimal lid size only needs to be computed in the case when the cycle contains some neutral region N_i of length at least $1/(2k)$. Then, the problem on the cycle C reduces to that on the closed segment $C \setminus N_i$. We have the following:

THEOREM 4.5. *Consider k robots patrolling a boundary cycle (resp., segment) with n vital regions. The robot trajectories which result in minimal idleness can be described using the combined strategy (resp., the partition strategy). Such a description can be computed using an $O(kn \log n)$ algorithm.* □

5. REFERENCES

[1] A. Aggarwal. *The Art Gallery Theorem and Algorithm.* PhD thesis, Johns Hopkins University, 1984.

[2] N. Agmon, S. Kraus, and G. A. Kaminka. Multi-robot perimeter patrol in adversarial settings. In *ICRA*, pages 2339–2345, 2008.

[3] A. Almeida, G. Ramalho, H. Santana, P. A. Tedesco, T. Menezes, V. Corruble, and Y. Chevaleyre. Recent advances on multi-agent patrolling. In *SBIA*, pages 474–483, 2004.

[4] E. M. Arkin, J. S. B. Mitchell, and C. D. Piatko. Minimum-link watchman tours. *IPL*, 86:203–207, 2003.

[5] S. Carlsson, B. J. Nilsson, and S. C. Ntafos. Optimum guard covers and m-watchmen routes for restricted polygons. *Int. J. Comp. Geom. Appl.*, 3:85–105, 1993.

[6] Y. Chevaleyre. Theoretical analysis of the multi-agent patrolling problem. In *IAT*, pages 302–308, 2004.

[7] W. Chin and S. C. Ntafos. Optimal watchman routes. *Inf. Proc. Lett.*, 28:39–44, 1988.

[8] W. Chin and S. C. Ntafos. Shortest watchman routes in simple polygons. *Discr. Comp. Geom.*, 6:9–31, 1991.

[9] W. Chin and S. C. Ntafos. The zookeeper route problem. *Inf. Sci.*, 63:245–259, 1992.

[10] J. Czyzowicz, P. Egyed, H. Everett, D. Rappaport, T. C. Shermer, D. L. Souvaine, G. T. Toussaint, and J. Urrutia. The aquarium keeper's problem. In *SODA*, pages 459–464, 1991.

[11] J. Czyzowicz, L. Gąsieniec, A. Kosowski, and E. Kranakis. Boundary patrolling by mobile agents with distinct maximal speeds. In *ESA 2011*, pages 701–712. Springer, 2011.

[12] M. Dror, A. Efrat, A. Lubiw, and J. S. B. Mitchell. Touring a sequence of polygons. In *STOC*, pages 473–482, 2003.

[13] A. Dumitrescu and C. Tóth. Watchman tours for polygons with holes. *Comput. Geom. Theory Appl.*, 45:326–333, 2012.

[14] K. Easton and J. W. Burdick. A coverage algorithm for multi-robot boundary inspection. In *ICRA*, pages 727–734. IEEE, 2005.

[15] S. Eidenbenz, C. Stamm, and P. Widmayer. Inapproximability results for guarding polygons and terrains. *Algorithmica*, 31(1):79–113, 2001.

[16] Y. Elmaliach, N. Agmon, and G. A. Kaminka. Multi-robot area patrol under frequency constraints. *Ann. Math. Artif. Intell.*, 57(3-4):293–320, 2009.

[17] Y. Elmaliach, A. Shiloni, and G. A. Kaminka. A realistic model of frequency-based multi-robot polyline patrolling. In *AAMAS (1)*, pages 63–70, 2008.

[18] Y. Elor and A. M. Bruckstein. Autonomous multi-agent cycle based patrolling. In *ANTS*, pages 119–130, 2010.

[19] F. V. Fomin, P. A. Golovach, A. Hall, M. Mihalák, E. Vicari, and P. Widmayer. How to guard a graph? *Algorithmica*, 61(4):839–856, 2011.

[20] F. V. Fomin and D. M. Thilikos. An annotated bibliography on guaranteed graph searching. *Theor. Comput. Sci.*, 399(3):236–245, 2008.

[21] Y. Gabriely and E. Rimon. Spanning-tree based coverage of continuous areas by a mobile robot. In *ICRA*, pages 1927–1933, 2001.

[22] S. K. Ghosh. Approximation algorithms for art gallery problems in polygons and terrains. In *WALCOM*, pages 21–34, 2010.

[23] N. Hazon and G. A. Kaminka. On redundancy, efficiency, and robustness in coverage for multiple robots. *Rob. and Autonom. Syst.*, 56:1102–1114, 2008.

[24] A. Kawamura and Y. Kobayashi. Fence patrolling by mobile agents with distinct speeds. In *ISAAC'12*, pages 598–608, 2012.

[25] G. D. Kazazakis and A. A. Argyros. Fast positioning of limited-visibility guards for the inspection of 2d workspaces. In *IEEE Int. Conf. on Intelligent Robots and Systems, Vol. 3*, pages 2843–2848, 2002.

[26] A. Machado, G. Ramalho, J.-D. Zucker, and A. Drogoul. Multi-agent patrolling: An empirical analysis of alternative architectures. In *MABS*, pages 155–170, 2002.

[27] A. Marino, L. E. Parker, G. Antonelli, and F. Caccavale. Behavioral control for multi-robot perimeter patrol: A finite state automata approach. In *ICRA*, pages 831–836, 2009.

[28] J. Mitchell. Geometric shortest paths and network optimization. In *Handbook of Computational Geometry, Chapter 15*, pages 633–701, 2000.

[29] B. J. Nilsson. *Guarding art galleries; Methods for mobile guards.* PhD thesis, Lund U., Sweden, 1995.

[30] B. J. Nilsson and D. Wood. Optimum watchmen route in spiral polygons. In *2nd Canadian Conf. Comput. Geometry*, pages 269–272, 1990.

[31] S. C. Ntafos. Watchman routes under limited visibility. *Comput. Geom.*, 1:149–170, 1991.

[32] J. O'Rourke. *Art Gallery Theorems and Algorithms.* Oxford University Press, 1987.

[33] E. Packer. Computing multiple watchman routes. In *WEA'08 Proc. 7th Workshop on Experimental Algorithms*, pages 114–128, 2008.

[34] F. Pasqualetti, A. Franchi, and F. Bullo. On optimal cooperative patrolling. In *CDC*, 2010.

[35] T. C. Shermer. Recent results in art galleries. In *Proc. of the IEEE*, volume 80, pages 1384–1399, 1992.

[36] M. Yamashita, H. Umemoto, I. Suzuki, and T. Kameda. Searching for mobile intruders in a polygonal region by a group of mobile searchers. *Algorithmica*, 31:208–236, 2001.

[37] V. Yanovski, I. A. Wagner, and A. M. Bruckstein. A distributed ant algorithm for efficiently patrolling a network. *Algorithmica*, 37(3):165–186, 2003.

Profitable Scheduling on Multiple Speed-Scalable Processors[*]

Peter Kling[†]
Heinz Nixdorf Institute &
Computer Science Department
University of Paderborn
peter.kling@upb.de

Peter Pietrzyk
Heinz Nixdorf Institute &
Computer Science Department
University of Paderborn
peter.pietrzyk@upb.de

ABSTRACT

We present a new online algorithm for profit-oriented scheduling on multiple speed-scalable processors. Moreover, we provide a tight analysis of the algorithm's competitiveness. Our results generalize and improve upon work by Chan et al. [10], which considers a single speed-scalable processor. Using significantly different techniques, we can not only extend their model to multiprocessors but also prove an enhanced and tight competitive ratio for our algorithm.

In our scheduling problem, jobs arrive over time and are preemptable. They have different workloads, values, and deadlines. The scheduler may decide not to finish a job but instead to suffer a loss equaling the job's value. However, to process a job's workload until its deadline the scheduler must invest a certain amount of energy. The cost of a schedule is the sum of lost values and invested energy. In order to finish a job the scheduler has to determine which processors to use and set their speeds accordingly. A processor's energy consumption is power $P_\alpha(s)$ integrated over time, where $P_\alpha(s) = s^\alpha$ is the power consumption when running at speed s. Since we consider the online variant of the problem, the scheduler has no knowledge about future jobs. This problem was introduced by Chan et al. [10] for the case of a single processor. They presented an online algorithm which is $\alpha^\alpha + 2e\alpha$-competitive. We provide an online algorithm for the case of multiple processors with an improved competitive ratio of α^α.

Categories and Subject Descriptors

F.2.2 [**Analysis of Algorithms and Problem Complexity**]: Nonnumerical Algorithms and Problems—*sequencing and scheduling*; F.1.2 [**Computation by Abstract Devices**]: Modes of Computation—*online computation, paral-*

lelism and concurrency; G.1.6 [**Numerical Analysis**]: Optimization—*convex programming*

Keywords

scheduling; energy; online algorithms; primal-dual; convex programming

1. INTRODUCTION

From an economical point of view, the value of energy has increased tremendously during the last decades. This applies not only to the energy consumed in small-scale computer systems but especially to the energy consumption in large data centers. According to current reports (e.g., Barroso and Hölzle [6]), the decisive factors regarding the costs of running a data center are mostly the cooling process and the actual computations rather than the acquisition of the necessary hardware. Thus, in order to maximize their revenue, data centers strive to minimize the energy consumption while still guaranteeing a sufficiently high quality of service to their customers. One way to approach this goal are technical solutions improving the involved hardware. However, coupling such solutions with canonical or standard algorithms wastes much potential. Only by designing sophisticated algorithms can one hope to fully exploit their power and possibilities. A prominent example for this is *dynamic speed scaling*, a technology that adapts a processor's speed according to the current workload (*Intel SpeedStep* or *AMD PowerNow!*). Simply decreasing the speed at times of small load may lower the total energy consumption substantially. However, a lower speed often also implies a lower quality of service, which in turn may impair the data center's revenue. One needs clever algorithms to fully utilize speed scaling and to achieve a provably good or even optimal profit.

But how exactly should a data center make use of speed scaling in order to maximize profit? On a relatively basic level, one can imagine a data center's situation as follows: Jobs of different sizes and values arrive over time at the data center. For finishing a customer's job in time, the data center receives a payment corresponding to the job's value. However, to finish a job the data center has to invest an amount of energy depending on the job's size and potential time constraints. Investing into low-value jobs that require much energy may lower the profit. Even processing jobs whose values seem to justify the energy investment may be bad, as this may hinder the efficient processing of more lucrative jobs that arrive later. Thus, one has to carefully choose not only how and when to process the different jobs but also

[†]Supported by the Graduate School on Applied Network Science (GSANS).
[*]This work is partially supported by the German Research Foundation (DFG) within the Collaborative Research Center "On-The-Fly Computing" (SFB 901).

which to process at all. We propose an algorithm that handles this scenario provably well and improves upon the former best known result. Moreover, we generalize the model to the important case of multiple processors (until now, only a single speed-scalable processor was considered). Our analysis is partly based on an intriguing new technique recently suggested by Gupta et al. [12]. We adapt and extend it to suit our problem and show its large potential compared to the classical analysis methods prevailing in this area (see "Our Contribution" later in this section). Because of space restrictions, most of the formal proofs reside in the appendix. As a convenience for the reader, a full version with all proofs incorporated can be found in [13].

Related Work.

There exists plenty of work concerning energy-efficient scheduling strategies in both theoretical and practical contexts. Dynamic speed scaling (also referred to as dynamic voltage scaling) is one of the most important technical tools to save energy in modern systems. It allows the scheduler to dynamically adapt the system's speed to the current workload. A recent survey by Albers [1] gives a good and compact overview on the state of the art of algorithmic research in this area. In the following, we concentrate on models for speed-scalable processors and jobs with deadline constraints. Theoretical work in this area has been initiated by Yao et al. [15]. They considered a single speed-scalable processor that processes preemptable jobs which arrive over time and come with different deadlines and workloads. Yao et al. studied the question of how to finish all the jobs in an energy-minimal way. In their seminal work [15], they modeled the power consumption $P_\alpha(s)$ of a processor running at speed s by a constant degree polynomial $P_\alpha(s) = s^\alpha$. Here, the energy exponent α is assumed to be a constant $\alpha \geq 2$. In classical CMOS-based systems $\alpha = 3$ usually yields a suitable approximation of the actual power consumption. Yao et al. developed an optimal offline algorithm, known as YDS, as well as the two online algorithms *Optimal Available* (OA) and *Average Rate* (AVR). Up to now, OA remains one of the most important algorithms in this area, being an essential part of many algorithms for both the original problem as well as for its manifold variations. Using a rather complex but elegant amortized potential function argument, Bansal et al. [3] proved that OA is exactly α^α-competitive. They also proposed a new algorithm, named BKP, which achieves a competitive ratio of essentially $2e^{\alpha+1}$. The algorithm qOA presented by Bansal et al. [5] is particularly well suited for low powers of α, where it outperforms both OA and BKP. In this work, the authors also proved that no deterministic algorithm can achieve a competitive ratio of better than $e^{\alpha-1}/\alpha$. In their recent work, Albers et al. [2] presented an optimal offline algorithm for the multiprocessor case. Moreover, using this algorithm, they were able to also extend OA to the multiprocessor case and proved the same competitive ratio of α^α as in the single processor case.

All results mentioned so far are concerned only with the energy necessary to finish *all* jobs. With respect to the profitability aspect, the two most relevant results for us are due to Chan et al. [10] and Pruhs and Stein [14]. Both proposed a model incorporating profitability into classical energy-efficient scheduling. In the simplest case, jobs have values and the scheduler is no longer required to finish all jobs. Instead, it can decide to not process jobs whose val-

ues do not justify the foreseeable energy investment necessary to complete them. The objective is to maximize the profit [14] or, similarly, to minimize the loss [10]. As argued by the authors, the latter model has the benefit of being a direct generalization of the classical model by Yao et al.. For maximizing the profit, Pruhs and Stein [14] showed that in order to achieve a bounded competitive ratio, resource augmentation is necessary and gave a scalable online algorithm. For minimizing the loss, Chan et al. [10] gave an $\alpha^\alpha + 2e\alpha$-competitive algorithm. Another very important and recent work is due to Gupta et al. [12] and considers the *Online Generalized Assignment Problem* (ONGAP). The authors showed an interesting relation to a multitude of problems in the context of speed-scalability (not only for scheduling). They developed a convex programming formulation of the problem and applied well-known techniques from convex optimization. Especially, they used a greedy primal-dual approach as known from linear programming (see, e.g., [9]). This way, they designed an online algorithm for the classical model by Yao et al. (no job values; one processor) which is very similar to OA and proved the exact same competitive ratio of α^α.

Our Contribution.

We develop and analyze a new online algorithm for scheduling valuable jobs on multiple speed-scalable processors. Our algorithm improves upon known results in two respects: For the single processor case it improves the best known competitive ratio from $\alpha^\alpha + 2e\alpha$ to α^α. Moreover, this constant competitive ratio holds even for the case of multiple processors. To the best of our knowledge, this is the first algorithm that is able to handle the multiprocessor case in this scenario. We also show that our analysis is tight in that the proven competitive ratio is optimal for our algorithm.

Our analysis is significantly different from the typical potential function argument which is dominant in the analysis of online algorithms in this research area. Instead, we make use of a framework recently suggested by Gupta et al. [12]. It utilizes well-known tools from convex optimization, especially duality theory and primal-dual algorithms. We develop a convex programming formulation and design a greedy primal-dual online algorithm for the problem at hand. Compared to the original framework, we have to overcome the additional issue of integral variables in our convex program that are caused by the new profitability aspect. Moreover, the handling of multiple processors proves to be a challenging task. It not only causes a much more complex objective function in the convex program but also makes it harder to grasp the structural properties of the resulting schedule. Our result shows that this technique is not only suitable for the classical energy-efficient scheduling model but also for more complex variations of it, as conjectured by Gupta et al.. It is interesting to note that, in terms of the analysis, this approach goes back to the roots of Yao et al.'s model, as the optimality proof of the YDS algorithm [4] is based on a similar convex programming formulation and the well-known KKT conditions from convex optimization [8]. Our algorithm can be seen as greedily increasing the convex program's variables while maintaining a relaxed version of these KKT conditions.

2. MODEL & PRELIMINARIES

We consider a system of m speed-scalable processors. That

is, each processor can be set to any speed $s \in \mathbb{R}_{\geq 0}$ (independently from the others). When running at speed s, the power consumption of a single processor is given by the *power function* $\mathrm{P}_\alpha(s) = s^\alpha$. Here, the constant parameter $\alpha \in \mathbb{R}_{>1}$ is called the *energy exponent*. A problem instance consists of a set $J = \{1, 2, \ldots, n\}$ of n jobs. Each job $j \in J$ is associated with a *release time* r_j, a *deadline* d_j, a *workload* w_j, and a *value* v_j. A *schedule* S describes if and how the different jobs are processed by the system. It consists of m speed functions $S_i \colon \mathbb{R}_{\geq 0} \to \mathbb{R}_{\geq 0}$ ($i \in \{1, 2, \ldots, m\}$) and a job assignment policy. The speed function S_i dictates the speed $S_i(t)$ of the i-th processor at time t. The job assignment policy decides which jobs to run on the processors. At any time t, it may schedule at most one job per processor, and each job can be processed by at most one processor at any given time (i.e., we consider nonparallel jobs). Moreover, jobs are preemptive: a running job may be interrupted at any time and continued later on, possibly on a different processor. The total work processed by processor i between time t_1 and t_2 is $\int_{t_1}^{t_2} S_i(t)\,\mathrm{d}t$. Similarly, the overall power consumed by this processor during the same time is $\int_{t_1}^{t_2} \mathrm{P}_\alpha(S_i(t))\,\mathrm{d}t$. Let $s_j(t)$ denote the speed used to process job j at time t. We say job j is *finished under schedule S* if S processes (at least) w_j units of j's work during the interval $[r_j, d_j)$. That is, if we have $\int_{r_j}^{d_j} s_j(t)\,\mathrm{d}t \geq w_j$.

A given schedule S may not finish all n jobs. In this case, the total value of unfinished jobs is considered as a loss. Thus, the cost of S is defined as the sum of the total energy consumption and the total value of unfinished jobs. More formally, if J_{rej} denotes the set of unfinished (aka rejected) jobs under schedule S, we define the *cost of schedule S* by

$$\mathrm{cost}(S) := \sum_{i=1}^{m} \int_0^\infty \mathrm{P}_\alpha(S_i(t))\,\mathrm{d}t + \sum_{j \in J_{\mathrm{rej}}} v_j. \tag{1}$$

Our goal is to construct a low-cost schedule in the *online scenario* of the problem. That is, the job set J is not known a priori, but rather revealed over time. Especially, we do not know the total number of jobs, and the existence as well as the attributes of a job $j \in J$ are revealed just when the job is released at time r_j. We measure the quality of algorithms for this online problem by their *competitive ratio*: Given an online algorithm A, let $A(J)$ denote the resulting schedule for job set J. The competitive ratio of A is defined as $\sup_J \frac{\mathrm{cost}(A(J))}{\mathrm{cost}(\mathrm{OPT}(J))}$, where $\mathrm{OPT}(J)$ denotes an optimal schedule for the job set J. Note that, by definition, the competitive ratio is at least one.

2.1 Convex Programming Formulation

In the following, we develop a convex programming formulation of the above (offline) scheduling problem to aid us in the design and analysis of our online algorithm (cf. Section 3). Following an idea by Bingham and Greenstreet [7], we partition time into *atomic intervals* T_k using the jobs' release times and deadlines. The goal of our convex program is to compute what portion of each job to process during the different atomic intervals in an optimal schedule. Once we have such a fixed *work assignment*, we use a deterministic algorithm by Chen et al. [11] to efficiently compute an energy-minimal way to process the corresponding work on the m processors in this interval. The energy consumption of the resulting schedule in the interval T_k can be written

$$\min_{\substack{0 \preceq x \\ y \in \{0,1\}^n}} \quad \sum_{k=1}^{N} \mathcal{P}_k(x_{1k}, x_{2k}, \ldots, x_{nk}) + \sum_{j \in J} (1 - y_j) v_j$$

$$\text{s.t.} \quad y_j - \sum_{k=1}^{N} c_{jk} x_{jk} \leq 0 \qquad , j \in J$$

Figure 1: Mathematical programming formulation (IMP) of our scheduling problem.

as a convex function $\mathcal{P}_k$ of the work assignment. This function plays a crucial role in the optimization objective of our convex program, and studying its properties and the corresponding schedule's structure is an important part of our analysis. We will elaborate on $\mathcal{P}_k$ once we have derived the convex program (see Section 2.2).

For a given job set J, let us partition the time horizon into $N \in \mathbb{N}$ atomic intervals T_k ($k \in \{1, 2, \ldots, N\}$) as follows. We define $T_k := [\tau_{k-1}, \tau_k)$ where $\tau_0 < \tau_1 < \ldots < \tau_N$ are chosen such that $\{\tau_0, \tau_1, \ldots, \tau_N\} = \{r_j, d_j \mid j \in J\}$. Let $l_k := \tau_k - \tau_{k-1}$ denote the length of interval T_k. Note that there are at most $2n-1$ intervals. To model the deadline constraint of job j, we introduce parameters $c_{jk} \in \{0, 1\}$ that indicate whether $T_k \subseteq [r_j, d_j)$ ($c_{jk} = 1$) or not ($c_{jk} = 0$). Our program uses two types of variables: *load variables* $x_{jk} \in [0, 1]$ for each job $j \in J$ and each atomic interval $k \in \{1, 2, \ldots, N\}$, and *indicator variables* $y_j \in \{0, 1\}$ for each job $j \in J$. The variable x_{jk} indicates what portion of j's workload is assigned to interval T_k and the variable y_j indicates whether job j is finished ($y_j = 1$) or not ($y_j = 0$). Figure 1 shows the complete (integral) mathematical program (IMP) for our scheduling problem. The first summand in the objective corresponds to the energy spent in the different intervals. The second summand charges costs for all unfinished jobs. The set of constraints ensures that a job can be declared as finished only if it has been completely assigned to intervals T_k lying in its release-deadline interval $[r_j, d_j)$. We use x and y to refer to the full vectors of variables x_{jk} and y_j, and we use the symbol "$\preceq$" for element-wise comparison.

If we relax the domain of (IMP) such that $0 \preceq y \preceq 1$, we get a convex program. We refer to this convex program as (CP). By introducing dual variables λ_j (also called *Lagrange multipliers*) for each constraint of (CP) we can write its *Lagrangian* $L(x, y, \lambda)$ as

$$\sum_{k=1}^{N} \mathcal{P}_k(x_{1k}, x_{2k}, \ldots, x_{nk})$$
$$+ \sum_{j \in J} (1 - y_j) v_j + \sum_{j \in J} \lambda_j \left(y_j - \sum_{k=1}^{N} c_{jk} x_{jk} \right). \tag{2}$$

It is a linear combination of the convex program's objective and constraints. Instead of prohibiting infeasible solutions (as done by the convex program), it charges a penalty for violated constraints (assuming positive λ_j). Now, the *dual function* of (CP) is defined as

$$g(\lambda) := \inf_{\substack{0 \preceq x \\ 0 \preceq y \preceq 1}} L(x, y, \lambda). \tag{3}$$

An important property of the dual function g is that for any

253

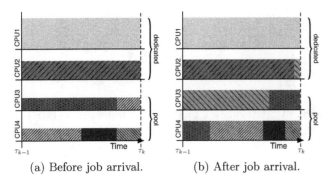

| (a) Before job arrival. | (b) After job arrival. |

Figure 2: Schedules of Chen et al.'s algorithm.

$\lambda \succeq 0$, the value $g(\lambda)$ is a lower bound on the optimal value of (CP). Moreover, since (CP) is a relaxation of (IMP), $g(\lambda)$ is also a lower bound on the optimal value of (IMP). See Boyd and Vandenberghe [8] for further details on these and similar known facts about (convex) optimization problems.

2.2 Power Consumption in Atomic Intervals

Let us give a more detailed description of the function $\mathcal{P}_k(x_{1k}, x_{2k}, \ldots, x_{nk})$. We defined $\mathcal{P}_k$ implicitly by mapping a given work assignment $x_{1k}, x_{2k}, \ldots, x_{nk}$ for interval T_k to the power consumption of Chen et al.'s algorithm [11] during T_k. This guarantees an energy-minimal schedule for the given work assignment. In the following, we give a concise description of this algorithm and derive a more explicit formulation as well as some properties of $\mathcal{P}_k$.

To ease the discussion, let us assume that the jobs are numbered such that $x_{1k}w_1 \geq x_{2k}w_2 \geq \cdots \geq x_{nk}w_n$. In a nutshell, Chen et al.'s algorithm can be described as follows. Define the job set

$$\psi(k) := \left\{ j \in J \;\middle|\; \begin{array}{l} j \leq m \,\wedge\, x_{jk} > 0 \\ \wedge\, x_{jk}w_j \geq \dfrac{\sum_{j'>j} x_{j'k}w_{j'}}{m-j} \end{array} \right\}. \tag{4}$$

These jobs are called *dedicated jobs* and are scheduled on their own *dedicated processor* using the energy-optimal (since minimal) speed $s_{jk} := \frac{x_{jk}w_j}{l_k}$. All remaining jobs, called *pool jobs*, are scheduled on the remaining *(pool) processors* in a greedy manner. The intuition is that dedicated jobs are larger than the remaining average workload and thus must be processed on a dedicated processor. See [7, Section 3.1] for a relatively short but more detailed description of the algorithm. Figure 2 illustrates the resulting schedule and how it may change due to the arrival of a new job. Using the above definition of dedicated jobs we can write $\mathcal{P}_k$ as

$$\mathcal{P}_k(x_{1k}, \ldots, x_{nk}) = \sum_{j \in \psi(k)} l_k \, \mathrm{P}_\alpha\!\left(\frac{x_{jk}w_j}{l_k}\right) \\ + (m - |\psi(k)|) l_k \, \mathrm{P}_\alpha\!\left(\frac{\sum_{j \notin \psi(k)} x_{jk}w_j}{(m - |\psi(k)|) l_k}\right). \tag{5}$$

The following proposition gathers some important properties concerning the power consumption function $\mathcal{P}_k$ of an atomic interval T_k.

PROPOSITION 1. *Consider an arbitrary atomic interval T_k together with its power consumption function $\mathcal{P}_k \colon \mathbb{R}_{\geq 0}^n \to \mathbb{R}$. This function has the following properties:*

(a) It is convex and $\mathcal{P}_k(0) = 0$.

(b) It is differentiable and the partial derivatives are given by $\frac{\partial \mathcal{P}_k}{\partial x_{jk}}(x_{1k}, \ldots, x_{nk}) = w_j \cdot \mathrm{P}'_\alpha(s_{jk})$. Here, s_{jk} denotes the speed used to schedule the workload $x_{jk}w_j$ in Chen et al.'s algorithm:

$$s_{jk} = \begin{cases} x_{jk}w_j / l_k & \text{, if } j \text{ is a dedicated job} \\ \dfrac{\sum_{j \notin \psi(k)} x_{jk}w_j}{(m - |\psi(k)|) l_k} & \text{, if } j \text{ is a pool job.} \end{cases} \tag{6}$$

We will also need to compare the result of Chen et al.'s algorithm before and after the arrival of a new job (cf. Figure 2). That is, how can the workloads on the processors change when a single entry of the work assignment changes from zero to some positive value?

PROPOSITION 2. *Consider Chen et al.'s algorithm called for some interval T_k with the two work assignments $x = (x_1, x_2, \ldots, x_n, 0)$ and $x' = (x_1, x_2, \ldots, x_n, z)$ (i.e., before and after the arrival of a new job). Let L_i and L'_i denote the total workload on the i-th fastest processor in the resulting schedules, respectively. Then, we have $0 \leq L'_i - L_i \leq z$.*

Proof sketches of both Proposition 1 and 2 can be found in the appendix.

3. ONLINE PRIMAL-DUAL ALGORITHM

The goal of this section is to use the convex programming formulation (CP) and its dual function $g \colon \mathbb{R}^n \to \mathbb{R}$ to derive a provably good online algorithm for our scheduling problem. We start by describing an algorithm that computes a solution to (CP) in an online fashion, but knowing the time partitioning T_k ($k \in \{1, 2, \ldots, n\}$). Subsequently, we explain how this solution is used to compute the actual schedule and how we handle the fact that the actual atomic intervals are not known beforehand. To solve (CP), we use a greedy primal-dual approach for convex programs as suggested by Gupta et al. [12]. Our algorithm extends their framework to the multiprocessor case and to profitable scheduling models. It shows how to incorporate rejection policies into the framework (handling the integral constraints in the convex program) and how to cope with more complex power functions of a system (in our case $\mathcal{P}_k$).

The Primal-Dual Algorithm.

Our primal-dual algorithm, in the following referred to as PD, maintains a set of primal variables (x, y) and a set of dual variables λ, all initialized with zero. Whenever a new job (i.e., a constraint in (CP)) arrives, we start to increase the primal variables x_{jk} ($k \in \{1, 2, \ldots, N\}$) in a greedy fashion until either the full job is scheduled (i.e., $\sum_k x_{jk} = 1$) or the planned energy investment for job j becomes too large compared to its value. In the latter case, the variables x_{jk} are reset to zero, λ_j is set to v_j, and y_j remains zero (the job is rejected). Otherwise, we set y_j to one (the job is finished) and λ_j to essentially the current rate of cost increase per job workload. When greedily increasing the primal variables, we assign the next infinitesimal small portion of job j to those atomic intervals that cause the smallest increase in costs. Essentially, these are the intervals where j's workload would

```
{executed each time a new job j ∈ J arrives}
init x_{jk}, y_j, and λ_j with zero for all k ∈ {1, 2, ..., N}
compute λ_{jk} := δ (∂𝒫_k / ∂x_{jk}) (x_{1k}, ..., x_{jk}, 0, ..., 0) for all T_k ⊆ [r_j, d_j)

let the set 𝒯_min contain all T_k with minimal λ_{jk}
for each T_k ∈ 𝒯_min in parallel:
    increase x_{jk} in a continuous way (which in turn raises λ_{jk}
        according to line 3)
    ensure that all λ_{jk} of intervals in 𝒯_min remain equal
    update 𝒯_min whenever the λ_{jk} reach a λ_{jk'} with T_{k'} ∉ 𝒯_min
    stop increasing once one of the following comes true
    (a) ∑ x_{jk} = 1:   set     y_j := 1, λ_j := λ_{jk}
    (b) λ_{jk} = v_j:   reset   x_{jk} := 0, λ_j := λ_{jk}
```

Listing 1: Primal-Dual Algorithm PS with parameter δ.

be scheduled with the slowest speed. See Listing 1 for the algorithm.

The described algorithm is similar to primal-dual algorithms known from linear programming, where primal or dual variables are raised at certain rates until the (relaxed) complementary slackness conditions are met. In fact, this algorithm is derived by using relaxed versions of the Karush-Kuhn-Tucker (KKT) conditions, essentially a generalization of the complementary slackness conditions for convex (or even general nonlinear) programs. The actual schedule used is the one computed by Chen et al.'s algorithm when applied to the current work assignment given by the primal variables x_{jk} for the atomic interval T_k.

Concerning the Time Partitioning.

Our algorithm formulation assumes a priori knowledge of the atomic intervals T_k. However, since the jobs arrive in an online fashion, the exact partitioning is actually not known to the algorithm. One can reformulate the algorithm such that it uses the intervals T'_k induced by the jobs $J' = \{1, 2, ..., j\} \subseteq J$ it knows so far. If a refinement of an atomic interval $T'_k = T_{k_1} \cup T_{k_2}$ occurs due to the arrival of a new job, the already assigned job portions are simply split according to the ratios $|T_{k_1}|/|T'_k|$ and $|T_{k_2}|/|T'_k|$. This reformulated algorithm produces an identical schedule. To see this, note that the algorithm with a priori knowledge of the refinement $T'_k = T_{k_1} \cup T_{k_2}$ treats both intervals T_{k_1} and T_{k_2} as identical (with respect to their relative size $|T_{k_i}|/|T'_k|$) up to the point when the job causing the refinement arrives.

4. ANALYSIS

In the following, let $(\tilde{x}, \tilde{y})$ and $\tilde{\lambda}$ denote the primal and dual variables computed by our algorithm PD. Remember that the final schedule computed by PD is derived by applying Chen et al.'s algorithm to the $\tilde{x}_{1k}, ..., \tilde{x}_{nk}$ values in each atomic interval T_k. We refer to this schedule as the $(\tilde{x}, \tilde{y})$-schedule or simply as the schedule PD. Our goal is to use $g(\tilde{\lambda})$ to bound the cost of this schedule (referred to as cost(PD)). Our main result is

THEOREM 3. *The competitive ratio of algorithm* PD *with the parameter* δ *set to* $\frac{1}{\alpha^{\alpha-1}}$ *is at most* α^α. *Moreover, there is a problem instance for which* PD *is exactly by a factor of* α^α *worse than an optimal algorithm. That is, our upper bound is optimal.*

For the upper bound, we show that cost(PD) $\leq \alpha^\alpha g(\tilde{\lambda})$.

Since, by duality, $g(\tilde{\lambda})$ is also a lower bound on the optimal value of (CP) and, thereby, on the optimal value of (IMP), we get $\frac{\text{cost(PD)}}{\text{cost(OPT)}} \leq \alpha^\alpha$. The lower bound follows from a known result for traditional energy-efficient scheduling (without job values but the necessity to finish all jobs) by setting the job values sufficiently high.

In the remainder, we develop the key ingredients for the proof of Theorem 3. We start in Section 4.1 and derive a more explicit formulation of the dual function value $g(\tilde{\lambda})$ by relating it to a certain (infeasible) solution to our convex program (CP) and a corresponding schedule. Section 4.2 further simplifies this formulation by expressing $g(\tilde{\lambda})$ solely in terms of the jobs (instead of their workloads in different atomic intervals). Based on this job-centric formulation, Section 4.3 develops different bounds for the dual function value depending on certain job characteristics. The proof of Theorem 3 is essentially a simple combination of these bounds. Because of space restrictions, we focus on the overall structure of the analysis. Detailed proofs of all the propositions and lemmas as well as of the main result can be found in the appendix.

4.1 Structure of Optimal Infeasible Solutions

First of all, note that the value $g(\tilde{\lambda}) = \inf L(x, y, \tilde{\lambda})$ (see Equation (3)) is finite and obtained by a pair $(\hat{x}, \hat{y})$ of primal variables. These primal variables can be interpreted as a (possibly infeasible) solution to the convex program (CP). Moreover, for our fixed dual variable $\tilde{\lambda}$, this solution is optimal in that it minimizes the sum of the objective cost and the penalty for violated constraints. In this sense, we refer to $(\hat{x}, \hat{y})$ as an *optimal infeasible solution*. Our goal is to understand the structure of this solution, which will eventually allow us to write $g(\tilde{\lambda})$ in a more explicit way. The results of this subsection are related to results from [12], but more involved due to the more complex nature of our objective function.

Note that $\hat{x}$ and $\hat{y}$ may differ largely from $\tilde{x}$ and $\tilde{y}$. However, the following lemmas show a strong correlation between this optimal infeasible solution and the feasible (partially integral) solution computed by algorithm PD.

LEMMA 4. *Consider an optimal infeasible solution* $(\hat{x}, \hat{y})$. *Without loss of generality, we can assume that it has the following properties:*

(a) $\hat{y} = \tilde{y}$

(b) *For any atomic interval* T_k, *there are at most* m *different jobs* j *with* $\hat{x}_{jk} > 0$.

Given an atomic interval T_k, we call the jobs j with $\hat{x}_{jk} > 0$ the *contributing jobs of* T_k and denote the corresponding job set by $\varphi(k)$. As done in the proof of Lemma 4, we can consider $\hat{x}$ as a work assignment for the atomic intervals T_k. By applying Chen et al.'s algorithm, we get a schedule whose energy cost in interval T_k is exactly $\mathcal{P}_k(\hat{x}_{1k}, ..., \hat{x}_{nk})$. We refer to this schedule as the $(\hat{x}, \hat{y})$-schedule. Using this terminology, the second statement of Lemma 4 essentially says that in this schedule at most m jobs are scheduled in any atomic interval T_k. Moreover, it follows immediately from the description of Chen et al.'s algorithm that all contributing jobs are dedicated jobs of the corresponding atomic interval.

We can derive a slightly more explicit characterization of the contributing jobs $\varphi(k)$ of an atomic interval T_k by exploiting that $(\hat{x}, \hat{y})$ is a minimizer of $(x, y) \mapsto L(x, y, \tilde{\lambda})$.

LEMMA 5. *Consider any atomic interval T_k and its contributing jobs $\varphi(k)$. Define the value $\hat{s}_j := (\tilde{\lambda}_j / \alpha w_j)^{\frac{1}{\alpha-1}}$ for any job j.*

(a) *For any $j \in \varphi(k)$ we have*

$$\hat{x}_{jk} = \frac{l_k}{w_j} \hat{s}_j = \frac{l_k}{w_j} (\tilde{\lambda}_j / \alpha w_j)^{\frac{1}{\alpha-1}}.$$

Moreover, j is scheduled at constant speed $\hat{s}_j$ in the $(\hat{x}, \hat{y})$-schedule.

(b) *The total contribution of all the $\hat{x}_{jk}$ variables to the dual function value $g(\tilde{\lambda})$ is given by*

$$(1 - \alpha) l_k \sum_{j \in \varphi(k)} \left(\frac{\hat{x}_{jk} w_j}{l_k} \right)^\alpha = (1 - \alpha) l_k \sum_{j \in \varphi(k)} \hat{s}_j^\alpha.$$

(c) *Let n_k denote the number of jobs available in an atomic interval T_k (i.e., jobs with $c_{jk} = 1$). The contributing jobs $\varphi(k)$ are the $\min(m, n_k)$ jobs with maximal $\hat{s}_j$-values under all available jobs.*

4.2 A Job-centric Formulated Dual Function

In the following, we assume that the optimal infeasible solution $(\hat{x}, \hat{y})$ adheres to Lemma 4. That is, we have $\hat{y} = \tilde{y}$ and we can relate the optimal infeasible solution to the $(\hat{x}, \hat{y})$-schedule which schedules in each atomic interval T_k exactly the $|\varphi(k)|$ ($\leq m$) available jobs with the largest $\hat{s}_j = (\tilde{\lambda}_j / \alpha w_j)^{\frac{1}{\alpha-1}}$-values, each on its own dedicated processor at speed $\hat{s}_j$. We use the somewhat lax notation $k \in \varphi^{-1}(j)$ to refer to the atomic intervals T_k to which j contributes. Our main goal in this section is to derive a formulation of the dual function value solely in terms of the jobs. We will also define and discuss the *trace* of a job, which helps to relate any job (even if unfinished) to a certain amount of energy consumed by our PD algorithm.

Given a job $j \in J$, let $l(j) := \sum_{k \in \varphi^{-1}(j)} l_k$ denote the total time it is scheduled in the $(\hat{x}, \hat{y})$-schedule. Moreover, let $E_{\tilde{\lambda}}(j)$ denote the total energy invested by the $(\hat{x}, \hat{y})$-schedule into job j. Now, we can formulate the following lemma.

LEMMA 6. *For any job $j \in J$, the total energy invested by the optimal infeasible solution into job j is $E_{\tilde{\lambda}}(j) = l(j) \hat{s}_j^\alpha$. Moreover, the dual function value $g(\tilde{\lambda})$ can be written as $g(\tilde{\lambda}) = (1 - \alpha) \sum_{j \in J} E_{\tilde{\lambda}}(j) + \sum_{j \in J} \tilde{\lambda}_j$.*

Tracing a Job.

Given a job j, we define its *trace* as a set of tuples (T_k, i) with $k \in \{1, 2, \dots, N\}$ and $i \in \{1, 2, \dots, m\}$. That is, a set of atomic intervals, each coupled with a certain processor. Our goal is to choose these such that we can account the energy $E_{\tilde{\lambda}}(j)$ used in the optimal infeasible solution on job j to the energy used by algorithm PD during j's trace (on the coupled processors). For the formal definition, let us first partition the contributing jobs $\varphi(k)$ of an interval T_k into the subset $\varphi_1(k) := \{ j \in \varphi(k) \mid \tilde{y}_j = 1 \}$ of jobs finished by PD and the subset $\varphi_2(k) := \{ j \in \varphi(k) \mid \tilde{y}_j = 0 \}$ of jobs unfinished by PD. Now, for any job $j \in J$ we define its *trace* $\mathrm{Tr}(j)$ as follows:

Case $\tilde{y}_j = 1$: $(T_k, i) \in \mathrm{Tr}(j) \iff \hat{s}_j$ is the i-th largest value[1] in $\{ \hat{s}_{j'} \mid j' \in \varphi_1(k) \}$

Case $\tilde{y}_j = 0$: $(T_k, |\varphi_1(k)| + i) \in \mathrm{Tr}(j) \iff \hat{s}_j$ is the i-th largest value in $\{ \hat{s}_{j'} \mid j' \in \varphi_2(k) \}$

That is, jobs that are finished by PD are mapped to the fastest processors in each atomic interval T_k for which they are contributing jobs, in decreasing order of their $\hat{s}_j$-values. Jobs contributing to T_k but which are unfinished by PD are mapped to the remaining processors (the exact order is not important in this case). Note that by this mapping, all traces $\mathrm{Tr}(j)$ are pairwise disjoint. We use the notation $E_{\mathrm{PD}}(j)$ to refer to the power consumption of PD during j's trace. That is, the power consumption on the i-th fastest processor in the atomic interval T_k for any $(T_k, i) \in \mathrm{Tr}(j)$. We use E_{PD} to denote the total power consumption of PD. Since the job traces are pairwise disjoint, we obviously have $E_{\mathrm{PD}} \geq \sum_{j \in J} E_{\mathrm{PD}}(j)$.

The following proposition formulates an important structural property of a job's trace. It gives us different lower bounds on the speed used by PD during a job's trace, depending on whether it is finished or not. To this end, let $\tilde{s}_j$ denote the speed PD planned to use for job j just before $\tilde{\lambda}_j$ got fixed (i.e., just before PD decides whether to finish j or not). If j is finished, we have

$$\tilde{\lambda}_j = \delta \frac{\partial \mathcal{P}_k}{\partial x_{jk}} (\tilde{x}_{1k}, \dots, \tilde{x}_{jk}, 0, \dots, 0) = \delta w_j \mathrm{P}_\alpha'(\tilde{s}_j)$$

(cf. algorithm description and Proposition 1). Solving this for $\tilde{s}_j$ yields $\tilde{s}_j = (\tilde{\lambda}_j / \delta \alpha w_j)^{1/\alpha - 1} = \delta^{-1/\alpha - 1} \hat{s}_j$. Similarly, we also get $\tilde{s}_j = \delta^{-1/\alpha - 1} \hat{s}_j$ for unfinished jobs. We use $\tilde{x}_j = \sum \tilde{x}_{jk} < 1$ to denote the corresponding portions of the unfinished job j planned to be scheduled by PD just before j was rejected.

PROPOSITION 7. *Consider $(T_k, i) \in \mathrm{Tr}(j)$ for a job $j \in J$. Let $s(i, k)$ denote the speed of the i-th fastest processor during T_k in the final schedule computed by PD. Then:*

(a) *If j is finished by PD, then $s(i, k) \geq \tilde{s}_j$.*

(b) *If j is not finished by PD, then $s(i, k) \geq \tilde{s}_j - \frac{\tilde{x}_{jk} w_j}{l_k}$.*

4.3 Balancing the Different Cost Components

As our goal is to lower-bound the dual function value $g(\tilde{\lambda}) = (1 - \alpha) \sum E_{\tilde{\lambda}}(j) + \sum \tilde{\lambda}_j$ by the cost of algorithm PD, we have to relate the values $E_{\tilde{\lambda}}(j)$ and $\tilde{\lambda}_j$ to the energy- and value- costs of PD. It depends on the job itself how this is done exactly. For example, in the case of finished jobs, both terms can be related to the actual energy consumption of PD in a relatively straightforward way. This becomes much harder if the job is not finished by PD: after all, in this case PD does not invest any energy into the job. The job's trace plays a crucial role in this case, as it allows us to account the energy investment of the optimal infeasible solution to the energy PD consumed during the trace. The next proposition gathers the most important relations to be used in the following proofs.

PROPOSITION 8. *Consider an arbitrary job $j \in J$:*

(a) $E_{\tilde{\lambda}}(j) = \tilde{\lambda}_j \frac{\hat{x}_j}{\alpha}$

---

[1] Ties are resolved arbitrarily but consistently.

(b) If j is finished by PD, then $E_{\tilde{\lambda}}(j) \leq \delta^{\frac{\alpha}{\alpha-1}} E_{\mathrm{PD}}(j)$.

(c) If j is not finished by PD and $\hat{x}_j > \delta^{\frac{1}{\alpha-1}}$, then $E_{\tilde{\lambda}}(j) <$
$\delta^{\frac{\alpha}{\alpha-1}} \left(1 - \frac{\delta^{\frac{1}{\alpha-1}}}{\hat{x}_j}\right)^{-\alpha} E_{\mathrm{PD}}(j)$.

Note that the bound for unfinished jobs in Proposition 8 has an additional factor > 1 compared to the one for finished jobs. However, for large enough $\hat{x}_j$ this factor becomes nearly one. Thus, we will apply this bound only in cases of large $\hat{x}_j$. If $\hat{x}_j$ is relatively small, we will instead bound $E_{\tilde{\lambda}}(j)$ only by its value. We continue by describing the different types of jobs we consider. In total, we differentiate between three job categories:

Finished Jobs These are all jobs j with $\tilde{y}_j = 1$ (i.e., jobs finished by PD). As mentioned above, we bound both components $E_{\tilde{\lambda}}(j)$ and $\tilde{\lambda}_j$ of $g(\tilde{\lambda})$ by the actual energy consumption of PD. We use $J_1 := \{\, j \in J \mid \tilde{y}_j = 1 \,\}$ to refer to this job category.

Unfinished, Low-yield Jobs We use the term *low-yield jobs* to refer to jobs not finished by PD and which have a relatively small $\hat{x}_j$. That is, jobs of which the optimal infeasible solution does not schedule too large a portion. Intuitively, the value of such jobs must be small, because otherwise it would have been beneficial to schedule a larger portion of them in the optimal infeasible solution. In this sense, these jobs are low-yield and we will exploit this fact by bounding both components $E_{\tilde{\lambda}}(j)$ and $\tilde{\lambda}_j$ of $g(\tilde{\lambda})$ by the job value PD is charged for not finishing j. More formally, this job category is $J_2 := \{\, j \in J \mid \tilde{y}_j = 0 \wedge \hat{x}_j \leq \frac{\alpha - \alpha^{1-\alpha}}{\alpha-1} \,\}$.

Unfinished, High-yield Jobs Correspondingly, the term *high-yield jobs* refers to jobs finished by PD and which have a relatively large $\hat{x}_j$. More exactly, this job category is $J_3 := \{\, j \in J \mid \tilde{y}_j = 0 \wedge \hat{x}_j > \frac{\alpha - \alpha^{1-\alpha}}{\alpha-1} \,\}$. This proves to be the most challenging case, as neither do the jobs feature a particularly small value nor does PD invest any energy into their execution. Instead, we use a mix of the job's value and the energy spent by PD during j's trace to account for its contribution. One has to carefully balance what portions of $E_{\tilde{\lambda}}(j)$ and $\tilde{\lambda}_j$ to bound by either $E_{\mathrm{PD}}(j)$ or by v_j.

In accordance with these job categories, we split the value of the dual function by the corresponding contributions. That is, $g(\tilde{\lambda}) = \sum_{i=1}^{3} g_i(\tilde{\lambda})$, where $g_i(\tilde{\lambda}) = (1-\alpha)\sum_{j \in J_i} E_{\tilde{\lambda}}(j) + \sum_{j \in J_i} \tilde{\lambda}_j$. The following lemmas bound each contribution separately.

LEMMA 9. *For finished jobs it holds that*
$$g_1(\tilde{\lambda}) \geq \delta E_{\mathrm{PD}} + (1-\alpha)\delta^{\frac{\alpha}{\alpha-1}} \sum_{j \in J_1} E_{\mathrm{PD}}(j).$$

LEMMA 10. *For unfinished, low-yield jobs it holds that*
$$g_2(\tilde{\lambda}) \geq \alpha^{-\alpha} \sum_{j \in J_2} v_j.$$

LEMMA 11. *For unfinished, high-yield jobs it holds that*
$$g_3(\tilde{\lambda}) \geq \frac{1-\alpha}{\alpha^\alpha} \sum_{j \in J_3} E_{\mathrm{PD}}(j) + \alpha^{-\alpha} \sum_{j \in J_3} v_j \quad , \text{if } \delta \leq \frac{1}{\alpha^{\alpha-1}}.$$

It remains to prove Theorem 3, our main result. Its proof is essentially a suitable combination of the bounds from the Lemmas 9 to 11 and can be found in the appendix.

5. CONCLUSION

We presented a new algorithm and an analysis based on duality theory for scheduling valuable jobs on multiple speed-scalable processors. The usage of duality theory to approach the analysis of energy-efficient scheduling algorithms was recently proposed by Gupta et al. [12]. Given that the first formal proof of the original offline algorithm's optimality was achieved by means of duality theory using the KKT conditions [4], it seems that this is a very natural way to approach this kind of problems. However, almost all results for online algorithms in this area use amortized competitiveness arguments similar to the original proof of OA's competitiveness, one of the first and most important online algorithms for energy-efficient scheduling. While this approach proved to be elegant and very powerful, designing suitable potential functions is difficult and needs a quite high amount of experience with the topic. Adapting these potential functions to new model variations and generalizations, or tuning them to narrow the gap to the known lower bounds is nontrivial and remains a challenging task. We think that using well-developed utilities from duality theory for convex programming may prove to be a worthwhile and promising alternative approach. Our results underline this conjecture, not only improving upon known results proved using the classical method but also generalizing them to the important case of multiple processors.

References

[1] S. Albers. Algorithms for dynamic speed scaling. In *Proceedings of the 28th Symposium on Theoretical Aspects of Computer Science*, pages 1–11. Schloss Dagstuhl, 2011.

[2] S. Albers, A. Antoniadis, and G. Greiner. On multi-processor speed scaling with migration. In *Proceedings of the 23rd ACM Symposium on Parallelism in Algorithms and Architectures (SPAA)*, pages 279–288, 2011.

[3] N. Bansal, T. Kimbrel, and K. Pruhs. Dynamic speed scaling to manage energy and temperature. In *Proceedings of the 45th IEEE Symposium on Foundations of Computer Science (FOCS)*, pages 520–529, 2004.

[4] N. Bansal, T. Kimbrel, and K. Pruhs. Speed scaling to manage energy and temperature. *Journal of the ACM*, 54(1):1–39, 2007.

[5] N. Bansal, H.-L. Chan, K. Pruhs, and D. Katz. Improved bounds for speed scaling in devices obeying the cube-root rule. In *Proceedings of the 36th International Colloquium on Automata, Languages and Programming (ICALP)*, pages 144–155. Springer, 2009.

[6] L. A. Barroso and U. Hölzle. The case for energy-proportional computing. *Computer*, 40(12): 33–37, 2007.

[7] B. D. Bingham and M. R. Greenstreet. Energy optimal scheduling on multiprocessors with migration. In *Proceedings of the 2008 IEEE International Symposium on Parallel and Distributed Processing with Applications (ISPA)*, pages 153–161. IEEE Computer Society, 2008.

[8] S. P. Boyd and L. Vandenberghe. *Convex*

Optimization. Cambridge University Press, 7 edition, 2004.

[9] N. Buchbinder and J. Naor. *The Design of Competitive Online Algorithms via a Primal-Dual Approach*. Now Publishers Inc., 2009.

[10] H.-L. Chan, T.-W. Lam, and R. Li. Tradeoff between energy and throughput for online deadline scheduling. In *WAOA*, pages 59–70. Springer, 2010.

[11] J.-J. Chen, H.-R. Hsu, K.-H. Chuang, C.-L. Yang, A.-C. Pang, and T.-W. Kuo. Multiprocessor energy-efficient scheduling with task migration considerations. In *Proc. of the 16th Euromicro Conference on Real-Time Systems*, pages 101–108, 2004.

[12] A. Gupta, R. Krishnaswamy, and K. Pruhs. Online primal-dual for non-linear optimization with applications to speed scaling. In *WAOA*, 2012.

[13] P. Kling and P. Pietrzyk. Profitable scheduling on multiple speed-scalable processors, 2012. arXiv:1209.3868.

[14] K. Pruhs and C. Stein. How to schedule when you have to buy your energy. In *APPROX/RANDOM*, pages 352–365. Springer, 2010.

[15] F. F. Yao, A. J. Demers, and S. Shenker. A scheduling model for reduced cpu energy. In *Proceedings of the 36th Annual Symposium on Foundations of Computer Science (FOCS)*, pages 374–382, 1995.

APPENDIX

Power Consumption in Atomic Intervals.

PROOF SKETCH PROPOSITION 1. (a) First, the equality $\mathcal{P}_k(0) = 0$ is obvious from the definition of $\mathcal{P}_k$. The convexity follows easily from [7, Lemma 3.2]. There, the authors proved the convexity of the function $(x_{1k}, \ldots, x_{nk}) \mapsto \mathcal{P}_k(x_{1k}/w_1, \ldots, x_{nk}/w_n)$ (a linear transformation of $\mathcal{P}_k$).

(b) The differentiability is obvious for all $(x_{1k}, \ldots, x_{nk})$ for which all the inequalities $x_{jk} w_j > \sum_{j' \geq j} x_{j'k} w_{j'}/(m-j)$ in Equation (2.2) are strict: For these, we have a small interval around x_{jk} such that the set $\psi(k)$ of dedicated jobs does not change. On these intervals, $\mathcal{P}_k$ is essentially a linear map of the differentiable function $\mathrm{P}_\alpha(s) = s^\alpha$. For other points, one can compute the left and right derivatives in x_{jk}, distinguishing whether job j switched between a dedicated processor and a pool processor, whether j stays on a dedicated processor, or whether j stays on a pool processor and some other jobs switch between processor types. All cases yield the same left and right derivatives as given in the statement. □

PROOF SKETCH PROPOSITION 2. We limit our analysis to the normalized case. That is, the case of unit workloads ($w_j = 1$ for all jobs) and an atomic interval of unit length ($l_k = 1$). The general case follows by a straightforward adaption. Without loss of generality, we furthermore assume $x_1 \geq x_2 \geq \cdots \geq x_n$. Note that we do not presume any relation between the newly arrived workload z and the remaining workloads. Let S and S' be the schedules produced by Chen et al.'s algorithm for the work assignments x and x', respectively. Similarly, we use d and d' to denote the number of dedicated processors, and L_{pool} and L'_{pool} for the workload of a pool processor in S and S', respectively. Remember that pool processors have the smallest workload. That is, we have $L_i \geq L_{\mathrm{pool}}$ and $L'_i \geq L'_{\mathrm{pool}}$ for all $i \in \{1, 2, \ldots, m\}$.

We start with the proof of $L'_i - L_i \geq 0$. Observe that the arrival of the workload z will not cause any of the former pool jobs to become a dedicated job (cf. Equation (4)). Moreover, by the same equation, for each dedicated processor that becomes a pool processor we also get a new pool job that has a workload of at least L_{pool}. Thus, the workload of pool processors from S can only increase. The workload of the i-th fastest dedicated processor in S is exactly x_i. If it becomes a pool processor, we have $x_i < L'_{\mathrm{pool}} = L'_i$, yielding $L_i = x_i < L'_i$. If it stays a dedicated processor, its workload is the i-th largest value in $\{x_1, \ldots, x_n, z\}$ and, thus, at least as large as the i-th largest value in $\{x_1, \ldots, x_n\}$, yielding $L_i \leq L'_i$. To prove the second statement, $L'_i - L_i \leq z$, let us assume $L'_i - L_i > z$ and seek a contradiction. We distinguish two cases, depending on the type (pool or dedicated) of the i-th fastest processor in S':

processor i is a pool processor in S' Note that the inequalities $z < L'_i - L_i \leq L'_i$ and i being a pool processor imply that z is also scheduled on a pool processor (cf. Equation (4)). As d' is the number of dedicated processors, we must have $i > d'$. Moreover, all the jobs with workload less than $L'_{d'}$ must be pool jobs in S'. These are exactly the jobs which are scheduled on the processors $d' + 1, \ldots, m$ in schedule S. Thus, the total workload of all pool processors in S' equals $(m - d')L'_i = z + \sum_{j > d'} L_j$. Using $i > d'$, $L'_{i'} - L_{i'} \geq 0$ for all $i' \in \{1, 2, \ldots, m\}$, and that all pool processors in S' have the same workload, we get $z = (m - d')L'_i - \sum_{j > d'} L_j = \sum_{j > d'}(L'_i - L_j) = \sum_{j > d'}(L'_j - L_j) \geq L'_i - L_i$. This contradicts our assumption.

processor i is a dedicated processor in S' Notice that our assumption implies $L'_i > L_i + z \geq z$. Together with i being a dedicated processor this yields $L'_i = x_i$ (because x_i remains the i-th largest value in the set $\{x_1, x_2, \ldots, x_n, z\}$). But the assumption also implies $L'_i > L_i + z \geq L_i \geq x_i$. We get the contradiction $x_i = L'_i > x_i$. □

Structure of Optimal Infeasible Solutions.

PROOF LEMMA 4. (a) Consider an arbitrary job $j \in J$ and remember that the domain for the variables $\hat{y}_j$ is restricted to $[0, 1]$. The contribution of variable $\hat{y}_j$ to $g(\tilde{\lambda}) = L(\hat{x}, \hat{y}, \tilde{\lambda})$ is exactly $\hat{y}_j(\tilde{\lambda}_j - v_j)$, as can be seen by considering Equation (2). If $\tilde{\lambda}_j < v_j$, this is minimized by choosing $\hat{y}_j$ maximal ($\hat{y}_j = 1$). Otherwise, we must have $\tilde{\lambda}_j = v_j$ (by the definition of algorithm PD). This allows us to choose $\hat{y}_j$ arbitrarily, such that we can set it to zero. Both choices correspond exactly to the way $\tilde{y}_j$ is set by algorithm PD.

(b) Assume there are more than m jobs with $\hat{x}_{jk} > 0$. We can assume $c_{jk} = 1$ for these jobs, because otherwise we could set $\hat{x}_{jk} = 0$ without increasing $g(\tilde{\lambda}) = L(\hat{x}, \hat{y}, \tilde{\lambda})$. Now, the values $\hat{x}_{1k}, \ldots, \hat{x}_{nk}$ correspond to a work assignment for the atomic interval T_k, as used by Chen et al.'s algorithm (cf. Section 2.2). By Equation (2), the contribution of these values to $g(\tilde{\lambda}) = L(\hat{x}, \hat{y}, \tilde{\lambda})$ is given by $\mathcal{P}_k(\hat{x}_{1k}, \ldots, \hat{x}_{nk}) - \sum_{j \in J} \tilde{\lambda}_j \hat{x}_{jk}$. Since there are more than m jobs j with a nonzero $\hat{x}_{jk}$, at least two of them must share a processor in the schedule computed by Chen et al.'s algorithm for this work assignment. In other words, there are two pool jobs $j, j' \in J \setminus \psi(k)$ with $\hat{x}_{jk}, \hat{x}_{j'k} > 0$. Together with Equation (5), we see that the contribution of $\hat{x}_{jk}$ and $\hat{x}_{j'k}$ to $g(\tilde{\lambda})$ consists of two terms: a convex term

$$(m - |\psi(k)|)l_k \, \mathrm{P}_\alpha\left(\frac{\sum_{j \notin \psi(k)} \hat{x}_{jk} w_j}{(m - |\psi(k)|)l_k}\right)$$

and a linear term $-\tilde{\lambda}_j \hat{x}_{jk} - \tilde{\lambda}_{j'} \hat{x}_{j'k}$. By changing $\hat{x}_{jk}$ and $\hat{x}_{j'k}$ along the line that keeps the sum $\hat{x}_{jk} w_j + \hat{x}_{j'k} w_{j'}$ constant, we can decrease one of the variables (say $\hat{x}_{jk}$) and increase the other such that the first (convex) term remains constant and the second (linear) term is not increased. This will not effect the type (dedicated or pool) of other jobs. The only job that may change its type is job j', as it may become a dedicated job. Once this happens, we iterate the process with two other pool jobs. As the number of dedicated jobs is upper bounded by m, this can happen only finitely often. Thus, at some point we can decrease $\hat{x}_{jk}$ all the way to zero without increasing the dual function value $g(\tilde{\lambda})$. We continue eliminating $\hat{x}_{jk}$ variables until at most m of them are nonzero. $\square$

PROOF LEMMA 5. (a) By definition, $\hat{x}$ is a minimizer of the function $x \mapsto L(x, \hat{y}, \tilde{\lambda})$. This implies $\frac{\partial L}{\partial x_{jk}}(\tilde{\lambda}, \hat{x}, \hat{y}) = 0$ for any contributing job $j \in \varphi(k)$. We get

$$0 = \frac{\partial L}{\partial x_{jk}}(\tilde{\lambda}, \hat{x}, \hat{y}) = \frac{\partial \mathcal{P}_k}{\partial x_{jk}}(\hat{x}_{1k}, \ldots, \hat{x}_{nk}) - \tilde{\lambda}_j$$
$$= w_j \cdot \mathrm{P}_\alpha'\left(\frac{\hat{x}_{jk} w_j}{l_k}\right) - \tilde{\lambda}_j = \alpha w_j \left(\frac{\hat{x}_{jk} w_j}{l_k}\right)^{\alpha - 1} - \tilde{\lambda}_j,$$

which yields the first statement by rearranging. The second statement follows by noticing that $\frac{\hat{x}_{jk} w_j}{l_k}$ is the speed used by Chen et al.'s algorithm for the (dedicated) job j.

(b) By definition of $g(\tilde{\lambda}) = L(\hat{x}, \hat{y}, \tilde{\lambda})$, we get that the total contribution of the $\hat{x}_{jk}$ variables is (there are no pool jobs!)

$$\mathcal{P}_k(\hat{x}_{1k}, \ldots, \hat{x}_{nk}) - \sum_{j \in \varphi(k)} \tilde{\lambda}_j \hat{x}_{jk}$$
$$= \sum_{j \in \varphi(k)} l_k \, \mathrm{P}_\alpha\left(\frac{\hat{x}_{jk} w_j}{l_k}\right) - \sum_{j \in \varphi(k)} \tilde{\lambda}_j \hat{x}_{jk}$$
$$= l_k \sum_{j \in \varphi(k)} \mathrm{P}_\alpha(\hat{s}_j) - \alpha l_k \sum_{j \in \varphi(k)} \frac{\tilde{\lambda}_j}{\alpha w_j} \hat{s}_j = (1 - \alpha) l_k \sum_{j \in \varphi(k)} \hat{s}_j^\alpha.$$

(c) The contributing jobs must be chosen such that their contribution is minimized. Using (b) and $\alpha > 1$, we see that this is the case when choosing the maximal number of available jobs (at most m) with the largest $\hat{s}_j$-values. $\square$

A Job-centric Formulated Dual Function.

PROOF LEMMA 6. The equality $E_{\tilde{\lambda}}(j) = l(j)\hat{s}_j^\alpha$ follows immediately from the above definitions, as j is processed by the $(\hat{x}, \hat{y})$-schedule at constant speed $\hat{s}_j$ for a total time of exactly $l(j)$. For the lemma's main statement, remember that $\hat{y}_j = 0$ if and only if $\tilde{\lambda}_j = v_j$. Otherwise we have $\hat{y}_j = 1$.

Thus, the contribution of $\hat{y}_j$ to $g(\tilde{\lambda})$ is exactly $(1 - \hat{y}_j)v_j + \tilde{\lambda}_j \hat{y}_j = \tilde{\lambda}_j$. As we have seen in Lemma 5 for a fixed k, the contribution of all $\hat{x}_{jk}$ to $g(\tilde{\lambda})$ is exactly $(1 - \alpha)l_k \sum_{j \in \varphi(k)} \hat{s}_j^\alpha$. Summing over all k, we get that the total contribution of the $\hat{x}$-variables equals

$$\sum_{k=1}^{N} (1 - \alpha) l_k \sum_{j \in \varphi(k)} \hat{s}_j^\alpha = (1 - \alpha) \sum_{k=1}^{N} \sum_{j \in \varphi(k)} l_k \hat{s}_j^\alpha$$
$$= (1 - \alpha) \sum_{j \in J} \sum_{k \in \varphi^{-1}(j)}^{N} l_k \hat{s}_j^\alpha = (1 - \alpha) \sum_{j \in J} l(j) \hat{s}_j^\alpha$$
$$= (1 - \alpha) \sum_{j \in J} E_{\tilde{\lambda}}(j).$$

Summing up the contributions of the $\hat{x}$- and $\hat{y}$-variables we get the desired statement. $\square$

PROOF PROPOSITION 7. (a) Remember that we have the equality $\tilde{s}_j = \delta^{-1/\alpha - 1} \hat{s}_j$. Because of this relation and the definition of $(T_k, i) \in \mathrm{Tr}(j)$, we must have that $\tilde{s}_j$ is the i-th largest value in $\{\tilde{s}_{j'} \mid j' \in \varphi_1(k)\}$. Now, together with Lemma 5(c), we even have that $\tilde{s}_j$ is the i-th largest value under all available jobs finished by PD. At the time τ_{k-1} (the start of interval T_k), all these available jobs j' have arrived. We consider two cases: If j is a dedicated job at this time, it is scheduled with a speed of exactly $\tilde{s}_j$. Moreover, all the $i - 1$ available jobs j' with $\tilde{s}_{j'} \geq \tilde{s}_j$ are dedicated jobs and are scheduled with a speed of $\tilde{s}_{j'}$, respectively. Thus, j is scheduled on the i-th fastest processor, yielding $s(i, k) \geq \tilde{s}_j$. If j is a pool job at this time, it is scheduled on one of the pool processors at a speed of at least $\tilde{s}_j$. But then, since pool processors are the slowest processors, the i-th fastest processor must also run at a speed of at least $\tilde{s}_j$.

(b) Remember that $\breve{x}_{jk}$ denotes the portion of job j PD planned to schedule in T_k just before j got rejected. If j was planned as a dedicated job, we have $l_k \tilde{s}_j = \breve{x}_{jk} w_j$. This trivially yields the desired statement because of $s(i, k) \geq 0$. If j was not planned as a dedicated job, it was to be processed on a pool processor. Let $L(i, k)$ denote the workload on the i-th fastest processor during T_k just after j was rejected (i.e., without $\breve{x}_{jk} w_j$). Similarly, let $L'(i, k)$ denote the workload on the i-th fastest processor during T_k just before j was rejected (i.e., including $\breve{x}_{jk} w_j$). Proposition 2 gives us $L'(i, k) - L(i, k) \leq \breve{x}_{jk} w_j$. Moreover, since j was planned as a pool job (which run at minimal speed), we must have $l_k \tilde{s}_j \leq L'(i, k)$. Combining these inequalities yields that the speed $L(i, k)/l_k$ on the i-th fastest processor during T_k at j's arrival was at least $\tilde{s}_j - \frac{\breve{x}_{jk} w_j}{l_k}$. As Proposition 2 also implies that the workload (and, thus, the speed) of the i-th fastest processor in an atomic interval can only increase due to the arrival of new jobs, we get the desired statement. $\square$

Balancing the Different Cost Components.

PROOF PROPOSITION 8. (a) We use the identities $\hat{s}_j = (\tilde{\lambda}_j / \alpha w_j)^{\frac{1}{\alpha - 1}}$ and $l(j)\hat{s}_j = \hat{x}_j w_j$ (cf. Lemma 5) and compute

$$E_{\tilde{\lambda}}(j) = l(j)\hat{s}_j^\alpha = l(j)\hat{s}_j \cdot \hat{s}_j^{\alpha - 1} = \hat{x}_j w_j \cdot \frac{\tilde{\lambda}_j}{\alpha w_j} = \tilde{\lambda}_j \frac{\hat{x}_j}{\alpha}.$$

(b) Assume j is finished by PD. Remember that $\tilde{s}_j$ denotes the speed assigned to j when it arrived and $\tilde{\lambda}_j$ got fixed.

We have the relation $\tilde{s}_j = \delta^{-1/\alpha - 1}\hat{s}_j$ (cf. Section 4.2). Let $s_{\min}$ denote the minimal speed of j's trace in the final $(\tilde{x}, \tilde{y})$-schedule produced by PD. That is, there is a tuple $(T_k, i) \in \mathrm{Tr}(j)$ such that the i-th fastest processor in T_k runs at speed $s_{\min}$ and $E_{\mathrm{PD}}(j) \geq l(j)s_{\min}^\alpha$. By Proposition 7 we must have $s_{\min} \geq \tilde{s}_j$. We compute

$$E_{\tilde{\lambda}}(j) = l(j)\hat{s}_j^\alpha = \delta^{\frac{\alpha}{\alpha-1}}l(j)\tilde{s}_j^\alpha \leq \delta^{\frac{\alpha}{\alpha-1}}l(j)s_{\min}^\alpha$$
$$\leq \delta^{\frac{\alpha}{\alpha-1}}E_{\mathrm{PD}}(j).$$

(c) Applying Proposition 7 to all $(T_k, i) \in \mathrm{Tr}(j)$ yields that the total workload L that is processed by PD during j's trace is at least $l(j)\tilde{s}_j - \check{x}_j w_j > l(j)\tilde{s}_j - w_j$. The minimum energy necessary to process this workload in $l(j)$ time units is $l(j)\left(L/l(j)\right)^\alpha$. We compute

$$E_{\mathrm{PD}}(j) \geq l(j)\left(\frac{L}{l(j)}\right)^\alpha > l(j)\left(\frac{l(j)\tilde{s}_j - w_j}{l(j)}\right)^\alpha$$
$$= l(j)\tilde{s}_j^\alpha\left(1 - w_j/\tilde{s}_j l(j)\right)^\alpha = \delta^{-\frac{\alpha}{\alpha-1}}E_{\tilde{\lambda}}(j)\left(1 - \frac{\delta^{\frac{1}{\alpha-1}}}{\hat{x}_j}\right)^\alpha.$$

Rearranging this inequality in a suitable way yields the desired statement. $\square$

PROOF LEMMA 9. We have $g_1(\tilde{\lambda}) = (1-\alpha)\sum_{j\in J_1}E_{\tilde{\lambda}}(j) + \sum_{j_1\in J}\tilde{\lambda}_j$. Using Proposition 8(b) and $\alpha > 1$ we bound the first summand by $(1-\alpha)\delta^{\frac{\alpha}{\alpha-1}}\sum_{j\in J_1}E_{\mathrm{PD}}(j)$. For the second summand, we get

$$\sum_{j\in J_1}\tilde{\lambda}_j = \sum_{j\in J_1}\sum_{k=1}^N \tilde{x}_{jk}\tilde{\lambda}_j$$
$$= \sum_{j\in J_1}\sum_{k=1}^N \tilde{x}_{jk}\delta\frac{\partial\mathcal{P}_k}{\partial x_{jk}}(\tilde{x}_{1k},\ldots,\tilde{x}_{jk},0,\ldots,0)$$
$$= \delta\sum_{k=1}^N\sum_{j\in J}\tilde{x}_{jk}\frac{\partial\mathcal{P}_k}{\partial x_{jk}}(\tilde{x}_{1k},\ldots,\tilde{x}_{jk},0,\ldots,0)$$
$$\geq \delta\sum_{k=1}^N\mathcal{P}_k(\tilde{x}_{1k},\ldots,\tilde{x}_{nk}) = \delta E_{\mathrm{PD}}.$$

The involved inequality is based on the fact that for any differentiable convex function $f: \mathbb{R}^n \to \mathbb{R}$ with $f(0) = 0$ and $x \in \mathbb{R}_{\geq 0}^n$ we have $\sum_{j=1}^n x_j \frac{\partial f}{\partial x_j}(x_1,\ldots,x_j,0,\ldots,0) \geq f(x)$ (see, e.g., [8, Chapter 3]). Together the bounds yield the lemma's statement. $\square$

PROOF LEMMA 10. Proposition 8(a) together with $\tilde{\lambda}_j = v_j$ for $j \in J_2$ yields $E_{\tilde{\lambda}}(j) = v_j\frac{\hat{x}_j}{\alpha}$. We get

$$g_2(\tilde{\lambda}) = \sum_{j\in J_2}(1-\alpha)E_{\tilde{\lambda}}(j) + \sum_{j\in J_2}\tilde{\lambda}_j$$
$$= \sum_{j\in J_2}\frac{1-\alpha}{\alpha}\hat{x}_j v_j + \sum_{j\in J_2}v_j = \sum_{j\in J_2}\left(1 - \frac{\alpha-1}{\alpha}\hat{x}_j\right)v_j$$
$$\overset{\mathrm{Def.}}{\underset{J_2}{\geq}} \sum_{j\in J_2}\left(1 - \frac{\alpha-\alpha^{1-\alpha}}{\alpha}\right)v_j = \alpha^{-\alpha}\sum_{j\in J_2}v_j. \quad \square$$

PROOF LEMMA 11. We make use of both Proposition 8(a) and Proposition 8(c). First note that the prerequisite $\delta \leq \frac{1}{\alpha^{\alpha-1}}$ together with $\alpha > 1$ and $j \in J_3$ gives us the relation $\delta^{\frac{1}{\alpha-1}} \leq \frac{1}{\alpha} \leq 1 \leq \frac{\alpha-\alpha^{1-\alpha}}{\alpha-1} < \hat{x}_j$. This allows us to apply

Proposition 8(c). The second summand of $g_3(\tilde{\lambda})$ is split into two parts, one of which is accounted for by energy invested by PD and the other one by values of unfinished jobs:

$$g_3(\tilde{\lambda}) = \sum_{j\in J_3}(1-\alpha)E_{\tilde{\lambda}}(j) + \sum_{j\in J_3}\tilde{\lambda}_j$$
$$= \sum_{j\in J_3}(1-\alpha)E_{\tilde{\lambda}}(j) + \sum_{j\in J_3}\left(1-\alpha^{-\alpha}\right)\tilde{\lambda}_j + \sum_{j\in J_3}\alpha^{-\alpha}\tilde{\lambda}_j$$
$$= \sum_{j\in J_3}(1-\alpha)E_{\tilde{\lambda}}(j) + \sum_{j\in J_3}\left(1-\alpha^{-\alpha}\right)\alpha E_{\tilde{\lambda}}(j)/\hat{x}_j + \sum_{j\in J_3}\alpha^{-\alpha}v_j$$
$$= \sum_{j\in J_3}(1-\alpha)E_{\tilde{\lambda}}(j)\left(1 - \frac{\alpha-\alpha^{1-\alpha}}{(\alpha-1)\hat{x}_j}\right) + \sum_{j\in J_3}\alpha^{-\alpha}v_j$$
$$> \sum_{j\in J_3}(1-\alpha)\delta^{\frac{\alpha}{\alpha-1}}E_{\mathrm{PD}}(j)\left(1 - \frac{\delta^{\frac{1}{\alpha-1}}}{\hat{x}_j}\right)^{-\alpha}\left(1 - \frac{\alpha-\alpha^{1-\alpha}}{(\alpha-1)\hat{x}_j}\right)$$
$$\quad + \sum_{j\in J_3}\alpha^{-\alpha}v_j$$
$$\geq \sum_{j\in J_3}(1-\alpha)\alpha^{-\alpha}\left(1 - \frac{1}{\alpha\hat{x}_j}\right)^{-\alpha}\left(1 - \frac{1}{\hat{x}_j}\right)E_{\mathrm{PD}}(j)$$
$$\quad + \sum_{j\in J_3}\alpha^{-\alpha}v_j \geq (1-\alpha)\alpha^{-\alpha}\sum_{j\in J_3}E_{\mathrm{PD}}(j) + \sum_{j\in J_3}\alpha^{-\alpha}v_j.$$

The first inequality applies Proposition 8(c), the penultimate inequality the relations deduced from the prerequisite, and the last inequality applies Bernoulli's inequality. $\square$

Main Result.

PROOF THEOREM 3. If we combine all the results from Lemma 9 to Lemma 11 we get

$$g(\tilde{\lambda}) \geq \alpha^{1-\alpha}E_{\mathrm{PD}} + (1-\alpha)\alpha^{-\alpha}\sum_{j\in J_1\cup J_3}E_{\mathrm{PD}}(j) + \alpha^{-\alpha}\sum_{j\in J_2\cup J_3}v_j$$
$$\geq \alpha^{1-\alpha}E_{\mathrm{PD}} + (1-\alpha)\alpha^{-\alpha}\sum_{j\in J}E_{\mathrm{PD}}(j) + \alpha^{-\alpha}\sum_{j\in J_2\cup J_3}v_j$$
$$\geq \left(\alpha^{1-\alpha} + (1-\alpha)\alpha^{-\alpha}\right)E_{\mathrm{PD}} + \alpha^{-\alpha}\sum_{j\in J_2\cup J_3}v_j$$
$$= \alpha^{-\alpha}\mathrm{cost}(\mathrm{PD}).$$

Now, let OPT denote an optimal schedule for the current problem instance. Moreover, let OPT′ denote an optimal solution to the relaxed mathematical program (CP). Obviously, it holds that $\mathrm{cost}(\mathrm{OPT}') \leq \mathrm{cost}(\mathrm{OPT})$. By duality, we know that $g(\tilde{\lambda}) \leq \mathrm{cost}(\mathrm{OPT}')$. By combining these inequalities we can bound PD's competitiveness by

$$\mathrm{cost}(\mathrm{PD}) \leq \alpha^\alpha g(\tilde{\lambda}) \leq \alpha^\alpha \mathrm{cost}(\mathrm{OPT}') \leq \alpha^\alpha \mathrm{cost}(\mathrm{OPT}).$$

For the lower bound, consider a single processor and assume the job values are high enough to ensure that PD finishes all jobs. We create a job instance of n jobs in the same way as done in [3] for the lower bound on OA and AVR. That is, job $j \in J = \{1, 2, \ldots, n\}$ arrives at time $j-1$ and has workload $(n-j+1)^{-1/\alpha}$. All jobs have the same deadline n. Now, whenever one of the jobs arrives, PD schedules all remaining jobs at the energy-optimal (i.e., minimal) speed as pool jobs. In other words, it computes a schedule that is optimal for the remaining known work. This is exactly what OA does (hence its name), which means that we get the same lower bound of α^α as for OA (cf. [3, Lemma 3.2]). $\square$

Nonclairvoyant Sleep Management and Flow-time Scheduling on Multiple Processors

Sze-Hang Chan
Department of Computer Science
University of Hong Kong
shchan@cs.hku.hk

Tak-Wah Lam[*]
Department of Computer Science
University of Hong Kong
twlam@cs.hku.hk

Lap-Kei Lee[†]
Department of Computer Science
University of Hong Kong
lklee@cs.hku.hk

Jianqiao Zhu
Department of Computer Sciences
University of Wisconsin-Madison
jianqiao@cs.wisc.edu

ABSTRACT

In large data centers, managing the availability of servers is often non-trivial, especially when the workload is unpredictable. Using too many servers would waste energy, while using too few would affect the performance. A recent theoretical study, which assumes the clairvoyant model where job size is known at arrival time, has successfully integrated sleep-and-wakeup management into multi-processor job scheduling and obtained a competitive tradeoff between flow time and energy [6]. This paper extends the study to the nonclairvoyant model where the size of a job is not known until the job is finished. We give a new online algorithm SATA which is, for any $\epsilon > 0$, $(1 + \epsilon)$-speed $O(\frac{1}{\epsilon^2})$-competitive for the objective of minimizing the sum of flow time and energy.

SATA also gives a new nonclairvoyant result for the classic setting where all processors are always on and the concern is flow time only. In this case, the previous work of Chekuri et al. [7] and Chadha et al. [8] has revealed that random dispatching can give a non-migratory algorithm that is $(1 + \epsilon)$-speed $O(\frac{1}{\epsilon^3})$-competitive, and any deterministic non-migratory algorithm is $\Omega(\frac{m}{s})$-competitive using s-speed processors [7], where m is the number of processors. SATA, which is a deterministic algorithm migrating each job at most four times on average, has a competitive ratio of $O(\frac{1}{\epsilon^2})$. The number of migrations used by SATA is optimal up to a constant factor as we can extend the above lower bound result.

[*]The research was supported by HKU-SPF 201109176197.

[†]Part of the work was done when working in MADALGO, Aarhus University, Denmark.

Categories and Subject Descriptors

C.4 [**Performance of Systems**]: Performance Attributes; F.2.0 [**Analysis of Algorithms and Problem Complexity**]: General

Keywords

Online scheduling; competitive analysis; sleep management; flow time; job migration

1. INTRODUCTION

Energy consumption is a major concern for large-scale data centers. Very often data centers are running more servers than necessary and wasting a lot of energy. When a processor is on, the power consumption is divided into *dynamic power* and *static power*; the former is consumed only when the processor is processing a job, while the latter is consumed constantly (due to leakage current) even when the machine is idle. For example, an Intel Xeon E5320 server requires 150W of power when idling and 240W when working [11]. The static power consumption is cut off only when a processor is put to sleep. From the energy viewpoint, a data center should let the servers sleep whenever they are idle; yet waking up the servers later requires extra energy, and it is energy inefficient to frequently switch servers on and off. It is nontrivial how to determine dynamically the appropriate number of working servers so as to strike a balance between energy usage and quality of service (QoS), especially when the workload is unpredictable. The past few years have witnessed a number of theoretical results on revisiting different scheduling problems to consider sleep management, QoS and energy consumption together (e.g., [6,14–16,18], see the survey [1]).

Multi-processor flow-time scheduling. A well-studied QoS measurement for job scheduling is the total flow time. The flow time (or simply the flow) of a job is the length of the duration from its arrival until its completion. We consider the online setting where jobs arrive at unpredictable times. There are $m > 1$ identical processors. Jobs are sequential (i.e., each can be executed on at most one processor at a time) and preemptive in nature. Flow-time scheduling on multiple processors is hard; competitive online algorithms can exist only when extra resource is given [17].

- For the clairvoyant model where job size is known at release time, it is known that both migratory and non-migratory algorithms can be $(1+\epsilon)$-speed $O(\frac{1}{\epsilon})$-competitive for flow time [3, 10].[1]

- From the viewpoint of operating systems, it is more natural to consider the nonclairvoyant model where the size of a job is not known until the job is finished. To minimize flow time on multi-processors, extra speed is not too useful if migration is not allowed; Chekuri et al. [7] showed that any deterministic non-migratory online algorithm that dispatches jobs at arrival times is $\Omega(\frac{m}{s})$-competitive when using s-speed processors. They also showed a randomized non-migratory algorithm that dispatches jobs randomly and is $(1+\epsilon)$-speed $O(\frac{1}{\epsilon^4}\log\frac{1}{\epsilon})$-competitive. Chadha et al. [8] improved the analysis of random dispatching and the competitive ratio to $O(\frac{1}{\epsilon^3})$. The recent work of Gupta et al. [13] on the other hand implies a deterministic migratory algorithm that is $(1+\epsilon)$-speed $O(\frac{1}{\epsilon^4})$-competitive; this algorithm migrates jobs after every infinitesimal time interval and requires unbounded number of migrations. Such migratory algorithm makes sense for multi-processors on a single chip, but may not be practical for a cluster of servers.

Sleep management and energy. We assume that a processor has two possible states, *awake* or *sleep*. When a processor is awake, it can process a job with energy consumed at the rate $\nu + \sigma$, where $\nu > 0$ is the dynamic power and $\sigma > 0$ is the static power. An awake processor can be idle, requiring only the static power σ. A processor can enter a sleep state to reduce its power consumption to zero, but a wake-up operation requires extra energy $\omega > 0$. A scheduler has to determine when and which processors should be put to sleep or waken up, and how the jobs are scheduled on the awake processors. Following the literature on optimizing flow time and energy, we consider the objective of minimizing the sum of flow time and energy (or in general, a linear combination of flow and energy)[2] [2]. Under the clairvoyant model, Chan et al. [6] have given a non-migratory algorithm that is $(1+\epsilon)$-speed $O(\frac{1}{\epsilon})$-competitive for flow time plus energy. They also showed that without faster processors, even a migratory algorithm is $\Omega(m)$-competitive.

Our contribution. Our main result is a nonclairvoyant algorithm called SATA (Scheduling with Arrival-Time-Alignment) for job scheduling with sleep management. SATA is a deterministic algorithm and $(1+\epsilon)$-speed $O(\frac{1}{\epsilon^2})$-competitive for the objective of minimizing flow time plus energy.

SATA also gives a new nonclairvoyant result for the classic setting where all processors are always on and the objective

is to minimize flow time only. In this case, SATA is $(1+\epsilon)$-speed $8(1+\frac{1}{\epsilon})^2$-competitive. It is interesting to compare SATA with existing nonclairvoyant algorithms. SATA is a deterministic migratory algorithm that guarantees each job being migrated at most 4 times on average. It has a better competitive ratio than the previous randomized non-migratory algorithm [8] and deterministic unbounded-migratory algorithm [13]. We also extend the lower bound result in [7] to show that if a job is allowed to migrate at most c times on average for any real $c < 1$, any deterministic nonclairvoyant s-speed algorithm for $s \geq 1$ has a competitive ratio $\Omega(\min(\frac{m}{s}, \frac{1}{\sqrt{cs}}))$. This lower bound holds even if jobs can be dispatched at any time.

Remarks on speed scaling. Another model for studying energy saving is the speed scaling model, in which a processor can dynamically scale its speed, and the power increases with the speed s according to a given power function $P(s)$. Online algorithms for minimizing flow time plus energy under the speed scaling model (without sleep management) have been studied extensively (e.g., [2, 4, 5, 12, 13], see [1] for a survey). In particular, the nonclairvoyant speed-scaling algorithm by Gupta et al. [13] is $(1+\epsilon)$-speed $O(\frac{1}{\epsilon^5})$-competitive. This algorithm requires unbounded number of migrations. We can extend SATA to support speed scaling (instead of sleep management) using some standard techniques [5, 12]; the resulting algorithm is $(1+\epsilon)$-speed $O(\frac{1}{\epsilon^3})$-competitive for flow plus energy and migrates each job at most 4 times on average. It is worth-mentioning that SATA assumes each processor to have the same speed-to-power function, while Gupta et al.'s algorithm [13] allows processors to be all different.

It is natural to consider a more general energy-saving model that exploits both speed scaling and sleep management. It is open how to adapt SATA or find another nonclairvoyant algorithm for this model. If clairvoyance is allowed, Chan et al. [6] have already given a non-migratory competitive algorithm that can exploit both sleep management and speed scaling for energy saving.

A glimpse of SATA. SATA processes a portion of the latest-arrived jobs (an idea from the parallel-job-algorithm[3] LAPS [9]), and runs k of them on each processor. The parameter k changes over time. We consider sequential jobs which can be executed on at most one processor at a time, so we may need to redistribute the jobs via migrations whenever the set of active jobs changes. This may appear to require a lot of migrations as each processor has to run exactly k of the km latest arrived jobs. Nevertheless, we derived a mechanism called the arrival-time-alignment property to ensure SATA can maintain this even job distribution by migrating at most two jobs when a job arrives or finishes. We can then analyze the SATA's competitiveness by a rather standard technique of potential analysis on the total flow-time incurred by SATA and the optimal algorithm OPT.

When processors can sleep, we extend SATA using two simple concepts: (1) use total flow time to trigger the next processor to wake up; and (2) use total idling energy to determine when to put an idle processor to sleep. The non-trivial part is extending the potential analysis. In our analysis we need to take into account the number of processors available to OPT. Without sleep management, this number

---

[1] An online algorithm A is said to be s-speed c-competitive if A's performance is at most c times the optimal offline algorithm OPT's performance when A is given processors s times faster than OPT's processors.

[2] From an economic point of view, both energy and flow time can be measured in terms of money and it can be assumed that users are willing to spend a certain units of energy for one unit of flow time; thus it makes sense to consider a linear combination of flow time and energy. By scaling the units of energy and time, we can assume they have the same relative weighting.

[3] The workload of a parallel job can be shared by multi-processors in parallel.

is always m. Our first attempt is to consider the number of OPT's awake processors at each time, yet this idea soon proves to be over precise. Our major trick here is to divide the time into intervals, each represents a cycle of SATA in which jobs and processors keep increasing and then both decrease to the bottom. A perhaps counter-intuitive idea here is to use the *maximum* number of OPT's awake processors within the interval, which turns out to be a sufficiently good estimate of OPT's available processors. Note that the potential analysis of the clairvoyant sleep management given in [6] is processor-based; it exploits a potential function that allows the best match-up of processors, then it becomes feasible to account for the progress of each pair of processors. However, such an approach only makes sense for non-migratory schedules.

To minimize flow time and energy on processors with the sleep state, SATA is $(1 + \epsilon)$-speed $32(1 + \frac{1}{\epsilon})^2$-competitive for flow time plus energy. We can extend the arrival-time-alignment property such that a job is migrated at most $(\ln m + 6)$ times on average. We need more migrations because SATA is always conservative and wakes up processors gradually; thus SATA needs to redistribute jobs to the newly awaken processor and this requires nonconstant number of migrations.

Organization of paper. Section 2 presents the algorithm SATA for minimizing flow time, and the lower bound result is given in Appendix A. Section 3 considers the sleep management model and extends SATA to minimize flow time plus energy. Section 4 discusses the extension to the speed scaling model.

2. SATA FOR NONCLAIRVOYANT FLOW-TIME SCHEDULING

In this section, we assume that all $m \geq 2$ processors are always awake (and ready to work). Jobs are sequential in nature (each can be processed by one processor at a time); preemption and migration are allowed. The objective is to minimize the total flow F, which is the sum over all jobs j of the time elapsed since job j arrives and until it is completed. It is useful to view the total flow as a quantity incurring at a rate equal to the number of active jobs (jobs released but not yet completed); i.e., $F = \int_0^\infty n(t) \, dt$ where $n(t)$ denotes the number of active jobs at time t. Below is the main result.

THEOREM 1. *For any $\epsilon > 0$, SATA is $(1 + \epsilon)$-speed $8(1 + \frac{1}{\epsilon})^2$-competitive for total flow time, and SATA migrates a job at most 4 times on average.*

At any time, let n_a be the number of active jobs of SATA. If $n_a < m$, SATA processes each job on a different processor. If $n_a \geq m$, SATA, using the idea of LAPS, processes at least $\lceil \beta n_a \rceil$ jobs that have the latest arrival times, where $\beta < 0.5$ is a constant (defined to be $\frac{\epsilon}{4(1+\epsilon)}$). Unlike LAPS, SATA exercises a tight control to require each of the m processors to run exactly k jobs, where $k \geq 1$ is the smallest integer such that $km \geq \lceil \beta n_a \rceil$ (note that $\beta < 0.5$ and thus $km \leq n_a$). In other words, SATA needs a nonclairvoyant technique that can evenly distribute the km latest-arrival jobs among the processors without migrating the jobs too often. This technique is rooted at the following property of job distribution when $n_a \geq m$.

Arrival-time-alignment property. Let $j_1, j_2, \ldots, j_{n_a}$ be all the active jobs ordered in ascending order of arrival

times. Define the *tail* jobs $J_{\text{tail}} = \{j_\tau, \ldots, j_{n_a}\}$ to be the $\lceil \beta n_a \rceil$ latest-arrival jobs (i.e., $\tau = n_a - \lceil \beta n_a \rceil + 1$). The following definitions are sensitive to the alignment width, defined to be the number of available processors, which always equals m in this section (Section 3 will consider arbitrary width $m_a \leq m$ and we need to replace m with m_a in the definitions). Define the *aligned jobs*, denoted J_{aln}, to be the m jobs (if exist) that arrived just before the tail jobs, i.e., $J_{\text{aln}} = \{j_{\max(1,\tau-m)}, \ldots, j_{\tau-1}\}$. Finally, let $x \in [0, m-1]$ be an integer such that $\lceil \beta n_a \rceil + x$ is a multiple of m. We call $j_{\tau-x}, \ldots, j_{\tau-1}$ the *boundary* jobs, denoted J_{bd}, which must all exist (because $\beta < 0.5$ and $\lceil \beta n_a \rceil + x \leq n_a$). A boundary job is also an aligned job. We say that the current job distribution satisfies the *arrival-time-alignment property* if the following conditions hold. Recall that k is the smallest integer such that $km \geq \lceil \beta n_a \rceil$.

- C1. Every aligned job is with a distinct processor.
- C2. Every processor hosting a boundary job must have exactly $k - 1$ tail jobs.
- C3. Every other processor must have exactly k tail jobs.

Figure 1 gives an example of these concepts. With the arrival-time-alignment property, SATA can let each processor run the boundary job (if present) and all the tail jobs. Over all processors, SATA is running x boundary jobs and $\lceil \beta n_a \rceil$ tail jobs, which together are the km latest-arrival jobs.

When $n_a < m$, SATA processes each job on a different processor, and dispatches any new job to a processor without jobs, so no job migration is needed when a job arrives or is completed. Once $n_a = m$, there should be exactly one job in each processor and the arrival-time-alignment property is immediately satisfied with $\lceil \beta n_a \rceil$ tail jobs and $m - \lceil \beta n_a \rceil$ boundary jobs. The arrival-time-alignment property will remain satisfied until a job arrives or is completed. Below we show that at most 2 migrations are needed to maintain the arrival-time-alignment property for each job arrival or completion. Suppose a job arrives or is completed at time t. Define $M_{<t}(j)$ or simply $M(j)$ to be the processor hosting job j just before time t (note that j may migrate to another processor at t). Below n_a and x also refer to the numbers just before t.

Dispatching and migration procedure due to job arrival: When a new job j_{NEW} arrives, the number of active jobs increases from n_a to n_a+1. By definition, the number of tail jobs (i.e., $|J_{\text{tail}}|$) becomes $\lceil \beta(n_a + 1) \rceil$, which is equal to $\lceil \beta n_a \rceil + 1$ or $\lceil \beta n_a \rceil$. To maintain the arrival-time-alignment property, we dispatch j_{NEW} and migrate at most two jobs as follows.

- Case 1: $|J_{\text{tail}}|$ increases by 1 (i.e., $\lceil \beta(n_a+1) \rceil = \lceil \beta n_a \rceil + 1$). By definition, J_{aln} is unchanged (and C1 holds), and $|J_{\text{bd}}|$ becomes $x - 1$ (precisely, $(x - 1) \mod m$). If $x \geq 1$, dispatch j_{NEW} to processor $M(j_{\tau-x})$; if $x = 0$, dispatch j_{NEW} to $M(j_{\tau-m})$. Then C2 and C3 hold.
- Case 2: $|J_{\text{tail}}|$ does not increase (i.e., $\lceil \beta(n_a + 1) \rceil = \lceil \beta n_a \rceil$). J_{aln} becomes $\{j_{\tau-m+1}, \ldots, j_\tau\}$, and j_τ replaces $j_{\tau-m}$ as an aligned job, and j_τ also replaces $j_{\tau-x}$ as a boundary job. To maintain C1, we migrate j_τ to processor $M(j_{\tau-m})$ as the new aligned job there. To maintain C2 and C3, we migrate an arbitrary tail job from $M(j_{\tau-m})$ to $M(j_\tau)$ (i.e., j_τ's hosting processor before j_{NEW} arrives), and dispatch j_{NEW} to $M(j_{\tau-x})$.

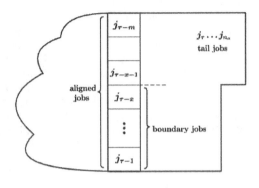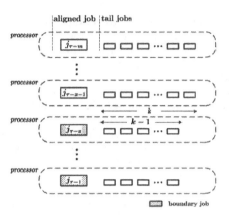

Figure 1: Arrival-time-alignment property

Migration procedure due to job completion: SATA only executes boundary or tail jobs. When a job j_{OLD} is completed, the number of active jobs becomes $n_a - 1$. We focus on the case $n_a - 1 \geq m$ (otherwise we stop maintaining the arrival-time-alignment property and each processor is currently hosting zero or one active job). By definition, $|J_{\text{tail}}|$ becomes $\lceil \beta(n_a - 1) \rceil$.

- **Case 1:** $|J_{\text{tail}}|$ decreases by 1. By definition, $|J_{\text{bd}}|$ becomes $x + 1$ (precisely, $(x + 1) \mod m$).

  (i) If j_{OLD} is a tail job, J_{aln} is unchanged (and C1 holds), and $j_{\tau - x - 1}$ becomes a boundary job. To maintain C2 and C3, we migrate an arbitrary tail job from $M(j_{\tau - x - 1})$ to $M(j_{\text{OLD}})$.

  (ii) If j_{OLD} is an aligned job, we make j_τ a new aligned job and migrate j_τ to $M(j_{\text{OLD}})$. Then C1 holds. To maintain C2 and C3, we migrate an arbitrary tail job from $M(j_{\tau - x - 1})$ to $M(j_\tau)$.

- **Case 2:** $|J_{\text{tail}}|$ does not decrease. In this case, $j_{\tau - m - 1}$ (if exists) should become a new aligned job, and we migrate $j_{\tau - m - 1}$ to maintain C1, as follows. If j_{OLD} is a tail job, then $j_{\tau - 1}$ becomes a tail job, and we migrate $j_{\tau - m - 1}$ to processor $M(j_{\tau - 1})$. Otherwise, j_{OLD} is an aligned job, and we migrate $j_{\tau - m - 1}$ to processor $M(j_{\text{OLD}})$. To maintain C2 and C3, we migrate a tail job from $M(j_{\tau - x - 1})$ to $M(j_{\text{OLD}})$.

LEMMA 2. *When a job arrives or is completed, it takes at most 2 migrations to maintain the arrival-time-alignment property.*

Algorithm SATA. We are ready to define SATA. Below n_a denotes the current number of active jobs (just before a job arrival or completion occurs). Whenever $n_a \geq m$, SATA maintains the arrival-time-alignment property.

Job arrival: When a job j arrives, if $n_a < m$, dispatch j to a processor without jobs; otherwise, dispatch j and migrate at most 2 jobs according to the job arrival procedure described above.

Job completion: When a job is completed, if $n_a \leq m$, no migration is needed; otherwise, migrate at most 2 jobs according to the job completion procedure described above.

Job scheduling:

- If $n_a < m$, each active job is processed on a different processor;

- If $n_a \geq m$, each processor shares its processing time equally among all its tail jobs and its boundary job (if present). Note that the m processors together are processing km latest-arrival jobs, where k is the smallest integer with $km \geq \lceil \beta n_a \rceil$.

Analysis of flow time. To analyze the flow time of SATA, we adapt the potential function analysis for LAPS [9]. The crux of the analysis is to define a suitable potential function $\Phi(t)$ that captures the difference of progress between SATA and OPT. Let $n_a(t)$ and $n_o(t)$ be the number of active jobs in SATA and OPT, respectively. At any time t, denote the active jobs in SATA as $j_1, j_2, \ldots, j_{n_a(t)}$, arranged in ascending order of release times. For each job j_i, let $q_a(j_i, t)$ and $q_o(j_i, t)$ be the remaining work of job j in SATA and OPT, respectively, and let $x_i = \max\{q_a(j_i, t) - q_o(j_i, t), 0\}$ which is the amount of work of j_i in SATA that is lagging behind OPT. We say a job j_i is *lagging* if $x_i > 0$. We define the potential function

$$\Phi(t) = \frac{2}{\epsilon} \cdot \sum_{i=1}^{n_a(t)} \max\left(1, \frac{i}{m}\right) \cdot x_i \ .$$

The definition of $\Phi(t)$ is similar to that of LAPS [9]; yet we give each job j_i the coefficient $\max(1, \frac{i}{m})$ instead of simply i as in [9]. This change is mainly because SATA is dealing with sequential jobs, while LAPS is dealing with parallel jobs that can be shared by multi-processors in parallel. Note that when $n_a < m$, SATA cannot fully utilize all the m processors as in LAPS. Furthermore, SATA is not running exactly $\lceil \beta n_a(t) \rceil$ jobs, the actual fraction varies over time which further complicates the analysis. When $t = 0$, $\Phi(t) = 0$. When a job arrives or is completed, Φ does not increase. Let $F(t)$ and $F^*(t)$ be the total flow incurred up to time t in SATA and OPT, respectively.

In the rest of this section we prove the following *running condition*, which relates the rate of increase of $F(t)$ to that of $F^*(t)$. Then Theorem 1 follows from integrating the running condition over time.

LEMMA 3. *At any time t when there is no job arrival or completion, $\frac{dF(t)}{dt} + \frac{d\Phi(t)}{dt} \leq 8(1 + \frac{1}{\epsilon})^2 \cdot \frac{dF^*(t)}{dt}$.*

PROOF. Consider a particular time t with no job arrival or completion by either SATA or OPT. For convenience, we drop t from all the notations. We divide the analysis into cases depending on n_a and m. In each case, $\frac{dF}{dt} = n_a$

and $\frac{dF^*}{dt} = n_o$. To bound the rate of change of Φ, we will consider how Φ changes in an infinitesimal amount of time (from t to $t + dt$). We may consider the rate of change of Φ due to SATA and OPT separately, which are denoted by $\frac{d\Phi_a}{dt}$ and $\frac{d\Phi_o}{dt}$, respectively. Note that $\frac{d\Phi}{dt} = \frac{d\Phi_a}{dt} + \frac{d\Phi_o}{dt}$. We call the term $\max\left(1, \frac{i}{m}\right)$ in the potential Φ the *coefficient* of job j_i. We also define a ratio ϕ such that SATA is currently processing ϕn_a lagging jobs.

Case 1: $n_a < m$. By definition, SATA is processing each active job on a different processor at speed $(1 + \epsilon)$, while OPT can process each job at speed at most 1. Therefore, for any lagging job j_i (i.e., $x_i > 0$), x_i is changing at rate at most $-(1 + \epsilon) + 1 = -\epsilon$; for any non-lagging job $j_{i'}$, $x_{i'}$ remains zero. We have $\frac{d\Phi}{dt} \le \frac{2}{\epsilon} \cdot \sum_{i:x_i>0} \max\left(1, \frac{i}{m}\right) \cdot (-\epsilon) = -2\sum_{i:x_i>0} 1 = -2\phi n_a$. There are $n_a - \phi n_a$ non-lagging active jobs, which must also be active in OPT, so $n_o \ge n_a - \phi n_a$. Then, $\frac{dF}{dt} + \frac{d\Phi}{dt} \le n_a - 2\phi n_a \le n_o = \frac{dF^*}{dt} \le 8(1 + \frac{1}{\epsilon})^2 \cdot \frac{dF^*}{dt}$.

Case 2: $n_a \ge m$. In this case, SATA is processing km ($k \ge 1$) latest-arrival jobs. We use L to denote these jobs. Since there are $(km - \phi n_a)$ non-lagging jobs in L, which must be active in OPT, we have $n_o \ge km - \phi n_a$. Recall that $\beta = \frac{\epsilon}{4(1+\epsilon)}$. We further consider two subcases depending on whether $n_a \le \frac{1}{2\beta}m$.

Case 2a: $n_a \le \frac{1}{2\beta}m$. In this case, $k = 1$, and thus SATA is running each job in L on a different processor at speed $(1 + \epsilon)$. Then, $\frac{d\Phi_a}{dt} \le \frac{2}{\epsilon} \cdot \sum_{i \in L:x_i>0} \max(1, \frac{i}{m}) \cdot (-(1+\epsilon)) \le \frac{2}{\epsilon} \cdot \phi n_a \cdot (-(1+\epsilon)) = -\frac{\phi}{2\beta}n_a$. OPT is processing at most n_o jobs, each at speed 1. Since the coefficient of j_{n_a} is the largest among all j_i's, we have $\frac{d\Phi_o}{dt} \le \frac{2}{\epsilon} \cdot \frac{n_a}{m} \cdot n_o \le \frac{2}{\epsilon} \cdot \frac{1}{2\beta} \cdot n_o = \frac{1}{\epsilon\beta}n_o$. Thus,

$$\frac{dF}{dt} + \frac{d\Phi}{dt} \le n_a - \frac{\phi}{2\beta}n_a + \frac{1}{\epsilon\beta}n_o$$
$$\le \frac{1}{2\beta}(km - \phi n_a) + \frac{1}{\epsilon\beta}n_o \quad \text{(as } n_a \le \frac{1}{2\beta}m \text{ and } k = 1\text{)}$$
$$\le \frac{1}{2\beta}n_o + \frac{1}{\epsilon\beta}n_o \le 8(1 + \frac{1}{\epsilon})^2 \cdot \frac{dF^*}{dt}.$$

Case 2b: $n_a > \frac{1}{2\beta}m$. In this case, each processor in SATA is running k jobs, each at speed $\frac{1+\epsilon}{k}$. Thus,

$$\frac{d\Phi_a}{dt} \le \frac{2}{\epsilon} \cdot \sum_{j_i \in L:x_i>0} \max(1, \frac{i}{m}) \cdot \frac{-(1+\epsilon)}{k}$$
$$\le -2(1 + \frac{1}{\epsilon}) \cdot \frac{1}{k} \cdot \sum_{j_i \in L:x_i>0} \frac{i}{m}$$
$$\le -2(1 + \frac{1}{\epsilon}) \cdot \frac{1}{k} \cdot \phi n_a(\frac{n_a-km}{m})$$
$$\text{(since any } j_i \in L \text{ has } i > n_a - km)$$
$$= -2(1 + \frac{1}{\epsilon}) \cdot \phi n_a(\frac{n_a}{km} - 1) = -\frac{\phi}{2\beta}n_a(\frac{n_a}{km} - 1).$$

OPT has m processors of speed 1, and the coefficient of j_{n_a} is the largest among all j_i's. We have $\frac{d\Phi_o}{dt} \le \frac{2}{\epsilon} \cdot \frac{n_a}{m} \cdot m \le \frac{2}{\epsilon}n_a$. Hence,

$$\frac{dF}{dt} + \frac{d\Phi}{dt} \le n_a - \frac{\phi}{2\beta}n_a(\frac{n_a}{km} - 1) + \frac{2}{\epsilon}n_a$$
$$\le n_a + \frac{\phi}{2\beta}n_a - \frac{\phi}{2\beta}n_a(\frac{n_a}{km}) + \frac{2}{\epsilon}n_a.$$

We now show that $\phi < 2\beta$ as follows. (1) If $n_a \le \frac{1}{\beta}m$, then $k = 1$ and $\phi n_a \le km = m$. Since $n_a > \frac{1}{2\beta}m$, we have $\phi n_a \le m < 2\beta n_a$ and $\phi < 2\beta$. (2) If $n_a > \frac{1}{\beta}m$, then $\phi n_a \le km < \beta n_a + m < 2\beta n_a$ and hence $\phi < 2\beta$.

In conclusion,

$$\frac{dF}{dt} + \frac{d\Phi}{dt} \le n_a + n_a - \frac{\phi}{2\beta}n_a(\frac{n_a}{km}) + \frac{2}{\epsilon}n_a \quad \text{(since } \phi < 2\beta\text{)}$$
$$= \frac{1}{2\beta}n_a - \frac{\phi}{2\beta}n_a(\frac{n_a}{km}) = \frac{1}{2\beta}(km - \phi n_a) \cdot (\frac{n_a}{km})$$
$$\le \frac{1}{2\beta^2}(km - \phi n_a) \quad \text{(as } km \ge \lceil \beta n_a \rceil \Rightarrow \frac{n_a}{km} \le \frac{1}{\beta}\text{)}$$
$$\le 8(1 + \frac{1}{\epsilon})^2 \cdot n_o = 8(1 + \frac{1}{\epsilon})^2 \cdot \frac{dF^*}{dt}. \qquad \square$$

3. SATA WITH SLEEP MANAGEMENT

This section considers scheduling in the sleep management model. In this model, a processor is in either the *awake* state or the *sleep* state. Only when it is awake, it can process a job and the energy is consumed at the rate $\nu + \sigma$, where $\nu > 0$ is the dynamic power and $\sigma > 0$ is the static power. An awake processor can be idle (i.e., not processing any job) and only requires the static power σ. A processor can enter the sleep state to reduce the power to zero. Initially, all processors are in the sleep state. Following the literature, we assume that state transition is immediate but requires energy. A *wake-up* from the sleep state requires ω units of energy, and the reverse takes zero.

This section shows how to extend SATA to handle sleep management of $m \ge 2$ processors and job scheduling on a variable number of processors. The aim is to minimize the total flow time F plus energy E. Intuitively, SATA has to maintain an appropriate number of awake processors and strike a balance between flow time and energy. We assume that SATA is using $(1 + \epsilon)$-speed processors for $\epsilon > 0$, which are $(1 + \epsilon)$ times faster than the optimal offline algorithm OPT while using the same power. Below is our main result.

THEOREM 4. *For any $\epsilon > 0$, SATA is $(1+\epsilon)$-speed $32(1 + \frac{1}{\epsilon})^2$-competitive for flow plus energy, and SATA migrates a job at most $(\ln m + 6)$ times on average.*

SATA uses two simple ideas to determine the appropriate number of awake processors: (1) total flow for waking up processors; and (2) total idling energy for putting processors to sleep. More specifically, SATA maintains two (real-value) counters C_f and C_e to keep track of the accumulated flow and idling energy, respectively (see the algorithm below for precise definition). We view them as two competing quantities: If C_f reaches ω first, we wake up a sleeping processor; otherwise, when C_e reaches ω, we put one awake processor to sleep. In either case, both counters are reset to 0 and the process is restarted. The idea looks simple, yet the potential analysis (of flow time plus energy) is more complicated than before and triggers us to come up with new insight.

With proper sleep management, SATA can then handle job dispatching, migrations and scheduling in the same way as in the previous section, except that the decisions are made with reference to m_a, the current number of awake processors, instead of m, the maximum number of processors. Let n_a denote the current number of active jobs. When $n_a < m_a$, SATA processes each job on a different awake processor, and dispatches any new job to an awake processor without jobs. In this case, SATA never migrates a job even if it wakes up a processor or puts it to sleep.

When $n_a \ge m_a$, SATA schedules the km_a latest-arrival jobs evenly on the m_a awake processors, where k is the smallest integer such that $km_a \ge \lceil \beta n_a \rceil$. SATA maintains the arrival-time-alignment property with alignment width m_a. This ensures that in each processor, the tail jobs and the boundary job (if present) sum up to k. This property remains satisfied over a maximal period in which m_a

remains unchanged and there are at least m_a active jobs. Within this period, for each job arrival and completion, SATA uses the procedures in Section 2 to maintain the arrival-time-alignment property (with alignment width m_a) using at most 2 migrations.

Migration due to a wake-up: When SATA wakes up a processor, the number of awake processors increases from m_a to $m_a + 1$. If n_a remains bigger than $m_a + 1$, the arrival-time-alignment property must be restored with alignment width $m_a + 1$. The wake-up does not change the active jobs and tail jobs. Denote the active jobs as $j_1, \cdots, j_{n_a}$, arranged in ascending order of arrival times. Since alignment width increases to $m_a + 1$, we need one more aligned job, which is job $j_{\tau - m_a - 1}$ (if exists) where $\tau = n_a - \lceil \beta n_a \rceil + 1$. To maintain C1, we send $j_{\tau - m_a - 1}$ to the new processor; to maintain C2 and C3, we migrate $\lceil \lceil \beta n_a \rceil / (m_a + 1) \rceil$ tail jobs from existing awake processors to the new processor.

The migration due to a wake-up can involve a lot of jobs. Nevertheless, a slightly tricky analysis shows that each job on average can be migrated $(\ln m + 2)$ times due to wake-up operations (see Lemma 14 in Appendix B). On the other hand, SATA is defined such that whenever $n_a \geq m_a$, SATA is not allowed to put an idle processor to sleep (see the algorithm below); thus, the number of awake processors and the alignment width will not decrease and cause any migration.

Algorithm Extended SATA. Below we give the details of extending SATA. Initially, all m processors are sleeping. Whenever $n_a \geq m_a$, SATA maintains the arrival-time-alignment property with alignment width m_a. Recall that σ and ω denote the static power and wake-up energy.

Wake up a processor: When $m_a < m$, increase C_f at rate of n_a; when $C_f = \omega$, wake up a sleeping processor, migrate jobs according to the wake-up procedure described above, and reset $C_f = C_e = 0$.

Put a processor to sleep: When $n_a < m_a$, increase C_e at rate of σ times the number of idle processors, i.e., $\sigma(m_a - n_a)$; when $C_e = \omega$, put an awake (idle) processor to sleep and reset $C_f = C_e = 0$.

Job arrival: When a job j arrives, if $n_a < m_a$, dispatch j to a processor without jobs; otherwise, dispatch j and migrate at most 2 jobs according to the job arrival procedure described above.

Job completion: When a job is completed, if $n_a \leq m_a$, no migration is needed; otherwise, migrate at most 2 jobs according to the job completion procedure described above.

Job scheduling:

- If $n_a < m_a$, each active job is processed on a different awake processor;

- If $n_a \geq m_a$, each awake processor shares its processing time equally among all its tail jobs and its boundary job (if present); note that the m_a processors together are processing the km_a latest-arrival jobs, where k is the smallest integer with $km_a \geq \lceil \beta n_a \rceil$.

It remains to show the competitive ratio of SATA stated in Theorem 4. Consider a schedule of SATA. We divide SATA's energy usage E into three parts: E_I is the *idling* energy (static energy incurred by processors when they are awake but idle), E_w the *working* energy (both dynamic and static energy incurred by processors when they are working on jobs), and U the wake-up energy. Denote F as SATA's

flow, and define SATA's total cost $G = F + E_w + E_I + U$. These notations of cost and energy are used for OPT in the same way, but marked with an asterisk. By the definition of SATA, we can upper bound SATA's energy by SATA's flow F and OPT's working energy E_w^*.

LEMMA 5. *(i)* $U \leq F$; *(ii)* $E_I \leq 2U$; *(iii)* $E_w \leq E_w^*$.

PROOF. (i) By definition, SATA wakes up a processor when C_f accumulates ω units of total flow, so the number of wake-ups times ω is at most the total flow F, i.e., $U \leq F$.

(ii) By definition, when SATA puts a processor to sleep, C_e accumulates ω units of idling energy; when SATA wakes up a processor, C_e accumulates at most ω units of idling energy before being reset to 0. Any idling energy would have been counted in C_e, so E_I is at most ω times the number of wake-up and sleep events. Note that all processors are asleep initially and after all jobs are completed. Thus, the number of sleep events equals the number of wake-ups and hence $E_I \leq 2U$.

(iii) Any two algorithms using processors of the same speed incur the same amount of working energy for completing all jobs. As SATA is using $(1+\epsilon)$-speed processors, E_w is indeed less than OPT's working energy, i.e., $E_w \leq E_w^*$. $\square$

The above lemma implies that SATA's total cost $G = F + E_w + E_I + U \leq 4F + E_w^*$. The rest of this section is devoted to analyzing the total flow F.

Intuitively, SATA's flow cannot be directly bounded by OPT's total cost. SATA often wakes up fewer processors than OPT and thus incurs more flow time. Such excess in flow is not related to OPT. To quantify it, our first attempt is to consider the flow incurred when SATA has fewer awake processors than OPT, yet this idea soon proves to be over precise. The number of awake processors in OPT can vary frequently. If SATA wakes up processors too slowly, then most of the excess in flow is incurred later when enough jobs have been accumulated. By that time, OPT may have less awake processors than SATA. Our major trick here is to give up an accurate accounting of OPT's number of processors. Instead we divide the time into some special intervals called S-interval. Roughly speaking, each S-interval represents a cycle of SATA in which jobs and processors keep increasing and then both decrease to the bottom. We use the maximum number of OPT's awake processors within the interval, which is more well-behaved and turns out to be a sufficiently good estimate of OPT's resource within the interval. We define *lazy flow* to be the flow incurred when SATA has fewer awake processors than such maximum number of OPT's processors (see precise definitions below).

S-intervals and lazy flow F_s. Let $m_a(t)$ and $m_o(t)$ be the number of awake processors in SATA and OPT at time t (after all wake-up and sleep events at time t), respectively. We partition the timeline into intervals called S-intervals as follows. Consider the sequence of wake-up and sleep events in SATA. Each S-interval starts with the last sleep event of the previous S-interval (except that the first starts at time 0), followed by a sequence of wake-ups and and then a maximal sequence of sleep events. By definition, two consecutive S-intervals overlap at one sleep event. For any time t during an S-interval I, we define $m_o^*(t) = \max_{t' \in I} m_o(t')$, which is the maximum number of awake processors used by OPT during I. At time t when two S-intervals overlap, SATA puts exactly one awake processor to sleep (by definition, only one processor of SATA can sleep at a time), and thus $n_a(t) \leq m_a(t)$. We define *lazy flow* F_s to be the total flow incurred at the times t when $m_a(t) < m_o^*(t)$, i.e., $F_s = \int_{t:m_a(t)<m_o^*(t)} n_a(t)\,dt$. Then, we can show Lemma 6 below, which involves two potential function analyses.

LEMMA 6. *(i)* $F \leq 8(1+\frac{1}{\epsilon})^2 F^* + (1+\frac{2}{\epsilon})F_s$; *(ii)* $F_s \leq 2(E_W^* + E_I^* + U^*)$.

Lemma 6 implies that $F \leq 8(1+\frac{1}{\epsilon})^2 F^* + 2(1+\frac{2}{\epsilon})(E_W^* + E_I^* + U^*)$. Together with Lemma 5, $G \leq 32(1+\frac{1}{\epsilon})^2 F^* + 8(1+\frac{2}{\epsilon})(E_W^* + E_I^* + U^*) + E_W^* \leq 32(1+\frac{1}{\epsilon})^2(F^* + E_W^* + E_I^* + U^*) = 32(1+\frac{1}{\epsilon})^2 G^*$. Theorem 4 follows.

3.1 Potential Analysis of Total Flow F

To show Lemma 6(i), we extend the potential analysis in Section 2 to allow SATA and OPT to use a variable number of processors. The potential function $\Phi(t)$ of Section 2 is modified so that the coefficient takes $m_a(t)$ and $m_o^*(t)$ into consideration. Recall that SATA's active jobs are arranged in ascending order of arrival times. For the i-th job j_i, we denote x_i as the amount of work of j_i in SATA that is lagging behind OPT (see Section 2 for the definitions). The new potential function is defined as follows:

$$\Phi(t) = \frac{2}{\epsilon} \cdot \sum_{i=1}^{n_a(t)} \max\left(1, \frac{i}{\max(m_a(t), m_o^*(t))}\right) \cdot x_i ,$$

where $\max\left(1, \frac{i}{\max(m_a(t), m_o^*(t))}\right)$ is called the *coefficient* of job j_i.

Initially, $\Phi(0) = 0$. When a job arrives or is completed, Φ does not increase. The way we integrate $m_a(t)$ and $m_o^*(t)$ into $\Phi(t)$ guarantees that when m_a and m_o^* changes, Φ cannot increase: When m_a increases, the coefficient of any job and thus Φ do not increase. When m_a decreases to $m_a - 1$ or when m_o^* changes, SATA puts one awake processor to sleep, which implies $n_a \leq m_a - 1$. The coefficients of all the n_a jobs remain exactly 1, so Φ does not change.

Let $F(t)$ be the total flow F incurred up to time t by SATA. Similarly, define $F^*(t)$ and $F_s(t)$ for OPT's total flow F^* and SATA's lazy flow F_s. It remains to show the following running condition. Lemma 6(i) then follows from integrating it over time.

LEMMA 7. *At any time t when there is no job arrival or completion or change on $m_a(t)$ or $m_o^*(t)$, $\frac{dF(t)}{dt} + \frac{d\Phi(t)}{dt} \leq 8(1+\frac{1}{\epsilon})^2 \cdot \frac{dF^*(t)}{dt} + (1+\frac{2}{\epsilon}) \cdot \frac{dF_s(t)}{dt}$.*

PROOF. At time t, let $n_a(t)$ and $n_o(t)$ be the number of jobs of SATA and OPT, respectively. For convenience, we drop t from all the notations. Note that $\frac{dF}{dt} = n_a$ and $\frac{dF^*}{dt} = n_o$. If $m_a < m_o^*$, $\frac{dF_s}{dt} = n_a$; otherwise, $\frac{dF_s}{dt} = 0$. To bound the rate of change of Φ, we will consider how Φ changes in an infinitesimal amount of time (from t to $t+dt$). If $n_a < m_a$, SATA processes each active job on a different awake processor. Similarly as in the proof of Lemma 3, we can show that $\frac{dF(t)}{dt} + \frac{d\Phi(t)}{dt} \leq 8(1+\frac{1}{\epsilon})^2 \cdot \frac{dF^*(t)}{dt}$. If $n_a \geq m_a \geq m_o^*$, $\max(m_a, m_o^*) = m_a$. The number of awake processors in OPT is $m_o \leq m_o^*$, which is at most m_a. Since only the processing of OPT can increase Φ, the worst case is that OPT is also using m_a awake processors as SATA. Then, similarly as in the proof of Lemma 3, we can show that $\frac{dF(t)}{dt} + \frac{d\Phi(t)}{dt} \leq 8(1+\frac{1}{\epsilon})^2 \cdot \frac{dF^*(t)}{dt}$.

It remains to consider $n_a \geq m_a$ and $m_o^* > m_a$. In this case, $\frac{dF_s}{dt} = n_a$. Since the processing of SATA can only

decrease Φ, it suffices to consider the change of Φ due to the processing of OPT. (Case 1) $n_a \geq m_o^*$: Since OPT has m_o awake processors of speed 1, and the coefficient of j_{n_a} is the largest among all j_i's, we have $\frac{d\Phi}{dt} \leq \frac{2}{\epsilon} \max(1, \frac{n_a}{\max(m_a, m_o^*)}) \cdot m_o = \frac{2}{\epsilon} \frac{n_a}{m_o^*} \cdot m_o \leq \frac{2}{\epsilon} n_a$. (Case 2) $n_a < m_o^*$: For any j_i, its coefficient is $\max(1, \frac{i}{\max(m_a, m_o^*)}) = 1$. Since OPT can process at most n_a jobs which are also active in SATA, and the speed for each job is at most 1, we have $\frac{d\Phi}{dt} \leq \frac{2}{\epsilon} n_a$. In both cases, $\frac{dF}{dt} + \frac{d\Phi}{dt} \leq n_a + \frac{2}{\epsilon} n_a = (1 + \frac{2}{\epsilon}) \cdot \frac{dF_s}{dt} \leq 8(1+\frac{1}{\epsilon})^2 \cdot \frac{dF^*}{dt} + (1+\frac{2}{\epsilon}) \cdot \frac{dF_s}{dt}$. □

3.2 Potential Analysis of Lazy Flow F_s

To prove Lemma 6(ii), we need another potential function to analyze F_s. Intuitively, if m_o^* is large in some S-interval, then OPT would have incurred more wake-up and static energy, and more lazy flow is incurred. We can relate the lazy flow against those OPT's energy. Yet OPT not necessarily wakes up the processors in the same S-interval in which a lot of lazy flow is incurred. Thus, we need the following potential function $\Phi(t)$ to account for the extra energy spent by OPT that has not yet been charged:

$$\Phi(t) = \omega \cdot \max(m_o(t) - m_a(t), 0) .$$

Let E_O^* be the total static energy incurred by processors in OPT, i.e., when they are working or idle. Then, $E_O^* \leq E_W^* + E_I^*$. We also assume that OPT pays ω units of energy when putting a processor to sleep, and the total amount is denoted by S^*. We have the same number of sleep and wake-up events, so $U^* = S^*$. We will compare SATA with such OPT, and show the following lemma.

LEMMA 8. *During each S-interval $I = [t_1, t_2]$, let $\Delta F_s = F_s(t_2) - F_s(t_1)$, and let $\Delta\Phi$, ΔU^*, ΔS^* and ΔE_O^* similarly for Φ, U^*, S^* and E_O^*. Then, $\Delta F_s + \Delta\Phi \leq \Delta U^* + \Delta S^* + 2 \cdot \Delta E_O^*$.*

Note that m_a, m_o and hence Φ start and end at 0. With Lemma 8, we can use induction over the S-intervals to show that $F_s \leq U^* + S^* + 2E_O^*$, which implies Lemma 6(ii) that $F_s \leq 2(E_W^* + E_I^* + U^*)$.

The rest of this section is devoted to proving Lemma 8. Recall that for any time $t \in I$, $m_o^*(t)$ is the maximum number of awake processors in OPT during I. Since $m_o^*(t)$ is fixed within I, we drop the parameter t. Similarly, we define m_a^* to be the maximum number of awake processor in SATA during I. By definition of S-intervals, I contains a sequence of wake-up events in SATA, followed by a sequence of sleep events in SATA. We split $I = [t_1, t_2]$ into two intervals: the *wake-up interval* I_w starts at t_1 and ends at the last wake-up of SATA in I; and the *sleep interval* I_s starts at the last wake-up of SATA in I and ends at t_2. Thus, m_a increases from $m_a(t_1)$ to m_a^* within I_w, and then decreases from m_a^* to $m_a(t_2)$ within I_s. We denote the lazy flow F_s incurred within I_w and I_s by $\Delta F_s(I_w)$ and $\Delta F_s(I_s)$, respectively. Note that $\Delta F_s = \Delta F_s(I_w) + \Delta F_s(I_s)$.

Consider the schedule of OPT. Let m_o^- be the *minimum* number of awake processors in OPT during I. Within I, m_o starts from $m_o(t_1)$, reaches the maximum m_o^* and the minimum m_o^- at different times, and finally ends up at $m_o(t_2)$. Therefore,

$$\Delta U^* \geq (m_o^* - m_o(t_1)) \cdot \omega + (m_o(t_2) - m_o^-) \cdot \omega \quad \text{and}$$

$$\Delta S^* \geq (m_o^* - m_o^-) \cdot \omega .$$

To prove Lemma 8, it suffices to show that $\Delta F_s(I_w) + \Delta F_s(I_s) + \Phi(t_2) \leq (m_o^* - m_o(t_1)) \cdot \omega + (m_o(t_2) - m_o^-) \cdot \omega + (m_o^* - m_o^-) \cdot \omega + 2 \cdot \Delta E_o^* + \Phi(t_1)$.

We relate $\Delta F_s(I_w)$ to SATA's wake-up energy incurred within I_w. By considering the wake-ups of SATA and OPT, the latter can be bounded by OPT's wake-up energy and all OPT's energy stored in Φ at t_1 (Lemma 9). We also relate $\Delta F_s(I_s)$ to SATA's idling energy incurred within I_s. By considering the sleep events of SATA and OPT, the latter can be bounded by OPT's sleeping energy and static energy (Lemma 10). Finally, we show that OPT has enough wake-up energy and static energy remaining to store back to Φ (i.e., at least $\Phi(t_2)$) for the next S-interval (Lemma 11).

LEMMA 9. $\Delta F_s(I_w) \leq (\min(m_a^*, m_o^*) - m_o(t_1)) \cdot \omega + \Phi(t_1)$.

PROOF. Recall that lazy flow is the flow incurred when $m_a(t) < m_o^*$. First, suppose $m_a(t_1) < m_o^*$. By definition of SATA, at time t_1 and at the end of I_w, both the counters C_e and C_f are zero. When C_f has accumulated ω units of flow, SATA wakes up a processor and resets C_f to zero. Therefore, $\Delta F_s(I_w)$ equals to the wake-up energy incurred by SATA within I_w, i.e., $(\min(m_a^*, m_o^*) - m_a(t_1)) \cdot \omega$. The latter is equal to $(\min(m_a^*, m_o^*) - m_o(t_1)) \cdot \omega + (m_o(t_1) - m_a(t_1)) \cdot \omega \leq (\min(m_a^*, m_o^*) - m_o(t_1)) \cdot \omega + \max(m_o(t_1) - m_a(t_1), 0) \cdot \omega$. Therefore, $\Delta F_s(I_w) \leq (\min(m_a^*, m_o^*) - m_o(t_1)) \cdot \omega + \Phi(t_1)$.

Now, suppose $m_a(t_1) \geq m_o^*$. Since m_a increases from $m_a(t_1)$ to m_a^* within I_w, which are always at least m_o^*, we have $\Delta F_s(I_w) = 0$. We consider two cases depending on whether $m_a^* \geq m_o(t_1)$.
Case 1: $m_a^* \geq m_o(t_1)$. Since $m_o^* \geq m_o(t_1)$ and Φ is always at least 0, we have

$$\Delta F_s(I_w) = 0 \leq (\min(m_a^*, m_o^*) - m_o(t_1)) \cdot \omega + \Phi(t_1) .$$

Case 2: $m_a^* < m_o(t_1)$. In this case, $m_a(t_1) \leq m_a^* < m_o(t_1) \leq m_o^*$. Thus,

$$\begin{aligned}\Delta F_s(I_w) = 0 &\leq (\min(m_a^*, m_o^*) - m_a(t_1)) \cdot \omega \\ &= (\min(m_a^*, m_o^*) - m_o(t_1) + m_o(t_1) - m_a(t_1)) \cdot \omega \\ &= (\min(m_a^*, m_o^*) - m_o(t_1)) \cdot \omega + \Phi(t_1) . \quad \Box\end{aligned}$$

LEMMA 10. $\Delta F_s(I_s) \leq (m_o^* - m_o^-) \cdot \omega + \Delta E_o^*$.

PROOF. If $m_a(t_2) \geq m_o^*$, since m_a decreases from m_a^* to $m_a(t_2)$ within I_s, we have $\Delta F_s(I_s) = 0 \leq (m_o^* - m_o^-) \cdot \omega + \Delta E_o^*$. Now, suppose $m_a(t_2) < m_o^*$. By definition of SATA, at the beginning of I_s and at time t_2, both the counters C_e and C_f are zero. Within I_s, whenever SATA puts a processor to sleep, C_e has accumulated ω units of idling energy; C_f has accumulated less than ω units of flow; and both C_e and C_f are reset to zero. Note also that if C_e is accumulating idling energy when $m_a(t) \leq m_o^-$, OPT would have accumulated at least the same amount of static energy. Therefore, we conclude that $\Delta F_s(I_s) < (\min(m_a^*, m_o^*) - \max(m_a(t_2), m_o^-)) \cdot \omega + \Delta E_o^* \leq (m_o^* - m_o^-) \cdot \omega + \Delta E_o^*$. $\Box$

LEMMA 11. $\Phi(t_2) \leq (m_o^* - \min(m_a^*, m_o^*)) \cdot \omega + (m_o(t_2) - m_o^-) \cdot \omega + \Delta E_o^*$.

PROOF. If $m_o(t_2) \leq m_a(t_2)$, it is trivial that $\Phi(t_2) = \max(m_o(t_2) - m_a(t_2), 0) \cdot \omega = 0 \leq (m_o^* - \min(m_a^*, m_o^*)) \cdot \omega + (m_o(t_2) - m_o^-) \cdot \omega + \Delta E_o^*$.

Now, consider the case that $m_o(t_2) > m_a(t_2)$ and we need to bound $\Phi(t_2) = (m_o(t_2) - m_a(t_2)) \cdot \omega$. Note that within I_s, whenever SATA puts a processor to sleep, C_e has accumulated ω units of idling energy; C_f has accumulated less

than ω units of flow; and both C_e and C_f are reset to zero. Note also that if C_e is accumulating idling energy when $m_a(t) \leq m_o^-$, OPT would have accumulated at least the same amount of static energy. Therefore, if $m_a^* \geq m_o(t_2)$,

$$\begin{aligned}&(m_o(t_2) - m_a(t_2)) \cdot \omega \\ &\leq (m_o(t_2) - \max(m_a(t_2), m_o^-)) \cdot \omega + \Delta E_o^* \\ &\leq (m_o(t_2) - m_o^-) \cdot \omega + \Delta E_o^* \\ &\leq (m_o^* - \min(m_a^*, m_o^*)) \cdot \omega + (m_o(t_2) - m_o^-) \cdot \omega + \Delta E_o^* .\end{aligned}$$

Similarly, if $m_a^* < m_o(t_2)$, we have $(m_a^* - m_a(t_2)) \cdot \omega \leq (m_a^* - \max(m_a(t_2), m_o^-)) \cdot \omega + \Delta E_o^*$. Thus, $(m_o(t_2) - m_a(t_2)) \cdot \omega = (m_o(t_2) - m_a^* + m_a^* - m_a(t_2)) \cdot \omega \leq (m_o^* - m_a^*) \cdot \omega + (m_a^* - \max(m_a(t_2), m_o^-)) \cdot \omega + \Delta E_o^*$, which, by $m_a^* < m_o(t_2)$, is less than $(m_o^* - \min(m_a^*, m_o^*)) \cdot \omega + (m_o(t_2) - m_o^-) \cdot \omega + \Delta E_o^*$. $\Box$

By Lemmas 9, 10 and 11, we obtain the desired inequality $\Delta F_s(I_w) + \Delta F_s(I_s) + \Phi(t_2) \leq (m_o^* - m_o(t_1)) \cdot \omega + (m_o(t_2) - m_o^-) \cdot \omega + (m_o^* - m_o^-) \cdot \omega + 2 \cdot \Delta E_o^* + \Phi(t_1)$, which implies $\Delta F_s + \Delta \Phi \leq \Delta U^* + \Delta S^* + 2 \cdot \Delta E_o^*$. Thus Lemma 8 is proven.

4. SATA WITH SPEED SCALING

This section considers scheduling in the speed scaling model. In this model, at any time t, each processor $i \in [1, m]$ can independently scale its speed $s_i(t) \in [0, T]$, where T is the maximum allowable speed, and the processor consumes power at rate $P(s_i(t))$. Without loss of generality, we can assume $P(0) = 0$, and P is defined, strictly increasing, strictly convex, continuous and differentiable at all speeds in $[0, T]$; if $T = \infty$, the speed range is $[0, \infty)$ and for any speed x, there exists x' such that $P(x)/x < P(s)/s$ for all $s > x'$ (otherwise the optimal speed scaling policy is to always run at the infinite speed and an optimal schedule is not well-defined). We use $Q(x)$ to denote $\min\{P^{-1}(x), T\}$. Note that Q is monotonically increasing and concave. E.g., if $P(s) = s^\alpha$ for some $\alpha > 1$, then $Q(x) = \min\{x^{1/\alpha}, T\}$.

This section shows how to extend SATA to the speed scaling model. The objective is to minimize the total flow time F plus energy E. Note that a $(1 + \epsilon)$-speed processor for any $\epsilon > 0$ can run at speed $(1 + \epsilon)s$ when given power $P(s)$. The following theorem shows that the extended SATA is $(1 + \epsilon)^2$-speed $O(\frac{1}{\epsilon^3})$-competitive.

THEOREM 12. For any $\epsilon > 0$, SATA is $(1 + \epsilon)^2$-speed $80(1 + \frac{1}{\epsilon})^3$-competitive for flow plus energy, and SATA migrates a job at most 4 times on average.

SATA handles job dispatching, migrations and selection in the same way as in Section 2. Let n_a be the current number of active jobs. Whenever $n_a \geq m$, SATA maintains the arrival-time alignment property with alignment width m. This ensures that each processor is processing exactly k jobs, where k is the smallest integer such that $km \geq \lceil \beta n_a \rceil$ where $\beta = \frac{\epsilon}{4(1+\epsilon)}$. After each job arrival and completion, SATA migrates up to 2 jobs to maintain the arrival-time-alignment property. SATA handles speed scaling as follows: At any time, each of the processors with active jobs works at the same speed. The total power of the processors is set to the number of active jobs n_a, except that when the processor speed exceeds the maximum speed T, it is capped at T. Below we give the details of extending SATA.

268

Job arrival: When a job j arrives, if $n_a < m$, dispatch j to a processor without jobs; otherwise, dispatch j and migrate at most 2 jobs according to the job arrival procedure in Section 2.

Job completion: When a job is completed, if $n_a \leq m$, no migration is needed; otherwise, migrate at most 2 jobs according to the job completion procedure in Section 2.

Job scheduling:

- If $n_a < m$, each active job is processed on a different processor running at speed $(1 + \epsilon)Q(1)$;
- If $n_a \geq m$, each processor runs at speed $(1 + \epsilon)Q(\frac{n_a}{m})$ and shares its processing time equally among all its tail jobs and its boundary job (if present). Note that the m processors together are processing km latest-arrival jobs, where k is the smallest integer with $km \geq \lceil \beta n_a \rceil$.

Restricting offline algorithm. It remains to show the competitive ratio of SATA stated in Theorem 12. We need to compare SATA against the optimal offline algorithm. To ease the analysis, we assume that OPT is the algorithm GKP [12], which is $(1 + \epsilon)$-speed $4(1 + \frac{1}{\epsilon})$-competitive for flow plus energy. GKP is clairvoyant and non-migratory in nature, and it always dispatches a job to a processor at release time. At any time t, GKP's processor $i \in [1, m]$ runs at speed $s_i^*(t) = Q(n_i^*(t))$, where $n_i^*(t)$ is the current number of active jobs assigned to processor i. This implies that if GKP has $n_o(t)$ active jobs at time t, i.e., $n_o(t) = \sum_{i=1}^{m} n_i^*(t)$, then the total speed over all processors of GKP is at most $m \cdot Q(\frac{n_o(t)}{m})$ if $n_o(t) \geq m$, and $n_o(t) \cdot Q(1)$ otherwise.[4] To show Theorem 12, it suffices to show that SATA is $(1 + \epsilon)$-speed $20(1 + \frac{1}{\epsilon})^2$-competitive against this restricted OPT.

Potential analysis of total flow F. The SATA's energy usage E is at most its total flow F because, by the definition of SATA, at any time, if $n_a < m$, the total power of all processors is $n_a \cdot P(Q(1)) \leq n_a \cdot P(P^{-1}(1)) = n_a$; and if $n_a \geq m$, the total power of all processors is $m \cdot P(Q(\frac{n_a}{m})) \leq m \cdot P(P^{-1}(\frac{n_a}{m})) = n_a$. Thus, it suffices to analyze SATA's flow time F. To this end, we adapt the potential function in Section 2 by taking speed scaling into account. Recall that SATA's active jobs are arranged in ascending order of arrival times. For the i-th job j_i, we denote x_i as the amount of work of j_i in SATA that is lagging behind OPT (see Section 2 for the definitions). Recall that $n_a(t)$ and $n_o(t)$ are the number of active jobs in SATA and OPT, respectively. The new potential function is defined as follows:

$$\Phi(t) = \frac{2}{\epsilon} \cdot \sum_{i=1}^{n_a(t)} \frac{\max\left(1, \frac{i}{m}\right)}{Q(\max\left(1, \frac{i}{m}\right))} \cdot x_i \,,$$

where $\max\left(1, \frac{i}{m}\right) / Q(\max\left(1, \frac{i}{m}\right))$ is called the *coefficient* of job j_i. In the full paper, we will prove the running condition $\frac{dF(t)}{dt} + \frac{d\Phi(t)}{dt} \leq 10(1 + \frac{1}{\epsilon})^2 \cdot \frac{dF^*(t)}{dt}$. Then Theorem 12 follows.

5. REFERENCES

[1] S. Albers. Energy-efficient algorithms. *Communications of the ACM*, 53(5):86–96, 2010.

[2] S. Albers, and H. Fujiwara. Energy-efficient algorithms for flow time minimization. *ACM Transactions on Algorithms*, 3(4):49, 2007.

[3] N. Avrahami, and Y. Azar. Minimizing total flow time and total completion time with immediate dispatching. *Algorithmica*, 47(3):253–268, 2007.

[4] N. Bansal, H. L. Chan, and K. Pruhs. Speed scaling with an arbitrary power function. In *Proc. SODA*, pages 693–701, 2009.

[5] S. H. Chan, T. W. Lam, and L. K. Lee. Non-clairvoyant speed scaling for weighted flow time. In *Proc. ESA*, pages 23–35, 2010.

[6] S. H. Chan, T. W. Lam, L. K. Lee, C. M. Liu, and H. F. Ting. Sleep management on multiple processors for energy and flow time. In *Proc. ICALP*, pages 219–231, 2011.

[7] C. Chekuri, A. Goel, S. Khanna, and A. Kumar. Multi-processor scheduling to minimize flow time with ϵ resource augmentation. In *Proc. STOC*, pages 363–372, 2004.

[8] J. Chadha, N. Garg, A. Kumar, and V. Muralidhara. A competitive algorithm for minimizing weighted flow time on unrelated processors with speed augmentation. In *Proc. STOC*, pages 679–684, 2009.

[9] J. Edmonds and K. Pruhs. Scalably scheduling processes with arbitrary speedup curves. In *Proc. SODA*, pages 685–692, 2009.

[10] K. Fox and B. Moseley. Online scheduling on identical processors using SRPT. In *Proc. SODA*, pages 120–128, 2011.

[11] A. Gandhi, V. Gupta, M. Harchol-Balter, and M. Kozuch. Optimality analysis of energy-performance trade-off for server farm management. *Performance Evaluation*, 67(11):1155–1171, 2010.

[12] A. Gupta, R. Krishnaswamy, and K. Pruhs. Scalably scheduling power-heterogeneous processors. In *Proc. ICALP*, pages 312–323, 2010.

[13] A. Gupta, S. Im, R. Krishnaswamy, B. Moseley, and K. Pruhs. Scheduling heterogeneous processors isn't as easy as you think. In *Proc. SODA*, pages 1242–1253, 2012.

[14] S. Irani, S. Shukla, and R. K. Gupta. Algorithms for power savings. *ACM Transactions on Algorithms*, 3(4):41, 2007.

[15] S. Khuller, J. Li, B. Saha. Energy efficient scheduling via partial shutdown. In *Proc. SODA*, pages 1360–1372, 2010.

[16] T. W. Lam, L. K. Lee, H. F. Ting, I. To, and P. Wong. Sleep with guilt and work faster to minimize flow plus energy. In *Proc. ICALP*, pages 665–676, 2009.

[17] S. Leonardi, and D. Raz. Approximating total flow time on parallel processors. *Journal of Computer and System Sciences*, 73(6):875–891, 2007.

[18] J. Li and S. Khuller. Generalized processor activation problems. In *Proc. SODA*, pages 80–94, 2011.

[19] R. Motwani, S. Phillips, and E. Torng. Nonclairvoyant scheduling. *Theor. Comput. Sci.*, 130(1):17–47, 1994.

[20] E. Torng and J. McCullough. SRPT optimally utilizes faster processors to minimize flow time. *ACM Transactions on Algorithms*, 5(1):1, 2008.

---

[4]By the concavity of Q, if $n_o(t) \geq m$, $\sum_{i=1}^{m} s_i^*(t) = \sum_{i=1}^{m} Q(n_i^*(t)) \leq mQ(\sum_{i=1}^{m} n_i^*(t)/m) = mQ(n_o(t)/m)$. Otherwise, GKP can use at most $n_o(t)$ processors, and similarly, $\sum_{i=1}^{m} s_i^*(t) \leq n_o(t)Q(n_o(t)/n_o(t)) = n_o(t)Q(1)$.

Appendix A: Lower Bound

In this appendix, we assume processors are always awake and consider nonclairvoyant scheduling that minimizes the total flow time. We give a lower bound result on deterministic nonclairvoyant algorithms that allows a job to be migrated $c < 1$ times on average. Below we do not assume that each job is dispatched at its arrival time.

THEOREM 13. *If at most $c < 1$ migration is allowed per job on average (or equivalently, the total number of migrations is at most cn where n is the number of jobs), the competitive ratio of any deterministic nonclairvoyant algorithm, when using s-speed processors for $s \geq 1$, is at least $\frac{1}{16}\min(\frac{m}{s}, \frac{1}{\sqrt{cs}})$ for minimizing total flow time.*

PROOF. Consider any nonclairvoyant online algorithm ONLINE that is using m s-speed processors, where $s \geq 1$. Let ADV be the offline adversary that is using m 1-speed processors. We will show that the competitive ratio of ONLINE is at least $\frac{m}{8sx}$, where $x = \lceil \sqrt{cm} \rceil$ if $c > 0$, and $x = 1$ if $c = 0$. Then Theorem 13 follows (when $c > 0$, $x = \lceil \sqrt{cm} \rceil \leq \max(2\sqrt{cm}, 1)$, and $\frac{m}{8sx} \geq \frac{m}{8s\max(2\sqrt{cm},1)} \geq \frac{1}{16}\min(\frac{m}{s}, \frac{1}{\sqrt{cs}})$; when $c = 0$, $x = 1$ and $\frac{m}{8sx} \geq \frac{m}{16s} = \frac{1}{16}\min(\frac{m}{s}, \frac{1}{\sqrt{cs}})$).

At time 0, ADV releases $n = m^3$ jobs $\{j_1, j_2, \ldots, j_{m^3}\}$. Define $\epsilon = \frac{1}{n^2}$. ADV will determine the sizes of all jobs at time 1. Consider ONLINE's schedule at time 1. Suppose ONLINE has processed $q(j_i)$ units of work for each job j_i.

- Let U be the set of jobs j_i that have $q(j_i) = 0$, i.e., ONLINE has not yet processed or dispatched them by time 1.
- Let P be a set of x processors to which ONLINE has dispatched most jobs.

We divide the proof into two cases based on a threshold $2mx^2$, which can be smaller, equal to, or bigger than n depending on the value of c.

Case 1. The total number of jobs in the x processors of P is less than $2mx^2$. In this case, ADV sets each job j_i to have size $q(j_i) + \epsilon$. Since ONLINE does not complete any job before time 1, ONLINE has total flow at least $1 \cdot n = n = m^3$. Consider ADV. ADV can first process ϵ units of work for each job on a single processor, and all jobs in U will be completed by time $n \cdot \epsilon = \frac{1}{n}$. ADV then simulates ONLINE's schedule on the other jobs from time 0 to time 1 (but working s times slower). Thus ADV has total flow at most $\frac{1}{n} \cdot n + s \cdot (n - |U|)$. Since the x processors of P are hosting most jobs dispatched by ONLINE, the total number of jobs that have been dispatched by ONLINE is at most $\min(2mx^2 \cdot \frac{m}{x}, n) = \min(2m^2x, n) \leq 2m^2x$ and thus $n - |U| \leq 2m^2x$. ADV has total flow at most $\frac{1}{n} \cdot n + s \cdot 2m^2x \leq 8m^2sx$. The competitive ratio of ONLINE is at least $\frac{m^3}{8m^2sx} = \frac{m}{8sx}$.

Case 2. The total number of jobs in the x processors of P is at least $2mx^2$. In this case, ADV selects $2mx^2$ jobs that are currently on P and set their size to sn. Note that $s < sn$. At time 1, ONLINE has processed any of these jobs for at most s units of work, and none of them is completed. Since ONLINE can only migrate at most cn jobs in total, at least $2mx^2 - cn$ jobs of size sn must be entirely run on the x processors in P. To minimize the flow, a best way for ONLINE is to process these jobs evenly on the x processors. Note that $x = 1$ if $c = 0$, and $x = \lceil \sqrt{cm} \rceil$ if $c > 0$. Then, we have $cn \leq mx^2$ and $2mx^2 - cn \geq mx^2$. Therefore, the total flow incurred by ONLINE is at least $x(1 + 2 + \cdots + \frac{mx^2}{x}) \cdot \frac{sn}{s} \geq \frac{1}{2}m^2x^3n$.

Consider ADV. ADV can first simulate ONLINE's schedule on all jobs except those with size sn, so these jobs would have been completed by time $s(1 + n \cdot \epsilon) = s(1 + \frac{1}{n})$. Then, ADV processes the $2mx^2$ jobs with size sn evenly on m processors. The total flow of ADV is at most $s(1 + \frac{1}{n}) \cdot n + m(1 + 2 + \cdots + \frac{2mx^2}{m}) \cdot sn \leq 2sn + m \cdot 3x^4sn \leq 4mx^4sn$ (since $m \geq 2$ and $x \geq 1$). Therefore, the competitive ratio of ONLINE is at least $\frac{\frac{1}{2}m^2x^3n}{4mx^4ns} = \frac{m}{8sx}$. $\square$

Appendix B: Migration Upper Bound (Section 3)

LEMMA 14. *Consider any sequence of wake-ups together and all the migrations involved in maintaining the arrival-time-alignment property. On average (over all jobs), a job is migrated at most $(\ln m + 2)$ times.*

PROOF. We consider each maximal sequence of consecutive wake-ups in SATA. Let t_1 be the time right after the last sleep event before this wake-up sequence; if such sleep event does not exist, let $t_1 = 0$. Let t_2 be the time right after the last wake-ups in the wake-up sequence. We will show that within the interval $I = [t_1, t_2]$, on average (over all jobs arriving in I), each job migrates at most $\ln m + 2$ times. Considering all such intervals I together, the average number of migrations per job is still at most $\ln m + 2$, and the lemma follows.

Consider the interval $I = [t_1, t_2]$. Suppose there are m_0 awake processors at t_1 and ℓ wake-ups within I. When SATA makes the i-th wakeup, let n_i be the current number of active jobs. Note that on the i-th wake-up, the number of awake processors becomes $m_i = m_0 + i$. If $n_i < m_i$, each job is hosted by a different processor, and no job needs to be migrated. Otherwise, we need to maintain the arrival-time-alignment property. We migrate job $j_{\tau - m - 1}$ (if exist) to the newly awaken processor as a new aligned job, so that property C1 holds. To maintain C2 and C3, we need to migrate $\lceil \lceil \beta n_i \rceil / m_i \rceil$ tail jobs from existing awake processors to the newly awaken processor. Let $k_i \geq 1$ be the smallest integer such that $k_i m_i \geq \lceil \beta n_i \rceil$. In other words, we need to migrate k_i tail jobs to the newly awaken processor. Since $n_i \geq m_i$ and $\beta < 0.5$, we have $k_i m_i \leq n_i$. Thus, the total number of migrations within I is at most

$$N = \sum_{1 \leq i \leq \ell: n_i \geq m_i} (1 + k_i) \leq \sum_{1 \leq i \leq \ell: n_i \geq m_i} \left(1 + \frac{n_i}{m_i}\right).$$

We can lower bound the number of jobs arriving in I, as follows. At time t_1, the number of active jobs must be no more than m_0 since there is a sleep event right before t_1 or $t_1 = 0$. Define $n^* = \max\{n_1, \ldots, n_l\}$. Then, the number of jobs arriving within I is at least $n^* - m_0$.

Now, we relate N with $(n^* - m_0)$. Let $r \leq \ell$ be the largest integer such that $n_r \geq m_r$. If such r does not exist, there is no migration within I. Otherwise, $N \leq \sum_{i=1}^{r}(1 + n_i/m_i)$ and $n_r \geq m_r = m_0 + r$. Note that $r \leq n_r - m_0 \leq n^* - m_0$, and $r \leq m$ (the wake-up sequence in I contains consecutive wake-ups). Also note that $n_i/m_i \leq n^*/m_i \leq (n^* - m_0)/(m_i - m_0) = (n^* - m_0)/i$. Therefore,

$$N \leq \sum_{i=1}^{r}\left(1 + \frac{n_i}{m_i}\right) \leq (n^* - m_0) \cdot \left(1 + \sum_{i=1}^{r}\frac{1}{i}\right)$$
$$\leq (n^* - m_0) \cdot (2 + \ln r) \leq (n^* - m_0) \cdot (2 + \ln m).$$

Therefore, the average number of migrations per job within I is at most $N/(n^* - m_0) \leq \ln m + 2$. $\square$

Reallocation Problems in Scheduling

Michael A. Bender
Computer Science,
Stony Brook University
and Tokutek, Inc.
USA
bender@cs.stonybrook.edu

Martin Farach-Colton
Computer Science,
Rutgers University
and Tokutek, Inc.
USA
farach@cs.rutgers.edu

Sándor P. Fekete
Computer Science
TU Braunschweig

Germany
s.fekete@tu-bs.de

Jeremy T. Fineman
Computer Science
Georgetown University
USA
jfineman@cs.georgetown.edu

Seth Gilbert
Computer Science
National University of Singapore
Singapore
seth.gilbert@comp.nus.edu.sg

ABSTRACT

In traditional on-line problems, such as scheduling, requests arrive over time, demanding available resources. As each request arrives, some resources may have to be irrevocably committed to servicing that request. In many situations, however, it may be possible or even necessary to *reallocate* previously allocated resources in order to satisfy a new request. This reallocation has a cost. This paper shows how to service the requests while minimizing the reallocation cost.

We focus on the classic problem of scheduling jobs on a multi-processor system. Each unit-size job has a time window in which it can be executed. Jobs are dynamically added and removed from the system. We provide an algorithm that maintains a valid schedule, as long as a sufficiently feasible schedule exists. The algorithm reschedules only $O(\min\{\log^* n, \log^* \Delta\})$ jobs for each job that is inserted or deleted from the system, where n is the number of active jobs and Δ is the size of the largest window.

Categories and Subject Descriptors

F.2.2 [**Analysis of Algorithms and Problem Complexity**]: Nonnumerical Algorithms and Problems—*Sequencing and scheduling*

Keywords

Scheduling, online problems, reallocation

This research was supported in part by NSF grants IIS 1247726, IIS 1247750, CCF 1114930, CCF 1217708, CCF 1114809, CCF 0937822, CCF 1218188, and by Singapore NUS FRC R-252-000-443-133.

1. INTRODUCTION

Imagine you are running a doctor's office. Every day, patients call and try to schedule an appointment, specifying a time period in which they are free. You respond by agreeing to a specific appointment time. Sometimes, however, there is no available slot during the period of time specified by the patient. What should you do? You might simply turn the patient away. Or, you can reschedule some of your existing patients, making room in the schedule.[1] Unfortunately, patients do not like being rescheduled. How do you minimize the number of patients whose appointments are rescheduled?

While scheduling a doctor's office may (or may not) seem a somewhat contrived motivating example, this situation arises with frequency in real-world applications. Almost any scenario that involves creating a schedule also requires the flexibility to later change that schedule, and those changes often have real costs (measured in equipment, computation, or tempers). For example, in the computational world, scheduling jobs on multiprocess machines and scheduling computation on the cloud lead to rescheduling. In the physical world, these problems arise with depressing regularity in scheduling airports and train stations. Real schedules are always changing.

In a tightly packed schedule, it can be difficult to perform this rescheduling efficiently. Each task you reschedule risks triggering a cascade of other reschedulings, leading to high costs (and unhappy patients). It is easy to construct an example where each job added or removed changes $\Omega(n)$ other jobs, even with constant-sized tasks. In this paper, we show that if there is slack in the schedule, then these rescheduling cascades can be collapsed, in fact down to $O(\log^* n)$ for unit-size jobs.

Reallocation Problems

We introduce a framework for studying the familiar topic of how to change resource allocations as problem instances change, with a goal of unifying results of this type, e.g., [16, 26, 29]. We call problems in this framework *reallocation problems*. A reallocation problem is online in the sense that requests arrive and the system responds. Unlike in the standard online setting where resources

---

[1]Before you get too skeptical about the motivation, this is exactly what M. F-C's ophthalmologist does.

are irrevocably assigned, in a reallocation problem, allocations may change. These reallocations, however, have a cost.

Reallocation lies somewhere between traditional notions of offline and online resource allocation. If the reallocation cost is 0, then there is no penalty for producing an optimal allocation after each request. In this case, a reallocation problem can be viewed as a sequence of offline problems. If the cost of reallocation is ∞, then no finite-cost reallocation is possible and the result is a traditional online problem. When there is a bounded but non-zero cost for reallocation, then there is a trade-off between the quality of an allocation and the cost of reallocation.

Many related questions have been asked in the scheduling community (explored more fully below), including: how can one design schedules that are robust to uncertain or noisy inputs (see, e.g., [22, 24]); how can one generate schedules that change in a limited way while still remaining close to optimal [28]; what is the computational cost of finding a new optimal schedule as the inputs change (e.g., [1, 2, 4, 10]). Our approach differs in that it is job-centered, meaning that we measure the cost of moving jobs rather than the cost of computing where jobs should move to.

Reallocation is a natural problem. Many existing algorithms, when looked in the right way, can be viewed as reallocation problems, e.g., reconfiguring FPGAs [14], maintaining a sparse array [9, 17, 31–33], or maintaining an on-line topological ordering (e.g., [8, 15, 21]). We believe that the framework developed in this paper will allow us to achieve new insights into classical scheduling and optimization problems and the cost of changing a good solution when circumstances change.

Our Problem

We focus on the reallocation version of a classical multiprocessor scheduling problem [18] (described more fully in Section 2). We are given a set of unit-length jobs to process on m machines. Each job has an arrival time and a deadline. The job must be assigned to a machine and processed at some point within the specified time window. Jobs are added and removed from the schedule dynamically. The goal is to maintain a feasible schedule at all times.

In order to process a request, it may be necessary to reschedule some previously scheduled jobs. There are two ways in which a job may be rescheduled: it may be *reallocated* to another time on the same machine, or it may be *migrated* to a different machine. The *migration cost* is the total number of jobs that are moved to different machines when new jobs are added or removed. The *reallocation cost* is the total number of jobs that are rescheduled, regardless of whether they are migrated or retained on the same machine. Our goal is to minimize both the migration cost and the total reallocation cost. We bound these costs separately, since we expect that a reallocation might be more expensive if it also entails a migration. (See [5, 7] for other work that considers migrations separately from other scheduling considerations, such as preëmptions.)

We call an algorithm that processes such a sequence of scheduling requests a *reallocating scheduler*. We show in Section 6 that a reallocating scheduler must allow for some job migrations and that there is no efficient reallocating scheduler without some form of resource augmentation; here we consider speed augmentation [20, 25]. We say that an instance is *γ-underallocated* if it is feasible even when all jobs sizes (processing times) are multiplied by γ. In other words, the offline scheduler is γ times slower than the online scheduler.

Results

This paper gives an efficient m-machine reallocating scheduler for unit-sized jobs with arrival times and deadlines. Informally, the paper shows that as long as there is sufficient slack (independent of m) in the requested schedule, then every request is fulfilled, the reallocation cost is small, and at most one job migrates across machines on each request. Specifically, this paper establishes the following theorem:

THEOREM 1. *There exists a constant γ as well as a reallocating scheduler for unit-length jobs such that for any m-machine γ-underallocated sequence of scheduling requests, we achieve the following performance. Let n_i denote the number of jobs in the schedule and Δ_i the largest window size when the ith reallocation takes place. Then the ith reallocation*

- *has cost $O(\min\{\log^* n_i, \log^* \Delta_i\})$, and*
- *requires at most one machine migration.*

We prove Theorem 1 in stages. In Sections 3 and 4, we assume that job windows are all nicely "aligned," by which we mean that all job windows are either disjoint, or else one is completely contained in the other. In Section 3, we show that the multi-machine aligned case can be reduced to the single-machine aligned case, sacrificing a constant-factor in the underallocation. In Section 4, we establish Theorem 1, assuming the windows are aligned and that $m = 1$. Finally, in Section 5, we remove the alignment assumption from Section 4, again sacrificing a constant-factor in the underallocation.

The crux of our new approach to scheduling appears in Section 4. This section gives a simple scheduling policy that is robust to changes in the scheduling instances. By contrast, most classical scheduling algorithms are brittle, where small changes to a scheduling instance can lead to a cascade of job reallocations even when the system is highly underallocated. This brittleness is certainly inherent to earliest-deadline-first (EDF) and least-laxity-first (LLF) scheduling policies, the classical greedy algorithms for scheduling with arrival times and deadlines. In fact, we originally expected that any greedy approach would necessarily be fragile. We show that this is not the case.

Our new scheduler is based upon a simple greedy policy ("reservation-based pecking-order scheduling"). Unlike most robust algorithms, which explicitly engineer redundancy, the resiliency of our scheduler derives from a basic combinatorial property of the underlying "reservation" system. In this sense, it feels different from typical mechanisms for achieving robustness in computer science or operations research.

Related Work

Here, we flesh out the details of related scheduling and resource allocation work.

Robust scheduling (or "robust planning") involves designing schedules that can tolerate some level of uncertainty. See [22, 24] for surveys and [11, 12, 19, 23] for applications to train and airline scheduling. The assumption in these papers is that the problem is approximately static, but there is some error or uncertainty, or that the schedule remains near optimal even if the underlying situation changes [28]. By contrast, we focus on an arbitrary, worst-case, sequence of requests that may lead to significant changes in the overall allocation of resources.

Researchers have also focused on finding a good fall-back plan ("reoptimization") when a schedule is forced to change. Given an optimal solution for an input, the goal is to compute a near-optimal solution to a closely related input [1,3,4,10]. These papers typically focus on the computational complexity of incremental optimization. By contrast, we focus on the cost of changing the schedule.

Shachnai et al. [27] introduced a framework that is most closely related to ours. They considered computationally intractable problems that admit approximation algorithms. When the problem instance changes, they would like to change the solution as little as possible in order to reestablish a desired approximation ratio. One difference between their framework and ours is that we measure the ratio of reallocation cost to allocation cost, whereas there is no notion of initial cost for them. Rather they measure the ratio of the transition cost to the optimal possible transition cost that will result in a good solution. Although their framework is an analogous framework for approximation algorithms, the particulars end up being quite different.

Davis et al. [13] propose a resource reallocation problem where the allocator must assign resources with respect to a user-determined set of constraints. The constraints may change, but the allocator is only informed when the solution becomes infeasible. The goals is to minimize communication between the allocator and the users.

Many other papers in the literature work within similar setting of job reallocations, but with different goals, restrictions, or scheduling problems in mind. Unal et al. [29] study a problem wherein an initial feasible schedule consisting of jobs with deadlines must be augmented to include a set of newly added jobs, minimizing some objective function on only the new jobs without violating any deadline constraints on the initial schedule. As in the present paper they observe that slackness in the original schedule facilitates a more robust schedule, but outside of the hard constraints they do not count the reallocation cost. Hall and Potts [16] allow a sequence of updates and aim to restrict the change in the schedule, but they evaluate the quality of their algorithm incrementally rather than with respect to a full sequence of updates or an offline objective.

More closely related to our setting, Westbrook [30] considers the total cost of migrating jobs across machines in an online load-balancing problem while also keeping the maximum machine load competitive with the current offline optimum, which is a different scheduling problem in a similar framework. Unlike in the present paper, Westbrook considers only migration costs and does not include the reallocation cost of reordering jobs on machines. Sanders et al. [26] consider a similar load-balancing problem with migration costs and no reallocation costs; their goal is to study the tradeoff between migration costs and the instantaneous competitive ratio.

2. REALLOCATION MODEL

Formally, an *on-line execution* consists of a sequence of scheduling requests of the following form: $\langle \text{INSERTJOB}, name, arrival, deadline \rangle$ and $\langle \text{DELETEJOB}, name \rangle$. A job j has integral arrival time a_j and deadline $d_j > a_j$, meaning that it must be scheduled in a timeslot no earlier than time a_j and no later than time d_j. We call the time interval $[a_j, d_j]$ the job's *window* W. We call $d_j - a_j$, denoted by $|W|$, the *window W's span*. We use *job j's span* as a shorthand for its window's span. Each job takes exactly one unit of time to execute.

At each step, we say that the *active jobs* are those that have already been inserted, but have not yet been deleted. Before each scheduling request, the scheduler must output a feasible schedule for all the active jobs. A feasible schedule is one in which each job is properly scheduled on a particular machine for a time in the the job's available window, and no two jobs on the same machine are scheduled for the same time. Notice that we are not concerned with actually *running* the schedule; rather, we construct a sequence of schedules subject to an on-line sequence of requests.

We define the *migration cost* of a request r_i to be the number of jobs whose machine changes when r_i is processed. We define the *reallocation cost* of a request r_i to be the number of jobs that must be rescheduled when r_i is processed.

When the scheduling instances do not have enough "slack" it may become impossible to achieve low reallocation costs. In fact, if there are n jobs currently scheduled, a new request may have reallocation cost $\Theta(n)$. Even worse, it may be that most reallocations require most jobs to be moved, as is shown in Lemma 12: for large-enough s, there exist length-s request sequences, in which $\Theta(s^2)$ reallocations are necessary. Moreover, for large-enough s, there exist length-s request sequences in which $\Theta(s)$ machine migrations are necessary (see Lemma 11).

Underallocated Schedules and Our Result

To cope with Lemmas 11 and 12, we consider schedules that contain sufficient slack, i.e., that are not fully subscribed. We say that a set of jobs is *m-machine γ-underallocated*, for $\gamma \geq 1$, if there is a feasible schedule for those jobs on m machines even when the job length (processing time) is multiplied by γ. This is equivalent to giving the offline scheduler a processing speed that is γ times slower than the online scheduler. When m is implied by context, we simply say *γ-underallocated*.

Overloading terminology, we say that a sequence of scheduling requests is *γ-underallocated* if after each request the set of active jobs is γ-underallocated.

Aligned-Windows Assumption

The assumption of aligned windows is used in Sections 3 and 4, but it is dropped in Section 5 to prove the full theorem. We say that a window W is *aligned* if (i) it has span 2^i, for some integer i, and (ii) it has a starting time that is a multiple of 2^i. If a job's window is aligned, we say that the job is *aligned*. We say that a set of windows (or jobs) are *recursively aligned* if every window (or job) is aligned.

Notice that recursive alignment implies that two jobs windows are either equal, disjoint, or one is contained in the other (i.e., the windows are laminar). Dealing with recursively aligned windows is convenient in part due to the following observation.

LEMMA 2. *If a recursively aligned set of jobs is m-machine γ-underallocated, then for any aligned window W there are at most $m|W|/\gamma$ jobs with span at most $|W|$ whose windows overlap W.*

PROOF. The window W comprises $|W|$ timeslots on each of m machines, for a total of $m|W|$ timeslots. By definition, a γ-underallocated instance is feasible even if the jobs' processing times are increased to γ. Thus, there may be at most $m|W|/\gamma$ jobs restricted to window W. Since the set of jobs is recursively aligned, if a job has window W' that overlaps W and $|W'| \leq |W|$, then W' is fully contained by W. Hence, there can be at most $m|W|/\gamma$ such jobs. □

3. REALLOCATING ALIGNED JOBS ON MULTIPLE MACHINES

This section algorithmically reduces the multiple-machine scheduling problem to a single-machine scheduling problem, assuming recursive alignment. The reduction uses at most one migration per request. We use m to denote the number of machines.

The algorithm is as follows. For every window W, record the number n_W of jobs having window W. (This number need only be recorded for windows that exist in the current instance, so there can be at most n relevant windows for n jobs.) The goal is to maintain the invariant that every machine has between $\lfloor n_W/m \rfloor$ and $\lceil n_W/m \rceil$ jobs with window W, with the extra jobs being assigned to the earliest machines. This invariant can be maintained simply by delegating jobs, for each window W, round-robin: if there are n_W jobs with window W, a new job with window W is delegated to machine $(n_W + 1) \mod m$. When a job with window W is deleted from some machine m_i, then a job is removed from machine $(n_w \mod m)$ and migrated to machine m_i. All job movements are performed via delegation to the single-machine scheduler on the specified machine(s).

The remaining question is whether the instances assigned to each machine are feasible. The following lemma says that they are.

LEMMA 3. *Consider any m-machine 6γ-underallocated recursively aligned set of jobs J, where γ is an integer. Consider a subset of jobs J' such that if J contains n_W jobs of window W, then J' contains at most $\lceil n_W / m \rceil$ jobs of window W. Then J' is 1-machine γ-underallocated.*

PROOF. Since J is underallocated, Lemma 2 says that there can be at most $m |W| / (6\gamma)$ jobs with window W or nested inside W. By definition, no window smaller than 6γ contains any jobs. The worry is that the ceilings add too many jobs to one machine. But there are at most $2 |W| / (6\gamma)$ windows nested inside W, and the ceilings add at most 1 job to each of these windows. So the total number of jobs in J' with windows inside W is at most $|W| / (6\gamma) + 2 |W| / (6\gamma) = |W| / (2\gamma)$. Even if all jobs are restricted to run at multiples of γ, a simple inductive argument shows that this many size-γ jobs can be feasibly scheduled. □

4. REALLOCATING ALIGNED JOBS ON ONE MACHINE

We now give a single machine, reallocating scheduler for unit-sized jobs. We assume a bound n on the number of jobs concurrently scheduled in the system, and relax this assumption at the end of the section.

Naïve Pecking-Order Scheduling is Logarithmic

We first give the naïve solution, which requires a logarithmic number of reallocations per job insert/delete. This solution uses what we call *pecking-order scheduling*, which means that a job k schedules itself without regard for jobs with longer span and with complete deference to jobs with shorter span. A job k with window W may get displaced by a job j with a shorter window (nested inside W), and k may subsequently displace a job ℓ with longer window.[2]

LEMMA 4. *Let n denote the maximum number of jobs in any schedule and let Δ denote the longest window span. There exists a greedy reallocating scheduler such that for every feasible sequence of recursively aligned scheduling requests, the reallocation cost of each insert/delete is $O(\min \{\log n, \log \Delta\})$.*

PROOF. To insert a job j with span 2^i, find any empty slot in j's window, and place j there. Otherwise, select any job k currently scheduled in j's window that has span $\geq 2^{i+1}$. If no such k exists, the instance is not feasible (as every job currently scheduled in j's window *must* be scheduled in j's window). If such a k exists, replace k with j and recursively insert k. This strategy causes cascading reallocations through increasing window spans, reallocating at most one job with each span. Since there are at most $\log \Delta$ distinct window spans in the aligned case, and moreover all jobs can fit within a window of span n, the number of cascading reallocations is $O(\min \{\log n, \log \Delta\})$. □

---

[2]At first glance, Lemma 4 seems to contradict the underallocation requirement given in Lemma 12. That lower bound, however, applies to the general case, whereas this lemma applies to the aligned case.

Pecking-Order Reallocation via Reservations Costs $O(\min \{\log^* n, \log^* \Delta\})$

We now give a more efficient reallocating scheduler, which matches Theorem 1 when the scheduling requests are recursively aligned. The algorithm is summarized for job insertions in Figure 4.

The intuition behind reservation scheduling manifests itself in the process of securing a reservation at a popular restaurant. If higher-priority diners already have reservations, then our reservation is waitlisted. Even if our reservation is "confirmed," a celebrity (or the President, for DC residents) may drop in at the last moment and steal our slot. If the restaurant is empty, or full of low-priority people like graduate students, then our reservation is fulfilled. The trick to booking a reservation at a competitive restaurant is to make several reservations in parallel. If multiple restaurants grant the reservation, we can select one to eat at. If a late arrival steals our slot, no problem, we have another reservation waiting.

Back to our scheduling problem, by spreading out reservations carefully, jobs will only interfere if they have drastically different spans. Our algorithm handles jobs with "long" windows and "short" windows separately, and only a "short" job can displace a long job. The scheduler itself is recursive, so "very short" jobs can displace "short" jobs which can displace "long" jobs, but the number of levels of recursion here will be $\log^* \Delta$, as opposed to $\log \Delta$ in the naive solution.

There are two components to the scheduler. The first component uses reservations to guarantee that jobs cannot displace (many) other jobs having "similar" span, so the reallocation cost if all jobs have similar spans is $O(1)$. These (over-)reservations, however, consume timeslots and amplify the underallocation requirements. Applying the scheduler recursively at this point is trivial to achieve a good reallocation cost, but the required underallocation would become nonconstant. The second component of the scheduler is to combine levels of granularity so that their effects on underallocation do not compound.

The remainder of the section is organized as follows. We first discuss an interval decomposition to separate jobs into different "levels" according to their spans. Then we present the scheduler with regards to a single job level. Finally we discuss how to incorporate multiple levels simultaneously.

Interval Decomposition

Our scheduler operates nearly independently at multiple levels of granularity. More precisely, we view these levels from bottom up by defining the threshold

$$L_{\ell+1} = \begin{cases} 2^5 & \text{if } \ell = 0 \\ 2^{L_\ell/4} & \text{if } \ell > 0 \end{cases}.$$

It is not hard to see that L is always a power of 2, growing as a tower function of $\sqrt[4]{2}$. It is often convenient to use the equivalent relationship $L_\ell = 4 \lg(L_{\ell+1})$—each threshold is roughly the lg of the next.

Our scheduler operates recursively according to these thresholds. The level-ℓ scheduler handles jobs and windows W with span $L_\ell < |W| \leq L_{\ell+1}$. We call a job (or window) a *level-ℓ job (window)* if its span falls in this range.

We partition level-ℓ windows into nonoverlapping, aligned subwindows called *level-ℓ intervals*, consisting of $L_\ell = 4 \lg L_{\ell+1}$ timeslots. The following observation is useful in our analysis:

$$(\text{\# of distinct level-}\ell\text{-window spans}) \leq \lg(L_{\ell+1}) = L_\ell/4 \quad (1)$$

The reallocation scheduler operates recursively within each interval to handle lower-level jobs. Because this is pecking-order scheduling, the recursive scheduler makes decisions without paying attention to the location of the higher-level jobs, guaranteeing only that each lower-level job is assigned a unique slot within its appropriate window. In doing so, it may displace a long job and invoke the higher-level scheduler.

Schedule Level-ℓ Jobs via Reservations

Consider a level-ℓ window W with span $2^k L_\ell$, for some integer $k \geq 1$ (i.e., W contains 2^k level-ℓ intervals). Let x denote the number of jobs having exactly window W.

The window W maintains a set of **reservations** for these x jobs, where each reservation is a *request for a slot in a given level-ℓ interval*. A reservation made by W can be **fulfilled**; this means that one slot from the requested interval is **assigned to W**, and the only level-ℓ jobs that may **occupy** that slot are any of the x jobs with window exactly W. Alternatively, a reservation can be **waitlisted**; this means that all the slots in the requested interval are already assigned to smaller windows than W. Which reservations are fulfilled and which are waitlisted may change over time as jobs get allocated and removed.

We now explain how these reservations are made. Initially, a level-ℓ window W makes one reservation for each enclosed level-ℓ interval. It makes two additional reservations for each job having window W. These reservations are spread out round-robin among the intervals within W (and independently of any jobs with any different windows). We maintain the following invariant:

INVARIANT 5. *If there are x jobs having level-ℓ window W with $|W| = 2^k L_\ell$, then W has exactly $2x + 2^k$ reservations in level-ℓ intervals.*

- *These reservations are assigned in round-robin order to the intervals in W.*
- *Each of the enclosed intervals contains either $\lfloor 2x/2^k \rfloor + 1$ or $\lfloor 2x/2^k \rfloor + 2$ of W's reservations, where the leftmost intervals have the most reservations and the rightmost intervals have the least reservations.*

To maintain Invariant 5, when a new job with window W is allocated, W makes two new reservations, and these are sent to the leftmost intervals that have the least number ($\lfloor 2x/2^k \rfloor + 1$) of W's reservations. When a job having window W is deleted, W removes one reservation each from the two rightmost intervals that have the most reservations.

We now describe the reservation process from the perspective of the interval, which handles reservation requests from the $< L_\ell/4$ level-ℓ windows that contain the interval (see Equation 1). The interval decides whether to fulfill or waitlist a reservation, prioritizing reservations made by shorter windows. Each interval I has an **allowance** $allowance(I)$, specifying which slots it may use to fulfill reservations. In the absence of lower-level jobs, the $|allowance(I)| = L_\ell$, since the interval has span L_ℓ. (When lower-level jobs are introduced, however, the allowance decreases—the allowance contains all those slots that are not *occupied* by lower-level jobs.) Thus, the interval sorts the window reservations with respect to span from shortest to longest, and fulfills the $|allowance(I)| \leq L_\ell$ reservations that originate from the shortest windows. A fulfilled reservation is assigned to a specific slot in the interval, while a waitlisted reservation has no slot. The interval maintains a list of these waitlisted reservations.

The set of fulfilled reservations changes dynamically as insertions/deletions occur. When a new reservation is made by window W, a longer window W' may lose a reserved slot as one of its fulfilled reservations is moved to the waitlist; if there is a job (of the same level) in that slot, it must be moved. When a job with window W is deleted, W has two fewer reservations, and so may lose two fulfilled slots. If there is a job in either of these slots, then that job must be moved. (In this case, a longer window W' may gain a fulfilled slot, but this does not require any job movement.) The following invariant is needed to establish the algorithm's correctness.

INVARIANT 6. *When a job having window W is newly allocated, W makes two new reservations. Then the job is assigned to any empty slot for which W has a fulfilled reservation. There will always be at least one such slot (proved by Lemma 8).*

Interestingly, as a consequence of pecking-order scheduling combined with round-robin reservations:

OBSERVATION 7. *Which reservations in which intervals are fulfilled and which are waitlisted is history independent. The actual placement of the jobs is not history independent.*

Scheduling Across All Levels

Consider inserting a level-ℓ job j. Suppose j's window is contained in a higher-level interval I'. We schedule j at its own level according to the pecking-order scheduler, without regard to higher-level schedulers. Recall that the first step of the insertion is placing two new reservations. Whenever the reservations cause another level-ℓ job j' to move from slot s to slot s', the allowance of all higher-level intervals must be updated to reflect the change in slot usage. However, since both $s \in I'$ and $s' \in I'$, and j' vacates the original slot s, there is no net change to $|allowance(I')|$. It is thus sufficient to swap s and s' for all higher-level intervals I', which may result in a total of one higher-level job movement.

After updating the reservations, the new job j is placed in one of its assigned slots s. This slot may either be empty, or it may contain a higher-level job h—the scheduler chooses s without regard to these possibilities. In either case, the slot s will be used by j, so it must be removed from $allowance(I')$ for any ancester interval I'—meaning the higher-level scheduler cannot use this slot. If the slot s was empty, then the job j is assigned to that slot and the insertion terminates. If the slot s was previously occupied by a higher-level job h, then h is displaced and a new slot must be found. Unlike in the case of reservations, $|allowance(I')|$ decreases here and we do not immediately have a candidate slot into which to place h. Instead, we reinsert h recursively using the scheduler at its level. This displacement and reinsertion may cascade to higher levels.

Observe that the higher-level scheduler is unaware of the reservation system employed by the lower-level scheduler. It only knows which slots are in its allowance. These slots are exactly those that are not *occupied* by short-window jobs. The interval does not observe the reservations occurring within nested intervals—only actual job placement matters. When a lower-level job is deleted, the allowance of the containing interval increases to include the slot that is no longer occupied.

Reservation Analysis

We now use the following lemma to establish Invariant 6, which claims that there are always enough fulfilled reservations. Since the reservations fulfilled by each interval are history independent (see Observation 7), this proof applies at all points during the execution of the algorithm.

LEMMA 8. *Suppose that a sequence of aligned scheduling requests 8-underallocated. If there are x jobs each having the same window W, then W has at least $x + 1$ fulfilled reservations.*

- Initially, each level-ℓ window W has one reservation in each level-ℓ interval contained in W.
- Initially, each interval I has $\text{allowance}(I) = I$.
- To insert a new level-ℓ job j with window W:
  1. Identify the two underloaded intervals I_1 and I_2 according to Invariant 5
  2. Call $\text{RESERVE}(I_1, W)$ and $\text{RESERVE}(I_2, W)$
  3. Call $\text{PLACE}(j)$

$\text{RESERVE}(I, W)$ // make a reservation in I for level-ℓ window W

1   **if** there is a slot $s \in \text{allowance}(I)$ that has not been assigned
2   **then** fulfill the reservation, assigning slot s to window W and **return**
3   let W' be the longest window with a fulfilled reservation in I, and let s be one of its slot
4   **if** $|W'| \leq |W|$
5   **then** waitlist the reservation for W
6   **else** waitlist the reservation for W' and take slot s from W'
7   **if** there is a level-ℓ job j' in slot s
8   **then** $\text{MOVE}(j')$
9   fulfill the reservation, assigning slot s to W
       // Note that though the reservation is fulfilled, the slot may be occupied by a higher-level job

---

$\text{MOVE}(j')$ // level-ℓ job j' lost the reservation to a slot it occupies

10   let W' be the window of j', and let s be the slot it occupies
11   let s' be a fulfilled slot, assigned to W', not containing any level-ℓ job   // exists by Lemma 8
12   **for** all ancestor intervals I' containing W'
13   **do** swap s and s' with regards to reservations and allowances for I' // both slots are inside I'
       // if a higher-level job h occupies s' then schedule h in s instead of s'
14   schedule j' in slot s'

$\text{PLACE}(j)$ // let W be j's window and let ℓ be j's level

15   let s be a fulfilled slot, assigned to W, not containing any level-ℓ job   // exists by Lemma 8
16   schedule j in s, potentially displacing a higher-level job h
17   remove s from the allowance of all higher-level intervals
18   **for** each ancestor interval whose allowance decreases   // s is only in allowances up to h's level
19   **do** adjust the reservations to reflect a smaller allowance, possibly waitlisting one reservation
20   **if** a newly waitlisted reservation is for a slot containing a job j'
21   **then** $\text{MOVE}(j')$
22   **if** there is a displaced job h
23   **then** $\text{PLACE}(h)$

Figure 1: Pecking-order scheduling with reservations.

PROOF. Let $|W| = 2^k L_\ell$ for level-ℓ window W. Let y be the number of level-ℓ jobs with windows nested inside W. Each of those windows makes 2 reservations for each job, plus an extra reservation to each of the 2^k intervals. So the total number of reservations in W is at most $2(x + y) + 2^k \lg W$. In addition, let z be the number of lower-level jobs nested inside W. Since we are 8-underallocated, we have $2(x + y) + z \leq 2(x + y + z) \leq |W|/4$ by Lemma 2. By Equation 1, we have $\lg W \leq L_\ell/4$, and hence $2^k \lg W \leq (2^k L_\ell)/4 = |W|/4$. Summing these up, we have that at most $|W|/2$ slots consumed by lower-level jobs and these reservations.

In order for a particular interval to waitlist even one of W's reservation requests, it would need to have strictly more than L_ℓ of these reservations or lower-level jobs assigned to it. But there are only $|W|/2$ slots consumed in total, so strictly less than $1/2$ the intervals can waitlist even one of W's reservations. Since window W reserves at least $\lfloor 2x/2^k \rfloor + 1$ slots in every one of the 2^k intervals by Invariant 5, it must therefore be granted strictly more than $(\lfloor 2x/2^k \rfloor + 1)(1/2)(2^k) \geq x$ fulfilled reservations. $\square$

Since each window W containing x jobs has at least $x + 1$ fulfilled reservations at intervals within W, there is always an appropriate slot to schedule a new belonging to this window. This ensures that there each operation leads to only $O(1)$ reallocations at each level.

Trimming Windows to n and Deamortization

Ideally, the reallocation cost for a request r should be a function of the number of active jobs n_r in the system when request r is made. To achieve this performance guarantee, we maintain a value n^* that is roughly the number of jobs in the current schedule. When the number of active jobs exceeds n^*, we double n^*; when the number of active jobs shrinks below $n^*/4$, we halve n^*.

For every job that has a window larger than $2\gamma n^*$, we trim its window—reducing it arbitrarily to size $2\gamma n^*$. The adjusted instance remains γ-underallocated, since there are at most n^* other jobs scheduled in the trimmed window of size $2\gamma n^*$.

To achieve good amortized performance, it is enough to rebuild the schedule from scratch each time we change the value of n^*. This rebuilding incurs an amortized $O(1)$ reallocation cost.

This amortized solution can be deamortized, as long as the scheduling instance is sufficiently underallocated that the following property holds: if each job is duplicated (i.e., inserted twice on inserts, deleted twice on delete), the resulting instance is γ-underallocated, for appropriate constant γ. This property holds as long as the initial (unduplicated) scheduling instance is 2γ-underallocated.

The idea is to rebuild the schedule gradually, performing a little update every time a new reallocation request is serviced. This approach is reminiscent to how one deamortizes the rebuilding of a hash table that is too full or too empty. We use the even (or odd) time slots for the old schedule and the odd (or even) time slots for the new schedule. Instead of rebuilding the schedule all at once, every time one job is added or deleted, two jobs are moved from the old schedule to the new schedule.

Wrapping Up

We conclude with the following lemma, which puts together the various results in this section:

LEMMA 9. *There exists a constant γ and a single-machine reallocating scheduler such that for any 1-machine γ-underallocated sequence of aligned scheduling requests, we achieve the following performance. Let n_i denote the number of jobs in the schedule and Δ_i the largest window size when the ith reallocation takes place. Then the ith reallocation has cost $O(\min\{\log^* n_i, \log^* \Delta_i\})$.*

PROOF. We consider the performance of the pecking-order scheduler with reservations, where we maintain an estimate n^* via deamortized shrinking and doubling and trim all windows to γn^*.

Lemma 8 shows that there is always a slot available to put a job (Invariant 6), and hence we observe that there are at most $O(1)$ reallocations at each level of the scheduler. Specifically, on insertion, the two reservations may result in two calls to MOVE for jobs at the same level as the one being inserted. Each MOVE results in one reallocation of the job being moved, plus at most one reallocation at a higher level. Then the call to PLACE may cascade across all levels, but it in aggregate it only includes one MOVE per level, each causing at most two reallocations.

If Δ_i is the largest job size when operation i occurs, there are no more than $O(\log^* \Delta_i)$ levels. Since $n_i^* \le 4n$, and all windows are trimmed to length γn^*, we also know that there are no more than $O(\log^*(4\gamma n_i))$ levels. From this the result follows. $\square$

5. REALLOCATING UNALIGNED JOBS ON MULTIPLE MACHINE

In this section, we generalize to jobs that are not aligned, removing the alignment assumptions that we made in Sections 3 and 4. We show that if S is a γ-underallocated sequence of scheduling requests, then we can safely *trim* each of the windows associated with each of the jobs, creating an aligned instance. Since the initial sequence of scheduling requests is underallocated, the resulting aligned sequence is also underallocated, losing only a constant factor.

We first define some terminology. If W is an arbitrary window, we say that ALIGNED(W) is a largest aligned window that is contained in W. (If there is more than one largest window, choose arbitrarily.) Notice that $|$ALIGNED(W)$| \ge |W|/4$. If J is a set of jobs, then ALIGNED(J) is the set of jobs in which the window W associated with each job is replaced with ALIGNED(W).

LEMMA 10. *Consider any m-machine 4γ-underallocated set of jobs J, where γ is an integer. Then ALIGNED(J) is m-machine γ-underallocated.*

PROOF. Assume for the sake of contradiction that ALIGNED(J) is not γ-underallocated. This implies that there must exist a window W that has $> m|W|/\gamma$ jobs with trimmed windows contained in W (as otherwise we could schedule the size γ jobs via a simple inductive argument). Let $J' \subseteq J$ be the jobs whose trimmed windows are contained in W.

Since J is 4γ-underallocated, we now examine an (unaligned) scheduling of the jobs in J' that satisfies the 4γ-underallocation requirement. We observe that all the jobs in J' are scheduled in a region of size at most $4|W|$. However, since the schedule is 4γ-underallocated, there can be at most $4m|W|/(4\gamma)$ jobs in this region of size $4|W|$. That is $|J'| \le m|W|/\gamma$, which is a contradiction. $\square$

From this we can conclude with the proof of Theorem 1:

PROOF OF THEOREM 1. Jobs are scheduled as follows: first, a new job has its window aligned; second, it is delegated to a machine in round-robin fashion; finally, it is scheduled via single-machine pecking-order scheduling with reservations. When a job is deleted, it is removed by the appropriate single-machine scheduler, and then there is at most one migration to maintain the balance of jobs across machines. This is the only time that jobs migrate.

Lemma 10 shows that the set of aligned jobs is m-machine $\gamma/4$-underallocated, and Lemma 3 shows that the jobs assigned to each machine are 1-machine $\gamma/24$-underallocated. Finally, Lemma 9 shows that each single-machine scheduler operation has cost $O(\min\{\log^* n_i, \log^* \Delta_i\})$—and each job addition or deletion invokes $O(1)$ single-machine scheduler operations. $\square$

6. WHAT HAPPENS WITHOUT UNDER-ALLOCATION?

This section explains what happens without underallocation and why migrations are necessary at all.

If migration cost is to be bounded only by reallocation cost and since jobs have unit size, it is trivial to transform a parallel instance to a single-machine instance my making a single machine go m times faster. Since migration cost across machines could be more expensive than rescheduling a single machine, we are interested in providing a tighter bound on the migration cost. The question then is: *are migrations necessary?* The following lemma shows that they are. In fact, the per-request migration cost must be $\Omega(1)$ in the worst-case for any deterministic algorithm.

LEMMA 11. *There exists a sufficiently large sequence of s job insertions/deletions on $m > 1$ machines, such that any deterministic scheduling algorithm has a total migration cost of $\Omega(s)$.*

PROOF. Without loss of generality, assume $6m$ divides s. Divide the s requests into $s/(6m)$ consecutive subsequences of $6m$ requests each. Each subsequence is as follows:

1. Insert $2m$ span-2 jobs with window $[0, 2]$.
2. Delete the m jobs scheduled on the first $m/2$ machines.
3. Insert m span-1 jobs with windows $[0, 1]$.
4. Delete all $2m$ remaining jobs.

After step 1, the only feasible schedule is to put two jobs on each machine. After step 2, half the machines have two jobs, and the other half of the machines have no jobs. The only feasible schedule after step 3 is to have on each machine a span-1 job starting at time 0, and a span-2 job starting at time 1. This means that half of the span-2 jobs must migrate across machines, causing $m/2$ migrations. There are thus $m/2$ migrations for every $6m$ requests, or a total of $s/12$ migrations. $\square$

It is also easy to see that for some sequences of scheduling requests, if they are not underallocated, it is impossible to achieve low reallocation costs, even if there exists a feasible schedule.

LEMMA 12. *There exists a sequence of s job inserts/deletions, such that any scheduling algorithm has a rescheduling cost of $\Omega(s^2)$.*

PROOF. Consider for example $\eta = s/2$ jobs numbered $0, 1, \ldots, \eta - 1$, where job j has window $[j, j+2]$. With the insertion of one additional job having window $[0, 1]$, forcing the job to be scheduled at time 0, all η other jobs are forced to schedule during their later slot. If that job is deleted and another unit-span job with window $[\eta, \eta + 1]$ is inserted, then all jobs are forced to schedule during their earlier slot. By toggling between these two options, all jobs are forced to move, resulting in cost $\Omega(\eta)$ to handle each request. Repeating η times gives a total cost of $\Omega(\eta^2) = \Omega(s^2)$. □

7. CONCLUSIONS AND OPEN QUESTIONS

The results in this paper suggest several followup questions. First, is it possible to generalize this paper's reallocation scheduler for the case where jobs are not unit-sized? Observe that we are limited by the computational difficulty of scheduling with arrival times and deadlines when jobs are not unit size; see [6] for recent results with resource augmentation. We are also limited by the following observation:

OBSERVATION 13. *Suppose there exist jobs of size 1 and jobs of size k, for any $k > 1$. For any reallocation scheduler, there is a sequence of $\Theta(n)$ scheduling requests that has aggregate reallocation cost $\Omega(kn)$, for $k \leq n$, even if the requests are γ-underallocated for any constant γ.*

PROOF. Consider a schedule of length $m = 2\gamma k$. Assume there are k unit-sized jobs that are each scheduled with a window beginning at 0 and ending at m. In addition, consider a single large job p that has size k and a window of span exactly k.

Initially, all k unit-size jobs are scheduled and they remain in the system throughout. The large job p is initially scheduled at time slot 0. It is then deleted from time slot 0 and re-inserted at time slot k, and then again at time slot $2k, 3k, \ldots, m - k$. The same sequence of 2γ insertions and deletions is then repeated n times.

During a single sequence of 2γ insertions and deletions, each of the k unit-sized jobs has to be rescheduled at least once, resulting in $\Omega(kn)$ reallocation cost. □

Does there exist a reallocation scheduler that handles jobs whose sizes are integers less than or equal to k and matching the bounds in Observation 13? There could be applications where jobs are not unit size, but where k is relatively small.

What happens if other types of reallocations are allowed, such as if new machines can be added or dropped from the schedule, or if machine speeds can change?

In this paper, γ is very large, and the paper does not attempt to optimize this constant, preferring clarity of exposition. How much can this constant be improved? Is there a reallocation scheduler where $\gamma = 1 + \varepsilon$?

Finally, what other scheduling and optimization problems lend themselves to study in the context of reallocation?

8. REFERENCES

[1] C. Archetti, L. Bertazzi, and M. G. Speranza. Reoptimizing the Traveling Salesman Problem. *Networks*, 42(3):154–159, 2003.

[2] C. Archetti, L. Bertazzi, and M. G. Speranza. Reoptimizing the 0-1 knapsack problem. *Discrete Appl. Math.*, 158(17):1879–1887, Oct. 2010.

[3] G. Ausiello, V. Bonifaci, and B. Escoffier. Complexity and approximation in reoptimization. In *Proccedings of CiE: Logic and Computation and Logic in the Real World*, 2007.

[4] G. Ausiello, B. Escoffier, J. Monnot, and V. T. Paschos. Reoptimization of minimum and maximum traveling salesman's tours. *J. Discrete Algorithms*, 7(4):453–463, 2009.

[5] B. Awerbuch, Y. Azar, S. Leonardi, and O. Regev. Minimizing the flow time without migration. *SIAM J. Comput.*, 31(5):1370–1382, 2002.

[6] N. Bansal, H.-L. Chan, R. Khandekar, K. Pruhs, C. Stein, and B. Schieber. Non-preemptive min-sum scheduling with resource augmentation. In *Proc. 48th Annual IEEE Symposium on Foundations of Computer Science (FOCS)*, pages 614–624, 2007.

[7] L. Becchetti, S. Leonardi, and S. Muthukrishnan. Average stretch without migration. *J. Comput. Syst. Sci.*, 68(1):80–95, 2004.

[8] M. A. Bender, J. T. Fineman, and S. Gilbert. A new approach to incremental topological ordering. In *Proc. 20th ACM-SIAM Symposium on Discrete Algorithms (SODA)*, pages 1108–1115, January 2009.

[9] M. A. Bender and H. Hu. An adaptive packed-memory array. *Transactions on Database Systems*, 32(4), 2007.

[10] H.-J. Böckenhauer, L. Forlizzi, J. Hromkovic, J. Kneis, J. Kupke, G. Proietti, and P. Widmayer. Reusing optimal TSP solutions for locally modified input instances. In *Proc. Fourth IFIP International Conference on Theoretical Computer Science (TCS)*, pages 251–270, 2006.

[11] A. Caprara, L. Galli, L. Kroon, G. Maróti, and P. Toth. Robust train routing and online re-scheduling. In T. Erlebach and M. Lübbecke, editors, *Proc. 10th Workshop on Algorithmic Approaches for Transportation Modelling, Optimization, and Systems*, volume 14 of *OpenAccess Series in Informatics (OASIcs)*, pages 24–33, Dagstuhl, Germany, 2010. Schloss Dagstuhl–Leibniz-Zentrum fuer Informatik.

[12] V. Chiraphadhanakul and C. Barnhart. Robust flight schedules through slack re-allocation. Submitted, 2011.

[13] S. Davis, J. Edmonds, and R. Impagliazzo. Online algorithms to minimize resource reallocations and network communication. In *APPROX-RANDOM*, pages 104–115, 2006.

[14] S. P. Fekete, T. Kamphans, N. Schweer, C. Tessars, J. C. van der Veen, J. Angermeier, D. Koch, and J. Teich. Dynamic defragmentation of reconfigurable devices. *ACM Trans. Reconfigurable Technol. Syst.*, 5(2):8:1–8:20, June 2012.

[15] B. Haeupler, T. Kavitha, R. Mathew, S. Sen, and R. E. Tarjan. Faster algorithms for incremental topological ordering. In *Proc. 35th International Colloquium on Automata, Languages, and Programming (ICALP)*, pages 421–433, July 2008.

[16] N. G. Hall and C. N. Potts. Rescheduling for new orders. *Operations Research*, 52(3), 2004.

[17] A. Itai, A. G. Konheim, and M. Rodeh. A sparse table implementation of priority queues. In *Proc. 8th Internationl Colloquium on Automata, Languages, and Programming (ICALP)*, volume 115 of *Lecture Notes in Computer Science*, pages 417–431, 1981.

[18] J. Jackson. Scheduling a production line to minimize maximum tardiness. Technical report, Management Science Research Project Research Report 43, University of California, Los Angeles, 1955.

[19] H. Jiang and C. Barnhart. Dynamic airline scheduling. *Transportation Science*, 43(3):336–354, 2009.

[20] B. Kalyanasundaram and K. Pruhs. Speed is as powerful as clairvoyance. *Journal of the ACM*, 47:214–221, 1995.

[21] I. Katriel and H. L. Bodlaender. Online topological ordering. In *Proc. 16th ACM-SIAM Symposium on Discrete Algorithms (SODA)*, pages 443–450, Vancouver, British Columbia, Canada, January 2005.

[22] P. Kouvelis and G. Yu. *Robust Discrete Optimization and Its Applications*. Kluwer, 1997.

[23] S. Lan, J.-P. Clarke, and C. Barnhart. Planning for robust airline operations: Optimizing aircraft routings and flight departure times to minimize passenger disruptions. *Transportation Science*, 40(1):15–28, 2006.

[24] J. M. Mulvey, R. J. Vanderbei, and S. A. Zenios. Robust optimization of large-scale systems. *Operations Research*, 43(2), 1995.

[25] C. A. Phillips, C. Stein, E. Torng, and J. Wein. Optimal time-critical scheduling via resource augmentation. *Algorithmica*, 32(2):163–200, 2002.

[26] P. Sanders, N. Sivadasan, and M. Skutella. Online scheduling with bounded migration. *Math. Oper. Res.*, 34(2):481–498, 2009.

[27] H. Shachnai, G. Tamir, and T. Tamir. A theory and algorithms for combinatorial reoptimization. In *Proc. 10th Latin American Symposium Theoretical Informatics (LATIN)*, pages 618–630, 2012.

[28] C. A. Tovey. Rescheduling to minimize makespan on a changing number of identical processors. *Naval Research Logistics*, 33:717–724, 1986.

[29] A. T. Unal, R. Uzsoy, and A. S. Kiran. Rescheduling on a single machine with part-type dependent setup times and deadlines. *Annals of Operations Research*, 70, 1997.

[30] J. Westbrook. Load balancing for response time. *Journal of Algorithms*, 35(1):1 – 16, 2000.

[31] D. Willard. Maintaining dense sequential files in a dynamic environment (extended abstract). In *Proc. 14th Annual Symposium on Theory of Computing (STOC)*, pages 114–121, 1982.

[32] D. E. Willard. Good worst-case algorithms for inserting and deleting records in dense sequential files. In *Proc. International Conference on Management of Data (SIGMOD)*, pages 251–260, 1986.

[33] D. E. Willard. A density control algorithm for doing insertions and deletions in a sequentially ordered file in good worst-case time. *Information and Computation*, 97(2):150–204, 1992.

Efficient Scheduling to Minimize Calibrations

Michael A. Bender[*]
Stony Brook University & Tokutek

David P. Bunde[†]
Knox College

Vitus J. Leung[‡]
Sandia National Laboratories

Samuel McCauley[*]
Stony Brook University

Cynthia A. Phillips[‡]
Sandia National Laboratories

ABSTRACT

Integrated Stockpile Evaluation (ISE) is a program to test nuclear weapons periodically. Tests are performed by machines that may require occasional calibration. These calibrations are expensive, so finding a schedule that minimizes calibrations allows more testing to be done for a given amount of money.

This paper introduces a theoretical framework for ISE. Machines run jobs with release times and deadlines. Calibrating a machine requires unit cost. The machine remains calibrated for T time steps, after which it must be recalibrated before it can resume running jobs. The objective is to complete all jobs while minimizing the number of calibrations.

The paper gives several algorithms to solve the ISE problem for the case where jobs have unit processing times. For one available machine, there is an optimal polynomial-time algorithm. For multiple machines, there is a 2-approximation algorithm, which finds an optimal solution when all jobs have distinct deadlines.

Categories and Subject Descriptors

F.2 [**Analysis of Algorithms and Problem Complexity**]: Nonnumerical Algorithms and Problems

Keywords

Integrated Stockpile Evaluation, approximation algorithms, calibration, resource allocation, scheduling.

[*]Supported in part by NSF grants IIS 1247726, CCF 1217708, CCF 1114809, and CCF 0937822. This work partially done while visiting Sandia National Laboratories. {bender,smccauley}@cs.stonybrook.edu.

[†]Partially supported by contract 899808 from Sandia National Laboratories. dbunde@knox.edu.

[‡]Sandia National Laboratories is a multi-program laboratory managed and operated by Sandia Corporation, a wholly owned subsidiary of Lockheed Martin Corporation, for the U.S. Department of Energy's National Nuclear Security Administration under contract DE-AC04-94AL85000. {vjleung, caphill}@sandia.gov.

1. INTRODUCTION

Integrated Stockpile Evaluation (**ISE**) is a program at Sandia National Laboratories to test nuclear weapons periodically to ensure that the weapons will continue to function according to their specifications [1]. These tests require a great deal of precision and dependability, and given the nuclear context, safety mistakes can have serious ramifications. Testing machines are expensive, and some must be calibrated on a regular basis. The calibrations themselves are also expensive—in a monetary though not necessarily temporal sense. Efficient scheduling of these tests and the calibrations necessary to perform them allows more weapons to be tested within a given budget. This paper gives a theoretical framework, motivated by the ISE problem, for scheduling tasks on machines that need to be calibrated periodically.

We model calibrations in a multi-machine setting as follows. We can **calibrate** a machine for unit cost. The machine stays **calibrated** for $T \geq 2$ time steps, after which it must remain idle until it is recalibrated. We refer to these T time steps following a calibration as an **interval**. Calibrating a machine is instantaneous, meaning that a machine can be recalibrated between two job executions running in successive time steps. Minimizing the number of calibrations helps minimize the total cost of an ISE instance.

We abstract the ISE problem by saying that we have a set of jobs $J = \{1, \ldots, n\}$, corresponding to weapons tests. Each job must be scheduled on one of P identical testing machines. A job j has a release time r_j, a due date d_j, and a processing requirement (length) p_j. If a job j is scheduled at time t, we must have $r_j \leq t$ and $t + p_j \leq d_j$. In most of this paper, we assume unit processing times, i.e., $p_j = 1$ for all j. This testing schedule is determined in advance, meaning that the jobs arrive offline.

Our objective is to find the feasible schedule that minimizes the number of calibrations. In the notation developed in [9], we denote the ISE problem as $P|r_j, d_j|\#\text{calibrations}$.

Related Work

One aspect of the ISE problem distinct from many classical scheduling problems is that it often makes sense to delay scheduling a job beyond its earliest feasible time step; see Figure 5. In contrast, for metrics such as minimizing maximum lateness or average completion time, scheduling a job later never helps; see e.g, [11]. This property that a job should be scheduled as early as possible often makes scheduling easier. For example, if the cost function has this property and jobs are restricted to unit size, the problem is polynomial even on multiple machines [5, 13].

One scheduling problem, somewhat reminiscent of the ISE problem, is that of minimizing the number of idle periods [2]. This problem can be solved in polynomial time for unit-sized jobs by dynamic programming. Minimizing idle periods captures the notion that it is expensive to turn on a machine that has been idle, whereas the ISE problem captures the notion that it is expensive to start a constant-sized period of activity. In [2] both machine activation and job processing time contribute to cost, whereas in the ISE problem only the activation intervals are important.

The restriction of unit size jobs can cause some otherwise NP-hard problems to become polynomial [4–6, 8, 12, 14, 18]. Other problems remain NP-hard; these include flow shop problems on multiple machines with a cost for switching machines [19], requiring additional resources for each job [3, 7, 8], or a partial ordering on the execution order of the jobs [16, 17]. It is not clear if the ISE problem remains NP-hard when restricted to unit-length jobs.

Results

We give the following results for the ISE problem with unit-sized jobs, and show that the problem is NP-complete with arbitrary-sized jobs:

- We give a greedy scheduler for any instance feasible on one machine.

- We show this single-machine solution remains optimal even if more machines become available. However, if an instance requires multiple machines, adding more machines may decrease the optimal cost.

- We give a polynomial-time 2-approximation algorithm for multi-machine ISE instances. This approximation algorithm gives an optimal solution for the special case where all jobs have distinct deadlines.

Overview

The rest of the paper is organized into single-machine results (Section 2) and multiple-machine results (Section 3). We conclude (Section 4) with generalizations that capture further aspects of the ISE application.

2. SINGLE-MACHINE ISE

In this section, we give an optimal algorithm for single-machine ISE. If a scheduling instance is feasible on a single machine, then the best single-machine schedule is optimal, even if more machines are available.

We focus on unit-sized jobs in this paper, since for arbitrary job lengths on any number of machines $P \geq 1$, the ISE problem is NP-hard.

THEOREM 1. *The ISE Problem is (weakly) NP-hard for any number of machines $P \geq 1$.*

PROOF. Hardness follows from a reduction from Partition. □

EDF Scheduling with Intervals

Our ISE algorithms run jobs based on the *Earliest Deadline First* (*EDF*) scheduling policy. Although Section 2 discusses the single-machine ISE, we also explain here how EDF works on multiple machines.

The EDF scheduler maintains a priority queue of jobs ordered by increasing deadline. If two jobs have the same deadline, the priority queue breaks ties arbitrarily but consistently.

EDF schedules jobs by iterating over time slots from earliest to latest. When EDF reaches a time slot t during which a new job j arrives ($r_j = t$), EDF adds j to the priority queue. Then EDF selects up to P jobs to run in time step t by popping these jobs from the priority queue.

LEMMA 2 ([10, 15]). *If jobs have unit size, EDF finds a feasible schedule on single or multiple machines if one exists.*

EDF also schedules optimally in the multi-machine ISE setting where machines can run only during specific active length-T intervals and otherwise must remain idle. To see why, create "dummy" jobs for each time step of each inactive machine, where each dummy job is constrained to run in its time step. Given the EDF schedule, we can permute the jobs among machines without changing their running time to create the proper intervals.

Optimal Single-Machine Algorithm

Although EDF always finds a feasible schedule, it may not minimize calibrations. We use EDF as a subroutine in another algorithm that we call *Lazy-Binning*. Lazy-Binning delays the start of an interval for as long as possible, until delaying it further would make it impossible to find a feasible schedule.

Before giving the algorithm, we define the notion of a *push*.

DEFINITION 3. *A push is a move of an interval from time t to $t + 1$. This may mean that later intervals on the same machine are recursively pushed, so that no two intervals overlap.*

Algorithm 1 Lazy-Binning

1: **for** Each time step t until all jobs are scheduled **do**
2:     **if** No working interval that contains time t **then**
3:         Run EDF starting at time step $t + 1$
4:         **if** EDF cannot find a feasible schedule **then**
5:             Begin a working interval at time t.
6:         **end if**
7:     **else**
8:         Schedule jobs in the current interval using EDF
9:     **end if**
10: **end for**

Lazy-Binning is the algorithm we obtain by performing all feasible pushes.

THEOREM 4. *Lazy-Binning is optimal.*

PROOF. To obtain a contradiction, assume that Lazy-Binning is not optimal. Consider the time $t \geq 0$ when Lazy-Binning first differs from every optimal schedule. In other words, from time 0 to $t - 1$, there exists at least one optimal schedule OPT that matches Lazy-Binning exactly, but no optimal schedule matches Lazy-Binning through time t. Furthermore, assume without loss of generality that OPT uses EDF to schedule jobs within an interval, as Lazy-Binning does. Thus, there are two ways for Lazy-Binning to differ from OPT:

- In Case A, Lazy-Binning starts an interval at time t while OPT remains idle.
- In Case B, Lazy-Binning does not start an interval at time t, OPT does.

We argue that neither of these cases is possible, leading to a contradiction.

Case A: Lazy-Binning starts an interval at time t, while OPT remains idle. This means that EDF failed to find a feasible schedule starting the next interval at time $t+1$ or later. But OPT is a feasible schedule that starts the next interval at time $t + 1$.

Case B: OPT starts an interval at time t, whereas Lazy-Binning remains idle. Consider a schedule OPT′ which has identical intervals to OPT, except that the interval that OPT starts at t is pushed.

OPT′ matches Lazy-Binning until time $t + 1$ so it cannot be an optimal schedule by our definition of t. Since OPT′ uses the same number of intervals as OPT, the cost for the schedule is the same, so it must be that OPT′ is infeasible; it cannot be suboptimal.

Let j be the first job that misses its deadline when EDF schedules jobs in OPT′. Any subsequent intervals that we add will be after j's deadline and cannot make OPT′ feasible. Therefore, j cannot be feasibly scheduled after the push, which means that Lazy-Binning starts an interval at t. □

We thus have an optimal algorithm for the single-machine case, as well as a test to see if a feasible schedule exists.

Lazy-Binning, as stated in Algorithm 1, runs in pseudopolynomial time, but the algorithm is easily modified to run in polynomial time. The issue is that if release times and deadlines have exponential values, Lazy-Binning may iterate through an exponential number of time steps. However, an interval need never start more than n time steps before the deadline of any job, giving a polynomial solution.

Why Adding Machines Does Not Help

We show that if an instance can be feasibly scheduled on one machine, adding more machines does not decrease the cost.

THEOREM 5. *If the ISE instance is feasible for a single machine, the one-machine schedule is optimal*

The following definitions and lemma are used to prove Theorem 5. A **configuration** C for a one-machine scheduling instance is a bit string where the tth bit is 1 if the machine is active at time t, and 0 if the machine is idle. The string indicates when the machine is working, but not which jobs are being executed. We say that a configuration is **feasible** if there exists a feasible schedule corresponding to that configuration.

LEMMA 6. *Consider a feasible one-machine scheduling instance on n jobs, and a feasible configuration C on jobs $1 \ldots n-1$ but not n, and a time t such that $r_n \le t < d_n$.*

If t is idle let $t_R = t$. Otherwise, let t_R be the earliest idle time step after t, and t_L be the latest idle time step before t. Then at least one of the following configurations for jobs $1, \ldots, n$ is feasible:

1. *C_L, which is identical to C except that t_L is an active time step.*
2. *C_R, which is identical to C except that t_R is an active time step.*

PROOF. Suppose that neither configuration is feasible. Let $X = t_R - t_L - 1$ denote the number of time slots between t_L and t_R. Note that this does not include t_L or t_R itself.

Because neither configuration is feasible, $r_n > t_L$ and $d_n \le t_R$. If this were not the case, job n could be scheduled in t_L or t_R, making C_L or C_R feasible, respectively.

Let EDF[C] denote the schedule obtained by assigning jobs to the active times in configuration C using EDF. Consider the time slots between t_L and t_R in EDF[C]. They are all full, so there must be X jobs running in these time steps; call this set of jobs J_X. There exists some job $i \in J_X$ such that $r_i \le t_L$ or $d_i > t_R$. Otherwise, $J_X \cup \{n\}$ is a set of $X + 1$ jobs that must be executed in X time steps, which is impossible in a feasible schedule on one machine. Let t_i be the time when i is scheduled in EDF[C]. Assume without loss of generality that i can be scheduled in t_R (if not analyze the mirror image of the schedule where time flows backwards and release times and deadlines trade roles).

There are three cases for t_i:
- Case 1: $t_L < r_n \le t_i < d_n \le t_R$.
- Case 2: $d_n \le t_i < t_R$.

Figure 1: Case 1 from the proof of Lemma 6. Job i can be scheduled in t_R, and job n can be scheduled in t_i where i was previously.

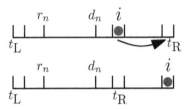

Figure 2: Case 2 from the proof of Lemma 6. Job i can be scheduled in t_R. Job n cannot be feasibly scheduled, but after a finite number of Case 2 instances we must get Case 1, when job n can be scheduled. The top of the figure depicts the schedule before the exchanges (denoted by arrows), and the bottom depicts the schedule after.

- Case 3: $t_L < t_i < r_n$.

The first two cases are shown in Figures 1 and 2, respectively. We prove that Case 1 means that C_R is feasible, Case 2 leads to a smaller instance of Lemma 6, allowing for a finite number of iterated steps until Case 1 is reached, and Case 3 can never occur. Note that we consider cases in order; Case 2 is only used if Case 1 does not apply, and Case 3 is only used if Cases 1 and 2 do not apply.

Case 1 (Figure 1): Schedule job n in time slot t_i and schedule i in t_R (feasible by definition of i). Keep all other jobs scheduled at the same time as in EDF[C]. Thus, C_R is feasible, contradicting our assumption.

Case 2 (Figure 2): Schedule i in t_R. Create a new configuration C' which is the same as C except time slot t_R is set to 1 and t_i is set to 0. Now C' is a new instance of Lemma 6 where t_i becomes the new t_R and t_L stays the same. Each time we hit Case 2, X decreases, so eventually Case 1 must occur (we will show Case 3 never occurs).

Case 3: If there are multiple jobs that meet the conditions for case 3 ($t_L < t_i < r_n$) that can be scheduled in t_R, let i be the one scheduled in the latest time slot in EDF[C].

Consider the set of jobs scheduled strictly between t_i and t_R; we must be able to schedule one in t_i. Otherwise, there are $t_R - t_i - 1$ jobs that cannot be scheduled in t_R or t_i, so each must be scheduled in $t_R - t_i - 1$ time steps. Job n must be scheduled between $r_n > t_i$ and $d_n \le t_R$, so it must be scheduled in one of these time steps as well. Then there are $t_R - t_i$ jobs that must be scheduled in one of $t_R - t_i - 1$ time steps, which cannot be feasible on one processor.

Let i' be the job that can be feasibly scheduled in t_i. This job has deadline before t_R, since we picked the i that can be scheduled

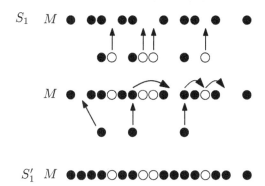

Figure 3: Moving jobs from I to M without increasing the cost. The Type 2 jobs, shown in white, can be moved over immediately, as shown on the first line of the figure. Afterwards, as shown on the second line, the Type 1 jobs shown in black must be moved over using Lemma 6, which may include shuffling some jobs scheduled on M. Finally we obtain S'_1, where all jobs from I are scheduled on M.

in t_R that is scheduled latest in EDF[C]. But then i' comes before i in EDF order, so when EDF reached t_i it would have scheduled i' instead of i. Contradiction. □

PROOF OF THEOREM 5: Given a schedule on multiple machines, we move all intervals one at a time to the first machine M. Each time we move an interval I, we only calibrate M one additional time at most. We diagram our strategy in Figure 3.

Suppose we are moving an interval I from machine M' to machine M. There are two types of jobs in I, those that have a job scheduled at the same time on M, which we call Type 1, and those that do not, which we call Type 2. First, move all jobs in I of Type 2 to M, which produces no infeasibility.

Let S_1 and S'_1 be the schedule of jobs on M before and after the jobs from I are added, respectively. Let t_F and t_L be the first and last time where S_1 and S'_1 differ.

Consider moving a type-1 job that ran at time t on machine M' to machine M. Because this is a type-1 job, machine M is busy at time t. Let t_1 be the last idle interval before t on machine M and let t_2 be the first idle time after t on Machine M. Use the algorithm from Lemma 6 to add a job with desired time t. This algorithm always places a job into either time t_1 or time t_2, extending the block of completely busy time covering time t. Thus the interval from t_F to t_L is completely busy on Machine M in configure S'_1. Therefore S'_1 requires at least $q = \lceil \frac{t_L - t_F + 1}{T} \rceil$ intervals to cover the active jobs in S_1 in from t_F through t_L. Because moving one interval from machine M' moves at most T jobs into the interval $t_F \ldots t_L$, configuration S_1 is inactive for at most T time steps in this interval. Therefore, configuration S_1 requires at least $q - 1$ intervals to cover jobs in $t_F \ldots t_L$ before receiving jobs from interval I.

To cover configuration S'_1, place one new interval at the first idle time in configuration S_1 not covered by an interval in configuration S_1 and push the following intervals as necessary, up to T time units, to eliminate interval overlap. The interval before t_F is covered by intervals as before in configuration S. The time between t_F and t_L is completely covered by q adjacent (touching) intervals.

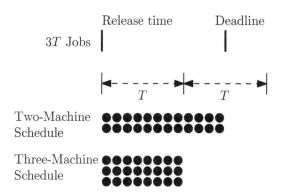

Figure 4: This schedule is feasible on two machines, but optimal on three. There are $3T$ jobs with a release time of zero and a deadline of $3T/2$. On two machines four calibrations are necessary, but with three matchines only three calibrations are necessary.

Each time after t_L that was covered in S_1 is still covered in S'_1. Either the original interval doesn't move, or it is pushed. But if an interval is pushed, then it is part of a set of adjacent intervals extending forward at least to t_F. Thus anything covered by the pushed interval is still covered by the new set of intervals. □

Theorem 5 does not extend to instances that require at least two machines for feasibility. With more machines, it is no longer true that using the minimum number of machines gives the optimal number of intervals. Consider an instance with kT jobs released at time 0 with common deadline $1.5T$, $k > 2$. These can be run on k machines with k intervals from 0 to T, but require $k + 1$ intervals on $k - 1$ machines. Figure 4 illustrates $k = 3$. Note that for $k = 2$, it is not feasible to go down to a single machine. By using this structure repeatedly, we see that removing a machine may increase the number of intervals by more than one.

3. ISE ON MULTIPLE MACHINES

We first characterize the structure of optimal solutions to the ISE problem on multiple machines. We then give a 2-approximation algorithm. We describe conditions under which our algorithms find optimal solutions.

Round Robin Machine Assignment

Let $\mathcal{I} = (I_1, I_2, \ldots, I_N)$ be a sequence of intervals, a partial solution for a set of jobs, ordered by increasing start time. Ties are broken consistently. For our multiple-machine algorithm, ties can be broken by interval creation time, since the algorithm is incremental. Without loss of generality, no two intervals in $\mathcal{I}$ on the same machine have start times within T of each other.

Each interval $I_j \in \mathcal{I}$ is scheduled on some machine P_j. Assigning intervals to machines can be done using a round-robin method for any feasible schedule.

LEMMA 7. *Given a feasible schedule S on P machines, there exists a schedule having the same cost and the same assignments of jobs to intervals where $P_j \equiv j \pmod{P}$.*

PROOF. We use an inductive argument on $N = |\mathcal{I}|$, the number of intervals. The lemma is true for $N = 1$, where we can place the first interval on the first machine.

Suppose we have legally placed the first k intervals. Let t denote the time when I_{k+1} begins. If scheduling I_{k+1} on machine $(k+1)$

(mod P) is not feasible, there exists another interval I_c scheduled at time t_c on P_{k+1} such that $t - T < t_c \leq t$. Since all previous intervals are scheduled using round-robin, there are $P - 1$ intervals starting between times t_c and t. Each of these must also be scheduled at or before t and after $t - T$, so in total there are $P+1$ intervals that must be scheduled in that range. Since there are P processors, two of the intervals must be scheduled concurrently on the same machine, which is infeasible. This contradicts the assumption that the schedule of the first k intervals is feasible. $\square$

Lemma 7 means that our algorithm need not explicitly determine an assignment of intervals to machines.

Our algorithm returns a sequence of interval start times. Given this sequence, we assign intervals to machines using round robin and schedule jobs within intervals using EDF.

Before proceeding, we further specify how EDF breaks ties.

INVARIANT 8. *When EDF removes job j from the priority queue to run at time step t, there may be multiple machines on which j could run. EDF breaks ties by assigning j to the first interval $I \in \mathcal{I}$ that does not yet have a job assigned at time slot t (but contains time slot t).*

Characterization of Pushes

When there are multiple machines, intervals can overlap provide they are on different machines. This leads to more subtlety in how we characterize a push.

DEFINITION 9. *A **push** is a move of an interval $I \in \mathcal{I}$ from time t to $t + 1$ that may recursively push later intervals in order to maintain the following:*
1. *The ordering of intervals in $\mathcal{I}$ does not change. Thus, any other interval that starts at t and is ordered after I in $\mathcal{I}$ is also pushed.*
2. *The intervals on each processor are nonoverlapping. Thus, any interval that starts at $t + T$ on the same processor as I is also pushed.*

Suppose the push of an interval results in a new set of intervals $\mathcal{I}'$ and let t be the latest start time of any interval in $\mathcal{I}'$. This push is *feasible* for an instance of jobs if by augmenting $\mathcal{I}'$ by zero or more intervals, each starting at time t or later, all jobs can be feasibly scheduled.

We categorize feasible pushes of the last currently-scheduled interval into four cases. Because we only consider pushing the last interval, we do not need to worry about cascades of pushes. There may be jobs in J that cannot be scheduled in any of the intervals.

DEFINITION 10. *Each feasible push of the last interval I fits one of four cases. When I is pushed, there may exist some job in I before the push that EDF no longer schedules after the push; denote this job j_{out}. Similarly, there may exist some job not scheduled before the push that EDF schedules after the push; denote this job j_{in}.*
- *Case 1: There exists no job j_{out}.*
- *Case 2: There exists a job j_{out} but no job j_{in}.*
- *Case 3: Job j_{out} is after j_{in} in EDF order.*
- *Case 4: Job j_{out} is before j_{in} in EDF order.*

Framework for Optimal Solutions

We extend Lazy-Binning to multiple machines.

DEFINITION 11. *A **push algorithm** repeatedly creates a new interval at the end of $\mathcal{I}$ and then pushes that interval. The algorithm*

- *performs all Case-1 and Case-3 pushes,*
- *never performs an infeasible push, and*
- *has the flexibility to choose which Case-2 and Case-4 pushes to perform.*

Once the algorithm stops pushing the interval, if there are remaining unscheduled jobs, the algorithm creates a new interval and begins pushing again.

At intermediate steps of a push algorithm, EDF assigns jobs to intervals only temporarily. EDF may assign some job j to some interval, but when an interval is pushed or a new interval is added to $\mathcal{I}$, re-running EDF may assign j to a different interval.

When $P = 1$, all feasible pushes are Case 1 and Case 3, so Lazy-Binning is a push algorithm. Theorem 4 proves a push algorithm is optimal for $P = 1$. Theorem 18 shows that an optimal push algorithm always exists for any number of processors.

Algorithm 2 Push Algorithm

1: $t \leftarrow 0$
2: **while** Not all jobs are scheduled **do**
3:     Remove all assignments of jobs to intervals
4:     **if** t is contained in P or more intervals **then**
5:         $t \leftarrow$ next time with $\leq P - 1$ intervals
6:     **end if**
7:     Create a new interval I at t
8:     Schedule jobs in all intervals with EDF
9:     **while** Pushing I is Case 1 or Case 3 **do**
10:         Push I
11:         $t \leftarrow t + 1$
12:     **end while**
13:     Perform 0 to T Case-2 or Case-4 pushes on I
14: **end while**

LEMMA 12. *A push of an interval I starting at t is of type Case 2 or Case 4 if and only if*
1. *before this push there is a $t_f \leq t + T$ such that jobs are scheduled in all calibrated time slots between t and t_f*
2. *each of these jobs is due no later than t_f, and*
3. *the push is feasible.*

The smallest such t_f has the property that $t_f - t \geq 2$ and at least two jobs are due exactly at t_f.

PROOF. We first explain why $t_f - t$ must be greater than 1. If $t_f - t = 1$ then there exists a job j that must be scheduled at time t, the first time step of I before the push. Scheduling j later would miss its deadline. Thus after the push, when I starts at $t + 1$, EDF does not schedule j in I. By Invariant 8, EDF schedules in the earliest possible interval in $\mathcal{I}$, so if j could be feasibly scheduled in an earlier interval it would be scheduled there before the push. Thus, j cannot be scheduled in an interval before I in $\mathcal{I}$. All later intervals must also start after the deadline of j by Definition 9, so j cannot be scheduled there either. Thus, if $f = 1$ the push is infeasible.

($\Leftarrow$) If these jobs do exist, there must be a j_{out}, because after we push I forward there are more jobs that must run between t and t_f than there are calibrated time steps between times t and t_f. The push cannot be Case 3 because before the push, any jobs released by time $t + T$ that precede j_{out} in EDF order would have been scheduled before j_{out} and they still will be after the push. If j_{in} is released at $t + T$, its deadline is at least $t + T + 1$. This is after j_{out} because j_{out} has deadline no later than $t_f \leq t + T$.

($\Rightarrow$) We now show that if there is a Case-2 or Case-4 push, such a t_f must exist. Let t_f be the deadline of j_{out}. We must have $t_f \leq t +$

T because if j_{out} could be scheduled at $t + T$, it could be scheduled in I after the push, ruling out Case 2. In Case 4, j_{out} is replaced in the set of scheduled jobs by a job later in EDF order. That would not happen if j_{out} could be feasibly scheduled in the new set of intervals.

After the push, all Y calibrated time slots from t to t_f must contain jobs since j_{out} cannot be scheduled. The configuration after the push is the same as before except that the slot in I at time t is replaced by a slot at time $t + T$. The EDF schedule is the same up to the slot at time t that is removed. This is the last slot in time t since I is the last interval. If there is no job in that slot, then the rest of the schedule can run as before and there is no j_{out}, which contradicts the type of push. The job j_b that ran at time t in I must compete with newly-released jobs at time $t + 1$. Some may have earlier deadlines than j_b so j_b may not recieve the very next slot. If j_b is never scheduled, it is j_{out} and all slots are full through t_f. Otherwise j_b is scheduled at some time $t < t_b \leq t_f$. By the same arguments as above, that slot must have held a job before the push. This job is either j_{out}, delayed by other jobs till past its deadline, or it displaces another till the cascade finally ends with the real j_{out}. All slots are then full until j_{out} fails to meet its deadline at time t_f.

All Y jobs the run between t and t_f in the pushed schedule also ran between t and t_f before the push. All jobs affected by the push (including j_{out}) ran no earlier than time t before the push. Every job in this set runs no earlier after the push (most at the same time except those involved in the cascade). All finish by t_f since only j_{out} was pushed later (to failure). Job j_{out} also ran before t_f before the push, since t_f is job j_{out}'s deadline. Thus, there were $Y + 1$ jobs running in the $Y + 1$ slots between time t and t_f before the push.

None of the $Y + 1$ jobs just described has a deadline later than t_f. Consider the discussion above about how the push affects the schedule. All jobs scheduled between times $t + 1$ and t_b, when the displaced job j_b is finally scheduled, had deadlines no larger than job j_b's deadline. This is because j_b was scheduled later by EDF. Job j_c, displaced by j_b, has a deadline no earlier than j_b's deadline and no earlier than the deadline for any job scheduled between t_b and l_c. Thus the displaced jobs have monotonically increasing deadlines and the current displaced job has a deadline no smaller than that of any job schedule since time t. Thus, job j_{out} has deadline no smaller than that of any job that ran between t and t_f.

We now show that at least two jobs are due exactly at the smallest t_f. Consider the smallest t_f. Because $t_f - t > 1$, there is at least one job scheduled at time $t_f - 1$ among the Y jobs described above (in interval I, for example). There is at least one job scheduled before $t_f - 1$ due after $t_f - 1$; otherwise $t_f - 1$ would satisfy the definition for t_f, violating the assumption that this is the smallest t_f. All jobs scheduled at $t_f - 1$ are due at t_f. There must be at least one such job in interval I. Thus, there are at least two jobs due at t_f. $\square$

COROLLARY 13. *Every push algorithm does no more than T Case-2 or Case-4 pushes on any interval.*

PROOF. Since there exists a job in I with deadline no later than t_f, by definition of the j_{out} for the push, I cannot be pushed past t_f. Otherwise that job could not be feasibly scheduled. Since $t_f \leq T$ the lemma follows. $\square$

LEMMA 14. *If intervals are added to a schedule, EDF schedules all jobs no later than without the added intervals.*

PROOF. Let S and S' be the schedule before and after the intervals are added. Assume the contrary: there exists a job j that is scheduled later in S' than in S. Let j be the first such job in EDF order and let t be the time when j is scheduled in S. When EDF reaches t in S', there must be some job j' before j in EDF order that has not been scheduled (otherwise EDF would schedule j). But j' must have already been scheduled when EDF reached t in S (otherwise EDF would schedule j' at t in S). Then j' is scheduled later in S' than in S, which contradicts our definition of j. $\square$

LEMMA 15. *Consider a Case-1 or Case-3 push of an interval I. If we remove any set of jobs J' from J, this will still be a Case-1 or Case-3 push.*

PROOF. It is immediate that removing jobs can never result in infeasibility.

We now show that removing jobs cannot cause a push to become Case 2 or Case 4. Assume the contrary, that the push of interval I at time t becomes Case 2 or Case 4 after removing J'. By Lemma 12, there must be some time step t_f where each calibrated time slot between t and t_f is running a job that must be scheduled before t_f. In each time slot, removing J' can only cause a job with a later deadline to be scheduled by EDF. Then before J' is removed, all calibrated time slots between t and t_f were already active with jobs with potentially earlier deadlines. Then this was a Case-2 or Case-4 push initially, leading to a contradiction. $\square$

LEMMA 16. *Performing Case-1 and Case-3 pushes can never increase the number of calibrations. That is, there is always an optimal schedule that performs a Case-1 or Case-3 push whenever one is available during the incremental schedule construction.*

PROOF. To obtain a contradiction, assume the contrary: no optimal schedule performs all available Case-1 and Case-3 pushes. Let OPT be the schedule that performs the most Case-1 and Case-3 pushes. We show that we can obtain a schedule that performs one more Case-1 or Case-3 push without increasing the cost, reaching a contradiction.

A Case-1 or Case-3 push is only defined on the last interval placed so far while we are making the schedule, so we refer to the push as Case 1 or Case 3 if the push is Case 1 or Case 3 with subsequent intervals removed. That is, EDF schedules jobs from the beginning after this removal to determine the case of the push.

We show that we can feasibly schedule all jobs in OPT after another Case-1 or Case-3 push on some interval I without increasing the number of intervals. Let t be the start time of the first interval I_1 in OPT that did not have all Case-1 or Case-3 pushes applied. So a push on I_1 is Case 1 or 3. Let I be the last interval started at time t. A push on I must also be Case 1 or 3. If it were Case 2 or 4, then by Lemma 12 there must be a time t_f before which all calibrated time slots must contain jobs with deadlines before t_f. But since EDF schedules in time slots in order by interval, all jobs in time slots before t_f in I_1 must also have deadlines before t_f. This means I_1 is Case 2 or 4, which contradicts our definition. Thus pushing I is Case 1 or 3. Furthermore, all subsequent intervals in OPT start at $t + 1$ or later, so pushing interval I preserves the ordering of the starting times of the intervals.

Let t be the time when I starts in OPT. For now, assume that all later intervals in OPT start strictly later than t. We will consider the case where one starts at t later in this proof.

We set the stage for an exchange argument. Schedule all jobs in OPT using EDF. There is a (possibly empty) set of jobs J' that are (1) scheduled between times t and $t + T - 1$ inclusive, and (2) scheduled in an interval after I in OPT. Figuratively, we remove these jobs and set their time slots as inactive. What we really do is peg these jobs to these time slots for our exchange, so that their positions in the schedule are not determined by rerunning EDF.

Perform the push on I in OPT with J' removed; now we have a sequence of intervals OPT'. When I was the last interval placed so far, the push was a Case-1 or Case-3 push. Now define j_{out} and j_{in} as in Definition 10. By Lemma 15, job j_{out}, if it exists, is released before j_{in} and has a deadline after j_{in} in EDF order. To summarize, j_{out} and j_{in} are defined, assuming that we run the schedule only allocating intervals up to I.

When we transform OPT into OPT$'$, we push I, and run EDF on OPT$'$ ignoring the jobs in J' and their time slots. Interval I ends at $t + T$. Let j'_{out} be a job scheduled before $t + T$ (in any interval) in OPT but after $t + T$ and not in I in OPT$'$; let j'_{in} be any job scheduled in an interval after $t + T$ in OPT but before $t + T$ or in I in OPT$'$.

Then j'_{in} is j_{in} and j'_{out} is j_{out} if it exists. This is because when I was the last interval, the push was Case 1 or Case 3. After adding subsequent intervals, none of the jobs scheduled in I are scheduled later than $t+T$, nor will a later job be scheduled in I or earlier than $t + T$.

Now we exchange jobs to show that OPT$'$ is feasible. We schedule the intervals up to the pushed I according to (the new) EDF. We schedule the jobs strictly after the interval I ends according the old EDF, except that in the slot where j'_{in} used to be, we replace that with j'_{out}. We keep the jobs J' exactly where they were before.

Then we have performed an extra Case-1 or Case-3 push of I without increasing the cost of the schedule, contradicting our assumption that we have the OPT with the most Case-3 pushes.

As described, this exchange argument leaves out an important detail. This argument applies when interval I has a gap before the next interval on the same processor. If there is no gap, that is, the two intervals are adjacent, then we need to adjust our argument slightly. A simple adjustment is just to view the adjacent intervals as one bigger interval and then to define the j'_{out} where j'_{in} according to this superinterval. □

LEMMA 17. *A set of k Case-2 pushes on an interval I can only be a part of an optimal push algorithm if, after the Case-2 pushes are performed, the next push would be a Case-4 push.*

PROOF. We will show that no job in J can be scheduled in the newly-calibrated time slots after the Case-2 pushes. Let J_I be the set of jobs feasibly scheduled by EDF in the first I intervals, before I is pushed. Let J'_I be the jobs that cannot be feasibly scheduled, so $J'_I = J \setminus J_I$. Since the pushes are Case 2, none of the jobs in J'_I can be scheduled in I after the Case-2 pushes on I. Adding subsequent intervals can only cause jobs to be scheduled earlier by Lemma 14, so no job in J_I is scheduled at a later point after we add intervals later than I in $\mathcal{I}$. Thus, no job in either J'_I or J_I can be scheduled in the newly-calibrated time slots.

By Lemma 12, after a Case-2 push, any further feasible pushes on the interval are Case 2 or Case 4.

Thus, any newly calibrated time slots due to the push remain inactive, and the pushes cannot decrease the cost of the remaining schedule unless there is a later Case-4 push. □

THEOREM 18. *There exists a sequence of Case-2 and Case-4 pushes such that the corresponding push algorithm is optimal.*

PROOF. This proof generalizes Theorem 4. All Case-1 pushes are identical to the single-machine case, and can still always occur without added cost. We show that Case-3 pushes never add to cost in Lemma 16. The remainder of the argument proceeds as in Theorem 4. □

2-Approximation Algorithm

We now give a 2-approximation algorithm (Algorithm 3). Algorithm 3 is not a push algorithm, though it has structural similarities. Observe that the algorithm also becomes Lazy-Binning if $P = 1$.

Algorithm 3 pushes intervals similarly to a push-algorithm. It never performs an infeasible push and performs all Case-1 and Case-3 pushes of each interval I. Whenever it sees an opportunity for an interval I to have a Case-4 push or a series of Case-2 pushes followed by a Case-4 push, Algorithm 3, instead, creates another interval I' right after I. These extra intervals are ignored for the purpose of determining the case of a push; otherwise the pushed interval may not be the last one scheduled. Like Lazy-Binning, this algorithm is pseudopolynomial as written. If release times and deadlines have exponential values, Algorithm 3 may iterate through an exponential number of time steps. However, an interval need never start more than n time steps before the deadline of any job. Incorporating this restriction makes Algorithm 3 run in polynomial time.

Algorithm 3 Lazy-Binning on Multiple Machines

1: $t \leftarrow 0; I \leftarrow \emptyset$
2: **while** Not all jobs are scheduled **do**
3:      Remove all assignments of jobs to intervals
4:      **if** P or more intervals overlap with I **then**
5:          $t \leftarrow$ next time with $\leq P - 1$ intervals
6:      **end if**
7:      Create a new interval I at t
8:      **while** Pushing I is Case 1 or Case 3 **do**
9:          Push I
10:          $t \leftarrow t + 1$
11:      **end while**
12:      $t' \leftarrow t$
13:      **while** Pushing I from t' is Case 2 **do**
14:          $t' \leftarrow t' + 1$
15:      **end while**
16:      **if** Pushing I is Case 4 **then**
17:          Create another interval at $t + T$
18:      **end if**
19: **end while**

LEMMA 19. *The set of jobs scheduled in the first i intervals of any push algorithm A can be feasibly scheduled after i rounds of Algorithm 3 (a round refers to an iteration of the while loop in Step 2).*

PROOF. By Corollary 13, any time when a time slot is calibrated in A's schedule, the corresponding time slot is also calibrated in Algorithm 3's schedule. Thus, for the first i intervals, we can copy the assignments of jobs to machines and times from A directly to time slots calibrated by Algorithm 3, giving a feasible schedule. □

COROLLARY 20. *Algorithm 3 gives a solution with cost no more than twice optimal, i.e. it is a 2-approximation.*

COROLLARY 21. *Algorithm 3 is optimal if all deadlines are distict.*

PROOF. From Lemma 12, a Case-4 push occurs only when multiple jobs have the same deadline. Thus, if no two jobs have the same deadline, Algorithm 3 adds no extra intervals and gives an optimal solution. □

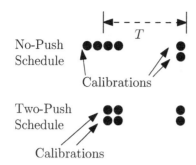

Figure 5: An example showing that both Case-2 and Case-4 pushes are sometimes necessary to obtain an optimal solution. This is also an example where Algorithm 3 gives a solution that is 3/2 times optimal. Four jobs have release time 0 and deadline 4. Two jobs have release time $2+T$ and deadline $3+T$. Algorithm 3 gives the solution shown in the top of the figure with a cost of three. Pushing the first interval twice (first a Case-2, then a Case-4 push) gives the solution shown in the bottom of the figure, with a cost of 2.

LEMMA 22. *Algorithm 3 is no better than a 3/2-approximation.*

PROOF. Consider an ISE instance with four jobs that have release time 0 and deadline 4, and two jobs that have release time $T + 2$ and deadline $T + 3$; see Figure 5. Algorithm 3 gives a solution with three intervals. However, the optimal solution pushes the first interval twice (a Case-2 and a Case-4 push) and gives a solution with two intervals. □

4. CONCLUSION

The complexity of the ISE problem with unit-sized jobs on multiple machines remains open. We suspect that the analysis of Algorithm 3 can be tightened, given that it performs better than twice optimal on all instances we have constructed.

As a next step we hope to generalize our model to capture more aspects of the actual ISE problem. For example, machines may not be identical, and calibrations may require machine time. Moreover, some jobs may not have unit size. We hope that efficient constant-factor approximations are still possible on more general instances of the ISE problem.

5. REFERENCES

[1] New integrated stockpile evaluation program to better ensure weapons stockpile safety, security, reliability, March 2006. http://www.sandia.gov/LabNews/060331.html.

[2] P. Baptiste. Scheduling unit tasks to minimize the number of idle periods: a polynomial time algorithm for offline dynamic power management. In *Proc. 17th Annual ACM-SIAM Symposium on Discrete Algorithms (SODA)*, pages 364–367, 2006.

[3] J. Blazewicz, J.K. Lenstra, and A.H.G. Rinnooy Kan. Scheduling subject to resource constraints: classification and complexity. *Discrete Applied Mathematics*, 5(1):11–24, 1983.

[4] P. Brucker. *Scheduling Algorithms*. Springer, New York, 2007.

[5] M.I. Dessouky, B.J. Lageweg, J.K. Lenstra, and S.L. van de Velde. Scheduling identical jobs on uniform parallel machines. *Statistica Neerlandica*, 44(3):115–123, 1990.

[6] M.M. Dessouky. Scheduling identical jobs with unequal ready times on uniform parallel machines to minimize the maximum lateness. *Computers and Industrial Engineering*, 34(4):793–806, 1998.

[7] M.M. Dessouky, M.I. Dessouky, and S.K. Verma. Flowshop scheduling with identical jobs and uniform parallel machines. *European Journal of Operational Research*, 109(3):620–631, 1998.

[8] M.R. Garey and D.S. Johnson. Complexity results for multiprocessor scheduling under resource constraints. *SIAM Journal on Computing*, 4(4):397–411, 1975.

[9] R.L. Graham, E.L. Lawler, J.K. Lenstra, and A.H.G. Rinnooy Kan. Optimization and approximation in deterministic sequencing and scheduling: a survey. *Annals of Discrete Mathematics*, 5(2):287–326, 1979.

[10] J.R. Jackson. Scheduling a production line to minimize maximum tardiness. Technical report, Management Science Research Project Research Report 43, University of California, Los Angeles, 1955.

[11] D. Karger, C. Stein, and J. Wein. Scheduling algorithms. *CRC Handbook of Computer Science*, 1997.

[12] W. Kern and W.N. Nawijn. Scheduling multi-operation jobs with time lags on a single machine. In *Twente Workshop on Graphs and Combinatorial Optimization*, pages 81–86, 1991.

[13] B.J. Lageweg, E.L. Lawler, J.K. Lenstra, and A.H.G. Rinnooy Kan. Computer aided complexity classification of deterministic scheduling problems. Technical Report BW 138/81, Stichting Mathematisch Centrum, Amsterdam, 1981.

[14] Y. Lin and W. Li. Parallel machine scheduling of machine-dependent jobs with unit-length. *European Journal of Operational Research*, 156(1):261–266, 2004.

[15] B. Simons and M. Sipser. On scheduling unit-length jobs with multiple release time/deadline intervals. *Operations Research*, 32(1):80–88, 1984.

[16] J.A. Stankovic, M. Spuri, M. Di Natale, and G.C. Buttazzo. Implications of classical scheduling results for real-time systems. *Computer*, 28(6):16–25, 1995.

[17] J. D. Ullman. Polynomial complete scheduling problems. *ACM SIGOPS Operating Systems Review*, 7(4):96–101, January 1973.

[18] W. Yu. *The two-machine flow shop problem with delays and the one-machine total tardiness problem*. PhD thesis, Department of Mathematics and Computer Science, Technische Universiteit Eindhoven, 1996.

[19] W. Yu, H. Hoogeveen, and J.K. Lenstra. Minimizing makespan in a two-machine flow shop with delays and unit-time operations is NP-hard. *Journal of Scheduling*, 7(5):333–348, 2004.

Non-Monetary Fair Scheduling — A Cooperative Game Theory Approach

Piotr Skowron
Faculty of Mathematics, Informatics and Mechanics
University of Warsaw
Warsaw, Poland
p.skowron@mimuw.edu.pl

Krzysztof Rzadca
Faculty of Mathematics, Informatics and Mechanics
University of Warsaw
Warsaw, Poland
krzadca@mimuw.edu.pl

ABSTRACT

We consider a multi-organizational system in which each organization contributes processors to the global pool but also jobs to be processed on the common resources. The fairness of the scheduling algorithm is essential for the stability and even for the existence of such systems (as organizations may refuse to join an unfair system).

We consider on-line, non-clairvoyant scheduling of sequential jobs. The started jobs cannot be stopped, canceled, preempted, or moved to other processors. We consider identical processors, but most of our results can be extended to related or unrelated processors.

We model the fair scheduling problem as a cooperative game and we use the Shapley value to determine the ideal fair schedule. In contrast to the current literature, we do not use money to assess the relative utilities of jobs. Instead, to calculate the contribution of an organization, we determine how the presence of this organization influences the performance of other organizations. Our approach can be used with arbitrary utility function (e.g., flow time, tardiness, resource utilization), but we argue that the utility function should be strategy resilient. The organizations should be discouraged from splitting, merging or delaying their jobs. We present the unique (to within a multiplicative and additive constants) strategy resilient utility function.

We show that the problem of fair scheduling is NP-hard and hard to approximate. However, for unit-size jobs, we present a fully polynomial-time randomized approximation scheme (FPRAS). We also show that the problem parametrized with the number of organizations is fixed parameter tractable (FPT). In cooperative game theory, the Shapley value is considered in many contexts as "the" fair solution. Our results show that, although the problem for the large number of organizations is computationally hard, this solution concept can be used in scheduling (for instance, as a benchmark for measuring fairness of heuristic algorithms).

Categories and Subject Descriptors

C.1.4 [**Computer Systems Organization**]: Processor Architectures—*Parallel Architectures*; F.2.2 [**Theory of Computation**]: Analysis of Algorithms and Problem Complexity—*Nonnumerical Algorithms and Problems*

Keywords

fair scheduling, cooperative game theory, Shapley value, cooperation, strategy resistance, approximation algorithms, inapproximability, fairness

1. INTRODUCTION

In multi-organizational systems, participating organizations give access to their local resources; in return their loads can be processed on other resources. The examples of such systems include PlanetLab, grids (Grid5000, EGEE), or organizationally distributed storage systems [16]. There are a few incentives for federating into consortia: the possibility of decreasing the costs of management and maintenance (one large system can be managed more efficiently than several smaller ones), but also the willingness to utilize resources more efficiently. Peak loads can be offloaded to remote resources. Moreover, organizations can access specialized resources or the whole platform (which permits e.g. testing on a large scale).

In the multi-organizational and multi-user systems fairness of the resource allocation mechanisms is equally important as its efficiency. Efficiency of BitTorrent depends on users' collaboration, which in turn requires the available download bandwidth to be distributed fairly [32]. Fairness has been also discussed in storage systems [4,14,15,17,40,41,44] and computer networks [42]. In scheduling, for instance, a significant part of the description of Maui [19], perhaps the most common cluster scheduler, focuses on the fair-share mechanism. Nevertheless there is no universal agreement on the meaning of fairness; next, we review approaches most commonly used in literature: distributive fairness and game theory.

In distributive fairness organizations are ensured a fraction of the resources according to *predefined (given) shares*. The share of an organization may depend on the perceived importance of the workload, payments [4,14,15,40]; or calculated to satisfy (predefined) service level agreements [17,21,44]. The literature on distributive fairness describes algorithms distributing resources according to the given shares, but does not describe how the shares should be set. In scheduling, distributive fairness is implemented through fair queuing mechanism: YFQ [1], SFQ and FSFQ [10,20], or their modifications [4,14,15,17,40,41,44,45].

A different approach is to optimize directly the performance (the utility) of users, rather than just the allocated resources. Kostreva el al. [23] proposes an axiomatic characterization of fairness based on multi-objective optimization; Rzadca et al. [34] applies this concept to scheduling in a multi-organizational system. Inoie et al. [18] proposes a similar approach for load balancing: a fair solution must be Pareto-optimal and the revenues of the players must be proportional to the revenues in Nash equilibrium.

While distributive fairness might be justified in case of centrally-managed systems (e.g. Amazon EC2 or a single HPC center), in our opinion it is inappropriate for consortia (e.g., PlanetLab or non-commercial scientific systems like Grid5000 or EGEE) in which there is no single "owner" and the participating organizations may take actions (e.g. rescheduling jobs on their resources, adding local resources, or isolating into subsystems). In case of such systems the shares of the participating organizations should depend both on their workload and on the owned resources; intuitively an organization that contributes many "useful" machines should be favored; similarly an organization that has only a few jobs.

Game theory is an established method for describing outcomes of decisions made by agents. If agents may form binding agreements, *cooperative game theory* studies the stability of resulting agreements (coalitions and revenues). There are well studied concepts of stability [30], like the *core*, the *kernel*, the *nucleolus*, the *stable set* or the *bargaining set*. The Shapley value [35] characterizes what is a *fair* distribution of the total revenue of the coalition between the participating agents.

The Shapley value has been used in scheduling theory but all the models we are aware of use the concept of money. The works of Carroll et at. [3], Mishra et al. [27], Mashayekhy and Grosu [26] and Moulin et al. [28] describe algorithms and the process of forming the coalitions for scheduling. These works assume that each job has a certain *monetary* value for the issuing organization and each organization has its initial monetary budget.

Money may have negative consequences on the stakeholders of resource-sharing consortia. Using (or even mentioning) money discourages people from cooperating [39]. This stays in sharp contrast with the idea behind the academic systems — sharing the infrastructure is a step towards closer cooperation. Additionally, we believe that using money is inconvenient in non-academic systems as well. In many contexts, it is not clear how to valuate the completion of the job or the usage of a resource (especially when workload changes dynamically). We think that the accurate valuation is equally important (and perhaps equally difficult) as the initial problem of fair scheduling. Although auctions [2] or commodity markets [22] have been proposed to set prices, these approaches implicitly require to set the reference value to determine profitability. Other works on *monetary* game-theoretical models for scheduling include [8,9,12,13,31]; monetary approach is also used for other resource allocation problems, e.g. network bandwidth allocation [43]. However, none of these works describes how to valuate jobs and resources.

In a non-monetary approach proposed by Dutot el al. [6] the jobs are scheduled to minimize the global performance metric (the makespan) with an additional requirement — the utility of each player cannot be worse than if the player would act alone. Such approach ensures the stability of the system against actions of any single user (it is not profitable for the user to leave the system and to act alone) but not to the formation of sub-coalitions.

In the selfish job model [38] the agents are the jobs that selfishly choose processors on which to execute. Similarly to our model the resources are shared and treated as common good; however, no agent contributes resources.

An alternative to scheduling is to allow jobs to share resources concurrently. In congestion games [5,29,33] the utility of the player using a resource R depends on the number of the players concurrently using R; the players are acting selfishly. Congestion games for divisible load scheduling were analyzed by Grosu and Chronopoulos [11] and Skowron and Rzadca [36].

In this paper we propose fair scheduling algorithms for systems composed of multiple organizations (in contrast to the case of multiple organizations using a system owned by a single entity). We model the organizations, their machines and their jobs as a cooperative game. In this game we do not use the concept of money. When measuring the contribution of the organization O we analyze how the presence of O in the grand coalition influences the completion times of the jobs of all participating organization. This contribution is expressed in the same units as the utility of the organization. In the design of the fair algorithm we use the concept of Shapley value. In contrast to simple cooperative game, in our case the value of the coalition (the total utility of the organizations in this coalition) depends on the underlying scheduling algorithm. This makes the problem of calculating the contributions of the organizations more involved. First we develop algorithms for arbitrary utilities (e.g. resource utilization, tardiness, flow time, etc.). Next we argue that designing the scheduling mechanism itself is not enough; we show that the utility function must be chosen to discourage organizations from manipulating their workloads (e.g. merging or splitting the jobs — similar ideas have been proposed for the money-based models [28]). We present an exponential scheduling algorithm for the strategy resilient utility function. We show that the fair scheduling problem is NP-hard and difficult to approximate. For a simpler case, when all the jobs are unit-size, we present a fully polynomial-time randomized approximation scheme (FPRAS). According to our experiments this algorithm is close to the optimum when used as a heuristics for workloads with different sizes of the jobs.

Our contribution is the following: (i) We derive the definition of the fair algorithm. Intuitively, fairness means that the utility for an organziation is close to its contribution i.e., its Shapley value. (ii) The Shapley value for an organization is derived based on the resources and the jobs the organization contributes — how the presence of the organization influences the processing times of the jobs of all organizations. The Shapley value is computed without any notion of money. (iii) We present an algorithm that computes a fair schedule for an arbitrary utility function (that might be a classical scheduling metric such as flow time, resource allocation, tardiness etc.). (iv) We observe that many utility functions are not strategy resistant, i.e. an organization can affect its utility by e.g. splitting its jobs into smaller pieces. We define the notion of strategy resistance and derive a strategy resistant utility function. (v) We show that the problem of calculating a fair schedule is NP-complete and hard to approximate. However, the problem parametrized by the number of organizations is fixed parameter tractable (FPT).

2. PRELIMINARIES

Organizations, machines, jobs. We consider a system built by a set of independent *organizations* $\mathcal{O} = \{O^{(1)}, O^{(2)}, \ldots O^{(k)}\}$ [6]. Each organization $O^{(u)}$ owns a *computational cluster* consisting of $m^{(u)}$ machines (*processors*) denoted as $M_1^{(u)}, M_2^{(u)}, \ldots M_{m^{(u)}}^{(u)}$ and produces its *jobs*, denoted as $J_1^{(u)}, J_2^{(u)}, \ldots$. Each job $J_i^{(u)}$ has *release time* $r_i^{(u)} \in \mathbb{T}$, where $\mathbb{T}$ is a discrete set of time moments. We consider an on-line problem in which each job is unknown until its release time. We consider a non-clairvoyant model i.e., the job's processing time is unknown until the job completes (hence we do not need to use imprecise [24] run-time estimates). For the sake of simplicity of the presentation we assume that machines are identical, i.e. each job $J_i^{(u)}$ can be executed at any machine and its processing always takes $p_i^{(u)}$ time units; $p_i^{(u)}$ is the *processing time*. Most of the results, however, can be extended to the case of related machines, where $p_i^{(u)}$ is a function of the schedule – the only exception make the results in Section 5.1, where we rely on the assumption that each job processed on any machine takes exactly one time unit. The results even generalize to the case of unrelated machines, however if we assume non-clairvoyant model with unrelated machines (i.e., we do not know the processing times of the jobs on any machine) then we cannot optimize the assignment of jobs to machines.

The jobs are sequential (this is a standard assumption in many scheduling models and, particularly, in the selfish job model [38]; an alternative is to consider the parallel jobs, which we plan to do in the future). Once a job is started, the scheduler cannot preempt it or migrate it to other machine (this assumption is usual in HPC scheduling because of high migration costs). Finally, we assume that the jobs of each individual organization should be started in the order in which they are presented. This allows organizations to have an internal prioritization of their jobs.

Cooperation, schedules. Organizations can cooperate and share their infrastructure; we say that organizations form a *coalition*. Formally, a coalition $\mathcal{C}$ is a subset of the set of all organizations, $\mathcal{C} \subseteq \mathcal{O}$. We also consider a specific coalition consisting of all organizations, which we call a *grand coalition* and denote as $\mathcal{C}_g$ (formally, $\mathcal{C}_g = \mathcal{O}$, but in some contexts we use the notation $\mathcal{C}_g$ to emphasize that we are referring to the set of the organizations that cooperate). A coalition must agree on the schedule of the jobs of its participants. A schedule $\sigma = \bigcup_{(u) \in \mathcal{C}} \bigcup_i \{(J_i^{(u)}, s_i^{(u)}, M(J_i^{(u)}))\}$ is a set of triples; a triple $(J_i^{(u)}, s_i^{(u)}, M(J_i^{(u)}))$ denotes a job $J_i^{(u)}$ started at time moment $s_i^{(u)} \geq r_i^{(u)}$ on machine $M(J_i^{(u)})$. Additionally, a machine executes at most one job at any time moment and each jobs is scheduled exactly once. We often identify a job $J_i^{(u)}$ with a pair $(s_i^{(u)}, p_i^{(u)})$; and a schedule with $\bigcup_{(u)} \bigcup_i \{(s_i^{(u)}, p_i^{(u)})\}$ (we do so for a more compact presentation of our results). The coalition uses all the machines of its participants and schedules consecutive tasks on available machines. We consider only greedy schedules: at any time moment if there is a free machine and a non-empty set of ready, but not scheduled jobs, some job must be assigned to the free machine. Since we do not know neither the characteristics of the future workload nor the duration of the started but not yet completed jobs, any non-greedy policy would be suboptimal. Also, such greedy policies are used in real-world schedulers [19].

Let $\mathfrak{J}$ denote the set of all possible sets of the jobs. An *online scheduling algorithm* (in short a scheduling algorithm) $\mathcal{A}$: $\mathfrak{J} \times \mathbb{T} \to \mathcal{O}$ is an online algorithm that continuously builds a schedule: for a given time moment $t \in \mathbb{T}$ such that there is a free machine in t and a set of jobs released before t but not yet scheduled: $\mathcal{J} \in \mathfrak{J}$, $\mathcal{A}(\mathcal{J}, t)$ returns the organization the task of which should be started. The set of all possible schedules produced by such algorithms is the set of *feasible schedules* and it is denoted by Γ. We recall that in each feasible schedule the tasks of a single organization are started in a FIFO order.

Objectives. We consider a *utility function* $\psi : \Gamma \times \mathcal{O} \times \mathbb{T} \to \mathbb{R}$ that for a given schedule $\sigma \in \Gamma$, an organization $O^{(u)}$, and a time moment t gives the value corresponding to the $O^{(u)}$ organization's satisfaction from a schedule σ until t. The examples of such utility functions that are common in scheduling theory are: flow time, resource utilization, turnaround, etc. Our scheduling algorithms will only use the notions of the utilities and do not require any external payments.

Since a schedule σ is fully determined by a scheduling algorithm $\mathcal{A}$ and a coalition $\mathcal{C}$, we often identify $\psi(\mathcal{A}, \mathcal{C}, O^{(u)}, t)$ with appropriate $\psi(\sigma, O^{(u)}, t)$. Also, we use a shorter notation $\psi^{(u)}(\mathcal{C})$ instead of $\psi(\mathcal{A}, \mathcal{C}, O^{(u)}, t)$ whenever the $\mathcal{A}$ and t are known from the context. We define the *characteristic function* $v : \Gamma \times \mathbb{T} \to \mathbb{R}$

describing the total utility of the organizations from a schedule: $v(\mathcal{A}, \mathcal{C}, t) = \sum_{O^{(u)} \in \mathcal{C}} \psi(\mathcal{A}, \mathcal{C}, O^{(u)}, t)$. As above, we can use an equivalent formulation: $v(\sigma, t) = \sum_{O^{(u)} \in \mathcal{C}} \psi(\sigma, O^{(u)}, t)$, also using a shorter notations $v(\mathcal{C})$ whenever it is possible. Note that the utilities of the organizations $\psi^{(u)}(\mathcal{C})$ constitute a division of the value of the coalition $v(\mathcal{C})$.

3. FAIR SCHEDULING BASED ON THE SHAPLEY VALUE

In this section our goal is to find a scheduling algorithm $\mathcal{A}$ that at each time t ensures a fair distribution of the coalition value $v(\mathcal{C})$ between the organizations. We will denote this desired fair division of the value v as $\phi^{(1)}(v), \phi^{(2)}(v), \ldots, \phi^{(k)}(v)$ meaning that $\phi^{(u)}(v)$ denotes the ideally fair revenue (utility) obtained by organization $O^{(u)}$. The goal of the algorithm is to produce a schedule in which the actual utilities $\psi^{(1)}(\mathcal{C}), \psi^{(2)}(\mathcal{C}), \ldots \psi^{(k)}(\mathcal{C})$ are close to the desired fair division $\phi^{(1)}(v(\mathcal{C})), \phi^{(2)}(v(\mathcal{C})), \ldots, \phi^{(k)}(v(\mathcal{C}))$ (we formalize this in Definitions 3.1 and 3.2).

We would like the values $\phi^{(u)}(v)$ to satisfy the following fairness properties (proposed by Shapley [35]):

1) efficiency: the total value $v(\mathcal{C})$ is distributed:

$$\sum_{O^{(u)} \in \mathcal{C}} \phi^{(u)}(v(\mathcal{C})) = v(\mathcal{C}).$$

2) symmetry: organizations $O^{(u)}$ and $O^{(u')}$ having indistinguishable contributions obtain the same profits:

$$\left(\forall_{\mathcal{C}' \subset \mathcal{C}: O^{(u)}, O^{(u')} \notin \mathcal{C}'} v(\mathcal{C}' \cup \{O^{(u)}\}) = v(\mathcal{C}' \cup \{O^{(u')}\})\right) \Rightarrow$$
$$\left(\phi^{(u)}(v(\mathcal{C})) = \phi^{(u')}(v(\mathcal{C}))\right).$$

3) additivity: for any two characteristic functions v and w and a function $(v+w)$: $\forall_{\mathcal{C}' \subseteq \mathcal{C}} (v+w)(\mathcal{C}') = v(\mathcal{C}') + w(\mathcal{C}')$ we have that $\forall_{\mathcal{C}' \subseteq \mathcal{C}} \forall_u : \phi^{(u)}((v+w)(\mathcal{C})) = \phi^{(u)}(v(\mathcal{C})) + \phi^{(u)}(w(\mathcal{C}))$.
Consider any two independent schedules σ_1 and σ_2 that together form a schedule $\sigma_3 = \sigma_1 \cup \sigma_2$ (σ_1 and σ_2 are independent iff removing any subset of the jobs from σ_1 does not influence the completion time of any job in σ_2 and vice versa). The profit of an organization that participates only in one schedule (say σ_1) must be the same in case of σ_1 and σ_3 (intuitively: the jobs that do not influence the current schedule, also do not influence the current profits). The profit of every organization that participates in both schedules should in σ_3 be the sum of the profits in σ_1 and σ_2. Intuitively: if the schedules are independent then the profits are independent too.

4) dummy: an organization that does not increase the value of any coalition $\mathcal{C}' \subset \mathcal{C}$ gets nothing:

$$\left(\forall_{\mathcal{C}' \subset \mathcal{C}} : v(\mathcal{C}' \cup \{O^{(u)}\}) = v(\mathcal{C}')\right) \Rightarrow \phi^{(u)}(v(\mathcal{C})) = 0.$$

Since the four properties are actually the axioms of the Shapley value [35], they fully determine the single mapping between the coalition values and the profits of organizations (known as the Shapley value). In game theory the Shapley value is considered the classic mechanism ensuring the fair division of the revenue of the coalition. The Shapley value can be computed by the following formula [35]:

$$\phi^{(u)}(v(\mathcal{C})) =$$
$$\sum_{\mathcal{C}' \subseteq \mathcal{C} \setminus \{O^{(u)}\}} \frac{\|\mathcal{C}'\|!(\|\mathcal{C}\| - \|\mathcal{C}'\| - 1)!}{\|\mathcal{C}\|!} (v(\mathcal{C}' \cup \{O^{(u)}\}) - v(\mathcal{C}')) \quad (1)$$

Algorithm 1: Fair algorithm for arbitrary utility function ψ.

Notation:
jobs$[\mathcal{C}][O^{(u)}]$ — list of waiting jobs of organization $O^{(u)}$.
$\phi[\mathcal{C}][O^{(u)}]$ — the contribution of $O^{(u)}$ in $\mathcal{C}$, $\phi^{(u)}(\mathcal{C})$.
$\psi[\mathcal{C}][O^{(u)}]$ — utility of $O^{(u)}$ from being in $\mathcal{C}$, $\psi(\mathcal{C}, O^{(u)})$.
v$[\mathcal{C}]$ — value of a coalition $\mathcal{C}$.
$\sigma[\mathcal{C}]$ — schedule for a coalition $\mathcal{C}$.
FreeMachine (σ, t) — returns true if and only if there is a free machine in σ in time t.

```
1
2   ReleaseJob(O^(u), J):
3   |  for C : O^(u) ∈ C do
4   |  |  jobs[C][O^(u)].push(J)
5
6   Distance(C, O^(u), t):
7   |  old ← σ[C];
8   |  new ← σ[C] ∪ {(jobs[C][O^(u)].first, t)};
9   |  Δψ ← ψ(new, O^(u), t) − ψ(old, O^(u), t);
10  |  return |φ[C][O^(u)] + Δψ/‖C‖ − ψ[C][O^(u)] − Δψ|
11  |  + ∑_{O^(u')} |φ[C][O^(u')] + Δψ/‖C‖ − ψ[C][O^(u')]|;
12
13  SelectAndSchedule(C, t):
14  |  u ← argmin_{O^(u)}(Distance(C, O^(u), t));
15  |  σ[C] ← σ[C] ∪ {(jobs[C][u].first, t)};
16  |  ψ[C][O^(u)] ← ψ(σ[C], O^(u), t);
17
18  UpdateVals(C, t):
19  |  foreach O^(u) ∈ C do
20  |  |  ψ[C][O^(u)] ← ψ(σ[C], O^(u), t);
21  |  |  φ[C][O^(u)] ← 0;
22  |  v[C] ← ∑_{O^(u)} ψ(σ[C], O^(u), t);
23  |  foreach C_sub : C_sub ⊆ C do
24  |  |  foreach O^(u) ∈ C_sub do
25  |  |  |  φ[C][O^(u)] ← φ[C][O^(u)]+
26  |  |  |  (v[C_sub] − v[C_sub \ {O^(u)}])
27  |  |  |  · (‖C_sub‖−1)!(‖C‖−‖C_sub‖)!/‖C‖! ;
28
29  FairAlgorithm(C):
30  |  foreach time moment t do
31  |  |  foreach job J_i^(u) : r_i^(u) = t do
32  |  |  |  ReleaseJob(O_i^(u), J_i^(u));
33  |  |  for s ← 1 to ‖C‖ do
34  |  |  |  foreach C' ⊂ C, such that ‖C'‖ = s do
35  |  |  |  |  UpdateVals(C', t);
36  |  |  |  |  while FreeMachine(σ[C'], t) do
37  |  |  |  |  |  SelectAndSchedule(C', t);
38  |  |  |  |  v[C] ← ∑_{O^(u)} ψ(σ[C], O^(u), t);
```

Let $\mathcal{L}_\mathcal{C}$ denote all orderings of the organizations from the coalition $\mathcal{C}$. Each ordering $\prec_c$ can be associated with a permutation of the set $\mathcal{C}$, thus $\|\mathcal{L}_\mathcal{C}\| = \|\mathcal{C}\|!$. For the ordering $\prec_c \in \mathcal{L}_C$ we define $\prec_c (O^{(i)}) = \{O^{(j)} \in \mathcal{C} : O^{(j)} \prec_c O^{(i)}\}$ as the set of all organizations from $\mathcal{C}$ that precede $O^{(i)}$ in the order $\prec_c$. The Shapley value can be alternatively expressed [30] in the following form:

$$\phi^{(u)}(v(\mathcal{C})) =$$
$$\frac{1}{\|\mathcal{C}\|!} \sum_{\prec_c \in \mathcal{L}_\mathcal{C}} \left(v(\prec_c (O^{(u)}) \cup \{O^{(u)}\}) - v(\prec_c (O^{(u)})) \right). \quad (2)$$

This formulation has an interesting interpretation. Consider the organizations joining the coalition $\mathcal{C}$ in the order $\prec_c$. Each organization $O^{(u)}$, when joining, contributes to the current coalition the value equal to $\left(v(\prec_c (O^{(u)}) \cup \{O^{(u)}\}) - v(\prec_c (O^{(u)})) \right)$. Intuitively, this value measures how the joining organization influences (decreases or increases) the total completion time of the jobs; $\phi^{(u)}(v(\mathcal{C}))$ is the expected contribution to the coalition $\mathcal{C}$, when the expectation is taken over the order in which the organizations join $\mathcal{C}$. Thus, we can identify the ideally fair utilities with the contributions of the organizations. Hereinafter we will call the value $\phi^{(u)}(v(\mathcal{C}))$ (or using a shorter notation $\phi^{(u)}$) as the *contribution* of the organization $O^{(u)}$.

Informally speaking, we would like the utility of each organization ψ to be as close to its contribution ϕ as possible. Ideally, the utilities of the organizations should be equal to the reference fair values, $\forall_u \psi^{(u)}(\mathcal{C}) = \phi^{(u)}(v(\mathcal{C}))$, but our scheduling problem is discrete so an algorithm guaranteeing this property may not exist. Thus, we will call as fair an algorithm that results in utilities close to contributions. We recall that the contribution is defined without a notion of money – the contribution of the organization measures how the presence of this organization affects the completion time of the jobs.

The following definition of a fair algorithm is in two ways recursive. First, we require an algorithm to be fair in all time moments t. Formally, a fair algorithm in time t must also be fair in all previous time moments $t' < t$ (point 1.) [1]. Second, to assess the contribution of the organization to the coalition $\mathcal{C}$ (its Shapley value) we need to know how this organization, when joining, changes the schedule of each subcoalition $\mathcal{C}' \subset \mathcal{C}$. However, to determine the schedule for a subcoalition $\mathcal{C}'$ we need to know how a fair scheduling algorithm works for $\mathcal{C}'$. In other words, to define what is a fair algorithm for a coalition $\mathcal{C}$ we need to know what is a fair algorithm for all subcoalitions $\mathcal{C}' \subset \mathcal{C}$ (point 4.). Finally, assuming we know the fair algorithms for all subcoalitions and we have the contributions of the organizations calculated (point 3.), we look for an algorithm that minimizes the distance between the utilities and the contributions of the organizations (the argmin expression).

Definition 3.1 *Set an arbitrary metric* $\| \cdot \|_d : 2^k \times 2^k \to \mathbb{R}_{\geq 0}$; *and set an arbitrary time moment* $t \in \mathbb{T}$. $\mathcal{A}$ *is a fair algorithm in* t *for coalition* $\mathcal{C}$ *in metric* $\| \cdot \|_d$ *if and only if:*

$$\mathcal{A} \in \text{argmin}_{\mathcal{A}' \in \mathcal{F}(<t)} \|\vec{\phi}(\mathcal{A}', \mathcal{C}, t) - \vec{\psi}(v(\mathcal{A}', \mathcal{C}, t)\|_d \quad , \text{where:}$$

1. $\mathcal{F}(< t)$ *is a set of algorithms fair in each point* $t' < t$; $\mathcal{F}(< 0)$ *is a set of all greedy algorithms,*

2. $\vec{\psi}(v(\mathcal{A}', \mathcal{C})$ *is a vector of utilities* $\langle \psi^{(u)}(v(\mathcal{A}', \mathcal{C})) \rangle$,

3. $\vec{\phi}(\mathcal{A}', \mathcal{C})$ *is a vector of contributions* $\langle \phi^{(u)}(v(\mathcal{A}', \mathcal{C})) \rangle$, *where* $\phi^{(u)}(v(\mathcal{A}', \mathcal{C}))$ *is given by Equation 1,*

4. *In Equation 1, for any* $\mathcal{C}' \subset \mathcal{C}$, $v(\mathcal{C}')$ *denotes* $v(\mathcal{A}_f, \mathcal{C}')$, *where* $\mathcal{A}_f$ *is any fair algorithm for* $\mathcal{C}'$.

---

[1] An alternative to being fair for all $t' < t$ would be to ensure asymptotic fairness; however, our formulation is more responsive and relevant for the online case. We want to avoid the case in which an organization is disfavored in one, possibly long, time period and favored in the next one.

Definition 3.2 *$\mathcal{A}$ is a fair algorithm for coalition $\mathcal{C}$ if and only if it is fair in each time $t \in \mathbb{T}$.*

Further on, we consider algorithms fair in the Manhattan metric (our analysis can be generalized to other distance functions): $\|\vec{v_1}, \vec{v_2}\|_M = \sum_{i=1}^{k} |v_1[i] - v_2[i]|$.

Based on Definition 3.2 we construct a fair algorithm for an arbitrary utility function ψ (Algorithm 1). The algorithm keeps a schedule for every subcoalition $\mathcal{C}' \subset \mathcal{C}$. For each time moment the algorithm complements the schedule starting from the subcoalitions of the smallest size. The values of all smaller coalitions $v[\mathcal{C}_s]$ are used to update the contributions of the organizations (lines 23-27) in the procedure UpdateVals. Before scheduling any job of the coalition $\mathcal{C}'$ the contribution and the utility of each organization in $\mathcal{C}'$ is updated (procedure UpdateVals). If there is a free machine and a set of jobs waiting for execution, the algorithm selects the job according to Definition 3.1, thus it selects the organization that minimizes the distance of the utilities $\vec{\psi}$ to their ideal values $\vec{\phi}$ (procedure SelectAndSchedule). Assuming the first job of the organization $O^{(u)}$ is tentatively scheduled, the procedure Distance computes a distance between the new values of $\vec{\psi}$ and $\vec{\phi}$. The procedure Distance works as follows. Assuming $O^{(u)}$ is selected the value $\Delta\psi$ denotes the increase of the utility of $O^{(u)}$ thanks to scheduling its first waiting job. This is also the increase of the value of the whole coalition. When procedure Distance$(\mathcal{C}, O^{(u)}, t)$ is executed, the schedules (and thus, the values) in time t for all subcoalitions $\mathcal{C}' \subset \mathcal{C}$ are known. The schedule, for coalition $\mathcal{C}$ is known only in time $(t - 1)$, as we have not yet decided which job should be scheduled in t. Thus, scheduling the job will change the schedule (and the value) only for a coalition $\mathcal{C}$. From Equation 1 it follows that if the value $v(\mathcal{C})$ of the coalition $\mathcal{C}$ increases by $\Delta\psi$ and the value of all subcoalitions remains the same, then the contribution $\phi^{(u')}$ of each organization $O^{(u')} \in \mathcal{C}$ to $\mathcal{C}$ will increase by the same value equal to $\Delta\psi/\|\mathcal{C}\|$. Thus, for each organization $O^{(u')} \in \mathcal{C}$ the new contribution of $O^{(u')}$ is $(\phi[\mathcal{C}][O^{(u')}] + \frac{\Delta\psi}{\|\mathcal{C}\|})$. The new utility for each organization $O^{(u')} \in \mathcal{C}$, such that $O^{(u')} \neq O^{(u)}$ is equal to $\psi[\mathcal{C}][O^{(u')}]$. The new utility of the organization $O^{(u)}$ is equal to $(\psi[\mathcal{C}][O^{(u)}] \| + \Delta\psi)$.

Theorem 3.3 *Algorithm 1 is a fair algorithm.*

PROOF. Algorithm 1 is a straightforward implementation of Definition 3.2. □

Proposition 3.4 *In each time moment t the time complexity of Algorithm 1 is $O(\|\mathcal{O}\|(2^{\|\mathcal{O}\|} \sum m^{(u)} + 3^{\|\mathcal{O}\|}))$.*

PROOF. Once the contribution is calculated, each coalition in t may schedule at most $\sum m^{(u)}$ jobs. The time needed for selecting each such a job is proportional to the number of the organizations. Thus, we get the $\|\mathcal{O}\|2^{\|\mathcal{O}\|} \sum m^{(u)}$ part of the complexity. For calculating the contribution of the organization $O^{(u)}$ to the coalition $\mathcal{C}$ the algorithm considers all subsets of $\mathcal{C}$ – there are $2^{\|\mathcal{C}\|}$ such subsets. Since there are $\binom{\|\mathcal{O}\|}{k}$ coalitions of size k, the number of the operations required for calculating the contributions of all organizations is proportional to:

$$\sum_{(u)} \sum_{k=0}^{\|\mathcal{O}\|} \binom{\|\mathcal{O}\|}{k} 2^k = \|\mathcal{O}\| \sum_{k=0}^{\|\mathcal{O}\|} \binom{\|\mathcal{O}\|}{k} 1^{\|\mathcal{O}\|-k} 2^k =$$

$$\|\mathcal{O}\|(1+2)^{\|\mathcal{O}\|} = \|\mathcal{O}\|3^{\|\mathcal{O}\|}.$$

This gives the $\|\mathcal{O}\|3^{\|\mathcal{O}\|}$ part of the complexity and completes the proof. □

Corollary 3.5 *The problem of finding fair schedule parametrized with the number of organizations is FPT.*

4. STRATEGY-PROOF UTILITY FUNCTIONS

There are many utility functions considered in scheduling, e.g. flow time, turnaround time, resource utilization, makespan, tardiness. However, it is not sufficient to design a fair algorithm for an arbitrary utility function ψ. Some functions may create incentive for organizations to manipulate their workload: to divide the tasks into smaller pieces, to merge or to delay them. This is undesired as an organization should not profit nor suffer from the way it presents its workload. An organization should present their jobs in the most convenient way; and should not play against other organizations. We show that in multi-organizational systems, as we have to take into account such manipulations, the choice of the utility functions is restricted.

For the sake of this section we introduce additional notation: let us fix an organzation $O^{(u)}$ and let σ_t denote a schedule of the jobs of $O^{(u)}$ in time t. The jobs $J_i(s_i, p_i)$ of $O^{(u)}$ are characterized by their start times s_i and processing times p_i. We are considering envy-free utility functions that for a given organization $O^{(u)}$ depend only on the schedule of the jobs of $O^{(u)}$. This means that there is no external economical relation between the organization (the organization O^u cares about O^v only if the jobs of O^v influence the jobs of O^u – in contrast to looking directly at the utility of O^v). We also assume the non-clairvoyant model – the utility in time t depends only on the jobs or the parts of the jobs completed before or at t. Let us assume that our goal is to maximize the utility function[2]. We start from presenting the desired properties of the utility function ψ (when presenting the properties we use the shorter notation $\psi(\sigma_t)$ for $\psi(\sigma_t, t)$):

1) Tasks anonymity (starting times) — improving the completion time of a single task with a certain processing time p by one unit of time is for each task equally profitable – for $s, s' \leq t - 1$, we require:

$$\psi(\sigma_t \cup \{(s, p)\}) - \psi(\sigma_t \cup \{(s + 1, p)\}) =$$
$$\psi(\sigma'_t \cup \{(s', p)\}) - \psi(\sigma'_t \cup \{(s' + 1, p)\}) > 0.$$

2) Tasks anonymity (number of tasks) — in each schedule increasing the number of completed tasks is equally profitable – for $s \leq t - 1$, we require:

$$\psi(\sigma_t \cup \{(s, p)\}) - \psi(\sigma_t) = \psi(\sigma'_t \cup \{(s, p)\}) - \psi(\sigma'_t) > 0.$$

3) Strategy-resistance — the organization cannot profit from merging multiple smaller jobs into one larger job or from dividing a larger job into smaller pieces:

$$\psi(\sigma_t \cup \{(s, p_1)\}) + \psi(\sigma_t \cup \{(s + p_1, p_2)\}) =$$
$$\psi(\sigma_t \cup \{(s, p_1 + p_2)\}).$$

In spite of dividing and merging the jobs, each organization can delay the release time of their jobs and artificially increase the size of the jobs. Delaying the jobs is however never profitable for the organization (by property 1). Also, the strategy-resistance property discourages the organizations to increase the sizes of their jobs (the utility coming from processing a larger job is always greater).

---

[2] We can transform the problem to the minimization form by taking the inverse of the standard maximization utility function

Algorithm 2: Function `SelectAndSchedule` for utility function ψ_{sp}.

```
1  SelectAndSchedule(C, t):
2  |   u ← argmin_{O^{(u)}}(ψ[C][O^{(u)}] − φ[C][O^{(u)}]) ;
3  |   σ[C] ← σ[C] ∪ {(jobs[C][u].first, t)};
4  |   ψ[C][O^{(u)}] ← ψ(σ[C], O^{(u)}, t);
```

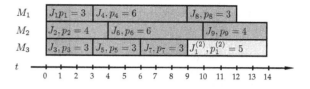

Figure 1: Consider 9 jobs owned by $O^{(1)}$ and a single job owned by $O^{(2)}$, all scheduled on 3 processors. We assume all jobs were released in time 0. In this example all jobs finish before or at time $t = 14$. The utility ψ_{sp} of the organization $O^{(1)}$ in time 13 does not take into account the last uncompleted unit of the job J_9, thus it is equal to: $3 \cdot (13 - \frac{0+2}{2}) + 4 \cdot (13 - \frac{0+3}{2}) + \cdots + 3 \cdot (13 - \frac{9+11}{2}) + 3 \cdot (13 - \frac{10+12}{2}) = 262$. The utility in time 14 takes into account all the parts of the jobs, thus it is equal to $3 \cdot (14 - \frac{0+2}{2}) + 4 \cdot (14 - \frac{0+3}{2}) + \cdots + 3 \cdot (14 - \frac{9+11}{2}) + 4 \cdot (14 - \frac{10+13}{2}) = 297$. The flow time in time 14 is equal to $3 + 4 + \cdots + 14 = 70$. If there was no job $J_1^{(2)}$, then J_9 would be started in time 9 instead of 10 and the utility ψ_{sp} in time 14 would increase by $4 \cdot (\frac{10+13}{2} - \frac{9+12}{2}) = 4$ (the flow time would decrease by 1). If, for instance, J_6 was started one time unit later, then the utility of the schedule would decrease by 6 (the flow time would decrease by 1), which shows that the utility takes into account the sizes of the jobs (in contrast to the flow time). If the job J_9 was not scheduled at all, the utility ψ_{sp} would decrease by 10, which shows that the schedule with more tasks has higher (more optimal) utility (the flow time would decrease by 14; since flow time is a minimization metric, this breaks the second axiom regarding the tasks anonymity).

To within a multiplicative and additive constants, there is only one utility function satisfying the aforementioned properties.

Theorem 4.1 *Let ψ be a utility function that satisfies the 3 properties: task anonymity (starting times); task anonymity (number of tasks); strategy-resistance. ψ is of the following form:*

$$\psi(\sigma, t) = \sum_{(s,p)\in\sigma_t} \min(p, t-s)\left(K_1 - K_2 \frac{s+\min(s+p-1, t-1)}{2}\right) + K_3$$

where

1. $K_1 = \psi(\sigma \cup \{(0,1)\}, t) - \psi(\sigma) > 0,$
2. $K_2 = \psi(\sigma \cup \{(s,p)\}, t) - \psi(\sigma \cup \{(s+1,p)\}, t) > 0,$
3. $K_3 = \psi(\emptyset).$

PROOF. Proof is in the full version of this paper [37]. □

We set the constants K_1, K_2, K_3 so that to simplify the form of the utility function and ensure that the utility is always positive. With $K_1 = 1$, $K_2 = t$ and $K_3 = 0$, we get the following strategy-proof utility function:

$$\psi_{sp}(\sigma, t) = \sum_{(s,p)\in\sigma:s\leq t} \min(p, t-s)\left(t - \frac{s+\min(s+p-1, t-1)}{2}\right) \tag{3}$$

ψ_{sp} can be interpreted as the task throughput. A task with processing time p_i can be identified with p_i unit-sized tasks starting in consecutive time moments. Intuitively, the function ψ_{sp} assigns to each such unit-sized task starting at time t_s a utility value equal to $(t - t_s)$; the higher the utility value, the earlier this unit-sized task completes. A utility of the schedule is the sum of the utilities over all such unit-sized tasks. ψ_{sp} is similar to the flow time except for two differences: (i) Flow time is a minimization objective, but increasing the number of completed jobs increases its value. E.g., scheduling no jobs results in zero (optimal) flow time, but of course an empty schedule cannot be considered optimal (breaking the second axiom); (ii) Flow time favors short tasks, which is an incentive for dividing tasks into smaller pieces (this breaks strategy-resistance axiom). The differences between the flow time and ψ_{sp} is also presented on example in Figure 1. The similarity of ψ_{sp} to the flow time is quantified by Proposition 4.2 below.

Proposition 4.2 *Let $\mathcal{J}$ be a fixed set of jobs, each having the same processing time p and each completed before t. Then, maximization of the ψ_{sp} utility is equivalent to minimization the flow time of the jobs.*

PROOF. Proof is in the full version of this paper [37]. □

5. FAIR SCHEDULING WITH STRATEGY-PROOF UTILITY

For the concrete utility ψ_{sp} we can simplify the `SelectAndSchedule` function in Algorithm 1. The simplified version is presented in Algorithm 2.

The algorithm selects the organization $O^{(u)}$ that has the largest difference $(\phi^{(u)} - \psi^{(u)})$ that is the organization that has the largest contribution in comparison to the obtained utility. One can wonder whether we can select the organization in polynomial time – without keeping the $2^{\|C\|}$ schedules for all subcoalitions. Unfortunately, the problem of calculating the credits for a given organization is NP-hard.

Theorem 5.1 *The problem of computing the contribution $\phi^{(u)}(C, t)$ for a given organization $O^{(u)}$ in coalition C in time t is NP-hard.*

PROOF. We present the reduction of the SUBSETSUM problem (which is NP-hard) to the problem of calculating the contribution for an organization. Let I be an instance of the SUBSETSUM problem. In I we are given a set of k integers $S = \{x_1, x_2, \ldots, x_k\}$ and a value x. We ask whether there exists a subset of S with the sum of elements equal to x. From I we construct an instance I_{con} of the problem of calculating the contribution for a given organization. Intuitively, we construct the set of $(\|S\| + 2)$ organizations: $\|S\|$ of them will correspond to the appropriate elements from S. The two dummy organizations a and b are used for our reduction. One dummy organization a has no jobs. The second dummy organization b has a large job that dominates the value of the whole schedule. The instance I_{con} is constructed in such a way that for each coalition C such that $b \in C$ and such that the elements of S corresponding to the organizations from C sum up to the value lower than x, the marginal contribution of a to C is $L + O(L)$, where $O(L)$ is small in comparison with L. The marginal contribution of a to other coalitions is small $(O(L))$. Thus, from the contribution of a, we can count the subsets of S with the sum of the elements lower than x. By repeating this procedure for $(x + 1)$ we can count the subsets of S with the sum of the elements lower than $(x + 1)$. By comparing the two values, we can find whether there exists the subset of S with the sum of the elements equal to x. The precise construction is described below.

Let $\mathcal{S}_{<x} = \{S' \subset S : \sum_{x_i \in S'} s_i < x\}$ be the set of the subsets of S, each having the sum of the elements lower than x. Let $n_{<x}(S) = \sum_{S' \in \mathcal{S}_{<x}} (\|S'\| + 1)!(\|S\| - \|S'\|)!$ be the number of the orderings (permutations) of the set $S \cup \{a, b\}$ that starts with some permutation of the sum of exactly one element of $\mathcal{S}_{<x}$ (which is some subset of S such that the sum of the elements of this subset is lower than x) and $\{b\}$ followed by the element a. In other words, if we associate the elements from $S \cup \{a, b\}$ with the organizations and each ordering of the elements of $S \cup \{a, b\}$ with the order of the organizations joining the grand coalition, then $n_{<x}(S)$ is the number of the orderings corresponding to the cases when organization a joins grand coalition just after all the organizations from $S' \cup \{b\}$, where S' is some element of $\mathcal{S}_{<x}$. Of course $\mathcal{S}_{<x} \subseteq \mathcal{S}_{<(x+1)}$. Note that there exists $S' \subset S$, such that $\sum_{x_i \in S'} x_i = x$ if and only if the set $\mathcal{S}_{<x}$ is a proper subset of $\mathcal{S}_{<(x+1)}$ (i.e. $\mathcal{S}_{<x} \subsetneq \mathcal{S}_{<(x+1)}$). Indeed, there exists S' such that $S' \notin \mathcal{S}_{<x}$ and $S' \in \mathcal{S}_{<(x+1)}$ if and only if $\sum_{x_i \in S'} x_i < x + 1$ and $\sum_{x_i \in S'} x_i \geq x$ from which it follows that $\sum_{x_i \in S'} x_i = x$. Also, $\mathcal{S}_{<x} \subsetneq \mathcal{S}_{<(x+1)}$ if and only if $n_{<(x+1)}(S)$ is greater than $n_{<(x)}(S)$ (we are doing a summation of the positive values over the larger set).

In I_{con} there is a set of $(k+2)$ machines, each owned by a different organization. We will denote the set of first k organizations as $\mathcal{O}_S$, the (k+1)-th organization as a and the (k+2)-th organization as b. Let $x_{tot} = \sum_{j=1}^{k} x_j + 2$. The i-th organization from $\mathcal{O}_S$ has 4 jobs: $J_1^{(i)}, J_2^{(i)}, J_3^{(i)}$ and $J_4^{(i)}$, with release times $r_1^{(i)} = r_2^{(i)} = 0$, $r_3^{(i)} = 3$ and $r_4^{(i)} = 4$; and processing times $p_1^{(i)} = p_2^{(i)} = 1$, $p_3^{(i)} = 2x_{tot}$ and $p_4^{(i)} = 2x_i$. The organization a has no jobs; the organization b has two jobs $J_1^{(b)}$ and $J_2^{(b)}$, with release times $r_1^{(b)} = 2$ and $r_2^{(b)} = (2x+3)$; and processing times $p_1^{(b)} = (2x+2)$ and $p_2^{(b)} = L = 4\|S\|x_{tot}^2((k+2)!) + 1$ (intuitively L is a large number).

Until time $t = 2$ only the organizations from $\mathcal{O}_S$ have some (unit-size) jobs to be executed. The organization b has no jobs till time $t = 2$, so it will run one or two unit-size jobs of the other organizations, contributing to all such coalitions that include b and some other organizations from $\mathcal{O}_S$. This construction allows to enforce that in the first time moment after $t = 2$ when there are jobs of some of the organizations from $\mathcal{O}_S$ and of b available for execution, the job of b will be selected and scheduled first.

Let us consider a contribution of a to the coalition $\mathcal{C}$ such that $a \notin \mathcal{C}$ and $b \in \mathcal{C}$. There are $(\|\mathcal{C} \cap \mathcal{O}_S\| + 2)$ machines in the coalition $\mathcal{C} \cup \{a\}$. The schedule in $\mathcal{C} \cup \{a\}$ after $t = 2$ looks in the following way (this schedule is depicted in Figure 2). In time $t = 2$ one machine (let us denote this machine as M') starts the job $J_1^{(b)}$ In time $t = 3$ some $\|\mathcal{C} \cap \mathcal{O}_S\|$ machines start the third jobs (the one with size $2x_{tot}$) of the organizations from $\mathcal{C} \cap \mathcal{O}$ and one machine (denoted as M'') starts the fourth jobs of the organizations from $\mathcal{C} \cap \mathcal{O}_S$; the machine M'' completes processing all these jobs in time $2y + 4$, where $y = \sum_{i:O^{(i)} \in \mathcal{C} \wedge O^{(i)} \in \mathcal{O}_S} x_i$ (of course $2y + 4 \leq 2x_{tot}$). In time $(2x+3)$, if $y < x$ the machine M'' starts processing the large job $J_2^{(b)}$ of the organization b; otherwise machine M'' in time $(2x + 3)$ still executes some job $J_4^{(i)}$ (as the jobs $J_4^{(i)}$ processed on M'' start in even time moments). In time $2x + 4$, if $y \geq x$, the large job $J_2^{(b)}$ is started by machine M' just after the job $J_1^{(b)}$ is completed, ($J_1^{(b)}$ completes in $(2x + 4)$); here we use the fact that after $t = 2$, b will be prioritized over the organizations from $\mathcal{O}_S$. To sum up: if $y < x$ then the large job $J_2^{(b)}$ is started in time $(2x + 3)$, otherwise it is started in time $(2x + 4)$.

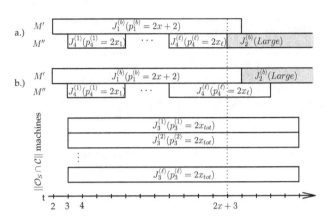

Figure 2: The schedules for the coalition $\mathcal{C} \cup \{a\}$ for two cases: a) $\sum_{i:O^{(i)} \in \mathcal{C} \wedge O^{(i)} \in \mathcal{O}_S} x_i \leq x$, **b)** $\sum_{i:O^{(i)} \in \mathcal{C} \wedge O^{(i)} \in \mathcal{O}_S} x_i > x$. **The two cases a) and b) differ only in the schedules on machines M' and M''. In the case a) the large job $J_2^{(b)}$ (marked as a light gray) is started one time unit earlier than in case b).**

If $y < x$ then by considering only a decrease of the starting time of the largest job, the contribution of a to the coalition $\mathcal{C}$ can be lower bounded by c_1:

$$c_1 = L\left(t - \frac{(2x+3) + (2x+3+L)}{2}\right) - L\left(t - \frac{(2x+4) + (2x+4+L))}{2}\right) = L,$$

The organization a causes also a decrease of the starting times of the small jobs (the jobs of the organizations from $\mathcal{O}_S$); each job of size smaller or equal to $2x_{tot}$. The starting time of each such small job is decreased by at most $2x_{tot}$ time units. Thus, the contribution of a in case $y < x$ can be upper bounded by c_2:

$$c_2 \leq L + 4\|S\|x_{tot}^2.$$

If $y \geq x$ then a causes only a decrease of the starting times of the small jobs of the organizations from $\mathcal{O}_S$, so the contribution of a to $\mathcal{C}$ in this case can be upper bounded by c_3:

$$c_3 \leq 4\|S\|x_{tot}^2.$$

By similar reasoning we can see that the contribution of a to any coalition $\mathcal{C}'$ such that $b \notin \mathcal{C}'$ is also upper bounded by $4\|S\|x_{tot}^2$.

The contribution of organization a, $\phi^{(a)}$, is given by Equation 1, with $u = a$ and $C = \{O^{(1)} \ldots O^{(k+2)}\}$. Thus:

$$\phi^{(a)} = \sum_{\mathcal{C}' \subseteq \mathcal{C} \setminus \{a\}} \frac{\|\mathcal{C}'\|!(k+1 - \|\mathcal{C}'\|)!}{(k+2)!} \mathrm{marg\_}\phi(\mathcal{C}', a),$$

where $\mathrm{marg\_}\phi(\mathcal{C}', a)$ is the contribution of a to coalition $\mathcal{C}'$. All the coalitions $\mathcal{C}'$ such that $a \notin \mathcal{C}', b \in \mathcal{C}'$ and $\sum_{i:O^{(i)} \in \mathcal{C}' \cap \mathcal{O}_S} x_i < x$ will contribute to $\phi^{(a)}$ the value at least equal to $\frac{n_{<x}(S)}{(k+2)!}c_1 = \frac{n_{<x}(S)L}{2(k+2)!}$ (as there is exactly $n_{<x}(S)$ orderings corresponding to the case when a is joining such coalitions $\mathcal{C}'$) and at most equal to $\frac{n_{<x}(S)}{(k+2)!}c_2 \leq \frac{n_{<x}(S)(L+8\|S\|x_{tot}^2)}{2(k+2)!}$. The other $(k+2)! - n_{<x}(S)$ orderings will contribute to $\phi^{(a)}$ the value at most equal to $\frac{((k+2)! - n_{<x}(S))}{(k+2)!}c_3 \leq \frac{((k+2)! - n_{<x}(S))(4\|S\|x_{tot}^2)}{(k+2)!}$. Also:

$$\frac{((k+2)! - n_{<x}(S))(4\|S\|x_{tot}^2)}{(k+2)!} + \frac{n_{<x}(S)(4\|S\|x_{tot}^2)}{(k+2)!} =$$

$$4\|S\|x_{tot}^2 < \frac{L}{(k+2)!},$$

which means that $\phi^{(a)}$ can be stated as $\phi^{(a)} = \frac{n_{<x}(S)L}{(k+2)!} + R$, where $0 \le R \le \frac{L}{(k+2)!}$. We conclude that $\lfloor \frac{(k+2)!\phi^{(a)}}{L} \rfloor = n_{<x}(S)$. We have shown that calculating the value of $\phi^{(a)}$ allows us to find the value $n_{<x}(S)$. Analogously, we can find $n_{<(x+1)}(S)$. By comparing $n_{<x}(S)$ with $n_{<(x+1)}(S)$ we find the answer to the initial SUBSETSUM problem, which completes the proof.

$\square$

We propose the following definition of the approximation of the fair schedule (similar definitions of the approximation ratio are used for multi-criteria optimization problems [7]):

Definition 5.2 *Let σ be a schedule and let $\vec{\psi}$ be a vector of the utilities of the organizations in σ. We say that σ is an α-approximation fair schedule in time t if and only if there exists a truly fair schedule σ^*, with the vector $\vec{\psi}^* = \langle \psi^{(u),*} \rangle$ of the utilities of the organizations, such that:*

$$\|\vec{\psi} - \vec{\psi}^*\|_M \le \alpha \|\vec{\psi}^*\|_M = \alpha \sum_u \psi^{(u),*} = \alpha \cdot v(\sigma^*, \mathcal{C}).$$

Unfortunately, the problem of finding the fair schedule is difficult to approximate. There is no algorithm better than 1/2 (the proof below). This means that the problem is practically inapproximable. Consider two schedules of jobs of m organizations on a single machine. Each organization has one job; all the jobs are identical. In the first schedule σ_{ord} the jobs are scheduled in order: $J_1^{(1)}, J_1^{(2)}, \dots J_1^{(m)}$ and in the second schedule σ_{rev} the jobs are scheduled in exactly reverse order: $J_1^{(m)}, J_1^{(m-1)}, \dots J_1^{(1)}$. The relative distance between σ_{ord} and σ_{rev} tends to 1 (with increasing m), so $(\frac{1}{2})$-approximation algorithm does not allow to decide whether σ_{ord} is truly better than σ_{rev}. In other words, $(\frac{1}{2})$-approximation algorithm cannot distinguish whether a given order of the priorities of the organizations is more fair then the reverse order.

Theorem 5.3 *For every $\epsilon > 0$, there is no polynomial algorithm for finding the $(\frac{1}{2} - \epsilon)$-approximation fair schedule, unless P = NP.*

PROOF SKETCH. Intuitively, we divide time in a number of independent batches. The jobs in the last batch are significantly larger than all the previous ones. We construct the jobs in all first batches so that the order of execution of the jobs in the last batch depends on whether there exists a subset $S' \subset S$ such that $\sum_{x_i \in S'} x_i = x$. If the subset does not exist the organizations are prioritized in some predefined order σ_{ord}; otherwise, the order is reversed σ_{rev}. The sizes of the jobs in the last batch are so large that they dominate the values of the utilities of the organizations. The relative distance between the utilities in σ_{ord} and in σ_{rev} is $(1 - \epsilon)$ so any $(\frac{1}{2} - \epsilon)$-approximation algorithm $\mathcal{A}$ would allow to infer the true fair schedule for such constructed instance, and so the answer to the initial SUBSETSUM problem. The precise construction is described the full version of this paper [37]. $\square$

5.1 Special case: unit-size jobs

In case when the jobs are unit-size the problem has additional properties that allow us to construct an efficient approximation (however, the complexity of this special case is open). However, the results in this section do not generalize to related or unrelated processors. For unit-size jobs, the value of each coalition $v(\mathcal{C})$ does not depend on the schedule:

Proposition 5.4 *For any two greedy algorithms $\mathcal{A}_1$ and $\mathcal{A}_2$, for each coalition $\mathcal{C}$ and each time moment t, the values of the coalitions $v(\mathcal{A}_1, \mathcal{C}, t)$ and $v(\mathcal{A}_2, \mathcal{C}, t)$ are equal, provided all jobs are unit-size.*

PROOF. We prove the following stronger thesis: for every time moment t any two greedy algorithms $\mathcal{A}_1$ and $\mathcal{A}_2$ schedule the same number of the jobs till t. We prove this thesis by induction. The base step for $t = 0$ is trivial. Having the thesis proven for $(t - 1)$ and, thus knowing that in t in both schedules there is the same number of the jobs waiting for execution (here we use the fact that the jobs are unit-size), we infer that in t the two algorithms schedule the same number of the jobs. Since the value of the coalition does not take into account the owner of the job, we get the thesis for t. This completes the proof. $\square$

As the result, we can use the randomized approximation algorithm for the scheduling problem restricted to unit-size jobs (Algorithm 3). The algorithm is inspired by the randomized approximation algorithm for computing the Shapley value presented by Liben-Nowell et al [25]. However, in our case, the game is not supermodular (which is shown in Proposition 5.5 below), and so we have to adapt the algorithm and thus obtain different approximation bounds.

Proposition 5.5 *In case of unit-size jobs the cooperation game in which the value of the coalition $\mathcal{C}$ is $v(\mathcal{C}) = \sum_{O^{(u)} \in \mathcal{C}} \psi(O^{(u)})$ is not supermodular.*

PROOF. Proof is in the full version of this paper [37]. $\square$

In this algorithm we keep simplified schedules for a random subset of all possible coalitions. For each organization $O^{(u)}$ the set $Subs[O^{(u)}]$ keeps $N = \frac{\|\mathcal{C}\|^2}{\epsilon^2} \ln\left(\frac{\|\mathcal{C}\|}{1-\lambda}\right)$ random coalitions not containing $O^{(u)}$; for each such random coalition $\mathcal{C}'$ which is kept in $Subs[O^{(u)}]$, $Subs'[O^{(u)}]$ contains the coalition $\mathcal{C}' \cup \{O^{(u)}\}$. For the coalitions kept in $Subs[O^{(u)}]$ we store a simplified schedule (the schedule that is determined by an arbitrary greedy algorithm). The simplified schedule allows us to find the value $v(\mathcal{C}')$ of the coalition $\mathcal{C}'$. Maintaining the whole schedule would require the recursive information about the schedules in the subcoalitions of $\mathcal{C}'$. However, as the consequence of Proposition 5.4 we know that the value of the coalition $v(\mathcal{C}')$ can be determined by an arbitrary greedy algorithm[3].

The third $foreach$ loop in procedure FairAlgorithm (line 26 in Algorithm 3) updates the values of all coalitions kept in $Subs$ and $Subs'$. From Equation 3 it follows that after one time unit if no additional job is scheduled, the value of the coalition increases by the number of completed unit-size parts of the jobs (here, as the jobs are unit size, finPerCoal$[\mathcal{C}']$ is the number of the completed jobs). In time moment t, all waiting jobs (the number of such jobs is $\|\text{jobs}[\mathcal{C}][O^{(u)}]\|$) are scheduled provided there are enough processors (the number of the processors is $\sum_{O^{(u)} \in \mathcal{C}'} m^{(u)}$). If n additional jobs are scheduled in time t then the value of the coalition in time t increases by n.

In the fourth $foreach$ loop (line 32 in Algorithm 3), once again we use the fact that the utility of the organization after one time unit increases by the number of finished jobs (finPerOrg$[O^{(u)}]$). In the last $foreach$ loop (line 35) the contribution of the organization

---

[3]In this point we use the assumption about the unit size of the jobs. The algorithm cannot be extended to the general case. In a general case, for calculating the value for each subcoalition we would require the exact schedule which cannot be determined polynomially (Theorem 5.1).

Algorithm 3: Fair algorithm for arbitrary utility function for utility function ψ_{sp} and for unit-size jobs.

Notation:
ϵ, λ — as in Theorem 5.6

```
1
2  Prepare(C):
3  |   N ← ⌈ ||C||²/ε² ln(||C||/(1-λ)) ⌉;
4  |   Γ ← generate N random orderings (permutations) of the
   |       set of all organizations (with replacement);
5  |   Subs ← Subs' ← ∅ ;
6  |   foreach ≺ ∈ Γ do
7  |   |   for u ← 1 to ||C|| do
8  |   |   |   C' ← {O^(i) : O^(i) ≺ O^(u)} ;
9  |   |   |   Subs ← Subs ∪ {C'};
   |   |   |   Subs' ← Subs' ∪ {C' ∪ {O^(u)}} ;
10
11 ReleaseJob(O^(u), J):
12 |   for C' ∈ Subs ∪ Subs' : O^(u) ∈ C' do
13 |   |   jobs[C'][O^(u)].push(J)
14
15 SelectAndSchedule(C, t):
16 |   u ← argmin_{O^(u)}(ψ[C][O^(u)] − φ[C][O^(u)]) ;
17 |   σ[C] ← σ[C] ∪ {(jobs[C][u].first, t)};
18 |   finPerOrg[O^(u)] ← finPerOrg[O^(u)] + 1;
19 |   φ[O^(u)] ← φ[O^(u)] + 1;
20
21 FairAlgorithm(C):
22 |   Prepare(C) ;
23 |   foreach time moment t do
24 |   |   foreach job J_i^(u) : r_i^(u) = t do
25 |   |   |   ReleaseJob(O_i^(u), J_i^(u));
26 |   |   foreach C' ⊂ Subs ∪ Subs' do
27 |   |   |   v[C'] ← v[C'] + finPerCoal[C'];
28 |   |   |   n ← min(∑_{O^(u)∈C'} m^(u), ||jobs[C][O^(u)]||) ;
29 |   |   |   remove first n jobs from jobs[C][O^(u)] ;
30 |   |   |   finPerCoal[C'] ← finPerCoal[C'] + n ;
31 |   |   |   v[C'] ← v[C'] + n ;
32 |   |   foreach O^(u) ∈ C do
33 |   |   |   ψ[O^(u)] ← ψ[O^(u)] + finPerOrg[O^(u)];
34 |   |   |   φ[O^(u)] ← 0;
35 |   |   |   foreach C' ∈ Subs : O^(u) ∉ C' do
36 |   |   |   |   marg_φ ← v[C' ∪ {O^(u)}] − v[C'] ;
37 |   |   |   |   φ[O^(u)] ← φ[O^(u)] + marg_φ · 1/N;
38 |   |   while FreeMachine(σ[C], t) do
39 |   |   |   SelectAndSchedule(C, t);
```

is approximated by summing the marginal contributions marg_ϕ only for the kept coalitions. Theorem 5.6 below gives the bounds for the quality of approximation.

Theorem 5.6 *Let $\vec{\psi}$ denote the vector of utilities in the schedule determined by Algorithm 3. If the jobs are unit-size, then $\mathcal{A}$ with the probability λ determines the ϵ-approximation schedule, i.e. gives guarantees for the bound on the distance to the truly fair solution:*
$$\|\vec{\psi} - \vec{\psi}^*\|_M \leq \epsilon |\vec{\psi}^*|.$$

PROOF. Proof is in the full version of this paper [37]. ☐

The complexity of Algorithm 3 is $\|\mathcal{O}\| \cdot N = \|\mathcal{O}\| \frac{\|C\|^2}{\epsilon^2} \ln\left(\frac{\|C\|}{1-\lambda}\right)$ times the complexity of the single-organization scheduling algorithm. As a consequence, we get the following result:

Corollary 5.7 *There exists an FPRAS for the problem of finding the fair schedule for the case when the jobs are unit size.*

In the full version of this paper [37] we show that Algorithm 3 can be used as a heuristic for the general case and that it produces more fair schedules than the round robin algorithm.

6. CONCLUSIONS

In this paper we define the fairness of the scheduling algorithm in terms of cooperative game theory which allows to quantify the impact of an organization on the system. We present a non-monetary model in which it is not required that each organization has accurate valuations of its jobs and resources. We show that classic utility functions may create incentives for workload manipulations. We thus propose a strategy resilient utility function that can be thought of as per-organization throughput.

We analyze the complexity of the fair scheduling problem. The general problem is NP-hard and difficult to approximate. Nevertheless, the problem parametrized with the number of organizations is FPT. Also, the FPT algorithm can be used as a reference for comparing the fairness of different algorithms on small instances. For a special case with unit-size jobs, we propose a FPRAS. In the full version of this paper [37] we show that the FPRAS can used as a heuristic algorithm; we also show another efficient heuristic. Our experimental evaluation indicates that the two algorithms produce reasonably fair schedules.

Since we do not require the valuation of the jobs, and we consider an on-line, non-clairvoyant scheduling, we believe the presented results have practical consequences for real-life job schedulers. In our future work we plan to use our fairness metric to experimentally assess standard scheduling algorithms, such as FCFS or fair-share. Also, we want to extend our model to parallel jobs.

Acknowledgements The research is funded by the Fundation for Polish Science "Homing Plus" Programme co-financed by the European Regional Development Fund (Innovative Economy Operational Programme 2007-2013). Piotr Skowron is partly supported by the European Union Human Capital Program "National PhD Programme in Mathematical Sciences" carried out at the University of Warsaw.

7. REFERENCES

[1] J. Bruno, J. Brustoloni, E. Gabber, B. Ozden, and A. Silberschatz. Disk scheduling with quality of service guarantees. In *ICMCS, Proc.*, page 400, 1999.

[2] R. Buyya, D. Abramson, and S. Venugopal. The grid economy. In *Special Issue on Grid Computing*, volume 93, pages 698–714, 2005.

[3] T. E. Carroll and D. Grosu. Divisible load scheduling: An approach using coalitional games. In *ISPDC, Proc.*, 2007.

[4] H. M. Chaskar and U. Madhow. Fair scheduling with tunable latency: a round-robin approach. *IEEE/ACM Trans. Netw.*, 11(4):592–601, 2003.

[5] G. Christodoulou and E. Koutsoupias. The price of anarchy of finite congestion games. In *STOC, Proc.*, pages 67–73, 2005.

[6] P.-F. Dutot, F. Pascual, K. Rzadca, and D. Trystram. Approximation algorithms for the multi-organization scheduling problem. *IEEE Transactions on Parallel and Distributed Systems*, 22:1888 – 1895, 2011.

[7] M. Ehrgott. Approximation algorithms for combinatorial multicriteria optimization problems. *International Transactions in Operational Research*, 7:2000, 2000.

[8] P. Ghosh, K. Basu, and S. K. Das. A game theory-based pricing strategy to support single/multiclass job allocation schemes for bandwidth-constrained distributed computing systems. *IEEE Transactions on Parallel and Distributed Systems*, 18(3):289–306, 2007.

[9] P. Ghosh, N. Roy, S. K. Das, and K. Basu. A pricing strategy for job allocation in mobile grids using a non-cooperative bargaining theory framework. *Journal of Parallel and Distributed Computing*, 65(11):1366 – 1383, 2005.

[10] P. Goyal, H. M. Vin, and H. Chen. Start-time fair queueing: a scheduling algorithm for integrated services packet switching networks. In *SIGCOMM, Proc.*, pages 157–168, 1996.

[11] D. Grosu and A. T. Chronopoulos. A game-theoretic model and algorithm for load balancing in distributed systems. In *IPDPS, Proc.*, pages 146–153, 2002.

[12] D. Grosu and A. T. Chronopoulos. A truthful mechanism for fair load balancing in distributed systems. In *NCA, Proc.*, 2003.

[13] D. Grosu and A. Das. Auction-based resource allocation protocols in grids. In *IPDCS, Proc.*, pages 20–27, 2004.

[14] A. Gulati and I. Ahmad. Towards distributed storage resource management using flow control. *SIGOPS Oper. Syst. Rev.*, 42(6):10–16, 2008.

[15] A. Gulati, I. Ahmad, and C. A. Waldspurger. PARDA: Proportional Allocation of Resources for Distributed Storage Access, Feb. 2009.

[16] R. Hasan, Z. Anwar, W. Yurcik, L. Brumbaugh, and R. Campbell. A survey of peer-to-peer storage techniques for distributed file systems. In *ITCC, Proc.*, pages 205–213, 2005.

[17] L. Huang, G. Peng, and T.-c. Chiueh. Multi-dimensional storage virtualization. *SIGMETRICS Perform. Eval. Rev.*, 32(1):14–24, 2004.

[18] A. Inoie, H. Kameda, and C. Touati. Pareto set, fairness, and nash equilibrium: A case study on load balancing. In *In Proc. of the 11th Intl. Symp. on Dynamic Games and Applications*, pages 386–393, 2004.

[19] D. B. Jackson, Q. Snell, and M. J. Clement. Core algorithms of the maui scheduler. In *JSSPP, Proc.*, pages 87–102, 2001.

[20] W. Jin, J. S. Chase, and J. Kaur. Interposed proportional sharing for a storage service utility. *SIGMETRICS Perform. Eval. Rev.*, 32(1):37–48, 2004.

[21] M. Karlsson, C. Karamanolis, and X. Zhu. Triage: Performance differentiation for storage systems using adaptive control. *Trans. Storage*, 1(4):457–480, 2005.

[22] C. Kenyon and G. Cheliotis. Grid resource commercialization: economic engineering and delivery scenarios. In *Grid resource management: state of the art and future trends*, pages 465–478. 2004.

[23] M. M. Kostreva, W. Ogryczak, and A. Wierzbicki. Equitable aggregations and multiple criteria analysis. *EJOR*, 158(2):362–377, 2004.

[24] C. Lee and A. Snavely. On the user–scheduler dialogue: studies of user-provided runtime estimates and utility functions. *International Journal of High Performance Computing Applications*, 20(4):495–506, 2006.

[25] D. Liben-Nowell, A. Sharp, T. Wexler, and K. Woods. Computing shapley value in supermodular coalitional games. In *COCOON, Proc.*, pages 568–579, 2012.

[26] L. Mashayekhy and D. Grosu. A merge-and-split mechanism

for dynamic virtual organization formation in grids. In *PCCC, Proc.*, pages 1–8, 2011.

[27] D. Mishra and B. Rangarajan. Cost sharing in a job scheduling problem using the shapley value. In *EC, Proc.*, pages 232–239, 2005.

[28] H. Moulin. On scheduling fees to prevent merging, splitting, and transferring of jobs. *Math. Oper. Res.*, 32(2):266–283, May 2007.

[29] N. Nisan, T. Roughgarden, E. Tardos, and V. V. Vazirani. *Algorithmic Game Theory*, chapter Routing Games. Cambridge University Press, 2007.

[30] M. J. Osborne and A. Rubinstein. *A Course in Game Theory*, volume 1 of *MIT Press Books*. The MIT Press, 1994.

[31] S. Penmasta and A. T. Chronopoulos. Price-based user-optimal job allocation scheme for grid systems. In *IPDPS, Proc.*, pages 336–336, 2006.

[32] R. Rahman, T. Vinkó, D. Hales, J. Pouwelse, and H. Sips. Design space analysis for modeling incentives in distributed systems. In *SIGCOMM, Proc.*, pages 182–193, 2011.

[33] A. Roth. The price of malice in linear congestion games. In *WINE, Proc.*, pages 118–125, 2008.

[34] K. Rzadca, D. Trystram, and A. Wierzbicki. Fair game-theoretic resource management in dedicated grids. In *CCGRID, Proc.*, 2007.

[35] L. S. Shapley. A value for n-person games. *Contributions to the theory of games*, 2:307–317, 1953.

[36] P. Skowron and K. Rzadca. Network delay-aware load balancing in selfish and cooperative distributed systems. In *IPDPS Workshops, Proc.*, 2013.

[37] P. Skowron and K. Rzadca. Non-monetary fair scheduling — cooperative game theory approach. *CoRR*, abs/1302.0948, http://arxiv.org/pdf/1302.0948, 2013.

[38] B. Vocking. Selfish load balancing. In N. Nisan, T. Roughgarden, E. Tardos, and V. V. Vazirani, editors, *Algorithmic Game Theory*. Cambridge University Press, 2007.

[39] K. D. Vohs, N. L. Mead, and M. R. Goode. The Psychological Consequences of Money. *Science*, 314(5802):1154–1156, Nov. 2006.

[40] Y. Wang and A. Merchant. Proportional-share scheduling for distributed storage systems, 2007.

[41] M. Welsh and D. Culler. Adaptive overload control for busy internet servers, 2003.

[42] A. Wierman. Fairness and scheduling in single server queues. *Surveys in Operations Research and Management Science*, 16:39–48, 2011.

[43] H. Yaïche, R. R. Mazumdar, and C. Rosenberg. A game theoretic framework for bandwidth allocation and pricing in broadband networks. *IEEE/ACM Trans. Netw.*, 8(5):667–678, Oct. 2000.

[44] J. Zhang, A. Sivasubramaniam, A. Riska, Q. Wang, and E. Riedel. An interposed 2-level i/o scheduling framework for performance virtualization. In *SIGMETRICS, Proc.*, pages 406–407, 2005.

[45] X. Zhu, M. Uysal, Z. Wang, S. Singhal, A. Merchant, P. Padala, and K. Shin. What does control theory bring to systems research? *SIGOPS Oper. Syst. Rev.*, 43(1):62–69, 2009.

Cloud Scheduling with Setup Cost

Yossi Azar [*]
Blavatnik School of Computer
Science, Tel-Aviv University
azar@tau.ac.il

Naama Ben-Aroya [†]
Blavatnik School of Computer
Science, Tel-Aviv University

Nikhil R. Devanur
Microsoft Research
Redmond, WA
nikdev@microsoft.com

Navendu Jain
Microsoft Research
Redmond, WA
navendu@microsoft.com

ABSTRACT

In this paper, we investigate the problem of online task scheduling of jobs such as MapReduce jobs, Monte Carlo simulations and generating search index from web documents, on cloud computing infrastructures. We consider the virtualized cloud computing setup comprising machines that host multiple identical virtual machines (VMs) under pay-as-you-go charging, and that booting a VM requires a constant setup time. The cost of job computation depends on the number of VMs activated, and the VMs can be activated and shutdown on demand. We propose a new bi-objective algorithm to minimize the maximum task delay, and the total cost of the computation. We study both the clairvoyant case, where the duration of each task is known upon its arrival, and the more realistic non-clairvoyant case.

Categories and Subject Descriptors

F.1.2 [**Computation by abstract devices**]: Modes of Computation—*Online computation*

General Terms

Algorithms, Theory

Keywords

online algorithms, scheduling, cloud computing, competitive ratio, clairvoyant, non-clairvoyant

1. INTRODUCTION

Scheduling problems involve jobs that must be scheduled on machines subject to certain constraints to optimize a

[*]Supported in part by the Israel Science Foundation (grant No. 1404/10).

[†]Supported in part by the Google Inter-university center.

given objective function. The goal is to compute a schedule that specifies when and on which machine each job is to be executed. In online scheduling, the scheduler receives jobs that arrive over time, and generally must schedule the jobs without any knowledge of the future.

Cloud Computing is a new paradigm for provisioning computing instances, i.e., virtual machines (VMs) to execute jobs in an on-demand manner. This paradigm shifts the location of the computing infrastructure from the user site to the network thereby reducing the capital and management costs of hardware and software resources [7]. Public cloud is available in a pay-as-you-go charging model that allows end-users to pay for VMs by the hour e.g., $0.12 per hour. Two key criteria determine the quality of the provided service: (a) the dollar price paid by the end-user for renting VMs and (b) the maximum delay among all given tasks of a job. The goal is to provide a scheduling algorithm that aims to minimize the delay and the production cost of executing a job. We consider arbitrary jobs such as MapReduce jobs, Monte Carlo simulations and generating search index from web documents.

In classical scheduling problems, the number of machines is fixed, and in sequence we have to decide which job to process on which machine. However, the cloud introduces a different model in which we can activate and release machines on demand, and thus control the number of machines being used to process the jobs. This highlights the trade-off between the number of machines used and the delay of processing the jobs. On one hand, if we didn't have to pay for each machine, we could use one machine for each task of the job, and reduce the delay to a minimum. On the other hand, if we want to minimize cost, we could only use a single machine for all tasks of the jobs in a work-conserving model.

In this paper we assume that all computing instances which are available for processing are initially inactive. In order to assign a task to any machine it should be activated first. To activate a machine there is a constant duration of setup until the machine is ready to process. Moreover, when a machine is no longer in use, it should be shut down, again, taking a constant duration for turning off. Both setup and shut down times are included in the production cost of this service, and therefore will be charged to the end-user. As a result, the number of machines allocated for a specific job has a major impact on the total cost.

Our goal is to minimize both the maximum delay (response time) and the total cost. The problem of finding the right balance between delay and cost is a bi-objective optimization problem. The solution to this problem is a set of Pareto optimal points. A solution is Pareto optimal if it is impossible to find a solution which improves on one or more of the objectives without worsening any of the others.

Our Results.

The performance of an algorithm will be described by competitive analysis where α is the cost ratio of the algorithm to the optimum cost and δ is the delay ratio (see section 2 for details).

- For the known-duration case (i.e. clairvoyant, task duration known upon its arrival), we present an optimal algorithm (up to a constant factor) with $\alpha = (1 + \epsilon)$, and at the same time $\delta = O\left(\frac{1}{\epsilon}\right)$.

- For the unknown-duration (i.e. non-clairvoyant) case, we present an optimal algorithm with $\alpha = (1 + \epsilon)$, and at the same time $\delta = O\left(\frac{\log \mu}{\epsilon}\right)$, where μ is the ratio of the longest task duration of any job to the shortest task duration of any job.

Related work.

Due to the importance of task scheduling and because they are often NP-hard, these kinds of problems have been much studied. Surveys on scheduling algorithms and online scheduling can be found in [9], [15] and [11]. Perhaps the most intuitive measure of Quality of Service (QoS) received by an individual job is the flow time. The flow time F_i of the ith job is the difference between its completion time and its release date. This measurement is equivalent to the delay attribute in our objective function. We next summarize some of the main prior results for minimizing the total and maximum flow time of n tasks on fixed number of m parallel identical machines.

Total flow time: Algorithm SRPT (shortest remaining processing time) has, within a constant factor, the best possible competitive ratio of any online algorithm for minimizing total flow time. It is $\Theta(min(\log \mu, \log n/m))$-competitive (where μ is the ratio between the maximum and the minimum processing time of a job), and this is known to be optimal within a constant factor [10]. SRPT uses both job migrations and pre-emptions to achieve its performance. Awerbuch, Azar, Leonardi, and Regev developed an algorithm without job migration (each job is processed on only one machine) that is $O(min(\log \mu, \log n))$-competitive [2]. Chekuri, Khanna, and Zhu developed a related algorithm without migration that is $O(min(\log \mu, \log n/m))$-competitive. These algorithms utilize a central pool to hold some jobs after their release date. Avrahami and Azar developed an algorithm without migration with immediate dispatch (each job is assigned to a machine upon its release) that is $O(min(\log \mu, \log n))$-competitive [1].

While SRPT and the related algorithms perform well on average, they may starve some jobs in order to serve most jobs well. The best results known for maximum flow time objective function come from Bender, Chakrabarti, and Muthukrishnan [4]. They show that FIFO (first in first out) is $(3 - 2/m)$-competitive, and provide a lower bound of $4/3$ for any non-preemptive algorithm for $m \geq 2$.

Non clairvoyant makespan: A general reduction theorem from [16] shows that in any variant of scheduling in online environment with makespan objective, any batch-style c-competitive algorithm can be converted into a $2c$-competitive algorithm in a corresponding variant which in addition allows release times. In [5] it is proved that for a certain class of algorithms the competitive ratio is increased only by additive 1, instead of the factor of 2 in the previous reduction; this class of algorithms includes all algorithms that use a greedy approach similar to List Scheduling. The intuition beyond these reductions is that if the release times are fixed, the optimal algorithm cannot do much before the last release time. In fact, if the online algorithm would know which job is the last one, it could wait until its release, then use the batch-style algorithm once, and achieve the competitive ratio of $c + 1$ easily.

In addition, since the late 1980s, a lot of research was made with bi-criteria objective function. A survey on such multicriteria scheduling can be found in [8]. However, none of these scheduling setups are applicable to the cloud environment.

Cloud scheduling: There has been little theoretical work on online scheduling on computational grids and clouds (where grids consists of a large number of identical processors that are divided into several machines at possibly multiple locations). Moreover, as far as we know, there are no previous results which differ from our model by only one parameter.

In [17], Tchernykh et al. addressed parallel jobs scheduling problem for computational grid systems. They concentrate on two-level hierarchy scheduling: at the first level, a broker allocates computational jobs to parallel computers. At the second level, each computer generates schedules of the parallel jobs assigned to it by its own local scheduler. Selection, allocation strategies, and efficiency of proposed hierarchical scheduling algorithms were discussed. Later, in [18], Tchernykh et al. addressed non-preemptive online scheduling of parallel jobs on two stage grids. They discussed strategies based on various combinations of allocation strategies and local scheduling algorithms. Finally, they proposed and analysed a scheme named adaptive admissible allocation. This includes a competitive analysis for different parameters and constraints. They showed that the algorithm is beneficial under certain conditions and allows for an efficient implementation in real systems. Furthermore, a dynamic and adaptive approach is presented which can cope with different workloads and grid properties.

Schwiegelshohn et al. [12] addressed non-clairvoyant and non-pre-emptive online job scheduling in grids. In their model, jobs have a fixed degree of parallelism, and the goal is to minimize the total makespan. They showed that the performance of Garey and Graham's list scheduling algorithm [6] is significantly worse in grids than in multiprocessors, and presented a grid scheduling algorithm that guarantees a competitive factor of 5.

In [13], Schwiegelshohn studied the case of non-clairvoyant scheduling on massively parallel identical processors. The author pointed out the disadvantages of commonly used metrics like makespan or machine utilization. Instead, he suggested to use the total weighted completion time metric. He showed that this metric exhibits many properties that are similar to the properties of the makespan objective. Later, in [14], he showed that no constant competitive factor exists for the extension of the problem to rigid parallel jobs.

Outline.

The remainder of this paper is as follows. Section 2 describes the scheduling models, the function for computing the quality of service (QoS), and a brief summary of our results. Section 3 presents the basic observations used throughout this paper. In sections 4 and 5 we present our algorithms, and give proofs for lower bound for the known-duration and unknown-duration cases, respectively.

2. THE MODEL

Input.

The job input consists of multiple tasks that need to be executed. Tasks arrive over time. A task i has an arrival time a_i and (possibly unknown) duration p_i. We denote by p the minimum duration of a task (we assume it is known) and by P the maximum duration. Let $\mu = P/p$.

Model.

Each task runs on a single machine (instance). Each machine can run a single task at a time. Tasks are non-preemptive, i.e., a task has to run continuously without interruptions. Let $e_i = a_i + p_i$ which is the earliest possible completion time of task i. Denote by c_i the actual completion time of task i and $d_i = c_i - e_i$ as the delay that the task encounters. We can activate or shut down machines at any time. In activation of a machine there is T_{setup} time until the machine is available for processing. In shut down there is $T_{shutdown}$ time to turn off the machine. For simplicity we may assume that there is only activation time $T_s = T_{setup} + T_{shutdown}$ and the shut-down is free.

We concentrate on the online problem where no information is known on future arrival of tasks, but that the arrivals of tasks are independent of the scheduling. We consider the known and unknown task duration model (i.e. clairvoyant and non-clairvoyant). In the clairvoyant case the duration of a task is known at its arrival. In the non-clairvoyant model the duration is unknown at its arrival and becomes known only once the task has been completed.

The Algorithm.

At any time t the algorithm needs to decide how many machines $M(t)$ to maintain (and hence to activate or to shut down machines). In addition it should decide for each task when and on which machine to run it. Since pre-emption is not allowed, once a task is started to be processed by a machine it has to run till completion without any interruption.

Goal function.

The goal function consists of two parts: cost and delay. Without loss of generality assume that the cost charged per machine per unit of time is one. Then

$$G = \int_t M(t)dt$$

is the dollar cost of the algorithm, and G_{Opt} is the dollar cost of the optimal algorithm. We would like to find an algorithm for which the dollar cost is close to the optimum while the the maximum delay of any task is small. Let D be the maximum delay of the online algorithm (i.e. $d_i \leq D$ for all tasks i), and D_{Opt} be the maximum delay of the optimal algorithm. Formally the performance of an algorithm will

be described by α - the cost ratio of the algorithm to the optimum cost ($\alpha = G/G_{Opt}$), and δ - the delay ratio ($\delta = D/D_{Opt}$). Let $W = \sum p_i$ be the total volume of the tasks. Clearly W is a lower bound for the cost. Actually, our online algorithm will be compared with the volume (as long as the volume is not too small). This corresponds to an optimal algorithm with no restriction on the delay (and hence the delay may be unbounded). On the other hand, the delay given by our algorithm will be compared to an aggressive algorithm with a maximum delay of only T_s which is the minimum possible (assuming at least one task needs to wait for the setup time). Surprisingly, we can provide an online algorithm whose performance compares favorably with the two optimal offline algorithms.

Remark: Let L be the difference between the latest and earliest release times. We assume that the total volume of tasks to process is at least the total duration of the process. Alternatively we may assume that the optimal algorithm is required to maintain at least one open machine at any time, and hence

$$G_{Opt} \geq L. \tag{1}$$

The case in which the volume is extremely small and there is no need to maintain one open machine is not of an interest (as the total work/cost is very small). If we insist in dealing with this case we can simply add an additive constant L. For the remainder of this paper we assume that the cost of the optimum is at least L.

3. BASIC OBSERVATIONS

We first show that it is not hard to have an algorithm with an optimal cost. Recall that W is the total volume of all tasks.

OBSERVATION 3.1. *For any algorithm (in particular the optimal algorithm) $G_{Opt} \geq W + T_s$. By (1) we also have $G_{Opt} \geq L$. Equality may be achieved only when a single machine is activated. Hence maintaining a single machine is optimal with respect to the cost (in a work-conserving system).*

The drawback of such extremely conservative algorithm is that the delays are not bounded. The queue of tasks as well as the delay of each task may go to infinity.

The other extreme possibility is to use a very aggressive algorithm with possibly low efficiency with respect to the cost but with a small delay in the completion of each task. Recall that p is the minimum duration of a task.

OBSERVATION 3.2. *An algorithm which activates a new machine for each task upon its arrival has a cost ratio of at most $T_s/p + 1$ and a maximum delay of T_s.*

The guarantee on the delay is excellent but the cost may be very large compared to the optimal cost. We are interested in achieving a much better efficiency, that is $1 + \epsilon$ approximation to the cost with reasonable delays. We note that if $T_s = 0$ then the optimal algorithm is trivial.

OBSERVATION 3.3. *If $T_s = 0$ then any algorithm with no idle machine is optimal with respect to the cost G_{Opt}. In particular, the algorithm which activates a new machine for each task upon its arrival is optimal. That is, the cost is the optimal cost (ratio of 1) and the delay of each task is 0 as task i is completed at e_i.*

4. KNOWN DURATION OF TASKS

In this section we first assume that the duration of each task p_i is known upon its arrival. Let $E = \frac{2T_s}{\epsilon}$ (for $0 < \epsilon < 1$). The following algorithm achieves a cost ratio of $(1 + \epsilon)$ and a delay ratio of $O\left(\frac{1}{\epsilon}\right)$.

Algorithm Clairvoyant

- Classify a task upon its arrival. It is a long task if $p_i \geq E$ and otherwise short.

- Upon the arrival of each new long task, activate a new machine.

- Accumulate short tasks. Activate a machine to process those tasks at the earliest between

  - case 1: the first time the volume of the accumulated tasks becomes above E. In this case, assign the tasks to a new allocated machine and restart the accumulation.

  - case 2: $(E - T_s)$ time passed from the earliest release time of those tasks. In this case, continue the accumulation until the machine is ready (at time E), assign the tasks to the machine, and then restart the accumulation. If the volume of the tasks exceeds E by the time the machine is ready, stop the accumulation and go to case 1 (these tasks will be classified as case 1).

- Process the tasks on their assigned machine according to their arrival order. Note that the volume assigned to a machine is below $2E$ and each task will start its processing within at most E time after the assigned machine is ready.

- Shut down a machine once it completes tasks assigned to it.

THEOREM 4.1. *The cost ratio of Algorithm Clairvoyant is at most $(1 + \epsilon)$. Moreover a long task will have a delay of T_s. The delay of a short task is at most $2E = \frac{4T_s}{\epsilon}$.*

PROOF. Let m be the number of machines opened for long tasks plus the number of machines opened to process tasks from case 1, whose accumulative volume was above E. Let r be the number of machines opened for the tasks from case 2, of which at least E time passed from the first task's release time until the release time of the first task in the next short tasks group. Clearly

$$G_{Opt} \geq W + T_s \geq mE + T_s = \frac{2mT_s}{\epsilon} + T_s$$

and as assumed in (1):

$$G_{Opt} \geq L \geq (r-1)E = \frac{2(r-1)T_s}{\epsilon}.$$

The total setup time for all machines is $(r + m)T_s$. Hence the cost ratio is at most

$$\frac{W+(r+m)T_s}{G_{Opt}} = \frac{W+T_s}{G_{Opt}} + \frac{(r-1)T_s}{G_{Opt}} + \frac{mT_s}{G_{Opt}}$$

$$\leq \frac{W+T_s}{W+T_s} + \frac{(r-1)T_s}{2(r-1)T_s/\epsilon} + \frac{mT_s}{2mT_s/\epsilon}$$

$$= 1 + \frac{\epsilon}{2} + \frac{\epsilon}{2} = 1 + \epsilon$$

as needed. Next we discuss the delays of the tasks. Once a long task arrives it will start running after the setup time and hence be delayed by at most T_s. A short task will get a machine after at most $E - T_s$ time, then the machine has T_s setup time and finally it will start running in at most additional E time. Hence its total delay is $2E$ as claimed. $\square$

We can further save cost and reduce the delay of Algorithm Clairvoyant although it does not improve the performance in the worst case. Specifically,

- Once a machine completed its assigned task it can process any waiting task. Shut down a machine once it becomes idle and there are no waiting tasks.

Next we show that if we insist on a total cost of at most $(1 + \epsilon)W$, then the loss in the delay ratio is required.

LEMMA 4.2. *If an online algorithm is limited to a cost of $(1 + \epsilon)W$, then its delay is at least $\frac{T_s}{\epsilon}$, and the delay ratio is $\frac{1}{\epsilon}$. This is true even if all of the tasks are of the same duration.*

PROOF. For $0 < \epsilon \leq \frac{1}{2}$: let $p = P = T_s\left(\frac{1}{\epsilon} - 1\right)$ (all the tasks have the same duration). We construct an instance of 4 tasks for which the maximum delay of an online algorithm would have to be at least $\frac{T_s}{\epsilon}$. We denote by W_t the total volume released by time t.

- At time 0, two tasks arrive ($W_0 = \frac{2(1-\epsilon)T_s}{\epsilon}$).

  The online algorithm can not activate more than one machine. If it activates two machines, its cost will be

  $$2T_s + W_0 > 2(1-\epsilon)T_s + W_0 = \epsilon W_0 + W_0 = (1+\epsilon)W_0.$$

  Hence, its cost will exceed the limitation. Therefore the online algorithm activates only one machine. At time T_s, this machine will start to process the first task, and at time $T_s + p$ it will process the second.

- At time $T_s + p$, the next two tasks arrive.

Note that the maximum delay of this scheduling is at least the delay of task 2, which is:

$$T_s + p = T_s + \frac{(1-\epsilon)T_s}{\epsilon} = \frac{T_s}{\epsilon}.$$

The offline algorithm, on the other hand, knows that $W = W_{T_s+p} = \frac{4(1-\epsilon)T_s}{\epsilon} \geq \frac{2T_s}{\epsilon}$ from the beginning of the process. Hence, it can open two machines on the arrival of tasks 1 and 2. The total cost is

$$2T_s + W \leq \epsilon W + W = (1+\epsilon)W.$$

Clearly, the delay of the first two tasks is T_s. The next two tasks can be scheduled immediately after their arrival, at time $T_s + p$, exactly after the completion of the first two tasks (one task for each machine). Therefore, the maximum delay of the offline algorithm is T_s, and the competitive ratio is at least $\delta = \frac{1}{\epsilon}$. $\square$

One may think that if we allow a total cost which is much higher than the total work then the delay ratio would become 1. We prove that this is not true. Specifically, if the cost is α times the total work, then the delay ratio is at least $1 + \frac{1}{2\alpha}$.

LEMMA 4.3. *If an online algorithm is limited to a cost of αW ($\alpha > 1$), its delay ratio is at least $1 + \frac{1}{2\alpha}$.*

PROOF. Let $p = P = \frac{T_s}{2(\alpha-1)}$ (all the tasks have the same duration). We construct an instance of 4 tasks for which the maximum delay of an online algorithm would have to be greater than the delay of an offline algorithm. We denote by W_t the total volume at time t.

- At time 0, two tasks arrive $\left(W_0 = \frac{T_s}{\alpha-1}\right)$.

  The online algorithm can not activate more than one machine. If it activates two machines, its cost will be

$$2T_s + W_0 = (\alpha-1)\frac{2T_s}{\alpha-1} + W_0 > (\alpha-1)W_0 + W_0 = \alpha W_0.$$

  Hence, its cost will exceed the limitation. Therefore the online algorithm activates only one machine. At time T_s, this machine will start to process the first task, and at time $T_s + p$ it will process the second.

- At time $T_s + p$, the next two tasks arrive.

The maximum delay of this scheduling is at least the delay of task 2, which is:

$$T_s + p = T_s + \frac{T_s}{2(\alpha-1)} \geq T_s\left(1 + \frac{1}{2\alpha}\right).$$

The offline algorithm knows that $W = \frac{2T_s}{\alpha-1}$ from the beginning of the process. Hence, it can open two machines on the arrival of tasks 1 and 2, with total cost of

$$2T_s + W = (\alpha-1)\frac{2T_s}{\alpha-1} + W = (\alpha-1)W + W = \alpha W.$$

and a delay of T_s. The next two tasks can be scheduled immediately after their arrival, at time $T_s + p$, exactly after the completion of the first two tasks (one task for each machine). Therefore, the maximum delay of the offline algorithm is T_s, and the competitive ratio is at least $1 + \frac{1}{2\alpha}$. $\square$

5. UNKNOWN DURATION OF TASKS

The algorithm Clairvoyant from section 4 depends on estimates of how long each task will run. However, user estimates of task duration compared to actual runtime are often inaccurate or overestimated [3]. In this section we focus on the non-clairvoyant case, where the task duration is known only on its completion.

Now we present our algorithm for the unknown duration case. We divide time into epochs and deal with the tasks in each epoch separately.

Algorithm Non-Clairvoyant

- Divide the time into epochs of $F = 4T_s/\epsilon$. Let B_0 be the set of tasks given initially (time 0) and for $k \geq 1$ let

$$B_k = \{i | (k-1)F < a_i \leq kF\}.$$

  All tasks B_k are handled at time kF separately from tasks of $B_{k'}$ for $k' \neq k$.

- Let $n_k = |B_k|$ be the number of tasks arrived in epoch k.

- Let $m_k = \lceil n_k p/F \rceil$ and activate m_k machines.

- Process tasks on machines in arbitrary order for $T_s + F$ time (this also includes setup times of newly activated machines) . If after $T_s + F$ time there are still waiting tasks then activate additional m_k machines set $m_k \leftarrow 2m_k$ and repeat this step (note that tasks that are already running will continue to run with no interruption).

- Shut down a machine once it becomes idle and there are no waiting tasks.

Recall that μ is the ratio of the longest to the shortest task duration.

LEMMA 5.1. *The cost ratio of Algorithm Non-Clairvoyant is $(1+\epsilon)$. Each task is delayed by at most $O\left(\frac{T_s \log \mu}{\epsilon}\right)$.*

PROOF. First we deal with the cost. Let W_k be the volume of tasks arrived in the kth epoch. Assume that doubling the number of machines happens $r_k \geq 0$ times until all these tasks are processed. Hence the final number of machines was $m_k 2^{r_k}$. The total setup times of the machines is $S_k = m_k 2^{r_k} T_s$. We first assume that $r_k \geq 1$. Since the tasks were not completed by $m_k 2^{r_k-1}$ machines it means that

$$W_k \geq m_k F(2^{r_k-1} + 2^{r_k-2} + \ldots + 2^0) \geq m_k F 2^{r_k-1}.$$

Hence

$$\frac{S_k}{W_k} = \frac{m_k 2^{r_k} T_s}{W_k} \leq \frac{m_k 2^{r_k} T_s}{m_k F 2^{r_k-1}} = \frac{2T_s}{F} = \frac{2T_s}{4T_s/\epsilon} = \frac{\epsilon}{2}.$$

We are left with the case that $r_k = 0$ i.e., all tasks were completed at the first round. Assume first that $n_k p/F > 1$ and hence $m_k \geq 2$. In this case $m_k = \lceil n_k p/F \rceil \leq 2n_k p/F$. Then

$$\frac{S_k}{W_k} = \frac{m_k T_s}{W_k} \leq \frac{m_k T_s}{n_k p} \leq \frac{2T_s n_k p/F}{n_k p} = \frac{2T_s}{F} = \frac{2T_s}{4T_s/\epsilon} = \frac{\epsilon}{2}.$$

The only remaining case is when $m_k = 1$ and $r_k = 0$ i.e., all tasks were completed by the single machine. In this case $S_k = T_s$.

Let K_1 be the set of k for which $m_k = 1$ and $r_k = 0$ and K_2 the set of all the other k's. Note that for every $k \in K_2$:

$$S_k \leq \frac{\epsilon}{2} W_k.$$

Hence

$$S = \sum_k S_k = \sum_{k \in K_1} S_k + \sum_{k \in K_2} S_k \leq \sum_{k \in K_1} T_s + \sum_{k \in K_2} \frac{\epsilon}{2} W_k.$$

Clearly, $\sum_{k \in K_2} W_k \leq W$. Recall that L is the difference between the latest and earliest release times. Since we divided that time to epochs of F we have $|K_1| \leq \lceil L/F \rceil$. We may assume that $L > F$ (otherwise we have only one epoch and one machine so it is easy) and hence $|K_1| \leq 2L/F$. Applying that, we get:

$$S \leq \sum_{k \in K_1} T_s + \sum_{k \in K_2} \frac{\epsilon}{2} W_k \leq \frac{2L}{F} T_s + \frac{\epsilon}{2} W.$$

Assigning the value of F, the assumptions of (1), and the fact that $G_{Opt} \geq W$:

$$S \leq \frac{2L}{F} T_s + \frac{\epsilon}{2} W \leq \frac{\epsilon}{2} G_{Opt} + \frac{\epsilon}{2} G_{Opt} = \epsilon G_{Opt}.$$

We conclude that the cost ratio is at most

$$\frac{G}{G_{Opt}} = \frac{W+S}{G_{Opt}} = \frac{W}{G_{Opt}} + \frac{S}{G_{Opt}} \leq \frac{W}{W} + \frac{\epsilon G_{Opt}}{G_{Opt}} = 1 + \epsilon$$

as needed.

Next we consider the delay. By volume consideration the number of machines in epoch k is at most $\lceil n_k P/F \rceil = \lceil n_k p\mu/F \rceil$, i.e., roughly μ times the initial number of machines for this epoch. Hence the doubling can happen at most $\log(\mu) + 1$ times. Hence the delay is at most $F + (F + T_s)(\log\mu + 2) = O\left(\frac{T_s \log\mu}{\epsilon}\right)$.

$\square$

LEMMA 5.2. *If an online non-clairvoyant algorithm is limited to a cost of $(1 + \epsilon)W$, then its delay ratio is $\Omega\left(\frac{\log\mu}{\epsilon}\right)$.*

PROOF. Let $p = \frac{T_s}{\epsilon(2\mu - 1)}$, and hence $P = p\mu$. We construct an instance of $n_0(\log\mu + 1)$ tasks for which the maximum delay of an online algorithm is $\Omega\left(\frac{T_s \log\mu}{\epsilon}\right)$ and the delay of an offline algorithm is T_s. We divide the tasks to $(\log\mu + 1)$ groups (each of size n_0). Tasks of group i (for $0 \le i \le \log\mu$) will be of length $p_i = p2^i$ and will arrive at $a_i = \sum_{k=0}^{i-1} p_k$ $(a_0 = 0)$.

A machine is alive at time t if it was activated before t and shut down after t. We denote by $m(t)$ the number of the live machines at time t. Clearly, the total cost of the online algorithm is at least $m(t)T_s + W$, for any t. Moreover, it is limited, by assumption, to $(1 + \epsilon)W$, and therefore

$$m(t) \le \frac{\epsilon}{T_s}W. \tag{2}$$

For any given time t^*, the online algorithm processed volume which is at most $\int_0^{t^*} m(t)\,dt$. At time t^* the online algorithm only knows the duration of the completed tasks. It may be possible that the duration of each of the remaining tasks is p. Therefore it may be possible that W is at most

$$pn_0(\log\mu + 1) + \int_0^{t^*} m(t)\,dt. \tag{3}$$

Assigning (3) in (2), we get that the maximum number of live machines is

$$m(t^*) \le \frac{\epsilon}{T_s}\left(n_0 p(\log\mu + 1) + \int_0^{t^*} m(t)\,dt\right). \tag{4}$$

Hence,

$$\frac{m(t^*)}{\left(n_0 p(\log\mu + 1) + \int_0^{t^*} m(t)\,dt\right)} \le \frac{\epsilon}{T_s}.$$

By integrating both sides over t^*

$$\ln\left(\frac{n_0 p(\log\mu + 1) + \int_0^{t^*} m(t)\,dt}{n_0 p(\log\mu + 1)}\right) \le \frac{\epsilon t^*}{T_s},$$

which yields

$$\frac{n_0 p(\log\mu + 1) + \int_0^{t^*} m(t)\,dt}{n_0 p(\log\mu + 1)} \le e^{\frac{\epsilon t^*}{T_s}},$$

and,

$$\frac{\epsilon}{T_s}\left(n_0 p(\log\mu + 1) + \int_0^{t^*} m(t)\,dt\right) \le \frac{\epsilon}{T_s}n_0 p(\log\mu + 1)e^{\frac{\epsilon t^*}{T_s}}. \tag{5}$$

By transitivity of (4) and (5),

$$m(t) \le \frac{\epsilon}{T_s}n_0 p(\log\mu + 1)e^{\frac{\epsilon t}{T_s}}.$$

By definition, $W = \sum_{i=0}^{\log\mu} n_0 p 2^i = n_0 p(2\mu - 1)$. Let C denote the completion time of the online algorithm. Hence we have the following:

$$
\begin{aligned}
n_0 p(2\mu - 1) \;=\; W &\le \int_0^C m(t)\,dt \\
&\le \int_0^C \frac{\epsilon}{T_s}n_0 p(\log\mu + 1)e^{\frac{\epsilon t}{T_s}}\,dt \\
&= n_0 p(\log\mu + 1)\left(e^{\frac{\epsilon C}{T_s}} - 1\right).
\end{aligned}
$$

Hence,

$$\frac{2\mu - 1}{\log\mu + 1} \le e^{\frac{\epsilon C}{T_s}} - 1$$

and therefore

$$\frac{T_s}{\epsilon}\ln\left(\frac{2\mu - 1}{\log\mu + 1} + 1\right) \le C.$$

The maximum delay of the online algorithm is at least the delay of the last completed task. Recall that $e_i = a_i + p_i$ is the earliest possible completion time of tasks of group i, and that $d_i = c_i - e_i$ is the delay that the task encounter. For each i

$$e_i \le \sum_{k=0}^{\log\mu - 1} p_k + p_{\log\mu} = p(2^{\log\mu+1} - 1) \le p(2\mu - 1) = \frac{T_s}{\epsilon}.$$

Therefore, the maximum delay D is at least

$$D \ge \frac{T_s}{\epsilon}\ln\left(\frac{2\mu - 1}{\log\mu + 1} + 1\right) - \frac{T_s}{\epsilon} = \Omega\left(\frac{T_s \log\mu}{\epsilon}\right).$$

The offline algorithm uses n_0 machines. Its total cost is

$$n_0 T_s + W = n_0 T_s \frac{\epsilon(2\mu - 1)}{\epsilon(2\mu - 1)} + W = n_0 p\epsilon(2\mu - 1) + W = (\epsilon + 1)W.$$

Hence, the cost is bounded as needed. Since the offline algorithm knows the real value of W, it uses all n_0 machines from the beginning of the scheduling. Each machine schedules exactly one task of each group. At time T_s each machine starts to process a task from group 0, at time $T_s + a_i$ it completes task from group $i - 1$, and starts to process task from group i. For each task in group i: $e_i = a_i + p_i$, and $c_i = T_s + a_i + p_i$. Therefore, each tasks is delayed by T_s, and the delay ratio is $\Omega\left(\frac{\log\mu}{\epsilon}\right)$ for all online algorithms with cost limited by $(1 + \epsilon)W$. $\square$

6. REFERENCES

[1] Nir Avrahami and Yossi Azar. Minimizing total flow time and total completion time with immediate dispatching. In *Proceedings of the fifteenth annual ACM symposium on Parallel algorithms and architectures*, pages 11–18, 2003.

[2] Baruch Awerbuch, Yossi Azar, Stefano Leonardi, and Oded Regev. Minimizing the flow time without migration. In *Proceedings of the thirty-first annual ACM symposium on Theory of computing*, pages 198–205, 1999.

[3] Cynthia Bailey Lee, Yael Schwartzman, Jennifer Hardy, and Allan Snavely. Are user runtime estimates inherently inaccurate? In *Job Scheduling Strategies for Parallel Processing*, volume 3277, pages 253–263. 2005.

[4] Michael A. Bender, Soumen Chakrabarti, and S. Muthukrishnan. Flow and stretch metrics for scheduling continuous job streams. In *Proceedings of the ninth annual ACM-SIAM symposium on Discrete algorithms*, pages 270–279, 1998.

[5] Anja Feldmann, Bruce Maggs, Jiri Sgall, Daniel D. Sleator, and Andrew Tomkins. Competitive analysis of call admission algorithms that allow delay, 1995.

[6] M. R. Garey and R. L. Graham. Bounds for multiprocessor scheduling with resource constraints. *SIAM Journal on Computing*, 4(2):187–200, 1975.

[7] Brian Hayes. Cloud computing. *Communications of the ACM*, 51(7):9–11, July 2008.

[8] Han Hoogeveen. Multicriteria scheduling. *European Journal of Operational Research*, 167(3):592 – 623, 2005.

[9] David Karger, Cliff Stein, and Joel Wein. Scheduling algorithms. *Algorithms and Theory of Computation Handbook*, 1997.

[10] Stefano Leonardi and Danny Raz. Approximating total flow time on parallel machines. In *Proceedings of the twenty-ninth annual ACM symposium on Theory of computing*, pages 110–119. ACM, 1997.

[11] Kirk Pruhs, Jiri Sgall, and Eric Torng. Online scheduling. pages 115–124, 2003.

[12] U. Schwiegelshohn, A. Tchernykh, and R. Yahyapour. Online scheduling in grids. In *Parallel and Distributed Processing, 2008. IPDPS 2008. IEEE International Symposium on*, pages 1 –10, april 2008.

[13] Uwe Schwiegelshohn. An owner-centric metric for the evaluation of online job schedules. *Proceedings of the 2009 multidisciplinary international conference on scheduling: theory and applications*, pages 557–569, 2009.

[14] Uwe Schwiegelshohn. A system-centric metric for the evaluation of online job schedules. *Journal of Scheduling*, 14:571–581, 2011.

[15] Jiri Sgall. On-line scheduling. In *Developments from a June 1996 seminar on Online algorithms: the state of the art*, pages 196–231, 1998.

[16] David B. Shmoys, Joel Wein, and David P. Williamson. Scheduling parallel machines on-line. In *Proceedings of the 32nd annual symposium on Foundations of computer science*, pages 131–140, 1991.

[17] Andrei Tchernykh, Juan Ram?rez, Arutyun Avetisyan, Nikolai Kuzjurin, Dmitri Grushin, and Sergey Zhuk. Two level job-scheduling strategies for a computational grid. In *Parallel Processing and Applied Mathematics*, volume 3911, pages 774–781. 2006.

[18] Andrei Tchernykh, Uwe Schwiegelshohn, Ramin Yahyapour, and Nikolai Kuzjurin. On-line hierarchical job scheduling on grids with admissible allocation. *Journal of Scheduling*, 13:545–552, 2010.

Efficient Online Scheduling for Deadline-Sensitive Jobs

[Extended Abstract]

Brendan Lucier
Microsoft Research
Cambridge, MA, USA
brlucier@microsoft.com

Ishai Menache
Microsoft Research
Redmond, WA, USA
ishai@microsoft.com

Joseph (Seffi) Naor[*]
CS Department, Technion
Haifa, Israel
naor@cs.technion.ac.il

Jonathan Yaniv
CS Department, Technion
Haifa, Israel
jyaniv@cs.technion.ac.il

ABSTRACT

We consider mechanisms for online deadline-aware scheduling in large computing clusters. Batch jobs that run on such clusters often require guarantees on their completion time (i.e., deadlines). However, most existing scheduling systems implement fair-share resource allocation between users, an approach that ignores heterogeneity in job requirements and may cause deadlines to be missed.

In our framework, jobs arrive dynamically and are characterized by their value and total resource demand (or estimation thereof), along with their reported deadlines. The scheduler's objective is to maximize the aggregate value of jobs completed by their deadlines. We circumvent known lower bounds for this problem by assuming that the input has *slack*, meaning that any job could be delayed and still finish by its deadline. Under the slackness assumption, we design a preemptive scheduler with a constant-factor worst-case performance guarantee. Along the way, we pay close attention to practical aspects, such as runtime efficiency, data locality and demand uncertainty. We evaluate the algorithm via simulations over real job traces taken from a large production cluster, and show that its actual performance is significantly better than other heuristics used in practice.

We then extend our framework to handle provider commitments: the requirement that jobs admitted to service must be executed until completion. We prove that no algorithm can obtain worst-case guarantees when enforcing the commitment decision to the job arrival time. Nevertheless, we design efficient heuristics that commit on job admission, in the spirit of our basic algorithm. We show empirically that these heuristics perform just as well as (or better than) the original algorithm. Finally, we discuss how our scheduling framework can be used to design *truthful* scheduling mechanisms, motivated by applications to commercial public cloud offerings.

*Work supported in part by the Technion-Microsoft Electronic Commerce Research Center, and by ISF grant 954/11.

Categories and Subject Descriptors

F.2.2 [**Analysis of Algorithms and Problem Complexity**]: Nonnumerical Algorithms and Problems—*sequencing and scheduling*; K.6.2 [**Management of Computing and Information Systems**]: Installation Management—*pricing and resource allocation*

General Terms

Algorithms

Keywords

Online Scheduling, Resource Allocation, Scheduling Algorithms, Truthful Mechanisms

1. INTRODUCTION

1.1 Background and Motivation

Batch processing constitutes a significant portion of the computing load across both large internal clusters and public clouds. Examples include data processing jobs (e.g., MapReduce, DryadLINQ, SCOPE), web search index updates, eScience applications, monte carlo simulations, and data analytics. Such jobs are often business-critical and time-sensitive, mandating strict service level agreements on completion time. Moreover, these jobs are not homogeneous in their timing requirements or value. For example, delays in updating website content must be minimized as they can lead to a significant loss in revenue, and financial trading firms must deliver the output of their analytics before the next trading day commences, but many simulation and rendering tasks are less urgent and can be completed at any time between two business days.

The promise of batch computing is that by centralizing the execution of diverse tasks, one can make efficient use of computing resources. For example, one could delay low-priority and time-insensitive tasks when usage peaks, responding dynamically as new jobs arrive in an online fashion. Unfortunately, resource allocation schemes currently used in practice do not live up to this promise. A common approach is to simply divide computing resources in some fair manner between applications (e.g., [7]), neglecting deadline awareness. Another approach is to give strict priority to deadline-sensitive jobs, but such heavy-handed schemes risk terminating low-priority jobs unnecessarily, lowering overall throughput; see [3] for an overview. Finally, external (i.e. paid) clouds generally eschew scheduling concerns, offloading the task of allocating sufficient resources for completing a job by its deadline to the customer.

The mismatch between current approaches and the evident need for *deadline-aware* scheduling mechanisms is due, in part, to the algorithmic difficulties of online scheduling. From a worst-case perspective, the problem of scheduling deadline-sensitive, online-arriving jobs with the goal of maximizing the value of completed jobs is inherently difficult. In its most general form, the problem admits a polylogarithmic lower bound on the competitive ratio of any randomized algorithm [2]. Previous works [12, 13, 2] have constructed algorithms with competitive ratios depending on the ratio κ between the maximal and minimal value, with the best one providing bound polylogarithmic in κ; however, as κ can be arbitrarily high, these bounds are unrealistic in practice. Constant competitive ratios are only known for special cases, e.g., identical job sizes [6], or job values which are proportional to their sizes [1]; yet both cases do not encompass realistic settings. A natural goal, then, is to develop constant-factor approximations under assumptions that can reasonably be assumed to hold for realistic input profiles in practice.

Any reasonable solution, in addition to overcoming the theoretical difficulty, must cope with practical constraints, such as inaccurate estimation of resource requirements, the need to complete admitted jobs (provider commitments), and resuming preempted jobs at the same physical location (to avoid large data transfers). This has lead the community to use heuristic methods, which do not have explicit worst-case guarantees but work well empirically, despite the known lower bounds. What aspects of practical input enable such heuristics to perform well? As it turns out, the lower bound demonstrated in [2] has an extreme property of requiring a job to start executing immediately upon arrival to meet its deadline. In "natural" inputs for which deadlines are not unreasonably tight, one might expect natural heuristics to perform reasonably well. The lack of completely tight deadlines is generally referred to as "slackness" in the input.

Our contribution is based on the following idea: if the existence of slackness in deadline constraints provides an empirical means of escape from worst-case lower bounds, then one can also revisit the theoretical problem under this assumption of slackness. Specifically, we assume that admissible jobs have lax time constraints, i.e., no job extremely pressures the system by requiring immediate and continuous execution in order to meet its deadline. This is a natural and justifiable assumption in practice. With this assumption, we find that a natural algorithmic approach provides strong theoretical guarantees, circumventing the prior polylogarithmic lower bound examples [2]. Moreover, our algorithmic approach performs well empirically, and is simple and robust enough for practical use. We therefore believe that this work provides an important step towards an efficient deadline-aware "ecosystem", which may capture complicated job models, as well as economic considerations such as user truthfulness.

We note that previous work by Garay et al. [4] considers online scheduling with input slackness, but under the assumption that the value of a job equals its size (for which constant factor approximations exist without slackness). Our work generalizes the scheduling model to incorporate arbitrary job values and demands (sizes), where it is necessary to circumvent the known barrier to constant factor approximation.

1.2 Our Results

We consider the following scheduling model. A service provider (scheduler), in charge of a computer cluster with multiple servers, receives processing requests of batch jobs that arrive online (over time); jobs are known to the system only upon arrival. Each job is characterized by a *value* for completion, the total resource *demand*

(or estimation thereof) and a *deadline*. The goal of the scheduler is to maximize the throughput of the system, i.e., the total value of fully-completed jobs. The main body of the paper focuses on the simplified case of a *single server* that has to be shared between multiple users. We do so to ease the exposition of the algorithm and proofs. The extension to multiple servers is elaborated on in Section 3.3.

The performance guarantees of our online algorithms depend on the *slackness* of the input jobs, denoted s, which is the minimum allowed ratio between a job's availability time (interval between arrival and deadline) and its minimal execution time. Our contribution can be classified into two domains, differing by the level of commitment required from the scheduler. A *committed* scheduler must finish executing any job that it begins to process, whereas a *non-committed* scheduler is not required to do so.

Non-Committed Scheduling. The main theoretical contribution we provide is a worst-case performance guarantee on the competitive ratio of our algorithm for online preemptive scheduling. Specifically, we design in Section 3 an algorithm $\mathcal{A}$ with a competitive ratio bounded by:

$$cr(\mathcal{A}) \leq \begin{cases} 3 + O\left(\frac{1}{(s-1)^2}\right) & 1 < s < 2 \\ 2 + O\left(\frac{1}{\sqrt[3]{s}}\right) & s \geq 2, \end{cases}$$

where we recall that s is the slack. We emphasize that algorithms obtaining constant competitive ratios for online preemptive scheduling under slackness assumptions with general job specifications have not been previously known, and that our work closes a large gap open for nearly a decade between positive and negative results related to this fundamental online scheduling problem.

To obtain the main result, we rely on a proof methodology we developed in our previous work [10] for offline scheduling with identical arrival times problem under slackness assumptions. In this work the scheduling problem is formulated as a linear program with strengthened constraints which are somewhat reminiscent of knapsack constraints. Using insights from [10], we approach the more challenging online scheduling problem and develop a novel algorithm for it. We note that although the online problem is completely different in its algorithmic nature from the offline version considered in [10], our proof techniques do share some common concepts. We provide performance guarantees for the online problem using the dual fitting technique together with sophisticated charging arguments tailored to this specific context.

From a practical viewpoint, our algorithm incorporates important design principles, which could be easily tracked and implemented in real systems. First, the job's value density (the ratio between the job value and demand) is the major factor which determines its precedence, rather than its deadline. Accordingly, an executing job j is preempted only if a newly arriving job has a value density which is at least γ times higher than the value density of j, where γ is a tunable *threshold* parameter of the algorithm. Further, due to input slackness, the scheduler need not decide whether to schedule a job right upon arrival, and may take a pre-defined lag for its decision. This principle is incorporated into our algorithm, by starting job execution only if the remaining time until its deadline is sufficiently large with respect to a *gap* parameter μ.

Committed Scheduling. In Section 4 we consider two variants of committed scheduling, in which the scheduler commits to jobs it decides to process: (1) *commitment on job arrival*, in which the scheduler decides upon job arrival whether it commits to the job or rejects it; for this model, we prove that no algorithm can provide any worst-case guarantee, even under a slackness assumption. (2) *commitment on job admission*, in which the scheduler guarantees job completion only once it begins processing it; that is, once a job is *admitted* (which need not happen immediately upon arrival), the scheduler must meet its deadline. Unfortunately, the theoretical guarantees we obtained for non-committed scheduling do not apply in this setting. Hence, we use insights gleaned from our theoretical result in order to design a heuristic solution. Specifically, we apply our original algorithm with a small change: we do not admit a new job whose execution would prevent the cluster from completing jobs to which it already committed to. While this heuristic does not have worst-case guarantees, we find that it performs very well in practice. We evaluate our solutions (both for non-committed and committed scheduling) through comprehensive simulations on empirical traces (extracted from a Microsoft cluster). Appealingly, our algorithms outperform other plausible heuristics, typically by $10 - 50$x.

Finally, we extend our heuristic for committed scheduling to accommodate economic considerations emerging from paid cloud service applications. We design a *truthful* scheduling mechanism, in which participants are incentivized not to manipulate the system for personal interest by misreporting their true job values and parameters (demands and deadlines). We show experimentally that our modified solution comes without utility loss for realistic input profiles.

1.3 Related Work

We provide a brief overview of recent related work in the context of datacenter resource allocation. Resource allocation is becoming a vital and central problem in today's large clusters. Quincy [8] is an algorithmic framework for assigning resources to batch jobs based on locality and fairness constraints. However, this work does not cover deadline considerations. Similarly, [5] the multi-resource allocation problem has been studied in the context of datacenters with fairness being the main performance criterion. Jockey [3] is a system that aims at finishing data-processing jobs (SCOPE) by their deadlines using dynamic allocation of CPU resources, based on offline and online profiling of jobs. However, Jockey focuses on the single job case, and does not explicitly address the scheduling of multiple jobs. Bazaar [11] considers the assignment of both bandwidth and CPU resources for meeting deadlines of multiple batch jobs. The basic idea is to profile jobs in advance and form an estimate of job completion time as a function of (bandwidth, CPU), then heuristically allocate these resources to maximize the number of jobs that complete by their deadlines. Unlike our model, all jobs are assumed to have equal value, and consequently resource allocation is kept static and job preemption is not required.

2. PRELIMINARIES

2.1 Problem Description

Job requests are submitted to a cluster consisting of C identical servers (resources), denoted $1, 2, \ldots, C$. All servers are fully available throughout time and each server can process at most one job at any given time. The cluster is managed by a service provider (scheduler), which also determines the resource allocation. The input is a finite set[1] of batch jobs, denoted $\mathcal{J}$. These jobs arrive to the system online, over the (continuous) time interval $\mathbb{R}^+ = [0, \infty)$. Every job $j \in \mathcal{J}$ is revealed to the system only upon its arrival

time a_j. Upon arrival, each job specifies its deadline, demand and value. The deadline d_j indicates the latest acceptable completion time for job j. The interval $W_j = [a_j, d_j]$ is called the *availability window* of job j.

The size D_j of job j, also referred to as the *demand* of the job, is the total resource amount required to complete the job (e.g., in CPU hours). In the bulk of the paper, we assume that D_j is deterministic. The case of demand uncertainty is treated separately in Appendix 3.4. A *value* of v_j is gained by the system if and only if job j is fully executed by its deadline (i.e., allocated D_j units of resource by time d_j). We emphasize that partial execution does not result in partial value. For any set of jobs $S \subseteq \mathcal{J}$, we denote by $v(S) = \sum_{j \in S} v_j$ its aggregate value. We denote $\rho_j \triangleq v_j/D_j$ as the *value-density* of job j (i.e., the ratio between its value and its demand). Value-densities will play a significant role in the design of our algorithms.

The goal of the scheduler is to maximize the *throughput*: total value of jobs fully completed by their deadlines. The scheduler is not required to complete all jobs. Specifically, if a job reaches its deadline without being completed, there is no benefit to allocating additional servers to it. We assume that at most k servers can be allocated to a single job at any given time. This parameter may stand for a common parallelism bound across jobs[2], or represent a management constraint such as a virtual cluster. For example, $k = 1$ means that every job can be processed on at most one server at any time. At any given time, the scheduler may allocate any number of servers between 0 and k to any job, subject to the capacity constraint C. In particular, jobs may be preempted. Execution of preempted jobs may be resumed from the point at which they were preempted (assuming proper checkpointing of intermediate states).

The performance guarantees of our online algorithms depend on a parameter $s \geq 1$ called the *slackness* of the input. We say that the input has slackness s if for each job j, $d_j - a_j \geq s \cdot (D_j/k)$. The slackness parameter s limits the tightness of a job's deadline with respect to its minimal execution time D_j/k. From a practical perspective, we can think of slackness either as a feature of the input or as a constraint imposed by the system (by declaring s). As we shall see, the performance of our algorithms improves as s increases.

2.2 Definitions

The following definitions refer to the execution of an online allocation algorithm $\mathcal{A}$ over an input set $\mathcal{J}$ of jobs. We drop $\mathcal{A}$ and $\mathcal{J}$ from notation when they are clear from context.

Competitive Ratio. For an online algorithm $\mathcal{A}$ and an input sequence of jobs $\mathcal{J}$, denote by $\mathcal{A}(\mathcal{J})$ the set of jobs that are fully completed by $\mathcal{A}$ over an online sequence of arriving jobs $\mathcal{J}$. The throughput gained by $\mathcal{A}$ is $v(\mathcal{A}(\mathcal{J}))$. Let $OPT(\mathcal{J})$ denote the set of jobs completed by an optimal offline allocation, i.e., one that has full knowledge of $\mathcal{J}$ in advance. We are interested in the worst-case performance guarantees of online algorithms, namely their competitive ratios:

$$\text{cr}(\mathcal{A}) = \max_{\mathcal{J}} \left\{ \frac{v(OPT(\mathcal{J}))}{v(\mathcal{A}(\mathcal{J}))} \right\}.$$

The competitive ratio is a standard measurement of the performance of online algorithms. Note that $\text{cr}(\mathcal{A}) \geq 1$, and that a smaller competitive ratio implies better performance guarantees.

---

[1] Algorithms described in this paper are well-defined for infinite job sequences; we assume finiteness for notational convenience.

[2] E.g., if jobs have different parallelism bounds, then k is the minimum thereof. We note that more involved parallelism models, such as Amdahl's law, are beyond the scope of our paper. Nevertheless, we believe that the insights and design principles obtained here may carry over to such models.

Job Allocations. Denote by $j_A^i(t)$ the job running on server i at time t and by $\rho_A^i(t)$ its value-density. We use $y_j^i(t)$ as a binary[3] variable indicating whether job j is running on server i at time t, i.e., whether $j = j_A^i(t)$ or not. We often refer to the function y_j^i as the *allocation* of job j on server i. Define $y_j(t) = \sum_{i=1}^C y_j^i(t)$ to be the total number of servers allocated to j at time t, and define Δ_j to be the overall amount of resources allocated to job j. The *starting point* $st(y_j^i) = \min\{\{t \mid y_j^i(t) = 1\} \cup \{\infty\}\}$ of job j on server i is the first time at which j is allocated to server i. If no such t exists, $st(y_j^i) = \infty$.

Job Availability and Status. For a job j, write $W_j^{-\mu}$ for the time interval $[a_j, d_j - \mu \cdot (D_j/k)]$. Note $W_j^0 = W_j$ is the availability window of j. Correspondingly, $A^{-\mu}(t) = \{j \in \mathcal{J} \mid t \in W_j^{-\mu}\}$ is defined as the set of jobs j at time t whose remaining availability time is at least μ times their minimal execution time D_j/k. The algorithms we design in this paper limit the starting time of jobs by selecting jobs to be processed only from the set $A^{-\mu}(t)$.

We divide the job set $\mathcal{J}$ into three sets, depending on the jobs' final execution status: (1) *completed (fully processed)* jobs $\mathcal{J}^F$, which have been completed by their corresponding job deadlines; (2) *partially processed* jobs $\mathcal{J}^P$, which have begun their execution but were not completed on time; and (3) *unprocessed (empty)* jobs $\mathcal{J}^E$, which have not been processed at all. We say that a job has been *admitted (allocated)* if it has begun execution, i.e., it is in $\mathcal{J} \setminus \mathcal{J}^E$. We denote by $\mathcal{J}_i^P$ the set of jobs that have been partially processed on server i.

2.3 The Dual Fitting Technique

A core element of our analysis is a dual fitting argument. Dual fitting is a common technique for bounding the performance of algorithms (the competitive ratio in our case). The technique uses weak duality, originating from optimization theory, to obtain an upper bound on the value gained by the optimal solution $OPT(\mathcal{J})$. In the field of algorithmic design, the dual fitting technique is typically applied over linear programming relaxations to combinatorial optimization problems. In our context, the relaxed formulation we use takes a slightly different form compared to standard linear programs, as a result of the non-discreteness of time. In the sequel we describe the dual fitting technique through its specific application to the scheduling model considered in the paper.

In the first step of this technique, we describe an optimization problem over linear constraints, called the *primal program*. The primal program is a *relaxed* formulation of the scheduling problem, i.e., every possible schedule of jobs in our scheduling problem is also a feasible solution to the primal program. The primal program may allow additional feasible solutions. As a consequence, the optimal solution to the primal program may have higher value than the optimal schedule. Formally, we denote by $OPT^*(\mathcal{J})$ the optimal solution to the primal program. This solution is super-optimal, meaning that $v(OPT(\mathcal{J})) \leq v(OPT^*(\mathcal{J}))$. We now describe the primal program used in context of our scheduling model.

Primal Program. The primal program is presented in equations (1)-(5). Notice that some of the constraints of the original problem were relaxed and replaced by a linear constraint. For example, the primal program does not constrain the variable $y_j(t)$ to be binary. Instead, the variable $y_j(t)$ may receive any number from the range $[0, 1]$. The objective function (1) represents the value gained from scheduled jobs. Notice that as a consequence of relaxing the vari-

ables $y_j(t)$, the objective function represents the total partial value gained from jobs. In other words, according to the primal program, the scheduler may gain partial value over partially completed jobs.

$$\max \quad \sum_{j \in \mathcal{J}} \rho_j \Delta_j \tag{1}$$

$$\Delta_j = \int_{a_j}^{d_j} \sum_{i=1}^C y_j^i(t)\,dt \; \leq \; D_j \qquad \forall j \tag{2}$$

$$\sum_{j: t \in W_j} y_j^i(t) \; \leq \; 1 \qquad \forall i, t \in \mathbb{R}^+ \tag{3}$$

$$\sum_{i=1}^C y_j^i(t) - k \cdot \frac{\Delta_j}{D_j} \; \leq \; 0 \qquad \forall j, t \in W_j \tag{4}$$

$$y_j^i(t) \geq 0 \qquad \forall j, i, t \in W_j \tag{5}$$

Recall that Δ_j represents the total amount of resources allocated to job j, and that the gain from a completed job is exactly $\rho_j D_j = v_j$. The primal program maximizes the throughput (1) under the following constraints: demand constraints (2), capacity constraints (3) and parallel execution constraints (4). Note that (3) implicitly requires that $y_j^i(t) \leq 1$. The last set of constraints, suggested by [9], are strengthened parallelism constraints. That is, instead of naturally bounding the amount of resources a job j may receive per time by k, we scale down the amount of servers the job may receive by Δ_j/D_j. Notice that a feasible solution to the relaxed formulation does not necessarily require that an executed job will necessarily be fully completed. Intuitively, according to these constraints, a job that is 50% completed may be allocated at most $0.5k$ servers at every moment. These set of strengthened constraints allow us to obtain better results, as we will see.

Dual Program. The dual optimization problem is associated with the primal program. By weak duality, every feasible solution to the dual program defines an upper bound to $v(OPT^*(\mathcal{J}))$.

$$\min \quad \sum_{j \in \mathcal{J}} D_j \alpha_j + \sum_{i=1}^C \int_0^\infty \beta_i(t)\,dt \tag{6}$$

$$\text{s.t.} \quad \alpha_j + \beta_i(t) + \pi_j(t) -$$
$$-\frac{k}{D_j} \int_{a_j}^{d_j} \pi_j(\tau)\,d\tau \; \geq \; \rho_j \qquad \forall j, i, t \in W_j \tag{7}$$

$$\alpha_j, \beta_i(t), \pi_j(t) \; \geq \; 0 \qquad \forall j, i, t \in W_j \tag{8}$$

For a solution (α, β, π) to the dual program, we refer to the value of the objective function induced by the solution as the *dual cost* of the solution. For every job j, the dual program defines a set of covering constraints (7) over its availability window W_j. We say that a constraint is *covered* by a solution if the constraint is satisfied.

There are three kinds of dual variables. Every job j has a variable α_j that appears in all of its covering constraints. Notice that by setting $\alpha_j = \rho_j$, all of the constraints of job j can be satisfied at a dual cost of $D_j \alpha_j = D_j \rho_j = v_j$. The second set of dual variables $\beta_i(t)$ are used to cover the remaining constraints, and can be thought of as a set of continuous functions $\beta_i : \mathbb{R}^+ \to \mathbb{R}^+$, one per server. The last set of variables $\pi_j(t)$ are a result of the gap decreasing constraints (4). These dual variables are used in the analysis for the case of multiple servers; in the analysis for a single server they will be set to 0.

---

[3]In Section 2.3 we extend the range of values $y_j^i(t)$ may receive. However, we will always treat it as an allocation indicator.

In Section 3 we present online algorithms for preemptive scheduling without commitments. To bound the competitive ratios of each algorithm, we will first consider the total value gained by the algorithm, $v(\mathcal{J}^F)$. We will then use the structure of $\mathcal{J}^F$ to construct a feasible solution to the dual program and evaluate its dual cost (the value of the solution according to the dual objective function). We will show that the constructed dual solution has cost $r \cdot v(\mathcal{J}^F)$ for some constant $r > 1$, which then implies (by the duality principle) that $v(OPT(\mathcal{J})) \leq r \cdot v(\mathcal{J}^F)$. This will allow us to conclude that the competitive ratio of the algorithm is at most r. We summarize our discussion in the following standard theorem.

THEOREM 2.1. *Let $\mathcal{A}$ be an online scheduling algorithm. If for every job input set $\mathcal{J}$ there exists a feasible solution (α, β, π) to the dual program with a dual cost of $r \cdot v(\mathcal{A}(\mathcal{J}))$, then $cr(\mathcal{A}) \leq r$.*

3. NON-COMMITTED SCHEDULING

In this section we present our main theoretical results: online algorithms for non-committed scheduling with guaranteed competitive ratio. We first present an algorithm for the single server case (Section 3.1) and analyze its performance Section 3.2. We then consider the extension to multiple servers in Section 3.3, and finally handle demand uncertainties in Section 3.4.

3.1 Single Server Algorithm

Throughout this subsection we assume there is a single server, so we drop the server index i from our notation. We define two parameters, each representing a simple principle that our scheduling algorithm will follow. The first principle incorporates the conditions for preempting a running job, and it is characterized by a *threshold parameter* $\gamma > 1$.

PRINCIPLE 3.1. *A pending job j' can preempt a running job j only if $\rho_{j'} > \gamma \rho_j$.*

Roughly, jobs are prioritized according to value-densities. This may seem counter-intuitive at first, since a small job can preempt a large job with much higher value. Presumably, such a scenario might lead to a great loss of value. However, we take advantage of the slackness assumption to compensate for the lost value. To do so, we incorporate a second principle, which restricts the starting time of jobs and is parameterized by a *gap parameter* μ ($1 \leq \mu \leq s$).

PRINCIPLE 3.2. *A job j cannot begin its execution after time $d_j - \mu D_j$.*

We provide brief intuition for the selection of these two principles. First, for a job j to be unprocessed, any job executed during $[a_j, d_j - \mu D_j]$ must have a value-density of at least ρ_j / γ. Second, for a job j to be partially processed (yet incomplete), any other job executed during $[d_j - \mu D_j, d_j]$ must have a value-density of at least $\gamma \rho_j$. This intuition will become more clear once we analyze the performance of the algorithm.

The algorithm $\mathcal{A}$ presented here for online preemptive single server scheduling (Algorithm 1) follows these two principles. The decision points of the algorithm occur at one of two events: either upon the arrival of a new job, or at the completion of the processed job. The algorithm handles both events similarly. When a new job arrives, the algorithm invokes a *threshold preemption rule*, which decides whether or not to preempt the currently running job. The preemption rule selects the pending job $j^* \in A^{-\mu}(t)$ of maximal value-density, and replaces the currently running job j with j^* only if $\rho_{j^*} > \gamma \rho_j$; ties broken arbitrarily. Note that it is always possible to complete any $j^* \in A^{-\mu}(t)$ before its deadline, since $\mu \geq 1$.

Algorithm 1: Single Server Algorithm $\mathcal{A}$

Event: On arrival of job j at time $t = a_j$:
  1. Call the threshold preemption rule.

Event: On job completion at time t:
  1. Resume execution of the preempted job with highest value-density.
  2. Call the threshold preemption rule.

Threshold Preemption Rule (t):
  1. $j \leftarrow$ job currently being processed.
  2. $j^* \leftarrow \arg\max \{\rho_{j^*} \mid j^* \in A^{-\mu}(t)\}$.
  3. if $(\rho_{j^*} > \gamma \cdot \rho_j)$
     3.1. Preempt j and run j^*.

When a job is completed, the second type of event, the preemption rule is also called. Here, j is selected as the preempted job with the highest value-density among the partially processed jobs. Before we proceed to analyze the competitive factor of $\mathcal{A}$, we summarize some of the properties of the algorithm in the following claim.

CLAIM 3.3. *The following properties of $\mathcal{A}$ hold:*

1. *Any allocated job $j \notin \mathcal{J}^E$ satisfies $st(y_j) \leq d_j - \mu D_j$.*

2. *For any t, let j be the job running at time t and let $j' \in A^{-\mu}(t)$ be a job that has not been completed by time t. Then $\rho_{j'} \leq \gamma \rho_j$.*

3. *Let $j' \in \mathcal{J}^P$ be a job partially processed by $\mathcal{A}$. Any job j running at some time t such that $st(y_{j'}) \leq t \leq d_{j'}$ satisfies $st(y_{j'}) < st(y_j)$.*

PROOF. Claim 1 follows directly from the threshold preemption rule. For the algorithm to start a job j at time t, job j must satisfy $j \in A^{-\mu}(t)$, which implies that $t \leq d_j - \mu D_j$.

To prove Claim 2, assume toward contradiction that $\rho_{j'} > \gamma \rho_j$. Consider the first time in the interval $[a_{j'}, t]$ that j is being processed. There must be such a time, since j is being processed at time t. This first time cannot be $a_{j'}$, since j' would preempt j at time $a_{j'}$ if j were being processed at that time. It is also impossible that j started its execution after $a_{j'}$, since j' is not complete by time t and j' would be preferred over j by the threshold preemption rule. Therefore, j must have been preempted before $a_{j'}$. This yields a contradiction, since j would not have resumed its execution as long as j' is present in the system.

For Claim 3, suppose for contradiction that $st(y_{j'}) \geq st(y_j)$. Since j continues executing at $t > st(y_{j'})$, this implies that j' was chosen for execution over j at time $st(y_{j'})$, and hence $\rho_{j'} > \rho_j$. However, since $j' \in \mathcal{J}^P$, it must be that j was chosen for execution over j' at time t, and hence $\rho_j \geq \rho_{j'}$, a contradiction. $\square$

3.2 Analysis of Single Server Algorithm

3.2.1 Competitive Ratio

Our competitive ratio analysis of the single server algorithm $\mathcal{A}$ relies on the dual fitting technique described in Section 2.3. Our analysis is post factum, that is, we retrospectively analyze the performance of the online algorithm after it has finished admitting jobs. Recall that $\rho_{\mathcal{A}}(t)$ represents the value-density of the job that was processed by $\mathcal{A}$ at time t. The analysis proceeds in two parts. In the first part of our analysis we show how to construct a feasible solution to the dual program, and bound its dual cost in terms of

$\int_0^\infty \rho_\mathcal{A}(t)dt$. Notice that time intervals in which incomplete jobs were processed do not contribute to the total value gained by the algorithm. Hence, the expression $\int_0^\infty \rho_\mathcal{A}(t)dt$ does not represent the throughput of the algorithm. Therefore, in the second part of our analysis, we bound the ratio between $\int_0^\infty \rho_\mathcal{A}(t)dt$ and the value $v(\mathcal{A}(\mathcal{J}))$ gained by the algorithm; the later can be simply written as $v(\mathcal{J}^F)$. The first part of our analysis is summarized in the following theorem.

THEOREM 3.4. *Consider an execution of $\mathcal{A}$ over an input set of arriving jobs $\mathcal{J}$. Let $\rho_\mathcal{A} : \mathbb{R} \to \mathbb{R}$ be a function representing the value-density of the job that was executed by $\mathcal{A}$ at every time t. Then, there exists a solution (α, β, π) to the dual program with a dual cost of at most:*

$$v(\mathcal{J}^F) + \gamma \cdot \frac{s}{s-\mu} \cdot \int_0^\infty \rho_\mathcal{A}(t)dt.$$

Before proving Theorem 3.4 we need to make several preliminary observations and develop additional machinery. The $\pi_j(t)$ variables are not necessary for the single server analysis of our algorithm, so for the remainder of this section we set them to 0. The dual constraints (7) then reduce to the following form:

$$\alpha_j + \beta(t) \geq \rho_j \qquad \forall j, t \in W_j \tag{9}$$

Our goal is to construct a feasible solution to the dual program, that is, a solution that covers (satisfies) all of the dual constraints (9). Notice that by setting $\alpha_j = \rho_j$ for each completed job $j \in \mathcal{J}^F$ we cover all of the dual constraints corresponding to j. This step increases the dual cost by exactly $\sum_{j \in \mathcal{J}^F} D_j \alpha_j = \sum_{j \in \mathcal{J}^F} D_j \rho_j = v(\mathcal{J}^F)$. To cover the remaining dual constraints of incomplete jobs, we use the β function. Notice that the variable $\beta(t)$ appears in all of the dual constraints (9) corresponding to time t. The β function allows us to cover the dual constraints of incomplete jobs $j \notin \mathcal{J}^F$ without having to pay for them separately using their corresponding α_j variables, as we did for completed jobs. To obtain a feasible solution to the dual program, we require that β satisfies for every time $t \in \mathbb{R}^+$: $\beta(t) \geq \max\{\rho_j \mid j \in A(t) \wedge j \notin \mathcal{J}^F\}$. Consider the following function $\beta^{-\mu} : \mathbb{R}^+ \to \mathbb{R}^+$, defined by:

$$\beta^{-\mu}(t) = \max\{\rho_j \mid j \in A^{-\mu}(t) \wedge j \notin \mathcal{J}^F\}. \tag{10}$$

The function $\beta^{-\mu}$ satisfies two useful properties. First, by Claim 3.3-2 we have $\beta^{-\mu}(t) \leq \gamma \cdot \rho_\mathcal{A}(t)$ for every time $t \in \mathbb{R}^+$. Second, the function $\beta^{-\mu}$ covers the dual constraints of every incomplete job $j \notin \mathcal{J}^F$ and time $t \in W_j^{-\mu} = [a_j, d_j - \mu D_j]$. This nearly completes the analysis, since we can cover most of the dual constraints (9) using the $\beta^{-\mu}$ function, and bound its cost in terms of $\rho_\mathcal{A}$. To cover the remaining constraints, we "stretch" the function $\beta^{-\mu}$ by using the following lemma.

LEMMA 3.5 (STRETCHING LEMMA). *Let $\beta^{-\mu} : \mathbb{R}^+ \to \mathbb{R}^+$ be a function satisfying: $\beta^{-\mu}(t) \geq \rho_j$ for every $j \notin \mathcal{J}^F$ and $t \in W_j^{-\mu}$. Then, there exists a function $\beta : \mathbb{R}^+ \to \mathbb{R}^+$ satisfying: $\beta(t) \geq \rho_j$ for every $j \notin \mathcal{J}^F$ and $t \in W_j$, such that*

$$\int_0^\infty \beta(t)dt \leq \frac{s}{s-\mu} \cdot \int_0^\infty \beta^{-\mu}(t)dt.$$

By combining the above observations with the stretching lemma, we construct a feasible solution to the dual program. The remaining details are given in the following proof.

PROOF OF THEOREM 3.4: Set $\alpha_j = \rho_j$ for every completed job $j \in \mathcal{J}^F$, and $\alpha_j = 0$ otherwise. To cover the remaining dual constraints, we apply the stretching lemma on the function $\beta^{-\mu}$ defined in (10) and obtain the function β. The $\pi_j(t)$ variables are all set to 0. The total cost of the dual solution (α, β, π) is bounded by:

$$\sum_{j \in \mathcal{J}} D_j \alpha_j + \int_0^\infty \beta(t)dt \leq v(\mathcal{J}^F) + \frac{s}{s-\mu} \int_0^\infty \beta^{-\mu}(t)dt$$

$$\leq v(\mathcal{J}^F) + \gamma \cdot \frac{s}{s-\mu} \int_0^\infty \rho_\mathcal{A}(t)dt.$$

The last inequality follows since $\beta^{-\mu}(t) \leq \gamma \cdot \rho_\mathcal{A}(t)$ for every $t \in \mathbb{R}^+$. $\square$

This completes the first part of the analysis. In the second part of the analysis, we bound the total cost of $\int_0^\infty \rho_\mathcal{A}(t)dt$ by applying a charging argument motivated by principles 3.1 and 3.2. This leads to the following theorem.

THEOREM 3.6. *Let $\mathcal{J}^F$ be the set of jobs completed by $\mathcal{A}$ with input $\mathcal{J}$, and let $v(\mathcal{J}^F)$ denote the total value gained by the algorithm. Let $\rho_\mathcal{A}(t)$ represent the value density of the job executed by $\mathcal{A}$ at time t. Then:*

$$\int_0^\infty \rho_\mathcal{A}(t)dt \leq v(\mathcal{J}^F) \cdot \left[\frac{(\gamma-1)(\mu-1)}{(\gamma-1)(\mu-1)-1} \cdot \right]$$

Our goal is to bound the expression $\int_0^\infty \rho_\mathcal{A}(t)dt$. We divide the timeline into two sets: $\mathcal{T}^F$, times during which the algorithm processed jobs that were eventually completed; and $\mathcal{T}^P$.

$$\mathcal{T}^F = \left\{ t \in \mathbb{R}^+ \mid j_\mathcal{A}(t) \in \mathcal{J}^F \right\} \quad ; \quad \mathcal{T}^P = \mathcal{T} \setminus \mathcal{T}^F$$

We can break the integral $\int_0^\infty \rho_\mathcal{A}(t)dt$ into two, according to $\mathcal{T}^F$ and $\mathcal{T}^P$. Notice that integrating $\rho_\mathcal{A}(t)$ over $\mathcal{T}^F$ gives us exactly $v(\mathcal{J}^F)$. Hence, it remains to bound $\int_{\mathcal{T}^P} \rho_\mathcal{A}(t)dt$. This expression represents the partial value that was lost over incomplete jobs, or formally: $\sum_{j \in \mathcal{J}^P} \rho_j \Delta_j$. Consider a partially processed job $j \in \mathcal{J}^P$. Define the *admission window* $Ad_j = [st(y_j), d_j]$ of job j as the interval between the job admission time (i.e., execution starting time) and its deadline. By Claim 3.3-1, the size of the admission window is at least μD_j. Let $I_j \subseteq Ad_j$ represent the times during which job j has been processed. Since job j has not been completed, its total execution time is at most D_j. Hence, the total time in Ad_j during which $\mathcal{A}$ processed jobs different than j is at least $(\mu-1)D_j$; denote this set of times by O_j. According to Claim 3.3-3, each of the jobs executed during O_j has a value-density at least γ times larger than ρ_j. Integrating $\rho_\mathcal{A}(t)$ over O_j gives us a total value of at least $\gamma(\mu-1)v_j$. Intuitively, the value gained during O_j can used to "pay" over the partial value $\rho_j \Delta_j \leq v_j$ that the algorithm lost by not completing job j. However, there is a flaw in the argument, since jobs that were processed during O_j have not necessarily been completed. To succeed, a more rigorous analysis is required.

We bound $\int_0^\infty \rho_\mathcal{A}(t)dt$ using a charging argument, which is motivated by the last paragraph. Initially, we charge every job running at some time t a value of $\rho_\mathcal{A}(t)$. We then apply a charging procedure that iteratively transfers charges away from incomplete jobs, until finally only completed jobs are charged. Finally, we bound the total amount each completed job is charged for (Lemma 3.7).

The Charging Procedure. Let $ch : \mathbb{R}^+ \to \mathbb{R}^+$ be a charging function, representing an amount charged from the job that has been processed per time t. Initially, we set $ch(t) = \rho_{\mathcal{A}}(t)$ for every time t. We describe a procedure that shifts values of $ch(t)$ towards completed jobs, that is, time slots in $\mathcal{T}^F$. After initializing ch, we sort the partially executed jobs in $\mathcal{J}^P$ according to their starting time $st(y_j)$. For each job $j \in \mathcal{J}^P$ in this order, we do the following:

1. Define: $I_j = \left\{ t \in \mathbb{R}^+ \mid j = j_{\mathcal{A}}(t) \right\}$.

2. Define: $O_j = Adj_j \setminus I_j$.

3. Let $\psi_j : I_j \to O_j$ be some bijection from I_j to O_j.

4. For every $t \in I_j$, increase $ch(\psi(t))$ by $(|I_j| / |O_j|) \, ch(t)$ and set $ch(t)$ to 0.

Let $ch'(t)$ denote the value of $ch(t)$ at the end of the procedure. At each iteration of the charging procedure, some incomplete job $j \in \mathcal{J}^P$ transfers all of the charges associated with it towards jobs that execute during O_j. Claim 3.3 implies that jobs processed in O_j have either been completed or have started executing after j. Since we sorted jobs by start times, this implies that after we transfer charges away from a job $j \in \mathcal{J}^P$, we never subsequently transfer charges back to j. This will imply that, at the end of the procedure, only jobs in $\mathcal{J}^F$ are charged. Our goal now is to obtain a good bound on $ch'(t)$ as a function of $ch(t)$. This goal is complicated by the fact that charges can be transferred multiple times, and along multiple paths, before reaching jobs from $\mathcal{J}^F$. The following is our main technical lemma, which analyzes the structure of the charging procedure in order to bound $ch'(t)$.

LEMMA 3.7. *At the end of the charging procedure:*

1. $\int_0^\infty \rho_{\mathcal{A}}(t)dt = \int_0^\infty ch'(t)dt$.

2. For every $t \in \mathcal{T}^F$, $ch'(t) \le \rho_{\mathcal{A}}(t) \cdot \frac{(\gamma-1)(\mu-1)}{(\gamma-1)(\mu-1)-1}$.

3. For every $t \notin \mathcal{T}^F$, $ch'(t) = 0$.

PROOF. Claim 1 holds since every iteration of the charging procedure (lines 1-4) does not change the value of $\int_0^\infty ch(t)dt$. We now prove Claim 3. Recall that the charging procedure sorts jobs in $\mathcal{J}^P$ according to their starting times. Every job $j \in \mathcal{J}^P$ transfers all of its charges towards jobs in Adj_j, which are either completed jobs or other jobs in $\mathcal{J}^P$. Claim 3.3-3 states that a job in $\mathcal{J}^P$ processed in Adj_j must have started after job j. This guarantees that at the end of the charging procedure, $ch'(t) = 0$ for every $t \notin \mathcal{T}^F$.

The rest of the proof is dedicated to proving Claim 2. Our goal is to bound the ratio between $ch'(t)$ and $\rho_{\mathcal{A}}(t)$ for every time $t \in \mathcal{T}^F$. Up until now we treated entries of the function $\rho_{\mathcal{A}}$ as value that has or has not been gained by the algorithm. However, the notion of value may be confusing in the current context of analyzing a charging argument. To avoid confusion, in this proof we refer to entries of $\rho_{\mathcal{A}}$ as *costs* that need to be paid for. Specifically, we are interested in costs that eventually affect $ch'(t)$.

Consider some time $t_i \in \mathcal{T}^P$. The role of i will be explained later on, and at this point can be ignored. Let j_i be the job that has been processed at time t_i. Consider the cost $\rho_{\mathcal{A}}(t_i)$. Initially, $ch(t_i)$ is charged for the cost of $\rho_{\mathcal{A}}(t_i)$. When the iterative loop of the charging procedure reaches job j_i, the cost $\rho_{\mathcal{A}}(t_i)$ is transferred to a different time $t_{i-1} = \psi_{j_i}(t_i)$ and scaled down by a factor of $1/(\mu-1)$, at least[4]. Let i represent how many times the cost $\rho_{\mathcal{A}}(t_i)$

----

[4] We note that the transferred value, $ch(t_i)$, may be larger than $\rho_{\mathcal{A}}(t_i)$, because of other costs transferred to t_i at an earlier stage. However, at this point in the analysis we are only interested in the portion of the transferred value corresponding to $\rho_{\mathcal{A}}(t_i)$.

has been transferred, and let t_i^F represent the final time to which the cost is transferred. By Claim 3, the job bring processed at t_i^F must have been completed by the algorithm.

Now consider an incomplete job $j' \in \mathcal{J}^P$, and some time t. We say that job j' *charges time t after i transfers* if there some time t_i for which $t_i^F = t$. We would like to understand how much of the final charge at t, $ch'(t)$, was transferred from job j'. A complication is that j' can charge time t in multiple ways. For example, it may be that $t \in O_{j'}$, so that the charge at t increases when j' is handled by the charging procedure. However, there may be another job incomplete j'' that was also being processed in the interval $O_{j'}$, which receives part of the charge of j'; when j'' is handled by the charging procedure, it might also transfer some of its charge – which includes charge received from j' – to time t. In general, charge may transfer from j' to time t via multiple paths of varying lengths; we will bound this transfer over all possible paths.

Let k be the number of incomplete jobs that have started between $st(y_{j'})$ and t (not including j'). We are interested in bounding the number of times that job j' charges t after i transfers. We claim this number is at most $\binom{k}{i-1}$. To see this, consider a cost $\rho_{\mathcal{A}}(t_i)$. Let $t_i \to t_{i-1} \to \cdots \to t_0 = t_i^F$ denote the path through which the cost $\rho_{\mathcal{A}}(t_i)$ is transferred, and by $j_i, j_{i-1}, \ldots, j_0$ the corresponding jobs processed during those times. Notice that the set $j_i, j_{i-1}, \ldots, j_0$ is unique for each such t_i, since every ψ is a bijection. Moreover, notice that the jobs j_i, j_{i-1}, j_1 must be sorted in ascending order of starting time, since by Claim 3.3-3 an incomplete job only charges jobs that have started after it. Hence, the number of options for such a t_i is the number of unique paths from j_i to j_0, which is the number of options to choose $j_{i-1}, \ldots, j_1$ out of k jobs. Notice that i can range between 1 and $k + 1$.

The last step of the proof is to bound $\rho_{j'}$. Without loss of generality, we assume that j' actually charges t after some amount of transfers, otherwise j' is irrelevant for the discussion. Consider the k incomplete jobs that started between $st(y_{j'})$ and t in ascending order of their starting times. Each job in this order must be contained in the admission window of its predecessor. By Claim 3.3-2, we get that $\rho_{j'} \le \rho_{\mathcal{A}}(t)/\gamma^{k+1}(\mu-1)^i$. Since each job j' is uniquely identified by the number k of jobs that start between time t and the start of j', and each path to such a j' from t has length at most $k + 1$, this gives us the following:

$$
\begin{aligned}
ch'(t) &\le \rho_{\mathcal{A}}(t) + \sum_{k=0}^{\infty} \sum_{i=1}^{k+1} \binom{k}{i-1} \frac{\rho_{\mathcal{A}}(t)}{\gamma^{k+1}(\mu-1)^i} \\
&= \rho_{\mathcal{A}}(t) + \sum_{k=0}^{\infty} \frac{\rho_{\mathcal{A}}(t)}{\gamma^{k+1}(\mu-1)} \sum_{i=1}^{k+1} \binom{k}{i-1} \frac{1}{(\mu-1)^{i-1}} \\
&= \rho_{\mathcal{A}}(t) + \sum_{k=0}^{\infty} \frac{\rho_{\mathcal{A}}(t)}{\gamma^{k+1}(\mu-1)} \left(1 + \frac{1}{\mu-1}\right)^k \\
&= \rho_{\mathcal{A}}(t) \left[1 + \frac{1}{\gamma(\mu-1)} \sum_{k=0}^{\infty} \left(\frac{\mu}{\gamma(\mu-1)}\right)^k\right] \\
&= \rho_{\mathcal{A}}(t) \left[1 + \frac{1}{\gamma(\mu-1)-\mu}\right] \\
&= \rho_{\mathcal{A}}(t) \left[\frac{(\gamma-1)(\mu-1)}{(\gamma-1)(\mu-1)-1}\right],
\end{aligned}
$$

which is exactly what was required in claim 2, thus completing the lemma. $\square$

Theorem 3.6 follows by simply integrating over t and applying Lemma 3.7. Combining Theorems 3.4 and 3.6 leads to our main result.

COROLLARY 3.8. *The competitive ratio of the single server algorithm $\mathcal{A}$ for online scheduling is at most:*

$$cr(\mathcal{A}) \leq 1 + \gamma \cdot \frac{s}{s-\mu} \cdot \left[\frac{(\gamma-1)(\mu-1)}{(\gamma-1)(\mu-1)-1} \right]. \quad (11)$$

Optimizing the bound. The bound on $cr(\mathcal{A})$ can be further optimized. A straightforward calculation shows that for any value of μ, the bound (11) is minimized for a unique optimal value of $\gamma^*(\mu) = \frac{\sqrt{\mu}}{\sqrt{\mu}-1}$; at this value, the bound becomes:

$$cr(\mathcal{A}) \leq 1 + \frac{s}{s-\mu} \cdot \frac{\sqrt{\mu}+1}{\sqrt{\mu}-1}.$$

There are two ways to interpret the above result. One may think of μ as a constraint set by the service provider. For example, by setting $\mu = s/2$, the service provider can limit the starting time of jobs to the first half of their availability window; as a result, the bound becomes $3 + O(1/\sqrt{s})$ for $s > 2$. On the other hand, the bound can be further optimized. By choosing $\mu \approx s^{2/3}$ for $s > 2$, or $\mu = (s+1)/2$ for $1 < s < 2$, we obtain the bounds stated in the introduction:

$$cr(\mathcal{A}) \leq \begin{cases} 3 + O\left(\frac{1}{(s-1)^2}\right) & 1 < s < 2 \\ 2 + O\left(\frac{1}{\sqrt[3]{s}}\right) & s \geq 2 \end{cases}$$

We note that one can optimize over μ and obtain more explicit bounds on the competitive ratio. We omit the details for brevity.

3.2.2 Bounding the Loss over Incomplete Jobs

In general, non-committed scheduling algorithms may begin processing jobs without having to complete them. This may lead to an undesired result, where the loss over incomplete jobs is relatively large compared to the gained value. To limit this loss, the service provider can incorporate the loss directly into the objective function. Let f be a penalty factor set by the service provider. Consider the following alternative objective:

$$\text{maximize } v(\mathcal{J}^F) - f \cdot v(\mathcal{J}^P). \quad (12)$$

We show that our algorithm maintains low loss compared to the value it gains. Proof details can be found in the full paper.

THEOREM 3.9. *For the objective (12), the competitive ratio of the non-committed algorithm $\mathcal{A}$ is at most:*

$$\left(1 + \gamma \cdot \frac{s}{s-\mu} \cdot \left[\frac{(\gamma-1)(\mu-1)}{(\gamma-1)(\mu-1)-1} \right] \right) \cdot$$
$$\cdot \left[1 - \frac{f}{(\gamma-1)(\mu-1)-1} \right]^{-1}. \quad (13)$$

3.3 Multiple Servers

The focus of this section is the 0-k Resource Allocation model for multiple identical servers, presented in Section 2. Here, each job may be allocated, at any point, any number of servers between 0 and a bound k set by the service provider. In this section, we construct a new algorithm called the NONCOMMITTED algorithm, which obtains the same competitive ratio as its single server counterpart, regardless of the values of k and C.

Our construction is incremental. We first consider the case of $k = 1$, in which each job may be allocated at most a single server at any time. Then, we generalize our solution to any value of k without incurring any loss in performance or runtime.

0-1 Resource Allocation. The algorithm for multiple servers with $k = 1$, which we denote by $\mathcal{M}$, is based on its single server counterpart $\mathcal{A}$. From an overall perspective, the algorithm $\mathcal{M}$ runs a local copy of the single server algorithm $\mathcal{A}$ on each of the C servers, under a restriction called the *job locality* restriction. According to the job locality restriction, a job preempted from server i may only resume its execution on server i; in other words, the algorithm prevents migration of preempted jobs between servers. The algorithm, given fully in Algorithm 2, executes this general approach in an efficient manner. When job j arrival at time t, we only invoke the threshold preemption rule on server $i_{\min}(t)$, which is the server running the job with lowest value-density (unused servers run idle jobs of value-density 0). Notice that it suffices to invoke the threshold preemption rule of server $i_{\min}(t)$: if job j is rejected, it would be rejected by the threshold preemption rule of any other server. When job j completes on server i, we first load the job with maximal value-density out of the jobs preempted from server i, and then invoke the threshold preemption rule.

Algorithm 2: Multiple Servers with $k = 1$

Event: On arrival of job j at time $t = a_j$:
1. Call Threshold Preemption Rule $(i_{\min}(t), t)$, with:
$$i_{\min}(t) = \arg\min \left\{ \rho_{\mathcal{M}}^i(t) \mid 1 \leq i \leq C \right\}.$$

Event: On job completion on server i at time t:
1. Resume execution of the preempted job with highest value-density among jobs preempted from server i.
2. Call Threshold Preemption Rule(i, t).

Threshold Preemption Rule (i, t):
1. $j \leftarrow$ job currently processed on server i.
2. $j^* \leftarrow \arg\max \left\{ \rho_{j^*} \mid j^* \in A^{-\mu}(t) \right\}$.
3. if ($\rho_{j^*} > \gamma \cdot \rho_j$)
    3.1. Preempt j and run j^* on server i.

Theorem 3.10 summarizes our analysis of the multiple server algorithm $\mathcal{M}$. The arguments used in the single server analysis can be extended to the multiple server case, without incurring any loss of guaranteed performance. Since the analysis is conceptually similar to its single server counterpart, we omit the full details from the proceedings version and only provide a high-level proof sketch.

THEOREM 3.10. *The algorithm $\mathcal{M}$ for multiple servers with no parallelized scheduling obtains a competitive ratio of at most:*

$$cr(\mathcal{M}) \leq 1 + \gamma \cdot \frac{s}{s-\mu} \cdot \left[\frac{(\gamma-1)(\mu-1)}{(\gamma-1)(\mu-1)-1} \right].$$

PROOF SKETCH. The analysis is relatively similar to its single server equivalent, apart from several adjustments. As before, the dual fitting analysis will provide a bound on the competitive ratio of $\mathcal{M}$. In the multiple server case, this bound depends on the expression $\sum_{i=1}^{C} \int_0^\infty \rho_{\mathcal{M}}^i(t) dt$, which represents the total value gained by the algorithm if it were to gain a partial value of $\rho_j \Delta_j$ for each partially processed job j. We can apply the proof of Lemma 3.7 on each server individually and sum across all servers, and as a result bound this expression by $v(\mathcal{J}^F) \cdot \left[\frac{(\gamma-1)(\mu-1)}{(\gamma-1)(\mu-1)-1} \right]$.

What complicates the proof is the dual fitting argument. Notice that now there is a dual constraint for each tuple (j, i, t), and all of them should be covered. To understand how to overcome the difficulties, we first explain why the single server analysis does not work in its current form. Consider a partially processed job j and consider some time t in which the job was processed. Let i be the server that processed job j at time t. Recall that we set $\alpha_j = 0$ for j. Since we did not use the π variables so far, the dual constraints corresponding to job j at time t can only be covered by the $\beta_i(t)$ variables. In the original analysis, the $\beta_i(t)$ variable has been set to the highest value-density of an unprocessed job at time t. However, setting $\beta_i(t)$ so does not necessarily cover the dual constraint of (j, i', t) for any server i'. Even by setting $\beta_i(t) = \gamma \cdot \rho_{\mathcal{M}}^i(t)$, we cannot guarantee that a constraint (j, i', t) for $i' \neq i$ will be covered. To overcome this problem, we use the $\pi_j(t)$ variables. The usage of these variables, and the necessary adjustments needed in order to correct the analysis, are both highly non-trivial and technical. We refer the reader to the full version of the paper for the complete analysis. $\square$

0-k Resource Allocation. Up to now we have restricted the execution of every job to at most one server at any time. In the following, we consider a more general model, in which each job may be processed simultaneously on any number of servers, up to a parallelism bound k set by the service provider. The service provider may flexibly change the resource usage of each job at any point.

Our solution reduces the problem to the 0-1 resource allocation case. We divide the C servers into C/k equal-sized "virtual clusters" (VCs). We assume k divides C for ease of exposition. In our solution, jobs are allocated to VCs rather than to individual servers. When a job is allocated to a VC, it runs on all of its k servers in parallel. Each VC runs a copy of the single server algorithm $\mathcal{A}$, under the job locality restriction, just as in Algorithm 2.

Algorithm 3: Multiple Servers

1. Divide the C servers into C/k equal-sized clusters.
2. Run Algorithm 2 under the following modifications:
   - Capacity: C/k.
   - Demand: D_j/k for each job j.

We prove that Algorithm 3 guarantees the same competitive ratio $cr(\mathcal{A})$ as for the single server case. The proof directly follows from our dual fitting analysis, therefore we leave it to the full version. We note that the algorithm we provide overcomes some concerns that may arise in practical settings. For example, the dynamic allocation of resources might in principle incur high network costs due to large data transfers. However, the job locality feature of our algorithm prevents jobs from migrating across VCs, thereby minimizing communication overheads. We emphasize that imposing this feature does not affect performance, as we guarantee the same competitive ratio of the single server algorithm. In other words, while our algorithm does not migrate jobs across VCs, and only ever allocates 0 or k resources to a job at any given time, our performance bounds are with respect to an optimal schedule without any such restrictions.

3.4 Demand Uncertainty

Up until now we have made a simplifying assumption that job resource requirements can be precisely specified by the job owner. Often times, however, the resource requirements may only be estimated, due to various reasons (unexpected data-processing overhead, outliers, etc.). We modify our algorithms to handle demand distributions with relatively low tail probability. Let α be the allowed deviation of the job resource requirement from the initial estimation (i.e., the expected demand). Formally, the resource demand may exceeds its expectation by a multiplicative factor of $(1 + \alpha)$, with probability at most β. We adjust our solution to

accommodate this uncertainty model, and show that the resulting algorithm exhibits low degradation of performance compared to the deterministic case.

THEOREM 3.11. *The algorithm for online preempted scheduling on multiple servers under uncertainty, where each job's true demand exceeds the reported demand by a factor of $(1 + \alpha)$ with probability at most β, assuming $\mu + \alpha + 1 < s$, obtains a competitive ratio of at most:*

$$\frac{1}{1 - \beta} \left(1 + \gamma \cdot \frac{s}{s - \alpha} \cdot \frac{s}{s - \mu} \cdot \left[\frac{(\gamma - 1)(\mu - 1)}{(\gamma - 1)(\mu - 1) - 1} \right] \right).$$

4. COMMITTED SCHEDULING

In the previous section we focused on non-committed preemptive scheduling, in which the scheduler is not required to complete jobs that had been admitted to the system. While this setting may be plausible in some applications, for example when all of the jobs belong to the same user, some applications do require a guarantee for completion. We therefore consider the design of *committed* online scheduling algorithms, whereby the algorithm guarantees that admitted jobs are completed by their deadlines. We distinguish between two models of commitment, differing by the timing of the commitment.

1. *Commitment on arrival*: jobs are notified upon arrival whether they will be completed or rejected.

2. *Commitment on admission*: a less restrictive model, in which the scheduling algorithm may delay the decision whether to commit to a job. However, once the job is admitted (begins execution), the scheduler is guaranteed to complete it by its deadline.

Due to space limitations, we omit our full analysis and empirical evaluation from this section. We refer the reader for the extended version of the paper for more details.

4.1 Commitment on Arrival

The strict requirement of making the scheduling decision upon arrival leads to the following negative result

THEOREM 4.1. *Any online algorithm that commits to jobs on arrival has an unbounded competitive ratio for any slackness parameter s.*

4.2 Commitment on Admission

We design a heuristic solution, called COMMITTED, for this less restrictive commitment model. Our heuristic is based on the algorithm developed in Section 3 for non-committed scheduling. Specifically, to ensure that all committed jobs are completed, we modify the original threshold preemption rule as follows. An unallocated job j^* that passes the threshold choice rule of a server i will be allocated (i.e. will preempt the currently running job) only if no commitments are violated as a result. That is, we simulate the future schedule on server i that would occur if all partially executed jobs on that server had their completion times pushed back by D_{j^*}/k. If one of the completion times is pushed beyond the deadline of the corresponding job, we reject job j^* from server i. It is an open question whether this heuristic (or any other online algorithm) admits a satisfactory competitive ratio. Consequently, we evaluate the performance of our solution through extensive simulations, see Section 4.4.

We note that the gap parameter μ provides a method for the service provider to interpolate between the extremes of commitment on arrival and commitment on admission. For example, if $\mu = s/2$ then the service provider will necessarily commit to accepting or rejecting each job by the halfway point of its admission window at the latest. Larger values of μ result in even earlier notification times (at the expense of throughput), up to the extreme of $\mu = s$ which corresponds to commitment on arrival.

4.3 Economic-Driven Mechanisms with Commitment on Allocation

The design of scheduling mechanisms for external applications, such as paid cloud services, involves additional complications derived from the selfish nature of participants. Such mechanisms must be sensitive to potential manipulation by customers, as users striving to maximize their personal gain may attempt to do so by reporting false values or job parameters. Our previous work considers economic aspects of deadline-sensitive scheduling in the offline setting [10]; however, we must extend the insights from those works to handle online job arrivals. Moreover, the algorithmic solutions on which these mechanisms rely must satisfy economic-driven properties, such as monotonicity.

We suggest a scheduling mechanism for online scheduling called TRUTHFULCOMMITTED, which satisfies desirable economic-driven properties. The algorithmic core of the mechanism is a simplification of the COMMITTED algorithm, obtained by setting $\mu = 1$. We prove that the general framework described in [10] can be applied in this context, which leads to the design of a mechanism that is *truthful in dominant strategies*, meaning that it is always in the best interest of a customer to report its real job value and parameters (demand, deadline). The proof of truthfulness can be found in the full paper; the evaluation is briefly discussed in Section 4.4.

4.4 Empirical Evaluation

We evaluate the performance of our heuristic solutions, by comparing them to the non-committed algorithm, as well as to straw man mechanisms that are used in practice. To that end, we test all the scheduling mechanisms on both synthetic and empirical traces (extracted from Microsoft's production cluster). The main goal of the experiments is to compare the obtained throughput across different solutions, and also examine the value of incomplete jobs under the non-committed scheduler. The main highlights of our empirical study are the following. We show that for reasonable values of the input slackness ($s > 2$), COMMITTED and TRUTHFULCOMMITTED achieve nearly identical performance to the non-committed algorithm, for which we proved worst-case performance guarantees. Moreover, our algorithms outperforms straw man mechanisms by an order of magnitude (typically 10-50x).

5. CONCLUDING REMARKS

This paper introduces novel solutions for deadline-aware scheduling in large computing clusters. Our solution methodology is built upon two plausible assumptions: that the input exhibits deadline slackness, and that the provider has some leeway on its required responsiveness. Using our methodology, we design a simple online algorithm and prove constant-factor approximation guarantees for its performance. Based on this algorithm, we design additional heuristics that address important practical concerns such as provider commitments, demand uncertainties, and economic constraints. Our experiments on both synthetic and real job traces demonstrate the dominance of our scheduling framework over other potential heuristics. We also discuss how our framework can be used to design a truthful mechanism for online scheduling.

Our results motivate future study of more sophisticated models and scenarios. Specifically, we plan to consider data-processing job models (e.g, Hadoop, COSMOS), in which the system could benefit from uneven and time-varying allocation of resources across jobs (e.g., allocate resources differently for different "phases" of the job). Another challenging direction is to extend our framework to multi-dimensional resource allocation problems, e.g. allocating both CPU and bandwidth; see e.g., [5, 11]. We believe that this paper provides guidelines for designing mechanisms for the above cases and beyond.

6. REFERENCES

[1] A. Bar-Noy, R. Canetti, S. Kutten, Y. Mansour, and B. Schieber. Bandwidth allocation with preemption. *SIAM J. Comput.*, 28(5):1806–1828, 1999.

[2] R. Canetti and S. Irani. Bounding the power of preemption in randomized scheduling. *SIAM J. Comput.*, 27(4):993–1015, 1998.

[3] A. Ferguson, P. Bodik, S. Kandula, E. Boutin, and R. Fonseca. Jockey: guaranteed job latency in data parallel clusters. In *Proceedings of the 7th ACM european conference on Computer Systems*, pages 99–112. ACM, 2012.

[4] J. A. Garay, J. Naor, B. Yener, and P. Zhao. On-line admission control and packet scheduling with interleaving. In *INFOCOM*, 2002.

[5] A. Ghodsi, V. Sekar, M. Zaharia, and I. Stoica. Multi-resource fair queueing for packet processing. In *Proceedings of the ACM SIGCOMM 2012 conference on Applications, technologies, architectures, and protocols for computer communication*, pages 1–12. ACM, 2012.

[6] M. T. Hajiaghayi, R. Kleinberg, M. Mahdian, and D. C. Parkes. Online auctions with re-usable goods. pages 165–174, 2005.

[7] H. Herodotou, F. Dong, and S. Babu. No one (cluster) size fits all: automatic cluster sizing for data-intensive analytics. In *Proceedings of the 2nd ACM Symposium on Cloud Computing*, page 18. ACM, 2011.

[8] M. Isard, V. Prabhakaran, J. Currey, U. Wieder, K. Talwar, and A. Goldberg. Quincy: fair scheduling for distributed computing clusters. In *Proceedings of the ACM SIGOPS 22nd symposium on Operating systems principles*, pages 261–276. ACM, 2009.

[9] N. Jain, I. Menache, J. Naor, and J. Yaniv. A truthful mechanism for value-based scheduling in cloud computing. *Algorithmic Game Theory*, pages 178–189, 2011.

[10] N. Jain, I. Menache, J. Naor, and J. Yaniv. Near-optimal scheduling mechanisms for deadline-sensitive jobs in large computing clusters. In *SPAA*, pages 255–266, 2012.

[11] V. Jalaparti, H. Ballani, P. Costa, T. Karagiannis, and A. Rowstron. Bridging the tenant-provider gap in cloud services. In *ACM Symposium on Cloud Computing*. ACM, 2012.

[12] G. Koren and D. Shasha. D^{over}; an optimal on-line scheduling algorithm for overloaded real-time systems. In *RTSS*, pages 290–299. IEEE Computer Society, 1992.

[13] G. Koren and D. Shasha. Moca: A multiprocessor on-line competitive algorithm for real-time system scheduling. *Theor. Comput. Sci.*, 128(1&2):75–97, 1994.

Locality-Aware Task Management for Unstructured Parallelism: A Quantitative Limit Study

Richard M. Yoo†
richard.m.yoo@intel.com

Christopher J. Hughes†
christopher.j.hughes
@intel.com

Changkyu Kim†
changkyu.kim@intel.com

Yen-Kuang Chen†
yen-kuang.chen
@intel.com

Christos Kozyrakis‡
christos@ee.stanford.edu

†Parallel Computing Laboratory
Intel Labs
Santa Clara, CA 95054

‡Pervasive Parallelism Laboratory
Stanford University
Stanford, CA 94305

ABSTRACT

As we increase the number of cores on a processor die, the on-chip cache hierarchies that support these cores are getting larger, deeper, and more complex. As a result, non-uniform memory access effects are now prevalent even on a single chip. To reduce execution time and energy consumption, data access locality should be exploited. This is especially important for task-based programming systems, where a scheduler decides when and where on the chip the code segments, i.e., tasks, should execute. Capturing locality for structured task parallelism has been done effectively, but the more difficult case, unstructured parallelism, remains largely unsolved—little quantitative analysis exists to demonstrate the potential of locality-aware scheduling, and to guide future scheduler implementations in the most fruitful direction.

This paper quantifies the potential of locality-aware scheduling for unstructured parallelism on three different many-core processors. Our simulation results of 32-core systems show that locality-aware scheduling can bring up to *2.39x* speedup over a randomized schedule, and *2.05x* speedup over a state-of-the-art baseline scheduling scheme. At the same time, a locality-aware schedule reduces average energy consumption by *55%* and *47%*, relative to the random and the baseline schedule, respectively. In addition, our 1024-core simulation results project that these benefits will only increase: Compared to 32-core executions, we see up to 1.83x additional locality benefits. To capture such potentials in a practical setting, we also perform a detailed scheduler design space exploration to quantify the impact of different scheduling decisions. We also highlight the importance of locality-aware stealing, and demonstrate that a stealing scheme can exploit significant locality while performing load balancing. Over randomized stealing, our proposed scheme shows up to *2.0x* speedup for stolen tasks.

Categories and Subject Descriptors

B.8.2 [**Hardware**]: Performance and Reliability—*performance analysis and design aids*; C.1.4 [**Computer Systems Organization**]: Processor Architectures—*parallel architectures*; D.1.3 [**Software**]: Programming Techniques—*concurrent programming*

Keywords

Task Scheduling; Task Stealing; Locality; Performance; Energy

1. INTRODUCTION

Limits on technology scaling highlights parallelism as the means to obtain sustainable performance. More cores are being packed on the same die, and the on-chip cache hierarchies that support these cores are getting larger, deeper, and more complex. As a result, non-uniform memory access (NUMA) effects are now common even on a single chip [4, 21]. Avoiding the high latency to access remote caches and main memory is increasingly critical for performance. The same holds for energy efficiency: Moving a word of data from a remote cache or from an off-chip memory requires 10 and 20 times, respectively, more energy than an arithmetic operation on that word [9]. Consensus exists [14, 7] that memory access locality should be exploited to reduce execution time and energy.

This is especially important for *task-based* programming systems [12, 25, 17, 5, 8, 26], where a computation is broken down into small code segments, *tasks*, and the underlying runtime *schedules* these tasks across threads for execution. Specifically, a scheduler generates a task schedule by *grouping* tasks to execute on the same thread, and by applying *ordering* across the tasks. For load balancing, the runtime may employ *stealing* to redistribute tasks from loaded threads to idle threads. To capture locality on a task-based system, the scheduling algorithm should be locality-aware.

The exact scheduling logic, however, depends on the type of parallelism exposed by the programming system: *structured* or *unstructured parallelism*. For *structured parallelism* (i.e., *task-parallel* programming systems [12, 31]), explicit data or control dependencies exist across tasks, and the runtime can leverage this information to exploit locality. A large body of work on capturing locality for structured parallelism exists [1, 13, 10, 29], and these schemes typically focus on exploiting producer-consumer locality (e.g., schedule consumer task close to producer).

On the contrary, for *unstructured parallelism* (i.e., *data-parallel programming systems* [25]), for each parallel section, tasks are all independent—they may execute on any thread at any time, and the computation result will still be valid. While they represent a significant class of parallel applications, exploiting locality for unstructured parallelism has been quite difficult: First, the lack of dependency information implies the scheduler must obtain additional information from the workload to synthesize locality structure. Without understanding what the crucial information is, run-time and storage overheads for collecting the information can be significant. Second, the larger degrees of freedom in scheduling increases algorithmic complexity. Having many degrees of freedom implies many grouping and ordering choices, and enumerating all combinations is prohibitive. Third, the complexity of many-core cache hierarchies makes the process all the more complicated. Grouping and ordering decisions must optimize locality across all cache levels, whether the hierarchy being *shared* or *private*.

As a result, capturing the locality of the applications utilizing unstructured parallelism is not well understood. In fact, many runtime systems retrofit the simple scheduling heuristics meant for structured parallelism (e.g., FIFO or LIFO [3]) to unstructured parallelism, and hope that the schedule will capture significant locality. More importantly, little quantitative analysis exists to demonstrate the potential of locality-aware scheduling, and to guide future locality-aware scheduler implementations in the most fruitful direction. While some compiler efforts that map unstructured parallelism onto the cache hierarchy have been reported [18], they (1) apply only to grid-based workloads, and (2) do not address stealing.

The contributions of our paper are as follows: (1) We provide results that **quantitatively demonstrate the potential of locality-aware scheduling** for unstructured parallelism. Specifically, we develop a locality analysis framework and an offline scheduler that takes workload profile information as input and generates schedules that are optimized for the target cache hierarchy. We then evaluate the effectiveness of the scheduler on **three specific many-core cache hierarchies** that represent distinct and very different points in the many-core design space. Our 32-core simulation results verify the importance of locality-aware scheduling, as we observe up to **2.39x** speedup over a randomized schedule and **2.05x** speedup over a state-of-the-art baseline scheduling scheme [6, 22]. By increasing the hit rates in the caches closer to the cores, a locality-aware schedule also saves energy: It reduces the average energy consumption in the memory hierarchy beyond the L1 caches by **55%** relative to the random schedule, and **47%** relative to the baseline. We also perform **1024-core simulations** to verify that the performance advantages of locality-awareness only increase with more cores, and see up to **1.83x** additional performance improvement.

(2) To capture such potentials in a practical setting, we also **perform a scheduler design space exploration** to quantify the impact of different design decisions. In particular, by selectively applying task grouping and ordering, we show that proper grouping alone brings up to 2.23x speedup over a random schedule, using a good ordering gives up to 1.17x additional speedup, and applying grouping and ordering across multiple cache levels gives up to 1.52x speedup over a single-level schedule. These results identify the most crucial information necessary to develop practical locality-aware schedulers.

Additionally, while the conventional wisdom says there exists an inherent tradeoff between locality and load balancing, we **show load balancing can exploit significant locality**. By honoring the task grouping and ordering specified by the schedule as it transfers tasks across threads, our locality-aware stealing implementation re-

Listing 1: **The core task-programming API.**

```
// Initialize task queue library
taskQInit(num_threads, max_tasks);

// Specify the parallel section by providing
// (1) task function and (2) task space
taskQEnqueue(task_fn, num_dims, size_arr);

// Execute the section in parallel
taskQWait();

// Finalize task queue library
taskQEnd();
```

duces task execution time for stolen tasks by up to a factor of **2.0x** over randomized stealing.

These results also demonstrate that application domains that traditionally refuted dynamic scheduling in favor of locality—e.g., high-performance computing—may employ dynamic task management without losing significant locality. Even for a dedicated system, interference due to shared resources on a large-scale many-core chip (e.g., caches and memory controllers) can introduce significant load imbalance [22], and statically orchestrating all computation and communication will be increasingly challenging.

2. LOCALITY-AWARE TASK SCHEDULING

The key to obtaining the results summarized above is to decouple workload locality analysis and schedule generation, to manage complexity. We first perform a graph-based locality analysis to understand inherent workload locality, and then utilize the analysis results to map computation onto a target cache hierarchy. This decoupling allows to generate schedules for various cache hierarchies using a common framework, and to systematically alter scheduling decisions to perform design space exploration.

2.1 Unstructured Parallelism: API and Workloads

Listing 1 shows the core task-programming API we use in this study, which assumes a task queue-based, software task manager [25, 22]. It shows one parallel section; a program may have many. When the user application invokes **taskQInit**(), the manager spawns worker threads in its thread pool, and creates a task queue for each thread. A user then specifies the parallel section by providing a *task function* and a *task space*—a Cartesian space of integers—to **taskQEnqueue**(). For each coordinate in the task space, the manager bundles the task function with the coordinate to create a task, and schedules it by enqueueing to one of the queues.

Calling **taskQWait**() triggers the parallel execution of tasks. At first, each thread repeatedly dequeues a task from its own queue, and executes it by invoking the task function with the coordinate as the argument. When its queue becomes empty, a thread tries to steal tasks from another queue. When the **taskQWait**() function returns, all the tasks have been executed, and the worker threads wait at the pool. Finally, **taskQEnd**() releases the allocated resources.

Note that the task manager assumes no dependencies among the tasks, and may arbitrarily group and order tasks across the queues; therefore, a task should be enqueued only after its dependencies have been satisfied. Since all the tasks in an unstructured parallel section are independent, large number of tasks can be created and enqueued in a single call to **taskQEnqueue**().

Table 1 summarizes the workloads we ported to the above API. Most of them are real C/C++ workloads originally written to stress test a commercial processor [28]; they are optimized to capture decent intra-task locality. Variants appear in [22, 27, 20] as well. In particular, notice that the applications utilize relatively fine-grained

Workload	Description	Task	Tasks that share data	Access pattern	# tasks	Task size	Input
hj	Probe phase of hash-join	Performs single row lookup	Look up same hash bucket (clustered sharing)	hash tables	4,096	157	4,460
bprj	Reconstruct a 3-D volume from 2-D images	Reconstructs a sub-volume	Work on sub-volumes mapping to overlapping pixels (clustered sharing)	3-D traversal	4,096	415	3,650
gjk	Collision detection	Operates on sets of object pairs	Work on overlapping object sets (clustered sharing)	pointer access	384	4,950	940
brmap	Map pixels in a 2-D image to another 2-D image	Maps pixels from a sub-image	Work on sub-images mapping to overlapping pixels (structured sharing)	trajectory-based	4,977	1,298	22,828
conv	2-D convolution filter (5x5) on image	Operates on square-shaped image block	Operate on overlapping pixels (structured sharing)	grid-based	1,056	9,487	26,400
mmm	Blocked matrix-matrix multiplication	Multiplies a pair of sub-matrices	Use common sub-matrix (clustered sharing)	grid-based	4,096	49,193	344,064
smvm	Sparse matrix-vector multiplication	Multiplies one row of matrix	Touch overlapping elements in a vector (clustered sharing)	sparse matrix	4,096	891	42,385
sp	Scalar pentadiagonal PDE solver	Solves a subset of equation lattice	Work on neighboring lattices (structured sharing)	grid-based	1,156	5,956	439

Table 1: **Workloads used in this study.** *Task size* **is the average dynamic instruction count.** *Input* **is the sum of all task footprints in KB.**

tasks, and are not necessarily organized in a cache oblivious [11] or recursive manner. As discussed, execution order of tasks in these workloads does not affect the computation result.

2.2 Graph-Based Locality Analysis

A locality-aware schedule should map tasks to cores, taking into account both locality and load balance. Two techniques to construct such a schedule are *task grouping* and *ordering*. Executing a set of tasks (a *task group*) on cores that share one or more levels of cache captures data reuse across tasks. Similarly, executing tasks in an optimal order minimizes the reuse distance of shared data between tasks, which makes it easier for caches to capture the temporal locality. Generating a locality-aware schedule depends on understanding how task groups should be formed, and when ordering will matter.

To understand the *inherent* locality patterns of workloads, we develop a *graph-based* locality analysis framework. The framework proceeds as follows: (1) We first profile each workload to collect data access traces at cache line granularity, and discard ordering information to obtain read and write sets for each task. (2) Using the set information, we construct a *task sharing graph*. In a task sharing graph $G(V, E)$, a *vertex* represents a task, and an *edge* denotes sharing. A *vertex weight* is the task size in terms of number of dynamic instructions, and an *edge weight* is the number of cache lines shared between the two tasks connected by the edge. (3) We then partition the graph to form task groups, and observe some metrics to determine the 'right' task group size and the impact of ordering.

Even with profile information about each task's read and write sets, creating an 'optimal' set of task groups is an *NP-hard* problem. We therefore use a heuristic graph partitioning tool (METIS [19]) to generate quality task groups. METIS divides the vertices from a task sharing graph into a given number of groups, while trying to (a) maximize the sum of edge weights internal to each group (i.e., data sharing captured by a task group), and (b) equalize the sum of vertex weights in each group (i.e., balance load).

Table 2 shows the framework output for some of our workloads. Using these results, we try to answer: (1) How should a task group be formed? and (2) When does ordering matter? In addition, we also discuss the implications of task size on locality. For now we discuss locality assuming a single core with a single cache. We later extend the analysis to multiple cores with complex, multi-level cache hierarchies.

Q1: How should a task group be formed?

In Table 2, *sum of footprints* denotes the average sum of individual task footprints for each task group, while *union of footprints*

denotes the average size of the union of individual task footprints (i.e., shared lines are counted only once)[1].

Intuitively, to maximize locality, a task group should be formed so that the *working set* of the group fits in cache. In that regard, the sum of footprints represents an upper bound on working set size (i.e., when a schedule fails to exploit any reuse across tasks), and the union of footprints represents a lower bound. For a fully-associative cache, the union of footprints should accurately track the working set. However, due to conflict misses and unaccounted runtime accesses, the actual cache capacity demand could be greater than the union of footprints. Hence, to capture the working set, task groups should be formed so that the cache size falls between the union and sum of task footprints. For example, in Table 2, for **smvm**, when generating a schedule for a 32 KB cache, a task group should contain 8 tasks so that the cache size is between 21 KB (= union of footprints) and 82 KB (= sum of footprints).

However, strictly following this rule may lead to other inefficiencies: For example, grouping too few tasks together might introduce high scheduling overhead, and too many could introduce load imbalance. Such issues can be avoided by performing multi-level grouping, or by executing tasks within a task group in parallel (see Section 2.3).

Q2: When does ordering matter?

We consider both *task ordering* and *group ordering*. *Task ordering* specifies the traversal order of vertices for a task group. Assuming a task queue-based task management system, task order denotes the *dequeue order* of tasks within the same group. *Group ordering* specifies the execution order of task groups. Both task ordering and group ordering can maximize temporal locality when reuse distance is minimized.

To assess when ordering matters, we define two metrics, *sharing degree* and *cut cost*, that dictate the importance of reuse distance on certain data. In Table 2, given a shared cache line, the *sharing degree* denotes the average number of tasks within a task group that share it. The table reports normalized sharing degree, so a degree of 1 means all the tasks within the task group share the cache line.

In terms of locality, sharing degree indicates the potential impact of task ordering. Specifically, a high sharing degree implies that data is shared by a large fraction of tasks. For example, in Table 2a, it can be seen that for task groups that would fit in a 32 KB cache (8 tasks per group), about 90% of the **smvm** tasks within a group

---

[1]Since read sharing is dominant in our workloads, we give equal weight to read and write sharing in computing our metrics. It is straightforward to assign different weights to reflect different costs for read and write sharing.

Table 2(a):

Relative task group size	1	1/2	$1/2^2$	$1/2^3$	$1/2^4$	$\mathbf{1/2^5}$	$1/2^6$	$1/2^7$	$1/2^8$	$\mathbf{1/2^9}$	$1/2^{10}$
# tasks / group	4,096	2,048	1,024	512	256	**128**	64	32	16	**8**	4
Sum of footprints (KB)	42,385	21,192	10,596	5,298	2,649	**1,324**	662	331	165	**82**	41
Union of footprints (KB)	4,946	2,618	1,408	757	400	**211**	110	59	34	**21**	14
Sharing degree	0.03	0.03	0.04	0.06	0.11	**0.21**	0.38	0.58	0.75	**0.90**	0.99
Cut cost (E+07)	0.00	2.04	3.13	3.68	3.98	**4.15**	4.27	4.41	4.77	**4.97**	5.08

(a) Statistics collected for **smvm**.

Relative task group size	1	1/2	$1/2^2$	$1/2^3$	$1/2^4$	$\mathbf{1/2^5}$	$1/2^6$	$\mathbf{1/2^7}$	$1/2^8$	$1/2^9$	$1/2^{10}$
# tasks / group	4,096	2,048	1,024	512	256	**128**	64	**32**	16	8	4
Sum of footprints (KB)	3,650	1,825	912	456	228	**114**	57	**28**	14	7	3
Union of footprints (KB)	177	91	51	29	16	**9**	5	**3**	1	1	1
Sharing degree	0.01	0.01	0.02	0.04	0.07	**0.13**	0.22	**0.38**	0.58	0.78	0.92
Cut cost (E+06)	0.00	4.19	6.31	7.37	7.91	**8.19**	8.36	**8.48**	8.61	8.71	8.77

(b) Statistics collected for **bprj**.

Table 2: **Framework output for** *smvm* **and** *bprj*. *Relative task group size* of 1 denotes the case where all the tasks are grouped into a single task group. *Sharing degree* of 1 means on average all the tasks within the task group share the cache line.

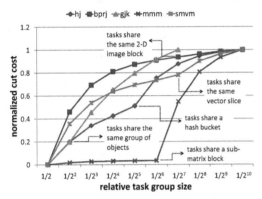

Figure 1: **Cut cost trend over different sizes of task groups. Cut costs are normalized to fit within the interval [0, 1].**

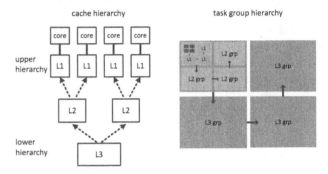

Figure 2: **Generating recursive task groups. Different levels of groups are sized to fit in a particular cache level. Colored arrows denote the group order determined over task groups.**

share any given shared cache line. Therefore, task ordering will have little impact on the reuse distance of shared data. On the other hand, when the sharing degree is low, task ordering could have a significant impact on locality. For **bprj** with 32 tasks per group, the sharing degree is 0.38, which is quite low compared to **smvm**. We can conjecture **bprj** is more sensitive to task ordering.

Next, in Table 2, the *cut cost* represents the sum of the edge weights for vertices in different groups (i.e., data sharing not captured within a single task group). Specifically, our workloads exhibited two distinct cut cost patterns: *clustered sharing* and *structured sharing*—relative importance of group ordering depends on this workload pattern.

Workloads with Clustered Sharing: When a task sharing graph is drawn for these workloads, the graph exhibits disjoint clusters or *cliques* of tasks that share the same data structure. For example, groups of **smvm** tasks share the same vector region, and **hj** tasks that access the same hash bucket.

Figure 1 plots the cut cost trend for the workloads of this type. As can be seen, these workloads exhibit an abrupt increase in cut cost—a *knee*—as we decrease the task group size. For some workloads, other cache lines are sporadically shared, so the knee is less visually striking; we determine knees by manual code analysis.

The sudden increase in cut cost means that the task group size became small enough that tasks sharing their key data structures have been separated into different groups. Ordering those task groups so that they execute consecutively will increase locality. For these workloads, assuming we group tasks so that each group fits in cache, the importance of group ordering depends on the *relative size of the cache to the task clique*. For example, we find that a task clique in **hj** exhibits a 128 KB footprint (where the knee is in Fig-

ure 1). On a 32 KB cache, **hj** would benefit from group ordering; on a 256 KB cache, group ordering would be less important.

Workloads with Structured Sharing: These workloads exhibit structured, regular sharing patterns. For example, for **conv**, a 2-D stencil operation, a task shares cache lines with its nearest 4 neighbors in the 2-D task space. For these workloads, cut cost is proportional to the number of groups, and no knee exists. Hence, group ordering is important *regardless of the cache size*; but a simple group ordering, such as assigning consecutive task groups to the same core, should capture reuse.

Now we discuss the implications of task size on a locality-aware schedule. In short, task size indirectly changes the relative importance of task grouping and ordering. For example, when the working set of a single task is larger than the cache, grouping tasks has little benefit, but ordering may help capture reuse from one task to the next. In general, smaller tasks give the scheduler more freedom. If a programmer breaks a large task into smaller tasks, and if the memory access pattern was originally suboptimal, better locality may be achieved via proper grouping and ordering.

2.3 Mapping Computation to Cache Hierarchy: Recursive Scheduling

We now leverage the framework analysis results to map computation onto an actual cache hierarchy. Specifically, we consider *recursive scheduling*, which (1) matches task group working sets and (2) applies ordering across all cache levels. The scheduling logic can be generically applied to arbitrary memory hierarchies; and by selectively applying task grouping and ordering, it can be used to perform scheduler design space exploration (see Section 3).

Creating an optimal order for tasks, however, is also an *NP-hard* problem. We therefore use a heuristic to provide high quality ordering. Specifically, we apply Prim's algorithm to construct a maximum spanning tree (MST), and use the order that the vertices are added to the MST. In architectural terms, Prim's algorithm accumulates the read and write sets of scheduled tasks, and picks the task whose read and write sets exhibit the maximum intersection with the cumulative sets as the next task to execute. To construct a task order, we apply MST on a task sharing graph. To construct a group order, we first map the task sharing graph to a *task group sharing graph*, where each *uber node* represents a task group; we then apply MST to the task group sharing graph.

Under recursive scheduling, to maximize the utility of every cache level, we start from the bottommost: We first group tasks so that the task group's working set fits in the last-level cache, and apply ordering over those groups. We then recursively apply this approach to each of the task groups, targeting one level up in the cache hierarchy each time. Figure 2 illustrates the procedure.

In the figure, we first perform grouping on the full set of tasks to create L3 groups, each of which matches the L3 size. Next, we order the L3 groups. For each L3 group, we then decompose it into tasks and create L2 groups to match the L2 size. Then we order the L2 groups. We proceed in this fashion until we finally generate L1 groups, order them, and order their component tasks.

Generating a schedule in this fashion results in a hierarchy of task groups. Moreover, since each task group also denotes a scheduling granularity, all the tasks in a group will be executed consecutively. Therefore, a task group will stay *resident* in its target cache from beginning to end. The existence of a hierarchy among these task groups guarantees that all the groups containing a given task stay resident at their corresponding level in the cache hierarchy, thus exploiting locality across all cache levels.

A slight complication arises when a system has private caches or caches shared by a subset of cores. In such a case, we should *pre-group* sets of task groups, so that groups with high sharing are assigned to the same cache. Specifically, recursive scheduling performs an additional operation whenever hitting a *branch* in the cache hierarchy: It first pre-groups the set of tasks according to the number of consumers one level above, and then performs grouping for each partition. For example, in Figure 2, with two L2 caches, before generating L2 groups it first divides the set of tasks in an L3 group into two partitions, one for each L2 cache. It then constructs a task sharing graph for each partition, and uses the graphs to create two sets of L2 groups. Each set of L2 groups is separately ordered. Due to the pre-grouping, the task schedule generated ensures that the tasks from a set of L2 groups go to the same L2—without this property, group ordering would not be effective. Pre-grouping can be done with the same graph partitioning algorithm that performs task grouping.

3. EVALUATION OF LOCALITY-AWARE TASK SCHEDULING

We now evaluate recursive schedules for specific many-core cache hierarchies that represent distinct points in the many-core design space, to quantify the potential of locality-aware scheduling and perform design space exploration.

3.1 Experiment Settings

As described in Table 3, we simulate three different many-core chip configurations[2]. The first configuration is a throughput computing processor we refer to as *Throughput Processor*. Each core has a private L1 and L2, so all caches are private. The combined L2 capacity is 8 MB, and coherence is maintained through a directory-based protocol. The ISA includes 512-bit SIMD instructions, and the applications have been tuned to use them; simple spatial locality is already captured, and exploiting the remaining locality is more challenging. For this configuration, we use an industrial simulator that models a commercial processor [28].

[2]Instruction caches are modeled in all simulations. However, since we pass function pointer, not the code, to schedule tasks, disruption due to scheduling is minimal.

Core	32 cores; dual issue in-order x86 16-wide 512-bit SIMD extensions Core-private 32 KB 8-way L1, 1-cycle Core-private 256 KB 16-way L2, 14-cycles Directory slice for L2 coherence
Interconnect	Ring network connects L2s, directory slices, and memory ctrls
Memory	4 memory ctrls, 120-cycles

(a) Throughput Processor Configurations

Core	32 cores; dual issue in-order SPARC v9 Core-private 32 KB 4-way L1, 1-cycle
Tile	4 cores per tile Tile-shared 4 MB 16-way banked L2, 10-cycles Directory slice, memory ctrl, and L3 bank
L3	16 MB per bank 16-way, 21-cycles
Interconnect	2-D flattened butterfly connects tiles
Memory	158-cycles

(b) Tiled Processor Configurations

Core	32 to 1024 cores; dual issue in-order x86 Core-private 32 KB 4-way L1, 1-cycle
Tile	1 core per tile Per-tile 512 KB 8-way L2, 12-cycles Directory slice and memory ctrl
Interconnect	2-D mesh connects tiles
Memory	100-cycles

(c) Futuristic Processor Configurations

Table 3: **Simulated system configurations.**

The second configuration is a tiled many-core processor we refer to as *Tiled Processor*. Each core has a private L1, and four cores form a tile. Each tile has a 4 MB L2 shared among the cores on the tile, and all tiles share a single L3 cache. We simulate this with the M5 simulator [2] coupled with the GEMS memory toolset [23].

In addition, to project the potential of locality-aware scheduling as the number of cores continues to increase, we employ a third configuration we refer to as *Futuristic Processor*. Each tile contains a core, core-private L1 and L2, and the tiles are connected through a mesh interconnect. We vary the number of cores from 32 to 1024. We model this configuration with a modified version of the Graphite parallel simulator [24].

Due to ISA and toolchain issues, we evaluate the Throughput Processor on all benchmarks except **sp** from Table 1, the Tiled Processor on the bottom four benchmarks, and the Futuristic Processor on all benchmarks except **gjk**.

As described in Section 2.1, we utilize a task queue-based software task management system [25, 22, 27]. In particular, task queues are pre-populated with offline-generated schedules right before the start of each parallel section. By default, randomized task stealing [3] is performed across queues for load balancing. We further study the implications of stealing on locality in Section 4.

By evaluating schedules from different scheduling policies, we can quantify the impact of various scheduling decisions on locality. Specifically, in addition to recursive schedules, we evaluate (a) random and (b) baseline schedules. We obtain a random schedule by assigning each task to a random core, and then randomly ordering the tasks for each core. We report the averages over 3 instances.

For the baseline schedule, we apply Parallel Depth First (PDF) scheduling [6]. Originally developed for structured parallelism, PDF hinges on the notion that many programs have been optimized for good sequential cache performance. Therefore, when a core completes a task, PDF assigns the task that the sequential program

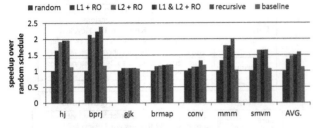

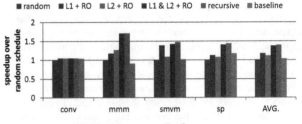

(a) Throughput Processor Performance	(b) Tiled Processor Performance

Figure 3: **Performance summary. Shows the speedup over a random schedule. For each workload, from left to right are: (1)** *random,* **(2)** *L1 grouping only,* **(3)** *L2 grouping only,* **(4)** *L1 and L2 grouping,* **(5)** *recursive schedule,* **and (6)** *baseline.* **Baseline represents the state-of-the-art PDF scheduling [6], and (2)~(4) use random ordering (***RO***) instead of MST ordering.**

Workload	# L2 grps	Tasks / L2 grp	Tasks / L1 grp	Sharing degree	L2 cut cost	L1 cut cost
hj	32	128	16	0.91	4.0E+06	7.1E+06
bprj	32	128	32	0.38	8.2E+06	8.5E+06
gjk	32	12	12	0.36	20,010	20,010
brmap	128	39	5	0.53	22,609	61,099
conv	32	33	4	0.55	10,036	27,620
mmm	512	8	1	N/A	1.3E+08	1.4E+08
smvm	32	128	8	0.90	4.2E+07	5.0E+07

Table 4: **Task groups determined by the recursive scheduler and per group statistics. Sharing degree is for L1.**

Workload	L1 MPKI			L2 MPKI		
	random	recursive	baseline	random	recursive	baseline
hj	16.05	**6.63**	13.74	12.64	**6.61**	11.36
bprj	12.93	**3.29**	10.35	10.16	**2.72**	6.91
gjk	8.35	7.55	7.31	8.10	7.39	7.16
brmap	18.66	14.97	14.53	18.48	14.60	14.48
conv	8.54	7.73	7.62	8.37	**5.30**	6.47
mmm	28.37	**17.05**	28.38	27.08	**14.29**	26.07
smvm	136.30	132.22	133.86	52.93	**23.29**	48.46

Table 5: **Measured MPKIs over different schedules. Bold figures denote where recursive schedule improves over baseline.**

would have executed next. Since many parallel programming systems support both structured and unstructured parallelism [25, 5, 8, 26], the same schedule is often applied to unstructured parallelism. For unstructured parallelism, PDF linearizes the task space along the innermost loop, and then evenly divides the tasks into as many chunks as cores, such that consecutive tasks fall in the same chunk. The scheduler then assigns one chunk per core.

Throughout the section, to isolate locality measurements from task management overheads, we use *the sum of the execution time of the tasks* as our primary locality metric. Management overheads can be mitigated through proposed hardware or hybrid methods [22, 20, 27]. Since it uses a simpler cache hierarchy, we focus on the Throughput Processor performance results first. In Section 3.3, we contrast the Tiled Processor results to highlight where different memory hierarchies affect scheduling; in Section 3.4, we project how locality benefits will scale with more cores.

3.2 Throughput Processor Performance Results

In this section, we first summarize the performance and energy benefits of recursive scheduling. Then we isolate the benefits of each feature of the recursive schedule. In particular, we answer the following questions: (1) How much does locality-aware scheduling matter? (2) How much does grouping matter? (3) How much does ordering matter? (4) How does task size affect the schedule? (5) How do single-level schedules compare?

For each workload, Table 4 shows the recursive scheduler's task groups for the Throughput Processor, and the corresponding statistics. Table 2 also highlights L2 and L1 groups.

Q1: How much does locality-aware scheduling matter?

Figure 3a presents the speedup of various schedules over a random schedule, measured in terms of the sum of the execution time of the tasks. For each workload, from left to right, different schedules activate different aspects of grouping and ordering, to arrive at recursive schedule. Here we focus on the performance of recursive schedules; we explain the rest in the following sections. Table 5 reports the measured misses per thousand instructions (MPKI).

The figure shows that a locality-aware schedule (i.e., from the recursive scheduler) improves performance significantly. On average, the speedup over the random schedule is 1.60x, and over the baseline is 1.43x. In particular, **hj**, **bprj**, and **mmm** see large speedups of 1.96x, 2.39x, and 2.00x, respectively. Table 5 shows that this speedup is obtained by improving the behavior at both cache levels, verifying that multiple levels of scheduling is important. **conv** and **smvm** also see significant speedups of 1.32x and 1.65x, respectively, from improved L2 behavior.

While **gjk** and **brmap** are fairly memory intensive (judging from their MPKIs), they see little benefit from locality-aware scheduling. These workloads have simple locality patterns that the baseline schedule is able to capture—grouping consecutive tasks captures most of the locality.

We now compare the energy consumption of different schedules. Specifically, we compute the energy for the *uncore*, i.e., the part of the memory hierarchy beyond the L1s[3], which includes the L2s, ring network, and memory: For each schedule we measure the total L2 accesses, network hops, and memory accesses, and use the model from [15] to derive energy. Figure 4 shows the results. For each workload, the first three pairs of bars show activity counts—L2 cache accesses, on-die interconnect hops, and memory accesses—and the last pair of bars shows energy consumption. Results are normalized to random schedule.

As expected, locality-aware schedule significantly reduces all three activity counts, and thus the energy consumption: On average, recursive schedule reduces energy by 55% relative to random schedule, and 47% relative to the baseline. Recursive schedules reduce L2 accesses by reducing the L1 miss rate (see Table 5), and likewise decrease on-die network and main memory activity by reducing the L2 miss rate. This shows that locality-aware scheduling, or *placing computation* near where data resides, could be a viable alternative to reducing energy through *migrating data* [16, 15] to the cores performing computation.

Q2: How much does grouping matter?

Recursive scheduling provides benefits through both grouping and ordering. Here, we isolate the benefits of grouping by disabling the ordering and pre-grouping parts of the recursive scheduler. We

---

[3][30] reports that on the chip level, Intel® many-core processors spend 40% of its power on the uncore.

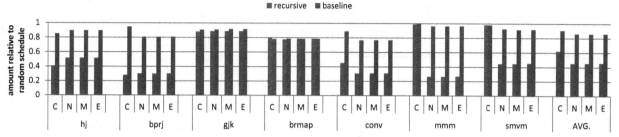

Figure 4: **Energy consumption and activity counts of the memory hierarchy beyond the L1 caches for various schedules.** *C*, *N*, and *M* denotes activity counts for L2 cache accesses, network hops, and memory accesses, respectively. *E* denotes the energy consumption.

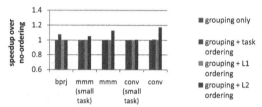

Figure 5: **Workload sensitivity to task, L1 group, and L2 group ordering. Speedup is relative to recursive grouping (with random ordering).**

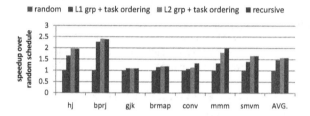

Figure 6: **Single-level schedule performance.**

also isolate the benefits of the two levels of grouping by disabling one of the two levels at a time.

Figure 3a shows the impact of various grouping policies. Compared to random schedules, performing both L1 and L2 grouping with random ordering (L1 & L2 + RO)—*recursive grouping*—provides 1.52x average speedup, capturing most of the benefit of full recursive schedules (1.60x). This shows that grouping captures significant locality, and ordering provides limited additional benefit on top of recursive grouping.

Due to its private-only cache hierarchy, on the Throughput Processor, applying only a single level of grouping can capture much of the locality benefits of recursive grouping: L1 grouping with random ordering (L1 + RO) or L2 grouping with random ordering (L2 + RO) provides 1.36x and 1.49x average speedup, respectively. Nevertheless, recursive grouping helps when different applications favor different cache levels.

Q3: How much does ordering matter?

We first consider ordering alone, and then when it can provide additional benefits over grouping. In a separate experiment where we applied MST ordering to each of the 32 task chunks generated by the baseline schedule, we observed 1.26x average speedup over random. So while ordering by itself does provide performance benefits, these are smaller than those from recursive grouping.

Next, in Figure 3a, comparing the performance of L1 and L2 grouping with random ordering (L1 & L2 + RO) against recursive scheduling shows that three workloads see benefits from ordering on top of grouping—1.07x, 1.17x, and 1.12x speedup on **bprj**, **conv**, and **mmm**, respectively.

Figure 5 shows **bprj**, **mmm**, and **conv** sensitivity to task, L1 group, and L2 group ordering. As can be seen, **bprj** benefits from

task ordering; **mmm** and **conv** on the other hand, benefit from ordering L2 groups. L1 group ordering is not as effective.

bprj benefits from task ordering since its first level working set is slightly larger than expected (due to runtime accesses), and its sharing degree is low (see Table 4). With task ordering, L1 MPKI for **bprj** reduces from 4.97 to 2.27, while L2 MPKI reduces from 2.37 to 1.90. **mmm** is a clustered sharing workload—its task groups exhibit affinity for a small number of other groups (see Section 2.2). It also has high L2 cut cost (see Table 4), meaning the affinity between L2 groups is very strong. Therefore, it benefits from ordering L2 groups. **conv** is a structured sharing workload—its task groups exhibit stencil-like affinity. It thus benefits from L2 ordering.

Q4: How does task size affect the schedule?

For regular, grid-based workloads such as **mmm** and **conv**, task size can be easily adjusted by changing blocking parameters. For **mmm**, a single task actually overflows an L1. We shrink each **mmm** task so that a dozen tasks can fit in a single L1 group. Likewise, we make each **conv** task smaller so that it fits in an L1. Figure 5 shows that the sensitivity to L2 ordering reduces for small tasks (we label the modified versions of workloads with small task). The workloads perform the same computation, independent of the task size; hence, the locality to be captured should remain the same. Task size then *alters at which cache level the locality is captured*.

Also, as discussed in Section 2.2, task size can affect performance by changing the scheduler's freedom to exploit locality. For the experiment above, the performance improvement of recursive scheduling over random increased from 2.00x to 3.08x as we decreased **mmm** task size. Since a task group amounts to a *scheduler-determined optimal task size*, users should express their tasks in the finest granularity possible to maximize scheduling freedom. Task scheduling overheads may limit task granularity, but they could be reduced with hardware or hybrid methods [22, 27].

Q5: How do single-level schedules compare?

A single-level schedule denotes performing grouping and ordering at a single level only: i.e., L1 or L2-sized task groups with MST task ordering, but random ordering across groups. Figure 6 compares the performance of L1 and L2 single-level schedules against recursive scheduling. As expected, recursive scheduling provides the best all-around performance. Specifically, for **conv** and **mmm**, neither single-level schedule alone matches the performance of the recursive schedule. For the other workloads, however, an L2 single-level schedule is on par with the recursive schedule—due in part to the flat cache hierarchy and L1 latency hiding through SIMD.

3.3 Tiled Processor Performance Results

Here we highlight where different cache hierarchies affect a locality-aware schedule. Specifically, we ported **conv**, **mmm**, **smvm**, and **sp** to the Tiled Processor[4], and conducted the same experiments.

---

[4]Vector instructions were replaced by scalar loops.

# cores	32	64	128	256	512	1024
Cache-to-cache	124.32	134.39	146.38	166.38	192.18	228.94
Mem-to-cache	184.61	186.70	199.13	208.93	220.83	246.30

Table 6: **Cache-to-cache and memory-to-cache transfer latency of a single cache line.**

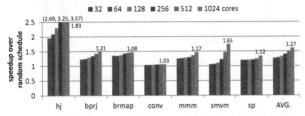

Figure 7: **Performance scalability up to 1024 cores. At each core count, speedup is over a random schedule. For each workload, the number on the rightmost bar denotes the additional locality benefits of 1024-core execution when compared to 32-core.**

Figure 3b summarizes the results. Similar to the Throughput Processor, recursive scheduling brings about a significant speedup: On average, the speedup over random is 1.40x, and over baseline is 1.35x. This demonstrates that a processor with a shared cache organization has similar potential for locality.

However, shared caches *alter the relative importance of grouping and ordering*. Similar to Figure 3a, Figure 3b compares different grouping schemes. In contrast to the Throughput Processor where L2 grouping alone (L2 + RO) provided most of the grouping benefits, for the Tiled Processor neither L1 nor L2 single-level grouping (i.e., L1 + RO and L2 + RO) consistently matches recursive grouping. With a complex cache organization, matching the task group hierarchy to the cache hierarchy becomes important.

For this hierarchy, we also see that ordering provides less benefit over grouping—the performance of L1 and L2 grouping with random ordering (L1 & L2 + RO) is very similar to recursive schedule. In particular, **conv** and **mmm**, which exhibit sensitivity to ordering on the Throughput Processor, now barely benefit from ordering. This can be attributed to the increased importance of recursive grouping: Recursive grouping amounts to applying *coarse ordering* over smaller groups, limiting the benefits of additional ordering.

As on the Throughput Processor, the benefits of ordering alone (i.e., applying MST to each task chunk generated by the baseline) are significant, but smaller than grouping alone: 1.15x speedup over random, compared to 1.37x.

3.4 Futuristic Processor Performance Results

As we add more cores on a processor die, the size of the on-die network increases, which results in larger access latencies for remote cache and memory. To quantify the impact of core scaling on locality-awareness, we vary the number of cores on the Futuristic Processor from 32 to 1024, and compare the performance of random and recursive schedules. Workload inputs were re-adjusted to fully utilize up to 1024 cores.

Table 6 first shows the measurements from a pointer-chasing microbenchmark; a producer core populates each cache line-wide entry of a list with a pointer to the next entry, then the consumer core chases the chain of pointers. The table reports the average latency to transfer a cache line from (1) one core's L2 cache to another core's L1, and (2) memory to an L1, as we increase the core count. Home nodes of the cache lines are spread uniformly, and the cache-to-cache transfer is between the cores farthest apart. As can be seen, remote cache access latency increases from 124 cycles at 32 cores to 229 cycles at 1024 cores. For the same configuration, the memory access cost increases from 185 cycles to 246 cycles.

Such an increase in latency in turn amplifies the impact of locality-aware scheduling. Figure 7 shows the speedup of recursive schedules over random schedules across varying core counts. With 32 cores, recursive schedule provides 1.27x average speedup over random (1.20x speedup over the baseline). As the number of cores increases, the benefit of locality-awareness increases across all workloads (at 1024 cores, 1.61x average speedup over random).

However, the exact degree depends on the workload locality pattern. In particular, for **hj** and **smvm**, which exhibit high L1 sharing degree (see Table 4), random schedules' poor task grouping generate many cache-to-cache transfers; and as the transfer latency increases, give recursive schedules significant performance advantage (compared to 32-core executions, 1.83x and 1.65x additional locality benefits with 1024 cores, respectively).

3.5 Summary: Guidelines for Practical Locality-Aware Task Schedulers

Locality-aware task scheduling can provide significant performance and energy efficiency improvements for unstructured parallelism, both on private and shared cache organizations. The importance of locality-awareness will only increase with larger core count. The relative importance of task grouping and ordering, however, is a function of the workload and the underlying cache hierarchy. Nevertheless, if a locality-aware scheduler were to implement only one scheme, it should be recursive grouping—recursively matching task group working set size across all cache levels. For a processor with (mostly) private cache hierarchy, a single-level schedule at the last-level cache can capture most of the locality.

4. LOCALITY-AWARE TASK STEALING

Dynamic task management comprises two components: (1) task scheduling, or initial assignment of tasks to threads, and (2) task stealing, or balancing load by transferring tasks from a loaded thread to an idle thread. In Sections 2 and 3, we explored locality-aware task scheduling. Here, we explore locality-aware task stealing.

4.1 Motivation

Intuitively, task stealing will benefit most from being locality-aware when many tasks are stolen. One major source of large load imbalance is multiprogramming: Software threads from applications compete for hardware contexts, and potentially large number of tasks may be stolen from a switched-out thread. Even for a dedicated system, interference due to shared resources on a many-core chip (e.g., caches and memory controllers) can introduce significant load imbalance [22].

Previously proposed stealing schemes, however, are *locality-oblivious*. The most widely adopted scheme, *randomized stealing* [3], chooses a victim at random, and steals one or more tasks (stealing multiple amortizes stealing overheads). It provides good characteristics such as even load distribution and theoretically bounded execution time, but its randomness renders it inherently locality-oblivious. In fact, if the task schedule is also locality-oblivious, we expect locality-oblivious stealing to have little impact on cache behavior. However, for a locality-aware schedule, this stealing policy may significantly decrease the performance of stolen tasks.

We verify this by inducing large amounts of task stealing. Specifically, we emulate context switching: After producing a task schedule for 32 threads (on the Throughput Processor), we offline a subset of the threads, and rely on stealing to redistribute tasks from the offlined threads.

Figure 8 shows the task performance trend of a random schedule and a recursive schedule for two workloads, normalized to the performance of a random schedule when no threads are offlined.

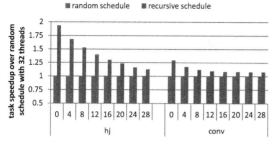

Figure 8: **Impact of locality-oblivious stealing on a locality-aware schedule. The numbers along the x-axis denote the number of threads offlined.**

We use the same randomized stealing policy for both schedules—it randomly selects a victim and tries to steal half of the victim's queue with a prescribed upper bound (an empirical value of 8 was used [22]). If it fails to steal anything, it visits the other potential victims in a round-robin fashion.

The case where no threads are offlined is the same data presented earlier. However, the benefit of recursive scheduling decreases as more threads are offlined, since the locality captured in the schedule is disrupted by randomized stealing. On the other hand, the performance with a random schedule is independent of the number of threads offlined. When tasks are scheduled in a locality-aware fashion, *locality-aware stealing* becomes important.

4.2 Locality Analysis of Task Stealing

We approach task stealing using a similar analysis methodology we used for scheduling. For this discussion, we assume a locality-aware task schedule created from a recursive scheduler. We explore the impact on locality of the two key design decisions for task stealing: (1) *Which* tasks to steal? and (2) *How many* tasks to steal?

Q1: Which tasks to steal?

Random victim selection fails to capture the locality between the tasks that have already executed and those that are to be stolen. Assuming a multi-level memory hierarchy, it would be the best if such locality is exploited through the highest-level cache (i.e., L1). If no such tasks are available, victim tasks should be chosen among those that will give sharing through the next level (i.e., L2), and so forth. In essence, a thief should look for tasks in a top-to-bottom fashion, so that the *stealing scope* gradually increases as we lower the cache level where sharing will take place.

Q2: How many tasks to steal?

The other locality to consider is the locality among the stolen tasks. A natural steal granularity that would provide good locality among victim tasks is a task group—after all, this is how recursive scheduling constructs groups. Stealing a task group at a time amortizes steal overheads, as well.

Stealing a *fixed amount or portions* of tasks each time may under- or overshoot a task group boundary, to break the group. Stealing an already-stolen task (i.e., *secondary stealing*) breaks locality within stolen task groups as well; secondary stealing from a group with strong internal sharing, e.g., an L1 group, may impair performance.

On the other hand, the level of task group stolen affects load balancing. Stealing a coarser granularity task group preserves more locality among stolen tasks, but could increase load imbalance, assuming we prohibit secondary stealing. One way to emulate the locality of stealing a coarser task group while maintaining flexibility is to steal smaller groups but enforce *steal ordering*: If a thread steals again, it follows the specified group order.

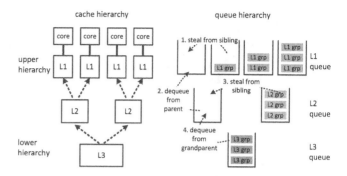

Figure 9: **Recursive stealing. The top-level queues (that hold tasks) are not shown. Colored numbers indicate the order that the leftmost core visits queues.**

4.3 Making Stealing Locality-Aware: Recursive Stealing

In this section we present a reference locality-aware stealing scheme, *recursive stealing*. Our discussion so far suggests that (1) stealing scope should recursively expand through the memory hierarchy, and that (2) stealing should be performed at the granularity of task groups. Figure 9 illustrates the scheme.

We maintain a hierarchy of queues, where a queue exists for each cache; these queues may be implemented as software or hardware components. A queue at a specific level holds task groups that fit in the cache for that level: an L3 queue holds L3 groups, an L2 queue holds L2 groups, etc. The order these task groups are stored reflects the *group order* determined by the recursive schedule. Not shown are the queues that hold actual tasks; for the example hierarchy, one task queue exists per L1 queue. Once a task group is dequeued and moved to an upper-level queue, it is logically broken down into upper-level groups. For example, when an L2 group is transferred to an L1 queue, it is decomposed into L1 groups.

To exploit as much locality as possible from the original recursive schedule, recursive stealing *interleaves* regular dequeues and steal operations. In our example (see Figure 9), tasks are replenished as follows. Once a task queue is empty, a thread attempts to dequeue from its L1 queue; if the L1 queue is empty, it attempts to steal from the sibling L1 queue (i.e., before it tries a regular dequeue from the L2 queue). We interleave steals with dequeues in this example because the L2 caches are shared: If a thread steals from a sibling L1 queue, it grabs an L1 group that shares data in the L2 cache with (a) the tasks it just executed, and (b) the tasks the sibling core(s) are currently executing; thus, we exploit the shared cache. If the L2 queue is empty as well, it climbs down the hierarchy and repeats the process: It attempts to steal from the sibling L2 queue, and then visits the L3 queue. When stealing, a thread grabs the task group at the tail of the victim queue, in the same way randomized stealing operates [3].

In addition, we do not allow stealing across task queues: The minimum steal granularity is an L1 group, and a stolen L1 group cannot be stolen again. For our workloads, this does not impose significant load imbalance, since a typical L1 group has 4 to 8 tasks.

In essence, recursive stealing exploits locality through two features: (1) by performing *recursive victim selection* to exploit locality across potentially multiple levels of shared caches, and (2) by stealing at minimum a whole L1 group to guarantee locality among the stolen tasks.

4.4 Performance Results

We first present the performance summary, and then isolate each feature of recursive stealing. In particular, we answer the follow-

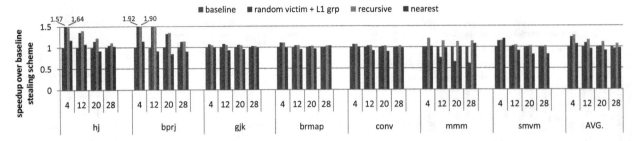

Figure 10: Performance improvement of stolen tasks. *baseline*, *recursive*, and *nearest* **represents randomized, recursive, and nearest-neighbor stealing, respectively.** *random victim + L1 grp* **disables the recursive victim selection in recursive stealing. The numbers along the x-axis indicate the number of threads offlined.**

ing questions: (1) How beneficial is locality-aware stealing? (2) How much does victim selection matter? (3) How much does steal granularity matter?

Q1: How beneficial is locality-aware stealing?

We implemented the recursive stealing scheme in Section 4.3 as a software library for our Throughput Processor configuration, and compared its performance against the baseline randomized stealing (see Section 4.1). For a given workload, we use the same recursive schedule in all experiments.

Figure 10 compares the performance of *stolen* tasks over various stealing schemes, as we offline some threads. Looking at the average, recursive stealing provides benefit across all numbers of offlined threads, but the average benefit decreases as more threads are offlined. When 4 threads are offlined, the average speedup over randomized stealing is 1.27x. The reason for the speedup decrease is that in general, executing the tasks on fewer cores (i.e., spreading an application's data across fewer caches) naturally captures more sharing. This is especially true for applications with small working sets. For this case, there is less potential for improving locality.

When we look at individual workload performance, we can see that those workloads that benefit the most from recursive scheduling, i.e., **hj**, **bprj**, and **mmm**, significantly benefit from recursive stealing. **hj** and **bprj**'s L1 groups are significantly larger than 8 tasks (the upper bound for the baseline stealing scheme), so stealing an L1 group at a time gives significant locality boost. When 28 threads are offlined, recursive stealing reduces the L1 miss rate by 1.28x and 1.39x, respectively. For **mmm**, however, an L1 group contains only a single task. Recursive stealing exploits locality through the L2 instead, and reduces the L2 miss rate by 1.56x (with 28 threads offlined). This verifies that both steal granularity and victim selection contribute to the benefits of recursive stealing.

smvm presents an interesting case. The workload benefits significantly from recursive scheduling, but the performance improvement due to recursive stealing is not as profound. By coincidence, random stealing's upper bound of 8 tasks matches the number of tasks within an L1 group. However, the baseline performs worse due to secondary stealing—**conv** behaves similarly. On the other hand, for **gjk** and **brmap**, which exhibit sharing through consecutive tasks, maintaining the task order is good enough to preserve most of the locality.

The source of randomized stealing's poor behavior is not that it chooses its victims at random, but that its victim selection is locality-oblivious. To demonstrate this, in Figure 10, we also show the performance of a nearest-neighbor stealing scheme. This scheme is the same as the baseline, except a thief always chooses its nearest-neighbor as the first victim. As can be seen, the scheme, which is also locality-oblivious, performs as poorly as randomized stealing.

Q2: How much does victim selection matter?

To isolate the benefits from recursive victim selection, we implement a stealing scheme which (1) selects a victim at random, but

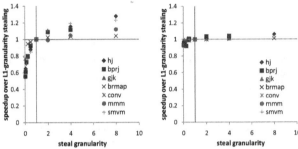

(a) High contention (4 threads   (b) Low contention (28 threads
off, 28 threads on)   off, 4 threads on)

Figure 11: Application sensitivity to steal granularity. Vertical and horizontal lines denote x = 1 and y = 1, respectively.

(2) steals an L1 group at a time. The random victim + L1 grp in Figure 10 shows its performance.

Most of our applications see the same performance from the random victim + L1 grp policy as recursive stealing. However, for workloads exhibiting strong sharing through L2, recursive victim selection is able to capture the locality. **mmm** shows this effect strongly, since its L1 group amounts to a single task—locality must be captured across L1 groups. In particular, as more threads are offlined, random victim selection exhibits deteriorating performance; offlining more threads means more victims to choose from, making it more likely that random victim selection fails to capture locality. While the baseline also uses random victim selection, it steals 8 tasks at a time, and captures some locality through L2.

Q3: How much does steal granularity matter?

Intuitively, if load balance is not an issue, stealing larger chunks of tasks will better exploit locality. Conversely, stealing a smaller number of tasks will fail to preserve the locality specified in the schedule. However, we find that sensitivity to steal granularity is regulated by the degree to which thieves contend over victim tasks.

In Figure 11, the x-axis denotes normalized steal granularity, where steal granularity of 1 denotes the case when a single L1 group is stolen at a time. The y-axis is the performance of a stolen task, normalized to the same case. When multiple L1 groups are stolen, they are stolen in an atomic fashion, and are not subject to secondary stealing.

Figure 11a shows the performance under high contention. In this configuration, 4 threads are offlined, and 28 online threads compete over the tasks assigned to the 4 offlined threads. When the contention is high, it becomes hard to preserve locality across multiple steal operations from the same thread. Therefore, performance is relatively sensitive to steal granularity. Specifically, we can see that reducing steal granularity below an L1 group results in a significant loss in locality, since the strong sharing within an L1 group is now broken. Conversely, increasing the steal granularity beyond a single L1 group gives sizeable locality improvements.

On the contrary, Figure 11b shows performance under low contention, when only 4 threads are online. These threads rarely contend over the tasks originally assigned to the 28 offlined threads, and recursive stealing improves inter-steal locality by preserving group order (see Section 4.2). In fact, recursive stealing effectively collects smaller task groups to emulate the effect of executing a larger granularity group. As a result, sensitivity to steal granularity is much smaller than the high contention case.

4.5 Summary

To preserve the locality exploited in task schedules while load balancing, task stealing should be made locality-aware. Two types of locality need to be captured: (a) locality between the tasks that have executed and that are to be stolen, and (b) locality among the stolen tasks. By adhering to the task grouping and ordering specified by the original schedule while transferring tasks, a stealing scheme can be made locality-compatible.

5. CONCLUSION

This paper provides a quantitative analysis of exploiting task locality for unstructured parallelism. Through a graph-based locality analysis framework and a generic, recursive scheduling scheme, we demonstrate that significant potential exists for locality-aware scheduling. Specifically, our simulation results of three distinct 32-core systems show significant performance improvement (up to 2.05x over a state-of-the-art baseline) and energy reduction (47% average reduction from the baseline). In addition, 1024-core simulation results project that with an increasing number of cores, benefits from locality-awareness will only increase (up to 1.83x additional benefits compared to 32-core executions). To capture this potential, we also explore the scheduler design space in detail. While we find the performance contributions of different scheduling decisions to be the function of the workload and the underlying cache hierarchy, matching the task group hierarchy to the cache hierarchy provides the most benefit. We also highlight the importance of locality-aware stealing when the tasks are scheduled in a locality-aware fashion, and demonstrate that a recursive stealing scheme can effectively exploit significant locality while load balancing (up to 2.0x speedup over randomized stealing).

6. ACKNOWLEDGMENTS

We thank the anonymous reviewers for the constructive feedback on the earlier version of this paper. Richard Yoo was supported in part by a David and Janet Chyan Stanford Graduate Fellowship. This work was supported in part by the Stanford Pervasive Parallelism Laboratory. Intel is a trademark of Intel Corporation in the U.S. and/or other countries.

7. REFERENCES

[1] Umut A. Acar, Guy E. Blelloch, and Robert D. Blumofe. The data locality of work stealing. In *Proc. of the 12th SPAA*, pages 1–12, 2000.

[2] Nathan L. Binkert, Ronald G. Dreslinski, Lisa R. Hsu, Kevin T. Lim, Ali G. Saidi, and Steven K. Reinhardt. The M5 simulator: Modeling networked systems. *IEEE Micro*, 26(4):52–60, 2006.

[3] Robert D. Blumofe and Charles E. Leiserson. Scheduling multithreaded computations by work stealing. In *Proc. of the 35th Annual Symposium on Foundations of Computer Science*, pages 356–368, 1994.

[4] Silas Boyd-Wickizer, Haibo Chen, Rong Chen, Yandong Mao, Frans Kaashoek, Robert Morris, Aleksey Pesterev, Lex Stein, Ming Wu, Yuehua Dai, Yang Zhang, and Zheng Zhang. Corey: An operating system for many cores. In *Proc. of the 8th OSDI*, pages 43–57, 2008.

[5] Philippe Charles, Christian Grothoff, Vijay Saraswat, Christopher Donawa, Allan Kielstra, Kemal Ebcioglu, Christoph von Praun, and Vivek Sarkar. X10:

[6] Shimin Chen, Phillip B. Gibbons, Michael Kozuch, Vasileios Liaskovitis, Anastassia Ailamaki, Guy E. Blelloch, Babak Falsafi, Limor Fix, Nikos Hardavellas, Todd C. Mowry, and Chris Wilkerson. Scheduling threads for constructive cache sharing on CMPs. In *Proc. of the 19th SPAA*, pages 105–115, 2007.

[7] Computing Community Consortium. 21st century computer architecture: A community white paper. 2012.

[8] Cray. Chapel Language Specification 0.796, 2010.

[9] William J. Dally. The future of GPU computing. In *the 22nd Annual Supercomputing Conference*, 2009.

[10] Kayvon Fatahalian, Daniel Reiter Horn, Timothy J. Knight, Larkhoon Leem, Mike Houston, Ji Young Park, Mattan Erez, Manman Ren, Alex Aiken, William J. Dally, and Pat Hanrahan. Sequoia: Programming the memory hierarchy. In *Proc. of the 2006 ACM/IEEE Conference on Supercomputing*, 2006.

[11] Matteo Frigo, Charles E. Leiserson, Harald Prokop, and Sridhar Ramachandran. Cache-oblivious algorithms. *Annual IEEE Symposium on Foundations of Computer Science*, 0:285–297, 1999.

[12] Matteo Frigo, Charles E. Leiserson, and Keith H. Randall. The implementation of the Cilk-5 multithreaded language. In *Proc. of the 1998 PLDI*, pages 212–223.

[13] Yi Guo, Jisheng Zhao, Vincent Cave, and Vivek Sarkar. SLAW: A scalable locality-aware adaptive work-stealing scheduler for multi-core systems. In *Proc. of the 2010 PPoPP*, pages 341–342.

[14] Mark Hill and Christos Kozyrakis. Advancing computer systems without technology progress. In *DARPA / ISAT Workshop*, 2012.

[15] Christopher J. Hughes, Changkyu Kim, and Yen-Kuang Chen. Performance and energy implications of many-core caches for throughput computing. *Micro, IEEE*, 30(6):25–35, 2010.

[16] Jaehyuk Huh, Changkyu Kim, Hazim Shafi, Lixin Zhang, Doug Burger, and Stephen W. Keckler. A NUCA substrate for flexible CMP cache sharing. *IEEE TPDS*, 18:1028–1040, 2007.

[17] Intel. Threading Building Blocks, http://www.threadingbuildingblocks.org.

[18] Mahmut Kandemir, Taylan Yemliha, Sai Prashanth Muralidhara, Shekhar Srikantaiah, Mary Jane Irwin, and Yuanrui Zhang. Cache topology aware computation mapping for multicores. In *Proc. of the 2010 PLDI*, pages 74–85.

[19] George Karypis and Vipin Kumar. A fast and high quality multilevel scheme for partitioning irregular graphs. In *Proc. of the 24th International Conference on Parallel Processing*, pages 113–122, 1995.

[20] John H. Kelm, Daniel R. Johnson, Matthew R. Johnson, Neal C. Crago, William Tuohy, Aqeel Mahesri, Steven S. Lumetta, Matthew I. Frank, and Sanjay J. Patel. Rigel: An architecture and scalable programming interface for a 1000-core accelerator. In *Proc. of the 36th ISCA*, pages 140–151, 2009.

[21] Changkyu Kim, Doug Burger, and Stephen W. Keckler. Nonuniform cache architectures for wire-delay dominated on-chip caches. *IEEE Micro*, 23:99–107, 2003.

[22] Sanjeev Kumar, Christopher J. Hughes, and Anthony Nguyen. Carbon: Architectural support for fine-grained parallelism on chip multiprocessors. In *Proc. of the 34th ISCA*, pages 162–173, 2007.

[23] Milo M. K. Martin, Daniel J. Sorin, Bradford M. Beckmann, Michael R. Marty, Min Xu, Alaa R. Alameldeen, Kevin E. Moore, Mark D. Hill, and David A. Wood. Multifacet's general execution-driven multiprocessor simulator (GEMS) toolset. *Computer Architecture News*, 33:92–99, 2005.

[24] Jason E. Miller, Harshad Kasture, George Kurian, Charles Gruenwald III, Nathan Beckmann, Christopher Celio, Jonathan Eastep, and Anant Agarwal. Graphite: A distributed parallel simulator for multicores. In *Proc. of the 16th HPCA*, pages 1–12, 2010.

[25] OpenMP Architecture Review Board. OpenMP Application Program Interface Version 3.1, 2011.

[26] Oracle. The Fortress Language Specification Version 1.0, 2008.

[27] Daniel Sanchez, Richard M. Yoo, and Christos Kozyrakis. Flexible architectural support for fine-grain scheduling. In *Proc. of the 15th ASPLOS*, pages 311–322, 2010.

[28] Larry Seiler, Doug Carmean, Eric Sprangle, Tom Forsyth, Michael Abrash, Pradeep Dubey, Stephen Junkins, Adam Lake, Jeremy Sugerman, Robert Cavin, Roger Espasa, Ed Grochowski, Toni Juan, and Pat Hanrahan. Larrabee: a many-core x86 architecture for visual computing. In *ACM SIGGRAPH 2008 Papers*, pages 18:1–18:15.

[29] Janis Sermulins, William Thies, Rodric Rabbah, and Saman Amarasinghe. Cache aware optimization of stream programs. In *Proc. of the LCTES 05*, pages 115–126.

[30] Avinash Sodani. Race to exascale: Opportunities and challenges. In *the 44th Annual IEEE / ACM International Symposium on Microarchitecture*, 2011.

[31] William Thies, Michal Karczmarek, and Saman P. Amarasinghe. StreamIt: A language for streaming applications. In *Proc. of the 11th CC*, pages 179–196, 2002.

An object-oriented approach to non-uniform cluster computing. In *Proc. of the 20th OOPSLA*, pages 519–538, 2005.

Balls-into-Bins with Nearly Optimal Load Distribution

Petra Berenbrink
Simon Fraser University
School of Comp. Science
8888 University Street
Burnaby, B.C., V5A 1S6
Canada
petra@cs.sfu.ca

Kamyar Khodamoradi
Simon Fraser University
School of Comp. Science
8888 University Street
Burnaby, B.C., V5A 1S6
Canada
kka50@cs.sfu.ca

Thomas Sauerwald
Max Planck Institute for
Informatics
Campus E1.4
66123 Saarbrücken
Germany
sauerwal@mpi-inf.mpg.de

Alexandre Stauffer
Department of Mathematical
Sciences
University Bath
Bath BA2 7AY
United Kingdom
astauffer@pobox.com

ABSTRACT

We consider sequential *balls-into-bins* processes that randomly allocate m balls into n bins. We analyze two allocation schemes that achieve a close to optimal maximum load of $\lceil m/n \rceil + 1$ and require only $\mathcal{O}(m)$ (expected) allocation time. These parameters should be compared with the classic d-choice-process which achieves a maximum load of $m/n + \log \log n/d + \mathcal{O}(1)$ and requires $m \cdot d$ allocation time.

Categories and Subject Descriptors

F.2.2 [**Analysis of Algorithms and Problem Complexity**]: Nonnumerical Algorithms and Problems—*Computations on discrete structures*; G.3 [**Probability and Statistics**]: Markov processes, Probabilistic algorithms (including Monte Carlo)

General Terms

Algorithms, Theory

Keywords

Balls-into-Bins, Load Balancing, Randomized Algorithms

1. INTRODUCTION

The goal of *balls-into-bins* processes is to allocate m balls into n bins. This is done by allowing each *ball* to choose its location among one or several randomly chosen bins. Two of the most important performance measures for these processes are the total number of random bin choices used for

the allocation (which is usually a good measure for the allocation time) and the maximum load. In this paper we consider two allocation schemes that are almost optimal in *both* criteria. Both protocols achieve a close to optimal maximum load of $\lceil m/n \rceil + 1$ and use only $\mathcal{O}(m)$ random bin choices. Balls-into-bins processes have a wide range of applications in the areas of hashing, load balancing, and resource allocation. In these applications, each ball represents a task or request, while each bin represents a server or processor.

The classical single-choice balls-into-bins process simply places each of the m balls into a bin chosen independently and uniformly at random. For $m = n$, it is well known that the expected maximum load is $\log n / \log \log n + \mathcal{O}(1)$ [14]. Karp et al. [11] observe that the maximum load can be vastly reduced if every ball is allowed to choose between several randomly chosen bins and is placed in the least loaded among them. This apparently small change reduces the maximum load to $\mathcal{O}(\log \log n)$ balls, with high probability, and has become widely known as "power of two choices". Azar et al. [4] analyze a process called GREEDY[d] where every ball is allowed to choose the bin with minimum load among d randomly chosen bins. They prove that this process achieves a maximum load of $\ln \ln n / \ln d + \mathcal{O}(1)$, with high probability. In [5], the authors extend these results to the heavily loaded case where the number of balls m is much larger than the number of bins n. They show that the maximum load is upper bounded by $m/n + \ln \ln n / \ln d + \mathcal{O}(1)$. For the case $m = n$, Vöcking [15] proves a general lower bound on the maximum load of $\ln \ln n /(d \cdot \ln \Phi_d)$, where $1.61 \leqslant \Phi_d \leqslant 2$, if every ball is allowed to choose d random bins. He also presents the LEFT[d] protocol that uses an asymmetric tie-breaking rule. Surprisingly, the maximal load achieved by this process matches his lower bound up to an additive constant. Mitzenmacher, Prabhakar and Shah [13] consider a balls-into-bins process (for $m = n$) where every ball has some memory. They consider the (d, k)-memory model where each ball chooses $d+k$ bins, d of which are selected uniformly at random, whereas the other k are the least loaded bins among the ones picked for the previous ball. The ball is then allocated into the least loaded among the $d + k$ bins. For $d = k = 1$, they show that the maximum load is at most $\ln \ln n / (2 \cdot \log(\Phi_2)) + \mathcal{O}(1)$, which matches the aforementioned lower bound by Vöcking [15] up to an additive constant.

Note that in all above protocols, if $m = n$, the allocation time is $dm = dn$ while the maximum load is at least $\Omega(\log \log n / d)$. Therefore a natural question is whether there are allocation protocols that achieve a better tradeoff between allocation time and maximum load, e.g., protocols that achieve a constant maximum load and an allocation time of $\mathcal{O}(n)$.

Czumaj and Stemann [7] study several balls-into-bins processes where the number of choices per ball depends on the load of the bins chosen by it. They show various tradeoffs between the average allocation time, maximum allocation time and the maximum load of a bin. For example, they consider the THRESHOLD protocol which is defined as follows. Every ball repeatedly samples bins until it finds a bin with load less than $m/n + 1$. For $m = n$ they show that the (total) allocation time is $(1.146 + o(1))m$ with high probability [7, Theorem 4].

Czumaj, Riley and Scheideler [6] consider an algorithm that first calculates an initial allocation using GREEDY[d]. Then the algorithm performs iteratively so-called self-balancing steps where balls may switch between the two initial bin choices. Their algorithm achieves a maximum load of $\lceil m/n \rceil$ and uses $\mathcal{O}(m) + n^{\mathcal{O}(1)}$ reallocation steps. Note that this algorithm relies on reallocations which are typically expensive. Other allocation schemes that achieve a nearly perfect maximum load and rely on reallocations of the balls are [3] and [12].

Similar reallocation schemes are also considered in the area of Cuckoo hashing. Here the goal is to allocate m data items (balls) into n buckets (bins) of size k, and to minimize kn. Every data item comes with d possible buckets. If a new data item arrives, it is allocated into one of its d bucket choices if one of them stores less than k items. Otherwise, one of the conflicting items, denote it by ℓ, is picked and reallocated. If, in turn, none of ℓ's other bucket choices $b_1, \ldots, b_k$ contains less than k items, another item in $b_1, \ldots, b_k$ is reallocated. The process stops if all items are allocated to a bucket. There are many results dealing with the best choices for d and k. For an overview of results in the area of Cuckoo hashing see, for example, [8].

1.1 Our Results

In this paper we consider two balls-into-bins protocols. First, we study a new protocol called ADAPTIVE which works as follows. The i-th ball samples bins uniformly at random until it finds a bin with load less than $i/n + 1$ and is then placed into that bin. From the definition of ADAPTIVE it follows directly that the maximum load is upper bounded by $\lceil m/n \rceil + 1$. We prove that ADAPTIVE requires only $\mathcal{O}(m)$ allocation time in expectation, which is asymptotically the same as THRESHOLD (Theorem 3.1). Hence, our new protocol is nearly optimal in terms of maximum load and allocation time. In contrast to THRESHOLD from [7], the ADAPTIVE protocol does not need to know the total number of balls m in advance. Instead, each ball must know how many balls have been already placed. This assumption is comparable to the (d, k)-memory model of [13], where every ball communicates with the ball that comes right after it. The

inherent weakness of this assumption is that having such information, a deterministic round-robin protocol can achieve a perfect load balance. However, although we never mention it explicitly, the ADAPTIVE protocol does not really need to know the exact number of balls, but only an upper bound of $\lceil i/n \rceil$ would suffice for our protocol to achieve the nearly optimal maximum load in $\mathcal{O}(m)$ allocation time.

In the second part of the paper, we extend the analysis of THRESHOLD from [7] to the case where m is much larger than n. Note that using the proof technique of [7], we only get an upper bound of $\mathcal{O}(m)$ on the allocation time of THRESHOLD for the cases where $m = \mathcal{O}(n)$. Here in this paper, we prove that the allocation time is $m + \mathcal{O}(m^{3/4} \cdot n^{1/4})$, (see Theorem 4.1), which is an improvement over the upper bound of [7]. From the definition of THRESHOLD it follows directly that the maximum load is $\lceil m/n \rceil + 1$. Hence, our result shows that, even for $m >> n$, THRESHOLD is nearly optimal both in terms of maximum load and allocation time.

Finally we compare the load distribution of both protocols. The analysis of the ADAPTIVE protocol reveals a result about the smoothness of the load distribution which might be of independent interest. We show that for the ADAPTIVE protocol the difference between the maximum and minimum load is at most $\mathcal{O}(\log n)$, (see Corollary 3.6). In contrast to that, the difference is polynomial in n for the THRESHOLD protocol (see Theorem 4.2).

We close the paper by presenting some experimental results indicating that in practice ADAPTIVE requires only a slightly larger allocation time than THRESHOLD, but achieves a much smoother load distribution.

2. ALGORITHMS AND NOTATION

We first recall the following protocol from [7] which we call THRESHOLD (see Figure 1). Clearly, the maximum load at the end of the THRESHOLD protocol is at most $\lceil m/n \rceil + 1$. We are interested in the *allocation time* of all balls, i.e., the total number of bins that have to be sampled in order to place all m balls.

---

for each ball i from 1 to m **do**
   repeat
      Choose a bin j independently and uniformly at random from $\{1, \ldots, n\}$
      if load of bin j is *strictly* less than $m/n + 1$ **then** place ball i into bin j
   until the ball is placed
end for

Figure 1: The THRESHOLD protocol from [7].

---

for each ball i from 1 to m **do**
   repeat
      Choose a bin j independently and uniformly at random from $\{1, \ldots, n\}$
      if load of bin j is *strictly* less than $i/n + 1$ **then** place ball i into bin j
   until the ball is placed
end for

Figure 2: Our new protocol called ADAPTIVE.

Algorithm	Expected Allocation Time	Maximum Load	Conditions on m and n
GREEDY$[d]$ [5]	$\Theta(md)$	$m/n + \frac{\ln\ln n}{\ln d} + \Theta(1)$	–
LEFT$[d]$ [15]	$\Theta(md)$	$m/n + \frac{\ln\ln n}{d\cdot\ln(\Phi_d)} + \Theta(1)$	–
[13]	$\Theta(m)$	$\frac{\ln\ln n}{\ln(\Phi_2)} + \Theta(1)$	$m = n$
[6]	$\mathcal{O}(m) + n^{\mathcal{O}(1)}$	$\lceil m/n\rceil$	$m = \omega(n^6 \log n)$
[6]	$m^{\mathcal{O}(1)}$	$\lceil m/n\rceil + 1$	$m = \mathcal{O}(n\log n)$
THRESHOLD [7, Thm. 4]	$1.146194m + o(m)$	$\lceil m/n\rceil + 1$	$m = n$
THRESHOLD [7, Thm. 11]	$\mathcal{O}(m)$	$\lceil m/n\rceil + 1$	$m = \mathcal{O}(n)$
ADAPTIVE ★	$\mathcal{O}(m)$	$\lceil m/n\rceil + 1$	–
THRESHOLD ★	$m + \mathcal{O}(m^{3/4}\cdot n^{1/4})$	$\lceil m/n\rceil + 1$	–

Table 1: Comparison of the expected allocation time and maximum load of various allocation schemes for m balls and n bins. The rows with ★ are our new results. Note that $1.6 < \Phi_d < 2$, see [5] for the precise definition.

The ADAPTIVE protocol (Figure 2) is very similar to the THRESHOLD protocol, except that the "threshold" is a function of the number of balls placed so far. Similar to the THRESHOLD protocol, the ADAPTIVE protocol ensures that the maximum load of any bin is bounded by $\lceil m/n\rceil + 1$. Note that if we replace in the ADAPTIVE protocol the threshold $i/n + 1$ by i/n, then the allocation time of each batch of n consecutive balls is basically a coupon collector process which translates into an overall allocation time of $\Theta((m/n)\cdot n\log n) = \Theta(m\log n)$.

We denote by $L(t) = (L_1(t), \ldots, L_n(t))$ the random vector giving the load distribution at the end of step t, i.e., $L_i(t) = \ell$ means that, among the first t balls, ℓ have been allocated to bin i. We will use $\ell(t) = (\ell_1(t), \ldots, \ell_n(t))$ to denote a fixed load distribution; i.e., $\ell(t)$ will be an instantiation of $L(t)$.

Throughout this paper, $\mathsf{Poi}(\lambda)$ denotes the Poisson distribution with parameter (and expected value) λ, and $\mathsf{Bin}(n, p)$ denotes the binomial distribution.

3. ANALYSIS OF ADAPTIVE

In the following we call a bin *underloaded* at the end of stage τ if its load is at most $\tau + 2 - C_1$ at the end of the stage, where $C_1 > 0$ is a constant that will be fixed later. A bis is called *overloaded* if its load is at least τ.

We assume in the following that $m = rn$, where r is lower bounded by a sufficiently large integer. Results for $r \notin \mathbb{N}$ can be easily obtained by resorting to the case $m = \lceil r\rceil n$. Moreover, results for the case r being bounded from above by an integer also follow directly from the observation that there are always at least $m/(r+1) = \Omega(n)$ bins in each step where a ball can be placed to.

Consider now the protocol ADAPTIVE. Since the load of every bin is an integer, the threshold of $i/n + 1$ in the line 4 of the protocol (Figure 2) only changes after n balls are allocated. Therefore, it is natural to divide the analysis into r stages of length n each. Stage τ ($1 \leqslant \tau \leqslant r$) is responsible for the allocation of the balls $(\tau - 1)\cdot n + 1, \ldots \tau n$.

We will use the following *exponential* potential function [10] for our analysis.

$$\Phi(\ell(t)) := \sum_{i=1}^{n} (1 + \varepsilon)^{\lceil t/n\rceil + 2 - \ell_i(t)}.$$

In this paper we choose $\varepsilon := 1/200$. Note that since $L_i(t +$

$1) \geqslant L_i(t)$, it always holds that

$$\Phi(L(t+1)) \leqslant (1 + \varepsilon) \cdot \Phi(L(t)).$$

We define $\Phi_i(\ell(t)) := (1 + \varepsilon)^{\lceil t/n\rceil + 2 - \ell_i(t)}$ as the potential of bin i. We also define $\Delta\Phi(L(\tau n)) := \Phi(L((\tau - 1)\cdot n)) - \Phi(L(\tau n))$ as the potential change in stage τ. We define $\Delta\Phi_i(L(\tau n)) := \Phi_i(L((\tau - 1)\cdot n)) - \Phi_i(L(\tau n))$.

In the rest of this section we show the following result.

THEOREM 3.1. *The expected allocation time of the ADAPTIVE protocol is* $\mathcal{O}(m)$.

PROOF. Let T_τ be the runtime of stage τ. To proof the theorem we show in Lemma 3.2 that $\mathbf{E}[T_\tau] = \mathcal{O}(n)$. Since $\mathbf{E}\left[\sum_{\tau=1}^{r} T_\tau\right] = \sum_{\tau=1}^{r} \mathbf{E}[T_\tau] = r \cdot \mathcal{O}(n) = \mathcal{O}(m)$, Theorem 3.1 follows from Lemma 3.2. □

In Section 3.1 (Corollary 3.6) we show that $\mathbf{E}[\Phi(L(t))] = \mathcal{O}(n)$. Note that this also means that the minimum load in step $t = m$ is with high probability at least $m/n - c\log n$ for some constant c. We will use these results for the proof of the following lemma.

LEMMA 3.2. *Let T_τ be the runtime of stage τ. Then it holds that* $\mathbf{E}[T_\tau] = \mathcal{O}(n)$.

PROOF. Fix any load distribution $L(t) = \ell(t)$ at the end of stage $\tau - 1$ with $t = (\tau - 1)n$. Define

$$\beta := \max\{(\Phi(\ell(t))/n, 16/\varepsilon^2\}.$$

Our goal is to prove that, with probability $1 - n^{-2}$, ADAPTIVE needs $\mathcal{O}(n \cdot (\mathbf{E}[\ln\beta]))$ steps to place the n balls of stage τ. Let $A_k := \{i \in \{1, \ldots, n\}: \ell_i(t) = \tau + 1 - k\}$ be the set of bins with k holes at time t. Then,

$$\beta \cdot n \geqslant \Phi(\ell(t)) = \sum_{k=0}^{\tau+1} \sum_{i \in A_k} (1 + \varepsilon)^{k+1},$$

so that $|A_k| \leqslant \beta n \cdot (1 + \varepsilon)^{-(k+1)} \leqslant 2^{-k\varepsilon} \cdot \beta n$.

The sum of the holes in bins having at least $4\lceil\ln(\beta)/\varepsilon\rceil$ holes is

$$\sum_{k=4\lceil\ln(\beta)/\varepsilon\rceil}^{\tau+1} |A_k| \cdot k \leqslant \sum_{k=4\lceil\ln(\beta)/\varepsilon\rceil}^{\tau+1} 2^{-k\varepsilon} \cdot \beta n \cdot k$$

$$= \frac{\beta n}{\varepsilon} \cdot \sum_{k=4\lceil\ln(\beta)/\varepsilon\rceil}^{\tau+1} 2^{-k\varepsilon} \cdot k\varepsilon$$

$$= \frac{\beta n}{\varepsilon} \cdot \sum_{k=4\lceil \ln(\beta)/\varepsilon \rceil}^{t+1} e^{-k\varepsilon/2} \cdot \left(\frac{4}{e}\right)^{-k\varepsilon/2} \cdot k\varepsilon$$

$$\leqslant 2 \cdot \frac{\beta n}{\varepsilon} \cdot \sum_{k=4\lceil \ln(\beta)/\varepsilon \rceil}^{t+1} e^{-k\varepsilon/2}$$

$$\leqslant 2 \cdot \frac{\beta n}{\varepsilon} \cdot \frac{e^{-2\ln(\beta)}}{1 - e^{-\varepsilon/2}}$$

$$\leqslant 8 \cdot \frac{\beta n}{\varepsilon} \cdot \frac{\beta^{-2}}{\varepsilon} = 8 \cdot \frac{n}{\beta \varepsilon^2},$$

where we used $(4/e)^{-x/2} \cdot x < 2$ for any $x \geqslant 0$ for the second inequality and the second last inequality holds since $e^{-x} \leqslant 1 - x/2$ for any $x \in (0, 1)$.

Now let

$$A' := \{i \in \{1, \ldots, n\} \colon \tau + 2 - 4\ln(\beta)/\varepsilon + 1 \leqslant \ell_i(t) \leqslant \tau + 1\}$$

be the set of bins with at least 1 and at most $4\lfloor \ln(\beta)/\varepsilon \rfloor - 1$ many holes at stage τ. Since at the beginning of every stage the total sum of holes is $2n$, it follows that at that time the sum of holes in bins of A' is at least $2n - 8n \cdot 1/(\beta \varepsilon^2) > (3/2) \cdot n$ by our choice of β. Hence, even after the allocation of the first $n-1$ balls of batch τ the total number of holes of the bins in A' will still be at least $(3/2) \cdot n - (n-1) \geqslant n/2$.

Each of these bins has at most $4\lfloor \ln(\beta)/\varepsilon \rfloor$ holes. It follows that even after the allocation of the first $n - 1$ balls of batch $\tau + 1$ there are still $\Omega(n/(\ln(\beta)/\varepsilon)) = \Omega(n/(\ln \beta))$ bins with at least one hole. Hence, the time to place n balls is stochastically smaller than the sum of n independent geometric random variables each with expectation $\mathcal{O}(\ln \beta)$. Therefore, Theorem 6.6 implies that

$$\mathbf{Pr}\left[T_{\tau+1} = \mathcal{O}(n \ln \beta)\right] \geqslant 1 - n^{-2}.$$

Next observe that, since $\Phi(\ell(t)) = \Omega(n)$, we have

$$\ln(\Phi(\ell(t))/n) = \Omega(\ln(\beta))$$

and therefore the above inequality implies that

$$\mathbf{Pr}\left[T_{\tau+1} = \mathcal{O}(n \ln(\Phi(\ell(t))/n))\right] \geqslant 1 - n^{-2}.$$

Let $\mathcal{S}$ be the (finite) set of possible values that $\Phi(\ell(t))$ can attain. Then (with $t = \tau n$)

$$\mathbf{E}\left[T_{\tau+1}\right]$$
$$= \sum_{k \in \mathcal{S}} \mathbf{Pr}\left[\Phi(\ell(t)) = k\right] \cdot \mathbf{E}\left[T_{\tau+1} \mid \Phi(t) = k\right]$$
$$\leqslant \sum_{k \in \mathcal{S}} \mathbf{Pr}\left[\Phi(\ell(t)) = k\right] \cdot (1 - n^{-2}) \cdot \mathcal{O}\left(n \cdot \ln\left(\frac{k}{n}\right)\right) + \frac{1}{n^2} \cdot n^2$$
$$= \mathcal{O}(n) \cdot \sum_{k \in \mathcal{S}} \mathbf{Pr}\left[\Phi(\ell(t)) = k\right] \cdot \log_{1+\varepsilon}\left(\frac{k}{n}\right) / \log_{1+\varepsilon}(e) + 1$$
$$= \mathcal{O}(n) \cdot \sum_{k \in \mathcal{S}} \mathbf{Pr}\left[\log_{1+\varepsilon}\left(\frac{\Phi(\ell(t))}{n}\right) = \log_{1+\varepsilon}\left(\frac{k}{n}\right)\right] \log_{1+\varepsilon}\left(\frac{k}{n}\right)$$
$$= \mathcal{O}(n) \cdot \mathbf{E}\left[\log_{1+\varepsilon}\left(\frac{\Phi(\ell(t))}{n}\right)\right].$$

Note that the last term in line two of the above equation stands for the worst case expected runtime, which is at most n per ball (all holes are in one bin) and n^2 for the whole batch. Corollary 3.6 (see Section 3.1) establishes that $\mathbf{E}[\Phi(\ell(t))] = \mathcal{O}(n)$. Using Jensen's inequality for concave

functions, we obtain that

$$\mathbf{E}\left[\log_{1+\varepsilon}(\Phi(\ell(t))/n)\right] \leqslant \log_{1+\varepsilon} \mathbf{E}\left[\Phi(\ell(t))/n\right]$$
$$\leqslant \log_{1+\varepsilon} \mathcal{O}(1) = \mathcal{O}(1).$$

Thus, at the beginning of the allocation of batch $\tau + 1$ we have that $\mathbf{E}\left[\log_{1+\varepsilon}(\Phi(\ell(t))/n)\right] = \mathcal{O}(1)$ and

$$\mathbf{E}\left[T_{\tau+1}\right] = \mathcal{O}(n) \cdot \mathcal{O}(1) = \mathcal{O}(n).$$

This finishes the proof. $\square$

3.1 Expected Potential Size

The goal of this section is to prove that the expected value of the potential function at any stage is $\mathcal{O}(n)$ (see Corollary 3.6). The first lemma shows that the expected number of balls allocated to bin i in stage $t+1$ is slightly larger than 1. Hence, bin i has a good chance of "catching up" with its load.

LEMMA 3.3. *Assume for $t = \tau n$ $L(t) = \ell(t)$ is fixed and let i be a bin with $\ell_i(t) \leqslant t + 2 - C_1$, where $C_1 > 0$ is a sufficiently large constant. Let $Y_i(\tau + 1)$ be the number of balls allocated to bin i in stage $\tau + 1$. Then for any $0 \leqslant k \leqslant C_1$,*

$$\mathbf{Pr}\left[Y_i(\tau + 1) \geqslant k \mid L(t) = \ell(t)\right]$$
$$\geqslant \mathbf{Pr}\left[\mathrm{Poi}(199/198) \geqslant k\right] - 2 \cdot 10^{-10}.$$

PROOF. Recall that $m = rn$ with r being an integer. We asssume that $t = \tau n, \tau \in \mathbb{N}$ balls have been allocated and we analyze the process of allocating the next n balls. Using the Pigeonhole Principle and the fact that $\ell_i(t) \leqslant t+1$ for every i, it follows that there are at least $(1/2) \cdot n$ bins j overloaded bins $\ell_j(t) \geqslant t$. Roughly speaking, the idea of the proof is now to show that the expected number of balls allocated to *underloaded* bins is larger than one since each overloaded bin can receive at most two additional balls.

Let us make this idea more formal. We divide the allocation of the next n balls into two phases, each phase allocates $n/2$ consecutive balls. Let $Y_i \in [0, n]$ be the number of balls that are placed into bin i during the execution of stage $\tau + 1$ (we drop the superscripts τ and $\tau + 1$ in the following for simplicity). Moreover, let $Y_i(1)$ and $Y_i(2)$ be the number of balls that are placed into bin i in the first and the second phase, so $Y_i = Y_i(1) + Y_i(2)$. Throughout we implicitly condition on $L(t)$ being equal to $\ell(t)$, but for simplicity we drop the conditioning.

Let us compute the probability that a particular bin j with $\ell_j = \tau$ reaches a load of $\tau + 2$ during the first phase. For each ball in the first phase, the probability of placing it into bin j is at least $1/n$, unless bin j has already reached a load of $\tau + 2$. Moreover, we need to sample at least $n/2$ bins randomly to place the first $n/2$ balls. Therefore,

$$\mathbf{Pr}\left[Y_j(1) = 2\right] \geqslant \mathbf{Pr}\left[\mathrm{Bin}\left(\frac{n}{2}, \frac{1}{n}\right) \geqslant 2\right]$$
$$\geqslant \binom{n}{2} \cdot \left(\frac{1}{n}\right)^2 \cdot \left(1 - \frac{1}{n}\right)^{n-2} \geqslant \frac{1}{20}.$$

The corresponding bound also holds for bins j with $\ell_j = \tau + 1$, i.e., $\mathbf{Pr}\left[Y_j(1) = 1\right] \geqslant 1/20$.

Hence the expected number of bins with load $\tau + 2$ after the first phase is at least $n/2 \cdot 1/20 = n/40$. Let $\mathcal{A}$ be the event that at least $n/100$ bins have load $\tau + 2$ after the first phase. To prove that $\mathcal{A}$ occurs with high probability, consider instead the event $\mathcal{B}$ that occurs if at least $n/100$ overloaded bins are chosen at least twice in the first $n/2$ samples of the incoming balls. Clearly, $\mathbf{Pr}\,[\mathcal{A}] \geqslant \mathbf{Pr}\,[\mathcal{B}]$. For bounding $\mathcal{B}$, we can use Azuma's inequality (Theorem 6.3 with all c_i's being 1) to obtain

$$\mathbf{Pr}\,[\mathcal{A}] \geqslant \mathbf{Pr}\,[\mathcal{B}] = 1 - e^{-\Omega(n)}.$$

Now we consider underloaded bins. Fix an arbitrary bin i with $\ell_i \leqslant \tau + 2 - C_1$, where $C_1 > 0$ is a sufficiently large constant to be specified later. Then for $0 \leqslant k \leqslant C_1 + 2$,

$\mathbf{Pr}\,[Y_i \geqslant k]$
$\geqslant \mathbf{Pr}\,[\mathcal{A}] \cdot \mathbf{Pr}\,[Y_i \geqslant k \mid \mathcal{A}] \geqslant \mathbf{Pr}\,[Y_i \geqslant k \mid \mathcal{A}] - \mathbf{Pr}\,[\neg\mathcal{A}]$

$\geqslant \displaystyle\sum_{k_1=0}^{C_1} \mathbf{Pr}\,[Y_i(1) = k_1 \wedge Y_i(2) \geqslant (k - k_1) \mid \mathcal{A}] - e^{-\Omega(n)}$

$= \displaystyle\sum_{k_1=0}^{C_1} \mathbf{Pr}\,[Y_i(1) = k_1 \mid \mathcal{A}]$
$\qquad \cdot \mathbf{Pr}\,[Y_i(2) \geqslant (k - k_1) \mid \mathcal{A} \wedge Y_i(1) = k_1] - e^{-\Omega(n)}$

$\geqslant \displaystyle\sum_{k_1=0}^{C_1} \mathbf{Pr}\,[Y_i(1) = k_1 \wedge \mathcal{A}]$
$\qquad \cdot \mathbf{Pr}\,\left[\mathsf{Bin}\left(\frac{n}{2}, \frac{1}{n - \frac{n}{100}}\right) \geqslant (k - k_1)\right] - e^{-\Omega(n)}$

$\geqslant \displaystyle\sum_{k_1=0}^{C_1} (\mathbf{Pr}\,[Y_i(1) = k_1] - \mathbf{Pr}\,[\neg\mathcal{A}])$
$\qquad \cdot \mathbf{Pr}\,\left[\mathsf{Bin}\left(\frac{n}{2}, \frac{1}{n - \frac{n}{100}}\right) \geqslant (k - k_1)\right] - e^{-\Omega(n)}$

$\geqslant \displaystyle\sum_{k_1=0}^{C_1} \mathbf{Pr}\,[Y_i(1) = k_1] \cdot \mathbf{Pr}\,\left[\mathsf{Bin}\left(\frac{n}{2}, \frac{1}{n - \frac{n}{100}}\right) \geqslant (k - k_1)\right]$
$\qquad - e^{-\Omega(n)} - n e^{-\Omega(n)},$

where the last line uses $\mathbf{Pr}\,[\neg\mathcal{A}] = e^{-\Omega(n)}$. Recall that for any $0 \leqslant r \leqslant C_1$, $\mathbf{Pr}\,[Y_i(1) \geqslant r] \geqslant \mathbf{Pr}\,[\mathsf{Bin}\left(\frac{n}{2}, \frac{1}{n}\right) \geqslant r]$. Since $\mathbf{Pr}\,\left[\mathsf{Bin}\left(\frac{n}{2}, \frac{1}{n - \frac{n}{100}}\right) \geqslant (k - k_1)\right]$ is increasing in k_1, we obtain that

$$\mathbf{Pr}\,[Y_i \geqslant k] \geqslant \sum_{k_1=0}^{C_1} \mathbf{Pr}\,\left[\mathsf{Bin}\left(\frac{n}{2}, \frac{1}{n}\right) = k_1\right]$$
$$\cdot \mathbf{Pr}\,\left[\mathsf{Bin}\left(\frac{n}{2}, \frac{1}{n - \frac{n}{100}}\right) \geqslant (k - k_1)\right]$$
$$- (n+1) \cdot e^{-\Omega(n)}.$$

Recall that for any three values a, b ($a \to \infty$) and k such that $a \cdot b$ and k are fixed, $\mathbf{Pr}\,[\mathsf{Bin}(a,b) = k] = \mathbf{Pr}\,[\mathsf{Poi}(ab) = k] + o(1)$. In particular, for any constant C, $\mathbf{Pr}\,[\mathsf{Bin}(a,b) \geqslant C] = \mathbf{Pr}\,[\mathsf{Poi}(a,b) \geqslant C] + o(1)$. Hence for $k \leqslant C_1$

$$\sum_{k_1=0}^{C_1} \mathbf{Pr}\,\left[\mathsf{Bin}\left(\frac{n}{2}, \frac{1}{n}\right) = k_1\right]$$
$$\cdot \mathbf{Pr}\,\left[\mathsf{Bin}\left(\frac{n}{2}, \frac{1}{n - \frac{n}{100}}\right) \geqslant (k - k_1)\right] - (n+1) \cdot e^{-\Omega(n)}$$

$$= \sum_{k_1=0}^{C_1} \mathbf{Pr}\,\left[\mathsf{Poi}\left(\frac{1}{2}\right) = k_1\right] \cdot \mathbf{Pr}\,\left[\mathsf{Poi}\left(\frac{100}{198}\right) \geqslant (k - k_1)\right]$$
$$- (C_1 + 1) \cdot o(1) - e^{-\Omega(n)}.$$

Now choose the constant $C_1 > 0$ large enough so that the inequality $\sum_{k_1=C_1+1}^{\infty} \mathbf{Pr}\,[\mathsf{Poi}\left(\frac{1}{2}\right) = k_1] \leqslant 10^{-10}$ holds. Then

$$\sum_{k_1=0}^{C_1} \mathbf{Pr}\,\left[\mathsf{Poi}\left(\frac{1}{2}\right) = k_1\right] \cdot \mathbf{Pr}\,\left[\mathsf{Poi}\left(\frac{100}{198}\right) \geqslant (k - k_1)\right]$$
$$- (C_1 + 1) \cdot o(1) - e^{-\Omega(n)}$$

$$= \sum_{k_1=0}^{\infty} \mathbf{Pr}\,\left[\mathsf{Poi}\left(\frac{1}{2}\right) = k_1\right] \cdot \mathbf{Pr}\,\left[\mathsf{Poi}\left(\frac{100}{198}\right) \geqslant (k - k_1)\right]$$
$$- \sum_{k_1=C_1+1}^{\infty} \mathbf{Pr}\,\left[\mathsf{Poi}\left(\frac{1}{2}\right) = k_1\right] \cdot \mathbf{Pr}\,\left[\mathsf{Poi}\left(\frac{100}{198}\right) \geqslant (k - k_1)\right]$$
$$- (C_1 + 3) \cdot o(1) - e^{-\Omega(n)}$$

$$\geqslant \sum_{k_1=0}^{\infty} \mathbf{Pr}\,\left[\mathsf{Poi}\left(\frac{1}{2}\right) = k_1\right] \cdot \mathbf{Pr}\,\left[\mathsf{Poi}\left(\frac{100}{198}\right) \geqslant (k - k_1)\right]$$
$$- 10^{-10} - o(1)$$

$$= \mathbf{Pr}\,\left[\mathsf{Poi}\left(\frac{199}{198}\right) \geqslant k\right] - 10^{-10} - o(1),$$

since $\mathsf{Poi}(\lambda_1) + \mathsf{Poi}(\lambda_2) = \mathsf{Poi}(\lambda_1 + \lambda_2)$. Hence for any $0 \leqslant k \leqslant C_1$ and $t = \tau n$

$$\mathbf{Pr}\,[Y_i(\tau + 1) \geqslant k \mid L(t) = \ell(t)]$$
$$\geqslant \mathbf{Pr}\,\left[\mathsf{Poi}\left(\frac{199}{198}\right) \geqslant k\right] - 2 \cdot 10^{-10}, \qquad (3.1)$$

as needed. $\square$

With the help of Lemma 3.3 and some algebraic manipulation we now prove that the potential contributed by underloaded bins decreases in stage $\tau + 1$ in expectation (recall that we choose $\varepsilon = 1/200$).

LEMMA 3.4. *Assume for $t = \tau n$ $L(t) = \ell(t)$ is fixed and let i be a bin with $\ell_i(t) \leqslant \tau + 2 - C_1$, where $C_1 > 0$ is the constant from Lemma 3.3. Then there is a constant $\kappa = \kappa(C_1) > 0$ with*

$$\mathbf{E}\,[\Delta\Phi_i(\ell((\tau + 1) \cdot n))] \geqslant (1 + \varepsilon)^{\tau + 2 - \ell_i(t)} \cdot \kappa = \Phi_i(\ell(t)) \cdot \kappa.$$

PROOF. Consider now the expected change of the potential Φ w.r.t. bin i, i.e.,

$\mathbf{E}\,[\Delta\Phi_i(\ell(t))]$
$= \Phi_i(\ell(t)) - \mathbf{E}\,[\Phi_i(L(t + n)) \mid L(t) = \ell(t)]$
$= (1 + \varepsilon)^{\tau + 2 - \ell_i(t)}$
$\qquad - \mathbf{E}\,\left[(1 + \varepsilon)^{\tau + 3 - \ell_i(t) - Y_i(\tau + 1)} \mid L(t) = \ell(t)\right]$
$= (1 + \varepsilon)^{\tau + 2 - \ell_i(t)}$
$\qquad - \displaystyle\sum_{k=0}^{\tau + 1 - \ell_i(t)} \mathbf{Pr}\,[Y_i(\tau + 1) = k \mid L(t) = \ell(t)] \cdot (1 + \varepsilon)^{\tau + 3 - \ell_i(t) - k}$
$= (1 + \varepsilon)^{\tau + 2 - \ell_i(t)} \cdot$
$\qquad \left(1 - \displaystyle\sum_{k=0}^{\tau + 1 - \ell_i(t)} \mathbf{Pr}\,[Y_i(\tau + 1) = k \mid L(t) = \ell(t)] \cdot (1 + \varepsilon)^{1 - k}\right).$

Now we define

$$p_k := \mathbf{Pr}\left[Y_i(\tau+1) = k \mid L(t) = \ell(t)\right],$$

$$r_k := (1+\varepsilon)^{1-k},$$

$$q_k := \mathbf{Pr}\left[\mathsf{Poi}\left(\frac{199}{198}\right) = k\right] + 2\cdot 10^{-10}.$$

Note that r_k is non-increasing in k. By inequality (3.1), for every $1 \leqslant k \leqslant C_1$,

$$\mathbf{Pr}\left[Y_i(\tau+1) \leqslant k-1 \mid L(t) = \ell(t)\right]$$

$$\leqslant \mathbf{Pr}\left[\mathsf{Poi}\left(\frac{199}{198}\right) \leqslant k-1\right] + 2\cdot 10^{-10}.$$

For every $0 \leqslant r \leqslant C_1 - 1$,

$$\mathbf{Pr}\left[Y_i(\tau+1) \leqslant r \mid L(t) = \ell(t)\right] = \sum_{k=0}^{r} p_k \leqslant \sum_{k=0}^{r} q_k.$$

We choose $C_1 > 0$ large enough such that the inequality $\sum_{k=0}^{C_1-1} \mathbf{Pr}\left[\mathsf{Poi}\left(\frac{199}{198}\right) = k\right] \geqslant 1 - 2\cdot 10^{-10}$ holds and therefore $\sum_{k=0}^{C_1-1} q_k \geqslant 1$. Since $\sum_{k=0}^{\tau+1-\ell_i(t)} p_k \leqslant 1$, we obtain that, for any $1 \leqslant r \leqslant \tau+3-\ell_i(t)$, $\sum_{k=0}^{r} p_k \leqslant \sum_{k=0}^{\max\{r,C_1-1\}} q_k$. Define $s_k := q_k$ for $0 \leqslant k \leqslant C_1 - 1$ and $s_k := 0$ otherwise. Hence, $\sum_{k=0}^{r} p_k \leqslant \sum_{k=0}^{r} s_k$. Applying now the second statement of Lemma 6.1 to the sequences p_k, r_k and s_k we conclude that

$$1 - \sum_{k=0}^{\tau+1-\ell_i(t)} \mathbf{Pr}\left[Y_i(\tau+1) = k \mid L(t) = \ell(t)\right] \cdot (1+\varepsilon)^{1-k}$$

$$\geqslant 1 - \sum_{k=0}^{C_1-1} \left(\mathbf{Pr}\left[\mathsf{Poi}\left(\frac{199}{198}\right) = k\right] + 2\cdot 10^{-10}\right) \cdot (1+\varepsilon)^{1-k}$$

$$\geqslant 1 - \sum_{k=0}^{C_1-1} e^{-\frac{199}{198}} \frac{\left(\frac{199}{198}\right)^k}{k!} \cdot (1+\varepsilon)^{1-k} - 2\cdot 10^{-10} \frac{1+\varepsilon}{1 - \frac{1}{1+\varepsilon}}$$

$$= 1 - e^{-\left(\frac{199}{198}\right)} \sum_{k=0}^{C_1-1} \frac{\left(\frac{199}{198}\right)^k}{k!} \cdot (1+\varepsilon)^{1-k} - 2\cdot 10^{-10} \cdot \frac{(1+\varepsilon)^2}{\varepsilon},$$

and since $\varepsilon = 1/200$,

$$= 1 - e^{-\frac{199}{198}} \cdot \sum_{k=0}^{C_1-1} \frac{(1+\varepsilon)\cdot\left(\frac{\left(\frac{199}{198}\right)}{1+\varepsilon}\right)^k}{k!} - 2\cdot 10^{-10} \cdot \frac{(1+\varepsilon)^2}{\varepsilon}$$

$$\geqslant 1 - e^{-\frac{199}{198}} \cdot \frac{201}{200} \cdot \sum_{k=0}^{C_1-1} \frac{\left(\frac{200}{201}\cdot\frac{199}{198}\right)^k}{k!} - 2\cdot 10^{-7}$$

$$\geqslant 1 - e^{-\frac{199}{198}} \cdot \frac{201}{200} \cdot e^{\frac{200}{201}\cdot\frac{199}{198}} - 2\cdot 10^{-7},$$

and an evaluation of these expressions numerically yields a lower bound of $\left(\beta - 2\cdot 10^{-7}\right)$, where $\beta > 0.000012\ldots > 2\cdot 10^{-7}$. $\square$

The next lemma shows that the potential decrease due to underloaded bins is already sufficient to conclude that $\mathbf{E}\left[\Phi(L(t+n)) \mid L(t) = \ell(t)\right] < \Phi(\ell(t))$, if $\Phi(\ell(t))$ is sufficiently large.

LEMMA 3.5. *Let $\rho_n := (\varepsilon+\kappa)/(\kappa/2) \cdot (1+\varepsilon)^{C_1} \cdot n$, where κ and C_1 are the constants from Lemma 3.4. For any load*

vector $\ell(t)$ with $\Phi(\ell(t)) \geqslant \rho_n$,

$$\mathbf{E}\left[\Phi(L(t+n)) \mid L(t) = \ell(t)\right] \leqslant \left(1 - \frac{\kappa}{2}\right)\cdot \Phi(\ell(t)).$$

PROOF. Consider now the beginning of stage $\tau+1$ (with $t = \tau n$) where $\Phi(\ell(t)) \geqslant \rho_n$, where $\rho_n := (\varepsilon+\kappa)/(\kappa/2)\cdot(1+\varepsilon)^{C_1}\cdot n$. Let $A \subseteq \{1,\ldots,n\}$ be the set of bins with a hole of size at most C_1, i.e. with load larger than $\tau+2-C_1$. Note that for every $i \in \{1,\ldots,n\}$, $\mathbf{E}\left[\Phi_i(L(t+n)) \mid L(t) = \ell(t)\right] \leqslant (1+\varepsilon)\cdot\Phi_i(\ell(t))$, and therefore,

$$\sum_{i\in A} \mathbf{E}\left[\Phi_i(L(t+n)) \mid L(t) = \ell(t)\right] \leqslant (1+\varepsilon)\cdot\sum_{i\in A}\Phi_i(\ell(t)).$$

On the other hand, for every bin $i \notin A$, Lemma 3.4 implies that

$$\mathbf{E}\left[\Phi_i(L(t+n)) \mid L(t) = \ell(t)\right] \leqslant (1-\kappa)\cdot\Phi_i(\ell(t)),$$

for some constant $\kappa < 1$. Hence,

$$\sum_{i\notin A} \mathbf{E}\left[\Phi_i(L(t+n)) \mid L(t) = \ell(t)\right]$$

$$\leqslant \sum_{i\notin A} (1-\kappa)\cdot\Phi_i(\ell(t)) = (1-\kappa)\cdot\sum_{i\notin A}\Phi_i(\ell(t))$$

$$= (1-\kappa)\cdot\left(\sum_{i=1}^{n}\Phi_i(\ell(t)) - \sum_{i\in A}\Phi_i(\ell(t))\right).$$

Putting everything together, we obtain

$$\mathbf{E}\left[\Phi(L(t+n)) \mid L(t) = \ell(t)\right]$$

$$= \sum_{i\in A} \mathbf{E}\left[\Phi_i(L(t+n)) \mid L(t) = \ell(t)\right]$$

$$+ \sum_{i\notin A} \mathbf{E}\left[\Phi_i(L(t+n)) \mid L(t) = \ell(t)\right]$$

$$\leqslant (1+\varepsilon)\cdot\sum_{i\in A}\Phi_i(\ell(t))$$

$$+ (1-\kappa)\cdot\left(\sum_{i=1}^{n}\Phi_i(\ell(t)) - \sum_{i\in A}\Phi_i(\ell(t))\right)$$

$$= (\varepsilon+\kappa)\cdot\sum_{i\in A}\Phi_i(\ell(t)) + (1-\kappa)\cdot\sum_{i=1}^{n}\Phi_i(\ell(t))$$

$$\leqslant (\varepsilon+\kappa)\cdot n\cdot(1+\varepsilon)^{C_1} + (1-\kappa)\cdot\Phi(\ell(t))$$

$$\leqslant \frac{\kappa}{2}\cdot\Phi(\ell(t)) + (1-\kappa)\cdot\Phi(\ell(t)) \leqslant \left(1 - \frac{\kappa}{2}\right)\cdot\Phi(\ell(t)),$$

where in the second to last line we used the lower bound on $\Phi(\ell(t))$. $\square$

Using the lemma above, we now establish that the (unconditional) expectation of the exponential potential function at any stage τ is $\mathcal{O}(n)$.

COROLLARY 3.6. *For any stage τ with $1 \leqslant \tau \leqslant r$, we show the followings:*

$$\mathbf{E}\left[\Phi(L(\tau n))\right] \leqslant (1+\varepsilon)^2 \rho_n/(\kappa/2) = \mathcal{O}(n),$$

where ρ_n is the value from Lemma 3.5.

PROOF. We show the result by induction on τ. The basic idea is that if the expected potential value is already small for step τn, then it can only increase by a factor of at most $(1+\varepsilon)$. On the other hand, if the expected potential value is large, then Lemma 3.5 implies that the expected potential will decrease in step $\tau + 1$. Combining these insights yields the first statement of Corollary 3.6.

Let us now turn to the formal proof. Clearly, $\mathbf{E}\left[\Phi(\ell(0))\right] = \mathcal{O}(n)$. Again we define $t = \tau n$. We break the proof into two cases:

Case 1. We assume that $\mathbf{E}\left[\Phi(L(t))\right] \geqslant (1 + \varepsilon) \cdot \rho_n / (\kappa/2)$ and let $\mathcal{S}$ be the set of possible values of $\Phi(L(t))$. Then using Lemma 3.5 we have

$\mathbf{E}\left[\Phi(L(t + n))\right]$

$= \sum_{k \in \mathcal{S}} \mathbf{Pr}\left[\Phi(L(t)) = k\right] \cdot \mathbf{E}\left[\Phi(L(t + n)) \mid \Phi(\ell(t) = k\right]$

$= \sum_{k \in \mathcal{S} : k \leqslant \rho_n}^{\rho_n} \mathbf{Pr}\left[\Phi(L(t)) = k\right] \cdot \mathbf{E}\left[\Phi(L(t + n)) \mid \Phi(\ell(t)) = k\right]$

$\quad + \sum_{k \in \mathcal{S} : k > \rho_n} \mathbf{Pr}\left[\Phi(L(t)) = k\right] \cdot \mathbf{E}\left[\Phi(L(t + n)) \mid \Phi(\ell(t)) = k\right]$

$\leqslant \sum_{k \in \mathcal{S} : k \leqslant \rho_n} \mathbf{Pr}\left[\Phi(L(t)) = k\right] \cdot (1 + \varepsilon) \cdot k$

$\quad + \sum_{k \in \mathcal{S} : k > \rho_n} \mathbf{Pr}\left[\Phi(L(t)) = k\right] \cdot (1 - \kappa) \cdot k$

$\leqslant (1 + \varepsilon) \cdot \rho_n + \sum_{k \in \mathcal{S} : k > \rho_n} \mathbf{Pr}\left[\Phi(L(t)) = k\right] \cdot (1 - \kappa) \cdot k$

$\leqslant (\kappa/2) \cdot \mathbf{E}\left[\Phi(L(t))\right] + (1 - \kappa) \cdot \sum_{k \in \mathcal{S}} \mathbf{Pr}\left[\Phi(L(t)) = k\right] \cdot k$

$\leqslant (1 - \kappa/2) \cdot \mathbf{E}\left[\Phi(L(t))\right],$

where the second last line uses our assumption saying that $\mathbf{E}\left[\Phi(L(t - 1))\right] \geqslant (1 + \varepsilon)\rho_n / (\kappa/2)$.

Case 2. We assume that $\mathbf{E}\left[\Phi(L(t)\right] \leqslant (1 + \varepsilon) \cdot \rho_n / (k/2)$. In this case,

$\mathbf{E}\left[\Phi(L(t + n))\right] \leqslant (1 + \varepsilon) \cdot \mathbf{E}\left[\Phi(L(t))\right] \leqslant (1 + \varepsilon)^2 \rho_n / (\kappa/2).$

Hence, using the inductive hypothesis we obtain the following for both cases: For all stages τ, the load vector $L(\tau n)$ at the end of stage τ fulfills $\mathbf{E}\left[\Phi(L(\tau n))\right] = \mathcal{O}(n)$, as $\rho_n = \mathcal{O}(n)$. This completes the proof. $\square$

4. ANALYSIS OF THRESHOLD

We now give our results for the THRESHOLD protocol. Due to space limitations, one proof of this section is omitted.

4.1 Upper Bound

In this part we extend the results from [7] for the case $m = \mathcal{O}(n)$ to the case where m is asymptotically greater than n.

THEOREM 4.1. *The allocation time of the* THRESHOLD *protocol is* $m + m^{3/4} \cdot n^{1/4} + n$, *with probability at least* $1 - 8n^{-2}$. *In particular, the expected allocation time is bounded by* $m + \mathcal{O}(m^{3/4} \cdot n^{1/4})$.

PROOF. Let $r := m/n$. We first observe that we can focus on the case where r is an integer. If r is not an integer, we can resort to the statement of theorem for $m = \lceil r \rceil \cdot n$. We can also assume that r is bounded from below by a sufficiently large constant for the following reason. As we stated before, if r is upper bounded by some constant, then one can easily prove that in each step t there are at least $m/(r + 1) = \Omega(n)$ bins with load less than $r + 1 = m/n + 1$. Hence the expected time to place m balls is stochastically

smaller than the sum of m geometric random variables each with constant mean.

For the proof we assume that all the bin choices of the balls are fixed in advance. Let C be a vector of infinite length. Every entry in C is a number in $[n]$ chosen uniformly and independently at random. The first ball uses the first i entries of C as random bin choices, until it is allocated to bin $C[i]$ (using the rules of THRESHOLD). The next ball then uses $C[i + 1], \ldots, C[i + j]$ until it is allocated to bin $C[i + j]$, and so on. Our goal is now to upper bound the number of entries of C that are used until THRESHOLD allocates all m balls into the n bins.

The main idea of our proof is to upper bound the total number of *holes* W_t in the bins at time t. The number of holes of a bin is defined as follows. A bin with ℓ balls has $r + 1 - \ell$ holes. If the number of remaining holes is less than or equal to n, then all m balls are allocated. Hence, at time t there are $(r + 1) \cdot n - W_t$ many balls allocated. We will show that after $T = \alpha n$ many steps (with $\alpha := r + r^{3/4} + 1$) we have $W_t \leqslant n$, with high probability. We note that our proof is inspired by the proof of the corresponding result from [7].

We define $X_1(t), \ldots, X_n(t)$ as the *access* distribution at the end of step t, i.e., $X_i(t) = x$ occurs x times in $C[1], \ldots, C[t]$. Moreover, let $L_1(t), \ldots, L_n(t)$ be the *load* distribution when the first t entries of C are used, i.e., $L_i(t) = x$ means that exactly x balls are allocated to bin i when we have gone through $C[1], \ldots, C[t]$. By definition of THRESHOLD

$$L_i(t) = \min\{r + 1, X_i(t)\}.$$

Our aim is to prove for our choice of T that w.h.p.

$$W_T = \sum_{i=1}^{n} (r + 1 - L_i(T)) = \sum_{i=1}^{n} \max\{r + 1 - X_i(T), 0\} \leqslant n.$$

Similar to the analysis of Czumaj and Stemann in [7] we use Poisson distributed random variables as an approximation for $X_1(t), \ldots X_n(t)$. We omit the superscript T in the following, as we only consider the access and load distribution at step T.

The expected number of requests that any bin receives in the first T steps is α. Let $Y_1, \ldots, Y_n$ be n independent Poisson random variables with expectation α. Using the Chernoff bound from Theorem 6.4 with $\varepsilon = r^{3/4}/\alpha$, $\alpha := r + r^{3/4} + 1$, we obtain for large enough r that for any i

$$\mathbf{Pr}\left[Y_i \leqslant r + 1\right] = \mathbf{Pr}\left[Y_i \leqslant \alpha - r^{3/4}\right]$$

$$= \mathbf{Pr}\left[Y_i \leqslant \left(1 - \frac{r^{3/4}}{\alpha}\right)\alpha\right]$$

$$\leqslant e^{-\left(\frac{r^{3/4}}{\alpha}\right)^2 \cdot \alpha/2} \leqslant e^{-\alpha^{1/2}/4}.$$

We proceed by a case distinction.

Case 1: $\alpha^{1/2} \geqslant 8 \log n$. Then the above probability is smaller than n^{-2}, so that with probability at least $1 - n^{-1}$ and by 6.7,

$$\mathbf{Pr}\left[\exists i : X_i \leqslant r + 1\right] \leqslant 4 \cdot \mathbf{Pr}\left[\exists i : Y_i \leqslant r + 1\right] \leqslant 4n^{-1}.$$

Case 2: $\alpha^{1/2} < 8 \log n$. Let

$$\mathcal{I} := \{i \in \{1, \ldots, n\} : Y_i \leqslant r + 1\}.$$

Then $|\mathcal{I}|$ is a random variable with $\mathbf{E}\left[|\mathcal{I}|\right] \leqslant n \cdot e^{-\alpha^{1/2}/4}$.

Using the inequality of Hoeffding, we obtain that

$$\mathbf{Pr}\left[|\mathcal{I}| \geqslant \mathbf{E}\left[|\mathcal{I}|\right] + \sqrt{n \log n}\right] \leqslant e^{-\frac{2(\sqrt{n \log n})^2}{n}} = n^{-2}.$$

Let $Y := \sum_{i=1}^{n} \max\{(r+1) - Y_i, 0\}$. Our goal is now to prove that Y is not too large with high probability. For $i \in \mathcal{I}$ define the random variable $Z_i := [(r+1) - Y_i \mid y_i \leqslant r+1]$. Then

$$\mathbf{Pr}\left[Z_i = k\right] = \frac{\mathbf{Pr}\left[Y_i = r+1-k\right]}{\mathbf{Pr}\left[Y_i \leqslant r+1\right]}. \qquad (4.1)$$

Further we define for any $1 \leqslant k \leqslant r+1$,

$$\begin{aligned}
p_k &:= \mathbf{Pr}\left[Z_i = k\right] \\
&= \frac{\mathbf{Pr}\left[Y_i = r+1-k\right]}{\mathbf{Pr}\left[Y_i \leqslant r+1\right]} \\
&= e^{-\alpha} \cdot \frac{\alpha^{r+1-k}}{(r+1-k)!} \cdot \frac{1}{\mathbf{Pr}\left[Y_i \leqslant r+1\right]}.
\end{aligned}$$

Hence,

$$\frac{p_k}{p_{k-1}} = \frac{r+2-k}{\alpha},$$

that is,

$$\begin{aligned}
p_k &= \frac{r+2-k}{\alpha} \cdot p_{k-1} \\
&\leqslant \frac{r+2}{r+r^{3/4}+2} \cdot p_{k-1} \leqslant (1 - r^{-1/4}/2) \cdot p_{k-1},
\end{aligned}$$

where the last inequality holds for sufficiently large r.

For any fixed set $\mathcal{I} \subseteq \{1, \ldots, n\}$, the random variables Z_i with $i \in \mathcal{I}$ satisfy the preconditions of Theorem 6.6 with $\delta = r^{-1/4}/2$, so that $\mathbf{E}\left[Z_i\right] \leqslant 2r^{1/4}$ and

$$\mathbf{Pr}\left[\sum_{i \in I} Z_i \geqslant (1+\varepsilon) \cdot |\mathcal{I}| \cdot 2r^{1/4}\right] \leqslant e^{-\varepsilon^2 |\mathcal{I}|/2(1+\varepsilon)}.$$

With $\alpha^{1/2} < 8 \log n$ and $\alpha = r + r^{3/4} + 1$ we have $n \geqslant 2 \cdot e^{-\alpha^{1/2}/4} \cdot n \cdot r^{1/4} + 2 \cdot \sqrt{n \log n} \cdot 2r^{1/4}$. Hence,

$$\begin{aligned}
&\mathbf{Pr}\left[Y \geqslant n\right] \\
&\leqslant \mathbf{Pr}\left[Y \geqslant 2 \cdot e^{-\alpha^{1/2}/4} \cdot n \cdot 2r^{1/4} + 2 \cdot \sqrt{n \log n} \cdot 2r^{1/4}\right] \\
&\leqslant \mathbf{Pr}\left[Y \geqslant 2 \cdot \mathbf{E}\left[|\mathcal{I}|\right] \cdot 2r^{1/4} + 2 \cdot \sqrt{n \log n} \cdot 2r^{1/4}\right] \\
&\leqslant \mathbf{Pr}\left[Y \geqslant 4r^{1/4} \cdot \left(\mathbf{E}\left[|\mathcal{I}|\right] + \sqrt{n \log n}\right)\right] \\
&\leqslant \mathbf{Pr}\left[|\mathcal{I}| \geqslant \mathbf{E}\left[|\mathcal{I}|\right] + \sqrt{n \log n}\right] \\
&\quad + \mathbf{Pr}\left[\begin{array}{l} Y \geqslant 4r^{1/4} \cdot \left(\mathbf{E}\left[|\mathcal{I}|\right] + \sqrt{n \log n}\right) \\ \mid |\mathcal{I}| \leqslant \mathbf{E}\left[|\mathcal{I}|\right] + \sqrt{n \log n} \end{array}\right] \\
&\leqslant n^{-2} + \mathbf{Pr}\left[\begin{array}{l} \sum_{i \in \mathcal{I}} Z_i \geqslant 2 \cdot |\mathcal{I}| \cdot 2r^{1/4} \\ \mid |\mathcal{I}| = \mathbf{E}\left[|\mathcal{I}|\right] + \sqrt{n \log n} \end{array}\right] \\
&\leqslant n^{-2} + e^{-\left(\mathbf{E}\left[|\mathcal{I}|\right] + \sqrt{n \log n}\right)/4} \leqslant 2 \cdot n^{-2},
\end{aligned}$$

where the first inequality uses the assumptions $\alpha^{1/2} \leqslant 8 \log n$, $\alpha \geqslant r$ and r being bounded below by a sufficiently large constant. Hence,

$$\begin{aligned}
&\mathbf{Pr}\left[Y \geqslant n\right] \\
&\leqslant \mathbf{Pr}\left[Y \geqslant n \mid |\mathcal{I}| > \mathbf{E}\left[|\mathcal{I}|\right] + \sqrt{n \log n}\right]
\end{aligned}$$

$$\begin{aligned}
&\quad \cdot \mathbf{Pr}\left[|\mathcal{I}| > \mathbf{E}\left[|\mathcal{I}|\right] + \sqrt{n \log n}\right] \\
&\quad + \mathbf{Pr}\left[Y \geqslant n \mid |\mathcal{I}| \leqslant \mathbf{E}\left[|\mathcal{I}|\right] + \sqrt{n \log n}\right] \\
&\quad \cdot \mathbf{Pr}\left[|\mathcal{I}| \leqslant \mathbf{E}\left[|\mathcal{I}|\right] + \sqrt{n \log n}\right] \\
&\leqslant \mathbf{Pr}\left[|\mathcal{I}| > \mathbf{E}\left[|\mathcal{I}|\right] + \sqrt{n \log n}\right] \\
&\quad + \mathbf{Pr}\left[Y \geqslant n \mid |\mathcal{I}| \leqslant \mathbf{E}\left[|\mathcal{I}|\right] + \sqrt{n \log n}\right] \\
&\leqslant n^{-2} + \mathbf{Pr}\left[\begin{array}{l} Y \geqslant 2 \cdot \left(\mathbf{E}\left[|\mathcal{I}|\right] + \sqrt{n \log n}\right) \cdot 2r^{1/4} \\ \mid |\mathcal{I}| \leqslant \mathbf{E}\left[|\mathcal{I}|\right] + \sqrt{n \log n} \end{array}\right] \\
&\leqslant n^{-2} + \mathbf{Pr}\left[\begin{array}{l} \sum_{i \in \mathcal{I}} Z_i \geqslant 2 \cdot |\mathcal{I}| \cdot 2r^{1/4} \\ \mid |\mathcal{I}| = \mathbf{E}\left[|\mathcal{I}|\right] + \sqrt{n \log n} \end{array}\right] \\
&\leqslant n^{-2} + e^{-\left(\mathbf{E}\left[|\mathcal{I}|\right] + \sqrt{n \log n}\right)/4} \leqslant 2 \cdot n^{-2},
\end{aligned}$$

By the relation between the Poisson model and the original balls-into-bins model (second statement in Lemma 6.7),

$$\begin{aligned}
&\mathbf{Pr}\left[\sum_{i=1}^{n} \max\{(r+1) - L_i, 0\} \geqslant n\right] \\
&\leqslant 4 \cdot \mathbf{Pr}\left[\sum_{i=1}^{n} \max\{(r+1) - Y_i, 0\} \geqslant n\right] \leqslant 8n^{-2}.
\end{aligned}$$

But from $\sum_{i=1}^{n} \max\{(r+1) - L_i, 0\} \leqslant n$, we can conclude that $\sum_{i=1}^{n} L_i \geqslant (r+1)n - n = rn = m$. Hence the THRESHOLD protocol finishes the placement of m balls before step T with probability at least $1 - 8n^{-2}$. This finishes the proof of the first statement. For the second statement, we simply divide the infinite vector C into consecutive sections of length αn. Then the probability that the choices in one section suffice to terminate the process is at least $1 - 8n^{-2}$, regardless of the outcomes in the previous sections. $\square$

4.2 Lower Bound

For our lower bounds we will also use the so-called *quadratic potential* [3], which is defined by

$$\Psi(\ell(t)) := \sum_{i=1}^{n} (\ell_i(t) - t/n)^2.$$

It is easy to verify that for any load vector $\ell(t)$ such that $\max_i \ell_i(t) \leqslant t/n + \mathcal{O}(1)$, $\Psi(\ell(t)) = \mathcal{O}(\Phi(\ell(t)))$. For simplicity we focus on the case $m = n^2$ here (similar lower bounds can be also obtained for other relations between m and n).

THEOREM 4.2. *Consider the* THRESHOLD *protocol with* $m = n^2$ *and let* $t = m$. *With probability at least* $1 - \exp(-\Omega(n^{1/2}))$, $L(t)$ *satisfies: (i)* $\Psi(L(t)) = \Omega(n^{9/8})$, *(ii)* $\max_{i,j}\left(L_i(t) - L_j(t)\right) = \Omega(n^{1/8})$, *and (iii)* $\Phi(L(t)) = 2^{\Omega(n^{1/8})}$.

This result should be compared to Corollary 3.6 for the ADAPTIVE protocol, showing that every bin has at most $O(\log n)$ holes.

5. EXPERIMENTS

We also compare the ADAPTIVE protocol to the THRESHOLD protocol by means of experiments (Figure 3). Inline with our theoretical results, we observe that the runtime of THRESHOLD quickly converges to m. Moreover, the runtime of ADAPTIVE seems to converge to a small constant times m.

To measure the smoothness of the final load distribution, we also compute the average values of the quadratic potential function. Here we observe that this value is significantly smaller for the ADAPTIVE protocol, as it converges quickly to a value that is independent of m (note that this principal convergence is also guaranteed by Lemma 3.5, since the quadratic potential function is asymptotically at most the exponential potential function).

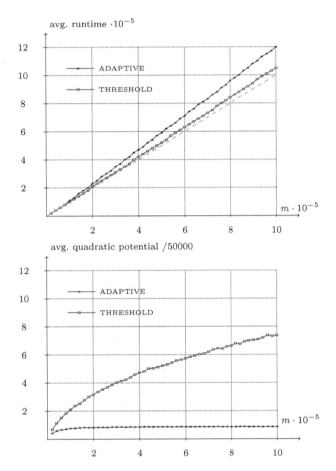

Figure 3: Empirical results for the THRESHOLD and ADAPTIVE protocol. Every point represents the average taken over 100 runs.

6. APPENDIX

We observe the following simple fact about convolution of sequences. Recall the definition of convolution: If $p = (p_k)_{k=0}^n$, $q = (q_k)_{k=0}^n$ are two sequences, then the sequence $p \star q = ((p \star q)_k)_{k=0}^{2n}$ defined by $(p \star q)_k := \sum_{i=\max\{0,k-n\}}^{\min\{k,n\}} p_i \cdot q_{k-i}$ is the convolution of p and q. We say that a sequence p majorizes a sequence q if for every $0 \leqslant j \leqslant n$, $\sum_{k=j}^n p_k \geqslant \sum_{k=j}^n q_k$.

LEMMA 6.1. *Let p, q and r three sequences of n numbers. If p majorizes q and r is non-increasing, then $\sum_{k=0}^n p_k \cdot r_k \leqslant \sum_{k=0}^n q_k \cdot r_k$.*

We also list several concentration inequalities that are used throughout the paper.

THEOREM 6.2   (HOEFFDINGS INEQUALITY). *Let $X_k, 1 \leqslant k \leqslant n$, be n independent binary random variables. Let $X := \sum_{k=1}^n X_k$. Then for any $\lambda > 0$,*

$$\mathbf{Pr}\left[|X - \mathbf{E}[X]| \geqslant \lambda\right] \leqslant 2e^{-\lambda^2/n}.$$

THEOREM 6.3   (AZUMA'S INEQUALITY). *Let $X_k, 0 \leqslant k \leqslant n$, be a martingale such that $|X_k - X_{k-1}| \leqslant c_k$ for every $1 \leqslant k \leqslant n$. Then for any $\varepsilon > 0$,*

$$\mathbf{Pr}\left[|X_n - X_0| \geqslant \varepsilon\right] \leqslant 2e^{-\frac{\varepsilon^2}{2\sum_{i=0}^n c_i^2}}.$$

THEOREM 6.4   ([2]). *Let $\mathsf{Poi}(\mu)$ be the Poisson distribution with mean μ. Then for any $\varepsilon > 0$,*

$$\mathbf{Pr}\left[\mathsf{Poi}(\mu) \leqslant (1-\varepsilon)\mu\right] \leqslant e^{-\varepsilon^2\mu/2}$$

$$\mathbf{Pr}\left[\mathsf{Poi}(\mu) \geqslant (1+\varepsilon)\mu\right] \leqslant \left[e^\varepsilon(1+\varepsilon)^{-(1+\varepsilon)}\right]^\mu$$

We note the following standard Chernoff bound for sum of geometric random variables which can be easily derived by using a Chernoff bound for a sum of Bernoulli random variables.

THEOREM 6.5   ([9]). *Suppose that $X_1, \ldots, X_n$ are independent geometric random variables on $\mathbb{N}$ with parameter δ, so $\mathbf{E}[X_i] = 1/\delta$ for each i. Let $X := \sum_{i=1}^n X_i$, $\mu = \mathbf{E}[X] = n/\delta$. Then it holds for any $\varepsilon > 0$ that*

$$\mathbf{Pr}\left[X \geqslant (1+\varepsilon)\mu\right] \leqslant e^{-\varepsilon^2 n/2(1+\varepsilon)}.$$

From Theorem 6.5 and a simple majorization argument, one can obtain the following extension:

THEOREM 6.6. *Suppose that $X_1, \ldots, X_n$ are independent random variables on $\mathbb{N}$, such that there is a value $0 < \delta < 1$ with $\mathbf{Pr}[X_i = k+1] \leqslant (1-\delta) \cdot \mathbf{Pr}[X_i = k]$ for all $k \geqslant 1$. Let $X := \sum_{i=1}^n X_i$, $\mu = \mathbf{E}[X]$. Then it holds for any $\varepsilon > 0$ that*

$$\mathbf{Pr}\left[X \geqslant (1+\varepsilon)\mu\right] \leqslant e^{-\varepsilon^2 n/2(1+\varepsilon)}.$$

Moreover, it also holds that $\mu \leqslant \frac{1}{\delta}$.

The following lemma due to Adler et al. is an extremely powerful tool for anlyzing balls-into-bins processes.

LEMMA 6.7   ([1, COROLLARY 13]). *Let process P_1 be the placement of m balls into n bins where each bin is chosen independently and uniformly at random. Let P_2 be the process where the load of every bin is an independent Poisson random variable with expectation m/n. Let $\mathcal{A}$ be any event concerning the final load distribution.*

(1) Then any event that occurs in P_2 with probability at most p, holds in P_1 with probability at most $p \cdot \sqrt{n}$.

(2) Moreover, any event that is increasing w.r.t. adding balls and holds in P_2 with probability at most p holds in P_1 with probability at most $4p$.

References

[1] M. Adler, S. Chakrabarti, M. Mitzenmacher, and L. E. Rasmussen. Parallel randomized load balancing. *Random Struct. Algorithms*, 13(2):159–188, 1998.

[2] N. Alon and J. Spencer. *The Probabilistic method.* Wiley-Interscience Series in Discrete Mathematics and Optimization. John Wiley & Sons, 2nd edition, 2000.

[3] B. Awerbuch, Y. Azar, S. A. Plotkin, and O. Waarts. Competitive routing of virtual circuits with unknown duration. In *SODA*, pages 321–327, 1994.

[4] Y. Azar, A. Z. Broder, A. R. Karlin, and E. Upfal. Balanced allocations. *SIAM J. Comput.*, 29(1):180–200, 1999.

[5] P. Berenbrink, A. Czumaj, A. Steger, and B. Vöcking. Balanced allocations: The heavily loaded case. *SIAM J. Comput.*, 35(6):1350–1385, 2006.

[6] A. Czumaj, C. Riley, and C. Scheideler. Perfectly balanced allocation. In *RANDOM*, pages 240–251, 2003.

[7] A. Czumaj and V. Stemann. Randomized allocation processes. *Random Struct. Algorithms*, 18(4):297–331, 2001.

[8] M. Dietzfelbinger, A. Goerdt, M. Mitzenmacher, A. Montanari, R. Pagh, and M. Rink. Tight thresholds for cuckoo hashing via XORSAT. In *ICALP (1)*, pages 213–225, 2010.

[9] D. Dubhashi and A. Panconesi. *Concentration of measure for the analysis of randomized algorithms.* Cambridge University Press, 2009.

[10] B. Ghosh, F. T. Leighton, B. M. Maggs, S. Muthukrishnan, C. G. Plaxton, R. Rajaraman, A. W. Richa, R. E. Tarjan, and D. Zuckerman. Tight analyses of two local load balancing algorithms. *SIAM J. Comput.*, 29(1):29–64, 1999.

[11] R. M. Karp, M. Luby, and F. Meyer auf der Heide. Efficient PRAM simulation on a distributed memory machine. *Algorithmica*, 16(4/5):517–542, 1996.

[12] R. Lüling and B. Monien. A dynamic distributed load balancing algorithm with provable good performance. In *SPAA*, pages 164–172, 1993.

[13] M. Mitzenmacher, B. Prabhakar, and D. Shah. Load balancing with memory. In *FOCS*, pages 799–808, 2002.

[14] M. Raab and A. Steger. "balls into bins" - a simple and tight analysis. In *RANDOM*, pages 159–170, 1998.

[15] B. Vöcking. How asymmetry helps load balancing. *J. ACM*, 50(4):568–589, 2003.

Author Index

www.ingramcontent.com/pod-product-compliance
Lightning Source LLC
Chambersburg PA
CBHW080152060326
40689CB00018B/3946